Continued on inside back cover

W9-APU-974

# INTERNATIONAL BUSINESS

## FIFTH EDITION

# INTERNATIONAL BUSINESS

## FIFTH EDITION

**Michael R. Czinkota**
*Georgetown University*

**Ilkka A. Ronkainen**
*Georgetown University*

**Michael H. Moffett**
*The American Graduate School of
International Management (Thunderbird)*

**THE DRYDEN PRESS**
HARCOURT BRACE COLLEGE PUBLISHERS

*Fort Worth Philadelphia San Diego New York Orlando
Austin San Antonio Toronto Montreal London Sydney Tokyo*

PUBLISHER  *George Provol*
ACQUISITIONS EDITOR  *John R. Weimeister*
DEVELOPMENTAL EDITOR  *Jennifer Sheetz Langer*
PROJECT EDITOR  *John Haakenson*
PRODUCTION MANAGER  *Eddie Dawson*
PRODUCT MANAGER  *Lisé Johnson*
ART DIRECTOR  *Bill Brammer*
PROJECT MANAGEMENT  *York Production Services*
COMPOSITOR  *York Graphic Services, Inc.*
TEXT TYPE  *10/12 New Baskerville*

ADDRESS FOR EDITORIAL CORRESPONDENCE: The Dryden Press, 301 Commerce Street, Suite 3700, Fort Worth, TX 76102

ADDRESS FOR ORDERS: The Dryden Press, 6277 Sea Harbor Drive, Orlando, FL 32887   1 (800) 782-4479 or 1 (800) 433-0001 (in Florida)

ISBN: 0-03-022378-4

Library of Congress Catalog Card Number: 98-28009

Printed in the United States of America

8 9 0 1 2 3 4 5 6 7   048   9 8 7 6 5 4 3 2 1

The Dryden Press
Harcourt Brace College Publishers

# The Dryden Press Series in Management

We are grateful for the leadership position the market has awarded to this book. We are keenly aware of the fact that best-selling status in the educational field also imposes an obligation to deliver cutting-edge innovations and improvements in terms of content as well as presentation. We honor your trust by doing our best to delight you through our presentation of conceptually sound, reality-based knowledge and by easing your task of teaching and learning about international business.

This textbook is unique in its approach to international business. Our direct corporate experience and advising of companies, both large and small, allows us to share with you the realities of the battle in the international marketplace. Due to our ongoing policy work with both national and international organizations, we are able to give you a firsthand perspective of government activities in international business. Through our research leadership we can provide you with insights at the forefront of global thinking. As a result, this book offers you the perspective of the multinational corporation as well as that of the small international start-up firm. It lets you understand how and why governments intervene in markets and suggests alternatives for working with governments to achieve corporate goals. This book provides you with a strong theory base but also fully reflects the managerial concerns of those who work on the front lines in the business world. Finally, ongoing improvements in pedagogy, presentation, and writing continue to make this book fun to teach with and learn from.

## Changes in the Fifth Edition

**Current Coverage**  In preparing this edition, we have listened closely to our market in order to deliver an outstanding product. We start out by presenting the impact of international business on countries, corporations, and individuals. In-depth attention is paid to the role of culture, policies, and politics. The dimensions of ethics, social responsibility, and diversity are fully reflected through examples and vignettes. Our research on antidumping allows us to demonstrate how companies are beginning to use this policy measure to obtain administrative shelter from their international competitors. We explore the sweatshop issue, highlight the need for acceptable working conditions around the globe, and report with an insider perspective on the latest international agreements to reduce bribery and corruption. We explain the increased use of arbitration procedures and show in the example of Bill Gates how companies lobby for changes in governmental policies.

**Greater Use of Worldwide Examples**  The global orientation of this book is reinforced by drawing on worldwide examples, trends, and data rather than just on U.S.-based information. We also ensure the reality and pragmatism of our content by always addressing the issue of "What does all this mean for firms in terms of implementing international business activities?" As an example, we explain how to use cultural variables for segmentation purposes in order to create new competitive tools.

**Technology and the Internet**  We have systematically developed electronic information sources and indicated relevant Web sites in the text so that the instructor and the student can go beyond the book and obtain further up-to-date information. In addition, Web-based questions and research tasks permit immersion in ongoing international business issues and communicate the excitement of rapid change. All references to the Web are highlighted with icons throughout the text. We have also included a quick reference guide on the inside cover. We also present thirty-four cases, more than 55 percent of them new or updated, in order to allow a clear linkage between theory and reality. By drawing case material from firms around the world, we offer truly global business scenarios ranging from Africa to Iceland, from dealing with Mad Cow Disease to operating a crocodile ranch. We also offer a special appendix on International Business and Geography.

**Blending Current Theory and Application**  Our theory section presents the latest thinking both from leading economists and business researchers. We also present the interdependence and linkages between the different theories so that the student gains an appreciation of the overall context of international business thought. All tables, figures, and maps were updated to present the most current information.

**Up-to-Date Coverage of EU, Asia, and Transition Economies**  In Part 3 we have streamlined the discussion of the international monetary system, included the issues surrounding the introduction of the EURO, and expanded the discussion of financial markets in order to reflect the financial turmoil in Asia. We provide in-depth coverage of the new developments in the European Union together with the changing roles of Mercosur and APEC. In discussing the latest changes in transition economies, we are, due to our direct involvement in founding three business learning institutions in Russia, able to highlight the human and leadership dimensions inherent in the change to a market economy.

**Increased Coverage of Research**  Part 4 has a greatly strengthened research chapter. An in-depth information appendix enhances the student's ability to conduct independent research, primarily by using Web sites and other resources of the Internet. We also focus on "born global" firms, which have a global orientation from their inception, and differentiate the levels of internationalization of the firm. We show how firms can receive export help from their governments and provide the Internet information for the leading export promotion organizations from around the globe. A new section highlights how leading-edge firms are developing "Export Complaint Management Systems" in order to stay close to their customers, adapt products quickly, and regain control of export channels.

**Strengthened Strategy Orientation**    Part 5 offers a strengthened strategy orientation. A new chapter on strategic planning presents a framework for planning, market choice, and a competitive strategy approach. An in-depth treatment of supply-chain management is offered to complement the logistics discussion. We deal with important implementation issues such as product tracking, electronic data interchange, and early supplier involvement. We also highlight the emergence of a new "post mortem" stage in the product life cycle, during which firms will have to engage in the reverse distribution of the products they have sold many years ago. A separate chapter on countertrade offers alternative ways of doing business in times of currency turmoil. Global community relations are addressed, including insights on corporate preparations for crisis situations. This section also offers the unique insights from a global delphi study conducted by the authors, the results of which are being used by several governments and corporations in structuring international trade strategies. Finally, a special section highlights the increasing role of women in international business leadership.

## Special Features

**Art and Photo Program**

In order to inspire the student's imagination, many color photographs are presented in this edition. Throughout the text, concepts are visually depicted through tables, figures, and graphics. Artwork is designed to reiterate key concepts as well as to provide a pleasing format for student learning.

**Organization**

The text is divided into five parts. The first part introduces the impact of international business on countries, firms, and individuals. The second part focuses on the theoretical foundations of international trade and investment and the economic activity of the nation. Part 3 concentrates on the economic and financial environment together with economic integration and economies in transition. Part 4 is devoted to the preparation for international business and market entry. Part 5 covers strategic management issues.

**Coverage**

The text covers the international business activities of small and medium-sized firms that are new to the international arena as well as those of giant multinational corporations. It also provides thorough coverage of the policy aspects of international business, reflecting the concerns of the U.S. government, foreign governments, and international institutions.

The text consistently adopts a truly global approach. Attention is given to topics that are critical to the international manager yet so far have eluded other international texts. This coverage includes chapters on countertrade, supply-chain management, international service trade, and doing business with newly emerging market economies under conditions of privatization.

**Geography**

To increase the geographic literacy of students, color maps have been redesigned and updated. They provide the instructor with the means to visually demonstrate concepts such as political blocs, socioeconomic variables, and transportation routes. In addition, a unique appendix focuses specifically on the topic of geography and international business. A list of maps appears on page xxix.

## Contemporary Realism

Each chapter offers a number of Global Perspectives that describe actual contemporary business situations. They are intended to serve as reinforcing examples, or minicases. As such, they will assist the instructor in stimulating class discussion and aid the student in understanding and absorbing the text material.

## Research Emphasis

A special effort has been made to provide current research information. Apart from sharing the results of our own research, and that of our colleagues, we offer at the end of each chapter a list of relevant recommended readings. These materials will enable the instructor and the student to go beyond the text whenever time permits. We also offer information about Web sites for research purposes so that the reader can go beyond the printed information.

## Cases and Video Support

All sections of the text are followed by cases, many written especially for this book. Of a total of thirty-four cases, six are also supported by video materials available to the instructor. Challenging questions accompany each case. They encourage in-depth discussion of the material covered in the chapters and allow students to apply the knowledge they have gained.

## Pedagogy

A textbook is about teaching, and we have made a major effort to strength the pedagogical value of this book.

- The listing of Web sites allows the student to go directly to the source and receive up-to-the-minute information.
- The use of color makes it easier to differentiate sections and improves the presentation of graphs and figures.
- The design of maps specific to chapters adds a visual dimension to the verbal explanation.
- The Global Perspectives bring concrete examples from the business world into the classroom.
- The video support materials enable better and more efficient instruction.
- A glossary has been provided for the student's benefit. Each key term is bold-faced and defined in the text where it first appears. A complete glossary is provided at the end of the text.

## Comprehensive Learning Package

## Instructor's Manual, Test Bank, and Transparency Masters

The text is accompanied by a completely revised *Instructor's Manual* designed to provide in-depth assistance to the professor. For this edition, this manual has been thoroughly updated and expanded with assistance from Amit Shah. For each chapter of the text, the manual provides suggested teaching notes, possible group projects, an overview of the chapter's objectives, and answers to all end-of-chapter Review and Discussion Questions. Answers are provided for all the questions that follow the end-of-part cases, and video teaching notes are provided for each video case that appears in the text. In addition, an annotated list of suggested films and videos is provided. The *Test Bank* portion of the manual provides a range of over 1,000 incisive multiple-choice, short answer, and essay questions for each chapter.

**Computerized Test Banks** are available for your use. The Dryden Press has software available in DOS, Macintosh, and Windows formats.

**Lecture Presentation Software** in MSPowerPoint is now available for your use. Chapter files include key concepts and can be customized by instructors for their lectures.

**Acetate Package** A full set of 100 four-color transparency acetates is available. Acetates are accompanied by detailed teaching notes that include summaries of key concepts.

The Dryden Press will provide complimentary supplements or supplement packages to those adopters qualified under our adoption policy. Please contact your sales representative to learn how you may qualify. If as an adopter or potential user you receive supplements you do not need, please return them to your sales representative or send them to:

Attn: Returns Department
Troy Warehouse
465 South Lincoln Drive
Troy, MO 63379

## Acknowledgements

We are grateful to a number of reviewers for their imaginative comments and criticisms and for showing us how to get it even more right:

Kamal M. Abouzeid
*Lynchburg College*
Yaur Aharoni
*Duke University*
Zafar U. Ahmed
*Minot State University*
Riad Ajami
*Rensselaer Polytechnic Institute*
Joe Anderson
*Northern Arizona University*
Robert Aubey
*University of Wisconsin—Madison*
David Aviel
*California State University*
Bharat B. Bhalla
*Fairfield University*
Julius M. Blum
*University of South Alabama*

Sharon Browning
*Northwest Missouri State University*
Peggy E. Chaudhry
*Villanova University*
Ellen Cook
*University of San Diego*
Luther Trey Denton
*Georgia Southern University*
Gary N. Dicer
*The University of Tennessee*
Peter Dowling
*University of Tasmania*
Derrick E. Dsouza
*University of North Texas*
Massoud Farahbaksh
*Salem State College*
Runar Framnes
*Norwegian School of Management*

Anne-Marie Francesco
*Pace University—New York*
Esra F. Gencturk
*University of Texas—Austin*
Debra Glassman
*University of Washington—Seattle*
Raul de Gouvea Neto
*University of New Mexico*
Antonio Grimaldi
*Rutgers, The State University of New Jersey*
John H. Hallaq
*University of Idaho*
Daniel Himarios
*University of Texas at Arlington*
Veronica Horton
*Middle Tennessee State University*
Basil J. Janavaras
*Mankato State University*
Michael Kublin
*University of New Haven*
Diana Lawson
*University of Maine*
Jan B. Luytjes
*Florida International University*
David McCalman
*Indiana University—Bloomington*
Tom Morris
*University of San Diego*
James Neelankavil
*Hofstra University*
Moonsong David Oh
*California State University—Los Angeles*
Sam C. Okoroafo
*University of Toledo*
Diane Parente
*State University of New York—Fredonia*

Jesus Ponce de Leon
*Southern Illinois University—Carbondale*
Jerry Ralston
*University of Washington—Seattle*
Peter V. Raven
*Eastern Washington University*
William Renforth
*Florida International University*
Martin E. Rosenfeldt
*The University of North Texas*
Tagi Sagafi-nejad
*Loyola College*
Rajib N. Sanyal
*Trenton State College*
Ulrike Schaede
*University of California—Berkeley*
John Stanbury
*Indiana University—Kokomo*
John Thanopoulos
*University of Akron*
Douglas Tseng
*Portland State University*
Betty Velthouse
*University of Michigan—Flint*
Heidi Vernon-Wortzel
*Northeastern University*
Steven C. Walters
*Davenport College*
James O. Watson
*Millikin University*
George H. Westacott
*SUNY—Binghamton*
Jerry Wheat
*Indiana University Southeast*
Kitty Y. H. Young
*Chinese University of Hong Kong*

Many thanks to those faculty members and students who helped us in sharpening our thinking by cheerfully providing challenging comments and questions. Several individuals had particular long-term impact on our thinking. These are Professor Bernard LaLonde, of the Ohio State University, a true academic mentor; the late Professor Robert Bartels, also of Ohio State; Professor Arthur Stonehill, of Oregon State University; Professor James H. Sood, of American University; Professor Arch G. Woodside, of Tulane University; Professor David Ricks, of Thunderbird; Professor Brian Toyne, of St. Mary's University; and Professor John Darling, of Mississippi State University. They are our academic ancestors.

Many colleagues, friends, and business associates graciously gave their time and knowledge to clarify concepts; provide us with ideas, comments, and suggestions; and deepen our understanding of issues. Without the direct links to business and policy that you have provided, this book could not offer its refreshing realism. In particular, we are grateful to Secretaries Malcolm Baldrige, C. William Verity, Clayton Yeutter, and William Brock for the opportunity to gain international business policy experience and to William Morris, Paul Freedenberg, H. P. Goldfield, and J. Michael Farrell for enabling its implementation. We also thank William Casselman, Lew Cramer of Media One, Joseph Lynch of ADI, and Reijo Luostarinen of HSE.

Valuable research assistance was provided by Laura Cooper and Peter Fitzmaurice, as well as Elaine Cowan and William Heuer, all of Georgetown University. We appreciate all of your work!

A very special word of thanks to the people at The Dryden Press. Thanks to John Weimeister for not dealing with suppliers and collaborating with authors, and to Jennifer Langer for her enthusiasm, creativity, and constructive feedback. Major assistance was also provided by the friendliness, expertise, and help of Karen Hill of Elm Street Publishing Services. Many thanks to Lisé Johnson who creatively markets *International Business*. Project management was provided by York Production Services.

Foremost, we are grateful to our families, who have had to tolerate late-night computer noises, weekend library absences, and curtailed vacations. The support and love of Ilona Vigh-Czinkota, Susan, Sanna, and Alex Ronkainen, Megan Murphy, and Caitlin Kelly gave us the energy, stamina, and inspiration to write this book.

Michael R. Czinkota
Ilkka A. Ronkainen
Michael H. Moffett
August, 1998

**Michael R. Czinkota** is on the faculty of marketing and international business of the Graduate School and the School of Business Administration at Georgetown University. From 1981 to 1986 he was the Chairman of the National Center for Export-Import Studies at the university. He has also held professorial appointments at universities in Asia, Australia, Europe, and the Americas.

From 1986 to 1989 Dr. Czinkota served in the U.S. government as Deputy Assistant Secretary of Commerce. He was responsible for macro trade analysis, departmental support of international trade negotiations and retaliatory actions, and policy coordination for international finance, investment, and monetary affairs. He also served as Head of the U.S. Delegation to the OECD Industry Committee in Paris and as Senior Trade Advisor for Export Controls.

Dr. Czinkota's background includes eight years of private sector business experience as a partner in an export-import firm and in an advertising agency and seventeen years of research and teaching in the academic world. He has been the recipient of research grants from various organizations, including the National Science Foundation, the National Commission of Jobs and Small Business, and the Organization of American States. He was listed as one of the three most published contributors to international business research in the *Journal of International Business Studies* and has written several books including *International Marketing, The Global Marketing Imperative,* and *Critical Issues in International Business.*

Dr. Czinkota served on the Board of Directors of the American Marketing Association and is on the Board of Governors of the Academy of Marketing Science and the editorial boards of the *Journal of Business Research, Journal of International Business Studies, International Marketing Review,* and *Asian Journal of Marketing.* He was named a Distinguished Fellow of the Academy of Marketing Science. For his work in international business and trade policy he has been awarded honorary degrees from the Universidad Poutificia Madre y Maestra in the Dominican Republic and the Universidad del Pacifico in Lima, Peru.

Dr. Czinkota has served as advisor to a wide range of individuals and institutions in the United States and abroad. He serves on several corporate boards; has worked with corporations such as AT&T, IBM, GE, Nestlé, and US WEST; and has assisted various governmental organizations in the structuring of effective trade promotion policies.

Dr. Czinkota was born and raised in Germany and educated in Austria, Scotland, Spain, and the United States. He studied law and business administration at the University of Erlangen–Nürnberg and was awarded a two-year Fullbright Scholarship. He holds an MBA in international business and a Ph.D. in logistics from The Ohio State University. He and his wife, Ilona, live in Luray, located in Virginia's Shenandoah Valley.

**Ilkka A. Ronkainen** is a member of the faculty of marketing and international business at the School of Business Administration at Georgetown University. From 1981 to 1986 he served as Associate Director and from 1986 to 1987 as Chairman of the National Center for Export-Import Studies.

Dr. Ronkainen serves as docent of international marketing at the Helsinki School of Economics. He was visiting professor at HSE during the 1987–1988 and 1991–1992 academic years and continues to teach in its Executive MBA, International MBA, and International BBA programs. Dr. Ronkainen holds a Ph.D. and a master's degree from the University of South Carolina as well as an M.S. (Economics) degree from the Helsinki School of Economics.

Dr. Ronkainen has published extensively in academic journals and the trade press. He is a co-author of *International Marketing*. He serves on the review boards of the *Journal of Business Research, International Marketing Review,* and *Journal of International Business Studies*. He served as the North American coordinator for the European Marketing Academy 1986–1990. He was a member of the board of the Washington International Trade Association from 1981 to 1986 and started the association's newsletter, Trade Trends.

Dr. Ronkainen has served as a consultant to a wide range of U.S. and international institutions. He has worked with entities such as IBM, the Rand Organization, and the Organization of American States. He maintains close relations with a number of Finnish companies and their internationalization and educational efforts.

## Michael H. Moffett is currently Associate Professor of Finance and International Business at the American Graduate School of International Management (Thunderbird). Dr. Moffett has a B.A. in Economics from the University of Texas at Austin (1977), an M.S. in Resource Economics from Colorado State University (1979), and M.A. and Ph.D. in International Economics from the University of Colorado–Boulder (1985).

Dr. Moffett has lectured at a number of universities around the world, including the Aarhus School of Business (Denmark), the Helsinki School of Economics and Business Administration (Finland), the Norwegian School of Economics (Norway), and the University of Ljubljana (Slovenia). Dr. Moffett has also lectured at a number of universities in the United States, including Trinity College, Washington D.C., and the University of Colorado–Boulder. He is a former visiting research fellow at the Brookings Institution, and he recently completed a two-year visiting professorship in the Department of International Business at the University of Michigan–Ann Arbor.

Michael Moffett's research publications have appeared in a number of academic journals, including the *Journal of International Money and Finance,* the *Journal of Financial and Quantitative Analysis, Contemporary Policy Issues,* and the *Journal of International Financial Management and Accounting*. He is co-author of *Multinational Business Finance,* eighth edition, 1998, with David Eiteman and Arthur Stonehill, as well as co-editor with Arthur Stonehill of *Transnational Financial Management* for the United Nations Centre for Transnational Corporations, 1993. He is a continuing contributor to numerous collective works in the fields of international finance and international business, including the *Handbook of Modern Finance* and the *International Accounting and Finance Handbook*. Dr. Moffett has also consulted with a number of private firms both in the United States and Europe.

# BRIEF CONTENTS

# CONTENTS

## 4  Politics and Laws    93

## PART 2  Theoretical Foundations    *151*

## 5  The Theory of International Trade and Investment    152

## 6 The International Economic Activity of the Nation: The Balance of Payments 182

## PART 3   The International Business Environment   *213*

## 9   Market Transitions and Development   286

# PART 4  International Business Preparation and Market Entry  *329*

## 10  International Business Research  330

## 11  International Business Entry  364

## 12  Multinational Corporations   391

## 16 International Logistics and Supply-Chain Management   537

## 17 Multinational Financial Mangement   572

## 18  Countertrade   608

## 19 International Accounting and Taxation 632

## 20 International Human Resource Management 659

# Maps

# THE IMPACT OF INTERNATIONAL BUSINESS

# PART 1

The globalization of business brings new opportunities and threats to governments, firms, and individuals. The challenge is to compete successfully in the global marketplace as it exists today and develops tomorrow.

Part 1 sets the stage by introducing the effects of international business and demonstrating the need to participate in international activities. In order to do so, one needs to be able to manage conflicts between cultures. This in turn requires an understanding of cultural differences in language, religion, values, customs, and education, so that one can develop cross-cultural competence. A chapter on culture addresses these dimensions.

In order to achieve an understanding of the political and legal dimensions which affect international business, this section highlights the policy issues surrounding the corporate decision maker and discusses the effect of politics and laws on business, together with the agreements, treaties, and laws that govern the relationships between home and host countries.

# CHAPTER 1

# The International Business Imperative

## LEARNING OBJECTIVES

◆ *To understand the history and importance of international business*

◆ *To learn the definition of international business*

◆ *To recognize the growth of global linkages today*

◆ *To understand the U.S. position in world trade and the impact international business has on the United States*

◆ *To appreciate the opportunities offered by international business*

## Cyberspace: The Trade Frontier

The Internet has burst onto the business scene, and its reach is global. The current trend toward electronic commerce poses serious challenges to the national and international agreements governing world trade. The rapid speed at which the Internet is evolving, combined with the explosion of business transactions in cyberspace, has raised doubts about whether governments will be able to provide order and stability in the sometimes chaotic electronic world. Some experts deem the Internet the "Wild West" of capitalism and argue that unless order is established, the projected growth in commercial transactions might not be as large as anticipated. They contend that the tenfold growth in world merchandise trade in the post–World War II era did not occur in a vacuum but under regulations brokered by the General Agreement on Tariffs and Trade and its successor, the World Trade Organization.

The significant growth of computer and Internet use has provided the impetus for a constantly changing business environment. Total trade in computers and software, the cornerstones of the new global information economy, currently exceeds $1 trillion and is forecast to exceed the $2 trillion mark within the next ten years. The Organization for Economic Cooperation and Development projects that within the next five to ten years up to $600 billion in purchases will be made annually on the Internet. The European Union predicted that electronic trade on the Internet and other electronic means could reach $100 billion annually by the year 2000 in the 15 EU states alone.

Internet supporters and skeptics alike agree that the faceless nature of cyberspace raises a host of policy questions, the most glaring of which is tax collection. The Internet eliminates not just national boundaries but also the identity of firms and individuals doing business, paving the way for exploitation of tax differences between nations. Since the Internet is not tied to a specific area, it is difficult to say which state or nation has tax jurisdiction. If a French consumer buys a software package from the local subsidiary of an American firm, for example, which country's tax applies? If the customer goes into a shop, the American firm's profit is taxed in France. If she downloads the software from the Internet, however, the lower American rates apply.

Issues such as these will plague government officials as the Internet increasingly expands its scope. Electronic trade, suggested one trade official, is likely to redefine the meaning of a traded good and cause massive problems in evaluating customs fees. Many experts believe that if the potential of the Internet is to be maximized, a framework of harmonized rules at both the national and international level must be developed.

*Sources:* "Taxes slip through the Net," *The Economist,* May 31, 1997 **http://www.economist.com;** John Zarocostas, "Limitations of Statutes," *The Journal of Commerce,* May 14, 1997: 1C.

WWW

## The Need For International Business

You are about to begin an exciting, important, and necessary task: the exploration of international business. International business is exciting because it combines the science and the art of business with many other disciplines, such as economics, anthropology, geography, history, language, jurisprudence, statistics, and demography. International business is important and necessary because economic isolationism has become impossible. Failure to become a part of the global market assures a nation of declining economic influence and a deteriorating standard of living for its citizens. Successful participation in international business, however, holds the promise of improved quality of life and a better society, even leading, some believe, to a more peaceful world.

International business offers companies new markets. Since the 1950s, the growth of international trade and investment has been substantially larger than the growth of domestic economies. As the opening vignette shows, technology continues to increase the reach and the ease of conducting international business, pointing to even larger growth potential in the future. A combination of domestic and international business, therefore, presents more opportunities for expansion, growth, and income than does domestic business alone. International business causes the flow of ideas, services, and capital across the world. As a result, innovations can be developed and disseminated more rapidly, human capital can be used better, and financing can take place more quickly. International business also offers consumers new choices. It can permit the acquisition of a wider variety of products, both in terms of quantity and quality, and do so at reduced prices through international competition. International business facilitates the mobility of factors of production—except land—and provides challenging employment opportunities to individuals with professional and entrepreneurial skills. Therefore, both as an opportunity and a challenge, international business is vital to countries, companies, and individuals.

## A Definition of International Business

International business consists of transactions that are devised and carried out across national borders to satisfy the objectives of individuals and organizations. These transactions take on various forms, which are often interrelated. Primary types of international business are export-import trade and direct foreign investment. The latter is carried out in varied forms, including wholly owned subsidiaries and joint ventures. Additional types of international business are licensing, franchising, and management contracts.

As the definition indicates, and as for any kind of domestic business, "satisfaction" remains a key tenet of international business. The fact that the transactions are *across national borders* highlights the difference between domestic and international business. The international executive is subject to a new set of macroenvironmental factors, to different constraints, and to quite frequent conflicts resulting from different laws, cultures, and societies. The basic principles of business still apply, but their application, complexity, and intensity may vary substantially.

The definition also focuses on international *transactions*. The use of this term recognizes that doing business internationally is an activity. Subject to constant change, international business is as much an art as a science. Yet success in the art of business depends on a firm grounding in its scientific aspects. Individual consumers, policymakers, and business executives with an understanding of both aspects will be able to incorporate international business considerations into their thinking and planning. They will be able to consider international issues and repercussions and make decisions related to questions such as these:

- How will our idea, good, or service fit into the international market?
- Should we enter the market through trade or through investment?
- What product adjustments are necessary to be responsive to local conditions?
- What threats from global competition should be expected?
- How can these threats be counteracted?

When management integrates these issues into each decision, international markets can provide growth, profit, and needs satisfaction not available to firms that limit their activities to the domestic marketplace. To aid in this decision process is the purpose of this book.

## A Brief History

Ever since the first national borders were formed, international business has been conducted by nations and individuals. In many instances, international business itself has been a major force in shaping borders and changing world history.

As an example, international business played a vital role in the formation and decline of the Roman Empire, whose impact on thought, knowledge, and development can still be felt today. Although we read about the marching of the Roman legions, it was not through military might that the empire came about. The Romans used the **Pax Romana,** or Roman peace, as a major stimulus. This ensured that merchants were able to travel safely and rapidly on roads built, maintained, and protected by the Roman legions and their affiliated troops. A second stimulus was the use of common coinage, which simplified business transactions and made them comparable throughout the empire. In addition, Rome developed a systematic law, central market locations through the founding of cities, and an effective communication system; all of these actions contributed to the functioning of the marketplace and a reduction of business uncertainty.

International business flourished within the empire, and the improved standard of living within the empire became apparent to those outside. Soon city-nations and tribes that were not part of the empire decided to join as allies. They agreed to pay tribute and taxes because the benefits were greater than the drawbacks.

Thus, the immense growth of the Roman Empire occurred mainly through the linkages of business. Of course, preserving this favorable environment required substantial effort. When pirates threatened the seaways, for example, Pompeius sent out a large fleet to subdue them. Once this was accomplished, the cost of international distribution within the empire dropped substantially because fewer shipments were lost at sea. Goods could be made available at lower prices, which in turn translated into larger demand.

Large firms are expanding around the globe. Once markets open up, multinational firms are quick to gain a foothold. Within a few years, PepsiCo has established itself in Vietnam.
*Source:* © Reuters/Corbis–Bettmann

The fact that international business was one of the primary factors that held the empire together can also be seen in the decline of Rome. When "barbaric" tribes overran the empire, again it was not mainly through war and prolonged battles that Rome had lost ground. Rather, outside tribes were attacking an empire that was already substantially weakened at its foundations because of infighting and increasing decadence. The Roman peace was no longer enforced, the use and acceptance of the common coinage had declined, and communications no longer worked as well. Therefore, affiliation with the empire no longer offered the benefits of the past. Former allies, who no longer saw any benefits in their association with Rome, willingly cooperated with invaders rather than face prolonged battles.

Similar patterns also can be seen in later eras. The British Empire grew mainly through its effective international business policy, which provided for efficient transportation, intensive trade, and an insistence on open markets.[1] More recently, the United States developed a world leadership position largely due to its championship of market-based business transactions in the Western world; the broad flow of ideas, goods, and services across national borders; and an encouragement of international communication and transportation. One could say the period from 1945 to 1990 was, for Western countries, characterized by a **Pax Americana,** an American peace.

Withholding the benefits of international business has also long been a tool of national policy. The use of economic coercion by nations or groups of nations, for example, can be traced back to the time of the Greek city-states and the Peloponnesian War. In the Napoleonic Wars, combatants used naval blockades to achieve their goal of "bringing about commercial ruin and shortage of food by dislocating trade."[2] Similarly, during the Civil War period in the United States, the North consistently pursued a strategy of denying international business opportunities to the South in order to deprive it of needed export revenues. More recently, the United Nations imposed a trade embargo against Iraq for its invasion and subsequent occupation of Kuwait in an attempt to ensure it had destroyed its chemical and biological weapons. Even though Iraq has resisted UN monitoring, its isolation from the trade community demonstrates the importance attributed to international business.

The importance of international business linkages was highlighted during the 1930s. At that time, the **Smoot-Hawley Act** raised import duties to reduce the volume of goods coming into the United States. The act was passed in the hope that it would restore domestic employment. The result, however, was retaliation by most trading partners. The ensuing worldwide depression and the collapse of the world financial system were instrumental in bringing about the events that led to World War II.

World trade and investment have assumed a heretofore unknown importance to the global community. In past centuries, trade was conducted internationally but not at the level or with the impact on nations, firms, and individuals that it has recently achieved. In the past 20 years alone, the volume of international trade in goods and services has expanded from $200 billion to more than $6.3 trillion.[3] As Figure 1.1 shows, the growth in the value of trade has greatly exceeded the level of overall world output growth.

During the same time, foreign direct investment grew fifteenfold, from $211 billion to more than $3.2 trillion in 1997.[4] **Multinational corporations** have invested in countries around the globe, with more than 800 of them having sales of more than $1 billion. Countries that had not been thought of as

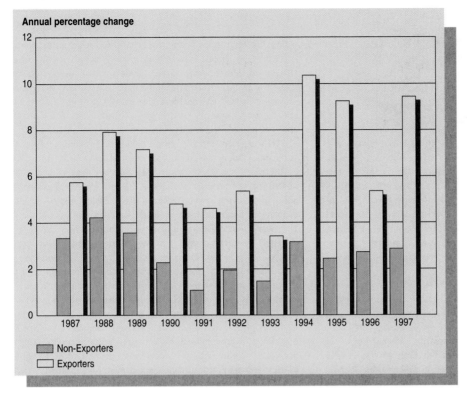

**Annual percentage change**

Non-Exporters
Exporters

**FIGURE 1.1**

**Growth of World Output and Trade, 1987–1997**
*Sources: World Economic and Social Survey 1997,* New York: United Nations, 1997, p. 44; UNCTAD, "World Investment Report," **http://www.unctad.org,** August 1997, and WTO, March 1998, **www.wto.org**.

major participants in international business have emerged as major economic powers. Individuals and firms have come to recognize that they are competing not only domestically but in a global marketplace. As a result, the international market has taken on a new dynamic, characterized by major change. Global Perspective 1.1 explains how this change offers both an opportunity and a threat.

## Global Linkages Today

International business had forged a network of **global linkages** around the world that binds us all—countries, institutions, and individuals—much closer than ever before. These linkages tie together trade, financial markets, technology, and living standards in an unprecedented way. They were widely recognized during the worldwide oil shock of the 1970s and have been apparent since then. A freeze in Brazil and its effect on coffee production are felt around the world. The sudden decline in the Mexican peso affected financial markets in the United States and reverberated throughout Poland, Hungary, and the Czech Republic. The economic turmoil in Asia affected stock markets, investments, and trade flows in all corners of the earth.

These linkages have also become more intense on an individual level. Communication has built new international bridges, be it through music or the watching of international programs transmitted by CNN **(www.cnn.com)**. New

# FREE TRADE NEEDS A DOMINANT CHAMPION

**T**he whole notion of reducing trade barriers is in serious trouble. Some of the sources of this trouble include the slow growth of most of the world's economies, increased competition from developing countries, global excess capacity in most industries, and, as a result of all of these forces, the politically disruptive weakness of job markets around the world. A little-noted problem may also undermine further attempts to negotiate trade pacts and even to keep commerce as open as it is now. No one is in a dominant position to impose free trade.

Only twice in history has free trade had such a powerful advocate, according to Susan B. Stanton, an economist at A. Gary Shilling & Co. She first cites the mid-nineteenth century, when Britain took advantage of its industrial head start and began liberalizing its trade in a search for markets for its greatly increased production. After a while, other industrializing nations followed Britain's path to prosperity and negotiated liberal trade agreements.

After World War II, Ms. Stanton writes, "The U.S., like 19th century Britain, was in a unique position to push for liberal trade." It had vastly expanded its industrial base during the war years, and it bore the cost of free trade to help rebuild other nations' economies and fortify Cold War allies.

But in the 1970s, the Bretton Woods monetary agreement and stable currency rates collapsed. Oil shocks and surging inflation further rattled financial markets. As other industrial nations, notably Japan, grew stronger, international competition sharpened. The ending of the Soviet threat weakened the Western alliance. And developing nations stepped up exports of manufactured goods. Now, the world's economies are facing this startling array of changes without a dominant nation able to uphold free trade.

"The sudden entry of three billion people from low-wage economies such as China, Mexico, and India into the global marketplace for goods, industries, and services is provoking new concerns among workers in the old industrial countries about their living standards," said David Hale, chief economist at Kemper Financial Companies. "Demographers project that practically all the growth in the world labor supply during the next half century will occur in developing nations." New technology will play a major role, too. The invasion of developing-world competitors into the marketplace will be facilitated by continuing improvements in worldwide communications. Almost across the board, technological change will keep wiping out old jobs while creating new ones.

Many people will blame the resulting turmoil in various industries and job markets on foreign competition. Without a dominant nation with the economic power and self-interest to demand free trade, these pressures, Ms. Stanton writes, will encourage protectionism and "the formation of inward-looking trade blocs" as "the individual domestic needs of countries overwhelm their international outlook." If protectionism spreads, unchecked by a strong, persistent free trade champion, the growth of international trade could slow down in coming decades and the world's economies would pay a heavy price.

*Source  Henry F. Meyers, "Free Trade Idea Needs a Dominant Champion," The Wall Street Journal, November 22, 1993, A1.*

products have attained international appeal and encouraged similar activities around the world—we wear blue jeans; we dance the same dances; we eat hamburgers, pizzas, and tacos.[5] Transportation linkages let individuals from different countries see and meet each other with unprecedented ease. Common cultural pressures result in similar social phenomena and behavior—for example, more dual-income families are emerging around the world, which leads to more frequent, but also more stressful, shopping.[6]

International business has also brought a global reorientation in production strategies. Only a few decades ago, for example, it would have been thought impossible to produce parts for a car in more than one country, assemble it in another, and sell it in yet other countries around the world. However, such global strategies, coupled with production and distribution sharing, are common today. Firms are also linked to each other through global supply agreements and joint undertakings in research and development. Figure 1.2 gives an example of how such linkages result in a final consumer product.

# FILTER

## BIG MAC UKRAINE

# Eat Locally, Spend Globally

Every three hours a new McDonald's opens somewhere on Earth. The menu varies somewhat from country to country—noodles in the Philippines, fries with mayo in the Netherlands—but there's one constant: the Big Mac, a towering illustration of the "glocal" economy at work. Whereas every Big Mac in the States is made from domestic ingredients (except for the sesame seeds), a foreign Big Mac uses ingredients from a variety of local and international suppliers. With over 21,000 restaurants in over a hundred countries, McDonald's relies on its overseas operations to generate half its $32 billion in sales. Here's a look at what goes into a Ukrainian Big Mac, and where it all comes from. —*Thomas Goetz*

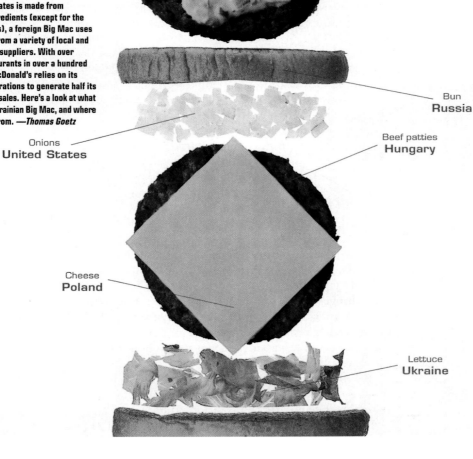

Sesame seeds
**Mexico**

Pickles
**Germany**

Special sauce
**Germany**

Bun
**Russia**

Onions
**United States**

Beef patties
**Hungary**

Cheese
**Poland**

Lettuce
**Ukraine**

## FIGURE 1.2

**The Global Components of a Big Mac in Ukraine**

Not only the production of goods has become global. Increasingly, service firms are part of the international scene. Banks, insurance companies, software firms, and universities are participating to a growing degree in the international marketplace. Firms and governments also are recognizing production's worldwide effects on the environment common to all. For example, high sulfur emissions in one area may cause acid rain in another. Pollution in one country may result in water contamination in another.

The level of **international investment** is at an unprecedented high. Multinational corporations conducting such investments have become corporate giants which, in terms of sales, can be bigger than entire nations. Ford's sales are greater than Saudi Arabia's and Norway's economies. Philip Morris's annual sales exceed New Zealand's gross domestic product.[7] Global investment strategies have had major effects on the patterns of trade. For example, many export and import flows are the result of multinational corporations shipping products to or from their subsidiaries. Such global investment also forces companies to recognize and play by new rules in areas such as business practices, legal requirements, and **ethics.** Global Perspective 1.2 explains some of this increase in complexity.

The United States, after having been a net creditor to the world for many decades, has been a world debtor since 1985. This means that the United States owes more to foreign institutions and individuals than they owe to U.S. entities. The shifts in financial flows have had major effects on international direct investment into plants as well. U.S. direct investment abroad in 1996 had a market value of more than $1.5 trillion; foreign investment in the United States had grown to $1.2 trillion. Currently one-third of the workers in the U.S. chemical industry toil for foreign owners.[8] Many U.S. office buildings are held by foreign landlords. The opening of plants abroad and in the United States increasingly takes the place of trade. All of these developments make us more and more dependent on one another.

This interdependence, however, is not stable. On an ongoing basis, realignments take place on both micro and macro levels that make past orientations at least partially obsolete. For example, for its first 200 years, the United States looked to Europe for markets and sources of supply. Despite the maintenance of this orientation by many individuals, firms, and policymakers, the reality of trade relationships has changed. U.S. two-way trade across the Pacific totalled $589 billion in 1997, $245 billion more than trade across the Atlantic.

At the same time, entirely new areas for international business activities have opened up. The East-West juxtaposition had for more than 40 years effectively separated the "Western" economies from the centrally planned ones. The lifting of the Iron Curtain presented a new array of trading and investment partners. As a result, trade and investment flows may again be realigned in different directions.

Concurrently, an increasing regionalization is taking place around the world, resulting in the split up of countries in some areas of the world and the development of country and trading blocs in others. Over time, firms may find that the free flow of goods, services, and capital encounters new impediments as regions become more inward looking.

Not only is the environment changing, but the pace of change is accelerating. "A boy who saw the Wright brothers fly for a few seconds at Kitty Hawk

## ETHICS AND INTERNATIONAL BUSINESS

**A**s the global economy becomes increasingly interdependent, cultural conflict becomes more prevalent. At the same time, societal concern for ethical corporate behavior is on the rise. These two forces intersect to highlight a particular problem of multinational businesses and any company involved in international trade or business. It is the problem of making ethical decisions when cultures have contradictory or inconsistent ethical perspectives.

Alternatives for responding to cross-cultural ethical conflict form a continuum, from complete adaptation to the host country's ethical standards to complete insistence on the application of home-country standards.

The view of adaptation encourages managers to become more familiar with a host culture, to avoid offending native sensibilities, and to build effective working relationships based on respect for the way things are done in the host country. Adaptation is also supported by the ethical stance of cultural relativism, which claims that the standards of each culture determine what is right in that culture.

On the other hand, many serious students of ethics are dissatisfied with any kind of relativism. They maintain that ethical standards are universal, and that cultural behavior that does not meet those standards should be identified as unethical. Thus, supporting governments that oppress their people or supporting ways of doing business that do not respect human life or that depend on deception are unacceptable, no matter what the culture.

In fact, neither adaptation nor relativism is satisfactory by itself. As managers face ethical conflicts, the appropriate strategies for dealing with them will depend on the nature of the specific ethical situation. The following is a range of possible responses to cross-cultural ethical conflict.

**Avoiding**—When a party simply chooses to ignore or not deal with the conflict; this response is often employed when the costs of dealing with the problem are high, due to, for example, massive legal fees or prolonged publicity.

**Forcing**—When one party forces its will upon another; often used when one part is stronger than the other, such a host country requiring payoffs.

**Education and Persuasion**—An attempt to convert others to one's position by providing information and through reasoning; for example, extolling the virtues of free enterprise.

**Infiltration**—Deliberately or not, by introducing values to another society an appealing idea may be spread.

**Negotiation and Compromise**—Both parties give up something yet one or both feel dissatisfied; for example, current U.S.–Japan trade negotiations.

**Accommodation**—One party adapts to the ethic of the other; for instance, an American business executive might learn to drink sake to do business in Japan.

**Collaboration and Problem Solving**—The parties work together to achieve a mutually satisfying solution, a win-win outcome, in which both their needs are met.

The appropriate response depends on the centrality of the values at stake, the degree of social consensus regarding the ethical issue, the decision maker's ability to influence the outcome, and the level of urgency surrounding the situation. Appropriate occasions exist for the use of each of these strategies.

*Source: John Kohls and Paul Buller, "Resolving Cross-Cultural Ethical Conflict: Exploring Alternative Strategies,"* Journal of Business Ethics *(1994): 31.*

in 1903 could have watched Apollo II land on the moon in 1969. The first electronic computer was built in 1946; today the world rushes from the mechanical into the electronic age. The double helix was first unveiled in 1953; today biotechnology threatens to remake mankind."[9]

These changes and the speed with which they come about significantly affect countries, corporations, and individuals. For example, the relative participation of countries in world trade is shifting. Over the past decades, the relative market share of Western Europe in trade has been declining. For the United States, the export share has declined while the import share has increased. Concurrent with these shifts, the global market shares of Japan, Southeast Asian countries, and China have increased.

# International Trade as a Percentage of Gross Domestic Product

Note: $\dfrac{\text{Exports} + \text{Imports}}{\text{GDP}}$ = International Trade Percentage

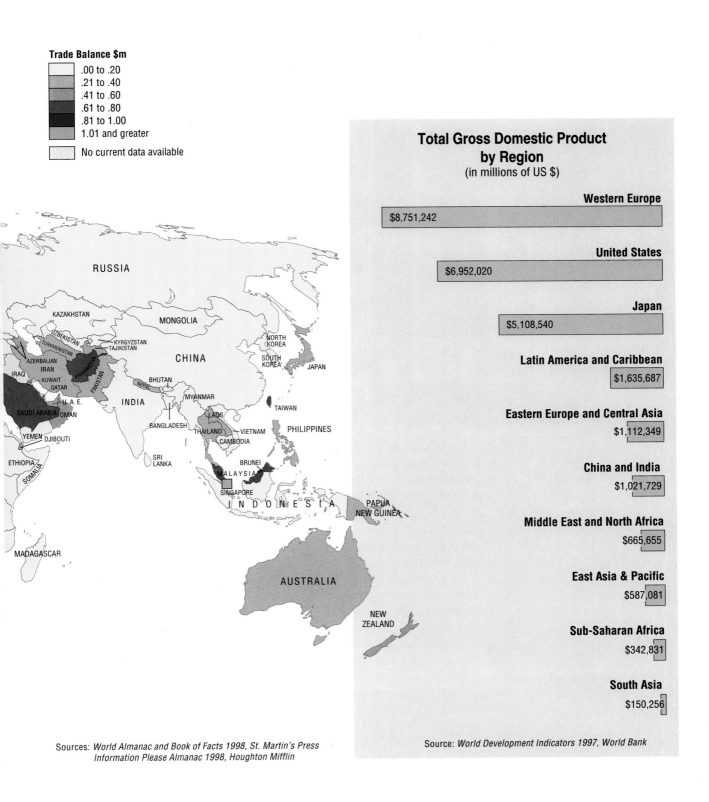

**Trade Balance $m**

- .00 to .20
- .21 to .40
- .41 to .60
- .61 to .80
- .81 to 1.00
- 1.01 and greater
- No current data available

## Total Gross Domestic Product by Region
(in millions of US $)

**Western Europe**
$8,751,242

**United States**
$6,952,020

**Japan**
$5,108,540

**Latin America and Caribbean**
$1,635,687

**Eastern Europe and Central Asia**
$1,112,349

**China and India**
$1,021,729

**Middle East and North Africa**
$665,655

**East Asia & Pacific**
$587,081

**Sub-Saharan Africa**
$342,831

**South Asia**
$150,256

Sources: *World Almanac and Book of Facts 1998*, St. Martin's Press
*Information Please Almanac 1998*, Houghton Mifflin

Source: *World Development Indicators 1997*, World Bank

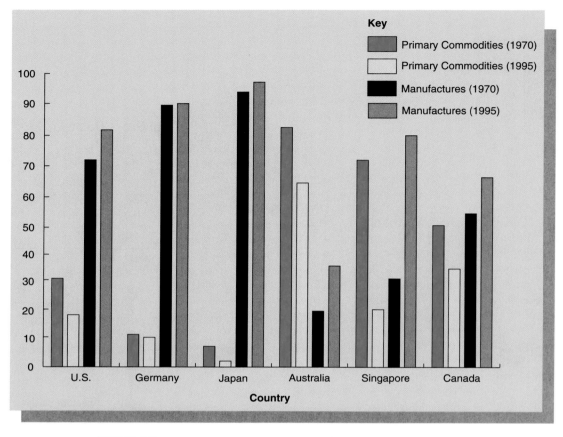

**FIGURE 1.3**

**The Changing Composition of Global Merchandise Exports**
*Source:* The World Bank, *World Development Report* 1996. **www.worldbank.org**

The **composition of trade** also has been changing. Figure 1.3 demonstrates the shift for some countries over time. In all instances, the role of primary commodities has dropped precipitously, while the importance of manufactured goods has increased, with major implications for farmers and industrial workers around the globe.

## The Current U.S. International Trade Position

From a global perspective, the United States has lost some of its importance as a supplier to the world but has gained in prominence as a market for the world. In spite of the decline in the global market share of U.S. exports, the international activities of the United States have not been reduced. On the contrary, exports have grown rapidly and successfully. However, many new participants have entered the international market. In Europe, firms in countries with war-torn economies following World War II have reestablished themselves.

In Asia, new competitors have aggressively obtained a share of the growing world trade. U.S. export growth was not able to keep pace with the total growth of world exports.

U.S. exports as a share of the GNP have grown substantially in recent years. However, this increase pales when compared with the international trade performance of other nations. Germany, for example, has consistently maintained an export share of more than 20 percent of GNP. Japan, in turn, which so often is maligned as the export problem child in the international trade arena, exports less than 10 percent of its GNP. Table 1.1 shows the degree to which the United States comparatively "underparticipates" in international business on a per capita basis, particularly on the export side.

Why should we worry about this underparticipation in trade? Why not simply concentrate on the large domestic market and get on with it? Why should it bother us that the largest portion of U.S. exports is attributed to only 2,500 companies? Why should it concern us that the U.S. Census Bureau estimates that less than two percent of all U.S. firms export?[10]

U.S. international business outflows are important on the **macroeconomic level** in terms of balancing the trade account. Lack of U.S. export growth has resulted in long-term trade deficits. In 1983, imports of products into the United States exceeded exports by more than $70 billion. This deficit rose to a record $171 billion in 1987. While in the ensuing years exports increased at a rapid rate, import growth also continued. As a result, in 1997, the U.S. merchandise trade deficit had risen $210 billion. Ongoing annual trade deficits in this range are still unsupportable in the long run. Such deficits add to the U.S. international debt, which must be serviced and eventually repaid. Exporting is not only good for the international trade picture but also a key factor in increasing employment. It has been estimated that $1 billion of exports supports the creation, on average, of 15,500 jobs and that by the turn of the century, more than 15 million U.S. jobs will be linked to exports.[11] Imports, in turn, bring a wider variety of products and services into a country. They exert competitive pressure for domestic firms to improve. Imports, therefore, expand the choices of consumers and improve their standard of living.

## The Impact of International Business on the United States

**TABLE 1.1**

**Exports and Imports per Capita for Selected Countries (1998)**

| Country | Exports per Capita | Imports per Capita |
|---|---|---|
| Canada | $6,903 | $6,484 |
| Germany | 6,236 | 5,384 |
| Japan | 3,341 | 2,683 |
| Mexico | 1,111 | 1,141 |
| Netherlands | 12,357 | 11,273 |
| Taiwan | 5,545 | 5,136 |
| United Kingdom | 4,844 | 5,311 |
| United States | 2,551 | 3,225 |

*Source:* Census Bureau, **www.census.gov** April 6, 1998; International Trade Administration **www.ita.doc.gov**, April 9, 1998; World Trade Organization, **www.wto.org**, March 19, 1998.

On the **microeconomic level,** participation in international business can help firms achieve economies of scale that cannot be achieved in domestic markets. Addressing a global market greatly adds to the number of potential customers. Increasing production lets firms ride the learning curve more quickly and therefore makes goods available more cheaply at home. Finally, and perhaps most important, international business permits firms to hone their competitive skills abroad by meeting the challenge of foreign products. By going abroad, firms can learn from their foreign competitors, challenge them on their ground, and translate the absorbed knowledge into productivity improvements back home. Firms that operate only in the domestic market are at risk of being surprised by the onslaught on foreign competition and thus seeing their domestic market share threatened. Research has shown that U.S. multinationals of all sizes and in all industries outperformed their strictly domestic counterparts—growing more than twice as fast in sales and earning significantly higher returns on equity and assets.[12] Workers also benefit. As Figure 1.4 shows, exporting firms of all sizes pay significantly higher wages than nonexporters.

The United States as a nation and as individuals must therefore seek more involvement in the global market. The degree to which Americans can successfully do business internationally will be indicative of their competitiveness and so help to determine their future standard of living.

As Global Perspective 1.3 shows, individual firms and entire industries are coming to recognize that in today's trade environment isolation is no longer possible. Both the willing and unwilling are becoming participants in global business affairs. Most U.S. firms are affected directly or indirectly by economic

**FIGURE 1.4**

**Average Plant Salary and Wages (Per Worker, Dollars per Hour)**
*Source: Business America,* Vol. 117, No. 9, September 1996, p. 9.

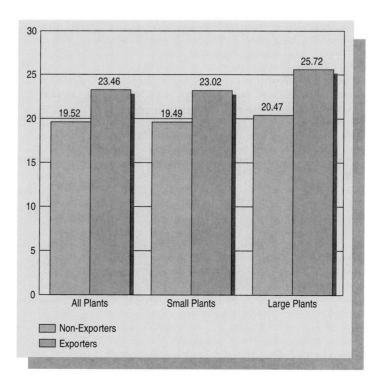

## SMALL U.S. FIRMS ARE MOVING FORWARD IN THE GLOBAL MARKETPLACE

**A** report by the United Nations confirms what the U.S. business community is all too aware of: Small and medium-sized companies in the United States are far behind their counterparts in other countries in setting up foreign operations. Compared with Japan and Western Europe, the United States has a relatively small percentage of corporate direct investment abroad from companies with fewer than 500 employees at their home sites. Small and medium-sized U.S. companies have $15 billion in foreign direct investments, 3 percent of the U.S. total. Similar size Japanese companies had $40 billion (15 percent) and developed European countries had about $43 billion (7.5 percent), according to the report.

Hopes are, however, that this tendency within the United States will shift as global business accelerates. There are some encouraging signs. The larger size of the U.S. marketplace was the main reason so many smaller companies tended to stay home, according to one of the authors of the report. Now, U.S. overseas presence has taken a big jump since the early 1980s because even small and medium-sized companies are beginning to feel competition from less developed countries. In addition, more firms are finding it easier to manage foreign operations or a joint venture because "recent technological developments in communications, transportation, and financial services have enabled firms of all sizes to better exploit international opportunities."

The growth in exports by U.S. companies of all sizes may well accelerate the pace of direct investments, according to John Williams, chief global economist of Bankers Trust Company. The weakness of the dollar, which makes U.S. goods cheaper for foreign customers, is giving many companies their first taste of foreign sales, he noted. "In the mid-1980s, when the dollar was much stronger, far fewer U.S. companies could compete."

Adds John Endean, vice president of the American Business Conference, "What we found with our members was that they start as exporters and move very quickly to rolling out direct investments to enhance or supplant their export strategy."

*Source: Fred R. Bleakley, "Smaller Firms in U.S. Avoid Business Abroad,"* The Wall Street Journal, *August 24, 1993, A7.*

and political developments in the international marketplace. Firms that refuse to participate actively are relegated to reacting to the global economy. Consider how the industrial landscape in the United States has been restructured in the past decade as a result of international business.

Many industries experience the need for international adjustments. U.S. farmers, because of high prices, increased international competition, trade-restricting government actions, and unfair foreign trade practices, have lost world market share. U.S. firms in technologically advanced industries, such as semiconductor producers, saw the prices of their products and their sales volumes drop precipitously because of global competition. As a result of competition, many industries have adjusted, but with great pain. Examples abound in the steel, automotive, and textile sectors of the U.S. economy.

Still other U.S. industries never fully recognized what had happened and, therefore, in spite of attempts to adjust, were not successful and have ceased to exist. VCRs are no longer produced domestically. Only a small percentage of motorcycles are manufactured in the United States. The shoe industry is in its death throes.

These developments demonstrate that it has become virtually impossible to disregard the powerful impact that international business now has on all of us. Temporary isolation may be possible and delay tactics may work for a while, but the old adage applies: You can run, but you cannot hide. Participation in the world market has become truly imperative.

Global activities offer many additional opportunities to business firms. Market saturation can be delayed by lengthening or rejuvenating the life of products in other countries. Sourcing policies that once were inflexible have become variable because plants can be shifted from one country to another and suppliers can be found on every continent. Cooperative agreements can be formed that enable each party to bring its major strength to the table and emerge with better goods, services, and ideas than it could on its own. Consumers all over the world can select from among a greater variety of products at lower prices, which enables them to improve their choices and lifestyles.

All of these opportunities need careful exploration if they are to be realized. What is needed is an awareness of global developments, an understanding of their meaning, and a development of the capability to adjust to change. Judging by the global linkages found in today's market and the rapid changes taking place, a background in international business is highly desirable for business students seeking employment. **Globalization** is the watchword that "describes the need for companies and their employees, if they are to prosper, to treat the world as their stage."[13]

## The Structure of the Book

This book in intended to enable you to become a better, more successful participant in the global business place. It is written for both those who want to attain more information about what is going on in international markets in order to be more well-rounded and better educated and for those who want to translate their knowledge into successful business transactions. The text melds theory and practice to balance conceptual understanding and knowledge of day-to-day realities. The book, therefore, addresses the international concerns of both beginning internationalists and multinational corporations.

The beginning international manager will need to know the answers to basic, yet important, questions: How can I find out whether demand for my product exists abroad? What must I do to get ready to market internationally? These issues are also relevant for managers in multinational corporations, but the questions they consider are often much more sophisticated. Of course, the resources available to address them are also much greater.

Throughout the book, public policy concerns are included in discussions of business activities. In this way, you are exposed to both macro and micro issues. Part 1 of the book introduces the importance of international business; discusses the interaction between international business and the nation-state; and addresses policy, political, legal, and cultural issues. Part 2 presents the theoretical dimensions of international trade and investment and explains the effect of international economic activities on a country. Part 3 covers the macroenvironment for international business and highlights the role of the international monetary system, economic integration, and economic development. Part 4 presents the research activities required to properly prepare for international business and lays out the options for market entry. Part 5 then addresses all the business management issues relevant to international business, using a strategic and applied perspective.

We hope that upon finishing the book, you will not only have completed another academic subject but also be well versed in the theoretical, policy, and strategic aspects of international business and therefore will be able to contribute to improved international competitiveness.

## Summary

International business has been conducted ever since national borders were formed and has played a major role in shaping world history. Growing in importance over the past three decades, it has shaped an environment that, due to economic linkages, today presents us with a global marketplace.

In the past two decades, world trade has expanded from $200 billion to more than $6.3 trillion, while international direct investment has grown from $211 billion to $3.2 trillion. The growth of both has been far more rapid than the growth of most domestic economies. As a result, nations are much more affected by international business than in the past. Global linkages have made possible investment strategies and business alternatives that offer tremendous opportunities. Yet these changes and the speed of change also can represent threats to nations and firms.

Over the past 30 years, the dominance of the U.S. international trade position has gradually eroded. Increasingly, new participants in international business compete fiercely for world market share, and U.S. firms have fallen behind in their global competitiveness.

Yet, times are changing. Individuals, corporations, and policymakers have awakened to the fact that international business is a major imperative and offers opportunities for future growth and prosperity. International business provides access to new customers, affords economies of scale, and permits the honing of competitive skills. Performing well in global markets is the key to improved standards of living, higher profits, and better wages. Knowledge about international business is therefore important to everyone, whether it is used to compete with foreign firms or simply to understand the world around us.

## Key Terms and Concepts

- Pax Romana
- Smoot-Hawley Act
- multinational corporation
- global linkages
- macroeconomic level
- microeconomic level
- Pax Americana
- international investment
- ethics
- composition of trade
- globalization

## Questions for Discussion

1. Will future expansion of international business be similar to that in the past?
2. Does increased international business mean increased risk?
3. Is it beneficial for nations to become dependent on one another?
4. Discuss the reasons for the decline in the U.S. world trade market share.
5. With wages in some countries at one-tenth of U.S. wages, how can America compete?

6. Compare and contrast domestic and international business.
7. Why do more firms in other countries enter international markets than do firms in the United States?
8. Using World Trade Organization data (shown on the International Trade page of its web site, **www.wto.org**), determine the following information: (a) the fastest growing traders, (b) the top ten exporters and importers in world merchandise trade, and (c) the top ten exporters or importers of commercial services.

## Recommended Readings

Czinkota, Michael R., and Masaaki Kotabe, eds. *Trends in International Business.* Oxford: Blackwell, 1998.

Czinkota, Michael R., Ilkka A. Ronkainen, and John J. Tarrant. *The Global Marketing Imperative.* Chicago: NTC, 1995.

Jones, Geoffrey. *The Evolution of International Business.* New York: Routledge, 1996.

Marquardt, Michael J., and Angus Reynolds. *The Global Learning Organization.* Burr Ridge, Ill.: Irwin, 1994.

Naisbitt, John. *Global Paradox.* New York: William Morrow, 1994.

Porter, Michael E. *The Competitive Advantage of Nations.* New York: The Free Press, 1990.

Reich, Robert B. *The Work of Nations: Preparing Ourselves for 21st-Century Capitalism,* New York: Random House, 1992.

Rodrik, Dani. *Has Globalization Gone Too Far?* Washington, DC: Institute for International Economics, 1997.

Svetlicic, Marjan, and H.W. Singer, eds. *The World Economy: Challenges of Globalization and Regionalization.* New York: St. Martin's Press, 1996.

## Notes

1. Paul R. Krugman, "What Do Undergraduates Need to Know about Trade?" AEA Papers and Proceedings, May 1993: 23–26.
2. Margaret P. Doxey, *Economic Sanctions and International Enforcement* (New York: Oxford University Press, 1980), 10.
3. World Trade Organization, "International Trade," **http://www.wto.org** December 1997.
4. UN Conference on Trade and Development, "World Investment Report," **http://www.unctad.org** August 1997.
5. Michael Marquardt and Angus Reynolds, *The Global Learning Organization* (Burr Ridge, Ill.: Irwin, 1994), vi.
6. Eugene H. Fram and Riad Ajami, "Globalization of Markets and Shopping Stress: Cross-Country Comparisons," *Business Horizons,* January-February 1994, 17–23.
7. Richard J. Barnet and John Cavanagh, *Global Dreams: Imperial Corporations and the New World Order* (New York: Simon and Schuster, 1994). 14.
8. Manufacturers Alliance, *Globalization of the Economy: Implications of Foreign Investment in U.S. Manufacturing* (Arlington, VA: Manufacturers Alliance), 1997.
9. Arthur M. Schlesinger, Jr., *The Cycles of American History* (Boston: Houghton Mifflin, 1986), XI.
10. *Characteristics of Business Owners,* US Bureau of the Census, Washington D.C., November 5, 1997.
11. *U.S. Jobs Supported by Exports of Goods and Services* (U.S. Department of Commerce, Washington D.C.), June 17, 1996; *U.S. Department of Commerce—The Big Emerging Markets: 1996 Outlook and Source Book* (Washington D.C., Bernan Press. 1996), 27.
12. Charles Taylor and Witold Henisz, *U.S. Manufacturers in the Global Market Place,* Report 1058, The Conference Board, 1994.
13. "Management Education," *The Economist,* March 2, 1991, 7.

# APPENDIX 1

# Geographical Perspectives on International Business[1]

The dramatic changes in the world of business have made geography indispensable for the study of international business. Without significant attention to the study of geography, critical ideas and information about the world in which business occurs will be missing.

Just as the study of business has changed significantly in recent decades, so has the study of geography. Once considered by many to be simply a descriptive inventory that filled in blank spots on maps, geography has emerged as an analytic approach that uses scientific methods to answer important questions.

Geography focuses on answering "Where?" questions. Where are things located? What is their distribution across the surface of the earth? An old aphorism holds, "If you can map it, it's geography." That statement is true, because one uses maps to gather, store, analyze, and present information that answers "Where?" questions. But identifying where things are located is only the first phase of geographic inquiry. Once locations have been determined, "Why?" and "How?" questions can be asked. Why are things located where they are? How do different things relate to one another at a specific place? How do different places relate to each other? How have geographic patterns and relationships changed over time? These are the questions that take geography beyond mere description and make it a powerful approach for analyzing and explaining geographical aspects of a wide range of different kinds of problems faced by those engaged in international business.

Geography answers questions related to the location of different kinds of economic activity and the transactions that flow across national boundaries. It provides insights into the natural and human factors that influence patterns of production and consumption in different parts of the world. It explains why patterns of trade and exchange evolve over time. And because a geographic perspective emphasizes the analysis of processes that result in different geographic patterns, it provides a means for assessing how patterns might change in the future.

---

[1]This appendix was contributed by Thomas J. Baerwald. Dr. Baerwald is deputy assistant director for the geosciences at the National Science Foundation in Arlington, Virginia. He is co-author of *Prentice Hall World Geography*—a best-selling geography textbook.

Geography has a rich tradition. Classical Greeks, medieval Arabs, enlightened European explorers, and twentieth-century scholars in the United States and elsewhere have organized geographic knowledge in many different ways. In recent decades, however, geography has become more familiar and more relevant to many people because emphasis has been placed on five fundamental themes as ways to structure geographic questions and to provide answers for those questions. Those themes are (1) location, (2) place, (3) interaction, (4) movement, and (5) region. The five themes are neither exclusive nor exhaustive. They complement other disciplinary approaches for organizing information, some of which are better suited to addressing specific kinds of questions. Other questions require insights related to two or more of the themes. Experience has shown, however, that the five themes provide a powerful means for introducing students to the geographic perspective. As a result, they provide the structure for this discussion.

## Location

For decades, people engaged in real estate development have said that the value of a place is a product of three factors: location, location, and location. This statement also highlights the importance of location for international business. Learning the location and characteristics of other places has always been important to those interested in conducting business outside their local areas. The drive to learn about other kinds of places, and especially their resources and potential as markets, has stimulated geographic exploration throughout history. Explorations of the Mediterranean by the Phoenicians; Marco Polo's journey to China; and voyages undertaken by Christopher Columbus, Vasco de Gama, Henry Hudson, and James Cook not only improved general knowledge of the world but also expanded business opportunities.

Assessing the role of location requires more than simply determining specific locations where certain activities take place. Latitude and longitude often are used to fix the exact location of features on the Earth's surface, but to simply describe a place's coordinates provides relatively little information about that place. Of much greater significance is its location relative to other features. The city of Singapore, for example, is between 1 and 2 degrees North latitude and is just west of 104 degrees East longitude. Its most pertinent locational characteristics, however, include its being at the southern tip of the Malay Peninsula near the eastern end of the Strait of Malacca, a critical shipping route connecting the Indian Ocean with the South China Sea. For nearly 150 years, this location made Singapore an important center for trade in the British Empire. After attaining independence in 1965, Singapore's leaders diversified its economy and complemented trade in its bustling port with numerous manufacturing plants that export products to nations around the world.

An understanding of how location influences business therefore is critical for the international business executive. Without clear knowledge of an enterprise's location relative to its suppliers, to its market, and to its competitors, an executive operates like the captain of a fog-bound vessel that has lost all navigational instruments and is heading for dangerous shoals.

## *Place*

In addition to its location, each place has a diverse set of characteristics. Although many of those characteristics are present in other places, the ensemble makes each place unique. The characteristics of places—both natural and human—profoundly influence the ways that business executives in different places participate in international economic transactions.

## Natural Features

Many of the characteristics of a place relate to its natural attributes. **Geologic characteristics** can be especially important, as the presence of critical minerals or energy resources may make a place a world-renowned supplier of valuable products. Gold and diamonds help make South Africa's economy the most prosperous on that continent. Rich deposits of iron ore in southern parts of the Amazon Basin have made Brazil the world's leading exporter of that commodity, while Chile remains a preeminent exporter of copper. Coal deposits provided the foundation for massive industrial development in the eastern United States, the Rhine River Basin of Europe, in western Russia, and in northeastern China. Because of abundant pools of petroleum beneath desert sands, standards of living in Saudi Arabia and nearby nations have risen rapidly to be among the highest in the world.

The geology of place also shapes its **terrain.** People traditionally have clustered in lower, flatter areas, because valleys and plains have permitted the agricultural development necessary to feed the local population and to generate surpluses that can be traded. Hilly and mountainous areas may support some people, but their population densities invariably are lower. Terrain also plays a critical role in focusing and inhibiting the movement of people and goods. Business leaders throughout the centuries have capitalized on this fact. Just as feudal masters sought control of mountain passes in order to collect tolls and other duties from traders who traversed an area, modern executives maintain stores and offer services near bridges and at other points where terrain focuses travel.

The terrain of a place is related to its **hydrology.** Rivers, lakes, and other bodies of water influence the kinds of economic activities that occur in a place. In general, abundant supplies of water boost economic development, because water is necessary for the sustenance of people and for both agricultural and industrial production. Locations like Los Angeles and Saudi Arabia have prospered despite having little local water, because other features offer advantages that more than exceed the additional costs incurred in delivering water supplies from elsewhere. While sufficient water must be available to meet local needs, overabundance of water may pose serious problems, such as in Bangladesh, where development has been inhibited by frequent flooding. The character of a place's water bodies also is important. Smooth-flowing streams and placid lakes can stimulate transportation within a place and connect it more easily with other places, while waterfalls and rapids can prevent navigation on streams. The rapid drop in elevation of such streams may boost their potential for hydroelectric power generation, however, thereby stimulating development of industries requiring considerable amounts of electricity. Large plants producing aluminum, for example, are found in the Tennessee and Columbia river valleys of the United States and in Quebec and British Columbia in Canada. These plants refine materials that originally were extracted elsewhere, especially bauxite and alumina from Caribbean nations like Jamaica and the Dominican Republic. Although the transport costs incurred in delivery of these materials to the plants is high, those costs are more than offset by the presence of abundant and inexpensive electricity.

**Climate** is another natural feature that has profound impact on economic activity within a place. Many activities are directly affected by climate. Locales blessed with pleasant climates, such as the Côte d'Azur of France, the Crimean Peninsula of Ukraine, Florida, and the "Gold Coast" of northeastern Australia, have become popular recreational havens, attracting tourists whose spending fuels the local economy. Agricultural production also is influenced by climate. The average daily and evening temperatures, the amount and timing of precipitation, the timing of frosts and freezing weather, and the variability of weather from one year to the next all influence the kinds of crops grown in an area. Plants producing bananas and sugar cane flourish in moist tropical areas, while cooler climates are more conductive for crops such as wheat and potatoes. Climate influences other industries, as well. The aircraft manufacturing industry in the United States developed largely in warmer, drier areas where conditions for test and delivery flights were most beneficial throughout the year. In a similar way, major rocket-launching facilities have been placed in locations where climatic conditions and trajectories are most favorable. As a result, the primary launch site of the European Space Agency is not in Europe at all but rather in the South American territory of French Guiana. Climate also affects the length of the work day and the length of economic seasons. For example, in some regions of the world, the construction industry can build only during a few months of the year because permafrost makes construction prohibitively expensive the rest of the year.

Variations in **soils** have a profound impact on agricultural production. The world's great grain-exporting regions, including the central United States, the Prairie Provinces of Canada, the "Fertile Triangle" stretching from central Ukraine through southern Russia into northern Kazakhstan, and the Pampas of northern Argentina, all have been blessed with mineral-rich soils made even more fertile by humus from natural grasslands that once dominated the landscape. Soils are less fertile in much of the Amazon Basin of Brazil and in central Africa, where heavy rains leave few nutrients in upper layers of the soil. As a result, few commercial crops are grown in those areas.

The **interplay between climate and soils** is especially evident in the production of wines. Hundreds of varieties of grapes have been bred to take advantage of the different physical characteristics of various places. The wines fermented from these grapes are shipped around the world to consumers, who differentiate among various wines based not only on the grapes but also on the places where they were grown and the conditions during which they matured.

## Human Features

The physical features of a place provide natural resources and influence the types of economic activities in which people engage, but its human characteristics also are critical. The **population** of a place is important because farm production may require intensive labor to be successful, as is true in rice-growing areas of eastern Asia. The skills and qualifications of the population also play a role in determining how a place fits into global economic affairs. Although blessed with few mineral resources and a terrain and climate that limit agricultural production, the Swiss have emphasized high levels of education and training in order to maintain a labor force that manufactures sophisticated products for export around the world. In recent decades, Japan and smaller nations such as South Korea and Taiwan have increased the productivity of their workers to become major industrial exporters.

As people live in a place, they modify it, creating a **built environment** that can be as or more important than the natural environment in economic terms. The most pronounced areas of human activity and their associated structures are in cities. In nations around the world, cities have grown dramatically during the twentieth century. Much of the growth of cities has resulted from the migration of people from rural areas. This influx of new residents broadens the labor pool and creates vast new demand for goods and services. As urban populations have grown, residences and other facilities have replaced rural land uses. Executives seeking to conduct business in foreign cities need to be aware that the geographic patterns found in their home cities are not evident in many other nations. For example, in the United States, wealthier residents generally have moved outward and as they established their residences, stores and services followed. Residential patterns in the major cities of Latin America and other developing nations tend to be reversed, with the wealthy remaining close to the city center while poorer residents are consigned to the outskirts of town. A store location strategy that is successful in the United States therefore may fail miserably if transferred directly to another nation without knowledge of the different geographic patterns of that nation's cities.

## Interaction

The international business professional seeking to take advantage of opportunities present in different places learns not to view each place separately. How a place functions depends not only on the presence and form of certain characteristics but also on interactions among those characteristics. Fortuitous combinations of features can spur a region's economic development. The presence of high-grade supplies of iron ore, coal, and limestone powered the growth of Germany's Ruhr Valley as one of Europe's foremost steel-producing regions, just as the proximity of the fertile Pampas and the deep channel of the Rio de la Plata combine to make Buenos Aires the leading economic center in southern South America.

Interactions among different features change over time within places, and as they do, so does that place's character and its economic activities. Human activities can have profound impacts on natural features. The courses of rivers and streams are changed, as dams are erected and meanders are straightened. Soil fertility can be improved through fertilization. Vegetation is changed, with naturally growing plants replaced by crops and other varieties that require careful management.

Many human modifications have been successful. For centuries, the Dutch have constructed dikes and drainage systems, slowly creating polders—land that once was covered by the North Sea but that now is used for agricultural production. But other human activities have had disastrous impacts on natural features. A large area in Ukraine and Belarus was rendered uninhabitable by radioactive materials leaked from the Chernobyl reactor in 1986. In countless other places around the globe, improper disposal of wastes has seriously harmed land and water resources. In some places, damage can be repaired, as has happened in rivers and lakes of the United States following the passage of measures to curb water pollution in the last three decades, but in other locales, restoration may be impossible.

Growing concerns about environmental quality have led many people in more economically advanced nations to call for changes in economic systems that harm the natural environment. Concerted efforts are under way, for example, to halt destruction of forests in the Amazon Basin, thereby preserving the vast array of different plant and animal species in the region and saving vegetation that can help moderate the world's climate. Cooperative ventures have been established to promote selective harvesting of nuts, hardwoods, and other products taken from natural forests. Furthermore, an increasing number of restaurants and grocers are refusing to purchase beef raised on pastures that are established by clearing forests.

Like so many other geographical relationships, the nature of human-environmental interaction changes over time. With technological advances, people have been able to modify and adapt to natural features in increasingly sophisticated ways. The development of air conditioning has permitted people to function more effectively in torrid tropical environments, thereby enabling the populations of cities such as Houston, Rio de Janeiro, and Jakarta to multiply many times over in recent decades. Owners of winter resorts now can generate snow artificially to ensure favorable conditions for skiers. Advanced irrigation systems now permit crops to be grown in places such as the southwestern United States, northern Africa, and Israel. The use of new technologies may cause serious problems over the long run, however. Extensive irrigation in large parts of the U.S. Great Plains has seriously depleted groundwater supplies. In central Asia, the diversion of river water to irrigate cotton fields in Kazakhstan and Uzbekistan has reduced the size of the Azal Sea by more than one-half since 1960. In future years, business leaders may need to factor into their decisions additional costs associated with the restoration of environmental quality after they have finished using a place's resources.

## Movement

Whereas the theme of interaction encourages consideration of different characteristics within a place, movement provides a structure for considering how different places relate to each other. International business exists because movement permits the transportation of people and goods and communication of information and ideas among different places. No matter how much people in one place want something found elsewhere, they cannot have it unless transportation systems permit the good to be brought to them or allow them to move to the location of the good.

The location and character of transportation and communication systems long have had powerful influences on the economic standing of places. Especially significant have been places on which transportation routes have focused. Many ports have become prosperous cities because they channeled the movement of goods and people between ocean and inland waterways. New York became the largest city in North America because its harbor provided sheltered anchorage for ships crossing the Atlantic; the Hudson River provided access leading into the interior of the continent. In eastern Asia, Hong Kong grew under similar circumstances, as British traders used its splendid harbor as an exchange point for goods moving in and out of southern China.

Businesses also have succeeded at well-situated places along overland routes. The fabled oasis of Tombouctou has been an important trading center for centuries because it had one of the few dependable sources of water in the Sahara. Chicago's ascendancy as the premier city of the U.S. heartland came when its early leaders engineered its selection as the termination point for a dozen railroad lines converging from all directions. Not only did much of the rail traffic moving through the region have to pass through Chicago, but passengers and freight passing through the city had to be transferred from one line to another, a process that generated numerous jobs and added considerably to the wealth of many businesses in the city.

In addition to the business associated directly with the movement of people and goods, other forms of economic activity have become concentrated at critical points in the transportation network. Places where transfers from one mode of transportation to another were required often were chosen as sites for manufacturing activities. Buffalo was the most active flour-milling center in the United States for much of the twentieth century because it was the point where Great Lakes freighters carrying wheat from the northern Great Plains and Canadian prairies were unloaded. Rather than simply transfer the wheat into rail cars for shipment to the large urban markets of the northeastern United States, millers transformed the wheat into flour in Buffalo, thereby reducing the additional handling of the commodity.

Global patterns of resource refining also demonstrate the wisdom of careful selection of sites with respect to transportation systems. Some of the world's largest oil refineries are located at places like Bahrain and Houston, where pipelines bring oil to points where it is processed and loaded onto ships in the form of gasoline or other distillates for transport to other locales. Massive refinery complexes also have been built in the Tokyo and Nagoya areas of Japan and near Rotterdam in the Netherlands to process crude oil brought by giant tankers from the Middle East and other oil-exporting regions. For similar reasons, the largest new steel mills in the United States are near Baltimore and Philadelphia, where iron ore shipped from Canada and Brazil is processed. Some of the most active aluminum works in Europe are beside Norwegian fjords, where abundant local hydroelectric power is used to process imported alumina.

Favorable location along transportation lines is beneficial for a place. Conversely, an absence of good transportation severely limits the potential for firms to succeed in a specific place. Transportation patterns change over time, however, and so does their impact on places. Some places maintain themselves because their business leaders use their size and economic power to become critical nodes in newly evolving transportation networks. New York's experience provides a good example of this process. New York became the United States's foremost business center in the early nineteenth century because it was ideally situated for water transportation. As railroad networks evolved later in that century, they sought New York connections in order to serve its massive market. During the twentieth century, a complex web of roadways and major airports reinforced New York's supremacy in the eastern United States. In similar ways, London, Moscow, and Tokyo reasserted themselves as transportation hubs for their nations through successive advances in transport technology.

Failure to adapt to changing transportation patterns can have deleterious impacts on a place. During the middle of the nineteenth century, business leaders in St. Louis discouraged railroad construction, seeking instead to maintain the supremacy of river transportation. Only after it became clear that railroads were the mode of preference did St. Louis officials seek to develop rail connections for the city, but by then it was too late; Chicago had ascended to a dominant position in the region. For about 30 years during the middle part of the twentieth century, airports at Gander, Newfoundland, Canada, and Shannon, Ireland, became important refueling points for trans-Atlantic flights. The development of planes that could travel nonstop for much longer distances returned those places to sleepy oblivion.

Continuing advances in transportation technology effectively have "shrunk" the world. Just a few centuries ago, travel across an ocean took harrowing months. As late as 1873, readers marveled then Jules Verne wrote of a hectic journal around the world in 80 days. Today's travelers can fly around the globe in less than 80 hours, and the speed and dependability of modern modes of transport have transformed the ways in which business is conducted. Modern manufacturers have transformed the notion of relationships among suppliers, manufacturers, and markets. Automobile manufacturers, for example, once maintained large stockpiles of parts in assembly plants that were located near the parts plants or close to the places where the cars would be sold. Contemporary auto assembly plants now are built in places where labor costs and worker productivity are favorable and where governments have offered attractive inducements. They keep relatively few parts on hand, calling on suppliers for rapid delivery of parts as they are needed when orders for new cars are received. This "just-in-time" system of production leaves manufacturers subject to disruptions caused by work stoppages at supply plants and to weather-related delays in the transportation system, but losses associated with these infrequent events are more than offset by reduced operating costs under normal conditions.

The role of advanced technology as a factor affecting international business is even more apparent with respect to advances in communications systems. Sophisticated forms of telecommunication that began more than 150 years ago with the telegraph have advanced through the telephone to facsimile transmissions and electronic mail networks. As a result, distance has practically ceased to be a consideration with respect to the transmission of information. Whereas information once moved only as rapidly as the person carrying the paper on which the information was written, data and ideas now can be sent instantaneously almost anywhere in the world.

These communication advances have had a staggering impact on the way that international business is conducted. They have fostered the growth of multinational corporations, which operate in diverse sites around the globe while maintaining effective links with headquarters and regional control centers. International financial operations also have been transformed because of communication advances. Money and stock markets in New York, London, Tokyo, and Frankfurt now are connected by computer systems that process transactions around the clock. As much as any other factor, the increasingly mobile forms of money have enabled modern business executives to engage in activities around the world.

## Regions

In addition to considering places by themselves or how they relate to other places, regions provide alternative ways to organize groups of places in more meaningful ways. A region is a set of places that share certain characteristics. Many regions are defined by characteristics that all of the places in the group have in common. When economic characteristics are used, the delimited regions include places with similar kinds of economic activity. Agricultural regions include areas where certain farm products dominate. Corn is grown throughout the "Corn Belt" of the central United States, for example, although many farmers in the region also plant soybeans and many raise hogs. Regions where intensive industrial production is a prominent part of local economic activity include the manufacturing belts of the northeastern United States, southern Canada, northwestern Europe, and southern Japan.

Regions can also be defined by patterns of movement. Transportation or communication linkages among places may draw them together into configurations that differentiate them from other locales. Studies by economic geographers of the locational tendencies of modern high-technology industries have identified complex networks of firms that provide products and services to each other. Because of their linkages, these firms cluster together into well-defined regions. The "Silicon Valley" of northern California, the "Western Crescent" on the outskirts of London, and "Technopolis" of the Tokyo region all are distinguished as much by connections among firms as by the economic landscapes they have established.

Economic aspects of movement may help define functional regions by establishing areas where certain types of economic activity are more profitable than others. In the early nineteenth century, German landowner Johann Heinrich von Thünen demonstrated how different costs for transporting various agricultural goods to market helped to define regions where certain forms of farming would occur. Although theoretically simple, patterns predicted by von Thünen can still be found in the world today. Goods such as vegetables and dairy products that require more intensive production and are more expensive to ship are produced closer to markets, while less demanding goods and commodities that can be transported at lower costs come from more remote production areas. Advances in transportation have dramatically altered such regional patterns, however. Whereas a New York City native once enjoyed fresh vegetables and fruit only in the summer and early autumn when New Jersey, upstate New York, and New England producers brought their goods to market, New Yorkers today buy fresh produce year-round, with new shipments flown in daily from Florida, California, Chile, and even more remote locations during the colder months.

Governments have a strong impact on the conduct of business, and the formal borders of government jurisdictions often coincide with the functional boundaries of economic regions. The divisive character of these lines on the map has been altered in many parts of the world in recent decades, however. The formation of common markets and free trade areas in Western Europe and North America has dramatically changed the patterns and flows of economic activity, and similar kinds of formal restructuring of relationships among nations likely will continue into the next century. As a result, business analysts increasingly need to consider regions that cross international boundaries.

Some of the most innovative views of regional organization essentially have ignored existing national boundaries. In 1981, Joel Garreau published a book titled *The Nine Nations of North America,* which subdivided the continent into a set of regions based on economic activities and cultural outlooks. Seven of Garreau's nine regions include territory in at least two nations. In the Southwest, "Mexamerica" recognized the bicultural heritage of Anglo and Hispanic groups and the increasingly close economic ties across the U.S.–Mexican border that were spurred by the *maquiladora* and other export-oriented programs. The evolution of this region as a distinctive collection of places has been accelerated by the passage of the North American Free Trade Agreement (NAFTA). Another cross-national region identified by Garreau is "The Islands," a collection of nations in the Caribbean for which Miami has become the functional "capital." Many business leaders seeking to tap into this rapidly growing area have become knowledgeable of the laws and customs of those nations. They often have done so by employing émigrés from those nations who may now be U.S. citizens but whose primary language is not English and whose outlook on the region is multinational.

In a similar vein, Darrell Delamaide's 1994 book entitled *The New Superregions of Europe* divides the continent into ten regions based on economic, cultural, and social affinities that have evolved over centuries. His vision of Europe challenges regional structures that persist from earlier times. Seen by many as a single region known as Eastern Europe, the formerly communist nations west of what once was the Soviet Union are seen by Delamaide as being part of five different "superregions": "The Baltic League," a group of nations clustered around the Baltic Sea; "Mitteleuropa," the economic heartland of northern Europe; "The Slavic Federation," a region dominated by Russia with a common Slavic heritage; "The Danube Basin," a melange of places along and near Europe's longest river; and "The Balkan Peninsula," a region characterized by political turmoil and less advanced economies.

Delamaide's book has been as controversial as Garreau's was a decade earlier. In both cases, however, the value of the ideas they presented was not measured in terms of the "accuracy" of the regional structures they presented, but rather by their ability to lead more people to take a geographic perspective of the modern world and how it functions. The regions defined by Garreau and Delamaide are not those described by traditional geographers, but they reflect the views of many business leaders who have learned to look across national boundaries in their search for opportunities. As business increasingly becomes international, the most successful entrepreneurs will be the ones who complement their business acumen with effective application of geographic information and principles.

## References Cited

Darrell Delamaide. *The New Superregions of Europe.* New York: Dutton, a division of Penguin Books, 1994.

Joel Garreau. *The Nine Nations of North America.* New York: Houghton Mifflin Co., 1981.

# CHAPTER 2

# Culture and International Business

### LEARNING OBJECTIVES

◆ *To define and demonstrate the effect of culture's various dimensions on international business*

◆ *To examine ways in which cultural knowledge can be acquired and individuals and organizations prepared for cross-cultural interaction*

◆ *To illustrate ways in which cultural risk poses a challenge to the effective conduct of business communications and transactions*

◆ *To suggest ways in which international businesses act as change agents in the diverse cultural environments in which they operate*

## Us and Them

**C**ultural diversity is everywhere. Managers both at home and abroad must plan strategies without assuming mutual understanding. People from different cultures share basic concepts but view them from different angles and perspectives, leading them to behave in ways that may seem irrational or even directly contradictory to what others consider appropriate. It is critical to remember that while all managers evaluate and criticize others' behavior, their own actions are also coming under scrutiny. The following perceptions of U.S. managers' practices highlight the point.

**Hans Riedel, Germany; Executive Vice President/**
**Sales and Marketing, Porsche AG**
We are coming from two different cultures, but we have to deal with each other. This starts with little things such as scheduling meetings on Thanksgiving. It does not show up in our [German] calendars or in our perceptions, but we should make it our business to know about this most important holiday. The same should go for Americans and German holidays.

**Jaime Zevada, Mexico; Manager of Investor Relations, Bufete Industrial, S.A.**
Time represents something else for an American than for a Mexican. If you have a meeting at 1:30, for a Mexican that could mean 1:45 or 2:00. It's a normal thing, everyone is late in Mexico, but it takes time for U.S. managers to understand this. In Mexico, we begin working at 9:00 or 9:30. We have breakfast meetings, with lots of food. Then we have a big lunch and siesta from 3:00 to 5:00. We are back at 5:00, then work until 9:00 or 10:00 at night. Similarly, the concept of law is different in Mexico. We try to tell our U.S. counterparts that here, when you handle relationships with the government, you invite their representatives for the weekend or you take them to dinner. To handle the union leader, it is the same thing. It is not written anywhere, but it is something you just do.

**Maciej Kosinski, Poland; Founder and President, EMTV/Euromedia**
Americans are intellectually open. If they do not understand where we are coming from, they are ready to listen. When we were working on the script for the Polish version of *Sesame Street,* we wanted to title one segment "Who is Afraid of the Black Beast?" The Americans were concerned, but for them it had racial connotations. But we explained that in Poland "The Black Beast" is a nursery rhyme, and it has nothing to do with race, which was accepted by the Americans. It is flexibility that Germans, for example, would never show. What does bother me, however, is the imperial tone that some of the big American companies adopt when they talk to us. It is always about how they know best and

how we should learn from them. We are really allergic to that in Central Europe, because for many years we had Big Brother on our backs.

**Hiroshi Tsujimura, Japan; Co-Chief Executive Officer,**
**Nomura Securities International**

Asians and Europeans are more interested in the long term while Americans are short term, meaning less than one year. If we have a project that is only going to be profitable in the long term, Americans are difficult to convince that it is worth doing. That affects what kind of deals get done with the Americans.

**Kim Samuel-Johnson, Canada; Director, The Samuel Group**

All Americans care about is size. Unless you are a huge company, with a well-known name, you are not worth their time.

*Source:* Stephan Herrera, "Damn Yankees," *Forbes* (March 10, 1997): 22–23; and Richard D. Lewis, *When Cultures Collide* (London: Nicholas Brealy Publishing, 1997): 2.

The ever-increasing level of world trade, opening of new markets, and intensifying competition have allowed—and sometimes forced—businesses to expand their operations. The challenge for managers is to handle the different values, attitudes, and behavior that govern human interaction. First, managers must ensure smooth interaction of the business with its different constituents, and second, they must assist others to implement programs within and across markets. It is no longer feasible to think of markets and operations in terms of domestic and international. Because the separation is no longer distinguishable, the necessity of culturally sensitive management and personnel is paramount.

As firms expand their operations across borders, they acquire new customers and new partners in new environments. Two distinct tasks become necessary: first, to understand cultural differences and the ways they manifest themselves and, second, to determine similarities across cultures and exploit them in strategy formulation. Success in new markets is very much a function of cultural adaptability: patience, flexibility, and appreciation of others' beliefs.[1] Recognition of different approaches may lead to establishing best practice; that is, a new way of doing things applicable throughout the firm. Ideally, this means that successful ideas can be transferred across borders for efficiency and adjusted to local conditions for effectiveness. Take the case of Nestlé. In one of his regular trips to company headquarters in Switzerland, the general manager of Nestlé Thailand was briefed on a summer coffee promotion from the Greek subsidiary, a cold coffee concoction called the Nescafe Shake. The Thai Group swiftly adopted and adapted the idea. It designed plastic containers to mix the drink and invented a dance, the Shake, to popularize the activity.[2]

Cultural competence must be recognized as a key management skill.[3] Cultural incompetence, or inflexibility, can easily jeopardize millions of dollars through wasted negotiations; lost purchases, sales, and contracts; and poor customer relations. Furthermore, the internal efficiency of a multinational corporation may be weakened if managers and workers are not "on the same wavelength." The tendency for U.S. managers is to be open and informal, but in some cultural settings that may be inappropriate. Similar hurdles are highlighted in the opening vignette. **Cultural risk** is just as real as political risk in the international business arena.

The intent of this chapter is to analyze the concept of culture and its various elements and then to provide suggestions for meeting the cultural challenge.

## Culture Defined

Culture gives an individual an anchoring point, an identity, as well as codes of conduct. Of the more than 160 definitions of culture analyzed by Kroeber and Kluckhohn, some conceive of culture as separating humans from nonhumans, some define it as communicable knowledge, and some as the sum of historical achievements produced by man's social life.[4] All of the definitions have common elements: Culture is learned, shared, and transmitted from one generation to the next. Culture is primarily passed on from parents to their children but also transmitted by social organizations, special interest groups, the government, schools, and churches. Common ways of thinking and behaving that are developed are then reinforced through social pressure. Geert Hofstede calls this the "collective programming of the mind."[5] Culture is also multidimensional, consisting of a number of common elements that are interdependent. Changes occurring in one of the dimensions will affect the others as well.

For the purposes of this text, culture is defined as an *integrated system of learned behavior patterns that are characteristic of the members of any given society.* It includes everything that a group thinks, says, does, and makes—its customs, language, material artifacts, and shared systems of attitudes and feelings.[6] The definition, therefore, encompasses a wide variety of elements from the materialistic to the spiritual. Culture is inherently conservative, resisting change and fostering continuity. Every person is encultured into a particular culture, learning the "right way" of doing things. Problems may arise when a person encultured in one culture has to adjust to another one. The process of **acculturation**—adjusting and adapting to a specific culture other than one's own—is one of the keys to success in international operations.

Edward T. Hall, who has made some of the most valuable studies on the effects of culture on business, makes a distinction between high- and low-context cultures.[7] In **high-context cultures,** such as Japan and Saudi Arabia, context is at least as important as what is actually said. The speaker and the listener rely on a common understanding of the context. In **low-context cultures,** however, most of the information is contained explicitly in the words. North American cultures engage in low-context communications. Unless one is aware of this basic difference, messages and intentions can easily be misunderstood. As an example, performance appraisals are typically a human resources function. If performance appraisals are to be centrally guided or conducted in a multinational corporation, those involved must be acutely aware of cultural nuances. One of the interesting differences is that the U.S. system emphasizes the individual's development, whereas the Japanese system focuses on the group within which the individual works. In the United States, criticism is more direct and recorded formally, whereas in Japan it is more subtle and verbal. What is not being said can carry more meaning than what is said.

Few cultures today are as homogeneous as those of Japan and Saudi Arabia. Elsewhere intracultural differences based on nationality, religion, race, or geographic areas have resulted in the emergence of distinct subcultures. The international manager's task is to distinguish relevant cross-cultural and intracultural differences and then to isolate potential opportunities and problems. Good examples are the Hispanic subculture in the United States and the Flemish and the Walloons in Belgium. On the other hand, borrowing and interaction among national cultures may narrow gaps between cultures. Here the international business entity acts as a **change agent** by introducing new products or ideas and practices. Although this may only shift consumption from one product brand to another, it may also lead to massive social change in the manner of consumption, the type of products consumed, and social organization. Consider, for example, that in the past ten years the international portion of McDonald's annual sales grew from 13 percent to 59 percent.[8] In markets such as Taiwan, 1 of the 106 countries entered, the entry of McDonald's and other fast-food entities dramatically changed eating habits, especially of the younger generation.

In bringing about change or in trying to cater to increasingly homogeneous demand across markets, the international business entity may be accused of "cultural imperialism," especially if the changes brought about are dramatic or if culture-specific adaptations are not made in management or marketing programs. Some countries, such as Brazil, Canada, France, and Indonesia, protect their "cultural industries" (such as music and motion pictures) through restrictive rules and subsidies. The 1993 GATT agreement that allows restrictions on exports of U.S. entertainment to Europe is justified by the Europeans as a cultural safety net intended to preserve national and regional identities.[9] Similarly, the example of Kentucky Fried Chicken in India illustrates the difficulties marketers may have in entering culturally complex markets. Even though the company opened its outlets in two of India's most cosmopolitan cities (Bangalore and New Delhi), it found itself the target of protests by a wide range of opponents. KFC could have alleviated or eliminated some of the anti-Western passions by tailoring its activities to the local conditions. First, rather than opting for more direct control, KFC should have allied itself with local partners for advice and support. Second, KFC should have tried to appear more Indian rather than using high-profile advertising with Western ideas. Indians are ambivalent towards foreign culture, and its ideas may not always work well there. Finally, KFC should have planned for competition, which came from small restaurants with political clout at the local level.[10]

## The Elements of Culture

The study of culture has led to generalizations that may apply to all cultures. Such characteristics are called **cultural universals,** which are manifestations of the total way of life of any group of people. These include such elements as bodily adornment, courtship rituals, etiquette, concept of family, gestures, jok-

**TABLE 2.1**

**Elements of Culture**

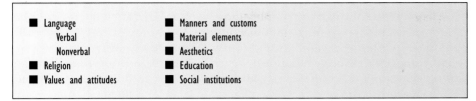

■ Language   ■ Manners and customs
    Verbal   ■ Material elements
    Nonverbal   ■ Aesthetics
■ Religion   ■ Education
■ Values and attitudes   ■ Social institutions

ing, mealtime customs, music, personal names, status differentiation, and trade customs.[11] These activities occur across cultures, but they may be uniquely manifested in a particular society, bringing about cultural diversity. Common denominators can indeed be found across cultures, but cultures may vary dramatically in how they perform the same activities.[12]

Observation of the major cultural elements summarized in Table 2.1 suggests that these elements are both material (such as tools) and abstract (such as attitudes). The sensitivity and adaptation to these elements by an international firm depends on the firm's level of involvement in the market—for example, licensing versus direct investment—and the good or service marketed. Naturally, some goods and services or management practices require very little adjustment, while some have to be adapted dramatically.

## Language

Language has been described as the mirror of culture. Language itself is multidimensional by nature. This is true not only of the spoken word but also of what can be called the nonverbal language of international business. Messages are conveyed by the words used, by how the words are spoken (for example, tone of voice), and through nonverbal means such as gestures, body position, and eye contact.

Very often mastery of the language is required before a person is acculturated to a culture other than his or her own. Language mastery must go beyond technical competency, because every language has words and phrases that can be readily understood only in context. Such phrases are carriers of culture; they represent special ways a culture has developed to view some aspect of human existence.

Language capability serves four distinct roles in international business.[13] Language is important in information gathering and evaluation. Rather than rely completely on the opinions of others, the manager is able to see and hear personally what is going on. People are far more comfortable speaking their own language, and this should be treated as an advantage. The best intelligence on a market is gathered by becoming part of the market rather than observing it from the outside. For example, local managers of a multinational corporation should be the firm's primary source of political information to assess potential risk. Second, language provides access to local society. Although English may be widely spoken and may even be the official company language, speaking the local language may make a dramatic difference. Third, language capability is increasingly important in company communications, whether within the corporate family or with channel members. Imagine the difficulties encountered by a country manage who must communicate with employees through an interpreter. Finally, language provides more than the ability to communicate. It extends beyond mechanics to the interpretation of contexts.

The manager's command of the national language(s) in a market must be greater than simple word recognition. Consider, for example, how dramatically different English terms can be when used in Australia, the United Kingdom, or the United States. In negotiations, U.S. delegates "tabling a proposal" mean that they want to delay a decision, while their British counterparts understand the expression to mean that immediate action is to be taken. If the British promise something "by the end of the day," this does not mean within 24 hours, but rather when they have completed the job. Additionally, they may say that negotiations "bombed," meaning that they were a success, which to an American could convey exactly the opposite message.

The two advertising campaigns presented in Figure 2.1 highlight the difficulties of transferring advertising campaigns across markets. Electrolux's theme for vacuum cleaners is taken literally in the United Kingdom, but in the United States, slang implications interfere with the intended message. With Lucky Goldstar, adaptation into Arabic was carried out without considering that Arabic reads from right to left. As a result, the creative concept in this executive was destroyed.

The role of language extends beyond that of a communication medium. Linguistic diversity often is an indicator of other types of diversity. In Quebec, the French language has always been a major consideration of most francophone governments, because it is one of the clear manifestations of the province's identity vis-à-vis the English-speaking provinces. The Charter of the

**FIGURE 2.1**

**Example of Ads That Transferred Poorly**

*Sources:* "Viewpoint," *Advertising Age,* June 29, 1987, 20; Mourad Boutros, "Lost in Translation," *M&M Europe,* September 1992, iv–v.

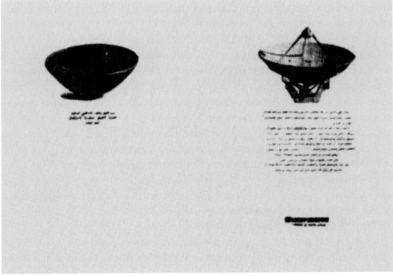

French Language states that the rights of the francophone collectivity are (1) the right of every person to have the civil administration, semipublic agencies, and business firms communicate with him of her in French; (2) the rights of workers to carry on their activities in French; and (3) the right of consumers to be informed and served in French. The Bay, a major Quebec retailer, spends $8 million annually on translation. It has even changed its name to La Baie in appropriate areas.

Dealing with language invariably requires local assistance. A good local advertising agency and a good local market research firm can prevent many problems. When translation is required, as when communicating with suppliers or customers, care should be taken in selecting the translator. The old saying, "If you want to kill a message, translate it," is true in that what needs to be conveyed is a feeling, which may require dramatically different terms than is achieved through a purely technical translation. To make sure, the simplest method of control is **backtranslation**—translating a foreign language version back to the original language by a different person than the one who made the first translation. This approach may be able to detect only omissions and blunders, however. To asses the quality of the translation, a complete evaluation with testing of the message's impact is necessary.[14]

## Nonverbal Language

Managers also must analyze and become familiar with the hidden language of foreign cultures.[15] Five key topics—time, space, material possessions, friendship patterns, and business agreements—offer a starting point from which managers can begin to acquire the understanding necessary to do business in foreign countries. In many parts of the world, time is flexible and not seen as a limited commodity; people come late to appointments or may not come at all. In Hong Kong, for example, it is futile to set exact meeting times, because getting from one place to another may take minutes or hours depending on the traffic situation. Showing indignation or impatience at such behavior would astonish an Arab, Latin American, or Asian. Understanding national and cultural differences in the concept of time is critical for an international business manager.

In some countries, extended social acquaintance and the establishment of appropriate personal rapport are essential to conducting business. The feeling is that one should know one's business partner on a personal level before transactions can occur. Therefore, rushing straight to business will not be rewarded, because deals are made on the basis of not only the best product or price but also the entity or person deemed most trustworthy. Contracts may be bound on handshakes, not lengthy and complex agreements—a fact that makes some, especially Western, businesspeople uneasy.

Individuals vary in the amount of space they want separating them from others. Arabs and Latin Americans like to stand close to people when they talk. If an American, who may not be comfortable at such close range, backs away from an Arab, this might incorrectly be taken as a negative reaction. Also, Westerners are often taken aback by the more physical nature of affection between Slavs—for example, being kissed squarely on the lips by a business partner, regardless of sex.

International body language must be included in the nonverbal language of international business. For example, an American manager may, after successful completion of negotiations, impulsively give a finger-and-thumb OK sign. In southern France, the manager would have indicated that the sale was worthless and, in Japan that a little bribe had been requested; the gesture would be grossly insulting to Brazilians. An interesting exercise is to compare and contrast the conversation styles of different nationalities. Northern Europeans are quite reserved in using their hands and maintain a good amount of personal space, whereas southern Europeans involve their bodies to a far greater degree in making a point.

**Religion**      In most cultures, people find in religion a reason for being and legitimacy in the belief that they are of a larger context. To define religion requires the inclusion of the supernatural and the existence of a higher power. Religion defines the ideals for life, which in turn are reflected in the values and attitudes of societies and individuals. Such values and attitudes shape the behavior and practices of institutions and members of cultures.

Religion has an impact on international business that is seen in a culture's values and attitudes toward entrepreneurship, consumption, and social organization. The impact will vary depending on the strength of the dominant religious tenets. While religion's impact may be quite indirect in Protestant Northern Europe, its impact in countries where Islamic fundamentalism is on the rise (such as Algeria) may be profound.

Religion provides the basis for transcultural similarities under shared beliefs and behavior. The impact of these similarities will be assessed in terms of the dominant religions of the world, Christianity, Islam, Hinduism, Buddhism, and Confucianism. While some countries may officially have secularism, such as Marxism-Leninism as a state belief (for example, China, Vietnam, and Cuba), traditional religious beliefs still remain a powerful force in shaping behavior.

International business managers must be aware of differences not only among the major religions but within those religions. The impact of the divisions may range from hostility, as in Sri Lanka, to barely perceptible historic suspicion, as in many European countries where Protestant and Catholic are the main divisions. With some religions, such as Hinduism, people may be divided into groups, and business managers need to understand the positions and the status of the groups to achieve efficient human resource management.

**Christianity** has the largest following among world religions, with more than 1.8 billion people.[16] While there are many subgroups within Christianity, the major division is between Catholicism and Protestantism. A prominent difference between the two is the attitude toward making money. While Catholicism has questioned it, the Protestant ethic has emphasized the importance of work and the accumulation of wealth for the glory of God. At the same time, frugality was emphasized and the residual accumulation of wealth from hard work formed the basis for investment. It has been proposed that the work ethic is responsible for the development of capitalism in the western world and the rise of predominantly Protestant countries into world economic leadership in the twentieth century.[17]

Major holidays are often tied to religion. Holidays are observed differently from one culture to the next, to the extent that the same holiday may have different connotations. Christian cultures observe Christmas and exchange gifts on either December 24 or December 25, with the exception of the Dutch, who exchange gifts on St. Nicholas Day, December 6. Tandy Corporation, in its first year in the Netherlands, targeted its major Christmas promotion for the third week of December with less than satisfactory results. The international manager must see to it that local holidays are taken into account in scheduling events ranging from fact-finding missions to marketing programs and in preparing local work schedules.

**Islam,** which reaches from the west coast of Africa to the Philippines and across a broad band that includes Tanzania, central Asia, western China, India, and Malaysia, has more than 1 billion followers.[18] Islam is also a significant minority religion in many parts of the world, including Europe. Islam has a pervasive role in the life of its followers, referred to as Muslims, through the Sharia (law of Islam). This is most obvious in the five stated daily periods of prayer, fasting during the holy month of Ramadan, and the pilgrimage to Mecca, Islam's holy city. While Islam is supportive of entrepreneurship, it nevertheless strongly discourages acts that may be interpreted as exploitation. Islam is also absent of discrimination, except those outside the religion. Some have argued that Islam's basic fatalism (that is, nothing happens without the will of Allah) and traditionalism have deterred economic development in countries observing the religion.

The role of women in business is tied to religion, especially in the Middle East, where women do not function as they would in the West. This affects the conduct of business in various ways; for example, the firm may be limited in its use of female managers or personnel in these markets, and women's role as consumers and influencers in the consumption process may be different. Access to women in Islamic countries may only be possible through the use of female sales personnel, direct marketing, and women's specialty shops.[19] Religion impacts goods and services, as well. When beef or poultry is exported to an Islamic country, the animal must be killed in the "halal" method and certified appropriately. Recognition of religious restrictions on products (for example, alcoholic beverages) can reveal opportunities, as evidenced by successful launches of several nonalcoholic beverages in the Middle East. Other restrictions may call for innovative solutions. A challenge for the Swedish firm that had the primary responsibility for building a traffic system to Mecca was that non-Muslims are not allowed access to the city. The solution was to use closed-circuit television to supervise the work. Given that Islam considers interest payments usury, bankers and Muslim scholars have worked to create interest-free banking that relies on lease agreements, mutual funds, and other methods to avoid paying interest.[20]

**Hinduism** has 750 million followers, mainly in India, Nepal, Malaysia, Guyana, Suriname, and Sri Lanka. It actually is not a religion, but a way of life predicated on the caste, or class to which one is born. While the caste system has produced social stability, its impact on business can be quite negative. For example, if it is difficult to rise above one's caste, individual effort is hampered. Problems in work force integration and coordination may become quite severe. Furthermore, the drive for business success may not be important if followers place value mostly on spiritual rather than materialistic achievement.

The family is an important element of Hindu society, with extended families being a norm. The extended family structure affects the purchasing power and consumption of Hindu families, and market researchers, in particular, must take this into account in assessing market potential and consumption patterns.

**Buddhism,** which extends its influence throughout Asia from Sri Lanka to Japan, has 334 million followers. Although it is an offspring of Hinduism, it has no caste system. Life is seen as filled with suffering, with achieving nirvana—a spiritual state marked by an absence of desire—as the solution. The emphasis in Buddhism is on spiritual achievement rather than worldly goods.

**Confucianism** has 150 million followers throughout Asia, especially among the Chinese, and has been characterized as a code of conduct rather than a religion. However, its teachings, which stress loyalty and relationships, have been broadly adopted. Loyalty to central authority and placing the good of a group before that of the individual may explain the economic success of Japan, South Korea, Singapore, and the Republic of China. It also has led to cultural misunderstandings: Western societies often perceive the subordination of the individual to the common good as a violation of human rights. The emphasis on relationships is very evident in developing business ties in Asia. Preparation may take years before understanding is reached and actual business transactions can take place.

## Values and Attitudes

Values are shared beliefs or group norms that have been internalized by individuals.[21] Attitudes are evaluations of alternatives based on these values. Differences in cultural values affect the way planning is executed, decisions are made, strategy is implemented, and personnel are evaluated. Table 2.2 provides examples of how U.S. values differ from other values around the world and how this, in turn, affects management functions. These cultural values have to be accommodated or used in the management of business functions.

The more rooted values and attitudes are in central beliefs (such as religion), the more cautiously one has to move. Attitude toward change is basically positive in industrialized countries, as is one's ability to improve one's lot in life; in tradition-bound societies, however, change is viewed with suspicion—especially when it comes from a foreign entity.

The Japanese culture raises an almost invisible—yet often unscalable—wall against all *gaijin* (foreigners). Many middle-aged bureaucrats and company officials believe that buying foreign products is downright unpatriotic. The resistance is not so much to foreign products as to those who produce and market them. Similarly, foreign-based corporations have had difficulty hiring university graduates or midcareer personnel because of bias against foreign employers. Even under such adverse conditions, the race can be run and won through tenacity, patience, and drive. As an example, Procter & Gamble has made impressive inroads with its products by adopting a long-term Japanese-style view of profits.

Cultural differences themselves can be a selling point suggesting luxury, prestige, or status. Occasionally, U.S. firms successfully use American themes abroad that would not succeed at home. In Japan, Levi Strauss promoted its popular jeans with a television campaign featuring James Dean and Marilyn Monroe, who represent the epitome of Japanese youths' fantasy of freedom from a staid, traditional society. The commercials helped establish Levi's as *the* prestige jeans, and status-seeking Japanese youth were willing to pay 40 percent more for them than local brands. Their authentic Levi's, however, are designed and mostly made in Japan, where buyers like a tighter fit. Similarly, many global

**TABLE 2.2**

**Effect of Value Differences On Management Practice**

| Value of U.S. Culture | Alternative Value | Management Functions Affected |
|---|---|---|
| The individual can influence the future (where there is a will there is a way). | Life follows a preordained course, and human action is determined by the will of God. | Planning and scheduling |
| We must work hard to accomplish our objectives (Protestant ethic). | Hard work is not the only prerequisite for success. Wisdom, luck, and time are also required. | Motivation and reward system |
| Commitments should be honored (people will do what they say they will do). | A commitment may be superseded by a conflicting request or an agreement may only signify intention and have little or no relationship to the capacity of performance. | Negotiating and bargaining |
| One should effectively use one's time (time is money that can be saved or wasted). | Schedules are important but only in relation to other priorities. | Long- and short-range planning |
| A primary obligation of an employee is to the organization. | The individual employee has a primary obligation to his family and friends. | Loyalty, commitment, and motivation |
| The best qualified persons should be given the positions available. | Family considerations, friendship, and other considerations should determine employment practices. | Employment, promotions, recruiting, selection, and reward. |
| Intuitive aspects of decision making should be reduced, and efforts should be devoted to gathering relevant information. | Decisions are expressions of wisdom by the person in authority, and any questioning would imply a lack of confidence in his judgment. | Decision-making process |
| Data should be accurate. | Accurate data are not as highly valued. | Record keeping |
| Company information should be available to anyone who needs it within the organization. | Withholding information to gain or maintain power is acceptable. | Organization communication, managerial style |
| Each person is expected to have an opinion and to express it freely even if his views do not agree with his colleagues. | Deference is to be given to persons in power or authority, and to offer judgment that is not in support of the ideas of one's superiors is unthinkable. | Communications, organizational relations |
| A person is expected to do whatever is necessary to get the job done (one must be willing to get one's hands dirty). | Various kinds of work are accorded low or high status and some work may be below one's "dignity" or place in the organization. | Assignment of tasks, performance, and organizational effectiveness |
| Change is considered an improvement and a dynamic reality. | Tradition is revered, and the power of the ruling group is founded on the continuation of a stable structure. | Planning, morale, and organization development |

*Source:* Adapted from Philip R. Harris and Robert T. Moran, *Managing Cultural Differences* (Houston, TX: Gulf Publishing, 1996), table 4.1

## Religions of the World: A Part of Culture

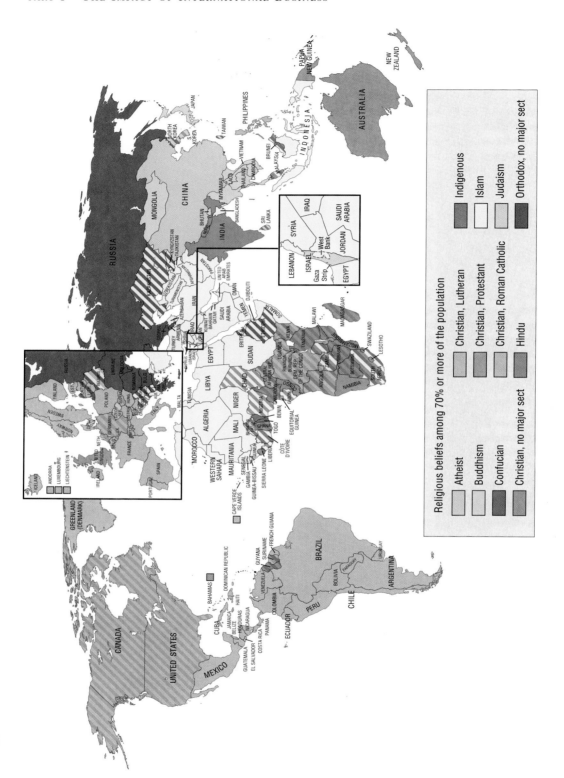

Source: *The World Factbook 1997–98*

brands, such as Nike and Reebok, are able to charge premium prices for their products due to loyal following.[22] At the same time, in the U.S. market, many companies have been successful emphasizing their foreign, imported image.

Changes occurring in manners and customs must be carefully monitored, especially in cases that seem to indicate a narrowing of cultural differences among peoples. Phenomena such as McDonald's and Coke have met with success around the world, but this does not mean that the world is becoming westernized. Modernization and westernization are not at all the same, as can be seen in Saudi Arabia, for example.

Understanding manners and customs is especially important in negotiations, because interpretations based on one's own frame of reference may lead to a totally incorrect conclusion. Universal respect is needed in cross-cultural negotiation, as seen in the Global Perspective 2.1. To negotiate effectively

**Manners and Customs**

---

## NEGOTIATING IN EUROPE: WATCH OUT FOR THE DIFFERENCES

**W**hile the European Union is an economic dynamo with 373 million people and economic power to match any other bloc, it is also a patchwork quilt of different languages and national customs, which makes it far less homogeneous than Japan, the United States, or even Asia as a whole. All of this can make negotiating in Europe a challenge. Businesspeople tend to be relatively reserved and quite formal (especially compared with their U.S. counterparts). One has to be prepared to wait for the work to begin and for an atmosphere of trust to be created. While any stereotyping of negotiators can be dangerous, broad characterizations do help negotiators as sensitization tools.

Even among Europeans, if two partners have not taken the trouble to get acquainted or complete their homework, the results can be disastrous. In one case, the Italian director of a construction company went to Germany to negotiate for a project. He began the discussion with a presentation of his company that vaunted its long history and its achievements. The German managers first looked startled, then they excused themselves and walked out the door, without even listening to the offer. The explanation: Germans typically do all the necessary background research before walking in the door. They thought the Italian manager was engaged in idle boasting about his company, and they found that offensive. Yet the Italian man-

ager thought he was engaged in a vague preliminary to any real negotiations. Real negotiating, as far as he was concerned, would not start at least for another day.

The example also illustrates the stark differences between the business styles of the northern and southern Europeans. Northern Europe, with its Protestant tradition and indoor culture, tends to emphasize the technical, the numerical, the tested. Southern Europe, on the other hand, with its Catholic background and open-air lifestyle, tends to favor personal networks, social context, innovation, and flair. Meetings in the south are often longer, but the total decision process may be faster.

The French do not neatly fit into the north-south dichotomy: One study found that the style of French negotiators was the most aggressive of thirteen diverse cultures studied. In a way, the French still embrace the art of diplomatic negotiating invented in France in the fourteenth century. French managers will have carefully prepared for the negotiations, but they generally will begin with some light, logical sparring. Throughout the preliminary and middle stages of negotiating, the French manager will judge the partners carefully on their intellectual skills and their ability to reply quickly and with authority. As one French manager put it: "Sometimes I am impressed more by brilliant savvy than by a well-reasoned argument." Because the French education system stresses mathematics and logic, doing business is a highly intellectual process for French managers. The details come last in French negotiations, so the final stage can prove to be tricky. French managers tend to slip in little extras when finalizing, like executive bonuses. It is therefore important to insist on what one wants at this stage, even if days have been spent getting to this point.

*Source: John L. Graham, "Vis-à-vis International Business Negotiations," Chap. 7 in* International Business Negotiations, *ed. Jean-Claude D. Usunier and Pervez N. Ghauri (London, U.K.: Dryden Press, 1996); "Negotiating in Europe,"* Hemispheres, *(July 1994): 43–47.*

abroad, all types of communication should be read correctly. Americans often interpret inaction and silence as negative signs. As a result, Japanese executives tend to expect that their silence can get Americans to lower prices or sweeten a deal. Even a simple agreement may take days to negotiate in the Middle East because the Arab party may want to talk about unrelated issues or do something else for a while. The abrasive style of Russian negotiators and their usual last-minute change requests may cause astonishment and concern on the part of ill-prepared negotiators. Some of the potential ways in which negotiators may not be prepared include (1) insufficient understanding of different ways of thinking; (2) insufficient attention to the necessity to save face; (3) insufficient knowledge and appreciation of the host country—its history, culture, government, and image of foreigners; (4) insufficient recognition of the decision-making process and the role of personal relations and personalities; and (5) insufficient allocation of time for negotiations.[23]

Managers must be concerned with differences in the ways products are used. Usage differences have to be translated into product form and promotional decisions. Maxwell House coffee is a worldwide brand name. It is used to sell coffee in both ground and instant form in the United States. In the United Kingdom, Maxwell House is available only in instant form. In France and Germany, it is sold in freeze-dried form only, while in the Scandinavian countries Maxwell House is positioned as the top-of-the-line entry. As a matter of fact, Maxwell House is called simply Maxwell in France and Japan, because "House" is confusing to consumers in those countries. In one South American market, a shampoo maker was concerned about poor sales of its entire product class. Research uncovered the fact that many women wash their hair with bars of soap and use shampoo only as a brief rinse or topper. Package sizes and labels must also be adapted in many countries to suit the needs of the particular culture. In Mexico, for example, Campbell's sells soup in cans large enough to serve four or five because families are generally large. In Britain, where consumers are more accustomed to ready-to-serve soups, Campbell's prints "one can makes two" on its condensed soup labels to ensure that shoppers understand how to use it.

Managers must be careful of myths and legends. One candy company had almost decided to launch a new peanut-packed chocolate bar in Japan, aimed at giving teenagers quick energy during cramming for exams. The company then found out about the Japanese old wives' tale that eating chocolate with peanuts can cause a nosebleed. The launch never took place. Similarly, approaches that would not be considered in the United States or Europe might be recommended in other regions; for example, when Conrad Hotels (the international division of Hilton Hotels) experienced low initial occupancy rates at its Hong Kong facility, they brought in a *fung shui* man. These traditional "consultants" are foretellers of future events and the unknown through occult means, and are used extensively by Hong Kong businesses.[24] In Hilton's case, the *fung shui* man suggested a piece of sculpture be moved outside the hotel's lobby because one of the characters in the statue looked like it was trying to run out of the hotel. The hotel's occupancy rate boomed. Meticulous research plays a major role in avoiding these types of problems. Concept tests determine the potential acceptance and proper understanding of a proposed new product. **Focus groups,** each consisting of 8 to 12 consumers representative of the proposed target audience, can be interviewed and their responses used as disaster checks and to fine-tune research findings. The most sensitive products, such as consumer packaged goods, require consumer usage and attitude studies as well as retail distribution studies and audits to analyze the movement of the product to retailers and eventually to households.

## Material Elements

Material culture refers to the results of technology and is directly related to how a society organizes its economic activity. It is manifested in the availability and adequacy of the basic economic, social, financial, and marketing infrastructure for the international business in a market. The basic **economic infrastructure** consists of transportation, energy, and communications systems. **Social infrastructure** refers to housing, health, and educational systems prevailing in the country of interest. **Financial** and **marketing infrastructures** provide the facilitating agencies for the international firm's operation in a given market—for example, banks and research firms. In some parts of the world, the international firm may have to be an integral partner in developing the various infrastructures before it can operate, whereas in others it may greatly benefit from their high level of sophistication.

The level of material culture can aid segmentation efforts if the degree of industrialization is used as a basis. For companies selling industrial goods, such as General Electric, this can provide a convenient starting point. In developing countries, demand may be highest for basic energy-generating products. In fully developed markets, time-saving home appliances may be more in demand.

Technological advances have been the major cause of cultural change in many countries. With technological advancement comes also **cultural convergence.** Black and white television sets extensively penetrated U.S. households more than a decade before similar levels occurred in Europe and Japan. With color television, the lag was reduced to five years. With video cassette recorders, the difference was only three years, but this time the Europeans and Japanese led the way while the United States was concentrating on cable systems. With the compact disc, penetration rates were equal in only one year. Today, with MTV available by satellite across Europe and the use of the Internet increasing, no lag exists.[25]

Material culture—mainly the degree to which it exists and how it is esteemed—has an impact on business decisions. Many exporters do not understand the degree to which Americans are package conscious; for example, cans must be shiny and beautiful. In foreign markets, packaging problems may arise due to the lack of materials, different specifications when the material is available, and immense differences in quality and consistency of printing ink, especially in South America and the Third World. Ownership levels of television sets and radios have an impact on the ability of media to reach target audiences.

## Aesthetics

Each culture makes a clear statement concerning good taste, as expressed in the arts and in the particular symbolism of colors, form, and music. What is and what is not acceptable may vary dramatically even in otherwise highly similar markets. Sex, for example, is a big selling point in many countries. In an apparent attempt to preserve the purity of Japanese womanhood, however, advertisers frequently turn to blond, blue-eyed foreign models to make the point.

In the same vein, Commodore International, the U.S.-based personal computer manufacturer, chose to sell computers in Germany by showing a naked young man in ads that ran in the German version of *Cosmopolitan*. Needless to say, approaches of this kind would not be possible in the United States because of regulations and opposition from consumer groups.

Color is often used as a mechanism for brand identification, feature reinforcement, and differentiation. In international markets, colors have more symbolic value than in domestic markets. Black, for instance, is considered the color of mourning in the United States and Europe, whereas white has the same symbolic meaning in Japan and most of the Far East. A British bank was interested in expanding its operations to Singapore and wanted to use blue and green as its identification colors. A consulting firm was quick to tell the client that green is associated with death in that country. Although the bank insisted on its original choice of colors, the green was changed to an acceptable shade.[26] Similarly, music used in broadcast advertisements is often adjusted to reflect regional differences.

International firms, such as McDonald's, have to take into consideration local tastes and concerns in designing their facilities. They may have a general policy of uniformity in building or office space design, but local tastes often warrant modifications. Respecting local cultural traditions may also generate goodwill towards the international marketer. For example, McDonald's painstakingly renovated a seventeenth-century building for their third outlet in Moscow.

## Education

Education, either formal or informal, plays a major role in the passing on and sharing of culture. Educational levels of a culture can be assessed using literacy rates, enrollment in secondary education, or enrollment in higher education available from secondary data sources. International firms also need to know about the qualitative aspects of education, namely, varying emphases on particular skills and the overall level of the education provided. Japan and South Korea, for example, emphasize the sciences, especially engineering, to a greater degree than do Western countries.

Educational levels also affect various business functions. For example, a high level of illiteracy suggests the use of visual aids rather than printed manuals. Local recruiting for sales jobs is affected by the availability of suitably trained personnel. In some cases, international firms routinely send locally recruited personnel to headquarters for training.

The international manager may also need to overcome obstacles in recruiting a suitable sales force or support personnel. For example, the Japanese culture places a premium on loyalty, and employees consider themselves members of the corporate family. If a foreign firm decides to leave Japan, its employees may find themselves stranded in midcareer, unable to find their place in the Japanese business system. Therefore, university graduates are reluctant to join any but the largest and most well known of foreign firms.[27]

If technology is marketed, the product's sophistication will depend on the educational level of future users. Product adaptation decisions are often influenced by the extent to which targeted customers are able to use the good or service properly.

Social institutions affect the ways people relate to each other. The family unit, which in Western industrialized countries consists of parents and children, in a number of cultures is extended to include grandparents and other relatives. This affects consumption patterns and must be taken into account, for example, when conducting market research.

The concept of kinship, or blood relations between individuals, is defined in a very broad way in societies such as those in sub-Saharan Africa. Family relations and a strong obligation to family are important factors to consider in human resource management in those regions. Understanding tribal politics in countries such as Nigeria may help the manager avoid unnecessary complications in executing business transactions.

The division of a particular population into classes is termed **social stratification.** Stratification ranges from the situation in northern Europe, where most people are members of the middle class, to highly stratified societies in which the higher strata control most of the buying power and decision-making positions.

An important part of the socialization process of consumers worldwide is **reference groups.**[28] These groups provide the values and attitudes that influence behavior. Primary reference groups include the family and coworkers and other intimate acquaintances, and secondary groups are social organizations where less-continuous interaction takes place, such as professional associations and trade organizations. In addition to providing socialization, reference groups develop a person's concept of self, which is manifested, for example, through the choice of products used. Reference groups also provide a baseline for compliance with group norms, giving the individual the option of conforming to or avoiding certain behaviors.

Social organization also determines the roles of managers and subordinates and how they relate to one another. In some cultures, managers and subordinates are separated explicitly and implicitly by various boundaries ranging from social class differences to separate office facilities. In others, cooperation is elicited through equality. For example, Nissan USA has no privileged parking spaces and no private dining rooms, everyone wears the same type of white coveralls, and the president sits in the same room with a hundred other white-collar workers. Fitting an organizational culture to the larger context of a national culture has to be executed with care. Changes that are too dramatic may disrupt productivity or, at the minimum, arouse suspicion.

Although Western business has impersonal structures for channeling power and influence—primarily through reliance on laws and contracts—the Chinese emphasize personal relationships to obtain clout. Things can get done without this human political capital, or *guanxi,* only if one invests enormous personal energy, is willing to offend even trusted associates, and is prepared to see it all melt away at a moment's notice.[29] For the Chinese, contracts form a useful agenda and a symbol of progress, but obligations come from relationships. McDonald's found this out in Beijing, where it was evicted from a central building after only 2 years despite having a 20-year contract. The incomer had a strong *guanxi,* whereas McDonald's had not kept its in good repair.[30]

# Social Institutions

## Sources of Cultural Knowledge

The concept of cultural knowledge is broad and multifaceted. Cultural knowledge can be defined by the way it is acquired. Objective or factual information is obtained from others through communication, research, and education. **Experiential knowledge,** on the other hand, can be acquired only by being involved in a culture other than one's own.[31] A summary of the types of knowledge needed by the international manager is provided in Table 2.3. Both factual and experiential information can be general or country-specific. In fact, the more a manager becomes involved in the international arena, the more he or she is able to develop a metaknowledge; that is, ground rules that apply whether in Kuala Lumpur, Malaysia, or Asunción, Paraguay. Market-specific knowledge does not necessarily travel well; the general variables on which the information is based do.

In a survey of managers on how to acquire international expertise, they ranked eight factors in terms of their importance, as shown in Table 2.4. The managers emphasized the experiential acquisition of knowledge. Written materials played an important but supplementary role, very often providing general or country-specific information before operational decisions were made. Interestingly, many of today's international managers have precareer experience in government, the Peace Corps, the armed forces, or missionary service. Although the survey emphasized travel, a one-time trip to London with a stay at a very large hotel and scheduled sightseeing tours does not significantly contribute to cultural knowledge. Travel that involves meetings with company personnel, intermediaries, facilitating agents, customers, and government officials, on the other hand, does contribute.[32]

However, from the corporate point of view, global capability is developed in more painstaking ways: foreign assignments, networking across borders, and the use of multicountry, multicultural teams to develop strategies and programs. At Nestlé, for example, managers move around a region (such as Asia or Latin America) at four- or five-year intervals and may serve stints at head-

**TABLE 2.3**

**Types of International Information**

| Source of Information | Type of Information | |
|---|---|---|
| | **General** | **Country Specific** |
| Objective | Examples: Impact of GDP Regional integration | Examples: Tariff barriers Government regulations |
| Experiential | Example: Corporate adjustment to internationalization | Examples: Product acceptance Program appropriateness |

**TABLE 2.4**

**Managers' Ranking of Factors Involved in Acquiring International Expertise**

| Factor | Considered Critical | Considered Important |
|---|---|---|
| 1. Business travel | 60.8% | 92.0% |
| 2. Assignments overseas | 48.8 | 71.2 |
| 3. Reading/television | 16.0 | 63.2 |
| 4. Training programs | 6.4 | 28.8 |
| 5. Precareer activities | 4.0 | 16.0 |
| 6. Graduate courses | 2.4 | 15.2 |
| 7. Nonbusiness travel | 0.8 | 12.8 |
| 8. Undergraduate courses | 0.8 | 12.0 |

*Source:* Stephen J. Kobrin, *International Expertise in American Business* (New York: Institute of International Education, 1984), 38.

quarters for two to three years between such assignments. Such broad experience allows managers to pick up ideas and tools to be used in markets where they have not been used or where they have not been necessary before. In Thailand, where supermarkets are revolutionizing consumer-goods marketing, techniques perfected elsewhere in the Nestlé system are being put to effective use. The experiences then, in turn, are used to develop newly emerging markets in the same region, such as Vietnam.

Managers have a variety of sources and methods to extend their knowledge of specific cultures. Most of these sources deal with factual information that provides a necessary basis for market studies. Beyond the normal business literature and its anecdotal information, specific-country studies are published by the U.S. government, private companies, and universities. The U.S. Department of Commerce's *Overseas Business Reports* cover more than 80 countries, while the Economist Intelligence Unit's *Country Reports* cover 180 countries. *Culturgrams,* which detail the customs of people in more than 100 countries, are published by the Center for International and Area Studies at Brigham Young University. Many agencies—such as accounting firms, advertising agencies, banks, and transportation companies—provide background information on the markets they serve for their clients. These range from the *International Business Guide* series published by Deloitte & Touche, which covers 107 countries and territories, the Hong Kong and Shanghai Banking Corporation's *Business Profile Series* for 20 countries in the Middle East and the Far East, to *World Trade* magazine's "Put Your Best Foot Forward" series, which covers Europe, Asia, Mexico/Canada, and Russia.

Blunders in foreign markets that could have been avoided with factual information are generally inexcusable. A manager who travels to Taipei without first obtaining a visa and is therefore turned back has no one else to blame. Other oversights may lead to more costly mistakes. For example, Brazilians are several inches shorter than the average American, but this was not taken into account when Sears erected American-height shelves that block Brazilian shoppers' view of the rest of the store.

International business success requires not only comprehensive fact finding and preparation but also an ability to understand and fully appreciate the nuances of different cultural traits and patterns. Gaining this **interpretive knowledge** requires "getting one's feet wet" over a sufficient length of time. Over the long run, culture can become a factor in the firm's overall success, as seen in Global Perspective 2.2.

## MAKING CULTURE WORK FOR YOU

**T**housands of European and U.S. companies have entered or expanded their operations in the fastest-growing region in the world—Asia. In the 1990s, the region outpaced the growth of the world's twenty-four leading industrial economies by more than six times. A total of 400 million Asian consumers have disposable incomes at least equal to the rich-world average.

Few companies have had as much experience—or success—as the 3M Company. The maker of everything from heart-lung machines to Scotch tape, the company's revenues for 1996 from international sales reached $7.6 billion (54 percent of total), with $900 million coming from the Asia-Pacific. At the root of the company's success are certain rules that allow it both to adjust to and exploit cultural differences.

■ **Embrace Local Culture**—3M's new plant near Bangkok, Thailand, is one example of how the company embraces local culture. A gleaming Buddhist shrine, wreathed in flowers, pays homage to the spirits Thais believe took care of the land prior to the plant's arrival. Showing sensitivity to local customs helps sales and builds employee morale, officials say. It helps the company understand the market and keeps it from inadvertently alienating people.

■ **Employ Locals to Gain Cultural Knowledge**—The best way to understand a market is to have grown up in it. Of the 7,500 3M employees in Asia, fewer than 10 are Americans. The rest are locals who know the customs and buying habits of their compatriots. 3M also makes grants of up to $50,000 available to its Asian employees to study product innovations, making them equals with their U.S. counterparts.

■ **Build Relationships**—3M executives started preparing for the Chinese market soon after President Nixon's historic visit in 1972. For ten years, company officials visited Beijing and invited Chinese leaders to 3M headquarters in St. Paul, Minnesota, building contacts and trust along the way. Such efforts paid off when, in 1984, the government made 3M the first wholly owned foreign venture on Chinese soil. 3Mers call the process FIDO ("first in defeats other"), a credo built on patience and a long-term perspective.

■ **Adapt Products to Local Markets**—Examples of how 3M adapts its products read like insightful lessons on culture. In the early 1990s, sales of 3M's famous Scotchbrite cleaning pads were languishing. Company technicians interviewed maids and housewives to determine why. The answer: Filipinos traditionally scrub floors by pushing a rough coconut shell around with their feet. 3M responded by making the pads brown and shaping them like a foot. In China, a big seller for 3M is a composite to fill tooth cavities. In the United States, dentists pack a soft material into the hole and blast it with a special beam of light, making it hard as enamel in five seconds. But in the People's Republic, dentists cannot afford the light. The solution is an air-drying composite that does the same thing in two minutes: it takes a little longer but is far less expensive.

■ **Help Employees Understand You**—At any given time, more than 30 Asian technicians are in the United States, where they learn the latest product advances while gaining new insight into how the company works. At the same time, they are able to contribute by infusing their insight into company plans and operations.

■ **Coordinate by Region**—When designers in Singapore discovered that consumers wanted to use 3M's Nomad household floor mats in their cars, they spread the word to their counterparts in Malaysia and Thailand. Today, the specially made car mats with easy-to-clean vinyl loops are big sellers across Southeast Asia. The company encourages its product managers from different Asian countries to hold regular meetings and share insights and strategies. The goal is to come up with regional programs and "Asianize" a product more quickly.

*Source: John R. Engen, "Far Eastern Front," World Trade (December 1994): 20–24; "A Survey of Asia," The Economist (October 30, 1993).* www.3m.com

## Cultural Analysis

To try to understand and explain differences among and across cultures, researchers have developed checklists and models showing pertinent variables and their interaction. An example of such a model is provided in Figure 2.2. Developed by Sheth and Sethi, this model is based on the premise that all international business activity should be viewed as innovation and as producing change.[33] After all, multinational corporations introduce management practices, as well as goods and services, from one country to others, where they are perceived to be new and different. Although many question the usefulness of such models, they do bring together all or most of the relevant variables on how consumers in different cultures may perceive, evaluate, and adopt new behaviors. However, any manager using such a tool should periodically cross-check its results against reality and experience.

The key variable of the model is propensity to change, which is a function of three constructs: (1) cultural lifestyle of individuals in terms of how deeply

**FIGURE 2.2**

**A Model of Cross-Cultural Behavior**

*Source:* Adapted by permission of the publisher from "A Theory of Cross-Cultural Buying Behavior," by Jagdish N. Sheth and S. Prakash Sethi, in *Consumer and Industrial Buyer Behavior,* eds. Arch G. Woodside, Jagdish N. Sheth, and Peter D. Bennett, 1977, 373. Copyright 1977 by Elsevier Science Publishing Co., Inc.

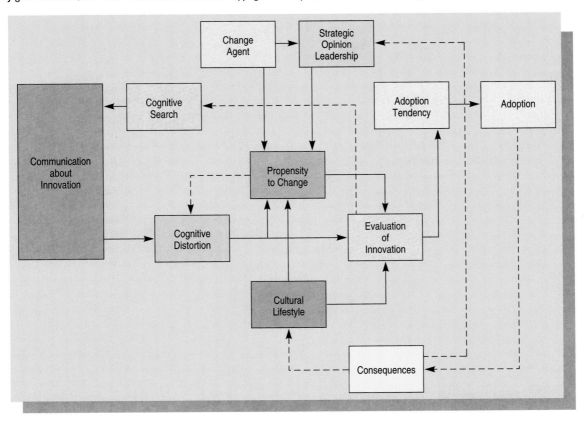

held their traditional beliefs and attitudes are, and also which elements of culture are dominant; (2) change agents (such as multinational corporations and their practices) and strategic-opinion leaders (for example, social elites); and (3) communication about the innovation from commercial sources, neutral sources (such as government), and social sources, such as friends and relatives.

It has been argued that differences in cultural lifestyle can be explained by four dimensions of culture.[34] The dimensions consist of (1) individualism ("I" consciousness versus "we" consciousness), (2) power distance (levels of equality in society), (3) uncertainty avoidance (need for formal rules and regulations), and (4) masculinity (attitude toward achievement, roles of men and women).

Knowledge of similarities along these four dimensions allows us to cluster countries and regions and establish regional and national marketing or business programs.[35] An example is provided in Table 2.5, in which the European market is segmented along cultural lines for the development of marketing programs. Cluster 2, consisting of Southern Europe, displays the highest un-

**TABLE 2.5**

**Culture-Based Segmentation**

| | Size (Million) | Cultural Characteristics | | | | Illustrative Marketing Implications |
| --- | --- | --- | --- | --- | --- | --- |
| | | Power Distance | Uncertainty Avoidance | Individualism | Masculinity | |
| Cluster 1 Austria, Germany, Switzerland, Italy, Great Britain, Ireland | 203 | Small | Medium | Medium-High | High | Preference for "high-performance" products; use "successful-achiever" theme in advertising; desire for novelty, variety, and pleasure; fairly risk-averse market |
| Cluster 2 Belgium, France, Greece, Portugal, Spain, Turkey | 182 | Medium | Strong | Varied | Low-Medium | Appeal to consumer's status and power position, reduce perceived risk in product purchase and use, emphasize product functionality |
| Cluster 3 Denmark, Sweden, Finland, Netherlands, Norway | 37 | Small | Low | High | Low | Relatively weak resistance to new products, strong consumer desire for novelty and variety, high consumer regard for "environmentally friendly" marketers and socially conscious firms |

*Source:* Sudhir H. Kale, "Grouping Euroconsumers: A Culture-Based Clustering Approach," *Journal of International Marketing* 3, 3 (1995): 42.

certainty avoidance and should therefore be targeted with risk-reducing marketing programs such as extended warranties and return privileges.[36]

Understanding the implications of the dimensions helps businesspeople prepare for international business encounters. For example, in negotiating in Germany one can expect a counterpart who is thorough, systematic, very well prepared, but also rather dogmatic and therefore less flexible and willing to compromise. Efficiency is emphasized. In Mexico, however, the counterpart may prefer to address problems on a personal and private basis rather than on a business level. This means more emphasis on socializing and conveying one's humanity, sincerity, loyalty, and friendship. Also, differences in the pace and business practices of a region have to be accepted.[37] Boeing Airplane Company found in its annual study on world aviation safety that countries with both low individualism and substantial power distances had accident rates 2.6 times greater than at the other end of the scale. The findings naturally have an impact on training and service operations of airlines.[38]

Communication about innovation takes place through the physical product itself (samples) or through experiencing a new company policy. If a new personnel practice, such as quality circles or flextime, is being investigated, results may be communicated in reports or through word of mouth by the participating employees. Communication content depends on the following factors: the good's or policy's relative advantage over existing alternatives; compatibility with established behavioral patterns; complexity; or the degree to which the good or process is perceived as difficult to understand and use; trialability, or the degree to which it may be experimented with without incurring major risk; and observability, which is the extent to which the consequences of the innovation are visible.

Before a good or policy is evaluated, information should be gathered about existing beliefs and circumstances. Distortion of data may occur as a result of selective attention, exposure, and retention. As examples, anything foreign may be seen in a negative light, another multinational company's efforts may have failed, or the government may discourage the proposed activity. Additional information may then be sought from any of the sources or from opinion leaders in the market.

Adoption tendency refers to the likelihood that the product or process will be accepted. Examples are advertising in the People's Republic of China and equity joint ventures with Western participants in Russia, both of them unheard of a decade ago. If an innovation clears the hurdles, it may be adopted and slowly diffused into the entire market. An international manager has two basic choices: to adapt company offerings and methods to those in the market or to try to change market conditions to fit company programs. In Japan, a number of Western companies have run into obstructions in the Japanese distribution system, where great value is placed on established relationships; everything is done on the basis of favoring the familiar and fearing the unfamiliar. In most cases, this problem is solved by joint ventures with a major Japanese entity that has established contacts. On occasion, when the company's approach is compatible with the central beliefs of a culture, the company may be able to change existing customs rather than adjust to them. Initially, Procter & Gamble's traditional hard-selling style in television commercials jolted most Japanese viewers accustomed to more subtle approaches. Now the ads are being imitated by Japanese competitors.

Although models such as the one in Figure 2.2 may aid in strategy planning by making sure that all variables and their interlinkages are considered, any analysis is incomplete without the basic recognition of cultural differences. Adjusting to differences requires putting one's own cultural values aside. James A. Lee proposes that the natural **self-reference criterion**—the unconscious reference to one's own cultural values—is the root of most international business problems.[39] However, recognizing and admitting this are often quite difficult. The following analytical approach is recommended to reduce the influence of cultural bias:

1. Define the problem or goal in terms of the domestic cultural traits, habits, or norms.
2. Define the problem or goal in terms of the foreign cultural traits, habits, or norms. Make no value judgments.
3. Isolate the self-reference criterion influence in the problem, and examine it carefully to see how it complicates the problem.
4. Redefine the problem without the self-reference criterion influence, and solve for the optimum-goal situation.

This approach can be applied to product introduction. If Kellogg's wants to introduce breakfast cereals into markets where breakfast is traditionally not eaten or where consumers drink very little milk, managers must consider very carefully how to instill the new habit. The traits, habits, and norms concerning the importance of breakfast are quite different in the United States, France, and Brazil, and they have to be outlined before the product can be introduced. In France, Kellogg's commercials are aimed as much at providing nutrition lessons as they are at promoting the product. In Brazil, the company advertised on a soap opera to gain entry into the market, because Brazilians often emulate the characters of these television shows.

Analytical procedures require constant monitoring of changes caused by outside events as well as the changes caused by the business entity itself. Controlling **ethnocentrism**—the tendency to consider one's own culture superior to others—can be achieved only by acknowledging it and properly adjusting to its possible effects in managerial decision making. The international manager needs to be prepared and able to put that preparedness to effective use.[40]

## The Training Challenge

International managers face a dilemma in terms of international and intercultural competence. The lack of adequate foreign language and international business skills have cost U.S. firms lost contracts, weak negotiations, and ineffectual management. A UNESCO study of 10- to 14-year-old students in nine countries placed Americans next to last in their comprehension of foreign cultures. Even when cultural awareness is high, there is room for improvement. For example, a survey of European executives found that a shortage of international managers was considered the single most important constraint on expansion abroad.[41] The increase in the overall international activity of firms has increased the need for cultural sensitivity training at all levels of the organization. Further, today's training must encompass not only outsiders to the firm but interaction within the corporate family as well. However inconsequential the degree of interaction may seem, it can still cause problems if proper understanding is lacking. Consider, for example, the date 11/12/98 on a telex; a European will interpret this as the 11th of December, an American as the 12th of November.

Some companies try to avoid the training problem by hiring only nationals or well-traveled Americans for their international operations. This makes sense for the management of overseas operations but will not solve the training need, especially if transfers to a culture unfamiliar to the manager are likely. International experience may not necessarily transfer from one market to another.

To foster cultural sensitivity and acceptance of new ways of doing things within the organization, management must institute internal education programs. The programs may include (1) culture-specific information (data covering other countries, such as videopacks and culturegrams), (2) general cultural information (values, practices, and assumptions of countries other than one's own), and (3) self-specific information (identifying one's own cultural paradigm, including values, assumptions, and perceptions about others).[42] One study found that Japanese assigned to the United States get mainly language training as preparation for the task. In addition, many companies use mentoring, whereby an individual is assigned to someone who is experienced and who will spend time squiring and explaining. Talks given by returnees and by visiting lecturers hired specifically for the task round out the formal part of training.[43]

The objective of formal training programs is to foster the four critical characteristics of preparedness, sensitivity, patience, and flexibility in managers and other personnel. The programs vary dramatically in terms of their rigor, involvement, and, of course, cost.[44] A summary of the programs is provided in Figure 2.3.

Environmental briefings and cultural-orientation programs are types of **area studies** programs. The programs provide factual preparation for a manager to operate in, or work with people from, a particular country. Area stud-

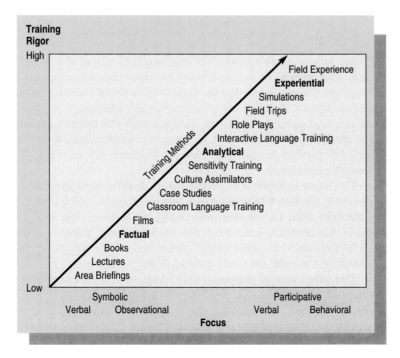

**FIGURE 2.3**

**Cross-Cultural Training Methods**

*Source:* J. Stewart Black and Mark Mendenhall, "A Practical but Theory-Based Framework for Selecting Cross-Cultural Training Methods," in *International Human Resource Management,* eds. Mark Mendenhall and Gary Oddou (Boston: PWS-Kent, 1991), 188.

ies should be a basic prerequisite for other types of training programs. Alone, area studies serve little practical purpose because they do not really get the manager's feet wet. Other, more involved, programs contribute context in which to put facts so that they can be properly understood.

The **cultural assimilator** is a program in which trainees must respond to scenarios of specific situations in a particular country. The programs have been developed for the Arab countries, Iran, Thailand, Central America, and Greece.[45] The results of the trainees' assimilator experience are evaluated by a panel of judges. This type of program has been used most frequently in cases of transfers abroad on short notice.

When more time is available, managers can be trained extensively in language. This may be required if an exotic language is involved. **Sensitivity training** focuses on enhancing a manager's flexibility in situations that are quite different from those at home. The approach is based on the assumption that understanding and accepting oneself is critical to understanding a person from another culture. Finally, training may involve **field experience,** which exposes a manager to a different cultural environment for a limited amount of time. While this approach is expensive, it is used by some companies, as seen in Global Perspective 2.3.

One field experience technique that has been suggested when the training process needs to be rigorous is the host-family surrogate. This technique places a trainee (and possibly his or her family) in a domestically located family of the nationality to which they are assigned.[46]

Regardless of the degree of training, preparation, and positive personal characteristics, a manager will always remain foreign. A manager should never rely on his or her own judgment when local managers can be consulted. In many instances, a manager should have an interpreter present at negotiations, especially if the manager is not completely bilingual. Overconfidence in one's language capabilities can create problems.

## *Summary*

Culture is one of the most challenging elements of the international marketplace. This system of learned behavior patterns characteristic of the members of a given society is constantly shaped by a set of dynamic variables: language, religion, values and attitudes, manners and customs, aesthetics, technology, education, and social institutions. To cope with this system, an international manager needs both factual and interpretive knowledge of culture. To some extent, the factual knowledge can be learned; its interpretation comes only through experience.

The most complicated problems in dealing with the cultural environment stem from the fact that one cannot learn culture—one has to live it. Two schools of thought exist in the business world on how to deal with cultural diversity. One is that business is business the world around, following the model of Pepsi and McDonald's. In some cases, globalization is a fact of life; however, cultural differences are still far from converging.

The other school proposes that companies must tailor business approaches to individual cultures. Setting up policies and procedures in each country has been compared to an organ transplant; the critical question centers around acceptance or rejection. The major challenge to the international manager is to make sure that rejection is not a result of cultural myopia or even blindness.

## LEARNING THE STRANGE FOREIGN WAYS

**S**amsung, Korea's largest conglomerate, has set a goal to become one of the world's top ten corporations by the year 2000 by achieving annual sales of $200 billion and to be among the top five electronics manufacturers, with annual sales of $56 billion. Samsung launched a "New Management" policy to achieve this ambitious goal. The directive to Samsung's 230,000 members is to do away with outdated practices and to initiate a new approach to the global environment. A generation of Korean managers came of age thinking that if they built it, they could sell it. Today's competitive environment requires players such as Samsung to contribute to local communities around the world by offering the best products and services everywhere.

The company wants to be culturally more sensitive, and not just to avoid gaffes. Programs developed for this purpose have taken many forms. For the last few years, Samsung has been sending its brightest junior employees overseas for a year. A total of 1,800 have completed such tours: 450 in Japan, 340 in North America, 100 in Central and South America, 240 in China, 340 in Europe, and 200 elsewhere in Asia. Their mission is not 100 percent business either. "International exposure is important, but you have to develop an appreciation of the foreign environment as well. You have to goof off at the mall, watch people, and develop international tastes," say Samsung officials. The program costs about $80,000 a year per person and takes key people out of circulation. But Samsung is convinced that cultural immersion will pay off in more astute judgments about what customers want. One concrete result is that the company is tailoring more products for specific overseas markets despite resistance of engineers in Seoul. "They want one model to sell to everyone. But they are accepting the concept now," state Samsung marketers. Much of that change has been attributed to people like Park Sang Jin, who had been overseas for 15 years, mostly in the United States. "If we do not do this type of concept, we will never catch up with our competitors," he states.

Overseas-bound managers attend a month-long boot camp where they are awakened at 5:50 A.M. for a jog, meditation, and then lessons on issues such as table manners or avoiding sexual harassment. For example, participants are taught not to ask female job applicants whether they are married, when they intend to marry, what their age or religion is.

Samsung employees coming back from overseas see much work to be done. After five years in Paris, Kim Jeong Kyu recognizes that time abroad has changed him. Now back in Seoul, he is trying to change Samsung—and having problems. "Even if I have a good idea, I will not suggest it too fast," Kim said. "They will say, 'He doesn't know the Korean situation. Maybe it will work in France, but not here.'"

*Source:* "*Sensitivity Kick,*" **The Wall Street Journal,** *December 30, 1992, 1, 4. Updated by interview, May 20, 1996.* **www.samsung.com**

*Fortune* examined the international performance of a dozen large companies that earn 20 percent or more of their revenue overseas.[47] The internationally successful companies all share an important quality: patience. They have not rushed into situations but rather built their operations carefully by following the most basic business principles. These principles are to know your adversary, know your audience, and know your customer.

WWW

## Key Terms and Concepts

| | | |
|---|---|---|
| cultural risk | Buddhism | experiential knowledge |
| acculturation | Confucianism | interpretive knowledge |
| high-context cultures | focus groups | self-reference criterion |
| low-context cultures | economic infrastructure | ethnocentrism |
| change agent | social infrastructure | area studies |
| cultural universals | financial infrastructure | cultural assimilator |
| backtranslation | marketing infrastructure | sensitivity training |
| Christianity | cultural convergence | field experience |
| Islam | social stratification | |
| Hinduism | reference groups | |

## Questions for Discussion

1. Comment on the assumption, "If people are serious about doing business with you, they will speak English."

2. You are on your first business visit to Germany. You feel confident about your ability to speak the language (you studied German in school and have taken a refresher course), and you decide to use it. During introductions, you want to break the ice by asking "Wie geht's?" and insisting that everyone call you by your first name. Speculate as to the reaction.

3. Q: "What do you call a person who can speak two languages?"
   A: "Bilingual."
   Q: "How about three?"
   A: "Trilingual."
   Q: "Excellent. How about one?"
   A: "Hmmmm. . . . American!"
   Is this joke malicious, or is there something to be learned from it?

4. What can be learned about a culture from reading and attending to factual materials?

5. Windham International is a global relocation consulting firm that provides cross-cultural training. The company's website (**http://www.windham-world.com/cross_3.html**) includes a cross-cultural IQ quiz. Take it.

6. Management at a U.S. company trying to market tomato paste in the Middle East did not know that, translated into Arabic, "tomato paste" is "tomato glue." How could it have known in time to avoid problems?

7. Provide examples of how the self-reference criterion might manifest itself.

8. Is any international business entity not a cultural imperialist? How else could one explain the phenomenon of multinational corporations?

## Recommended Readings

Axtell, Roger E. *Do's and Taboos Around the World*. New York: John Wiley & Sons, 1993.

Bache, Ellyn. *Culture Clash*. Yarmouth, Maine: Intercultural Press, 1990.

Brislin, R. W., W. J. Lonner, and R. M. Thorndike. *Cross-Cultural Research Methods*. New York: Wiley, 1973.

Catlin, Linda, and Thomas White. *Cultural Sourcebook and Case Studies*. Cincinnati: South-Western, 1994.

Copeland, Lennie, and Lewis Griggs. *Going International: How to Make Friends and Deal Effectively in the Global Marketplace*. New York: Random House, 1985.

Fisher, Glen. *International Negotiation*. Yarmouth, Maine: Intercultural Press, 1986.

Hall, Edward T., and Mildred Reed Hall. *Understanding Cultural Differences*. Yarmouth, Maine: Intercultural Press, 1990.

Lewis, Richard D. *When Cultures Collide*. London, England: Nicholas Brealey Publishing, 1996.

O'Hara-Devereaux, Mary, and Robert Johansen. *Global Work: Bridging Distance, Culture, and Time*. San Francisco: Jossey-Bass Publishers, 1994.

Terpstra, Vern, and Keith David. *The Cultural Environment of International Business*. Cincinnati: South-Western, 1991.

Trompenaars, Fons. *Riding the Waves of Culture*. New York: Irwin, 1994.

U.S. Department of Commerce. *International Business Practices*. Washington, D.C.: U.S. Government Printing Office, 1993.

Weiss, Joseph. *Regional Cultures, Managerial Behavior, and Entrepreneurship*. Westport, Conn.: Quorum Books, 1988.

## Notes

1. "Rule No. 1: Don't Diss the Locals," *Business Week*, May 15, 1995, 8.

2. Carla Rapoport, "Nestlé's Brand-Building Machine," *Fortune*, September 19, 1994, 147–156.

3. Mary O'Hara-Devereaux and Robert Johansen, *Global Work: Bridging Distance, Culture, and Time* (San Francisco: Jossey-Bass Publishers, 1994), 11.

4. Alfred Kroeber and Clyde Kluckhohn, *Culture: A Critical Review of Concepts and Definitions* (New York: Random House, 1985), 11.

5. Geert Hofstede, "National Cultures Revisited," *Asia-Pacific Journal of Management* 1 (September 1984): 22–24.

6. Robert L. Kohls, *Survival Kit for Overseas Living* (Chicago: Intercultural Press, 1979), 3.

7. Edward T. Hall, *Beyond Culture* (Garden City, N.Y.: Anchor Press, 1976), 15.

8. See http://www.mcdonalds.com

9. Michael T. Malloy, "America, Go Home," *The Wall Street Journal,* March 26, 1993. R7.

10. Marita von Oldenborgh, "What's Next for India?" *International Business* (January 1996): 44–47; and Ravi Vijh, "Think Global, Act Indian," *Export Today* (June 1996): 27–28.

11. George P. Mundak, "The Common Denominator of Cultures," in *The Science of Man in the World,* ed. Ralph Linton (New York: Columbia University Press, 1945), 123–142.

12. Philip R. Harris and Robert T. Moran, *Managing Cultural Differences* (Houston: Gulf, 1996), 201.

13. David A. Ricks, *Big Business Blunders* (Homewood, Ill.: Irwin, 1983), 4.

14. Margareta Bowen, "Business Translation," *Jerome Quarterly* (August-September 1993): 5–9.

15. Edward T. Hall, "The Silent Language of Overseas Business," *Harvard Business Review* 38 (May–June 1960): 87–96.

16. *Statistical Abstract of the United States* (Washington, D.C.: U.S. Government Printing Office, 1994): 855.

17. David McClelland, *The Achieving Society* (New York: Irvington, 1961): 90.

18. *World Almanac and the Book of Facts* (Mahwah, N.J.: Funk & Wagnalls, 1995), 734.

19. Mushtaq Luqmami, Zahir A. Quraeshi, and Linda Delene, "Marketing in Islamic Countries: A Viewpoint," *MSU Business Topics* 23 (Summer 1980): 17–24.

20. "Islamic Banking: Faith and Creativity," *New York Times,* April 8, 1994, D1, D6.

21. James F. Engel, Roger D. Blackwell, and Paul W. Miniard, *Consumer Behavior* (Hinsdale, Ill.: Dryden, 1995), 443.

22. "Latest Sneakers Fly Off Tokyo Shelves Even at $1,300 a Pair," *The Washington Post,* November 7, 1996, A1, A10.

23. Sergey Frank, "Global Negotiations: Vive Les Differences!" *Sales and Marketing Management* 144 (May 1992): 64–69.

24. "Fung Shui Man Orders Sculpture Out of Hotel," *South China Morning Post,* July 27, 1992, 4.

25. Kenichi Ohmae, "Managing in a Borderless World," *Harvard Business Review* 67 (May–June 1989): 152–161.

26. Joe Agnew, "Cultural Differences Probed to Create Product Identity," *Marketing News,* October 24, 1986, 22.

27. Joseph A. McKinney, "Joint Ventures of United States Firms in Japan: A Survey," *Venture Japan* 1 (1988): 14–19.

28. Engel, Blackwell, and Miniard, *Consumer Behavior,* 716.

29. Peter McGinnis, "Guanxi or Contract: A Way to Understand and Predict Conflict Between Chinese and Western Senior Managers in China-Based Joint Ventures," in *Multinational Business Management and Internationalization of Business Enterprises,* ed. Daniel E. McCarthy and Stanley J. Hille (Nanjing, China: Nanjing University Press, 1993), 354–351.

30. Tim Ambler, "Reflections in China: Re-Orienting Images of Marketing," *Marketing Management* 4 (Summer, 1995): 23–30.

31. James H. Sood and Patrick Adams, "Model of Management Learning Styles as a Predictor of Export Behavior and Performance," *Journal of Business Research* 12 (June 1984): 169–182.

32. Stephen J. Kobrin, *International Expertise in American Business* (New York: Institute of International Education, 1984), 36.

33. Jagdish N. Sheth and S. Prakash Sethi, "A Theory of Cross-Cultural Buying Behavior," in *Consumer and Industrial Buying Behavior,* eds. Arch G. Woodside, Jagdish N. Sheth, and Peter D. Bennett (New York: Elsevier North-Holland, 1977), 369–386.

34. Geert Hofstede, *Culture's Consequences: International Differences in Work-Related Values* (Beverly Hills, Calif.: Sage Publications, 1984), Chapter 1.

35. Simcha Ronen and Oded Shenkar, "Clustering Countries on Attitudinal Dimensions: A Review and Synthesis," *Academy of Management Journal* 28 (September, 1985): 440–452.

36. For applications of the framework, see Sudhir H. Kale, "Culture-Specific Marketing Communications," *International Marketing Review* 8, No. 2 (1991): 18–30; and Sudhir H. Kale, "Distribution Channel Relationships in Diverse Cultures," *International Marketing Review* 8, No. 3 (1991): 31–45.

37. Frank, "Global Negotiations: Vive Les Differences!"

38. "Building a 'Cultural Index' to World Airline Safety," *The Washington Post,* August 21, 1994, A8.

39. James A. Lee, "Cultural Analysis in Overseas Operations," *Harvard Business Review* 44 (March-April 1966): 106–114.

40. Peter D. Fitzpatrick and Alan S. Zimmerman, *Essentials of Export Marketing* (New York: American Management Organization, 1985), 16.

41. "Expansion Abroad: The New Direction for European Firms," *International Management* 41 (November 1986): 20–26.

42. W. Chan Kim and R. A. Mauborgne, "Cross-Cultural Strategies," *Journal of Business Strategy* 7 (Spring 1987): 28–37.

43. Mauricio Lorence, "Assignment USA: The Japanese Solution," *Sales and Marketing Management* 144 (October 1992): 60–66.

44. Rosalie Tung, "Selection and Training of Personnel for Overseas Assignments," *Columbia Journal of World Business* 16 (Spring 1981): 68–78.

45. Harris and Moran, *Managing Cultural Differences,* 267–295.

46. Simcha Ronen, "Training the International Assignee," in *Training and Career Development,* ed. I. Goldstein (San Francisco: Jossey-Bass, 1989), 426–440.

47. Kenneth Labich, "America's International Winners," *Fortune,* April 14, 1986, 34–46.

# CHAPTER 3

# National Trade and Investment Policies

### LEARNING OBJECTIVES

◆ *To see how trade and investment policies have historically been a subset of domestic policies*

◆ *To examine how historical attitudes toward trade and investment policies are changing*

◆ *To see how global linkages in trade and investment have made policymakers less able to focus solely on domestic issues*

◆ *To understand that nations must cooperate closely in the future to maintain a viable global trade and investment environment*

## Are U.S. States Overstepping Their Boundaries?

**H**ow often should trade be used as a weapon? Where should lines be drawn for the sake of free trade? Restrictions on trade emanating from the politically motivated U.S. Congress often draw fire from other countries, most recently concerning the Cuban Liberty and Democratic Solidarity Act (the "Helms-Burton" Act) and the Iran-Libya Sanctions Act. Both acts impose sanctions on foreign firms for doing business with countries politically opposed to the United States. Now foreign businesses have another reason to criticize zealous American legislators. In a 1997 report on U.S. trade barriers, the European Commission highlights what it calls "a worrying new trend" in U.S. trade restrictions. It cites a Massachusetts law directed at human rights abuses in Burma as an example of the trend toward "sub-federal purchasing laws restricting the ability of EU and other companies doing business with specific countries to bid for contracts in various states and cities."

The 1996 Massachusetts Burma Law bars state purchases of goods from companies doing business in military-ruled Burma (now renamed Myanmar), effectively barring around 150 foreign companies from government contracts in the state. Although other states, including California, Connecticut, and Texas, have proposed or adopted similar laws, the Massachusetts law has gained international notoriety. The European Union argues that the law violates a World Trade Organization provision committing countries to open all government contracts to international bidding. Japan has also entered the fray; Japanese officials have criticized the law and voiced support for taking the United States to the WTO over the issue.

The EU and other countries see the Burma law a part of a disturbing trend in U.S. policy making. They point to a "multiplication of such initiatives," including U.S. sanctions directed against foreign companies doing business in Cuba, Iran, or Syria. All of these initiatives seek to regulate economic actors operating beyond U.S. jurisdiction, according to critics of U.S. policy. Not surprisingly, foreign firms were not pleased to hear that some members of the U.S. Congress are now exploring a sanctions act on the national level aimed at companies doing business in Burma. ▨

*Sources:* Leen Van Parys, "EU complains of US overstepping its boundaries," *The Journal of Commerce* (July 30, 1997): 3A; "Japan may join EU-US talks on Massachusetts law against Burma," *Agence France Presse,* July 8, 1997.

This chapter discusses the policy actions taken by countries. All nations have international trade and investment policies. The policies may be publicly pronounced or kept secret, they may be disjointed or coordinated, or they may be applied consciously or determined by a laissez-faire attitude. Trade policy actions become evident when measures taken by governments affect the flow of trade and investment across national borders. As the opening vignette illustrates, nations and even parts of nations can and will take actions to achieve particular policy goals. Since it often is not possible to directly interfere with a country's policies, trade measures are a frequently used vehicle to precipitate policy changes abroad.

## Rationale and Goals of Trade and Investment Policies

Government policies are designed to regulate, stimulate, direct, and protect national activities. The exercise of these policies is the result of **national sovereignty,** which provides a government with the right and burden to shape the environment of the country and its citizens. Because they are "border bound," governments focus mainly on domestic policies. Nevertheless, many policy actions have repercussions on other nations, firms, and individuals abroad and are therefore a component of a nation's trade and investment policy.

Government policy can be subdivided into two groups of policy actions that affect trade and investment. One affects trade and investment directly, the other indirectly. The domestic policy actions of most governments aim to increase the **standard of living** of the country's citizens, to improve the **quality of life,** to stimulate national development, and to achieve full employment. Clearly, all of these goals are closely intertwined. For example, an improved standard of living is likely to contribute to national development. Similarly, quality of life and standard of living are closely interlinked. Also, a high level of employment will play a major role in determining the standard of living. Yet all of these policy goals will also affect international trade and investment indirectly. For example, if foreign industries become more competitive and rapidly increase their exports, employment in the importing countries may suffer. Likewise, if a country accumulates large quantities of debt, which at some time must be repaid, the present and future standard of living will be threatened.

In more direct ways, a country may also pursue policies of increased development that mandate either technology transfer from abroad or the exclusion of foreign industries to the benefit of domestic infant firms. Also, government officials may believe that imports threaten the culture, health, or standards of the country's citizens and thus the quality of life. As a result, officials are likely to develop regulations to protect the citizens.

Nations also institute **foreign policy** measures designed with domestic concerns in mind but explicitly aimed to exercise influence abroad. One major goal of foreign policy may be national security. For example, nations may develop alliances, coalitions, and agreements to protect their borders or their spheres of interest. Similarly, nations may take measures to enhance their national security preparedness in case of international conflict. Governments also wish to improve trade and investment opportunities and to contribute to the security and safety of their own firms abroad.

Policy aims may be approached in various ways. For example, to develop new markets abroad and to increase their sphere of influence, nations may give foreign aid to other countries. This was the case when the United States generously awarded Marshall Plan funds for the reconstruction of Europe. Governments may also feel a need to restrict or encourage trade and investment flows in order to preserve or enhance the capability of industries that are important to national security.

Each country develops its own domestic policies, and therefore policy aims will vary from nation to nation. Inevitably, conflicts arise. For example, full employment policies in one country may directly affect employment policies in another. Similarly, the development aims of one country may reduce the development capability of another. Even when health issues are concerned, disputes may arise. One nation may argue that its regulations are in place to protect its citizens, whereas other nations may interpret the regulations as market barriers. An example of the latter situation is the celebrated hormone dispute between the United States and the European Union. U.S. cattle are treated with growth hormones. While the United States claims that these hormones are harmless to humans, many Europeans find them scary. Given the differences in perspectives, there is much room for conflict when it comes to trade policies, particularly when the United States wants to export more beef and the European Union attempts to restrict such beef imports.

The trade disagreement between the United States and Japan in the automotive sector is another example. While the U.S. claimed that Japanese firms prevent the importation and sale of U.S.-made auto parts, Japan's government blamed quality concerns and lack of effort by U.S. firms. Such disagreements can quickly escalate into major trade conflicts.

Differences among national policies have always existed and are likely to erupt into occasional conflict. Yet, the closer economic linkage among nations has made the emergence of such conflicts more frequent and the disagreements more severe. In recognition of this development, efforts have been made since 1945 to create a multilateral institutional arrangement that can help to resolve national conflicts, harmonize national policies, and facilitate increased international trade and investments.

## Global Trade Regulation Since 1945

In 1945, the United States led in the belief that international trade and investment flows were a key to worldwide prosperity. Many months of international negotiations in London, Geneva, and Lake Success (New York) culminated on March 24, 1948, in Havana, Cuba, with the signing of the Havana Charter for the **International Trade Organization(ITO).** The charter represented a series of agreements among 53 countries. It was designed to cover international commercial policies, restrictive business practices, commodity agreements, employment and reconstruction, economic development and international investment, and a constitution for a new United Nations agency to administer the whole.[1]

Even though the International Trade Organization incorporated many farsighted notions, most nations refused to ratify its provisions. They feared the power and bureaucratic size of the new organization—and the consequent threats to national sovereignty. As a result, this most forward-looking approach to international trade and investment was never implemented. However, other organizations conceived at the time have made major contributions toward improving international business. An agreement was initiated for the purpose of reducing tariffs and therefore facilitating trade. In addition, international institutions such as the United Nations, the World Bank, and the International Monetary Fund were negotiated.

The **General Agreement on Tariffs and Trade (GATT)** has been called a "remarkable success story of a postwar international organization that was never intended to become one."[2] It started out in 1947 as a set of rules to ensure nondiscrimination, transparent procedures, the settlement of disputes, and the participation of the lesser-developed countries in international trade. To increase trade GATT uses tariff concessions, through which member countries agree to limit the level of tariffs they will impose on imports from other GATT members. An important tool is the **Most-Favored Nation (MFN)** clause, which calls for each member country to grant every other member country the same most favorable treatment which it accords to any other country with respect to imports and exports.[3] MFN in effect, provides for equal, rather than special, treatment.

The GATT was not originally intended to be an international organization. Rather, it was to be a multilateral treaty designed to operate under the International Trade Organization (ITO). However, because the ITO never came into being, the GATT became the governing body for settling international trade disputes. Gradually it evolved into an institution that sponsored various successful rounds of international trade negotiations. Headquartered in Geneva, Switzerland, the GATT Secretariat conducts its work as instructed by the representatives of its member nations. Even though the GATT had no independent enforcement mechanism and relied entirely on moral suasion and on frequently wavering membership adherence to its rules, it achieved major progress for world trade.

Early in its history, the GATT accomplished the reduction of duties for trade in 50,000 products, amounting to two-thirds of the value of the trade among its participants. In subsequent years, special GATT negotiations such as the Kennedy Round, named after John F. Kennedy, and the Tokyo Round, named after the location where the negotiations were agreed upon, further reduced trade barriers and improved dispute-settlement mechanisms. The GATT also developed better provisions for dealing with subsidies and more explicit definitions of roles for import controls. Table 3.1 provides an overview of the different GATT rounds.

The latest GATT negotiations, called the Uruguay Round, were initiated in 1987. Even though tariffs still were addressed in these negotiations, their importance has been greatly diminished due to the success of earlier agreements. The main thrust of negotiations had become the sharpening of dispute-settlement rules and the integration of the trade and investment areas that were outside of the GATT. After many years of often contentious negotiations, a new accord was finally ratified in early 1995. The GATT was supplanted by a new institution, the **World Trade Organization (WTO),** which now administers international trade and investment accords. These accords will gradually reduce governmental subsidies to industries and will convert nontariff barriers into more transparent tariff barriers. The textile and clothing industries eventually will be brought into the WTO regime, resulting in decreased subsidies

WWW

**TABLE 3.1**

**Negotiations in the GATT**

| Round | Dates | Numbers of Countries | Value of Trade Covered | Average Tariff Cut | Average Tariffs Afterward |
|---|---|---|---|---|---|
| Geneva | 1947 | 23 | $10 billion | 35% | n/a |
| Annecy | 1949 | 33 | Unavailable | | n/a |
| Torquay | 1950 | 34 | Unavailable | | n/a |
| Geneva | 1956 | 22 | $2.5 billion | | n/a |
| Dillon | 1960–1961 | 45 | $4.9 billion | | n/a |
| Kennedy | 1962–1967 | 48 | $40 billion | 35% | 8.7% |
| Tokyo | 1973–1979 | 99 | $155 billion | 34% | 4.7% |
| Uruguay | 1986–1994 | 124 | $300 billion | 38% | 3.9% |

*Sources:* John H. Jackson *The World Trading System* (Cambridge, Mass.: MIT Press. 1989), and *The GATT: Uruguay Round Final Act should Produce Overall U.S. Economic Gains.* U.S. General Accounting Office, Report to Congress, Washington, D.C., July 1994. **www.gao.gov**

and fewer market restrictions. An entire new set of rules was designed to govern the service area, and agreement also was reached on new rules to encourage international investment flows.

The GATT and now the WTO have made major contributions to improved trade and investment flows around the world. The latest round alone is predicted to increase global exports by more than $755 billion by the year 2002.[4] The success of the GATT and the resulting increase in welfare has refuted the old postulate that "the strong is most powerful alone." Nations have increasingly come to recognize that international trade and investment activities are important to their own economic well-being.

Nations also have come to accept that they must generate sufficient outgoing export and incoming investment activities to compensate for the inflow of imports and outgoing investment. In the medium and long term, the balance of payments must be maintained. For short periods of time, gold or capital transfers can be used to finance a deficit. Such financing, however, can continue only while gold and foreign assets last or while foreign countries will accept the IOUs of the deficit countries, permitting them to pile up foreign liabilities. This willingness, of course, will vary. Some countries, such as the United States, can run up deficits of hundreds of billions of dollars because of political stability, acceptable rates of return, and perceived economic security. Yet, over the long term, all nations are subject to the same economic rules.

## Changes in the Global Policy Environment

Three major changes have occurred over time in the global policy environment: a reduction of domestic policy influence, a weakening of traditional international institutions, and a sharpening of the conflict between industrialized and developing nations. These three changes in turn have had a major effect on policy responses in the international trade and investment field.

The effects of growing global linkages on the domestic economy have been significant. Policymakers have increasingly come to recognize that it is very difficult to isolate domestic economic activity from international market events. Again and again, domestic policy measures are vetoed or counteracted by the activities of global market forces. Decisions that were once clearly in the domestic purview now have to be revised due to influences from abroad. Global Perspective 3.1 shows how international factors can shape or direct domestic economic policy. At the same time, the clash between the fixed geography of nations and the nonterritorial nature of many of today's problems and solutions continues to escalate. Nation-states may simply no longer be the natural problem-solving unit. Local government may be most appropriate to address some of the problems of individuals, while transnational or even global entities are required to deal with larger issues such as economics, resources, or the environment.[5]

Agricultural policies, for example—historically a domestic issue—have been thrust into the international realm. Any time a country or a group of nations such as the European Union contemplates changes in agricultural subsidies, quantity restrictions, or even quality regulations, international trade partners are quick to speak up against the resulting global effects of such changes. When countries contemplate specific industrial policies that encourage, for example, industrial innovation or collaboration, they often encounter major opposition from their trading partners, who believe that their own industries are jeopardized by such policies. Those reactions and the resulting constraints are the result of growing interdependencies among nations and a closer linkage between industries around the world. The following examples highlight the penetration of U.S. society by international trade considerations.

- One of every six American manufacturing jobs is in the export sector.[6]
- One of every three U.S. farm acres produces crops for export.[7]
- U.S. firms that export experience 20 percent faster employment growth and are 9 percent less likely to go out of business than are nonexporting firms.[8]
- Wages for U.S. jobs supported by merchandise exports are 20 percent higher than the national average.[9]
- Foreign central banks and private investors hold over 28 percent of the total number of outstanding U.S. Treasury securities.[10]

To some extent, the economic world as we knew it has been turned upside down. For example, trade flows used to determine **currency flows** and therefore the exchange rate. In the more recent past, currency flows have taken on a life of their own, increasing from an average daily trading volume of $18 billion in 1980 to almost $2 trillion in the late 1990s. As a result, they have begun to set the value of exchange rates independent of trade. These exchange rates in turn have now begun to determine the level of trade. Governments that want to counteract these developments with monetary policies find that currency flows outnumber trade flows by more than ten to one. Also, private sector financial flows vastly outnumber the financial flows that can be marshaled by governments, even when acting in concert. The interactions between global and domestic financial flows have severely limited the freedom for governmental action. For example, if the European Central Bank or the Federal Reserve of the United States changes interest rate levels, these changes will not

## Reduction of Domestic Policy Influences

# THE EFFECT OF GLOBAL LINKAGES

**P**oliticians have historically blamed economic ills on enemies ranging form monopolists and trade unionists to fascists and communists. Now some politicians are using the same dramatic rhetoric for what they see as a new enemy—the electronic army of currency and bond traders. Some critics argue that today national economic sovereignty is being eroded by massive international capital flows, leaving governments powerless to defend their own economic interests.

The past two decades have witnessed a revolution, as domestic financial markets have opened up to massive global capital flows, beyond the control of any government. The shifts in this vast pool of capital can often spell the difference between the success or failure of an economic policy. Alarmists suggest that irrational and selfish currency speculators are dictating economic policy. Malaysian Prime Minister Mahathir Mohamad, reeling from a 20 percent devaluation of his country's currency in the span of a few months, vehemently denounced currency speculators, including financier and philanthropist George Soros. Mahathir denounced currency trading as "unnecessary, unproductive and immoral," warning developing nations that they could "be suddenly manipulated and forced to bow to the great fund managers who have now come to be the people to decide who should prosper and who shouldn't."

Recent bouts of financial instability, such as the Mexican peso crisis and the turmoil suffered by Thai and Malaysian economies in 1997, demonstrate how cruelly global financial markets can punish countries whose policies they deem inadequate. James Carville, one of President Clinton's campaign advisors, sums up a common view of the bond market: "I used to think that if there was reincarnation, I wanted to come back as the president or the pope. But now I want to be the bond market: you can intimidate everybody." More telling, perhaps, is the graffiti seen on a wall in Poland that reads:

"We wanted democracy, but we ended up with the bond market."

Such fears have driven government efforts to try to curb the market's power. Government impotence, especially at a time of financial turbulence, brings forth greater calls for governments to subdue markets by such methods as closer international policy coordination and the imposition of capital controls or transaction taxes. Are such demands warranted? Financial liberalization has produced huge benefits. A liberal capital market ensures that savings are directed to the most productive investments, without regard for national boundaries. Increased competition has fostered greater efficiency in the financial system, offering better opportunities for savers and lower costs for borrowers. The end result of these influences is higher investment and growth.

The price that governments have to pay for these benefits is a weakening of their traditional economic ammunition, in terms of both policy choices and the effectiveness of the weapons they can use. It is possible, however, that this added constraint on government policy has been beneficial all around. Liberal markets often provide a healthy discipline, which in the long term will encourage better economic policies and performance.

A liberalized and globalized capital market, argues Richard O'Brien, an economist at Global Business Network, limits government's ability to abuse their traditional base of economic power: the ability to tax, the ability to print money, and the ability to borrow. If a government borrows recklessly or allows inflation to creep up, for example, investors will seek refuge in another currency. All that is being lost is the power to pursue damaging policies. As Soros put it, "Foreign financial institutions can play a useful role because closed financial systems tend to be inefficient, corrupt and bound up in politics," although he admits that "foreign capital is notoriously fickle."

As global financial markets become more integrated, the reward for pursuing the right policies will become bigger. The danger of the growing capital market may not be the market itself, but government's temptation to respond to market excesses by trying to force the global capital market into a straitjacket.

*Sources: Pam Woodall, "Who's in the Driver's Seat?," **The Economist** (October 7, 1995); Sandra Sugawara, "Halt Urged On Speculative Money Trades," September 21, 1997 and "Soros opposes currency trade limits," September 22, 1997, **The Washington Post**.*

only influence domestic activities, but also trigger international flows of capital that may reduce, enhance, or even negate the domestic effects. Similarly, rapid technological change and vast advances in communication permit firms and countries to quickly emulate innovation and counteract carefully designed plans. As a result, governments are often powerless to implement effective policy measures, even when they know what to do.

Governments also find that domestic regulations often have major international repercussions. In the United States, for example, the breakup of AT&T resulted in significant changes in the purchasing practices of the newly formed Bell companies. Overnight, competitive bids became decisive in a process that previously was entirely with the firm. This change opened up the U.S. market to foreign suppliers of telecommunications equipment, with only limited commensurate market developments abroad for U.S. firms. Therefore, U.S. telecommunications firms found themselves suddenly under much greater competitive pressures than did their foreign counterparts.

Legislators around the world are continually confronted with such international linkages. In some countries, the implications are understood, and new legislation is devised with an understanding of its international consequences. In other nations, particularly in the United States, national sovereignty expectations often relegate international repercussions to the status of side effects that can be ignored. Yet, given the linkages among economies, this is an unwarranted and sometimes even dangerous view. It threatens to place firms at a competitive disadvantage in the international marketplace or may make it easier for foreign firms to compete in the domestic market.

Even when policymakers want to take decisive steps, they are often unable to do so. In the late 1980s, for example, the United States decided to impose **punitive tariffs** of 100 percent on selected Japanese imports to retaliate for Japanese nonadherence to a previously reached semiconductor agreement. The initial goal was clear. Yet the task became increasingly difficult as the U.S. government developed a list of specific imports to be targeted. In many instances, the U.S. market was heavily dependent on the Japanese imports, which meant that U.S. manufacturers and consumers would be severely affected by punitive tariffs. As Figure 3.1 shows, many Japanese products are actually produced or assembled in the United States. To halt the importing of components would throw Americans out of work.

Other targeted products were not actually produced in Japan. Rather, Japanese firms had opened plants in third countries, such as Mexico. Penalizing these product imports would therefore punish Mexican workers and affect Mexican employment, an undesirable result.

More and more products were eliminated from the list before it was published. In two days of hearings, additional linkages emerged. For example, law enforcement agencies testified that if certain fingerprinting equipment from Japan were sanctioned, law enforcement efforts would suffer significantly. Of the $1.8 billion worth of goods initially considered for the sanctions list, the government was barely able to scrape together $300 million worth. Figure 3.2 illustrates how far such linkages have progressed in the aircraft industry. With so many product components being sourced from different countries around the world, it becomes increasingly difficult to decide what constitutes a domestic product. In light of this uncertainty, policy actions against foreign products becomes more difficult as well.

Policymakers find themselves with increasing responsibilities, yet with fewer and less effective tools to carry them out. More segments of the domestic economy are vulnerable to international shifts at the same time that they are becoming less controllable. To regain some power to influence policies, some governments have sought to restrict the influence of world trade by erecting barriers, charging tariffs, and implementing import regulations. However, these

**FIGURE 3.1**

**Japanese Products Can Drive the U.S. Economy**
*Sources:* Toyota Motor Company

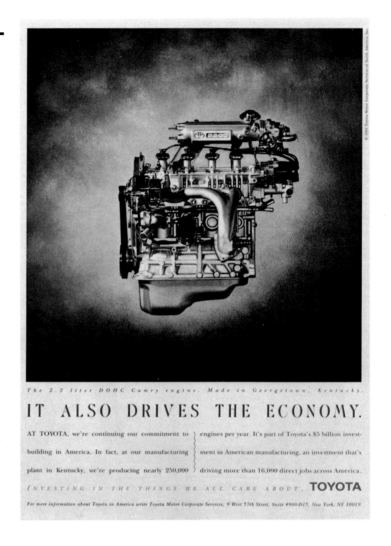

*The 2.2 liter DOHC Camry engine. Made in Georgetown, Kentucky.*

## IT ALSO DRIVES THE ECONOMY.

AT TOYOTA, we're continuing our commitment to } engines per year. It's part of Toyota's $5 billion invest-

building in America. In fact, at our manufacturing } ment in American manufacturing, an investment that's

plant in Kentucky, we're producing nearly 250,000 } driving more than 16,000 direct jobs across America.

*INVESTING IN THE THINGS WE ALL CARE ABOUT.* **TOYOTA**

*For more information about Toyota in America write Toyota Motor Corporate Services, 9 West 57th Street, Suite 4900-D15, New York, NY 10019.*

measures too have been restrained by the existence of international agreements forged through institutions such as the WTO or bilateral negotiations. World trade has therefore changed many previously held notions about the sovereignty of nation-states and extraterritoriality. The same interdependence that made us all more affluent has also left us more vulnerable.

**Weakening International Institutions**

The intense linkages among nations and the new economic environment resulting from new market entrants and the encounter of different economic systems are weakening the traditional international institutions and are therefore affecting their roles.

The ratification of the Uruguay Round and the formation of the WTO have provided the former GATT with new impetus. However, the organization is confronted with many difficulties. One of them is the result of the organi-

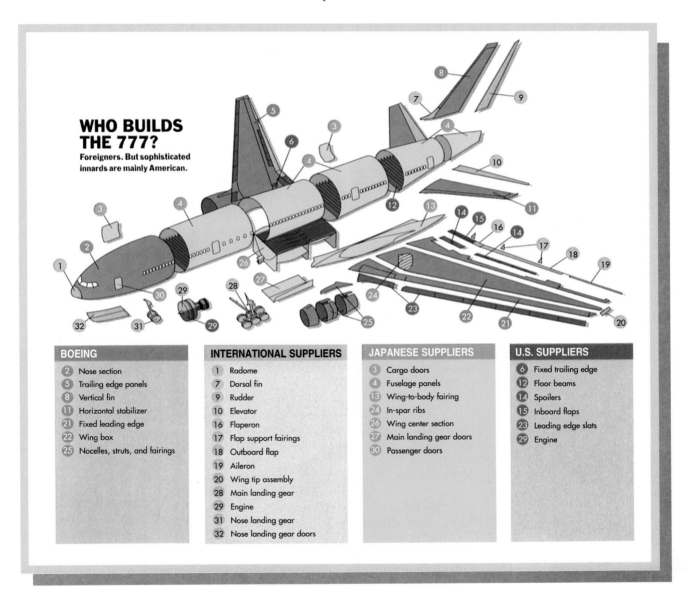

**FIGURE 3.2**

**Who Builds the Boeing 777?**

*Source:* Boeing as appeared in *Fortune* (April 20, 1992): 140. 1992 Time Inc. All rights reserved.

zation's success. Historically, a key focus of the WTO's predecessor was on reducing tariffs. With tariff levels at an unprecedented low level, however, attention now has to rest with areas such as nontariff barriers, which are much more complex and indigenous to nations. In consequence, any emerging dispute is likely to be more heatedly contested and more difficult to resolve. A second traditional focus rested with the right to establishment in countries. Given today's technology, however, the issue has changed. Increasingly, firms will clamor for the right to operations in a country without seeking to establish themselves there. For example, given the opportunities offered by telecommunications, one can envision a bank becoming active in a country without establishing a single office or branch.

Another key problem area results from the fact that many disagreements were set aside for the sake of concluding the negotiations. Disputes in such areas as entertainment and intellectual property rights protection are likely to resurface in the near term and cause a series of trade conflicts among nations. If the WTO's dispute settlement mechanism is then applied to resolve the conflict, outcries in favor of national sovereignty may cause nations to withdraw from the agreement whenever a country loses in a dispute.

A final major weakness of the WTO may result from the desire of some of its members to introduce "social causes" into trade decisions. It is debated, for example, whether the WTO should also deal with issues such as labor laws, competition, and emigration freedoms. Other issues, such as freedom of religion, provision of health care, and the safety of animals are being raised as well. It will be very difficult to have the WTO remain a viable organization if too many nongermane issues are loaded onto the trade and investment mission. The 132 governments participating in the WTO have diverse perspectives, histories, relations, economies, and ambitions. Many of them fear that social causes can be used to devise new rules of protectionism against their exports. Then there is also the question of how much companies—which, after all, are the ones doing the trading and investing—should be burdened with concerns outside of their scope.

To be successful, the WTO needs to be able to focus on its core mission, which deals with international trade and investment. The addition of social causes may appear politically expedient, but will be a key cause for divisiveness and dissent, and thus will inhibit progress on further liberalization of trade and investment. Failure to achieve such progress would leave the WTO without teeth and would negate much of the progress achieved in the Uruguay Round negotiations. It might be best to leave the WTO free from such pressures and look to increased economic ties to cross-pollinate cultures, values, and ethics and to cause changes in the social arena.[11]

Similar problems have befallen international financial institutions. For example, although the IMF has functioned well so far, it is currently under severe challenge by new substantial financial requirements. So far, the IMF has been able to smooth over the most difficult problems, but has not found ways to solve them. For example, in the 1995 peso crisis of Mexico, the IMF was able to provide some relief through a stand-by credit. Yet, given the financial needs of many other nations such as South Korea, Malaysia, Indonesia, Thailand, and Russia, the nations of central Europe, and many countries in Latin America, the IMF simply does not have enough funds to satisfy such needs. In cases of multiple financial crises, it then is unable to provide its traditional function of calming financial markets in turmoil.

Apart from its ability to provide funds, the IMF must also rethink its traditional rules of operations. For example, it is quite unclear whether stringent economic rules and benchmark performance measures are equally applicable to all countries seeking IMF assistance. New economic conditions that have not been experienced to date may require different types of approaches. The linkage between economic and political stability also may require different considerations, possibly substantially changing the IMF's mission.

Similarly, the World Bank **www.worldbank.org** successfully met its goal of aiding the reconstruction of Europe but has been less successful in furthering the economic goals of the developing world and the newly emerging market economies in the former Soviet bloc. Therefore, at the same time when domestic policy measures have become less effective, international institutions that could help to develop substitute international policy measures have been weakened by new challenges to their traditional missions and insufficient resources to meet such challenges.

## Sharpening of the Conflict between Industrialized and Developing Nations

In the 1960s and 1970s it was hoped that the developmental gap between industrialized nations and many countries in the less-developed world could gradually be closed. This goal was to be achieved with the transfer of technology and the infusion of major funds. Even though the 1970s saw vast quantities of petrodollars available for recycling and major growth in borrowing by some developing nations, the results have not been as expected. Although several less-developed nations have gradually emerged as newly industrialized countries (NICs), even more nations are facing grim economic futures.

In Latin America, many nations are still saddled with enormous amounts of debt, rapidly increasing populations, and very fragile economies. The newly emerging democracies in central Europe and the former Soviet Union also face major debt and employment problems. In view of their shattered dreams, policymakers in these nations have become increasingly aggressive in their attempts to reshape the ground rules of the world trade and investment flows. Although many policymakers share the view that major changes are necessary to resolve the difficulties that exist, no clear-cut solutions have emerged.

Lately, an increase in environmental awareness has contributed to a further sharpening of the conflict. As Global Perspective 3.2 shows, developing countries may place different emphasis on environmental protection. If they are to take measures that will assist the industrialized nations in their environmental goals, they expect to be assisted and rewarded in these efforts. Yet, many in the industrialized world view environmental issues as "global obligation," rather than as a matter of choice, and are reluctant to pay.

## Policy Responses to Changing Conditions

The word *policy* conjures up an image of a well-coordinated set of governmental activities. Unfortunately, in the trade and investment sector, as in most of the domestic policy areas, this is rarely the case. Policymakers need to respond too often to short-term problems, need to worry too much about what is politically salable to multiple constituencies, and in some countries, are in office too short a time to formulate a guiding set of long-term strategies. All too often, because of public and media pressures, policymakers must be concerned with current events—such as monthly trade deficit numbers and investment flow figures—that may not be very meaningful in the larger picture. In such an environment, actions may lead to extraordinarily good tactical measures but fail to achieve long-term success.

## The Global Environment: A Source of Conflict
## Between Developed and Less-Developed Nations

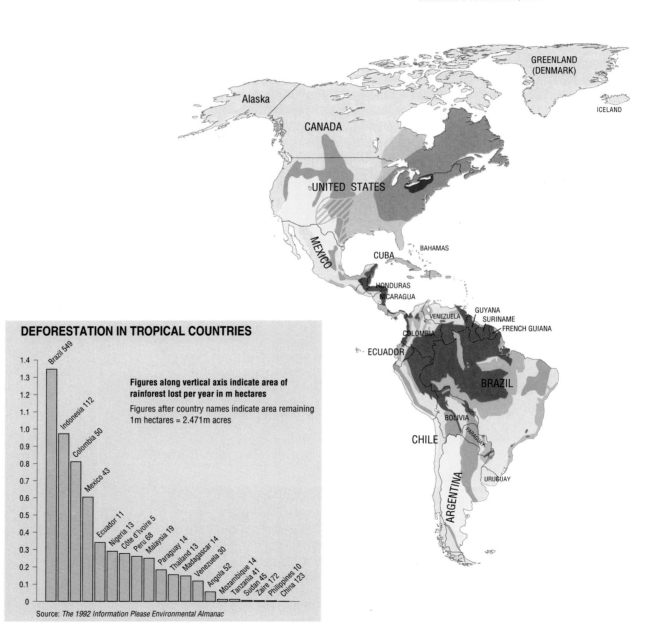

**DESERTIFICATION**

Areas with risk of desertification

Existing deserts

Source: *Atlas of the Environment, 2nd Ed.*

**DEFORESTATION IN TROPICAL COUNTRIES**

**Figures along vertical axis indicate area of
rainforest lost per year in m hectares**

Figures after country names indicate area remaining
1m hectares = 2.471m acres

Source: *The 1992 Information Please Environmental Almanac*

**RAINFOREST DESTRUCTION**

Present distribution of forest area

Area originally forested

Source: *Atlas of the Environment,  2nd Ed.*

**ACID DEPOSITION**
**Estimated acidity of precipitation in Europe (1988) and  North America (1985)**

**ph**

4.6–5.0 (less acidic)

4.2–4.6

4.2 (more acidic)

Source: *Atlas of the Environment,  2nd Ed.*

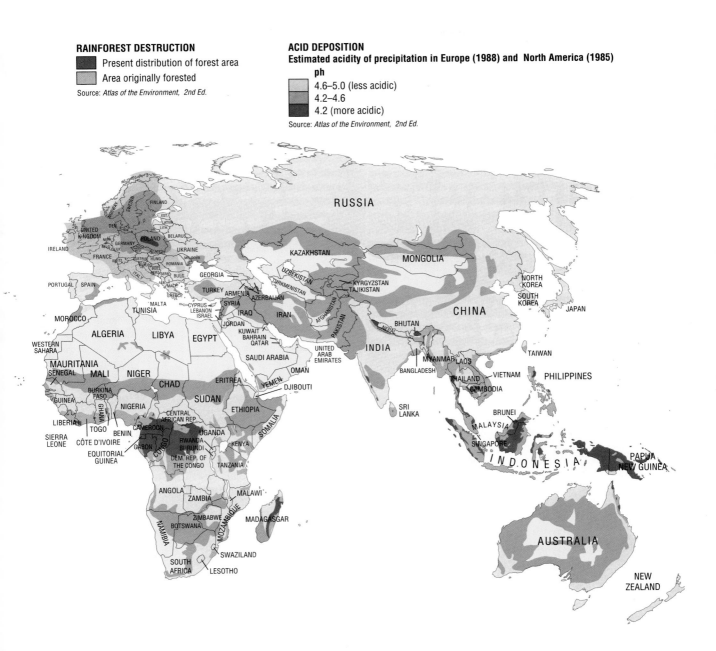

Source: *Atlas of the Environment,  2nd Ed.*

## STALEMATE AFTER THE EARTH SUMMIT: NORTH VERSUS SOUTH

Ozone depletion, acid rain, and global warming make headlines daily. But different countries have different concerns. World leaders met in Rio de Janeiro for a United Nations–sponsored Earth Summit to discuss the health of the planet. At the meetings, the developing world voiced two essential concerns: their lack of money and technology. The industrialized nations in turn focused primarily on the environment, wanting to do something about potential threats such as global warming.

The two viewpoints often clash. Said Jessica Ocaya-Lakidi of Uganda: "We don't yet have the big industries. We are lagging so far behind that we don't talk of industrial pollution." Maximo Kalaw, Jr., for Manila added: "The message is, if you cannot help us on debt, forget about the environmental conservation of our forests, because it is too much of a burden to handle." In essence, the developing countries are suggesting a straightforward bargain: If we get money, they say to the industrialized world, we will protect the environmental resources you claim to value so highly.

By contrast, the developed world sees a common responsibility of humanity that developing nations have to help fulfill. For example, the rosy periwinkle, a pink shrub found only in Madagascar, can be used to make drugs that have proved effective in fighting childhood leukemia and Hodgkin's disease. Plant genes found in Africa can also be used to improve varieties of wheat, corn, rice, and tomatoes. Therefore, it is important to maintain as much biodiversity as possible, a goal that requires the protection of natural resources. Some companies have already taken action to help. BankAmerica Corp., for example, forgave $6 million of its outstanding loans to Latin American countries in exchange for the debtor nations' promise to conserve ecologically critical rain forests.

In spite of the wide praise for such debt-for-nature swaps, many developing nations see them as a potential threat to their sovereignty. There is concern that these swaps are an attempt to somehow put areas of sovereign territory off limits to domestic control.

Meeting again five years after the Earth Summit, world leaders found themselves still stalemated over the same North-South divisions that created conflict in 1992. At the Earth Summitt+5, many of the same opinions were voiced. Minister Msuya Waldi Mangachi of Tanzania, speaking for the "Group of 77" representing 132 developing countries, said that conflict occurred because "developing countries were expecting reaffirmation of commitments for financial support made at Rio, while developed-country partners came to fine tune [Rio's plan of action for environmental preservation] and add new areas." A stalemate resulted, he said, since "we saw those new areas as additional obligations, with no means proposed by donors for implementation and no movement on redressing unfulfilled commitments."

*Sources: Eugene Robinson, "At the Earth Summit, South Aims to Send Bill North,"* **The Washington Post,** *June 1, 1992, A1, A14; "Earth Summit Review Ends with Few Commitments," United Nations press release, July 1997.*
*UN Division for Sustainable Development:* **www.un.org/dpcsd/dsd**

## Restrictions of Imports

**WWW**

In the United States, the Congress has increasingly focused on trade issues and provided the president with additional powers to affect trade. Unfortunately, apart from the consent to the NAFTA and WTO trade agreements, most of these new powers provide only for an increasing threat against foreign importers and investors, not for better conditions for U.S. exporters of goods, services, or capital. As a result, the power of the executive branch of government to improve international trade and investment opportunities for U.S. firms through international negotiations and the relaxation of rules, regulations, and laws has become increasingly restricted over time.

Worldwide, most countries maintain at least a surface-level conformity with international principles. However, many exert substantial restraints on free trade through import controls and barriers. Some of the more frequently encountered barriers are listed in Table 3.2. They are found particularly in countries that suffer from major trade deficits or major infrastructure problems,

**TABLE 3.2**

**Trade Barriers**

There are literally hundreds of ways to build a barrier. The following list provides just a few of the trade barriers that exporters face.

- Restrictive licensing
- Special import authorization
- Global quotas
- Voluntary export restraints
- Temporary prohibitions
- Advance import deposits
- Taxes on foreign exchange deals
- Preferential licensing applications
- Excise duties
- Licensing fees
- Statistical taxes
- Sales taxes
- Consumption taxes
- Discretionary licensing

- Licenses for selected purchases
- Country quotas
- Seasonal prohibitions
- Health and sanitary prohibitions
- Foreign exchange licensing
- Licenses subject to barter and countertrade
- Customs surcharges
- Stamp taxes
- Consular invoice fees
- Taxes on transport
- Service charges
- Value-added taxes
- Turnover taxes
- Internal taxes

*Source:* Mark Magnier, "Blockades to Food Exports Hide Behind Invisible Shields," *The Journal of Commerce* (September 18, 1989): 5A. Reprinted with permission.

causing them to enter into voluntary restraint agreements with trading partners or to selectively apply trade-restricting measures such as tariffs, quotas, or nontariff barriers against trading partners.

**Tariffs** are taxes based primarily on the value of imported goods and services. **Quotas** are restrictions on the number of foreign products that can be imported. **Nontariff barriers** consist of a variety of measures such as testing, certification, or simply bureaucratic hurdles that have the effect of restricting imports. All of these measures tend to raise the price of imported goods. They therefore constitute a transfer of funds from the buyers (or, if absorbed by them, the sellers) of imports to the government, and—if accompanied by price increases of competing domestic products—to the domestic producers of such products.

**Voluntary restraint agreements** are designed to help domestic industries reorganize, restructure, and recapture production prominence. Even though officially voluntary, these agreements are usually implemented through severe threats against trading partners. Due to their "voluntary" nature, the agreements are not subject to any previously negotiated bilateral or multilateral trade accords.

When nations do not resort to the subtle mechanism of voluntary agreements to affect trade flows, they often impose tariffs and quotas. Many countries use **antidumping** laws to impose tariffs on imports. Antidumping laws are designed to help domestic industries that are injured by unfair competition from abroad due to products being "dumped" on them. Dumping may involve selling goods overseas at prices lower than those in the exporter's home market or at a price below the cost of production or both. The growing use of antidumping measures by governments around the world complicates the pricing decisions of exporters. Large domestic firms, on the other hand, can use the antidumping process to obtain strategic shelter from foreign competitors.[12]

For example, in 1983 the International Trade Commission imposed a five-year tariff on Japanese heavy motorcycles imported into the United States. The 49.4 percent duty was granted at the request of Harley-Davidson, which could no longer compete with the heavily discounted bikes being imported by companies such as Honda and Kawasaki. The gradually declining tariff gave Harley-Davidson the time to enact new management strategies without worrying about the pressure of the Japanese imports. Within four years, Harley-Davidson was back on its feet and again had the highest market share in the heavyweight class of bikes. In 1987, Harley-Davidson officials requested that the tariff be lifted a year early. As a result, the policy was labeled a success. However, at no time were the costs of these measures to U.S. consumers even considered.

The third major method by which imports have been restricted is nontariff barriers. These consist of buy-domestic campaigns, preferential treatment for domestic bidders compared with foreign bidders, national standards that are not comparable to international standards, and an emphasis on the design rather than the performance of products. Global Perspective 3.3 gives and example of how Japan designed new domestic regulations to reduce the import success of foreign rice. Such nontariff barriers are often the most insidious obstacles to free trade, since they are difficult to detect, hard to quantify, and demands for their removal are often blocked by references to a nation's cultural and historic heritage.

One other way in which imports are sometimes reduced is by tightening market access and entry of foreign products through involved procedures and inspections. Probably the most famous are the measures implemented by France. In order to stop or at least reduce the importation of foreign video recorders, the French government ruled that all of them had to be sent to the customs station at Poitiers. This customshouse was located away from major transport routes, woefully understaffed, and open only a few days each week. In addition, the few customs agents at Poitiers insisted on opening each package separately to inspect the merchandise. Within a few weeks, imports of video recorders came to halt. Members of the French government, however, were able to point to the fact that they had not restrained trade at all; rather, they had only made some insignificant changes in the procedures of domestic governmental actions.

The discussion of import restrictions has focused thus far on merchandise trade. Similar restrictions are applicable to investment flows and, by extension, to international trade in services. In order to protect ownership, control, and development of domestic industries, many countries impose varying restrictions on investment capital flows. Most frequently, they are in the form of investment-screening agencies that decide whether any particular foreign investment project is sufficiently meritorious to warrant execution. Canada, for example, has "Investment Canada" an agency that scrutinizes foreign investments.[13] So do most developing nations, where special government permission must be obtained for investment projects. This permission frequently carries with it certain conditions, such as levels of ownership permitted, levels of dividends that can be repatriated, numbers of jobs that must be created, or the extent to which management can be carried out by individuals from abroad.

# CAN CALIFORNIA RICE STICK IN JAPAN?

**A**pparently, the nationality of rice matters. A bad summer reduced the 1993 Japanese rice harvest, and Japan was forced to import foreign rice. So the government tried to prevent imports from undermining the market for domestic rice, and encouraged Japanese consumers to keep buying subsidized, expensive Japanese rice.

The rice accord under GATT ruled out import quotas or other nontariff barriers. Therefore, Japan's Ministry of Agriculture designed a more subtle means to maintain control of the market. Hiding behind a superficial argument of "national equality," the ministry announced in early 1994 that no specific rice could be sold separately. All rice—domestic and imported—had to be mixed, so that the resulting rice did not have a "nationality." The directive prescribed a mix formula of 30 percent Japanese; 50 percent Californian, Chinese, and Australian combined; and 20 percent Thai rice.

Different rices have different uses. For instance, the Californian variety works well when steamed, while the Chinese or Thai variety is needed for a Chinese dish, and the Japanese goes very well with sushi. As no doubt was intended, the resultant nationless mix was appalling. You simply cannot steam a Californian/Thai mix.

The ministry's thinking: Given a choice, every Japanese in his right mind would buy the homegrown, nonmixed product as soon as it hit the market again. There would be no need for import quotas or other nontariff barriers. While the initial reaction to the mixed rice policy was what the ministry was looking for, it wasn't long before outrage over the restrictive policies grew so strong that retailers were able to ignore the mixing directive without fearing ministry action. It had become clear that the citizens sufficiently disliked Thai rice and had not developed a taste for Chinese rice either; thus the ministry declared that foreign rice could now be sold just by itself—with one exception. The most popular of all imports, the sticky Californian rice, still could not be sold in its pure form. It was mixed with rice from other states and sold under the name "American." The official reason for this mixing was that there was not enough Californian rice for everyone. But retailers openly admitted that the rice was mixed in order to lower its quality so that they could also sell the less popular Chinese and Thai grains.

In addition to being the object of this quality-reducing policy, the "American" mix was subject to a 580 percent tariff, making it exactly as expensive as medium-quality Japanese rice ($15 a pound), thereby removing any price advantage. The Japanese government was able to take in revenue of $2.7 billion from its rice-import tariffs. The revenue was used to subsidize Japanese rice farmers and improve their irrigation systems. The idea was that as the new GATT "minimum-access rule" kicks in over a seven-year period beginning in 1995, Japanese farmers would become price competitive.

Since the minimum-access rule took effect, Japan has been forced to comply with the GATT agreement by importing an increasing amount of foreign rice each year, despite recent bumper harvests of the domestic crop. The government has been stockpiling as much as 2.5 million tons of surplus rice. Faced with the glut of rice, Japan's Food Agency has been using imported rice in processed food, like crackers. Imported rice rarely finds its way to direct sales at supermarkets. But Japanese farmers fear that imported rice will become more competitive after the year 2000, when rice tariffs will be discussed at WTO agriculture negotiations.

*Sources: Ulrike Schaede, "Japan Rice Move Leaves 'Em Steaming," **The Wall Street Journal**, June 1, 1994, A14; Hirotaka Terai, "Shaky Agriculture Policy Feeding Rice Glut," **The Daily Yomiuri**, October 23, 1997, p. 13.*

The United States restricts foreign investment in instances where national security or related concerns are at stake. Major foreign investments may be reviewed by the **Committee on Foreign Investments in the United States (CFIUS).** CFIUS became active, for example, during the intended purchase of Fairchild Semiconductor Industries by Fujitsu of Japan. The review precipitated a major national discussion and resulted in the withdrawal of the Fujitsu purchase offer. Prior to that, national attention was focused on investment strategies of Arab firms, governments, and individuals in the United States. The concern was that, because of their increased oil income in the 1970s, Arab countries and nationals would be able to take over significant portions of U.S. industry and real estate. Yet the fears of being bought out were never justified, because investor perceptions of the potential political backlash resulted in a self-regulatory mechanism.

Foreign direct investment restrictions are often debated in many countries. Frequently, nations become concerned about levels of foreign direct investment and the "selling out" of the patrimony. However, the bottom line is that although the restriction of investments may permit more domestic control over industries, it also denies access to foreign capital. This in turn can result in a tightening up of credit markets, higher interest rates, and less impetus for innovation.

**The Effects of Import Restriction**  Policymakers are faced with several problems when trying to administer import controls. First, most of the time such controls exact a huge price from domestic consumers. Import controls may mean that the most efficient sources of supply are not available. The result is either second-best products or higher costs for restricted supplies, which in turn cause customer service standards to drop and consumers to pay significantly higher prices. Even though these costs may be widely distributed among many consumers and are less obvious, the social cost of these controls may be damaging to the economy and subject to severe attack from individuals. However, these attacks are countered by pressure from protected groups that benefit from import restrictions. For example, while citizens of the European Union may be forced by import controls to pay an elevated price for all the agricultural products they consume, agricultural producers in the region benefit from higher incomes. Achieving a proper trade-off is often difficult, if not impossible, for the policymaker.

A second major problem resulting from import controls is the downstream change in the composition of imports that may result. For example, if the importation of copper ore is restricted, through either voluntary restraints or quotas, producing countries may opt to shift their production systems and produce copper wire instead, which they can export. As a result, initially narrowly defined protectionistic measures may snowball in order to protect one downstream industry after another.

Another major problem that confronts the policymaker is that of efficiency. Import controls designed to provide breathing room to a domestic industry so it can either grow or recapture its competitive position often do not work. Rather than improve the productivity of an industry, such controls may provide it with a level of safety and a cushion of increased income, subsequently causing it to lag behind in technological advancements.

One must also be aware of the corporate response to import restrictions. Corporations faced with such restrictions can encourage their governments to erect similar barriers to protect them at home. The result is a gradually escalating set of trade obstacles. In addition, corporations can make strategic use of such barriers by incorporating them into their business plans and exploiting them in order to gain market share. For example, some multinational corporations have pressed governments to initiate antidumping actions against their competitors when faced with low-priced imports. In such instances, corporations may substitute adroit handling of government relations for innovation and competitiveness.

Finally, corporations also can circumvent import restrictions by shifting their activities. For example, instead of conducting trade, corporations can shift to foreign direct investment. The result may be drop in trade inflow, yet the domestic industry may still be under strong pressure from foreign firms. The investments of Japanese car producers in the United States serve as an example. However, due to the job-creation effects of such investment, such shifts may have been the driving desire on the part of the policymakers who implemented the import controls.

In addition to imposing restraints on imports, nations also control their exports. The reasons are short supply, national security and foreign policy purposes, or the desire to retain capital.

**Restrictions of Exports**

The United States, for example, regards trade as a privilege of the firm, granted by government, rather than a right or a necessity. As will be explained in more detail in Chapter 4, U.S. legislation to control exports focuses on **national security** controls—that is, the control of weapons exports or high-technology exports that might adversely affect the safety of the nation. In addition, exports can be controlled for reasons of foreign policy and short supply. These controls restrict the international business opportunities of firms if a government believes that such a restriction would send a necessary foreign policy message to another country. Such action may be undertaken regardless of whether the message will have any impact or whether similar products can easily be supplied by companies in other nations. Although perhaps valuable as a tool of international relations, such policies give a country's firms the reputation of being unreliable suppliers and may divert orders to firms in other nations.

Many nations also restrict exports of capital, because **capital flight** is a major problem for them. Particularly in situations where countries lack necessary foreign exchange reserves, governments are likely to place restrictions on capital outflow. In essence, government claims to have higher priorities for capital than its citizens. They in turn, often believe that the return on investment or the safety of the capital is not sufficiently ensured in their own countries. The reason may be governmental measures or domestic economic factors, such as inflation. These holders of capital want to invest abroad. By doing so, however, they deprive their domestic economy of much-needed investment funds.

Once governments impose restrictions on the export of funds, the desire to transfer capital abroad only increases. Because companies and individuals are ingenious in their efforts to achieve capital flight, governments, particularly in developing countries, continue to suffer. In addition, few new outside investors will enter the country because they fear that dividends and profits will not be remitted easily.

**Export Promotion Efforts**

The desire to increase participation in international trade and investment flows has led nations to implement export promotion programs. These programs are designed primarily to help domestic firms enter and maintain their position in international markets and to match or counteract similar export promotion efforts by other nations.

Most governments supply some support to their firms participating or planning to participate in international trade. Typically, this support falls into one of four categories: export information and advice, production support, marketing support, or finance and guarantees. While such support is widespread and growing, its intensity varies by country. For example, the United States spends 3 cents per $1000 of GDP on export promotion, compared with Germany's and Japan's expenditures of 5 cents, Great Britain's 7 cents, France's 18 cents, and Canada's 33 cents.[14] Figure 3.3 shows the different degree of export credit support offered by various countries.

**U.S. Export Promotion**    Given the deterioration of the U.S. trade balance, U.S. government trade policy is focusing on export programs to improve the international trade performance of U.S. firms. The Department of Commerce offers information services that provide data on foreign trade and market developments. The department's Foreign Commercial Service posts hundreds of professionals around the world to gather information and to assist business executives in their activities abroad.

A national export strategy has been formulated in order to coordinate the activities of diverse federal agencies. For the first time, the federal government has officially recognized that "American firms will simply not thrive at home unless they take full advantage of the tremendous opportunities abroad."[15] As a result of these efforts, a national network of export assistance centers has been created, capable of providing one-stop shops for exporters in search of export counseling and financial assistance. In addition, an official interagency advocacy network was created that helps U.S. companies win overseas contracts for large government purchases abroad. A variety of agencies have formed the

**FIGURE 3.3**

**Export Credit Agency Financing as a Percent of Exports, 1995**

*Sources:* The U.S. Trade Finance Agencies: A Special Report by the Trade Promotion Coordinating Committee, (US Government Printing Office, Washington, D.C.) June 1997: 16; **www.oecd.org**, May 1998 **www.exim.gov**, May 1998.

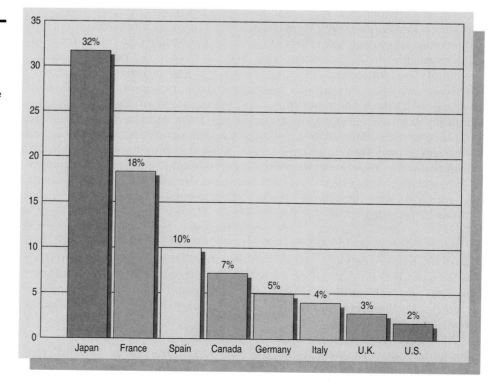

Trade Promotion Coordination Committee in order to continue improving services to U.S. exporters. A listing of these agencies together with their web sites is provided in the appendix to this chapter so that readers can obtain the most up-to-date information about trade policy changes and export assistance.

Another area of activity by the U.S. government is export financing. The Export-Import Bank of the United States provides U.S. firms with long-term loans and loan guarantees so that they can bid on contracts where financing is a key issue. In response to actions by foreign competitors, the bank has, on occasion also resorted to offering **mixed aid credits.** The credits, which take the form of loans composed partially of commercial interest rates and partially of highly subsidized developmental aid interest rates, result in very low interest loans to exporters.

Tax legislation that inhibited the employment of Americans by U.S. firms abroad has also been altered. In the past, U.S. nationals living abroad were, with some minor exclusion, fully subject to U.S. federal taxation. The cost of living abroad can often be quite high—for example, rent for a small apartment can approach $5,000 per month—so this tax structure often imposed a significant burden on U.S. firms and citizens abroad. As a result, companies frequently were not able to send U.S. employees to their foreign subsidiaries. However, a revision of the tax code now allows a substantial amount of income (up to 74,000 in 1999) to remain tax-free. More Americans can now be posted abroad. In their work they may specify the use of U.S. products, thus enhancing the competitive position of U.S. firms.

Any export promotion raises several questions. One concerns the justification of the expenditure of public funds for what is essentially an activity that should be driven by profits. It appears, however, that the start-up cost for international operations, particularly for smaller firms, may be sufficiently high to warrant some kind of government support.[16] A second question focuses on the capability of government to provide such support. Both for the selection and reach of firms as well as the distribution of support, government is not necessarily better equipped than the private sector to do a good job. A third issue concerns competitive export promotion. If countries provide such support to their firms, they may well distort the flow of trade. If other countries then increase their support of firms in order to counteract the effects, all that results is the same volume of trade activity, but at subsidized rates. It is therefore important to carefully evaluate export promotion activities as to their effectiveness and competitive impact. Perhaps such promotion is only beneficial when it addresses existing market gaps.

## Import Promotion Efforts

Some countries have also developed import promotion measures. The measures are implemented primarily by nations that have accumulated and maintained large balance-of-trade surpluses. They hope to allay other nations' fears of continued imbalances and to gradually redirect trade flows.

Japan, for example, has completely refurbished the operations of the Japan External Trade Organization (JETRO). This organization, which initially was formed to encourage Japanese exports, has now begun to focus on the promotion of imports to Japan. It organizes trade missions of foreign firms coming to Japan, hosts special exhibits and fairs within Japan, and provides assistance and encouragement to potential importers.

Many countries are also implementing policy measures to attract foreign direct investment. These policies can be the result of the needs of poorer countries to attract additional foreign capital to fuel economic growth without taking out more loans that call for fixed schedules of repayment.[17] Industrialized nations also participate in these efforts since governments are under pressure to provide jobs for their citizens and have come to recognize that foreign direct investment can serve as a major means to increase employment and income. Global Perspective 3.4 reports on some of the investment promotion efforts undertaken in the EU. Increasingly, even state and local governments are participating in investment promotion. Some U. S. states, for example, are sending out "Invest in the USA" missions on a regular basis. Others have opened offices abroad to inform local businesses about the beneficial investment climate at home.

Incentives used by policymakers to facilitate such investments are mainly of three types: fiscal, financial, and nonfinancial. **Fiscal incentives** are specific tax measures designed to attract the foreign investor. They typically consist of special depreciation allowances, tax credits or rebates, special deductions for capital expenditures, tax holidays, and the reduction of tax burdens on the in-

---

## COURTING FOREIGN INVESTORS FOR JOBS

**E**urope faces unemployment rates double the U.S. level, creating pressure for European politicians to come up with innovative ways to create jobs. Increasingly, European governments are turning to multinational corporations with incentives linked to the number of jobs the company will create by investing in the country. The more jobs a multinational manufacturer promises, the more subsidies the government will provide it. European countries thus find themselves competing with each other for multinationals' investment.

Britain, the leader in this race with 40 percent of all foreign investment in the European Union, paid $48,600 for each of the 6,100 jobs created in 1996 when LG, a south Korean firm, invested in an electronics complex. According to Britain's Trade and Industry Ministry, more than 285,000 jobs were created or preserved through foreign investment from 1994 to 1997. The subsidized jobs in turn created nonsubsidized jobs through local suppliers and improved the quality of local sourcing.

As European firms themselves seek to lower operations

costs by building plants abroad—including in Central and Eastern Europe—Germany, France, and Switzerland often have to play the foreign investment game with European companies. For example, France paid over $55,000 per job to get Mercedes-Benz's Swatch auto plant to locate in its eastern region of Lorraine. But this phenomenon is not limited to Europe—individual U.S. states have investment agencies in Europe that court foreign investors, offering cash incentives for job creation. For every job Mercedes-Benz created at its Alabama factory, it reaped around $165,000; at its Spartanburg, South Carolina plant, BMW received more than $100,000 per job. American companies investing in Europe have also benefited from the practice: In 1995 Ford got a $104 million grant for a new Jaguar plant in Birmingham, U.K., and the auto maker later used similar tactics when it threatened to close its assembly plant in Liverpool unless it received a government grant toward the cost of building a new model there.

Governments use the subsidies to induce investment not only from auto firms but, at even greater cost, from high-tech computer and electronics companies. With countries engaged in a bidding war for multinationals' investment, smaller nations face the prospect of being outspent by bigger competitors. Despite the high cost of the handouts, in this buyer's market, no country wants to miss the opportunity to gain job growth and modernized industry, especially when they plagued by high unemployment.

*Sources: Bruce Barnard, "A Buyer's Job Market," **The Journal of Commerce** (February 12, 1997): 1C, 23C.*

vestor. **Financial incentives** offer special funding for the investor by providing, for example, land or building, loans, and loan guarantees. **Nonfinancial incentives** can consist of guaranteed government purchases; special protection from competition through tariffs, import quotas, and local content requirements; and investments in infrastructure facilities.

All of these incentives are designed primarily to attract more industry and therefore create more jobs. They may slightly alter the advantage of a region and therefore make it more palatable for the investor to choose to invest in that region. By themselves, they are unlikely to spur an investment decision if proper market conditions do not exist.

Investment promotion policies may succeed in luring new industries to a location and in creating new jobs, but they may also have several drawbacks. For example, when countries compete for foreign investment, several of them may offer more or less the same investment package. The slight advantage that the incentives of one country may have over another's package generally makes little difference in the investment site selected.[18] Moreover, investment policies aimed at attracting foreign direct investment may occasionally place established domestic firms at a disadvantage if they do not receive any support.

## A Strategic Outlook For Trade and Investment Policies

All countries have international trade and investment policies. The importance and visibility of these policies have grown dramatically as international trade and investment flows have become more relevant to the well-being of most nations. Given the growing linkages among nations, it will be increasingly difficult to consider domestic policy without looking at international repercussions.

### A U.S. Perspective

The U.S. need is for a positive trade policy rather than reactive, ad hoc responses to specific situations. Protectionistic legislation can be helpful, provided it is not enacted. Proposals in Congress, for example, can be quite useful as bargaining chips in international negotiations. If passed and signed into law, however, protectionistic legislation can result in the destruction of the international trade and investment framework.

It has been suggested that a variety of regulatory agencies could become involved in administering U.S. trade policy. Although such agencies could be useful from the standpoint of addressing narrowly defined grievances, they carry the danger that commercial policy will be determined by a new chorus of discordant voices. Shifting the power of setting trade and investment policy from the executive branch to agencies or even states could give the term *New Federalism* a quite unexpected meaning and might cause progress at the international negotiation level to grind to a halt. No U.S. negotiator can expect to retain the goodwill of foreign counterparts if he or she cannot place issues on the table that can be negotiated without constantly having to check back with various authorities.

In light of continuing large U.S. trade deficits, there is much disenchantment with past trade policies. The disappointment with past policy measures, particularly trade negotiations, is mainly the result of overblown expectations.

Too often, the public has mistakenly expected successful trade negotiations to affect the domestic economy in a major way, even though the issue addressed or resolved was only of minor economic importance. Yet, in light of global changes, U.S. trade policy does need to change. Rather than treating trade policy as a strictly "foreign" phenomenon, it must be recognized that it is mainly domestic economic performance that determines global competitiveness. Therefore, trade policy must become more domestically oriented at the same time that domestic policy must become more international in vision. Such a new approach should pursue at least four key goals. First, the nation must improve the quality and amount of information government and business share to facilitate competitiveness. Second, policy must encourage collaboration among companies in such areas as goods and process technologies. Third, American industry collectively must overcome its export reluctance and its short-term financial orientation. And, fourth, America must invest in its people, providing education and training suited to the competitive challenges of the next century.[19]

## An International Perspective

From an international perspective, trade and investment negotiations must continue. In doing so, trade and investment policy can take either a multilateral or bilateral approach. **Bilateral negotiations** are carried out mainly between two nations, while **multilateral negotiations** are carried out among a number of nations. The approach can also be broad, covering a wide variety of products, services, or investments, or it can be narrow in that it focuses on specific problems.

In order to address narrowly defined trade issues, bilateral negotiations and a specific approach seem quite appealing. Very specific problems can be discussed and resolved expediently. However, to be successful on a global scale, negotiations need to produce winners. Narrow-based bilateral negotiations require that there be, for each issue, a clearly identified winner and loser. Therefore, such negotiations have less chance for long-term success, because no one wants to be the loser. This points toward multilateral negotiations on a broad scale, where concessions can be traded off among countries, making it possible for all participants to emerge and declare themselves as winners. The difficulty lies in devising enough incentives to bring the appropriate and desirable partners to the bargaining table.

Policymakers must be willing to trade off short-term achievements for long-term goals. All too often, measures that would be beneficial in the long term are sacrificed to short-term expediency to avoid temporary pain and the resulting political cost. Given the increasing linkages among nations and their economies, however, such adjustments are inevitable. In the recent past, trade and investment volume continued to grow for everyone. Conflicts were minimized and adjustment possibilities were increased manyfold. As trade and investment policies must be implemented in an increasingly competitive environment, however, conflicts are likely to increase significantly. Thoughtful economic coordination will therefore be required among the leading trading nations. Such coordination will result to some degree in the loss of national sovereignty.

New mechanisms to evaluate restraint measure will also need to be designed. The beneficiaries of trade and investment restraints are usually clearly defined and have much  to gain, whereas the losers are much less visible, which will make coalition building a key issue. The total cost of policy measures affecting trade and investment flows must be assessed, must be communicated, and must be taken into consideration before such measures are implemented.[20]

The affected parties need to be concerned and join forces. The voices of retailers, consumers, wholesalers and manufacturers all need to be heard. Only then will policymakers be sufficiently responsive in setting policy objectives that increase opportunities for firms and choices for consumers.

## Summary

Trade and investment policies historically have been a subset of domestic policies. Domestic policies in turn have aimed primarily at maintaining and improving the standard of living, the developmental level, and the employment level within a nation. Occasionally, foreign policy concerns also played a role. Increasingly, however, this view of trade and investment policies is undergoing change. While the view was appropriate for global developments that took place following World War II, changes in the current world environment require changes in policies.

Increasingly, the capability of policymakers simply to focus on domestic issues is reduced because of global linkages in trade and investment. In addition, traditional international institutions concerned with these policies have been weakened, and the developmental conflict among nations has been sharpened. As a result, there is a tendency by many nations to restrict imports either through tariff or nontariff barriers. Investment restrictions also are used to control influences from abroad. Yet, all these actions have repercussions that negatively affect industries and consumers.

Nations also undertake efforts to promote exports through information and advice, production and marketing support, and financial assistance. While helpful to the individual firm, in the aggregate, such measures may only assist firms in efforts that the profit motive would encourage them to do anyway. Yet, for new entrants to the international market such assistance may be useful. Governments also promote imports and foreign direct investment in order to receive needed products or to attract economic activity.

In the future, nations must cooperate closely. They must view domestic policy-making in the global context in order to maintain a viable and growing global trade and investment environment. Policies must be long term in order to ensure the well-being of nations and individuals.

## Key Terms and Concepts

national sovereignty

standard of living

quality of life

foreign policy

International Trade Organization (ITO)

General Agreement on Tariffs and Trade (GATT)

Most-Favored Nation (MFN)

International Monetary Fund (IMF)

World Bank

World Trade Organization (WTO)

tariffs

quotas

nontariff barriers

voluntary restraint agreements

antidumping

Committee on Foreign Investments in the United States (CFIUS)

national security

capital flight

mixed aid credits

fiscal incentives

financial incentives

nonfinancial incentives

currency flows

punitive tariff

bilateral negotiations

multilateral negotiations

### Questions for Discussion

1. Discuss the role of voluntary import restraints in international business.
2. What is meant by multilateral negotiations?
3. Discuss the impact of import restrictions on consumers.
4. Why would policymakers sacrifice major international progress for minor domestic policy gains?
5. Discuss the varying inputs to trade and investment restrictions by beneficiaries and by losers.
6. Why are policymakers often oriented to the short term?
7. Discuss the effect of foreign direct investment on trade.
8. Which organization in the U.S. Department of Commerce could be compared with Japan's External Trade Organization (JETRO)? How do the functions of the two organizations differ according to the descriptions given on their web sites? (Look at JETRO's description under the site **www.jetro.go.jp** and at the description of the different agencies in the Department of Commerce at **www.doc.gov.**)

### Recommended Readings

Cavusgil, S. Tamer, and Michael R. Czinkota, eds. *International Perspectives on Trade Promotion and Assistance.* New York: Quorum, 1990.

Czinkota, Michael R., ed. *Improving U.S. Competitiveness.* Washington, D.C.: Government Printing Office, 1988.

Frazier, Michael. *Implementing State Government Export Programs.* New York: Praeger, 1992.

Hindley, Brian. *Antidumping Industrial Policy: Legalized Protectionism in the WTO and What To Do About It.* Washington, D.C.: AEI Press, 1996.

Hufbauer, Gary Clyde, and Kimberly Ann Elliott. *Measuring the Costs of Protection in the United States.* Washington, D.C.: Institute for International Economics, 1994.

Krugman, Paul, and Alasdair Smith, eds. *Empirical Studies of Strategic Trade Policy.* Chicago: The University of Chicago Press, 1994.

Qureshi, Asif H. *The World Trade Organization: Implementing International Trade Norms.* Manchester: Manchester University Press, 1996.

Schott, Jeffrey. *WTO 2000: Setting the Course for World Trade.* Washington, D.C.: Institute for International Economics, 1996.

Special Issue on Export Promotion of *The International Trade Journal* Vol. 11, No. 1 (Spring 1997).

### Notes

1. Michael R. Czinkota, "The World Trade Organization: Perspectives and Prospects," *Journal of International Marketing* 3, 1 (1995), 85–92.
2. Thomas R. Graham, "Global Trade: War and Peace," *Foreign Policy* 50 (Spring 1983): 124–127.
3. Edwin L. Barber III, "Investment-Trade Nexus," in *U.S. International Policy,* ed. Gary Clyde Hufbauer (Washington, D.C.: The International Law Institute, 1982), 9–4.
4. "Uruguay Round Results to Expand Trade by $755 Billion," *Focus: GATT Newsletter* (May 1994): 6.
5. Jessica T. Mathews, "Power Shift," *Foreign Affairs* (January/February 1997): 50–66.
6. Federal News Service (September 16, 1997).
7. *The Washington Post,* October 13, 1996.
8. J. David Richardson and Karin Rindal, *Why Exports Matter: More!* (Washington, D.C.: The Institute for International Economics and The Manufacturing Institute, February 1996).
9. Department of Commerce, Office of Trade and Economic Analysis, *Business America* (May 1997).
10. 1995 data, reported in *Investor's Business Daily* (December 30, 1996).
11. Michael R. Czinkota, "The World Trade Organization: Perspectives and Prospects," 85–92.
12. Michael R. Czinkota and Masaaki Kotabe, "A Marketing Perspective of the U.S. International Trade Commission's Antidumping Actions—An Empirical Inquiry," *Journal of World Business* 32, 2 (1997): 169–187.
13. *Canada: A Guide for Foreign Investors* (2nd Ed), Coopers and Lybrand, Ottawa, Canada, 1997.

14. U. S. Department of Commerce, *National Export Strategy* (Washington D.C.: U.S. Government Printing Office), October 1996.

15. *National Export Strategy,* Fourth Annual Report to the United States Congress, Trade Promotion Coordinating Committee (U.S. Government Printing Office: Washington D.C., October 1996), 8.

16. Masaaki Kotabe and Michael R. Czinkota, "State Government Promotion of Manufacturing Exports: A Gap Analysis," *Journal of International Business Studies* (Winter 1992): 637–658.

17. Stephen Guisinger, "Attracting and Controlling Foreign Investment," *Economic Impact* (Washington, D.C.: United States Information Agency, 1987), 18.

18. Ibid., 20.

19. Michael R. Czinkota and Masaaki Kotabe, "America's New World Trade Order," *Marketing Management* 1, 3 (1992): 46–54.

20. Michael R. Czinkota, ed., *Proceedings of the Conference on the Feasibility of a Protection Cost Index,* August 6, 1987 (Washington, D.C.: Department of Commerce, 1987), 7.

# Appendix

# Members of the U.S. Trade Promotion Coordination Committee (TPCC)

Information on both individual TPCC agency programs and the National Export Strategy is available on the Internet. The TPCC's official repository of export promotion information is the National Trade Data Bank available from STAT-USA. Information about individual TPCC agency programs can be obtained by using the following Internet addresses:

- National Trade Data Bank **(http://www.stat-usa.gov)**
- Agency for International Development **(http://www.usaid.gov)**
- Council of Economic Advisers **(http://www.whitehouse.gov/wh/eop/cea)**
- Department of Agriculture **(http://www.fas.usda.gov)**
- Department of Commerce **(http://www.ita.dox.gov)**
- Department of Defense **(http://www.dtic.dla.mil)**
- Department of Energy **(http://www.osti.gov)**
- Department of Interior **(http://www.doi.gov)**
- Department of Labor **(http://www.dol.gov)**
- Department of State **(http://www.state.gov)**
- Department of Transportation **(http://www.dot.gov)**
- Department of the Treasury **(http://www.ustreas.gov)**
- Environmental Protection Agency **(http://www.epa.gov)**
- Ex-Im Bank of the United States **(http://www.exim.gov)**
- National Economic Council **(http://www.whitehouse.gov/wh/eop/nec)**
- Office of the U.S. Trade Representative **(http://www.ustr.gov)**
- Office of Management and Budget **(http://www.whitehouse.gov/wh/eop/omb)**
- Overseas Private Investment Corporation **(http://www.opic.gov)**
- Small Business Administration **(http://www.sba.gov)**
- U.S. Information Agency **(http://www.usia.gov)**
- U.S. Trade and Development Agency **(http://www.tda.gov)**

*Source: National Export Strategy,* Fourth Annual Report to the United States Congress (Washington, D.C.: U. S. Government Printing Office1996), 54.

# C H A P T E R 4

# Politics and Laws

## LEARNING OBJECTIVES

◆ *To understand the importance of the political and legal environments in both the home and host countries to the international business executive*

◆ *To learn how governments affect business through legislation and regulations*

◆ *To see how the political actions of countries expose firms to international risks*

◆ *To examine the differing laws regulating international trade found in different countries*

◆ *To understand how international political relations, agreements, and treaties can affect international business*

## Sweatshop Economics

International corporations cringe at accusations of sweatshop labor practices, and policymakers seek to legislate international labor standards. But both find that sweatshop conditions linger in factories around the world. Often industrialized nations are shocked to find sweatshop conditions in their own backyard. Revelations of harsh labor conditions in areas under Western legal jurisdiction or under the eyes of a Western multinational corporation typically lead to a flurry of legislation and new policy proclamations. But human rights activists are usually dissatisfied with the level of response to their outrage, whether they blame government oversight or multinational corporations.

Even a nation that claims the moral high ground on safe labor laws can find itself unwittingly playing host to sweatshop labor practices. The Northern Mariana Islands, located 600 miles off China, have been a U.S. commonwealth since 1986. They are the twentieth-largest supplier of clothing to the U.S. market, and their goods are marked "Made in the U.S.A." But their close ties to the United States have not allowed for the enforcement of American labor standards, much to the dismay of human rights activists. In fact, even though the Marianas do not face U.S. duties or quotas, their labor laws are not in line with U.S. standards.

Due to loose immigration laws, companies on the islands employ around 35,000 foreign laborers alongside 25,000 local citizens; an additional 2,000 to 6,000 workers are believed to work there illegally. The appalling work conditions have shocked U.S. officials: Workers toil during eighteen-hour days in factories surrounded by barbed wire; foreign workers often are not allowed to join unions, attend religious services, marry, or quit their jobs; and the minimum wage is about $2 less than the U.S. mainland wage. In a belated response to the situation, the U.S. Congress is working on legislation to extend U.S. immigration, naturalization, and minimum wage laws to the Mariana Islands. It remains to be seen whether such legal changes will create a work environment equivalent to that in the United States.

The private sector record of dealing with the enforcement of international labor standards seems mixed at best, according to human rights activists. International corporations, often accused of perpetuating sweatshop conditions in factories abroad, seem unable to solve the problem through mere policy changes. A report by two respected Hong Kong human rights organizations documented the use of child labor in shoe factories in China. The Asia Monitor Resource Center and the Hong Kong Christian Industrial Committee charged that Nike and Reebok's monitoring systems "have been completely ineffective" in detecting flagrant violations of basic Chinese labor law as well as their own codes of conduct. They cited routine instances of forcing underage

WWW

children to work overtime with less pay than China's legal minimum wage, along with significant health and safety problems in the factories.

The human rights organizations' accusations contrasted with the optimistic tone of President Clinton's antisweatshop task force, in which both companies agreed to help establish guidelines for American companies that manufacture clothing and shoes in low-wage countries. But persistent criticism by human rights groups points to the need for multinationals, in conjunction with government actors, to develop new strategies for dealing with sweatshops. After all, the media spotlight on sweatshop practices will only intensify over time, increasing pressure on government officials and threatening corporate public relations.

*Sources:* Paula L. Green, "Marianas a haven for Asian makers," *The Journal of Commerce* (September 25, 1997): 1A, 5A; Tim Shorrock, "Groups fault Reebok, Nike on child labor," *The Journal of Commerce* (September 22, 1997): 3A.

Politics and laws play a critical role in international business. Even the best plans can go awry as a result of unexpected political or legal influences, and the failure to anticipate these factors can be the undoing of an otherwise successful business venture.

Of course, a single international political and legal environment does not exist. The business executive has to be aware of political and legal factors on a variety of levels. For example, while it is useful to understand the complexities of the host country's legal system, such knowledge may not protect against sanctions imposed by the home country. The firm, therefore, has to be aware of conflicting expectations and demands in the international arena, and work together with governments to maintain viable international business practices, as we saw in the example that opened the chapter.

This chapter will examine politics and laws from the manager's point of view. The two subjects are considered together because laws generally are the result of political decisions. The chapter discussion will break down the study of the international political and legal environment into three segments: the politics and laws of the home country; those of the host country; and the bilateral and multilateral agreements, treaties, and laws governing the relations among host and home countries.

## The Home-Country Perspective

No manager can afford to ignore the rules and regulations of the country from which he or she conducts international business transactions. Many of the laws and regulations may not specifically address international business issues, yet they can have a major impact on a firm's opportunities abroad. Minimum-wage legislation, for example, has a bearing on the **international competitiveness** of a firm using production processes that are highly labor intensive. The cost of domestic safety regulations may significantly affect the pricing policies of firms. For example, U.S. legislation creating the Environmental Superfund requires payment by chemical firms based on their production volume, regardless of whether the production is sold domestically or exported. As a result, these firms are at a disadvantage internationally when exporting their commodity-type products. They are required to compete against firms that have a cost advantage because their home countries do not require payment into an environmental fund.

Other legal and regulatory measures, however, are clearly aimed at international business. Some may be designed to help firms in their international efforts. For example, governments may attempt to aid and protect the business efforts of domestic companies facing competition from abroad by setting standards for product content and quality.

The political environment in most countries tends to provide general support for the international business efforts of firms headquartered within the country. For example, a government may work to reduce trade barriers or to increase trade opportunities through bilateral and multilateral negotiations. Such actions will affect individual firms to the extent that they improve the international climate for free trade.

Often governments also have specific rules and regulations that restrict international business. Such regulations are frequently political in nature and are based on governmental objectives that override commercial concerns. The restrictions are particularly sensitive when they address activities outside the country. Such measures challenge the territorial sovereignty of other governments and raise the issue of **extraterritoriality**—meaning a nation's attempt to set policy outside its territorial limits. Yet actions implying such extraterritorial reach are common, because nations often argue that their citizens and products maintain their nationality wherever they may be, and they therefore continue to be subject to the rules and laws of their home country.

Three main areas of governmental activity are of major concern to the international business manager. They are embargoes or trade sanctions, export controls, and the regulation of international business behavior.

**Embargoes and Sanctions**

The terms **sanction** and **embargo** as used here refer to governmental actions that distort free flows of trade in goods, services, or ideas for decidedly adversarial and political, rather than economic, purposes. Sanctions tend to consist of specific coercive trade measures such as the cancellation of trade financing or the prohibition of high-technology trade, while embargoes are usually much broader in that they prohibit trade entirely. For example, the United States imposed sanctions against some countries by prohibiting the export of weapons to them, but it initiated an embargo against Cuba when all but humanitarian trade was banned. To understand sanctions and embargoes better, it is useful to examine the auspices and legal justifications under which they are imposed.

Trade embargoes have been used quite frequently and successfully in times of war or to address specific grievances. For example, in 1284, the Hansa, an association of north German merchants, believed that its members were suffering from several injustices by Norway. On learning that one of its ships had been attacked and pillaged by the Norwegians, the Hansa called an assembly

Iraq continues to live under a United Nation's trade embargo which began following Iraq's invasion of Kuwait. While devastating Iraq's economy, it has not-proved effective in curbing international military confrontations during the 1990s.

*Source:* © Reuters/Corbis–Bettmann

of its members and resolved an economic blockade of Norway. The export of grain, flour, vegetables, and beer was prohibited on pain of fines and confiscation of the goods. The blockade was a complete success. Deprived of grain from Germany, the Norwegians were unable to obtain it from England or elsewhere. As a contemporary chronicler reports: "Then there broke out a famine so great that they were forced to make atonement." Norway was forced to pay indemnities for the financial losses that had been caused and to grant the Hansa extensive trade privileges.[1]

Over time, economic sanctions and embargoes have become a principal tool of the foreign policy for many countries. Often, they are imposed unilaterally in the hope of changing a country's government or at least changing its policies. Between 1914 and 1983, there were 99 incidents in which sanctions were used to pursue political goals, 46 of which occurred after 1970.[2] Reasons for the impositions have varied, ranging from the upholding of human rights to attempts to promote nuclear nonproliferation or antiterrorism.

After World War I, the League of Nations set a precedent for the legal justification of economic sanctions by subscribing to a covenant that contained penalties or sanctions for breaching its provisions. The members of the League of Nations did not intend to use military or economic measures separately, but the success of the blockades of World War I fostered the opinion that "the economic weapon, conceived not as an instrument of war but as a means of peaceful pressure, is the greatest discovery and most precious possession of the League."[3] The basic idea was that economic sanctions could force countries to behave peacefully in the international community.

The idea of multilateral use of economic sanctions was again incorporated into international law under the charter of the United Nations, but greater emphasis was placed on the enforcement process. Sanctions decided on are mandatory, even through each permanent member of the Security Council can veto efforts to impose them, The charter also allows for sanctions as enforcement actions by regional agencies, such as the Organization of American States, the Arab League, and the Organization of African Unity, but only with the Security Council's authorization.

The apparent strength of the United Nations' enforcement system was soon revealed to be flawed. Stalemates in the Security Council and vetoes by permanent members often led to a shift of discussions to the General Assembly, where sanctions are not enforceable. Also, concepts such as "peace and "breach of peace" were seldom perceived in the same context by all members, and thus no systematic sanctioning policy developed under the United Nations.[4]

Another problem with sanctions is that frequently their unilateral imposition has not produced the desired result. Sanctions may make the obtaining of goods more difficult or expensive for the sanctioned country, yet their purported objective is almost never achieved. In order to work, sanctions need to be imposed multilaterally and affect goods that are vital to the sanctioned country—goals that are clear, yet difficult to implement. On rare occasions, however, global cooperation can be achieved. For example, when Iraq invaded Kuwait in August of 1990, virtually all members of the United Nations condemned this hostile action and joined a trade embargo against Iraq. Typically, individual countries have different relationships with the country subject to the sanctions due to geographic or historic reasons, and therefore cannot or do not want to terminate trade relations. In this instance, however, both major and minor Iraqi trading partners—including many Arab nations—honored the United Nations trade embargo and ceased trade with Iraq in the attempt to force it to withdraw its troops from Kuwait. Agreements were made to financially compensate those countries most adversely affected by the trade measures.

This close multinational collaboration has straightened the sanctioning mechanism of the United Nations greatly. It may well be that sanctions will reemerge as a powerful and effective international political tool in the world. When one considers that sanctions may well be the middle ground between going to war or doing nothing, their effective functioning can represent a powerful arrow in the quiver of international policy measures.

Sanctions imposed by governments usually mean significant loss of business, and the issue of compensating the domestic firms and industries affected by these sanctions is always raised. Yet, trying to impose sanctions slowly or making them less expensive to ease the burden on these firms undercuts their ultimate chance for success. The international business manager is often caught in this political web and loses business as a result. Frequently, firms try to anticipate sanctions based on their evaluations of the international political climate. Nevertheless, even when substantial precautions are taken, firms may still suffer substantial losses due to contract cancellations. However, the reputation of a supplier unable to fill a contractual obligation will be damaged much more seriously than that of an exporter who anticipates sanctions and realizes it cannot accept the offer in the first place.[5]

## Export Controls

Many nations have **export control systems,** which are designed to deny or at least delay the acquisition of strategically important goods by adversaries. In the United States, the export control system is based on the Export Administration Act and the Munitions Control Act. These laws control all export of goods, services, and ideas from the United States. The determinants for controls are national security, foreign policy, short supply, and nuclear nonproliferation.

For any export from the United States to take place, the exporter needs to obtain an **export license** from the Department of Commerce, which administers the Export Administration Act.[6] In consultation with other government agencies—particularly the Departments of State, Defense, and Energy—the Commerce Department has drawn up a list of commodities whose export is considered particularly sensitive. In addition, a list of countries differentiates nations according to their political relationship with the United States. Finally, a list of individual firms that are considered to be unreliable trading partners because of past trade-diversion activities exists for each country.

After an export license application has been filed, specialists in the Department of Commerce match the commodity to be exported with the **critical commodities list,** a file containing information about products that are either particularly sensitive to national security or controlled for other purposes. The product is then matched with the country of destination and the recipient company. If no concerns regarding any of the three exist, an export license is issued. Control determinants and the steps in the decision process are summarized in Figure 4.1.

This process may sound overly cumbersome, but it does not apply in equal measure to all exports. Many international business activities can be carried out with a **general license,** which provides blanket permission to export. Under such a license, which is not even a piece of paper, exports can be freely shipped to most trading partners provided that neither the product not the country involved is considered sensitive. However, the process becomes more complicated and cumbersome when products incorporating high-level technologies and countries not friendly to the United States are involved. The exporter must then apply for a **validated export license,** which consists of written authorization to send a product abroad.

The international business repercussions of export controls are important. It is one thing to design an export control system that is effective and that restricts those international business activities subject to important national concerns. It is, however, quite another when controls lose their effectiveness and when one country's firms are placed at a competitive disadvantage with firms in other counties whose control systems are less extensive or even nonexistent.

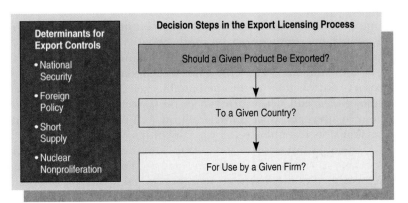

**FIGURE 4.1**

**U.S. Export Control System**

## A Changed Environment for Export Controls

Six major changes have fundamentally altered the parameters of the traditional export control regime.[7] The most important change has been the collapse of the Iron Curtain and the subsequent disappearance of the Soviet Union and the Eastern Bloc. As a result, both the focus and the principal objective of export controls have been altered. It makes little sense today to still speak of "Soviet adversaries," nor is the singular objective of maintaining the "strategic balance of power" still valid.

A second change derives directly from the first. Nowadays, the principal focus of export controls must rest on the Third World. Quite a number of countries from this region want chemical and nuclear weapons and the technology to make use of them. For example, a country such as Libya can do little with its poison gas shells without a suitable delivery system.[8] As a result, export controls have moved from a "strategic balance" to a "tactical balance" approach. Nevertheless, even though the political hot spots addressed may be less broad in terms of their geographic expanse, the peril emanating from regional disintegration and local conflict may be just as dangerous to the world community as earlier strategic concerns with the Soviet Union.[9]

A third major change consists of the loosening of mutual bonds among allied nations. It used to be that the United States, Western Europe, and Japan, together with emerging industrialized nations, held a generally similar strategic outlook. This outlook was driven by the common desire to reduce, or at least contain, the influence of the Soviet Union. With the disappearance of the Soviet Union, however, individual national interests that had been subsumed by the overall strategic objective gained in importance. As a consequence, differences in perspectives, attitudes, and outlooks can now lead to ever-growing conflicts among the major players in the trade field.

Major change has also resulted from the increased **foreign availability** of high technology products. In the past decade, the number of participants in the international trade field has grown rapidly. High technology products are available worldwide from many sources. The broad availability makes any denial of such products more difficult to enforce. If a nation does control the exports of widely available products, it imposes a major competitive burden on its firms.

The speed of change and the rapid dissemination of information and innovation around the world also has shifted. For example, the current life cycle of computer chips is only 18 months. More than 70 percent of the data processing industry's sales resulted from the sale of devices that did not exist two years earlier.[10] This enormous technical progress is accompanied by a radical change in computer architecture. Instead of having to replace a personal computer or a workstation with a new computer, it is possible now to simply exchange microprocessors or motherboards with new, more efficient ones. Futhermore, today's machines can be connected to more than one microprocessor and users can customize and update configurations almost at will. Export controls that used to be based largely on capacity criteria have become almost irrelevant because they can no longer fulfill the function assigned to them. A user simply acquires additional chips, from whomever, and uses expansion slots to enhance the capacity of his or her computer.

The question arises as to how much of the latest technology is required for a country to engage in "dangerous" activity. For example, nuclear weapons and sophisticated delivery systems were developed by the United States and the Soviet Union long before supercomputers became available. Therefore, it is reasonable to assert that researchers in countries working with equipment that is less than state of the art, or even obsolete, may well be able to achieve a threat capability that can result in major destruction and affect the world order.

From a control perspective, there is also the issue of equipment size. Due to their size, supercomputers and high technology items used to be fairly difficult to hide and any movement of such products was easily detectable. Nowadays, state-of-the-art technology has been miniaturized. Much leading-edge technological equipment is so small that it can fit into a briefcase, and most equipment is no larger than the luggage compartment of a car. Given these circumstances, it has become difficult, if not impossible, to closely supervise the transfer of such equipment.

There are four key export control problem areas for firms and policymakers. First is the continuing debate about what constitutes military-use products, civilian-use products, and **dual-use products.** Increasingly, goods are of the dual-use nature, meaning that they are commercial products that have potential military applications. The classic example is a pesticide factory that, some years later, is revealed to be a poison gas factory.[11] It is difficult enough to clearly define weapons. It is even more problematic to achieve consensus among nations regarding dual-use goods. For example, what about quite harmless screws if they are to be installed in rockets or telecommunications equipment used by the military? The problem becomes even greater with attempts to classify and list subcomponents and regulate their exportation. Individual country lists will lead to a distortion of competition if they deviate markedly from each other. The very task of drawing up any list is itself fraught with difficulty when it comes to components that are assembled. For example, the Patriot missile, which was deployed in the Persian Gulf War, consists, according to German law, only of simple parts whose individual export is permissible.

Even if governments were to agree on lists and continuously updated them, the resulting control aspects would be difficult to implement. Controlling the transfer of components within and among companies across economic areas such as NAFTA or the European Union (EU) would significantly slow down business. Even more importantly, to subject only the export of physical goods to surveillance is insufficient. The transfer of knowledge and technology is of equal or greater importance. Weapons-relevant information easily can be exported via books, periodicals, and disks, therefore, their content also would have to be controlled. Foreigners would need to be prevented from gaining access to such sources during visits or from making use of data networks across borders. Attendance at conferences and symposia would have to be regulated, the flow of data across national borders would have to be controlled and today's communication systems and highways such as Internet would have to be scrutinized. All these concerns have lead to the emergence of controls of **deemed exports.** These controls address people rather than products in those instances where knowledge transfer could lead to a breach of export restrictions. Global Perspective 4.1 explains some of the issues surrounding the concept.

Conflicts also result from the desire of nations to safeguard their own economic interests. Due to different industrial structures, these interest vary across nations. For example, Germany, with a strong world market position in machine tools, motors, and chemical raw materials, will think differently about

**Export Control Problems and Conflicts**

## NATIONAL SECURITY VERSUS ECONOMIC COMPETITIVENESS

**W**hat does a U.S. company exporting sensitive technology to an unfriendly country have in common with one hiring a foreigner from that country to work on the technology? Both will face stiff penalties from the U.S. government if they fail to obtain an export license. While most export control rules govern the shipment of sensitive products to foreign countries, the regulation of "deemed exports" involves controlling the flow of technology to foreign individuals. U.S. companies must obtain a license before hiring a nonresident alien to work on a technology requiring license for export to his or her country. The wide reach of deemed export regulations could even extend to foreign students attending American universities or foreign professors participating in U.S. conferences. In effect, the United States treats foreign engineers or scientists as if they were foreign countries.

High-tech firms are seeking the abolition of the regulation, calling it "bureaucratic overkill" and a "leftover from the Cold War," which stalls the hiring of specialists who are in demand. A sympathetic Commerce Department official admitted, "These companies need those scientists to help maintain U.S. competitiveness," with high-tech industry trying to fill 170,000 jobs — a number expected to rise to 700,000 by the year

2000. The companies argue that the technologies are adequately safeguarded without the deemed export regulations. They point out that exporters face separate regulations requiring them to act if they know an illegal transfer is about to occur, and companies jealously guard their own technologies, singing nondisclosure agreements with employees.

The frustration of the companies is compounded by the fact that the deemed export rule became more stringent after 1994, when the industry itself asked for clarification of the rule. Before, firms only needed a license if they had knowledge of an "intent to export." Now, a license is required even if no export takes place. Industry advocates now seek at least a return to the pre-1994 form of the regulation, if not its outright elimination.

Even though many commentators heralded the end of the Cold War as an opportunity for U.S. policymakers to elevate economic competitiveness to the top of their priority list, the State Department, Congress, and the Pentagon often seem preoccupied with fears of China and other threats to nuclear proliferation. With an anti-China mood pervading the Capitol, government regulation of deemed exports probably won't disappear anytime soon. Given the political climate, Silicon Valley recruiters looking to hire an Iranian engineer or a Chinese scientist in the near future can only hope for an acceleration of the licensing process, which now often drags on for months. Meanwhile, as the world's technology leader and vanguard against nuclear proliferation, the United States continues to grapple with the dilemmas of its competing economic and security interests.

**Source:** *Michael S. Lelyveld, "'Deemed Export' Rule Deemed Nuisance," The Journal of Commerce* (June 16, 1997): 1A, 5A.

controls than a country such as the United States will, which sees computers as an area of its competitive advantage. Adjustments in industrial structure add fuel to the fire. For example, as nations reduce their defense industries in size, many firms see exports as the road to survival. Yet, concerns about the export of military equipment and know-how lead to disagreements between and within nations.

These problems and conflicts seem to ensure that dissent and disagreement in the export control field are unlikely to decrease, but rather will multiply in the future. As long as regulations are not harmonized internationally, firms will need to be highly sensitive to different and perhaps rapidly changing export control regimens.

## Regulating International Business Behavior

Home countries may implement special laws and regulations to ensure that the international business behavior of firms headquartered within them is conducted within moral and ethical boundaries considered appropriate. The definition of appropriateness may vary from country to country and from government to government. Therefore, the content of such regulations, their enforcement, and their impact on firms may vary substantially among nations. As a result, the international manager must walk a careful line, balancing the expectations held in different countries.

One major area in which nations attempt to govern international business activities involves **boycotts.** As an example, Arab nations developed a blacklist of companies that deal with Israel. Further, Arab customers frequently demand assurance that products they purchase are not manufactured in Israel and that the supplier company does not do any business with Israel. The goal of these actions clearly is to impose a boycott on business with Israel. U.S. political ties to Israel caused the U.S. government to adopt antiboycott laws to prevent U.S. firms from complying with the boycott. The laws include a provision to deny foreign income tax benefits to companies that comply with the boycott. They also require notifying the U.S. government if boycott requests are received. U.S. firms that comply with the boycott are subject to heavy fines and to denial of export privileges. As Global Perspective 4.2 shows, firms and even governments can be confronted with major difficulties when they are even perceived to comply with boycotts.

Caught in a web of governmental activity, firms may be forced either to lose business or to pay substantial fines. This is especially true if the firm's products are competitive yet not unique, so that the supplier can opt to purchase them elsewhere. The heightening of such conflict can sometimes force companies to search for new ways to circumvent the law, which may be very risky, or to totally withdraw operations from a country.

---

## ADAPTATION ABROAD CAN SPELL TROUBLE AT HOME

**A**dapting business practices to a foreign culture can place a firm in the delicate position of trying to accommodate foreign preferences. But it can also result in a backlash at home if accommodation goes too far or is not well justified, as the Pentagon discovered in a discrimination case involving a contractor. This unusual case illustrates a conflict between domestic U.S. laws and policy and an attempt to do business abroad.

The U.S. government hired CACI, Inc. to microfilm millions of documents in Saudi Arabia to help prepare for the defense of a lawsuit against the United States by Boeing Co. At a briefing by Air Force officers, CACI and Justice Department employees were told that no Jews would be allowed to go to Saudi Arabia for the project. After a complaint by the Anti-Defamation League of B'nai B'rith, the Commerce Department launched an investigation into whether the policy violated the U.S. prohibition on complying with the Arab boycott of Israel. The case also brought into question the possibility of violations of federal bias laws.

The Commerce Department eventually reached settlements with the Air Force, Justice Department, CACI, and the individuals involved, and the Air Force lawyer received a letter of reprimand. Strangely, however, the investigation didn't turn up any satisfying evidence for the motivation behind the discriminatory policy. The Commerce Department reported no indication that the restriction stemmed from a Saudi request; the only reasons given by the Air Force involved concern for the safety of Jewish employees. The CACI operations manual framed the policy in the context of "cultural differences between Moslems and Jews." Questions remain about the extent to which cultural misunderstanding played a role in adopting the policy of discrimination.

**Source:** *Michael S. Lelyveld, "Air Force's 'no Jews' case brings letter of reprimand,"* **The Journal of Commerce** *(July 17, 1997): 5A.*

Another area of regulatory activity affecting the international business efforts of firms is **antitrust laws.** These laws often apply to international operations as well as to domestic business. In many countries, antitrust agencies watch closely when a firm buys a company, engages in a joint venture with a foreign firm, or makes an agreement abroad with a competing firm in order to ensure that the action does not result in restraint of competition.

Given the increase in worldwide cooperation among companies, however, the wisdom of extending antitrust legislation to international activities is being questioned. Some limitations to these tough antitrust provisions were already implemented decades ago. For example, in the United States the **Webb-Pomerene Act** of 1918 excludes from antitrust prosecution firms cooperating to develop foreign markets. This law was passed as part of an effort to aid export efforts in the face of strong foreign competition by oligopolies and monopolies. The exclusion of international activities from antitrust regulation was further enhanced by the Export Trading Company Act of 1982, which ensures that cooperating firms are not exposed to the threat of treble damages. Further steps to loosen the application of antitrust laws to international business are under consideration because of increased competition from state-supported enterprises, strategic alliances, and global megacorporations.

Firms operating abroad are also affected by laws against **bribery** and **corruption.** In many countries, payments or favors are a way of life, and "a greasing of the wheels" is expected in return for government services. As a result, many companies doing business internationally routinely pay bribes or do favors for foreign officials in order to gain contracts. Even in the late 1990s, the British Chamber of Commerce reported that bribery and corruption was a problem for 14 percent of exporters.[12] In the 1970s, a major national debate erupted in the United States about these business practices, led by arguments that U.S. firms have an ethical and moral leadership obligation and that contracts won through bribes do not reflect competitive market activity. As a result, the **Foreign Corrupt Practice Act** was passed in 1977, making it a crime for U.S. executives of publicly traded firms to bribe a foreign official in order to obtain business.

A number of U.S. firms have complained about the act, arguing that it hinders their efforts to compete internationally against companies whose home countries have no such antibribery laws. The problem is one of ethics versus practical needs and, to some extent, of the amounts involved. For example, it may be hard to draw the line between providing a generous tip and paying a bribe in order to speed up a business transaction. Many business executives believe that the United States should not apply its moral principles to other societies and cultures in which bribery and corruption are endemic. To compete internationally, executives argue, they must be free to use the most common methods of competition in the host country.

On the other hand, applying different standards to executives and firms based on whether they do business abroad or domestically is difficult to do. Also, bribes may open the way for shoddy performance and loose moral standards among executives and employees and may result in a spreading of general unethical business practices. Unrestricted bribery could result in firms concentrating on how to bribe best rather than on how to best produce and market their products. Typically, international businesses that use bribery fall into three categories: those who bribe to counterbalance the poor quality of their products or their high price; those who bribe to create a market for their unneeded goods; and, in the bulk of cases, those who bribe to stay competitive with other firms that bribe.[13] In all three of these instances, the customer is served poorly, the prices increase, and the transaction does not reflect economic competitiveness.

The international manager must carefully distinguish between reasonable ways of doing business internationally—that is, complying with foreign expectations—and outright bribery and corruption. To assist the manager in this task, the 1988 Trade Act clarifies the applicability of the Foreign Corrupt Practices legislation. The revisions outline when a manager is expected to know about violation of the act, and they draw a distinction between the facilitation of routine governmental actions and governmental policy decisions. Routine actions concern issues such as the obtaining of permits and licenses, the processing of governmental papers (such as visas and work orders), the providing of mail and phone service, and the loading and unloading of cargo. Policy decisions refer mainly to situations in which the obtaining or retaining of a contract is at stake. While the facilitation of routine actions is not prohibited, the illegal influencing of policy decisions can result in the imposition of severe fines and penalties. The risks inherent in bribery have grown since 1997, when the Organization for Economic Cooperation and Development (OECD) adopted a treaty criminalizing the bribery of foreign public officials, moving well beyond its previous discussions, which only sought to outlaw the tax deductibility of improper payments. The Organization of American States (OAS) has also officially condemned bribery. Similarly, the World Trade Organization has decided to consider placing bribery rules on its agenda. It appears that after twenty years of calling in the wilderness, the U.S. policy stance is being accepted by other countries as well.

**WWW**

All of these issues of governmental regulation pose difficult and complex problems, for they place managers in the position of having to choose between home-country regulations and foreign business practices. This choice is made even more difficult because diverging standards of behavior are applied to businesses in different countries. However, the gradually emerging consensus among international organizations may eventually level the playing field.

A final, major issue that is critical for international business managers is that of general standards of behavior and ethics. Increasingly, public concerns are raised about such issues as environmental protection, global warming, pollution, and moral behavior. However, these issues are not of the same importance in every country. What may be frowned upon or even illegal in one nation may be customary or at least acceptable in others. For example, the cutting down of the Brazilian rain forest may be acceptable to the government of Brazil, but scientists and concerned consumers may object vehemently because of the effect on global warming and other climatic changes. The export of U.S. tobacco products may be legal but results in accusations of exporting death to developing nations. China may use prison labor in producing products for export, but U.S. law prohibits the importation of such products. Mexico may permit the use of low safety standards for workers, but they buyers of Mexican products may object to the resulting dangers.

International firms must understand the conflicts and should assert leadership in implementing change. Not everything that is legally possible should be exploited for profit. By acting on existing, leading-edge knowledge and standards, firms will be able to benefit in the long term through consumer good-will and the avoidance of later recriminations.

## Host Country Political and Legal Environment

Politics and laws of a host country affect international business operations in a variety of ways. The good manager will understand these dimensions of the countries in which the firm operates so that he or she can work within existing parameters and can anticipate and plan for changes that may occur.

**Political Action and Risk**

Firms usually prefer to conduct business in a country with a stable and friendly government, but such governments are not always easy to find. Managers must therefore continually monitor the government, its policies, and its stability to determine the potential for political change that could adversely affect corporate operations.

There is **political risk** in every nation, but the range of risks varies widely from country to country. In general, political risk is lowest in countries that have a history of stability and consistency. Political risk tends to be highest in nations that do not have this sort of history. In a number of countries, however, consistency and stability that were apparent on the surface have been quickly swept away by major popular movements that drew on the bottled-up frustrations of the population. Three major types of political risk can be encountered: **ownership risk,** which exposes property and life; **operating risk,** which refers to interference with the ongoing operations of a firm; and **transfer risk,** which is mainly encountered when attempts are made to shift funds between countries. Firms can be exposed to political risk due to government actions or even actions outside the control of governments. The type of actions and their effects are classified in Figure 4.2.

A major political risk in many countries is that of conflict and violent change. A manager will want to think twice before conducting business in a country in which the likelihood of such change is high. To begin with, if conflict breaks out, violence directed toward the firm's property and employees is a strong possibility. Guerrilla warfare, civil disturbances, and terrorism often take an anti-industry bent, making companies and their employees potential targets. International corporations are often subject to major threats, even in countries that boast great political stability. Sometimes the sole fact that a firm is market oriented is sufficient to attract the wrath of terrorists. For example, in the spring of 1991, Detlev Rohwedder, chairman of the German Treuhand (the institution in charge of privatizing the state-owned firms of the former East Germany), was assassinated at his home in Germany by the Red Army Faction because of his "representation of capitalism."

International terrorists have frequently targeted U.S. corporate facilities, operations, and personnel abroad for attack in order to strike a blow against the United States and capitalism. U.S. firms, by their nature, cannot have the elaborate security and restricted access of U.S. diplomatic offices and military bases. As a result, United States businesses are the primary target of terrorists worldwide, and remain the most vulnerable targets in the future.[14] The meth-

| | **Loss May Be the Result of:** | |
|---|---|---|
| **Contingencies May Include:** | The actions of legitimate government authorities | Events caused by factors outside the control of government |
| The involuntary loss of control over specific assets without adequate compensation | • Total or partial expropriation<br>• Forced divestiture<br>• Confiscation<br>• Cancellation or unfair calling of performance bonds | • War<br>• Revolution<br>• Terrorism<br>• Strikes<br>• Extortion |
| A reduction in the value of a stream of benefits expected from the foreign-controlled affiliate | • Nonapplicability of "national treatment"<br>• Restriction in access to financial, labor, or material markets<br>• Controls on prices, outputs, or activities<br>• Currency and remittance restrictions<br>• Value-added and export performance requirements | • Nationalistic buyers or suppliers<br>• Threats and disruption to operations by hostile groups<br>• Externally induced financial constraints<br>• Externally imposed limits on imports or exports |

**FIGURE 4.2**

**Exposure to Political Risk**

*Source:* José de la Torre and David H. Neckar, "Forecasting Political Risks for International Operations," in H. Vernon-Wortzel and L. Wortzel. *Global Strategic Management: The Essentials,* 2nd ed. (New York: John Wiley and Sons, 1990), 195.

ods used by terrorists against business facilities include bombing, arson, hijacking, and sabotage. To obtain funds, the terrorists resort to kidnapping executives, armed robbery, and extortion.[15]

In many countries, particularly in the developing world, **coups d'état** can result in drastic changes in government. The new government often will attack foreign firms as remnants of a Western-dominated colonial past, as has happened in Cuba, Nicaragua, and Iran. Even if such changes do not represent an immediate physical threat, they can lead to policy changes that may have drastic effect. The past few decades have seen coups in Ghana, Ethiopia, Iraq, and Iran, for example, that have seriously impeded the conduct of international business.

Less drastic, but still worrisome, are changes in government policies that are not caused by changes in the government itself. These occur when, for one reason or another, a government feels pressured to change its policies toward foreign businesses. The pressure may be the result of nationalist or religious factions or widespread anti-Western feeling.

A broad range of policy changes is possible as a result of political unrest. All of the changes can affect the company's international operations, but not all of them are equal in weight. Except for extreme cases, companies do not usually have to fear violence against their employees, although violence against company property is quite common. Also common are changes in policy that result from a new government or a strong new stance that is nationalist and opposed to foreign investment. The most drastic public steps resulting from such policy changes are usually expropriation and confiscation.

**Expropriation** is the transfer of ownership by the host government to a domestic entity. According to the World Bank, from the early 1960s through 1970s, a total of 1,535 firms from 22 different countries were expropriated in 511 separate actions by 76 nations.[16] Expropriation was an appealing action to many countries because it demonstrated their nationalism and transferred a certain amount of wealth and resources from foreign companies to the host country immediately. It did have costs to the host country, however, to the extent that it made other firms more hesitant to invest there. Expropriation does not relieve the host government of providing compensation to the former owners. However, these compensation negotiations are often protracted and frequently result in settlements that are unsatisfactory to the owners. For example, governments may offer compensation in the form of local, nontransferable currency or may base compensation on the book value of the firm. Even though firms that are expropriated may deplore the low levels of payment obtained, they frequently accept them in the absence of better alternatives.

The use of expropriation as a policy tool has sharply decreased over time. In the mid-1970s, more than 83 expropriations took place in a single year. By the turn of the century, the annual average had declined to fewer than 3. Apparently, governments have come to recognize that the damage they inflict on themselves through expropriation exceeds the benefits they receive.[17]

**Confiscation** is similar to expropriation in that it results in a transfer of ownership from the firm to the host country. It differs in that it does not involve compensation for the firm. Some industries are more vulnerable than others to confiscation and expropriation because of their importance to the host country's economy and their lack of ability to shift operations. For this reason, such sectors as mining, energy, public utilities, and banking have frequently been targets of such government actions.

Confiscation and expropriation constitute major political risk for foreign investors. Other government actions, however, are equally detrimental to foreign firms. Many countries are turning from confiscation and expropriation to more subtle forms of control, such as **domestication.** The goal of domestication is the same—that is, to gain control over foreign investment—but the method is different. Through domestication, the government demands transfer of ownership and management responsibility. It can impose **local content** regulations to ensure that a large share of the product is locally produced or demand that a larger share of the profit is retained in the country. Changes in labor laws, patent protection, and tax regulations are also used for purposes of domestication.

Domestication can have profound effects on an international business operation for a number of reasons. If a firm is forced to hire nationals as managers, poor cooperation and communication can result. If domestication is imposed within a very short time span, corporate operations overseas may have to be headed by poorly trained and inexperienced local managers. Domestic content requirements may force a firm to purchase its supplies and parts locally. This can result in increased costs, less efficiency, and lower-quality products. Export requirements imposed on companies may create havoc for their international distribution plans and force them to change or even shut down operations in third countries.

Finally, domestication usually will shield an industry within one country from foreign competition. As a result, inefficiencies will be allowed to thrive due to a lack of market discipline. This will affect the long-run international competitiveness of an operation abroad and may turn into a major problem when, years later, domestication is discontinued by the government.

If government action consists of weakening or not enforcing **intellectual property right** (IPR) protection, companies run the risk of losing their core competitive edge. Such steps may temporarily permit domestic firms to become quick imitators. Yet, in the longer term, they will not only discourage the ongoing transfer of technology and knowledge by multinational firms, but also reduce the incentive for local firms to invest in innovation and progress.

Poor IPR legislation and enforcement in the otherwise lucrative markets of Asia illustrate a clash between international business interests and developing nations' political and legal environments. Businesses attempting to enter the markets of China, Indonesia, Malaysia, Singapore, Taiwan, Thailand, and the Philippines face considerable risk in these countries, which have the world's worst records for copyright piracy and intellectual property infringements. But these newly industrialized countries argue that IPR laws discriminate against them because they impede the diffusion of technology and artificially inflate prices. They also point to the fact that industrialized nations such as the United States and Japan violated IPR laws during earlier stages of development. In fact, the United States became a signatory to the Berne Convention on copyrights only in 1989—around one hundred years after its introduction—and Japan disregarded IPR laws in adapting Western technologies during the 1950s. Futhermore, although newly industrialized nations are becoming increasingly aware that strong IPR protection will encourage technology transfer and foreign investment, the weak nature of these countries' court structures and the slow pace of legislation often fail to keep pace with the needs of their rapidly transforming economies.[18]

## Economic Risk

Most businesses operating abroad face a number of other risks that are less dangerous, but probably more common, than the drastic ones already described. A host government's political situation or desires may lead it to impose economic regulations or laws to restrict or control the international activities of firms.

Nations that face a shortage of foreign currency will sometimes impose controls on the movement of capital into and out of the country. Such controls may make it difficult for a firm to remove its profits or investments from the host country. Sometimes **exchange controls** are also levied selectively against certain products or companies in an effort to reduce the importation of goods that are considered to be a luxury or to be sufficiently available through domestic production. Such regulations often affect the importation of parts, components, or supplies that are vital to production operations in the country. They may force a firm either to alter its production program or, worse yet, to shut down its entire plant. Prolonged negotiations with government officials

# The Risk of Terrorist Activity: A Factor in International Business Decisions

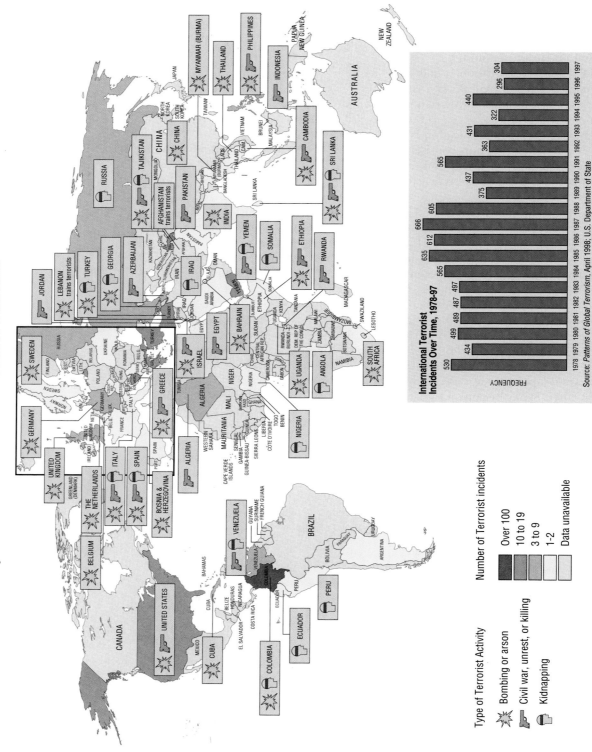

**International Terrorist Incidents Over Time, 1978–97**

| Year | Frequency |
|------|-----------|
| 1978 | 530 |
| 1979 | 434 |
| 1980 | 499 |
| 1981 | 489 |
| 1982 | 487 |
| 1983 | 497 |
| 1984 | 565 |
| 1985 | 635 |
| 1986 | 612 |
| 1987 | 666 |
| 1988 | 605 |
| 1989 | 375 |
| 1990 | 437 |
| 1991 | 565 |
| 1992 | 363 |
| 1993 | 431 |
| 1994 | 322 |
| 1995 | 440 |
| 1996 | 296 |
| 1997 | 304 |

Source: *Patterns of Global Terrorism*, April 1998; U.S. Department of State

**Number of Terrorist incidents**
- Over 100
- 10 to 19
- 3 to 9
- 1–2
- Data unavailable

**Type of Terrorist Activity**
- Bombing or arson
- Civil war, unrest, or killing
- Kidnapping

Source: *Patterns of Global Terrorism*, April 1998; U.S. Department of State

may be necessary to reach a compromise on what constitutes a "valid" expenditure of foreign currency resources. Because the goals of government officials and corporate managers are often quite different, such compromises, even when they can be reached, may result in substantial damage to the international operations of the firm.

Countries may also use **tax policy** toward foreign investors in an effort to control multinational corporations and their capital. Tax increases may raise much-needed revenue for the host country, but they can severely damage the operations of foreign investors. This damage, in turn, will frequently result in decreased income for the host country in the long run. The raising of tax rates needs to be carefully differentiated from increased tax scrutiny of foreign investors. Many governments believe that multinational firms may be tempted to shift tax burdens to lower-tax countries by using artificial pricing schemes between subsidiaries. In such instances, governments are likely to take measures to obtain their fair contribution form multinational operations. In the United States, for example, increased focus on the taxation of multinational firms demanded by President Clinton has resulted in various back-tax payments by foreign firms and the development of corporate pricing policies in collaboration with the Internal Revenue Service.[19]

The international executive also has to worry about **price controls.** In many countries, domestic political pressures can force governments to control the prices of imported products or services, particularly in sectors considered highly sensitive from a political perspective, such as food or health care. A foreign firm involved in these areas is vulnerable to price controls because the government can play on citizens' nationalistic tendencies to enforce the controls. Particularly in countries that suffer from high inflation, frequent devaluations, or sharply rising costs, the international executive may be forced to choose between shutting down the operation or continuing production at a loss in the hope of recouping profits when the government loosens or removes its price restrictions. Price controls can also be administered to prevent prices from being too low. As explained in more detail in Chapter 14, governments have enacted antidumping laws, which prevent foreign competitors from pricing their imports unfairly low in order to drive domestic competitors out of the market. Since dumping charges depend heavily on the definition of "fair" price, a firm can sometimes become the target of such accusations quite unexpectedly. Proving that no dumping took place can become quite onerous in terms of time, money, and information disclosure.

## Managing the Risk

Managers face the risk of confiscation, expropriation, domestication, or other government interference whenever they conduct business overseas, but ways exist to lessen the risk. Obviously, if a new government comes into power and is dedicated to the removal of all foreign influences, there is little a firm can do. In less extreme cases, however, managers can take actions that will reduce the risk, provided they understand the root causes of the host country's policies.

Adverse governmental actions are usually the result of nationalism, the deterioration of political relations between home and host country, the desire for independence, or opposition to colonial remnants. If a host country's citizens feel exploited by foreign investors, government officials are more likely to take antiforeign action. To reduce the risk of government intervention, the international firm needs to demonstrate that it is concerned with the host country's society and that it considers itself an integral part of the host country, rather than simply an exploitative foreign corporation. Ways of doing this include intensive local hiring and training practices, better pay, contributions to charity, and societally useful investments. In addition, the company can form joint ventures with local partners to demonstrate that it is willing to share its gains with nationals. Although such actions will not guarantee freedom from political risk, they will certainly lessen the exposure.

Another action that can be taken by corporations to protect against political risk is the close monitoring of political developments. Increasingly, private sector firms offer such monitoring assistance, permitting the overseas corporation to discover potential trouble spots as early as possible and to react quickly to prevent major losses.

Firms can also take out insurance to cover losses due to political and economic risk. Most industrialized countries offer insurance programs for their firms doing business abroad. In Germany, for example, Hermes Kreditanstalt provides exporters with insurance. In the Untied States, the Overseas Private Investment Corporation (OPIC) can cover three types of risk insurance: Currency inconvertibility insurance, which covers the inability to convert profits, debt service, and other remittances from local currency into U.S. dollars; Expropriation insurance, which covers the loss of an investment due to expropriation, nationalization or confiscation by a foreign government; and political violence insurance, which covers the loss of assets or income due to war, revolution, insurrection, or politically motivated civil strife, terrorism and sabotage.[20] The cost of coverage varies by country and type of activity, but it averages $0.60 for $100 of coverage per year to protect against inconvertibility, $0.60 to protect against expropriation, and $1.05 to compensate for damage to business income and assets from political violence.[21] Usually the policies do not cover commercial risks and, in the event of a claim, cover only the actual loss—not lost profits. In the event of a major political upheaval, however, risk insurance can be critical to a firm's survival.

The discussion to this point has focused primarily on the political environment. Laws have been mentioned only as they appear to be the direct result of political change. However, the laws of host countries need to be considered on their own to some extent, for the basic system of law is important to the conduct of international business.

## Legal Differences and Restraints

Countries differ in their laws as well as in their use of the law. For example, over the past decade the United States has become an increasingly litigious society in which institutions and individuals are quick to initiate lawsuits. Court battles are often protracted and costly, and even the threat of a court case can reduce business opportunities. In contrast, Japan's tradition tends to minimize the role of the law and of lawyers. On a per capita basis, Japan has only about 5 percent of the number of lawyers that the United States has.[22] Whether the number of lawyers is cause or effect, the Japanese tend not to litigate. Litigation in Japan means that the parties have failed to compromise, which is contrary to Japanese tradition and results in loss of face. A cultural predisposition therefore exists to settle conflicts outside the court system, as shown in Global Perspective 4.3.

## TWO AIR DISASTERS, TWO CULTURES, TWO REMEDIES

**W**hen two jumbo jets crashed 10 days apart in Dallas and in the mountains near Tokyo, Americans and Japanese shared a common bond of shock and grief. Soon, however, all parties in Japan—from the airline to the employers of victims—moved to put the tragedy behind them. In the United States, legal tremors will continue for years.

Lawyers hustled to the scene of the Delta Air Lines accident at Dallas–Ft. Worth Airport and set up shop at an airport hotel. Proclaimed San Francisco attorney Melvin Belli: "I'm not an ambulance chaser—I get there before the ambulance." "We always file the first suit," bragged Richard Brown, a Melvin Belli associate who flew to Dallas "to get to the bottom of this and to make ourselves available." But he adds: "We never solicited anyone directly. We were called to Texas by California residents who lost their loved ones." Within 72 hours, the first suit against Delta was filed. Insurance adjusters working for Delta went to work quickly as well.

Seven thousand miles away, Japan Air Lines (JAL) President Yasumoto Takagi humbly bowed to families of the 520 victims and apologized "from the bottom of our hearts." He vowed to resign once the investigation was complete. Next of kin received "condolence payments" and negotiated settlements with the airline. Traditionally, few if any lawsuits are filed following such accidents.

Behind these differences lie standards of behavior and corporate responsibility that are worlds apart. "There is a general Japanese inclination to try to settle any disputes through negotiations between the parties before going to court," said Koichiro Fujikura, Tokyo University law professor. Added Carl Green, a Washington, D.C., attorney and specialist on Japanese law. "There is an assumption of responsibility. In our adversarial society, we don't admit responsibility. It would be admitting liability."

After a JAL jet crashed into Tokyo Bay in 1982, killing 24, JAL President Takagi visited victims' families, offered gifts, and knelt before funeral altars. JAL offered families about $2,000 each in condolence payments, then negotiated settlements reported to be worth between $166,000 and $450,000, depending on the age and earning power of each victim. Only one family sued.

Japanese legal experts expected settlements in the 1985 crash to be as high as 500 million yen—about $2.1 million—apiece. Negotiations may be prolonged. But if families believe that JAL is sincerely sorry, "I think their feelings will be soothed," predicted attorney Takeshi Odagi.

Japan's legal system encourages these traditions. "Lawyers don't descend in droves on accident scenes because they barely have enough time to handle the suits they have," says John Haley, a law professor at the University of Washington who has studied and worked in Japan. "There are fewer judges per capita than there were in 1890," Haley added. Only 500 lawyers are admitted to the bar each year.

Source: *Clemens P. Work, Sarah Peterson, and Hidehiro Tanakadate, "Two Air Disasters, Two Cultures, Two Remedies," U.S. News and World Report (August 26, 1985): 25–26.*

Over the millenia of civilization, many different laws and legal systems have emerged. King Hammurabi of Babylon codified a series of decisions by judges into a body of laws. Legal issues in many African tribes were settled through the verdicts of clansmen. A key legal perspective that survives today is that of theocracy. For example, Hebrew law was the result of the dictates of God. Islamic law, or the sharia, is the result of scripture, prophetic utterances and practices, and scholarly interpretations.[23] These legal systems have faith and belief as their key focus and are a mix of societal, legal, and spiritual guidelines.

While legal systems are important to society, from an international business perspective, the two major legal systems worldwide can be categorized into common law and code law. **Common law** is based on tradition and depends less on written statutes and codes than on precedent and custom. Common law originated in England and is the system of law in the United States. **Code**

**law,** on the other hand, is based on a comprehensive set of written statutes. Countries with code law try to spell out all possible legal rules explicitly. Code law is based on Roman law and is found in the majority of the nations of the world.

In general, countries with the code law system have much more rigid laws than those with the common law system. In the latter, courts adopt precedents and customs to fit cases, allowing a better idea of basic judgment likely to be rendered in new situations. The differences between code law and common law and their impact on international business, while wide in theory, are not as broad in practice. One reason is that many common-law countries, including the United States, have adopted commercial codes to govern the conduct of business.

Host countries may adopt a number of laws that affect the firm's ability to do business. Tariffs and quotas, for example, can affect the entry of goods. Special licenses for foreign goods may be required.

Other laws may restrict entrepreneurial activities. In Argentina, for example, pharmacies must be owned by the pharmacist. This legislation prevents an ambitious businessperson from hiring druggists and starting a pharmacy chain. Similarly, the law prevents the addition of a drug counter to an existing business such as a supermarket and thus the broadening of the product offering to consumers.

Specific legislation may also exist regulating what does and does not constitute deceptive advertising. Many countries prohibit specific claims that compare products to the competition, or they restrict the use of promotional devices. Even when no laws exist, regulations may hamper business operations. For example, in some countries, firms are required to join the local chamber of commerce or become a member of the national trade association. These institutions in turn may have internal sets of rules that specify standards for the conduct of business that may be quite confining.

Seemingly innocuous local regulations that may easily be overlooked can have a major impact on the international firm's success. For example, Japan had an intricate process regulating the building of new department stores or supermarkets. The government's desire to protect smaller merchants brought the opening of new, large stores to a virtual standstill. Since department stores and supermarkets serve as the major conduit for the sale of imported consumer products, the lack of new stores severely affected opportunities for market penetration of imported merchandise.[24] Only after intense pressure from the outside did the Japanese government decide in early 1991 to reconsider the regulations.

Finally, the interpretation and enforcement of laws and regulations may have a major effect on international business activities. As Global Perspective 4.4 shows, the interpretation given by courts to the meaning of a name can affect consumer perceptions and sales of products.

## The Influencing of Politics and Laws

To succeed in a market, the international manager needs much more than business know-how. He or she must also deal with the intricacies of national politics and laws. Although to fully understand another country's legal political system will rarely be possible, the good manager will be aware of its im-

## HOW SWISS IS THE SWISS ARMY KNIFE?

American soldiers returning from Europe after World War II coined the phrase "Swiss Army knife" to describe the ingenious pocketknives produced in Switzerland and used by the Swiss military. Today, the knife is practically a celebrity: displayed at the New York Museum of Modern Art, sent into outer space, offered as gifts by U.S. presidents.

A federal court in Washington, D.C., has decided that the Chinese can sell cheap imitations of the famous Swiss knives—and even call them by the Swiss Army name. "It hurt," said James Kennedy, chairman of the Forschner Group in Connecticut, which has imported the Swiss-made knives since the 1950s and lost the court fight to stop the Chinese sales. Forschner had argued the sales and reputation of the superior, original Swiss Army knife could be damaged by the inferior Chinese version. "Why don't they call it a 'Chinese Army Knife?'" asked one Swiss military official.

The Swiss-Chinese duel is part of an increasingly contentious debate in U.S. business law: Who owns geographic designations in popular product names? Is "Swiss Army knife" a generic term like Swiss cheese, Bermuda shorts, or French fries? Market research performed by University of Florida professor Joel Cohen showed that 43 percent of consumers shown the Chinese-made knife—without knowing its origin—assumed it was of high quality and Swiss origin because of its design and the "Swiss Army" name. "That's the key issue," said Cohen. "Here the Swiss Army knife with an outstanding reputation for quality, and here's somebody who's copying their product and relying on the fact that consumers are going to make that inference about quality."

Arrow Trading Company, the seller of the Chinese-made knives and winner of the court ruling, declares that what it is selling is really not such a bad product. "It's a product that sells for a much lower price than the Swiss product sells for, and its quality is commensurate with its price," said lawyer Louis Ederer. An Arrow Trading Co. legal brief declared, "It's not false advertising to call a particular type of cheese 'Swiss cheese' even if it is made in Wisconsin."

Last year a federal judge found that the Chinese version misled the public. The judge, likening the Swiss version to a Rolls-Royce and the Chinese knife to a Yugo, ordered Arrow Trading to stop the sales. But in the most recent decision, an appeals court reversed that decision, agreeing with Arrow Trading that "Swiss Army knives" were more akin to "English muffins" or "French horns." The court did send the case back to the trial court to decide whether the "Made in China" label should be more prominent.

**Source:** *Benjamin Weiser, "It Slices, It Dices, It Outrages the Swiss," The Washington Post, July 30, 1994, F1.*

portance and will work with people who do understand how to operate within the system.

Many areas of politics and law are not immutable. Viewpoints can be modified or even reversed, and new laws can supersede old ones. Therefore, existing political and legal restraints do not always need to be accepted. To achieve change, however, some impetus for it—such as the clamors of a constituency—must occur. Otherwise, systemic inertia is likely to allow the status quo to prevail.

The international manager has various options. One is to simply ignore prevailing rules and expect to get away with it. Pursuing this option is a high-risk strategy because the possibility of objection and even prosecution exists. A second, traditional, option is to provide input to trade negotiators and expect any problem areas to be resolved in multilateral negotiations. The drawbacks to this option are, of course, the quite time-consuming process involved and the lack of control by the firm.

A third option involves the development of coalitions and constituencies that can motivate legislators and politicians to consider and ultimately implement change. This option can be pursued in various ways. First of all, direct linkages and their costs and benefits can be explained to legislators and politicians. For example, a manager can explain the employment and economic effects of certain laws and regulations and demonstrate the benefits of change. The picture can be enlarged by including indirect linkages. For example, suppliers, customers, and distributors can be asked to help explain to decision makers the benefit of change. In addition, the public at large can be involved through public statements or advertisements. Figure 4.3 provides an example of such an explanatory effort by Bill Gates in favor of free trade negotiations.

Developing such coalitions is not an easy task. Companies often seek assistance in effectively influencing the government decision-making process. Such assistance is particularly beneficial when narrow economic objectives or single-issue campaigns are involved. Typically, **lobbyists** provide this assistance. Usually, there are well-connected individuals and firms that can provide access to policymakers and legislators in order to communicate new and pertinent information.

Many U.S. firms have representatives in Washington, D.C., as well as in state capitals and are quite successful at influencing domestic policies. Often, however, they are less adept at ensuring proper representation abroad. For example, a survey of U.S. international marketing executives found that knowledge and information about foreign trade and government officials was ranked lowest among critical international business information needs. This low ranking appears to reflect the fact that many U.S. firms are far less successful in their interactions with governments abroad and far less intensive in their lobbying efforts than are foreign entities in the United States.[25]

Foreign countries and companies have been particularly effective in their lobbying in the United States. As an example, Brazil has retained nearly a dozen U.S. firms to cover and influence trade issues. Brazilian citrus exporters and computer manufacturers have hired U.S. legal and public relations firms to provide them with information on relevant U.S. legislative activity. The Banco do Brasil also successfully lobbied for the restructuring of Brazilian debt and favorable U.S. banking regulations.

Although representation of the firm's interests to government decision makers and legislators is entirely appropriate, the international manager must also consider any potential side effects. Major questions can be raised if such representation becomes very overt. Short-term gains may be far outweighed by long-term negative repercussions if the international firm is perceived as exerting too much political influence.

There are major public concerns about the representation of foreign firms in Washington, D.C. Particularly the issue of representation by former government officials has come under public scrutiny, and many complaints have been voiced about the "revolving door." Legislation has therefore been passed that provides for cooling off periods during which former policymakers cannot return to their agencies to represent clients. The ethics provisions implemented by President Clinton have tightened the restrictions even more, with a focus on the representation of foreign firms. Yet, some opponents have argued that these provisions are overly harsh, since they deprive former policymakers of employment, discriminate against foreign firms, and prevent individuals from seeking to serve in government.

**FIGURE 4.3**

**A Lobbying Ad**
*Source: The Washington Post,*
November 7, 1997, p. A22.

WWW

# "We Live In A Globally Connected Age..."

An Open Letter to the Members of the 105th Congress

Before the Congress adjourns for the year, Members will cast an important vote — one with tremendous significance for America's continuing prosperity. A vote to support extension of "fast track" trade negotiating authority is a vote to affirm the essential strength and vitality of the American economy.

**Foreign trade and foreign sales translate into strong American industries.** The American economy is the strongest it has been in a generation. American exports have built an economic engine that has created hundreds of thousands of new jobs and thousands of new businesses. One example is the U.S. software industry, where foreign sales account for roughly half of all revenues. American companies have three-quarters of the global software market, provide over 600,000 direct U.S. jobs, and are growing more than twice as fast as the overall U.S. economy. This success story is being repeated across countless other industries.

**We live in a globally connected age.** The way to continue this historic growth is to negotiate agreements that remove barriers to American goods and services. The new agreements negotiated under fast track aren't needed to give other countries access to the American market — we already have an open economy. But future trade agreements are needed to give American industries expanded access to world markets and to create more jobs and more economic growth here at home.

**Without the ability to negotiate, we forfeit the ability to protect.** Much of America's economic growth is dependent on intellectual property. Software programs, movies, books and music, biotechnology, pharmaceuticals, and an exploding array of information services all rely on the ability to protect patents, copyrights and trademarks in order to stay in business. Here in the U.S., our intellectual property industries benefit from strong legal protection. But internationally, theft of intellectual property has become an increasing concern. The single best tool we have to encourage other governments' respect for our intellectual property is negotiated trade agreements, ratified and signed by national leaders. Take away the agreement, and we risk undermining the protection. Reduce the protection, and our industries will stall. But with strong agreements, negotiated under fast track authority, we can protect these growing industries and the millions of Americans they employ.

American innovation is fueling new industries and creating jobs at an unprecedented pace. Our industries are producing at record rates. The road ahead is a global picture: connected, open, free and informed. America's free-enterprise system is a model for the world economy. We should be proud of our success and welcome the future. Extending fast track is the way to do it.

*Bill Gates*

Bill Gates

**Microsoft**

## International Relations and Laws

In addition to understanding the politics and laws of both home and host countries, the international manager must also consider the overall international political and legal environment. This is important because policies and events occurring among countries can have a profound impact on firms trying to do business internationally.

### International Politics

The effect of politics on international business is determined by both the bilateral political relations between home and host countries and by multilateral agreements governing the relations among groups of countries.

The government-to-government relationship can have a profound influence in a number of ways, particularly if it becomes hostile. Among numerous examples in recent years of the relationship between international politics and international business, perhaps the most notable involves U.S.–Iranian relations following the 1979 Iranian revolution. Although the internal political changes in the aftermath of that revolution certainly would have affected any foreign firm doing business in Iran, the deterioration in U.S.–Iranian political relations that resulted from the revolution had a significant additional impact on U.S. firms. Following the revolution, U.S. firms were injured not only by the physical damage caused by the violence, but also by the anti-American feelings of the Iranian people and their government. The resulting clashes between the two governments subsequently destroyed business relationships, regardless of corporate feelings or agreements on either side.

International political relations do not always have harmful effects. If bilateral political relations between countries improve, business can benefit. One example is the improvement in Western relations with Central Europe following the official end of the Cold War. The political warming opened the potentially lucrative former Eastern bloc markets to Western firms.

The overall international political environment has effects, whether good or bad, on international business. For this reason, the good manager will strive to remain aware of political currents and relations worldwide and will attempt to anticipate changes in the international political environment so that his or her firm can plan for them.

### International Law

**International law** plays an important role in the conduct of international business. Although no enforceable body of international law exists, certain treaties and agreements are respected by a number of countries and profoundly influence international business operations. For example, the World Trade Organization (WTO) defines internationally acceptable economic practices for its member nations. Although it does not directly deal with individual firms, it does affect them indirectly by providing some predictability in the international environment.

International law also plays a major role in protecting intellectual property rights. Rights to intellectual property involve rights to inventions, **patents, trademarks,** and industrial designs, and copyrights for literary, musical, artistic, pho-

WWW

tographic, and cinematographic works. Currently, these types of intellectual property are not completely defined by any international treaty, and the laws differ from country to country on several important points. Thus the rights granted by one country's patent, trademark, or copyright may confer no protection abroad.

Some international agreements exist to ease the task of filing for intellectual property rights in those countries in which a firm wants to conduct business or ensure protection. The **Paris Convention for the Protection of Industrial Property,** to which 96 countries are party, sets minimum standards of protection and provides the right of national treatment and the right of priority. This means that members will not discriminate against foreigners and that firms have one year (six months for a design or trademark) in which to file an application.

The Patent Cooperation Treaty (PCT) provides procedures for filing one international application designating countries in which a patent is sought, which has the same effect as filing national applications in each of those countries. Similarly, the European Patent Office examines applications and issues national patents in any of its member countries. Other regional offices include the African Industrial Property Office (ARIPO), the French-speaking African Intellectual Property Organization (OAPI), and one in Saudi Arabia for six countries in the Gulf region.

Much more needs to be done to protect intellectual property. Knowledge is often the firm's most precious competitive advantage, and violation of those rights can have significant financial repercussions.

International organizations such as the United Nations and the Organization for Economic Cooperation and Development have also undertaken efforts to develop codes and guidelines that affect international business. These include the Code on International Marketing of Breast-milk Substitutes, which was developed by the World Health Organization (WHO), and the UN Code of Conduct for Transnational Corporations. Even though there are thirty-four such codes in existence, the lack of enforcement ability hampers their full implementation.

In addition to multilateral agreements, firms are affected by bilateral treaties and conventions between the countries in which they do business. For example, a number of countries have signed bilateral Treaties of Friendship, Commerce, and Navigation (FCN). The agreements generally define the rights of firms doing business in the host country. They normally guarantee that firms will be treated by the host country in the same manner in which domestic firms are treated. While these treaties provide for some sort of stability, they can also be canceled when relations worsen.

The international legal environment also affects the manager to the extent that firms must concern themselves with jurisdictional disputes. Because no single body of international law exists, firms usually are restricted by both home and host country laws. If a conflict occurs between contracting parties in two different countries, a question arises concerning which country's laws are to be used and in which court the dispute is to be settled. Sometimes the contract will contain a jurisdictional clause, which settles the matter with little problem. If the contract does not contain such a clause, however, the parties to the dispute have a few choices. They can settle the dispute by following the laws of the country in which the agreement was made, or they can resolve it by obeying the laws of the country in which the contract will have to be fulfilled. Which laws to use and in which location to settle the dispute are two different decisions. As a result, a dispute between a U.S. exporter and a French importer could be resolved in Paris but be based on New York State law. The importance of such provisions was highlighted by the lengthy jurisdictional disputes surrounding the Bhopal incident in India.

In cases of disagreement, the parties can choose either arbitration or litigation. Litigation is usually avoided for several reasons. It often involves extensive delays and is very costly. In addition, firms may fear discrimination in foreign countries. Therefore, companies tend to prefer conciliation and **arbitration,** because they result in much quicker decisions. Arbitration procedures are often spelled out in the original contract and usually provide for an intermediary who is judged to be impartial by both parties. Frequently, intermediaries will be representatives of chambers of commerce, trade associations, or third-country institutions. One nongovernmental organization handling international commercial disputes is the International Court of Arbitration, founded in 1923 by the International Chamber of Commerce. The Court is composed of members from 48 countries. Each year it handles arbitrations in some 25 different countries with arbitrators of some 50 different nationalities. Arbitration usually is faster and less expensive than litigation in the courts. In addition, the limited judicial recourse available against arbitral awards, as compared with court judgments, offers a clear advantage. Parties that use arbitration rather than litigation know that they will not have to face a prolonged and costly series of appeals. Finally, arbitration offers the parties the flexibility to set up a proceeding that can be conducted as quickly and economically as the circumstances allow. For example, a multimillion dollar ICC arbitration was completed in just over two months.

WWW

## Summary

The political and legal environment in the home and host countries and the laws and agreements governing relationships among nations are important to the international business executive. Compliance is mandatory in order to do business successfully abroad. To avoid the problems that can result from changes in the political and legal environment, it is essential to anticipate changes and to develop strategies for coping with them. Whenever possible, the manager must avoid being taken by surprise and letting events control business decisions.

Governments affect international business through legislation and regulations, which can support or hinder business transactions. An example is when export sanctions or embargoes are imposed to enhance foreign policy objectives. Similarly, export controls are used to preserve national security. Nations also regulate the international business behavior of firms by setting standards that relate to bribery and corruption, boycotts, and restraint of competition.

Through political actions such as expropriation, confiscation, or domestication, countries expose firms to international risk. Management therefore needs to be aware of the possibility of such risk and alert to new developments. Many private sector services are available to track international risk situations. In the event of a loss, firms may rely on insurance for political risk or they may seek redress in court. International legal action, however, may be quite slow and may compensate for only part of the loss.

Managers need to be aware that different countries have different laws. One clearly pronounced difference is between code law countries, where all possible legal rules are spelled out, and common law countries such as the United States, where the law is based on tradition, precedent, and custom.

Managers must also pay attention to international political relations, agreements, and treaties. Changes in relations or rules can mean major new opportunities and occasional threats to international business.

## Key Terms and Concepts

| | | |
|---|---|---|
| international competitiveness | Webb-Pomerene Act | lobbyist |
| | bribery | international law |
| extraterritoriality | transfer risk | patent |
| sanction | coups d'état | corruption |
| embargo | expropriation | Foreign Corrupt |
| export control system | confiscation | Practices Act |
| export license | domestication | political risk |
| critical commodities list | local content | ownership risk |
| general license | intellectual property | operating risk |
| validated export license | rights | trademark |
| foreign availability | exchange controls | Paris Convention for the |
| dual-use products | tax policy | Protection of |
| deemed exports | price controls | Industrial Property |
| boycott | common law | arbitration |
| antitrust laws | code law | |

## Questions for Discussion

1. Discuss this potential dilemma: "High political risk requires companies to seek a quick payback on their investments. Striving for a quick payback, however, exposes firms to charges of exploitation and results in increased political risk."
2. How appropriate is it for governments to help drum up business for their countries' companies abroad? Shouldn't commerce be completely separate from politics?
3. Discuss this statement: "The national security that our export control laws seek to protect may be threatened by the resulting lack of international competitiveness of U.S. firms."
4. Discuss the advantages and disadvantages of common law and code law.
5. Research some examples of multinational corporations that have remained untouched by waves of expropriation. What was their secret to success?
6. The United States has been described as a litigious society. How does frequent litigation affect international business?
7. After you hand your passport to the immigration officer in country X, he misplaces it. A small "donation" would certainly help him find it again. Should you give him the money? Is this a business expense to be charged to your company? Should it be tax deductible?
8. What are your views on lobbying efforts by foreign firms?
9. According to the anticorruption monitoring organization Transparency In-

ternational, which countries have the highest levels of corruption? Which have the lowest levels? (Use the Corruption Perception Index found at **www.transparency.de**) What problems might an exporter have in doing business in a country with high levels of corruption?

10. What are some of the countries suspected of proliferation by the United States? What type of exports might be barred from these countries? (Use the U.S. Bureau of Export Administration's "List of Entities of Proliferation Concern" from the web site, **www.bxa.doc.gov**)

## Recommended Readings

Czinkota, Michael R. and Erwin Dichtl., "Export Controls and Global Changes," *Der Markt* 3 (1996) 148–155.

Elliott, Kimberly Ann, editor. *Corruption and the Global Economy.* Washington D.C.: Institute for International Economics, 1997.

Erickson, G. Scott. "Export Controls: Marketing Implications of Public Policy Choices," *Journal of Public Policy and Marketing* 16, no. 1 (Spring 1997).

Hufbauer, Gary Clyde, Jeffrey J. Schott, and Kimberly Ann Elliott. *Economic Sanctions Reconsidered.* Washington, D.C.: Institute for International Economics, 1990.

Moody, George. *Grand Corruption: How Business Bribes Damage Developing Countries.* Oxford: World View Publishing, 1997.

Organization for Economic Cooperation and Development. *OECD Convention on Combatting Bribery of Foreign Public Officials in International Business Transactions,* Paris: Organization for Economic Cooperation and Development, November, 1997.

Political Risk Services. *Political Risk Yearbook.* Syracuse, N.Y.: Political Risk Services, 1997.

Trade Information Center. *Export Programs: A Business Guide to Federal Export Assistance Programs.* Washington D.C.: Trade Information Center, 1996.

Heidi Vernon-Wortzel, and Lawrence H. Wortzel, editors. *Strategic Management in the Global Economy* 3rd ed. New York: John Wiley, 1997.

## Notes

1. Quoted in Philippe Dollinger, *The German Hansa* (Stanford, CA: Stanford University Press, 1970), 49.
2. Gary Clyde Hufbauer and Jeffery J. Schott, "Economic Sanctions: An Often Used and Occasionally Effective Tool of Foreign Policy," in *Export Controls,* ed. Michael R. Czinkota (New York: Praeger, 1984), 18–33.
3. Robin Renwick, *Economic Sanctions* (Cambridge, Mass.: Harvard University Press, 1981), 11.
4. Margaret P. Doxey, *Economic Sanctions and International Enforcement* (New York: Oxford University Press, 1980), 10.
5. G. Scott Erickson, "Export Controls: Marketing Implications of Public Policy Choices," *Journal of Public Policy and Marketing* 16, 1 (Spring 1997): 83.
6. Robert M. Springer, Jr., "New Export Law an Aid to International Marketers," *Marketing News,* January 3, 1986, 10, 67.
7. This section has been adapted from: Michael R. Czinkota and Erwin Dichtl, "Export Controls: Providing Security in a Volatile Environment," *The International Executive* 37, 5 (1995): 485–497.
8. Erwin Dichtl, "Defacto Limits of Export Controls:

The Need for International Harmonization," paper presented at the 2nd Annual CiMar Conference, Rio de Janeiro, August 1994.
9. Allen S. Krass, "The Second Nuclear Era: Nuclear Weapons in a Transformed World," in *World Security: Challenges for a New Century,* 2d ed., M. Klare and D. Thomas, eds. (St. Martin's Press, 1994), 85–105.
10. Paul Freedenberg, testimony before the Subcommittee on International Finance and Monetary Policy of the Committee on Banking, Housing, and Urban Affairs, United States Senate, Washington, D.C., February 3, 1994, 2.
11. E.M. Hucko, *Aussenwirtschaftsrecht-Kriegswaffenkontrollrecht, Textsammlung mit Einführung,* 4th ed. (Cologne, 1993).
12. "Bribery a Problem with Overseas Customers," *Management Accounting* 75, 6 (June 1997): 61.
13. George Moody, *Grand Corruption: How Business Bribes Damage Developing Countries* (Oxford: World View Publishing, 1997): 23.
14. Michael G. Harvey, "A Survey of Corporate Programs for Managing Terrorist Threats," *Journal of International Business Studies* (Third Quarter 1993): 465–478.

15. Harvey J. Iglarsh, "Terrorism and Corporate Costs," *Terrorism* 10 (1987): 227–230.

16. Joseph V. Miscallef, "Political Risk Assessment," *Columbia Journal of World Business* 16 (January 1981): 47.

17. Michael Minor, "LDCs, TNCs, and Expropriations in the 1980s," *The CYC Reporter* (Spring 1988): 53.

18. Shengliang Deng, Pam Townsend, Maurice Robert, and Normand Quesnel, "A Guide to Intellectual Property Rights in Southeast Asia and China," *Business Horizons* (November-December 1996): 43–50.

19. Paul Blustein, "Kawasaki to Pay Additional Taxes to U.S.," *The Washington Post,* December 11, 1992, D1.

20. *OPIC Annual Report,* Washington, D.C., 1998

21. *Investment Insurance Handbook* (Washington, D.C.: Overseas Private Investment Corporation, 1991).

22. Federal News Service, *Hearing of the House Judiciary Committee,* April 23, 1997.

23. Surya Prakash Sinha, *What Is Law? The Differing Theories of Jurisprudence* (New York: Paragon House, 1989).

24. Michael R. Czinkota and Jon Woronoff, *Unlocking Japan's Market* (Chicago: Probus Publishing, 1991).

25. Michael R. Czinkota, "International Information Needs for U.S. Competitiveness," *Business Horizons* 34, 6 (November/December 1991): 86–91.

# International Vendor Relations at Pier 1 Imports

Over 200,000 pieces of stainless steel flatware are just sitting in a Pier 1 Imports warehouse. Where did these come from? Most recently they were stocked in Pier 1 stores—that is until a couple of customers informed store managers that the stainless steel pieces rusted. The company response? After a very rapid testing process that confirmed the customers' observations, the offending product was pulled from all stores and sent to its "resting place"—all within a two-week period.

The people in merchandising at company headquarters in Fort Worth, Texas, and the local Pier 1 agent in China now have ascertained that while there are 47 different types of stainless steel, only one—referred to as 18-8—can be used to make serviceable flatware that won't rust. This newly recognized quality specification has been quickly communicated to all other company agents who purchase flatware assuring that this product quality issue will not arise again.

It is John Baker's responsibility to oversee the network of corporate buyers and on-site agents who are directly responsible for finding, choosing, and assuring the quality of merchandise imported from around the world. Baker, the Senior Manager of Merchandise Compliance, accepted a position at Pier 1 Imports over twenty years ago after working for various department stores purchasing "tabletop" and kitchen wares. When he first came on board as a buyer, he spent nearly six months of the year on the road, working with the agent network and finding new vendors for Pier 1 merchandise. Today, Baker also handles the increasingly complex area of government regulations of merchandise.

Because such a high percentage of Pier 1 Imports' merchandise is imported (over 85 percent), it is especially critical that U.S. government regulations regarding various product categories be studied and communicated to the manufacturers in other countries. These government regulations form one of the two measures of qual-ity assurance for Pier 1 products. The second is that the products must conform to aesthetic standards that guarantee that the product fits the Pier 1 image and Pier 1 customer desires. It is in large part the buyer's expertise that assures that these standards are met.

What is the process for finding and selecting vendors in countries other than the United States? First of all, Pier 1 depends upon a well- and long-established network of agents in every country from which they import. In some lesser-developed regions, Pier 1 agents work with governments to help locate professional exporters. Some exporters are found at international trade fairs as well. The bulk of Pier 1 agents are native to the country in which they work, and some have been in place for as long as thirty years with their children now taking over the local positions.

The agents' jobs include finding local producers of handcrafted items that fit the Pier 1 customer needs. Buyers look for new sources of products at local craft fairs and even flea markets. Right now, for example, local agents in several countries are looking for sources of wooden furniture—primarily chests and tables—because Pier 1 would like to add to this in-store category. Based upon the location of raw materials, in this case in Italy, South America, Indonesia, and Thailand, agents are searching for just the right manufacturers to be brought to the buyers' attention.

Because it is the agents based within the various exporting countries who must enforce quality requirements, it is critical that John Baker and his colleagues carefully communicate both governmental and aesthetic product requirements to the agents. The agents can then "sit down at the table" with the manufacturers and work out the quality issues. If misunderstandings occur, Pier 1 is always ready to accept some of the responsibility because they view their manufacturers and agents as their partners in this business.

Because Pier 1 Imports has carefully carved out a unique niche in the specialty retail store industry, buyers are hard to hire from outside the company. As Baker noted, "The bulk of our staff has come out of our stores. It is easy for a buyer to move from Macy's to Hudson's—the products are the same as are most of the vendors. The Pier 1 buyer, however, must understand the Pier 1 store in order to be able to effectively and efficiently buy for it." These Pier 1 buyers, along with their agents on-site around the globe, serve as the company's primary link to product quality.

### Questions for Discussion

1. What are the implications for sales, customer satisfaction, and profits for companies like Pier 1 (http://www.pier1.com) when low quality merchandise is not identified early in the purchasing process?
2. Do you think that Pier 1 might have avoided this problem if it had a very aggressive quality assurance program, i.e., ISO 9000, in place?

# The Global Car Market: The European Battleground

Cars are as essential to people as the clothes they wear; after a home, a car is the second-largest purchase for many. The car provides more than just instant and convenient personal transportation: it can be a revered design or a sign of success. Developers estimate that 200 yards is the maximum distance an American is prepared to walk before getting into a car. When the Berlin Wall came down, one of the first exercises of a newfound freedom for the former East Germans was to exchange their Trabants and Wartburgs for Volkswagens and Opels.

Western Europe is the largest car market in the world (see Figure 1). But while the car markets of Western Europe, North America, and Japan account for 90 percent of the vehicles sold, these markets are quite saturated. By the year 2000, for example, there will probably be one car per person aged 20–64 in North America.

Two general approaches will become evident. First, car manufacturers need to sell fewer cars, but more profitably. Secondly, they need to look for new markets. In the coming decades market growth will come from Asia, Eastern and Central Europe, and Latin America. China

*Sources: This case was prepared by Ilkka A. Ronkainen. It is largely based on "The Endless Road," The Economist (October 17, 1992): 1–18; "On Guard, Europe," Business Week (December 14, 1992): 54–55; Carla Rapoport, "Europe Takes on the Japanese," Fortune (January 11, 1993): 14–18; "Back to the Way We Were," The Economist (November 6, 1993): 83–84; and Louis Kraar, "Korea's Automakers," Fortune (March 6, 1995): 152–164.*

and India will eventually provide millions of new drivers. These new realities will have a profound impact on the car market and its players in the future.

In 1986, the Massachusetts Institute of Technology started a study that was published in a book, *The Machine that Changed the World*. The results showed that the Japanese took less time to make a car with fewer defects than the Americans or the Europeans. The main differences were due to the way factories were organized, as shown in Figure 2. The higher productivity of the Japanese has given them an overwhelming advantage: though they have not used it to cut prices, it has given them more profit per car than competitors get. As earnings mount, they can spend more to develop better cars or build the sales networks they need to expand sales. With huge overcapacity in the European car market, inefficiencies and redundancies have been inevitable with devastating results; for example, Renault lost $850 million in 1996.

## The European Car Market

The "1992" process was to have opened up the European car market to competition by December 31, 1992. However, largely due to the performance gap between the Europeans and the Japanese producers, the European Commission has pushed the dismantling of trade barriers to the end of 1999. This has taken the form of voluntary quotas, which for 1994 was 993,000 cars. The Europeans fear that while all the Japanese carmakers together just barely equal the share of number two General Motors, things could change rapidly in a market where no one company has even 20 percent market share (see Figure 3).

Japanese car manufacturers are also hindered in Europe due to exclusive dealerships; that is, dealers are not allowed to sell competing brands. Car manufacturers argue that such arrangements are critical in protecting the character, quality, and service of their cars. In practice, this means that outsiders would have to develop distribution systems from scratch. The European Commission has granted a block exemption for this practice from the antitrust provisions of the Treaty of Rome.

Behind the protectionism is that European carmakers want to avoid the fate of their American counterparts a decade earlier, when Japanese market share jumped from 20 percent to 32 percent in the United States. By the end of the 1990s, the Japanese could be producing more than 1.5 million cars in Europe. Added to growing imports from Japan, Japanese market share could grow from 12 percent to 18 percent of the market. The prospect

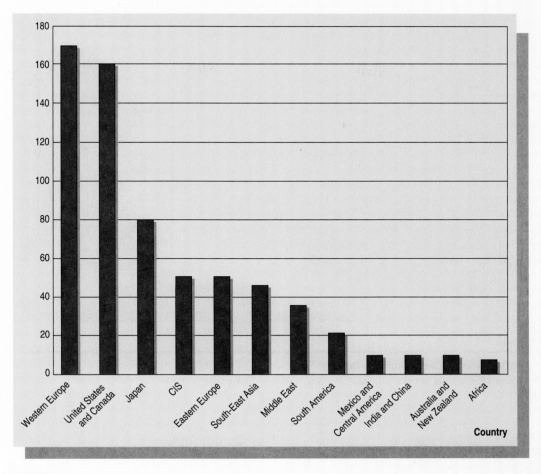

**FIGURE 1**

**World Car Sales by Region, 1992–2002 (in Millions of Cars)**
*Source:* "The Car Industry: In Trouble Again," *The Economist* (October 17, 1992): 4.

has stirred both protectionist impulses, especially in France and Italy, and new competitiveness by the European producers.

Both in France and in Italy, the car industry is one of the national champions that have fared well in protected markets but are relative weaklings in the global marketplace. Italy's Fiat, for example, produces about 4 percent of the country's GNP, which makes it impossible for the government to let it go down. In France, Jacques Calvet, the chairman of PSA (producer of Peugeot and Citron) has repeatedly called for prohibiting new Japanese transplant factories in Europe, strict quotas, and freezing Japanese market share within the European Union.

More alarming for the Europeans is their loss of share outside of Europe. France's Renault and PSA have completely written off the U.S. market, believing that they can prosper with a strong European base while holding off the Japanese. Even some of the European specialists, such as Mercedes Benz and Volvo, have been steadily losing share in the growing luxury segment of the U.S. market. Some have faith in their own markets. One auto executive forecast by saying: "The French are, well, so French. I don't think foreign cars, especially Japanese cars will do well in France. Not in our lifetime."

### Questions for Discussion

1. The CEO of BMW, Eberhard von Kuenheim, commented on the Japanese threat by saying: "Where is the rule that the Japanese must win? The story of their endless success just may be ending." Is he realistic?

|  | | Average* for car plants in: | |
| --- | :---: | :---: | :---: |
|  | Japan | United States | Europe |
| **Performance** | | | |
| Productivity (hours per car) | 16.8 | 25.1 | 36.2 |
| Quality (defects per 100 cars) | 60 | 82 | 97 |
| **Layout** | | | |
| Factory space (per sq ft per car per year) | 5.7 | 7.8 | 7.8 |
| Size of repair area (as % of assembly space) | 4.1 | 12.9 | 14.4 |
| Stocks** | 0.2 | 2.9 | 2 |
| **Employees** | | | |
| Workforce in teams (%) | 69.3 | 17.3 | 0.6 |
| Suggestions (per employee per year) | 61.6 | 0.4 | 0.4 |
| Number of job classifications | 12 | 67 | 15 |
| Training of new workers (hours) | 380 | 46 | 173 |
| **Automation (% of process automated)** | | | |
| Welding | 86 | 76 | 77 |
| Painting | 55 | 34 | 38 |
| Assembly | 2 | 1 | 3 |

*1989
**for eight sample parts
*Source:* "The Secrets of the Production Line," *The Economist,* October 17, 1992, 6.

**FIGURE 2**

**Differences in Car Manufacturing**

*Source:* "The Secrets of the Production Line," *The Economist* (October 17, 1992): 6.

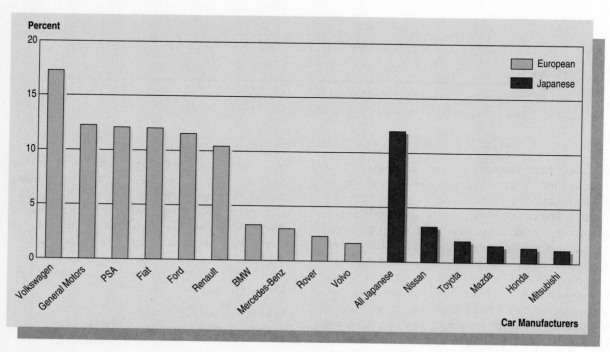

**FIGURE 3**

**Europe's Fiercely Contested Car Market**

*Source:* Carla Rapoport, "Europe Takes on the Japanese," *Fortune* (January 11, 1993): 14.

2. What must the European car manufacturers do to face the global realities of their industry to survive and succeed?

3. Two of the largest car manufacturers in Europe are General Motors and Ford. Neither has been targeted by European Commission moves and are not generally seen as a threat. Why?

# IKEA: Furnishing the World

IKEA, the world's largest home furnishings retail chain, was founded in Sweden in 1943 as a mail-order company and opened its first showroom ten years later. From its headquarters in Almhult, IKEA has since expanded to worldwide sales of $5 billion from 131 outlets in 27 countries (see Table 1). In fact, the second store that IKEA built was in Oslo, Norway. Today, IKEA operates large warehouse showrooms in Sweden, Norway, Denmark, Holland, France, Belgium, Germany, Switzerland, Austria, Finland, Italy, Canada, the United States, Saudi Arabia, Spain, and the United Kingdom. It has smaller stores in Kuwait, United Arab Emirates, Australia, Hong Kong, Singapore, Malaysia, Taiwan, the Canary Islands, and Iceland. A store near Budapest, Hungary, opened in 1990, followed by outlets in Poland and the Czech Republic in 1991 and Slovakia in 1992. Stores were opened in China in 1997. The

IKEA Group's new organization has three regions: Europe, North America, and Asia-Pacific.

The international expansion of IKEA has progressed in three phases, all of them continuing at the present time: Scandinavian expansion, begun in 1963; West European expansion, begun in 1973; and North American expansion, begun in 1976. Of the individual markets, Germany is the largest, accounting for 29.9, followed by Sweden at 10.6 percent of company sales. The phases of expansion are detectable in the worldwide sales shares depicted in

*Source: This case, prepared by Ilkka A. Ronkainen, is based on "Furnishing the World,"* The Economist *(November 19, 1994): 79; Richard Norman and Rafael Ramirez, "From Value Chain to Value Constellation: Designing Interactive Strategy,"* Harvard Business Review *71 (July/August 1993): 65–77; "IKEA's No-Frills Strategy Extends to Management Style,"* Business International *(May 18, 1992): 149–150; Bill Saporito, "IKEA's Got 'Em Lining Up,"* Fortune *(March 11, 1991): 72; Rita Martenson, "Is Standardization of Marketing Feasible in Culture-Bound Industries? A European Case Study,"* International Marketing Review *4 (Autumn 1987): 7–17; Eleanor Johnson Tracy, "Shopping Swedish Style Comes to the U.S.,"* Fortune, *(January 27, 1986): 63–67; Mary Krienke, "IKEA—Simple Good Taste,"* Stores *(April 1986): 58; Jennifer Lin, "IKEA's U.S. Translation,"* Stores *(April 1986): 63; "Furniture Chain Has a Global View,"* Advertising Age *(October 26, 1987): 58; Bill Kelley, "The New Wave from Europe,"* Sales & Marketing Management *(November 1987): 46–48. Updated information provided directly by IKEA U.S., Inc. For more information, see* **http://www.ikea.com**.

**TABLE 1**

**IKEA's International Expansion**

| Year | Outlets[a] | Countries[a] | Coworkers[b] | Catalog Circulation[c] | Turnover in Swedish Crowns[d] |
|------|---------|-----------|-----------|------------------------|-------------------------------|
| 1954 | 1 | 1 | 15 | 285,000 | 3,000,000 |
| 1964 | 2 | 2 | 250 | 1,200,000 | 79,000,000 |
| 1974 | 10 | 5 | 1,500 | 13,000,000 | 616,000,000 |
| 1984 | 66 | 17 | 8,300 | 45,000,000 | 6,770,000,000 |
| 1988 | 75 | 19 | 13,400 | 50,535,000 | 14,500,000,000 |
| 1990 | 95 | 23 | 16,850 | n.a. | 19,400,000,000 |
| 1992 | 119 | 24 | 23,200 | n.a. | 24,275,000,000 |
| 1995 | 131 | 27 | 30,500 | n.a. | 38,557,000,000 |
| 1997 | 142 | 28 | 36,400 | n.a. | 45,820,000,000 |

[a]Stores/countries being opened by 1998.
[b]36,400 coworkers are equivalent to 27,000 full-time workers.
[c]17 languages, 39 editions; exact number no longer made available.
[d]Corresponding to net sales of the IKEA group of companies.

*Source:* IKEA U.S., Inc.

Figure 1. "We want to bring the IKEA concept to as many people as possible," IKEA officials have said. The company estimates that over 100 million people visit its showrooms annually.

## The IKEA Concept

Ingvar Kamprad, the founder, formulated as IKEA's mission to "offer a wide variety of home furnishings of good design and function at prices so low that the majority of people can afford to buy them." The principal target market of IKEA, which is similar across countries and regions in which IKEA has a presence, is composed of people who are young, highly educated, liberal in their cultural values, white-collar workers, and not especially concerned with status symbols.

IKEA follows a standardized product strategy with a universally accepted assortment around the world. Today, IKEA carries an assortment of thousands of different home furnishings that range from plants to pots, sofas to soup spoons, and wine glasses to wallpaper. The smaller items are carried to complement the bigger ones. IKEA does not have its own manufacturing facilities but designs all of its furniture. The network of subcontracted manufacturers numbers nearly 2,487 in 71 different countries.

IKEA's strategy is based on cost leadership secured by contract manufacturers, many of which are in low-labor-cost countries and close to raw materials, yet accessible to logistics links. High-volume production of standardized items allows for significant economies of scale. In exchange for long-term contracts, leased equipment, and technical support from IKEA, the suppliers manufacture exclusively at low prices for IKEA. IKEA's designers work with the suppliers to build savings-generating features into the production and products from the outset.

Manufacturers are responsible for shipping the components to large distribution centers, for example, to the central one in Almhult. These twelve distribution centers then supply the various stores, which are in effect mini-warehouses.

IKEA consumers have to become "prosumers"—half producers, half consumers—because most products have

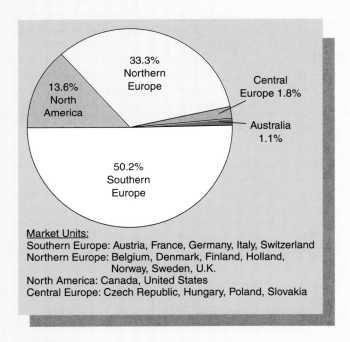

**FIGURE 1**

**IKEA's Worldwide Sales Expressed as Percentages of Turnover by Market Unit**

to be assembled. The final distribution is the customer's responsibility as well. Although IKEA expects its customers to be active participants in the buy-sell process, they are not rigid about it. There is a "moving boundary" between what consumers do for themselves and what IKEA employees will do for them. Consumers save the most by driving to the warehouses themselves, putting the boxes on the trolley, loading them into their cars, driving home, and assembling the furniture. Yet IKEA can arrange to provide these services at an extra charge. For example, IKEA cooperates with car rental companies to offer vans and small trucks at reasonable rates for customers needing delivery service. Additional economies are reaped from the size of the IKEA outlets; for example, the Philadelphia store is 169,000 square feet (15,700 square meters). IKEA stores include babysitting areas and cafeterias and are therefore intended to provide the value-seeking, car-borne consumer with a complete shopping destination. IKEA managers state that their competitors are not other furniture outlets but all attractions vying for the consumers' free time. By not selling through dealers, the company hears directly from its customers.

Management believes that its designer-to-user relationship affords an unusual degree of adaptive fit. IKEA has "forced both customers and suppliers to think about value in a new way in which customers are also suppliers (of time, labor information, and transportation), suppliers are also customers (of IKEA's business and technical services), and IKEA itself is not so much a retailer

as the central star in a constellation of services." Figure 2 provides a presentation of IKEA's value chain.

Although IKEA has concentrated on company-owned, larger-scale outlets, franchising has been used in areas in which the market is relatively small or where uncertainty may exist as to the response to the IKEA concept. These markets include Hong Kong and the United Arab Emirates. IKEA uses mail order in Europe and Canada but has resisted expansion into the United States, mainly because of capacity constraints.

IKEA offers prices that are 30 to 50 percent lower than fully assembled competing products. This is a result of large-quantity purchasing, low-cost logistics, store location in suburban areas, and the do-it-yourself approach to marketing. IKEA's prices do vary from market to market, largely because of fluctuations in exchange rates and differences in taxation regimes, but price positioning is kept as standardized as possible.

IKEA's promotion is centered on the catalog. The IKEA catalog is printed in thirteen languages and has a worldwide circulation of well over 50 million copies. The catalogs are uniform in layout except for minor regional differences. The company's advertising goal is to generate word-of-mouth publicity through innovative approaches. The IKEA concept is summarized in Table 2.

## IKEA in the Competitive Environment

IKEA's strategy positioning is unique. As Figure 3 illustrates, few furniture retailers anywhere have engaged in

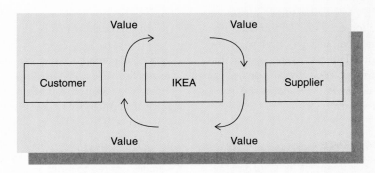

**FIGURE 2**

**IKEA's Value Chain**

*Source:* Richard Norman and Rafael Ramirez, "From Value Chain to Value Constellation: Designing Interactive Strategy," *Harvard Business Review* 71 (July/August 1993): 72.

**TABLE 2**

**The IKEA Concept**

| | |
|---|---|
| Target market: | "Young people of all ages" |
| Product: | IKEA offers the same products worldwide. The number of active articles is 11,400. The countries of origin of these products are: Nordic countries (32 percent), Western Europe (30 percent), Eastern Europe (13 percent), Far East (20 percent), and North America (5 percent). Most items have to be assembled by the customer. The furniture design is modern and light. |
| Distribution: | IKEA has built its own distribution network. Outlets are outside the city limits of major metropolitan areas. Products are not delivered, but IKEA cooperates with car rental companies that offer small trucks. IKEA offers mail order in Europe and Canada. |
| Pricing: | The IKEA concept is based on low price. The firm tries to keep its price-image constant. |
| Promotion: | IKEA's promotional efforts are mainly through its catalogs. IKEA has developed a prototype communications model that must be followed by all stores. Its advertising is attention-getting and provocative. Media choices vary by market. |

long-term planning or achieved scale economies in production. European furniture retailers, especially those in Sweden, Switzerland, Germany, and Austria, are much smaller than IKEA. Even when companies have joined forces as buying groups, their heterogeneous operations have made it difficult for them to achieve the same degree of coordination and concentration as IKEA. Because customers are usually content to wait for the delivery of furniture, retailers have not been forced to take purchasing risks.

The value-added dimension differentiates IKEA from its competition. IKEA offers limited customer assistance but creates opportunities for consumers to choose (for example, through informational signage), transport, and assemble units of furniture. The best summary of the competitive situation was provided by a manager at another firm: "We can't do what IKEA does, and IKEA doesn't want to do what we do."

## IKEA in the United States

After careful study and assessment of its Canadian experience, IKEA decided to enter the U.S. market in 1985 by establishing outlets on the East Coast and, in 1990, one in Burbank, California. In 1996, a total of twelve stores (six in the Northeast, four in California, one in Seattle, and one in Texas) generated sales of over $350 million.

The stores employ 2,300 workers. The overwhelming level of success in 1987 led the company to invest in a warehousing facility near Philadelphia that receives goods from Sweden as well as directly from suppliers around the world. Plans call for two to three additional stores annually over the next twenty-five years, concentrating on the north-eastern United States and California.

Success today has not come without compromises. "If you are going to be the world's best furnishing company, you have to show you can succeed in America, because there is so much to learn here," said Goran Carstedt, head of North American operations. Whereas IKEA's universal approach had worked well in Europe, the U.S. market proved to be different. In some cases, European products conflicted with American tastes and preferences. For example, IKEA did not sell matching bedroom suites that consumers wanted. Kitchen cupboards were too narrow for the large dinner plates needed for pizza. Some Americans were buying IKEA's flower vases for glasses.

Adaptations were made. IKEA managers adjusted chest drawers to be an inch or two deeper because consumers wanted to store sweaters in them. Sales of chests increased immediately by 40 percent. In all, IKEA has redesigned approximately a fifth of its product range in North America. Today, 45 percent of the furniture in the stores in North America is produced locally, up from 15 percent in the early 1990s. In addition to not having to

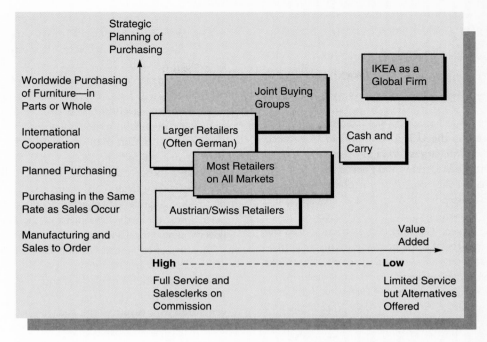

**FIGURE 3**

**Competition in Furniture Retailing**

*Source:* Rita Martenson, "Is Standardization of Marketing Feasible in Culture-Bound Industries? A European Case Study." *International Marketing Review* 4 (Autumn 1987): 14.

pay expensive freight costs from Europe, this has also helped in cut stock-outs. And because Americans hate standing in lines, store layouts have been changed to accommodate new cash registers. IKEA offers a more generous return policy in North America than in Europe, as well as next-day delivery service.

In hindsight, IKEA executives are saying they "behaved like exporters, which meant not really being in the country. . . . It took us time to learn this." IKEA's adaptation has not meant destroying its original formula. Their approach is still to market the streamlined and contemporary Scandinavian style to North America by carrying a universally accepted product range but with a mind on product lines and features that appeal to local preferences. The North American experience has caused the company to start remixing its formula elsewhere as well. Indeed, now that Europeans are adopting some Ameri-

can furnishing concepts (such as sleeper sofas), IKEA is transferring some American concepts to other markets such as Europe.

**Questions for Discussion**

1. What has allowed IKEA to be successful with a relatively standardized product and product line in a business with strong cultural influence? Did adaptations to this strategy in the North American market constitute a defeat to their approach?
2. Which features of the "young people of all ages" are universal and can be exploited by a global/regional strategy?
3. Is IKEA destined to succeed everywhere it cares to establish itself?

# Substituting U.S. Tobacco Exports for Domestic Consumption

Tobacco and its related products have traditionally played an important role in the U.S. economy. In 1997, tobacco represented the fifth largest cash crop in the United States. Twenty-three U.S. states and Puerto Rico grow tobacco, twenty-one states manufacture tobacco products, thirty-three states export tobacco, and all fifty states are engaged in the marketing of tobacco products.

In 1964, the *Surgeon General's Report* documented the adverse health effects of smoking. Since then, many medical experts have repeatedly warned the public that smoking causes lung cancer, low birth weights, and other health problems. As a result of increased awareness of the consequences of smoking, U.S. cigarette consumption, as well as other forms of tobacco use, have been gradually decreasing. Although health considerations played an important role in discouraging smoking, other factors such as higher cigarette prices, steeper federal and local taxes, and governmental restrictions on smoking in public places also contributed to this decline. Since reaching a peak in 1981, total domestic cigarette consumption declined by nearly 22 percent, and per capita consumption by nearly 31 percent. However, in 1995, there were still about 50 million cigarette consumers in the U.S. who bought over 485 billion pieces of cigarettes for $45 billion.

## The Importance of Tobacco for the U.S. Economy

Taxes on tobacco products contribute significantly to government income and help reduce the budget deficit. As the number of smokers has declined, the government has

*Source: This study was prepared by Michael R. Czinkota and Veronika Cveckova, using the following background material: Foreign Agricultural Service statistics; "World Cigarette Situation" by the FAS; "Tobacco Industry Profile 1995" by the Tobacco Institute; Glenn Frankel, "U.S. Aided Cigarette Firms in Conquests Across Aisa," The Washington Post, November 17, 1996; Saundra Torry and John Schwartz, "Contrite Tobacco Executives Admit Health Risks Before Congress," Washington Post, January 30, 1998: A14; Chip Jones, "Cigarette Farmers to Buy Less Leaf," Richmond Times-Dispatch, December 3, 1997; A1; John M. Broder, "Cigarette Makers Reach $368 Billion Accord," New York Times, June 21, 1997.*

raised the cigarette tax in order to preserve the level of tax revenues from smoking. The cigarette tax was raised from 8 cents per pack of twenty cigarettes in the period between 1951 and 1982 to 16 cents from 1983 to 1990, 20 cents from 1991 to 1992 and, finally, 24 cents per pack as of January 1993. In 1995, the tobacco production and related industries contributed over $35 billion to government revenues in excise, sales, personal income, and corporate taxes. Out of this amount, nearly $6 billion (25 percent of total federal excise taxes) was generated by the federal excise tax on tobacco and $9 billion by state and local excise taxes. This means that about 31 percent of the retail price of tobacco products in the United States ends up in the treasuries of the federal and local governments (see Figure 1).

According to a study by the Tobacco Merchants Association, the tobacco industry, including growers, manufacturers, distributors, and core suppliers, employed over 690,000 people in 1996. In addition, 2.4 million jobs were generated as a result of the tobacco industry's expenditures such as promotion and transportation.

## The Importance of Tobacco Exports

In the face of their diminishing domestic market, U.S. tobacco companies are vigorously promoting cigarette exports. Developing countries are the home to most of the world's smokers and are therefore the number one target for cigarette exports (see Table 1). The international cigarette market is dominated by U.S. brands (see Table 2). However, U.S. companies would be able to sell even more cigarettes in developing countries if their products were free of import restrictions.

In 1996, the U.S. tobacco industry produced 754 billion pieces of cigarettes. In the same year cigarette exports totaled about 241 billion pieces. The exports of tobacco and tobacco manufactures resulted in a $5.3 billion surplus in the 1996 trade balance for this group of products, about one-fourth of the surplus in all agricultural products (see Figure 2). U.S. firms exported cigarettes to 113 countries. The leading destinations for these exports were Belgium-Luxembourg (from there, cigarettes are distributed to individual EU countries), Japan, Saudi Arabia, Lebanon, and Singapore.

## U.S. Trade Policy

Tobacco-related revenue is an important source of income for the governments of many countries. As a result, many nations have traditionally blocked the import

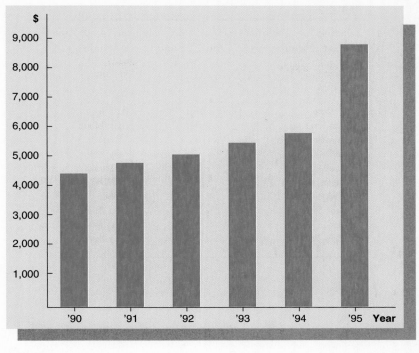

**FIGURE 1**

**Federal Excise and Sales Tax Collections on Domestic Tobacco Sales (in Millions of Dollars)**

of cigarettes by imposing high import tariffs, discriminatory taxes, and restrictive marketing and distribution practices. Japan, China, South Korea, and Thailand even set up state monopolies to produce cigarettes. Throughout the 1980s, the Asian tigers were running huge trade surpluses with the United States. When the U.S. annual trade deficit reached a record high of $123 billion in 1984, the Reagan administration turned to the Office of the U.S. Trade Representative (USTR), a federal agency under the Executive Office of the president. Section 301 of the

1974 Trade Act empowered the USTR to investigate unfair trading practices by foreign countries toward U.S. exporters and required that the U.S. government impose sanctions if the foreign government found at fault in its trade policy toward U.S. firms does not make changes within one year.

As U.S. tobacco products were among the most restricted goods, the USTR soon turned its attention to this case of foreign trade discrimination. The scrutiny was aided by the fact that Japan, South Korea, and Thailand

**TABLE 1**

**Estimated Number of Smokers (in Millions of Persons)**

|  | Men | Women |
| --- | --- | --- |
| Developed Countries | 200 | 100 |
| Developing Countries | 700 | 100 |

**TABLE 2**

**Leading International Brands Sold outside the North American Market (Manufactured in the U.S. and Other Countries)**

| Brand | Producer |
|-------|----------|
| Marlboro | Philip Morris |
| Mild Seven | Japan Tobacco |
| Winston | R.J. Reynolds |
| L&M | Philip Morris |
| Camel | R.J. Reynolds |
| Benson & Hedges | PM/BAT/AB |
| Gaulloise | Gaulloise |
| Bond Street | Philip Morris |
| SE555 | British American Tobacco |
| Philip Morris | Philip Morris |

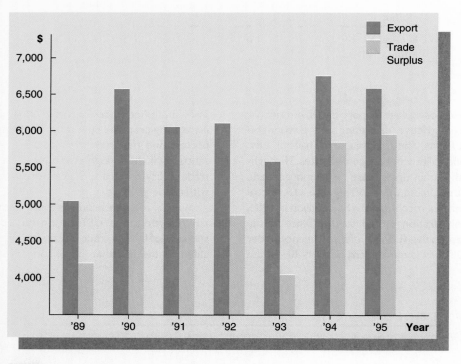

**FIGURE 2**

**U.S. Trade in Tobacco and Tobacco Manufactures (SITC Product Group No. 12) (in Millions of Dollars)**

were signatories to the General Agreement on Tariffs and Trade (GATT), and Taiwan was interested in joining as well. By their discriminatory policies toward U.S. cigarette imports, these countries violated the free trade principles they had agreed to respect under the GATT. In September 1985, the White House filed a complaint with the USTR under the Section 301 against Japanese restrictions on the sale of cigarettes. After a long series of negotiations and mounting pressure from the U.S. government, in September 1986, Japan gave in and allowed imports of U.S. cigarettes. Almost immediately, cigarettes rose from the fortieth to the second most-advertised product on Tokyo television. Imported brands currently control 21 percent of the Japanese market with $7 billion in annual sales.

In January 1988, the U.S. tobacco industry filed a 301 complaint with the USTR against South Korea. The USTR's efforts were supported by members of Congress from tobacco states. In July 1987, even before the USTR initiated its investigation, senators Dole (Kansas), Helms (North Carolina), Gore (Tennessee), and others wrote to the president of South Korea and demanded that U.S. companies be allowed to import and advertise tobacco products. The pressure on the South Korean government was intensified by a strong lobby in Seoul paid for by R.J. Reynolds and Philip Morris. In May 1988, Seoul agreed to the import of U.S. cigarettes and lifted its ban on cigarette advertising. Within one year, U.S. companies acquired more than 6 percent of the South Korean cigarette market. Taiwan was a similar story. Foreign brands went from 1 percent of the market to 20 percent within two years of the country's opening to cigarette imports in 1986. Thailand liberalized the market for imported cigarettes in August 1991. As a result, imports of foreign brands doubled in 1992 and rose again by 43 percent in 1993.

China is the world's largest cigarette producer with 1.7 trillion pieces produced in 1994. There are 350 million smokers in China today who consume 30 percent of the annual world cigarette production, which was 5.49 trillion pieces in 1994. China is also one of only a few countries where cigarette consumption is on the rise. All Chinese cigarettes are produced by a state monopoly. Because the Chinese government is eager to acquire advanced technology and marketing know-how from the West, it offered limited partnerships to a few foreign cigarette producers, including R.J. Reynolds and Philip Morris. Taxes from cigarette sales raise 12 percent of the Chinese government's annual revenue. As a

consequence, the government wants to continue to protect its state monopoly from foreign competition. In 1992, the USTR negotiated an agreement under which China promised to eliminate tariffs and other trade barriers on U.S. cigarette imports within two years. However, the Chinese government has not enforced the agreement. In light of the current hostility on the part of the Clinton administration toward cigarette consumption, the U.S. tobacco industry has not asked the USTR to intervene against China's continuing restrictions on cigarette imports.

With the opening of the markets of the former Soviet Union and Eastern Europe at the beginning of the 1990s, U.S. tobacco manufacturers found new opportunities for expansion. With 60 percent of their populations smoking, Hungary, Poland, Bulgaria, the former Yugoslav republics, the Czech Republic, and Slovakia are among the top ten nations in per capita cigarette consumption. Armenia, Georgia, Azerbaijan, Russia, Ukraine, and Moldova rank among the top twenty. Unlike in Asia in the 1980s, U.S. companies are welcomed here as contributors of new technology and scarce investment funds. As part of the privatization process in the formerly communist countries, U.S. cigarette producers were able to buy previously state-owned cigarette factories and are quickly gaining ground in these new markets. Some analysts project that over the next decade, Western tobacco manufacturers will gain control over the entire East European cigarette market, which will more than make up for the revenues lost at home.

In addition to these market developments, the conclusion of the Uruguay Round in 1992 and the founding of the World Trade Organization (WTO) brought a number of positive developments for the U.S. tobacco export industry: the European Union agreed to cut export subsidies and reduce tariffs on both unmanufactured and manufactured tobacco, Japan promised to maintain zero duty on cigarettes and to lower duty on cigars, and New Zealand reduced its tariff on cigarettes.

## Government Support of the Tobacco Industry

The U.S. Department of Agriculture (USDA) administers laws to stabilize tobacco production and prices. According to the Tobacco Institute, without this regulation, more tobacco would be produced and prices would be lower. In 1994, the Commodity Credit Corporation, an agency established in 1933 to administer commodity stabilization programs for the USDA, made new loans to tobacco farmers of $351 million. These loans are to be repaid with interest as collateral tobacco is sold. The only direct cost incurred to the taxpayers is the administrative cost of this program.

Until the late 1980s, the U.S. government was in strong support of the tobacco industry. It funded three export promotion programs: the Foreign Market Development Program (also known as the Cooperator Program), the Targeted Export Assistance Program, and the Export Credit Guarantee programs. The most important of these were the Export Credit Guarantee Programs administered by the Commodity Credit Corporation (CCC) of the Department of Agriculture. Under these programs, the CCC underwrote credit extended by the private banking sector in the United States to approved foreign banks, to pay for tobacco and other agricultural products sold by U.S. firms to foreign buyers. Between October 1985 and September 1989, sixty-six companies received guarantees of credits under these programs for the sale of 127 million pounds of tobacco with a market value of $214 million. The Targeted Export Assistance Program's purpose was to counteract the adverse effects of subsidies, import quotas, or other unfair trade practices on U.S. agricultural products. Under this program, Tobacco Associates, a private organization entrusted to carry out this endeavor, received $5 million in funding in 1990 to provide certain countries with the technical know-how, training, and equipment to manufacture cigarettes that use U.S. tobacco. In addition, Tobacco Associates received funds from the USDA to promote market development activities for U.S. tobacco products.

Currently, the U.S. government no longer funds export promotion programs related to tobacco and tobacco manufactures. All government programs that used to help the U.S. tobacco industry to enter foreign markets have been eliminated since 1990, under the Bush and Clinton administrations. For example, although the CCC still funds agricultural exports in general, it no longer assists in the exports of tobacco.

## Conflicting Objectives

The past involvement of the U.S. government in furthering the export of tobacco has generated controversy within the United States. The U.S. government, spear-

headed by the Department of Health and Human Services, has been actively discouraging smoking on the domestic scene. In addition, the United States is a strong supporter of the worldwide antismoking movement. The Department of Health and Human Services serves as a collaborating headquarters for the United Nations World Health Organization and maintains close relationships with other health organizations around the world in sharing information on the detrimental health effects of smoking.

During congressional hearings in April 1994, top executives from R.J. Reynolds, Philip Morris, and U.S. Tobacco stated under oath their belief that nicotine was not addictive. In contrast, in 1996, the Food & Drug Administration concluded that nicotine was addictive and should be classified as a drug. In August 1996, President Clinton announced that the FDA will begin regulating cigarette and smokeless tobacco advertising and sales in the United States. During the same speech he said: "Cigarette smoking is the most significant public health problem facing our people. More Americans die every year from smoking-related diseases than from AIDS, car accidents, murders, suicides, and fires combined. The human cost doesn't begin to calculate the economic cost."

In 1998, the turnaround in the U.S. debate over domestic tobacco policy was evident in the conciliatory testimony of tobacco industry officials admitting before Congress that smoking is hazardous and addictive. Their statements followed four years in which attorneys general and private lawyers in forty-one states mounted lawsuits against the industry, and tobacco industry executives agreed to pay $368.5 billion in a legislative proposal to settle the major lawsuits. If Congress approves the proposal, the industry would also agree to restrict marketing, do away with advertising figures like Joe Camel and the Marlboro man, pay fines if youth smoking did not fall to specific levels, and submit to FDA jurisdiction.

Although the Clinton administration has been the most antismoking administration in U.S. history, the government has not initiated any concrete steps to reduce U.S. tobacco exports and U.S. investment in cigarette production abroad. This is partly due to the fact that many in government believe that U.S. tobacco products are merely capturing an existing market share now or previously controlled by state monopolies. In contrast to this claim, the National Bureau of Economic Research estimated that U.S. entry in the 1980s into countries previously closed to cigarette imports pushed up the average per capita cigarette consumption by almost 10 percent in the targeted countries. This occurred due to increased advertising and price competition caused by the entry of U.S. products.

This situation reflects a conflict between morality and economics. Projections show that the declining U.S. cigarette consumption can be easily replaced by foreign markets over the next decade. Thus, by pursuing an antismoking policy only at home, the U.S. government is not risking too much. On the contrary, a smaller number of U.S. smokers will significantly reduce the U.S. health system's expenditures on the treatment of smoking-related illnesses. However, the U.S. policy of permissiveness toward cigarette exports is at odds with government's involvement in the worldwide campaign to reduce smoking for health reasons. Conflicting opinions can be heard from different representatives of the government. While Representative Henry A. Waxman of California and former U.S. Surgeon General C. Everett Koop continue to be staunch supporters of the antismoking campaign and principal opponents of U.S. tobacco exports, Representative Thomas J. Bliley of Virginia and Senator Jessie Helms of North Carolina continue to fight against government regulation of tobacco sales and are key supporters of tobacco exports. The dividing force is economics: North Carolina is the number one tobacco-growing state with annual cash receipts from tobacco crops of $1.05 billion, Virginia is the sixth largest tobacco grower with $187 million in receipts in 1997.

## Questions for Discussion

1. Should U.S. exports of tobacco products be permitted in light of the domestic campaign against smoking?
2. Should the U.S. government be involved in tearing down foreign trade barriers to U.S. tobacco? Should the personal preference of the president affect U.S. trade policy?
3. Should export promotion support be provided to U.S. tobacco producers? What about such support for the export of U.S. beef, which may cause obesity abroad?
4. To what degree should ethics influence government policy or corporate decision making in the case of tobacco exports?

# The Once and Future Ivory Trade

## Introduction

International trade in endangered species products is valued at an estimated $10–15 billion annually. Much of this trade, including the sale of rhinoceros, panda, turtle, and tiger products, is either partially or completely outlawed under the United Nations Convention on International Trade in Endangered Species (CITES), a U.N. organization established in 1973. Perhaps the most controversial animal covered by the treaty is the African elephant. In response to a halving of the African elephant population between the late–1970s and the mid–1980s, CITES imposed an unconditional ban on the international trade in African elephant products, most notably ivory, in 1989.

Backed strongly by the United States, Europe, and certain nations of central and eastern Africa, the ban has come under growing scrutiny as its opponents argue that certain African countries with stable or growing elephant populations, should be afforded the opportunity to profit from existing ivory stockpiles. Without applying a tangible value to the African elephant, through means such as ivory sales, opponents of the ban believe that the endangered animal's preservation will fall victim to neglect. Conversely, supporters of the ban believe that any liberalization of the current rules will send the message that protection of the African elephant is no longer important. This will lead to a reintroduction of the worst as-

*Source: This case was written by Peter Fitzmaurice, under the supervision of Professor Michael R. Czinkota. Sources include: Lynne Duke, "Limited Trade in Ivory Approved,"* The Washington Post, *June 20, 1997: A16; Guy Gugliotta, "Hunting the Elephant in AID's Budget,"* The Washington Post, *February 18, 1997: A11; Kevin A. Hill, "Conflicts Over Development and Environmental Values: The International Ivory Trade in Zimbabwe's Historical Context,"* http://www.fiu.edu/~khill/elephant.htm; *Michael Satchell, "Save the Elephant: Start Shooting Them,"* U.S. News & World Report *(November 25, 1996): 51; Ken Wells, "The Hot New Slogan in Africa Game Circles Is 'Use It Or Lose It',"* The Wall Street Journal, *January 7, 1997: A1; Saving the Elephant: Nature's Great Masterpiece,"* The Economist, *July 1, 1989): 15, "Tiger Economics,"* Far Eastern Economic Review *(August 1993): 19.*

pects of the international ivory trade, they argue, including uncontrollable poaching and smuggling.

The debate culminated in June 1997 at a worldwide CITES conference in Harare, Zimbabwe. After a week's worth of testimony and cajoling from both sides, Botswana, Namibia, and Zimbabwe, home to over a quarter of all African elephants and among the most successful countries at protecting their elephant populations, were granted the right to sell 120 tons of stockpiled ivory to Japan under strict guidelines. While the debate over the ban was anything but congenial in the months prior to the CITES meeting, this decision to allow a brief resumption of the sale of ivory after nearly a decade, supported by over 75 percent of CITES member countries, raised the debate to a new level. Opponents of the ban have new hope that deserving African countries may once again be able to profit from one of their most unique natural resources. Conversely, ban supporters fear that subsequent exceptions will be granted by CITES and the world will once again witness a vast shrinkage of the African elephant population.

## Building Up to a Ban

The African elephant's misfortune is its tusks. Asian elephants have small tusks and have been trained by humans for over 4,000 years. The African elephant, however, has remained a creature of the wild. Its primary commercial worth for centuries, therefore, has been its ivory tusks. In 1930 there were between 5 and 10 million elephants roaming the African plains and jungles. By the time the first true census was conducted in 1979, there were only 1.2 million remaining. The fundamental problem is that elephants need a lot of room to live, and in this respect, humans have become their direct competitors. The tropical and subtropical realms where the African elephants dwell are precisely where human populations have been exploding the fastest, quadrupling in number since the turn of the century and claiming more and more elephant range for cropland, pastureland, and timber.

As economic and political instability became more the rule than the exception, in many African countries during the 1960s and 1970s the illegal killing of elephants grew. Traditionally, elephants in Africa have always been hunted for meat and to eliminate problem animals. But increasingly killings were for hard cash from ivory. Tusks became an underground currency, like drugs, spreading webs of corruption from remote villages to urban centers throughout the world. The 1970s saw the price of ivory skyrocket. Suddenly, to a herder or subsistence

farmer, this was no longer an animal but a walking fortune, worth more than a dozen years of honest toil. To currency-strapped governments and revolutionaries alike, ivory was a way to pay for more firearms and supplies. In the 1980s, Africa had nearly ten times the weapons than a decade earlier, which encouraged more poaching. Ivory was running above a hundred dollars per pound, and everyone from poorly paid park rangers to high-ranking wildlife ministers had joined the poaching network.[1]

Total exports of unworked ivory from Africa rose from between 200 and 400 tons per year in the 1950s, to around 1,000 tons in 1980, increasing by about 10 percent per year. Throughout the 1980s, annual export levels ranged between 700 and 1,000 tons (see Figure 1). Such steady export levels hide the true impact on the African elephant population. By 1987, most mature bull elephants had been shot, leaving only the smaller tusks of elephant cows and calves to be traded. For this reason, one ton of traded ivory by the late 1980s represented approximately 113 dead elephants, up from an average of 54 in 1979.

At the beginning of the 1980s, there existed an estimated 1.2 million elephants in Africa, including 376,000 in Zaire and 204,000 in Tanzania (see Figure 2). As poaching accelerated over the next several years, the elephant population dropped to approximately 600,000 by 1988, with Zaire's total falling to 103,000 and Tanzania's to 75,000. To better control the declining populations, an ivory quota system was established in 1986 under the authority of CITES. Under the system, all ivory exports were to be authorized by CITES. During the system's first year of operation, a global quota of 108,000 tusks was set. Though estimates can be extremely difficult to gauge, experts determined that this figure, which was thought by some conservationists to be ten times too high, was easily exceeded thanks to smugglers not interested in the paperwork of securing an authorization and unhindered by poaching laws that were not enforced.

As elephant populations continued to fall over the next two years, CITES convened in Switzerland in October 1989 under tremendous pressure to impose a full global ban on ivory and other elephant products. When the votes of the more than 100 CITES member countries were counted, supporters of the ban had won a very emotional and significant victory. However, one-third

---

[1]This brief account of the African elephant's changing circumstances is excerpted from Douglas H. Chadwick, "Out of Time, Out of Space: Elephants," *National Geographic* (May 1991).

| WHO EXPORTS IVORY | | |
|---|---|---|
| tonnes | exports 1986 | cumulative exports 1979–87 |
| Burundi | 90 | 488 |
| Botswana | 0 | 58 |
| Chad | 0 | 111 |
| Cent. Af. Rep. | 19 | 1,136 |
| Congo | 17 | 917 |
| Cameroon | 1 | 28 |
| Kenya | 2 | 131 |
| Namibia | 1 | 37 |
| Somalia | 61 | 105 |
| South Africa | 41 | 329 |
| Sudan | 78 | 1,452 |
| Tanzania | 70 | 653 |
| Uganda | 36 | 424 |
| Zaire | 23 | 640 |
| Zambia | 10 | 149 |
| Zimbabwe | 8 | 94 |
| Total (incl. other countries) | 663 | 6,828 |
| Source: Wildlife Trade Monitoring Unit, London Environmental Economics Centre | | |

**FIGURE I**

**Who Exports Ivory**
*Source:* "Saving the Elephant: Nature's Great Masterpiece," *The Economist* (July 1, 1989): 17.

of the African countries most affected by the measure had voted against the ban. The agreement regulates only international ivory sales, and permits member countries to opt out of any commitment without sanction. Several southern African countries have done just that, continuing to permit big-game hunting under strict rules. However, with most nations adhering closely to the ban, the legal ivory trade has been decimated and the value of this natural resource for range countries has been vastly diminished.

Several southern African countries, including those recently permitted to sell stockpiled ivory, proposed at the 1989 convention an exception to the ban for countries that had developed sustainable culling programs. The proposal was shelved, largely as a result of opposition from Western conservationists and east African countries, such as Kenya and Tanzania, which were experiencing rapidly declining elephant populations. In the aftermath of the

1989 meeting, a war of words between the two factions "escalated to proportions rarely seen at scientific or diplomatic conferences," according to one participant. CITES convened again in 1992, with similar calls for a loosening of the ban, and similar rejection by most countries outside southern Africa. It wasn't until 1997 that the majority of CITES member countries agreed that an exception to the ban was justified. This change in stance was largely affected by a growing belief, particularly among African wildlife and government officials, that a recommercialization of the ivory trade would enable nations to benefit economically from the elephant, creating a practical incentive to protect the species, something missing under the current ban.

## A Market Approach to Preservation

Supporters of the ban argue that a legalized ivory trade would once again facilitate a thriving illegal parallel market. Only by making all ivory trade illegal will it become easier to police poaching, a major culprit of the African elephant's rapid population decline. But critics argue that a complete ban is simply inappropriate for saving the elephant. A much more probable effect of the ban, they say, will be an ever-rising price for ivory. Many who previously bought ivory legally would now buy the smuggled product. If the legal supply is choked off, but poaching continues, as it undoubtedly will, the increased demand for smuggled tusks will raise the black market value. This, in turn, will raise the profitability of poaching, and increase the risks poachers will be willing to take. The ban, they conclude, will only drive the ivory trade underground, making it as hard to police as cocaine smuggling from the forests of Latin America.

Critics of the ban propose an alternative approach to preserving the elephant. Summed up in the title of a front page January 1997 *Wall Street Journal* article on the subject, "use it or lose it" has become the rallying cry for supporters of legalized trade for ivory and other endangered species products. The argument goes as follows: Few of the species that man finds useful have become endangered so long as their commercialization was possible. When the Europeans came to North America there were no chickens, but millions of passenger pigeons. Today this type of pigeon is extinct, while millions of chickens are harvested each day. The reason is clear say some: the demand for chickens ensures that there is a healthy profit in breeding them. Likewise, there is no danger that man will soon run out of cows, sheep, ducks, or goats.

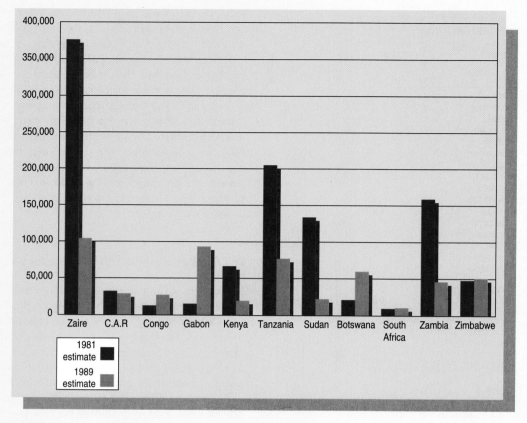

**FIGURE 2**

**Elephant Population by Selected Country**
*Source:* "Saving the Elephant: Nature's Great Masterpiece," *The Economist* (July 1, 1989): 16.

Markets are irresistible forces, it is argued, and demand creates supply. Vast smuggling networks exist because of a growing demand that the market is prohibited from meeting. Today's problem, trade-ban critics argue, is that growing restrictions on the trade in ivory and other such products threaten to remove the profit from legitimate traders and increase the price and incentives for poachers who ignore the law.

Unable to utilize the tremendous value in elephants, few "locals" will bother with serious preservation efforts. "Unless we can make wildlife conservation profitable for all peoples, we cannot save our elephants for the future," according to Richard Leakey, a noted anthropologist and director of wildlife management for Kenya. Some have proposed an international regulatory system, or "Ivory Exchange," which would create an enforceable producers' cartel enabling open but limited trade in ivory. Either way, a legal ivory trade will recognize the economic value

of the elephant, therefore creating a stake in its survival for those living among the animal and best able to promote its preservation. Coupled with this type of regulated trade should be the strong enforcement of poaching laws, an absolutely vital aspect of preservation. This combination of legal trade and strict enforcement of poaching laws is the environment within which the elephant has the best chances for long-term survival, critics of the ban contend.

Zimbabwe, Botswana, Namibia, and South Africa are in the forefront of efforts to implement such an approach. They argue that they have established very successful conservation programs, and should be permitted to profit from their elephants. If impoverished communities are prevented from profiting, "(the elephant) becomes a nuisance, people grow to detest it and feel that they have no stake in its survival," says Peter Kunjeku, director of the Wildlife Society of Zimbabwe. Support for a lifting of the ban is not a stance "against the traditional elephant in the traditional national park," says Kay Muir, a University of Zimbabwe economist and game specialist. Rather, it is a recognition that as rising human populations make new public parks impossible and put pressures on existing ones, animals and their protectors will increasingly have to assume the "true costs of paying their way." Gilbert Grosvenor, Chairman of the National Geographic Society, proclaimed a year after the ban went into effect that "all agree that elephants must earn their keep . . . the day of the free-roaming elephant is over."

## Preservation Success Stories

Unless African countries properly manage their elephant stocks and enforce anti-poaching laws, nothing other countries may do will have much of an effect on the elephant's survival, say critics of the ban. In many countries, game scouts are vastly underpaid, poorly equipped, and unmotivated to do their job. Some scouts even choose to join the other side. The elephant's rate of decline, however, has never been consistent across Africa. Some range countries, particularly those in the south, have adeptly managed their elephant populations before and since the 1989 ban, and now actually contend with oftentimes problematic surpluses. South Africa's world famous Kruger National Park has recently begun the first-ever elephant contraceptive program to control the park's burgeoning pachyderm population. The park removes an average of 600 elephants per year, primarily through culling, but more recently through relocation, in order to keep the population at its carrying capacity of 7,500 elephants. Left to its own devices, the park's elephant population could double in 15 years.

Botswana's elephant population is increasing by 5 percent per year, and is now estimated at 80,000, up from 20,000 in 1980 and 58,000 in 1989. "That's elephants, not chickens," says Ketumile Masire, Botswana's president. "Many are starving and in some areas are destroying their own habitat. We fear they will do irreparable harm to the ecosystem. We would like to reduce our herds and market the ivory," he said. Zimbabwe, with 70,000 elephants, has over twice its carrying capacity. "It's not as if we're against preserving the elephant or that we're ungrateful for the help of the West," says Jon Hutton, director of Africa Resources Trust. He says, however, that Western conservationists need to take into account countries like Zimbabwe "that have a good track record of looking after their elephants."

These countries argue, by way of example, that there are successful models of government preservation programs that do not require the assistance (or hindrance many would argue) of a trade ban. They point to Kenya, which arguably has the most at stake in the elephant's survival due to its huge safari industry, as an example of a failing approach to elephant protection. Kenya criminalized poaching in 1976, and has since seen over half of its elephant population killed off.

## Profit Equals Protection

One vastly misunderstood aspect of the elephant issue is the utter antipathy that exists between the animal and African farmers and villagers. To put it in the words of Tony Prior, U.S. Agency for International Development's (AID) natural resources policy advisor for Africa "elephants take up a lot of ecological space." An elephant can consume as much as 900 pounds of leaves and branches in a day and can be quite partial to maize fields. The overall effect is that elephants can decimate healthy vegetation and leave barren otherwise valuable land. In Zimbabwe, an average of ten farmers per year are trampled to death trying to defend their crops. One Zimbabwe elephant expert recently developed a mortarlike device that launches canisters of pepper spray at approaching elephants. "Elephants are the darlings of the Western world, but they are enemy number one in Kenya," says David Western, head of the Kenya Wildlife Service. "The African farmer's enmity toward elephants is as visceral as Western mawkishness is passionate," he says. Close to 400 Kenyans have been killed by wildlife, primarily elephants, since 1990. "You really have to pity these farmers," says Dourga Albert, a wildlife official in Cameroon. "See them weep after elephants have raided their crops. It's like a plague had befallen them." The typical result in villages throughout Africa is that the marauding invaders are killed, either by locals or, with the locals' gracious approval, poachers.

This condition, however, is changing in many areas of southern Africa. Damaged land and crop losses are not only being tolerated, but villages are doing their best to guard against poachers. This surprising change in behavior is due to the proliferation of government programs that dispense licenses to villages, enabling locals, or paying hunters, to cull an allotted number of elephants each year. One such program in Zimbabwe is known as CAMPFIRE (Communal Areas Management Program for Indigenous Resources). Begun the year the ivory ban came into effect, the program operates on the belief that if big game animals are to survive—both in and out of preserves—people who share the land must benefit. Participants of CAMPFIRE, usually individual villages, are able to sell permits under strict control to big-game trophy hunters, or cull the elephants themselves for hides, tusks, and meat. A single elephant can net a local community $20,000–$50,000. CAMPFIRE earns about $2.5 million a year from sport hunting, which is dispersed among 600,000 people living on communal lands. In one Zimbabwe village, residents received an annual payment of $25 apiece, significant when it is considered that the average Zimbabwean earns approximately $100–$150 per year. Revenues from the program have financed two grinding mills, a water line, and a small school for the village.

As for poaching, CAMPFIRE's spokesman Tawona Tavengwa says that it has dropped sharply in participating areas since the program began. "Local people now have an interest in preserving their wildlife." In many cases it has prompted local villages that had turned some of their own lands into economically doubtful cattle farms, to convert them back into game lands. "If you are taking lands that are marginally productive and putting them to a productive use, and game benefits, that's a plus," he says.

CAMPFIRE depends upon a $28 million multiyear AID grant for its operation. "This is a resource management project, not a wildlife project," according to Tony Prior, AID's overseer for the program. AID believes it is demonstrating to Zimbabweans that a properly managed environment is a renewable and lucrative resource. However, the Humane Society of the United States thinks the program is just an excuse to let Zimbabweans profit from the killing of endangered elephants. Prior says the goal of CAMPFIRE is to get people to see wildlife and the environment as income sources. "We want to make maintaining the wildlife population a matter of self-interest," Prior says. In response to the Humane Society and other conservation groups that have hurled accusations of mismanagement and corruption at CAMPFIRE, Prior responds by saying environmental projects take time to mature and AID is attempting "to put in place the conditions for long-term change." Elephant hunting is not the problem, he concludes, not with the threat of "30,000 elephants dying from drought."

Irrespective of the controversy, locals are grateful for the opportunity to share in the profit from their own resources. The program has brought the Zimbabwe village of Mahenya full circle. Villagers once hated nearby Gonarezhou Park because they were forced off the land thirty years ago to create the preserve and were forbidden to hunt the animals that had sustained them for centuries. "Now we use the skills and knowledge of our elders to conserve wildlife as they once did," says one villager. "Once again animals are a part of our livelihood." CAMPFIRE, emulated in other southern African countries, is expected to be funded at least through 1999, despite a fight by some members of Congress to abolish the program.

## Eco-Imperialism?

After all the arguing and exchanging of information and statistics, those calling for a legalization of the ivory trade simply feel they should not have to obtain the approval of other countries in order to harvest their own natural resources. A University of Zimbabwe game economist states that Westerners, in not viewing the elephant firsthand, have no idea of the "lost opportunity costs" to villagers who are often asked to forego development of their lands and accept crop losses, damaged housing, and sometimes loss of life for the sake of the elephant. "Would citizens of industrialized countries choose the survival of the whale, panda or bear . . . at the expense of their lives, the education of their children, or their pensions?" she asks. "I doubt it. Yet they ask Africans to give up very substantial needs in order to ensure that wildlife prospers." A Zimbabwe newspaper, referring to the controversy, denounced "well-fed and prosperous Europeans and North Americans, wearing leather shoes and tucking into high-priced meat dishes, telling African peasants that basically they are only on earth as picturesque extras in a huge zoo."

Much of the debate boils down to differences in culture and values. Opponents of the ivory trade fear that the doctrine of "consumptive use," taken to extremes, is ultimately harmful because it reduces the value of all animals to mere economics. "I don't like the idea of turning everything into a cow," says Josh Ginsberg of the Wildlife Conservation Society. Teresa Telecky, a top zoologist with the Humane Society, believes "it's insane to try to assign an economic value to every animal on Earth." In Africa, however, those who have managed to nurture their elephant populations see no reason why they should not be able to profit as a result. CITES Deputy Secretary-General Jacques Berney neatly phrased the distinction: "On the one side you have those who believe in . . . utilization of wildlife as an economic resource; on the other you have those who believe purely in protection . . . who would still like to ban the ivory trade tomorrow even if there were three million elephants in Africa instead of 650,000."

## The Future

So how has the ivory ban worked? It's difficult to tell. Statistics on elephant populations are extremely difficult to collect—the animal does not stay in one place, or one country for that matter, very long. Additionally, some of the largest populations reside in very dense jungle. Many experts, agree, however, that the rapid slaughter of elephants in the 1980s has been largely reduced in the 1990s—though hardly ended. Two hundred tuskless elephant carcasses were found in Congo in late 1996. A Korean national arriving home from Gabon that same year was caught transporting over 100 kilograms of ivory and ivory products in a washing machine and sofa. More recently, in June 1997 Taiwanese officials seized 130 kilograms of ivory and ivory products, as well as two 300-kilogram ivory sculptures, from members of a South African–Taiwan smuggling ring.

A 1995 study on the effectiveness of the ban concluded "the answer to this question (of effectiveness) remains . . . inconclusive." In assuming the ban has brought about a significant drop in poaching, critics characterize such an outcome as only temporary. Poaching or no poaching, the African elephant population is likely to continue to decline due to the encroachment of humans upon elephant habitat.

Supporters of the ban can rest assured that even a partial return to a normalized ivory trade is years away. The one-time ivory sales made possible by the 1997 CITES decision alone will take 2–3 years to complete, due to the significant documentation and conditions imposed by CITES. The implications of the CITES decision, however, are unmistakable; as African countries continue to exert pressure and make their case to the international community, and as elephant populations continue to rise in those nations with successful preservation programs, additional exceptions are likely to be granted and the current ban will come under increased scrutiny.

### Questions for Discussion

1. Critique the following argument: "Successful protection of the African elephant (or any other endangered species) requires a profit incentive."
2. If the United States and other nations are going to refuse ivory imports, should they compensate impoverished exporting nations by opening markets wider for other products?
3. Should elephant range countries direct their economic potential and limited resources towards more growth-related, higher-skilled industries?

4. Assess the implications of the 1997 CITES decision to permit limited ivory exports as it relates to trade in other types of endangered wildlife.

# Attracting Foreign Direct Investment: German Luxury Cars in the USA

Two southern U.S. states, South Carolina and Alabama, received what many view as just rewards for their hospitality, generosity, and probusiness environment. These rewards came in the form of multimillion-dollar investments for new automobile plants. The Germany luxury car legends BMW and Mercedes-Benz both chose to invest in new production sites in the southern United States. For BMW, the search ended in the summer of 1992, when management decided to locate its plant in the Greenville-Spartanburg area of South Carolina. Mercedes concluded its closely watched search in the fall of 1993, choosing tiny Vance, Alabama, as home for its new plant.

The German investments represent two key facets of a very competitive industry: the need to cut costs and easy access to target markets. U.S. wages are, on average, 60 percent lower than in Germany. Both German carmakers are competing head-to-head with Japanese producers that are already well ensconced on the U.S. production scene.

*Source: This case was written by Michael R. Czinkota and Peter Fitzmaurice based on the following sources: "Bayerische Motoren Werke AG: Investment in U.S. Plant to Increase by $200 Million,"* The Wall Street Journal, *February 28, 1996, B6; Bill McAllister,* "BMW Plant Becomes Symbol for Free Trade," The Washington Post, *March 1, 1996, A9; Chris Burritt,* "BMW Eases Boom and Bust of Textiles," Atlanta Journal and Atlanta Constitution, *April 14, 1996, H9; Allen Myerson,* "O Governor, Won't You Buy Me a Mercedes Plant," The New York Times, *September 1, 1996, 3:I;* "Porsche, Mercedes Talk of Sharing Ala. Output," Atlanta Journal and Atlanta Constitution, *July 5, 1996, E3:* "Why Mercedes Is Alabama Bound," Business Week *(October 11, 1993): 138–139;* "Alabama Steers Mercedes South," ENR *(October 11, 1993): 6–7;* "Mercedes-Benz Parks $300 Million Plant in Alabama," Site Selection *(December 1993): 1292;* "Europe Loves Dixie," Europe *(October 1992): 30–36;* "The Beemer Spotlight Falls on Spartanburg, USA," Business Week *(July 6, 1992): 38;* "The Boom Belt," Business Week *(September 27, 1993): 98–104. For more information, see* www.daimlerbenz.com, www.daimlerchrysler.com, www.bmw.com

Both South Carolina and Alabama are celebrating the hard-fought battle that won them thousands of future jobs, potential financial returns in the billions, and the prestige of having landed such world-class companies. These developments are also expected to make other potential investors take a long, hard look at the two states as well.

Each investment decision was based on different details; however, the underlying case of trying to land a world-class investor at seemingly whatever means possible is present in both examples. A closer look at the two foreign direct investments provides the opportunity to view some of the different details and circumstances, as well as the similarities, that exist in luring a desirable investment.

## The BMW Decision

Over three years, BMW looked at 250 locations in ten countries. When it was clear that BMW planned on locating its facility in the United States, a race ensued between competing states to win the cherished investment. In the end, the choice came down to Nebraska and South Carolina.

South Carolina Governor Carroll Campbell put up a strong recruiting effort, visiting BMW in Germany and making offers that were hard to refuse. In order to obtain the $640 million plant and the expected 6,000 new state jobs, a bit of southern finesse was added. For instance, the site most desired by BMW had 134 separate landowners. In order to ease land acquisition problems, Gov. Campbell secured a $25 million appropriation from the state legislature to buy the property. He personally telephoned reluctant sellers and within fourteen weeks, the state and local governments had spent $36.6 million to buy every single property—including a home that one family had just finished building two weeks before they were approached. To sweeten the deal, new roads and site improvements were included, and the runway at the local airport was to be extended to accommodate BMWs cargo planes. The state also offered a $41 million property tax break to BMW. Furthermore, the local airport's free-trade-zone status was extended to include the 900-acre plant site, meaning BMW will not have to pay duties on parts imported from Germany or elsewhere until cars actually leave the plant for sale in the United States.

One of the big determinants for BMW was South Carolina's excellent technical school system. Under the investment agreement, the state will customize its training program for the company, even sending instructors to Munich to study the equipment that will be used. In all, the state has promised to spend $3 million to train workers for BMW alone, a considerable sum when one takes into account that in 1992 South Carolina spent $5.8 million on technical training for the entire state. In addition, local businesses offered to pay up to $3 million for additional training.

The constant stream of amenities and special treatment that South Carolina extended to BMW was especially critical to completing this deal, according to industry analysts, given the fact that BMW is considered to be a conservative corporation not prone to bold moves. The firm does not just want to be accepted, it wants to be welcomed. Carl Flescher, a vice president with BMW North America states: "I've only been down there for about ten or fifteen days and I am very impressed. The embracing of this whole thing is incredible. You go to the Holiday Inn and there is a sign that says 'Welcome BMW.' You pulled up to the Hertz rental car and they know who you are. People are genuinely friendly, open, and elated." Gov. Campbell sums up the whole mission best: "The name BMW is generally associated with excellence and quality and that by itself is a benefit. Other companies will say, 'Well, wait a minute, BMW is rated as one of the best, and they chose South Carolina. So, they must be doing something right.' "

When BMW chose to locate in South Carolina, it was joining a group of European firms (including BASF, Rieter, Marzoli International, and Michelin) that had already discovered the state's comparatively cheaper and skilled workforce, as well as the hospitable, probusiness atmosphere. In fact, South Carolina's Spartanburg County, the home of BMW's plant, hosts over 100 foreign-affiliated companies, and about half of South Carolina's workers are employed by foreign-owned firms, one of the highest percentages in the country.

In 1995, BMW began U.S. production of a new, more affordable model aimed at the American market, specifically graying baby boomers. The plant was up and running ahead of schedule and producing 300 cars a day within several months of start-up. By 1996, suppliers had invested more than $70 million in the county and hired over 600 people. The plant's success resulted in some unexpected attention during South Carolina's 1996 Republican presidential primary. A few leading candidates chose the plant as a showcase of their free-trade stances in this highly internationalized state. Bob Dole, on site, commented: "This is one perfect example of what can happen when you trade." In the late 90s, BMW announced a $200 million, 300,000-square-foot expansion to the plant, expected to result in an additional 500 jobs and 100 cars a day in capacity. This will accelerate the company's plan to push capacity to almost 100,000 cars a year by the end of the decade.

## The Daimler Benz Investment

In the case of Daimler Benz, its automobile division Mercedes was searching for a U.S. location to construct a $300 million plant to manufacture its new sport utility vehicle, which was expected to offer stiff competition to the Ford Explorer and the Jeep Grand Cherokee. Initially, Mercedes' search included 170 sites in thirty states. Alabama knew that to win the investment, its offer would have to be outstanding. One state official recalls the message from a Mercedes consulting firm representative: "Everyone knows what South Carolina gave BMW. My client feels they are better than BMW!"

So the race was on, and in the end, Alabama won the "industrial crown jewel," as Governor Jim Folsom, Jr., referred to it. Mercedes was impressed by the entrepreneurial, nonbureaucratic attitude of Alabama's state government. The firm also liked the access to interstate highways, railroads, and ports; adequate available labor; proximity to schools; quality of life; and, of course, a lucrative package of financial incentives. Here is a partial list of these incentives: $92.2 million to buy and develop the site, create a foreign trade zone, and build an employee training center; $77.5 million to extend water, gas, and sewer lines along with other infrastructure; $75 million to purchase 2,500 of the new vehicles for use by state employees; $60 million in government funds to train Mercedes employees, suppliers, and workers in related industries, enriched by $15 million from the private sector; $8.7 million in tax breaks, in all, a total of more than $300 million.

The plant began production in early 1997. Annual volume is 70,000 cars, half of which are sold in the United States. Direct employment generated from the plant is expected to reach 1,500 by the end of the decade. New employment will also come via suppliers. According to the Economic Development Partnership of Alabama, the plant has already created over 1,100 new jobs among seven major suppliers. Further job growth could come from a pending agreement between Mercedes and fellow German automaker Porsche AG to produce Porsche's own version of a sport utility vehicle at the Alabama plant. Under the proposed agreement, the Porsche vehicles would be sold outside the United States, protecting Mercedes against additional competition in the United States.

If reached, the agreement could mean the production of an additional 8,000 cars a year at the plant.

Alabama believes it invested wisely. One study found that the $300 million used to lure the German investment will yield shining returns of $365 million during the first year of operation and $7.3 billion over the next twenty years. But there are limits to the lure of state incentives. One state official commented: "Ultimately it comes down to the company's personal choice." Says Mercedes project leader Andreas Renschler: "Whether you get $10 million more or less in one state doesn't make any difference. We sensed a much higher dedication to our project."

Many experts contend that states are "buying" industry at too steep a price. The financial incentives necessary to land the BMW plant, including a $1 per year land lease, will cost South Carolina $130 million over thirty years. Then—North Carolina governor Jim Hunt criticized much of Alabama's incentives package to Mercedes, saying, "We do not need to risk the future of the franchise to recruit star players." In particular, Hunt pointed to what some refer to as the "Benz Bill," which allows 5 percent of corporate income tax from the plant and 5 percent of the plant employees' taxes to be used to retire Mercedes debt. The cost of incentives for the Mercedes plant, on a per new job basis, is eighteen times what Tennessee paid for a Nissan plant in 1980 and four times what Kentucky paid for a Toyota plant in 1985.

Some economists argue that rich incentives often fail to yield adequate returns for a city or state. Corporate welfare, they say, diverts money better spent attracting businesses through improved infrastructure and schools. "It is nothing but a zero-sum game," said former U.S. Labor Secretary Robert Reich. "Resources are moved around; Peter is robbed to pay Paul." Proposals to halt the growth in financial incentives offered to large corporations, often foreign, include a tax on all incentives received by a corporation to move facilities.

The attitude of "not giving away the franchise," however, is increasingly being seen by decision makers as detrimental, especially in this day of corporate downsizing, whereby politicians are judged on how many jobs they create in the private sector. A report by an international site-selection consultant, commissioned by North Carolina after losing the chance to land BMW, read that the state "is increasingly seen as a nonparticipant in incentive practices at a time when incentives are growing in importance." So the question "How much is too much?" is complicated by the fact that growing expectations and necessities may seemingly warrant the types of grandiose offers that are portrayed in the Mercedes and BMW cases.

## Questions for Discussion

1. Do you believe that states should encourage foreign direct investment? Why or why not?
2. Do incentives determine whether or not a company will invest in a particular country?
3. How should a state government determine the upper limit of its investment support?
4. Do FDI incentives place locally established firms at a disadvantage?

# Harley-Davidson (A): Protecting Hogs

On September 1, 1982, Harley-Davidson Motor Company and Harley-Davidson York, Inc., filed a petition for "relief," or protection, with the U.S. International Trade Commission (ITC). The filing, a request under Section 201 of the U.S. Trade Act of 1974, was a request for escape clause relief from the damaging imports of heavyweight motorcycles into the United States. Harley-Davidson Motor Company, and more specifically its traditional large engine motorcycle, the hog,[1] was facing dwindling domestic market share. This was a last desperate act for survival.

## Import Penetration

Throughout most of the first half of the twentieth century, there were more than 150 different manufacturers of motorcycles in the United States. By 1978, however, there were only three, and only one, Harley-Davidson, was U.S.–owned. The other two U.S. manufacturers were Japanese-owned, Kawasaki and Honda America.

By the early 1980s, Harley-Davidson was in trouble.

SOURCE; *This case was written by Michael H. Moffett. This case is intended for class discussion purposes only and does not represent either efficient or inefficient management practices.*

[1] The motorcycles produced and sold by Harley-Davidson have traditionally been known as hogs. The nickname is primarily in reference to their traditional large size, weight, and power. See **http://www.harley-davidson.com**.

Imports held a 60 percent share of the total heavyweight motorcycle market by 1980, and they continued to grow. Harley's difficulties worsened as its products suffered increasing quality problems, with labor and management facing off against one another instead of against the competition. By the end of 1982, in a total domestic market that had seen no growth in three years, import market share rose to 69 percent.

The declining market share of domestic producers in a flat market translated into a fight of Harley against all competitors, because Harley was up against two domestic competitors who were really not domestic. Kawasaki and Honda America were producing in the United States essentially the same products as those being imported. In fact, Harley argued that the two domestic competitors were only assembling foreign-made parts in the United States and were therefore not domestic producers at all.

## The Harley Law

What has become known as the "Harley Law" was the resulting finding of the ITC that imports were a contributing cause of injury to the domestic heavyweight motorcycle industry. The ITC recommended to then–President Ronald Reagan that import duties be increased for a period of five years. Duties were to be raised to 45 percent the first year (1983), with the duty declining steadily over each following year until reaching 10 percent in the fifth and final year of protection (1988).

The president and his staff agreed with the finding but wanted a tariff rate quota (TRQ) instead of a straight tariff increase. A TRQ is a combination of tariffs and quotas; in this case, the increased tariff rates would be imposed only on imports (by volume) above a specific number per year. This was intended to allow specific small foreign producers to have continued access to the U.S. markets, while still providing Harley with protection from the large-volume importers who were rapidly gaining domestic market share. Table 1 provides a listing of the major tariff rate quotas as specified by the ITC.

The domestic industry that was to be protected was defined as those motorcycles "with a total piston displacement of over 700 cc."[2] This was strategic success for Harley, in that most of its motorcycle sales were actually 1000 cc and higher. This meant Harley was able to hinder competitor sales in product categories other than those reflecting the head-to-head competition. Harley had

[2] Hufbauer, 1986, 263.

**TABLE 1**

Tariff Rate Quotas for Heavyweight Motorcycles

| Country | Pre-1983 Share[2] | 1983 Quota[1] | 1983 Share | 1988 Quota[3] |
|---------|-------------------|---------------|------------|---------------|
| West Germany | .4% | 5,000 | 33.3% | 10,000 |
| Japan | 93.0% | 6,000 | 40.0% | 11,000 |
| Others | 6.6% | 4,000 | 26.7% | 9,000 |

Notes:
[1] These quotas and tariff schedules applicable to motorcycles with engine displacement of 700 cubic centimeters and greater, only. Volume quotas are per engine.

[2] Pre-1983 shares are percentage of total imports into the United States originating from that country.

[3] All quota shares rise 1,000 units per year after 1983, with the terminal quotas of 1988 being effective only for that final year (after which there would be no further Tariff Rate Quotas).

*Source:* Adapted from *Trade Protection in the United States: 31 Case Studies* (Washington, D.C.: Institute for International Economics, 1986), 263–264.

also requested that the imported parts that were being used by its two domestic competitors also be subject to tariff restrictions. Harley argued that the lower-cost product that was damaging the domestic industry was composed of the same parts, whether assembled in Japan or in the United States by Kawasaki and Honda America. On this last point, however, they were unsuccessful. Domestic producers would be protected against final product sales only, and no restrictions would be placed on imported parts.

## Competitive Response: Competitors

TRQs were implemented for the 1983 through 1988 period. As seen in Table 2, the first two years of protection did have the desired result: import market share fell precipitously. Imports fell from a high of 69 percent in 1982

to just 24 percent in 1984. It is also interesting to note, however, that total market sales fell dramatically over this same period. After two years of significant protection, domestic production had increased only 20 percent (from 100,000 to 121,000 units per year), although the total market had fallen by 130,000 from 1982 to 1983 alone (and 1983 was a year of rapid economic growth in the United States following the severe recession of 1981–1982).

The response of Harley's major competitors to the TRQs was rapid and predictable. First, the two major domestic producers, Kawasaki and Honda America, immediately stepped up production of heavyweight motorcycles within the United States. The ITC estimates that imports of parts other than engines increased 82 percent in the first year of protection (1983) and more than 200 percent in the second year (1984). The ITC also es-

**TABLE 2**

Import and Domestic Heavyweight Motorcycle Market Shares (thousands of units)

| Year | Total Sales[1] | Domestic Share (%) | Import Share (%) |
|------|----------------|--------------------|--------------------|
| 1980 | 326 (100%) | 130 (40%) | 196 (60%) |
| 1981 | 327 (100%) | 125 (38%) | 202 (62%) |
| 1982 | 324 (100%) | 100 (31%) | 224 (69%) |
| 1983 (TRQ) | 194 (100%) | 100 (52%) | 94 (48%) |
| 1984 (TRQ) | 159 (100%) | 121 (76%) | 38 (24%) |

[1] Total sales is the sum of domestic production and imports; exports were negligible over the subject period.

*Source:* Adapted from *Trade Protection in the United States: 31 Case Studies* (Washington, D.C.: Institute for International Economics, 1986, and various publications of the U.S. International Trade Commission)

timates that between 50 and 70 percent of the final value of the domestically produced Kawasaki and Honda America motorcycles was imported as parts. Second, the same Japanese-owned producers altered the product manufactured outside the United States, primarily in Japan, to reduce engine displacement from the designed 750 cc to between 690 and 700 cc in order to fall below the TRQ coverage. Third, the Japanese government, on behalf of its own producers, filed a complaint under Article XIII of the General Agreement on Tariffs and Trade (GATT) that the European competitors (Germany) were receiving discriminatory treatment (although filed, there were no formal findings ever made on this complaint).

## Competitive Response: Harley

Harley-Davidson used the period of import relief to restructure, retool, and retrain. Two specific actions were taken to strengthen Harley to once again be a competitive firm.

1. **A Rededication to Quality**—Although Harley had instituted quality circles in manufacturing as early as 1976, renewed efforts in quality monitoring and labor involvement dramatically improved the quality of the product.[3] By 1988, Harley had 117 quality circles in operation with more than 50 percent of all employees involved in the improvement of their own product. The implementation of a just-in-time materials-management program, which Harley termed "materials as needed," also aided greatly in reducing costs of production.

2. **Diversification of Earnings**—In 1986, Harley purchased Holiday Rambler Corporation of Wakarusa, Indiana. Holiday Rambler is a recreational vehicle manufacturer that was expected to provide Harley with broadened earnings flows as the domestic motorcycle industry was increasingly stagnant in growth. Harley has also continued to increase production and sales of other products, such as metal bomb casings and liquid-fuel rocket engines for the U.S. Department of Defense.

Harley's measures were indeed effective in returning the company to profitability and competitiveness. In 1987,

a year ahead of schedule, Harley requested that the tariff rate quotas be removed from imported motorcycles.

### Questions for Discussion

1. Were the tariff rate quotas (TRQs) really effective in protecting Harley-Davidson against Japanese manufacturers' import penetration? What was the role of imported parts in this effectiveness of protection?
2. Did Harley-Davidson "adjust" to changing market conditions during the period in which the U.S. government afforded it protection from foreign competition? Do you believe it responded to the expectations of public policymakers to reclaim competitiveness on world markets?

### References

Beals, Vaughn. "Harley-Davidson: An American Success Story." *Journal for Quality & Participation* 11, 2 (June 1988): A19–A23.

Gelb, Thomas. "Overhauling Corporate Engine Drives Winning Strategy." *Journal of Business Strategy* 10, 6 (November/December 1989): 8–12.

Grant, Robert M., R. Krishnan, Abraham B. Shani, and Ron Baer. "Appropriate Manufacturing Technology: A Strategic Approach." *Sloan Management Review* 33, 1 (Fall 1991): 43–54.

Hackney, Holt. "Easy Rider." *Financial World* 159, 18 (September 4, 1990): 48–49.

"How Harley Beat Back the Japanese." *Fortune* (September 25, 1989): 155–164.

Hufbauer, Gary Clyde, Diane T. Berliner, and Kimberly Ann Elliot. *Trade Protection in the United States: 31 Case Studies.* Washington, D.C.: The Institute for International Economics, 1986.

"Mounting the Drive for Quality." *Manufacturing Engineering* 108, 1 (January 1992): 92, 94.

Muller, E. J. "Harley's Got the Handle on Inbound." *Distribution* 88, 3 (March 1989): 70, 74.

Pruzin, Daniel R. "Born to be Verrucht." *World Trade* 5, 4 (May 1992): 112–117.

Reid, Peter C. *Well-Made in America.* New York: McGraw-Hill, 1989.

Rudin, Brad. "Harley Revs Up Image Through Diversifying." *Pensions & Investment Age* 15, 3 (February 9, 1987): 21–23.

Sepehri, Mehran. "Manufacturing Revitalization at Harley-Davidson Motor Co." *Industrial Engineering* 19, 8 (August 1987): 86–93.

---

[3]When the first quality circles were created in 1976, it was estimated that the first 100 motorcycles off the production line were costing an additional $100,000 to "repair" before they were up to standards for sale. This had to change.

# THEORETICAL FOUNDATIONS

## PART 2

Part 2 provides theoretical background for international trade and investment activities. Classical concepts such as absolute and comparative advantage are explained. Key emphasis rests with modern-day theoretical developments that are presented in light of the realities of international business. In addition, the international economic activity of nations are discussed.

# CHAPTER 5

# The Theory of International Trade and Investment

## LEARNING OBJECTIVES

◆ *To understand the traditional arguments of how and why international trade improves the welfare of all countries*

◆ *To review the history and compare the implications of trade theory from the original work of Adam Smith to the contemporary theories of Michael Porter*

◆ *To examine the criticisms of classical trade theory and examine alternative viewpoints of which business and economic forces determine trade patterns between countries*

◆ *To explore the similarities and distinctions between international trade and international investment*

## Heavyweight Currency Squeezes Czech Trade

The Czech government is casting around for ways of cutting back its soaring trade deficit without devaluing the koruna—something it was committed to avoid. The cabinet met this week to discuss a range of measures, including boosting export promotion and research and development and curbing public sector wage growth. The deficit, which totaled Kc100.9 billion ($3.7 billion) in the eight months to August 1996 was forecast to reach 7 percent of gross domestic product that year.

Senior policymakers agreed on the need to increase domestic competitiveness and exports, which were flagging mainly because of the strength of the koruna and a slowdown in economic activity in the country's main export markets. Economic ministers and the head of the central bank firmly ruled out a currency devaluation or import surcharges to cut the deficit.

Vaclav Klaus, the prime minister, said the strength of the koruna was not the root cause of the problem and promised no change to the long-running policy of fixed exchange rates, which has become an article of faith for the government. However, he said the government wanted to prevent wage growth from exceeding labor productivity and would seek to curb public sector wage rises.

Analysts backed the stance on the koruna, but the currency continued to rise against the U.S. dollar and the D-Mark, further exacerbating the problems of exports. The country is importing capital goods for investment while exports are growing more slowly than imports because of strong demand at home. But the benefits of the imports of technology have still to result in higher exports of better-quality goods.

*Source:* "Heavyweight Currency Squeezes Czech Trade," Vincent Boland, *Financial Times,* Friday October 18, 1996, p. 2.

The debates, the costs, the benefits, and the dilemmas of international trade have in many ways not changed significantly from the time when Marco Polo crossed the barren wastelands of Eurasia to the time of the expansion of U.S. and Canadian firms across the Rio Grande into Mexico under the North American Free Trade Agreement. At the heart of the issue is what the gains—and the risks—are to the firm and the country as a result of a seller from one country servicing the needs of a buyer in a different country. If a Spanish firm wants to sell its product to the enormous market of mainland China, whether it produces at home and ships the product from Cadiz to Shanghai (international trade) or actually builds a factory in Shanghai (international investment), the goal is still the same: To sell a product for profit in the foreign market.

This chapter provides a directed path through centuries of thought on why and how trade and investment across borders occurs. Although theories and theorists come and go with time, a few basic questions have dominated this intellectual adventure:

- Why do countries trade?
- Do countries trade or do firms trade?
- Do the elements that give rise to the competitiveness of a firm, an industry, or a country as a whole, arise from some inherent endowment of the country itself, or do they change with time and circumstance?
- Once identified, can these sources of competitiveness be manipulated or managed by firms or governments to the benefit of the traders?

International trade is expected to improve the productivity of industry and the welfare of consumers. Let us learn how and why we still seek the exotic silks of the Far East.

## The Age of Mercantilism

The evolution of trade into the form we see today reflects three events: the collapse of feudal society, the emergence of the mercantilist philosophy, and the life cycle of the colonial systems of the European nation-states. Feudal society was a state of **autarky,** a society that did not trade because all of its needs were met internally. The feudal estate was self-sufficient, although hardly "sufficient" in more modern terms, given the limits of providing entirely for oneself. Needs literally were only those of food and shelter, and all available human labor was devoted to the task of fulfilling those basic needs. As merchants began meeting in the marketplace, as travelers began exchanging goods from faraway places at the water's edge, the attractiveness of trade became evident.

In the centuries leading up to the Industrial Revolution, international commerce was largely conducted under the authority of governments. The goals of trade were, therefore, the goals of governments. As early as 1500 the benefits of trade were clearly established in Europe, as nation-states expanded their influence across the globe in the creation of colonial systems. To maintain and expand their control over these colonial possessions, the European nations needed fleets, armies, food, and all other resources the nations could muster. They needed wealth. Trade was therefore conducted to fill the governments' treasuries, at minimum expense to themselves but to the detriment of their captive trade partners. Although colonialism normally is associated with the exploitation of those captive societies, it went hand in hand with the evolving exchange of goods among the European countries themselves, **mercantilism.**

Mercantilism mixed exchange through trade with accumulation of wealth. Since government controlled the patterns of commerce, it identified strength with the accumulation of **specie** (gold and silver) and maintained a general policy of exports dominating imports. Trade across borders—exports—was considered preferable to domestic trade because exports would earn gold. Import duties, tariffs, subsidization of exports, and outright restriction on the importation of many goods were used to maximize the gains from exports over the costs of imports. Laws were passed making it illegal to take gold or silver out of the country, even if such specie was needed to purchase imports to produce their own goods for sale. This was one-way trade, the trade of greed and power.

The demise of mercantilism was inevitable given class structure and the distribution of society's product. As the Industrial Revolution introduced the benefits of mass production, lowering prices and increasing the supplies of goods to all, the exploitation of colonies and trading partners came to an end. However, governments still exercise considerable power and influence on the conduct of trade.

## Classical Trade Theory

The question of why countries trade has proven difficult to answer. Since the second half of the eighteenth century, academicians have tried to understand not only the motivations and benefits of international trade, but also why some countries grow faster and wealthier than others through trade. Figure 5.1 provides an overview of the evolutionary path of trade theory since the fall of mercantilism. Although somewhat simplified, it shows the line of development of the major theories put forward over the past two centuries. It also serves as an early indication of the path of modern theory: the shifting focus from the country to the firm, from cost of production to the market as a whole, and from the perfect to the imperfect.

### The Theory of Absolute Advantage

Generally considered the father of economics, Adam Smith published *The Wealth of Nations* in 1776 in London. In this book, Smith attempted to explain the process by which markets and production actually operate in society. Smith's two main areas of contribution, *absolute advantage* and the *division of labor,* were fundamental to trade theory.

Production, the creation of a product for exchange, always requires the use of society's primary element of value, human labor. Smith noted that some countries, owing to the skills of their workers or the quality of their natural resources, could produce the same products as others with fewer labor-hours. He termed this efficiency **absolute advantage.**

Adam Smith observed the production processes of the early stages of the Industrial Revolution in England and recognized the fundamental changes that were occurring in production. In previous states of society, a worker performed all stages of a production process, with resulting output that was little more than sufficient for the worker's own needs. The factories of the industrializing world were, however, separating the production process into distinct stages, in which each stage would be performed exclusively by one individual, the **division of labor.** This specialization increased the production of workers and industries. Smith's pin factory analogy has long been considered the recognition of one of the most significant principles of the industrial age.

> To take an example, therefore, from a very trifling manufacture; but one in which the division of labour has been very often taken notice of the trade of the pin-maker; a workman not educated to this business . . . could scarce, perhaps, with his utmost industry, make one pin in a day, and certainly could not make twenty. But in a way in which this business is now carried on, not only the whole work is a peculiar trade, but it is divided in to a number of branches, of which the greater part are

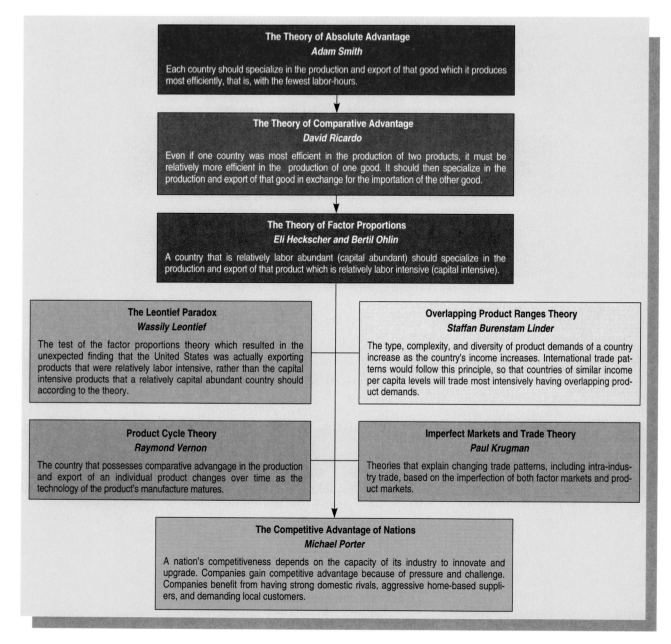

**FIGURE 5.1**

**The Evolution of Trade Theory**

likewise peculiar trades. One man draws out the wire, another straights
it, a third cuts it, a fourth points it, a fifth grinds it at the top for receiving the head: to make the head requires two or three distinct operations; to put it on is a peculiar business . . . I have seen a small man-
ufactory of this kind where ten men only were employed, and where

some of them consequently performed two or three distinct operations. But though they were very poor, and therefore but indifferently accommodated with the necessary machine, they could, when they exerted themselves, make among them about twelve pounds of pins in a day. There are in a pound upwards of four thousand pins of a middling size.[1]

Adam Smith then extended his division of labor in the production process to a division of labor and specialized product across countries. Each country would specialize in a product for which it was uniquely suited. More would be produced for less. Thus, by each country, specializing in products for which it possessed **absolute advantage,** countries could produce more in total and exchange products—trade—for goods that were cheaper in price than those produced at home.

## The Theory of Comparative Advantage

Although Smith's work was instrumental in the development of economic theories about trade and production, it did not answer some fundamental questions about trade. First, Smith's trade relied on a country possessing absolute advantage in production, but did not explain what gave rise to the production advantages. Second, if a country did not possess absolute advantage in any product, could it (or would it) trade?

David Ricardo, in his 1819 work entitled *On the Principles of Political Economy and Taxation,* sought to take the basic ideas set down by Smith a few steps further. Ricardo noted that even if a country possessed absolute advantage in the production of two products, it still must be relatively more efficient than the other country in one good's production than the other. Ricardo termed this the **comparative advantage.** Each country would then possess comparative advantage in the production of one of the two products, and both countries would then benefit by specializing completely in one product and trading for the other.

## A Numerical Example of Classical Trade

To fully understand the theories of absolute advantage and comparative advantage, consider the following example. Two countries, France and England, produce only two products, wheat and cloth (or beer and pizza, guns and butter, and so forth). The relative efficiency of each country in the production of the two products is measured by comparing the number of labor-hours needed to produce one unit of each product. Table 5.1 provides an efficiency comparison of the two countries.

England is obviously more efficient in the production of wheat. Whereas it takes France four labor-hours to produce one unit of wheat, it takes England only two hours to produce the same unit of wheat. France takes twice as many labor-hours to produce the same output. England has absolute advantage in the production of wheat. France needs two labor-hours to produce a unit of cloth that it takes England four labor-hours to produce. England therefore requires two more labor-hours than France to produce the same unit of cloth. France has absolute advantage in the production of cloth. The two countries are exactly opposite in relative efficiency of production.

David Ricardo took the logic of absolute advantages in production one step further to explain how countries could exploit their own advantages and gain

**TABLE 5.1**

Absolute Advantage and Comparative Advantage*

| Country | Wheat | Cloth |
|---------|-------|-------|
| England | 2 | 4 |
| France | 4 | 2 |

- England has absolute advantage in the production of wheat. It requires fewer labor-hours (2 being less than 4) for England to produce one unit of wheat.
- France has absolute advantage in the production of cloth. It requires fewer labor-hours (2 being less than 4) for France to produce one unit of cloth.
- England has comparative advantage in the production of wheat. If England produces one unit of wheat, it is forgoing the production of 2/4 (0.50) of a unit of cloth. If France produces one unit of wheat, it is forgoing the production of 4/2 (2.00) of a unit of cloth. England therefore has the lower opportunity cost of producing wheat.
- France has comparative advantage in the production of cloth. If England produces one unit of cloth, it is forgoing the production of 4/2 (2.00) of a unit of wheat. If France produces one unit of cloth, it is forgoing the production of 2/4 (0.50) of a unit of wheat. France therefore has the lower opportunity cost of producing cloth.

*Labor-hours per unit of output.

from international trade. Comparative advantage, according to Ricardo, was based on what was given up or traded off in producing one product instead of the other. In this numerical example England needs only two-fourths as many labor-hours to produce a unit of wheat as France, while France needs only two-fourths as many labor-hours to produce a unit of cloth. England therefore has comparative advantage in the production of wheat, while France has comparative advantage in the production of cloth. A country cannot possess comparative advantage in the production of both products, so each country has an economic role to play in international trade.

## National Production Possibilities

If the total labor-hours available for production within a nation were devoted to the full production of either product, wheat or cloth, the **production possibilities frontiers** of each country can be constructed. Assuming both countries possess the same number of labor-hours, for example 100, the production possibilities frontiers for each country can be graphed, as in Figure 5.2. If England devotes all labor-hours (100) to the production of wheat (which requires 2 labor-hours per unit produced), it can produce a maximum of 50 units of wheat. If England devotes all labor to the production of cloth instead, the same 100 labor-hours can produce a maximum of 25 units of cloth (100 hours/4 hours per unit of cloth). If England did not trade with any other country, it could only consume the products that it produced itself. England would therefore probably produce and consume some combination of wheat and cloth such as point A in Figure 5.2 (15 units of cloth, 20 units of wheat).

France's production possibilities frontier is constructed in the same way. If France devotes all 100 labor-hours to the production of wheat, it can produce

**FIGURE 5.2**

**Production Possibility Frontiers, Specialization of Production, and the Benefits of Trade**

**England**

1. Initially produces and consumes at point A.
2. England chooses to specialize in the production of wheat and shifts production from point A to point B.
3. England now exports the unwanted wheat (30 units) in exchange for imports of cloth (30 units) from France.
4. England is now consuming at point C, where it is consuming the same amount of wheat but 15 more units of cloth than at original point A.

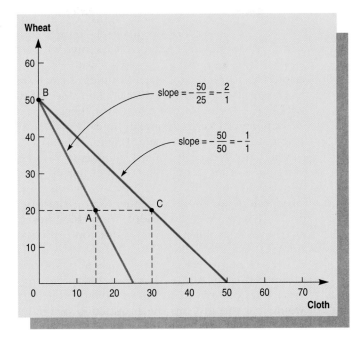

**France**

1. Initially produces and consumes at point D.
2. France chooses to specialize in the production of cloth and shifts production from point D to point E.
3. France now exports the unwanted cloth (30 units) in exchange for imports of wheat (30 units) from England.
4. France is now consuming at point F, where it is consuming the same amount of cloth but 15 more units of wheat than at original point D.

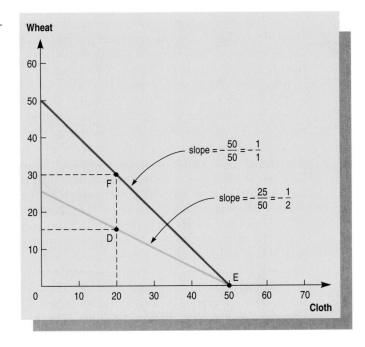

a maximum of 25 units (100 labor hours/4 hours per unit of wheat). If France devotes all 100 labor-hours to cloth, the same 100 labor-hours can produce a maximum of 50 units of cloth (100 labor/hours/2 hours per unit of cloth). If France did not trade with other countries, it would produce and consume at some point such as point D in Figure 5.2 (20 units of cloth, 15 units of wheat).

These frontiers depict what each country could produce in isolation—without trade (sometimes referred to as *autarky*). The slope of the production possibility frontier of a nation is a measure of how one product is traded off in production with the other (moving up the frontier, England is choosing to produce more wheat and less cloth). The slope of the frontier reflects the "trade-off" of producing one product over the other; the trade-offs represent prices, or **opportunity costs.** Opportunity cost is the forgone value of a factor of production in its next-best use. If England chooses to produce more units of wheat (in fact, produce only wheat), moving from point A to point B along the production possibilities frontier, it is giving up producing cloth to produce only wheat. The "cost" of the additional wheat is the loss of cloth. The slope of the production possibilities frontier is the ratio of product prices (opportunity costs). The slope of the production possibilities frontier for England is $-50/25$, or $-2.00$. The slope of the production possibilities frontier for France is flatter, $-25/50$, or $-0.50$.

The relative prices of products also provide an alternative way of seeing comparative advantage. The flatter slope of the French production possibilities frontier means that to produce more wheat (move up the frontier), France would have to give up the production of relatively more units of cloth than would England, with its steeper sloped production possibilities frontier.

## The Gains from International Trade

Continuing with Figure 5.2, if England were originally not trading with France (the only other country) and it was producing at its own maximum possibilities (on the frontier and not inside the line), it would probably be producing at point A. Since it was not trading with another country, whatever it was producing it must also be consuming. So England could be said to be consuming at point A also. Therefore, without trade, you consume what you produce.

If, however, England recognized that it has comparative advantage in the production of wheat, it should move production from point A to point B. England should specialize completely in the product it produces best. It does not want to consume only wheat, however, so it would take the wheat it has produced and trade with France. For example, England may only want to consume 20 units of wheat, as it did at point A. It is now producing 50 units, and therefore has 30 units of wheat it can export to France. If England could export 30 units of wheat in exchange for imports of 30 units of cloth (a 1:1 ratio of prices), England would clearly be better off than before. The new consumption point would be point C, where it is consuming the same amount of wheat as point A, but is now consuming 30 units of cloth instead of just 15. More is better; England has benefited from international trade.

France, following the same principle of completely specializing in the product of its comparative production advantage, moves production from point D to point E, producing 50 units of cloth. If France now exported the unwanted cloth, for example 30 units, and exchanged the cloth with England for imports of 30 units of wheat (note that England's exports are France's imports), France too is better off as a result of international trade. Each country would do what it does best, exclusively, and then trade for the other product.

But at what prices will the two countries trade? Since each country's production possibilities frontier has a different slope (different relative product prices), the two countries can determine a set of prices between the two domestic prices. In the above example, England's price ratio was $-2:1$, while France's domestic price ratio was $-1:2$. Trading 30 units of wheat for 30 units of cloth is a price ratio of $-1:1$, a slope or set of prices between the two domestic price ratios. The dashed line in Figure 5.2 illustrates this set of trade prices.

Are both countries better off as a result of trade? Yes. The final step to understanding the benefits of classical trade is to note that the point where a country produces (point B for England and point E for France in Figure 5.2) and the point where it consumes are now different. This allows each country to consume beyond their own production possibilities frontier. Society's welfare, which is normally measured in its ability to consume more wheat, cloth, or any other goods or services, is increased through trade.

## Concluding Points about Classical Trade Theory

Classical trade theory contributed much to the understanding of how production and trade operates in the world economy. Although like all economic theories they are often criticized for being unrealistic or out of date, the purpose of a theory is to simplify reality so that the basic elements of the logic can be seen. Several of these simplifications have continued to provide insight in understanding international business.

- **Division of Labor.** Adam Smith's explanation of how industrial societies can increase output using the same labor-hours as in preindustrial society is fundamental to our thinking even today. Smith extended this specialization of the efforts of a worker to the specialization of a nation.
- **Comparative Advantage.** David Ricardo's extension of Smith's work explained for the first time how countries that seemingly had no obvious reason for trade could individually specialize in producing what they did best and trade for products they did not produce.
- **Gains from Trade.** The theory of comparative advantage argued that nations could improve the welfare of their populations through international trade. A nation could actually achieve consumption levels beyond what it could produce by itself. To this day this is one of the fundamental principles underlying the arguments for all countries to strive to expand and "free" world trade.

## Factor Proportions Trade Theory

Trade theory changed drastically in the first half of the twentieth century. The theory developed by the Swedish economist Eli Heckscher and later expanded by his former student Bertil Ohlin formed the theory of international trade that is still widely accepted today, **factor proportions theory.**

# Current Account Balances as a Percentage of Gross Domestic Product

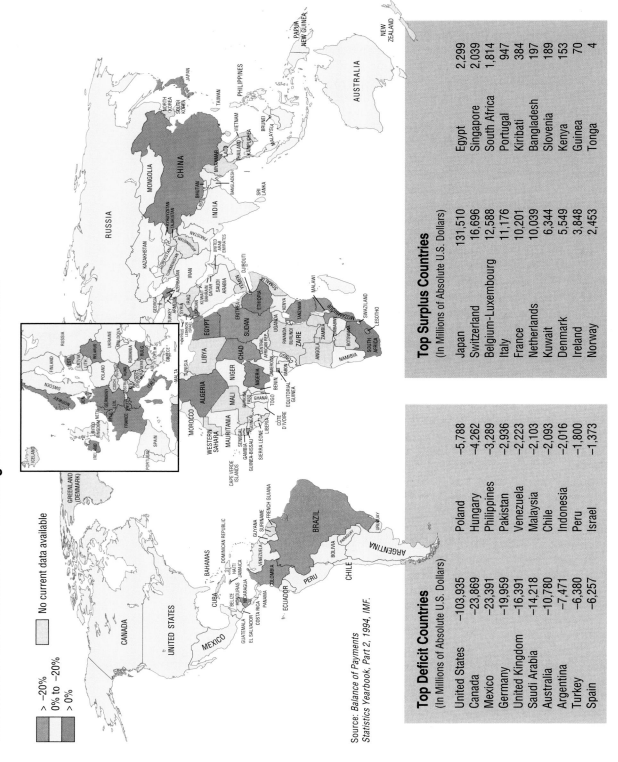

Legend:
- > −20%
- 0% to −20%
- > 0%
- No current data available

Source: *Balance of Payments Statistics Yearbook, Part 2, 1994, IMF.*

**Top Surplus Countries**
(In Millions of Absolute U.S. Dollars)

|  |  |
|---|---|
| Japan | 131,510 |
| Switzerland | 16,696 |
| Belgium-Luxembourg | 12,588 |
| Italy | 11,176 |
| France | 10,201 |
| Netherlands | 10,039 |
| Kuwait | 6,344 |
| Denmark | 5,549 |
| Ireland | 3,848 |
| Norway | 2,453 |
| Egypt | 2,299 |
| Singapore | 2,039 |
| South Africa | 1,814 |
| Portugal | 947 |
| Kiribati | 384 |
| Bangladesh | 197 |
| Slovenia | 189 |
| Kenya | 153 |
| Guinea | 70 |
| Tonga | 4 |

**Top Deficit Countries**
(In Millions of Absolute U.S. Dollars)

|  |  |
|---|---|
| United States | −103,935 |
| Canada | −23,869 |
| Mexico | −23,391 |
| Germany | −19,959 |
| United Kingdom | −16,391 |
| Saudi Arabia | −14,218 |
| Australia | −10,780 |
| Argentina | −7,471 |
| Turkey | −6,380 |
| Spain | −6,257 |
| Poland | −5,788 |
| Hungary | −4,262 |
| Philippines | −3,289 |
| Pakistan | −2,936 |
| Venezuela | −2,223 |
| Malaysia | −2,103 |
| Chile | −2,093 |
| Indonesia | −2,016 |
| Peru | −1,800 |
| Israel | −1,373 |

Heckscher and Ohlin noted that countries are endowed with varying degrees of productive resources and contended that the production of goods is a function of the most intensive use of those resources. DeKalb Genetics Corporation, an international marketer of seed products, is the leading supplier of corn, grain sorghum, and sunflower seeds to Argentina, where the growing season is the opposite of the United States'. Seasonal conditions are a significant factor in the high volume of corn production in Argentina.

*Source:* Courtesy of DeKalb Genetics Corporation

## Factor Intensity in Production

The Heckscher-Ohlin theory considered two **factors of production,** labor and capital. Technology determines the way they combine to form a good. Different goods required different proportions of the two factors of production.

Figure 5.3 illustrates what it means to describe a good by its factor proportions. The production of one unit of good X requires 4 units of labor and 1 unit of capital. At the same time, to produce 1 unit of good Y requires 4 units of labor and 2 units of capital. Good X therefore requires more units of labor per unit of capital (4 to 1) relative to Y (4 to 2). X is therefore classified as a

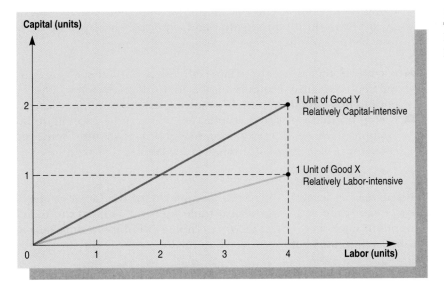

**FIGURE 5.3**

**Factor Proportions in Production**

relatively labor-intensive product, and Y is relatively capital intensive. These **factor intensities,** or **proportions,** are truly relative and are determined only on the basis of what product X requires relative to product Y and not to the specific numbers of labor to capital.

It is easy to see how the factor proportions of production differ substantially across goods. For example, the manufacturing of leather footwear is still a relatively labor-intensive process, even with the most sophisticated leather treatment and patterning machinery. Other goods, such as computer memory chips, however, although requiring some highly skilled labor, require massive quantities of capital for production. These large capital requirements include the enormous sums needed for research and development and the manufacturing facilities needed for clean production to ensure the extremely high quality demanded in the industry.

According to factor proportions theory, factor intensities depend on the state of technology, the current method of manufacturing a good. The theory assumed that the same technology of production would be used for the same goods in all countries. It is not, therefore, differences in the efficiency of production that will determine trade between countries as it did in classical theory. Classical theory implicitly assumed that technology or the productivity of labor is different across countries. Otherwise, there would be no logical explanation why one country requires more units of labor to produce a unit of output than another country. Factor proportions theory assumes no such productivity differences.

## Factor Endowments, Factor Prices, and Comparative Advantage

If there is no difference in technology or productivity of factors across countries, what then determines comparative advantage in production and export? The answer is that factor prices determine cost differences. And these prices are determined by the endowments of labor and capital the country possesses. The theory assumes that labor and capital are immobile; factors cannot move across borders. Therefore, the country's endowment determines the relative costs of labor and capital as compared with other countries.

Using these assumptions, factor proportions theory stated that a country should specialize in the production and export of those products that use intensively its relatively abundant factor.

- A country that is relatively labor abundant should specialize in the production of relatively labor-intensive goods. It should then export those labor-intensive goods in exchange for capital-intensive goods.
- A country that is relatively capital abundant should specialize in the production of relatively capital-intensive goods. It should then export those capital-intensive goods in exchange for labor-intensive goods.

## Assumptions of the Factor Proportions Theory

The increasing level of theoretical complexity of the factor proportions theory, as compared with the classical trade theory, increased the number of assumptions necessary for the theory to "hold." It is important to take a last look at the assumptions before proceeding further.

1. The theory assumes two countries, two products, and two factors of production, the so-called 2×2×2 assumption. Note that if both countries were

producing all of the output they could and trading only between themselves (only two countries), both countries would have to have balances in trade!

2. The markets for the inputs and the outputs are perfectly competitive. The factors of production, labor, and capital were exchanged in markets that paid them only what they were worth. Similarly, the trade of the outputs (the international trade between the two countries) was competitive so that one country had no market power over the other.

3. Increasing production of a product experiences diminishing returns. This meant that as a country increasingly specialized in the production of one of the two outputs, it eventually would require more and more inputs per unit of output. For example there would no longer be the constant "labor-hours per unit of output" as assumed under the classical theory. Production possibilities frontiers would no longer be straight lines but concave. The result was that complete specialization would no longer occur under factor proportions theory.

4. Both countries were using identical technologies. Each product was produced in the same way in both countries. This meant the only way that a good could be produced more cheaply in one country than in the other was if the factors of production used (labor and capital) were cheaper.

Although a number of additional technical assumptions were necessary, these four highlight the very specialized set of conditions needed to explain international trade with factor proportions theory. Much of the trade theory developed since has focused on how trade changes when one or more of these assumptions is not found in the real world.

## The Leontief Paradox

One of the most famous tests of any economic or business theory occurred in 1950, when economist Wassily Leontief tested whether the factor proportions theory could be used to explain the types of goods the United States imported and exported. Leontief's premise was the following.

> A widely shared view on the nature of the trade between the United States and the rest of the world is derived from what appears to be a common sense assumption that this country has a comparative advantage in the production of commodities which require for their manufacture large quantities of capital and relatively small amounts of labor. Our economic relationships with other countries are supposed to be based mainly on the export of such "capital intensive" goods in exchange for forgoing products which—if we were to make them at home—would require little capital but large quantities of American labor. Since the United States possesses a relatively large amount of capital—so goes this oft-repeated argument—and a comparatively small amount of labor, direct domestic production of such "labor intensive" products would be uneconomical; we can much more advantageously obtain them from abroad in exchange for our capital intensive products.[2]

Leontief first had to devise a method to determine the relative amounts of labor and capital in a good. His solution, known as **input-output analysis,** was an accomplishment on its own. Input-output analysis is a technique of decomposing a good into the values and quantities of the labor, capital, and other potential factors employed in the good's manufacture. Leontief then used this methodology to analyze the labor and capital content of all U.S. merchandise imports and exports. The hypothesis was relatively straightforward: U.S. exports should be relatively capital intensive (use more units of capital relative to labor) than U.S. imports. Leontief's results were, however, a bit of a shock.

Leontief found that the products that U.S. firms exported were relatively more labor intensive than the products the United States imported.[3] It seemed that if the factor proportions theory were true, the United States is a relatively labor-abundant country! Alternatively, the theory could be wrong. Neither interpretation of the results was acceptable to many in the field of international trade.

A variety of explanations and continuing studies have attempted to solve what has become known as the **Leontief Paradox.** At first, it was thought to have been simply a result of the specific year (1947) of the data. However, the same results were found with different years and data sets. Second, it was noted that Leontief did not really analyze the labor and capital contents of imports but rather the labor and capital contents of the domestic equivalents of these imports. It was possible that the United States was actually producing the products in a more capital-intensive fashion than were the countries from which it also imported the manufactured goods.[4] Finally, the debate turned to the need to distinguish different types of labor and capital. For example, several studies attempted to separate labor factors into skilled labor and unskilled labor. These studies have continued to show results more consistent with what the factor proportions theory would predict for country trade patterns.

## Linder's Overlapping Product Ranges Theory

The difficulties in empirically validating the factor proportions theory led many in the 1960s and 1970s to search for new explanations of the determinants of trade between countries. The work of Staffan Burenstam Linder focused, not on the production or supply side, but instead on the preferences of consumers, the demand side. Linder acknowledged that in the natural resource-based industries, trade was indeed determined by relative costs of production and factor endowments.

However, Linder argued, trade in manufactured goods was dictated not by cost concerns but rather by the similarity in product demands across countries. Linder's was a significant departure from previous theory and was based on two principles:

1. As income, or more precisely per-capita income, rises, the complexity and quality level of the products demanded by the country's residents also rises. The total range of product sophistication demanded by a country's residents is largely determined by its level of income.
2. The entrepreneurs directing the firms that produce society's needs are more knowledgeable about their own domestic market than about foreign markets. An entrepreneur could not be expected to effectively serve a foreign market that is significantly different from the domestic market because competitiveness comes from experience. A logical pattern would be for an entrepreneur to gain success and market share at home first then expand to foreign markets that are similar in their demands or tastes.

International trade in manufactured goods would then be influenced by similarity of demands. The countries that would see the most intensive trade are those with similar per-capita income levels, for they would possess a greater likelihood of overlapping product demands.

So where does trade come in? According to Linder, the overlapping ranges of product sophistication represent the products that entrepreneurs would know well from their home markets and could therefore potentially export and compete in foreign markets. For example, the United States and Canada have almost parallel sophistication ranges, implying they would have a lot of common ground, overlapping product ranges, for intensive international trade and competition. They are quite similar in their per-capita income levels. But Mexico and the United States, or Mexico and Canada, would not. Mexico has a significantly different product sophistication range as a result of a different per capita income level.

The overlapping product ranges described by Linder would today be termed market segments. Not only was Linder's work instrumental in extending trade theory beyond cost considerations, but it has also found a place in the field of international marketing. As illustrated in the theories following the work of Linder, many of the questions that his work raised were the focus of considerable attention in the following decades.

## International Investment and Product Cycle Theory

A very different path was taken by Raymond Vernon in 1966 concerning what is now termed **product cycle theory.** Diverging significantly from traditional approaches, Vernon focused on the product (rather than the country and the technology of its manufacture), not its factor proportions. Most striking was the appreciation of the role of information, knowledge, and the costs and power that go hand in hand with knowledge.

> . . . we abandon the powerful simplifying notion that knowledge is a universal free good, and introduce it as an independent variable in the decision to trade or to invest.

Using many of the same basic tools and assumptions of factor proportions theory, Vernon added two technology-based premises to the factor-cost emphasis of existing theory:

1. Technical innovations leading to new and profitable products require large quantities of capital and highly skilled labor. These factors of production are predominantly available in highly industrialized capital-intensive countries.
2. These same technical innovations, both the product itself and more importantly the methods for its manufacture, go through three stages of maturation as the product becomes increasingly commercialized. As the manufacturing process becomes more standardized and low-skill labor-intensive, the comparative advantage in its production and export shifts across countries.

Product cycle theory is both supply-side (cost of production) and demand-side (income levels of consumers) in its orientation. Each of these three stages that Vernon described combines differing elements of each.

**The Stages of the Product Cycle**

**Stage I: The New Product**   Innovation requires highly skilled labor and large quantities of capital for research and development. The product will normally be most effectively designed and initially manufactured near the parent firm and therefore in a highly industrialized market due to the need for proximity to information; the need for communication among the many different skilled-labor components required.

In this development stage, the product is nonstandardized. The production process requires a high degree of flexibility (meaning continued use of highly skilled labor). Costs of production are therefore quite high.

The innovator at this stage is a monopolist and therefore enjoys all of the benefits of monopoly power, including the high profit margins required to repay the high development costs and expensive production process. Price elasticity of demand at this stage is low; high-income consumers buy it regardless of cost.

**Stage II: The Maturing Product:**   As production expands, its process becomes increasingly standardized. The need for flexibility in design and manufacturing declines, and therefore the demand for highly skilled labor declines. The innovating country increases its sales to other countries. Competitors with slight variations develop, putting downward pressure on prices and profit margins. Production costs are an increasing concern.

As competitors increase, as well as their pressures on price, the innovating firm faces critical decisions on how to maintain market share. Vernon argues that the firm faces a critical decision at this stage, either to lose market share to foreign-based manufacturers using lower-cost labor or to invest abroad to maintain its market share by exploiting the comparative advantages of factor costs in other countries. This is one of the first theoretical explanations of how trade and investment become increasingly intertwined.

**Stage III: The Standardized Product**   In this final stage, the product is completely standardized in its manufacture. Thus, with access to capital on world capital markets, the country of production is simply the one with the cheapest unskilled labor. Profit margins are thin, and competition is fierce. The product has largely run its course in terms of profitability for the innovating firm.

The country of comparative advantage has therefore shifted as the technology of the product's manufacture has matured. The same product shifts in its location of production. The country possessing the product during that stage enjoys the benefits of net trade surpluses. But such advantages are fleeting, according to Vernon. As knowledge and technology continually change, so does the country of that product's comparative advantage.

## Trade Implications of the Product Cycle

**Product cycle theory** shows how specific products were first produced and exported from one country but, through product and competitive evolution, shifted their location of production and export to other countries over time. Figure 5.4 illustrates the trade patterns that Vernon visualized as resulting from the maturing stages of a specific product cycle. As the product and the market for the product mature and change, the countries of its production and export shift.

The product is initially designed and manufactured in the United States. In its early stages (from time $t_0$ to $t_1$), the United States is the only country producing and consuming the product. Production is highly capital intensive

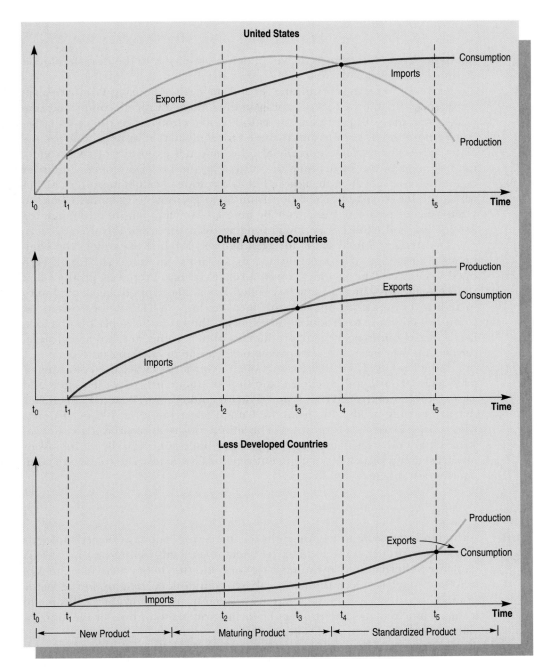

**FIGURE 5.4**

**Trade Patterns and Product Cycle Theory**

Source: Raymond Vernon, "International Investment and International Trade in the Product Cycle,"
*Quarterly Journal of Economics* (May 1966): 199.

and skilled labor intensive at this time. At time $t_1$ the United States begins exporting the product to Other Advanced Countries, as Vernon classified them. These countries possess the income to purchase the product in its still New Product Stage, in which it was relatively high priced. These Other Advanced Countries also commence their own production at time $t_1$ but continue to be net importers. A few exports, however, do find their way to the Less Developed Countries at this time as well.

As the product moves into the second stage, the Maturing Product Stage, production capability expands rapidly in the Other Advanced Countries. Competitive variations begin to appear as the basic technology of the product becomes more widely known, and the need for skilled labor in its production declines. These countries eventually also become net exporters of the product near the end of the stage (time $t_3$). At time $t_2$ the Less Developed Countries begin their own production, although they continue to be net importers. Meanwhile, the lower cost of production from these growing competitors turns the United States into a net importer by time $t_4$. The competitive advantage for production and export is clearly shifting across countries at this time.

The third and final stage, the Standardized Product Stage, sees the comparative advantage of production and export now shifting to the Less Developed Countries. The product is now a relatively mass-produced product that can be made with increasingly less-skilled labor. The United States continues to reduce domestic production and increase imports. The Other Advanced Countries continue to produce and export, although exports peak as the Less Developed Countries expand production and become net exporters themselves. The product has run its course or life cycle in reaching time $t_5$.

A final point: Note that throughout this product cycle, the countries of production, consumption, export, and import are identified by their labor and capital levels, not firms. Vernon noted that it could very well be the same firms that are moving production from the United States to Other Advanced Countries to Less Developed Countries. The shifting location of production was instrumental in the changing patterns of trade but not necessarily in the loss of market share, profitability, or competitiveness of the firms. The country of comparative advantage could change.

## The Contributions of Product Cycle Theory

Although interesting in its own right for increasing emphasis on technology's impact on product costs, product cycle theory was most important because it explained international investment. Not only did the theory recognize the mobility of capital across countries (breaking the traditional assumption of factor immobility), it shifted the focus from the country to the product. This made it important to match the product by its maturity stage with its production location to examine competitiveness.

Product cycle theory has many limitations. It is obviously most appropriate for technology-based products. These are the products that are most likely to experience the changes in production process as they grow and mature. Other products, either resource-based (such as minerals and other commodities) or services (which employ capital but mostly in the form of human capital), are not so easily characterized by stages of maturity. And product cycle theory is most relevant to products that eventually fall victim to mass production and therefore cheap labor forces. But, all things considered, product cycle theory served to breach a wide gap between the trade theories of old and the intellectual challenges of a new, more globally competitive market in which capital, technology, information, and firms themselves were more mobile.

## The New Trade Theory

Global trade developments in the 1980s led to much criticism of the existing theories of trade. First, although there was rapid growth in trade, much of it was not explained by current theory. Secondly, the massive size of the merchandise trade deficit of the United States—and the associated decline of many U.S. firms in terms of international competitiveness—served as something of a country-sized lab experiment demonstrating what some critics termed the "bankruptcy of trade theory." Academics and policymakers alike looked for new explanations.

Two new contributions to trade theory were met with great interest. Paul Krugman, along with several colleagues in the mid-1980s, developed a theory of how trade is altered when markets are not perfectly competitive, or when production of specific products possess economies of scale. A second and very influential development was the growing work of Michael Porter, who examined the competitiveness of industries on a global basis, rather than relying on country-specific factors to determine competitiveness.

### Economies of Scale and Imperfect Competition

Paul Krugman's theoretical developments once again focused on cost of production and how cost and price drive international trade. Using theoretical developments from microeconomics and market structure analysis, Krugman focused on two types of economics of scale, *internal economies of scale* and *external economies of scale.*[5]

**Internal Economies of Scale**   When the cost per unit of output depends on the size of an individual firm, the larger the firm the greater the scale benefits, and the lower the cost per unit. A firm possessing internal economies of scale could potentially monopolize an industry (creating an *imperfect market*), both domestically and internationally. If it produces more, lowering the cost per unit, it can lower the market price and sell more products, because it *sets* market prices.

The link between dominating a domestic industry and influencing international trade comes from taking this assumption of imperfect markets back to the original concept of comparative advantage. For this firm to expand sufficiently to enjoy its economies of scale, it must take resources away from other domestic industries in order to expand. A country then sees its own range of products in which it specializes narrowing, providing an opportunity for other countries to specialize in these so-called abandoned product ranges. Countries again search out and exploit comparative advantage.

A particularly powerful implication of internal economies of scale is that it provides an explanation of intra-industry trade, one area in which traditional trade theory had indeed seemed bankrupt. **Intra-industry trade** is when a country seemingly imports and exports the same product, an idea that is obviously inconsistent with any of the trade theories put forward in the past three centuries. According to Krugman, internal economies of scale may lead a firm to specialize in a narrow product line (to produce the volume necessary for economies of scale cost benefits); other firms in other countries may produce products that are similarly narrow, yet extremely similar: *product differentiation*. If consumers in either country wish to buy both products, they will be importing and exporting products that are, for all intents and purposes, the same.[6]

Intra-industry trade has been studied in detail in the past decade. Intra-industry trade is measured with the Grubel-Lloyd Index, the ratio of imports and exports of the same product occurring between two trading nations. It is calculated as follows:

$$\text{Intra-Industry Trade Index}_i = \frac{|X_i - M_i|}{(X_i + M_i)},$$

where i is the product category and $|X - M|$ is the absolute value of net exports of that product (exports−imports). For example, if Sweden imports 100 heavy machines for its forest products industry from Finland, and at the same time exports to Finland 80 of the same type of equipment, the intra-industry trade (IIT) index would be:

$$\text{IIT} = \frac{|80 - 100|}{(80 + 100)} = 1 - .1111 = .89.$$

The closer the index value to 1, the higher the level of intra-industry trade in that product category. The closer the index is to 0, the more one-way the trade between the countries exists, as traditional trade theory would predict.

**External Economies of Scale**  When the cost per unit of output depends on the size of an industry, not the size of the individual firm, the industry of that country may produce at lower costs than the same industry that is smaller in size in other countries. A country can potentially dominate world markets in a particular product, not because it has one massive firm producing enormous quantities (for example, Boeing), but rather because it has many small firms that interact to create a large, competitive, critical mass (for example, fine crystal glassware in eastern Germany). No one firm need be all that large, but several small firms in total may create such a competitive industry that firms in other countries cannot ever break into the industry on a competitive basis.[7]

Unlike internal economies of scale, external economies of scale may not necessarily lead to imperfect markets, but they may result in an industry maintaining its dominance in its field in world markets. This provides an explanation as to why all industries do not necessarily always move to the country with the lowest-cost energy, resources, or labor. What gives rise to this critical mass of small firms and their interrelationships is a much more complex question. The work of Michael Porter provides a partial explanation of how these critical masses are sustained.

## The Competitive Advantage of Nations

The focus of early trade theory was on the country or nation and its inherent, natural, or endowment characteristics that may give rise to increasing competitiveness. As trade theory evolved, it shifted its focus to the industry and product level, leaving the national-level competitiveness question somewhat behind. Recently, many have turned their attention to the question of how coun-

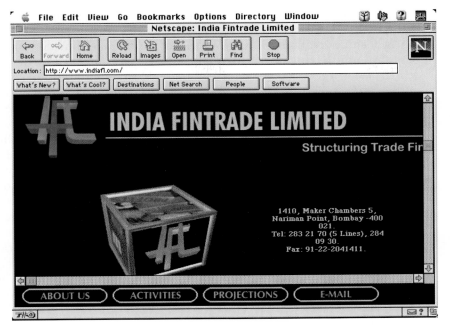

India is trying to increase its competitive advantage by creating new organizations to support the financial needs of its industries. India Fintrade Limited exists as a complementary financial entity to the banking sector for the purpose of promoting and structuring international trade finance in India.
Source: **http://indiafl.com/**

tries, governments, and even private industry can alter the conditions within a country to aid the competitiveness of its firms.

The leader in this area of research has been Michael Porter of Harvard. As he states:

> National prosperity is created, not inherited. It does not grow out of a country's natural endowments, its labor pool, its interest rates, or its currency's values, as classical economics insists.
>
> A nation's competitiveness depends on the capacity of its industry to innovate and upgrade. Companies gain advantage against the world's best competitors because of pressure and challenge. They benefit from having strong domestic rivals, aggressive home-based suppliers, and demanding local customers.
>
> In a world of increasingly global competition, nations have become more, not less, important. As the basis of competition has shifted more and more to the creation and assimilation of knowledge, the role of the nation has grown. Competitive advantage is created and sustained through a highly localized process. Differences in national values, culture, economic structures, institutions, and histories all contribute to competitive success. There are striking differences in the patterns of competitiveness in every country; no nation can or will be competitive in every or even most industries. Ultimately, nations succeed in particular industries because their home environment is most forward-looking, dynamic, and challenging.[8]

Porter argued innovation is what drives and sustains competitiveness. A firm must avail itself of all dimensions of competition, which he categorized into four major components of "the diamond of national advantage":

1. **Factor Conditions:** The appropriateness of the nation's factors of production to compete successfully in a specific industry. Porter notes that although these factor conditions are very important in the determination of trade, they are not the only source of competitiveness as suggested by the classical, or factor proportions, theories of trade. Most importantly for Porter, it is the ability of a nation to continually create, upgrade, and deploy its factors (such as skilled labor) that is important, not the initial endowment.

2. **Demand Conditions:** The degree of health and competition the firm must face in its original home market. Firms that can survive and flourish in highly competitive and demanding local markets are much more likely to gain the competitive edge. Porter notes that it is the character of the market, not its size, that is paramount in promoting the continual competitiveness of the firm. And Porter translates *character* as demanding customers.

3. **Related and Supporting Industries:** The competitiveness of all related industries and suppliers to the firm. A firm that is operating within a mass of related firms and industries gains and maintains advantages through close working relationships, proximity to suppliers, and timeliness of product and information flows. The constant and close interaction is successful if it occurs not only in terms of physical proximity but also through the willingness of firms to work at it.

4. **Firm Strategy, Structure, and Rivalry:** The conditions in the home-nation that either hinder or aid in the firm's creation and sustaining of international competitiveness. Porter notes that no one managerial, ownership, or operational strategy is universally appropriate. It depends on the fit and flexibility of what works for that industry in that country at that time.

These four points, as illustrated in Figure 5.5, constitute what nations and firms must strive to "create and sustain through a highly localized process" to ensure their success.

Porter's emphasis on innovation as the source of competitiveness reflects an increased focus on the industry and product that we have seen in the past

**FIGURE 5.5**

**Determinants of National Competitive Advantage: Porter's Diamond**

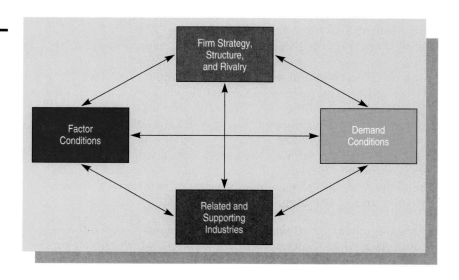

three decades. The acknowledgment that the nation is "more, not less, important" is to many eyes a welcome return to a positive role for government and even national-level private industry in encouraging international competitiveness. Including factor conditions as a cost component, demand conditions as a motivator of firm actions, and competitiveness all combine to include the elements of classical, factor proportions, product cycle, and imperfect competition theories in a pragmatic approach to the challenges that the global markets of the twenty-first century present to the firms of today.

## The Theory of International Investment

Trade is the production of a good or service in one country and its sale to a buyer in another country. In fact, it is a firm (not a country) and a buyer (not a country) that are the subjects of trade, domestically or internationally. A firm is therefore attempting to access a market and its buyers. The producing firm wants to utilize its competitive advantage for growth and profit and can also reach this goal by international investment.[9]

Although this sounds easy enough, consider any of the following potholes on the road to investment success. Any of the following potholes may be avoided by producing within another country.

■ Sales to some countries are difficult because of tariffs imposed on your good when it is entering. If you were producing within the country, your good would no longer be an import.

■ Your good requires natural resources that are available only in certain areas of the world. It is therefore imperative that you have access to the natural resources. You can buy them from that country and bring them to your production process (import) or simply take the production to them.

■ Competition is constantly pushing you to improve efficiency and decrease the costs of producing your good. You therefore may want to produce where it will be cheaper—cheaper capital, cheaper energy, cheaper natural resources, or cheaper labor. Many of these factors are still not mobile, and therefore you will go to them instead of bringing them to you.

There are thousands of reasons why a firm may want to produce in another country, and not necessarily in the country that is cheapest for production or the country where the final good is sold.

The subject of international investment arises from one basic idea: the mobility of capital. Although many of the traditional trade theories assumed the immobility of the factors of production, it is the movement of capital that has allowed **foreign direct investments** across the globe. If there is a competitive advantage to be gained, capital can and will get there.

### The Foreign Direct Investment Decision

Consider a firm that wants to exploit its competitive advantage by accessing foreign markets as illustrated in the decision-sequence tree of Figure 5.6.

The first choice is whether to exploit the existing competitive advantage in new foreign markets or to concentrate their resources in the development

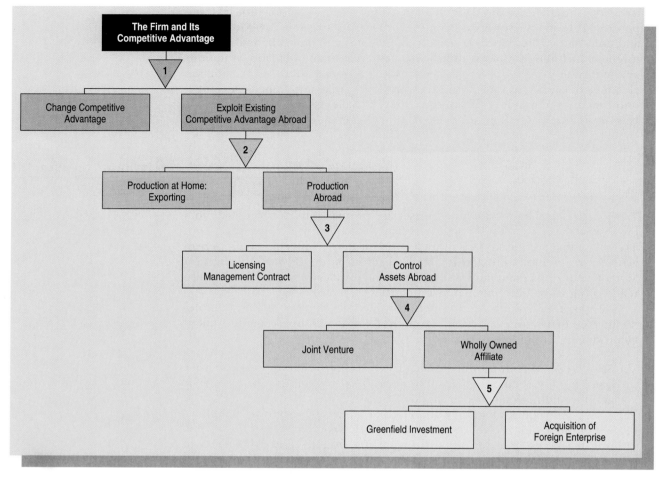

**FIGURE 5.6**

**The Direct Foreign Investment Decision Sequence**

*Source:* Adapted from Gunter Dufey and R. Mirus, "Foreign Direct Investment: Theory and Strategic Considerations," unpublished, University of Michigan, May 1985.

of new competitive advantages in the domestic market. Although many firms may choose to do both as resources will allow, more and more firms are choosing to go international as at least part of their expansion strategies.

Second, should the firm produce at home and export to the foreign markets, or produce abroad? The firm will choose the path that will allow it to access the resources and markets it needs to exploit its existing competitive advantage. But it will also consider two additional dimensions of each foreign investment decision: (1) the degree of control over assets, technology, information, and operations and (2) the magnitude of capital that the firm must risk. Each decision increases the firm's control at the cost of increased capital outlays.

After choosing to produce abroad, the firm must decide how. The distinctions among different kinds of foreign direct investment (branch 3 and downward in Figure 5.6), licensing agreements to greenfield construction (building a new facility from the ground up), vary by degrees of ownership. The licensing management contract is by far the simplest and cheapest way to produce abroad. Another firm is licensed to produce the product, but with your firm's technology and know-how. The question is whether the reduced capital investment of simply licensing the product to another manufacturer is worth the risk of loss of control over the product and technology.

The firm that wants direct control over the foreign production process next determines the degree of equity control: to own the firm outright, or as a joint investment with another firm. Trade-offs with joint ventures continue the debate over control of assets and other sources of the firm's original competitive advantage. Many countries try to ensure the continued growth of local firms and investors by requiring that foreign firms operate jointly with local firms.

The final decision branch between a "greenfield investment"—building a firm from the ground up—and the purchase of an existing firm, is often a question of cost. A greenfield investment is the most expensive of all foreign investment alternatives. The acquisition of an existing firm is often lower in initial cost but may also contain a number of customizing and adjustment costs that are not apparent at the initial purchase. The purchase of a going concern may also have substantial benefits if the existing business possesses substantial customer and supplier relationships that can be used by the new owner in the pursuit of its own business.

## The Theory of Foreign Direct Investment

What motivates a firm to go beyond exporting or licensing? What benefits does the multinational firm expect to achieve by establishing a physical presence in other countries? These are the questions that the theory of foreign direct investment has sought to answer. As with trade theory, the questions have remained largely the same over time, while the answers have continued to change. With hundreds of countries, thousands of firms, and millions of products and services, there is no question that the answer to such an enormous question will likely get messy.

The following overview of investment theory has many similarities to the preceding discussion of international trade. The theme is a global business environment that attempts to satisfy increasingly sophisticated consumer demands, while the means of production, resources, skills, and technology needed become more complex and competitive. A more detailed analysis of foreign direct investment theory is presented in Chapter 12.

## Firms as Seekers

A firm that expands across borders may be seeking any of a number of specific sources of profit or opportunity.

1. **Seeking Resources:** There is no question that much of the initial foreign direct investment of the eighteenth and nineteenth centuries was the result of firms seeking unique and valuable natural resources for their products. Whether it be the copper resources of Chile, the linseed oils of Indonesia, or the petroleum resources spanning the Middle East, firms establishing permanent presences around the world are seeking access to the resources at the core of their business.

2. **Seeking Factor Advantages:** The resources needed for production are often combined with other advantages that are inherent in the country of production. The same low-cost labor at the heart of classical trade theory provides incentives for firms to move production to countries possessing these factor advantages. As noted by Vernon's Product Cycle, the same firms may move their own production to locations of factor advantages as the products and markets mature.

3. **Seeking Knowledge:** Firms may attempt to acquire other firms in other countries for the technical or competitive skills they possess. Alternatively, companies may locate in and around centers of industrial enterprise unique to their specific industry, such as the footwear industry of Milan or the semiconductor industry of the Silicon Valley of California.

4. **Seeking Security:** Firms continue to move internationally as they seek political stability or security. For example, Mexico has experienced a significant increase in foreign direct investment as a result of the tacit support of the United States, Canada, and Mexico itself as reflected by the North American Free Trade Agreement.

5. **Seeking Markets:** Not the least of the motivations, the ability to gain and maintain access to markets is of paramount importance to multinational firms. Whether following the principles of Linder, in which firms learn from their domestic market and use that information to go international, or the principles of Porter, which emphasize the character of the domestic market as dictating international competitiveness, foreign market access is necessary.

## Firms as Exploiters of Imperfections

Much of the investment theory developed in the past three decades has focused on the efforts of multinational firms to exploit the imperfections in factor and product markets created by governments. The work of Hymer, Kindleberger, and Caves noted that many of the policies of governments create imperfections.[10] These market imperfections cover the entire range of supply and demand of the market: trade policy (tariffs and quotas), tax policies and incentives, preferential purchasing arrangements established by governments themselves, and financial restrictions on the access of foreign firms to domestic capital markets.

1. **Imperfections in Access.:** Many of the world's developing countries have long sought to create domestic industry by restricting imports of competitive products in order to allow smaller, less competitive domestic firms to grow and prosper—so-called **import substitution policies.** Multinational firms have sought to maintain their access to these markets by establishing their own productive presence within the country, effectively bypassing the tariff restriction.

2. **Imperfections in Factor Mobility:** Other multinational firms have exploited the same sources of comparative advantage identified throughout this chapter—the low-cost resources or factors often located in less-developed countries or countries with restrictions on the mobility of labor and capital. However, combining the mobility of capital with the immobility of low-cost labor has characterized much of the foreign direct investment seen throughout the developing world over the past 50 years.

3. **Imperfections in Management:** The ability of multinational firms to successfully exploit or at least manage these imperfections still relies on their ability to gain an "advantage." Market advantages or powers are seen in international markets as in domestic markets: cost advantages, economies of scale and scope, product differentiation, managerial or marketing technique and knowledge, financial resources and strength.

All these imperfections are the things of which competitive dreams are made. The multinational firm needs to find these in some form or another to justify the added complexities and costs of international investments.

## Firms as Internalizers

The question that has plagued the field of foreign direct investment is, Why can't all of the advantages and imperfections mentioned be achieved through management contracts or licensing agreements (the choice available to the international investor at Step 3 in Figure 2.8)? Why is it necessary for *the firm itself* to establish a physical presence in the country? What pushes the multinational firm further down the investment decision tree?

The research of Buckley and Casson, and Dunning has attempted to answer these questions by focusing on nontransferable sources of competitive advantage—proprietary information possessed by the firm and its people.[11] Many advantages firms possess center around their hands-on knowledge of producing a good or providing a service. By establishing their own multinational operations they can internalize the production, thus keeping confidential the information that is at the core of the firm's competitiveness. **Internalization** is preferable to the use of arms-length arrangements such as management contracts or licensing agreements. They either do not allow the effective transmission of the knowledge or represent too serious a threat to the loss of the knowledge to allow the firm to successfully achieve the hoped-for benefits of international investment.

## *Summary*

The theory of international trade has changed drastically from that first put forward by Adam Smith. The classical theories of Adam Smith and David Ricardo focused on the abilities of countries to produce goods more cheaply than other countries. The earliest production and trade theories saw labor as the major factor expense that went into any product. If a country could pay that labor less, and if that labor could produce more physically than labor in other countries, the country might obtain an absolute or comparative advantage in trade.

Subsequent theoretical development led to a more detailed understanding of production and its costs. Factors of production are now believed to include labor (skilled and unskilled), capital, natural resources, and other potentially significant commodities that are difficult to reproduce or replace, such as energy. Technology, once assumed to be the same across all countries, is now seen as one of the premier driving forces in determining who holds the competitive edge or advantage. International trade is now seen as a complex combination of thousands of products, technologies, and firms that are constantly innovating to either keep up with or get ahead of the competition.

## BOEING SAYS ASIAN CRISIS MAY DELAY 60 DELIVERIES

The Boeing Co. said Asian airlines may delay taking delivery of as many as 60 jetliners over the next three years because the region's economic problems are slowing growth in airline traffic. The world's biggest aircraft maker could see as many as 20 Asian deliveries a year delayed through 2000, said Gordon McHenry, director of airline industry analysis for Boeing. Boeing still expects to deliver the jetliners, starting in 2001, when an economic rebound is predicted in the region, he said.

A loss of 20 deliveries a year would be small compared with the company's expected delivery of 550 planes next year, McHenry said. Yet analysts said Boeing's report didn't eliminate their concerns about the uncertainties of doing business in Asia.

"This would be good news if I had a high degree of confidence that this is all it's going to entail," said Peter Jacobs, an analyst with Ragen MacKenzie. "The reality is that no one knows what news is going to come out of the region tomorrow."

The company has orders from airlines in South Korea, Malaysia, Thailand, Indonesia, the Philippines, and Japan, all of which have seen estimates of their economic growth shrink as Asia's currency and stock markets have foundered. The Asian financial crisis started in the summer when Thailand gave up efforts to prop up its currency, as investors bailed out of the nation's stocks and bonds. The currency plunged, creating a crisis of confidence that had ripple effects throughout the region's financial markets. The Boeing models most likely to see deliveries delayed are the 747, 777, and 767.

Modern trade theory has looked beyond production cost to analyze how the demands of the marketplace alter who trades with whom and which firms survive domestically and internationally. The abilities of firms to adapt to foreign markets, both in the demands and the competitors that form the foreign markets, have required much of international trade and investment theory to search out new and innovative approaches to what determines success and failure.

Finally, as world economies grew and the magnitude of world trade increased, the simplistic ideas that guided international trade and investment theory have had to grow with them. The choices that many firms face today require them to directly move their capital, technology, and know-how to countries that possess other unique factors or market advantages that will help the firm keep pace with market demands. Even then, as illustrated by Global Perspective 5.1, world business conditions constitute changing fortunes.

### Key Terms and Concepts

- mercantilism
- specie
- absolute advantage
- division of labor
- comparative advantage
- production possibilities frontier
- autarky

- opportunity cost
- factor proportions theory
- factors of production
- factor intensities
- input-output analysis
- Leontief Paradox
- product cycle theory

- intra-industry trade
- competitive advantage
- product differentiation
- economies of scale
- foreign direct investment
- import substitution
- internalization

## Questions for Discussion

1. According to the theory of comparative advantage as explained by Ricardo, why is trade always possible between two countries, even when one is absolutely inefficient compared to the other?

2. The factor proportions theory of international trade assumes that all countries produce the same product the same way. Would international competition cause or prevent this from happening?

3. What, in your opinion, were the constructive impacts on trade theory resulting from the empirical research of Wassily Leontief?

4. Product cycle theory has always been a very "attractive theory" to many students. Why do you think that is?

5. If the product cycle theory were accepted for the basis of policy-making in the United States, what should the U.S. government do to help U.S. firms exploit the principles of the theory?

6. Many trade theorists argue that the primary contribution of Michael Porter has been to repopularize old ideas, in new, more applicable ways. To what degree do you think Porter's ideas are new or old?

7. How would you analyze the statement that "international investment is simply a modern extension of classical trade"?

8. How can a crisis in Asia impact jobs and profits in the United States?

9. The differences across multinational firms is striking. Using a sample of firms such as those listed here, pull from their individual web pages the proportions of their incomes that are earned outside their country of incorporation.

| | |
|---|---|
| Walt Disney | **http://www.disney.com/** |
| Nestlé S.A. | **http://www.nestle.com/html/home.html** |
| Intel | **http://www.intel.com/** |
| Daimler-Benz | **http://www.daimler-benz.com/index_e.htm** |
| Mitsubishi Motors | **http://www.mitsubishi-motors.co.jp/** |

Also note the way in which international business is now conducted via the Internet. Several of the above home pages allow the user to choose the language of the presentation viewed. Others, like Daimler-Benz, report financial results in two different accounting frameworks, those used in Germany and the Generally Accepted Accounting Practices (GAAP) used in the United States.

10. There is no hotter topic in business today than corporate governance, the way in which firms are controlled by management and ownership across countries. Use the following sites to view recent research, current events and news items, and other information related to the relationships between a business and its stakeholders.

| | |
|---|---|
| Corporate Governance Net | **http://www.corpgov.net/** |
| Corporate Governance Research | **http://www.irrc.org/proxy/cgs.html** |

## Recommended Readings

Bhagwati, Jagdish, and Arvind Panagariya, eds. *The Economics of Preferential Trade Agreements*. Washington, D.C.: American Enterprise Institute, 1996.

Buckley, Peter J., and Mark Casson. *The Future of the Multinational Enterprise*. London: Macmillan, 1976.

Caves, Richard E. International Corporations: The Industrial Economics of Foreign Investment. *Economica* (February 1971): 1–27.

Dunning, John H. Trade Location of Economic Activity and the MNE: A Search for an Eclectic Approach. In *The International Allocation of Economic Activity,* edited by Bertil Ohlin, Per-Ove Hesselborn, and Per Magnus Wijkman. New York: Homes and Meier, 1977, 395–418.

Heckscher, Eli. The Effect of Foreign Trade on the Distribution of Income. In *Readings in International Trade,* edited by Howard S. Ellis and Lloyd A. Metzler. Philadelphia: The Blakiston Company, 1949.

Helpman, Elhaman, and Paul Krugman. *Market Structure and Foreign Trade.* Cambridge, Mass.: MIT Press, 1985.

Husted, Steven, and Michael Melvin. *International Economics.* 4th ed. Reading, Mass.: Addison-Wesley Publishing, 1997.

Hymer, Stephen H. *The International Operations of National Firms: A Study of Direct Foreign Investment.* Cambridge, Mass.: MIT Press, 1976.

Linder, Staffan Burenstam. *An Essay on Trade and Transformation.* New York: John Wiley & Sons, 1961.

Maskus, Keith E., Deborah Battles, and Michael H. Moffett. Determinants of the Structure of U.S. Manufacturing Trade with Japan and Korea, 1970–1984. In *The Internationalization of U.S. Markets,* edited by David B. Audretch and Michael P. Claudon. New York: New York University Press, 1989, 97–122.

Ohlin, Bertil. *Interregional and International Trade.* Boston: Harvard University Press, 1933.

Porter, Michael. "The Competitive Advantage of Nations." *Harvard Business Review* (March–April 1990).

Ricardo, David. *The Principles of Political Economy and Taxation.* Cambridge, United Kingdom: Cambridge University Press, 1981.

Root, Franklin R. *International Trade and Investment.* 6th ed. Chicago: South-Western Publishing, 1990.

Smith, Adam. *The Wealth of Nations.* New York: The Modern Library, 1937.

Todaro, Michael P. *Economic Development.* 6th ed. Reading, Mass.: Addison-Wesley Publishing, 1997.

Vernon, Raymond. International Investment and International Trade in the Product Cycle. *Quarterly Journal of Economics* (1966): 190–207.

Wells, Louis T., Jr. A Product Life Cycle for International Trade? *Journal of Marketing* 22 (July 1968): 1–6.

## Notes

1. Adam Smith, *An Inquiry into the Nature and Causes of the Wealth of Nations* (New York: E.P. Dutton & Company, 1937), 4–5.

2. Wassily Leontief, "Domestic Production and Foreign Trade: the American Capital Position Re-Examined," *Proceedings of the American Philosophical Society,* 97, no. 4 (September 1953), as reprinted in Wassily Leontief, *Input-Output Economics* (New York: Oxford University Press, 1966), 69–70.

3. In Leontief's own words: "These figures show that an average million dollars' worth of our exports embodies considerably less capital and somewhat more labor than would be required to replace from domestic production an equivalent amount of our competitive imports. . . . The widely held opinion that—as compared with the rest of the world—the United States' economy is characterized by a relative surplus of capital and a relative shortage of labor proves to be wrong. As a matter of fact, the opposite is true." Leontief, 1953, 86.

4. If this were true, it would defy one of the basic assumptions of the factor proportions theory, that all products are manufactured with the same technology (and therefore same proportions of labor and capital) across countries. However, continuing studies have found this to be quite possible in our imperfect world.

5. For a detailed description of these theories see Elhanan Helpman and Paul Krugman, *Market Structure and Foreign Trade* (Cambridge, MIT Press, 1985).

6. This leads to the obvious debate as to what constitutes a "different product" and what is simply a cosmetic difference. The most obvious answer is found in the field of marketing: If the consumer believes the products are different, then they are different.

7. There are a variety of potential outcomes from external economies of scale. For additional details see Paul R. Krugman and Maurice Obstfeld, *International Economics: Theory and Policy,* 3d ed. (Harper-Collins, 1994).

8. Michael E. Porter, "The Competitive Advantage of Nations," *Harvard Business Review* (March-April 1990): 73–74.

9. The term *international investment* will be used in this chapter to refer to all nonfinancial investment. International financial investment includes a number of forms beyond the concerns of this chapter, such as the purchase of bonds, stocks, or other securities issued outside the domestic economy.

# CHAPTER 6

# The International Economic Activity of the Nation: The Balance of Payments

## LEARNING OBJECTIVES

◆ *To understand the fundamental principles of how countries measure international business activity, the balance of payments*

◆ *To examine the similarities of the current and capital accounts of the balance of payments*

◆ *To understand the critical differences between trade in merchandise and services, and why international investment activity has recently been controversial in the United States*

◆ *To review the mechanical steps of how exchange rate changes are transmitted into altered trade prices and eventually trade volumes*

◆ *To understand how countries with different government policies toward international trade and investment, or different levels of economic development, differ in their balance of payments*

## Finding a Scapegoat

**W**hen things go wrong, there is nothing like finding a scapegoat, ideally a fabulously wealthy foreigner. So when the topic of turbulence in regional currency markets came up at the annual meeting in Malaysia of the Association of South-East Asian Nations (ASEAN), there seemed an obvious case of villains: international speculators, led by an American financier, George Soros. Malaysia's prime minister, Mahathir Mohammad, was characteristically forthright, repeatedly naming Mr. Soros as the guilty man.

It would be more useful to look closer to home. Self-criticism, alas, would be less rhetorically satisfying. It would also require pointing fingers directly at the leaders who have led their countries into such turmoil. For Thailand to blame Soros for its plight is rather like condemning an undertaker for burying a suicide. A decade of economic growth averaging around 8 percent a year had blinded policymakers to signs of impending crisis, many of which were related to the baht's peg to a basket of currencies dominated by the dollar. Export growth stalled as the dollar strengthened last year. Local companies and financial institutions, meanwhile, had piled up dollar debts because interest rates were low, and there appeared to be no exchange risk. On July 28, 1997, it [Thailand] announced it was entering talks with the International Monetary Fund (IMF) about a standby line of credit to stem a slide into national bankruptcy. ■

*Source:* Abstracted from "Of crashes and conspirators," *The Economist,* August 2, 1997, 57–58.

International business transactions occur in many different forms over the course of a year. The measurement of all international economic transactions between the residents of a country and foreign residents is called the **balance of payments (BOP).**[1] Government policymakers need such measures of economic activity to evaluate the general competitiveness of domestic industry, to set exchange-rate or interest-rate policies or goals, and for many other purposes. Individuals and businesses use various BOP measures to gauge the growth and health of specific types of trade or financial transactions by country and regions of the world against the home country.

International transactions take many forms. Each of the following examples is an international economic transaction that is counted and captured in the U.S. balance of payments.

- U.S. imports of Honda automobiles, which are manufactured in Japan.
- A U.S.-based firm, Bechtel, is hired to manage the construction of a major water-treatment facility in the Middle East.
- The U.S. subsidiary of a French firm, Saint Gobain, pays profits (dividends) back to the parent firm in Paris.

■ Daimler-Benz, the well-known German automobile manufacturer, purchases a small automotive parts manufacturer outside Chicago, Illinois.
■ An American tourist purchases a hand-blown glass figurine in Venice, Italy.
■ The U.S. government provides grant financing of military equipment for its NATO (North Atlantic Treaty Organization) military ally, Turkey.
■ A Canadian dentist purchases a U.S. Treasury bill through an investment broker in Cleveland, Ohio.

These are just a small sample of the hundreds of thousands of international transactions that occur each year. The balance of payments provides a systematic method for the classification of all of these transactions. There is one rule of thumb that will always aid in the understanding of BOP accounting: Watch the direction of the movement of money.

The balance of payments is composed of a number of subaccounts that are watched quite closely by groups as diverse as investors on Wall Street, farmers in Iowa, politicians on Capital Hill, and in boardrooms across America. These groups track and analyze the two major subaccounts, the **current account** and the **capital account,** on a continuing basis. Before describing these two subaccounts and the balance of payments as a whole, it is necessary to understand the rather unusual features of how balance of payments accounting is conducted.

## *Fundamentals of Balance of Payments Accounting*

The balance of payments must balance. If it does not, something has either not been counted or counted properly. It is therefore improper to state that the BOP is in disequilibrium. It cannot be. The supply and demand for a country's currency may be imbalanced, but that is not the same thing. Subaccounts of the BOP, such as the merchandise trade balance, may be imbalanced, but the entire BOP of a single country is always balanced.

There are three main elements to the process of measuring international economic activity: (1) identifying what is and is not an international economic transaction; (2) understanding how the flow of goods, services, assets, and money creates debits and credits to the overall BOP; and (3) understanding the bookkeeping procedures for BOP accounting, called double entry.

**Defining International Economic Transactions**

Identifying international transactions is ordinarily not difficult. The export of merchandise, goods such as trucks, machinery, computers, telecommunications equipment, and so forth, is obviously an international transaction. Imports such as French wine, Japanese cameras, and German automobiles are also clearly international transactions. But this merchandise trade is only a portion of the thousands of different international transactions that occur in the United States or any other country each year.

Many other international transactions are not so obvious. The purchase of a glass figure in Venice, Italy, by an American tourist is classified as a U.S. merchandise import. In fact, all expenditures made by American tourists around the globe that are for goods or services (meals, hotel accommodations, and so forth) are recorded in the U.S. balance of payments as imports of travel services in the current account. The purchase of a U.S. Treasury bill by a foreign resident is an international financial transaction and is dutifully recorded in the capital account of the U.S. balance of payments.

## The BOP as a Flow Statement

The BOP is often misunderstood because many people believe it to be a balance sheet, rather than a cash flow statement. By recording all international transactions over a period of time, it is tracking the continuing flow of purchases and payments between a country and all other countries. It does not add up the value of all assets and liabilities of a country like a balance sheet does for an individual firm.

There are two types of business transactions that dominate the balance of payments:

1. **Real Assets.** The exchange of goods (for example, automobiles, computers, watches, textiles) and services (for example, banking services, consulting services, travel services) for other goods and services (barter) or for the more common type of payment, money.
2. **Financial Assets.** The exchange of financial claims (for example, stocks, bonds, loans, purchases or sales of companies) in exchange for other financial claims or money.

Although assets can be separated as to whether they are real or financial, it is often easier to simply think of all assets as being goods that can be bought and sold. An American tourist's purchase of a handwoven area rug in a shop in Bangkok is not all that different from a Wall Street banker buying a British government bond for investment purposes.

## BOP Accounting: Double-Entry Bookkeeping

The balance of payments employs an accounting technique called **double-entry bookkeeping.** Double-entry bookkeeping is the age-old method of accounting in which every transaction produces a debit and a credit of the same amount. Simultaneously. It has to. A debt is created whenever an asset is increased, a liability is decreased, or an expense is increased. Similarly, a credit is created whenever an asset is decreased, a liability is increased, or an expense is decreased.

An example clarifies this process. A U.S. retail store imports from Japan $2 million worth of consumer electronics. A negative entry is made in the merchandise-import subcategory of the current account in the amount of $2 million. Simultaneously, a positive entry of the same $2 million is made in the capital account for the transfer of a $2 million bank account to the Japanese manufacturer. Obviously, the result of hundreds of thousands of such transactions and entries should theoretically result in a perfect balance.

That said, it is now a problem of application, and a problem it is. The measurement of all international transactions in and out of a country over a year is a daunting task. Mistakes, errors, and statistical discrepancies will occur. The primary problem is that although double-entry bookkeeping is employed in theory, the individual transactions are recorded independently. Current and capital account entries are recorded independent of one another, not together as double-entry bookkeeping would prescribe. It must then be recognized that there will be serious discrepancies (to use a nice term for it) between debits and credits, and the possibility in total that the balance of payments may not balance!

The following section describes the various balance of payment accounts, their meanings, and their relationships, using the United States as the example. The chapter then concludes with a discussion—and a number of examples—of how different countries with different policies or levels of economic development may differ markedly in their balance of payment accounts.

## The Accounts of the Balance of Payments

The balance of payments is composed of two primary subaccounts, the *Current Account* and the *Financial/Capital Account.* In addition, the *Official Reserves Account* tracks government currency transactions, and a fourth statistical subaccount, the *Net Errors and Omissions Account,* is produced to preserve the balance in the BOP. The international economic relationships between countries do, however, continue to evolve, as the recent revision of the major accounts within the BOP discussed below indicates.[2]

**The Current Account**

The *Current Account* includes all international economic transactions with income or payment flows occurring within the year, the *current* period. The *Current Account* consists of four subcategories:

1. **Goods Trade:** This is the export and import of goods. Merchandise trade is the oldest and most traditional form of international economic activity. Although many countries depend on imports of many goods (as they should according to the theory of comparative advantage), they also normally work to preserve either a balance of goods trade or even a surplus.
2. **Services Trade:** This is the export and import of services. Some common international services are financial services provided by banks to foreign importers and exporters, travel services of airlines, and construction services of domestic firms in other countries. For the major industrial countries, this subaccount has shown the fastest growth in the past decade.
3. **Income:** This category is predominantly *current income* associated with investments that were made in previous periods. If a U.S. firm created a subsidiary in South Korea to produce metal parts in a previous year, the proportion of net income that is paid back to the parent company in the current year (the dividend) constitutes current investment income. Additionally, wages and salaries paid to nonresident workers is also included in this category.
4. **Current Transfers:** Transfers are the financial settlements associated with the change in ownership of real resources or financial items. Any transfer between countries that is one-way, a gift, or a grant, is termed a *current transfer.* A common example of a current transfer would be funds provided by the United States government to aid in the development of a less-developed nation. Transfers associated with the transfer of fixed assets are included in a new separate account, the Capital Account, which now follows the Cur-

rent Account. The contents of what previously had been called the capital account are now included within the *Financial Account.*

All countries possess some amount of trade, most of which is merchandise. Many smaller and less-developed countries have little in the way of service trade, or items that fall under the income or transfers subaccounts.

The Current Account is typically dominated by the first component described—the export and import of merchandise. For this reason, the *Balance on Trade* (BOT), which is so widely quoted in the business press in most countries, refers specifically to the balance of exports and imports of goods trade only. For a larger industrialized country, however, the BOT is somewhat misleading because service trade is not included; it may be opposite in sign on net, and it may actually be fairly large as well.

Table 6.1 summarizes the Current Account and its components for the United States for the 1993–95 period. As illustrated, the U.S. goods trade balance has consistently been negative, but has been partially offset by the continuing surplus in services trade. The U.S. Current Account was in deficit in the identical amount for both 1994 and 1995—$148 billion.

**Goods Trade**    Figure 6.1 places the current account values of Table 6.1 in perspective over time by dividing the current account into its two major components: (1) goods trade and (2) services trade and investment income. The first and most striking message is the magnitude of the goods trade deficit in the 1990s (a continuation of a position created in the early 1980s). The balance on services and income, although not large in comparison to net goods trade, has with few exceptions run a surplus over the past two decades.

**TABLE 6.1**

**The United States Current Account, 1993–95 (billions of U.S. dollars)**

|  | 1993 | 1994 | 1995 |
|---|---|---|---|
| Goods exports | 459 | 505 | 578 |
| Goods imports | −590 | −669 | −750 |
| Goods trade balance (BOT) | −131 | −165 | −172 |
| Services trade credits | 184 | 194 | 209 |
| Services trade debits | −124 | −132 | −140 |
| Services trade balance | 60 | 61 | 68 |
| Income receipts | 120 | 142 | 183 |
| Income payments | −111 | −147 | −192 |
| Income balance | 9 | −5 | −9 |
| Current transfers, credits | 5 | 5 | 6 |
| Current transfers, debits | −43 | −44 | −41 |
| Net transfers | −37 | −39 | −35 |
| **Current Account Balance** | **−100** | **−148** | **−148** |

*Source:* Based on The International Monetary Fund, *Balance of Payments Statistics Yearbook,* 1996, p. 823.
*Note:* Totals may not add due to rounding.

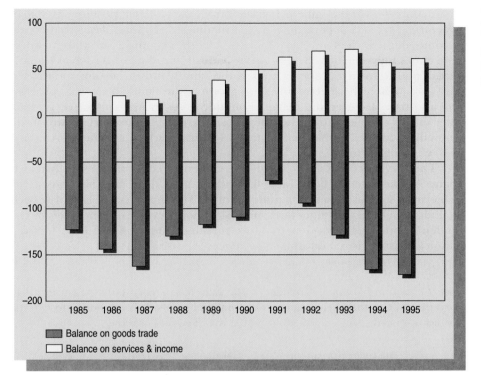

**FIGURE 6.1**

**The U.S. Goods Trade Balance & Balance on Services and Income, 1985– 95 (billions of U.S. dollars)**

The deficits in the BOT of the past decade have been an area of considerable concern for the United States, in both the public and private sectors. Merchandise trade is the original core of international trade. The manufacturing of goods was the basis of the industrial revolution, and the focus of the theory of international trade described in the previous chapter. Manufacturing is traditionally a sector of the economy that employs most of a country's workers. The goods trade deficit of the 1980s saw a decline in the U.S. in the traditional heavy industries that have over history employed many of America's workers. Declines in the net trade balance in areas such as steel, automobiles, automotive parts, textiles, shoe manufacturing, and others have caused massive economic and social disruption. The problems of dealing with these shifting trade balances will be discussed in detail in a later chapter.

The most encouraging news for U.S. manufacturing trade is the growth of exports in the latter half of the 1980s and the early years of the 1990s. A number of factors contributed to the growth of U.S. exports, such as the weaker dollar (which made U.S.-manufactured goods cheaper in terms of the currencies of other countries) and more rapid economic growth in Europe in the latter part of the 1980s. Understanding merchandise import and export performance is much like understanding the market for any single product. The demand factors that drive both imports and exports are income, the economic growth rate of the buyer, and price (the price of the product in the eyes of the consumer after passing through an exchange rate). For example, U.S. merchandise imports reflect the income level and growth of American consumers and industry. As income rises, so does the demand for imports.

Exports follow the same principles but in the reversed position. U.S. manufacturing exports depend not on the incomes of U.S. residents, but on the incomes of the buyers of U.S. products in all other countries around the world. The major markets for U.S. exports are industrialized nations such as Canada, Japan, and western Europe, as well as the rapidly industrializing countries of East Asia. When these economies are growing, the demand for U.S. products will also rise. However, the recent economic crises in Asia (discussed in detail later in this chapter) now raise questions regarding U.S. export growth in the immediate future. Global Perspective 6.1 illustrates how significant Asia is to U.S. export growth.

The service component of the U.S. current account is one of mystery to many. As illustrated in both Table 6.1 and Figure 6.1, the U.S. has consistently achieved a surplus in services trade income. The major categories of services include travel and passenger fares, transportation services, expenditures by U.S. students abroad and foreign students pursuing studies in the U.S., telecommunications services, and financial services.

## The Capital and Financial Account

The *Capital and Financial Account* of the balance of payments measures all international economic transactions of financial assets. It is divided into two major components, the *capital account* and the *financial account*.

## U.S. EXPORTS TO ASIA: HOW IMPORTANT ARE THEY?

**T**he Asian economic crisis, which began in the summer of 1997, has had significant repercussions for all nations, regardless of whether they are within the region itself or not. For example, the United States exports significant amounts of goods to many of the countries in the Asian Pacific region. According to the United States International Trade Administration, the 1995 U.S. trade balance, export sales, and export rank for affected Asian countries was the following.

| Country | 1995 U.S. Bilateral Trade Balance | U.S. Exports to Each Country in 1995 | Export Rank |
|---------|-----------------------------------|--------------------------------------|-------------|
| Japan | (59,280) | 583,865 | 2 |
| Korea | 1,230 | 25,413 | 5 |
| Taiwan | (9,680) | 19,295 | 7 |
| Singapore | (3,246) | 15,318 | 9 |
| Hong Kong | 3,926 | 14,220 | 11 |
| China | (33,807) | 11,748 | 13 |
| Malaysia | (8,666) | 8,818 | 17 |
| Thailand | (4,949) | 6,402 | 18 |
| Philippines | (1,712) | 5,294 | 23 |
| Indonesia | (4,081) | 3,356 | 29 |

*Date abstracted from United States Trade Representative.* **http://www.ustr.gov/reports/hte/1996/appendix.htm** *(January 1998).*

■ **The Capital Account:** The *capital account* is made up of transfers of financial assets and the acquisition and disposal of nonproduced/nonfinancial assets. This account has been introduced as a separate component in the International Monetary Fund's balance of payments just in the past two years. The magnitude of capital transactions covered is of relatively minor amount, and will be included in principle in all of the following discussions of the financial account.

■ **The Financial Account:** The financial account consists of three components: *direct investment, portfolio investment,* and *other asset investment.* Financial assets can be classified in a number of different ways including the length of the life of the asset (its maturity) and by the nature of the ownership (public or private). The Financial Account, however, uses a third way. It is classified by the degree of control over the assets or operations the claim represents: *portfolio investment,* where the investor has no control, or *direct investment,* where the investor exerts some explicit degree of control over the assets. (The contents of the Financial Account are for all intents and purposes the same as those of the Capital Account under the IMF's BOP accounting framework used until 1996.)

Table 6.2 shows the major subcategories of the U.S. capital account balance from 1993–95, *direct investment, portfolio investment,* and *other long-term and short-term capital.*

1. **Direct Investment:** This is the net balance of capital dispersed out of and into the United States for the purpose of exerting control over assets. For example, if a U.S. firm either builds a new automotive parts facility in another country or actually purchases a company in another country, this

**TABLE 6.2**

**The United States Financial Account and Components, 1993–95**
**(billions of U.S. dollars)**

|  | 1993 | 1994 | 1995 |
|---|---|---|---|
| **Direct Investment** | | | |
| Direct investment abroad | −78 | −54 | −96 |
| Direct investment in the United States | 43 | 50 | 60 |
| Net direct investment | −35 | −5 | −35 |
| **Portfolio Investment** | | | |
| Equity securities, net | −42 | −47 | −34 |
| Debt securities, net | 0 | 78 | 128 |
| Net portfolio investment | −42 | 31 | 93 |
| **Other Investment** | | | |
| Other investment assets | 31 | −41 | −104 |
| Other investment liabilities | 36 | 104 | 66 |
| Net other investment | 67 | 63 | −37 |
| **Net Financial Account Balance** | −11 | 89 | 21 |

*Source:* Based on The International Monetary Fund, *Balance of Payments Statistics Yearbook,* 1996, p. 823.
*Note:* Totals may not add due to rounding.

would fall under *direct investment* in the U.S. balance of payments accounts. When the capital flows out of the U.S., it enters the balance of payments as a negative cash flow. If, however, foreign firms purchase firms in the U.S. (for example Sony of Japan purchased Columbia Pictures in 1989) it is a capital inflow and enters the balance of payments positively. Whenever 10 percent or more of the voting shares in a U.S. company is held by foreign investors, the company is classified as the U.S. affiliate of a foreign company, and a *foreign direct investment*. Similarly, if U.S. investors hold 10 percent or more of the control in a company outside the United States, that company is considered the foreign affiliate of a U.S. company.

2. **Portfolio investment:** This is net balance of capital that flows in and out of the United States, but does not reach the 10 percent ownership threshold of direct investment. If a U.S. resident purchases shares in a Japanese firm, but does not attain the 10 percent threshold, it is considered a *portfolio investment* (and in this case an outflow of capital). The purchase or sale of debt securities (like U.S. Treasury bills) across borders is also classified as *portfolio investment* because debt securities by definition do not provide the buyer with ownership or control.

3. **Other Investment Assets/Liabilities:** This final category consists of various short-term and long-term trade credits, cross-border loans from all types of financial institutions, currency deposits and bank deposits, and other accounts receivable and payable related to cross-border trade.

**Direct Investment**   Figure 6.2 shows how the major subaccounts of the U.S. capital account, *net direct investment, portfolio investment,* and *other investment* have changed since 1985.

The boom in foreign investment into the United States, or foreign resident purchases of assets in the U.S., during the 1980s was extremely controversial. The source of concern over foreign investment in any country, including the United States, focuses on two topics—**control** and **profit.** Most countries possess restrictions on what foreigners may own in their country. This is based on the premise that domestic land, assets, and industry in general should be held by residents of the country. For example, up until 1990 it was not possible for a foreign firm to own more than 20 percent of any company in Finland. This rule is the norm, rather than the exception. The United States has traditionally had few restrictions on what foreign residents or firms can own or control in the U.S.; most restrictions that remain today are related to national security concerns. As opposed to many of the traditional debates over whether international trade should be free or not, there is not the same consensus that international investment should necessarily be free. This is a question that is still very much a domestic political concern first, and an international economic issue second. As illustrated in Figure 6.2, however, the debate has been subdued in the 1990s as a result of the net direction; net direct investment has been flowing out of the U.S. regularly since 1990.

The second major source of concern over foreign direct investment is who receives the profits from the enterprise. Foreign companies owning firms in the United States will ultimately profit from the activities of the firms, or put another way, from the efforts of American workers. In spite of evidence that foreign firms in the United States reinvest most of the profits in the United States (in fact at a higher rate than domestic firms), the debate has continued

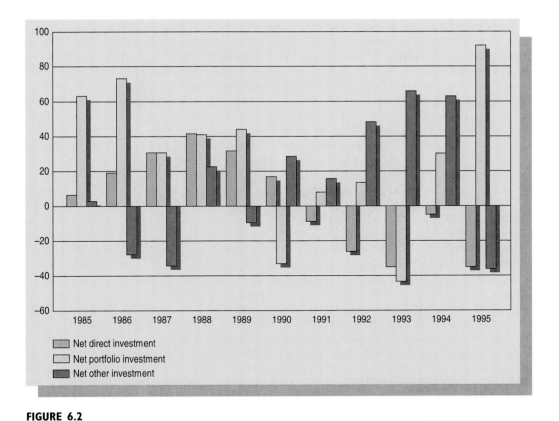

**FIGURE 6.2**

**The United States Financial Account, 1985–96 (billions of U.S. dollars)**

on possible profit drains. Regardless of the actual choices made, workers of any nation feel the profits of their work should remain in the hands of their own citizens. Once again, this is in many ways a political and emotional concern more than an economic one.

The choice of words used to describe foreign investment can also influence public opinion. If these massive capital inflows are described as "capital investments from all over the world showing their faith in the future of American industry," the net capital surplus is represented as decidedly positive. If, however, the net capital surplus is described as resulting in "the United States as the world's largest debtor nation," the negative connotation is obvious. Both are essentially spins on the economic principles at work. Capital, whether short-term or long-term, flows to where it believes it can earn the greatest return for the level of risk. Although in an accounting sense that is "international debt," when the majority of the capital inflow is in the form of direct investment and a long-term commitment to jobs, production, services, technological, and other competitive investments, the impact on the competitiveness of American industry (an industry located within the United States) is increased. The "net debtor" label is misleading in that it invites comparison with large debt crisis conditions suffered by many countries in the past, like Mexico and Brazil. As described later in this chapter, there are fundamental differences.

**FIGURE 6.3**

Current and
Financial/Capital Account
Balances for Germany,
Japan, and the United
States, 1988–95 (billions of
U.S. dollars)

Germany

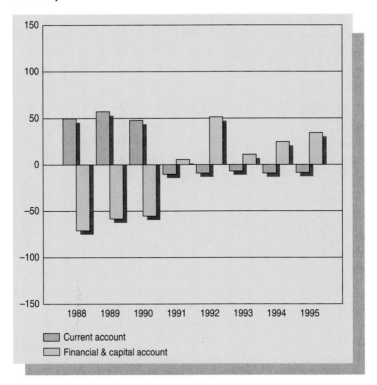

Japan

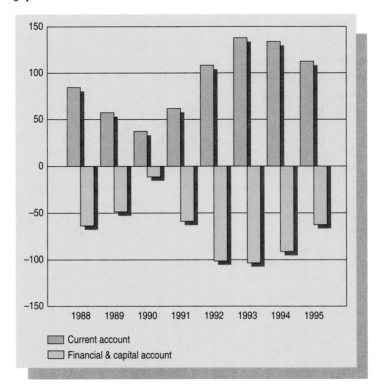

**United States**

**FIGURE 6.3**

**Continued**

**Portfolio Investment**   Portfolio investment is capital invested in activities that are purely profit-motivated (return), rather than ones made in the prospect of controlling or managing the investment. Investments that are purchases of debit securities, bonds, interest-bearing bank accounts, and the like are only intended to earn a return. They provide no vote or control over the party issuing the debt. Purchases of debt issued by the U.S. government (U.S. Treasury bills, notes, and bonds) by foreign investors constitutes net portfolio investment in the United States.

As illustrated in Figure 6.2, portfolio investment has shown a much more volatile behavior than net direct investment over the past decade. Many U.S. debt securities, such as U.S. Treasury securities and corporate bonds, were in high demand in the late 1980s, while surging emerging markets in both debt and equities caused a reversal in direction in the 1990s. The motivating forces for portfolio investment flows are always the same, *return* and *risk*. This theoretical fact, however, does not make them any the more predictable.

**Current and Financial Account Balance Relationships**   Figure 6.3 illustrates the current and financial account balances for Germany, Japan, and the United States over recent years. They are all presented on the same scale so that relative magnitudes are comparable across the three countries. What the figure shows is one of the basic economic and accounting relationships of the balance of payments: *the inverse relationship between the Current and Financial accounts.* This inverse relationship is not accidental. The methodology of the balance of payments, double-entry bookkeeping, requires that the current and financial accounts be offsetting. Countries experiencing large current account deficits "finance" these purchases through equally large surpluses in the financial account and vice versa.

## Net Errors and Omissions

As noted before, because Current Account and Financial Account entries are collected and recorded separately, errors or statistical discrepancies will occur. The *net errors and omissions account* (this is the title used by the International Monetary Fund) makes sure that the BOP actually balances.

## Official Reserves Account

The official reserves account is the total currency and metallic reserves held by official monetary authorities within the country. These reserves are normally composed of the major currencies used in international trade and financial transactions (so-called "hard currencies" like the U.S. dollar, German mark, and Japanese yen) and gold.

The significance of official reserves depends generally on whether the country is operating under a **fixed exchange rate** regime or a **floating exchange rate** system. If a country's currency is fixed, this means that the government of the country officially declares that the currency is convertible into a fixed amount of some other currency. For example, for many years the South Korean won was fixed to the U.S. dollar at 484 won equal to 1 U.S. dollar. It is the government's responsibility to maintain this fixed rate (also called *parity rate*). If for some reason there is an excess supply of Korean won on the currency market, to prevent the value of the won from falling, the South Korean government must support the won's value by purchasing won on the open market (by spending its hard currency reserves, its *official reserves*) until the excess supply is eliminated. Under a floating rate system, the government possesses no such responsibility and the role of official reserves is diminished.

## The Balance of Payments in Total

Table 6.3 provides the official balance of payments for the United States as presented by the International Monetary Fund (IMF), the multinational organization that collects these statistics for over 160 different countries around the globe. Now that the individual accounts and the relationships among the accounts have been discussed, Table 6.3 gives a comprehensive overview of how the individual accounts are combined to create some of the most useful summary measures for multinational business managers.

The current account (line A in Table 6.3), the capital account (line B), and the financial account (line C) combine to form the *basic balance (Total, Groups A Through C)*. This is one of the most frequently used summary measures of the BOP. It is used to describe the international economic activity of the nation as determined by market forces, not by government decisions (such as currency market intervention). The U.S. *basic balance* totaled a deficit of $127 billion in 1995. A second frequently used summary measure, the overall balance, also called the official settlements balance *(Total of Groups A Through D in Table 6.3)*, was at a deficit of $96 billion in 1995.

**TABLE 6.3**

**The United States Balance of Payments, Analytic Presentation, 1988–95 (billions of U.S. dollars)**

| | 1988 | 1989 | 1990 | 1991 | 1992 | 1993 | 1994 | 1995 |
|---|---|---|---|---|---|---|---|---|
| **A. Current Account** | **−127.71** | **−104.27** | **−94.26** | **−9.26** | **−61.35** | **−99.72** | **−147.77** | **−148.23** |
| Goods: exports fob | 320.23 | 362.16 | 389.31 | 416.91 | 440.35 | 458.73 | 504.55 | 577.82 |
| Goods: imports fob | −447.19 | −477.30 | −498.34 | −490.98 | −536.45 | −590.10 | −669.15 | −749.81 |
| Balance on goods | −126.96 | −115.14 | −109.03 | −74.07 | −96.10 | −131.37 | −164.60 | −171.99 |
| Services: credit | 111.16 | 127.72 | 147.35 | 163.67 | 177.14 | 184.09 | 193.62 | 208.55 |
| Services: debit | −98.53 | −102.54 | −117.64 | −118.46 | −118.29 | −123.62 | −132.23 | −140.43 |
| Balance on Goods and Services | −114.33 | −89.96 | −79.32 | −28.86 | −37.25 | −70.90 | −103.21 | −103.87 |
| Income: credit | 129.20 | 152.65 | 160.42 | 137.14 | 119.21 | 120.05 | 141.87 | 182.85 |
| Income: debit | −116.69 | −139.68 | −140.54 | −122.33 | −109.04 | −111.42 | −147.17 | −192.02 |
| Balance on Goods, Services, and Income | −101.82 | −76.99 | −59.44 | −14.05 | −27.08 | −62.27 | −108.51 | −113.04 |
| Current transfers: credit | 3.66 | 4.09 | 8.79 | 46.84 | 6.50 | 5.20 | 5.22 | 5.65 |
| Current transfers: debit | −29.55 | −31.37 | −43.61 | −42.05 | −40.77 | −42.65 | −44.48 | −40.84 |
| **B. Capital Account** | **0.23** | **0.24** | **0.26** | **0.28** | **0.43** | **−0.20** | **−0.61** | **0.10** |
| Capital account: credit | 0.23 | 0.24 | 0.26 | 0.28 | 0.43 | 0.47 | 0.47 | 0.53 |
| Capital account: debit | | | | | | −0.67 | −1.08 | −0.43 |
| **Total, Groups A plus B** | **−127.48** | **−104.03** | **−94.00** | **−8.98** | **−60.92** | **−99.92** | **−148.38** | **−148.13** |
| **C. Financial Account** | **103.38** | **63.44** | **13.76** | **13.75** | **35.33** | **−10.72** | **88.95** | **20.70** |
| Direct investment abroad | −16.18 | −36.83 | −29.95 | −31.38 | −42.66 | −78.17 | −54.47 | −95.53 |
| Direct investment in the United States | 57.27 | 67.73 | 47.92 | 22.01 | 17.58 | 43.01 | 49.76 | 60.23 |
| Portfolio investment assets | −7.88 | −22.10 | −28.80 | −45.69 | −49.17 | −146.26 | −60.29 | −98.96 |
| Equity securities | −0.92 | −17.22 | −7.41 | −30.64 | −32.40 | −63.38 | −48.09 | −50.70 |
| Debt securities | −6.96 | −4.88 | −21.39 | −15.05 | −16.77 | −82.88 | −12.20 | −48.26 |
| Portfolio investment liabilities | 48.18 | 65.60 | −4.20 | 53.30 | 62.20 | 103.83 | 91.11 | 192.38 |
| Equity securities | −0.48 | 6.96 | −14.52 | 9.47 | −4.17 | 20.92 | 0.91 | 16.41 |
| Debt securities | 48.66 | 58.64 | 10.32 | 43.83 | 66.37 | 82.91 | 90.20 | 175.97 |
| Other investment assets | −73.28 | −83.40 | −13.73 | 13.82 | 17.79 | 31.19 | −41.31 | −103.63 |
| Monetary authorities | | | | | | | | |
| General government | 1.84 | 2.39 | 1.71 | 3.32 | −3.16 | −0.34 | −0.35 | −0.28 |
| Banks | −46.74 | −40.12 | 15.53 | −15.08 | 23.82 | 29.95 | −8.16 | −69.14 |
| Other sectors | −28.38 | −45.67 | −30.97 | 25.58 | −2.87 | 1.58 | −32.80 | −34.21 |
| Other investment liabilities | 95.27 | 72.44 | 42.52 | 1.69 | 29.59 | 35.68 | 104.15 | 66.21 |
| Monetary authorities | | | | | | 2.59 | −2.35 | 5.28 |
| General government | −0.47 | 0.16 | 1.87 | 1.36 | 2.19 | 1.71 | 2.34 | 1.08 |
| Banks | 61.92 | 50.25 | −2.04 | 2.75 | 10.30 | 20.92 | 111.54 | 25.28 |
| Other sectors | 33.82 | 22.03 | 42.69 | −2.42 | 17.10 | 10.46 | −7.38 | 34.57 |
| **Total, Groups A Through C** | **−24.10** | **−40.59** | **−80.24** | **4.77** | **−25.59** | **−110.64** | **−59.43** | **−127.43** |
| **D. Net Errors and Omissions** | **−11.73** | **55.83** | **46.54** | **−26.83** | **−23.11** | **43.55** | **13.71** | **31.54** |
| **Total, Groups A Through D** | **−35.83** | **15.24** | **−33.70** | **−22.06** | **−48.70** | **−67.09** | **−45.72** | **−95.89** |
| **E. Reserves and Related Items** | **35.83** | **−15.24** | **33.70** | **22.06** | **48.70** | **67.09** | **45.72** | **95.89** |
| Reserve assets | −3.92 | −25.26 | −2.24 | 5.75 | 3.93 | −1.40 | 5.34 | −9.74 |
| Use of Fund credit and loans | | | | | | | | |
| Liabilities constituting for author's reserves | 39.75 | 10.02 | 35.94 | 16.31 | 44.77 | 68.49 | 40.38 | 105.63 |
| Exceptional financing | | | | | | | | |

*Source:* Based on The International Monetary Fund, *Balance of Payments Statistics Yearbook,* 1996, p. 823. Values may not match original source due to rounding.

The meaning of the balance of payments has changed over the past 30 years. As long as most of the major industrial countries were still operating under fixed exchange rates, the interpretation of the BOP was relatively straightforward. A surplus in the BOP implied that the demand for the country's currency exceeded the supply, and that the government should then allow the currency value to increase *(revalue)* or to intervene and accumulate additional foreign currency reserves in the Official Reserves Account. This would occur as the government sold its own currency in exchange for other currencies, thus building up its stores of hard currencies. A deficit in the BOP implied an excess supply of the country's currency on world markets, and the government would then either *devalue* the currency or expend its official reserves to support its value. But the transition to floating exchange rate regimes in the 1970s (described in the following chapter) changed the focus from the total BOP to its various subaccounts like the Current and Financial Account balances. These are the indicators of economic activities and currency repercussions to come. The recent crises in Mexico (1994) and Asia (1997) highlight the continuing changes in the role of the balance of payments. Global Perspective 6.2 illustrates that, in the case of Asia, private sector debt was a significant contributor to the problem. Global Perspective 6.3 presents Moody's ratings off the web for sovereign borrowers worldwide.

## The Balance of Payments and Economic Crises

The sum of cross-border international economic activity, the balance of payments, can be used by international managers to forecast economic conditions, and in some cases, economic crisis. The mechanics of international economic crisis often follow a similar path of development:

## PRIVATE SECTOR DEBT AND FORECASTING THE ASIAN CRISIS

Fitch IBCA, Europe's largest credit rating agency, yesterday admitted that it and its large rivals, Standard & Poors and Moody's Investors Service of the United States, had largely failed to predict the recent turmoil in Asia. The admission, accompanied by an attack on the International Monetary Fund

for its allegedly poor forecasting record in Asia, followed widespread criticism of the three big agencies over their handling of the Asian upheavals. The agencies came in for particularly fierce criticism for their treatment of South Korea. The country was rated at the same level as Italy and Sweden as recently as last October, but has since been downgraded to junk bond status.

The agency said it and its competitors had underestimated the spread of "market contagion" in Asia. It had also failed to fully appreciate the impact that high levels of external private sector debt would have on the creditworthiness of sovereign borrowers.

*Source: Adapted from "Credit Agency Accepts Criticisms Over Asia," by Edward Luce,* **Financial Times,** *January 14, 1998, p. 15.* http://www.FT.com

The Inter-American Development Bank is the oldest and largest regional multilateral development institution established to help finance economic growth and social development in Latin America and the Caribbean. The Bank's operations cover the entire spectrum of economic and social development. The Bank's membership includes 26 Latin American and Caribbean countries, Canada, and the United States.
Source: http://www.iadb.org

1. A country that experiences rapidly expanding current account deficits will simultaneously build financial account surpluses (the inverse relationship noted previously).
2. The capital that flows into a country, while strong and steady, may be able to offset or "finance" the current account deficits for long periods of time.
3. Frequently, however, if domestic economic conditions worsen (or it appears that they are about to), the capital that is so critical to maintaining the balance of the country's BOP flows out. This sudden outflow results in a severe deficit in the overall balance of payments, and the country's currency may be suddenly and severely devalued.

International debt crises have occurred for as long as there has been international trade and commerce. Each crisis has its own particular characteristics, but all follow the economic fundamentals described above. A sampling of the more highly visible crises of the past twenty years bears this out.

## The Latin American Debt Crisis

Beginning in the late 1970s, the governments of a number of major Latin American countries (Mexico, Argentina, and Brazil most notably), borrowed billions of U.S. dollars on world markets to finance more rapid economic development in their countries. The debt was acquired primarily through syndicates of banking institutions from around the world, and more than 90 percent of the debt obligations were in U.S. dollars. Many of these countries possessed massive quantities of natural resources and other factors that would aid in rapid development. Their access to more capital was thought to constitute a sound policy for more rapid economic growth. At the same time, slower economic growth among the largest industrial countries produced large quantities of capital that could

# MOODY'S INVESTORS SERVICE RATINGS

http://www.moodys.com/repldata/ratings

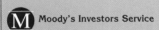

**Moody's Investors Service**

| Moody's | Ratings | Research |
|---------|---------|----------|
| Economics | Data | Directory |

http://www.moodys.com/repldata/ratings

*Ratings* & ratings actions · · · · · · · · · · ·

Rating Actions | Sovereign Ratings | Rating Coverage
How to Use Ratings | Rating Definitions

## Sovereign Ceilings for Foreign-Currency Ratings
*as of Jan 18, 1998, 06:03 EST*

| | Bonds and Notes | | Bank Deposits | |
|---|---|---|---|---|
| | Long-Term | Short-Term[1] | Long-Term | Short-Term[1] |
| Alsderny | Aaa | P-1 | Aaa | P-1 |
| Andorra | Aa2 | P-1 | Aa2 | P-1 |
| Argentina | Ba3 | NP | B1 | NP |
| Australia | Aa2 | P-1 | Aa2 | P-1 |
| Austria | Aaa | P-1 | Aaa | P-1 |
| Bahamas | A3 | P-2 | A3 | P-2 |
| Bahamas - Off Shore Banking Center | Aaa | P-1 | Aaa | P-1 |
| Bahrain | Ba1 | NP | Ba2 | NP |
| Bahrain - Off Shore Banking Center | A3 | P-2 | A3 | P-2 |
| Barbados | Ba1 | NP | Ba2 | NP |
| Belgium | Aa1 | P-1 | Aa1 | P-1 |
| Bermuda | Aa1 | P-1 | Aa1 | P-1 |
| Brazil | B1 | NP | B2 | NP |
| Bulgaria | B2 | NP | B3 | NP |
| Canada | Aa2 | P-1 | Aa2 | P-1 |
| Cayman Islands | Aa3 | P-1 | Aa3 | - |
| Cayman Islands - Off Shore Banking Center | Aaa | P-1 | Aaa | P-1 |
| Chile | Baa1 | P-2 | Baa1 | P-2 |
| China | A3 | P-2 | Baa2 | P-3 |
| Colombia | Baa3 | - | Ba1 | NP |
| Costa Rica | Ba1 | NP | Ba2 | NP |
| Croatia | Baa3 | P-3 | Ba1 | NP |
| Cyprus | A2 | P-1 | A2 | P-1 |
| Czech Republic | Baa1 | P-2 | Baa1 | P-2 |
| Denmark | Aa1 | P-1 | Aa1 | P-1 |
| Dominican Republic | B1 | NP | B2 | NP |
| Ecuador | B1 | NP | B2 | NP |
| Egypt | Ba1 | NP | Ba2 | NP |
| El Salvador | Baa3 | P-3 | Baa3 | P-3 |
| Estonia | Baa1 | P-2 | Baa1 | P-2 |
| Finland | Aa1 | P-1 | Aa1 | P-1 |
| France | Aaa | P-1 | Aaa | P-1 |
| Germany | Aaa | P-1 | Aaa | P-1 |
| Gibraltar | Aaa | P-1 | Aaa | P-1 |
| Greece | Baa1 | P-2 | Baa1 | P-2 |
| Guatemala | Ba2 | NP | Ba3 | NP |
| Guernsey | Aaa | P-1 | Aaa | P-1 |
| Hong Kong | A3 | P-1** | A3 | P-1** |
| Hungary | Baa3 | P-3 | Ba1 | NP |
| Iceland | Aa3 | P-1 | Aa3 | P-1 |
| India | Baa3** | P-3** | Ba1** | NP |
| Indonesia | B2 | NP | Caa1 | NP |
| Ireland | Aa1 | P-1 | Aa1 | P-1 |
| Isle of Man | Aaa | P-1 | Aaa | P-1 |
| Israel | A3 | P-2 | A3 | P-2 |
| Italy | Aa3 | P-1 | Aa3 | P-1 |
| Japan | Aaa | P-1 | Aaa | P-1 |
| Jersey | Aaa | P-1 | Aaa | P-1 |
| Jordan | Ba3 | NP | B1 | NP |
| Kazakstan | Ba3 | NP | B1 | NP |
| Korea | Ba1** | NP | Caa1 | NP |
| Kuwait | Baa1 | P-2 | Baa1 | P-2 |
| Latvia | Baa2 | P-3 | Baa3 | P-3 |
| Lebanon | B1 | NP | B2 | NP |
| Liechtenstein | Aaa | P-1 | Aaa | P-1 |

# MOODY'S
# INVESTORS
# SERVICE
# RATINGS

http://www.moodys.com/repldata/ratings

| | | | | |
|---|---|---|---|---|
| Lithuania | Ba1 | NP | Ba2 | NP |
| Luxembourg | Aaa | P-1 | Aaa | P-1 |
| Macau | Baa1 | P-2 | Baa1 | P-2 |
| Malaysia | A2 | P-2 | Baa1 | P-2 |
| Malta | A2 | P-1 | A2 | P-1 |
| Mauritius | Baa2 | P-2 | Baa2 | P-2 |
| Mexico | Ba2 | NP | B1 | NP |
| Moldova | Ba2 | NP | Ba3 | NP |
| Monaco | Aaa | P-1 | Aaa | P-1 |
| Netherlands | Aaa | P-1 | Aaa | P-1 |
| New Zealand | Aa1 | P-1 | Aa1 | P-1 |
| Norway | Aaa | P-1 | Aaa | P-1 |
| Oman | Baa2 | P-2 | Baa2 | P-2 |
| Pakistan | B2 | NP | B3** | NP |
| Panama | Baa1 | P-2 | Baa2 | P-2 |
| Panama - Off Shore Banking Center | Aa2 | P-1 | Aa2 | P-1 |
| Peru | B2 | NP | B3 | NP |
| Philippines | Ba1 | NP | Ba2 | NP |
| Poland | Baa3 | - | Ba1 | NP |
| Portugal | Aa3 | P-1 | Aa3 | P-1 |
| Qatar | Baa2 | P-2 | Baa2 | P-2 |
| Romania | Ba3 | NP | B1 | NP |
| Russia | Ba2 | NP | Ba3 | NP |
| San Marino | Aa3 | P-1 | Aa3 | P-1 |
| Sark | Aaa | P-1 | Aaa | P-1 |
| Saudi Arabia | Baa3 | P-3 | Baa3 | P-3 |
| Singapore | Aa1 | P-1 | Aa1 | P-1 |
| Slovakia | Baa3 | - | Ba1 | NP |
| Slovenia | A3 | P-2 | A3 | P-2 |
| South Africa | Baa3 | - | Ba1 | NP |
| Spain | Aa2 | P-1 | Aa2 | P-1 |
| Sweden | Aa3 | P-1 | Aa3 | P-1 |
| Switzerland | Aaa | P-1 | Aaa | P-1 |

http://www.moodys.com/repldata/ratings

| | | | | |
|---|---|---|---|---|
| Taiwan | Aa3 | P-1 | Aa3 | P-1 |
| Thailand | Ba1 | NP | B1 | NP |
| Trinidad & Tobago | Ba1 | NP | Ba2 | NP |
| Tunisia | Baa3 | - | Ba1 | NP |
| Turkey | B1 | NP | B2 | NP |
| Turkmenistan | B2 | NP | B3 | NP |
| United Arab Emirates | A2 | P-2 | A2 | P-2 |
| United Kingdom | Aaa | P-1 | Aaa | P-1 |
| United States of America | Aaa | P-1 | Aaa | P-1 |
| Uruguay | Baa3 | P-3 | Baa3 | P-3 |
| Venezuela | Ba2 | NP | Ba3 | NP |
| Vietnam | Ba3 | NP | B1 | NP |

[1]  Commercial Paper of Banks/Bank Holding Companies falls under the bank deposit ceiling.
\*   Under review for possible upgrade.
\*\*  Under review for possible downgrade.

| Moody's | Ratings | Research | Data | Economic | Directory |
|---|---|---|---|---|---|
| | E-Mail | Site Map | Search | Home | |

Please direct *technical comments or questions* to Moody's WebMaster.
This site is designed to accommodate a *wide range of browsers* to ensure broad *compatibility and accessibility*.
© *Copyright* 1998 by Moody's Investors Service, 99 Church Street, New York, NY 10007

not find profitable uses at home, but was anxiously searching new investment opportunities abroad, as those afforded by the Latin American nations.

Ordinarily, the ability of a borrower to repay a domestic loan, regardless of whether the borrower is a firm, a public utility, or even a national government, is dependent on their ability to generate income and sufficient cash flow in the same currency as the borrower's business. But the debt of the Latin American borrowers was in U.S. dollars. The fact is that a country obtains foreign currency only one way—by exporting. When Mexico or Brazil or Argentina exports products to world markets, it can request payment in a currency that is readily convertible on world markets, such as the U.S. dollar, Japanese yen, or German mark. But in order for the country to service rising foreign currency debt burdens, it must not only continue to export, but also refrain from using hard currency earnings for import purchases. Only by running a trade surplus can a country such as Brazil hope to earn the hard currency needed for debt repayment.

Although the Latin American countries had traditionally been strong exporters, the combination of enormous debt burdens with worldwide recession in the early 1980s caused a massive shortfall in earnings. Debt payments came due, and the day came in 1982 when borrowers were unable to repay (for Mexico it actually fell due on Friday August 13). Capital fled their economics, currency values plummeted, and the economy began a spiral downward.

Due to the scale of the problem, both in terms of the magnitude of debt and the number of individual banks and institutions around the world with whom negotiations and debt restructurings needed to take place, the International Monetary Fund took on an increasingly central role in the Latin American debt crisis. In addition to providing much of the bailout lending throughout the 1980s, in many cases the IMF also served as chief negotiator and economic manager. This constituted a sizeable increase in the power and visibility of the IMF, an institution originally formed only to serve as a lender to countries experiencing short-term balance of payments problems (which of course the Latin American countries were experiencing). Only through long years of restructuring, rebalancing, and severe economic sacrifice, were most of the Latin American countries able to recover from the devastation of the debt crisis of 1982.

## The Mexican Peso Devaluation of 1994 and the Tequila Effect

With the passage of the North American Free Trade Agreement (NAFTA) in 1992, the Latin American crisis of the 1980s seemed a thing of the past. Economic growth was strong and stable, and with the establishment of a New Peso on January 1, 1993, Mexico was on its way up. With renewed economic stability and the promise of access to the large consumer markets of the United States and Canada via NAFTA, Mexico enjoyed massive infusions of capital in the early 1990s. As illustrated in Figure 6.4, net portfolio investment rose to more than $27 billion in 1993 (up from a net deficit of $4 billion in 1990), and direct investment ballooned in 1994 to $11 billion.

The infusion of capital into Mexico was the result of two fundamental changes: first, the willingness of the Mexican government and people to open Mexico for foreign investors and foreign ownership; and second, the willingness of foreign investors to put large quantities of capital at risk in a country with a less than sterling investment history. There were early signs of trouble, however, that many multinational companies heeded. First, the magnitude of the capital investment was in the form of portfolio investment, which was predominantly money invested in securities, not in factories, farms, and other fixed

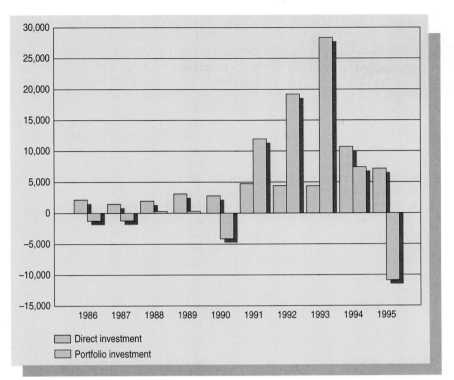

FIGURE

Mexico'

Capital:

versus P

(million

204

assets for long-term economic growth (see Figure 6.4). Secondly, the Mexican current account deficit was expanding rapidly as Mexican consumers, long-term captives of an economy trying to work its way out of the earlier debt crisis, were now able to enjoy the fruits of the world marketplace. The BOP pressures boiled over in December 1994, as the peso was devalued by more than 20 percent overnight to avoid a complete economic collapse. The prosperity of the early 1990s had indeed proven to be too much too soon. Global Perspective 6.4, focuses on possible solutions to the crisis.

One of the most worrisome results of the Mexican peso crisis of 1994 was the way in which international investors fled from markets throughout Latin America, not just those of Mexico. The so-called tequila effect reflected what many consider panic on the part of international investors who saw Mexico as only the first domino in a long series of failures to come. The flight of capital from many of the other Latin countries, though in the long-run not overly destructive, was a cost that many countries continued to pay for past wrongs (previous debt crises) and newfound economic success.

The spring and summer of 1997 brought yet another example of the dangers of rapid economic growth, expanding current account deficits, and the seemingly false security afforded borrowers on international capital markets. Like the Latin American borrowers of the '70s and '80s, the countries of East Asia have enjoyed rapid economic growth and rapid increases in their standards of living for a number of years. And like the Latin American borrowers before them, they were in many ways "blinded . . . to signs of impending crisis" to quote the vignette that opened this chapter.

**The Currency Crisis of 1997 and the Asian Flu**

## SPENDING AT CORE OF MEXICO'S WOES

**W**ashington—Here are answers to some basic questions about the Mexican financial crisis:

Question: How did Mexico get into this mess?

Answer: For years, both the Mexican government and the Mexican people have been spending beyond their means. The country's trade deficit is high, and the government relies too much on money borrowed from foreigners. In December, a renewed peasant uprising in Chiapas state made investors nervous, with the result that they dumped pesos and called in their debts, causing the currency's value to begin dropping on international markets. The government did not have enough foreign currency reserves to buy pesos and halt the decline. It had to call on its allies for help.

Q: So why is this a problem for the United States?

A: Sales of U.S. goods in Mexico could plunge because the prices of our products are soaring there. This could cost thousands of U.S. jobs as exports are slowed. Also, with the peso's value plunging, more U.S. jobs could shift to Mexico because wages and production costs would be lower there. And many U.S. investors who purchased Mexican stocks or mutual funds holding Mexican stocks could lose much of their investments. There also could be political problems in the United States if the peso remained weak, because a sharp rise in illegal immigration would be expected as more and more Mexicans tried to get dollar-paying jobs.

Q: What are we going to do to help?

A: Originally, President Clinton wanted to extend loan guarantees of $40 billion to Mexico, much the same way the government bailed out Chrysler Corp. But Congress refused to support the idea because it would impose too much of a financial risk on U.S. taxpayers. Clinton is bypassing Congress and going straight to the U.S. Treasury, using his executive power to commit $20 billion for emergency assistance to Mexico. This is not foreign aid or a grant. Instead, it is expected to take the form of currency swaps: The Treasury will exchange dollars for pesos with an agreement to swap them back in the future as a way of pumping dollars into Mexican coffers.

Q: How much will this cost U.S. taxpayers?

A: There's no direct cost. But there is a risk for the Treasury, which will be committing billions of its reserves to the proposition that the value of the peso will stabilize.

Q: What about Mexico's other allies?

A: The International Monetary Fund and Bank of International Settlements will kick in $27 billion in loans, while the Bank of Canada will provide a $1 billion line of credit.

Q: What will Mexico do with the money?

A: Investor confidence has been so shaken that Mexico needs to be able to commit billions of dollars to cover all its obligations if bondholders decide to take the money and run. Hopefully, that won't be necessary. But the Mexican government has to be prepared for the worst.

Q: Is this a bailout for Wall Street?

A: Many in Congress think so. But unlike a Mexican debt crisis in 1982, when just a few big commercial banks were holding bad loans, this crisis has many more potential victims, including millions of Americans who have invested money in bond funds for "emerging nations." According to some estimates, U.S. investors hold as much as $100 billion in Mexican stocks and bonds.

Q: Did the North American Free Trade Agreement cause this crisis?

A: Indirectly. During debate over the agreement in 1993, President Clinton and Mexico's then-President Carlos Salinas de Gortari emphasized the progress Mexico had made in opening and reforming its economy, not its shortcomings. Salinas could have taken steps to reduce imports and pay Mexico's soaring foreign debt, but that would have meant higher inflation and a recession.

*Source: Knight-Ridder Tribune,* **The Arizona Republic,** *February 1, 1995, p. A7.*

Table 6.4 illustrates how the current accounts of many of the East Asian nations consistently deteriorated in the early to mid-1990s. Many so-called experts were surprised to find that the very nations that are so often admired for their ability to export and penetrate other-country markets were themselves building larger and larger trade deficits and financing it though borrowing on international markets. In fact, through 1995, the financial account surpluses were more than enough to sustain the current account deficits. Many firms in Thailand, Indonesia, Malaysia, and the Philippines had grown so used to sta-

**TABLE 6.4**

**The Asian Flu: Current Account Trends in East Asia, 1988–96 (millions in U.S. dollars)**

| Country | 1988 | 1989 | 1990 | 1991 | 1992 | 1993 | 1994 | 1995 |
|---|---|---|---|---|---|---|---|---|
| **Deficit Countries** | | | | | | | | |
| Indonesia | −1,397 | −1,108 | −2,988 | −4,260 | −2,780 | −2,106 | −2,792 | −7,023 |
| Korea | 14,538 | 5,387 | −1,745 | −8,291 | −3,939 | 1,016 | −3,855 | −8,251 |
| Malaysia | 1,867 | 315 | −870 | −4,183 | −2,167 | −2,809 | −4,147 | −5,000 |
| Philippines | −390 | −1,456 | −2,695 | −1,034 | −1,000 | −3,016 | −2,950 | −1,980 |
| Thailand | −1,654 | −2,498 | −7,281 | −7,571 | −6,303 | −6,364 | −8,085 | −13,554 |
| Subtotal | 12,964 | 640 | −15,579 | −25,339 | −16,189 | −13,279 | −21,829 | −35,808 |
| **Surplus Countries** | | | | | | | | |
| China | −3,802 | −4,317 | 11,997 | 13,272 | 6,401 | −11,609 | 6,908 | 1,618 |
| Singapore | 1,882 | 2,923 | 3,097 | 4,884 | 5,615 | 4,205 | 11,284 | 15,093 |
| Subtotal | −1,920 | −1,394 | 15,094 | 18,156 | 12,016 | −7,404 | 18,192 | 16,711 |

*Source:* Data abstracted from the IMF's *Balance of Payments Statistics Yearbook,* 1996. Hong Kong and Taiwan are not listed, as they are not current standing separate members of the IMF.

ble exchange rates that rarely varied in value against the U.S. dollar, they no longer differentiated in their minds or their balances sheets as to whether the capital they borrowed was baht or rupiah or ringgit or U.S. dollars; they were increasingly seen as one and the same. They were not. As in the case of Mexico a mere three years previous, the financial and economic repercussions of this crisis continue to flow across East Asia. This *Asian flu,* will take years to resolve. For now, regional governments work tirelessly with the IMF to reestablish access to badly-needed sources of capital to lubricate the engines of East Asia's economies. Global Perspective 6.5 comments on the predictability of the Asian crisis, and the credit study of these countries after the fact (January 1998).

## Summary

The balance of payments is the summary statement of all international transactions between one country and all other countries. The balance of payments is a flow statement, summarizing all the international transactions that occur across the geographic boundaries of the nation over a period of time, typically a year. Because of its use of double-entry bookkeeping, the BOP must always balance in theory, though in practice there are substantial imbalances as a result of statistical errors and misreporting of current account and capital account flows.

The two major subaccounts of the balance of payments, the current account and the capital account, summarize the current trade and international capital flows of the country. Due to the double-entry bookkeeping method of accounting, the current account and capital account are always inverse on balance, one in surplus while the other experiences deficit. Although most nations strive for current account surpluses, it is not clear that a balance on current or capital account, or a surplus on current account, is either sustainable or desirable. The monitoring of the various subaccounts of a country's balance

## IMF BAIL OUTS: TRUTH AND FICTION

IMF assistance to Korea, Indonesia, and Thailand has been criticized for "bailing out" specific groups—such as commercial banks and private investors—at the expense of other, less favored groups and taxpayers. In fact, IMF assistance has been provided in support of programs that are designed to deal with the causes and consequences of economy-wide, structural imbalances and the potential threats these imbalances pose to the international monetary system. Under the conditions of these programs, commercial banks and private investors are not being protected from financial losses, as outlined below.

Equity holders and owners of other publicly traded instruments have suffered losses. In U.S. dollar terms, as of December 17, 1997:

- Korea's stock market had declined 67 percent since August 11
- Indonesia's stock market had declined 75 percent since July 30
- Thailand's stock market had declined 63 percent since July 29

There are no provisions in IMF-supported programs for public sector guarantees, subsidies, or support for *nonfinancial* institutions that are facing financial difficulties and may be forced into bankruptcy. When *financial* sectors are restructured, shareholders and, as far as possible, also creditors of *insolvent* institutions should bear the losses they would have sustained in the context of liquidations under bankruptcy procedures. Under the programs:

- No liquidity support is to be given to insolvent institutions.
- No special treatment is provided for shareholders of institutions that have lost their capital—any payments they receive will be in strict conformity with applicable laws.
- In cases where national authorities had granted guarantees to certain categories of depositors or creditors prior to entering into policy negotiations with the IMF, the authorities must ensure that any likely recourse to official support can be met while still achieving a sustainable fiscal position in the medium term.

Liquidity support may be provided to financial institutions that are undercapitalized but *solvent.* However, under the programs:

- Such support is conditional upon the institutions being recapitalized and undertaking incisive restructuring programs to restore them to full financial health.
- Whenever public resources are used to support the restructuring of institutions whose operations have been suspended or placed under conservatorship, previous owners should be removed (through writing down their equity) and management replaced.
- The potential cost of liquidity support to the public purse should be minimized through measures that (a) improve the institution's financial health (and thereby their capacity to repay liquidity support) and (b) strengthen the economy so that creditors have much less reason to wish to unwind their exposures.

*Source:* **http://www.imf.org/**, *January 1998.*

of payments activity is helpful to decision makers and policymakers at all levels of government and industry in detecting the underlying trends and movements of fundamental economic forces driving a country's international economic activity.

## Key Terms and Concepts

- balance of payments
- current account
- capital account
- double-entry bookkeeping
- goods trade
- service trade

- investment income
- current transfer
- direct investment account
- portfolio investment account
- control

- profit
- net errors and omissions account
- official reserves account
- official settlements balance
- floating exchange rate
- fixed exchange rate

## Questions for Discussion

1. Why must a country's balance of payments always be balanced in theory?
✓2. What is the difference between the merchandise trade balance (BOT) and the current account balance?
3. What is service trade?
4. Why is foreign direct investment so much more controversial than foreign portfolio investment? How does this relate to Mexico in the 1990s?
5. Should the fact that the United States may by the world's largest net debtor nation be a source of concern for government policymakers? Is the United States like Finland?
6. While the United States "suffered" a current account deficit and a capital account surplus in the 1980s, what were the respective balances of Japan doing?
7. What does it mean for the United States to be one of the world's largest indebted countries?
8. How do exchange rate changes alter trade so that the trade balance actually improves when the domestic currency depreciates?
9. How have trade balances in Asia contributed to the cause of the current Asian crisis?
10. The IMF, World Bank, and United Nations are only a few of the major world organizations that track, report, and aid international economic and financial development. Using these web sites and others that may be linked to them, briefly summarize the economic outlook for the developed and emerging nations of the world. For example, the full text of chapter 1 of the *World Economic Outlook* published annually by the World Bank is available through the IMF's web page.

**WWW**

| International Monetary Fund | **http://www.imf.org/** |
| United Nations | **http://www.unsystem.org/** |
| The World Bank Group | **http://www.worldbank.org/** |
| Europa (EU) Homepage | **http://europa.eu.int/** |
| Bank for International Settlements | **http://www.bis.org/** |

11. Current economic and financial statistics and commentaries are available via the IMF's web page under "What's New," "Fund Rates," and the "IMF Committee on Balance of Payments Statistics." For an in-depth examination of the IMF's ongoing initiative on the validity of these statistics, termed metadata, visit the IMF's Dissemination Standards Bulletin Board listed below.

| International Monetary Fund | **http://www.imf.org/** |
| IMF's Dissemination Standards Bulletin Board | **http://dsbb.imf.org/** |

12. Visit Moody's sovereign ceilings and foreign currency ratings service site on the web to evaluate what progress is being made in the nations of the Far East on recovering their perceived creditworthiness.

| Moody's Sovereign Ceilings | **http://www.moodys.com/repldata/ratings/ratsov.htm** |

## Recommended Readings

Agenor, Pierre-Richard, Jagdeep S. Bhandari, and Robert P. Flood. Speculative Attacks and Models of Balance of Payments Crises. *International Monetary Fund Staff Papers*, 39, 2 (June 1992) 357–394.

Bergsten, C. Fred, ed. *International Adjustment and Financing: The Lessons of 1985–1991*. Washington, D.C.: Institute for International Economics, 1991.

Eiteman, David K., Arthur I. Stonehill, and Michael H. Moffet. *Multinational Business Finance*. 8th ed. Reading, Mass.: Addison Wesley Longman, 1998.

Evans, John S. *International Finance: A Markets Approach*. New York: Dryden Press, 1992.

Eun, Cheol S., and Bruce G. Resnick. *International Financial Management*. Boston, Mass.: Irwin McGraw-Hill, 1998.

Giddy, Ian H. *Global Financial Markets*. Lexington, Mass.: Elsevier, 1994.

Grabbe, J. Orlin. *International Financial Markets*. 2d edition. New York: Elsevier, 1991.

*Handbook of International Trade and Development Statistics*, New York: United Nations, 1989.

Husted, Steven, and Michael Melvin. *International Economics*. 4th ed. Reading, Mass.: Addison Wesley Longman, 1997.

*IMF Balance of Payments Yearbook*, Washington, D.C.: International Monetary Fund, annually.

Root, Franklin R. *International Trade and Investment*. 6th ed. Chicago: South-Western Publishing, 1990.

*62nd Annual Report*. Basle, Switzerland: Bank for International Settlements, June 15, 1992.

## Notes

1. The official terminology used throughout this chapter, unless otherwise noted, is that of the International Monetary Fund (IMF). Since the IMF is the primary source of similar statistics for balance of payments and economic performance worldwide, it is more general than other terminology forms, such as that employed by the U.S. Department of Commerce.

2. All balance of payment data used in this chapter is drawn from the International Monetary Fund's *Balance of Payments Statistics Yearbook*. This source is used because the IMF presents the balance of payments statistics for all member countries on the same basis and in the same format, allowing comparison across countries. The U.S. Department of Commerce also publishes the balance of payments and other international transaction statistics for the United States alone in the *Survey of Current Business*. Unfortunately, the U.S. Department of Commerce uses a different organization for the various subaccounts than that used by the IMF. Also—unfortunately—the U.S. Department of Commerce is much quicker in its publication of statistics (for the United States alone) than the IMF is (for the hundreds of member countries). When this book went to press in September 1998, the most recent *Balance of Payments Statistics Yearbook* had been published in December 1996 and included data ending 1995.

   This results in a dilemma for textbook authors: to use the most recent data for whichever country is the subject of discussion from whatever sources, or to use a single consistent source across all countries. We have chosen to stay with the single source, the IMF, and risk appearing one year out of data statistically on publication. For the purposes of edification and consistency, we feel the IMF's balance of payments statistics are preferable. For those readers interested in the most recent data for any specific country, the central bank bulletin of most countries reports balance of payments statistics typically four to six months previous to those of the IMF. But, the reader must also be forewarned of the varying formats of statistical presentation.

# Music: America's Booming Export

International trade is imperative in today's world because the global nature of the economy makes economic isolationism impossible. Failure to participate successfully in the global market will reduce a nation's economic influence and standard of living. Full participation can improve the quality of life.

While U.S. exports have not dropped in recent years, U.S. export growth has not kept pace with the total growth of world exports. Firms in economies torn by World War II have reestablished themselves and have obtained a share of the growing world trade for themselves.

Not all news about the U.S. trade position is bad news. An exception to the reduction in demand for American automobiles, steel, and television sets is the world's insatiable appetite for American entertainment. Some estimate that it is the country's second-largest export behind aircraft, but ahead of such staples as soybeans and coal.

Foreign sales account for two-thirds of the music market, and there is plenty of room for growth. Deregulation of broadcasting in Europe and around the world is expected to open up new outlets for music to air, and, presumably, young consumers will rush to the nearest record store with open wallets.

The industry is particularly interested in the former Soviet Union and China. Michael Jackson's album *Bad* sold half a million albums in China, a figure that looks very attractive to the music industry. The head of a major record company was asked why recorded American music sells so well. "If you had an on-street interview any place in the world, and you asked the kid or the twenty-five-year-

old to name the first ten artists that come to mind, I think that at least six of those ten are going to be artists that had their beginnings in the United States," said Robert Summer, president of CBS Records International.

This broad appeal is not just for consumption. It is also attracting foreign companies to purchase U.S. record companies. Bertelsmann, a giant German conglomerate, owns RCA Records. Sony paid $2 billion for CBS Records. Thorn-EMI, which owns Capital Records, is British, and so is Polygram. Only two of the six major record companies are U.S.-owned, MCA and Warner. And while the music industry searches out its next batch of superstars, some worry that those stars and the companies that earn money for them will be foreign. Entertainment executives were asked: Will the United States let this business slip offshore as so many other businesses have or is there something uniquely American about this product that will preclude limitations?

"I don't think the creative edge is going to be taken over until our cultural appeal worldwide is superseded," commented Sam Holdsworth, president of Billboard Entertainment Group.

Robert Huziak, president of RCA records, added, "I don't think that the United States will ever be without that creative motivation for the young people and hence we will always be able to continue to grow."

Joe Smith, president of Capital-EMI Music, was more pessimistic. He predicted a wave of Russian rock and roll to surface sometime before the end of this century. "Then those guys that make these VCRs and the television sets are soon going to turn creative, and one day somebody in China is going to say 'let's rock'n roll too.' I don't believe we can keep the edge unless we continue to develop our talent and do it," he said. "And that's my concern about the corporatization of rock and roll."

When asked whether the purchase of American record companies by Japanese and German firms will have an impact on the quality of the product, Smith said it depends on the dedication of the companies. "It won't have a great impact on our music unless they squeeze down on us and say, 'Well, don't sign so many new acts next year.' You only keep the edge by signing new talent, by mining what is the best in the country," said Smith. "In

SOURCE: This case was drawn from the Public Broadcasting System's television program Adam Smith, which aired on March 10, 1989. Producer: Alvin H. Perlmutter, Inc.

this country, a combination of blues and country and rock and roll got started here. We've still got the edge, but we can lose it because all that is very copyable."

"Somebody just with a headset and a CD can pick up every riff that Chuck Berry ever played or Joe Walsh, or Clapton," Smith said. "They can pick all that stuff up very quickly."

## Questions for Discussion

1. How can the world demand for U.S.-produced entertainment, particularly in the music industry, have an effect on a macroeconomic level? On a microeconomic level? In your answer, define these two terms.
2. Explain the concept of "global linkages." Describe linkages that could be tied to the music industry on an international basis.
3. Should the United States be concerned about an increasing foreign presence within the American music industry? Why or why not? Will it affect the quality of the product? Explain.
4. What changes have occurred in the U.S. music industry since this PBS program was aired?

# One Afternoon at the United States International Trade Commission

*Chairwoman Stern:* We turn now to investigation TA–201–55 regarding nonrubber footwear. Staff has assembled. Are there any questions? Vice Chairman Liebeler has a question. Please proceed.

*Vice Chairman Liebeler:* My questions are for the Office of Economics, Mr. Benedick. Do foreign countries have a comparative advantage in producing footwear?

*Mr. Benedick:* Yes, foreign producers generally have a comparative advantage vis-à-vis the domestic producers in producing footwear. Footwear production generally involves labor-intensive processes which favor the low-wage countries such as Taiwan, Korea, and Brazil, which are the three largest foreign suppliers by volume. For in-

SOURCE: Official Transcript Proceedings before the U.S. International Trade Commission, *meeting of the Commission, June 12, 1985, Washington, D.C.*

stance, the hourly rate for foreign footwear workers in these countries ranges from about one-twelfth to one-fourth of the rate for U.S. footwear workers.

*Vice Chairman Liebeler:* Is it likely that this comparative advantage will shift in favor of the domestic industries over the next several years?

*Mr. Benedick:* It is not very likely. There seems to be little evidence that supports this. The domestic industry's generally poor productivity performance over the last several years, which includes the period 1977 to 1981, roughly corresponding to the period of OMAs (Orderly Marketing Arrangements) for Taiwan and Korea, suggests that U.S. producers must significantly increase their modernization efforts to reduce the competitive advantage of the imported footwear.

*Vice Chairman Liebeler:* Have you calculated the benefits and costs of import relief using various assumptions about the responsiveness of supply and demand to changes in price?

*Mr. Benedick:* Yes. On the benefit side, we estimated benefits of import restrictions to U.S. producers, which included both increased domestic production and higher domestic prices. We also estimated the terms of trade benefits resulting from import restrictions. These latter benefits result from an appreciation of the U.S. dollar as a result of the import restrictions.

On the cost side, we estimated cost to consumers of the increase in average prices on total footwear purchases under the import restrictions and the consumer costs associated with the drop in total consumption due to the higher prices.

*Vice Chairman Liebeler:* In your work, did you take into account any retaliation by our trading partners?

*Mr. Benedick:* No.

*Vice Chairman Liebeler:* What was the 1984 level of imports?

*Mr. Benedick:* In 1984, imports of nonrubber footwear were approximately 726 million pairs.

*Vice Chairman Liebeler:* If a 600 million pair quota were imposed, what would the effect on price of domestic and foreign shoes be, and what would the market share of imports be?

*Mr. Benedick:* At your request, the Office of Economics estimated the effects of the 600 million pair quota. We estimate that prices of domestic footwear would increase by about 11 percent, and prices of imported footwear would increase by about 19 percent.

The import share, however, would drop to about 59 percent of the market in the first year of the quota.

*Vice Chairman Liebeler:* What would aggregate cost to consumers be of that kind of quota?

*Mr. Benedick:* Total consumer cost would approach 1.3 billion dollars in each year of such a quota.

*Vice Chairman Liebeler:* What would be the benefit to the domestic industry of this quota?

*Mr. Benedick:* Domestic footwear production would increase from about 299 million pairs for 1984, to about 367 million pairs, or by about 23 percent. Domestic sales would increase from about $3.8 billion to about $5.2 billion, an increase of about 37 percent.

*Vice Chairman Liebeler:* How many jobs would be saved?

*Mr. Benedick:* As a result of this quota, domestic employment would rise by about 26,000 workers over the 1984 level.

*Vice Chairman Liebeler:* What is the average paid to those workers?

*Mr. Benedick:* Based on questionnaire responses, each worker would earn approximately $11,900 per year in wages and another $2,100 in fringe benefits, for a total of about $14,000 per year.

*Vice Chairman Liebeler:* So what then would be the cost to consumers of each of these $14,000-a-year jobs?

*Mr. Benedick:* It would cost consumers approximately $49,800 annually for each of these jobs.

*Vice Chairman Liebeler:* Thank you very much, Mr. Benedick.

*Commissioner Eckes:* I have a question for the General Counsel's representative. I heard an interesting phrase a few moments ago, "comparative advantage." I don't recall seeing that phrase in Section 201. Could you tell me whether it is there and whether it is defined?

*Ms. Jacobs.* It is not.

*Chairwoman Stern:* I would like to ask about cost/benefit analysis. Perhaps the General Counsel's Office again might be the best place to direct this question. It is my understanding that the purpose of Section 201 is to determine whether a domestic industry is being injured, the requisite level for requisite reasons, imports being at least as important a cause of the serious injury as any other cause, and then to recommend a remedy which we are given kind of a short menu to select from to remedy the industry's serious injury.

Are we to take into account the impact on the consumer?

Are we to do a cost/benefit analysis when coming up with the remedy which best relieves the domestic industry's serious injury?

*Ms. Jacobs:* As the law currently stands, it is the responsibility of the commission to determine that relief which is a duty or import restriction which is necessary to prevent or remedy the injury that the commission has determined to exist. The president is to weigh such considerations as consumer impact, etc. The commission is not necessarily responsible for doing that. Of course, the commission may want to realize that, knowing the president is going to consider those factors, they might want to also consider them, but in fact, that it is not the responsibility of the commission. It is the responsibility of the commission only to determine that relief which is necessary to remedy the injury they have found.

*Chairwoman Stern:* I can understand our reporting to the president other materials which aren't part of our consideration, but nevertheless necessary for the president in his consideration, but having that information and providing it to the president is different from its being part of the commission's consideration in its recommendations.

*Ms. Jacobs:* That's right. Your roles are quite different in that respect.

*Vice Chairman Liebeler:* Nations will and should specialize in production of those commodities in which they have a comparative advantage. Fortunately, our country has a large capital stock which tends to provide labor with many productive employments. Our comparative advantage is in the production of goods that use a high ratio of capital to labor. Shoes, however, are produced with a low ratio of capital to labor.

Therefore, American footwear cannot be produced as cheaply as foreign footwear. The availability of inexpensive imports permits consumers to purchase less expensive shoes and it allows the valuable capital and labor used in this footwear industry to shift to more productive pursuits.

This situation is not unique to the footwear industry. The classic example is agriculture, where the share of the labor force engaged in farming declined from 50 percent to 3 percent over the last 100 years. This shift did not produce a 47 percent unemployment rate. It freed that labor to produce cars, housing, and computers.

The decline of the American footwear industry is part of this dynamic process. This process is sometimes very painful. Congress, by only providing for temporary relief, has recognized that our continued prosperity depends on our willingness to accept such adjustments.

The industry has sought this so-called "temporary import relief" before. The ITC has conducted approximately 170 investigations relating to this industry. This is the fourth footwear case under Section 201, and so far the industry has gotten relief twice. The 1975 petition resulted in adjustment assistance. The 1976 case resulted in orderly marketing agreements with Taiwan and Korea.

In spite of the efforts of the domestic industry to suppress imports, the industry has been shrinking. Between 1981 and 1984, 207 plants closed; 94 of these closings occurred just last year. The closing of unprofitable plants is a necessary adjustment. Import relief at this stage will retard this process and encourage entry into a dying industry.

Because there is no temporary trade restriction that would facilitate the industry's adjustment in foreign competition, I cannot recommend any import barrier.

*Chairwoman Stern:* The intent of the General Import Relief law is to allow a seriously injured industry to adjust to global competition. The commission must devise a remedy which corresponds to the industry and the market forces it must face.

No other manufacturing sector of our economy faces stiffer competition from abroad than the U.S. shoe industry. Imports have captured three-fourths of our market. No relief program can change the basic conditions of competition that this industry must ultimately face on its own. The best that we as a commission can do—and under Section 201 that the president can do—is to give the industry a short, predictable period of relief to allow both large and small firms to adjust, coexist, and hopefully prosper.

I am proposing to the president an overall quota on imports of 474 million pairs of shoes in the first year. Shoes with a customs value below $2.50 would not be subject to this quota. The relief would extend for a full five years.

*Commissioner Lodwick:* Section 201 is designed to afford the domestic industry a temporary respite in order to assist it in making an orderly adjustment to import competition. The fact that the law limits import relief to an initial period of up to five years, to be phased down after three years to the extent feasible, indicates that Congress did not intend domestic producers to find permanent shelter from import competition under the statute.

Accordingly, I intend to recommend to the president a five-year quota plan which affords the domestic non-rubber footwear industry ample opportunity to implement feasible adjustment plans which will facilitate, as the case may be, either the orderly transfer of resources to alternative uses or adjustments to new conditions of competition.

*Commissioner Rohr:* In making my recommendation, I emphasize the two responsibilities which are placed on the commission by statute. First, it must provide a remedy which it believes will effectively remedy the injury which is found to exist.

Secondly, Congress has stated that we, as commissioners, should attempt, to the extent possible, to develop a remedy that can be recommended to the president by a majority of the commission. I have taken seriously my obligations to attempt to fashion a remedy with which at least a majority of my colleagues can agree. Such remedy is a compromise.

I am concurring in the remedy proposal which is being presented today by a majority of the commission. This majority recommendation provides for an overall limit on imports of 474 million pairs; an exclusion from such limitation of shoes entering the United States with a value of less than $2.50 per pair; a growth in such limitation over a five-year period of 0 percent, 3 percent, and 9 percent; and the sale of import licenses through an auctioning system.

*Commissioner Eckes:* It is my understanding that a majority of the commission has agreed on these points. I subscribe to that and will provide a complete description of my views in my report to the president.

## Questions for Discussion

1. What are your views of the ITC recommendation?
2. Should the principle of comparative advantage always dictate trade flows?
3. Why are the consumer costs of quotas so often neglected?
4. Discuss alternative solutions to the job displacement problem.
5. How would you structure a "temporary relief program"?

# THE INTERNATIONAL BUSINESS ENVIRONMENT

## PART 3

O perating internationally requires managers to be aware of a highly complex environment. Domestic and international environmental factors and their interaction have to be recognized and understood. In addition, ongoing changes in these environments have to be appreciated.

Part 3 delineates the macroenvironmental factors and institutions affecting international business. It explains the workings of the international monetary system and financial markets and highlights the increasing trend toward economic integration around the world. This section concludes with a chapter on doing business in emerging markets. Particular focus rests on the new market orientation of nations whose economies used to be centrally planned, such as the former Soviet Union.

# CHAPTER 7

# International Financial Markets

### LEARNING OBJECTIVES

◆ *To understand how currencies are traded and quoted on world financial markets*

◆ *To examine the linkages between interest rates and exchange rates*

◆ *To understand the similarities and differences between domestic sources of capital and international sources of capital*

◆ *To examine how the needs of individual borrowers have changed the nature of the instruments traded on world financial markets in the past decade*

◆ *To understand how the debt crises of the 1980s and 1990s are linked to the international financial markets and exchange rates*

## Finance officials trade insults in Hong Kong

**H**ONG KONG—At this kind of meeting, people don't usually get hot under their starched collars. And they certainly don't call each other names in public.

But at the annual World Bank conference over the weekend, two men on opposite sides of the region's economic crisis—the speculator vs. the states-man—had a showdown, firing off words like "moron" and "menace."

"It's *High Noon* in Hong Kong," a World Bank official said.

George Soros, an American financier who once made $1 billion in a day betting against the British pound, has drawn the ire of Malaysian Prime Minister Mahathir Mohammed after his speculative attack on weak currencies in Southeast Asia.

Suddenly, the central bankers' main theme this week has become how to stop the meltdown of the Asian miracle.

Mahathir, 71, who has overseen Malaysia's growth during his 16-year rule, charged that Soros aimed to stop the fast-growing region in its tracks.

"All these countries have spent 40 years trying to build up their economies," Mahathir said before the conference, "and a moron like Soros comes along with a lot of money" and undermines them.

Since July, Malaysia's ringgit has lost 20 percent of its value. Although experts say the country's economic policies invited such a correction, the prime minister said Malaysia is the victim of a costly game.

"Currency trading," Mahathir declared in a speech Saturday evening, "is unnecessary, unproductive and immoral. . . . It should be illegal."

Soros denied that his hedge fund, the $9.1 billion Quantum Fund, had a role in devaluing the ringgit; in his own speech, he said that, ironically, it was buying Malaysian currency during the crash that helped buffer the impact. Mahathir, he said, was using him "as a scapegoat for his own mistakes."

"Dr. Mahathir," Soros added, "is a menace to his own country."

*Source:* Maggie Farley, *Los Angeles Times*

International financial markets serve as links between the financial markets of each individual country and as independent markets outside the jurisdiction of any one country. The market for currencies is the heart of this international financial market. International trade and investment are often denominated in a foreign currency, so the purchase of the currency precedes the purchase of goods, services, or assets.

This chapter provides a detailed guide to the structure and functions of the foreign currency markets, the international money markets, and the international securities markets. All firms striving to attain or preserve competitiveness will need to work with and within these international financial markets in the 1990s.

## The Market for Currencies

The price of any one country's currency in terms of another country's currency is called a foreign currency exchange rate. For example, the exchange rate between the U.S. dollar (USD) and the German mark (deutschemark, or DEM) may be "1.5 marks per dollar," or simply abbreviated DEM 1.5000/USD. This is the same exchange rate as when stated USD 1.00 = DEM 1.50. Since most international business activities require at least one of the two parties to first purchase the country's currency before purchasing any good, service, or asset, a proper understanding of exchange rates and exchange rate markets is very important to the conduct of international business.

A word on symbols. As already noted, the symbols USD and DEM are often used as the symbols for the U.S. dollar and the German mark. The field of international finance suffers, however, from a lack of agreement when it comes to currency abbreviations. This chapter will use the computer symbols used by the Telerate news service for the sake of consistency (although any other set would work just as well). As a practitioner of international finance, as with all fields, stay on your toes. Every market, every country, every firm, has its own set of symbols. For example, the symbol for the British pound sterling can be £ (the pound symbol), GBP (Great Britain pound), STG (sterling), or UKL (United Kingdom pound).

### Exchange Rate Quotations and Terminology

The order in which the foreign exchange (FX) rate is stated is sometimes confusing to the uninitiated. For example, when the rate between the U.S. dollar and the German mark was stated above, a **direct quotation** on the German mark was used. This is simultaneously an **indirect quotation** on the U.S. dollar. The direct quote on any currency is the form when that currency is stated first; an indirect quotation refers to when the subject currency is stated second. Figure 7.1 illustrates both forms, direct and indirect quotations, for major world currencies for Friday December 19, 1997. The daily currency quotations from *The Wall Street Journal* are the most commonly seen set of exchange rate quotations in use today.

Most of the quotations listed in Figure 7.1 are **spot rates.** A spot transaction is the exchange of currencies for immediate delivery. Although it is defined as immediate, in actual practice settlement actually occurs two business days following the agreed-upon exchange. The other time-related quotations listed in Figure 7.1 are the **forward rates.** Forward exchange rates are contracts that provide for two parties to exchange currencies on a future date at an agreed-upon exchange rate. Forwards are typically traded for the major volume currencies for maturities of 30, 90, 120, 180, and 360 days (from the present date). The forward, like the basic spot exchange, can be for any amount of currency. Forward contracts serve a variety of purposes, but their primary purpose is to allow a firm to lock in a future rate of exchange. This is a valuable tool in a world of continually changing exchange rates.

# CURRENCY TRADING

## EXCHANGE RATES

Friday, December 19, 1997

The New York foreign exchange selling rates below apply to trading among banks in amounts of $1 million and more, as quoted at 4 p.m. Eastern time by Dow Jones and other sources. Retail transactions provide fewer units of foreign currency per dollar.

| Country | U.S. $ equiv. Fri | U.S. $ equiv. Thu | Currency per U.S. $ Fri | Currency per U.S. $ Thu |
|---|---|---|---|---|
| Argentina (Peso) | 1.0001 | 1.0005 | .9999 | .9995 |
| Australia (Dollar) | .6530 | .6514 | 1.5314 | 1.5352 |
| Austria (Schilling) | .08024 | .08017 | 12.462 | 12.474 |
| Bahrain (Dinar) | 2.6525 | 2.6525 | .3770 | .3770 |
| Belgium (Franc) | .02736 | .02723 | 36.550 | 36.720 |
| Brazil (Real) | .8980 | .8986 | 1.1136 | 1.1129 |
| Britain (Pound) | 1.6700 | 1.6663 | .5988 | .6001 |
| 1-month forward | 1.6679 | 1.6642 | .5996 | .6009 |
| 3-months forward | 1.6630 | 1.6593 | .6013 | .6027 |
| 6-months forward | 1.6560 | 1.6522 | .6039 | .6053 |
| Canada (Dollar) | .6988 | .7012 | 1.4311 | 1.4262 |
| 1-month forward | .6995 | .7020 | 1.4295 | 1.4246 |
| 3-months forward | .7005 | .7029 | 1.4276 | 1.4227 |
| 6-months forward | .7013 | .7035 | 1.4259 | 1.4214 |
| Chile (Peso) | .002277 | .002282 | 439.15 | 438.25 |
| China (Renminbi) | .1203 | .1203 | 8.3100 | 8.3100 |
| Colombia (Peso) | .0007704 | .0007772 | 1298.00 | 1286.74 |
| Czech. Rep. (Koruna) | | | | |
| Commercial rate | .02936 | .02921 | 34.057 | 34.238 |
| Denmark (Krone) | .1480 | .1479 | 6.7555 | 6.7615 |
| Ecuador (Sucre) | | | | |
| Floating rate | .0002283 | .0002283 | 4380.00 | 4380.00 |
| Finland (Markka) | .1870 | .1865 | 5.3462 | 5.3629 |
| France (Franc) | .1681 | .1682 | 5.9485 | 5.9450 |
| 1-month forward | .1684 | .1685 | 5.9365 | 5.9330 |
| 3-months forward | .1690 | .1691 | 5.9168 | 5.9130 |
| 6-months forward | .1699 | .1700 | 5.8868 | 5.8832 |
| Germany (Mark) | .5632 | .5635 | 1.7755 | 1.7745 |
| 1-month forward | .5643 | .5646 | 1.7721 | 1.7712 |
| 3-months forward | .5662 | .5665 | 1.7662 | 1.7651 |
| 6-months forward | .5691 | .5693 | 1.7573 | 1.7565 |
| Greece (Drachma) | .003577 | .003578 | 279.60 | 279.47 |
| Hong Kong (Dollar) | .1290 | .1290 | 7.7500 | 7.7490 |
| Hungary (Forint) | .004976 | .004961 | 200.97 | 201.56 |
| India (Rupee) | .02544 | .02546 | 39.310 | 39.275 |
| Indonesia (Rupiah) | .0001961 | .0001934 | 5100.00 | 5170.00 |
| Ireland (Punt) | 1.4579 | 1.4552 | .6859 | .6872 |
| Israel (Shekel) | .2827 | .2829 | 3.5371 | 3.5347 |
| Italy (Lira) | .0005741 | .0005737 | 1742.00 | 1743.00 |
| Japan (Yen) | .007732 | .007768 | 129.33 | 128.73 |
| 1-month forward | .007771 | .007807 | 128.68 | 128.09 |
| 3-months forward | .007838 | .007875 | 127.59 | 126.99 |
| 6-months forward | .007947 | .007986 | 125.83 | 125.23 |
| Jordan (Dinar) | 1.4134 | 1.4134 | .7075 | .7075 |
| Kuwait (Dinar) | 3.2830 | 3.2841 | .3046 | .3045 |
| Lebanon (Pound) | .0006547 | .0006547 | 1527.50 | 1527.50 |
| Malaysia (Ringgit) | .2621 | .2642 | 3.8153 | 3.7853 |
| Malta (Lira) | 2.5608 | 2.5575 | .3905 | .3910 |
| Mexico (Peso) | | | | |
| Floating rate | .1233 | .1238 | 8.1130 | 8.0750 |
| Netherland (Guilder) | .4994 | .5001 | 2.0026 | 1.9998 |
| New Zealand (Dollar) | .5820 | .5796 | 1.7182 | 1.7253 |
| Norway (Krone) | .1373 | .1380 | 7.2843 | 7.2473 |
| Pakistan (Rupee) | .02296 | .02296 | 43.560 | 43.560 |
| Peru (new Sol) | .3710 | .3713 | 2.6955 | 2.6935 |
| Philippines (Peso) | .02522 | .02469 | 39.650 | 40.500 |
| Poland (Zloty) | .2855 | .2854 | 3.5030 | 3.5033 |
| Portugal (Escudo) | .005503 | .005510 | 181.72 | 181.48 |
| Russia (Ruble) (a) | .0001682 | .0001683 | 5945.00 | 5943.00 |
| Saudi Arabia (Riyal) | .2666 | .2666 | 3.7505 | 3.7506 |
| Singapore (Dollar) | .5979 | .5974 | 1.6725 | 1.6740 |
| Slovak Rep. (Koruna) | .02916 | .02907 | 34.294 | 34.396 |
| South Africa (Rand) | .2058 | .2058 | 4.8600 | 4.8595 |
| South Korea (Won) | .0006452 | .0006754 | 1550.00 | 1480.50 |
| Spain (Peseta) | .006645 | .006658 | 150.48 | 150.20 |
| Sweden (Krona) | .1289 | .1286 | 7.7575 | 7.7754 |
| Switzerland (Franc) | .6969 | .6957 | 1.4350 | 1.4375 |
| 1-month forward | .6995 | .6983 | 1.4295 | 1.4320 |
| 3-months forward | .7043 | .7030 | 1.4199 | 1.4224 |
| 6-months forward | .7116 | .7102 | 1.4053 | 1.4080 |
| Taiwan (Dollar) | .03095 | .03106 | 32.311 | 32.200 |
| Thailand (Baht) | .02230 | .02265 | 44.850 | 44.150 |
| Turkey (Lira) | .00000498 | .00000499 | 200725.00 | 200550.00 |
| United Arab (Dirham) | .2723 | .2723 | 3.6725 | 3.6725 |
| Uruguay (New Peso) | | | | |
| Financial | .1002 | .1002 | 9.9800 | 9.9800 |
| Venezuela (Bolivar) | .001988 | .001990 | 502.92 | 502.55 |
| | | | --- | |
| SDR | 1.3586 | 1.3561 | .7360 | .7374 |
| ECU | 1.1133 | 1.1140 | | |

Special Drawing Rights (SDR) are based on exchange rates for the U.S., German, British, French , and Japanese currencies. Source: International Monetary Fund.

European Currency Unit (ECU) is based on a basket of community currencies.

a-fixing, Moscow Interbank Currency Exchange.

The Wall Street Journal daily foreign exchange data for 1996 and 1997 may be purchased through the Readers' Reference Service (413) 592-3600.

# Key Currency Cross Rates  Late New York Trading Dec 19, 1997

| | Dollar | Pound | SFranc | Guilder | Peso | Yen | Lira | D-Mark | FFranc | CdnDlr |
|---|---|---|---|---|---|---|---|---|---|---|
| Canada | 1.4311 | 2.3899 | .99728 | .71462 | .17640 | .01107 | .00082 | .80603 | .24058 | .... |
| France | 5.9485 | 9.9340 | 4.1453 | 2.9704 | .73321 | .04599 | .00341 | 3.3503 | .... | 4.1566 |
| Germany | 1.7755 | 2.9651 | 1.2373 | .88660 | .21885 | .01373 | .00102 | .... | .29848 | 1.2407 |
| Italy | 1742.0 | 2909.1 | 1213.9 | 869.87 | 214.72 | 13.469 | .... | 981.13 | 292.85 | 1217.2 |
| Japan | 129.33 | 215.98 | 90.125 | 64.581 | 15.941 | .... | .07424 | 72.841 | 21.742 | 90.371 |
| Mexico | 8.1130 | 13.549 | 5.6537 | 4.0512 | .... | .06273 | .00466 | 4.5694 | 1.3639 | 5.6691 |
| Netherlands | 2.0026 | 3.3443 | 1.3955 | .... | .24684 | .01548 | .00115 | 1.1279 | .33666 | 1.3993 |
| Switzerland | 1.4350 | 2.3964 | .... | .71657 | .17688 | .01110 | .00082 | .80822 | .24124 | 1.0027 |
| U.K. | .59880 | .... | .41728 | .29901 | .07381 | .00463 | .00034 | .33726 | .10066 | .41842 |
| U.S. | .... | 1.6700 | .69686 | .49935 | .12326 | .00773 | .00057 | .56322 | .16811 | .69876 |

Source: Dow Jones

**FIGURE 7.1**

**Exchange Rate and Cross Rate Tables**

*Source: The Wall Street Journal,* Monday December 20, 1997, p. C21.

Foreign exchange traders at banks can move millions of dollars, yen, or marks around the world with a few keystrokes on their networked computes. The deregulation of international capital flows contributes to faster, cheaper transactions in the currency markets.

*Source:* Courtesy of Republic National Bank of New York

The quotations listed will also occasionally indicate if the rate is applicable to business trade (the commercial rate) or for financial asset purchases or sales (the financial rate). Countries that have government regulations regarding the exchange of their currency may post official rates, while the markets operating outside their jurisdiction will list a floating rate. In this case, any exchange of currency that is not under the control of its government is interpreted as a better indication of the currency's true market value.

## Direct and Indirect Quotations

*The Wall Street Journal* quotations list the rates of exchange between major currencies, both in direct and indirect forms. The exchange rate for the German mark versus U.S. dollar, in the third column shown, is DEM 1.7755/USD. This is a direct quote on the German mark or indirect quote on the U.S. dollar. The inverse of this spot rate is listed in the first column, the indirect quote on the German mark or direct quote on the U.S. dollar, USD .5632./DEM. The two forms of the exchange rate are of course equal, one being the inverse of the other.[1]

$$\frac{1}{1.7755} = \text{USD } .5632/\text{DEM}$$

Luckily, world currency markets do follow some conventions to minimize confusion. With only a few exceptions, most currencies are quoted in direct quotes versus the U.S. dollar (DEM/USD, YEN/USD, FFR/USD), also known as **European terms.** The major exceptions are currencies at one time or another associated with the British Commonwealth, including the Australian dollar and, of course, the British pound sterling. These are customarily quoted as USD per pound sterling or USD per Australian dollar, known as **American terms.** Once again, it makes no real difference whether you quote U.S. dollars per Japanese yen or Japanese yen per U.S. dollar, as long as you know which is being used for the transaction.

Figure 7.2, the foreign currency quotations from the *Financial Times* of London, provides wider coverage of the world's currencies, including many of the lesser known and traded. These quotes are also for Friday, December 19, 1997, the same day as the quotes from *The Wall Street Journal* in Figure 7.1. However, even though the currency quotations are for the same day, they are not necessarily the same, reflecting the differences in the time zones, the local markets, and even the actual banks surveyed for newspaper quotation purposes.

## Cross Rates

Although it is common among exchange traders worldwide to quote currency values against the U.S. dollar, it is not necessary. Any currency's value can be stated in terms of any other currency. When the exchange rate for a currency is stated without using the U.S. dollar as a reference, it is referred to as a **cross rate.** For example, if the German mark and Japanese yen are both quoted versus the U.S. dollar, they would appear as DEM 1.7755/USD and YEN 129.33/USD. But if the YEN/DEM cross rate is needed, it is simply a matter of division:

$$\frac{\text{YEN } 129.33}{\text{DEM } 1.7755} = \text{YEN } 72.841/\text{DEM}$$

The YEN/DEM cross rate of 72.841 is the third leg of the triangle, which must be true if the first two exchange rates are known. If one of the exchange rates changes due to market forces, the others must adjust for the three exchange rates again to align. If they are out of alignment, it would be possible to make a profit simply by exchanging one currency for a second, the second for a third, and the third back to the first. This is known as **triangular arbitrage.** Besides the potential profitability of arbitrage that may occasionally occur, cross rates have become increasingly common in a world of rapidly expanding trade and investment. The world's financial markets no longer revolve around the U.S. dollar.

## Percentage Change Calculations

The quotation form is important when calculating the percentage change in an exchange rate. For example, if the spot rate between the Japanese yen and the U.S. dollar changed from YEN 125/USD to YEN 150/USD, the percentage change in the value of the Japanese yen is:

$$\frac{\text{YEN } 125/\text{USD} - \text{YEN } 150/\text{USD}}{\text{YEN } 150/\text{USD}} \times 100 = -16.67\%$$

## FT GUIDE TO WORLD CURRENCIES

The table below gives the latest available rates of exchange (rounded) against four key currencies on Friday, December 19, 1997 . In some cases the rate is nominal. Market rates are the average of buying and selling rates except where they are shown to be otherwise. In some cases market rates have been calculated from those of foreign currencies to which they are tied.

| Country | Currency | £ STG | US $ | D-MARK | YEN (X 100) |
|---|---|---|---|---|---|
| Afghanistan | (Afghani) | 7925.61 | 4750.00 | 2685.44 | 3683.03 |
| Albania | (Lek) | 243.608 | 146.000 | 82.5418 | 113.205 |
| Algeria | (Dinar) | 96.7098 | 57.9604 | 32.7682 | 44.9410 |
| Andorra | (French Fr) | 9.8887 | 5.9265 | 3.3506 | 4.5953 |
| | (Sp Peseta) | 250.366 | 150.050 | 84.8315 | 116.345 |
| Angola | (Readj Kwanza) | 429030.8 | 257128.0 | 145368.6 | 199370.4 |
| Antigua | (E Carib $) | 4.5051 | 2.7000 | 1.5265 | 2.0935 |
| Argentina | (Peso) | 1.6683 | 0.9998 | 0.5652 | 0.7752 |
| Armenia | (Dram) | 834.058o | 499.870 | 282.604 | 387.586 |
| Aruba | (Florin) | 2.9867 | 1.7900 | 1.0120 | 1.3879 |
| Australia | (Aus $) | 2.5521 | 1.5295 | 0.8647 | 1.1860 |
| Austria | (Schilling) | 20.7639 | 12.4443 | 7.0354 | 9.6489 |
| Azerbaijan | (Manat) | 6590.77o | 3950.00 | 2233.15 | 3062.73 |
| Azores | (Port Escudo) | 303.593 | 181.950 | 102.866 | 141.079 |
| Bahamas | (Bahama $) | 1.6686 | 1 | 0.5654 | 0.7754 |
| Bahrain | (Dinar) | 0.6291 | 0.3770 | 0.2131 | 0.2923 |
| Balearic Is | (Sp Peseta) | 250.366 | 150.050 | 84.8315 | 116.345 |
| Bangladesh | (Taka) | 75.8357 | 45.4500 | 25.6954 | 35.2408 |
| Barbados | (Barb $) | 3.3560 | 2.0113 | 1.1371 | 1.5595 |
| Belarus | (Rouble) | 67442.8o | 40420.0 | 22851.7 | 31340.6 |
| Belgium | (Belg Fr) | 60.9105 | 36.5050 | 20.6383 | 28.3050 |
| Belize | (B $) | 3.3371 | 2.0000 | 1.1307 | 1.5508 |
| Benin | (CFA Fr) | 988.870 | 592.650 | 335.058 | 459.526 |
| Bermuda | (Bermudian $) | 1.6686 | 1 | 0.5654 | 0.7754 |
| Bhutan | (Ngultrum) | 65.3905 | 39.1900 | 22.1563 | 30.3869 |
| Bolivia | (Boliviano) | 8.9268 | 5.3500 | 3.0246 | 4.1483 |
| Botswana | (Pula) | 6.2973 | 3.7736 | 2.1334 | 2.9259 |
| Brazil | (Real) | 1.8592 | 1.1143 | 0.6299 | 0.8640 |
| Brunei | (Brunei $) | 2.7882 | 1.6710 | 0.9447 | 1.2957 |
| Bulgaria | (Lev) | 2939.98 | 1762.00 | 996.156 | 1366.21 |
| Burkina Faso | (CFA Fr) | 988.870 | 592.650 | 335.058 | 459.526 |
| Burma | (Kyat) | 10.4313 | 6.2517 | 3.5344 | 4.8474 |
| Burundi | (Burundi Fr) | 675.629 | 404.920 | 228.924 | 313.965 |
| Cambodia | (Riel) | 5743.15 | 3442.00 | 1945.95 | 2668.84 |
| Cameroon | (CFA Fr) | 988.870 | 592.650 | 335.058 | 459.526 |
| Canada | (Canadian $) | 2.3887 | 1.4316 | 0.8093 | 1.1100 |
| Canary Is | (Sp Peseta) | 250.366 | 150.050 | 84.8315 | 116.345 |
| Cp. Verde | (CV Escudo) | 159.030 | 95.3100 | 53.8840 | 73.9009 |
| Cayman Is | (CI $) | 1.3819 | 0.8282 | 0.4682 | 0.6422 |
| Cent. Afr. Rep | (CFA Fr) | 988.870 | 592.650 | 335.058 | 459.526 |
| Chad | (CFA Fr) | 988.870 | 592.650 | 335.058 | 459.526 |
| Chile | (Chilean Peso) | 732.911 | 439.250 | 248.332 | 340.583 |
| China | (Yuan) | 13.8151 | 8.2797 | 4.6810 | 6.4199 |
| Colombia | (Col Peso) | 2148.93 | 1287.90 | 728.121 | 998.604 |
| Comoros | (Fr) | 741.337 | 444.300 | 251.187 | 344.499 |
| Congo | (CFA Fr) | 988.870 | 592.650 | 335.058 | 459.526 |
| Congo (DemRep) | (Zaire)(2) | 229425.5 | 137500.0 | 77736.3 | 106613.9 |
| Costa Rica | (Colon) | 405.833 | 243.225 | 137.509 | 188.590 |
| Côte d'Ivoire | (CFA Fr) | 988.870 | 592.650 | 335.058 | 459.526 |
| Croatia | (Kuna) | 10.3862 | 6.2247 | 3.5191 | 4.8264 |
| Cuba | (Cuban Peso)(1) | 38.3767 | 23.0000 | 13.0032 | 17.8336 |
| Cyprus | (Cyprus £) | 0.8663 | 0.5192 | 0.2935 | 0.4026 |
| Czech Rep. | (Koruna) | 57.2230 | 34.2950 | 19.3889 | 26.5915 |
| Denmark | (Danish Krone) | 11.2462 | 6.7401 | 3.8105 | 5.2261 |
| Djibouti Rep | (Djib Fr) | 296.535 | 177.720 | 100.475 | 137.800 |
| Dominica | (E Carib $) | 4.5051 | 2.7000 | 1.5265 | 2.0935 |
| Dominican Rep | (D Peso) | 24.3608 | 14.6000 | 8.2542 | 11.3205 |
| Ecuador | (Sucre) | 7439.23o | 4458.50 | 2520.64 | 3457.01 |
| | (Sucre) | 7425.04a | 4450.00 | 2515.83 | 3450.41 |
| Egypt | (Egyptian £) | 5.6773 | 3.4025 | 1.9236 | 2.6382 |
| El Salvador | (Colon) | 14.6082 | 8.7550 | 4.9497 | 6.7884 |
| Equat'l Guinea | (CFA Fr) | 988.870 | 592.650 | 335.058 | 459.526 |
| Estonia | (Kroon) | 23.6087 | 14.1492 | 7.9993 | 10.9709 |
| Ethiopia | (Ethiopian Birr) | 11.1760 | 6.6980 | 3.7868 | 5.1935 |
| Falkland Is | (Falk £) | 1 | 0.5993 | 0.3388 | 0.4647 |
| Faroe Is | (Danish Krone) | 11.2462 | 6.7401 | 3.8105 | 5.2261 |
| Fiji Is | (Fiji $) | 2.5572 | 1.5326 | 0.8665 | 1.1883 |
| Finland | (Markka) | 8.9205 | 5.3463 | 3.0225 | 4.1453 |
| France | (Fr) | 9.8887 | 5.9265 | 3.3506 | 4.5953 |
| Fr. Cty/Africa | (CFA Fr) | 988.870 | 592.650 | 335.058 | 459.526 |
| Fr. Guiana | (Local Fr) | 9.8887 | 5.9265 | 3.3506 | 4.5953 |
| Fr. Pacific Is | (CFP Fr) | 179.716 | 107.708 | 60.8933 | 83.5140 |
| Gabon | (CFA Fr) | 988.870 | 592.650 | 335.058 | 459.526 |
| Gambia | (Dalasi) | 16.8086 | 10.0738 | 5.6953 | 7.8109 |
| Germany | (D-Mark) | 2.9513 | 1.7688 | 1 | 1.3715 |
| Ghana | (Cedi) | 3743.40 | 2243.50 | 1268.37 | 1739.55 |

| Country | Currency | £ STG | US $ | D-MARK | YEN (X 100) |
|---|---|---|---|---|---|
| Gibraltar | (Gib £) | 1 | 0.5993 | 0.3388 | 0.4647 |
| Greece | (Drachma) | 464.458 | 278.360 | 157.372 | 215.833 |
| Greenland | (Danish Krone) | 11.2462 | 6.7401 | 3.8105 | 5.2261 |
| Grenada | (E Carib $) | 4.5051 | 2.7000 | 1.5265 | 2.0935 |
| Guadeloupe | (French Fr) | 9.8887 | 5.9265 | 3.3506 | 4.5953 |
| Guam | (US $) | 1.6686 | 1 | 0.5654 | 0.7754 |
| Guatemala | (Quetzal) | 10.3767 | 6.2190 | 3.5159 | 4.8221 |
| Guinea | (Fr) | 1892.97 | 1134.50 | 641.395 | 879.662 |
| Guinea-Bissau | (CFA Fr)(3) | 988.870 | 592.650 | 335.058 | 459.526 |
| Guyana | (Guyanese $) | 238.269 | 142.800 | 80.7327 | 110.723 |
| Haiti | (Gourde) | 28.0033 | 16.7830 | 9.4884 | 13.0131 |
| Honduras | (Lempira) | 22.0249 | 13.2000 | 7.4627 | 10.2349 |
| Hong Kong | (HK $) | 12.9313 | 7.7500 | 4.3815 | 6.0091 |
| Hungary | (Forint) | 335.254 | 200.925 | 113.594 | 155.792 |
| Iceland | (Icelandic Krona) | 119.343 | 71.5250 | 40.4370 | 55.4586 |
| India | (Indian Rupee) | 65.3905 | 39.1900 | 22.1563 | 30.3869 |
| Indonesia | (Rupiah) | 8509.65 | 5100.00 | 2883.31 | 3954.41 |
| Iran | (Rial) | 5005.65u | 3000.00 | 1696.07 | 2326.12 |
| Iraq | (Iraqi Dinar) | 0.5188o | 0.3109 | 0.1758 | 0.2411 |
| Iraq | (Iraqi Dinar) | 2002.26m | 1200.00 | 678.426 | 930.449 |
| Irish Rep | (Punt) | 1.1436 | 0.6854 | 0.3875 | 0.5314 |
| Israel | (Shekel) | 5.8924 | 3.5315 | 1.9965 | 2.7382 |
| Italy | (Lira) | 2897.19 | 1736.35 | 981.654 | 1346.32 |
| Jamaica | (Jamaican $) | 58.1490 | 34.8500 | 19.7026 | 27.0218 |
| Japan | (Yen) | 215.193 | 128.970 | 72.9138 | 100 |
| Jordan | (Jordanian Dinar) | 1.1864 | 0.7110 | 0.4020 | 0.5513 |
| Kazakhstan | (Tenge) | 126.551 | 75.8450 | 42.8794 | 58.8083 |
| Kenya | (Kenya Shilling) | 104.451 | 62.6000 | 35.3912 | 48.5384 |
| Kiribati | (Australian $) | 2.5521 | 1.5295 | 0.8647 | 1.1860 |
| Korea North | (Won) | 3.6708 | 2.2000 | 1.2438 | 1.7058 |
| Korea South | (Won) | 2627.97 | 1575.00 | 890.434 | 1221.21 |
| Kuwait | (Kuwaiti Dinar) | 0.5082 | 0.3046 | 0.1722 | 0.2361 |
| Laos | (New Kip) | 1898.81 | 1138.00 | 643.374 | 882.376 |
| Latvia | (Lats) | 0.9740 | 0.5838 | 0.3300 | 0.4526 |
| Lebanon | (Lebanese £) | 2548.71 | 1527.50 | 863.580 | 1184.38 |
| Lesotho | (Maluti) | 8.1117 | 4.8615 | 2.7485 | 3.7695 |
| Liberia | (Liberian $) | 1.6686 | 1 | 0.5654 | 0.7754 |
| Libya | (Libyan Dinar) | 0.6399 | 0.3835 | 0.2168 | 0.2974 |
| Liechtenstein | (Swiss Fr) | 2.3845 | 1.4291 | 0.8079 | 1.1081 |
| Lithuania | (Litas) | 6.6717 | 3.9985 | 2.2606 | 3.1003 |
| Luxembourg | (Lux Fr) | 60.9105 | 36.5050 | 20.6383 | 28.3050 |
| Macao | (Pataca) | 13.3571 | 8.0052 | 4.5258 | 6.2070 |
| Macedonia | (Denar) | 91.6164 | 54.9078 | 31.0424 | 42.5741 |
| Madagascar | (MG Fr) | 8342.75 | 5000.00 | 2826.78 | 3876.87 |
| Madeira | (Port Escudo) | 303.593 | 181.950 | 102.866 | 141.079 |
| Malawi | (Kwacha) | 34.5306 | 20.6950 | 11.7000 | 16.0464 |
| Malaysia | (Ringgit) | 6.3822 | 3.8250 | 2.1625 | 2.9658 |
| Maldive Is | (Rufiya) | 19.6388 | 11.7700 | 6.6542 | 9.1262 |
| Mali Rep | (CFA Fr) | 988.870 | 592.650 | 335.058 | 459.526 |
| Malta | (Maltese Lira) | 0.6511 | 0.3902 | 0.2206 | 0.3026 |
| Martinique | (Local Fr) | 9.8887 | 5.9265 | 3.3506 | 4.5953 |
| Mauritania | (Ouguiya) | 278.090 | 166.665 | 94.2249 | 129.228 |
| Mauritius | (Maur Rupee) | 36.9167 | 22.1250 | 12.5085 | 17.1552 |
| Mexico | (Mexican Peso) | 13.5804 | 8.1390 | 4.6014 | 6.3108 |
| Moldova | (Leu) | 7.8088 | 4.6800 | 2.6459 | 3.6288 |
| Monaco | (French Fr) | 9.8887 | 5.9265 | 3.3506 | 4.5953 |
| Mongolia | (Tugrik) | 1309.41 | 784.760 | 443.668 | 608.483 |
| Montserrat | (E Carib $) | 4.5051 | 2.7000 | 1.5265 | 2.0935 |
| Morocco | (Dirham) | 16.0590 | 9.6245 | 5.4413 | 7.4626 |
| Mozambique | (Metical) | 19180.0 | 11495.0 | 6498.76 | 8912.93 |
| Namibia | (S A Rand) | 8.1117 | 4.8615 | 2.7485 | 3.7695 |
| Nauru Is | (Australian $) | 2.5521 | 1.5295 | 0.8647 | 1.1860 |
| Nepal | (Nepalese Rupee) | 95.0239 | 56.9500 | 32.1970 | 44.1576 |
| Netherlands | (Guilder) | 3.3263 | 1.9935 | 1.1270 | 1.5457 |
| N'nd Antilles | (A/Guilder) | 2.9867 | 1.7900 | 1.0120 | 1.3879 |
| New Zealand | (NZ $) | 2.8618 | 1.7151 | 0.9697 | 1.3299 |
| Nicaragua | (Gold Cordoba) | 16.5730 | 9.9326 | 5.6155 | 7.7015 |
| Niger Rep | (CFA Fr) | 988.870 | 592.650 | 335.058 | 459.526 |
| Nigeria | (Naira) | 36.5179o | 21.8860 | 12.3734 | 16.9698 |
| | (Naira) | 126.560m | 75.8500 | 42.8822 | 58.8121 |
| Norway | (Nor. Krone) | 12.0976 | 7.2504 | 4.0990 | 5.6217 |
| Oman | (Rial Omani) | 0.6424 | 0.3850 | 0.2176 | 0.2985 |

| Country | Currency | £ STG | US $ | D-MARK | YEN (X 100) |
|---|---|---|---|---|---|
| Pakistan | (Pak. Rupee)(4) | 73.4262 | 44.0060 | 24.8790 | 34.1211 |
| Panama | (Balboa) | 1.6686 | 1 | 0.5654 | 0.7754 |
| Papua New Guinea | (Kina) | 2.9325 | 1.7575 | 0.9936 | 1.3627 |
| Paraguay | (Guarani) | 3837.66 | 2300.00 | 1300.32 | 1783.36 |
| Peru | (New Sol) | 4.5276 | 2.7135 | 1.5341 | 2.1040 |
| Philippines | (Peso) | 65.5241 | 39.2700 | 22.2015 | 30.4489 |
| Pitcairn Is | (£ Sterling) | 1 | 0.5993 | 0.3388 | 0.4647 |
| | (NZ $) | 2.8618 | 1.7151 | 0.9697 | 1.3299 |
| Poland | (Zloty) | 5.8429 | 3.5018 | 1.9797 | 2.7152 |
| Portugal | (Escudo) | 303.593 | 181.950 | 102.866 | 141.079 |
| Puerto Rico | (US $) | 1.6686 | 1 | 0.5654 | 0.7754 |
| Qatar | (Riyal) | 6.0755 | 3.6412 | 2.0585 | 2.8233 |
| Reunion Is. de la | (F/Fr) | 9.8887 | 5.9265 | 3.3506 | 4.5953 |
| Romania | (Leu) | 13381.8 | 8020.00 | 4534.15 | 6218.50 |
| Russia | (Rouble) | 9886.99m | 5925.50 | 3350.01 | 4594.48 |
| Rwanda | (Fr) | 578.137 | 346.491 | 195.890 | 268.660 |
| St Christopher | (E Carib $) | 4.5051 | 2.7000 | 1.5265 | 2.0935 |
| St Helena | (£) | 1 | 0.5993 | 0.3388 | 0.4647 |
| St Lucia | (E Carib $) | 4.5051 | 2.7000 | 1.5265 | 2.0935 |
| St Pierre & Miquelon | (F/Fr) | 9.8887 | 5.9265 | 3.3506 | 4.5953 |
| St Vincent | (E Carib $) | 4.5051 | 2.7000 | 1.5265 | 2.0935 |
| San Marino | (Italian Lira) | 2897.19 | 1736.35 | 981.654 | 1346.32 |
| Sao Tome | (Dobra) | 3987.83 | 2390.00 | 1351.20 | 1853.14 |
| Saudi Arabia | (Riyal) | 6.2581 | 3.7506 | 2.1204 | 2.9081 |
| Senegal | (CFA Fr) | 988.870 | 592.650 | 335.058 | 459.526 |
| Seychelles | (Rupee) | 8.5263 | 5.1100 | 2.8890 | 3.9622 |
| Sierra Leone | (Leone) | 1376.55 | 825.000 | 466.418 | 639.684 |
| Singapore | ($) | 2.7882 | 1.6710 | 0.9447 | 1.2957 |
| Slovakia | (Koruna) | 57.0160 | 34.1710 | 19.3187 | 26.4953 |
| Slovenia | (Tolar) | 278.001 | 166.612 | 94.1949 | 129.187 |
| Solomon Is | ($) | 7.7649 | 4.6537 | 2.6310 | 3.6084 |
| Somali Rep | (Shilling) | 4371.60 | 2620.00 | 1481.23 | 2031.48 |
| South Africa | (Rand) | 8.1117 | 4.8615 | 2.7485 | 3.7695 |
| Spain | (Peseta) | 250.366 | 150.050 | 84.8315 | 116.345 |
| Spanish Ports In N Africa | (Sp Peseta) | 250.366 | 150.050 | 84.8315 | 116.345 |
| Sri Lanka | (Rupee) | 102.699 | 61.5500 | 34.7976 | 47.7243 |
| Sudan Rep | (Dinar) | 238.436 | 142.900 | 80.7892 | 110.801 |
| Surinam | (Guilder) | 669.088 | 401.000 | 226.707 | 310.925 |
| Swaziland | (Lilangeni) | 8.1117 | 4.8615 | 2.7485 | 3.7695 |
| Sweden | (Krona) | 12.9268 | 7.7473 | 4.3800 | 6.0071 |
| Switzerland | (Fr) | 2.3845 | 1.4291 | 0.8079 | 1.1081 |
| Syria | (£) | 66.7420 | 40.0000 | 22.6142 | 31.0150 |
| Taiwan | ($) | 53.9443 | 32.3300 | 18.2779 | 25.0678 |
| Tanzania | (Shilling) | 1033.67 | 619.500 | 350.238 | 480.344 |
| Thailand | (Baht) | 76.9202 | 46.1000 | 26.0629 | 35.7447 |
| Togo Rep | (CFA Fr) | 988.870 | 592.650 | 335.058 | 459.526 |
| Tonga Is | (Pa'anga) | 2.5521 | 1.5295 | 0.8647 | 1.1860 |
| Trinidad/Tobago | ($) | 10.3450 | 6.2000 | 3.5052 | 4.8073 |
| Tunisia | (Dinar) | 1.8883 | 1.1317 | 0.6398 | 0.8775 |
| Turkey | (Lira) | 337689.5 | 202385.0 | 114419.4 | 156924.1 |
| Turks & Caicos | (US $) | 1.6686 | 1 | 0.5654 | 0.7754 |
| Tuvalu | (Australian $) | 2.5521 | 1.5295 | 0.8647 | 1.1860 |
| Uganda | (New Shilling) | 1882.12 | 1128.00 | 637.721 | 874.622 |
| Ukraine | (Hryvna) | 3.2287 | 1.9350 | 1.0940 | 1.5004 |
| U A E | (Dirham) | 6.1284 | 3.6729 | 2.0765 | 2.8479 |
| United Kingdom | (£) | 1 | 0.5993 | 0.3388 | 0.4647 |
| United States | (US $) | 1.6686 | 1 | 0.5654 | 0.7754 |
| Uruguay | (Peso Uruguayo) | 16.6438 | 9.9750 | 5.6394 | 7.7344 |
| Vanuatu | (Vatu) | 205.257 | 123.015 | 69.5472 | 95.3826 |
| Vatican | (Lira) | 2897.19 | 1736.35 | 981.654 | 1346.32 |
| Venezuela | (Bolivar) | 839.214v | 502.960 | 284.351 | 389.982 |
| Vietnam | (Dong) | 20503.1 | 12288.0 | 6947.08 | 9527.80 |
| Virgin Is-British | (US $) | 1.6686 | 1 | 0.5654 | 0.7754 |
| Virgin Is-US | (US $) | 1.6686 | 1 | 0.5654 | 0.7754 |
| Western Samoa | (Tala) | 4.5952 | 2.7540 | 1.5570 | 2.1354 |
| Yemen (Rep of) | (Rial) | 206.900r | 124.000 | 70.1040 | 96.1464 |
| Yugoslavia | (New Dinar) | 9.7792 | 5.8609 | 3.3135 | 4.5444 |
| Zambia | (Kwacha) | 2373.52 | 1422.50 | 804.218 | 1102.97 |
| Zimbabwe | ($) | 29.2415 | 17.5250 | 9.9078 | 13.5884 |
| ECU | (ECU) | 1.4928 | 0.8947 | 0.5058 | 0.6937 |
| SDR | (SDR) | 1.22100 | 0.737409 | 0.415324 | 0.578814 |

Abbreviations: (a) Free rate; (m) Market rate; (o) Official rate; (r) Parallel rate (t) Tourist rate (u) Currency fixed against the US Dollar (v) Floating rate (1) Market rate now shown for Cuba (2) Name changed from Zaire on May 19th 1997, currency scheduled to change to Congolese Francs (3) Guinea-Bissau adopted the CFA Franc to replace the Peso on 1/8/97 (4) Pakistan Rupee devalued by 8% on 16/10/97: FT enquiries to Business Research Centre 0171 256 5130. Some data derived from THE WM/REUTERS CLOSING SPOT RATES & Bank of America, Economics Department, London Trading Centre. Enquiries: 0171 634 4365. **To obtain a copy of this table by Fax from the Cityline service dial 0891 437001. Calls are charged at 50p per minute at all times. FT Cityline apologises for the recent suspension in service. We are now pleased to inform users that the service is once again fully operational.**

**Friday, December 19, 1997**

**FIGURE 7.2**

**Guide to World Currencies**

*Source: The Financial Times,* December 19, 1997.

The Japanese yen has declined in value versus the U.S. dollar by 16.67 percent. This is consistent with the intuition that it now requires more yen (150) to buy a dollar than it used to (125).

The same percentage change result can be achieved by using the inverted forms of the same spot rates (indirect quotes on the Japanese yen), if care is taken to also "invert" the basic percentage change calculation. Using the inverse of YEN 125/USD (USD 0.0080/YEN) and the inverse of YEN 150/USD (USD 0.0067/YEN), the percentage change is still −16.67 percent:

$$\frac{USD\ 0.0067/YEN\ -\ USD\ 0.0080/YEN}{USD\ 0.0080/YEN} \times 100 = -16.67\%$$

If the percentage changes calculated are not identical, it is normally the result of rounding errors introduced when inverting the spot rates. Both methods are identical, however, when calculated properly.

## Foreign Currency Market Structure

The market for foreign currencies is a worldwide market that is informal in structure. This means that it has no central place, pit, or floor like the floor of the New York Stock Exchange, where the trading takes place (or in an alley as described in Global Perspective 7.1). The "market" is actually the thousands of telecommunications links among financial institutions around the globe, and it is open twenty-four hours a day. Someone, somewhere, is nearly always open for business.

For example, Table 7.1 reproduces a computer screen from one of the major international financial information news sources, Reuters. This is the spot exchange screen, called FXFX, which is available to all subscribers to the Reuters news network. The screen serves as a bulletin board, where all financial institutions wanting to buy or sell foreign currencies can post representative prices. Although the rates quoted on these computer screens are indicative of current prices, the buyer is still referred to the individual bank for the latest quotation due to the rapid movement of rates worldwide. There also are hundreds of banks operating in the markets at any moment that are not listed on the brief sample of Reuters FXFX page.[2] The speed with which this market moves, the multitude of players playing on a field that is open twenty-four hours a day, and the circumference of the earth with its time and day differences produce many different "single prices."

One way to put this ever-changing market in perspective is to think of the FX market as a never-ending horse race. The winner is the one that is ahead at one point on the track, at one point in time, from the viewpoint of where in the stands the audience is sitting. The markets continue, as would the theoretical horses, forever. The rates quoted by Bankers Trust or Telerate are therefore only daily snapshots of the race, the daily photo finish from the individual bank's seat in the stands.

## Currency Bid and Offer Quotes

The individual spot quotes shown in Table 7.1 have both bid and offer quotations for the currencies listed. For example, DG Bank (Deutsche Bank) in Frankfurt, Germany, posted a spot quote on the German mark (DEM) of 1.8528/33 at 13:07 (1:07 p.m. London time). These bid and offer quotes are

## DIALING FOR DINARS: IRAQIS TURN ON RADIO TO SET EXCHANGE RATE

To check the health of the Iraqi economy, forget about visiting the Central Bank of the Ministry of Finance. Take a walk down a narrow side street behind the Shorja outdoor market instead, and watch the blackmarket money-changers hawk crumpled Ben Franklins.

"I've got a book," shouts a changer, using code for the clutch of 100 hundred-dollar bills he is hoisting. "Who wants it for 12 million?" Several prospective buyers huddling on the sidewalk call out, and one man grabs the changer by the elbow, hustling him away with an anxious glance over his shoulder. The deal is done behind a parked Toyota. Then the changer, struggling under the weight of three burlap sacks packed with Iraqi currency makes his way back to his closet-sized storefront, where he masquerades as a cigarette merchant, to tune in to the foreign news on his shortwave radio. What he hears out of Washington or New York, and how he interprets it, will decide what he offers for dollars during his next venture onto the street-side trading floor.

### Bad News Bulls

A U.S. missile strike? That will boost the dollar by 800 Iraqi dinars at least. A visit to the city by the United Nations weapons-inspection team? That's possibly good news, and merits about a 10-dinar decrease. (After the team departs, and makes it inevitable negative report to the U.N., the dinar goes 20 points in the other direction.) A statement by Madeline Albright, U.S. ambassador to the U.N., on the suspended pact to allow Iraq to sell oil to buy food? Hardly worth trading on. ("We call her Not-So-Bright," says a trader.) A speech about Iraq by President Clinton? Little effect, unless Mr. Clinton makes an especially colorful threat.

### Great Expectations

The dinar fluctuates so wildly because its worth is based on Iraqis' wavering expectations of when the country will be able again to export crude oil—the nation's vital foreign-currency earner—and because Iraq imports so many of its products. When oil flows, Iraq is awash in dollars, which the government sells to the people at inexpensive rates (more than three dollars to a dinar, for example, before the 1991 Gulf War). So the less likely it appears that oil will flow again soon, the more despondent people become and the more determined they are to buy ever-scarcer dollars on the black market. Which means bad news makes the dollar rise against the dinar; good news makes it fall.

Does the system work? Western diplomats who live in Baghdad think so. "The only difference between what goes on here and what goes on in New York is that there they're worried about what the Deutsche Bank or Federal Reserve might do, and here they're looking at Bill Clinton and Saddam Hussein," says one diplomat who has himself made a few underground money trades. "And of course here they don't have computers or ticker tape."

*Source: "Dialing for Dinars: Iraqis Turn On Radio To Set Exchange Rate," **The Wall Street Journal**, Friday September 20, 1996, p. A8.*

for either the purchase (bid) or sale (offer) of German marks in exchange for U.S. dollars.

| Bid: | DEM 1.8528/USD | The spot rate of exchange at which the bank is willing to purchase U.S. dollars, or sell German marks. |
| Offer: | DEM 1.8533/USD | The spot rate of exchange at which the bank is willing to sell U.S. dollars, or buy German marks. |

The quote is stated with only the last two digits of the offer rate listed separately. Every exchange rate has a customary number of digits used. In the case of the DEM/USD, all quotes are carried to the fourth decimal place. These are referred to as "basis points" or "pips."[3] The individual bank makes its profit on a single trade on the **spread,** the difference between the bid and offer quotes (if it simultaneously bought and sold dollars for marks at the quoted rates). Global Perspective 7.2 illustrates how trading occurs between traders themselves.

**TABLE 7.1**

Typical Foreign Currency Quotations on a Reuters Screen

| 13:07 | CCY | Page | Name | *Reuters Spot Rates* | CCY | | HI* Euro** | Lo FXFX |
|-------|-----|------|------|------------|-----|-----|----------|---------|
| 13.06 | DEM | DGXX | DG BANK | FFT | 1.8528/33 | * DEM | 1.8538 | 1.8440 |
| 13.06 | GBP | AIBN | AL IRISH | N.Y. | 1.7653/63 | * GBP | 1.7710 | 1.7630 |
| 13.06 | CHF | CITX | CITYBANK | ZUR | 1.5749/56 | * CHF | 1.5750 | 1.5665 |
| 13.06 | JPY | CHNY | CHEMICAL | N.Y. | 128.53/58 | * JPY | 128.70 | 128.23 |
| 13.07 | FRF | MGFX | MORGAN | LDN | 6.3030/60 | * FRF | 6.3080 | 6.2750 |
| 13.06 | NLG | MGFX | MORGAN | LDN | 2.0920/30 | * NLG | 2.0925 | 2.0815 |
| 13.00 | ITL | MGFX | MORGAN | LDN | 1356.45/6.58 | * ITL | 1356.45 | 1349.00 |
| 13.02 | XEV | PRBX | PRIVAT | COP | 1.1259/68 | * XEV | 1.1304 | 1.1255 |

Column 1: Time of entry of the lastest quote to the nearst minute (British Standard time).

Column 2: Currency of quotation (bilateral with the U.S. dollar); quotes are currency per USD, except for the British pound sterling (dollars per unit of pound) and the European Currency Unit (dollars per unit of XEV). The currency symbols are as follows: DEM—German mark; GBP—British pound sterling; CFH—Swiss franc; JPY—Japanese yen; FRF—French franc; NGL—Netherlands guilder; ITL—Italian lira; XEV—European Currency Unit.

Column 3: Mnemonic of inputting bank. Allows the individual trader to dial up the correct page (by this mnemonic) where the trader could see the full set of spot and forward quotes for this and other currencies being offered by this bank.

Column 4: Name of the inputting bank.

Column 5: Branch location of that bank from which the quote has emanated (so that an inquiring trader can telephone the correct branch); FFT—Frankfurt; N.Y.—New York; ZUR—Zurich; LDN—London; COP—Copenhagen.

Column 6: Spot exchange rate quotation, bid quote, then offer quote.

Column 7: Recent high price for this specific quote.

Column 8: Recent low price for this specific quote.

*Source:* Adapted from C. A. E. Goodhart and L. Figliuoli, "Every Minute Counts in Financial Markets," *Journal of International Money and Finance,* 10, 1991, pp. 23–52.

## Market Size and Composition

Until recently there was little data on the actual volume of trading on world foreign currency markets. Starting in the spring of 1986, however, the Federal Reserve Bank of New York, along with other major industrial countries' central banks through the auspices of the Bank for International Settlements (BIS), started surveying the activity of currency trading every three years. Some of the principal results are shown in Figure 7.3.

Growth in foreign currency trading has been nothing less than astronomical. The survey results for the month of April 1995 indicate that daily foreign currency trading on world markets exceeded $1,000,000,000,000 (a trillion with a *t*). In comparison, the annual (not daily) U.S. government budget deficit has never exceeded $300 billion, and the U.S. merchandise trade deficit has never topped $200 billion.

The majority of the world's trading in foreign currencies is still taking place in the cities where international financial activity is centered: London, New York, and Tokyo. A recent survey by the U.S. Federal Reserve of currency trading by financial institutions and independent brokers in New York reveals additional information of interest. Approximately 66 percent of currency trading occurs in the morning hours (Eastern Standard Time), with 29 percent be-

## THE LINGUISTICS OF CURRENCY TRADING

| | |
|---|---|
| *"Yoshi, it's Maria in New York. May I have a price on twenty cable?"* | *"Yoshi, it's Maria in New York. I am interested in either buying or selling 20 million British pounds.* |
| *"Sure. One seventy-five, twenty-thirty."* | *"Sure. I will buy them from you at 1.7520 dollars to each pound or sell them to you at 1.7530 dollars to each pound."* |
| *"Mine twenty."* | *"I'd like to buy them from you at 1.7530 dollars to each pound."* |
| *"All right. At 1.7530, I sell you twenty million pounds."* | *"All right. I sell you 20 million pounds at 1.7530 dollars per pound."* |
| *"Done."* | *"The deal is confirmed at 1.7530."* |
| *"What do you think about the Swiss franc? It's up 100 pips."* | *"Is there any information you can share with me about the fact that the Swiss franc has risen one-one hundredth of a franc against the U.S. dollar in the past hour?"* |
| *"I saw that. A few German banks have been buying steadily all day . . . ."* | *"Yes, German banks have been buying Swiss francs all day, causing the price to rise a little . . . ."* |

*Source:* **Adapted from The Basics of Foreign Trade and Exchange,** *by Adam Gonelli,* **The Federal Reserve Bank of New York, Public Information Department,** *1993, p. 34.*

tween noon and 4 P.M., and the remaining 5 percent between 4 P.M. and 8 A.M. the next day.

Three reasons typically given for the enormous growth in foreign currency trading are

1. **Deregulation of International Capital Flows**—It is easier than ever to move currencies and capital around the world without major governmental restrictions. Much of the deregulation that has characterized government policy over the past ten to fifteen years in the United States, Japan, and the now European Union has focused on financial deregulation.
2. **Gains in Technology and Transaction Cost Efficiency**—It is faster, easier, and cheaper to move millions of dollars, yen, or marks around the world than ever before. Technological advancements not only in the dissemination of information, but also in the conduct of exchange or trading, have added greatly to the ability of individuals working in these markets to conduct instanteous arbitrage (some would say speculation).
3. **The World Is a Risky Place**—Many argue that the financial markets have become increasingly volatile over recent years, with larger and faster swings in financial variables such as stock values and interest rates adding to the motivations for moving more capital at faster rates.

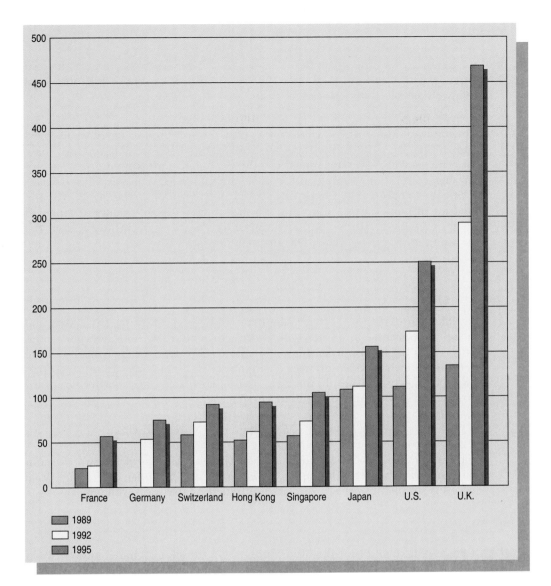

**FIGURE 7.3**

**Daily Foreign Currency Trading on World Markets (billions of U.S. dollars)**

*Source:* Adapted by authors from Federal Reserve Bank of New York's *Summary of Results of U.S. Foreign Exchange Market Turnover Survey,* April 1995, and the Bank for International Settlements 63rd Annual Report.

## The Purpose of Exchange Rates

If countries are to trade, they must be able to exchange currencies. To buy wheat, or corn, or videocassette recorders, the buyer must first have the currency in which the product is sold. An American firm purchasing consumer electronic products manufactured in Japan must first exchange its U.S. dollars for Japanese yen, then purchase the products. And each country has its own currency.[4] The exchange of one country's currency for another should be a relatively simple transaction, but it's not.

## What Is a Currency Worth?

At what rate should one currency be exchanged for another currency? For example, what should the exchange rate be between the U.S. dollar and the Japanese yen? The simplest answer is that the exchange rate should equalize purchasing power. For example, if the price of a move ticket in the United States is $6, the "correct" exchange rate would be one that exchanges $6 for the amount of Japanese yen it would take to purchase a movie ticket in Japan. If ticket prices are ¥540 (a common symbol for the yen is ¥) in Japan, then the exchange rate that would equalize purchasing power would be:

$$\frac{¥540}{$6} = ¥90/$.$$

Therefore, if the exchange rate between the two currencies is ¥90/$, she or he can purchase a ticket regardless of which country the movie goer is in. This is the theory of **purchasing power parity (PPP),** generally considered the definition of what exchange rates ideally should be. The purchasing power parity exchange rate is simply the rate that equalizes the price of the identical product or service in two different currencies:

$$\text{Price in Japan} = \text{Exchange rate} \times \text{Price in U.S.}$$

If the price of the same product in each currency is $P^¥$ and $P^\$$, and the spot exchange rate between the Japanese yen and the U.S. dollar is $S^{¥/\$}$, the price in yen is simply the price in dollars multiplied by the spot exchange rate,

$$P^¥ = S^{¥/\$} \times P^\$.$$

If this is rearranged (dividing both sides by $P^\$$), the spot exchange rate between the Japanese yen and the U.S. dollar is the ratio of the two product prices,

$$S^{¥/\$} = \frac{P^¥}{P^\$}.$$

These prices could be the price of just one good or service, such as the move ticket mentioned previously, or they could be price indices for each country that cover many different goods and services. Either form is an attempt to find comparable products in different countries (and currencies) in order to determine an exchange rate based on purchasing power parity. The question then is whether this logical approach to exchange rates actually works in practice.

## The Law of One Price

The version of purchasing power parity that estimates the exchange rate between two currencies using just one good or service as a measure of the proper exchange for all goods and services is called the **Law of One Price.** To apply the theory to actual prices across countries, we need to select a product that is identical in quality and content in every country. To be truly theoretically correct, we would want such a product to be produced entirely domestically, so that there are no import factors in its construction.

Where would one find such a perfect product? McDonald's. Table 7.2 presents what *The Economist* magazine calls the "Big Mac Index of Currencies." What it provides is a product that is essentially the same the world over and is produced and consumed entirely domestically.

The Big Mac Index compares the actual exchange rate with the exchange rate implied by the purchasing power parity measurement of comparing Big Mac prices across countries. For example, say the average price of a Big Mac in the United States on a given date is $2.42. On the same date, the price of a Big Mac in Canada, in Canadian dollars, is C$2.88. This then is used to calculate the PPP exchange rate as before:

$$\frac{\text{C\$2.88 per Big Mac}}{\text{\$2.42 per Big Mac}} = \text{C\$1.19/\$}.$$

The exchange rate between the Canadian dollar and the U.S. dollar should be C$1.19/$ according to a PPP comparison of Big Mac prices. The actual exchange rate on the date of comparison (April 7, 1997) was C$1.39/$. This means that each U.S. dollar was actually worth 1.39 Canadian dollars, when the index indicates that each U.S. dollar should have been worth 1.19 Canadian dollars. Therefore, if one is to believe in the Big Mac index, the Canadian dollar was undervalued by 14 percent.

## Monetary Systems of the Twentieth Century

The mixed fixed/floating exchange rate system operating today is only the latest stage of a continuing process of change. The systems that have preceded the present system varied between gold-based standards (**The Gold Standard**) and complex systems in which the U.S. dollar largely took the place of gold (**The Bretton Woods Agreement**). To understand why the dollar, the mark, and the yen are floating today, it is necessary to return to the (pardon the pun) *golden oldies*.

Although there is no recognized starting date, the gold standard as we call it today began sometime in the 1880s and extended up through the outbreak of the First World War. The gold standard was premised on three basic ideas:

**The Gold Standard**

1. a system of fixed rates of exchange existed between participating countries;
2. "money" issued by member countries had to be backed by reserves of gold; and
3. gold would act as an automatic adjustment, flowing in and out of countries, and automatically altering the gold reserves of that country if imbalances in trade or investment did occur.

Under the gold standard, each country's currency would be set in value per ounce of gold. For example, the U.S. dollar was defined as $20.67 per

**TABLE 7.2**

### The Law of One Price: The Big Mac Hamburger Standard

| Country | (1) Big Mac Price in Local Currency | (2) Actual Exchange Rate 4/7/97 | (3) Big Mac Prices in Dollars | (4) Implied PPP of the Dollar | (5) Local Currency under (−)/over (+) Valuation |
|---|---|---|---|---|---|
| United States | $ 2.42 | — | 2.42 | — | — |
| Argentina | Peso 2.50 | 1.00 | 2.50 | 1.03 | +3 |
| Australia | A$2.50 | 1.29 | 1.94 | 1.03 | −20 |
| Austria | Sch34.00 | 12.0 | 2.82 | 14.0 | +17 |
| Belgium | BFr109 | 35.3 | 3.09 | 45.0 | +28 |
| Brazil | Real2.97 | 1.06 | 2.81 | 1.23 | +16 |
| Britain | £1.81 | 1.63 | 2.95 | 1.34 | +22 |
| Canada | C$2.88 | 1.39 | 2.07 | 1.19 | −14 |
| Chile | Peso1,200 | 417 | 2.88 | 496 | +19 |
| China | Yuan9.70 | 8.33 | 1.16 | 4.01 | −52 |
| Czech Republic | CKr53.0 | 29.2 | 1.81 | 21.9 | −25 |
| Denmark | DKr25.75 | 6.52 | 3.95 | 10.6 | +63 |
| France | FFr17.5 | 5.76 | 3.04 | 7.23 | +26 |
| Germany | DM4.90 | 1.71 | 2.86 | 2.02 | +18 |
| Hong Kong | HK$9.90 | 7.75 | 1.28 | 4.09 | −47 |
| Hungary | Forint271 | 178 | 1.52 | 112 | −37 |
| Israel | Shekel1.15 | 3.38 | 3.40 | 4.75 | +40 |
| Italy | Lire4,600 | 1,683 | 2.73 | 1,901 | +13 |
| Japan | ¥294 | 126 | 2.34 | 121 | −3 |
| Malaysia | M$3.87 | 2.50 | 1.55 | 1.60 | −36 |
| Mexico | Peso14.9 | 7.90 | 1.89 | 6.16 | −22 |
| Netherlands | Fl5.45 | 1.92 | 2.83 | 2.25 | +17 |
| New Zealand | NZ$3.25 | 1.45 | 2.24 | 1.34 | −7 |
| Poland | Zloty4.30 | 3.10 | 1.39 | 1.78 | −43 |
| Russia | Rouble11,000 | 5.739 | 1.92 | 4,545 | −21 |
| Singapore | S$3.00 | 1.44 | 2.08 | 1.24 | −14 |
| South Africa | Rand7.80 | 4.43 | 1.76 | 3.22 | −27 |
| South Korea | Won2,300 | 894 | 2.57 | 950 | +6 |
| Spain | Pta375 | 144 | 2.60 | 155 | +7 |
| Sweden | SKr26.0 | 7.72 | 3.37 | 10.7 | +39 |
| Switzerland | SFr5.90 | 1.47 | 4.02 | 2.44 | +66 |
| Taiwan | NT$68.0 | 27.6 | 2.47 | 28.1 | +2 |
| Thailand | Baht46.7 | 26.1 | 1.79 | 19.3 | −26 |

Column (1): Prices in local currency; may vary by location.
Column (2): Actual exchange rate on April 7, 1997 (London quotes).
Column (3): column (1) ÷ column (2)
Column (4): column (1) ÷ $2.42 (price of Big Mac in United States).
Column (5): column (4) ÷ column (2).

*Source:* Adapted from "Big MacCurrencies," *The Economist,* April 12, 1997, p. 71. Original quotations courtesy of McDonald's. United States Big Mac price is the average of New York, Chicago, San Francisco, and Atlanta. British exchange rate and implied PPP rates quoted in U.S. dollar per pound.

ounce, while the British pound sterling was defined as £4.2474 per ounce. Once each currency was defined versus gold, the determination of the exchange rate between the two currencies (or any two currencies) was simple:

$$\frac{\$20.67/\text{ounce of gold}}{£4.2474/\text{ounce of gold}} = \$4.8665/£.$$

The use of gold as the pillar of the system was a result of historical tradition, and not anything inherently unique to the metal gold itself. It was shiny, soft, rare, and generally acceptable for payment in all countries.

## The Interwar Years, 1919–1939

The 1920s and 1930s were a tumultuous period for the international monetary system. The British pound sterling, the dominant currency prior to World War I, survived the war but was greatly weakened. The U.S. dollar returned to the gold standard in 1919, but gold convertibility was largely untested across countries throughout the 1920s, as world trade took long to recover from the destruction of the war. With the economic collapse and bank runs of the 1930s, the U.S. was forced to once again abandon gold convertibility.

The economic depression of the 1930s was worldwide. As all countries came under increasingly desperate economic conditions, many countries (including the United States) resorted to isolationist policies and protectionism. World trade slowed to a trickle, and with it the general need for currency exchange. It was not until the latter stages of the Second World War that international trade and commerce once again demanded a system for currency convertibility and stability.

## The Bretton Woods Agreement, 1944–1971

The governments of forty-four of the Allied Powers gathered together in Bretton Woods, New Hampshire, in 1944 to plan for the postwar international monetary system. The British delegation, headed by Lord John Maynard Keynes, the famous economist, and the U.S. delegation, headed by Secretary of the Treasury Henry Morgenthau, Jr., and director of the Treasury's monetary research department, Harry D. White, labored long and hard to reach an agreement. In the end, all parties agreed that a postwar system would be stable and sustainable only if it was able to provide sufficient liquidity to countries during periods of crisis. Any new system had to have facilities for the extension of credit for countries to defend their currency values.

After weeks of debate, the Bretton Woods Agreement was reached. The plan called for the following:

1. Fixed exchange rates between member countries, termed an "adjustable peg"
2. The establishment of a fund of gold and currencies available to members for stabilization of their respective currencies (the **International Monetary Fund**)
3. The establishment of a bank that would provide funding for long-term development projects (the **World Bank**)

Like the gold standard at the turn of the century, all participants were to establish par values of their currencies in terms of gold. Unlike the prior sys-

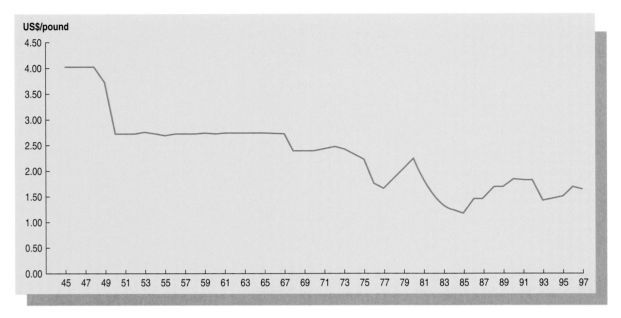

**FIGURE 7.4**

**The U.S. Dollar–British Pound Exchange Rate, 1945–1998**

tem, however, there was little if any convertibility of currencies for gold expected; convertibility was versus the U.S. dollar ("good as gold"). In fact, the only currency officially convertible to gold was the U.S. dollar (pegged at \$35/ounce). It was this reliance on the value of the dollar and the reliance on the economic stability of the U.S. economy, in fact, which led to twenty-five years of relatively stable currency and to the system's eventual collapse.

One indicator of the success of the Bretton Woods system is the stability that it provided the major world currencies throughout the 1950s and 1960s (the long flat line in Figure 7.4). The U.S. dollar–British pound exchange rate enjoyed its longest period of stability at this time, and has certainly not experienced such either before or since.

**Times of Crisis, 1971–1973**

On August 15, 1971, President Richard M. Nixon of the United States announced that "I have instructed [Treasury] Secretary [John B.] Connally to suspend temporarily the convertibility of the dollar into gold or other assets." With this simple statement, President Nixon effectively ended the fixed exchange rates established at Bretton Woods, New Hampshire, more than twenty-five years earlier.

In the weeks and months following the August announcement, world currency markets devalued the dollar, although the United States had only ended gold convertibility, not officially declared the dollar's value to be less. In late 1971, the Group of Ten finance ministers met at the Smithsonian Institution in Washington, D.C., to try to piece together a system to keep world markets operational. First, the dollar was officially devalued to \$38/ounce of gold (as if anyone had access to gold convertibility). Secondly, all other major world currencies were revalued against the dollar (the dollar was relatively devalued), and all would now be allowed to vary from their fixed parity rates by plus/minus 2.25 percent from the previous 1.00 percent.

Without convertibility of at least one of the member currencies to gold, the system was doomed from the start. Within weeks, currencies were surpassing their allowed deviation limits; revaluations were occurring more frequently; and the international monetary system was not a "system," it was chaos. Finally, world currency trading nearly ground to a halt in March 1973. The world's currency markets closed for two weeks. When they reopened, major currencies (particularly the U.S. dollar) were simply allowed to float in value. In January 1976, the Group of Ten once again met, this time in Jamaica, and the Jamaica Agreement officially recognized what the markets had known for years—the world's currencies were no longer fixed in value.

## Floating Exchange Rates, 1973–Present

Since March of 1973, the world's major currencies have floated in value versus each other. This flotation poses many problems for the conduct of international trade and commerce, problems that are themselves the subject of entire courses of study (*currency risk management* for one). The inability of a country, a country's government to be specific, to control the value of its currency on world markets has been a harsh reality for most.

Throughout the 1970s, if a government wished to alter the current value of its currency, or even slow or alter a trending change in the currency's value, the government would simply buy or sell its own currency in the market using its reserves of other major currencies. This process of **direct intervention** was effective as long as the depth of the government's reserve pockets kept up with the volume of trading on currency markets. For these countries—both then and today—the primary problem is maintaining adequate foreign exchange reserves.

By the 1980s, however, the world's currency markets were so large that the ability of a few governments (the United States, Japan, and Germany to name three) to move a market simply through direct intervention was over. The major tool now left was for government (at least when operating alone) to alter economic variables such as interest rates—to alter the *motivations* and *expectations* of market participants for capital movements and currency exchange. During periods of relative low inflation (a critical assumption), a country that wishes to strengthen its currency versus others might raise domestic interest rates to attract capital from abroad. Although relatively effective in many cases, the downside of this policy is that it raises interest rates for domestic consumers and investors alike, possibly slowing the domestic economy. The result is that governments today must often choose between an external economic policy action (raising interest rates to strengthen the currency) and a domestic economic policy action (lowering interest rates to stimulate economic activity).

There is, however, one other method of currency value management that has been selectively employed in the past fifteen years, termed **coordinated intervention.** After the U.S. dollar had risen in value dramatically over the 1980 to 1985 period, the Group of Five or G5 nations (France, Japan, West Germany, United States, and United Kingdom) met at the Plaza Hotel in New York in September 1985 and agreed to a set of goals and policies, the **Plaza Agreement.**

These goals were to be accomplished through coordinated intervention among the central banks of the major nations. By the Bank of Japan (Japan), the Bundesbank (Germany), and the Federal Reserve (United States) all simultaneously intervening in the currency markets, they hoped to reach the combined strength level necessary to push the dollar's value down. Their actions were met with some success in that instance, but there have been few occasions since then of coordinated intervention.

## Fixed and Floating Currencies Today

Although the current floating exchange rate system, if it is indeed a "system" in any real way, has suffered through periods of volatility and crisis, it is at present the way the world works. Or is it? If one were to look at all of the world's currencies today, as in the International Monetary Fund's Exchange Rates Arrangements table (Table 7.3), it is obviously not easy to simply state what type of currency system the world operates under. There are a variety of different fixed, floating, managed floating, etc., systems at work. We now turn our attention to one of the most topical systems, the European Monetary System (EMS) and its current transition to a single currency.

## The European Monetary System and the Euro

In the week following the suspension of dollar convertibility to gold in 1971, the finance ministers of a number of the major countries of western Europe discussed how they might maintain the fixed parities of their currencies independent of the U.S. dollar. By April 1972, they had concluded an agreement that was termed the "snake within the tunnel." The member countries agreed to fix parity rates between currencies with allowable trading bands of 2.25 percent variance. As a group they would allow themselves to vary by 4.5 percent versus the U.S. dollar. Although the effort was well intentioned, the various pressures and crises that rocked international economic order in the 1970s, such as the OPEC price shock of 1974, resulted in a relatively short life for the "snake."

In 1979 a much more formalized structure was put in place among many of the major members of the European Community. The **European Monetary System (EMS)** officially began operation in Mach 1979 and once again established a grid of fixed parity rates among member currencies. The EMS was a much more elaborate system for the management of exchange rates than its predecessor "snake." The EMS consisted of three different components that would work in concert to preserve fixed parities (also termed central rates).

First, all countries that were committing their currencies and their efforts to the preservation of fixed exchange rates entered the **Exchange-Rate Mechanism (ERM).** Although all the currencies of the countries of the European Union would be used in the calculation of important indices for management purposes, several countries chose not to be ERM participants. Participation in the ERM technically required that countries accept bilateral responsibility of maintaining the fixed rates.

The second element of the European Monetary System was the actual grid of bilateral exchange rates with their specified band limits. As under the Smith-

## TABLE 7.3

**Exchange Rate Arrangements as of September 30, 1997[1]**

| Currently pegged to | | | | | Flexibility limited in terms of a single currency or group of currencies | | More flexible | |
|---|---|---|---|---|---|---|---|---|
| U.S. dollar | French franc | Other currency | SDR | Other composite[2] | Single currency[3] | Cooperative arrangements[4] | Other managed floating | Independently floating |
| Angola | Benin | Bhutan | Libya | Bangladesh | Bahrain | Austria | Algeria | Afghanistan, |
| Antigua & Barbuda | Burkina Faso | (Indian rupee) | Myanmar | Botswana | Qatar | Belgium | Belarus | Islamic State of |
| Argentina | Cameroon | Bosnia and | | Burundi | Saudi Arabia | Denmark | Brazil | Albania |
| Bahamas, The | C. African Rep. | Herzegovina | | Cape Verde | United Arab | Finland | Cambodia | Armenia |
| Barbados | Chad | (deutsche mark) | | Cyprus | Emirates | France | Chile | Australia |
| | | Brunei Darussalam | | | | | | Azerbaijan |
| Belize | Comoros | (Singapore | | Fiji | | Germany | China, P.R. | |
| Djibouti | Congo, Rep. of | dollar) | | Iceland | | Ireland | Colombia | Bolivia |
| Dominica | Côte d'Ivoire | Bulgaria | | Jordan | | Italy | Costa Rica | Canada |
| Grenada | Equatorial | (deutsche mark) | | Kuwait | | Luxembourg | Croatia | Congo, Dem. Rep. |
| Iraq | Guinea | Estonia | | Malta | | Netherlands | Czech Republic | Ethiopia |
| | Gabon | (deutsche mark) | | | | | | Gambia, The |
| Liberia | | | | Morocco | | Portugal | Dominican Rep. | |
| Lithuania | Guinea-Bissau | Kiribati | | Samoa | | Spain | Ecuador | Ghana |
| Marshall Islands | Mali | (Australian | | Seychelles | | | Egypt | Guatemala |
| Micronesia, | Niger | dollar) | | Slovak Republic | | | El Salvador | Guinea |
| Fed. States of | Senegal | Lesotho | | Solomon Islands | | | Eritrea | Guyana |
| Nigeria | Togo | (South African | | | | | | Haiti |
| | | rand) | | Tonga | | | Georgia | |
| Oman | | Namibia | | Vanuatu | | | Greece | India |
| Panama | | (South America | | | | | Honduras | Indonesia |
| St. Kitts & Nevis | | rand) | | | | | Hungary | Jamaica |
| St. Lucia | | Nepal | | | | | Iran, I.R. of | Japan |
| St. Vincent and the | | (Indian rupee) | | | | | | Kazakhstan |
| Grenadines | | San Marino | | | | | Israel | |
| Syrian Arab Rep. | | (Italian lira) | | | | | Korea | Kenya |
| | | Swaziland | | | | | Kyrgyz Rep. | Lebanon |
| | | (South African | | | | | Lao P.D. Rep | Madagascar |
| | | rand) | | | | | Latvia | Malawi |
| | | | | | | | | Mauritania |
| | | | | | | | Macedonia | |
| | | | | | | | FYR of | Mexico |
| | | | | | | | Malaysia | Moldova |
| | | | | | | | Maldives | Mongolia |
| | | | | | | | Mauritius | Mozambique |
| | | | | | | | Nicaragua | New Zealand |
| | | | | | | | | |
| | | | | | | | Norway | Papua New Guinea |
| | | | | | | | Pakistan | Paraguay |
| | | | | | | | Poland | Peru |
| | | | | | | | Russia | Philippines |
| | | | | | | | Singapore | Romania |
| | | | | | | | | |
| | | | | | | | Slovenia | Rwanda |
| | | | | | | | Sri Lanka | São Tomé and |
| | | | | | | | Sudan | Principe |
| | | | | | | | Suriname | Sierra Leone |
| | | | | | | | Thailand | Somalia |
| | | | | | | | | South Africa |
| | | | | | | | Tunisia | |
| | | | | | | | Turkmenistan | Sweden |
| | | | | | | | Turkey | Switzerland |
| | | | | | | | Urkaine | Tajikistan, Rep. of |
| | | | | | | | Uruguay | Tanzania |
| | | | | | | | | Trinidad and |
| | | | | | | | Uzbekistan | Tobago |
| | | | | | | | Venezuela | |
| | | | | | | | Vietnam | Uganda |
| | | | | | | | | United Kingdom |
| | | | | | | | | United States |
| | | | | | | | | Yemen, Republic of |
| | | | | | | | | Zambia |
| | | | | | | | | |
| | | | | | | | | Zimbabwe |

| Classification status[1] | 1991 | 1992 | 1993 | 1994 | 1995 QI | QII | QIII | QIV | 1996 QI | QII | QIII | QIV | 1997 QI | QII | QIII |
|---|---|---|---|---|---|---|---|---|---|---|---|---|---|---|---|
| Currency pegged to | | | | | | | | | | | | | | | |
| U.S. dollar | 24 | 24 | 21 | 23 | 23 | 23 | 23 | 22 | 21 | 20 | 20 | 21 | 21 | 21 | 21 |
| French franc | 14 | 14 | 14 | 14 | 14 | 14 | 14 | 14 | 14 | 14 | 14 | 14 | 14 | 15 | 15 |
| Russian ruble | — | 6 | — | — | — | — | — | — | — | — | — | — | — | — | — |
| Other currency | 4 | 6 | 8 | 8 | 8 | 7 | 7 | 8 | 9 | 9 | 9 | 9 | 9 | 9 | 11 |
| SDR | 6 | 5 | 4 | 4 | 3 | 3 | 3 | 3 | 3 | 2 | 2 | 2 | 2 | 2 | 2 |
| Other currency composite | 33 | 29 | 26 | 21 | 20 | 20 | 20 | 19 | 19 | 20 | 20 | 20 | 20 | 18 | 17 |
| Flexibility limited vis-à-vis a | | | | | | | | | | | | | | | |
| single currency | 4 | 4 | 4 | 4 | 4 | 4 | 4 | 4 | 4 | 4 | 4 | 4 | 4 | 4 | 4 |
| Cooperative arrangements | 10 | 9 | 9 | 10 | 10 | 10 | 10 | 10 | 10 | 10 | 10 | 12 | 12 | 12 | 12 |
| Adjusted according to a | | | | | | | | | | | | | | | |
| set of indicators | 5 | 3 | 4 | 3 | 3 | 3 | 3 | 2 | 2 | 2 | 2 | 2 | — | — | — |
| Managed floating | 27 | 23 | 29 | 33 | 35 | 39 | 38 | 44 | 44 | 45 | 46 | 45 | 48 | 49 | 48 |
| Independently floating | 29 | 44 | 56 | 58 | 59 | 56 | 57 | 54 | 55 | 55 | 54 | 52 | 51 | 51 | 51 |
| Total | 156 | 167 | 175 | 178 | 179 | 179 | 179 | 180 | 181 | 181 | 181 | 181 | 181 | 181 | 181 |

[1]For members with dual or multiple exchange markets, the arrangement shown is that in the major market.
[2]Comprises currencies that are pegged to various "baskets" of currencies of the members' own choice, as distinct from the SDR basket.
[3]Exchange rates of all currencies have shown limited flexibility in terms of the U.S. dollar.
[4]Refers to the cooperative arrangement maintained under the European Monetary System.
[5]Starting May 24, 1994, the Azerbaijan authorities ceased to peg the manat to the Russian ruble and the exchange arrangement was reclassified to "Independently floating."

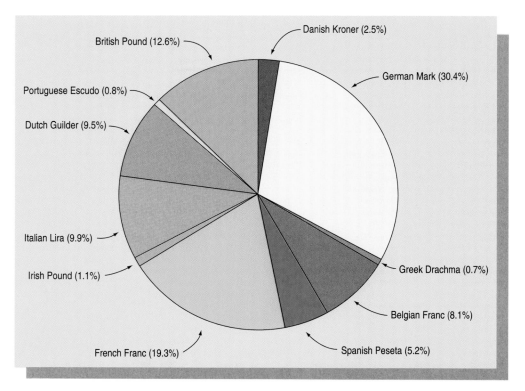

**FIGURE 7.5**

**The Composition of the European Currency Unit**

*Source:* "The ECU and Its Role in the Process towards Monetary Union," *European Economy,* No. 48, September 1991, p. 125.

sonian Agreement and the former snake, member currencies were allowed to deviate ±2.25 percent from their parity rate. Some currencies, however, such as the Italian lira, were originally allowed larger bands (±10 percent variance) due to their more characteristic volatility.

The third and final element of the European Monetary System was the creation of the European Currency Unit (ECU). As illustrated in Figure 7.5, the ECU is a weighted average index of the currencies that are part of the EMS. Each currency is weighted by a value reflecting the relative size of that country's trade and gross domestic product. This allows each currency to be defined in units per ECU. The ECU can also serve as a method of value accounting among EMS members without showing preference by using one individual currency.

## Events and Performances of the EMS

The need for fixed exchange rates within Europe is clear. The countries of western Europe trade among themselves to a degree approaching interstate commerce in the United States. It is therefore critical to the economies and businesses of Europe that exchange rates be as stable as possible. Although it had its critics, the EMS generally was successful in providing exchange rate stability.

The EMS, however, has recently experienced several setbacks. A number of the political and economic forces that have driven European economies in the past decade have started to put new and exceptional pressures on the EMS.

- **Deutschemark dominance.** Most EMS realignments have resulted in the revaluation of the German mark and the devaluation of most other member currencies. The rapid growth of German industry and trade has resulted in the deutschemark growing in its proportion of world currency trading. The EMS is often now referred to as the "DMZ" or "DM Zone."
- **EMS membership expansion.** Although not formally a part of the European Union, the EMS is a parallel organization in terms of membership. As the EU has expanded to include Greece (1981) and Portugal and Spain (1986), so has the EMS. The British pound has long been included in the calculation of the ECU, but it was not until the autumn of 1990 that Great Britain joined the ERM. Although all countries are not ERM participants, the expansion of more countries, economies, and their currencies into the EMS has introduced considerable pressure on the system.
- **German reunification.** The merging of West Germany and East Germany in 1989 significantly increased inflationary and budgetary pressures in Germany. The West German currency, the deutschemark, was exchanged for the East German currency, the ostmark, at fixed rates that were artificially high for the ostmark. This caused major monetary policy actions that threatened the internal stability of the EMS as the dominance of the deutschemark within the EMS was only seen to increase.
- **Maastricht and a single currency for Europe.** The continuing movements toward European integration (the **Maastricht Treaty**) have resulted in a specific time schedule for the eventual creation of a single currency to replace the individual currencies of the EMS/EU members.

## The Maastricht Treaty

In an attempt to maintain the momentum of European integration, the members of the European Union concluded the Maastricht Treaty in December 1991. The treaty, besides laying out long-term goals of harmonized social and welfare policies in the Union, specified a timetable for the adoption of a single currency to replace all individual currencies. This was a very ambitious move. The Maastricht Treaty called for the integration and coordination of economic and monetary policy so that few financial differences would exist by the time of currency unification in 1997. For a single currency to work, there could be only one monetary policy across all countries. Otherwise, different monetary policies would lead to different interest rates. Differences in interest rates often lead to large capital flows.

The first major hurdle for the single currency was the acceptance of the treaty. Denmark had been successful in gaining the right to conduct a popular vote of its citizens to determine whether the degree of integration described by Maastricht was indeed desirable. In May 1992, the Danes voted "nej" (no). The Irish and French immediately scheduled popular votes in their own countries. The Irish vote resulted in a relatively strong show of support, while the French vote conducted on September 20 was an extremely narrow yes vote. The French result was immediately dubbed "le petit oui."

**The Euro**

On January 1, 1999, the member states of the European Union will initiate European Monetary Unification, the creation of a single currency for the EU, called the **euro.** This new currency will eventually replace all the individual currencies of the participating member states, resulting in a single, simple, efficient medium of exchange for all trade and investment activities. The explicit schedule for the various stages of euro introduction and expansion is described in Table 7.4.

The actual process of putting a single currency in place in the European Union has been, and will continue to be, complex. As mentioned previously in our discussion on monetary systems in the twentieth century, in order for the individual currencies to first be irrevocably locked in their rates of exchange

**TABLE 7.4**

**Euro Calendar: What Will Happen and When**

By 30 June 1997
■ Legislation establishing the euro as a currency
■ Stability and growth pact
■ Exchange Rate Mechanism Mk II. by the EMI
■ Blueprint on future monetary policy instruments by the EMI [1]
■ Design of euro coins

As soon as possible in 1998
■ Decision on participating Member States European Council

During 1998
■ Creation of the ECB [2] and appointment of its executive board
■ Start production of euro banknotes and coins
■ Adoption of necessary secondary legislation

January 1, 1999
■ Conversion rates are irrevocably fixed and various legislations come into force, notably on the legal status of the euro
■ Definition and execution of the single monetary policy in euro by the ESCB [3]
■ Foreign exchange operations start in euro by the ESCB [3]
■ New public debt issued in euro by Member States, European Investment Bank, Commission

January 1, 1999 to January 1, 2002 (at the latest)
■ Changeover to the euro by the banking and finance industry
■ Assist the whole economy in an orderly changeover, by the Commission and Member States

January 1, 2002 (at the latest)
■ Start circulation of euro banknotes by the ESCB [3]
■ Start circulation of euro coins in Member States
■ Complete changeover to the euro in public administration by the Member States

July 1, 2002 (at the latest)
■ Cancel the legal tender status of national banknotes and coins by the Member States, ESCB [3]

[1] EMI—European Monetary Institute, precursor of the ECB
[2] ECB—European Central Bank
[3] ESCB—European System of Central Banks
[4] on a recommendation from the Council of Ministers on the basis of reports and recommendations from the Commission and the EMI

*Source:* **http://europa.eu.int/euro/en/calendar.asp** (January 1998)

amongst themselves (as the various currencies will be at some point in 1998), there must be a single monetary policy conducted throughout the European Union participating states. This has been accomplished in a two-step process: first, by the establishment of the European Monetary Institute (EMI), which both studied and established the monetary preconditions of a single currency; and secondly, with the formation of a single central-banking institution for the European Union, the European Central Bank (ECB). The ECB will be responsible for both the formulation and implementation of a single monetary policy for the EU. This is the single most important requirement for a stable and workable euro.

Although there continue to be many critics and opponents to the euro, the European Union has continued to move forward and maintain its basic schedule for single currency implementation. A number of the member states will not achieve the required economic criteria for immediate entry into participation, which has led to a proposal of a multispeed, or staged member, entry. There also remains much debate over the relationship between those countries who wish to participate, the "ins," and those who do not, the "outs." Only time will tell if the system is workable, but time is now short.

## International Money Markets

A money market traditionally is defined as a market for deposits, accounts, or securities that have maturities of one year or less. The international money markets, often termed the Eurocurrency markets, constitute an enormous financial market that is in many ways outside the jurisdiction and supervision of world financial and governmental authorities.

### Eurocurrency Markets

A **Eurocurrency** is any foreign currency-denominated deposit or account at a financial institution outside the country of the currency's issuance. For example, U.S. dollars that are held on account in a bank in London are termed **Eurodollars.** Similarly, Japanese yen held on account in a Parisian financial institution would be classified as Euroyen. The *Euro* prefix does not mean these currencies or accounts are only European, as German marks on account in Singapore would also be classified as a Eurocurrency, a Euromark account.

### Eurocurrency Interest Rates

What is the significance of these foreign currency-denominated accounts? Simply put, it is the purity of value that comes from no governmental interference or restrictions with their use. Eurocurrency accounts are not controlled or managed by governments (for example, the Bank of England has no control over Eurodollar accounts), therefore, the financial institutions pay no deposit insurance, hold no reserve requirements, and normally are not subject to any interest rate restrictions with respect to such accounts. Eurocurrencies are one of the purest indicators of what these currencies should yield to terms of interest. Sample Eurocurrency interest rates for 1995 are shown in Table 7.5.

There are hundreds of different major interest rates around the globe, but the international financial markets focus on a very few, the **interbank interest rates.** Interbank rates charged by banks to banks in the major international fi-

**TABLE 7.5**

**Exchange Rates and Eurocurrency Interest Rates**

| Exchange/Interest Rate | Maturity | U.S. Dollar (USD) | German Mark (DEM/USD) | Japanese Yen (JAP/USD) |
|---|---|---|---|---|
| Spot Exchange Rate | — | | 1.5496 | 99.61% |
| Eurocurrency Deposit Rate | | | | |
| London bid rates; | 1 month | 5.8750% | 5.0625% | 2.2813% |
| percent per annum | 3 months | 6.3750% | 5.1875% | 2.3438% |
| | 6 months | 6.8750% | 5.3750% | 2.3438% |
| | 12 months | 7.6250% | 5.7500% | 2.5938% |
| Forward Exchange Rate | | | | |
| | 1 month | — | 1.5486 | 99.36 |
| | 3 months | — | 1.5451 | 98.62 |
| | 6 months | — | 1.5384 | 97.43 |
| | 12 months | — | 1.5226 | 94.95 |

*Source:* Adapted from *Harris Bank Foreign Exchange Weekly Review,* Harris Trust and Savings Bank, Chicago, December 30, 1994.

nancial centers such as London, Frankfurt, Paris, New York, Tokyo, Singapore, and Hong Kong are generally regarded as "the interest rate" in the respective market. The interest rate that is used most often in international loan agreements is the Eurocurrency interest rate on U.S. dollars (Eurodollars) in London between banks: the London Interbank Offer Rate (LIBOR). Because it is a Eurocurrency rate, it floats freely without regard to governmental restrictions on reserves or deposit insurance or any other regulation or restriction that would add expense to transactions using this capital. The interbank rates for other currencies in other markets are often named similarly, PIBOR (Paris interbank offer rate), MIBOR (Madrid interbank offer rate), HIBOR (either Hong Kong or Helsinki interbank offer rate), SIBOR (Singapore interbank offer rate). While **LIBOR** is the offer rate—the cost of funds "offered" to those acquiring a loan—the equivalent deposit rate in the **Euromarkets** is LIBID, the London InterBank Bid Rate, the rate of interest other banks can earn on Eurocurrency deposits. Global Perspective 7.3 illustrates how low interest rates can get.

How do these international Eurocurrency and interbank interest rates differ from domestic rates? Answer: not by much. They generally move up and down in unison, by currency, but often differ by the percentage by which the restrictions alter the rates of interest in the domestic markets. For example, because the Euromarkets have no restrictions, the spread between the offer rate and the bid rate (the loan rate and the deposit rate) is substantially smaller than in domestic markets. This means the loan rates in international markets are a bit lower than domestic market loan rates, and deposit rates are a bit higher in the international markets than in domestic markets. This is, however, only a big-player market. Only well-known international firms, financial or non-financial, have access to the quantities of capital necessary to operate in the Euromarkets. But as described in the following sections on international debt

## RUN ON 'FREE' MONEY IN JAPAN CRIPPLES THE YEN

**T**here is a reason why the Japanese yen comes across as the weakling of the currency markets these days: Japan, with its struggling economy, frail stock market, and cheap funds has become a place to borrow, not invest. "Here in Japan you are in an extraordinary situation, and that extraordinary factor is that money is free," said Jesper Koll, an economist at J.P. Morgan Securities Asia Ltd. With rock-bottom interest rates essentially offset by inflation, he continued, money has become a free commodity. "As a result," he quickly added, "it is flowing out of the country. Are we not now just witnessing the making of another bubble?"

So while some in the United States are preoccupied with how strong the dollar should be, here in Japan the headache is how weak the yen will get. Every few days, a Japanese official utters fretful remarks about the decline of the yen, which, in percentage terms, traveled twice as far against the dollar in January [1997] as it had moved on average each month last year. Yet, Japanese officials might be relieved that investors have only recently acted on an increasingly legitimate reason for a weaker yen: the gap in interest rates between their country and the United States. People are pumping money out of Japan in search of higher yields, fueling the stock and bond markets in New York and overseas, several economists say. Investors come to Japan to raise funds, then convert their yen borrowings into dollars. When such activity turns into a flood, the value of the yen slides.

The role of interest rates becomes crucial. Japan's official discount rate, the interest rate the central bank charges commercial banks for overnight funds, stands at a record low 0.1 percent, and the rate for overnight funds secured with bonds has often hovered below that level. Factor in an inflation rate of 0.5 percent, and borrowed funds here are in theory not merely free, but offer a dividend.

*Source: "Run on 'Free' Money in Japan Cripples the Yen," International Herald Tribune, February 22–23, 1997, 1.*

and equity markets, more and more firms are gaining access to the Euromarkets to take advantage of deregulated capital flows.

## Linking Eurocurrency Interest Rates and Exchange Rates

Eurocurrency interest rates also play a large role in the foreign exchange markets themselves. They are, in fact, the interest rates used in the calculation of the forward rates we noted earlier. Recall that a forward rate is a contract for a specific amount of currency to be exchanged for another currency at a future date, usually 30, 60, 90, 180, or even 360 days in the future. Forward rates are calculated from the spot rate in effect on the day the contract is written along with the respective Eurocurrency interest rates for the two currencies.

For example, to calculate the 90-day forward rate, multiply the spot rate on that date by the ratio of the two Eurocurrency interest rates. Note that it is important to adjust the interest rates for the actual period of time needed, 90 days (3 months) of a 360-day financial year:

$$\text{90-Day Forward} = \text{Spot} \times \left[ \frac{1 + \left( i_{90}^{DEM} \times \frac{90}{360} \right)}{1 + \left( i_{90}^{USD} \times \frac{90}{360} \right)} \right]$$

Now, plugging in the spot exchange rate of DEM 1.5496/USD and the two 90-day (3-month) Eurocurrency interest rates from Table 7.5 (5.1875 percent for the DEM and 6.3750 percent for the USD), the 90-day forward exchange rate is

$$\text{DEM } 1.5496/\text{USD} \times \left( \frac{1 + \left(.051875 \times \frac{90}{360}\right)}{1 + \left(.06375 \times \frac{90}{360}\right)} \right) = \text{DEM } 1.5451/\text{USD}$$

The forward rate of DEM 1.5451/USD is a "stronger rate" for the German mark than the current spot rate. This is because it takes 1.5496 marks to buy one dollar spot, but will only take 1.5451 marks to buy one dollar at the forward rate 90 days in the future. The German mark is said to be "**selling forward** at a premium," meaning that the forward rate for purchasing marks is more expensive than the spot rate.

Why is this the case? The reason is that the Eurocurrency interest rate on the German mark for 90 days is lower than the Eurocurrency interest rate on the U.S. dollar. If it were the other way around—if the German mark interest rate were higher than the U.S. dollar interest rate—the German mark would be "selling forward at a discount." The forward rates quoted in the foreign exchange markets, and used so frequently in international business, simply reflect the difference in interest rates between the two currencies.

Businesses frequently use forward exchange-rate contracts to manage their exposure to currency risk. As Chapter 17 will detail, corporations use many other financial instruments and techniques beyond forward contracts to manage currency risk, but forwards are still the mainstay of industry.

Banks around the world are very active in International Capital Markets. Lloyd's Bank in the United Kingdom has been recognized as a global leader in the banking and insurance industries.

Source: http://www.lloydsbank.co.uk

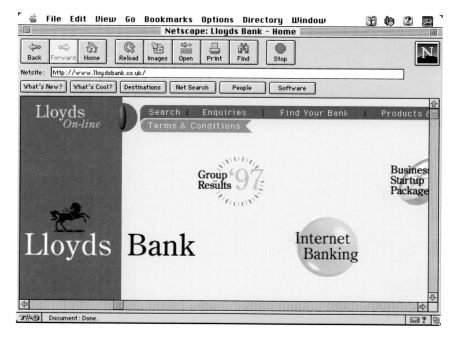

## International Capital Markets

Just as with the money markets, the international capital markets serve as links among the capital markets of individual countries, as well as constituting a separate market of its own, the capital that flows into the Euromarkets. Firms can now raise capital, debit or equity, fixed or floating interest rates, in any of a dozen currencies, for maturities ranging from one month to thirty years, in the international capital markets. Although the international capital markets traditionally have been dominated by debt instruments, international equity markets have shown considerable growth in recent years.

The international financial markets can be subdivided in a number of ways. The following sections describe the international debt and equity markets for securitized and nonsecuritized capital. This is capital that is separable and tradable, like a bond or a stock. *Nonsecuritized,* a fancy term for bank loans, was really the original source of international capital (as well as the international debt crisis).

The definition of what constitutes an international financial transaction is dependent on two fundamental characteristics: (1) whether the borrower is domestic or foreign, and (2) whether the borrower is raising capital denominated in the domestic currency or a foreign currency. These two characteristics form four categories of financial transactions, as illustrated in Figure 7.6.

**Defining International Financing**

**FIGURE 7.6**

**Categorizing International Financial Transactions: Issuing Bonds in London**

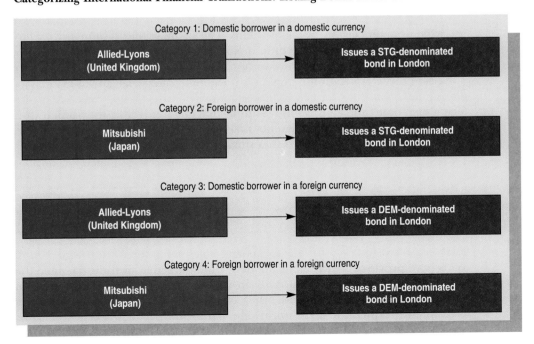

- **Category 1: Domestic Borrower/Domestic Currency**—This is a traditional domestic financial market activity. A borrower who is resident within the country raises capital from domestic financial institutions denominated in local currency. All countries with basic market economies have their own domestic financial markets, some large and some quite small. This is still by far the most common type of financial transaction.
- **Category 2: Foreign Borrower/Domestic Currency**—This is when a foreign borrower enters another country's financial market and raises capital denominated in the local currency. The international dimension of this transaction is based only on who the borrower is. Many borrowers, both public and private, increasingly go to the world's largest financial markets to raise capital for their enterprises. The ability of a foreign firm to raise capital in another country's financial market is sometimes limited by that government's restrictions on who can borrow, as well as the market's willingness to lend to foreign governments and companies that it may not know as well as domestic borrowers.
- **Category 3: Domestic Borrower/Foreign Currency**—Many borrowers in today's international markets need capital denominated in a foreign currency. A domestic firm may actually issue a bond to raise capital in its local market where it is known quite well, but raise the capital in the form of a foreign currency. This type of financial transaction occurs less often than the previous two types because it requires a local market in foreign currencies, a Eurocurrency market. A number of countries, such as the United States, highly restrict the amount and types of financial transactions in foreign currency. International financial centers such as London and Zurich have been the traditional centers of these types of transactions.
- **Category 4: Foreign Borrower/Foreign Currency**—This is the strictest form of the traditional Eurocurrency financial transaction, a foreign firm borrowing foreign currency. Once again, this type of activity may be restricted by which borrowers are allowed into a country's financial markets and which currencies are available. This type of financing dominates the activities of many banking institutions in the **offshore banking** market.

Using this classification system, it is possible to categorize any individual international financial transaction. For example, the distinction between an international bond and a Eurobond is simply that of a Category 2 transaction (foreign borrower in a domestic currency market) and a Category 3 or 4 transaction (foreign currency denominated in a single local market or many markets).

## International Banking and Bank Lending

Banks have existed in different forms and roles since the Middle Ages. Bank loans have provided nearly all of the debt capital needed by industry since the start of the Industrial Revolution. Even in this age in which securitized debt instruments (bonds, notes, and other types of tradable paper) are growing as sources of capital for firms worldwide, banks still perform a critical role by providing capital for medium-sized and smaller firms, which dominate all economies.

## Structure of International Banking

Similar to the direct foreign investment decision sequence discussed in Chapter 5, banks can expand their cross-border activities in a variety of ways. Like all decisions involving exports and direct investment, increasing the level of international activity and capability normally requires placing more capital and knowledge at risk to be able to reap the greater benefits of expanding markets.

A bank that wants to conduct business with clients in other countries but does not want to open a banking operation in that country can do so through correspondent banks or representative offices. A **correspondent bank** is an unrelated bank (by ownership) based in the foreign country. By the nature of its business, it has knowledge of the local market and access to clients, capital, and information, which a foreign bank does not.

A second way that banks may gain access to foreign markets without actually opening a banking operation there is through representative offices. A **representative office** is basically a sales office for a bank. It provides information regarding the financial services of the bank, but cannot deliver the services itself. It cannot accept deposits or make loans. The foreign representative office of a U.S. bank will typically sell the bank's services to local firms that may need banking services for trade or other transactions in the United States.

If a bank wants to conduct banking business within the foreign country, it may open a branch banking office, a banking affiliate, or even a wholly owned banking subsidiary. A branch banking office is an extension of the parent bank and is not independently financed from the parent. The branch office is not independently incorporated, and therefore is commonly restricted in the types of banking activities that it may conduct. Branch banking is by far the most common form of international banking structure used by banks, particularly by banks based in the United States.

A foreign banking affiliate or banking subsidiary is a locally and separately incorporated bank from the parent bank. If the local bank is wholly owned by the parent, it is a subsidiary; if only partially owned, it is an affiliate. For all intents and purposes, these are local banks, and they usually can provide the same financial services provided by any other bank in that country. Despite this freedom, many foreign banking subsidiaries find it difficult to compete with true local banks due to long-standing business relationships and corporate-banking ties that may date back for decades or longer. Among the major industrial countries today, however, many foreign banking affiliates and subsidiaries are so highly integrated into local financial markets that they are indistinguishable from local banks.

## Offshore Banking

Most governments regulate the degree of financial activity in a foreign currency that can take place. This has encouraged the growth of what is generally referred to as offshore banking. Offshore banking is the name given to Category 4 transactions, foreign borrowers of foreign currencies.

The primary motivation of offshore banking is avoiding regulation. Governments do not normally regulate banking activity that does not affect their domestic markets, so countries that have historically allowed unregulated foreign banking activity have been the centers of offshore banking. Many tropical islands, such as the Caymans, the Bahamas, and the Netherlands Antilles, have been the centers of much of offshore banking activity, although countries such as Luxembourg and Switzerland have also provided many of the same services. Although transactions are officially "booked" through the offshore cen-

# The Locations of the World's International Financial Centers (IFCs) and International Offshore Financial Centers (IOFCs)

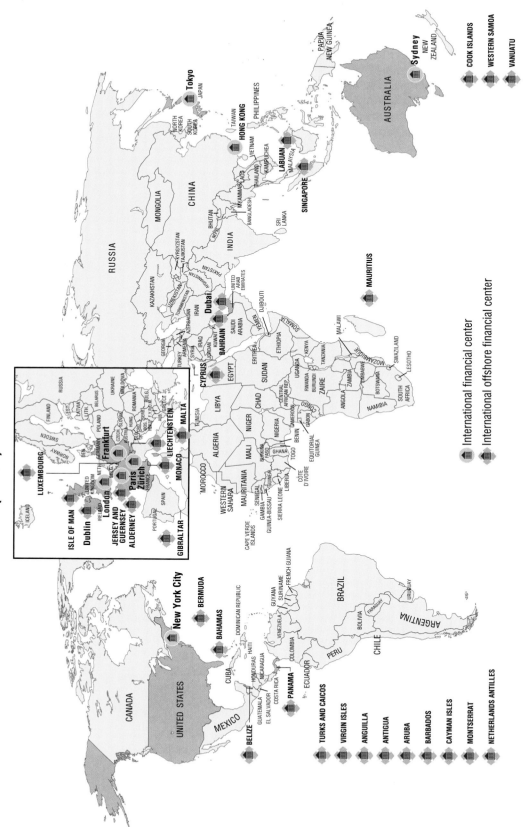

Note: *International Financial Centers (IFCs)* are the traditional centers of international financial activity, and normally include the conduct of both domestic and international financial transactions. *International Offshore Financial Centers (IOFCs)* are centers of offshore financial activities only (no interaction is allowed with the domestic financial or business community), and normally exist because of specific tax laws and provisions which encourage their establishment and allow them special treatment.

● International financial center

◆ International offshore financial center

Source: *Multinational Business Finance*, 7th Ed., Eiteman, Stonehill, and Moffet.

ters, most of the activity is on paper or via telex only; most of the capital never reaches the remote locales.

Most of the appeal of the offshore centers had been avoiding taxes on income earned abroad, thus offshore banking centers were often referred to as "tax havens." The centers can shield income from taxes because capital can be held unbeknownst to the owner's home country tax authorities. For the most part, these "Wild West" days of international finance are over, and it is generally no longer possible to shield income in tax havens.

## International Bank Lending

Bank lending internationally consists of two types of financial credits: (1) loans extended by a single bank, and (2) loans extended by a collection or syndicate of banks. These loans are international loans if they are extended to a foreign borrower or are denominated in a foreign currency.

International bank lending has grown significantly since the early 1980s when net lending was dominated by syndicated loans extended to developing countries. After the decline of the syndicated loan market in the mid-1980s, the growth in international bank lending was in the more traditional form of a simple loan arranged between a single bank and a corporate (not government) borrower.

**Syndicated Loans**   A **syndicated loan,** sometimes called a syndicated credit, is an arrangement in which between twenty and fifty banks in many different countries contribute to the funding of a single large loan. Originally a market that transferred capital from the richer industrial countries to the less developed countries in need of development capital, the market has changed to one that recycles capital among the industrial countries. The market now focuses on lending not to less-developed country governments, but to corporations. Additionally, the capital no longer is targeted at long-term development projects, but rather for the financing of a large proportion of the merger and acquisition financing needed for corporate takeovers in the United States and the United Kingdom.

## International Security Markets

Although banks continue to provide a large portion of the international financial needs of government and business, it is the international debt securities markets that have experienced the greatest growth in the past decade. The market is composed of the **Euronote** market and the **international bond** market.

## The Euronote Market

The Euronote market is a collective term for a variety of short- to medium-term types of financing. The original types of financing were termed *note issuance facilities* (NIFs) and *revolving underwriting facilities* (RUFs). These "facilities" were arrangements that would allow a firm to borrow capital as needed but at a predetermined rate of interest through notes that were guaranteed to be purchased by a group of financial institutions.

The true source of sustained financing in the Euronote market came from a financial export of the United States, commercial paper (CP). Commercial paper is a short-term note, typically 30, 60, 90, or 180 days in maturity, sold directly into the financial markets by large corporations. The market originated in the United States in the 1970s when a number of major firms realized they were actually larger and more creditworthy than many of the banks from which they were borrowing. The solution was to sell their own debt notes directly to the market and bypass the costs of banks. These notes were called commercial paper.

The international version, **Euro commercial paper (ECP),** arrived in the European markets with a splash in the early 1980s. One of the primary reasons for its rapid growth was the lack of anything similar in most national financial markets.[5] Although the growth of domestic CP markets has taken a little steam out of the Euro-CP market of late, it has continued to provide the majority of the financing in the general Euronote market since the mid-1980s.

The third and final type of financing available in the Euronote market is the Euromedium-term note (EMTN). Another export of the rapidly innovating financial markets in the United States, the EMTN is the Euromarket version of a method of selling short- to medium-maturity bonds when needed. Unlike a bond issue, which is the sale of a large quantity of long-term debt all at one time, medium-term notes can be sold gradually into the market as the firm decides it needs additional debt financing. This is the result of having a "shelf-registration," in which the government authorities (the Securities and Exchange Commission in the United States) allow a large quantity of debt (the notes) to be registered but to be held "on the shelf" and sold as needed by the firm.

## The International Bond Market

Even with all these strange and innovative ways of raising capital in the international financial markets, it is still the international bond market that provides the bulk of financing.

The four categories of international debt financing discussed previously particularly apply to the international bond markets. Foreign borrowers have been using the large, well-developed capital markets of countries such as the United States and the United Kingdom for many years. These issues are classified generally as **foreign bonds** as opposed to Eurobonds. Each has gained its own pet name for foreign bonds issued in that market. For example, foreign bond issues in the United States are called Yankee bonds, in the United Kingdom Bulldogs, in the Netherlands Rembrandt bonds, and in Japan they are called Samurai bonds. When bonds are issued by foreign borrowers in these markets, they are subject to the same restrictions that apply to all domestic borrowers. If a Japanese firm issues a bond in the United States, it still must comply with all rules of the U.S. Securities and Exchange Commission, including the fact that they must be dollar-denominated.

Bonds that fall into Categories 3 and 4 are termed **Eurobonds.** The primary characteristic of these instruments is that they are denominated in a currency other than that of the country where they are sold. For example, many U.S. firms may issue Euro-yen bonds on world markets. These bonds are sold in international financial centers such as London or Frankfurt, but they are denominated in Japanese yen. Because these Eurobonds are scattered about the global markets, most are a type of bond known as a **bearer bond.** A bearer bond is owned officially by whoever is holding it, with no master registration list being held by government authorities who then track who is earning interest income from bond investments.[6] Bearer bonds have a series of small coupons that border the bond itself. On an annual basis, one of the coupons is cut or "clipped" from the bond and taken to a banking institution that is one of the listed paying agents. The bank will pay the holder of the coupon the interest payment due, and usually no official records of payment are kept.

## International Equity Markets

Firms are financed with both debt and equity. Although the debt markets have been the center of activity in the international financial markets over the past three decades, there are signs that international equity capital is becoming more popular.

Again using the same categories of international financial activities, the Category 2 transaction of a foreign borrower in a domestic market in local currency is the predominant international equity activity. Foreign firms often issue new shares in foreign markets and list their stock on major stock exchanges such as those in New York, Tokyo, or London. The purpose of foreign issues and listings is to expand the investor base in the hope of gaining access to capital markets in which the demand for shares of equity ownership is strong.

A foreign firm that wants to list its shares on an exchange in the United States does so through American Depository Receipts. These are the receipts to bank accounts that hold shares of the foreign firm's stock in that firm's country. The equities are actually in a foreign currency, so by holding them in a bank account and listing the receipt on the account on the American exchange, the shares can be revalued in dollars and redivided so that the price per share is more typical of that of the U.S. equity markets ($20 to $60 per share frequently being the desired range).

There has been considerable growth in the 1990s in the Euro-equity markets. A Euro-equity issue is the simultaneous sale of a firm's shares in several different countries, with or without listing the shares on an exchange in that country. The sales take place through investment banks. Once issued, most Euro-equities are listed at least on the computer screen quoting system of the International Stock Exchange (ISE) in London, the SEAQ. As of late 1994, the Frankfurt stock exchange was the most globalized of major equity exchanges, with more than 45 percent of the firms listed on the exchange being foreign. At the same time, 18.8 percent of the firms on the London exchange were foreign, New York was a distant third with 7.6 percent foreign firms, with Tokyo fourth with less than 6 percent. Figure 7.7 illustrates a recent announcement, a "tombstone" as it is called in the investment banking industry, of a global offering by Deutsche Telekom, a German company.

## Private Placements

One of the largest and largely unpublicized capital markets is the **private placement** market. A private placement is the sale of debt or equity to a large investor. The sale is normally a one-time-only transaction in which the buyer of the bond or stock purchases the investment and intends to hold it until maturity (if debt) or until repurchased by the firm (if equity). How does this differ from normal bond and stock sales? The answer is that the securities are not resold on a secondary market such as the domestic bond market or the New York or London stock exchanges. If the security was intended to be publicly

## Deutsche Telekom 𝕋 ▪ ▪

# 85,000,000 Ordinary Shares
### (nominal value DM 5 per Share)
# in the form of American Depositary Shares or Shares

Deutsche Telekom AG, a stock corporation organized under the laws of the Federal Republic of Germany, is offering hereby, through the several Americas Underwriters, 85 million Ordinary Shares, nominal value DM 5 each, of the Company in the form of (i) American Depositary Shares, each representing one Share, or (ii) Shares, as part of the Global Offering described herein. The ADSs are evidenced by American Depositary Receipts. In addition to the Shares being offered in the Americas Offering, the Global Offering includes (i) an offering of 402 million Shares in the German Offering and (ii) an offering of 113 million Shares in the aggregate, in the form of ADSs or Shares, in the Asia-Pacific/Rest of World Offering, the Rest of Europe Offering and the U.K. Offering. In addition to the Global Offering, the Company has reserved 23.7 million Shares for issuance to employees of Deutsche Telekom and its German subsidiaries. The Company will offer certain incentives to retail investors in the German Offering and to such employees. See "The Global Offering."

Upon completion of the Global Offering and the Employee Offering, the Federal Republic of Germany will own 2.03 billion Shares, representing approximately 76.5% of the share capital of the Company (assuming no exercise of the Underwriters' over-allotment option).

Prior to the Global Offering there has been no public market for the ADSs or the Shares. The Shares have been approved for listing on the Frankfurt Stock Exchange as well as the other German stock exchanges under the symbol "DTE". The ADSs have been approved for listing, subject to official notice of issuance, on the New York Stock Exchange under the symbol "DT". Application has also been made to list the Shares on the Tokyo Stock Exchange. In addition, it is expected that the Shares and the ADSs will be eligible for quotation and trading through SEAQ International. See "The Global Offering."·

**THESE SECURITIES HAVE NOT BEEN APPROVED OR DISAPPROVED BY THE SECURITIES AND EXCHANGE COMMISSION OR ANY STATE SECURITIES COMMISSION NOR HAS THE SECURITIES AND EXCHANGE COMMISSION OR ANY STATE SECURITIES COMMISSION PASSED UPON THE ACCURACY OR ADEQUACY OF THIS PROSPECTUS. ANY REPRESENTATION TO THE CONTRARY IS A CRIMINAL OFFENSE.**

|  | Initial Public Offering Price | Underwriting Discount(1) | Proceeds to the Company(2) |
|---|---|---|---|
| Per ADS(3) | $18.89 | $0.472 | $18.418 |
| Per Share | DM 28.50 | DM 0.713 | DM 27.787 |
| Total(4) | $1,605,650,000 | $40,120,000 | $1,565,530,000 |

(1) The Company has agreed to indemnify the Underwriters against certain liabilities, including liabilities under the U.S. Securities Act of 1933.
(2) Before deducting expenses allocable to the Americas Offering payable by the Company estimated to be $12,500,000.
(3) Based on an exchange rate of DM 1.5085 = $1.00.
(4) Assumes that all the Shares sold in the Americas Offering are sold in the form of ADSs. The Company has granted the Underwriters an option, exercisable by the Global Coordinators on their behalf, from November 18 to December 31, 1996, to purchase up to an additional 90 million Shares (of which 12.75 million Shares relate to the Americas Offering) at the initial public offering price, less a discount of DM 0.570 per Share or $0.378 per ADS, as the case may be, solely to cover over-allotments, if any. If such option is exercised in full, the total initial public offering price, discounts and proceeds to the Company from the Americas Offering will be $1,846,497,500, $44,939,500, and $1,801,558,000, respectively. See "Underwriting."

### Global Coordinators

**Deutsche Bank**
Aktiengesellschaft

**Dresdner Bank**
Aktiengesellschaft

**Goldman, Sachs & Co.**

The ADSs and the Shares offered hereby are offered severally by the Americas Underwriters, as specified herein, subject to receipt and acceptance by them and subject to their right to reject any order in whole or in part. It is expected that the Shares will be delivered in book-entry form through the facilities of the Deutscher Kassenverein AG and the ADRs evidencing the ADSs will be ready for delivery through the facilities of The Depository Trust Company on or about November 20, 1996, against payment therefor in immediately available funds.

**Goldman, Sachs & Co.**

**Deutsche Morgan Grenfell**

**Merrill Lynch & Co.**

**Morgan Stanley & Co.**
Incorporated

**Salomon Brothers Inc**

**ABN AMRO Rothschild**
A Division of ABN AMRO Securities (USA) Inc.

**CS First Boston**

**Dresdner Kleinwort Benson**
North America LLC

The date of this Prospectus is November 17, 1996.

---

**FIGURE 7.7**

**An Announcement of a Global Equity Offering**
*Source:* Dresdner Bank, New York, January 1998.

traded, the issuing firm would have to meet a number of disclosure and registration requirements with the regulatory authorities. In the United States, this would be the Securities and Exchange Commission.

Historically, much of the volume of private placements of securities occurred in Europe, with a large volume being placed with large Swiss financial institutions and large private investors. But in recent years the market has grown substantially across all countries as the world's financial markets have grown and as large institutional investors (particularly pension funds and insurance firms) have gained control over increasing shares of investment capital.

Although the international markets are large and growing, this does not mean they are for everyone. For many years, only the largest of the world's multinational firms could enter another country's capital markets and find acceptance. The reasons are information and reputation.

Financial markets are by definition risk-averse. This means they are very reluctant to make loans to or buy debt issued by firms that they know little about. Therefore, the ability to gain access to the international markets is dependent on a firm's reputation, its ability to educate the markets about what it does, how successful it has been, and its patience. The firm must in the end be willing to expend the resources and effort required to build a credit reputation in the international markets. If successful, the firm may enjoy the benefits of new, larger, and more diversified sources of the capital it needs.

The individual firm, whether it be a chili dog stand serving the international tastes of office workers at the United Nations Plaza or a major multinational firm such as Honda of Japan, is affected by exchange rates and international financial markets. Although the owner of the chili dog stand probably has more important and immediate problems than exchange rates to deal with, it is clear that firms such as Honda see the movements in these markets as critically important to their long-term competitiveness.

## Gaining Access to International Financial Markets

## Summary

This chapter has spanned the breadth of the international financial markets from currencies to capital markets. As illustrated by the "plan" for solving the Asian crisis shown in Global Perspective 7.4, the two are forever interrelated. The world's currency markets expanded threefold in only six years, and there is no reason to believe this growth will end. It is estimated that more than $1 trillion worth of currencies change hands daily, and the majority of it is either U.S. dollars, German marks, or Japanese yen. These are the world's major floating currencies.

But the world's financial markets are much more than currency exchanges. The rapid growth in the international financial markets—both on their own and as linkages between domestic markets—has resulted in the creation of a large and legitimate source of finance for the world's multinational firms. The recent expansion of market economics to more and more of the world's countries and economies sets the stage for further growth for the world's currency and capital markets, but also poses the potential for new external debt crises.

## SOLVING THE ASIAN CRISIS

# The Plan

*How to stop the currency crisis and get Asia growing again*

### I. A NEW TEAM

Create a task force of top private bankers, IMF officials, accountants, and central bankers from the G-8 nations and Asia. Their mandate: hammer out a regionwide solution. An Asian heads the team. The task force would work in tandem with the IMF, and, if necessary, supersede it.

### 2. COME CLEAN

The task force's first job is to get all the bad news out on hidden debts and corporate basket cases in all of Asia's trouble spots.

### 3. TRIAGE

The task force moves fast to stabilize the currencies. Steps include:

■ Coordinating a regional policy of punishingly high interest rates to stop capital flight. This is a short-term policy only.

■ Restoring confidence and liquidity fast. The main step here is to roll over the short-term debt of core banks in Korea, Indonesia, Malaysia, Thailand, and the Philippines. This debt could be securitized through bonds with longer repayment schedules. Interest payments might be guaranteed by governments themselves, or an outside

institution such as the IMF. The workout must inflict a cost on the foreign leaders.

■ Encouraging a swift private workout between outside lenders and the region's corporations and finance companies. Western banks can swap debt for equity or grant easier repayment terms. The emphasis is on speed—everyone takes losses.

■ Establishing an additional stabilization fund of about $100 billion. This money would help meet emergency liquidity needs. G-8 nations and rich Asian countries would chip in.

### 4. NEW FRAMEWORK

Western and Asian leaders will agree to an Asian agency to prevent similar crises. Among its features:

■ An Asian Reconstruction Fund staffed by top technocrats that would sell bad assets in the region and rebuild liquidity when private workouts need assistance. The fund would speed up workouts to strengthen corporate balance sheets and restart capital flows.

■ A new regulatory authority to introduce uniform regional rules that insure full disclosure in central bank accounts, update bankruptcy laws, introduce real supervision of banks, and improve local accounting systems and securities laws.

### 5. NEW COOPERATION

At an APEC meeting later this year, the world's leaders publicly endorse the workout. In return, G-8 nations (especially Japan) pledge to maintain growth and preserve open markets for Asia.

## Key Terms and Concepts

| | | |
|---|---|---|
| direct quotation | International Monetary Fund | Euromarkets |
| indirect quotation | World Bank | selling forward |
| spot rates | direct intervention | offshore banking |
| forward rates | coordinated intervention | correspondent banks |
| European terms | Plaza Agreement | representative office |
| American terms | European Monetary System (EMS) | syndicated loan |
| cross rates | | Euronote |
| triangular arbitrage | Exchange Rate Mechanism (ERM) | international bond |
| spread | | Euro commercial paper (ECP) |
| purchasing power parity (PPP) | Maastricht Treaty | |
| | euro | foreign bond |
| law of one price | Eurocurrency | Eurobond |
| gold standard | Eurodollars | bearer bond |
| Bretton Woods Agreement | interbank interest rates | private placement |
| | LIBOR | |

## Questions for Discussion

1. How and where are currencies traded?
2. Does it matter whether a currency is quoted as DEM/USD or USD/DEM?
3. What is a forward rate? How do banks set forward rates?
4. What is a Eurocurrency?
5. What is a Eurocurrency interest rate? Is it different from LIBOR?
6. What makes a currency sell forward at a discount?
7. What is the difference between an international bond and a Eurobond?
8. How are the currencies of the Far East linked to the borrowing of private firms in the Far East?
9. The IMF, World Bank, and United Nations are only a few of the major world organizations that track, report, and aid international economic and financial development. Using these web sites and others that may be linked to them, briefly summarize the economic outlook for the developed and emerging nations of the world. For example, the full text of chapter 1 of the *World Economic Outlook*, published annually by the World Bank, is available through the IMF's web page.

   | | |
   |---|---|
   | International Monetary Fund | **http://www.imf.org/** |
   | United Nations | **http://www.unsystem.org/** |
   | The World Bank Group | **http://www.worldbank.org/** |
   | Europa (EU) Homepage | **http://europa.eu.int/** |
   | Bank for International Settlements | **http://www.bis.org/** |

10. Current economic and financial statistics and commentaries are available via the IMF's web page under "What's New," "Fund Rates," and the "IMF Committee on Balance of Payments Statistics." For an in-depth examination of the IMF's ongoing initiative on the validity of these statistics, termed *metadata,* visit the IMF's Dissemination Standards Bulletin Board listed below.

    | | |
    |---|---|
    | International Monetary Fund | **http://www.imf.org/** |
    | IMF's Dissemination Standards Bulletin Board | **http://dsbb.imf.org/** |

11. Visit Moody's sovereign ceilings and foreign currency ratings service site on the web to evaluate what progress is being made in the nations of the Far East on recovering their perceived creditworthiness.

    Moody's Sovereign Ceilings

    **http://www.moodys.com/repldata/ratings/ratsov.htm**

12. American Depository Receipts (ADRs) now make up more than 10 percent of all equity trading on U.S. stock exchanges. As more companies based outside of the United States list on U.S. markets, the need to understand the principle forces that drive ADR values increases with each trading day. Beginning with Deutsch Morgan Grenfell's detailed description of the ADR process and current ADR trading activity, prepare a briefing for senior management in your firm encouraging them to consider internationally diversifying the firm's liquid asset portfolio with ADRs.

    Deutsche Morgan Grenfell

    **http://www.adr-dmg.com/adr-dmg/welcome.html**

## Recommended Readings

Bank for International Settlements. *Annual Report.* Basle, Switzerland, annually.

Black Wednesday: The Campaign for Sterling. *The Economist* (January 9, 1993): 52, 54.

Commission of the European Communities. The ECU and Its Role in the Process Towards Monetary Union. *European Economy* 48 (September 1991): 121–138.

Dewey, Davis Rich. *Financial History of the United States.* 2d Edition. New York: Longmans, Green, and Company, 1903.

Driscoll, David D. *What Is the International Monetary Fund?* Washington, D.C.: External Relations Department, International Monetary Fund, November 1992.

Eiteman, David, Arthur Stonehill, and Michael H. Moffett. *Multinational Business Finance.* 8th edition. Reading, Mass.: Addison-Wesley, 1998.

Federal Reserve Bank of New York. *Summary of Results of the U.S. Foreign Exchange Market Turnover Survey,* April 1995.

The Financial Times. *FT Guide to World Currencies,* January 20, 1997.

Funabashi, Yuichi. *Managing the Dollar: From the Plaza to the Louvre.* Washington, D.C.: Institute of International Economics, 1988.

Giddy, Ian. *Global Financial Markets.* Lexington, Mass.: Heath, 1993.

Goodhart, C.A.E., and L. Figliuoli. "Every Minute Counts in Financial Markets." *Journal of International Money and Finance* 10 (1991): 23–52.

Grabbe, J. Orlin. *International Financial Markets.* 2d edition. New York: Elsevier, 1991.

International Monetary Fund. *International Financial Statistics.* Washington, D.C., monthly.

Morgan Guaranty. *World Financial Markets,* New York, various issues.

The New Trade Strategy. *Business Week* (October 7, 1985): 90–93.

The Paris Pact May Not Buoy the Dollar for Long. *Business Week* (March 9, 1987): 40–41.

Rivalries Beset Monetary Pact. *Business Week* 776 (July 15, 1944): 15–16.

Tran, Hung Q., Larry Anderson, and Ernst-Ludwig Drayss. Eurocapital Markets. Chap. 8 in *International Finance and Investing.* The Library of Investment Banking, edited by Robert Lawrence Kuhn. Homewood, Ill.: Dow Jones-Irwin, 1990, 129–160.

Treasury and Federal Reserve Foreign Exchange Operations. *Federal Reserve Bulletin* (October 1971): 783–814.

Ungerer, Horst, Jouko J. Hauvonen, Augusto Lopez-Claros, and Thomas Mayer. *The European Monetary System: Developments and Perspectives.* Washington, D.C.: International Monetary Fund, 1990.

Van Dormael, Armand. *Bretton Woods.* New York: Holmes & Meier, 1978.

*The Wall Street Journal.* Foreign Exchange Rates, January 20, 1997, C21.

The World Bank. *World Debt Tables, 1991–92.* Washington, D.C., 1992.

## Notes

1. Rounding errors are solved quite simply with exchange rates. With a few notable exceptions, all active trading takes place using direct quotations on foreign currencies versus the U.S. dollar (DEM 1.5152/USD, YEN 99.36/USD) and for a conventional number of decimal places. These are the base rates that are then used if needed for the calculation of the inverse indirect quotes on the foreign currencies.

2. A currency trader once remarked to the authors that the spot quotes listed on such a screen were no more and no less accurate to the "true price" than the sticker price on a showroom automobile. Of course, this may no longer be true since the introduction of the Saturn, which sells at sticker price only!

3. Exchange rate "basis points" should not be confused with interest rate basis points, where a single basis point is 1/100th of a percent.

4. Actually there are a few exceptions. Panama, for example, has used the U.S. dollar for many years.

5. Domestic commercial paper markets were legalized in many major countries only in the middle to late 1980s: France in 1985, the United Kingdom in 1986, Japan in 1987, Belgium in 1990, and Germany in 1991.

6. Bearer bonds were issued by the U.S. government up until the early 1980s, when discontinued. Even though they were called bearer bonds, a list of bond registration numbers was still kept and recorded in order to tax investors holding the bearer instruments.

# CHAPTER 8

# Economic Integration

## Building Blocs (or Stumbling Blocs?) of Worldwide Free Trade

**R**egional groupings based on economics will become increasingly important in the 1990s. Countries around the globe are making efforts to suppress national interests in favor of regional ones. A total of thirty-two such groupings is estimated to be in existence: three in Europe, four in the Middle East, five in Asia, and ten each in Africa and the Americas. With respect to the three major blocs, the American, European, and Asian, trade inside these blocs has grown at a rapid pace, while trading among these blocs or with outsiders is either declining or growing far more moderately.

Some of these groupings around the world have the superstructure of nation-states (such as the European Union), some (such as the ASEAN Free Trade Area) are multinational agreements that may be more political arrangements than cohesive trading blocs at present. Some arrangements are not trading blocs per se, but work to further them. The Free Trade Area of the Americas is a foreign policy initiative designed to further democracy in the region through incentives to capitalistic development and trade liberalization. The Andean Common Market and Mercosur have both indicated an intention to negotiate with the parties of the North American Free Trade Agreement (NAFTA) to create a hemispheric market. Regional economic integration in Asia has been driven more by market forces than by treaties and by a need to maintain balance in negotiations with Europe and North America. Broader formal agreements are in formative stages; for example, the Asia Pacific Economic Coop-

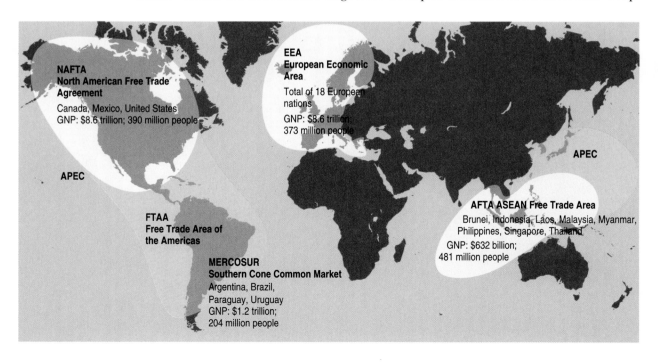

**NAFTA**
**North American Free Trade Agreement**

Canada, Mexico, United States
GNP: $8.6 trillion; 390 million people

**APEC**

**EEA**
**European Economic Area**

Total of 18 European nations

GNP: $8.6 trillion; 373 million people

**APEC**

**FTAA**
**Free Trade Area of the Americas**

**MERCOSUR**
**Southern Cone Common Market**
Argentina, Brazil, Paraguay, Uruguay
GNP: $1.2 trillion; 204 million people

**AFTA ASEAN Free Trade Area**
Brunei, Indonesia, Laos, Malaysia, Myanmar, Philippines, Singapore, Thailand
GNP: $632 billion; 481 million people

eration (APEC) initiated in 1988 would bring together partners from multiple continents. AFTA members are joined by such economic powerhouses as China, South Korea, Taiwan, and the United States.

Regional groupings are constantly in a state of development. In 1995, informal proposals were made to create a new bloc between NAFTA and EU members called TAFTA, the Transatlantic Free Trade Area. Since the elimination of the Soviet Union in 1991, 12 former republics have tried to forge common economic policies, but thus far only Belarus, Kazakhstan, and Russia are signatories to a free-trade pact.

Regional groupings will mean that companies are facing ever-intensifying competition and trading difficulties for sales inside a bloc. In the long term, firms will come under pressure to globalize and source locally. Actions of these global companies may also allay fears that regional blocs are nothing but protectionism on a grander scale.

*Source:* "American Politics, Global Trade," *The Economist,* September 27, 1997, 23–26. Ilkka A. Ronkainen, "Trading Blocs: Opportunity or Demise for International Trade?" *Multinational Business Review* 1(Spring 1993): 1–9; Paivi Vihma, "Gatt Kittuu, Kauppablokit Nousevat," *Talouselama,* number 11, 1992, 42–43; and Joseph L. Brand, "The New World Order," *Vital Speeches of the Day* 58(December): 155–160.

The benefits of free trade and stable exchange rates are available only if nation-states are willing to give up some measure of independence and autonomy. This has resulted in increased economic integration around the world with agreements among countries to establish links through movement of goods, services, capital, and labor across borders. Some predict, however, that the regional **trading blocs** of the new economic world order will divide into a handful of protectionist superstates that, although liberalizing trade among members, may raise barriers to external trade.

Economic integration is best viewed as a spectrum. At one extreme we might envision a truly global economy in which all countries share a common currency and agreed to a free flow of goods, services, and factors of production. At the other extreme would be a number of closed economies, each independent and self-sufficient. The various integrative agreements in effect today lie along the middle of this spectrum. The most striking example of successful integration is the historic economic unification that is taking place around the world today. These developments were discussed in the chapter's opening vignette. Some countries, however, give priority to maintaining economic self-sufficiency and independence. Their ranks have thinned considerably in the 1990s with countries such as Vietnam becoming heavily involved in international trade and investment. Even North Korea is now considered as a possible future market by companies such as Coca-Cola.

This chapter will begin with an explanation of the various levels of economic integration. The level of integration defines the nature and degree of economic links among countries. The major arguments both for and against economic integration will be reviewed. Next, the European Union, the North American Free Trade Agreement, Asia Pacific Economic Cooperation, and other economic alliances will be discussed. Finally, possible strategic moves by international managers in response to integration are outlined.

# Levels of Economic Integration

A trading bloc is a preferential economic arrangement among a group of countries. The forms it may take are shown in Table 8.1. From least to most integrative, they are the free trade area, the customs union, the common market, and the economic union.[1]

## The Free Trade Area

The **free trade area** is the least restrictive and loosest form of economic integration among countries. In a free trade area, all barriers to trade among member countries are removed. Therefore, goods and services are freely traded among member countries in much the same way that they flow freely between, for example, South Carolina and New York. No discriminatory taxes, quotas, tariffs, or other trade barriers are allowed. Sometimes a free trade area is formed only for certain classes of goods and services. An agricultural free trade area, for example, implies the absence of restrictions on the trade of agricultural products only. The most notable feature of a free trade area is that each country continues to set its own policies in relation to nonmembers. In other words, each member is free to set any tariffs, quotas, or other restrictions that it chooses on trade with countries outside the free trade area. Among such free trade areas the most notable are the European Free Trade Area (EFTA) and the North American Free Trade Agreement (NAFTA).

## The Customs Union

The **customs union** is one step further along the spectrum of economic integration. Like the members of a free trade area, members of a customs union dismantle barriers to trade in goods and services among themselves. In addition, however, the customs union establishes a common trade policy with respect to nonmembers. Typically, this takes the form of a common external tariff, where imports from nonmembers are subject to the same tariff when sold

**TABLE 8.1**

**Forms of International Economic Integration**

| Stage of Integration | Abolition of Tariffs and Quotas among Members | Common Tariff and Quota System | Abolition of Restrictions on Factor Movements | Harmonization and Unification of Economic Policies and Institutions |
|---|---|---|---|---|
| Free trade area | Yes | No | No | No |
| Customs union | Yes | Yes | No | No |
| Common market | Yes | Yes | Yes | No |
| Economic union | Yes | Yes | Yes | Yes |

*Source:* Franklin R. Root, *International Trade and Investment,* Cincinnati, Ohio: South-Western Publishing Company, 1992, 254.

to any member country. Tariff revenues are then shared among members according to a prespecified formula.

Further still along the spectrum of economic integration is the **common market.** Like the customs union, a common market has no barriers to trade among members and has a common external trade policy. In addition, however, factors of production are also mobile among members. Factors of production include labor, capital, and technology. Thus restrictions on immigration, emigration, and cross-border investment are abolished. The importance of **factor mobility** for economic growth cannot be overstated. When factors of production are freely mobile, then capital, labor, and technology may be employed in their most productive uses. To see the importance of factor mobility, imagine the state of the U.S. economy if unemployed steelworkers in Pittsburgh were prevented from migrating to the growing Sunbelt in search of better opportunities. Alternatively, imagine that savings in New York banks could not be invested in profitable opportunities in Chicago.

    Despite the obvious benefits, members of a common market must be prepared to cooperate closely in monetary, fiscal, and employment policies. Furthermore, while a common market will enhance the productivity of members in the aggregate, it is by no means clear that individual member countries will always benefit. Because of these difficulties, the goals of common markets have proved to be elusive in many areas of the world, notably Central America and Asia. However, the objective of the **Single European Act** was to have a full common market in effect within the EU at the end of 1992. While many of the directives aimed at opening borders and markets were implemented on schedule, major exceptions do still exist. A prime example is in automobiles.

The creation of a true **economic union** requires integration of economic policies in addition to the free movement of goods, services, and factors of production across borders. Under an economic union, members would harmonize monetary policies, taxation, and government spending. In addition, a common currency would be used by all members. This could be accomplished de facto, or in effect, by a system of fixed exchange rates. Clearly, the formation of an economic union requires nations to surrender a large measure of their national sovereignty. Needless to say, the barriers to full economic union are quite strong. Our global political system is built on the autonomy and supreme power of the nation-state, and attempts to undermine the authority of the state will undoubtedly always encounter opposition. As a result, no true economic unions are in effect today. The European Union is committed to European unity, in name at least, through the Maastricht Treaty. The aim is to achieve full monetary union by 1999 with a single European currency in use by 2002.

## The Common Market

## The Economic Union

## *Arguments Surrounding Economic Integration*

A number of arguments surround economic integration. They center on (1) trade creation and diversion; (2) the effects of integration on import prices, competition, economies of scale, and factor productivity; and (3) the benefits of regionalism versus nationalism.

## Trade Creation and Trade Diversion

Economist Jacob Viner first formalized the economic costs and benefits of economic integration.[2] Chapter 5 illustrated that the classical theory of trade predicts a win-win result for countries participating in free trade. The question is whether similar benefits accrue when free trade is limited to one group of countries. The case examined by Viner was the customs union. The conclusion of Viner's analysis was that either negative or positive effects may result when a group of countries trade freely among themselves but maintain common barriers to trade with nonmembers.

Viner's arguments can be highlighted with a simple illustration. In 1986, Spain formally entered the European Union (EU) as a member. Prior to membership, Spain—like all nonmembers such as the United States, Canada, and Japan—traded with the EU and suffered the common external tariff. Imports of agricultural products from Spain or the United States had the same tariff applied to their products, for example, 20 percent. During this period, the United States was a lower-cost producer of wheat compared to Spain. U.S. exports to EU members may have cost $3.00 per bushel, plus a 20 percent tariff of $0.60, for a total of $3.60 per bushel. If Spain at the same time produced wheat at $3.20 per bushel, plus a 20 percent tariff of $0.64 for a total cost to EU customers of $3.84 per bushel, its wheat was more expensive and therefore less competitive.

But when Spain joined the EU as a member, its products were no longer subject to the common external tariffs; Spain had become a member of the "club" and therefore enjoyed its benefits. Spain was now the low-cost producer of wheat at $3.20 per bushel, compared to the price of $3.60 from the United States. Trade flows changed as a result. The increased export of wheat and other products by Spain to the EU as a result of its membership is termed **trade creation.** The elimination of the tariff literally created more trade between Spain and the EU. At the same time, because the United States was still outside of the EU, its products suffered the higher price as a result of tariff application. U.S. exports to the EU fell. When the source of trading competitiveness is shifted in this manner from one country to another, it is termed **trade diversion.**

Whereas trade creation is distinctly positive in moving toward freer trade, and therefore lower prices for consumers within the EU, the impact of trade diversion is negative. Trade diversion is inherently negative because the competitive advantage has shifted away from the lower-cost producer to the higher-cost producer. The benefits of Spain's membership are enjoyed by Spanish farmers (greater export sales) and EU consumers (lower prices). The two major costs are reduced tariff revenues collected and costs borne by the United States and its exports as a result of lost sales.

From the perspective of nonmembers such as the United States, the formation or expansion of a customs union is obviously negative. Most damaged will naturally be countries that may need to have trade to build their economies, such as the countries of the Third World. From the perspective of members of the customs union, the formation or expansion is only beneficial if the trade creation benefits exceed trade diversion costs.

## Reduced Import Prices

When a small country imposes a tariff on imports, the price of the goods will typically rise because sellers will increase prices to cover the cost of the tariff. This increase in price, in turn, will result in lower demand for the imported goods. If a bloc of countries imposes the tariff, however, the fall in demand for the imported goods will be substantial. The exporting country may then be forced to reduce the price of the goods. The possibility of lower prices for imports results from the greater market power of the bloc relative to that of a single country. The result may then be an improvement in the trade position of the bloc countries. Any gain in the trade position of bloc members, however, is offset by a deteriorating trade position for the exporting country. Again, unlike the win-win situation resulting from free trade, the scenario involving a trade bloc is instead win-lose.

## Increased Competition and Economies of Scale

Integration increases market size and therefore may result in a lower degree of monopoly in the production of certain goods and services.[3] This is because a larger market will tend to increase the number of competing firms, resulting in greater efficiency and lower prices for consumers. Moreover, less energetic and productive economies may be spurred into action by competition from the more industrious bloc members.

Many industries, such as steel and automobiles, require large-scale production in order to obtain economies of scale in production. Therefore, certain industries may simply not be economically viable in smaller, trade-protected countries. However, the formation of a trading bloc enlarges the market so that large-scale production is justified. The lower per-unit costs resulting from scale economies may then be obtained. These lower production costs resulting from greater production for an enlarged market are called **internal economies of scale.**

In a common market, **external economies of scale** may also be present. Because a common market allows factors of production to flow freely across borders, the firm may now have access to cheaper capital, more highly skilled labor, or superior technology. These factors will improve the quality of the firm's good or service or will lower costs or both.

## Higher Factor Productivity

When factors of production are freely mobile, the wealth of the common market countries, in aggregate, will likely increase. The theory behind this contention is straightforward: factor mobility will lead to the movement of labor and capital from areas of low productivity to areas of high productivity. In addition to the economic gains from factor mobility, there are other benefits not so easily quantified. The free movement of labor fosters a higher level of communication across cultures. This, in turn, leads to a higher degree of cross-cultural understanding; as people move, their ideas, skills, and ethnicity move with them.

Again, however, factor mobility will not necessarily benefit each country in the common market. A poorer country, for example, may lose badly needed investment capital to a richer country, where opportunities are perceived to be more profitable. Another disadvantage of factor mobility that is often cited is the brain-drain phenomenon. A poorer country may lose its most talented workers when they are free to search out better opportunities.

## Regionalism versus Nationalism

Economists have composed elegant and compelling arguments in favor of the various levels of economic integration. It is difficult, however, to turn these arguments into reality in the face of intense nationalism. The biggest impedi-

## LABOR PAINS OF INTEGRATION

**E**conomic integration will not make everyone happy, despite promises of great benefits from the free flow of people, goods, services, and money. More developed countries, such as the United States and France, fear a hemorrhage of jobs as companies shift their operations to less prosperous regions with lower wages or fewer governmental controls.

Under NAFTA, cross-border controls on trucking were to be eliminated by the end of 1995, allowing commercial vehicles to move freely in four U.S. and six Mexican states of the border region. But U.S. truckers, many of whom are members of the Teamsters Union, would have none of it. Mexican trucks were accused of being dirty, dangerous, and exceeding weight limits. President Clinton, eager for union support, has delayed implementation of the agreement. The problem is that over 85 percent of the $190 billion in U.S.-Mexican trade moves on trucks, and with no agreement, delays and red tape are com-

mon. Governors of U.S. border states and Mexican authorities are upset. "We simply cannot afford to have this archaic, inefficient system at the border hold up our multibillion dollar trade," said Herminio Blanco, Mexico's trade minister.

In Europe, politicians blame other member countries for job losses. U.S. vacuum cleaner maker Hoover decided to relocate its production facilities from France's Burgundy region to Scotland, axing 600 jobs in the process. The move has sparked controversy in France on whether the single European market will strip the country of jobs. France has accused Britain of "social dumping"—eroding workers' rights in a bid to attract foreign direct investment. As a part of the deal, Hoover's Scottish workers agreed to accept new working practices, including limits on strike action. Yet Hoover has done nothing wrong. To remain competitive in what is fast becoming a global business, the company believes it must concentrate vacuum cleaner production in Europe in a single plant. It also needs a flexible work force, which is a big competitive advantage in many industries. By shifting production bases, Hoover is estimated to cut costs by a quarter. Part of this savings will come from economies of scale, the rest from lower wages.

*Source: "The Trucks that Hold Back NAFTA," The Economist (December 13, 1997): 23–24; "A Singular Market," The Economist (October 22, 1994): 10–16; "French Say United Europe Promotes 'Job Poaching,'" The Washington Post, February 10, 1993; and "Labour Pains," The Economist (February 6, 1993): 71.*

ment to economic integration remains in the reluctance of nations to surrender a measure of their autonomy. Integration, by its very nature, requires the surrender of national power and self-determinism. An example of this can be seen in Global Perspective 8.1

## European Integration

### Economic Integration in Europe from 1948 to the Mid-1980s

The period of the Great Depression from the late 1920s through World War II was characterized by isolationism, protectionism, and fierce nationalism. The economic chaos and political difficulties of the period resulted in no serious attempts at economic integration until the end of the war. From the devastation of the war, however, a spirit of cooperation gradually emerged in Europe.

The first step in this regional cooperative effort was the establishment of the Organization for European Economic Cooperation (OEEC) in 1948 to administer Marshall Plan aid from the United States. Although the objective of the OEEC was limited to economic reconstruction following the war, its success set the stage for more ambitious integration programs.

In 1952, six European countries (West Germany, France, Italy, Belgium, the Netherlands, and Luxembourg) joined in establishing the European Coal

**TABLE 8.2**

**Membership of the European Union**

| 1957 | | 1993 | | 1995 | | 2001+ |
|---|---|---|---|---|---|---|
| France | | Great Britain (1973) | | Austria (1995) | | Czech Republic |
| West Germany | | Ireland (1973) | + | Finland (1995) | | Cyprus |
| Italy | | Demark (1973) | | Sweden (1995) | + | Estonia |
| Belgium | + | Greece (1981) | | | | Hungary |
| Netherlands | | Spain (1986) | | | | Poland |
| Luxembourg | | Portugal (1986) | | | | Slovenia |

and Steel Community (ECSC). The objective of the ECSC was the formation of a common market in coal, steel, and iron ore for member countries. These basic industries were rapidly revitalized into competitive and efficient producers. The stage was again set for further cooperative efforts.

In 1957, the European Economic Community (EEC) was formally established by the **Treaty of Rome.** In 1967, ECSC and EEC as well as the European Atomic Energy Community (EURATOM) were merged to form the European Community (EC). Table 8.2 shows the founding members of the community in 1957, members who have joined since, as well as those invited to join early in the twenty-first century. The Treaty of Rome is a monumental document, composed of more than 200 articles. The main provisions of the treaty are summarized in Table 8.3 The document was (and is) quite ambitious. The cooperative spirit apparent throughout the treaty was based on the premise that the mobility of goods, services, labor, and capital—the "four freedoms"—was of paramount importance for the economic prosperity of the region. Founding members envisioned that the successful integration of the European economies would result in an economic power to rival that of the United States.

Some countries, however, were reluctant to embrace the ambitious integrative effort of the treaty. In 1960, a looser, less integrated philosophy was endorsed with the formation of the European Free Trade Association (EFTA) by eight countries: United Kingdom, Norway, Denmark, Sweden, Austria, Finland,

**TABLE 8.3**

**Main Provisions of the Treaty of Rome**

1. Formation of a free trade area: the gradual elimination of tariffs, and other barriers to trade among members
2. Formation of a customs union: the creation of a uniform tariff schedule applicable to imports from the rest of the world
3. Formation of a common market: the removal of barriers to the movement of labor, capital, and business enterprises
4. The adoption of common agricultural policies
5. The creation of an investment fund to channel capital from the more advanced to the less developed regions of the community

Portugal, and Switzerland. Barriers to trade among member countries were dismantled, although each country maintained its own policies with nonmember states. Since that time EFTA has lost much of its original significance due to its members joining the European Union (Denmark and the United Kingdom in 1973, Portugal in 1986, and Austria, Finland, and Sweden in 1995). EFTA countries have cooperated with the EU through bilateral free trade agreements, and, since 1994, through the European Economic Area (EEA) arrangement, which allows for free movement of people, goods, services, and capital within the combined area of the EU and EFTA. Of the EFTA countries, Iceland and Liechtenstein (which joined the EEA only in May 1995) have decided not to apply for membership in the EU. Norway was to have joined in 1995, but after a referendum declined membership, as it did in 1973. Switzerland's decision to stay out of the EEA has stalled its negotiations with the EU.

A conflict that intensified throughout the 1980s was between the richer and more industrialized countries and the poorer countries of the Mediterranean region. The power of the bloc of poorer countries was strengthened in the 1980s when Greece, Spain, and Portugal became EU members. Many argue that the dismantling of barriers between the richer and poorer countries will benefit the poorer countries by spurring them to become competitive. However, it may also be argued that the richer countries have an unfair advantage and therefore should accord protection to the poorer members before all barriers are dismantled.

Another source of difficulty that intensified in the 1980s was the administration of the community's **common agricultural policy (CAP).** Most industrialized countries, including the United States, Canada, and Japan, have adopted wide-scale government intervention and subsidization schemes for the agriculture industry. In the case of the EU, however, these policies have been implemented on a community-wide, rather than national, level. The CAP includes (1) a price-support system whereby EU agriculture officials intervene in the market to keep farm product prices within a specified range, (2) direct subsidies to farmers, and (3) rebates to farmers who export or agree to store farm products rather than sell them within the community. The implementation of these policies absorbs about two-thirds of the annual EU budget.

The CAP has caused problems both within the EU and in relationships with non-members. Within the EU, the richer, more industrialized countries resent the extensive subsidization of the more agrarian economies. Outside trading partners, especially the United States, have repeatedly charged the EU with unfair trade practices in agriculture.

## The European Union Since the Mid-1980s

By the mid-1980s, a sense of "Europessimism" permeated most discussions of European integration. Although the members remained committed in principle to the "four freedoms," literally hundreds of obstacles to the free movement of goods, services, people, and capital remained. For example, there were cumbersome border restrictions on trade in many goods, and although labor was theoretically mobile, the professional certifications granted in one country were often not recognized in others.

Growing dissatisfaction with the progress of integration, as well as threats of global competition from Japan and the United States, prompted the Europeans to take action. A policy paper published in 1985 (now known as the **1992 White Paper**) exhaustively identified the remaining barriers to the four freedoms and proposed means of dismantling them.[4] It listed 282 specific measures designed to make the four freedoms a reality.

The implementation of the White Paper proposals began formally in 1987 with the passage of the **Single European Act,** which stated that "the community shall adopt measures with the aim of progressively establishing the internal market over a period expiring on 31 December 1992." The Single European Act envisaged a true common market where goods, people, and money could move between Germany and France with the same ease that they move between Wisconsin and Illinois.

Progress toward the goal of free movement of goods has been achieved largely due to the move from a "common standards approach" to a "mutual recognition approach." Under the common standards approach, EU members were forced to negotiate the specifications for literally thousands of products, often unsuccessfully. For example, because of differences in tastes, agreement was never reached on specifications for beer, sausage, or mayonnaise. Under the mutual recognition approach, the laborious quest for common standards is in most cases no longer necessary. Instead, as long as a product meets legal and specification requirements in one member country, it may be freely exported to any other, and customers serve as final arbiters of success.

Less progress toward free movement of people in Europe has been made than toward free movement of goods. The primary difficulty is that EU members have been unable to agree on a common immigration policy. As long as this disagreement persists, travelers between countries must pass through border checkpoints. Some countries—notably Germany—have relatively lax immigration policies, while others—especially those with higher unemployment rates—favor strict controls on immigration. A second issue concerning the free movement of people is the acceptability of professional certifications across countries. In 1993, the largest EU member countries passed all of the professional worker directives. This means that workers' professional qualifications will be recognized throughout the EU, guaranteeing them equal treatment in terms of employment, working conditions, and social protection in the host country.

Attaining free movement of capital within the EU entails several measures. First, citizens will be free to trade in EU currencies without restrictions. Second, the regulations governing banks and other financial institutions will be harmonized. In addition, mergers and acquisitions will be regulated by the EU rather than by national governments. Finally, securities will be freely tradable across countries.

A key aspect of free trade in services is the right to compete fairly to obtain government contracts. Under the 1992 guidelines, a government should not give preference to its own citizens in awarding government contracts. However, little progress has been made in this regard. Open competition in public procurement has been calculated to save $10 billion a year. Yet the nonnational share of contracts has been 5 percent since 1992. Worse still, few unsuccessful bidders complain, for fear that they would be ignored in future bids.[5]

Project 1992 has always been part of a larger plan and a process more so than a deadline.[6] Many in the EU bureaucracy argued that the 1992 campaign required a commitment to **economic and monetary union (EMU)** and subsequently to political union. These sentiments were confirmed at the Maastricht summit in December 1991, which produced various recommendations to that effect. The ratification of the **Maastricht Treaty** in late 1993 by all of the 12 member countries of the EC created the **European Union** starting January 1, 1994. The treaty calls for a commitment to economic and monetary union and a move toward political union with common foreign and security policy.[7] (The European Monetary System, its history, and future are discussed in detail in Chapter 7.)

Despite the uncertainties about the future of the EU, new countries want to join. Most EFTA countries have joined or are EU applicants in spite of the fact that the EEA treaty gives them most of the benefits of a single market. They also want to have a say in the making of EU laws and regulations. Although no timetable for final membership has been set, the EU invited the Czech Republic, Cyprus, Estonia, Hungary, Poland, and Slovenia to begin membership negotiations in March 1998. Five other central European countries (Bulgaria, Latvia, Lithuania, Romania, and Slovakia) were given precandidate status.[8] The two-tier process was devised because some countries were deemed to have prepared their democratic institutions and economies better and faster than others. Turkey's application has been hindered by its poor human rights record, its unresolved dispute with Greece over Cyprus, and internal problems with Kurdish separatists. In the meanwhile, these countries will enjoy preferential trade rights through association membership with the EU. Access to EU markets is essential for growth in central Europe. The EU hopes, furthermore, that the promise of membership and access to its markets will result in greater political stability in the region.[9] The arrangement will also create investment opportunities for firms and cheaper goods for consumers in the EU.

## Organization of the EU

The executive body of the EU is the European Commission, headquartered in Brussels. The commission may be likened to the executive branch of the U.S. government. It is composed of 20 commissioners (two from each larger member country and one from each smaller member). The commissioners oversee 23 directorates (or departments), such as agriculture, transportation, and ex-

The European Union has several governing bodies, one of which is the EU Parliament. The Parliament has 626 members elected by popular vote in their home nation. The Parliament has power to veto membership applications and trade agreements with non-EU countries.  Source: Reuters/Vincent Kessler/Archive Photos.

ternal relations. The commissioners are appointed by the member states, but according to the Treaty of Rome, their allegiance is to the community, not to their home country.

The Council of Ministers has the final power to decide EU actions. There are a total of 87 votes in the council. The votes are allocated to the representatives of member countries on the basis of country size. Some of the most important provisions of the Single European Act expanded the ability of the council to pass legislation. The number of matters requiring unanimity was reduced, and countries' ability to veto legislation was weakened substantially. The Presidency of the Council rotates among the member states every six months.

The Court of Justice is somewhat analogous to the judicial branch of the U.S. government. The court is composed of 15 judges and is based in Luxembourg. The court adjudicates matters related to the European Constitution, especially trade and business disputes. Judicial proceedings may be initiated by member countries, as well as by firms and individuals.

The European Parliament is composed of 626 members elected by popular vote in member countries. The Parliament is essentially an advisory body with relatively little power. The fact that the only elected body of the EU has little policymaking power has led many to charge that the EU suffers from a "democratic deficit." In other words, decisions are made bureaucratically rather than democratically. However, the Single European Act empowered the Parliament to veto EU membership applications as well as trade agreements with non-EU countries. Many observers believe that the Parliament will gain new powers as European integration proceeds.

The entities and the process of decision making are summarized in Figure 8.1

## Implications of the Integrated European Market

Perhaps the most important implication of the four freedoms for Europe is the economic growth that is expected to result.[10] Several specific sources of increased growth have been identified. First, there will be gains from eliminating the transaction costs associated with border patrols, customs procedures, and so forth. Second, economic growth will be spurred by the economies of scale that will be achieved when production facilities become more concentrated. Third, there will be gains from more intense competition among EU companies. Firms that were monopolists in one country will now be subject to competition from firms in other EU countries. Economists have estimated that the reforms will cause an increase in European gross domestic product of about 5 percent over the medium term and 2 million new jobs will be created.

The proposals have important implications for firms within and outside Europe. There will be substantial benefits for those firms already operating in Europe. Those firms will gain because their operations in one country can now be freely expanded into others, and their products may be freely sold across borders. In a borderless Europe, firms will have access to many more millions of consumers. In addition, the free movement of capital will allow the firms to sell securities, raise capital, and recruit labor throughout Europe. Substantial economies of scale in production and marketing will also result. The extent of these economies of scale will depend on the ability of the managers to find panregional segments or to homogenize tastes across borders through their promotional activity.

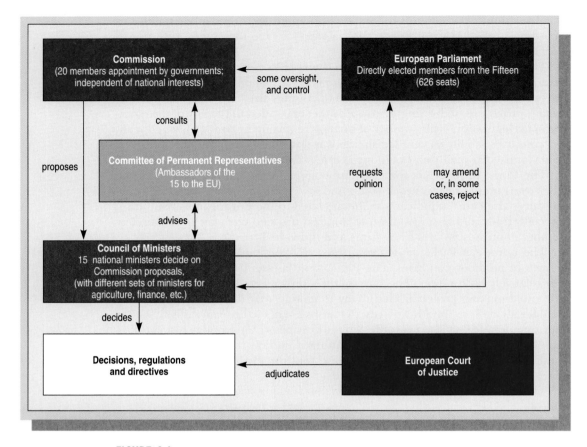

**FIGURE 8.1**

**Organization and Decision Making of the EU**
*Source:* Adapted from "My, How You've Grown," *The Economist,* January 25, 1992, 31–32.

For firms from nonmember countries, European integration presents various possibilities depending on the firm's position within the EU.[11] Table 8.4 provides four different scenarios with proposed courses of action. Well-established U.S.-based multinational marketers such as H.J. Heinz and Colgate-Palmolive will be able to take advantage of the new economies of scale. For example, 3M plants earlier turned out different versions of the company's products for various markets. Now, the 3M plant in Wales, for example, makes videotapes and videocassettes for all of Europe.[12] Colgate-Palmolive has to watch out for competitors, such as Germany's Henkel, in the brutally competitive detergent market. At the same time, large-scale retailers, such as France's Carrefour and Germany's Aldi group, are undertaking their own efforts to exploit the situation with hypermarkets supplied by central warehouses with computerized inventories. Their procurement policies have to be met by companies such as Heinz. Many multinationals are developing pan-European strategies to exploit the emerging situation; that is, they are standardizing their products and processes to the greatest extent possible without compromising local input and implementation.

**TABLE 8.4**

**Proposed Company Responses to European Markets**

| Company Status | Challenges | Response |
|---|---|---|
| Established multinational in one market/multiple markets | Exploit opportunities from improved productivity | |
| | Meet challenge of competitors | Pan-European strategy |
| | Cater to customers/ intermediaries doing same | |
| Firm with one European subsidiary | Competition | Expansion |
| | Loss of niche | Strategic alliances |
| | | Rationalization |
| | | Divestment |
| Exporter to Europe | Competition | European branch |
| | Access | Selective acquisition |
| | | Strategic alliance |
| No interest in Europe | Competition at home | Entry |
| | Lost opportunity | |

*Source:* Material drawn from John F. Magee, "1992 Moves Americans Must Make." *Harvard Business Review* 67 (May–June 1989): 78–84.

A company with a foothold in only one European market is faced with the danger of competitors who can use the strength of multiple markets. Furthermore, the elimination of barriers may do away with the company's competitive advantage. For example, more than half of the forty-five major European food companies are in just one or two of the individual European markets and seriously lag behind broader-based U.S. and Swiss firms. Similarly, automakers PSA and Fiat are nowhere close to the cross-manufacturing presence of Ford and GM. The courses of action include expansion through acquisitions or mergers, formation of strategic alliances (for example, AT&T's joint venture with Spain's Telfónica to produce state-of-the-art microchips), rationalization by concentrating only on business segments in which the company can be a pan-European leader, and finally, divestment.

Exporters will need to worry about maintaining their competitive position and continued access to the market. Companies with a physical presence may be in a better position to assess and to take advantage of the developments. Some firms, such as Filament Fiber Technology Inc. of New Jersey, have established production units in Europe. Digital Microwave Corporation of California decided to defend its market share in Europe by joining two British communications companies and setting up a digital microwave radio and optical-fiber plant in Scotland.[13] In some industries, marketers do not see a reason either to be in Europe at all or to change from exporting to more involved modes of entry. Machinery and machine tools, for example, are in great demand in Europe, and marketers in these companies say they have little reason to manufacture there.

The term **Fortress Europe** has been used to describe the fears of many U.S. firms about a unified Europe. The concern is that while Europe dismantles internal barriers, it will raise external ones, making access to the European market difficult for U.S. and other non-EU firms. In a move designed to protect European farmers, for example, the EU has occasionally banned the import of certain agricultural goods from the United States. The EU has also called on members to limit the number of American television programs broadcast in Europe. Finally, many U.S. firms are concerned about the relatively strict domestic content rules recently passes by the EU. These rules require certain products sold in Europe to be manufactured with European inputs. One effect of the perceived threat of Fortress Europe has been an increased direct investment in Europe by U.S. firms. Fears that the EU will erect barriers to U.S. exports and of the domestic content rules governing many goods have led many U.S. firms to initiate or expand European direct investment.

## North American Economic Integration

Although the EU is undoubtedly the most successful and well-known integrative effort, integration efforts in North America, although only a few years old, have gained momentum and attention. What started as a trading pact between two close and economically well-developed allies has already been expanded conceptually to include Mexico, and long-term plans call for further additions. However, in North American integration the interest is purely economic; there are no constituencies for political integration.

### U.S.–Canada Free Trade Agreement

After three failed tries this century, the United States and Canada signed a free trade agreement that went into effect January 1, 1989. The agreement created a $5 trillion continental economy.[14] The two countries had already had sectoral free trade arrangements; for example, one for automotive products has existed for 23 years. Even before the agreement, however, the United States and Canada were already the world's largest trading partners, and there were relatively few trade barriers. The new arrangement eliminated duties selectively in three stages over the 1989–1999 period.[15] For example, the first round eliminated a 3.9 percent tariff on U.S. computers shipped to Canada as well as 4.9–22 percent duties on trade in whiskey, skates, furs, and unprocessed fish. The sensitive sectors, such as textiles, steel, and agricultural products, will not be liberalized until the latter part of the transitionary period. Both countries see the free-trade agreement as an important path to world competitiveness. Although there have been some dislocations, due to production consolidation, for example, the pact is expected to create 750,000 jobs in the United States and 150,000 in Canada. It is also expected to add as much as 1 percent in growth to both countries' economies as it takes effect in various stages. Trade between the United States and Canada hit $290 billion in 1996, up more than 50 percent since 1988.

### North American Free Trade Agreement

Negotiations on a North American Free Trade Agreement (NAFTA) began in 1991 to create the world's largest free market, with 390 million consumers and a total output of 8.6 trillion.[16] The pact marked a bold departure: never before have industrialized countries created such a massive free trade area with a developing country neighbor.

NAFTA opened North America to trade causing a flood of activity between the United States and Mexico. To deal with complaints about differences in environmental standards and worker protections between countries, the North American Agreement on Labor Cooperation and the Commission on Environmental Compliance were established.   Source: © 1995 Todd Bigelow/Black Star

Since Canada stands to gain very little from NAFTA (its trade with Mexico is 1 percent of its trade with the United States), much of the controversy has centered on the gains and losses for the United States and Mexico. Proponents have argued that the agreement will give U.S. firms access to a huge pool of relatively low-cost Mexican labor at a time when demographic trends are indicating labor shortages in many parts of the United States. At the same time, many new jobs are created in Mexico. The agreement will give firms in both countries access to millions of additional consumers, and the liberalized trade flows will result in faster economic growth in both countries. Overall, the corporate view toward NAFTA is overwhelmingly positive.

Opposition to NAFTA has been on issues relating to labor and the environment. Unions in particular worried about job loss to Mexico given lower wages and work standards, some estimating that six million U.S. workers were vulnerable to job loss. A distinctive feature of NAFTA is the two side agreements that were worked out to correct perceived abuses in labor and in the environment in Mexico. The North American Agreement on Labor Cooperation (NAALC) was set up to hear complaints about worker abuse. Similarly, the Commission on Environmental Compliance was established to act as a public advocate on the environment. The side agreements have, however, had little impact, mainly because the mechanisms they created have almost no enforcement power.[17]

After a remarkable start in increased trade and investment, NAFTA suffered a serious setback due to significant devaluation of the Mexican peso in early 1995 and the subsequent impact on trade. Critics of NAFTA argued that too much was expected too fast of a country whose political system and economy were not ready for open markets. In response, advocates of NAFTA argued that there was nothing wrong with the Mexican real economy and that the peso crisis was a political one that would be overcome with time. As a matter of fact, with the help of the United States and the IMF, Mexico's economy started a strong recovery in 1996.

Trade between Canada, Mexico, and the United States has increased by 43 percent since NAFTA took effect, with total trade exceeding $421 billion in 1996. Reforms have turned Mexico into an attractive market in its own right. Mexico's gross domestic product has been expanding by more than 3 percent every year since 1989, and exports to the United States have risen 72 percent since 1986 to $73 billion in 1996. By institutionalizing the nation's turn to open markets, the free-trade agreement has attracted considerable new foreign investment. The United States has benefited from Mexico's success. U.S. exports to Mexico surpass those to Japan at $57 billion in 1996. While the surplus of $1.3 billion in 1994 had turned to a deficit of $16.2 billion in 1996 mainly due to Mexico's financial crisis, these imports have helped in Mexico's recovery and will, therefore, strengthen NAFTA in the long term. Furthermore, U.S. imports from Mexico have been shown to have much higher U.S. content than imports from other countries.[18] Among the U.S. industries to benefit are computers, autos, petrochemicals, and financial services. In 1990, Mexico opened its computer market by eliminating many burdensome licensing requirements and cutting the tariff from 50 percent to 20 percent. As a result, exports surged 23 percent in that year alone. IBM, which makes personal and mid-sized computers in Mexico, anticipates sales growth to about $1 billion from that country. In Mexico's growth toward a more advanced society, manufacturers of consumer goods will also stand to benefit. NAFTA has already had a major impact in the emergence of new retail chains, many established to handle new products from abroad. The top twenty exports and imports between Mexico and the United States are in virtually the same industries, indicating intra-industry trade in complementary products. This is evidence of industry specialization and building of economies of scale for global competitiveness.[19]

Free trade does produce both winners and losers. Although opponents concede that the agreement is likely to spur economic growth, they point out that segments of the U.S. economy will be harmed by the agreement. Overall wages and employment for unskilled workers in the United States will fall because of Mexico's low-cost labor pool. U.S. companies have been moving operations to Mexico since the 1960s. The door was opened when Mexico liberalized export restrictions to allow for more so-called **maquiladoras,** plants that make goods and parts or process food for export back to the United States. The supply of labor is plentiful, the pay and benefits are low, and the work regulations are lax by U.S. standards. The average maquiladora wage equals $1.73 per hour, compared with $2.17 an hour for Mexican manufacturers.[20] The maquiladora industry has grown remarkably within NAFTA, constituting 38.5 percent of Mexico's manufactured exports.[21] The investment mix within the industry is changing, however, with the arrival of Asian consumer-electronics producers, such as SONY and Samsung.[22]

A 1993 International Trade Commission assessment estimates that while NAFTA would create a net gain of 35,000 to 93,500 U.S. jobs by 1995, it would also cause U.S. companies to shed as many as 170,000 jobs.[23] Recent studies have put job gain or loss as almost a washout. The good news is that free trade has created higher skilled and better paying jobs in the United States as a result of growth in exports. As a matter of fact, jobs in exporting firms tend to pay 10 to 15 percent more than the jobs they replace. Losers have been U.S. manufacturers of auto parts, furniture, and household glass; sugar, peanut, and citrus growers; and seafood and vegetable producers. The fact that job losses have been in more heavily unionized sectors has made these losses politically charged. In most cases, high Mexican shipping and inventory costs will continue to make it more efficient for many U.S. industries to serve their home market from U.S. plants.

Countries dependent on trade with NAFTA countries are concerned that the agreement will divert trade and impose significant losses on their economies. Asia's continuing economic success depends largely on easy access to the North American markets, which account for more than 25 percent of annual export revenue for many Asian countries. Lower-cost producers in Asia are likely to lose some exports to the United States if they are subject to tariffs while Mexican firms are not and may, therefore, have to invest in NAFTA.[24] Similarly, many in the Caribbean and Central America fear that the apparel industries of their regions will be threatened, as would much-needed investments.[25]

NAFTA may be the first step toward a hemispheric bloc, but nobody expects it to happen any time soon. It took more than three years of tough bargaining to reach an agreement between the United States and Canada, two countries with parallel economic, industrial, and social systems.[26] The challenges of expanding free trade throughout Latin America will be significant. However, many of Latin America's groupings are making provisions to join NAFTA and create a hemispheric trade regime.[27] As a first step, Chile was scheduled to join as a fourth member in 1997. However, Chile's membership has not materialized due to U.S. political maneuvering, which, in turn, has jeopardized economic integration in the Americas, as shown in Global Perspective 8.2

## Other Economic Alliances

The world's developing countries have perhaps the most to gain from successful integrative efforts. Because many of these countries are also quite small, economic growth is difficult to generate internally. Many of these countries have adopted policies of **import substitution** to foster economic growth. With an import substitution policy, new domestic industries produce goods that were formerly imported. Many of these industries, however, can be efficient producers only with a higher level of production than can be consumed by the domestic economy. Their success, therefore, depends on accessible export markets made possible by integrative efforts.

### Integration in Latin America

Before the signing of the U.S.–Canada Free Trade Agreement, all of the major trading bloc activity in the Americas had taken place in Latin America. One of the longest-lived integrative efforts among developing countries was the Latin America Free Trade Association (LAFTA), formed in 1961. As the name suggests, the primary objective of LAFTA was the elimination of trade barriers. The 1961 agreement called for trade barriers to be gradually dismantled, leading to completely free trade by 1973. By 1969, however, it was clear that a pervasive protectionist ideology would keep LAFTA from meeting this objective, and the target date was extended to 1980. In the meantime, however, the

# WILL HEMISPHERIC TRADE REGIME WAIT FOR THE UNITED STATES?

The United States has long regarded Latin America as its business backyard and NAFTA as the model for Western Hemispheric integration. However, this thinking and the goal of creating a free-trade bloc covering the hemisphere by the year 2005 have run into considerable problems, some created by the United States and some by others.

The Clinton Administration failed to gain "fast track" negotiating authority from the U.S. Congress (that is, to broker deals that Congress could vote up or down but not amend). This was to be the major tool in extending NAFTA to the rest of Latin America and to boost U.S. exports there by eliminating local tariffs, which typically run from 10 to 13 percent. Without this authority, Latin Americans fear that any agreements negotiated could be turned down later or amended to have unacceptable terms by the U.S. Congress. "No fast track, no concrete negotiations," says Jose Botafogo, the Brazilian Foreign Ministry's subsecretary general of commerce. Rejecting the opinion that they are protectionist, the majority in the U.S. Congress argue that they want trade deals to include tough new requirements for U.S. trading partners to raise their labor and environmental standards. The alternative is that the U.S.'s standards might be dragged down.

The effects have been significant. Fed up with the wait to join NAFTA, Chile has moved closer to Europe and its own neighbors. It has joined MERCOSUR as an associate member, has free trade agreements with both Mexico (1992) and Canada (1996), and has begun formal talks on a separate trade deal with the EU. U.S. companies are reporting trade deals lost to their Canadian competitors who are free of Chile's average 11 percent tariffs. A number of U.S. companies have started shipping goods from plants in Canada and Mexico to Chile. Until 1997, Chrysler had been selling minivans in Chile that were made at its St. Louis, Missouri, plant. Now they've switched to importing those made at their plant in Ontario to capitalize on lower tariffs.

The failure to win fast track is likely to strengthen the hand of MERCOSUR, especially Brazil, in setting the terms of regional integration. A MERCOSUR-led move to hemispheric free trade could lead to slower efforts to remove barriers to U.S. exports and instead favor trade among South American nations. MERCOSUR's trade with the United States was $30 billion in 1996, while intra-bloc trade was $16 billion.

MERCOSUR's biggest trading partners, however, are the Europeans, who are expected to improve their positions dramatically as a result of U.S. inactivity. Their trade in 1996 exceeded $40 billion. By 1999 the EU and MERCOSUR are expected to begin talks that could lead to a free-trade area. EU politicians are striving to make the European flavor of Latin America even stronger. Europeans have won many of the top privatization deals since the early 1990s when governments in South America started opening up their markets. Spain's Telefónica de España, for example, has spent $5 billion buying telephone companies in Brazil, Chile, Peru, and Argentina, where France Télécom and STET of Italy are active as well. France's Electricité de France and Lyonnaise des Eaux have taken over state-owned facilities. In Brazil, 7 of the 10 largest private companies are European-owned, while just two are controlled by U.S. interests. Europeans dominate huge sectors in the economy, from automakers Volkswagen and Fiat to French supermarket chain Carrefour to Anglo-Dutch personal-care products group Gesy-Lever.

United States' trading partners in Latin America are perceiving that the U.S. government is willing to subjugate its international obligations to domestic political concerns. If trade is increasingly being sacrificed for the ultimate purpose of gaining political votes, access to the U.S. market may lose some of its value as the ultimate prize. MERCOSUR, for example, is arguing that NAFTA is not the only game in the region.

*Source: "Chile Takes Its Trade Elsewhere,"* The Washington Post, *December 25, 1997, A29, A38; "In Backyard of the U.S., Europe Gains Ground In Trade, Diplomacy,"* The Wall Street Journal, *September 18, 1997, A1, A8; "Is Europe Elbowing the U.S. Out of South America?"* Business Week, *August 4, 1997, 56; "Ah, Pan-American Free Trade,"* The Economist, *March 1, 1997, 43; "Latin America Becomes USA's Lost Horizon,"* Crossborder Monitor, *February 5, 1997, 1; "Hemispheric Trade Regime May Not Wait for USA,"* Crossborder Monitor, *November 13, 1996, 1–2.*

global debt crisis, the energy crisis, and the collapse of the Bretton Woods system prevented the achievement of LAFTA objectives. Dissatisfied with LAFTA, the group made a new start as the Latin American Integration Association (LAIA) in 1980. The objective is a higher level of integration than that envisioned by LAFTA; however, the dismantling of trade barriers remains a necessary and elusive first step.

The Central American Common Market (CACM) was formed by the Treaty of Managua in 1960. The CACM has often been cited as a model integrative effort for other developing countries. By the end of the 1960s, the CACM had succeeded in eliminating restrictions on 80 percent of trade among members. A continuing source of difficulty, however, is that the benefits of integration have fallen disproportionately to the richer and more developed members. Political difficulties in the area have also hampered progress. However, the member countries renewed their commitment to integration in 1990.

Integration efforts in the Caribbean have focused on the Caribbean Community and Common Market formed in 1968. Caribbean nations (as well as Central American nations) have benefited from the **Caribbean Basin Initiative (CBI),** which, since 1983, has extended trade preferences and granted access to the markets of the United States. Under NAFTA the preferences are lost, which means that the countries have to cooperate more closely among each other. Mexico and CACM have already started planning for a free-trade agreement. Proposals have also been made in the United States to extend unilaterally NAFTA benefits to CBI countries to protect them from investment and trade diversion.

None of the activity in Latin America has been hemispheric; the Central Americans have had their structures, the Caribbean nations theirs, and the South Americans had their own different forms. However, in a dramatic transformation, these nations are now looking for free trade as a salvation from stagnation, inflation and debt.[28] In response to the recent developments, Brazil, Argentina, Uruguay, and Paraguay set up a common market with completion by the end of 1994 called MERCOSUR (Mercado Comun del Sur).[29] Bolivia, Colombia, Ecuador, Peru, and Venezuela have formed the Andean Common Market (ANCOM). Many Latin nations are realizing that if they do not unite, they will become decreasingly important in the global market.

Recent foreign policy of the United States has also responded to Latin American regionalism. The **Enterprise for the Americas Initiative (EAI)** was designed in 1990 to further democracy in the region by providing incentives to capitalistic development and trade liberalization. The ultimate goal is a free-trade zone from Point Barrow, Alaska, to Patagonia. The argument is that free trade throughout the Americas would channel investment and technology to Latin nations and give U.S. firms a head start in those markets. If Latin America grows as estimated at an average of 4 percent annually during the 1990s under trade liberalization, imports will increase by $170 billion, of which U.S. firms can capture as much as 40 percent. However, before it can become a reality, many political (such as democratization) and economic (such as market-oriented policies) changes have to take place. The first step to such a zone was taken in December 1994, when leaders of 34 countries in the Americas agreed to work toward a hemispheric trade zone, **Free Trade Area of the Americas (FTAA),** by 2005. Ministerials held since have established working groups to gather data and make recommendations in preparation for the FTAA negotiations.

Changes in corporate behavior have been swift. Free-market reforms and economic revival have had companies ready to export and to invest in Latin America. For example, Brazil's opening of its computer market has resulted in Hewlett-Packard establishing a joint venture to produce PCs. Companies are also changing their approaches with respect to Latin America. In the past, Kodak dealt with Latin America through eleven separate country organizations.

It has since streamlined its operations to five "boundariless" companies organized along product lines and, taking advantage of trade openings, created centralized distribution, thereby making deliveries more efficient and decreasing inventory-carrying costs.[30]

## Integration in Asia

The development in Asia has been quite different from that in Europe and in the Americas. While European and North American arrangements have been driven by political will, market forces may compel politicians in Asia to move toward formal integration. While Japan is the dominant force in the area and might seem the choice to take leadership in such an endeavor, neither the Japanese themselves nor the other nations want Japan to do it. The concept of a "Co-Prosperity Sphere" of fifty years ago has made nations wary of Japan's influence.[31] Also, in terms of economic and political distance, the potential member countries are far from each other, especially compared to the EU. However, Asian interest in regional integration is increasing for pragmatic reasons. First, European and American markets are significant for the Asian producers, and some type of organization or bloc may be needed to maintain leverage and balance against the two other blocs. Second, given that much of the growth in trade for the nations in the region is from intra-Asian trade, having a common understanding and policies will become necessary. A future arrangement will most likely use the frame of the most established arrangement in the region, the Association of Southeast Asian Nations (ASEAN). Before late 1991, ASEAN had no real structures, and consensus was reached through information consultations. In October 1991, ASEAN members (Brunei, Indonesia, Malaysia, Philippines, Singapore, Thailand, Vietnam and since 1997, Myanmar and Laos) announced the formation of a customs union called ASEAN Free Trade Area (AFTA), with completion expected by 2003. The Malaysians have pushed for the formation of the East Asia Economic Group (EAEG), which would add Hong Kong, Japan, South Korea, and Taiwan to the list. This proposal makes sense; without Japan and the rapidly industrializing countries of the region such as South Korea and Taiwan, the effect of the arrangement would be small. Japan's reaction has been generally negative toward all types of regionalization efforts, mainly because it has had the most to gain from free-trade efforts. However, part of what has been driving regionalization has been Japan's reluctance to foster some of the elements that promote free trade, such as reciprocity.[32] Should the other trading blocs turn against Japan, its only resort may be to work toward a more formal trade arrangement in Pacific Asia.

Another formal proposal for cooperation would start building bridges between two emerging trade blocs. Some individuals have publicly called for a U.S.–Japan common market. Given the differences on all fronts between the two, the proposal may be quite unrealistic at this time. Negotiated trade liberalization will not open Japanese markets due to major institutional differences, as seen in many rounds of successful negotiations but totally unsatisfactory results. The only solution for the U.S. government is to forge better cooperation between the government and the private sector to improve competitiveness.[33]

In 1998, Australia proposed the Asia Pacific Economic Cooperation (APEC) as an annual forum. The proposal called for ASEAN members to be joined by Australia, New Zealand, Japan, China, Hong Kong, Taiwan, South Korea, Canada, and the United States. It was initially modeled after the Organization for Economic Cooperation and Development (OECD), which is a center for research and high-level discussion. Since then, APEC's goals have become more ambitious. At present, APEC has eighteen members with a combined GNP of $15 trillion and has the third largest economy of the world. The key objective of APEC are to liberalize trade by 2020, to facilitate trade by harmonizing standards, and to build human capacities for realizing the region's ambitions. The trade-driven economies of the region have the world's largest pool of savings, the most advanced technologies, and fastest growing markets. Therefore, companies with interests in the region are observing and supporting APEC-related developments closely as shown in the Global Perspective 8.3

However, the future actions of the other two blocs will determine how quickly and in what manner the Asian bloc, whatever it is, will respond. Also, the stakes are the highest for the Asian nations since their traditional export markets have been in Europe and in North America and, in this sense, very dependent on free access.

Economic integration has also taken place on the Indian subcontinent. In 1985, seven nations of the region (India, Pakistan, Bangladesh, Sri Lanka,

---

## WORKING FOR FREE TRADE IN ASIA

General Motors—and all the major car makers—is driving into Asia. The world's largest industrial company has found the environmental challenges considerable despite the lure of substantial market potential made possible by the growing middle class. In addition to distribution challenges and aggressive competition from other manufacturers, both local and foreign, the most daunting ones are barriers to free trade. For example, in Indonesia, GM faces competition from a local model, the Timor, which costs substantially less due to government supports (that is, lower duties on imported components). Before President Suharto's resignation, the company was run by one of his sons.

To overcome distribution difficulties, GM will invest $450 million in a regional manufacturing facility in Rayong Province to build the specially designed and engineered Opel "Car for Asia" beginning early in the twenty-first century. The Thai facility is the culmination of GM's buildup in Asia that started in 1990 with the establishment of a regional office in Hong Kong and representative offices in Bangkok, Jakarta, Kuala Lumpar, and Beijing. In 1994, the GM's Asia headquarters was moved from Detroit to Singapore. While Singapore will provide co-

ordination and support, GM will tailor manufacturing, sales, and distribution strategies to meet local requirements. It established GM China in 1994 as a separate entity, and in Japan it bought a 37.5 percent equity stake in Isuzu. The Asian economic crisis, which hit Thailand especially hard, made GM scale down the investment in Thailand from $750 million and to change the product from a $15,000 Astra to a considerably cheaper model.

To combat protectionism and further the cause of free trade, GM has developed a three-prong strategy. The first approach focuses on executives working with government representatives from the United States, European Union, and Japan to dismantle what GM regards as the largest flaws. The company uses its clout as a major investor, but it can also call on support from industries that follow it into a new market, such as component manufacturers. On the second level, GM works within existing frameworks to balance the effects of nationalistic policies. In countries such as Indonesia and Malaysia, it develops company-specific plans to preserve avenues of sales even under challenging circumstances. Finally, GM is also pursuing its business strategy in Asia's free-trade areas. Since it will be a long time before barriers are taken down in the Asia Pacific Economic Cooperation Forum (APEC), its immediate focus is on the ASEAN Free Trade Area (AFTA). GM is hopeful that the automotive sector will be a beneficiary of tariff reductions—provided that member governments can be persuaded that such cuts are in their best interests.

*Source: "GM Delays Plans to Open Big Thai Plant," The Wall Street Journal, January 6, 1998, A2; and "GM Presses for Free Trade in Asia," Crossborder Monitor, January 15, 1997, 1, 9.*

Nepal, Bhutan, and the Maldives) launched the South Asian Association for Regional Cooperation (SAARC). Cooperation is limited to relatively noncontroversial areas, such as agriculture and regional development. Elements such as the formation of a common market have not been included.

## Integration in Africa and the Middle East

Africa's economic groupings range from currency unions among European nations and their former colonies to customs unions among neighboring states. In 1975, sixteen west African nations attempted to create a megamarket large enough to interest investors from the industrialized world and reduce hardship through economic integration. The objective of the Economic Community of West African States (ECOWAS) was to form a customs union and eventual common market. Although many of its objectives have not been reached, its combined population of 160 million represents the largest economic entity in sub-Saharan Africa. Other entities in Africa include the Afro-Malagasy Economic Union, the East Africa Customs Union, the West African Economic Community, and the Maghreb Economic Community. Many of these, however, have not been successful due to the small size of the members and lack of economic infrastructure to produce goods to be traded inside the blocs.

Countries in the Arab world have made some progress in economic integration. The Gulf Cooperation Council (GCC) is one of the most powerful, economically speaking, of any trade groups. The per-capita income of its six member states (Bahrain, Kuwait, Oman, Qatar, Saudi Arabia, and the United Arab Emirates) is in the ninetieth percentile in the world. The GCC was formed in 1980 mainly as a defensive measure due to the perceived threat from the Iran–Iraq war. Its aim is to achieve free trade arrangements with the EU and EFTA as well as bilateral trade agreements with western European nations.

A listing of the major regional trade agreements is provided in Table 8.5.

## Economic Integration and the International Manager

Regional economic integration creates opportunities and challenges for the international manager. Economic integration may have an impact on a company's entry mode by favoring direct investment, since one of the basic rationales for integration is to generate favorable conditions for local production and interregional trade. By design, larger markets are created with potentially more opportunity. Harmonization efforts may result in standardized regulations, which can positively affect production and marketing efforts.

The international manager must, however, make assessments and decisions regarding integrating markets from four points of view.[34] The first task is to create a vision of the outcome of the change. Change in the competitive landscape can be dramatic if scale opportunities can be exploited in relatively homogeneous demand conditions. This could be the case, for example, for industrial goods and consumer durables, such as cameras and watches, as well as for professional services. The international manager will have to take into consideration varying degrees of change readiness within the markets themselves; that is, governments and other stakeholders, such as labor unions, may oppose the liberalization of competition in all market segments. For example, while plans have called for liberalization of air travel and automobile marketing in Europe, EU members have found loopholes to protect their own companies.

**TABLE 8.5**

**Major Regional Trade Associations**

| | |
|---|---|
| **AFTA** | **ASEAN Free Trade Area** |
| | Brunei, Indonesia, Malaysia, Philippines, Singapore, Thailand, Vietnam |
| **ANCOM** | **Andean Common Market** |
| | Bolivia, Colombia, Ecuador, Peru, Venezuela |
| **APEC** | **Asia Pacific Economic Cooperation** |
| | Australia, Brunei, Canada, Chile, China, Hong Kong, Indonesia, Japan, Malaysia, Mexico, New Zealand, Papua New Guinea, Philippines, Singapore, South Korea, Taiwan, Thailand, United States |
| **CACM** | **Central American Common Market** |
| | Costa Rica, El Salvador, Guatemala, Honduras, Nicaragua, Panama |
| **CARICOM** | **Caribbean Community** |
| | Antigua and Barbuda, Bahamas, Barbados, Belize, Dominica, Grenada, Guyana, Jamaica, Montserrat, St. Kitts-Nevis, St. Lucia, St. Vincent and the Grenadines, Suriname, Trinidad-Tobago |
| **ECOWAS** | **Economic Community of West African States** |
| | Benin, Berkina Faso, Cape Verde, Gambia, Ghana, Guinea, Guinea-Bissau, Ivory Coast, Liberia, Mali, Mauritania, Niger, Nigeria, Senegal, Sierra Leone, Togo |
| **EU** | **European Union** |
| | Austria, Belgium, Denmark, Finland, France, Germany, Greece, Ireland, Italy, Luxembourg, Netherlands, Portugal, Spain, Sweden United Kingdom |
| **EFTA** | **European Free Trade Association** |
| | Iceland, Liechtenstein, Norway, Switzerland |
| **GCC** | **Gulf Cooperation Council** |
| | Bahrain, Kuwait, Oman, Qatar, Saudi Arabia, United Arab Emirates |
| **LAIA** | **Latin American Integration Association** |
| | Argentina, Bolivia, Brazil, Chile, Colombia, Ecuador, Mexico, Paraguay, Peru, Uruguay, Venezuela |
| **MERCOSUR** | **Southern Common Market** |
| | Argentina, Brazil, Paraguay, Uruguay |
| **NAFTA** | **North American Free Trade Agreement** |
| | Canada, Mexico, United States |

For information see **http://www.aseansec.org; http://www.apec.org;
http://www.caricom.org; http://www.eurunion.org; http://www.nafta.org**

WWW

The international manager then will have to develop a strategic response to the new environment to maintain a sustainable long-term competitive advantage. Those companies already present in an integrating market should fill in gaps in goods and market portfolios through acquisitions or alliances to create a balanced panregional company. Those with a weak presence, or none at all, may have to create alliances for distribution with established firms.[35] To take advantage of the new situation in Europe, James River Corporation from the United States, Nokia from Finland, and Cragnotti & Partners from Italy launched a pan-European papermaking joint venture called Jamont. Before 1992, papermaking was highly fragmented in Europe but the joint-venture partners saw a chance to develop a regional manufacturing and marketing strategy. A total of thirteen companies in ten countries were acquired and pro-

# International Groupings

**OECD** Organization for Economic Co-operation and Development
**OPEC** Organization of the Petroleum Exporting Countries
**Commonwealth**

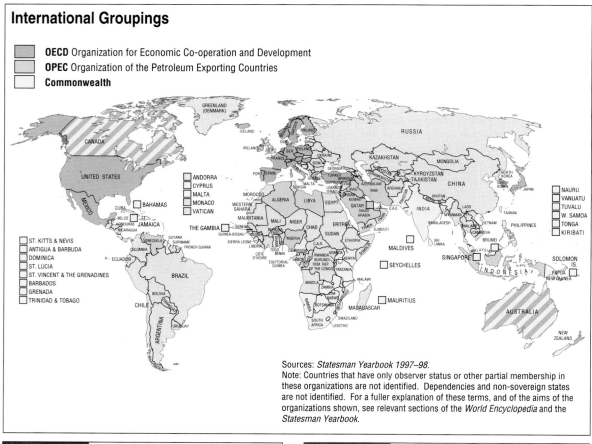

Sources: *Statesman Yearbook 1997–98.*
Note: Countries that have only observer status or other partial membership in these organizations are not identified. Dependencies and non-sovereign states are not identified. For a fuller explanation of these terms, and of the aims of the organizations shown, see relevant sections of the *World Encyclopedia* and the *Statesman Yearbook.*

**MIDDLE-EAST**

**OAPEC** Organization of Arab Petroleum Exporting Countries
**Gulf Co-operation Council**
**The Arab League**

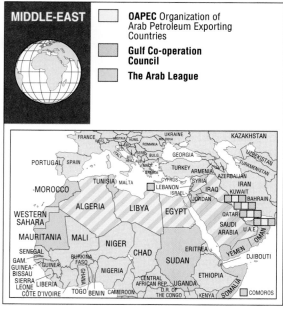

**EUROPE-TRADE**

**EU** European Union
**EFTA** European Free Trade Association
**Association membership in EU**

**PACIFIC BASIN**

**AFTA** ASEAN (Association of South East Asian Nations) Free Trade Area

**AMERICAS**

**NAFTA** North American Free Trade Agreement

**ANCOM** Andean Common Market

**MERCOSUR** Southern Common Market

**CARICOM** Caribbean Community and Common Market

**CACM** Central American Common Market

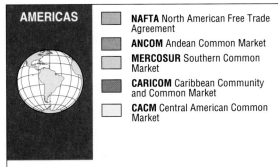

**AFRICA**

**OAU** *non*-members of the Organization for African Unity

**\*Franc Zone** currency linked to the French Franc

**SADCC** Southern Africa Development Co-ordination Conference

**COMESA** Common Market for East and Southern Africa (formerly **PTA**)

**ECOWAS** Economic Community of West African States

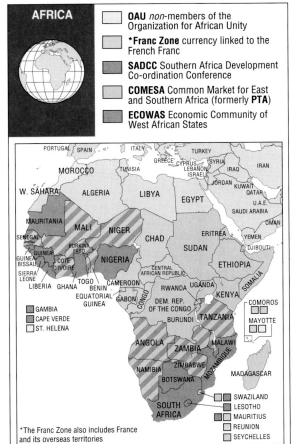

*The Franc Zone also includes France and its overseas territories

duction was consolidated. For example, before the new strategy, each company made deep-colored napkins; now all of Jamont's products come from one plant in Finland.[36] An additional option for the international manager is leaving the market altogether in response to the new competitive conditions or the level of investment needed to remain competitive. Bank of America sold its operations in Italy to Deutsche Bank once it determined the high cost of becoming a pan-European player.

Whatever the changes, they will call for company reorganization.[37] Structurally, authority will have to be more centralized so regional programs can be executed. In staffing, focus will have to be on individuals who understand the subtleties of consumer behavior across markets and therefore are able to evaluate the similarities and differences among cultures and markets. In developing systems for the planning and implementation of regional programs, adjustments will have to be made to incorporate views throughout the organization. If, for example, decisions on regional advertising campaigns are made at headquarters without consultation with country operations, resentment by the local staff will lead to less-than-optimal execution. Companies may even move corporate or divisional headquarters from the domestic market to be closer to the customer; AT&T estimates that several of its units may have their headquarters abroad, especially in Europe. Similarly, companies have moved their headquarters for Latin American operations from the United States to cities such as Caracas, Venezuela.

Finally, economic integration will involve various powers and procedures, such as the EU's Commission and its directives. The international manager is not powerless to influence both of them; a passive approach may result in competitors gaining an advantage or a disadvantageous situation emerging for the company. For example, it was very important for the U.S. pharmaceutical industry to obtain tight patent protection as part of the NAFTA agreement and substantial time and money was spent on lobbying both the executive and legislative branches of the U.S. government in the effort to meet its goal. Often policymakers rely heavily on the knowledge and experience of the private sector in carrying out its own work. Influencing change will therefore mean providing policymakers with industry information such as test results. Lobbying will usually have to take place at multiple levels simultaneously; within the EU, this means the European Commission in Brussels, the European Parliament in Strasbourg, or the national governments within the EU. Managers with substantial resources have established their own lobbying offices in Brussels, while smaller companies get their voices heard through joint offices or their industry associations. In terms of lobbying, U.S. firms have been at an advantage given their experience in their home market; however, for many non–U.S. firms, lobbying is a new, yet necessary, skill to be acquired. At the same time, managers in two or more blocs can work together to produce more efficient trade through, for example, mutual recognition agreements (MRAs) on standards.[38]

## Cartels and Commodity Price Agreements

An important characteristic that distinguishes developing countries from industrialized countries is the nature of their export earnings. While industrialized countries rely heavily on the export of manufactured goods, technology, and services, the developing countries rely chiefly on the export of primary products and raw materials—for example, copper, iron ore, and agricultural products. This distinction is important for several reasons. First, the level of price competition is higher among sellers of primary goods, because of the typically larger number of sellers and also because primary goods are homogeneous. This can be seen by comparing the sale of computers with, for example, copper. Only three of four countries are a competitive force in the computer market, whereas at least a dozen compete in the sale of copper. Furthermore, while goods differentiation and therefore brand loyalty are likely to exist in the market for computers, buyers of copper are likely to purchase on the basis of price alone. A second distinguishing factor is that supply variability will be greater in the market for primary goods because production often depends on uncontrollable factors such as weather. For these reasons, market prices of primary goods—and therefore developing country export earnings—are highly volatile.

Responses to this problem have included cartels and commodity price agreements. A **cartel** is an association of producers of a particular good. While a cartel may consist of an association of private firms, our interest is in the cartels formed by nations. The objective of a cartel is to suppress the market forces affecting its good in order to gain greater control over sales revenues. A cartel may accomplish this objective in several ways. First, members may engage in price fixing. This entails an agreement by producers to sell at a certain price, eliminating price competition among sellers. Second, the cartel may allocate sales territories among its members, again suppressing competition. A third tactic calls for members to agree to restrict production, and therefore supplies, resulting in artificially higher prices.

The most widely known cartel is the Organization of Petroleum Exporting Countries (OPEC). OPEC became a significant force in the world economy in the 1970s. In 1973, the Arab members of OPEC were angered by U.S. support for Israel in the war in the Mideast. In response, the Arab members declared an embargo on the shipment of oil to the United States and quadrupled the price of oil—from approximately \$3 to \$12 per barrel. OPEC tactics included both price fixing and production quotas. Continued price increases brought the average price per barrel to nearly \$35 by 1981. The cartel has experienced severe problems since, however. First, the demand for OPEC oil declined considerably as the result of conservation, the use of alternative sources, and increased oil production by nonmembers. OPEC's market share has declined from its 55 percent peak in 1974 to 40 percent at present.[39] All of these factors also contributed to sharp declines in the price of oil. Second, the cohesiveness among members diminished. Sales often occurred at less than the agreed-upon price, and production quotas were repeatedly violated. The members of OPEC convened following the Persian Gulf was in early 1991 in an attempt to regain control over oil prices, but it remains to be seen whether OPEC will regain its influence as a major force in the world economy.

International **commodity price agreements** involve both buyers and sellers in an agreement to manage the price of a certain commodity. Often, the free market is allowed to determine the price of the commodity over a certain range. However, if demand and supply pressures cause the commodity's price to move outside that range, an elected or appointed manager will enter the market to buy or sell the commodity to bring the price back into the range. The manager controls the **buffer stock** of the commodity. If prices float downward, the manager purchases the commodity and adds to the buffer stock. Under upward pressure, the manager sells the commodity from the buffer stock. This system is somewhat analogous to a managed exchange rate system such as the EMS, in which authorities buy and sell to influence exchange rates. International commodity agreements are currently in effect for sugar, tin, rubber, cocoa, and coffee.

## Summary

Economic integration involves agreements among countries to establish links through the movements of goods, services, and factors of production across borders. These links may be weak or strong depending on the level of integration. Levels of integration include the free-trade area, customs union, common market, and full economic union.

The benefits derived from economic integration include trade creation, economies of scale, improved terms of trade, the reduction of monopoly power, and improved cross-cultural communication. However, a number of disadvantages may also exist. Most importantly, economic integration may work to the detriment of non-members by causing deteriorating terms of trade and trade diversion. In addition, no guarantee exists that all members will share the gains from integration. The biggest impediment to economic integration is nationalism. There is strong resistance to surrendering autonomy and self-determinism to cooperative agreements.

The most successful example of economic integration is the European Union. The EU has succeeded in eliminating most barriers to the free flow of goods, services, and factors of production. In addition, the EU has made progress toward the evolution of a common currency and central bank, which are fundamental requirements of an economic union. In the Americas, NAFTA is paving the way for a hemispheric trade bloc.

A number of regional economic alliances exist in Africa, Latin America, and Asia, but they have achieved only low levels of integration. Political difficulties, low levels of development, and problems with cohesiveness have impeded integrative progress among many developing countries. However, many nations in these areas are seeing economic integration as the only way to prosperity in the future.

International commodity price agreements and cartels represent attempts by producers of primary products to control sales revenues and export earnings. The former involves an agreement to buy or sell a commodity to influence prices. The latter is an agreement by suppliers to fix prices, set production quotas, or allocate sales territories. OPEC had inestimable influence on the global economy during the 1970s, but its importance has since diminished.

## Key Terms and Concepts

| | | |
|---|---|---|
| trading bloc | common market | economic union |
| free trade area | factor mobility | trade creation |
| customs union | Single European Act | trade diversion |

internal economies
  of scale
external economies
  of scale
Treaty of Rome
common agricultural
  policy (CAP)
1992 White Paper
Single European Act

economic and monetary
  union (EMU)
Maastricht Treaty
European Union
Fortress Europe
maquiladoras
import substitution
Caribbean Basin
  Initiative (CBI)

Enterprise for the
  Americas Initiative (EAI)
Free Trade Area of the
  Americas (FTAA)
cartel
commodity price
  agreement
buffer stock

NAFTA

## Questions for Discussion

1. Explain the difference between a free-trade area and a customs union. Speculate why negotiations were held for a North American Free Trade Agreement rather than for a North American Common Market.
2. What problems might a member country of a common market be concerned about?
3. Construct an example of a customs union arrangement resulting in both trade creation and trade diversion.
4. Distinguish between external and internal economies of scale resulting from economic integration.
5. Are economic blocs (such as the EU and NAFTA) building blocs or stumbling blocs as far as worldwide free trade is concerned?
6. Suppose that you work for a medium-sized manufacturing firm in the Midwest. Approximately 20 percent of your sales are to European customers. What threats and opportunities does your firm face as a result of an integrated European market?
7. Compare and contrast two different points of view on expanding NAFTA by accessing the websites of America Leads on Trade, an industry coalition promoting increased access to world markets (**http://www.fasttrack.org**), and the AFL-CIO, American Federation of Labor–Congress of Industrial Organizations (**http://www.aflcio.org**).
8. What type of adjustments will U.S. firms make as a result of NAFTA?

## Recommended Readings

*The Arthur Andersen North American Business Sourcebook.* Chicago: Triumph Books, 1994.

Bannister, Rebecca R. *The NAFTA Success Story: More Than Just Trade.* Washington, D.C.: Progressive Policy Institute, 1997.

Buiter, William, and Richard Marston. *International Economic Policy Coordination.* Cambridge, England: Cambridge University Press, 1987.

Cooper, Richard. *Economic Policy in an Interdependent World.* Cambridge, Mass.: MIT Press, 1987.

EC Commission. *Completing the Internal Market: White Paper from the Commission to the European Council.* Luxembourg: EC Commission, 1985.

Fair, D.E., and C. de Boissieu, eds. *International Monetary and Financial Integration—The European Dimension.* Norwell, Mass.: Kluwer, 1987.

Ryans, John K., Jr., and Pradeep A. Rau. *Marketing Strategies for the New Europe: A North American Perspective on 1992.* Chicago: American Marketing Association, 1990.

Sapir, Andre, and Alexis Jacquemin, eds. *The European Internal Market.* Oxford, England: Oxford University Press, 1990.

Schott, Jeffrey, *United States–Canada Free Trade: An Evaluation of the Agreement.* Washington, D.C.: Institute for International Economics, 1988.

Stoeckel, Andrew, David Pearce, and Gary Banks. *Western Trade Blocs*. Canberra, Australia: Centre for International Economics, 1990.

Suriyamongkol, Majorie L. *Politics of ASEAN Economic Cooperation*. Oxford, England: Oxford University Press, 1988.

*Trade Liberalization: Western Hemisphere Trade Issues Confronting the United States* Washington, D.C.: United States General Accounting Office, 1997.

United Nations. *From the Common Market to EC92: Integration in the European Community and Transnational Corporations*. New York: United Nations Publications, 1992.

## Notes

1. The discussion of economic integration is based on the pioneering work by Bela Balassa, *The Theory of Economic Integration* (Homewood, Ill.: Richard D. Irwin, 1961).
2. Jacob Viner, *The Customs Union Issue* (New York: Carnegie Endowment for International Peace, 1950).
3. J. Waelbroeck, "Measuring Degrees of Progress in Economic Integration," in *Economic Integration, Worldwide, Regional, Sectoral*, ed. F. Machlop (London: Macmillan, 1980).
4. EC Commission, *Completing the Internal Market: White Paper from the Commission to the European Council* (Luxembourg: EC Commission, 1985).
5. "A Singular Market," *The Economist* (October 22, 1994): 10–16.
6. Various aspects of the 1992 Common Market are addressed in André Sapir and Alexis Jacquemin, eds., *The European Internal Market* (Oxford, England: Oxford University Press, 1990).
7. "The Maths of Post-Maastricht Europe," *The Economist* (October 16, 1993): 51–52.
8. "Ex-Communist Nations Receive Nod From EU," *The Washington Post*, December 14, 1997, A28.
9. "Will More Be Merrier?" *The Economist* (October 17, 1992): 75.
10. Economic growth effects are discussed in Richard Baldwin, "The Growth Effects of 1992," *Economic Policy* (October 1989): 248–281; or Rudiger Dornbusch, "Europe 1992: Macroeconomic Implications," *Brookings Papers on Economic Activity* 2 (1989): 341–362.
11. John F. Magee, "1992: Moves Americans Must Make," *Harvard Business Review 67* (May–June 1989): 72–84.
12. Richard I. Kirkland, "Outsider's Guide to Europe in 1992," *Fortune* (October 24, 1988): 121–127.
13. "Should Small U.S. Exporters Take the Plunge?" *Business Week* (November 14, 1988): 64–68.
14. "Getting Ready for the Great American Shakeout," *Business Week* (April 4, 1988): 44–46.
15. "Summary of the U.S.-Canada Free Trade Agreement," *Export Today* 4 (November–December 1988): 57–61.
16. Raymond Ahearn, *Trade and the Americas* (Washington, D.C.: Congressional Research Service, 1997), 3–4.
17. "NAFTA's Do-Gooder Side Deals Disappoint," *The Wall Street Journal* October 15, 1997, A19.
18. "U.S. Trade with Mexico During the Third NAFTA Year," *International Economic Review* (Washington, D.C.: International Trade Commission, April 1997): 11.
19. Sidney Weintraub, *NAFTA at Three: A Progress Report* (Washington, D.C.: Center for Strategic and International Studies, 1997), 17–18.
20. Jim Carlton, "The Lure of Cheap Labor," *The Wall Street Journal*, September 14, 1992, R16.
21. "Mexico's NAFTA Trade Surge Led by Maquiladoras," *Crossborder Monitor* (July 23, 1997): 1–2.
22. "Localizing Production," *Global Commerce* (August 20, 1997): 1.
23. "A Noose Around NAFTA," *Business Week* (February 22, 1993): 37.
24. Andrew Stoeckel, David Pearce, and Gary Banks, *Western Trade Blocs* (Canberra, Australia: Centre for International Economics, 1990).
25. Jose De Cordoba, "Alarm Bells in the Caribbean," *The Wall Street Journal*, September 24, 1992, R8.
26. "A Giant Step Closer to North America Inc." *Business Week* (December 5, 1988): 44–45.
27. "Next Stop South," *The Economist* (February 25, 1995): 29–30.
28. Thomas Kamm, "Latin Links," *The Wall Street Journal*, September 24, 1992, R6.
29. "The World's Newest Trading Bloc," *Business Week* (May 4, 1992): 50–51.
30. "Ripping Down the Walls Across the Americas," *Business Week* (December 26, 1994): 78–80.
31. Emily Thornton, "Will Japan Rule a New Trade Bloc?" *Fortune* (October 5, 1992): 131–132.
32. Paul Krugman, "A Global Economy Is Not the Wave of the Future," *Financial Executive* 8 (March/April 1992): 10–13.
33. Michael R. Czinkota and Masaaki Kotabe, "America's New World Trade Order," *Marketing Management* 1 (Summer 1992): 49–56.
34. Eric Friberg, Risto Perttunen, Christian Caspar, and

Dan Pittard, "The Challenges of Europe 1992," *The McKinsey Quarterly* 21, 2 (1988): 3–15.

35. John A. Quelch, Robert D. Buzzell, and Eric R. Salama, *The Marketing Challenge of 1992* (Reading, Mass.: Addison-Wesley, 1990), Chapter 13.

36. "A Joint-Venture Papermaker Casts Net Across Europe," *The Wall Street Journal,* December 7, 1992, B4.

37. Gianluigi Guido, "Implementing a Pan-European Marketing Strategy," *Long Range Planning* 24, 5 (1991): 23–33.

38. "TABD Uses Virtual Organization for Trade Lobbying," *Crossborder Monitor* (July 2, 1997): 1.

39. "OPEC's Joyride Was Great While It Lasted," *Business Week* (June 3, 1996): 52.

# CHAPTER 9

# Market Transitions and Development

## LEARNING OBJECTIVES

◆ *To understand the special concerns that must be considered by the international manager when dealing with emerging market economies*

◆ *To survey the vast opportunities for trade offered by emerging market economies*

◆ *To understand why economic change is difficult and requires much adjustment.*

◆ *To become aware that privatization offers new opportunities for international trade and investment*

## Emerging Countries Produce New Competitors

In the 1980s Americans in both the private and public sector were very concerned about U.S. competitiveness. American companies, it was perceived, were falling behind their foreign rivals—especially the Japanese. Today, however, U.S. companies have bounced back and their technology is again the envy of the world.

For Michael Porter, a Harvard Business School professor, sizing up U.S. companies against competitors in the Group of Seven (Canada, France, Germany, Great Britain, Italy, Japan, and the United States) is yesterday's battle. The most competitive rivals will increasingly be global and can emerge from almost anywhere. Some of the new entrants Porter sees are Brazil, Chile, China, India, and Malaysia. Big competitors will likely spring from these newly emerging markets.

A survey of American executives by the Council on Competitiveness found that nearly 50 percent of them saw the toughest foreign competition in the future coming from emerging countries outside of the G-7. Developing countries are increasingly turning out world-class goods and services. Some of these goods come from outposts of U.S., Japanese, and European multinational enterprises that have invested heavily in the emerging economies. Increasingly, though, world-class companies are home grown.

In a recent Morgan Stanley & Co. report on the paper and pulp industry, for example, three out of the twelve most competitive companies were based in developing nations. India is emerging as a powerhouse in steel, chemicals, pharmaceuticals, and computer software. Many emerging countries are penetrating the markets of other developing countries before attempting entry into that more competitive G-7 markets. South Korea's auto industry has done just that in countries such as Venezuela and Poland.

The chief economist at Cigna Retirement & Investment Services, Edward Guay, provides some insight into these recent trends: "You can't forget that countries like Malaysia, Taiwan, Brazil, [and] Chile have sent their managers to the best schools in the U.S." American universities have been training foreign scientists and managers for years.

If there is any danger to American companies, suggests Porter, it is that many developing countries are getting better in quality while remaining much cheaper in terms of wages and other costs. "The challenge facing the U.S. is how do we justify our wages?" he says. "The answer is to remain innovative, to use American creativity to continue inventing things of greater value, specialty steels instead of basic steels, the next drugs, the new semiconductor chips, the financial services never thought of by anyone before." ▪

*Source:* Bernard Wysocki Jr., "Emerging Nations Win Major Exporting Role," *The Wall Street Journal,* February 24, 1997.

This chapter addresses major societal, economic, and ideological shifts that are occurring in the global economy. The focus is on the emerging democracies of central Europe and the new countries that were the former Soviet Union, due to significant shifts in ideology and economic thinking that have taken place there. In addition, economic changes in large emerging markets such as China, Southeast Asia, and Latin America are presented and the role of privatization is discussed. Finally, the role of international business in development is presented.

The emergence of new players in world trade has important implications for the international business manager both in terms of opportunities and of risks, as this chapter's opening vignette showed. Privatization is addressed because the increasing transition of corporations from government ownership into private hand presents a substantial shift in market orientation and offers new opportunities for trade and investment. Developmental issues are presented to reflect the special needs of large regions of the world and the resulting special responsibilities of international business.

## Doing Business With Emerging Market Economies

The major market economies emerging out of formerly centrally planned economies are Russia and the now independent states of the former Soviet Union, East Germany (now unified with West Germany), the eastern and central European nations (Albania, Bulgaria, the Czech and Slovak Republics, Hungary, Poland, and Romania), and the People's Republic of China.

It is a common belief that business ties between the Western world and these nations are a recent phenomenon. That is not the case. In the 1920s, for example, General Electric and RCA helped develop the Soviet electrical and communications industries. Ford constructed a huge facility in Nizhni Novgorod to build Model A cars and buses. DuPont introduced its technology to Russia's chemical industry. However, since the late 1940s, former centrally planned economies and Western corporations engaged in international business had rather limited contact.[1]

Socialist countries perceived international corporations as "aggressive business organizations developed to further the imperialistic aims of Western, especially American, capitalists the world over."[2] Furthermore, may aspects of capitalism, such as the private ownership of the means of production, were seen as exploitative and antithetical to communist ideology. Western managers, in turn, often saw socialism as a threat to the market system and the Western world in general.

**A Brief Historic Review**

Due to differing politics and ideology, the trade history of socialist countries is quite different from that of the United States and the West. The former Soviet system of foreign trade dates to a decree signed by Lenin on April 22, 1918. It established that the state would have a monopoly on foreign trade and that all foreign trade operations were to be concentrated in the hands of organizations specifically authorized by the state. This system of a state-controlled mo-

The opening of Eastern Europe to international trade has provided vast opportunities for the expansion of international marketing activities.
Source: © Filip Horvat/SABA

nopoly was also adopted by the East European satellites of the Soviet Union and by the People's Republic of China.

In effect, this trade structure isolated the firms and consumers in socialist economies from the West and unlinked demand from supply. Rigid state bureaucracies regulated the entire economy. Over time, domestic economic problems emerged. The lack of attention to market forces resulted in misallocated resources, and the lack of competition promoted inefficiency. Centralized allocation prevented the emergence of effective channels of distribution. Managers of plants were more concerned with producing the quantities stipulated by a rigid **central plan** (often five-year plans, one following another) than with producing the products and the quality desired. Entrepreneurship was disdained, innovation risky. Consequently, socialist economies achieved only lackluster growth, and their citizens fell far behind the West in their standard of living.

In the mid-1980s, the Soviet Union developed two new political and economic programs: **perestroika** and **glasnost.** Perestroika was to fundamentally reform the Soviet economy by improving the overall technological and industrial base as well as the quality of life for Soviet citizens through increased availability of food, housing, and consumer goods. Glasnost was to complement those efforts by encouraging the free exchange of ideas and discussion of problems, pluralistic participation in decision making, and increased availability of information.[3]

The major domestic steps were followed shortly by legislative measures that thoroughly reformed the Soviet foreign-trade apparatus. In a major move away from previous trade centralization, national agencies, large enterprises, and research institutes were authorized to handle their own foreign transactions directly.

Concurrent with the steps taken in the Soviet Union, other socialist countries also initiated major reforms affecting international business. China began to launch major programs of modernization and developed multinational corporations of its own. Virtually all socialist countries began to invite foreign investors to form joint ventures in their countries to help satisfy both domestic and international demand and started to privatize state enterprises.

## The Demise of The Socialist System

By late 1989, all the individual small shifts resulted in the emergence of a new economic and geopolitical picture. With an unexpected suddenness, the Iron Curtain disappeared, and, within less than three years, the Communist empire ceased to exist. Virtually overnight, Eastern Europe and the former Soviet Union, with their total population of 400 million and a combined GNP of $3 trillion,[4] shifted their political and economic orientations toward a market economy. The former socialist satellites shed their communist governments. Newly elected democratic governments decided to let market forces shape their economies. East Germany was unified with West Germany. In March 1992, Hungary was admitted as an associate member of the European Union. By then, the entire Soviet Union had disappeared. Individual regions within the Commonwealth of Independent States reasserted their independence and autonomy, resulting in a host of emerging nations, often heavily dependent on one another, but now separated by nationalistic feelings and political realities.

The political changes were accompanied by major economic action. Externally, trade flows were redirected from the former Soviet Union toward the European Union, as Figure 9.1 shows. Internally, austerity programs were introduced and prices of subsidized products were adjusted upward to avoid distorted trade flows due to distorted prices. Wages were kept in check to reduce inflation. Entire industries were either privatized or closed down. These steps led to a significant decrease in the standard of living of the population. Initially, the support for the internal economic transformation continued, demonstrating the great desire on the part of individuals and governments to participate in the world marketplace and the hope that these transformations would achieve a better standard of living. Over time, however, increasing economic difficulties precipitated large levels of discontent, and, by some, a desire for a return to the old days. As a result, some countries have experienced civil and political strife, and the reemergence of political hard-liners. Economic progress will be a crucial component of democratic political stability. But these nations need to determine for themselves whether they want to continue on the arduous path toward liberalization. They will have to decide whether the pain of transition is worth the promise of democracy and free markets.[5]

Due to military intervention, China did not undergo such radical political shifts. However, its economic changes were of similar significance. New enterprise zones were opened, designed to produce products targeted for export. Foreign investors were invited into the country. Individuals were permitted to translate their entrepreneurial skills into action and keep the profits.

From a Western perspective, all these changes indicated the end of the Cold War. After the ebbing of initial euphoria, it was also learned and understood that the shouts for democracy were, to a large degree, driven not only by political but also by economic desires. Freedom meant not only the right to free elections but also the expectation of an increased standard of living in the form of color televisions, cars, and the many benefits of a consumer society. To sustain the drive toward democracy, these economic desires had to appear attainable. Therefore, it was in the interest of the Western world as a whole to contribute to the democratization of the former Communist nations by searching for ways to bring them "the good life."

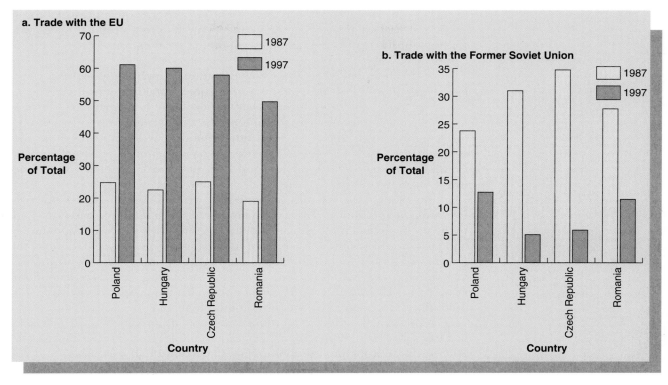

**FIGURE 9.1**

**A Redirection of Trade Flows**
*Source: Direction of Trade Statistics,* International Monetary Fund, Washington, D.C.: September 1997.

For Western firms, the political and economic shifts converted a latent but closed market into a market offering very real and vast opportunities. Yet the shifts are only the beginning of a process. The announcement of an intention to change does not automatically result in change itself. For example, the abolition of a centrally planned economy does not create a market economy. Laws permitting the emergence of private sector entrepreneurs do not create entrepreneurship. The reduction of price controls does not immediately make goods available or affordable. Deeply ingrained systemic differences between the emerging democracies and Western firms continue. Highly prized, fully accepted fundamentals of the market economy, such as the reliance on competition, support of the profit motive, and the willingness to live with risk on a corporate and personal level, are not yet fully accepted. Major changes still need to take place. It is therefore useful to review the major economic and structural dimensions of the emerging democracies to identify major shortcomings and opportunities for international business.

Many of the newly emerging democracies (NEDs) face major **infrastructure shortages.** Transportation systems, particularly those leading to the West, are either nonexistent or in disrepair. The housing stock is in need of total overhaul. Communication systems will take years to improve. Market intermediaries often do not exist. Payments and funds-transfer systems are inadequate.

## The Realities of Economic Change

Even though major efforts are under way to improve the infrastructure—evidenced, for example, by Hungary's success in installing a cellular telephone system—infrastructure shortcomings will inhibit economic growth for years to come.

Capital shortages are also a major constraint. Catching up with the West in virtually all industrial areas will require major capital infusions. In addition, a new environmental consciousness will require large investments in environmentally sound energy-generation and production facilities. Even though major programs are being designed to attract hidden personal savings into the economies, NEDs must rely to a large degree on attracting capital from abroad. Continued domestic uncertainties and high demand for capital around the world make this difficult.

Firms doing business with the emerging democracies encounter interesting demand conditions. Buyers, in many instances, have never been exposed to the problem of decision making; their preferences are vague and undefined, and they are therefore poorly trained in making market choices.[6] Little accurate market information is available. For example, knowledge about pricing, advertising, research, and trading is virtually nonexistent, and few institutions are able to accurately research demand and channel supply. As a result, it is quite difficult for corporations to respond to demand.

To the surprise of many investors, the emerging democracies have substantial knowledge resources to offer. For example, it is claimed that Russia and Central Europe possess about 35 to 40 percent of all researchers and engineers in the world.[7] At the same time, however, these nations suffer from the disadvantages imposed by a lack of management skills. In the past, management mainly consisted of skillful maneuvering within the allocation process. Central planning, for example, required firms to request tools seven years in advance; material requirements needed to be submitted two years in advance. Ordering was done haphazardly, since requested quantities were always reduced, and surplus allocations could always be traded with other firms. The driving mechanism for management was therefore not responsiveness to existing needs, but rather plan fulfillment through the development of a finely honed **allocation mentality,** which waits for instructions from above.

Commitment by managers and employees to their work is difficult to find. Many employees are still caught up in old work habits, which consisted of never having to work a full shift due to other commitments and obligations. The notion that "they pretend to pay us, and we pretend to work" is still very strong. The current dismantling of the past policy of the "Iron Rice Bowl," which made layoffs virtually impossible, is further reducing rather than increasing such commitment.

The new environment also complicates managerial decision making. Because of the total lack of prior market orientation, even simple reforms require an almost unimaginable array of decisions about business licenses, the setting of optimal tax rates, rules of business operation, definitions of business expense for taxation purposes, safety standards, and rules concerning nondiscrimination and consumer protection.[8]

To cope with all these new challenges, NEDs need trained managers. Since no large supply of such individuals exists, much of the training must be newly developed. Simply applying established Western guidelines to such training is inappropriate due to the differences in the people to be trained. Business learn-

**TABLE 9.1**

**Russian Attitudes toward Business Learning**

| Attitude | Dimension |
|---|---|
| Pride | We are educated people, but our views are totally discounted. |
| Fear | This new order is more dangerous than the Cold War since it has no rules. This new international competition is coming in, and we are without shelter. |
| Suspicion | How do we know the market is good for us? Why should Americans tell Russians how to run their business? |
| Credibility | Schools are pushing courses like used carpets. Has training made people more successful? |
| Specificity | Expertise is only valuable in the context of Russia. |
| Compatibility | We understand the words but have no mental image of their meaning. |
| Complexity | Having fun during learning is not Russian. Complex ideas should be taught in a complex way. |
| Longevity | Will our learning truly make a difference? |
| Desire | We need to learn how to do civilized business. We must learn to care, break loose from old patterns. |

*Source:* Michael R. Czinkota "Russia's Transition to a Market Economy: Learning about Business, *Journal of International Marketing* 5, 4 (1997): 73–93.

ing in transition economies must focus on key business issues such as marketing, strategic planning, international business, and financial analysis. However, it must not just focus on the transmission of knowledge, but also aim to achieve behavioral change. Given the lack of market orientation in the previous business environment, managers must adapt their behavior in areas such as problem solving, decision making, the development of customer orientation, and team building. In addition, the attitudes held by managers toward business and Western teaching approaches must be taken into consideration. As Table 9.1 shows, these attitudes can be quite inhibiting to the acceptance of new knowledge.

## Adjusting to Global Change

Both institutions and individuals tend to display some resistance to change. The resistance grows if the speed of change increases. It does not necessarily indicate a preference for the earlier conditions but rather a concern about the effects of adjustment and a fear of the unknown. In light of the major shifts that have occurred both politically and economically in central Europe and the former Soviet Union and the accompanying substantial dislocations, resistance should be expected. Deeply entrenched interests and traditions are not easily supplanted by the tender and shallow root of market-oriented thinking. The understanding of linkages and interactions cannot be expected to grow overnight. For example, greater financial latitude for firms also requires that inefficient firms be permitted to go into bankruptcy—a concept not cherished by many. The need for increased efficiency and productivity causes sharp reductions in employment—a painful step for the workers affected. The growing ranks of unemployed are swelled by the members of the military who have been brought home or demobilized. Concurrently, wage reforms threaten to relegate blue-collar workers, who were traditionally favored by the socialist system, to second-class status, while permitting the emergence of a new entrepreneurial class of the rich, an undesirable result for those not participating in the upswing. Retail price reforms endanger the safety net of larger population segments, and widespread price changes introduce inflation. It is difficult to accept a system where there are winners and losers, particularly for those on the losing side. As a result, an increase in ambivalence and uncertainty may well produce rapid shifts in economic and political thinking, which in turn may produce another set of unexpected results.

But it is not just in the emerging democracies that major changes have come about. The shifts experienced there also have major impact on the established market economies of the West. Initially, the immediate changes in the West were confined to the reduction of the threat of war and a redefinition of military and political strategy. Over time, however, Western governments are discovering that the formation of new linkages and dismantling of old ones will also cause major dislocations at home. For example, the change in military threat has affected military budgets. Budget changes in turn have changed the production of military goods and the employment level in the defense sector.

Major changes also result from the reorientation of trade flows. With traditional and "forced" trade relationships vanishing and the need for income from abroad increasing, many more countries exert major efforts to become partners in global trade. They attempt to export much more of their domestic production. Many of the exports are in product categories such as agriculture, basic manufacturing, steel, aluminum, and textiles, which are precisely the economic sectors in which the industrialized nations are already experiencing surpluses. As a result, the threat of displacement is high for traditional producers in industrialized nations.

Due to domestic economic dislocations, the pressure is on Western governments to restrict the inflow of trade from the East. Giving in to such pressure, however, would be highly detrimental to the further development of these new market economies. The countries in transition need assistance in their journey. Providing them with open markets is the best form of assistance, much more valuable than the occasional transfer of aid funds. Rapid changes and substantial economic dislocation have caused many individuals and policy makers in the East to become suspicious and wary of Western business approaches. Unless Western governments and businesses are able to convincingly demonstrate how competition, variety, trade, and freedom of choice can improve the quality of life, the opportunity to transform postsocialist societies will be lost.[9] As Global Perspective 9.1 describes, the West must share the burden of global economic adjustment.

## International Business Challenges and Opportunities

The pressure of change also presents vast opportunities for the expansion of international business activities. Large populations offer new potential consumer demand and production supply. Many opportunities arise out of the en-

## THE CORESPONSIBILITY OF THE WEST

**E**astern Europe has undergone almost incomprehensible change. The Czech Republic was deeply involved in the change and its president, Vaclav Havel, has spoken very candidly about what has happened and what is at stake, for all the nations on Earth:

"The world used to be so simple: There was a single adversary who was more or less understandable, who was directed from a single center, and whose sole aim in its final years was to maintain the status quo. At the same time, the existence of this adversary drew the West together as well, because faced with this global and clearly defined danger, it could always somehow agree on a common approach. All that has vanished. The world has suddenly become unusually complex and far less intelligible. The old order has collapsed, but no one has yet created a new one.

" . . . The 'postcommunist world' is constantly springing new surprises on the West: Nations hitherto unheard of are awakening and want countries of their own. Highly improbable people from God knows where are winning elections. It is not even clear whether the very people who four years ago so astonishingly roused themselves from their torpor and overthrew communism do not actually miss that system today. . . . How much easier it must have been for Western politicians when they were faced with a homogenous Soviet mass and didn't have to worry about distinguishing one nation from another.

" . . . Now that the Cold War is over, the impression is that the headaches it caused are over. But the headaches are never over. . . . Our countries must deal with their own immense problems themselves. The 'non-postcommunist West,' however, should not look on as though it were a mere visitor at a zoo or the audience at a horror movie, on edge to know how it will turn out. It should perceive these processes at the very least as something that intrinsically concerns it, and that somehow decides its own fate, that demands its own active involvement and challenges it to make sacrifices in the interests of a bearable future for us all.

" . . . To make my point briefly and simply: it seems to me that the fate of the so-called West is today being decided in the so-called East. If the West does not find a key to us, who were once violently separated from the West, it will ultimately lose the key to itself."

**Source: Vaclav Havel ,"A Call for Sacrifice: The Coresponsibility of the West," Foreign Affairs (March/April 1994): 2–7.**

thusiasm with which a market orientation is embraced in some nations. Companies that are able to tap into the desire for an improved standard of living can develop new demand on a large scale. Global Perspective 9.2 presents some of the opportunities in the automotive sector.

When trying to respond to demand, a major challenge encountered by firms is the lack of information about end users. Business strives to satisfy the needs and wants of individuals and organizations. Due to a lack of available research, the international manager must often use hearsay, educated guesses, and the opinions of intermediaries in making business decisions.

Another major difficulty encountered is the frequent unavailability of convertible currency. Products, however, necessary, often cannot be purchased by emerging market economies because no funds are available to pay for them. As a result, many of the countries resort to barter and countertrade. This places an additional burden on the international manager, who must not only market products to the clients but must also market the products received in return to other consumers and institutions. However, as Chapter 18 will explain, new methods of countertrade are being developed by the world business community to reduce the impact of this problem.

Problems also have arisen from the lack of protection some of the countries afford to intellectual property rights. Firms have complained about frequent illegal copying of films, books, and software, and about the counterfeit-

## RUSSIA'S UNTAPPED AUTO MARKET

In the showroom of a Moscow auto dealership, Volodya Dmitriev eyes the sleek design of a Skoda Felicia, a Volkswagen built in the Czech Republic. "It's a great car," he says. "Still . . ." He glances over at a Russian-made Lada, which starts at about half the $10,500 sticker price of the Volkswagen. The Russian leaves the dealership undecided, but Volkswagen and other foreign car dealers are boosting their efforts to lure car shoppers like Dmitriev back. Soon Volkswagen will start assembling Skodas in Russia and Belarus in an attempt to avoid import tariffs that account for 30 percent of the sticker price.

General Motors and Daewoo (a South Korean firm) are already manufacturing cars in the former Soviet Union. Even with the lowered costs of domestic assembly, these foreign cars will still cost thousands more than the best-selling Russian models. But foreign producers are gambling that their appealing designs and superior quality will win over customers. If their gamble pays off, they will be in the running for one of the world's greatest untapped auto markets.

In Russia only 83 of every 1,000 people own their own car, less than half the ownership rate in Eastern Europe. Many who do are itching to trade in their Soviet clunkers for a car with superior foreign engineering. In 1996, Russian drivers snapped up 50,000 new imported cars—twice the number from the previous year. Analysts suggest that the market will grow at least 4 percent annually through the end of the decade. These statistics translate into increased foreign sales, especially of the spacious American cars preferred by most Russian drivers.

Still, most foreign automakers are investing only moderately in the former Soviet Republics. Ford, GM, and Skoda are setting up operations that will cost about $20 million and will produce no more than a few thousand units a year. Companies are holding back investment mainly because of the region's unstable economy and because they haven't yet established a solid distribution and sales network. Yet no one wants to be left out of the potentially lucrative market. "Once the economic situation stabilizes, the former Soviet Union can be a market of major size," says Wayne Booker, Ford vice-chairman for emerging markets. "It is absolutely essential that we be there."

Foreign car makers still have difficult hurdles to overcome, though. In a region that often lacks the rule of law, many Russians feel that foreign-made cars will become targets of thieves and bribe-hungry traffic police. Consumer tastes are also very hard to predict in the new market economies. After his survey of the foreign models at the dealership, customer Akhmed Mirzoyev announces that he has decided on the Russian Lada. "I just needed something for running errands around town," he explains.

*Source: Carol Matlock, "Ready to Burn Rubber in Russia," Business Week (March 31, 1997).*

ing of brand-name products. Unless importers can be assured that government safeguards will protect their property, trade and technology transfer will be severely inhibited.

Problems also can be encountered when attempting to source products from emerging market economies. Many firms have found that selling is not part of the economic culture in some of the countries. The few available descriptive materials are often poorly written and devoid of useful information. Obtaining additional information about a product may be difficult and time-consuming.

The quality of the products obtained can also be a major problem. In spite of their great desire to participate in the global marketplace, many producers still tend to place primary emphasis on product performance and neglect, to a large extent, issues of style and product presentation. Therefore, the international manager needs to forge agreements that require the manufacturer to improve quality, provide for technical control, and ensure prompt delivery before sourcing products from emerging market economies.

Nevertheless, sufficient opportunities exist to make consideration of such international business activities worthwhile. Some emerging market economies

A bus shelter in Moscow's
Red Square advertising foreign products is evidence of
business opportunities in an
open economy.
*Source:* Robert Harding
Picture Library/London

have products that are unique in performance. While they were nontradable
during a time of ideological conflict, they are becoming successful global products in an era of new trade relations. For example, research shows that Russian tractors can be sold successfully in the United States. A study found that
many of the previously held negative attitudes about imports from the region
have been modified by the improved political climate.[10] Many countries offer
low labor costs and, in some instances, a great availability of labor. These nations can offer consumers in industrialized nations a variety of products at low
costs.

Currently, most sourcing opportunities from Eastern Europe and the Commonwealth of Independent States are for industrial products, which reflects
the past orientation of research and development expenditures. Over time,
however, consumer products may play a larger role. In addition, there are also
substantial opportunities for technology transfer. For example, the former Soviet training program for cosmonauts, which prepared space travelers for long
periods of weightlessness, actually provides quite useful information for U.S.
manufacturers of exercise equipment. Therefore, even if not interested in entering the emerging market economies, the international business executive
would be wise to maintain relationship with them in order not to lose a potentially valuable source of supply.

## State Enterprises and Privatization

One other area where the international business executive must deal with a
period of transition is that of state-owned enterprises. These firms represent a
formidable pool of international suppliers, customers, and competitors. Many
of them are currently being converted into privately owned enterprises. This
transition also presents new opportunities.

## Reasons for the Existence of State-Owned Enterprises

A variety of economic and noneconomic factors has contributed to the existence of state-owned enterprises. Two primary ones are national security and economic security. Many countries believe that, for national security purposes, certain industrial sectors must be under state control. Typically, these sectors include telecommunications, airlines, banking, and energy.

Economic security reasons are primarily cited in countries that are heavily dependent on specific industries for their economic performance. This may be the case when countries are heavily commodity dependent. Governments frequently believe that, given such heavy national dependence on a particular industrial sector, government control is necessary to ensure national economic health.

Other reasons also contributed to the development of state-owned enterprises. On occasion, the sizable investment required for the development of an industry is too large to come from the private sector. Therefore, governments close the gap between national needs and private sector resources by developing these industries themselves. In addition, governments often decide to rescue failing private enterprises by placing them in government ownership. In doing so, they fulfill important policy objectives, such as the maintenance of employment, the development of depressed areas, or the increase of exports.

Some governments also maintain that state-owned firms may be better for the country than privately held companies because they may be more societally oriented and therefore contribute more to the greater good. This was particularly the case in areas such as telecommunications and transportation, where profit maximization, at least from a governmental perspective, was not always seen as the appropriate primary objective.

## The Effect of State-Owned Enterprises on International Business

Three types of activities where the international manager is likely to encounter state-owned enterprises are market entry, the sourcing or marketing process, and international competition. On occasion, the very existence of a state-owned enterprise may inhibit or prohibit foreign market entry. For reasons of development and growth, governments frequently make market entry from the outside quite difficult so that the state-owned enterprise can perform according to plan. Even if market entry is permitted, the conditions under which a foreign firm can conduct business are often substantially less favorable than the conditions under which state-owned enterprises operate. Therefore, the international firm may be placed at a competitive disadvantage and may not be able to perform successfully even though economic factors would indicate success.

The international manager also faces a unique situation when sourcing from or marketing to state-owned enterprises. Even though the state-owned firm may appear to be simply another business partner, it is ultimately an extension of the government and its activities. This may mean that the state-owned enterprise conducts its transactions according to the overall foreign policy of the country rather than according to economic rationale. For example, political considerations can play a decisive role in purchasing decisions. Contracts may be concluded for noneconomic reasons rather than be based on product offering and performance. Contract conditions may depend on foreign policy outlook, prices may be altered to reflect government displeasure, and delivery performance may change to "send a signal." Exports and imports may be delayed or encouraged depending on the current needs of government. Even though an economic rationale appears to exist within a state-owned enterprise, the interests and concerns of the owner—the state—may lead it to be driven by politics.[11]

This also holds true when the international firm encounters international competition from state-owned enterprises. Very often, the concentration of the firms is not in areas of comparative advantage, but rather in areas that at the time are most beneficial for the government owning the firm. Input costs often are much less important than policy objectives. Sometimes, state-owned enterprises may not even know the value of the products they buy and sell because prices in themselves have such a low priority. As a result, the international manager may be confronted with competition that is very tough to beat.

Nonetheless, many firms have begun to form joint ventures with state-owned enterprises. As Global Perspective 9.3 shows, such ventures can be suc-

## How to Win in China

**A** sparkling IBM service center stands amid the turmoil around the Beijing West Railway Station and its slew of frantic passengers trying to catch the next train to Shanghai. The outlet, one of forty IBM has set up around China in a venture with the Railways Ministry, is one element of an aggressive effort that has catapulted IBM to the top of China's booming personal-computer market after a decade of disappointment. It's the kind of success that offers a glimmer of hope to those who question whether China will ever pay off for Western investors.

The Chief Executive of Northern Telecom Ltd., Jean C. Montey, has a different story. In spite of investing $130 million in a giant state-of-the-art factory, forging several research and development ties with government institutions, and securing a solid foothold in China's $13 billion telecom-equipment market, Nortel is barely breaking even. One problem for the company is that many of its rivals have set up similar plants. Instead of the five competitors Montey expected, there are now twelve. He doesn't foresee any improvement in the situation.

It seems as though there are two Chinas: One is a frustrating bottomless pit and the other is the biggest emerging market in the world. On the one hand, there is the old China, where remnants of the Communist party planning apparatus pile excessive demands on multinationals, especially in politically sensitive areas such as cars, chemicals, and telecommunications equipment. In this China, companies are besieged by local officials, tormented by policy swings, and railroaded into bad partnerships. With a mushrooming $39.5 billion U.S. trade deficit with China, investor's woes have gained added sympathy from those in the United States who favor a tougher policy stance toward the Communist state.

These critics should pay heed, however, to the new market-driven China that is emerging quicker than the spread of wildfire. Consumer sectors from fast food to shampoo are now extremely free. Barriers to entry in more tightly guarded areas are diminishing as provincial authorities, rival ministries, and even the military compete with Beijing for authority. Here are a few strategies that successful firms have employed to win in the largest of all emerging markets:

■ **Choose the right partners.** Winning companies avoid teaming up with inept and inefficient state enterprises or relying too heavily on in top-level "connections" in Beijing. Increasingly, successful companies are searching for partners from entrepreneurial companies owned by local governments or the military. They also insist on management control.

■ **Focus on the basics.** Foreign investment is often plagued by poor business planning. Smart players make money by focusing on the fundamentals, such as marketing, distribution, and sales.

■ **Guard technology.** Resisting government pressure to transfer key business know-how lessens the opportunities for future competitors. Winners typically hand over only the knowledge necessary to ensue that their Chinese ventures are competitive, while keeping next-generation technology at home. They also fight aggressively against theft of intellectual property.

■ **Fly low.** Huge, costly, and high-profile projects often become bogged down in red tape, national politics, and bureaucratic turf wars. Successful companies launch a series of small ventures associated with more cooperative local governments.

*Source: Mark Clifford, "How You Can Win in China," **Business Week** (May 26, 1997), p. 66.*

cessful as long as business success rather than politics plays the major role. Otherwise, government interference can play havoc with a firm's business plans.

## Privatization

Beginning in the mid-1980s governments and citizens came to recognize the drawbacks of government control of enterprises. Competition was restrained, which resulted in lower quality of goods and reduced innovation. Domestic citizens were deprived of lower prices and of choice. The international competitiveness of state-controlled enterprises was suffering, which often resulted in the need for growing government subsidies. In addition, rather than focusing on the business aspects, many government-controlled corporations had become grazing grounds for political appointees or vote winners through job allocations. As a result, many government-owned enterprises excelled in losing money.[12]

Governments are increasingly recognizing that it is possible to reduce the cost of governing by changing their role and involvement in the economy. Through **privatization,** governments can cut their budget costs and still ensure that more efficient—not fewer—services are provided to their citizens. Privatized goods and services are often more competitive and more innovative. The conversion of government monopolies into market-driven activities tends to attract foreign investment capital, bringing additional know-how and financing to enterprises. Finally, governments can use proceeds from privatization to fund other pressing domestic needs.

In the mid-1970s, the United States reduced government involvement in industry by deregulating domestic industries that had been tightly controlled and regulated, such as telephone service and airlines. Within a decade, deregulation spread across many industrialized and developing nations, resulting in more consumer choice and lower rates. Britain pioneered the concept of privatization in 1979 by converting 20 state firms into privately owned companies. In the 1980s, Chile privatized 470 enterprises, which had produced 24 percent of the country's value added.[13] By the mid-1990s, privatization had become a key element in governmental economic strategy around the world. Global privatization proceeds exceed $240 billion and encompass a wide variety of industries and countries, as Figure 9.2 shows. In addition to Asia, Africa, Latin America, and the Eastern European nations, Western Europe entered the privatization field on a large scale. As a result of these efforts, many new private companies that were large by global standards emerged and provided, on a local level, unprecedented levels of innovation and quality.

The methods of privatization vary from country to country. Some nations come up with a master plan for privatization, whereas others deal with it on a case-by-case basis. The Treuhandanstalt of Germany, for example, which was charged with disposing of most East German state property, aimed to sell firms but also to maximize the number of jobs retained. In other countries, ownership shares are distributed to citizens and employees. Some nations simply sell to the highest bidder in order to maximize the proceeds. For example, Mexico has used most of its privatization proceeds to amortize its internal debt, resulting in savings of nearly $1 billion a year in interest payments.

The purpose of most privatization programs is to improve productivity, profitability, and product quality and to shrink the size of government. As companies are exposed to market forces and competition, they are expected to produce better goods and services at lower costs. Privatization also intends to attract new capital for these firms so that they can carry out necessary adjustments

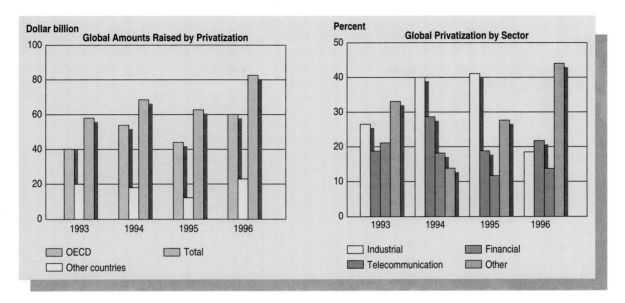

**FIGURE 9.2**

**Trends in Global Privatization**

*Source:* Organization for Economic Cooperation and Development, *Financial Market Trends,* 64 (June 1996).

and improvements. Since local capital is often scarce, privatization efforts increasingly aim to attract foreign capital investment. Privatization, however, is no magic wand, as Global Perspective 9.4 shows. Its key benefits come from corporate adjustment, which is often quite painful.

The trend toward privatization offers unique opportunities for international managers. Existing firms, both large and small, can be acquired at low cost, often with governmental support through tax exemptions, investment grants, special depreciation allowances, and low-interest-rate credits. The purchase of such firms enables the international firm to expand operations without having to start from scratch. In addition, since wages are often low in the countries where privatization takes place, there is a major opportunity to build low-cost manufacturing and sourcing bases. Furthermore, the international firm can also act as a catalyst by accelerating the pace of transferring business skills and technology and by boosting trade prospects. In short, the very process of change offers new opportunities to the adept manager.

## The Role of the Multinational Firm*

All problems aside, the market potential of transition economies is enormous. It is this promise that is paramount to understanding the developing role of multinational firms in transition economies. They enter because they see enor-

*The authors gratefully acknowledge the valuable input of Professor Viktoria Dalko to this section.

## PRIVATIZATION IN AFRICA

The manager of the state-owned Tanzanian Brewery used to spend his mornings dealing with a long line of people outside his office. Most carried notes that read along these lines: "The bearer of this note is my friend. I am having a funeral at my brother's house this weekend. Please ensure that there is an adequate supply of beer." The note would usually be signed by a government minister or some other important official.

The Tanzanian Brewery was build with a capacity of 1.3 million liters of beer a day but produced only 400,000. It had a 25 percent share of the market but provided a bad-tasting product. A privatization drive by the Tanzanian government enabled South African Breweries to buy a 50 percent stake in the defunct state-run operation. After obtaining a five-year management contract, the South Africans cut the workforce, built a new brewery, improved the taste, and grabbed 75 percent of the market. Just recently the brewery turned its first profit.

Tanzania has privatized 138 companies, including cashew and tobacco farms, mines, a cigarette factory, and the brewery.

But they are only halfway there and have the most difficult part ahead. The 121 companies left to be privatized include such operations as decrepit state-run utilities that will be difficult to transfer to private hands because they are such unattractive investments. The problem is complicated by the government's desire to see a large portion of these companies in the hands of its citizens. The fact is that few people in Tanzania have the necessary capital to invest in these companies. Thus, instead of selling off companies outright, the government is retaining a share for later sale to the Tanzanians.

In theory the state has made strides to open up the country for business. In practice, investing in Tanzania is more like riding a roller coaster. Frequent power failures and shoddy telephone networks demonstrate the country's lack of investment in its infrastructure. Both foreign and local business people complain about the labyrinthlike tax system with over thirty different taxes from different authorities. Permits and licenses arrive late or not at all unless certain palms are greased.

Clearly, privatization provides a mechanism for greater efficiency in emerging economies. Unfortunately, governments cannot simply wave a magic wand that makes privatization a reality. The task is overwhelming, especially in former socialist countries like Tanzania where an entrenched bureaucracy and other vested interests are an ingrained part of the society.

*Source: Dares Salam, "Private Sector Beer is Best," The Economist (November 2, 1996) p 46.*

mous profit potential. This potential, however, may not be attained quickly, and they must time their entry and activity to pace themselves for the long race.

The experience to date in many transition economics has been mixed in terms of business success. Many of the newly formed purely domestic businesses have experienced relatively short life spans often characterized by rapid growth and significant profitability, albeit short lived in duration. The causes of failure typically are: problems in general business management; the institution of new government regulations or taxes; or regulatory failures.

Multinational firms, however, have experienced higher rates of success in transition economies for a variety of reasons. First, foreign firms have had a tendency to enter—at least initially—service sectors that allowed high profit potential with minimal capital investments. This permits a first-stage entry of little capital at risk as noted in Global Perspective 9.2, which showed that automakers such a GM and Daewoo are entering the Russian market with very little capital. Many of these service-sector market niches, such as insurance, internet-based telecommunication services, security sales and brokerage services, and management consulting, to name a few, are "markets" that simply did not exist under the prior economic system. Many multinational firms have found these segments enormously profitable to date and have quickly gained a foothold in transition economies.

As multinational firms gain experience and knowledge of the local markets, they may then increase the size of their capital investments, for example in the form of acquisitions or greenfield investments. The local market is then used as a export base to neighboring or other transition economies, taking advantage of long-standing linkages across countries for trade and commerce. At this point, the domestic market is not the focus of the firm's activity. With few exceptions, the profit potential is seen as cost-based access to other external markets.

This export orientation of the multinational firm is quite consistent with the economic policy goals of the transition economies. They are often sorely in need of export earnings. Having a multinational firm use their economic system as "base camp" for export-led development adds employment and infrastructure support. This is also one of the factors contributing to the special privileges accorded foreign multinationals by host governments in transition, such as preferential import duties, corporate tax breaks, and subsidized labor. In fact, many multinationals quickly find their access to local capital through the rapidly developing domestic financial sector to be easier than that of other domestic borrowers, since many domestic companies are effectively excluded from accessing necessary capital. This is in many ways an unfortunate result of the lower-risk profile of the multinational firm compared to recently established domestic enterprises. If not balanced by encouragement for domestic firms, this disadvantage may result in growing criticism of multinational firms and their impact on transition economies. It can also lead to renewed nationalist pressures on governments and reduce the ability of multinational firms to expand their activities in transition economies.

Finally, as multinational firms mature in transition economies, many find that the domestic market itself represents a legitimate market opportunity on a stand-alone basis. Although this is the commonly assumed goal of economic *privatization* or *marketization*, it is not always achieved. For example, as global firms expand their presence in transition economies, expanding their offerings in industrial and retail products and services, they may quickly become net importers of capital equipment and other necessary inputs for providing the high level of economic goods demanded by the populace. Due to simultaneous investments by many firms, they may also find many more competitors in this new market than they had expected.

Many transition economies now recognize that if they are to develop businesses that are *world-class competitors* and not just poor domestic copies of foreign firms, they must somehow tap the knowledge base already thriving within successful global firms. Frequently multinational firms are invited to begin joint ventures only with domestic parties. This in itself is often difficult, given that these domestic businesses or entities rarely have significant capital to contribute, but rather bring to the table nonquantifiable contributions such as market savvy and emerging business networks.

For example, in the global telecommunications industry, access to capital is only one of the many needs for industrial development. The technical know-how of the world's key global players is also needed for the development of a first-class industry. Countries like Hungary, Indonesia, and Brazil have invited foreign companies in conjunction with domestic parties to form international joint ventures to bid for the rights to develop large segments or geographic areas within their borders. This requirement is intended to serve as a way of tapping the enormous technical and market knowledge base and commitment of established multinational firms. Without their cooperation, the ability to close the gap with the leading global competitors may be impossible.

Often the multinational firm is invited into a transition economy to bring capital and technical and market know-how to help improve existing second-class companies. For example, in the early 1990s, General Motors negotiated extensively with the Polish government on the establishment of a joint venture with one of the government-owned automobile manufacturers. GM would contribute capital and technology, while the Polish automobile manufacturer contributed its own existing asset base, workers already in place, and access to a potentially large market. The problem confronted by GM and so many other multinational firms in similar circumstances is that they view the contributions of their domestic partner to be less significant than the potential loss of technical and intellectual property, and the risks associated with maintaining the multinational firm's own reputation and quality standards. In addition, it is frequently more expensive to retool an existing manufacturing facility than it is to simply start fresh with a greenfield facility. These are difficult partnerships, and each and every one requires extended discussion, negotiation, and special "chemistry" for success.

## Summary

Special concerns must be considered by the international manager when dealing with former centrally planned economies in transition. Although the emerging market economies offer vast opportunities for trade, business practices may be significantly different from those to which the executive is accustomed.

In the emerging market economies, the key to international business success will be an understanding of the fact that societies in transition require special adaptation of business skills and time to complete the transformation. Due to their growing degree of industrialization, other economies are also becoming part of the world trade and investment picture. It must be recognized that these global changes will, in turn, precipitate adjustments in industrialized nations, particularly in the trade sector. Adapting early to these changes can offer new opportunities to the international firm.

Often the international manager is also faced with state-owned enterprises that have been formed in noncommunist nations for reasons of national or economic security. These firms may inhibit foreign market entry, and they frequently reflect in their transactions the overall domestic and foreign policy of the country rather than any economic rationale. The current global trend toward privatization offers new opportunities to the international firm, either through investment or by offering business skills and knowledge to assist in the success of privatization.

## Key Terms and Concepts

| | | |
|---|---|---|
| central plan | infrastructure shortages | state-owned enterprise |
| perestroika | allocation mentality | privatization |
| glasnost | | |

## Questions for Discussion

1. Planning is necessary, yet central planning is inefficient. Why?
2. Discuss the observation that "Russian products do what they are supposed to do—but only that."
3. How can and should the West help eastern European countries?
4. How can central European managers be trained to be market oriented?
5. Where do you see the greatest potential in future trade between emerging market economies and the West?
6. What are the benefits of privatization?
7. Why do most transition economy governments require foreign multinationals to enter business via joint ventures with existing domestic firms?
8. Why do foreign multinationals often have advantaged access to capital in transition economies over purely domestic companies.
9. What programs and information services are offered to U.S. exporters operating in the former Soviet Union through the U.S. Department of Commerce? (Refer to Commerce's Business Information Service for the Newly Independent States, **http://www.itaiep.doc.gov/bisnis/bisnis.html**.)
10. What role does the European Bank for Reconstruction and Development play in transforming the formerly communist economies of Eastern Europe and the Soviet Union? (Refer to their web site, **www.ebrd.com**.)

## Recommended Readings

Bateman, Milford, ed. *Business Cultures in Central and Eastern Europe.* Oxford: Butterworth-Heinemann, 1997.

Boecker, Paul M., ed. *Latin America's Turnaround: The Paths to Privatization and Foreign Investment.* San Francisco: ICS Press, 1993.

Fogel, Daniel S. *Managing in Energy Market Economies: Cases from the Czech and Slovak Republics.* Boulder, Colo.: Westview Press, 1994.

Kaminski, Bartlomiej, ed. *Economic Transition in Russia and the New States of Eurasia.* Armonk, NY: M.E. Sharpe, 1996.

Lieberman, Ira W., Stilpon S. Nestor, and Raj M. Desai, eds. *Between State and Market: Mass Privatization in Transition Economies.* Washington, D.C.: World Bank, 1997.

Liew, Leong, H. *The Chinese Economy in Transition: From Plan to Market.* Cheltenham, UK: Edward Elgar, 1997.

Puffer, Sheila M., et al. *Business and Management in Russia.* Cheltenham, UK: Elgar, 1996.

Wood, Adrien. *North-South Trade, Employment and Inequality: Changing Fortunes in a Skill-Driven World.* Oxford: Oxford University Press, 1994.

## Notes

1. Richard M. Hammer, "Dramatic Winds of Change," *Price Waterhouse Review* 33 (1989): 23–27.
2. Peter G. Lauter and Paul M. Dickie, "Multinational Corporations in Eastern European Socialist Economies," *Journal of Marketing* 25 (Fall 1975): 40–46.
3. Eugene Theroux and Arthur L. George, *Joint Ventures in the Soviet Union: Law and Practice,* rev. ed. (Washington, D.C.: Baker & McKenzie, 1989), 1.
4. *The World Factbook 1994* (Washington, D.C.: Central Intelligence Agency, 1994).
5. Thomas Pickering, "Russia and America at Mid-Transition," *SAIS Review* (Winter/Spring 1995): 81–92.
6. Johny K. Johansson, *Marketing, Free Choice and the New International Order* (Washington, D.C.: Georgetown University, March 2, 1990). 10.
7. Mihaly Simai, *East-West Cooperation at the End of the 1980s: Global Issues, Foreign Direct Investments, and Debts* (Budapest: Hungarian Scientific Council for World Economy, 1989), 21.
8. Jerry F. Hough, *Opening Up the Soviet Economy* (Washington, D.C.: The Brookings Institution, 1988), 46.
9. Michael R. Czinkota, Helmut Gaisbauer, and Reiner

Springer, "A Perspective of Marketing in Central and Eastern Europe," *The International Executive* 39, 6 (November/December 1997): 831–848.

10. Johny K. Johansson, Ilkka A. Ronkainen, and Michael R. Czinkota, "Negative Country of Origin Effects: The Case of the New Russia," *Journal of International Business Studies* 25, 1 (1994): 157–176.

11. Renato Mazzolini, "European Government-Controlled Enterprises: An Organizational Politics View," *Journal of International Business Studies* 11 (Spring-Summer 1980): 48–58.

12. "European Privatization: Two Half Revolutions," *The Economist* (January 22, 1994): 55, 58.

13. "Owners Are the Only Answer," *The Economist* (September 21, 1991): 10.

# A Taste of the West

In the mid-1980s, Mikhail Gorbachev introduced a new program called "perestroika" in the Soviet Union. Perestroika was to fundamentally reform the Soviet economy by improving the overall technological and industrial base as well as improving the quality of life for Soviet citizens through increased availability of food, housing, and consumer goods. It was hoped that this program would stimulate the entrepreneurial spirit of Soviet citizens and help the country and its government overcome crucial shortcomings. These shortcomings were the result of decades of communist orientation, which had led to significant capital and management shortages and inhibited the development of a market orientation and of consumer-oriented technology.

In subsequent years, a number of joint ventures between Western firms and Soviet institutions were either contemplated or even formed. However, many of the ventures, due to internal difficulties, met with only limited success. Nevertheless, the efforts of one firm, McDonald's—an icon of free enterprise—were hailed as a spectacular success.

The January 31, 1990, grand opening of McDonald's in the center of Moscow represented an important milestone for McDonald's Corporation and for the food-service industry in the Soviet Union. The state-of-the-art renovated building, formerly a cafe and a cultural gathering place, has indoor seating for more than 700 people, has outside seating for 200, and is fully accessible to the handicapped. It currently employs more than 1,000 people—the largest McDonald's crew in the world—and has served more than 30,000 people per day. The original plans were to serve between 10,000 and 15,000 customers per day. The Soviet Union became the fifty-second country to host the world's largest quick-service food restaurant company, and the Russian language is the twenty-eighth working language in which the company operates. McDonald's Corporation, based in Oak Brook, Illinois, serves more than 22 million people daily in 11,000 restaurants in 52 countries. The Soviet population of more than 291 million represented a major potential market of new customers for McDonald's.

## The Negotiations

George A. Cohon, vice chairman of Moscow McDonald's and president and chief executive officer of McDonald's Restaurants of Canada, Limited, provided the leadership for the company's successful venture. His personal commitment and energy were irreplaceable during the long period of joint-venture discussions with the Soviet Union. Cohon's Canadian team spent more than 12 years negotiating the agreement for McDonald's to enter into the Soviet market. In April 1988, agreement was reached on the largest joint venture ever made between a food company and the Soviet Union. This concluded the longest new-territory negotiation by the company since it was founded in 1955.

Cohon and his Canadian team had spent thousands of hours in Moscow making presentations to hundreds of senior trade officials, staff at various ministries, and countless other groups within the Soviet Union. Despite numerous setbacks and requests for endless submissions of and revisions to their proposals, Cohon persisted because many Soviets appeared to genuinely want to establish closer ties with the West. According to Cohon, McDonald's negotiations "outlived three Soviet premiers."

The historic joint-venture contract provided for an initial 20 McDonald's restaurants in Moscow and a state-of-the-art food production and distribution center to supply the restaurants. McDonald's accepts only rubles;

*SOURCES: McDonald's corporate information, 1994: "A Month Later, Moscow McDonald's Is Still Drawing Long and Hungry Lines," Houston Post, March 1, 1990; background information from McDonald's Restaurants of Canada, Ltd.; Jeffrey A. Tannenbaum. "Franchisers See a Future in East Bloc," The Wall Street Journal, June 5, 1990. B1; Kevin Maney and Diane Rinehart. "McDonald's in Moscow Opens Today," USA Today, January 31, 1990, B1: "McDonald's on the Volga," Employment Review 3 (1990): Moscow McDonald's videotape produced for Dryden Press. 1990: Oliver Wates. "Crowds Still Gather at Lenin's Tomb, but Lineups are Longer at McDonald's," London Free Press, June 9, 1990.*

future restaurants may accept hard currency. McDonald's Canada is managing the new venture in partnership with the Food Service Administration of the Moscow City Council in a 51 to 49 percent Soviet-Canadian partnership.

## International Technology Transfer

Cohon stated that what ultimately sold the Soviets on McDonald's was the food technology it had to offer. In addition, the company's emphasis on quality, service, cleanliness, and value convinced the Moscow city officials that McDonald's could work in their city. Vladimir Malyshkov, chairman of the board of Moscow McDonald's, stated that McDonald's "created a restaurant experience like no other in the Soviet Union. It demonstrates what can be achieved when people work together."

Moscow McDonald's was clearly an international venture. McDonald's personnel from around the world helped prepare for the opening. Dutch agricultural consultants assisted in improving agricultural production. For example, they helped plant and harvest a variety of potato needed to make french fries that met McDonald's quality standards. Other international consultants assisted in negotiating contracts with farmers throughout the country to provide quality beef and other food supplies, including onions, lettuce, pickles, milk, flour, and butter. Once the Soviet farmers learned to trust the consultants, they became eager to learn about the new Western production technologies.

The technology transfer provided important long-term benefits to the Soviet citizenry. For example, through the transfer of agricultural technology and equipment, the Soviet potato farm Kishira increased its yield by 100 percent. According to the Kishira chairman, farmers from all over the Soviet Union requested technical training in production methods to increase their crop yields. Also, since the Soviet machinery lagged fifteen to twenty years behind Western technology, new machinery from Holland was used to harvest the potatoes used to make french fries. However, according to a Dutch agricultural consultant, because of the McDonald's venture, it may not take the Soviets twenty years to catch up to Western production methods.

The development of a 10,000-square-meter food production and distribution center, located in the Moscow suburb of Solntsevo, was also an international effort involving equipment and furnishings from Austria, Canada, Denmark, Finland, Germany, Holland, Italy, Japan, Spain, Sweden, Switzerland, Taiwan, Turkey, the United Kingdom, the United States, and Yugoslavia. The center provides a state-of-the-art food-processing environment that meets McDonald's rigid standards.

At full capacity, the center employs more than 250 workers. Also at full capacity, the meat line produces 10,000 patties per hour from locally acquired beef. Milk delivered in McDonald's refrigerated dairy trucks from a local farm is pasteurized and processed at the center. Flour, yeast, sugar, and shortening are used to produce more than 14,000 buns per hour on the center's bakery line. Storage space at the center holds 3,000 tons of potatoes, and the pie line produces 5,000 apple pies per hour, made from fruit from local farmers.

## Management Training

Training for McDonald's crew and managers is essential to the customer service that the company provides. According to Bob Hissink, vice president of operations for Moscow McDonald's, hiring was just the beginning of assembling the largest McDonald's crew in the world. More than 25,000 applications were sorted, and 5,000 of the most qualified candidates were interviewed. Finally, the 630 new members of the first Moscow McDonald's team were selected. Initial training sessions were compressed into a four-week period with four or five shifts twelve hours a day. Seasoned McDonald's staff from around the world assisted the Soviet managers with crew training. The new crew of 353 women and 277 men was trained to work in several different capacities at the restaurant and had accumulated more than 15,000 hours of skills development by opening day. During restaurant operating hours, about 200 crew members at a time are on duty.

The training requirements were more extensive for McDonald's managers. Four Soviets selected as managers of Moscow McDonald's spent more than nine months in North American training programs that must be completed by any McDonald's manager in the world. The Soviets graduated from the Canadian Institute of Hamburgerology after completing more than 1,000 hours of training. Their studies included classroom instruction, equipment-maintenance techniques, and on-the-job restaurant management.

Their training also included a two-week, in-depth study program at Hamburger University, McDonald's international training center in Oak Brook, Illinois. With more than 200 other managers from around the world, they completed advanced restaurant operations studies in senior management techniques and operating procedures.

The Soviet managers were thus qualified to manage any McDonald's restaurant in the world.

## The Gradual Expansion

Initially, McDonald's Corporation had expected a rather quick expansion of restaurants. However, political and economic difficulties slowed progress. In 1991, the Soviet Union ceased to exist. From then on, the firm had to deal with the new Russian government. But at the original McDonald's on Pushkin Square, the twenty-seven cash registers at the seventy-foot service counter kept on ringing. In spite of all the political changes, by June 1993, more than 50 million customers had been served at a rate of 40,000 to 50,000 a day. The original staff of 630 had grown to 1,500, and the initial 80 expatriates working in Moscow had dwindled to less than a dozen.

On June 1, 1993, the McDonald's office building opened in Moscow. The twelve-story building had cost the equivalent of $50 million. It was the most modern office building in Moscow and had prestige tenants such as Coca-Cola, American Express, Mitsui, and the Upjohn Company. On its main floor was the second McDonald's restaurant, which was opened by Russian President Boris Yeltsin. Only one month later, the third McDonald's restaurant opened in Moscow's Arbat district. Like its predecessors, this restaurant too accepted only rubles. Ten thousand people waited in line for the opening to taste the food and see the restoration of the historic building in which the restaurant was located. By the end of the first day, this new restaurant had served 60,000 people. The day's receipts, an estimated 50 million rubles, were presented to Mrs. Yeltsin, in support of child health care.

## The Long-Term Vision

According to Cohon, "McDonald's is a business, but also is a responsible member of the communities it serves. The joint venture should help foster cooperation between nations and a better understanding among people. When individuals from around the world work shoulder-to-shoulder, they learn to communicate, to get along, and to be part of a team. That's what we call burger diplomacy." There is a Russian expression that says that you must eat many meals with a person before you come to know him. At 70,000 meals per day, it may not take long for the Russians to better understand the West through its corporate ambassador, McDonald's.

## Questions for Discussion

1. Was Cohon's negotiation effort worth the success? Why or why not?
2. Discuss the extent of infrastructural investment necessary to start the first McDonald's restaurant in Moscow.
3. What is the effect of the "ruble only" policy?
4. How can McDonald's use the acquired rubles?

# Mad Cow Disease

## Background

Bovine spongiform encephalopathy (BSE),[1] or Mad Cow Disease, is a fatal neurological illness found in cattle. It causes afflicted animals to exhibit aggressive behavior, eventually leading to disorientation and death. While a few hundred cases have been reported throughout continental Europe since the disease's identification in 1986, BSE has overwhelmingly struck herds in Britain, where over 160,000 cases have been confirmed on over 33,000 farms over the past ten years.

*This case was written by Peter Fitzmaurice under the supervision of Professor Michael R. Czinkota. Sources used were: "All of Europe Seems to Be Shunning Beef," The Wall Street Journal, March 29, 1996, A8; "Mad Cows and Englishmen," The Economist (March 30, 1996): 25; "Burnt by the Steak," The Economist (April 6, 1996): 57; "Burning Steaks," The Economist (April 20, 1996): 47; Fred Barbash, "Britain Threatens Trade War," The Washington Post, April 23, 1996, A12; Fred Barbash, "Britain Fights Back Over Ban on Beef," The Washington Post, May 22, 1996, A27; Warren Hoge, "British Call Halt to Cow Slaughter Demanded by European Union," The New York Times, September 20, 1996, A11; Warren Hoge, "For the Farming Life Now, Who'll Give Tuppence?," The New York Times, October 23, 1996, A4; Warren Hoge, "Major, Feeling Political Heat, Plans to Step Up Slaughter of Cows," The New York Times, December 17, 1996, A15; "Bracing for a Mad Cow Epidemic," Business Week (January 27, 1997): 38; Richard Rhodes, "Mad Cows and Americans," The Washington Post Magazine, March 9, 1997, 13. Various Issues of the U.S. Department of Agriculture, Foreign Agricultural Service Attache Reports, 3/96–2/97.*

[1]*BSE is one of several diseases known as spongiform encephalopathies. Most types of diseases are caused by bacteria and viruses that need their own proteins to survive. Such proteins can usually be attacked and destroyed by a host's immune system. Encephalopathies are different in that the infection seems to depend on the infected host's own proteins. Lacking any foreign proteins, encephalopathic infections go unnoticed by the host's immune system.*

Despite various theories, experts cannot fully explain the cause of Britain's misfortune. One widely held theory points to the parallel incidence in Britain of a related disease found in sheep, known as scrapie. British cow feed processors, in order to provide a more nutritious feed, traditionally "cooked" sheep and other animal remains at unusually low temperatures (100°C, as compared to 130° to 140°C in other countries), perhaps too low to kill the scrapie protein thought to be transmitted to cows. Furthermore, due to the lack of available soybean (the other widely-used cow feed supplement) in Britain, the diets of British herds consist of a greater proportion of sheep and other animal-derived feed than do those of herds in other countries. These and other factors have been linked by experts to Britain's BSE epidemic. Conclusive answers to the most basic of questions regarding BSE, however, remain a mystery. After more than ten years of research, experts cannot even agree on how to dispose of frozen, diseased carcasses.

In the 1980s, concerns over the spread of BSE resulted in most European countries banning all types of animal-derived cow feed. France and Ireland took the further precaution of destroying entire herds that experienced one or more cases of BSE. In the United States, where there has never been a reported case of BSE, an effort to head off an outbreak resulted in a ban on the importation of live British calves and cattle products. Britain responded to the new discovery by making BSE an identifiable disease in 1988. As a means of avoiding a spread of the disease, a ban was instituted within Britain on the use of cow-derived cow feed. Despite these developments, herds of British-born cattle continued to be raised in numerous countries, including France and the Netherlands, which together imported an estimated 400,000 British calves in 1995. Overall, Britain's beef industry remained strong during the first half of the 1990s, generating nearly 1 million metric tons of product in 1995 (see Figure 1).

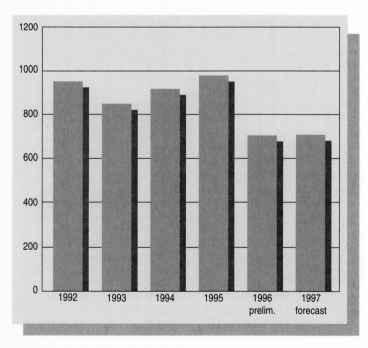

**FIGURE 1**

**British Beef Production ('000s of metric tons)**

*Source:* U.S. Department of Agriculture, Foreign Agricultural Service, Beef and Veal Production 1992–1997
(**http://ffas.usda.gov/fasprograms/f...ity/dip/mar97circular/beefprod. txt**).

## A Possible Link to Humans

The possibility that BSE could be transmitted to humans through consumption of beef was always a lingering question. It was not until 1996, however, that the likelihood of such a link was scientifically identified. A British government health commission reported in March of that year that ten recent deaths in the United Kingdom attributed to a human spongiform encephalopathy known as Creutzfeldt-Jakob disease (CJD) may have been caused by the consumption of BSE-contaminated beef.

While the evidence for such a link was only circumstantial, the effect on the public in Britain and throughout most beef-consuming nations was one of immediate alarm. Media reaction to the news was "widespread and at times hysterical," according to a U.S. embassy report. Beef consumption and production throughout Europe dropped significantly within days of the commission's announcement, buoying sales of pork, poultry, fish, and vegetarian burgers. The multinational fast-food chains McDonald's and Burger King immediately switched to non-British beef. McDonald's action alone was expected to cost British beef producers $38 million in lost sales for 1996. British consumers were generally unable to differentiate between domestic and imported beef, prompting supermarkets and restaurants to hastily adopt national origin labeling policies in order to maintain sales.

The promises of European butchers and meat merchants not to sell British beef allayed few fears, as consumers questioned the extent of the spread of BSE throughout Europe. In the large German farming state of Bavaria, the market for beef practically collapsed. A major Munich slaughterhouse reported within days of the announcement that the number of cattle being prepared for slaughter had dropped by 80 percent. In addition to beef, consumers were careful to avoid all sorts of other cattle-derived products. Processed cow fats are sometimes used to make cookies and salty snacks taste rich and to make lipsticks glide smoothly. Cow proteins show up in shampoo. Collagen, extracted from the inner layer of cattle hide, is used to balm wounds and cosmetically puff up lips. Gelatin, refined from cattle hide and bones, is found in such foods as ice cream, gummy candies, and marshmallows—as well as the capsules encasing drugs. While no evidence exists that CJD or BSE can be transmitted through these various products, consumers reacted with extreme caution. Tesco, a large British supermarket chain, pledged to label all of its products to indicate whether they contained any British cattle products.

## The Government Reaction

The British government immediately sought to reassure consumers and announced that it was prepared, if necessary, to destroy all 11 million cows in Britain. This drastic solution was soon downplayed, and government officials began a campaign of stressing the "extremely low" risk of contracting an illness from beef. "It isn't the cows that are mad, it's the people," said Britain's Secretary of State for Health Stephen Dorrell. "I eat beef, and I let my children eat beef." The British Agriculture Minister went so far as to feed a hamburger to his four-year-old daughter on live television.

Despite the British government's pleas for "reasonable" measures, concerned foreign governments immediately imposed various restrictions on British cattle and beef products. Russia and South Africa, which had been key markets for British beef, turned primarily to Australia for shipments. Denmark compiled a blacklist of products made from British beef, ranging from foodstuffs to cosmetics. In the Middle East, fears that Irish herds might also be contaminated led Iran to halt Irish beef imports. Egyptian authorities turned away three shiploads of Irish cattle, stranding the herds offshore for several days. Egypt also banned British leather, while Jordan refused British and Irish dairy products. Hong Kong banned frozen and chilled British beef imports, and Taiwan, which banned most British beef products in 1990, added canned British beef products to the list. In Costa Rica, as in other Latin American countries, customs officers searched tourists' bags for contraband steaks. Ghana and Libya banned imports of all European beef, regardless of origin.

The complete ban on British cattle and beef products instituted by the Commission of the European Union, however, sent the greatest shockwaves. "Hasty, ill-prepared, disproportionate and unscientific," was the reaction from Keith Meldrum, Britain's top veterinary official. Britain expected a quick lifting of the ban in exchange for steps designed to confine the disease. "A slaughter policy is not excluded (from consideration). Clearly that is a matter we need to consider," said the British Agriculture Minister in late March. By April, the EU issued its preliminary conditions for having the ban lifted. Under the plan, all British cattle (the majority of which are dairy cows) over thirty months in age would be slaughtered and incinerated at the end of their useful life. This program, termed the "thirty-month cull," would serve to keep the meat of 4.6 million cows born and raised prior to 1993–1994 (the beginning of Britain's most comprehensive BSE preventive measures), out of the food chain. In addition, under what was designated the "selective cull," Britain was required to slaughter for incineration several tens of thousands of additional younger cattle that were identified as "high risk," including those from herds that had experienced a case of BSE. In recognition of the significant costs to be incurred by British farmers and renderers, the EU agreed to cover 70 percent of related costs, the same level used to compensate Germany during its 1994 outbreak of swine fever.

By mid-April, Britain released its response to the EU proposal, containing most of the details requested by the EU, but falling short in some respects, including the number of cows to be included under the selective cull. Several EU governments were unsatisfied with Britain's proposal, suggesting that the ban remain in place until the next review, six weeks hence. The European Commission conferred, explaining that Britain would have to undertake more drastic measures before a lifting of the ban could be considered. Despite the disagreement, Britain began the culling program.

## The Ensuing "Beef War"

What followed has been described as one of the most serious strains in Britain's historically frayed relationship with the rest of Europe. Repeated attempts by Britain throughout the first half of 1996 to have the costly EU ban lifted failed. Elections in 1997 were fast approaching and the economic impact of the ban was building. British trade unions reported that over 8,000 beef industry workers had lost their jobs in a period of a few weeks. Experts stated that the United Kingdom economy as a whole was poised to lose 1 percent of annual growth and 100,000 jobs, while sustaining nearly 2 percent of added inflation due to higher beef, milk, and related prices. Some suggested that Britain was facing its worst economic catastrophe since the pound had to be bailed out by the IMF in 1976.

After a month, the crisis escalated to threats of a trade war. Advisors to then prime minister John Major let it be known that he was "incandescent" with rage and "fuming" over European leaders' unwillingness to lift the ban. The British government warned that a retaliatory ban on an unspecified list of European imports would be seriously considered. For good measure, Britain brought its case before the European Court of Justice in the hopes of proving the ban illegal. "This is quite a serious crisis," said Kenneth Minogue, a political scientist at the London

School of Economics. "(It could) lead to a serious rupture" of British–EU relations.

When many thought the friction could get no worse, the EU's agriculture minister, Franz Fischler, stated in mid-April that the ban was inspired largely by concern for the European beef market, rather than by health fears. He remarked, "(I) wouldn't hesitate to eat beef in England." Other EU officials also conceded that the ban was in response to the health of the market, rather than that of the public. Even McDonald's, in announcing its intentions to halt the use of British beef in its U.K. outlets, stated that British beef is safe, but it could not disregard the growing unease of its customers. The president of McDonald's British operations stated, "This is about public confidence and I have to tell you that people are not feeling confident about British beef right now."

One month after Fischler's admission, in conjunction with additional failed attempts at having the ban lifted, the British government begun a strategy of "noncooperation" within the EU governing bodies. Prime Minister Major accused fellow EU members of "willful" behavior and a "breach of faith" in maintaining the two-month-old ban. Addressing the House of Commons, he said Britain "cannot be expected to continue to cooperate normally" in the business of the EU. "We cannot continue business as usual with Europe when we are faced with this clear disregard by some of our partners of reason, common sense and Britain's national interest." The government's primary targets were EU decisions that required unanimous approval from members countries. The first casualty of this noncooperation was a new set of Europewide bankruptcy rules. After month's time, Britain managed to block more than seventy policy decisions, bog down an intergovernmental conference on the EU's future, and disrupt plans for a June EU summit meeting.

Adding to the British government's frustration was the continuing domestic slump in beef retail sales. For the three-month period ending June 5, 1996, consumption of beef in the United Kingdom was down about 24 percent over the prior-year period. By May, the number of British households purchasing beef declined by 13 percent. Major supermarkets had begun refusing "clean" beef from slaughterhouses that were also active in the government's new culling program. One supermarket executive said the government was "naive" to believe that material from culled cattle would not find its way into the food chain. In a unique move, Britain's ASDA supermarket chain announced its support of domestic beef by refusing to sell foreign beef. ASDAs CEO stated,

"British beef is the best and safest in the world and our shoppers want to buy it."

## A Tenuous Compromise

By June of 1996, the British-imposed paralysis of EU decision making and the prospects of a deepening European crisis, finally prompted an agreement between Britain and the EU to have the beef ban gradually lifted in exchange for various measures by Britain, designed to isolate the risks of BSE and assure the global beef market.

Under the agreement, Britain would be required to fully implement corrective measures already underway, as well as to meet several new EU demands. In addition to the complete implementation of the thirty-month cull, the EU imposed an increase of Britain's selective cull, which would now target 147,000 cattle, up from the previous number of 80,000. In addition, the new agreement required Britain to establish a new system to identify cattle and their movements; the removal of meat and bone meal from feed mills and farms; new regulations on farm and equipment cleaning; and tighter controls on the British rendering industry. Despite predictions by John Major that conditions would be met and the ban would be lifted by early 1997, no firm dates or time frames were specified in the agreement.

Though EU decision making was restored with Britain's suspension of its nonparticipation tactics, relations remained strained between European partners. With the announcement of the June agreement, French farmers set fires, blocked roads, and prevented British ships from docking. Throughout Europe, farmers and others registered their anger, blaming Britain for the crisis and claiming that the risk to health and jobs remained. One French cattle breeder explained, "You have animals, you keep feeding them, and no one comes to buy them. This is a living product. We are very worried today because there is no market for our product." Strong criticism came not only from other Europeans— then-British opposition leader Tony Blair voiced these harsh words: "There is a humiliation in this deal. There is ignominy in this deal. In fact, it is not a deal at all, it is a rout."

The British government was initially hopeful that the repeal of the ban would begin by autumn of 1996, despite a July setback by the EU's High Court, which found that the EU was justified in imposing the restriction. It soon became apparent, however, that fellow EU governments were in no hurry to have the ban lifted and that it could be many months, if not years, before most British beef would be eligible for import. This realization, coupled with new findings by Oxford University scientists that BSE would run its course by the year 2001 even without the proposed wholesale slaughter, resulted in the decision by Britain in September to amend its commitment under the June agreement. It would now be willing to slaughter 22,000 cattle under the selective cull, as opposed to the agreed upon 147,000. The British government stated, "For the present, (we) are not proceeding with the selective cull, but will return to cull options in the light of the developing science." An EU spokesman responded, "There are some perplexing thoughts in Brussels about what is actually happening in the UK. We don't actually understand why it appears from time to time that the Government of the U.K. appears to want to go it alone."

It was December before Britain had a change of heart, and decided to restart the selective cull of thousands of cows from BSE-infected herds. In a reversal of attitudes, the Agriculture Minister stated, "Unless we commit ourselves to the selective cull, the entire ban will remain in place for the foreseeable future." The change of heart was largely rooted in domestic politics. The region of the U.K. to benefit first from an initial lifting of the ban would most likely be Northern Ireland, which has the most grass-fed herds and has suffered the fewest cases of BSE. Interestingly, the Prime Minister had just lost his majority in the House of Commons, and his Government's survival depended on the nine votes of the Ulster (Northern Ireland) Unionist Party.

## Assessment and the Future

By the end of 1996, Britain had slaughtered 1.5 million cattle under the culling programs. British beef production and consumption for 1996 had declined 27 and 16 percent, respectively. British beef exports had dropped by over 80 percent from 1995 levels. Other EU beef producers were also caught in the downturn. Reduced world demand forced EU producers to store beef. Beef inventories increased from 8,810 tons at the beginning of 1996 to 417,932 tons by year's end. Beef consumption for the year was down 8 percent in France, 10 percent in Germany, and 25 percent in Italy. Market returns for EU beef deteriorated precipitously, despite expanded intervention and slaughter programs. Reference prices for beef in Europe's major markets dropped significantly for the period of March to August 1996 (see Figures 2–4).

**FIGURE 2**

**British Beef Exports ('000s of metric tons)**

*Source:* U.S. Department of Agriculture, Foreign Agricultural Service, Beef and Veal Production 1992–1997 (**http://ffas.usda.gov/fasprograms/f...ity/dip/mar97 circular/beexpo.txt**).

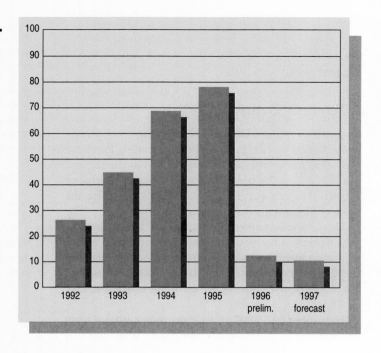

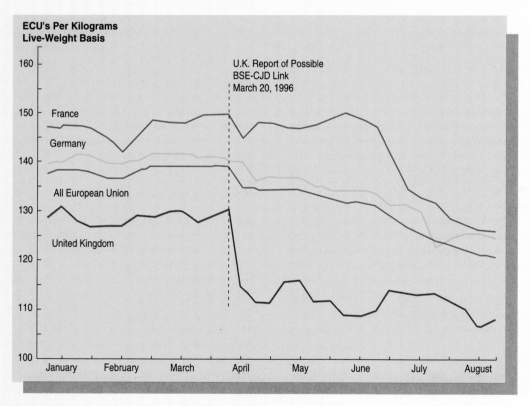

**FIGURE 3**

**Beef Reference Prices in the European Union, 1996; Week Ending August 15, 1996**

*Source:* **http://ffas.usda.gov/fasprograms/f...mmodity/dip/nov96circular/bsel.gif**

**FIGURE 4**

**European Union Beef Consumption**
**('000s of metric tons)**

*Source:* U.S. Department of Agriculture, Foreign Agricultural
Service, Beef and Veal Production 1992–1997
(http://ffas.usda.gov/fa...97circular/beefcons.txt).

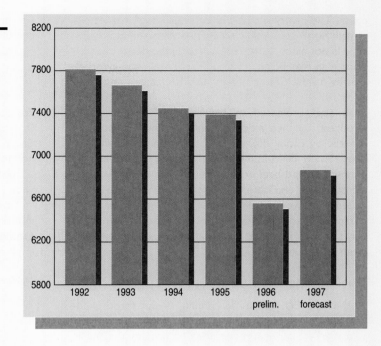

British farmers were growing increasingly wary as the new year passed and a lifting of the ban was not in sight. "The farmer finds it depressing to have a herd and not be able to have any control over it. It gets under people's agricultural skin," according to one British auctioneer. Property listings in farming areas throughout Britain became full of notices of farm and herd sales. "There already was a move off the small family farm, but this thing has turbocharged it," said one industry expert.

Slaughterhouses quickly became overloaded throughout 1996, requiring cattle farmers and dairymen to feed and house condemned cows through the winter and into the spring, creating shortages for younger, productive cattle. Though most expenses were being covered with public funds, the British government proposed in February 1997 that the subsidies paid to renderers be withdrawn by March 1998. The Agriculture Ministry assumed in the proposal that a substantial portion of the extra costs would be passed back to producers, resulting in a drop in gross margins for beef farmers of between 5 and 25 percent. The proposal stated that it is not the government's objective to provide support to avoid business closures or rationalization as support is removed, but rather to aid the transition back to a market-driven system.

Through mid-1997, there had been practically no easing of the global ban. The agreed-upon slaughter program continued, as did consultations between London and Brussels. Although Britain ultimately agreed to the EU conditions, most observers believe it unlikely that the ban will be lifted swiftly. It is more likely that exports of live calves and beef from certified BSE-free herds will be permitted first, followed by a gradual lifting of the overall ban. Consumer resistance in importing countries and newly imposed EU-wide country-of-origin labeling requirements will likely constrain any large-scale resumption of exports.

Due to improving consumer confidence, beef consumption in Britain is expected to partially rebound in 1997, though beef production and exports are expected to be flat. The EU beef market is anticipated to see a 1–2 percent increase in beef production in 1997, with exports rebounding significantly from Ireland and France. Projections of EU beef consumption for 1997 are approximately 6.8 million tons, an improvement over 1996 but still shy of 1995's level of 7.4 million tons.

The final outcome of BSE and its full impact on the European beef industry will be unknown for years. Many adjustments have been made thus far by the EU and individual member states to rid their herds of BSE and its disabling effects. Expectations for a sizable jump in consumer confidence and beef consumption are dependent upon the measures put forward by the various governments. The reality is that the European beef market will remain highly susceptible to BSE scares in the future. Europe is not alone, however. Fears that the death of an Indiana man may be linked to BSE sent grain and livestock futures on the Chicago Mercantile Exchange tumbling in April 1997.

A study released in January 1997 provided the strongest evidence yet that people can and have become infected by eating BSE-tainted beef. Even if transmission is extremely difficult, millions of Britons may have been exposed to bad beef before the government introduced measures to eradicate the disease in 1988. The study stated that, given the disease can take a decade or more to manifest itself in those infected, slight increases in cases may signal an epidemic that could eventually affect hundreds of thousands of Britons.

### Questions for Discussion

1. Was the EU justified in banning British cattle products? Was the immediate intent of the ban to prevent a market collapse, rather than to protect the public from BSE?
2. Evaluate the British government's strategy of non-cooperation within the EU.
3. How might this case have been different had the EU not existed?
4. Research other cases in which trade barriers were imposed by governments on behalf of health concerns. Compare and contrast these cases with the EU's ban on British beef.

# Ecological Cooling: The Fridge from Eastern Germany

In March of 1993, mass production of the world's first refrigerator that works without damaging the earth's vital ozone layer began in Niederschmiedeberg, the hometown of a small eastern German firm. FORON Domes-

*SOURCE: This case was written by Michael R. Czinkota based on discussions with Dr. Juergen Lembke, head of marketing, FORON GmbH, and reports by German and U.S. media. Financial and logistical support from the U.S. Information Agency (USIA) is gratefully acknowledged.*

tic Appliances GmbH offers the first "green" refrigerator, completely free of chlorofluorocarbons (CFCs). The road to this achievement, however, was not easy.

## CFCs and the Montreal Agreement

For decades, chlorofluorocarbons (CFCs) were the refrigerants of choice worldwide. They were nontoxic, nonflammable, and energy-efficient. The price of $.57 per pound in 1980 also made CFCs quite inexpensive. Introduced in the 1930s, by 1985 CFCs represented a worldwide market of $1.5 billion a year.

Since 1974, scientists had theorized that CFCs could deplete the earth's ozone layer, which shields the earth from the sun's harmful ultraviolet rays. As a result of these implications, and due to public pressure, the U.S. government banned the use of CFCs in aerosol propellants in 1978. Due to the nonavailability of reasonable substitutes, however, the use of CFCs in refrigerators and air conditioners continued to be permitted.

After scientists observed a hole in the ozone layer over Antarctica, nations from around the world enacted the 1987 Montreal Protocol, which called for a 50 percent cut in CFC use by mid-1988. Given the growing public concern with environmental issues, the protocol was subsequently revised twice: in 1990, it was agreed that the 50 percent reduction in most CFCs was to be achieved by 1995 and the 1992 revision banned all CFC use by 1996.

The ban had chilling effect on the producers of cooling devices since they depended heavily on CFCs. For example, to reduce energy consumption, refrigerators are insulated with polyurethane foam. During manufacture, the foam is saturated with 300 to 600 grams of CFCs. The gas remains in the foam and because it insulates better than air, the gas provides for heat insulation. The disadvantage of CFC-foamed polyurethane is that the CFCs gradually diffuse out of the foam and are replaced by air. The CFC escapes into the atmosphere and destroys the ozone layer. The energy efficiency of the refrigerators also deteriorates considerably over the years due to the CFC–air exchange.

CFCs also contribute to the actual refrigeration process. Due to their thermodynamic properties, CFCs are highly temperature responsive to compression and expansion, therefore allowing an efficient cooling process to take place. Even though hermetically sealed, a leaky pipe or uncontrolled disposal can result in the gradual release of up to 250 grams of CFCs.

## dkk Scharfenstein

Deutsche Klima and Kraftmaschinen AG was founded in the German state of Saxony in 1927. The firm concentrated on producing heating and cooling devices together with compressors. In the 1950s the East German communist regime took over the firm as state property and renamed it dkk Scharfenstein. As the only firm in Eastern Europe producing both refrigerators and compressors, dkk Scharfenstein (DKK) soon achieved a leadership position in the region. By 1989, the firm's 5,200 employees produced more than 1 million refrigerators and 1.5 million compressors. Every apartment built by the East Germany regime had a refrigerator made by DKK. Ten million East German households had a DKK fridge; 80 percent of households had its freezers.

With the fall of the Berlin Wall on November 9, 1989, and the collapse of communism in Eastern Europe, DKK's markets collapsed as well. Long-term export contracts were rescinded. At the same time, domestic demand declined precipitously as stylish new products from West Germany became available. By 1992, production had declined to 200,000 refrigerators, and employment had shrunk to 1,000. In light of the continuing decline of its business, dkk Scharfenstein was taken over by Germany's Treuhandanstalt, the German government's privatization arm.

## Development of The Eco-Fridge

dkk Scharfenstein had been familiar with the ecological problems of CFCs since the mid-eighties. At that time, the firm had considered a switch to hydrofluorocarbon (HFC) 134a. This new chemical did not contain chlorine, but still made use of fluor, which contributes to the greenhouse effect and to global warming. However, these plans were abandoned for two reasons. First, the price of HFC 134a was far more than that of CFC. Second, unlike its Western counterparts, Scharfenstein was unable to obtain the product from Western markets due to export control regulations promulgated by the Multilateral Committee for Export Controls (COCOM). While HFC 134a was available in the Soviet Union, only very limited quantities were offered for sale.

After 1990, HFC 134a became freely available in eastern Germany. By that time, however, the Scharfenstein staff already was working on a different project. In conjunction with Professor Harry Rosin, head of the Dortmund Institute for Hygiene, Scharfenstein had focused on a mix of butane and propane gases to cool its refrigerators. The ingredients were environmentally friendly and, with newly designed compressors, the equipment operated with less electrical power.

Management presented the new product to Treuhand, in an effort to stave off the liquidation of the firm. Treuhand attempted to interest a consortium consisting of the German firms Bosch and Siemens in acquiring Scharfenstein. After a cursory review, however, both firms decided that the new technology was too radical, unproven, and flammable and withdrew from all discussions. They, like major competitors such as Whirlpool and AEG, would continue to concentrate on HFC 134a research and production. Although expensive, HFC 134a now was competitive because new taxes had increased CFC prices to more than $5 per pound. In addition, major investments had already been made into HFC production. For example, in its race against DuPont and Elf Atochem, the British firm Imperial Chemical Industries PLC alone already had invested nearly $500 million into HFC development. To ensure that retailers would share their perspective, major producers of refrigerators supplied leaflets that warned about the dangers of explosion of fridges filled with propane and butane.

Treuhand did not approve the production of the new fridge. In light of mounting losses, an additional 360 Scharfenstein employees were laid off and Treuhand announced plans to liquidate the firm.

Facing the shutdown of its operations, Scharfenstein's management decided to go public with its new product. Information on the CFC-free fridge was sent to all manufacturers of refrigeration equipment, none of whom showed any interest. However, interest did materialize from unexpected quarters: The leadership of the Greenpeace organization. This worldwide environmental nonprofit group quickly recognized the benefits of the new fridge. It commissioned ten prototype models to be produced, and after finding them satisfactory, mounted a $300,000 advertising campaign in favor of the production of "greenfreeze." Intense negotiations with retailers brought in orders and options for 70,000 of the refrigerators.

The future of Scharfenstein brightened immediately. The German Ministry for the Environment supported a capital infusion of $3 million into the company. Shortly thereafter, Treuhand rescinded the layoffs that had been announced. By 1993, the firm was acquired by a consortium of British, Kuwaiti, and German investors and renamed FORON Household Appliances GmbH.

Since then, FORON has received various environmental prizes and labels. The firm was awarded the government's coveted Blue Angel symbol for environmental friendliness. The German Technical Society awarded its safety seal of approval. The business magazine *DM* named the fridge its product of the year.

The giant German appliance manufacturers, which once scorned the new technology as "impossible, dangerous and too energy-consuming," now are scrambling to put out their own green refrigerators. Major efforts for CFC-free refrigerators are also being undertaken by U.S. and Japanese manufacturers. In the United States, a group of utilities offered $30 million to the manufacturer that designed the most energy efficient refrigerator without using CFCs.

FORON expects to produce more than 160,000 ecofridges per year and actively is exploring the possibility of exports. Inquiries have been received from China, Japan, the United States, India, Australia, and New Zealand. Even though the product is priced some 5 to 10 percent more than conventional models, the firm believes that "consumers who are environmentally aware will pay the price."

### Questions for Discussion

1. Why is the acceptance of innovation sometimes inhibited by established industry players?
2. Evaluate the role of Greenpeace in promoting the ecofridge. Is such an activity appropriate for a nonprofit organization?
3. What motivated Scharfenstein's investment in environmentally friendly technology?
4. How can governments encourage the development of environmentally responsive technology?

# Otjiwarongo Crocodile Ranch

In the hot and humid hatchery of his crocodile ranch in the small Namibian town of Otjiwarongo, Mr. van Dyk was worriedly stacking the plastic crates containing 1,350 newly laid crocodile eggs into the limited space. It was December 10, 1993 and he knew that he had to expand the hatching and nursing facilities of his crocodile ranch before January 1996 in order to provide the necessary space to accommodate twice the present production of eggs expected in the 1996 breeding season.

To finance this expansion, Mr. van Dyk hoped to enter a stable and regular market for his supply of crocodile skins. With his limited experience in marketing, he was not sure as to how and where to start exporting.

Mr. van Dyk was also considering the option of exporting processed crocodile skin products, like handbags, shoes and belts. Without the resources to construct his own tannery, he would have to find processing and manufacturing facilities. There was the possibility to send the skins to South Africa for processing into finished products before exporting them. Thinking about options to finance the expansion, Mr. van Dyk also remembered the proposal for a partnership he had received from an investor in Europe who could process the skins into quality products: during a visit in September 1993, a German tourist had expressed interest in investing in Mr. van Dyk's crocodile ranch.

Stepping out of the hatchery into the equally hot, but less humid, nursery where he raised the young crocodiles, Mr. van Dyk knew he had to take some action well before the 1996 breeding season.

## Background

Mr. van Dyk started the Otjiwarongo Crocodile Ranch in 1986. Prior to this, he had his own motor service station and bakery in Khorixas, a town in the far north of Namibia. He had also farmed with cattle and sheep, but due to droughts and a high theft rate, he abandoned his farming operations. He sold his business and made the decision to start up a crocodile ranch because he considered himself to be a farmer at heart and also because he was very interested in tourism. He visited various crocodile farms in South Africa and Botswana, where he made a thorough study of crocodile farming during 1985.

Mr. van Dyk chose Otjiwarongo as the ideal location for his business. The climate of Otjiwarongo—hot during summer months and warm in winter—was favourable

*This case was written by Daan Strauss, Coordinator, Small Enterprise Development, Institute for Management and Leadership Training (IMLT), Namibia, under the ITC/PRODEC Project for Improving International Business Training at selected African Institutions. The case is intended for use in training programmes and is not meant to illustrate correct or incorrect handling of business situations. 1995.*

Source: African Cases in International Business, *International Trade Centre and PRODEC, Geneva 1995.*

for crocodile farming. It was on the main tourism route of Namibia, and he could find a regular supply of meat to feed the crocodiles as the Otjiwarongo abattoir was prepared to supply him with unborn calves.

Breeding crocodiles was a capital intensive venture. A hatchery and nursery were built next to the breeding yard to ensure that the eggs could be hatched and the crocodiles raised in ideal conditions. The buildings on Mr. van Dyk's property were valued at N$800,000 in 1988. The planned expansion was expected to cost about N$600,000 (US$1.00 = N$3.60).

Mr. van Dyk had also built a curio shop which served as entrance to the ranch. In the curio shop, he kept various crocodile products like eggshells, skulls and skeletons, along with a few crocodile skin products made from skins he had sent to South Africa to be manufactured into shoes and belts. Mr. van Dyk and his wife regretted the fact that they could not stock the shop with more products, but supplies had to be kept at a minimum due to the lack of funds.

Ever since they started the crocodile ranch, Mr. van Dyk and his wife had been inviting tourists to visit the ranch in Otjiwarongo, in the Northern highlands of central Namibia. The crocodile ranch received an average of 1,000 tourists per month. The visitors' entry fees represented a substantial means of income before exports of crocodile skins started in 1991. In 1993, tourists still contributed N$6,000 per month to Mr. van Dyk's income, although exporting crocodile skins had become the main source of income.

Additional income for the crocodile ranch was earned by selling crocodile meat to interested restaurants in Namibian towns. During 1993, Mr. van Dyk sold 1,100kg of crocodile meat. He planned to slaughter 600 crocodiles in 1994, which would mean that he could sell 15,000kg of meat. There was a possibility for exporting crocodile meat to Singapore, but the dealer he spoke to in Singapore wanted at least four tons of meat at a time. This meant that Mr. van Dyk would have had to slaughter at least 1,500 crocodiles at a time to be able to fill up a container for exporting purposes, which was not possible for him in 1993. He planned to start exporting meat by 1998.

Mr. van Dyk was a member of the Transvaal Crocodile Breeders' Association in Pretoria, South Africa. In 1991, he obtained his license to trade in endangered species from CITES (Convention on International Trade in Endangered Species of Wild Fauna and Flora) in Lausanne, Switzerland, which had a membership of 112 countries world-wide. Membership of CITES was a condition for exporting crocodile skins, as most crocodilians were on the endangered species list of the CITES.

According to an article published in the "Industrie du cuir" in Paris in February 1992, raising was considered a good method of preserving those species which had become rare while continuing trading in their skins. Two types of "farming" crocodilians had been developed:

- "Ranches," particularly in Southern Africa (notably Zimbabwe), which tended to concentrate on Nile crocodiles. Eggs were taken from the wild and the young were raised in captivity until the commercial length of 1.5m to 2m was attained, when they were slaughtered.
- "Farms," which, in general, handled the whole reproduction cycle. There were numerous "farms" in Thailand and the United States.

The article assumed that 80 percent of the current world supply of crocodile skins, estimated at around 400,000 per annum, were sourced from farms. Ten years earlier, before legislation on the protection of endangered species had been passed in many countries, the figure of world supply had been around 2 million skins per year.

## Crocodile Breeding

Mr. van Dyk bought his original breeding stock of 49 adult Nile crocodiles from a farmer in Botswana in 1986 for N$220,000. The hatchlings from the first eggs were kept and after spending four years in the nursery, these 58 female crocodiles were housed in a second breeding yard that Mr. van Dyk had been developing since 1987. These females were expected to start producing in the 1996 breeding season.

Having adapted to their new environment, the production of eggs by the adult crocodiles increased steadily. Mr. van Dyk managed to successfully hatch crocodile eggs as follows:

| | | |
|---|---|---|
| 1986 | 58 hatchlings out of | 71 eggs |
| 1987 | 364 hatchlings out of | 408 eggs |
| 1988 | 488 hatchlings out of | 530 eggs |
| 1989 | 540 hatchlings out of | 630 eggs |
| 1990 | 630 hatchlings out of | 714 eggs |
| 1991 | 705 hatchlings out of | 838 eggs |
| 1992 | 936 hatchlings out of | 1,273 eggs |
| 1993 | 1,050 hatchlings out of | 1,356 eggs |

During the mating season, outside temperatures influenced the fertility rate of the eggs. In 1993, 12 percent of the eggs were unfertilized, while the figure for 1992 was 23 percent.

The amount of eggs laid by a female crocodile depended on her age. The younger ones laid on average 21 per breeding season and the mature ones could lay up to 75. This gave an average of 48 eggs per female. As soon as the female crocodiles laid their eggs, they were packed into crates and taken to the hatchery. To further ensure successful hatching of the eggs, they had to be stacked into the crates in exactly the same position as they had been laid.

To maximize profits, Mr. van Dyk had to ensure that he produced first-grade skins. The newly hatched crocodiles were kept in a nursery for two and a half years, at which age they were about 1.4m long and provided skins of 35cm wide, fetching the best price. The nursery was free of stones to avoid scratches on the crocodiles' skins. Maintenance of high humidity and ideal temperatures, a regular supply of vitamins to the young crocodiles, and clean and hygienic conditions were necessary to keep the young crocodiles healthy, which in turn meant a more favourable environment to ensure first-grade skins.

At the slaughter-age of two and a half years, the crocodiles would normally start to fight among each other, resulting in skins being scratched or damaged, and thus reducing their value. This was also the age at which they became dangerous and would attack workers cleaning the nursery.

Being extremely sensitive creatures, the young crocodiles could easily be upset by loud noise, sudden movements, light and vibrations. Because of the influence tourists had on the crocodiles, Mr. van Dyk kept only 10 percent of the young crocodiles on view for visiting purposes, and the tourists were always requested to keep their voices low and move slowly.

## Costs and Revenues

Mr. van Dyk raised start-up capital for the crocodile ranch through a commercial bank and through a development corporation in Namibia. In 1993, he was still indebted to both institutions for loans taken in 1988, payable over a 5- and 13-year period respectively.

Mr. van Dyk's monthly expenses in the last quarter of 1993 were as follows:

| | |
|---|---|
| Water and electricity: | N$2,200 |
| Crocodile feeding: | N$4,000 |
| Wages: | N$2,000 |
| Veterinarian costs: | N$ 150 |
| Administrative costs: | N$ 100 |
| Other (including his salary): | N$5,000 |
| Installments and interest: | N$5,000 |

For December 1993, Mr. van Dyk expected the following revenues:

| | |
|---|---|
| Export of 150 skins: | N$30,000 |
| Sales of meat: | N$ 8,000 |
| Tourists' entry fees: | N$ 6,000 |

December 1993 was, however, an exceptional month because of a planned initial export of 150 skins to Germany, an order which had not yet been confirmed. The average monthly income was N$20,000.

## Marketing

The constitution of the Transvaal Crocodile Breeders' Association stipulated that each individual breeder was responsible for the marketing of his own products. This left the responsibility for marketing and selling with Mr. van Dyk, who did not have much experience in this field.

Although the Otjiwarongo Crocodile Ranch was the only one of its kind in Namibia, it faced worldwide competition for exports of crocodile skins. Crocodilians, including caimans and gharials, alligators and crocodiles, were to be found all around the world: caimans in Central and South America, alligators in the southeast of the United States and in China. The more than 20 different species of crocodiles were scattered far more widely: North of Australia, Africa, Southeast Asia, India, Central and South America and the West Indies. Size of the crocodilians varied with the species, from 1.5m to 2m in dwarf species, such as the dwarf crocodile and Schneider's caiman, up to 5m to 7m for the Nile and Indopacific crocodiles. In Southern Africa alone there were 23 competitors breeding crocodiles, most of them in the province of Natal, South Africa, but also in Zimbabwe, Zambia, Botswana, Malawi and Mozambique. Zimbabwe was the leading exporter of Nile Crocodile skins in Southern Africa and was the second largest producer after the United States of America.

Other exotic hides, like ostrich and buffalo skins formed part of the competition Mr. van Dyk faced. The trade in exotic skins was subject to fashion trends. Mr. van Dyk considered this to be one reason for the fluctuating prices, which ranged from US$9.00 per centimeter in 1991 to US$3.00 in 1993 for first-grade skins of 30cm wide.

Because of his limited funds, Mr. van Dyk did not advertise. "I have to first look after my crocodiles before I can find the money to advertise," he stated.

Mr. van Dyk had started exporting crocodile skins in December 1991. Quantities and destinations of exports were as follows:

| 1991 | 163 skins to Spain | (Direct transaction) |
| 1992 | 250 skins to Spain | (Direct transaction) |
| 1993 | 100 skins to Singapore | (Direct transaction) |
| 1993 | 150 skins to Singapore | (Through a South African agent) |

In November 1993, he managed to secure an order from a German buyer for an initial 150 skins followed by 50 skins per month through an agent in South Africa. The German buyer indicated that he would be in South Africa by the beginning of December 1993, but failed to turn up. This left Mr. van Dyk quite unsure as to whether the deal would go through.

The few times that he had exported skins, he contracted embassies in Windhoek for addresses of potential buyers, or alternatively was contacted by buyers who had come to know about him.

The most recent order from Germany in November 1993 quoted the following prices per centimeter for first-grade skins:

| 20–24 cm: | US$1.80 |
| 25–29 cm: | US$2.80 |
| 30–34 cm: | US$3.50 |
| 35 cm + 1: | US$5.00 |

Prices for second grade skins were 25 percent less, while third grade skins were not accepted on the market.

For international business, Mr. van Dyk preferred to deal with German buyers. As Namibia had historical links with Germany, most of the tourists visiting the crocodile ranch were German speaking. Mr. van Dyk also communicated well in German and found direct communication with other countries difficult. If he were to enter into a partnership, he would prefer a German or Swiss partner. This preference, however, did not prevent him from selling to non-German buyers.

To do business with buyers abroad, Mr. van Dyk would either deal with them directly, through an agent or eventually through a prospective foreign partner. However, both Mr. van Dyk and his wife were very reluctant to enter into a partnership because of a previous unpleasant incident with a partner abroad, who became disinterested when revenues were not as quickly forthcoming as he thought they would. While still considering this as an alternative, the van Dyks were not sure whether the advantages outweighed the disadvantages. The potential German investor had indicated that he would visit them

in January 1994 to take up further discussions, and Mr. and Mrs. van Dyk were thinking about the terms and conditions they should propose for an eventual partnership. Mr. van Dyk hoped to enter into an agreement where the partner would be responsible for all marketing activities, while he himself would see to the smooth running of the ranch and the visiting tourists.

Because of the pressing need for funds to finance expansion, Mr. van Dyk also thought about the possibility of exporting processed crocodile skin products. This could be done through a tannery in South Africa, but he knew that this would be expensive because of the time-span between sending of the skins for processing and eventual sales of the finished products. He would have to carry the costs for the tanning and manufacturing of the products in the meantime. In 1993, the cost of tanning alone was N$2.50 per centimeter, amounting to approximately N$75.00 per skin. He also considered selling the products in his curio shop at the ranch, but these up-market products did not sell fast enough in Otjiwarongo. It was only the occasional well-off tourist that would buy some of the products, but it was a possible source of income nonetheless. The other option was to have the skins processed through the intended partner in Europe, so that the finished products would be nearer to the user.

There was another possibility to do business with an Italian buyer who had announced his visit to the ranch for January 1994. This was not definite as yet and Mr. van Dyk was worried about dealings with buyers who did not seem to be reliable. However, he had got some information on the Italian market (see appendix) and was ready to explore any business opportunities.

In December 1993, Mr. van Dyk had 600 crocodiles ready for the market out of the 2,100 growing young crocodiles in the nursery. He forecasted a production of 2,000 hatchlings for 1994 and 3,000 hatchlings for 1995. As from 1996 he could double this production, when the females in the second breeding yard started producing. This implied that he would have to find a way to build the second hatchery and nursery before 1996. His average monthly income was only adequate to ensure the smooth running of the ranch. His forecasts for 1996 onwards promised enough income for expansion, but if the necessary facilities were not ready before 1996, he would not be in a position to cater to the increased production.

Being the only crocodile farmer in Namibia and responsible for his own marketing, Mr. van Dyk wondered what action he should take to ensure the necessary expansion of his operations before 1996.

## Questions for Discussion

1. What are the advantages and disadvantages of options open to Mr. van Dyk?
2. Which criteria should Mr. van Dyk use in selecting his market(s)?
3. Depending on the suggested selection criteria, what additional information would Mr. van Dyk need to formulate his marketing strategy?
4. What should be the most urgent steps in Mr. van Dyk's export marketing action plan?

# Appendix: International Trade in Nile Crocodile Skins

## The Crocodile Skin Markets in Italy and France[*]

### Overview

World prices for Nile crocodile skins dropped tremendously since the late 1980s and demand was steeply going down. Changes in fashion trends and consumer tastes as well as the world recession had greatly contributed to this decline in demand for farmed skins of the crocodylus niloticus (the Nile crocodile from Africa).

[*]Excerpts from the PRODEC Market Research Report No. 12/91 by Ms. Queen Sachile "The markets for Zambian wet-salted crocodile skins in Italy and France," Helsinki 1991. Published by the Programme for Development Cooperation at the Helsinki School of Economics (PRODEC), Töölönkatu 11A, 00100 Helsinki, Finland.

Competition in the supply of wet-salted Nile crocodile skin was reported to come from Zimbabwe, Zambia, Malawi, Botswana and Mozambique and also from Ethiopia, Kenya, Madagascar and Tanzania who had a reservation on the species and therefore traded under a specified annual export quota system. As indicated in the table below, Zimbabwe was the leading exporter to Nile crocodile skins and the second largest producer of crocodile or alligator skins after the United States.

Since the 1990s, competition from the United States was increasing, flooding the market with cheaper skins from its farms. South America was also providing large quantities of wild skins of the caiman crocodiles.

Skins from the United States were cheaper than African skins, with an average price of about US$3.00/cm in the early 1990s, while skins from South America were larger and therefore preferred for the production of handbags which required skins of more than 35cm across the belly.

### The Italian Market

Italy imported crocodile skins from various sources around the globe.

According to the views of the tanners interviewed, the erratic import figures were a reflection of limited availability from the supplying countries, which forced the tanners to buy the maximum of available quantities from any source available the demand for the commodity was very high at the time.

All the interviewed tanners said they were currently operating about 50 percent below capacity due to declining demand, and were getting most of their raw skins

**Exports of African Countries (in number of skins)**

| Country | 1986 | 1987 | 1988 | 1989 |
|---|---|---|---|---|
| Zimbabwe | 7,216 | 7,924 | 11,609 | 10,647 |
| Malawi | 684 | 1,173 | 1,329 | 2,104 |
| Tanzania | 763 | 1,724 | 2,311 | 1,715 |
| South Africa | 87 | 758 | 1,905 | 4,326 |
| Madagascar | 673 | 4,338 | 3,177 | 4,543 |
| Kenya | — | 150 | 1,400 | 2,499 |
| Mozambique | — | 529 | 795 | 1,554 |
| Botswana | 10 | 65 | 69 | 204 |
| Zambia | 3,117 | 3,235 | 3,738 | 2,389 |

Source: CITES Annual Returns.

**World Imports of Nile Crocodile Skins**
**(in number of skins)**

| Year | World Imports |
| --- | --- |
| 1986 | 18,753 |
| 1987 | 24,147 |
| 1988 | 29,524 |
| 1989 | 35,515 |

*Source:* CITES Annual Returns.

from South America and the United States, which were cheaper sources. In addition, skins from South America were also larger. None of the interviewed processors was interested in a joint venture for the production of crocodylus niloticus skins.

Most crocodile skins were imported into Italy by tanneries who processed the skins and treated them into different colours as specified by manufacturers of crocodile items. Items included belts, handbags, wallets and shoes for sale either in the local market or for export.

The majority of Italian tanners imported directly from farmers in the export countries. The import of raw skins did not attract any duty regardless of source of supply. Skins were airfreighted into Italy packed in double jute bags with labels indicating the number of skins and the weight.

The average CIF price indicated by CITES in 1990 for different types of skins were:

| | |
| --- | --- |
| Nile crocodile | US$12–14/cm |
| Porosus | US$12–14/cm |
| Caiman crocodile | US$45–48/per sq.ft |
| Mississippi alligator | US$6–8/cm |

CITES estimated that these prices had fallen by 50 percent in 1991.

### The French Market

Due to the oversupply of the French market with farmed skins from the United States at a lower price than that offered by African farmers, a competitive factor had been introduced which hitherto had been totally absent. African farmers faced a steadily increasing price competition among different African countries producing crocodylus niloticus skins, as well as strong price competition from the United States.

Most French tanners were buying from the United States not only for the lower prices but also because of the assured United States market for the processed skins and items. French importers sourced their skins directly from farmers by air. Companies interviewed for the report were interested in importing farmed skins from Africa in the future, but at a price lower than US$5.00/cm. In 1991, skins from the United States were sourced in France at US$2.50/cm for skin sizes 18–24cm, US$4.50/cm for skin sizes 25–35cm and US$10.00/cm for skins above 35cm.

With respect to joint ventures in Africa, French companies felt that market requirements regarding delivery time, quality, and color specifications of crocodile items would make a tanning operation located in Africa difficult to manage. Their position was that they would get in touch with African farmers when the demand situation in Europe improved.

## The Banana Wars

The European Union (EU) is the main market in the world for bananas, constituting 37.5 percent of all world trade (see Figure 1). That is why a decision by the EU Farm Council in December of 1992 attracted attention among banana-producing nations. Up until the decision, different EU countries had different policies regarding imports of bananas. While Germany, for example, had no restrictions at all, countries such as the United Kingdom, France, and Spain restricted their imports to favor those from their current and former African, Caribbean, and Pacific (ACP)

SOURCE: *This case was prepared by Ilkka A. Ronkainen. It is based on* "Caribbean, U.S. Blame Each Other in Banana Split," The Journal of Commerce, *October 15, 1997, 4A;* "Caribbean Could Wonder Where the Yellow Went," The Washington Post, *March 19, 1997, C9, C12;* "Banana Trouble," The Washington Times, *November 6, 1994, A13–14;* "Banana Regulations Split the European Community," The Journal of Commerce *(October 22, 1993): 1;* "The Banana War," International Business Chronicle 4 *(February 1–15, 1993): 22; Organization of American States,* "OAS Takes Note of Regional Statements on the Marketing of Bananas in Europe," Report on the OAS Permanent Council Meeting, *February 24, 1993; and Joseph L. Brand,* "The New World Order," Vital Speeches of the Day 58 *(December 1991): 155–160. The help of Gladys Navarro with an earlier version of this case is appreciated. For more information on bananas and trade in bananas, see* **http://www.chiquita.com**, **http://www.dole.com**, *and* **http://www.fyffes.com**. *For different points of view on the banana dispute, see* **http://www.cbea.org**, **http://www.sice.oas.org**, *and* **http://www.ustr.gov/reports/**.

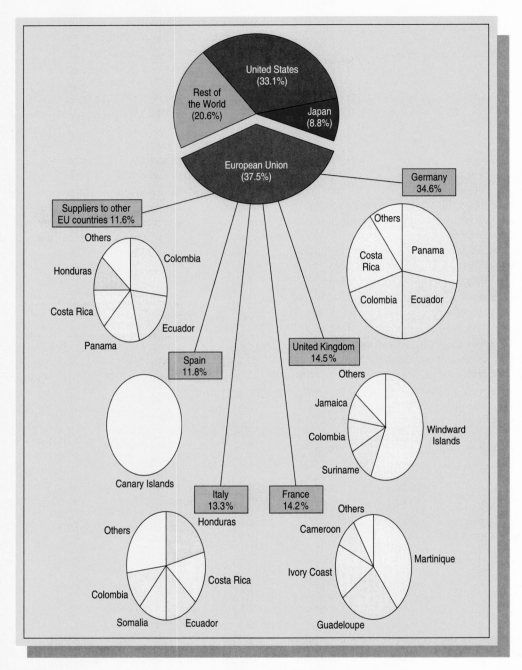

**FIGURE I**

**Trade in Bananas: EU Country Imports by Source**

*Source:* Brent Borrell and Sandy Cuthbertson, *EC Banana Policy 1992,* Center for International Economics, Sydney, Australia, 1991, chart 2.1.

colonies. (This preferential trading agreement is known as the Lomé Convention.) The decision called for a quota of 2.2 million tons with a 20 percent tariff for all banana imports from Latin America ($126 per ton), rising to 170 percent for quantities over that limit ($1,150 per ton). Since Latin American exports to Europe were approximately 2.7 million tons in 1992, the quota has effectively cut almost 25 percent of the countries' exports to the EU.

The main stated reason for imposing the quota and the tariffs is to protect former colonies by allowing them to enjoy preferential access to the EU market. Other reasons implied have been the $300 million in tariff revenue resulting from the measures as well as moving against the "banana dollar" (reference to the U.S. control of the Latin American banana trade through its multinationals). Belgium, Germany, and Holland have objected to the measures not only because of the preference given to higher-cost, lower-quality bananas from current and former colonies, but also because of the economic impact. The Belgians estimated an immediate loss of 500 jobs in its port cities, which traditionally have handled substantial amounts of Latin American banana imports. Twice, the European Court of Justice has rejected Germany's challenge to the EU's banana policy. Even in the United Kingdom, where the preferential treatment has enjoyed widespread support, there has been criticism of the decision.

The conflict escalated into one of the most complicated trade wars in the history of international trade. It has pitted EU members against one another, the United States against the EU, U.S. multinationals against their European counterparts, U.S. investment interests against U.S. foreign policy concerns, Guatemala against Costa Rica, Latin American growers against Caribbean growers, and the U.S. government against four major Latin American nations.

On two separate occasions in 1993 and 1994 panels of the General Agreement on Tariffs and Trade (GATT) found EU banana rules to be unfair and tried to convince the EU to reform its discriminatory and burdensome banana rules. As a result of EU's failure to do anything, a case was initiated with GATT's successor, the World Trade Organization (WTO), in 1996. The WTO agreed in 1997 with the complaint and turned down a subsequent EU appeal later in the same year.

## History of the Banana

Bananas can be traced back thousands of years to ancient manuscripts by the Chinese and Arabs. European experience starts in 327 B.C. with Alexander the Great's conquest of India. Bananas were introduced to the Americas by Spanish explorers in 1516. From that point on, many tropical regions with average temperatures of 80°F (25°C) and annual rainfall of 78–98 inches (2300–2900 mm) have benefitted from bananas as a source of food and, increasingly, trade. Trade in bananas started only in earnest with the introduction of the steam engine and refrigeration enabling transportation quicker and in better condition to Europe and North America. Consumers in the United States were first introduced to bananas at the Philadelphia Centennial Exhibition in 1876.

## The Latin American Position

Bananas are the world's most-traded fruit, and the $5.1 billion in banana trade makes it second only to coffee among foodstuffs. The major banana producers in the world are presented in Figure 2. For countries such as Ecuador, Costa Rica, Colombia, and Honduras the restrictions would cost $1 billion in revenues and 170,000 jobs. For countries such as Costa Rica, banana exports are vital. Bananas represent 8 percent of the country's domestic product, bring in $500 million in hard-currency earnings, and employ one-fifth of the labor force.

The presidents of Colombia, Costa Rica, Ecuador, Guatemala, Honduras, Nicaragua, Panama, and Venezuela held a summit February 11, 1993, in Ecuador and issued a declaration rejecting the EU banana-marketing guidelines as a violation of GATT and principles of trade liberalization. However, following the formal adoption of the banana decision by the EU in July 1993, the EU and four Latin American nations (Costa Rica, Colombia, Nicaragua, and Venezuela) cut a deal in March 1994. The four countries agreed to drop their GATT protest in exchange for modifications in the restrictions they face. Guatemala refused to sign the agreement and Ecuador, Panama, and Mexico lodged protests.

The economics of production are clearly in favor of the Latin producers. The unit-cost of production in the Caribbean is nearly 2.5 times what it is for Latin American producers. For some producers, such as Martinique and Guadeloupe, the cost difference is even higher. The EU quota therefore results in major trade diversion.

The affected Latin nations have used various means at the international level to get the EU to modify its position. In addition to the summit, many are engaged in lobbying in Brussels as well as the individual EU-member capitals. They have also sought the support of the United States, given its interests both in terms of U.S. multinational corporations' involvement in the ba-

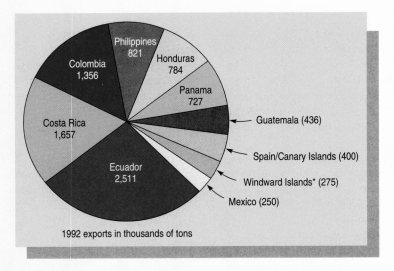

1992 exports in thousands of tons

**FIGURE 2**

**Leading Banana Producers**

\* Includes Dominica, Grenada, Saint Lucia, Saint Vincent and Grenadines.

*Source:* United Nations Food and Agriculture Organization, Intergovernmental Group on Bananas.

nana trade as well as its investment in encouraging economic growth in the developing democracies of Latin America.

## The U.S. Position

Initial U.S. reaction was that of an interested observer. The United States provided support and encouragement for the Latin Americans in their lobbying efforts in Geneva, Brussels, and the European capitals. However, in October 1994, U.S. Trade Representative Mickey Kantor announced plans to start a year-long investigation of the EU's banana restrictions, with sanctions against European imports as a possibility. This action broke new ground in trade disputes. While governments traditionally have started trade wars as a means of protecting domestic jobs and key industries, the banana dispute involves U.S. investment and overseas markets more than it does jobs at home. The probe was requested by Chiquita, the world's largest banana marketer, and the Hawaii Banana Industry Association, whose 130 small family farms constitute the entire banana-growing contingent. Although only 7,000 of the company's 45,000 employees are in the United States, Chiquita officials argued that the value

added by the company's U.S. workers—marketers, shippers, and distributors—make it a major agricultural priority.

The U.S. challenge was "not politically prudent," complained Gerard Kiely spokesperson for the EU Agricultural Commissioner, by noting that the United States does not even export bananas. However, 12 senators sent a letter to Mr. Kantor warning against the dangerous precedent if the EU banana regime went unchallenged. Unless deterred, the EU could possibly employ similar measures it is using for bananas for other agricultural products, especially those that the United States does export.

The United States is, however, in favor of a WTO waiver to the EU to provide support to its former colonies. The contention is that the EU feels that it can within this waiver take any measures it deems necessary regardless of the impact on other WTO members. The United States and the other four countries filing the complaint argued for a more narrow interpretation, which would mean a simple system of tariff protection supported by aid to increase the efficiency of some producers and help the remainder to retire or diversify. The tariff would, in effect, offset some of the cost differences in the EU markets.

The United States argues that many ACP producers are not competitive because of their special circumstances (such as small average farm size of 5 acres/ 2 hectares) as well as a result of the EU preferences, which have given the ACP nations a disincentive to become competitive or to diversify.

## The Caribbean Position

For many nations banana exports are the mainstay of their economies. For example, for the tiny West Indies island of St. Lucia, which sells its banana to its former colonial master, the United Kingdom, banana dependence is 70 percent of the national income. Furthermore, the industry employs four out of five St. Lucians.

Therefore it was not surprising that heads of government of the thirteen-member Caribbean Community (CARICOM) approved a resolution February 24, 1993, supporting the EU guidelines. "No one country in this hemisphere is as dependent on bananas for its economic survival as the Windward Islands," declared Ambassador Joseph Edsel Edmunds of Saint Lucia. Referring to the criticism of the EU decision by the Latin nations, he added: "Are we being told that, in the interest of free trade all past international agreements between the Caribbean and friendly nations are to be dissolved, leaving us at the mercy of Latin American states and megablocs?" He noted that Latin American banana producers command 95 percent of the world market and more than two-thirds of the EU market.

Ambassador Kingsley A. Layne of Saint Vincent and the Grenadines asserted that the issue at stake "is nothing short of a consideration of the right of small states to exist with a decent and acceptable standard of living, self-determination, and independence. The same flexibility and understanding being sought by other powerful partners in the WTO in respect of their specific national interests must also be extended to the small island developing states."

After the WTO decision was rendered, the Caribbean nations have tried to strengthen alliances with European parliamentarians and have mobilized international opinion to continue to challenge the WTO ruling. "The decision represents a failure by the WTO, in its blind pursuit of free trade, to take into account the interests of small developing countries," said Marshall Hall, chairman of the Caribbean Banana Exporters Association. The Windward Islands, especially, are worried that the WTO ruling will further discourage farmers in the region who are already reducing quantities of fruit for export.

## The Corporate Position

The dispute has also pitted U.S. multinationals (Chiquita, Dole, and Del Monte) against the Europeans (Geest and Fyffes). Since 1996, the U.K.–based Geest has been owned jointly by the Windward Island Banana Development Company and the Irish Fyffes. The two European multinationals control between them virtually all of the banana shipping and marketing from such markets as Belize, Suriname, Jamaica, and the Windward Islands. Chiquita, in particular, complains that the EU is arranging insider deals for Geest and Fyffes to exempt them from export licensing fees imposed by Latin American nations that have agreed with the EU, or even to secure them a slice of the export business from Latin American markets where they have no foothold at present. The EU's licensing system has transferred 50 percent or more of U.S. or Latin American companies import rights principally to EU firms. The Caribbean nations and the EU assert that the United States is taking its action solely to support the world's largest banana trader, Chiquita, because it wields great political influence.

### Questions for Discussion

1. If you were a member of the Organization of American States (of which all of the Caribbean and Latin American countries mentioned in the case are members) and its Permanent Council (which must react to two opposing statements concerning the EU decision), with which one would you side?
2. Given the WTO's decision, what are the alternatives for the EU and the Caribbean banana growers?
3. What types of strategic moves will an international marketing manager of a Latin American banana exporter have to take in light of the quota and the tariffs?

# INTERNATIONAL BUSINESS PREPARATION AND MARKET ENTRY

## PART 4

In order to operate successfully abroad, firms must prepare for their market entry. Key in the preparation is the conduct of research to build a knowledge base of country specific issues and market specific opportunities and concerns.

Once such a base is established, the country can enter international markets, initially through exporting and international intermediaries. Over time, expansion can occur through foreign direct investment and lead to the formation of the multinational corporation.

# CHAPTER 10

# International Business Research

## LEARNING OBJECTIVES

◆ To gain an understanding of the need for research

◆ To explore the differences between domestic and international research

◆ To learn where to find and how to use sources of secondary information

◆ To gain insight into the gathering of primary data

◆ To examine the need for international management information systems

## Electronic Information Sources on the EU

**W**ith the expanding economic and political union occurring within Europe, official information resources are becoming more centralized. A short sampling of government sources of information helpful to international managers targeting the EU are reviewed below.

### EUROPA

Located at **http:/europa.eu.int** is the main server that provides access to bibliographic, legal, and statistical databases offered by the European Commission. Many databases are available on Europa including RAPID, SCAD, EUROCRON, and ECLAS. RAPID provides full text of press releases issued daily by the European Commission, Council of Ministers, Court of Justice, Court of Auditors, Economic and Social Committee and the Committee of the Regions. In addition to the texts, a list of items released each day may be downloaded. SCAD is a bibliographic database with references to official legislative documents and publications, as well as secondary periodical literature on the EU. EUROCRON provides a menu-guided presentation of general macroeconomic statistics and farm data. ECLAS is an on-line catalog of the Central Library of the Commission.

### EUROSTAT

The Statistical Office of the European Communities (EUROSTAT), which is located at **http:/europa.eu.int/en/comm/eurostat/serven/part6/6som.htm** provides information on diskettes, tapes, and CD-ROMs. This site offers a wide selection of electronic information as well as software for graphics using COMEXT, along with map and graphic capabilities.

### EPOQUE

EPOQUE is the documentary database of the European Parliament. Its files cover the status of legislation in progress; citations for sessions documents, debates, resolutions and opinions; bibliographic references to studies done by Parliament; and a catalog of the Parliament's library. Please note, this is a restricted database, but **http:/www.europarl.eu.int** offers free and timely information regarding the European Parliament.

The single most important cause for failure in international business is insufficient preparation and information. The failure of managers to comprehend cultural disparities, the failure to remember that customers differ from country to country, and the lack of investigation into whether or not a market exists prior to market entry has made international business a high-risk activity.[1] International business research is therefore instrumental to international business success since it permits the firm to take into account different environments, attitudes, and market conditions. Fortunately, such research has become less complicated. As the opening vignette shows, information from around the globe can be obtained quite easily.

This chapter discusses data collection and provides a comprehensive overview of how to obtain general screening information on international markets, to evaluate business potential, and to assess current or potential opportunities and problems. Data sources that are low cost and that take little time to accumulate—in short, secondary data—are considered first. The balance of the chapter is devoted to more sophisticated forms of international research, including primary data collection and the development of an information system.

## International and Domestic Research

The tools and techniques of international research are the same as those of domestic research. The difference is in the environment to which the tools are applied. The environment determines how well the tools, techniques, and concepts work. Although the objectives of research may be the same, the execution of international research may differ substantially from that of domestic research. The four primary reasons for this difference are new parameters, new environmental factors, an increase in the number of factors involved, and a broader definition of competition.

### New Parameters

In crossing national borders, a firm encounters parameters not found in domestic business. Examples include duties, foreign currencies and changes in their value, different modes of transportation, and international documentation. New parameters also emerge because of differing modes of operating internationally. For example, the firm can export, it can license its products, it can engage in a joint venture, or it can carry out foreign direct investment. The firm that has done business only domestically will have had little or no experience with the requirements and conditions of these types of operations. Managers must therefore obtain information in order to make good business decisions.

### New Environmental Factors

When going international, a firm is exposed to an unfamiliar environment. Many of the domestic assumptions on which the firm and its activities were founded may not hold true internationally. Management needs to learn the culture of the host country, understand its political systems and level of stability, and comprehend the existing differences in societal structures and language. In addition, it must understand pertinent legal issues in order to avoid violating local laws. The technological level of the society must also be incorporated in the business plan. In short, all the assumptions that were formulated over the years based on domestic business activities must now be reevaluated. This crucial point is often neglected because most managers are born in the environment of their domestic operations and only subconsciously learn to understand the constraints and opportunities of their business activities. The situation is analogous to learning one's native language. Even without much formal training, native speakers may use the language correctly. Only when attempting to learn a foreign language will they begin to appreciate the structure of language and the need for grammatical rules.

## The Number of Factors Involved

Environmental relationships need to be relearned whenever a firm enters a new international market. The number of changing dimensions increases geometrically. Coordination of the interaction among the dimensions becomes increasingly difficult because of their sheer number. Such coordination, however, is crucial to the international success of the firm for two reasons. First, in order to exercise some central control over its international operations, a firm must be able to compare results and activities across countries. Otherwise, any plans made by headquarters may be inappropriate. Second, the firm must be able to learn from its international operations and must find ways to apply the new lessons learned to different markets. Without coordination, such learning cannot take place in a systematic way. The international research process can help in this undertaking.

## Broader Definition of Competition

The international market exposes the firm to a much greater variety of competition than that found in the home market. For example, a firm may find that ketchup competes against soy sauce. Similarly, firms that offer labor-saving devices domestically may suddenly be exposed to competition from cheap manual labor. As a result, the firms must determine the breadth of the competition, track competitive activities, and evaluate their actual and potential impact on company operations.

## Recognizing the Need for International Research

Many firms do little research before they enter a foreign market. Often, decisions concerning entry and expansion in overseas markets and selection and appointment of distributors are made after a cursory, subjective assessment of the situation. The research done is often less rigorous, less formal, and less quantitative than for domestic activities. Furthermore, once a firm has entered a foreign market, it is likely to discontinue researching that market.

A major reason why managers are reluctant to engage in international research is their lack of sensitivity to differences in culture, consumer tastes, and market demands. Often managers assume that their methods are both best and acceptable to all others. Fortunately, this is not true. What a boring place the world would be if it were!

A second reason is a limited appreciation for the different environments abroad. Often firms are not prepared to accept that labor rules, distribution systems, the availability of media, or advertising regulations may be entirely different from those in the home market. Due to pressure to satisfy short-term financial goals, managers are unwilling to spend money to find out about the differences.

A third reason is lack of familiarity with national and international data sources and inability to use international data once they are obtained. As a result, the cost of conducting international research is perceived to be prohibitively high and therefore not a worthwhile investment relative to the benefits to be gained.

Finally, firms often build their international business activities gradually, frequently based on unsolicited orders. Over time, actual business experience in a country or with a specific firm may then be used as a substitute for organized research.

Despite the reservations firms have, research is as important internationally as it is domestically. Firms must learn where the opportunities are, what customers want, why they want it, and how they satisfy their needs and wants so that the firm can serve them efficiently. Firms must obtain information about the local infrastructure, labor market, and tax rules before making a plant location decision. Doing business abroad without the benefit of research places firms, their assets, and their entire international future at risk.

Research allows management to identify and develop international strategies. The task includes the identification, evaluation, and comparison of potential foreign business opportunities and the subsequent target market selection. In addition, research is necessary for the development of a business plan that identifies all the requirements necessary for market entry, market penetration, and expansion. On a continuing basis, research provides the feedback needed to fine-tune various business activities. Finally, research can provide management with the intelligence to help anticipate events, take appropriate action, and adequately prepare for global changes.

## Determining Research Objectives

Before research can be undertaken, research objectives must be determined. They will vary depending on the views of management, the corporate mission of the firm, the firm's level of internationalization, and its competitive situation.

**Going International— Exporting**

A frequent objective of international research is that of foreign market opportunity analysis. When a firm launches its international activities, it will usually find the world to be uncharted territory. Fortunately, information can be accumulated to provide basic guidelines. The aim is not to conduct a painstaking and detailed analysis of the world on a market-by-market basis, but instead to utilize a broad-brush approach. Accomplished quickly and at low cost, this approach will narrow the possibilities for international business activities.

Such an approach should begin with a cursory analysis of general variables of a country, including total and per capita GNP, mortality rates, and population figures. Although these factors in themselves will not provide any detailed information, they will enable the researcher to determine whether corporate objectives might be met in the market. For example, high-priced consumer products are unlikely to be successful in the People's Republic of China, as their price may be equal to a significant proportion of the customer's annual salary, the customer benefit may be minimal, and the government is likely to prohibit their importation. Similarly, the offering of computer software services may be of little value in a country where there is very limited use of computers. Such a cursory evaluation will help reduce the number of markets to be considered to a more manageable number—for example, from 225 to 25.

As a next step, the researcher will require information on each individual country for a preliminary evaluation. Information typically desired will highlight the fastest growing markets, the largest markets for a particular product or service, demand trends, and business restrictions. Although precise and detailed information may not be obtainable, information is available for general product categories or service industries. Again, this overview will be cursory but will serve to quickly evaluate markets and further reduce their number.

At this stage, the researcher must select appropriate markets for in-depth evaluation. The focus will now be on opportunities for a specific type of service, product, or brand, and will include an assessment as to whether demand already exists or can be stimulated. Even though aggregate industry data may have been obtained previously, this general information is insufficient to make company-specific decisions. For example, the demand for sports equipment should not be confused with the potential demand for a specific brand. The research now should identify demand and supply patterns and evaluate any regulations and standards. Finally, a **competitive assessment** needs to be made, matching markets to corporate strengths and providing an analysis of the best potential for specific offerings. A summary of the various stages in the determination of market potential is provided in Figure 10.1.

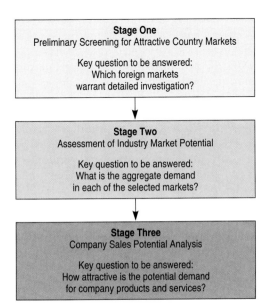

**FIGURE 10.1**

**A Sequential Process of Researching Foreign Market Potentials**

*Source:* S. Tamer Cavusgil, "Guidelines for Export Market Research," *Business Horizons* 28 (November–December 1985): 29. Copyright 1985 by the Foundation for the School of Business at Indiana University. Reprinted by permission.

### Going International— Importing

When importing, the major focus shifts from supplying to sourcing. Management must identify markets that produce supplies or materials desired or that have the potential to do so. Foreign firms must be evaluated in terms of their capabilities and competitive standing.

Just as management would want to have some details on a domestic supplier, the importer needs to know, for example, about the reliability of a foreign supplier, the consistency of its product or service quality, and the length of delivery time. Information obtained through the subsidiary office of a bank or an embassy can prove very helpful.

In addition, foreign rules must be scrutinized as to whether exportation is possible. As examples, India may set limits on the cobra handbags it allows to be exported, and laws protecting a nation's cultural heritage may prevent the exportation of pre-Columbian artifacts from Latin American countries.

The international manager must also analyze domestic restrictions and legislation that may prohibit the importation of certain goods into the home country. Even though a market may exist at home for foreign umbrella handles, for example, quotas may restrict their importation to protect domestic industries. Similarly, even though domestic demand may exist for ivory, its importation may be illegal because of legislation enacted to protect wildlife worldwide.

### Market Expansion

Research objectives include obtaining more detailed information for business expansion or monitoring the political climate so that the firm successfully can maintain its international operation. Information may be needed to enable the international manager to evaluate new business partners or assess the impact of a technological breakthrough on future business operations. The better defined the research objective is, the better the researcher will be able to determine information requirements and thus conserve the time and financial resources of the firm.

## Conducting Secondary Research

### Identifying Sources of Data

Typically, the information requirements of firms will cover both macro information about countries and trade, as well as micro information specific to the firm's activities. Table 10.1 provides an overview of the types of information that, according to a survey of executives, are most crucial for international business. If each firm had to go out and collect all the information needed on-site in the country under scrutiny, the task would be unwieldy and far too expensive. On many occasions, however, firms can make use of **secondary data,** that is, information that already has been collected by some other organization. A wide variety of sources present secondary data. The principal ones are governments, international institutions, service organizations, trade associations, directories, and other firms. This section provides a brief review of major data sources. Details on selected monitors of international issues are presented in Appendix 10A at the end of the chapter.

**Governments**   Most countries have a wide array of national and international trade data available. Typically, the information provided by governments ad-

**TABLE 10.1**

**Critical International Information**

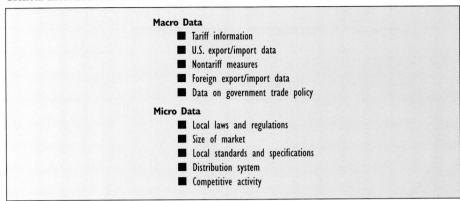

> **Macro Data**
> - ■ Tariff information
> - ■ U.S. export/import data
> - ■ Nontariff measures
> - ■ Foreign export/import data
> - ■ Data on government trade policy
>
> **Micro Data**
> - ■ Local laws and regulations
> - ■ Size of market
> - ■ Local standards and specifications
> - ■ Distribution system
> - ■ Competitive activity

*Source:* Michael R. Czinkota, "International Information Needs for U.S. Competitiveness," *Business Horizons* 34, 6 (November–December 1991): 86–91.

dresses either macro and micro issues or offers specific data services. Macro information includes data on population trends, general trade flows among countries, and world agriculture production. Micro information includes materials on specific industries in a country, their growth prospects, and their foreign trade activities.

Unfortunately, the data are often published only in their home countries and in their native languages. The publications mainly present numerical data, however, and so the translation task is relatively easy. In addition, the information sources are often available at embassies and consulates, whose mission includes the enhancement of trade activities. The commercial counselor or commercial attaché can provide the information as can government sponsored web sites. The user should be cautioned, however, that the information is often dated and that the industry categories used abroad may not be compatible with industry categories used at home.

**International Organizations**   Some international organizations provide useful data for the researcher. The *Statistical Yearbook* produced by the United Nations (UN) contains international trade data on products and provides information on exports and imports by country. However, because of the time needed for worldwide data collection, the information is often quite dated. Additional information is compiled and made available by specialized substructures of the United Nations. Some of these are the United Nations Conference on Trade and Development (UNCTAD), which concentrates primarily on international issues surrounding developing nations, such as debt and market access, and the United Nations Center on Transnational Corporations. The *World Atlas* published by the World Bank provides useful general data on population, growth trends, and GNP figures. The Organization for Economic Cooperation and Development (OECD) also publishes quarterly and annual trade data on its member countries. Organizations such as the International Monetary Fund (IMF) and the World Bank publish summary economic data and occasional staff papers that evaluate region- or country-specific issues in depth.

WWW

Coa Cola markets its products around the globe by diversifying the flavors it offers. Their fruit flavored soft drink, Fanta, which is a red punch flavor in the USA is peach in Botswana, passion fruit in France, and flower-flavored in Japan.
Source: **http://www.lloydsbank.co.uk**

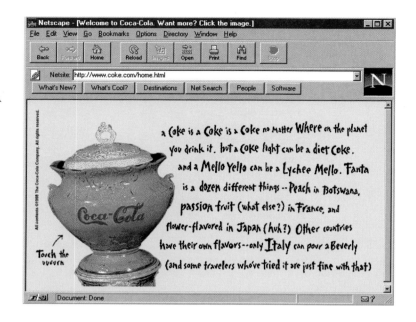

**Service Organizations**   A wide variety of service organizations that provide information include banks, accounting firms, freight forwarders, airlines, international trade consultants, research firms, and publishing houses located around the world. Frequently they are able to provide information on business practices, legislative or regulatory requirements, and political stability, as well as trade and financial data. As Figure 10.2 shows, often such service providers also can accumulate a wide variety of data from different countries and therefore offer one-stop shopping to the researcher.

**Trade Associations**   Associations such as world trade clubs and domestic and international chambers of commerce (such as the American Chamber of Commerce abroad) can provide good information on local markets. Often files are maintained on international trade flows and trends affecting international managers. Valuable information can also be obtained from industry associations. These groups, formed to represent entire industry segments, often collect a wide variety of data from their members that are then published in an aggregate form. Most of these associations represent the viewpoints of their member firms to the government, so they usually have one or more publicly listed representative in the capital. The  information provided is often quite general, however, because of the wide variety of clientele served.

**Directories and Newsletters**   A large number of industry directories are available on local, national, and international levels. The directories primarily serve to identify firms and to provide very general background information, such as the name of the chief executive officer, the level of capitalization of the firm, the location, the address and telephone number, and some description of the firm's products. A host of newsletters discuss specific international business issues, such as international trade finance, legislative activities, countertrade, international payment flows, and customs news. Usually these newsletters cater to narrow audiences but can provide important information to the firm interested in a specific area.

**FIGURE 10.2**

**An Advertisement for International Information Services**

*Source: Financial Times*, September 21, 1994, II (special survey).

**Electronic Information Services**   Obtaining trade information rapidly is often the key to success in the international market. With the proliferation of new technologies, such information is now more readily available than ever before. In light of the vast quantity of information available, making use of technology becomes essential. Just consider, "roughly 1,000 specialized periodicals hit the mail every year, progressively examining narrower and narrower subjects. Publishers print 1,000 new book titles each day, and the sum of printed information doubles every eight years. Currently, 40 percent of the U.S. work force helps create, process, or transmit information, and 40 percent of all business investments go into information technology".[2]

When information is needed, managers cannot spend a lot of time, energy, or money finding, sifting through, and categorizing it. Consider laboring through every copy of a trade publication to find out the latest news on how environmental concerns are affecting marketing decisions in Mexico. With electronic information services, search results can be obtained within minutes. International on-line computer database services, numbering in the thousands, can be purchased to supply information external to the firm, such as exchange rates, international news, and import restrictions. Most database hosts do not charge any sign-up fee and request payment only for actual use. The selection of initial database hosts depends on the choice of relevant databases, taking into account their product and market limitations, language used, and geographical location. Global Perspective 10.1 shows how easily information on Latin American markets can be obtained. A large number of databases, developed by analysts who systematically sift through a wide range of periodicals, reports, and books in different languages, provide information on given products and markets. Many of the main news agencies now have information available through on-line databases, providing information on events that affect certain markets. Some databases cover extensive lists of companies in given countries and the products they buy and sell. A large number of databases exist that cover various categories of trade statistics. The main economic indicators of the UN, IMF, OECD, and EU are available on-line. Standards institutes in most of the G7 nations provide on-line access to their databases of technical standards and trade regulations on specific products.[3]

Compact Disk/Read-Only Memory (CD-ROM) technology allows for massive amounts of information (the equivalent of 300 books of 1,000 pages each, or 1,500 floppy disks) to be stored on a single 12-centimeter plastic disk. The technology increasingly is used for storing and distributing large volumes of information, such as statistical databases. Typically, the user pays no user fees but instead invests in a CD-ROM "reader" and purchases the actual CDs.

A CD-ROM service widely used in the United States is the National Trade Data Bank (NTDB), a monthly product issued by the U.S. Department of Commerce's Office of Business Analysis. The NTDB includes more than 170,000 documents, including full-text market research reports, domestic and foreign economic data, import and export statistics, trade information and country studies, all compiled from twenty-six government agencies.[4] The NTDB can also provide profiles of screened businesses that are interested in importing U.S. products.

Using data services for research means that professionals do not have to leave their offices, going from library to library to locate the facts they need. Many on-line services have late-breaking information available within twenty-four hours to the user. These techniques of research are cost-effective as well. Stocking a company's library with all the books needed to have the same amount of data that is available on-line or with CD-ROM would be too expensive and space-consuming. A listing of selected databases useful for international business is presented in the appendix to this chapter.

## Selection of Secondary Data

Just because secondary information has been found to exist does not mean that it must be used. Even though one key advantage of secondary data over primary research is that they are available relatively quickly and inexpensively,

## THE LATIN WEB OF INFORMATION

For investors in Latin America, the growth of the Internet has provided a wealth of business research tools at their fingertips. Although the rapid expansion of global Web sites has received much publicity, now there are also many lesser-known region-specific databases and timely information sources on the Web. Companies, financial institutions, and governments alike have discovered that the Web is a valuable yet inexpensive way to provide updated information to a wide and geographically diverse audience.

A Mexican government program provides one example of the timeliness of the Web as an information provider for investors in Latin America. When Mexico announced a new program for financing development, it was able to give instant access to an extensive report on the program at the same time that the announcement appeared in media reports. Businesses had immediate access to primary-source information that otherwise would have been difficult and time-consuming to acquire.

However, the swift growth and dynamic nature of Internet-based information sources has magnified the fundamental problem facing researchers using the Web: the Internet has little structure to organize its abundance of information, and it has no filter to determine the quality of information. As a result, business researchers often need explicit knowledge of the information they are seeking, the sources for that information, and their Web addresses before beginning research. Language skills also are a plus; as with many region-specific Web sites that are printed in the local language, Latin American Web sites often bury a lot of the English-language material under pages of Spanish. Nevertheless, the following sites give an indication of the quality and timeliness of information available to researchers on Latin American investment opportunities:

- *Stock Exchanges.* All major Latin American exchanges are now online, providing same-day closing prices of traded shares. Many provide daily bulletins with company announcements. Peru's Bolsa de Valores de Lima even has quotes available throughout the day with only a three-minute delay and financial statements for every listed company on the exchange. The Bolsa Electrónica de Chile provides real-time share prices and a historical database of transactions.

- *Official Economic Statistical Agencies.* A potential investor can now find all the basic details about Latin American economies quickly over the Web. Inflation, unemployment, industrial production, and other figures are often available on the Web even before they are published in the press. Argentina's Instituto Nacional de Estadística y Censos (INDEC) and Brazil's Instituto de Geografia e Estatística (IBGE) offer extensive historical demographic and economic data.

- *Central Banks and Regulatory Agencies.* These sites provide recent data on interest rates, foreign exchange movements, and financial sector performance. Most central banks or main banking regulatory agency sites offer downloadable material and economic and statistical analyses. The Bank for International Settlements serves as the Latin American "central bank's banker" and it has a site that publishes international financial data relating to Latin America.

- *Company Web Sites.* One study concluded that 30 percent of the major Latin American companies now have Web sites. Although they vary in depth and quality, many contain production, export, and services information as well as press releases.

*Selected sites:*
Chile: Bolsa Electrónica de Chile—**www.bolchile.cl/**
Peru: Bolsa de Valores de Lima—**www.bvl.com.pe/homepage.html**
Argentina: Instituto Nacional de Estadística y Censos (INDEC)—**www.indec.mecon.ar/**
Brazil: Instituto de Geografia e Estatística (IBGE)—**www.ibge.gov.br/**
International: Bank for International Settlements (BIS)—**www.bis.org/**

*Source: Christopher Tilley and Mary Gwynn, "The Internet Advantage," LatinFinance, 89 (September 1997): pp. 57-9.*

the researcher should still assess the effort and benefit of using them. Secondary data should be evaluated regarding the quality of their source, their recency, and their relevance to the task at hand. Clearly, since the information was collected without the current research requirements in mind, there may well be difficulties in coverage, categorization, and comparability. For example, an "engineer" in one country may differ substantially in terms of training and responsibilities from a person in another country holding the same title. It is therefore important to be careful when getting ready to interpret and analyze data.

## Interpretation and Analysis of Secondary Data

Once secondary data have been obtained, the researcher must creatively convert them into information. Secondary data were originally collected to serve another purpose than the one in which the researcher is currently interested. Therefore, they can often be used only as **proxy information** in order to arrive at conclusions that address the research objectives. For example, the market penetration of television sets may be used as a proxy variable for the potential demand for video recorders. Similarly, in an industrial setting, information about plans for new port facilities may be useful in determining future containerization requirements.

The researcher must often use creative inferences, and such creativity brings risks. Therefore, once interpretation and analysis have taken place, a consistency check must be conducted. The researcher should always cross-check the results with other possible sources of information or with experts. Yet, if properly implemented, such creativity can open up one's eyes to new market potential, as Global Perspective 10.2 shows.

## Conducting Primary Research

Even though secondary data are useful to the researcher, on many occasions primary information will be required. **Primary data** are obtained by a firm to fill specific information needs. Firms specialize in primary international research, even under difficult circumstances as indicated in Figure 10.3. Although the research may not be conducted by the company with the need, the work must be carried out for a specific research purpose in order to qualify as primary research. Typically, primary research intends to answer such clear-cut questions as:

- What is the sales potential for our measuring equipment in Malaysia?
- How much does the typical Greek consumer spend on fast food?
- What effect will our new type of packaging have on our green consumers in Norway?
- What service standards do industrial customers expect in Japan?

The researcher must have a clear idea of what the population under study should be and where it is located before deciding on the country or region to investigate. Conducting research in an entire country may not be necessary if, for example, only urban centers are to be penetrated. Multiple regions of a country need to be investigated, however, if a lack of homogeneity exists because of different economic, geographic, or behavioral factors. One source reports of the failure of a firm in Indonesia due to insufficient geographic dispersion of its research. The firm conducted its study only in large Indonesian cities during the height of tourism season, but projected the results to the en-

## CREATIVE RESEARCH

**W**hen American entrepreneur Peter Johns went to Mexico to do business, he couldn't buy what he needed most: information. So he dug it up himself. Johns wanted to distribute mail-order catalogs for upscale U.S. companies to consumers in Mexico. He thought that a large market was there just waiting to be tapped. However, when he tried to test his theory against hard data, he ran into a big blank.

Johns, who has spent 30 years in international marketing, couldn't find a useful marketing study for Mexico City. Government census reports weren't much help because they stop breaking down income levels at about $35,000, and they give ranges, rather than precise numbers, on family size.

So Johns embarked on some primary research. He went into the affluent neighborhoods and found just what he had suspected: satellite dishes, imported sports cars, and women carrying Louis Vuitton handbags. He reached his own conclusions about the target market for his catalogs. "There is no question there is a sense of consumer deprivation in the luxury market of Mexico City," said Johns.

After deciding to pursue his new enterprise, Johns reached another obstacle. His new enterprise, Choices Unlimited, has obtained rights from about twenty U.S. companies to distribute their catalogs in Mexico City. Now, he needed mailing lists, and he could not find them. Owners of mailing lists do not like to sell them because buyers tend to recycle the lists without authorization. Some of those that are available are expensive and may not include information such as zip codes, important barometers of household wealth.

Johns asked his local investors for membership lists of the city's exclusive golf clubs. He also obtained directories of the parents of students at some of the city's exclusive private schools. Johns received these lists for free. "That's called grassroots marketing intelligence," said Johns.

Down the road, Johns hopes to have a Mexican customer base of 7,500 families spending an average of $600 a year on his products. By then, he should have another product to sell: his customer list.

**Source: Dianna Solis, "Grass-Roots Marketing Yields Clients in Mexico City," The Wall Street Journal, October 24, 1991, B2.**

tire population. When the company set up large production and distribution facilities to meet the expected demand, it realized only limited sales to city tourists.[5]

The discussion presented here will focus mainly on the research-specific issues. Application dimensions such as market choice and market analysis will be covered in Chapter 14.

## Industrial versus Consumer Sources of Data

The researcher must decide whether research is to be conducted in the consumer or the industrial product area, which in turn determines the size of the universe and respondent accessibility. Consumers usually are a very large group, whereas the total population of industrial users may be limited. Cooperation by respondents may also vary. In the industrial setting, differentiation between users and decision makers may be important because their personalities, their outlooks, and their evaluative criteria may differ widely. Determining the proper focus of the research is therefore of major importance to its successful completion.

## Determining the Research Technique

Selection of the research technique depends on a variety of factors. First, the objectivity of the data sought must be determined. Standardized techniques are more useful in the collection of objective data than of subjective data. Also,

**FIGURE 10.3**

**An Example of Primary Research under Difficult Conditions**

*Source:* Reprinted by permission of Research International, The Leading Worldwide Research Company.

## THE INTERVIEWING IS EASY...
## IF THIS MAN DOESN'T SHOOT YOU FIRST

**TASK :**

Interview Afghans who fled across the border into Pakistan to see if they're listening to the BBC. Problem: you have to get past the local warlords who control the area.

Hand this problem to any old research company claiming to do international research, and you're in trouble. The BBC turned to Research International.

**KNOWING WHAT WORKS**

In today's competitive world, companies are increasingly looking toward off-shore markets. And that means good information is essential, even in developed markets.

But international research isn't just a case of taking what you do here and transplanting it there.

A national probability sample in Brazil will have you climbing a palm tree. "I will buy" on a scale in Japan doesn't mean the same thing in Spain. In tax-shy Italy, quota sampling on the basis of income won't get you very far!

**GLOBAL PERSPECTIVE + LOCAL INSIGHT**

We have Research International offices on the ground in 38 of the world's most important markets, from France to Argentina, the USA to Russia, London to Singapore. All our companies are leaders in their markets.

Our professional staff know their markets because they live there—not through visits or by reading the statistics.

We have conducted more than 4,000 international projects. In the last two years alone, we've worked in over 100 countries.

We know what works. And what doesn't. We know what research should cost. We know how to insure comparable high quality standards worldwide.

**RESEARCH INTERNATIONAL IN NORTH AMERICA**

You may be surprised to know that Research International has 6 companies and 9 offices in this region. Whether it's large scale survey work, product testing, customer satisfaction research, qualitative or observational research, we can help.

We can put together an unrivaled team drawing on Research International resources in place in New York, Boston, San Francisco, Chicago, Toronto, Mexico City and in San Juan.

**COMMITMENT TO INNOVATION WORLDWIDE**

Being on the ground all around the world also means that we have access to the best brains and the best thinking around the globe. Which means that we can offer our clients innovative, powerful techniques regardless of place of origin.

Our commitment to R. & D. runs very deep. Each year, we spend more of our own money on basic research than most of our competitors bring to the bottom line.

**RESEARCH INTERNATIONAL**

the degree of structure sought in the data collection needs to be determined. Unstructured data will require more open-ended questions and more time than structured data. Whether the data are to be collected in the real world or in a controlled environment must be determined. Finally, it must be decided whether to collect historical facts or information about future developments. This is particularly important for consumer research, because firms frequently want to determine the future intentions of consumers about buying a certain product.

Once the structure of the type of data sought is determined, the researcher must choose a research technique. As in domestic research, the types available are interviews, focus groups, observation, surveys, and experimentation. Each one provides a different depth of information and has its own unique strengths and weaknesses.

**Interviews** with knowledgeable people can be of great value for the corporation that wants international information. Bias from the individual may be part of the findings, so the intent should be to obtain not a wide variety of data, but rather in-depth information. When specific answers are sought to very narrow questions, interviews can be particularly useful.

**Focus Groups** are a useful research tool resulting in interactive interviews. A group of knowledgeable people is gathered for a limited period of time (two to four hours). Usually, seven to ten participants is the ideal size for a focus group. A specific topic in introduced and thoroughly discussed by all group members. Because of the interaction, hidden issues are sometimes raised that would not have been detected in an individual interview. The skill of the group leader in stimulating discussion is crucial to the success of a focus group. Focus groups, like in-depth interviews, do not provide statistically significant information; however, they can be helpful in providing information about perceptions, emotions, and attitudinal factors. In addition, once individuals have been gathered, focus groups are a highly efficient means of rapidly accumulating a substantial amount of information.

When planning international research using focus groups, the researcher must be aware of the importance of language and culture in the interaction process. Major differences may exist already in preparing for the focus group. In some countries, participants can simply be asked to show up at a later date at a location where they will join the focus group. In other countries, participants have to be brought into the group immediately because commitments made for a future date have little meaning. In some nations, providing a payment to participants is sufficient motivation for them to open up in discussion. In other countries, one first needs to host a luncheon or dinner for the group so that members get to know each other and are willing to interact.

Once the focus group is started, the researcher must remember that not all societies encourage frank and open exchange and disagreement among individuals. Status consciousness may result in the opinion of one participant being reflected by all others. Disagreement may be seen as impolite, or certain topics may be taboo. Unless a native focus group leader is used, it also is possible to completely misread the interactions among group participants and to miss out on nuances and constraints participants feel when commenting in the group situation. One of this book's authors, for example, used the term *group discussion* in a focus group with Russian executives, only to learn that the translated meaning of the term was *political indoctrination session*.[6]

**Observation** requires the researcher to play the role of a nonparticipating observer of activity and behavior. In an international setting, observation can be extremely useful in shedding light on practices not previously encountered or understood. This aspect is especially valuable to the researcher who has no knowledge of a particular market or market situation. It can help in understanding phenomena that would have been difficult to assess with other techniques. For example, Toyota sent a group of its engineers and designers to southern California to nonchalantly observe how women get into and operate their cars. They found that women with long fingernails have trouble opening the door and operating various knobs on the dashboard. Toyota engineers and designers were able to comprehend the women's plight and redesign some of their automobile exteriors and interiors, producing more desirable cars.[7]

All the research instruments discussed so far are useful primarily for the gathering of qualitative information. The intent is not to amass data or to search for statistical significance, but rather to obtain a better understanding of given situations, behavioral patterns, or underlying dimensions. The researcher using these instruments must be cautioned that even frequent repetition of the measurements will not lead to a statistically valid result. However, statistical validity often may not be the major focus of corporate research. Rather, it may be the better understanding, description, and prediction of events that have an impact on decision making. When quantitative data are desired, surveys, and experimentation are more appropriate research instruments.

**Surveys**   Survey research is useful in quantifying concepts. In the social sciences, it is generally accepted that the cross-cultural survey is scientifically the most powerful method of hypothesis testing.[8] **Surveys** are usually conducted via questionnaires that are administered personally, by mail, or by telephone. Use of the survey technique presupposes that the population under study is accessible and able to comprehend and respond to the question posed through the chosen medium. As Global Perspective 10.3 shows, this may not always be the case. Particularly for mail and telephone surveys, a major precondition is the feasibility of using the postal system or the widespread availability of telephones. Obviously, this is not a given in all countries. In many nations only limited records about dwellings, their location, and their occupants are available. In Venezuela, for example, most houses are not numbered but rather are given individual names such as Casa Rosa or El Retiro. In some countries, street maps are not even available. As a result, reaching respondents by mail is virtually impossible. In other countries, obtaining a correct address may be easy, but the postal system may not function well.

Telephone surveys may also be inappropriate if telephone ownership is rare. In such instances, any information obtained would be highly biased even if the researcher randomized the calls. In some cases, inadequate telephone networks and systems, frequent line congestion, and a lack of telephone directories may also prevent the researcher from conducting surveys.

Since surveys deal with people who in an international setting display major differences in culture, preference, education, and attitude, just to mention a few factors, the use of the survey technique must be carefully examined. For example, in some regions of the world, recipients of letters may be illiterate. Others may be very literate, but totally unaccustomed to some of the standard research scaling techniques used in the United States and therefore may be unable to respond to the instrument. Other recipients of a survey may be reluctant to respond in writing, particularly when sensitive questions are asked. This sensitivity, of course, also varies by country. In some nations, any questions about income, even in categorical form, are considered highly proprietary; in others the purchasing behavior of individuals is not readily divulged.

The researcher needs to understand such constraints and prepare a survey that is responsive to them. For example, surveys can incorporate drawings or even cartoons to communicate better. Personal administration or collaboration with locally accepted intermediaries may improve the response rate. Indirect questions may need to substitute for direct ones in sensitive areas. Questions may have to be reworded to ensure proper communication. Figure 10.4 provides an example of a rating scale developed by researchers to work with a diverse population with relatively little education. In its use, however, it was

## MARKET RESEARCH IN RUSSIA

**W**estern firms can spend years of frustration and mistakes trying to navigate the often chaotic markets of economies in transition. Market research companies can often help steer them back on track by giving valuable insight into market characteristics and customer tastes. Exporters operating in Russia are finding market researchers crucial to solving the riddle of Russian economic activity and consumer preferences. Reporting on even basic facts about the Russian economy is murky, so market research firms in Russia work to establish reliable databases on everything from the number of firms operating in a given area to apartment sales.

Market research companies in Russia are filling the gap between academic research and conventional wisdom about Russian businesses. For example, a statement widely reported by economists claims that official Russian statistics understate the rapid growth of the economy by not counting small service-sector companies the elude tax authorities. These academics claim there are 300,000 private commercial companies in Moscow. But one market research firm, Mobile, found that only 8,000 of the companies in Moscow actually advertise or do business, indicating that tax avoidance gives the impression of more private commercial activity than exists in reality. This firm also uses electricity consumption data to measure production and consumption in different regions.

Mobile's analysis of apartment sales in Moscow helped one supermarket chain determine where to locate its three next outlets. The client found the Mobile study that broke down apartment sales by metro station particularly useful, finding that the most profitable sales occurred around a few central metro stations. Other services offered by Mobile include tracking product sales and polling dealers. Out of their databases, Mobile analysts produce weekly bulletins summarizing the markets for computers, home appliances, office equipment, real estate, medicine, and construction. Major Mobile clients include Apple, Matsushita, Samsung, Daewoo, Hitachi, Philips, Sharp, Canon, Rank Xerox, and Deloitte & Touche.

Russian Market Research Co. is another firm that helps Western exporters understand the Russian market. The firm's director, Greg Thain, believes that a major difficulty facing market researchers in Russia is the lack of understanding of basic business concepts among Russians. This creates problems in training interviewers and even in interpreting survey results. Thain emphasized the need to find market researchers with a Western understanding of sales and marketing problems.

Product research can clear away other more basic obstacles to doing business in Russia. For instance, Russian Market Research Co. tested U.S.–made mayonnaise with Russian focus groups. Their difficulties in translating the concept of American mayonnaise in a country where mayonnaise is a cream used in apple pie and in soups, not just in salads, alerted Western manufacturers to the need to reformulate their mixtures in the Russian market.

Whether the problem facing Western exporters in Russia is a matter of determining consumer tastes, tracking sales, or exploring investment possibilities in a region, market research firms can help solve the puzzle of a market in the country Winston Churchill once described as "a riddle wrapped in a mystery inside an enigma."

*Source: John Helmer, "The Russian Riddle,"* **The Journal of Commerce** *April 30, 1997: 1C, 27C.*

found that the same scale aroused negative reactions among better-educated respondents, who considered the scale childish and insulting to their intelligence.

In spite of all the potential difficulties, the survey technique remains a useful one because it allows the researcher to rapidly accumulate a large quantity of data amenable to statistical analysis. With constantly expanding technological capabilities, international researchers will be able to use this technique even more in the future.

**Experimentation**   Experimental techniques determine the effect of an intervening variable and help establish precise cause-and-effect relationships. However, **experimentation** is difficult to implement in international research. The researcher faces the task of designing an experiment in which most variables are held constant or are comparable across cultures. For example, an experiment to determine a causal effect within the distribution system of one coun-

**FIGURE 10.4**

**The Funny Faces Scale**

*Source:* C. K. Corder, "Problems and Pitfalls in Conducting Marketing Research in Africa," *Marketing Expansion in a Shrinking World,* ed. Betsy Gelb. Proceedings of American Marketing Association Business Conference (Chicago: AMA, 1978), pp. 86–90.

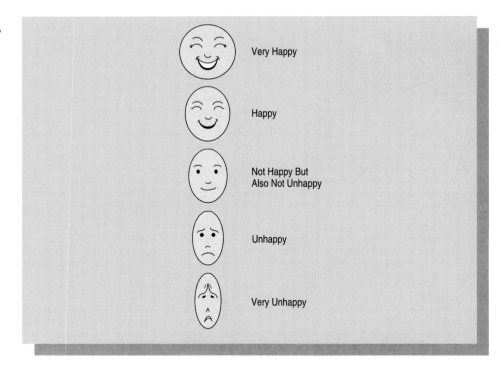

try may be very difficult to transfer to another country because the distribution system may be quite different. For this reason, experimental techniques are only rarely used, even though their potential value to the international researcher is recognized.

## The International Information System

Many organizations have data needs that go beyond specific international research projects. Most of the time, daily decisions must be made for which there is neither time nor money for special research. An **information system** can provide the decision maker with basic data for most ongoing decisions. Defined as "the systematic and continuous gathering, analysis, and reporting of data for decision-making purposes,"[9] such a system serves as a mechanism to coordinate the flow of information to corporate managers.

To be useful to the decision maker, the system must have certain attributes. First of all, the information must be *relevant*. The data gathered must have meaning for the manager's decision-making process. Only rarely can corporations afford to spend large amounts of money on information that is simply "nice to know." Any information system will have to continuously address the balance to be struck between the expense of the research design and process and the value of the information to ongoing business activities. Second, the information must be *timely*. Managers derive little benefit if decision information needed today does not become available until a month from now. To be of use to the international decision maker, the system must therefore feed from a variety of international sources and be updated frequently. For multinational corporations, this means a real-time linkage between international subsidiaries and a broad-based ongoing data input operation. Third, information must be *flexible*—that is, it must be available in the form needed by management. An information system must therefore permit manipulation of the format and combination of the data. Fourth, information contained in the system must be *accurate*. This is especially important in international research because information quickly becomes outdated as a result of major environmental changes. Fifth, the system's information bank must be reasonably *exhaustive*. Factors that may influence a particular decision must be appropriately represented in the information system because of the interrelationships among variables. This means that the information system must be based on a wide variety of factors. Sixth, the collection and processing of data must be *consistent*. This is to hold down project cost and turnaround time, while ensuring that data can be compared regionally. This can be achieved by centralizing the management under one manager who oversees the system's design, processing, and analysis.[10] Finally, to be useful to managers, the system must be *convenient* to use. Systems that are cumbersome and time-consuming to reach and to use will not be used enough to justify corporate expenditures to build and maintain them.

One area where international firms are gradually increasing the use of information system technology is in the export field. In order to stay close to their customers, proactive firms are developing **export complaint systems.** These systems allow customers to contact the original supplier of a product in order to inquire about products, to make suggestions, or to present complaints. Firms are finding that about 5 percent of their customers abroad are dissatisfied with the product. By establishing direct contact via E–mail, a toll-free telephone number, or a web site, firms do not need to rely on the filtered feedback from channel intermediaries abroad and can learn directly about product failures, channel problems, or other causes of customer dissatisfaction. The development of such an export complaint system requires substantial resources, intensive planning, and a high degree of cultural sensitivity. Customers abroad must be informed of how to complain, and their cost of complaining must be minimized, for example, by offering an interactive web site. The response to complaints must also be tailored to the culture of the complainant. For example, to some customers, the speed of reply matters most, while to others the thoughtfulness of the reply is of key concern. As a result, substantial resources must be invested into personnel training so the system works in harmony with customer expectations. Most important, however, is a firm's ability to aggregate and analyze complaints and to make use of them internally. Complaints are often the symptom for underlying structural problems of a product or a process. If used properly, an export complaint system can become a rich source of information for product improvement and innovation.

To build an information system, corporations use the internal data that are available from divisions such as accounting and finance and also from various subsidiaries. In addition, many organizations put mechanisms in place to enrich the basic data flow to information systems. Three such mechanisms are environmental scanning, Delphi studies, and scenario building.

**Environmental Scanning** Any changes in the business environment, whether domestic or foreign, may have serious repercussions on the activities of the firm. Corporations therefore understand the necessity for tracking new developments. Although this can be done implicitly in the domestic environment, the remoteness of international markets requires a continuous information flow. For this purpose, some large multinational organizations have formed environmental scanning groups.

**Environmental scanning** activities provide continuous information on political, social, and economic affairs internationally; on changes of attitudes of public institutions and private citizens; and on possible upcoming alterations. Environmental scanning models can be used for a variety of purposes, ranging from the development of long-term strategies and getting managers to broaden their horizons to the structure of action plans. Obviously, the precision required for environmental scanning varies with its purpose. The more immediate and precise the application will be within the corporation, the greater the need for detailed information. On the other hand, heightened precision may reduce the usefulness of environmental scanning in strategic planning, which is long term.

Environmental scanning can be performed in various ways. One consists of obtaining factual input on a wide variety of demographic, social, and economic characteristics of foreign countries. Frequently, managers believe that factual data alone are insufficient for their information needs. Particularly when forecasting future developments, other methods are used to capture underlying dimensions of social change. One significant method is that of media analysis. A wide array of newspapers, magazines, and other publications are scanned worldwide in order to pinpoint over time the gradual evolution of new views or trends. Corporations also use the technique of media analysis to pinpoint upcoming changes in their line of business. For example, the Alaskan oil spill by the Exxon *Valdez* and the rash of oil spills that followed resulted in entirely new international concern about environmental protection and safety, reaching far beyond the actual incidents and participants.

With the current heightened awareness of environmental and ethical issues such as pollution, preservation of natural resources, and animal testing, firms are increasingly looking for new opportunities to expand their operations while remaining within changing moral and environmental boundaries.

Environmental scanning is conducted by a variety of groups within and outside the corporation. Quite frequently, small corporate staffs are created at headquarters to coordinate the information flow. In addition, subsidiary staff can be used to provide occasional intelligence reports. Groups of volunteers are also formed to gather and analyze information worldwide and feed their individual analyses back to corporate headquarters, where the "big picture" can then be constructed. Rapidly growing use of the Internet also allows firms to find out about new developments in their fields of interests and permits them to gather information through bulletin boards and discussion groups. For example, some firms use search engines to comb through thousands of newsgroups for any mention of a particular product or application. If they find frequent references, they can investigate further to see what customers are saying.[11]

**Delphi Studies**   To enrich the information obtained from factual data, corporations and governments frequently resort to the use of creative and highly qualitative data-gathering methods. One approach is through **Delphi studies.**

These studies are particularly useful in the international environment because they are "a means for aggregating the judgments of a number of . . . experts . . . who cannot come together physically."[12] This type of research clearly aims at qualitative measures by seeking a consensus from those who know, rather than average responses from many people with only limited knowledge.

Typically, Delphi studies are carried out with groups of about thirty well-chosen participants who possess expertise in an area of concern, such as future developments of the international trade environment. The participants are asked to identify the major issues in the given area of concern. They are also requested to rank order their statements according to importance and explain the rationale behind the order. The aggregated information and comments are then sent to all participants in the Delphi group. Group members are encouraged to agree or disagree with the various rank orders and the comments. This allows statements to be challenged. In another round, the participants respond to the challenges. Several rounds of challenges and responses result in a reasonably coherent consensus.

The Delphi technique is particularly valuable because it uses mail, facsimile, or electronic communication to bridge large distances and therefore makes experts quite accessible at a reasonable cost. It avoids the drawback of ordinary mail investigations, which lack interaction among participants. Several rounds may be required, however, so substantial time may elapse before the information is obtained. Also, a major effort must be expended in selecting the appropriate participants and in motivating them to participate in the exercise with enthusiasm and continuity. When carried out on a regular basis, Delphi studies can provide crucial augmentation of the factual data available for the information system. For example, a large portion of this book's last chapter was written based on an extensive Delphi study carried out by the authors.

**Scenario Building**   The information obtained through environmental scanning or Delphi studies can then be used to conduct a scenario analysis. One approach involves the development of a series of plausible scenarios that are constructed from trends observed in the environment. Another method consists of formally reviewing assumptions built into existing business plans and positions.[13] Subsequently, some of these key assumptions such as economic growth rates, import penetration, population growth, and political stability, can be varied. By projecting variations for medium- to long-term periods, completely new environmental conditions can emerge. The conditions can then be analyzed for their potential domestic and international impact on corporate strategy.

The identification of crucial variables and the degree of variation are of major importance in **scenario building**. Scenario builders also need to recognize the nonlinearity of factors. To simply extrapolate from currently existing situations is insufficient, since extraneous factors often enter the picture with significant impact. The possibility of **joint occurrences** must be recognized as well, because changes may not come about in isolated fashion but instead may spread over wide regions. For example, given large technological advances, the possibility of wholesale obsolescence of current technology must be considered. Quantum leaps in computer development and new generations of computers may render obsolete the entire technological investment of a corporation.

For scenarios to be useful, management must analyze and respond to them by formulating contingency plans. Such planning will broaden horizons and may prepare managers for unexpected situations. Through the anticipation of possible problems, managers hone their response capability and in turn shorten response times to actual problems.

The development of an international information system is of major importance to the multinational corporation. It aids the ongoing decision process and becomes a vital tool in performing the strategic planning task. Only by observing global trends and changes will the firm be able to maintain and improve its competitive position. Much of the data available are quantitative in nature, but researchers must also pay attention to qualitative dimensions. Quantitative analysis will continue to improve as the ability to collect, store, analyze, and retrieve data increases as a result of computer development. Nevertheless, the qualitative dimension will remain a major component for corporate research and planning activities.

## Summary

Constraints of time, resources, and expertise are the major inhibitors to international research. Nevertheless, firms need to carry out planned and organized research in order to explore foreign market opportunities and challenges successfully. Such research must be linked closely to the decision-making process.

International research differs from domestic research in that the environment—which determines how well tools, techniques, and concepts apply—is different abroad. In addition, the international manager must deal with duties, exchange rates, and international documentation; a greater number of interacting factors; and a much broader definition of the concept of competition.

When the firm is uninformed about international differences in consumer tastes and preferences or about foreign market environments, the need for international research is particularly great. Research objectives need to be determined based on the corporate mission, the level of international expertise, and the business plan. These objectives will enable the research to identify the information requirements.

Given the scarcity of resources, companies beginning their international effort must rely on data that have already been collected. These secondary data are available from sources such as governments, international organizations, directors, or trade associations.

To fulfill specific information requirements, the researcher may need to collect primary data. An appropriate research technique must be selected to collect the information. Sensitivity to different international environments and cultures will aid the researcher in deciding whether to use interviews, focus groups, observation, surveys, or experimentation as data-collection techniques.

To provide ongoing information to management, an information system is useful. Such a system will provide for the continuous gathering, analysis, and reporting of data for decision-making purposes. Data gathered through environmental scanning, Delphi studies, or scenario building enable management to prepare for the future and hone its decision-making abilities.

## Key Terms and Concepts

| | | |
|---|---|---|
| competitive assessment | focus groups | environmental scanning |
| secondary data | observation | export complaint systems |
| proxy information | surveys | Delphi studies |
| primary data | experimentation | scenario building |
| interviews | information system | joint occurrence |

## Questions for Discussion

1. What is the difference between domestic and international research?
2. You are employed by National Engineering, a firm that designs subways. Because you have had a course in international business, your boss asks you to spend the next week exploring international possibilities for the company. How will you go about this task?
3. Discuss the possible shortcomings of secondary data.
4. Why should a firm collect primary data in its international research?
5. Of all the OECD countries, which one(s) derives the largest share of its GDP from the services sector? from agriculture? from industry? (these figures can be downloaded from the OECD in Figures on the site **www. oecd.org**).
6. What are the top ten trading partners for the United States? What was the U.S.'s top commodity import from France? What was the U.S.'s top commodity export to Japan (use the U.S. Foreign Trade Highlights tables on the Department of Commerce's International Trade Administration site, **www.ita.doc.gov**)?
7. What are some of the products and services the World Bank offers to firms doing business in the developing world (refer to the World Bank's web page "Doing Business with the Bank," through **www.worldbank.org**)?
8. What are some of the economic trends in transition economies, according to the European Bank for Reconstruction and Development (refer to the "About the Region" section of its site, **www.ebrd.com**)?
9. To which group of countries are NAFTA members most likely to export (use the Inter-American Development Bank's exports tables under the "Research and Statistics" database section of its web page, **www.iadb.org**)?
10. What are the latest statistical news releases from the European Union EUROSTAT web page (see **http://europa.eu.int**)?

## Recommended Readings

Barbuta, Domenica M. *The International Financial Statistics Locator: A Research and Information Guide.* New York: Garland Publishers, 1995.

Churchill, Gilbert A., Jr. *Marketing Research: Methodological Foundations.* 7th ed. Fort Worth, Tex.: Dryden Press, 1999.

*Directory of Online Databases.* Santa Monica, Calif.: Cuadra Associates, published annually.

*GreenBook International Directory of Marketing Research Companies and Services.* New York: American Marketing Association, 1997. **www.greenbook.org**

Hassan, Salah S., and Roger D. Blackwell. *Global Marketing: Perspectives and Cases.* Fort Worth, Tex.: Dryden Press, 1994.

Palvia, Prashant, Anil Kumar, Nadesan Kumar, and Rebecca Hendon. "Information Requirements of a Global EIS: An Exploratory Macro Assessment." *Decisions Support Systems* 16, 2 (1996): 169–179.

Patzer, Gordon L. *Using Secondary Data in Marketing Research: United States and Worldwide.* Westport, Conn.: Quorum Books, 1995.

Schreiber, Mae N. *International Trade Sources: A Research Guide.* New York: Garland Publishers, 1997.

Zuckerman, Amy. *International Standards Desk Reference: Your Passport to World Markets, ISO 9000, CE Mark, QS-9000, SSM, ISO 14000, Q 9000 American, European, and Global Standards Systems.* New York: American Management Association, 1997.

## Notes

1. David A. Ricks, *Blunders in International Business* (Cambridge, Mass.: Blackwell, 1993).
2. Peter D. Moore, "Looking Ahead: The Information Age Has a Flip Side," *The Los Angeles Times,* May 2, 1990.
3. Bernard Ancel and Sonia Srivastava, "Market Information at Your Fingertips," *International Trade Forum* (April 1993): 12–17.
4. "National Trade Data Bank," Government Documents Department: Lauinger Library, Georgetown University, 1998.
5. Ricks, *Blunders in International Business,* 134.
6. Michael R. Czinkota, "Russia's Transition to a Market Economy: Learning about Business," *Journal of International Marketing* 5, 4 (Fall, 1997): 73–93.
7. Michael R. Czinkota and Masaaki Kotabe, "Product Development the Japanese Way," in M. Czinkota and M. Kotabe, *Trends in International Business: Critical Perspectives* (Oxford: Blackwell Publishers, 1998), 153–158.
8. Lothar G. Winter and Charles R. Prohaska, "Methodological Problems in the Comparative Analysis of International Marketing Systems," *Journal of the Academy of Marketing Science* 11 (Fall 1983): 421.
9. Thomas C. Kinnear and James R. Taylor, *Marketing Research: An Applied Approach,* 5th ed. (New York: McGraw-Hill, 1996).
10. Joseph Marinelli and Anastasia Schleck, "Collecting, Processing Data for Marketing Research Worldwide," *Marketing News* 31, 17 (August 18, 1997): 12, 14.
11. David A. Andelman, "Betting on the Net." *Sales and Marketing Management* (June 1995): 47–59.
12. Andrel Delbecq, Andrew H. Van de Ven, and David H. Gustafson, *Group Techniques for Program Planning* (Glenview, Ill.: Scott Foresman, 1975), 83.
13. William H. Davidson, "The Role of Global Scanning in Business Planning," *Organizational Dynamics* (Winter 1991): 5–16.

A P P E N D I X  **10A**

# Monitors of International Issues

## Selected Organizations

- **American Bankers Association**
  1120 Connecticut Avenue NW
  Washington, DC 20036
  www.aba.com
- **American Bar Association**
  750 N. Lake Shore Drive
  Chicago, IL 60611
  *and*
  1800 M Street NW
  Washington, DC 20036
  www.abanet.org/intlaw/home
  .html
- **American Management Association**
  440 First Street NW
  Washington, DC 20001
  www.amanet.org
- **American Marketing Association**
  250 S. Wacker Drive Suite 200
  Chicago, IL 60606
  http://ama.org
- **American Petroleum Institute**
  1220 L Street NW
  Washington, DC 20005
  www.api.org
- **Asia-Pacific Economic Cooperation**
  Secretariat
  438 Alexandra Road
  #14-00, Alexandra Road
  Singapore 119958
  www.apecsec.org.sg
- **Asian Development Bank**
  2330 Roxas Boulevard
  Pasay City, Philippines
  www.asiandevbank.org

- **Association of South East Asian Nations (ASEAN)**
  Publication Office
  c/o The ASEAN Secretariat
  70A, Jalan Sisingamangaraja
  Jakarta 11210
  Indonesia
  www.asean.or.id
- **Chamber of Commerce of the United States**
  1615 H Street NW
  Washington, DC 20062
  www.uschamber.org
- **Commission of the European Communities to the United States**
  2100 M Street NW
  Suite 707
  Washington, DC 20037
- **Conference Board**
  845 Third Avenue
  New York, NY 10022
  *and*
  1755 Massachusetts Avenue
  NW Suite 312
  Washington, DC 20036
  www.conference-board.org
- **Deutsche Bundesbank**
  Wilhelm-Epstein-Str. 14
  P.O.B. 10 06 02
  D-60006 Franfurt am Main
  www.bundesbank.de
- **Electronic Industries Association**
  2001 Pennsylvania Avenue
  NW
  Washington, DC 20004
  www.eia.org

- **European Bank for Reconstruction and Development**
  One Exchange Square
  London EC2A 2EH
  United Kingdom
  www.ebrd.com
- **European Union**
  200 Rue de la Lio
  1049 Brussels, Belgium
  *and*
  2100 M Street NW 7th Floor
  Washington, DC 20037
- **Export-Import Bank of the United States**
  811 Vermont Avenue NW
  Washington, DC 20571
  www.exim.gov
- **Federal Reserve Bank of New York**
  33 Liberty Street
  New York, NY 10045
  www.ny.frb.org
- **Inter-American Development Bank**
  1300 New York Avenue NW
  Washington, DC 20577
  www.iadb.org
- **International Bank for Reconstruction and Development (World Bank)**
  1818 H Street NW
  Washington, DC 20433
  www.worldbank.org
- **International Monetary Fund**
  700 19th Street NW
  Washington, DC 20431
  www.imf.org

■ **International Telecommunication Union**
Place des Nations
Ch-1211 Geneva 20
Switzerland
**http://info.itu.int**

■ **Marketing Research Society**
111 E. Wacker Drive Suite 600
Chicago, IL 60601

■ **National Association of Manufacturers**
1331 Pennsylvania Avenue
Suite 1500
Washington, DC 20004
**www.nam.org**

■ **National Federation of Independent Business**
600 Maryland Avenue SW
Suite 700
Washington, DC 20024
**www.nfib.org**

■ **Organization for Economic Cooperation and Development**
2 rue Andre Pascal
75775 Paris Cedex Ko, France
*and*
2001 L Street NW Suite 700
Washington, DC 20036
**www.oecd.org**

■ **Organization of American States**
17th and Constitution Avenue NW
Washington, DC 20006
**www.oas.org**

■ **Society for International Development**
1401 New York Avenue NW
Suite 1100
Washington, DC 20005
**www.aed.org/sid**

■ **Transparency International**
Otto-Suhr-Allee 97-99
D-10585 Berlin / Germany
**www.transparency.de**

■ **World Trade Centers Association**
1 World Trade Center Suite 7701
New York, NY 10048
**www.wtca.org**

## European Union

■ **Europa**
The umbrella server for all institutions
**http://europa.eu.int**

■ **ISPO (Information Society Project Office)**
Information on telecommunications and information market developments
**http://www.ispo.cec.be**

■ **I'M – EUROPE**
Information on telematics, telecommunications, copyright, IMPACT program for the information market
**http://www2.echo.lu**

■ **CORDIS**
Information on EU research programs
**http://www.cordis.lu**

■ **EUROPARL**
Information on the European Parliament's activities
**http://europarl.eu.int**

■ **Delegation of the European Commission to the US**
Press releases, EURECOM: Economic and Financial News, EU-US relations, information on EU policies and Delegation programs
**http://www.eurunion.org**

■ **Citizens Europe**
Covers rights of citizens of EU member states
**http://citizens.eu.int**

■ **EUDOR (European Union Document Repository)**
Bibliographic database
**http://www.eudor.com**

■ **Euro**
The Single Currency
**http://euro.eu.int**

■ **European Agency for the Evaluation of Medicinal Products**
Information on drug approval procedures and documents of the Committee for Proprietary Medicinal Products and the Committee for Veterinary Medicinal Products
**http://www.eudra.org/emea.html**

■ **European Centre for the Development of Vocational Training**
Under construction, with basic information on the Centre and contact information
**http://www.cedefop.gr**

■ **European Environment Agency**
Information on the mission, products and services, and organizations and staff of the EEA
**http://www.eea.dk**

■ **European Investment Bank**
Press releases and information on borrowing and loan operations, staff, and publications
**http://www.eib.org**

■ **European Monetary Institute**
Related Treaty provisions setting up the Institute, rules of procedure, function and staff, list of publications
**http://europa.eu.int/emi/emi.html**

■ **European Training Foundation**
Information on vocational education and training programs in Central and Eastern Europe and Central Asia
**http://www.etf.it**

■ **Office for Harmonization in the Internal Market**
Guidelines, application forms, and other information related to registering an EU trademark
**http://europa.eu.int/agencies/ohim/ohim.htm**

■ **Council of the European Union**
Information and news from the Council, with sections

covering Common Foreign and Security Policy (CFSP) and Justice and Home Affairs; under construction
http://ue.eu.int

- **Court of Justice**
Overview, press releases, publications, and full-text proceedings of the Court; full text coverage of recent case-law is planned
http://europa.eu.int/cj/en/index.htm

- **Court of Auditors**
Information notes, annual reports, and other publications
http://www.eca.eu.int

## United Nations
www.un.org

- **Conference of Trade and Development**
Palais des Nations
1211 Geneva 10
Switzerland
www.unicc.unctad.org

- **Department of Economic and Social Affairs**
1 United Nations Plaza
New York, NY 10017
www.un.org/ecosocdev/

- **Industrial Development Organization**
1660 L Street NW
Washington, DC 20036
*and*
Post Office Box 300
Vienna International Center
A-1400 Vienna, Austria
www.unido.org

- **UN Publications**
Room 1194
1 United Nations Plaza
New York, NY 10017
www.un.org/pubs/

- **Statistical Yearbook**
1 United Nations Plaza
New York, NY 10017

## Indexes to Literature

- **Business Periodical Index**
H.W. Wilson Co.
950 University Avenue
Bronx, NY 10452

- **New York Times Index**
University Microfilms
International
300 N. Zeeb Road
Ann Arbor, MI 48106
http://www.nytimes.com

- **Public Affairs Information Service Bulletin**
11 W. 40th Street
New York, NY 10018
http://www.pais.internet

- **Reader's Guide to Periodical Literature**
H.W. Wilson Co.
950 University Avenue
Bronx, NY 10452
http://www.tulane.edu/~horn.rdg.html

- **Wall Street Journal Index**
University Microfilms
International
300 N. Zeeb Road
Ann Arbor, MI 48106
http://www/wsj.com

## Directories

- **American Register of Exporters and Importers**
38 Park Row
New York, NY 10038

- **Arabian Year Book**
Dar Al-Seuassam Est. Box 42480
Shuwahk, Kuwait

- **Directories of American Firms Operating in Foreign Countries**
World Trade Academy Press
Uniworld Business
Publications Inc.
50 E. 42nd Street
New York, NY 10017

- **The Directory of International Sources of Business Information**

Pitman
128 Long Acre
London, WC2E 9AN,
England

- **Encyclopedia of Associations**
Gale Research Co.
Book Tower
Detroit, MI 48226

- **Polk's World Bank Directory**
R.C. Polk & Co.
2001 Elm Hill Pike
P.O. Box 1340
Nashville, TN 37202

- **Verified Directory of Manufacturer's Representatives**
MacRae's Blue Book Inc.
817 Broadway
New York, NY 10003

- **World Guide to Trade Associations**
K.G. Saur & Co.
175 Fifth Avenue
New York, NY 10010

## Encyclopedias, Handbooks, and Miscellaneous

- **A Basic Guide to Exporting**
U.S. Government Printing
Office
Superintendent of
Documents
Washington, DC 20402

- **Doing business in . . . Series**
Price Waterhouse
1251 Avenue of the Americas
New York, NY 10020

- **Economic Survey of Europe**
The United Nations
United Nations
Publishing Division
1 United Nations Plaza
Room DC2-0853
New York, NY 10017

■ **Economic Survey of Latin America**
United Nations
United Nations
Publishing Division
1 United Nations Plaza
Room DC2-0853
New York, NY 10017

■ **Encyclopedia Americana, International Edition**
Grolier Inc.
Danbury, CT 06816

■ **Encyclopedia of Business Information Sources**
Gale Research Co.
Book Tower
Detroit, MI 48226

■ **Europa Year Book**
Europa Publications Ltd.
18 Bedford Square
London WC1B 3JN, England

■ **Export Administration Regulations**
U.S. Government
Printing Office
Superintendent of Documents
Washington, D.C. 20402

■ **Exporters' Encyclopedia– World Marketing Guide**
Dun's Marketing Services
49 Old Bloomfield Rd.
Mountain Lake, NJ 07046

■ **Export-Import Bank of the United States Annual Report**
U.S. Government
Printing Office
Superintendent of Documents
Washington, D.C. 20402

■ **Exporting for the Small Business**
U.S. Government
Printing Office
Superintendent of Documents
Washington, D.C. 20402

■ **Exporting to the United States**
U.S. Government
Printing Office
Superintendent of Documents
Washington, D.C. 20402
Export Shipping Manual

■ **U.S. Government Printing Office**
Superintendent of Documents
Washington, D.C. 20402

■ **Foreign Business Practices: Materials on Practical Aspects of Exporting, International Licensing, and Investing**
U.S. Government
Printing Office
Superintendent of Documents
Washington, D.C. 20402

■ **A Guide to Financing Exports**
U.S. Government Printing
Office
Superintendent of Documents
Washington, D.C. 20402

■ **Handbook of Marketing Research**
McGraw-Hill Book Co.
1221 Avenue of the Americas
New York, NY 10020

## Periodic Reports, Newspapers, Magazines

■ **Advertising Age**
Crain Communications Inc.
740 N. Rush Street
Chicago, IL 60611
http://www.adage.com

■ **Advertising World**
Directories International Inc.
150 Fifth Avenue Suite 610
New York, NY 10011

■ **Arab Report and Record**
84 Chancery Lane
London WC2A 1DL, England

■ **Barron's**
University Microfilms
International
300 N. Zeeb Road
Ann Arbor, MI 48106
http://www.barrons.com

■ **Business America**
U.S. Department
of Commerce
14th Street and Constitution
Avenue N.W.
Washington, D.C. 20230

■ **Business International**
Business International Corp.
One Dag Hammarskjold Plaza
New York, NY 10017

■ **Business Week**
McGraw-Hill Publications Co.
1221 Avenue of the Americas
New York, NY 10020
http://www.businessweek.com

■ **Commodity Trade Statistics**
United Nations Publications
1 United Nations Plaza
Room DC2-0853
New York, NY 10017

■ **Conference Board Record**
Conference Board Inc.
845 Third Avenue
New York, NY 10022

■ **Customs Bulletin**
U.S. Customs Service
1301 Constitution
Avenue N.W.
Washington, D.C. 20229

■ **Dun's Business Month**
Goldhirsh Group
38 Commercial Wharf
Boston, MA 02109

■ **The Economist**
Economist Newspaper Ltd.
25 St. James Street
London SW1A 1HG, England
http://www.economist.com

■ **Europe Magazine**
2100 M Street N.W. Suite 707
Washington, D.C. 20037

■ **The Financial Times**
Bracken House
10 Cannon Street
London EC4P 4BY, England
http://www.ft-se.co.uk

■ **Forbes**
Forbes, Inc.
60 Fifth Avenue
New York, NY 10011
http://www.forbes.com

■ **Fortune**
Time, Inc.
Time & Life Building
1271 Avenue of the Americas

New York, NY 10020
**http://pathfinder.com/fortune**
■ **Global Trade**
North American Publishing
Co.
401 N. Broad Street
Philadelphia, PA 19108
■ **Industrial Marketing**
Crain Communications, Inc.
740 N. Rush Street
Chicago, IL 60611
■ **International Financial
Statistics**
International Monetary Fund
Publications Unit
700 19th Street N.W.
Washington, D.C. 20431
**http://www.imf.com**
■ **Investor's Daily**
Box 25970
Los Angeles, CA 90025
Journal of Commerce
110 Wall Street
New York, NY 10005
■ **Sales and Marketing
Management**
Bill Communications Inc.
633 Third Avenue
New York, NY 10017
■ **Wall Street Journal**
Dow Jones & Company
200 Liberty Street
New York, NY 10281
**http://www.wsj.com**
■ **World Agriculture Situation**
U.S. Department of
Agriculture
Economics Management Staff
**http://www.econ.ag.gov**
■ **Pergamon Press Inc.**
Journals Division
Maxwell House
Fairview Park
Elmsford, NY 10523
■ **World Trade Center
Association (WTCA) Directory**
World Trade Centers
Association
1 World Trade Center
New York, NY 10048

■ **International Encyclopedia of
the Social Sciences**
Macmillan and the Free Press
866 Third Avenue
New York, NY 10022
■ **Marketing and
Communications Media
Dictionary**
Media Horizons Inc.
50 W. 25th Street
New York, NY 10010
■ **Market Share Reports**
U.S. Government
Printing Office
Superintendent of Documents
Washingon, D.C. 20402
■ **Media Guide International:
Business/Professional
Publications**
Directories International Inc.
150 Fifth Avenue Suite 610
New York, NY 10011
■ **Overseas Business Reports**
U.S. Government
Printing Office
Superintendent of Documents
Washington, D.C. 20402
■ **Trade Finance**
U.S. Department of Commerce
International Trade
Administration
Washington, D.C. 20230
■ **World Economic Conditions in
Relation to Agricultural Trade**
U.S. Government Printing
Office
Superintendent of Documents
Washington, D.C. 20402
■ **Yearbook of International
Trade Statistics**
United Nations
United Nations
Publishing Division
1 United Nations Plaza
Room DC2-0853
New York, NY 10017

## Selected Trade Databases[1]
**News agencies**
Comline—Japan Newswire*

Dow Jones News
Nikkei Shimbun News
Database Omninews
Reuters Monitor
UPI
**Trade publication references with
bibliographic keywords**
Agris*
Biocommerce Abstracts &
Directory
Findex
Frost {short} Sullivan Market
Research Reports
Marketing Surveys Index
McCarthy Press Cuttings Service
Paperchem
PTS F & S Indexes*
Trade and Industry Index*
**Trade publication references with
summaries**
ABI/Inform*
Arab Information Bank
Asia-Pacific
BFAI
Biobusiness
CAB Abstracts*
Chemical Business Newsbase
Checmical Industry Notes
Caffeeline
Delphes
InfoSouth Latin American Infor-
mation System*
Management Contents
NTIS Bibliographic Data Base*
Paperchem
PIRA Abstract*
PSTA
PTS Marketing & Advertising
Reference Service
PTS Promt*Rapra Abstracts*
Textline
Trade & Industry ASAP
World Textiles

**Full text of trade publications**
Datamonitor Market Reports
Dow Jones News
Euromonitor Market Direction
Federal News Service*
Financial Times Business Report

File
Financial Times Fulltext*
Globefish
ICC Key Notes Market Research
Investext*
McCarthy Press Cuttings Service
PTS Promt*
Textline
Trade & Industry ASAP

**Satistics**
Agrostat (diskette only)
ARI Network/CNS
Arab Information Bank
Comext/Eurostat*
Comtrade
FAKT-German Statistics
Globefish
IMF Data
OECD Data
Piers Imports
PTS Forecasts
PTS Time Series
Reuters Monitor
Trade Statistics
Tradstat World Trade Statistics
TRAINS (CD-ROM being developed)
US I/E Maritime Bills of Lading
US Imports for Consumption
World Bank Statistics

**Price information**
ARI Network/CNS
Chemical Business Newsbase
COLEACP
Commodity Options
Commodities 2000

Market News Service of ITC
Nikkei Shimbun News Database
Reuters Monitor
UPI
US Wholesale Prices

**Company registers**
ABC Europe Production Europe*
Biocommerce Abstracts & Directory
CD-Export (CD-ROM only)
Cerved*Company Intelligence*
D&B Duns Market Identifiers (U.S.A.)
D&B European Marketing File
D&B Eastern Europe
Dun's Electronic Business Directory
Firmexport/Firmimport*
Hoppenstedt Austria*
Hoppenstedt Germany*
Hoppenstedt Benelux
Huco-Hungarian Companies
ICC Directory of Companies
Kompass Asia/Pacific
Kompass Europe (EKOD)*
Mexican Exporters/Importers
Piers Imports
Polu-Polish Companies
SDOE
Thomas Register*
TRAINS (CD-ROM being developed)
UK Importers
UK Importers (DECTA)
US Directory of Importers
US I/E Maritime Bills of Lading
World Trade Center Network

**Trade opportunities, tenders**
Business
Federal News Service
Huntech-Hungarian Technique
Scan-a-Bid
Tenders Electronic Daily
World Trade Center Network

**Tariffs and trade regulations**
Celex*
ECLAS
Justis Eastern Europe (CD-ROM only)
Scad*
Spearhead*
Spcers Centre for Europe
TRAINS (CD-ROM being developed)
US Code of Federal Regulations
US Federal Register
US Harmonized Tariff Schedule

**Standards**
BSI Standardline
Noriane/Perinorm*
NTIS Bibliographic Data base*
STandards Infodisk ILI (CD-ROM only)

**Shipping information**
Piers Imports
Tradstat World Trade Statistics
US I/E Maritime Billd of Lading

**Others**
Fairbase
Ibiscus

---

*Available on CD-ROM as well.
[1]International Trade FORUM, International Trade Centre. UNCTAD/GATT. April 1993, 15.

# Selected U.S. Government Publications and Services

## Macrodata

*World Population* is issued by the U.S. Bureau of the Census, which collects and analyzes worldwide demographic data. Information is provided about total population, fertility, mortality, urban population, growth rate, and life expectancy. Also published are detailed demographic profiles, including an analysis of the labor force structure of individual countries.

*Foreign Trade Highlights* are annual reports published by the Department of Commerce. They provide basic data on U.S. merchandise trade with major trading partners and regions. They also contain brief analyses of recent U.S. trade developments.

*Foreign Trade Report FT410* provides a monthly statistical record of shipments of all merchandise from the United States to foreign countries, including both the quantity and dollar value of exports to each country. It also contains cumulative export statistics from the first of the calendar year.

*World Agriculture,* a publication of the U.S. Department of Agriculture, provides production information, data, and analyses by country along with review of recent economic conditions and changes in agricultural and trade policies. Frequent supplements provide an outlook of anticipated developments for the coming year.

## Country Information

*National Trade Data Bank,* a key product of the U.S. Department of Commerce, provides monthly CD-ROM disks that contain overseas market research, trade statistics, contact information, and other reports that may assist U.S. exporters in their international marketing efforts.

*Country Commercial Guides* report on a particular country's commercial environment including economic, political, and market analysis.

*Industry SubSector Analyses* are market research reports, ranging from 5 to 20 pages, on specific product categories, for example, electromedical equipment in one country.

*Background Notes,* prepared by the Department of State, present a survey of a country's people, geography, economy, government, and foreign policy: The reports also include important national economic and trade information.

## Product Information

*Export Statistics Profiles* analyze exports for a single industry, product by product, country by country, over a five-year period. Data are rank-ordered by dollar value for quick identification of the leading products and industries. Tables show the sales of each product to each country as well as competitive information, growth, and future trends. Each profile also contains a narrative analysis that highlights the industry's prospects, performance, and leading products.

*SBA Automated Trade Locator Assistance System (SBAtlas),* available through the U.S. Small Business Administration, provides small businesses with product reports which rank the top 35 import and export markets for a particular good or service and country reports which identify the top 20 products most frequently traded in a target market.

## Services

*Agent Distributor Service (ADS):* The Foreign Commercial Service (FCS) provides a customized search for interested and qualified foreign representatives for a firm's product.

*Aglink:* Collaborative effort between the Foreign Agricultural Service and the Small Business Administration to match foreign buyers with U.S. agribusiness firms.

*Business Briefings and Technical Symposia:* The U.S. Trade and Development Agency sponsors technical seminars abroad designed to promote sales of sophisticated products and technology.

*Catalog Exhibitions:* The Department of Commerce organizes displays of product literature and videotape presentations overseas.

*Customized Market Analysis:* The FCS provides a custom foreign market survey on a product's overall marketability, names of competitors, comparative prices, and customary business practices.

*Economic Bulletin Board:* The Department of Commerce provides access to the latest economic data releases, including trade opportunities, for on-line users.

*Foreign Agricultural Service:* Employees of the U.S. Department of Agriculture, stationed both abroad and in the United States with the Mission to facilitate agricultural exports from the United States. Provides counseling, research, general market information, and market introduction services.

*International Buyer Program:* The FCS brings foreign buyers to U.S. trade shows for industries with high export potential.

*International Company Profile:* The FCS publishers background research conducted by FCS officers abroad on potential trading partners, such as agents, distributors, and licensees.

*Matchmaker Events:* The Department of Commerce introduces U.S. companies to new markets through short visits abroad to match the U.S. firm with a representative or prospective partner.

*Trade Missions:* Groups of U.S. business executives, led by Commerce Department staff, meet with potential foreign buyers, agents, and distributors.

*Trade Opportunity Program:* The FCS daily collection of trade opportunities worldwide is published and electronically distributed to subscribers.

For further information on U.S. Department of Commerce exporter assistance programs and trade information, contact them at 1-800-872-8223.

# CHAPTER 11

# International Business Entry

## LEARNING OBJECTIVES

◆ *To learn how firms gradually progress through an internationalization process*

◆ *To examine the differing reasons why firms internationalize*

◆ *To understand the strategic effects of internationalization on the firm*

◆ *To study the various modes of entering the international market*

◆ *To understand the role and functions of international intermediaries*

◆ *To learn about the opportunities and challenges of licensing and franchising*

## Cracking the Global Market Is No Piece of Cake

Increasingly, the place to do business is in the global market. Recent trends have ushered in an era of unprecedented export opportunities. The collapse of communism, the completion of NAFTA, the foundation of the World Trade Organization, and the embrace of freer markets by much of the developing world have all combined to push the growth of world trade to twice that of the world economy. For individual companies, exporting can translate into a more diversified stream of revenue, faster sales growth, and, of course, fatter profits. Workers benefit as well; wages for workers in jobs supported by merchandise exports are 20 percent higher than the national average. "Over time, you learn that the more people you can trade with, the more money you can make," suggests Abby Shapiro, head of International Strategies, Inc., an electronic publisher of global business information.

Sound too good to be true? Perhaps it is. The risks associated with exporting can be just as huge as the benefits. Fluctuating currencies, impenetrable cultures, faraway customers, delayed payments, and archaic business practices can torment the unseasoned exporter. "Small business sees the growth prospects outside the U.S., but the international market can burn and kill you in terms of cost," cautions Browing Rockwell, president of Horizon Trading Co., an international trading company based in Washington. "Just because the U.S. is part of the global economy doesn't mean all—or any—of the 200-plus countries in the world are interested in your products," adds Roger Prestwich, director of education at the Minnesota Trade office.

Even with good preparation and international know-how, going abroad can prove hazardous. The experience of Anthony A. Batarse Jr., a California auto dealer, illustrates the difficulties of going global. In 1992 he heard that the government of Cameroon was looking to buy 500 customized vehicles and a service center—a deal worth $24 million. Over the next few years, Batarse got financing from the Export-Import Bank, took out his savings, refinanced his home, and even checked the human rights record of Cameroon with Amnesty International. He sent engineers to Cameroon to start preliminary work on the service center and ordered the special cars from General Motors. The deal was killed however, when the State Department reversed its previous stand approving trade with Cameroon, citing Cameroon's poor credit record and the risk that the government's abusive police would use the cars. Batarse was forced to sell two of his dealerships to repay the $750,000 he had spent and is still burdened with debt.

Though international business will always entail risks, the following steps can be taken to improve chances of success.

- Do lots of homework at the beginning.
- Plan on investing heavily on your overseas expansion.
- Tap into the network of professionals well versed in the nuances of international trade.
- Understand that going global is a long-term commitment.

*Source:* Christopher Farrell and Edith Updike, "So You Think the World is Your Oyster," *Business Week,* (June 9, 1997): 4.

International business holds out the promise of large new market areas, yet firms cannot simply jump into the international marketplace and expect to be successful. They must adjust to needs and opportunities abroad, have quality products, understand their customers, and do their homework. They must also understand the vagaries of international markets, as this chapter's opening vignette shows. The rapid globalization of markets, however, reduces the time available to adjust to new market realities.

This chapter is concerned with the activities of firms preparing to enter international markets. Primary emphasis is placed on export activities. The chapter focuses on the role of management in starting up international operations and describes the basic stimuli for international activities. Entry modes for the international arena are highlighted, and the problems and benefits of each mode are discussed. Finally, the role of facilitators and intermediaries in international business is described.

## The Role of Management

The type and quality of its management are keys to a firm's success in the international marketplace. Management dynamism and commitment are crucial in the first steps toward international operations. Managers of firms with a strong international performance typically are active, aggressive, and display a high degree of international orientation.[1] Such an orientation is indicated by substantial global awareness and cultural sensitivity.[2] Conversely, the managers of firms that are unsuccessful or inactive internationally usually exhibit a lack of determination or devotion to international business. The issue of **managerial commitment** is a critical one because foreign market penetration requires a vast amount of market development activity, sensitivity toward foreign environments, research, and innovation. Regardless of what the firm produces or where it does business internationally, managerial commitment is crucial for enduring stagnation and sometimes even setbacks and failure.[3] To obtain such a commitment, it is important to involve all levels of management early on in the international planning process and to impress on all players that the effort will only succeed with a commitment that is companywide.[4]

Initiating international business activities takes the firm in an entirely new direction, quite different from adding a product line or hiring a few more people. Going international means that a fundamental strategic change is taking place. The decision to export usually comes from the highest levels of management, typically the owner, president, chairman, or vice president of marketing.[5]

The carrying out of the decision—that is, the initiation of international business transactions and their implementation—is then the primary responsibility of marketing personnel. It is important to establish an organizational structure in which someone has the specific responsibility for international activities. Without such a responsibility center, the focus necessary for success can easily be lost. Such a center need not be large. For example, just one person assigned part time to international activities can begin exploring and entering international markets.

The first step in developing international commitment is to become aware of international business opportunities. Management must then determine the degree and timing of the firm's internationalization. For instance, a German corporation that expands its operation into Austria, Switzerland, Belgium, and the Netherlands is less international than a German corporation that launches operations in Japan and Brazil. Moreover, if a German-based corporation already has activities in the United States, setting up a business in Canada does not increase its degree of internationalization as much as if Canada was the first "bridgehead" in North America[6] Management must decide the timing of when to start the internationalization process and how quickly it should progress. For example, market entry might be desirable as soon as possible because clients are waiting for the product or because competitors are expected to enter the market shortly. In addition, it may desire to either enter a market abroad selectively or to achieve full market coverage from the outset. Decisions on these timing issues will determine the speed with which management must mobilize and motivate the people involved in the process.[7] It must be kept in mind that a firmwide international orientation does not develop overnight, but rather needs time to grow. Internationalization is a matter of learning, of acquiring experiential knowledge. A firm must learn about foreign markets and institutions, but also about its own internal resources in order to know what it is capable of when exposed to new and unfamiliar conditions.[8]

Management is often much too preoccupied with short-term, immediate problems to engage in sophisticated long-run planning. As a result, many firms are simply not interested in international business. Yet certain situations may lead a manager to discover and understand the value of going international and to decide to pursue international business activities. Trigger factors frequently are foreign travel, during which new business opportunities are discovered, or the receipt of information that leads management to believe that such opportunities exist. Unsolicited orders from abroad are an example. Managers who have lived abroad and have learned foreign languages or are particularly interested in foreign cultures are more likely to investigate whether international business opportunities would be appropriate for their firms.

New management or new employees can also bring about an international orientation. For example, managers entering a firm may already have had some international business experience and may try to use this experience to further the business activities of the firm where they are currently employed.

## Motivations to Go Abroad

Normally, management will consider international activities only when stimulated to do so. A variety of motivations can push and pull individuals and firms along the international path. An overview of the major motivations that have been found to make firms go international is provided in Table 11.1. Proactive motivations represent stimuli for firm-initiated strategic change. Reactive motivations describe stimuli that result in a firm's response and adaptation to changes imposed by the outside environment. In other words, firms with proactive motivations go international because they want to; those with reactive motivations have to go international.

**Proactive Motivations**

Profits are the major proactive motivation for international business. Management may perceive international sales as a potential source of higher profit margins or of more added-on profits. Of course, the profitability perceived when planning to go international is often quite different from the profitability actually obtained. Particularly in international start-up operations, initial profitability may be quite low.[9] The gap between perception and reality may be especially large when the firm has not previously engaged in international business. Despite thorough planning, unexpected influences can change the profit picture substantially. Shifts in exchange rates, for example, may drastically affect profit forecasts.

Unique products or a technological advantage can be another major stimulus. A firm may produce goods or services that are not widely available from international competitors. Again, real and perceived advantages must be differentiated. Many firms believe that they offer unique products or services, even though this may not be the case internationally. If products or technologies are unique, however, they certainly can provide a competitive edge. What needs to be considered is how long such an advantage will last. The length of time is a function of the product, its technology, and the creativity of competitors. In the past, a firm with a competitive edge could often count on being the sole supplier to foreign markets for years to come. This type of ad-

**TABLE 11.1**

**Major Motivations to Internationalize Small and Medium-Sized Firms**

| Proactive | Reactive |
| --- | --- |
| Profit advantage | Competitive pressures |
| Unique products | Overproduction |
| Technological advantage | Declining domestic sales |
| Exclusive information | Excess capacity |
| Managerial commitment | Saturated domestic markets |
| Tax benefit | Proximity to customers and ports |
| Economies of scale | |

Nike began marketing in the Pacific Rim by creating a partnership with Nissho Iwai. Nike's Asia Pacific revenues reached $1.2 billion by the end of 1997. Nike achieved this extraordinary growth by connecting the Nike brand to consumers emotionally, culturally, and with local relevance.
© John McDermott

vantage has shrunk dramatically because of competing technologies and the frequent lack of international patent protection.

Special knowledge about foreign customers or market situations may be another proactive stimulus. Such knowledge may result from particular insights by a firm, special contacts an individual may have, in-depth research, or simply from being in the right place at the right time (for example, recognizing a good business situation during a vacation trip). Although such exclusivity can serve well as an initial stimulus for international business, it will rarely provide prolonged motivation because competitors—at least in the medium run—can be expected to catch up with the information advantage. Only if firms build up international information advantage as an ongoing process, through, for example, broad market scanning or assured informational exclusivity, can prolonged corporate strategy be based on this motivation.

Another motivation reflects the desire, drive, and enthusiasm of management toward international business activities. The managerial commitment can exist simply because managers like to be part of a firm that engages in international business. (It sounds impressive.) Further, such activity can often provide a good reason for international travel—for example, to call on a major customer in the Bahamas during the cold winter months. Often, however, the managerial commitment to internationalize is simply the reflection of a general entrepreneurial motivation, that is, a desire for continuous growth and market expansion.[10]

Tax benefits can also play a major motivating role. Many governments use preferential tax treatment to encourage exports. In the United States, for example, a tax mechanism called a foreign sales corporation (FSC) provides firms with certain tax deferrals and makes international business activities more profitable. (More detail on the FSC is presented in Chapter 19.) As a result of the tax benefits, firms either can offer their product at a lower cost in foreign markets or can accumulate a higher profit.

A final major proactive motivation involves economies of scale. International activities may enable the firm to increase its output and therefore rise more rapidly on the learning curve. The Boston Consulting Group has shown that the doubling of output can reduce production costs up to 30 percent. Increased production for international markets can therefore help to reduce the cost of production for domestic sales and make the firm more competitive domestically as well.[11]

## Reactive Motivations

A second type of motivation, primarily characterized as reactive, influences firms to respond to environmental changes and pressures rather than to attempt to blaze trails. Competitive pressures are one example. A company may fear losing domestic market share to competing firms that have benefited from the economies of scale gained through international business activities. Further, it may fear losing foreign markets permanently to competitors that have decided to focus on these markets. Since market share usually is most easily retained by firms that initially obtain it, some companies may enter the international market head over heels. Quick entry, however, may result in equally quick withdrawal once the firm recognizes that its preparation has been inadequate.

Similarly, overproduction can result in a major reactive motivation. During downturns in the domestic business cycle, foreign markets have historically provided an ideal outlet for excess inventories. International business expansion motivated by overproduction usually does not represent full commitment by management, but rather a safety-valve activity. As soon as domestic demand returns to previous levels, international business activities are curtailed or even terminated. Firms that have used such a strategy once may encounter difficulties when trying to employ it again because many foreign customers are not interested in temporary or sporadic business relationships.

Declining domestic sales, whether measured in sales volume or market share, have a similar motivating effect. Goods marketed domestically may be at the declining stage of their product life cycle. Instead of attempting to push back the life cycle process domestically, or in addition to such an effort, firms may opt to prolong the product life cycle by expanding the market. In the past, such efforts by firms in industrialized countries often met with success because customers in less-developed countries only gradually reached the level of need and sophistication already obtained by customers in the developed countries. Increasingly, however, because of global competition, these lags are shrinking.

Excess capacity can also be a powerful motivator. If equipment for production is not fully utilized, firms may see expansion abroad as an ideal way to achieve broader distribution of fixed costs. Alternatively, if all fixed costs are assigned to domestic production, the firm can penetrate foreign markets with a pricing scheme that focuses mainly on variable cost. Yet such a view is feasible only for market entry. A market-penetration strategy based on variable cost alone is unrealistic because, in the long run, fixed costs have to be recovered to replace production equipment.

The reactive motivation of a saturated domestic market has similar results to that of declining domestic sales. Again, firms in this situation can use the international market to prolong the life of their good and even of their organization.

A final major reactive motivation is that of proximity to customers and ports. Physical and psychological closeness to the international market can often play a major role in the international business activities of the firm. For example, a firm established near a border may not even perceive itself as going abroad if it does business in the neighboring country. Except for some firms close to the Canadian or Mexican border, however, this factor is much less prevalent in the United States than in many other nations. Most European firms automatically go abroad simply because their neighbors are so close.

In general, firms that are most successful in international business are usually motivated by proactive—that is, firm internal—factors. Proactive firms are also frequently more service oriented than reactive firms. Further, proactive firms tend to be more marketing and strategy oriented than reactive firms, which have as their major concern operational issues. The clearest differentiation between the two types of firms can probably be made ex post facto by determining how they initially entered international markets. Proactive firms are more likely to have solicited their first international order, whereas reactive firms frequently begin international activities after receiving an unsolicited order from abroad.

## Concerns and Problems of Going International

Going international presents the firm with new environments, entirely new ways of doing business, and a host of new problems. The problems have a wide range. They can consist of strategic considerations, such as service delivery and compliance with government regulations. The firm needs to determine its preparedness for internationalization by assessing its internal strengths and weaknesses. This preparedness has to be evaluated in the context of the globalization of the industry within which the firm operates, since this context will affect the competitive position and strategic options available to the firm.[12] In addition, the firm has to focus on start-up issues, such as how to find and effectively communicate with customers and operational matters, such as information flows and the mechanics of carrying out an international business transaction. This involves a variety of new documents, including commercial invoices, bills of lading, consular invoices, inspection certificates, and shipper's export declarations. The paperwork is necessary to comply with various domestic, international, or foreign regulations. The regulations may be designed to control international business activities, to streamline the individual transaction, or, as in the case of the shipper's export declaration, to compile trade statistics.

## Strategic Effects of Going International

As a firm goes international, unusual things can happen to both risk and profit. Management's perception of risk exposure grows in light of the gradual development of expertise, the many concerns about engaging in a new activity,

**FIGURE 11.1**

**Profit and Risk During Early Internationalization**

*Source:* Michael R. Czinkota, "A National Export Development Policy for New and Growing Businesses," *Journal of International Marketing* 2, 1 (1994): 95.

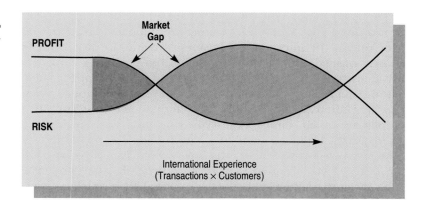

and uncertainty about the new environment it is about to enter. Domestically, the firm has gradually learned about the market and therefore managed to decrease its risk. In the course of international expansion, the firm now encounters new and unfamiliar factors, exposing it to increased risk. At the same time, because of the investment needs required by a serious international effort, immediate profit performance may slip. In the longer term, increasing familiarity with international markets and the diversification benefits of serving multiple markets will decrease the firm's risk below the previous "domestic only" level and increase profitability as well. In the short term, however, managers may face an unusual, and perhaps unacceptable, situation: rising risk accompanied by decreasing profitability. In light of this reality, which is depicted in Figure 11.1, many executives are tempted to either not initiate international activities or to discontinue them.[13]

Understanding the changes in risk and profitability can help management overcome the seemingly prohibitive cost of going international, since the negative developments may be only short term. Yet, success does require the firm to be a risk taker, and firms must realize that satisfactory international performance will take time.[14] Satisfactory performance can be achieved in three ways: effectiveness, efficiency, and competitive strength. Effectiveness is characterized by the acquisition of market share abroad and by increased sales. Efficiency is manifested later by rising profitability. Competitive strength refers to the firm's position compared to other firms in the industry, and is, due to the benefits of international experience, likely to grow. The international executive must appreciate the time and performance dimensions associated with going abroad in order to overcome short-term setbacks for the sake of long-term success.

## Alternative Entry Strategies

Conceivably, a new firm could create large-scale subsidiaries abroad or could even be formed for international business purposes. However, four forms of entry strategies are used by the majority of firms that initiate international business activities: indirect exporting and importing, direct exporting and importing, licensing, and franchising. These alternatives are discussed in this chapter in more detail. Other modes of entry, such as direct foreign investment, management contracts, contract manufacturing, and turnkey operations, are mostly used by larger and more experienced firms and are therefore addressed in Chapter 12.

Firms can be involved in exporting and importing in an indirect or direct way. Indirect involvement means that the firm participates in international business through an intermediary and does not deal with foreign customers or firms. Direct involvement means that the firm works with foreign customers or markets with the opportunity to develop a relationship. The end result of exporting and importing is similar whether the activities are direct or indirect. In both cases, goods and services either go abroad or come to the domestic market from abroad, and goods may have to be adapted to suit the targeted market. However, the different approaches have varying degrees of impact on the knowledge and experience levels of firms. The less direct the involvement of the firm, the less likely is the internal development of a storehouse of information and expertise on how to do business abroad, information that the firm can draw on later for further international expansion. Therefore, while indirect activities represent a form of international market entry, they are unlikely to result in growing management commitment to international markets or increased capabilities in serving them.

Many firms are indirect exporters and importers, often without their knowledge. As an example, merchandise can be sold to a domestic firm that in turn sells it abroad. This is most frequently the case when smaller suppliers deliver products to large multinational corporations, which use them as input to their foreign sales. Foreign buyers may also purchase products locally and then send them immediately to their home country. More examples of "exporting in your own backyard" are given in Table 11.2. While indirect exports may be the result of unwitting participation, some firms also choose this method of inter-

## Indirect Exporting and Importing

**TABLE 11.2**

**Exporting in Your Own Backyard: A Dozen Segments for Indirect Exporters**

1. Large companies purchasing goods for their own foreign affiliates
2. Large design and construction firms purchasing goods for foreign projects awarded to them
3. Branches of gigantic foreign trading companies purchasing goods for their affiliates
4. Export merchants buying for their own account
5. Large foreign companies purchasing goods through their domestic buying office or agents
6. Military purchasing for use abroad
7. Exporters seeking goods to round out their own lines
8. United Nations members purchasing for development projects
9. Foreign governments purchasing goods
10. Foreign department stores purchasing goods through buying offices
11. Foreign buyers on purchasing trips
12. Government-financed transactions requiring domestic goods

*Source:* Nelson Joyner, Georgetown University, teaching notes, 1998.

## MAKING A QUIET SPLASH ABROAD

For small businesses size can be an unexpected strength in tackling overseas markets. Export giants once seemed to have all the right advantages to enter new markets: well-established distribution systems and plenty of money, personnel, and political clout. But small companies have a personal touch, putting foreign clients in direct contact with the chief executive seeking a sale. They also have the ability to fly in under the radar without getting noticed and to make a quiet splash.

Several small companies in the midwestern state of Indiana are proving that the growth of U.S. exports doesn't just come from household names like Motorola or General Electric, but rather from companies like Red Spot Paint & Varnish Co., which sells paint and other coatings to auto makers. International sales used to be so rare for that company that its president would handle them on Saturday mornings, but now four full-time employees cover exports, which comprise 20 percent of the company's annual sales of $90 million. On its overseas journey, Red Spot learned some basic lessons about selling abroad,

according to their director of international sales. The major one: Personal contact works best. One Argentinean customer was impressed enough by the hospitality Red Spot offered on his visit to offer a $100,000 contract—an insignificant amount in the eyes of Red Spot's competitors.

Gaining a client base abroad has certainly been hard work for the small company; it courted a German auto parts maker for seven years before winning its business. But now that account is giving Red Spot additional business in Germany and Mexico. And Red Spot maintains that its research and development for new products will give it a further edge in international competition.

Other Indiana companies seeking to enter the global market have found help from their state government. The Indiana Department of Commerce has eight offices around the world that provide legal advice, transportation, and interpreters. Other services include booking foreign hotel rooms for executives and providing free workspace, telephones, and fax services. Indiana state commerce officials also meet with local businesses to discuss practical issues of foreign business trips ranging from how to catch a cab in Mexico City to which gastrointestinal medicine works best.

As more small businesses realize the gains to be found in fast-moving international markets, their contribution to U.S. overall exports will continue to rise. They will be banking on the increased foreign appetite for American goods.

*Source: Robert L. Rose and Carl Quintanilla, "Tiptoeing Abroad: More Small U.S. Firms Take Up Exporting, with Much Success,"* The Wall Street Journal, *December 20, 1996: A1, A8.*

national entry as a strategic alternative that conserves effort and resources while still taking advantage of foreign opportunities.

At the same time, many firms that perceive themselves as buying domestically may in reality buy imported products. They may have long-standing relations with a domestic supplier who, because of cost and competitive pressures, has begun to source products from abroad rather than to produce them domestically. In this case, the buyer firm has become an indirect importer.

**Direct Exporting and Importing**

Firms that opt to export or import directly have more opportunities ahead of them. As Global Perspective 11.1 shows, they learn more quickly the competitive advantages of their products and can therefore expand more rapidly. They also have the ability to control their international activities better and can forge relationships with their trading partners, which can lead to further international growth and success.

However, the firms also are faced with obstacles. These hurdles include identifying and targeting foreign suppliers and/or customers and finding retail space, processes that can be very costly and time-consuming. Some firms are overcoming such barriers through the use of mail-order catalogs ("storeless" distribution networks) or video brochures. In Japan, for example, "high-cost rents, crowded shelves, and an intricate distribution system have made launching new products via conventional methods an increasingly difficult and expensive proposition. Direct marketing via catalog short-circuits the distribution train and eliminates the need for high-priced shop space."[15]

## International Intermediaries

Both direct and indirect importers and exporters frequently make use of intermediaries who can assist with troublesome yet important details such as documentation, financing, and transportation. The intermediaries also can identify foreign suppliers and customers and help the firm with long- or short-term market penetration efforts. Three major types of international intermediaries are export management companies, Webb-Pomerene associations, and trading companies. Together with export facilitators, the intermediaries can bring the global market to the domestic firm's doorstep and help overcome financial and time constraints. Table 11.3 shows those areas in which intermediaries have been found to be particularly helpful.

It is the responsibility of the firm's management to decide how to use the intermediaries. Options range from using their help for initial market entry to developing a long-term strategic collaboration. It is the degree of corporate involvement in and control of the international effort that determines whether the firm operates as an indirect or direct internationalist.

## Export Management Companies

Firms that specialize in performing international business services as commission representatives or as distributors are known as **export management companies (EMCs)**. Most EMCs are quite small. Many were formed by one or two principals with experience in international business or in a particular geographic area. Their expertise enables them to offer specialized services to domestic corporations.

EMCs have two primary forms of operation: they take title to goods and operate internationally on their own account, or they perform services as

**TABLE 11.3**

---

**How a Trade Intermediary Can Offer Assistance**

1. Knows foreign market competitive conditions
2. Has personal contacts with potential foreign buyers
3. Evaluates credit risk associated with foreign buyers
4. Has sales staff to call on current foreign customers in person
5. Assumes responsibility for physical delivery of product to foreign buyer

*Source:* Richard M. Castaldi, Alex F. De Noble, and Jeffrey Kantor, "The Intermediary Service Requirements of Canadian and American Exporters," *International Marketing Review* 9, 2 (1992): 21–40.

agents. They often serve a variety of clients, thus their mode of operation may vary from client to client and from transaction to transaction. An EMC may act as an agent for one client and as a distributor for another. It may even act as both for the same client on different occasions.

**The EMC as an Agent** When working as an agent, the EMC is primarily responsible for developing foreign business and sales strategies and establishing contacts abroad. Because the EMC does not share in the profits from a sale, it depends heavily on a high sales volume, on which it charges commission. The EMC may therefore be tempted to take on as many products and as many clients as possible to obtain a high sales volume. As a result, the EMC may spread itself too thin and may be unable to adequately represent all the clients and products it carries. The risk is particularly great with small EMCs.

In addition to its international activities, this type of EMC must concentrate a substantial amount of effort on the development of domestic clients. The clients often are exactly the firms that are unwilling to commit major resources to the international business effort. They must be convinced that it is worthwhile to consider international business. To develop and expand its clientele, the EMC must divert some of its limited resources to that task.

EMCs that have specific expertise in selecting markets because of language capabilities, previous exposure, or specialized contacts appear to be the ones most successful and useful in aiding client firms in their international business efforts. For example, they can cooperate with firms that are already successful in international business but have been unable to penetrate a specific region. By sticking to their area of expertise and representing only a limited number of clients, such agents can provide quite valuable services.

**The EMC as a Distributor** When operating as a distributor, the EMC purchases products from the domestic firm, takes title, and assumes the trading risk. Selling in its own name, it has the opportunity to reap greater profits than when acting as an agent. The potential for greater profit is appropriate, because the EMC has drastically reduced the risk for the domestic firm while increasing its own risk. The burden of the merchandise acquired provides a major motivation to complete an international sale successfully. The domestic firm selling to the EMC is in the comfortable position of having sold its merchandise and received its money without having to deal with the complexities of the international market. On the other hand, it is less likely to gather much international business expertise.

**Compensation of EMCs** The mechanism of an EMC may be very useful to the domestic firm if such activities produce additional sales abroad. However, certain services must be performed that demand resources for which someone must pay. As an example, a firm must incur market development expenses to enter foreign markets. At the very least, products must be shown abroad, visits must be arranged, or contacts must be established. Even though it may often not be discussed, the funding for these activities must be found.

One possibility is a fee charged to the manufacturer by the EMC for market development, sometimes in the form of a retainer and often on an annual basis. The retainers vary and are dependent on the number of products represented and the difficulty of foreign market penetration. Frequently, manufacturers are also expected to pay all or part of the direct expenses associated with foreign market penetration. These expenses may involve the production and translation of promotional product brochures, the cost of attending trade shows, the provision of product samples, or trade advertising.

Alternatively, the EMC may demand a price break for international sales. In one way or another, the firm that uses an EMC must pay the EMC for the international business effort. Otherwise, despite promises, the EMC may simply add the firm and product in name only to its product offering and do nothing to achieve international success. Management needs to be aware of this cost and the fact that EMCs do not offer a free ride. Depending on the complexity of a product and the necessity to carry out developmental research, promotion, and services, management must be prepared to part with some portion of the potential international profitability to compensate the EMC for its efforts.

**Power Conflicts between EMCs and Clients**   The EMC in turn faces the continuous problem of retaining a client once foreign market penetration is achieved. Many firms use an EMC's services mainly to test the international arena, with the clear desire to become a direct participant once successful operations have been established. Of course, this is particularly true if foreign demand turns out to be strong and profit levels are high. The conflict between the EMC and its clients, with one side wanting to retain market power by not sharing too much international business information, and the other side wanting to obtain that power, often results in short-term relationships and a lack of cooperation. Since international business development is based on long-term efforts, this conflict frequently leads to a lack of success.

For the concept of an export management company to work, both parties must fully recognize the delegation of responsibilities, the costs associated with those activities, and the need for information sharing, cooperation, and mutual reliance. Use of an EMC should be viewed just like a domestic channel commitment, requiring a thorough investigation of the intermediary and the advisability of relying on its efforts, a willingness to cooperate on a relationship rather than on a transaction basis, and a willingness to properly reward its efforts. The EMC in turn must adopt a flexible approach to managing the export relationship. It must continue to upgrade the levels of services offered, constantly highlighting for the client the dimensions of postsales service and providing in-depth information, since those are its biggest sources of differential advantage.[16] By doing so, the EMC lets the client know that the cost is worth the service and thereby reduces the desire for circumvention.

## Webb-Pomerene Associations

Legislation enacted in 1918 led to **Webb-Pomerene associations** that permit U.S. firms to cooperate in terms of international sales allocation, financing, and pricing information. The associations must take care not to engage in activities that would reduce competition within the United States. To more successfully penetrate international markets, however, they can allocate markets, fix quotas, and select exclusive distributors or brokers.

In spite of this early effort to encourage joint activities by firms in the international market, the effectiveness of Webb-Pomerene associations has not been substantial. At their peak, from 1930 to 1934, fifty Webb-Pomerene associations accounted for about 12 percent of U.S. exports. By 1997 only 15 associations were active and accounted for less than 1 percent of U.S. exports.[17] In addition, it appears that most of the users of this particular form of export intermediary are not the small and medium-sized firms the act was initially intended to assist, but rather the dominant firms in their respective industries.

The lack of success of this particular intermediary has mainly been ascribed to the fact that the antitrust exemption granted was not sufficiently ironclad. Further, specialized export firms are thought to have more to offer to a domestic firm than does an association, which may be particularly true if the association is dominated by one or two major competitors in an industry. Such dominance makes joining the association undesirable for smaller firms.

## Trading Companies

A third major intermediary is the trading company. The concept was originated by the European trading houses such as the Fuggers of Augsburg. Later on, monarchs chartered traders to form corporate bodies that enjoyed exclusive trading rights and protection by the naval forces in exchange for tax payments. Examples of such early trading companies are the Oost-Indische Compagnie of the Netherlands, formed in 1602, followed shortly by the British East India Company and La Compagnie des Indes chartered by France.[18] Today, the most famous trading companies are the **sogoshosha** of Japan. Names such as Mitsubishi, Mitsui, and C. Itoh have become household words around the world. The nine trading company giants of Japan act as intermediaries for about one-third of the country's exports and two-fifths of its imports.[19] The general trading companies play a unique role in world commerce by importing, exporting, countertrading, investing, and manufacturing. Their vast size allows them to benefit from economies of scale and perform their operations at high rates of return, even though their profit margins are less than 2 percent.

Four major reasons have been given for the success of the Japanese sogoshosha. First, by concentrating on obtaining and disseminating information about market opportunities and by investing huge funds in the development of information systems, the firms have the mechanisms and organizations in place to gather, evaluate, and translate market information into business opportunities. Second, economies of scale permit the firms to take advantage of their vast transaction volume to obtain preferential treatment by, for example, negotiating transportation rates or even opening up new transportation routes and distribution systems. Third, the firms serve large internal markets, not only in Japan but also around the world, and can benefit from opportunities for countertrade. Finally, sogoshosha have access to vast quantities of capital, both within Japan and in the international capital markets. They can therefore carry out transactions that are too large or risky to be palatable or feasible for other firms.[20] In spite of changing trading patterns, these giants continue to succeed by shifting their strategy to expand their domestic activities in Japan, entering more newly developing markets, increasing their trading activities among third countries, and forming joint ventures with non-Japanese firms. Global Perspective 11.2 explains some of the new business activities of the sogoshosha.

**Expansion of Trading Companies**   For many decades, the emergence of trading companies was commonly believed to be a Japan-specific phenomenon. Japanese cultural factors were cited as the reason that such intermediaries could

## JAPANESE TRADING COMPANIES DEVELOP NEW VENTURES

**W**hen Japan rebuilt itself in the wake of World War II, its immense trading companies provided big business with badly needed conduits of trade. Today, as Japan's economy restructures once again, trading companies serve a relatively new function: providers of badly needed capital to international business ventures.

The trading companies' new role has benefited small businesses and start-ups like CareNet Inc., a cable broadcasting company that will feature programs and televised conferences for Japan's medical community. When Japanese banks dismissed the idea as too risky, CareNet's founders turned to Hitoshi Suga, president of the venture capital arm of trading giant Mitsui & Co. A few weeks later, Mr. Suga invested 30 million yen ($237,500) in the enterprise.

Since Japanese banks have been bogged down in debt, trading companies have evolved as one of the few credible sources of financing for local start-ups. "The times are changing," says Mitsuo Kurobe, a managing director of Salomon Brothers Japan. "I've been involved in many start-ups in need of financing, and the trading companies are easily spending tens of millions of dollars on them."

Throughout Japan's history, trading companies have led the economy through new and unexplored waters. At the turn of the century, trading companies were the foundation upon which many of Japan's big businesses were based when the country modernized. They established the overseas distribution channels that served as conduits for the country's export machine after World War II. They also ushered in many of the speculative investments that fueled Japan's economy a decade ago.

However, technological changes combined with the economic slowdown of the early '90s began to eliminate many of the costly middleman functions upon which the Japanese trading companies had thrived. Sales from operations of Japan's major trading companies have been stagnant for much of this decade because manufacturers are beginning to replace traditional distribution channels with their own sales networks.

"Taking a product and distributing it is no longer adequate," says Hiro Satake, president of Itochu Techno-Science Corp. "The information revolution has made many products accessible without middlemen, so we've been forced to find niches." Japanese trading companies appear to have found such a niche in venture capital.

*Source: Steve Glain, "Japan's Trading Giants Spark Venture Capital," The Wall Street Journal, May 15, 1997, A18.*

operate successfully only from that country. In the last few decades, however, many other governments have established trading companies. In countries so diverse as Korea, Brazil, and Turkey, trading companies are now handling large portions of national exports.[21] The reason these firms have become so large is due, in good measure, to special and preferential government incentives, rather than market forces alone. Therefore, they may be vulnerable to changes in government policies.

In the United States, **export trading company (ETC)** legislation designed to improve the export performance of small and medium-sized firms was implemented in 1982. To improve export performance, bank participation in trading companies was permitted, and the antitrust threat to joint export efforts was reduced through precertification of planned activities by the U.S. Department of Commerce. Businesses were encouraged to join together to export or offer export services.

Permitting banks to participate in ETCs was intended to allow ETCs better access to capital and therefore permit more trading transactions and easier receipt of title to goods. The relaxation of antitrust provisions in turn was meant to enable firms to form joint ventures more easily. The cost of developing and penetrating international markets would then be shared, with the proportional share being, for many small and medium-sized firms, much easier to bear. As an example, in case a warehouse is needed in order to secure foreign market penetration, one firm alone does not have to bear all the costs. A consortium of firms can jointly rent a foreign warehouse. Similarly, each firm need not station a service technician abroad at substantial cost. Joint funding of a service center by several firms makes the cost less prohibitive for each one. The trading company concept also offers a one-stop shopping center for both the firm and its foreign customers. The firm can be assured that all international functions will be performed efficiently by the trading company, and at the same time, the foreign customer will have to deal with few individual firms.

**Trading Company Activities**   Although ETCs seem to offer major benefits to many U.S. firms that want to go abroad, they have not been very extensively used. By 1998 only 167 individual ETC certificates had been issued by the U.S. Department of Commerce. Since some of the certificates covered all the members of trade associations, a total of 5,000 companies were part of an ETC.[22]

Yet, given the current market structure, in which most exporters are small and fragmented and unable to avail themselves of international markets due to a lack of resources and information, the opportunity for collaboration is still useful. ETCs may still become the major vehicle for the generation of new international business entry activities by small and medium-sized firms. The concepts of synergism and cooperation certainly make sense in terms of enhancing the international competitiveness of firms. Yet the focus of ETCs should perhaps not be pure exporting. Importing and third-country trading may also generate substantial activity and profit. Through the carrying out of a wide variety of business transactions, international market knowledge is obtained. The management and consulting expertise may in itself be a salable service.

## International Facilitators

Facilitators are entities outside the firm that assist in the process of going international by supplying knowledge and information but not participating in the transaction. Such facilitators can come both from the private and the public sector.

### Private Sector Facilitators

Major encouragement and assistance can result from the statements and actions of other firms in the same industry. Information that would be considered proprietary if it involved domestic operations is often freely shared by competing firms when it concerns international business. The information not only has source credibility but is viewed with a certain amount of fear, because a too-successful competitor may eventually infringe on the firm's domestic business.

A second, quite influential group of private sector facilitators is distributors. Often a firm's distributors are engaged, through some of their business activities, in international business. To increase their international distribution volume, they encourage purely domestic firms to participate in the international market. This is true not only for exports but also for imports. For example, a major customer of a manufacturing firm may find that materials available from abroad, if used in the domestic production process, would make the product available at lower cost. In such instances, the customer may approach the supplier and strongly encourage foreign sourcing.

Banks and other service firms, such as accounting and consulting firms, can serve as major facilitators by alerting their clients to international opportunities. While these service providers historically follow their major multinational clients abroad, increasingly they are establishing a foreign presence on their own. Frequently, they work with domestic clients on expanding market reach in the hope that their service will be used for any international transaction that results. Given the extensive information network of many service providers—banks, for example, often have a wide variety of correspondence relationships—the role of these facilitators can be major. Like a mother hen, they can take firms under their wings and be pathfinders in foreign markets.

Chambers of commerce and other business associations that interact with firms can frequently heighten their interest in international business. Yet, in most instances, such organizations function mainly as secondary intermediaries, because true change is brought about by the presence and encouragement of other managers.

## Public Sector Facilitators

Government efforts can also facilitate the international efforts of firms. In the United States, for example, the Department of Commerce provides major export assistance, as do other federal organizations such as the Small Business Administration and the Export-Import Bank. Most countries maintain similar export support organizations. Table 11.4 provides the names of selected export promotion agencies from around the globe, together with their web addresses. Employees of these organizations typically visit firms and attempt to analyze their international business opportunities. Through rapid access to government resources, these individuals can provide data, research reports, counseling, and financing information to firms. Government organizations can also sponsor meetings that bring interested parties together and alert them to new business opportunities abroad. Key governmental facilitation also occurs when firms are abroad. By receiving information and assistance from their embassies, many business ventures abroad can be made easier. Table 11.5 shows the areas in which U.S. embassies abroad receive the most requests for assistance from companies.

Increasingly, organizations at the state and local level also are active in encouraging firms to participate in international business. Many states and provinces have formed agencies for economic development that provide information, display products abroad, conduct trade missions, and sometimes even offer financing. Similar services can also be offered by state and local port authorities and by some of the larger cities. State and local authorities can be a major factor in facilitating international activities because of their closeness to firms.

Educational institutions such as universities and community colleges can also be major international business facilitators. They can act as trade information clearing houses, facilitate networking opportunities, provide client counseling and technical assistance, and develop trade education programs.[23]

**TABLE 11.4**

**Selected Export Promotion Agencies around the Globe**

**Australia:** Australian Trade Commission
http://www.austrade.gov.au
**Canada:** Export Development Corporation
http://www.edc.ca/
**France:** Centre Français du Commerce Extérieur
http://www.cfce.fr/
**Germany:** Federal Office of Foreign Trade Information (BfAI)
http://www.bfai.com
**India:** India Trade Promotion Organisation (ITPO)
http://economictimes.com/etonline/itpo
**Japan:** Japan External Trade Organization (JETRO)
http://www.jetro.go.jp
**Singapore:** Trade Development Board
http://www.gov.sg/mti/tdb1.html
**South Korea:** Trade-Investment Promotion Agency (KOTRA)
http://www.kotra.or.kr/
**United Kingdom:** Overseas Trade Services
http://www.dti.gov.uk/ots/
**United States:** Export-Import Bank
http://www.exim.gov
International Trade Administration
http://www.ita.doc.gov
Foreign Agricultural Service
http://www.fas.usda.gov

They can also develop course projects that are useful to firms interested in international business. For example, students may visit a firm and examine its potential in the international market as a course requirement. With the skill and supervision of faculty members to help the students develop the final report, such projects can be useful to firms with scarce resources, while they expose students to real-world problems.

**TABLE 11.5**

**Most Frequent Requests for Business Assistance from U.S. Embassies**

1. Business analysis of the foreign country
2. Introduction to local business leadership
3. Scheduling appointments with foreign government officials
4. Information about export/import regulations
5. Embassy intervention with foreign governments on contracts
6. Information about government contracts
7. Information on investment or tax incentives

*Source:* U.S. Department of State, Foreign Service Institute, Washington, D.C., 1993.

## Other Forms of International Market Entry and Expansion

Licensing and franchising are two forms of international market entry and expansion in addition to direct and indirect exporting. They are strategies that can be used by themselves or in conjunction with export activities.

Under a **licensing agreement,** one firm permits another to use its intellectual property for compensation designated as **royalty.** The recipient firm is the licensee. The property licensed might include patents, trademarks, copyrights, technology, technical know-how, or specific business skills. For example, a firm that has developed a bag-in-the-box packaging process for milk can permit other firms abroad to use the same process. Licensing therefore amounts to exporting intangibles.

**Licensing**

**Assessment of Licensing**   Licensing has intuitive appeal to many would-be international managers. As an entry strategy, it requires neither capital investment nor detailed involvement with foreign customers. By generating royalty income, licensing provides an opportunity to exploit research and development already conducted. After initial costs, the licensor can reap benefits until the end of the license contract period. Licensing also reduces the risk of expropriation because the licensee is a local company that can provide leverage against government action.

Licensing may help to avoid host-country regulations applicable to equity ventures. Licensing also may provide a means by which foreign markets can be tested without major involvement of capital or management time. Similarly, licensing can be used as a strategy to preempt a market before the entry of competition, especially if the licensor's resources permit full-scale involvement only in selected markets.

Licensing is not without disadvantages. It is a very limited form of foreign market participation and does not in any way guarantee a basis for future expansion. As a matter of fact, quite the opposite may take place. In exchange for the royalty, the licensor may create its own competitor not only in the market for which the agreement was made but for third-country markets as well.

Licensing has also come under criticism from many governments and supranational organizations. They have alleged that licensing provides a mechanism for corporations in industrialized countries to capitalize on older technology. These accusations have been made even though licensing offers a foreign entity the opportunity for immediate market entry with a proven concept. It therefore eliminates the risk of R&D failure, the cost of designing around the licensor's patents, or the fear of patent-infringement litigation.

Some companies are increasingly hesitant to enter licensing agreements. For example, Japanese firms are delighted to sell goods to China but are unwilling to license the Chinese to produce the goods themselves. They fear that, because of the low wage structure in China, such licenses could create a powerful future competitor in markets presently held by Japan.

**Principal Issues in Negotiating Licensing Agreements**   The key issues in negotiating licensing agreements include the scope of the rights conveyed, compensation, licensee compliance, dispute resolution, and the term and termination of the agreement.[24] The more clearly these issues are spelled out, the more trouble free the association between the two parties can be.

The rights conveyed are product and/or patent rights. Defining their scope involves specifying the technology and know-how or show-how to be included. In addition, the transfer process must be negotiated. For example, an agreement should specify whether or not manuals will be translated into the licensee's language.

Compensation for the license is a second major issue. The licensor will want the agreement to cover (1) **transfer costs,** namely all variable costs incurred in transferring technology to a licensee and all ongoing costs of maintaining the agreement; (2) **R&D costs** incurred in developing the licensed technology; and (3) **opportunity costs** incurred in the foreclosure of other sources of profit, such as exports or direct investment. The licensor wants a share of the profits generated from the use of the license.

Licensees usually do not want to include allowances for opportunity costs and often argue that the R&D costs have already been covered by the licensor. License payments, or royalties, are therefore a function both of the licensor's minimum necessary return and the cost of the licensee's next best alternative. The methods of compensating the licensor typically take the form of running royalties—such as 5 percent of license sales—and/or up-front payments, service fees, and disclosure fees (for proprietary data).

Licensee compliance should be stipulated in the agreement. Some areas of compliance are technology transfer regulations, confidentiality of information provided, record keeping and audit provisions, and quality standards. Provisions for dispute resolution will center on the choice of law for contract interpretation and conflict resolution. Often these provisions include arbitration clauses that allow a third, neutral party to resolve any disputes that arise.

Finally, the term, termination, and survival rights of licenses must be specified. Government regulations in the licensee's market must be studied. A waiver should be applied for if the conditions are not favorable (for example, in terms of the maximum allowed duration).

A special form of licensing is **trademark licensing,** which has become a substantial source of worldwide revenue for companies that can trade on well-known names and characters. Trademark licensing permits the names or logos of designers, literary characters, sports teams, or movie stars to appear on clothing, games, foods and beverages, gift and novelties, toys, and home furnishings. Licensors can make millions of dollars with little effort, while licensees can produce a brand or product that consumers will recognize immediately. Trademark licensing is possible, however, only if the trademark name indeed conveys instant recognition.

## Franchising

A fourth international entry strategy, **franchising,** is the granting of the right by a parent company (the franchisor) to another, independent entity (the franchisee) to do business in a prescribed manner. The right can take the form of selling the franchisor's products; using its name, production, and marketing techniques; or using its general business approach.[25] Usually franchising involves a combination of many of those elements. The major forms of franchising are manufacturer-retailer systems (such as car dealerships), manufac-

Franchising is one way to expand into international markets. An example is this Dunkin' Donuts franchise in Thailand.

*Source:* Courtesy of Allied Lyons

turer-wholesaler systems (such as soft drink companies), and service firm–retailer systems (such as lodging services and fast-food outlets).

Typically, to be successful in international franchising, the firm must be able to offer unique products or unique selling propositions. If such uniqueness can be offered, growth can be rapid and sustained. With its uniqueness, a franchise must offer a high degree of standardization. In most cases, standardization does not require 100 percent uniformity, but rather, international recognizability. Concurrent with this recognizability, the franchisor can and should adapt to local circumstances. Food franchisors, for example, will vary the products and product lines offered depending on local market conditions and tastes.

International franchising has grown strongly in the past decade. In 1998, more than 400 U.S. franchisers maintained more than 20,000 franchises in more than 100 countries. These operations generated a net royalty flow of more than $425 million and generated exports of $6 billion.[26] Franchising by non-U.S. firms has grown even more spectacularly. While only 13 percent of U.S. franchisers have international operations, 30 percent of French franchisers and 29 percent of Austrian franchisers are active abroad.[27] Overall, there are more than 750,000 franchise operations worldwide. Global Perspective 11.3 discusses some of the international expansion efforts of the McDonald's franchise.

The reasons for international expansion of franchise systems are market potential, financial gain, and saturated domestic markets. Global market de-

## FEEDING JAPAN'S APPETITE FOR BURGERS

McDonald's felt a slump in U.S. sales when it failed to lure more adults with its new hamburgers and chicken and fish sandwiches, which were touted as more sophisticated than the standard Big Mac. With the U.S. market for hamburgers seemingly saturated, McDonald's turned to its international franchises in search of sales growth. In 1996, the operating income of McDonald's foreign franchises expanded by 10 percent, while its domestic restaurants' operating income declined by 9 percent. Franchising in Japan has provided McDonald's with its second largest market, with 2,000 restaurants compared with 12,000 in the United States. And sales in Japan have been rising, in contrast to U.S. restaurants' performance.

McDonald's franchises in Japan have found success under local market conditions. In seeking to expand their share of the Japanese market, McDonald's adopted a strategy of price cuts designed to compete with typical lunches in Japan, which can run around $10 for rice, noodles, and tea. McDonald's prices plain hamburgers in Japan at only $1. The price-cutting has had an impact on burger-slinging rivals in Japan; its nearest competitor, Mos Burger, saw its sales fall in the wake of McDonald's price slashing. In fact, McDonald's (Japan)—a joint venture with the Japanese trading company Fujita & Co.—is Japan's largest burger chain with 60 percent of the market.

But McDonald's in Japan could soon face the same problems it has in the United States with winning new adult customers. In Japan, the restaurant chain is even more of a hangout for kids than it is in the United States. Japanese tend to try to escape tiny apartments by spending more time in restaurants and coffee shops than Americans. For teenagers, McDonald's is often the only affordable hangout. One Japanese analyst commented, "These customers are simply paying for a cheap place to hang out. It probably wouldn't matter if the product wasn't a hamburger."

However, McDonald's in Japan faces high rent costs and the expense of importing beef and other ingredients. These high costs combined with the price cutting have led to a decrease in profit growth. McDonald's continues to build new restaurants in Japan at a furious pace—500 per year—but it will need to find new and more affluent customers to continue to thrive. That will mean finding a new strategy besides price cutting to expand its appeal beyond teenagers. Otherwise McDonald's will find itself with another saturated market, and it will need to look for another country that still has an appetite for burgers to continue its international franchising success.

*Source: "McDonald's Banks On Japan Burger Appetite," South China Morning Post, March 25, 1997.*

mand is also very high for franchises. From a franchisee's perspective, the franchise is beneficial because it reduces risk by implementing a proven concept. From a governmental perspective, there are also major benefits. The source country does not see a replacement of exports or an export of jobs. The recipient country sees franchising as requiring little outflow of foreign exchange, since the bulk of the profits generated remains within the country.[28]

Even though franchising has been growing rapidly, problems are often encountered in international markets. A major problem is foreign government intervention. In the Philippines, for example, government restrictions on franchising and royalties hindered ComputerLand's Manila store from offering a broader range of services, leading to a separation between the company and its franchisee. Selection and training of franchisees represents another problem area. Many franchise systems have run into difficulty by expanding too quickly and granting franchises to unqualified entities. Although the local franchisee knows the market best, the franchisor still needs to understand the market for product adaptation and operational purposes. The franchisor, in order to remain viable in the long term, needs to coordinate the efforts of individual franchisees—for example, to share ideas and engage in joint undertakings, such as cooperative advertising.

## A Comprehensive View of International Expansion

The central driver of internationalization is the level of managerial commitment. This commitment will grow gradually from an awareness of international potential to the adaptation of international business as a strategic business direction. It will be influenced by the information, experience, and perception of management, which in turn is shaped by motivations, concerns, and the activities of change agents.

Management's commitment and its view of the capabilities of the firm will then trigger various international business activities, which can range from indirect exporting and importing to more direct involvement in the global market. Eventually, the firm may then expand further through measures such as joint ventures, strategic alliances, or foreign direct investment. The latter activities are discussed in the next chapter.

All of the developments, processes, and factors involved in the overall process of going international are linked to each other. A comprehensive view of these linkages is presented schematically in Figure 11.2.

**FIGURE 11.2**

**A Comprehensive Model of International Entry and Expansion**

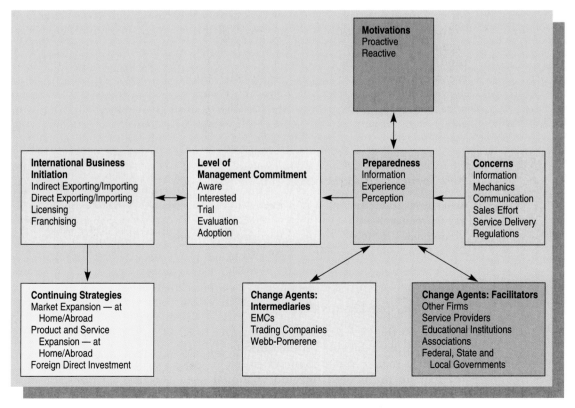

## Summary

Firms do not become experienced in international business overnight, but rather progress gradually through an internationalization process. The process is triggered by different motivations to go abroad. The motivations can be proactive or reactive. Proactive motivations are initiated by aggressive management, whereas reactive motivations are the defensive response of management to environmental changes and pressures. Firms that are primarily stimulated by proactive motivations are more likely to enter international business and succeed.

In going abroad, firms encounter multiple problems and challenges, which range from a lack of information to mechanics and documentation. In order to gain assistance in its initial international experience, the firm can make use of either intermediaries or facilitators. Intermediaries are outside companies that actively participate in an international transaction. They are export management companies, Webb-Pomerene associations, or trading companies. In order for these intermediaries to perform international business functions properly, however, they must be compensated. This will result in a reduction of profits.

International facilitators do not participate in international business transactions, but they contribute knowledge and information. Increasingly, facilitating roles are played by private sector groups, such as industry associations, banks, accountants, or consultants and by universities and federal, state, and local government authorities.

Apart from indirect and direct exporting and importing, alternatives for international business entry are licensing and franchising. The basic advantage of licensing is that it does not involve capital investment or knowledge of foreign markets. Its major disadvantage is that licensing agreements typically have time limits, are often proscribed by foreign governments, and may result in creating a competitor. The use of franchising as a means of expansion into foreign markets has increased dramatically. Franchisors must learn to strike a balance between, on the one hand, adapting to local environments and, on the other, standardizing to the degree necessary to maintain international recognizability.

## Key Terms and Concepts

| | | |
|---|---|---|
| managerial commitment | export trading company | R&D costs |
| export management | (ETC) | opportunity costs |
| companies (EMCs) | licensing agreement | trademark licensing |
| Webb-Pomerene association | royalty | franchising |
| sogoshosha | transfer costs | |

## Questions for Discussion

1. Discuss the difference between a proactive and a reactive firm, focusing your answer on international business.
2. Why is management commitment so important to export success?
3. Explain the benefits that international sales can have for domestic business activities.

4. Discuss the benefits and the drawbacks of treating international market activities as a safety-valve mechanism.
5. Give some of the reasons why distributors would want to help a firm gain a greater foothold in the international market.
6. Comment on the stance that "licensing is really not a form of international involvement because it requires no substantial additional effort on the part of the licensor."
7. Suggest reasons for the explosive international expansion of U.S.-based franchise systems.
8. What is the purpose of export intermediaries?
9. How can an export intermediary avoid circumvention by a client or customer?
10. What makes an export agent different from any other channel member?
11. Is there a need for trading companies?
12. What forms of export assistance are offered by the Small Business Administration and the Export-Import Bank (consult their web sites at **www.sba.gov** and **www.exim.gov.**)?

13. What market research tools does the web site TradePort (**www.tradeport.org.**) offer to first-time exporters? Which ones do you find most valuable.

## Recommended Readings

Agmon, Tamir, and Richard Drobnick. *Small Firms in Global Competition.* New York: Oxford University Press, 1994.

Bell, John. *Single or Joint Venturing?: A Comprehensive Approach to Foreign Entry Mode Choice.* Brookfield, Vt.: Avebury, 1996.

*Craighead's International Business, Travel and Relocation Guide to 81 Countries 1998-99.* 9th ed. Detroit: Gale, 1997.

Czinkota, Michael R. *Export Development Strategies: U.S. Promotion Policy.* New York: Praeger, 1982.

Czinkota, Michael R., Ilkka Ronkainen, and John Tarrant. *The Global Marketing Imperative.* Lincolnwood, Ill.: NTC Business Books, 1995.

Darling, John R. "Doing Business in Foreign Markets: Keys for Success of the Small Business Firm." *Journal of Managerial Issues* 9, 2 (Summer 1997): 145–161.

*The Export Yellow Pages.* Washington, D.C.: U.S. West, 1997.

Leonidou, Leonidas C., and Constantine S. Katsikeas. "The Export Development Process: An Integrative Review of Empirical Models." *Journal of International Business Studies* 27, 3 (1996): 517–552.

Mascarenhas, Briance. "The Order and Size of Entry into International Markets." *Journal of Business Venturing* 12, 4 (July 1997): 287–299.

Morrison, Teresa C. *Dun & Bradstreet's Guide to Doing Business around the World.* Englewood Cliffs, N.J.: Prentice Hall, 1997.

Perry, Anne C. *The Evolution of Selected U.S. Trade Intermediaries.* Westport, Conn.: Quorum Books, 1992.

Sarkar, Mitrabarun, and S. Tamer Cavusgil. "Trends in International Business Thought and Literature: A Review of International Market Entry Mode Research: Integration and Synthesis." *International Executive* 38, 6 (November/December 1996): 825–847.

Tomas, Michael J., and Donald G. Howard. "The Export Trading Company Act: An Update." *Journal of Marketing Channels* 2, 1 (1993): 105–119.

## Notes

1. Hartmut Holzmüller and Barbara Stöttinger, "Structural Modeling of Success Factors in Exporting: Cross-Validation and Further Development of an Export Performance Model," *Journal of International Marketing* 4, 2 (1996): 29–55.

2. Brendan J. Gray, "Profiling Managers to Improve Export Promotion Targeting," *Journal of International Business Studies* 28, 2 (1997): 387–420.

3. Anthony C. Koh and James Chow, "An Empirical Investigation of the Variations in Success Factors in

Exporting by Country Characteristics," *Midwest Review of International Business Research,* ed. Tom Sharkey, Vol. VII (Toledo, 1993).

4. S. Tamer Cavusgil, "Preparing for Export Marketing," *International Trade Forum* 2 (1993): 16–30.

5. Michael R. Czinkota, *Export Development Strategies* (New York: Praeger, 1982), 10.

6. Michael Kutschker and Iris Bäuerle, "Three Plus One: Multidimensional Strategy of Internationalization," *Management International Review* 37, 2 (1997): 103–125.

7. Michael Kutschker, Iris Bäuerle, and Stefan Schmid, "International Evolution, International Episodes, and International Epochs—Implications for Managing Internationalization," *Management International Review,* Special Issue 2 (1997): 101–124.

8. Kent Eriksson, Jan Johanson, Anders Majkgard, and D. Deo Sharma, "Experiential Knowledge and Cost in the Internationalization Process," *Journal of International Business Studies* 28, 2 (1997): 337–360.

9. Masaaki Kotabe and Michael R. Czinkota, "State Government Promotion of Manufacturing Exports: A Gap Analysis," *Journal of International Business Studies* (Winter 1992): 637–658.

10. Yoo S. Yang, Robert P. Leone, and Dana L. Alden, "A Market Expansion Ability Approach to Identify Potential Exporters," *Journal of Marketing* 56 (January 1992): 84–96.

11. Michael R. Czinkota and Michael L. Ursic, "An Experience Curve Explanation of Export Expansion," in *International Marketing Strategy* (Fort Worth: Dryden Press, 1994), 133–141.

12. Carl Arthur Solberg, "A Framework for Analysis of Strategy Development in Globalizing Markets," *Journal of International Marketing* 5, 1 (1997): 9–30.

13. Michael R. Czinkota, "A National Export Development Policy for New and Growing Businesses," *Journal of International Marketing* 2, 1 (1994): 91–101.

14. Van Miller, Tom Becker, and Charles Crespy, "Contrasting Export Strategies: A Discriminant Analysis Study of Excellent Exporters," *The International Trade Journal* 7, 3 (1993): 321–340.

15. "New 'Storeless' Market Gateways," *Focus Japan,* August 1989, 3.

16. Daniel C. Bello, David J. Urban, and Bronislaw J. Verhage, "Evaluating Export Middlemen in Alternative Channel Structures," *International Marketing Review* 8 (1991): 49–64.

17. John Hoagland, Federal Trade Commission, December 5, 1997.

18. Dong-Sung Cho, *The General Trading Company: Concept and Strategy* (Lexington, Mass.: Lexington Books, 1987), 2.

19. Lee Smith, "Does the World's Biggest Company Have a Future?" *Fortune* (August 7, 1995): 125.

20. Yoshi Tsurumi, *Sogoshosha: Engines of Export-Based Growth* (Montreal: The Institute for Research on Public Policy, 1980).

21. Atilla Dicle and Ulku Dicle, "Effects of Government Export Policies on Turkish Export Trading Companies," *International Marketing Review* 9, 3 (1992): 62–76.

22. Vanessa Bachman, Office of Export Trading Companies, U.S. Department of Commerce, Washington, D.C., Jan. 7, 1998.

23. Nancy Lloyd Pfahl, "Using a Partnership Strategy to Establish an International Trade Assistance Program," *Economic Development Review* (Winter 1994): 51–59.

24. Martin F. Connor, "International Technology Licensing" (Washington, D.C.: Seminars in International Trade, National Center for Export-Import Studies, 1985), Teaching Notes.

25. Donald W. Hackett, "The International Expansion of U.S. Franchise Systems," in *Multinational Product Management,* ed. Warren J. Keegan and Charles S. Mayer (Chicago: American Marketing Association, 1979), 61–81.

26. Josh Martin, "Profitable Supply Chain" *The Journal of Commerce,* March 11, 1998, 1 C, 23 C.

27. Arthur Andersen, "Franchise Services," 1997, JAM Research. **www.arthurandersen.com** and International Franchise Association, **www.franchise.org** .

28. Nizamettin Aydin and Madhav Kacker, "International Outlook of U.S.-Based Franchisers," *International Marketing Review* 7 (1990): 43–53.

# CHAPTER 12

# Multinational Corporations

## LEARNING OBJECTIVES

◆ *To define the concept of a multinational corporation and assess its various dimensions*

◆ *To compare arguments for and against foreign direct investment from the viewpoints of firms, nation-states, and other interest groups*

◆ *To examine the role of technology transfer in foreign direct investment and the operations of the multinational corporation*

◆ *To analyze the various modes of operation and cooperation available to a multinational corporation*

## The Stateless Corporation

**A**s cross-border trade and investment flows reach new heights, big global companies are effectively making decisions with little regard to national boundaries. The European, U.S., and Japanese giants heading in this direction are learning how to juggle multiple identities and multiple loyalties. Worried by the emergence of regional trading blocs in Europe, North America, and east Asia, these world corporations are building insider capabilities no matter where they operate. At the same time, factories and laboratories are moved around the world freely. Given the wave of mergers, acquisitions, and strategic alliances, the question of national control has become even more unclear. Technological change is blurring other boundaries as well. For example, the internet allows professionals in India to perform routine architectural or audit work for clients in New York or London at sizable savings.

A fitting example of such a corporation is ABB (Asea Brown Boveri), a $36 billion electrical engineering giant. From headquarters in Zurich, Swedish, German, and Swiss managers shuffle assets around the globe, keep the books in dollars, and conduct most of their business in English. Yet the companies that make up their far-flung operations tailor ABB's turbines, transformers, robots, and high-speed trains to local markets so successfully that ABB looks like an established domestic player everywhere.

Statelessness does provide certain environmental advantages. Among the benefits are the ability to avoid trade and political problems, to sidestep regulatory hurdles, to achieve labor concessions, to balance costs, and to win technology breakthroughs.

The Canadian telecommunications giant, Nortel, has moved so many of its manufacturing functions to the United States that it can win Japanese contracts on the basis of being a U.S. company. Japan favors U.S. over Canadian telecommunications companies because of the politically sensitive U.S.–Japanese trade gap.

When Germany's BASF launched biotechnology research at home, it confronted legal and political challenges from the environmentally conscious green movement. As a result, the company moved its cancer and immune-system research to Cambridge, Massachusetts, because of the availability of engineers and scientists and because the state had better resolved controversies involving safety, animal rights, and the environment.

One of the main factors that prompted U.S. pharmaceutical maker Smith-Kline and Britain's Beecham to merge was that they needed to guarantee that they could avoid licensing and regulatory hassles in their largest markets, western Europe and the United States. The company can now identify itself as an inside player on both sides of the Atlantic.

When Xerox Corp. started moving copier rebuilding work to Mexico, its union in Rochester, New York, objected. The risk of job loss was clear, and the union agreed to undertake the changes in work style and productivity needed to keep the jobs.

Some world companies make almost daily decisions on where to shift production. When Dow Chemical saw European demand for a certain solvent decline recently, the company scaled back its production in Germany and shifted to producing another chemical there, one previously imported from Louisiana and Texas.

Otis Elevator Inc.'s latest product, the Elevonic 411, benefited from the company's global operations. The elevator was developed by six research centers in five countries. Otis's group in Farmington, Connecticut, handled the systems integration, Japan designed the special motor drives that make the elevators ride smoothly, France perfected the door systems, Germany handled the electronics, and Spain took care of the small-geared components. The international process saved more than $10 million in design costs and cut the development cycle from four years to two.

Multinational corporations are usually better than their more local rivals at creating, gathering, and cross-fertilizing knowledge. They enjoy access to a larger pool of management talent, a wider range of skills, and a greater variety of perspectives, and they are likely to know more about such things as consumer trends, technological needs, and competitors' moves.

Some analysts have suggested that today's global firms will be superseded by a new form, the "relationship enterprise." These are networks of strategic alliances among big firms, spanning different industries and countries, but held together by common goals that encourage them to act almost as a single firm. For example, early in the twenty-first century, Boeing, British Airways, Siemens, TNT (an Australian parcel-delivery firm), and SNECMA (a French aircraft-engine maker) might together win a deal to build new airports in China. British Airways and TNT would receive preferential routes and landing slots, Boeing and SNECMA would win aircraft contracts, and Siemens would provide the air traffic control systems.  ▪

*Source:* "Perspective: The Heart of the New World Economy," *Financial Times,* October 1, 1997, 1; "Big Is Back," *The Economist,* June 24, 1995. A Survey of Multinationals, 1–24; Peter Norman, "World Economy and Finance," *Financial Times,* September 30, 1994, 1, 32; "The Global Firm: R.I.P.," *The Economist,* February 6, 1993, 69; "Cooperation Worth Copying," *The Washington Post,* December 13, 1992, H1, H6; and "The Stateless Corporation," *Business Week,* May 14, 1990, 98–106; **http://www.nortel.com**; **http://www.abb.com**; **http://www.basf.com**; **http://www.sb.com**; **http://www.xerox.com**; **http://www.dow.com**; **http://www.otis.com**.

**WWW**

Once a firm establishes a production facility abroad, its international operations take on new meaning. The firm has typically evolved to this stage through exporting and/or licensing, which by themselves can no longer satisfy its growth objectives. Many companies have found their exports dramatically curtailed because of unfavorable changes in exchange rates or trade barriers. Moreover, for firms in small domestic markets, physical presence through manufacturing is a must in the world's largest markets if the firm is to survive in the long term. Direct investment makes the firm's commitment to the international marketplace more permanent.

At the same time, the firm also becomes a corporate citizen in another nation-state, subject to its laws and regulations as well as its overall environmental influences. To remain effective and efficient as an entity, the firm has to coordinate and control its activities in multiple environments, making decisions that may not be optimal for one or more of the markets in which it operates. As a result, the firm may come under scrutiny by private and public organizations, ranging from consumer groups to supranational organizations such as the United Nations.

In today's environment—with no single country dominating the world economy or holding a monopoly on innovation—technologies, capital, and talents flow in many different directions, driving the trend toward a form of "stateless" corporation, as seen in the chapter's opening vignette.

This chapter will outline the basics of the multinational corporate phenomenon. It will compare the arguments for and against foreign direct investment from the viewpoints of firms, nation-states, and other interest groups. Further, it will analyze alternative arrangements available to multinational corporations in their operations in the world marketplace.

## The Multinational Corporate Phenomenon

Multinational entities have played a role in international trade for more than 300 years. The beginnings of these operations can be traced to the British and Dutch trading companies and, after their decline, to European overseas investments, mainly in the extractive industries. The phenomenon as it is known today is the result of the lead taken by U.S.–based companies in the post–World War II period and later followed by western European and Japanese entities.[1] By 1998 the total number of multinationals exceeded 45,000 with 280,000 affiliates around the world.[2] They are engaged in activities from the extractive to the manufacturing sectors, and they account for a significant share of the world's output. The global sales of foreign affiliates of multinationals are estimated to be $7 trillion, far greater than world exports at $5 trillion. The largest 600 multinationals are estimated to generate between one-fifth and one-fourth of the value added in the production of goods and services.[3]

### The Multinational Corporation Defined

Different terms abound for the multinational corporation. They include global, world, transnational, international, supernational, and supranational corporation. The term *multinational enterprise* is used by some when referring to internationally involved entities that may not be using a corporate form. In this text, the term *multinational corporation (MNC)* will be used throughout.

Similarly, there is an abundance of definitions. The United Nations defines multinational corporations as "enterprises that own or control production or service facilities outside the country in which they are based."[4] Although this definition has been criticized as being oriented too much to the economist,[5] it nevertheless captures the quantitative and qualitative dimensions of many of the other definitions proposed.

Quantitatively, certain minimal criteria have been proposed that firms must satisfy before they can be regarded as multinational. The number of countries of operation is typically two, although the Harvard multinational enterprise project required subsidiaries in six or more nations.[6] Another measure is the proportion of overall revenue generated from foreign operations. Although no agreement exists regarding the exact percentage to be used, 25 to 30 percent is most often cited.[7] One proposal is that the degree of involvement in foreign markets has to be substantial enough to make a difference in decision making. Another study proposed that several nations should be owners of the corporation, as is the case with Royal Dutch Shell Group and Unilever or as in the merger between Swiss Brown Boveri and Swedish Asea to form ABB.[8]

However, production abroad does not necessarily indicate a multinational corporation. Qualitatively, the behavior of the firm is the determining factor. If the firm is to be categorized as a multinational corporation, its management must consider it to be multinational and must act accordingly. In terms of management philosophies, firms can be categorized as **ethnocentric** (home-market oriented), **polycentric** (oriented toward individual foreign markets), or **regiocentric** or **geocentric** (oriented toward larger areas, even the global marketplace).[9] Even ethnocentric firms would qualify as multinational corporations if production were the sole criterion. However, the term should be reserved for firms that view their domestic operation as a part of worldwide (or regionwide) operations and direct an integrated business system. The definition excludes polycentric firms, which may be comparable to holding companies.

Both quantitative and qualitative criteria are important in the defining task. Regardless of the definition, the key criteria are that the firm controls its production facilities abroad and manages them (and its domestic operations) in an integrated fashion in pursuit of global opportunities.

## The World's Multinational Corporations

Many of the world's largest corporate entities, listed in Table 12.1, are larger economically than most of their host nations. Some operate in well over 100 countries; for example, IBM has operations in 132 nations. Of the 25 firms listed, 10 are headquartered in the United States, 8 in western Europe, and 7 in east Asia. The economic power they command is enormous; according to one estimate, the 500 largest industrial corporations account for 80 percent of the world's direct investment and ownership of foreign affiliates.[10]

Although dominated by certain countries, the multinational corporate phenomenon has spread worldwide. For example, corporate headquarters for the 500 largest industrial corporations are in 32 different nations. Direct investment by firms from Africa, Asia, and Latin America has increased dramatically, especially by firms from more industrialized nations such as the Republic of Korea, Mexico, and Brazil.[11] Among the largest in 1997 were Daewoo from Korea, a diversified industrial conglomerate, as well as Petroleos de Venezuela, a state-owned oil company. Of these companies, Pan-American Beverages of Mexico has the highest share of sales outside its home country, 73 percent.[12]

**TABLE 12.1**

**The 25 Largest Industrial Corporations Ranked By Sales: 1996**

| Rank | Company | Country | Sales in $ millions | Foreign Revenue (% of total) | Foreign Profit (% of Total) |
|------|---------|---------|---------------------|------------------------------|------------------------------|
| 1. | General Motors | US | 168369.0 | 31 | 31 |
| 2. | Ford | US | 146991.0 | 32.7 | 5 |
| 3. | Royal Dutch/Shell Group | UK/Neth | 128174.5 | N/A | 87.7 |
| 4. | Exxon | US | 119434.0 | 76.8 | 68.6 |
| 5. | Toyota Motor | JPN | 108702.0 | 47.4 | N/A |
| 6. | Wal-Mart | US | 106147.0 | 4.8 | .4 |
| 7. | General Electric | US | 79179.0 | 29.5 | 21.9 |
| 8. | Nippon Telephone and Telegraph | JPN | 78320.7 | N/A | N/A |
| 9. | IBM | US | 75947.0 | 61.3 | 65.2 |
| 10. | Hitachi | JPN | 75669.0 | 31 | N/A |
| 11. | AT&T | US | 74525.0 | N/A | N/A |
| 12. | Mobil | US | 72267.0 | 67.2 | 61.1 |
| 13. | Daimler-Benz | Ger | 71589.3 | 63.1 | N/A |
| 14. | British Petroleum | UK | 69851.9 | N/A | N/A |
| 15. | Matsushita Electric | JPN | 68147.5 | 47.2 | N/A |
| 16. | Volkswagen | Ger | 66527.5 | N/A | N/A |
| 17. | Daewoo | Sth Korea | 65160.2 | 21.3 | N/A |
| 18. | Siemens | Ger | 63704.7 | 33.94 | 46 |
| 19. | Chrysler | US | 61397.0 | 13.4 | 9.0 |
| 20. | Nissan Motor | JPN | 59118.2 | 48.7 | 14.4 |
| 21. | Philip Morris | US | 54553.0 | 36 | 25.5 |
| 22. | Unilever | UK/Neth | 52067.4 | 51.35 | 46.8 |
| 23. | Fiat | Italy | 50509.0 | N/A | N/A |
| 24. | Sony | JPN | 50277.9 | 71.9 | 29.9 |
| 25. | Nestlé | Switz | 48932.5 | N/A | N/A |

*Source:* "The International 500," *Forbes* (July 28, 1997): 218; "The Global 500," *Fortune* (August 4, 1997): F-2; and various 1996 and 1997 annual reports. See also **http://www.forbes.com** and **http://www.pathfinder.com/fortune/**.

The impact of multinationals varies by industry sector and by country. In oil, multinational corporations still command 30 percent of production, despite strong national efforts by some countries. Their share in refining and marketing is still 45 percent. In several agribusiness sectors, such as pineapples, multinationals account for approximately 60 percent of the world output. Similarly, the contribution of multinational corporations' affiliates may account for more than one-third of the output of the marketing sector in certain countries. For example, U.S. companies owned 32 percent of the paper and pulp industry, 36 percent of the mining and smelting industry, and 39 percent of manufacturing overall in Canada before the foreign direct investment climate changed in the early 1980s.[13] Despite a tightening of investment regulations, 40 percent of Canadian manufacturing is foreign owned with U.S. firms accounting for 80 percent of that share.

The importance of the world marketplace to multinational corporations also varies. The foreign sales share of total sales for the world's largest industrial corporations has increased steadily. The percentage will naturally vary by industry (for example, oil company ratios are well over half) and by the country of origin. For many European-based companies, domestic sales may be less than 10 percent of overall sales. In 1997, for example, as a percentage of total worldwide sales, Philips's sales in Holland were 4 percent, SKF's sales in Sweden were 4 percent, and Sandoz's sales in Switzerland were a mere 2 percent. Comparable figures for U.S.–based companies, such as Johnson & Johnson and 3M, are about 50 percent.

The 1980s saw an increasing multinationalization of service companies, mainly in the finance and trade-related services, although other service MNCs such as accounting and advertising firms established considerable numbers of affiliates abroad.

## Foreign Direct Investment

To understand the multinational corporate phenomenon, one must analyze the rationale for foreign direct investment. Foreign direct investment represents one component of the international business flow and includes start-ups of new operations as well as purchases of more than 10 percent of existing companies. The other component is portfolio investment—that is, the purchase of stocks and bonds internationally—which was discussed in Chapter 7.

Foreign direct investment has only recently received adequate attention. In 1974, for example, no comprehensive list of foreign firms investing in the United States was available, no one knew which firms were indeed foreign owned, and major shortcomings existed in the foreign direct investment data available.[14] In view of the fact that the U.S. data-gathering system is highly sophisticated, much less information about foreign direct investment was probably available in other countries.

Recent concerted data-gathering and estimation efforts by organizations such as the Organization for Economic Cooperation and Development (OECD) and the International Monetary Fund (IMF) indicate that foreign direct investments have grown tremendously. The total value of such global investment, which in 1967 was estimated at $105 billion, had climbed to an estimated $596 billion by 1984[15] and $3.2 trillion by 1998.[16] Foreign direct investment has clearly become a major avenue for foreign market entry and expansion. Foreign direct investment in the United States, for example, totaled $630 billion in 1996, up from a meager $6.9 billion in 1970.[17] At the same time, U.S. direct investment abroad totaled $796 billion.

## Reasons for Foreign Direct Investment

Firms expand internationally for a variety of reasons. An overview of the major determinants of foreign direct investment is provided in Table 12.2.

**Marketing Factors**  Marketing considerations and the corporate desire for growth are major causes of the increase in foreign direct investment. Even a sizable domestic market may present limitations to growth. Firms therefore need to seek wider market access in order to maintain and increase their sales. Laidlaw Transportation Ltd., the biggest school bus operator in Canada, moved

**TABLE 12.2**

**Major Determinants of Direct Foreign Investment**

**Marketing Factors**
1. Size of market
2. Market growth
3. Desire to maintain share of market
4. Desire to advance exports of parent company
5. Need to maintain close customer contact
6. Dissatisfaction with existing market arrangements
7. Export base
8. Desire to follow customers
9. Desire to follow competition

**Barriers to Trade**
1. Government-erected barriers to trade
2. Preference of local customers for local products

**Cost Factors**
1. Desire to be near source of supply
2. Availability of labor
3. Availability of raw materials
4. Availability of capital/technology
5. Lower labor costs
6. Lower other production costs
7. Lower transport costs
8. Financial (and other) inducements by government
9. More favorable cost levels

**Investment Climate**
1. General attitude toward foreign investment
2. Political stability
3. Limitation on ownership
4. Currency exchange regulations
5. Stability of foreign exchange
6. Tax structure
7. Familiarity with country

**General**
1. Expected higher profits
2. Other

*Source:* Adapted from Organization for Economic Cooperation and Development, *International Investment and Multinational Enterprises* (Paris: OECD, 1983), 41.

south of the border, where it saw considerably more room to grow. Business has quadrupled, and the company now draws 60 percent of its revenue from the United States.[18] Some firms make investments in order to be closer to and better serve some of their major clients, such as Siemens with its $4.3 billion investment in the U.S. market. The growth objective can be achieved most quickly through the acquisition of foreign firms. In 1994, for example, the value of cross-border deals was $239 billion, with U.S. firms leading in the efforts by buying 1,173 companies abroad and selling 668 companies to non–U.S. entities.[19] One of the companies that has made the largest acquisitions in the U.S. market in recent years is Nestlé, which has acquired companies such as Carnation and Alcon Laboratories. Other reasons for foreign direct investment include the desire to gain know-how and the need to add to existing sales force strength.

A major cause for the recent growth in foreign direct investment is derived demand. Often, as large multinational firms move abroad, they are quite interested in maintaining their established business relationships with other firms. Therefore, they frequently encourage their suppliers to follow them and continue to supply them from the new foreign location. For example, advertising agencies often move abroad in order to service foreign affiliates of their domestic clients. Similarly, engineering firms, insurance companies, and law firms often are invited to provide their services abroad. Yet not all of these developments come about from co-optation by client firms. Often firms invest abroad for defensive reasons, out of fear that their clients may find other sources abroad, which also eventually might jeopardize their status even in the domestic market. To preserve quality, Japanese automakers have urged more than forty of their suppliers from Japan to establish production in the United States.[20]

For similar reasons, firms follow their competitors abroad. Competitive firms influence not only their engaging in foreign direct investment, but even where the investments are made.[21] Many firms have found that even their competitive position at home is affected by their ability to effectively compete in foreign markets.

**Barriers to Trade**   Foreign direct investment permits firms to circumvent barriers to trade and operate abroad as domestic firms, unaffected by duties, tariffs, or other import restrictions. The enormous amount of U.S. investment would not have been originally attracted to Canada had it not been for the barriers to trade erected by the Canadian government to support domestic industry. At the same time, with the worldwide reduction in tariffs, foreign direct investment behavior is changing. In Australia, the tariff on imported cars has fallen from 57.5 percent to 22.5 percent, while the number of imported cars has increased from 15 percent to half of the sales. One large car maker, Nissan, has abandoned local manufacturing as a result, and others have threatened to follow unless the pace of tariff reductions slows down.[22]

In addition to government-erected barriers, barriers may also be imposed by customers through their insistence on domestic goods and services, either as a result of nationalistic tendencies or as a function of cultural differences. Futhermore, local buyers may want to buy from sources that they perceive to be reliable in their supply, which means buying from local producers. For some products, country-of-origin effects may force a firm to establish a plant in a country that has a built-in positive stereotype for product quality.[23]

**Cost Factors**   Servicing markets at sizable geographic distances and with sizable tariff barriers has made many exporters' offerings in foreign markets prohibitively expensive. Many manufacturing multinationals have established plants overseas to gain cost advantages in terms of labor and raw materials. For example, many of the border plants in Mexico provide their U.S. parents with low-cost inputs and components through the maquiladora program.

Foreign direct investment occurs not only horizontally, by firms acquiring or establishing similar firms abroad, but also vertically. Some firms engage in foreign direct investment to secure their sources of supply for raw materials and other intermediary goods. This usually secures supply and may provide it at a lower cost as well.

All in all, cost factors are not necessarily the primary attraction for manufacturers to make foreign direct investments, as seen in Global Perspective 12.1. The need for highly skilled labor and developed communication, transportation, and institutional infrastructures has increased.[24] The emergence of manufacturing technologies such as flexible manufacturing systems and total quality management have increased the importance of worker education and skill. Just-in-time logistics systems increase dependence on suppliers and the reliability of the transportation infrastructure. While manufacturing sites may be chosen due to proximity to technological resources, such as Motorola's decision to produce cellular phones in the "Silicon Glen" area of Scotland, choosing a site for a distribution center in integrated markets will be influenced by the countries' logistics platforms (as seen in Chapter 16). For example, Bausch & Lomb's European distribution center is located at Schipol Airport in Amsterdam, Holland, due not only to its central geographic location but also to the excellent logistics network.

**Investment Climate**   Foreign direct investment by definition implies a degree of control over the enterprise.[25] Yet this may be unavailable because of environmental constraints, even if the firm owns 100 percent of the subsidiary. The general attitude toward foreign investment and its development over time may be indicative of the long-term prospects for investment. For example, if asked to choose, 48 percent of Americans would discourage Japanese investment and only 18 percent would encourage it.[26] In many countries, foreign direct investment tends to arouse nationalistic feelings. Political risk has to be defined broadly to include not only the threat of political upheaval but also the likelihood of arbitrary or discriminatory government action that will result in financial loss. This could take the form of tax increases, price controls, or measures directed specifically at foreign firms such as partial divestment of ownership, local-content requirements, remittance restrictions, export requirements, and limits on expatriate employment.[27] The investment climate is also measured in terms of foreign currency risk. The evaluations will typically focus on possible accounting translation exposure levels and cashflows in foreign currency.

In a survey of 108 U.S.–based multinational corporations, foreign direct investment was found to be profit and growth driven.[28] The influence of the other variables will vary depending on the characteristics of the firm and its management, on its objectives, and on external conditions.

## The Host-Country Perspective

The host government is caught in a love-hate relationship with foreign direct investment. On the one hand, the host country has to appreciate the various contributions, especially economic, that the foreign direct investment will make. On the other hand, fears of dominance, interference, and dependence are often voiced and acted on. The major positive and negative impacts are summarized in Table 12.3.

# SEARCH FOR THE RIGHT MANUFACTURING PLAN

**A** study by Ernst & Young finds that only one-third of 650 projects announced by U.S. public companies went to countries with low-cost labor and that the majority were placed in targeted industrialized markets. Getting as close as possible to customers now outweighs all other variables. Although producing close to customers is not new, it has taken on added significance as competitive pressures have escalated and manufacturing processes constantly have changed.

Just two of the ten countries that attracted the most U.S. investments, Mexico and Russia, have cheap labor (defined by the U.S. Labor Department as less than 25 percent of U.S. wages). Altogether, only 196 new projects (30 percent) were destined for low-cost-labor nations. The most popular sites for new projects were Canada, the United Kingdom, Germany, and France.

The main reasons U.S. manufacturers locate overseas is to gain footholds in prime markets. Many U.S. companies are looking to build market share in industrialized countries by gaining access to customers, technology, and skills, as opposed to choosing a country due to the availability of cheap labor. Other important factors, particularly for first-time investors, are financial incentives and low corporate tax rates. The importance of labor costs naturally is affected by the type of business. Labor-intensive industries such as textiles are still looking for cheap employment. But even those industries will think first about producing in countries that have both low labor costs and big markets.

Europe, mainly the EU, was the most popular site for U.S. investment (357 projects). Asia attracted 20 percent of all the projects, and four-fifths of the projects in Asia were joint ventures. Only 22 projects were announced for South America and the Caribbean, 6 for the Middle East, and only 1 for Africa.

The opening of markets has complicated the decision on production locations. Costs themselves are ever changing, making today's Vietnam tomorrow's Hong Kong. The reality of an investment decision may be shaped by how quickly a location can be changed. Similarly, the opening of markets may mean that manufacturing (and its location) has to be structured so that products can be adapted to serve different markets within a region. Investments in production facilities may also be made to drive different objectives; for example, a facility in Japan may be necessary to contribute to product development, while the facility in China will be charged with mass production on a worldwide basis.

**Top U.S. Investment Locations**

| Country* | Number of Projects |
|---|---|
| Canada | 84 |
| United Kingdom | 72 |
| Germany | 60 |
| France | 59 |
| MEXICO | 56 |
| Japan | 43 |
| RUSSIA | 20 |
| Australia | 17 |
| Italy | 17 |
| Netherlands | 16 |
| Spain | 16 |
| Ireland | 15 |
| CHINA | 14 |
| HUNGARY | 14 |
| POLAND | 12 |
| INDIA | 11 |
| Belgium | 10 |
| South Korea | 10 |
| Brazil | 8 |
| INDONESIA | 8 |

\* Uppercase indicates countries with low rates for hourly labor.

*Source: "Lowest Cost Isn't Always the Answer,"* Financial Times, *October 15, 1997, 10–11; Carla Kruytbosch, "Where in the World to Make It,"* International Business, *February 1994, 53–76; and Gregory Sandler, "NAFTA Aims Spotlight at Border Site,"* Export Today 8 *(November/December 1992): 19. See also* http://www.ey.com.

**The Positive Impact**   Foreign direct investment has contributed greatly to world development in the past forty years. Said Lord Lever, a British businessman who served in the cabinets of Harold Wilson and James Callaghan, "Europe got twenty times more out of American investment after the war than the multinationals did; every country gains by productive investment.[29]

**WWW**

**TABLE 12.3**

**Positive and Negative Impacts of Foreign Direct Investment on Host Countries**

**Positive Impact**
1. Capital formation
2. Technology and management skills transfer
3. Regional and sectoral development
4. Internal competition and entrepreneurship
5. Favorable effect on balance of payments
6. Increased employment

**Negative Impact**
1. Industrial dominance
2. Technological dependence
3. Disturbance of economic plans
4. Cultural change
5. Interference by home government of multinational corporation

*Sources:* Jack N. Behrman, *National Interests and the Multinational Enterprise* (Englewood Cliffs. N.J.: Prentice-Hall, 1970), Chapters 2 through 5; Jack N. Behrman, *Industrial Policies: International Restructuring and Transnationals* (Lexington, Mass.: Lexington Books, 1984), Chapter 5; and Christopher M. Korth, *International Business* (Englewood Cliffs, N.J.: Prentice-Hall 1985), Chapters 12 and 13.

Capital flows are especially beneficial to countries with limited domestic sources and restricted opportunities to raise funds in the world's capital markets. In addition, foreign direct investment may attract local capital to a project for which local capital alone would not have sufficed.

The role of foreign direct investment has been seen as that of **technology transfer.**[30] Technology transfer includes the introduction of not only new hardware to the market but also the techniques and skills to operate it. In industries where the role of intellectual property is substantial, such as pharmaceuticals or software development, access to parent companies' research and development provides benefits that may be far greater than those gained through infusion of capital. This explains the interest that many governments have expressed in having multinational corporations establish R&D facilities in their countries.

An integral part of technology transfer is managerial skills, which are the most significant labor component of foreign direct investment. With the growth of the service sector, many economies need skills rather than expatriate personnel to perform the tasks.

Foreign direct investment can be used effectively in developing a geographical region or a particular industry sector. Foreign direct investment is one of the most expedient ways in which unemployment can be reduced in chosen regions of a country. Futhermore, the costs of establishing an industry are often too prohibitive and the time needed too excessive for the domestic industry, even with governmental help, to try it on its own. In many developing countries, foreign direct investment may be a way to diversify the industrial base and thereby reduce the country's dependence on one or a few sectors.

At the company level, foreign direct investment may intensify competition and result in benefits to the economy as a whole as well as to consumers through increased productivity and possibly lower prices. Competition typically introduces new techniques, goods and services, and ideas to the markets. It may improve existing patterns of how business is done.

The major impact of foreign direct investment on the balance of payments is long term. Import substitution, export earnings, and subsidized imports of technology and management all assist the host nation on the trade account side of the balance of payments. Not only may a new production facility substantially decrease the need to import the type of products manufactured, but it may start earning export revenue as well. Several countries, such as Brazil, have imposed export requirements as a precondition for foreign direct investment. On the capital account side, foreign direct investment may have short-term impact in lowering a deficit as well as long-term impact in keeping capital at home that otherwise could have been invested or transferred abroad. However, measurement is difficult because significant portions of the flows may miss—or evade—the usual government reporting channels. In 1990, more than half of foreign investment was "unidentified," in that experts could not figure out what type it was or where it came from.[31]

Jobs are often the most obvious reason to cheer about foreign direct investment. Foreign companies directly employ three million Americans, or about 3 percent of the workforce, and indirectly create opportunities for millions more. The benefits reach far beyond mere employment. Salaries paid by multinational corporations are usually higher than those paid by domestic firms. The creation of jobs translates also into the training and development of a skilled work force. Consider, for example, the situation of many Caribbean states that are dependent on tourism for their well-being. In most cases, multinational hotel chains have been instrumental in establishing a pool of trained hospitality workers and managers.

All of the benefits discussed are indeed possible advantages of foreign direct investment. Their combined effect can lead to an overall enhancement in the standard of living in the market as well as an increase in the host country's access to the world market and its international competitiveness. It is equally possible, however, that the impact can be negative rather than positive.

**The Negative Impact**   Although some of the threats posed by multinational corporations and foreign direct investment in terms of stunted economic development, low levels of research and development, and poor treatment of local employees are exaggerated, in many countries some industrial sectors are dominated by foreign-owned entities. In France, for example, three-fourths of the computer and data-processing equipment sector was dominated by foreign affiliates in the 1980s.[32] In Belgium, oil refining (78 percent) and electrical engineering (87 percent) showed the highest rates of foreign participation.[33]

Foreign direct investment most often is concentrated in technology-intensive industries, therefore, research and development is another area of tension. Multinational corporations usually want to concentrate their R&D efforts, especially their basic research. With its technology transfer, the multinational corporation can assist the host country's economic development, but it may leave the host country dependent on flows of new and updated technology. Futhermore, the multinational firm may contribute to the **brain drain** by attracting scientists from host countries to its central research facility. Many countries have demanded and received research facilities on their soil, where they can better control results. Many countries are weary of the technological dominance of the United States and Japan and view it as a long-term threat. Western European nations, for example, are joining forces in basic research and development under the auspices of the so-called EUREKA project, which is a pan-European pooling of resources to develop new technologies with both governmental and private sector help.

Many of the economic benefits of foreign direct investment are controversial as well. Capital inflows may be accompanied by outflows in a higher degree and over a longer term than is satisfactory to the host government. For example, many of the hotels built in the Caribbean by multinational chains were unable to find local suppliers and had to import supplies and thus spend much-needed foreign currency. Many officials also complain that the promised training of local personnel, especially for management positions, has never taken place. Rather than stimulate local competition and encourage entrepreneurship, multinationals with their often superior product offering and marketing skills have stifled competition. Many countries, including the United States, have found that multinational companies do not necessarily want to rely on local suppliers but rather bring along their own from their domestic market.

Many governments see multinationals as a disturbance to their economic planning. Decisions are made concerning their economy over which they have little or no control. Host countries do not look favorably on a multinational that may want to keep the import content of a product high, especially when local suppliers may be available.

Multinational companies are, by definition, change agents. They bring about change not only in the way business my be conducted but also, through the products and services they generate and the way they are marketed, cause change in the lifestyles of the consumers in the market. The extent to which this is welcomed or accepted varies by country. For example, the introduction of fast-food restaurants to Taiwan dramatically altered eating patterns, especially of teenagers, who made these outlets extremely popular and profitable. Concern has been expressed about the apparent change in eating patterns and the higher relative cost of eating in such establishments.

The multinational corporation will also have an impact on business practices. Although multinationals usually pay a higher salary, they may also engage in practices that are alien to the local work force, such as greater flexibility in work rules. Older operators in Japan, for example, may be removed from production lines to make room for more productive employees. In another country where the Japanese firm establishes a plant, tradition and union rules may prevent this.[34]

Some host nations have expressed concern over the possibility of interference, economically and politically, by the home government of the multinational corporation; that is, they fear that the multinational may be used as an instrument of influence.[35] The United States has used U.S.–based corporations to extend its foreign policy in areas of capital flows, technology controls, and competition. Foreign direct investment regulations were introduced in the United States in the 1960s to diminish capital outflows from the country and thus to strengthen the country's balance-of-payment situation. If the actions of affiliates of U.S.–based companies are seen to have a negative impact on competition in the U.S. market, antitrust decrees may be used to change

# The Operations & Structure of a Multinational Firm

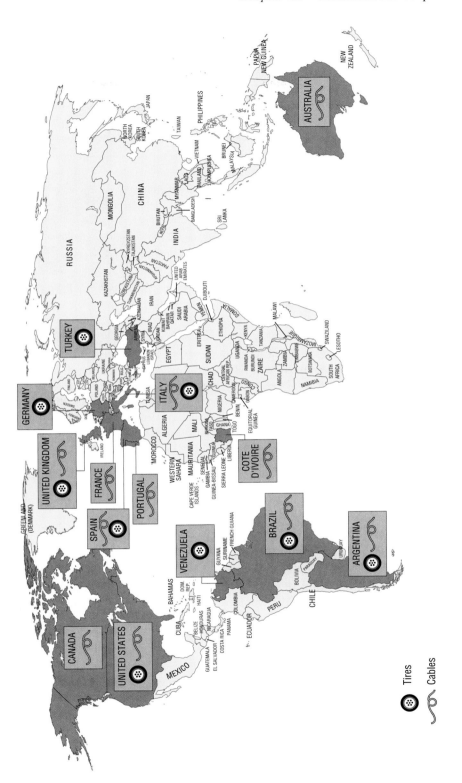

Tires
Cables

Source: Pirelli Group

Foreign direct investment creates jobs. The United States benefits from additional employment opportunities provided by foreign investment in production facilities such as the Toyota-GM plant in California.

*Source:* Courtesy of New United Motor Manufacturing, Inc.

the situation. Increasingly, major foreign direct investments are screened by the Committee for Foreign Investments in the United States (CFIUS). Concerns have been raised mainly in terms of national security and the large number of investors from a particular country, whether they are from the United States or Japan.

Of course, the multinational is available not only to the home government as a political or economic instrument but to the host government and other groups as well. Fixed investments by multinationals can be held hostage by a host country in trying to win concessions from other governments. In an increasing number of cases, host governments insist on quid pro quo deals in which foreign direct investment is contingent on adherence to specified requirements, such as export targets. Many United Nations sanctions, although approved by governments, have to be carried out through the compliance of multinational companies, as was the case with the divestment that took place to force the South African government to abandon the policy of apartheid.

Countries engage in informal evaluation of foreign direct investment, both outbound and inbound. Canada, for example, uses the Foreign Investment Review Agency to determine whether foreign-owned companies are good corporate citizens. Sweden reviews outbound foreign direct investment in terms of its impact on the home country, especially employment.

## The Home-Country Perspective

Most of the aspects of foreign direct investment that concern host countries apply to the home country as well. Foreign direct investment means addition to the home country's gross national product from profits, royalties, and fees remitted by affiliates. In many cases, intracompany transfers bring about additional export possibilities.[36] Many countries, in promoting foreign direct investment, see it as a means to stimulate economic growth—an end that would expand export markets and serve other goals, such as political motives, as well. For example, the **Overseas Private Investment Corporation** provides insurance for new U.S. foreign direct investment in friendly developing countries against currency inconvertibility, expropriation, and political violence.[37] Some countries, such as Japan, have tried to gain preferential access to raw materials through firms that owned the deposits. Other factors of production can be obtained through foreign direct investment as well. Companies today may not have the luxury of establishing R&D facilities wherever they choose but must locate them where human power is available. This explains, for example, why Northern Telecom, the Canadian telecommunications giant, has more than 500 of its roughly 2,000 R&D people based in the United States, mostly in California.

The major negative issue centers on employment. Many unions point not only to outright job loss but also to the effect on imports and exports. The most controversial have been investments in plants in developing countries that export back to the home countries. Multinationals such as electronics manufacturers, who have moved plants to southeast Asia and Mexico, have justified this as a necessary cost-cutting competitive measure.

Another critical issue is that of technological advantage. Some critics state that, by establishing plants abroad or forming joint ventures with foreign entities, the country may be giving away its competitive position in the world marketplace. This is especially true when the recipients may be able to avoid the time and expense involved in developing new technologies.

The U.S. government has also taken a position on the behavior of U.S.–based firms overseas. The Foreign Corrupt Practices Act was passed in 1977, and a section of it deals with bribery. Although clear-cut bribery of elected officials is universally banned, the United States is the only country in the world that has legislation as extensive as the Foreign Corrupt Practices Act guiding the conduct of its firms abroad. Many U.S. firms have indeed complained about the negative impact that compliance has in some markets of the world where facilitating payments are common.[38] However, the international arena as a whole is changing in this regard. A total of thirty-four countries signed the Convention on Combating Bribery of Foreign Public Officials in International Business Transactions in 1997. The International Monetary Fund (IMF) is tying its loans to good governance—transparency and accountability—and has canceled loans due to lack of action against corruption by recipient governments.[39]

## Management of the Relationship

Arguments for and against foreign direct investment are endless. Costs and benefits must be weighed. Only the multinational corporation itself can assess expected gains against perceived risks in its overseas commitments. At the same time, only the host and home countries can assess benefits realized against costs in terms of their national priorities. If these entities cannot agree on objectives because their most basic interests are in conflict, they cannot agree on the means either. In most cases, the relationship between the parties is not necessarily based on logic, fairness, or equity, but on the relative bargaining power of each.[40] Futhermore, political changes may cause rapid changes in host government–MNC relations, as seen in Global Perspective 12.2.

The bargaining positions of the multinational corporation and the host country change over time. The course of these changes is summarized in Figure 12.1. The multinational wields its greatest power before the investment is

# THE RUSSIAN INVESTMENT DILEMMA

**B**usinesspeople from around the world have flocked to Moscow since 1986 when Soviet President Mikhail Gorbachev encouraged them to seek joint ventures with Soviet partners. Gorbachev's strategy was to revitalize the Soviet economy by introducing modern technology and Western business methods. The foreign companies were attracted by the huge untapped markets. After the breakup of the Soviet Union in December 1991, most of the interest focused on Russia as the largest of the new states.

By 1995, there were 18,000 joint ventures in Russia and more than $10 billion in foreign direct investment. Companies from the United States had the largest number of joint ventures in Russia, followed by Germany, Finland, and Austria. Large U.S. industrials are there, including IBM, GE, Kodak, Playtex, and AT&T. In 1993, PepsiCo. Signed a $3 billion multiyear trade pact, and in 1989–1990 McDonald's invested $50 million in a food-processing plant in Moscow. Thousands of small and mid-sized ventures also have arrived. Most of the joint ventures have been in software, tourism, and heavy industrial production. Significant growth has occurred in research and development. Companies such as Bell Labs are working with Russian scientists to study space, electronics, optics, lasers, and nuclear energy.

Some estimate that only 8 percent of the joint ventures have been successful due to conflicts with partners, capitalization problems, and clashes with bureaucracy. Once in Russia, a company has to live with a bewildering array of legal, economic, and political uncertainties. The struggle to introduce capitalism has produced a hodgepodge of commercial laws and regulations that are often vague, bizarre, or contradictory. Rules may change overnight. And it is frequently impossible to know which official is responsible for what decision. Companies may have to face more or less independent "substates" that decide which federal laws are accepted and which are not. One U.S. company spent several months preparing bids for a project after it had been assured that foreign bids would be considered. When the time came for the authorities to make the decision, however, they reversed themselves and allowed only Russian companies to bid. The pervasiveness of crime throughout the Russian economy will have a crippling effect on future prospects.

Among the biggest pitfalls is the uncertainty over property rights. Power struggles as to who controls physical assets may leave the Western entity in limbo. Otis Elevator Company, which has formed four joint ventures in Russia, obtains written statements from the highest public officials possible and then hopes for the best. "If a company needs a cast-iron guarantee that everything is in compliance with all laws and regulations, it will be very difficult to get things done," one company executive noted.

Other Western investors cut through legal tangles by persuading political leaders to issue decrees on their behalf. For example, a decree from Boris Yeltsin helped France's Elf Aquitane set up an oil exploration venture in Russia. Forming strong personal connections with regional leaders also will help. A high level of involvement will help convince the leaders and their constituents that the company's intent is not only to profit from Russia, but also to improve life in the community. In establishing an operation in Moscow, Coca-Cola shipped $650,000 of medical supplies for local hospital. In some cases, only tougher measures will help. When a $5 per barrel surcharge was imposed on Conoco after a deal was signed to develop pipeline and infrastructure projects in three Russian oil and gas regions, the company was able to get an exemption from the surcharge by threatening to cancel its plans to develop another field. Acer Computers, the world's fifth largest maker of personal computers, decided to establish an assembly plant in Finland from which it would then send its product across the border to the Russian market mainly to avoid many of the problems and let their distributors worry about them.

Despite the concerns, many are convinced that no one or nothing can lead Russia astray from the road to market-oriented reforms, for the simple reason that there is no other path. Says Jim Tilley, head of Conoco's Moscow office, "There will be ups and downs; it is just a matter of how far those downs go." Michael Adams, CEO of Young & Rubicam/Sovero, an advertising joint venture, said, "This is a lousy business environment, but there is great growth potential. Right now, most people are happy if they aren't bleeding to death." Many have concluded that not investing poses the greater risk. By the turn of the century, an environment will have been created in which businesses can, if not prosper, at least do business.

*Sources: "Surprise: The Economy in Russia is Clawing out of Deep Recession,"* The Wall Street Journal, *January 28, 1998, A1, A11;* "A Culture of Criminals," Newsweek *(January 19, 1998):* "Laptops from Lapland," The Economist, *September 6, 1997, 67–68; "Russian Investment Dilemma," Harvard Business Review 72 (May–June 1994); 35–44; Vladmir Kvint, "Don't Give Up on Russia," Harvard Business Review 72 (March–April 1994): 62–74; and Paul Hofheinz, "Russia 1993: Europe's Timebomb," Fortune (January 25, 1993): 106–108. See also* http://www.pepsico.com; **http://www.mcdonalds.com;** **http://www.otis.com;** **http://www.acer.com;** **http://www.coca-cola.com;** **http://www.conoco.com.**

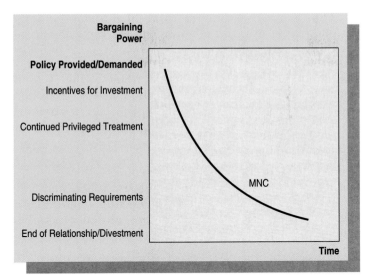

**FIGURE 12.1**

**Bargaining Position of Multinational Corporation (MNC) and Host Country**
*Sources:* Christopher M. Korth, *International Business* (Englewood Cliffs. N.J.: Prentice-Hall, 1985), 350; and Thomas A. Poynter, "Managing Government Intervention: A Strategy for Defending the Subsidy," *Columbia Journal of World Business* 21 (Winter 1986): 55–65.

actually made; in the negotiation period, it can require a number of incentives over a period of time. Whether or not the full cycle of events takes place depends on developments in the market as well as the continued bargaining strength of the multinational.

The multinational corporation can maintain its bargaining strength by developing a local support system through local financing, procurement, and business contracts as well as by maintaining control over access to technology and markets. The first approach attempts to gain support from local market entities if discriminating actions by the government take place. The second approach aims to make the operation of the affiliate impossible without the contribution of the parent.

Host countries, on the other hand, try to enhance their role by instituting control policies and performance requirements. Governments attempt to prevent the integration of activities among affiliates and control by the parent. In this effort, they exclude or limit foreign participation in certain sectors of the economy and require local participation in the ownership and management of the entities established. The extent of this participation will vary by industry, depending on how much the investment is needed by the host economy. Performance requirements typically are programs aimed at established foreign investors in an economy. These often are such discriminatory policies as local content requirements, export requirements, limits on foreign payments (especially profit repatriation), and demands concerning the type of technology transferred or the sophistication and level of operation engaged in. In some cases, demands of this type have led to firms' packing their bags. For example, Coca-Cola left India when the government demanded access to what the firm considered to be confidential intellectual property. Only India's free-market reforms have brought Coca-Cola amongst many other investors back to the country. Cadbury Schweppes sold its plant in Kenya because price controls made its operation unprofitable.[41] On their part, governments can, as a last resort, expropriate the affiliate, especially if they see that the benefits are greater than the cost.[42]

The approaches and procedures that have been discussed are quite negative by nature. However, relations between the firm and its host country, or the home country for that matter, by no means need to be adversarial. The multinational corporation can satisfy its own objectives and find local acceptability by implementing activities that contribute to the following six goals: (1) efficiency, by applying appropriate technologies to different markets; (2) equity, by reinvesting earnings; (3) participation, by establishing local training programs; (4) creativity, by introducing indigenous R&D capabilities in local affiliates; (5) stability, by consistently and openly explaining behavior; and (6) diversity, by developing product lines specifically for local demand.[43] Communication of the goals to various constituents an take place through advertising. The approaches taken by BASF and ENRON are provided in Figure 12.2.

Environmental concerns are emerging as an important part of a multinational's normal business operations. Multinationals have extensive involvement in many pollution-intensive industries and have, by definition, mobility to seek attractive locations for production sites. However, multinationals give rise to higher expectations and often are expected to assume leadership roles in environmental protection due to their financial, managerial, and technological strength. Studies have found that although multinationals may have adopted lower environmental standards in their operations in developing countries, overall they maintain a better record than their local counterparts.[44]

A number of efforts have been made in the past twenty-five years to establish guidelines for the conduct of multinational corporations. The major ones are those drafted by the Organization of Economic Cooperation and Development and by the United Nations. Most multinationals, such as Johnson & Johnson and Apple Computer, have drafted their own versions of codes of conduct as well as value systems.[45]

## Dealing with Other Constituents

Multinational corporations also have to manage their relations with various other constituencies. This is crucial because even small, organized groups of stockholders may influence control of the firm, particularly if the ownership base is wide. Companies must, therefore, adopt policies that will allow them to effectively respond to pressure and criticism, which will continue to surface. Oliver Williams suggested that these policies have the following traits: (1) openness about corporate activities with a focus on how the activities enhance social and economic performance; (2) preparedness to utilize the tremendous power of the multinational corporation in a responsible manner and, in the case of pressure, to counter criticisms swiftly; (3) integrity, which very often means that the corporation must avoid not only actual wrongdoing but the mere appearance of it; and (4) clarity, because it will help ameliorate hostility if a common language is used with those pressuring the corporation.[46] He proposed that the corporation's role is one of enlightened self-interest: Reasonable critics understand that the business cannot compromise the bottom line.

Complicating the situation often is the fact that groups in one market criticize what the marketer is doing in another market. For example, the Interfaith Center on Corporate Responsibility urged Colgate-Palmolive to stop marketing Darkie toothpaste under that brand name in Asia because of the term's offensiveness elsewhere in the world. Darkie toothpaste was sold in Thailand, Hong Kong, Singapore, Malaysia, and Taiwan, packaged in a box that features a likeness of Al Jolson in blackface.[47]

## ASEAN and BASF
## BRINGING OUT THE BEST

**Expanding operations in ASEAN**
BASF investments are boosting regional economies

**Making a fashion statement**
BASF produces dyes such as indigo contributing to the universal popularity of blue jeans

**... committed to improving our quality of life.**

BASF's remarkably successful partnerships with ASEAN nations confirm the wisdom of "working local, going global."

Today the world over, you'll find thousands of excellent products in homes, offices, farms and industries made in ASEAN with components from BASF. A world leader in chemicals.

**Developing the best out of people**
BASF's commitment to training and further education is an investment in human resources.

**Making medicine work better**
BASF ideas and products are improving the effectiveness of modern pharmaceuticals.

For more information, contact
BASF South East Asia
Regional Headquarters Pte. Ltd.
7 Temasek Boulevard
#35-01 Suntec Tower One
Singapore 038987
Tel   : (65) 4323666
Fax  : (65) 4323261
http  : www.basf.com

**Providing environment-friendly crop protection agents**
BASF is concerned with raising agricultural yields while conserving the environment.

**Applying water-based coatings to cars**
BASF is constantly searching for the most ecologically friendly solutions to industrial problems.

**ASEAN and BASF.
Bringing out the best.**

**BASF**

For the industrious Filipinos, power losses were so common that work shifts were planned around them. So they acted. By breaking tradition and creating an electricity grid fit for a global competitor. Together we built two power stations, which are now generating a steady flow of electricity and foreign investors. What's on your energy wish list? 1-888-55-ENRON, www.enron.com.

Natural gas. Electricity. Endless possibilities.

---

**FIGURE 12.2**

**Developing a Local Image**
*Source: Newsweek* (January 26, 1998), 21; and *The Economist* (April 26, 1997), 37. See also **http://www.basf.com** and **http://www.enron.com**.

## Transfer of Technology

To a great extent, the role of foreign direct investment is that of technology transfer. Technology transfer is the transfer of systematic knowledge for the manufacture of a product, for the application of a process, or for the rendering of a service and does not extend to the mere sale or lease of goods.[48] Multinational corporations are one of the major vehicles for channeling technology to other countries.

**WWW**

## The Basics of Technology Transfer

The essential requirements for the transfer of technology are: (1) the availability of suitable technology, (2) social and economic conditions favoring transfer, and (3) the willingness and ability of the receiving party to use and adapt the technology. In industrialized countries, sophisticated processes can be applied economically, with specialists available to solve problems and develop techniques. The problems arise in smaller developing countries with little industrial experience. Production facilities must be scaled down for small series; machinery and procedures must be simplified to cope with the lack of skill and training. Yet, in most cases, the quality has yet to meet worldwide standards. To overcome these kinds of problems, the Dutch electronics giant Philips has created a special pilot plant. The plant sees to it that the many elements constituting an industrial activity are properly adapted to local circumstances and that the necessary know-how and other elements are transferred to developing countries. The elements of the transfer are summarized in Table 12.4. Through people and capital, the necessary personnel, software, and hardware are combined for the transfer of appropriate manufacturing technology. The transfer cannot be accomplished by sending machinery and manuals; it is achieved as technicians show the recipients what should be done and how.

Technology transfer can occur both formally and informally. Formal channels include licensing, foreign direct investment, and joint ventures. Informal channels include reverse engineering, diversions, and industrial espionage. Most of the technology trade has traditionally taken place among developed countries. A significant proportion of the trade has also occurred through traditional equity interactions (subsidiaries or joint ventures) and nonequity interactions, such as licensing agreements between nonaffiliated entities.[49] The informal channels' share of the market, although difficult to determine, is of concern to both the governments and the entities generating technology.

Technology transfer is likely to increase considerably with increased industrialization, which will generate not only new technological needs but also more sophisticated processes and technologies in existing sectors. Many countries no longer are satisfied to receive as much know-how as possible as quickly as possible; they want to possess technology themselves and to generate technology indigenously.

**TABLE 12.4**

**Elements of Technology Transfer**

| Personnel | Software | Hardware |
|---|---|---|
| Product know-how | Manuals | Buildings |
| Manufacturing know-how | Procedures | Assembly lines |
| Equipment know-how | Documentation | Equipment |
| Training | Information | Tools |
| | | Components |
| | | Raw materials |

*Source:* J.C. Ramaer and P.H. Pijs, "Adapting Technology," undated working paper, Utrecht, The Netherlands: Philips.

Technology has to be adapted to factors that are often contradictory. For example, three standards for color television are in use in the world: NTSC in the Americas (except for Brazil) and Japan; PAL in Europe, British Commonwealth Countries, the Middle East, and Brazil; and SECAM in France, former French colonies, and eastern and central Europe. The standards differ from each other in terms of the numbers of fields and lines in the picture. Videotapes from the NTSC, PAL, or SECAM standards cannot be played on the others' machines. In some cases, performance requirements at the transfer location may even be more challenging; for example, machinery may have to be operated in a facility where it is not completely protected from the elements. If the multinational corporation has multiple production bases, technology may have to be adjusted at each one and still meet worldwide quality standards. Often the quantities to be produced are a factor in technology transfer. For example, producing 7,000 sets in Thailand is considerably different from producing 700,000 in Holland.

Of critical concern in preparing the transfer are the strengths and weaknesses of the people who will be involved in production, including their practical knowledge, experience, abilities, and attitudes. Machinery may need to be simplified and on-site maintenance may need to be provided. Moreover, technology from countries such as the United States and Japan may be inappropriate if the recipient wants labor-intensive technology to create employment and income-earning opportunities. In such cases, the adjustment may consist of backward invention whereby a technically simplified version of the product is developed. Technology transfer also involves providing management and staff with advance information about conditions they will find in the transfer location. Costs of the various input elements for the production process such as labor, energy, materials, and components will vary from one market to the next and thus call for differing specifications in the technology transferred.

The quality of the infrastructure requires special attention. For example, frequent power outages may be characteristic of the area in which machinery is to be used; this would indicate the need for features in the technology to avoid variations in output and quality. Some industries, such as home electronics, spend as much as 50 percent of each dollar earned on the purchase of component parts. Yet, in smaller developing countries, the few existing suppliers may need extensive technical assistance to produce what is needed. The designs for components often must be simplified to allow for local production. The assistance may be critical because of government regulation of component imports. Other government policies may affect payment for technology, types of technology that can be transferred, and foreign involvement in the process through, for example, work permits for foreigners.

## Adapting Technology to Local Conditions

## Modes of Operation

In carrying out its foreign direct investment, a multinational corporation has a variety of ownership choices, ranging from 100 percent ownership to a minority interest. With international competition intensifying, risks in market entry and goods development escalating, and the need for global strategy increasing, many companies rely on interfirm cooperation as a means of survival.

When the investment alternative is not attractive or feasible, management contracts provide a mode of foreign market participation.

## Full Ownership

For many firms, the foreign direct investment decision is, initially at least, considered in the context of 100 percent ownership. The reason may have an ethnocentric basis; that is, management may believe that no outside entity should have an impact on corporate decision making. Alternatively, it may be based on financial concerns. For example, the management of IBM until very recently held the belief that by relinquishing a portion of its ownership abroad, it would be setting a precedent for shared control with local partners that would cost more than that which could possibly be gained.[50] In some cases, IBM withdrew operations from countries rather than agree to government demands for local ownership.

In order to make a rational decision about the extent of ownership, management must evaluate the extent to which total control is important to the success of its international marketing activities. Often full ownership may be a desirable, but not a necessary, prerequisite for international success. At other times it may be essential, particularly when strong linkages exist within the corporation. Interdependencies between and among local operations and headquarters may be so strong that nothing short of total coordination will result in an acceptable benefit to the firm as a whole.[51]

Increasingly, however, the international environment is hostile to full ownership by multinational firms. Government action through outright legal restrictions or discriminatory actions is making the option less attractive. The choice is either to abide by existing restraints and accept a reduction in control or to lose the opportunity to operate in the country. In addition to formal action by the government, the general conditions in the market may make it advisable for the firm to join forces with local entities, with them being in charge of government relations.

## Interfirm Cooperation

The world is too large and the competition too strong for even the largest multinational corporations to do everything independently. Technologies are converging and markets becoming integrated, thus making the costs and risks of both goods and market development ever greater. Partly as a reaction to and partly to exploit the developments, management in multinational corporations has become more pragmatic about what it takes to be successful in global markets. The result has been the formation of **strategic alliances** with suppliers, customers, competitors, and companies in other industries to achieve multiple goals.

A strategic alliance (or partnership) is an informal or formal arrangement between two or more companies with a common business objective. It is something more than the traditional customer-vendor relationship but something less than an outright acquisition. The alliances can take forms ranging from informal cooperation to joint ownership of worldwide operations. For example, Texas Instruments has reported agreements with companies such as IBM, Hyundai, Fujitsu, Alcatel, and L. M. Ericsson using such terms as "joint development agreement," "cooperative technical effort," "joint program for development," "alternative sourcing agreement," and "design/exchange agreement for cooperative product development and exchange of technical data."[52]

**Reasons for Interfirm Cooperation** Strategic alliances are being used for many different purposes by the partners involved. Market development is one common focus. Penetrating foreign markets is a primary objective of many companies. In Japan, Motorola is sharing chip designs and manufacturing facilities with Toshiba to gain greater access to the Japanese market. Some alliances are aimed at defending home markets. With no orders coming in for nuclear power plants, Bechtel Group has teamed up with Germany's Siemens to service existing U.S. plants.[53] Another focus is the spreading of the cost and risk inherent in production and development efforts. Texas Instruments and Hitachi have teamed up to develop the next generation of memory chips. The costs of developing new jet engines are so vast that they force aerospace companies into collaboration; one such consortium was formed by United Technologies' Pratt & Whitney division, Britain's Rolls-Royce, Motoren-und-Turbinen Union from Germany, Fiat of Italy, and Japanese Aero Engines (made up of Ishikawajima Heavy Industries and Kawasaki Heavy Industries).[54] Some alliances are formed to block and co-opt competitors.[55] For example, Caterpillar formed a heavy equipment joint venture with Mitsubishi in Japan to strike back at its main global rival, Komatsu, in its home market. In the case of new technologies, companies have joined forces to win over markets to their operating standard. Toshiba and Time-Warner jointly developed the DVD (double-sided, digital videodisc) to compete against another format developed by Sony and Philips in an effort to establish the world standard for interactive compact disks.[56]

The most successful alliances are those that match the complementary strengths of partners to satisfy a joint objective. Often the partners have different product, geographic, or functional strengths that the partners build on, rather than use to fill gaps.[57] Some of the major alliances created on this basis are provided in Figure 12.3.

**Types of Interfirm Cooperation** Each form of alliance is distinct in terms of the amount of commitment required and the degree of control each partner has. The equity alliances—minority ownership, joint ventures, and consortia—feature the most extensive commitment and shared control. The types of strate-

**FIGURE 12.3**

**Complementary Strengths Create Value**

*Source:* Joel Bleeke and David Ernst, "Is Your Strategic Alliance Really a Sale?" *Harvard Business Review* 73 (January–February 1995): 97–105; and Melanie Wells, "Coca-Cola Proclaims Nestea Time for CAA." *Advertising Age,* January 30, 1995, 2. See also **http://www.pepsico.com**; **http://www.lipton.com**; **http://www.cocacola.com**; **http://www.nestle.com**; **http://www.kfc.com**; **http://www.siecor.com**; **http://www.ericsson.com**; and **http://www.hp.com**.

| Partner *Strength...* + | Partner *Strength...* = | Joint Objective |
|---|---|---|
| **Pepsico** *marketing clout for canned beverages* | **Lipton** *recognized tea brand and customer franchise* | *To sell canned iced tea beverages jointly* |
| **Coca-Cola** *marketing clout for canned beverages* | **Nestle** *recognized tea brand and customer franchise* | *To sell canned iced tea beverages jointly* |
| **KFC** *established brand and store format, and operations skills* | **Mitsubishi** *real estate and site-selection skills in Japan* | *To establish a KFC chain in Japan* |
| **Siemens** *presence in range of telecommunications markets worldwide and cable-manufacturing technology* | **Corning** *technological strength in optical fibers and glass* | *To create a fiber-optic-cable business* |
| **Ericsson** *technological strength in public telecommunications networks* | **Hewlett-Packard** *computers, software, and access to electronics-channels* | *To create and market network management systems* |

**FIGURE 12.4**

**Forms of Interfirm
Cooperation**

*Source:* Adapted with permission
from Bernard L. Simonin, *Transfer
of Knowledge of International
Strategic Alliances: A Structural
Approach,* unpublished
dissertation, the University of
Michigan, Ann Arbor, 1991.

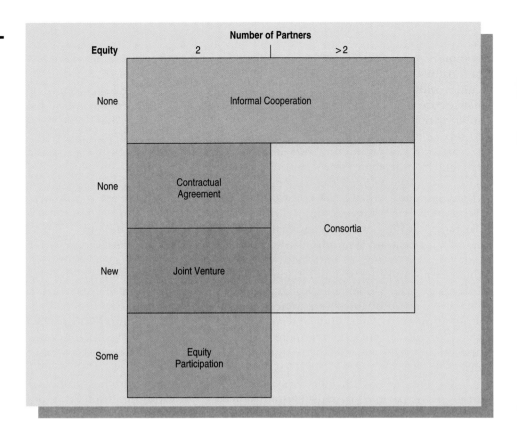

gic alliances are summarized in Figure 12.4, using the extent of equity involved and the number of partners in the endeavor as defining characteristics. More detailed discussion of the various alliances follows.

*Informal Cooperation*   In informal cooperative deals, partners work together without a binding agreement. This arrangement often takes the form of visits to exchange information about new products, processes, and technologies or may take the more formal form of the exchange of personnel for limited amounts of time. Often such partners are of no real threat in each other's markets and of modest size in comparison to the competition, making collaboration necessary.[58] The relationships are based on mutual trust and friendship, and they may lead to more formal arrangements, such as contractual agreements or joint projects.

*Contractual Agreements*   Strategic alliance partners may join forces for joint R&D, joint marketing, or joint production. Similarly, their joint efforts might include **licensing,** cross-licensing or **cross-marketing activities.** Nestlé and General Mills have signed an agreement whereby Honey Nut Cheerios and Golden Grahams are made in General Mills's U.S. plants, shipped in bulk to Europe for packaging at a Nestlé plant, and then marketed in France, Spain, and Portugal by Nestlé[59] This arrangement—complementary marketing (also known as piggybacking)—allows firms to reach objectives that they cannot reach efficiently by themselves.[60] Firms also can have a reciprocal arrangement whereby each partner provides the other access to its markets for a product. AT&T and Olivetti have had such a cross-marketing agreement covering the United States and Europe. In the service sector, international airlines have started to share hubs, coordinate schedules, and simplify ticketing. United Airlines, Lufthansa, Air Canada, SAS, Thai Airways International, and Varig formed the "Star Alliance" to provide worldwide coverage for their customers both in the travel and shipping communities.

Contractual agreements also exist for outsourcing; for example, General Motors buys cars and components from South Korea's Daewoo, and Siemens buys computers from Fujitsu. As corporations look for ways to simultaneously grow and maintain their competitive advantage, outsourcing has become a powerful new tool for achieving those goals. **Contract manufacturing** allows the corporation to separate the physical production of goods from the research and development and marketing stages, especially if the latter are the core competencies of the firm. Such contracting is popular in the footwear and garment industries as seen in the Global Perspective 12.3. The benefits of such contracting are to improve company focus on higher value-added activities, to gain access to world-class capabilities, and to reduce operating costs. Contract manufacturing has been criticized because of the pressure it puts on the contractors to cut prices and thereby labor costs. However, such work does provide many companies, especially in developing countries, the opportunity to gain the necessary experience in product design and manufacturing technology to allow them to function in world markets. Some have even voiced concerns that the experience eventually may make them competitors of their former developed-country partners.

In some parts of the world and in certain industries, governments insist on complete or majority ownership of firms, which has caused multinational companies to turn to an alternative method of enlarging their overseas business.[61] The alternative is a **management contract,** in which the firm sells its expertise in running a company while avoiding the risk or benefit of ownership. Depending on the extensiveness of the contract, it may even permit some measure of control. As an example, the manufacturing process may have to be relinquished to foreign firms, yet international distribution may be required for the product. A management contract could serve to maintain a strong hold on the operation by ensuring that all distribution channels remain firmly controlled.

Management contracts may be more than a defensive measure. Although they are used to protect existing investment interests when they have been partly expropriated by the local government, an increasing number of companies are using them as a profitable opportunity to sell valuable skills and resources. For example, companies in the service sector often have independent entities with the sole task of seeking out opportunities and operating management contracts.[62]

Often a management contract is the critical element in the success of a project. For example, financial institutions may gain confidence in a project because of the existence of a management contract and may sometimes even make it a precondition for funding.[63]

## OUTSOURCING: JUST DO IT!/?

**N**ike, the footwear company based in Beaverton, Oregon, is expanding in international markets in both sales and production. While international sales currently account for one-third of Nike's total, 100 percent of its footwear is produced by subcontractors, most of them outside the United States. Nike's own people focus on the services part of the production process, including design, product development, marketing, and distribution. For example, through its "Futures" inventory control system, Nike knows exactly what it needs to order early enough to plan production accordingly. This avoids excess inventory and assures better prices from its subcontractors.

To achieve both stability and flexibility in its supplier relationships, Nike has three distinct groups of subcontractors in its network:

■ Developed partners, the most important group, participate in joint product development and concentrate on the production of the newest designs. Traditionally, they have been located in the People's Republic of China and Republic of China but, given rising labor costs, some of the more labor-intensive activities have been moved out. The developed partners typically have worked exclusively for Nike on a minimum monthly order basis.
■ The second group of Nike's suppliers are called developing sources and offer low labor costs and the opportunity for Nike to diversify assembly sites. Currently, they

are located in the People's Republic of China, Indonesia, and Thailand. Nearly all are exclusive suppliers to Nike and as such receive considerable assistance from the company with a view of upgrading their production. They will be the next generation of developed partners for Nike.
■ The third group, volume producers, are large-scale factories serving a number of other independent buyers. They generally manufacture a specific product for Nike, but they are not involved in any new product because of fears they could leak proprietary information to competitors. Orders from Nike for suppliers in this group fluctuate, with variations of 50 percent between monthly orders.

Nike's outsourcing activity over time follows a geographic pattern, as does its overall market participation. As a matter of fact, a "Nike index" has been developed by Jardine Fleming to track a country's economic development. Development starts when Nike products' manufacturing starts there (e.g., Indonesia in 1989, Vietnam in 1996). Second stage is reached when labor starts flowing from basic industries, such as footwear, to more advanced ones, such as automobiles and electronics (Hong Kong in 1985, South Korea in 1990). An economy is fully developed when a country is developed as a major market (Japan in 1984, Singapore in 1991, and South Korea in 1994).

Outsourcing has, especially since 1995, been the focus of concern. In Indonesia, for example, where Nike has 70 million shoes produced annually by contract manufacturers in 12 factories, complaints about low wages and inhumane working conditions have sparked debate. Nike's response has been a code of conduct and its enforcement in countries where it has outsourcing activity.

*Sources: "Pangs of Conscience," Business Week (July 29, 1996), 46–47; "Can Nike Just Do It?" Business Week (April 18, 1994, 86–90): and United Nations, World Investment Report 1994: An Executive Summary (New York: United Nations, 1994), 15. See also* http://www.nikeworkers.com *and* http://www.nike.com.

One specialized form of management contract is the **turnkey operation.** Here, the arrangement permits a client to acquire a complete international system, together with skills investment sufficient to allow unassisted maintenance and operation of the system following its completion.[64] The client need not search for individual contractors or subcontractors or deal with scheduling conflicts or with difficulties in assigning responsibilities or blame. Instead, a package arrangement permits the accumulation of responsibility in one entity, thus greatly easing the negotiation and supervision requirements and subsequent accountability. When the project is running, the system will be totally owned, controlled, and operated by the customer. An example of such an arrangement is the Kama River truck plant in Russia, built mainly by U.S. firms.

Management contracts have clear benefits for the client. They provide organizational skills not available locally, expertise that is immediately available rather than built up, and management assistance in the form of support services that would be difficult and costly to replicate locally. For example, hotels managed by the Sheraton Corporation have access to Sheraton's worldwide reservation system. Management contracts today typically involve training locals to take over the operation after a given period.

Similar advantages exist for the supplier. The risk of participating in an international venture is substantially lowered, while significant amounts of control are still exercised. Existing know-how that has been built up through substantial investment can be commercialized, and frequently the impact of fluctuations in business volume can be reduced by making use of experienced personnel who otherwise would have to be laid off. In industrialized countries such as the United States, with economies that are increasingly service based, accumulated service knowledge and comparative advantage should be used internationally. Management contracts permit firms to do so.

Management contracts require an attitude change on two accounts: Control must be shared, and the time involvement may be limited. Establishing a working relationship with the owner in which both understand and respect their roles is essential. Even though the management contractor may be training local personnel to eventually take over, this by no means signifies the end of the relationship. For example, the hotel once managed by Sheraton may well remain in the system to buy reservation services, thus providing Sheraton with additional revenue.

From the client's perspective, the main drawbacks to consider are overdependence and potential loss of some essential control. For example, if the management contractor maintains all of the international relationships, little if any experience may be passed on to the local operation. Instead of a gradual transfer of skills leading to increasing independence, the client may have to rely more and more on the performance of the contractor.

*Equity Participation* Many multinational corporations have acquired minority ownerships in companies that have strategic importance for them to ensure supplier ability and build formal and informal working relationships. An example of this is Ford Motor Company's 33.4 percent share of Mazda. The partners continue operating as distinctly separate entities, but each enjoys the strengths the other partner provides. For example, thanks to Mazda, Ford has excellent support in the design and manufacture of subcompact cars, while Mazda has improved access to the global marketplace. The recipient of the investment will benefit as well. GM's purchase of 50 percent of Saab helped Saab not only to become profitable but also enhanced its competitiveness through sharing parts with other GM models. Without GM's resources, Saab also could not have afforded the development of new models.[65] Equity ownership in an innovator may give the investing company first access to any new technology developed. Geoworks is a leading company developing operating systems specifically for smart phones. Through its 7 percent ownership, Nokia is given priority when new systems become available.[66]

Another significant reason for equity ownership is market entry and support of global operations. Telefonica de Espana has acquired varying stakes in Latin American telecommunications systems—a market that is the fastest growing region of the world after Asia.[67]

*Joint Ventures*   A joint venture can be defined as the participation of two or more companies in an enterprise in which each party contributes assets, owns the entity to some degree, and shares risk.[68] The venture is also considered long term. The reasons for establishing a joint venture can be divided into three groups: (1) government suasion or legislation, (2) one partner's needs for other partners' skills, and (3) one partner's needs for other partners' attributes or assets.[69] Equality of the partners is not necessary. In some joint ventures, each partners' contributions—typically consisting of funds, technology, plant, or labor—also vary.

The key to a joint venture is the sharing of a common business objective, which makes the arrangement more than a customer-vendor relationship but less than an outright acquisition. The partners' rationales for entering into the arrangement may vary. An example is New United Motor Manufacturing Inc. (NUMMI), the joint venture between Toyota and GM. Toyota needed direct access to the U.S. market, while GM benefited from the technology and management approaches provided by its Japanese partner.

Joint ventures may be the only way in which a firm can profitably participate in a particular market. For example, India restricts equity participation in local operations by foreigners to 40 percent. Other entry modes may limit the scale of operation substantially; for example, exports may be restricted because of tariff barriers. Many Western firms are using joint ventures to gain access to eastern and central European markets.

Joint ventures are valuable when the pooling of resources results in a better outcome for each partner than if each were to conduct its activities individually. This is particularly true when each partner has a specialized advantage in areas that benefit the venture. For example, a firm may have new technology yet lack sufficient capital to carry out foreign direct investment on its own. Through a joint venture, the technology can be used more quickly and market penetration achieved more easily. Similarly, one of the partners may have a distribution system already established or have better access to local suppliers, either of which permits a greater volume of sales in a shorter period of time.

Joint ventures also permit better relationships with local government and other organizations such as labor unions. Government-related reasons are the major rationale for joint ventures in less-developed countries four times more frequently than in developed countries.[70] Particularly if the local partner is the government, or the local partner is politically influential, the new venture may be eligible for tax incentives, grants, and government support. Negotiations for certifications or licenses may be easier because authorities may not perceive themselves as dealing with a foreign firm. Relationships between the local partner and the local financial establishment may enable the joint venture to tap local capital markets. The greater experience (and therefore greater familiarity) with the local culture and environment of the local partner may enable the joint venture to benefit from greater insights into changing market conditions and needs.

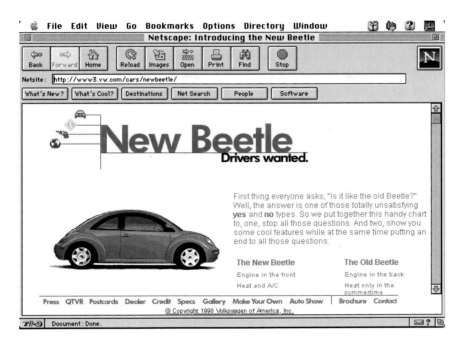

Cooperation between international divisions has enabled Volkswagen to reintroduce their famous beetle bug car back into the market. Crucial for success is a reliable communication flow between German headquarters, manufacturing plants in Mexico and dealerships around the world.
Source: **http://www3.vw.com/ cars/newbeetle/**

A final major commercial reason to participate in joint ventures is the desire to minimize the risk of exposing long-term investment capital, while at the same time maximizing the leverage on the capital that is invested.[71] Economic and political conditions in many countries are increasingly volatile. At the same time, corporations tend to shorten their investment planning time span more and more. This financial rationale therefore takes on more importance.

Seven out of ten joint ventures have been found to fall short of expectations and/or are disbanded.[72] The reasons typically relate to conflicts of interest, problems with disclosure of sensitive information, and disagreement over how profits are to be shared—in general—to lack of communication before, during, and after formation of the venture. In some cases, managers have been more interested in the launching of the venture than the actual running of the enterprise. Many of the problems stem from a lack of careful consideration in advance of how to manage the new endeavor. A partnership works on the basis of trust and commitment or not at all. Actually, if either or both partners insist on voting on critical matters, the venture has already failed.

Typical disagreements cover the whole range of business decisions, including strategy, management style, accounting and control, marketing policies and strategies, research and development, and personnel. The joint venture may, for example, identify a particular market as a target only to find that one of the partners already has individual plans for it. U.S. partners have frequently complained that their Japanese counterparts do not send their most competent personnel to the joint venture; instead, because of their lifetime employment practice, they get rid of less competent managers by sending them to the new entities.

Similarly, the issue of profit accumulation and distribution may cause discontent. If one partner supplies the joint venture with a good, the partner will prefer that any profits accumulate at headquarters and accrue 100 percent to one firm rather than at the joint venture, where profits are divided according to equity participation. Such a decision may not be greeted with enthusiasm by the other partner. Further, once profits are accumulated, their distribution may lead to dispute. For example, one partner may insist on a high payout of dividends because of financial needs, whereas the other may prefer the reinvestment of profits into a growing operation.

*Consortia*   A new drug can cost $500 million to develop and bring to market; a mainframe computer or a telecommunications switch can require $1 billion. Some $7 billion goes into creating a generation of computer chips. To combat the high costs and risks of research and development, research consortia have emerged in the United States, Japan, and Europe. For example, IBM, Siemens and Toshiba—three of the world's largest electronics companies— have teamed up to develop 256-megabite memory chips.[73] Since the passage of the **Joint Research and Development Act** of 1984 (which allows both domestic and foreign firms to participate in joint basic research efforts without the fear of antitrust action), well over 100 consortia have been registered in the United States. The consortia pool their resources for research into technologies ranging from artificial intelligence to those needed to overtake the Japanese lead in semiconductor manufacturing. (The major consortia in those fields are MCC and Sematech.)[74] In the automotive sector, Chrysler, GM, and Ford formed CAR (Consortium for Automotive Research) for basic development work on issues such as safety and powering cars in the future. The Europeans have five mega-projects to develop new technologies registered under the names EUREKA, ESPRIT, BRITE, RACE, and COMET. The Japanese consortia have worked on producing the world's highest-capacity memory chip and advanced computer technologies. On the manufacturing side, the formation of Airbus Industrie secured European production of commercial jets. The consortium, backed by France's Aerospatiale, German's Messerschmitt Boklow Blohm, British Aerospace, and Spain's Construcciones Aeronauticas, has become a prime global competitor.

*Managerial Considerations*   The first requirement of interfirm cooperation is to find the right partner. Partners should have an orientation and goals in common and should bring complementary and relevant benefits to the endeavor. The venture makes little sense if the expertise of both partners is in the same area; for example, if both have production expertise but neither has distribution know-how. Patience should be exercised; a deal should not be rushed into, nor should the partners expect immediate results. Learning should be paramount in the endeavor while at the same time, partners must try not to give away core secrets to each other.[75]

Second, the more formal the arrangement, the greater care that needs to be taken in negotiating the agreement. In joint venture negotiations, for example, extensive provisions must be made for contingencies. The points to be explored should include, depending on the partner, and the venture: (1) clear definition of the venture and its duration; (2) ownership, control, and management; (3) financial structure and policies; (4) taxation and fiscal obligation; (5) employment and training; (6) production; (7) government assistance; (8) transfer of technology; (9) marketing arrangements; (10) environmental protection; (11) record keeping and inspection; and (12) settlement of disputes.[76] The issues have to be addressed before the formation of the venture; otherwise, they eventually will surface as points of contention. A joint venture agreement, although comparable to a marriage agreement, should contain the elements of a divorce contract. In case the joint venture cannot be maintained to the satisfaction of partners, plans must exist for the dissolution of the agreement and for the allocation of profits and costs. Typically, however, one of the partners buys out the other partner(s) when partners decide to part ways.

A strategic alliance, by definition, also means a joining of two corporate cultures, which can often be quite different. To meet this challenge, partners must have frequent communication and interaction at three levels of the organization: the top management, operational leaders, and workforce levels. Trust and relinquishing control are difficult not only at the top but also at levels where the future of the venture is determined. A dominant partner may determine the corporate culture, but even then the other partners should be consulted. The development of specific alliance managers may be advised to forge the net of relationships both within and between alliance partners and, therefore, to support the formal alliance structure.[77]

Strategic alliances operate in a dynamic business environment and must therefore adjust to changing market conditions. The agreement between partners should provide for changes in the original concept so that the venture can flourish and grow. The trick is to have an a priori understanding as to which party will take care of which pains and problems so that a common goal is reached.

Government attitudes and policies have to be part of the environmental considerations of corporate decision makers. While some alliances may be seen as a threat to the long-term economic security of a nation, such as the cancelled equity investment by Taiwan Aerospace in McDonnell-Douglas's commercial airframe operation, in some cases links with foreign operators may be encouraged. For example, the U.S. government urged major U.S. airlines to form alliances with foreign carriers to gain access to emerging world markets, partly in response to the failure to achieve free access to all markets for U.S. airlines through so-called "open-skies" agreements.[78]

## Summary

Multinational corporations are probably among the most powerful economic institutions of all time. They not only have production facilities in multiple countries but also look beyond their own domestic markets for opportunities. They scan the globe to expand their operations. Multinational corporations are no longer the monopoly of the United States, western Europe, and Japan; many developing countries have a growing amount of foreign direct investment.

Foreign direct investment is sought by nations and firms alike. Nations are looking to foreign direct investment for economic development and employment, firms for new markets, resources, and increased efficiency. The relationships among the entities involved—the firm, the host government, and the home government—have to be managed to attain each benefit. The critical role of foreign direct investment is technology transfer, which means the transfer of a combination of hardware, software, and skills for production processes.

Different operational modes are possible for the multinational corporation. Full ownership is becoming more unlikely in many markets as well as industries, and the firm has to look at alternative approaches. The main alternative is interfirm cooperation, in which the firm joins forces with other business entities, possibly even a foreign government. In some cases, when the firm may not want to make a direct investment, it will offer its management expertise for sale in the form of management contracts.

## Key Terms and Concepts

| | | |
|---|---|---|
| ethnocentric | Overseas Private Investment | management contract |
| polycentric | Corporation | turnkey operation |
| regiocentric | strategic alliances | Joint Research and |
| geocentric | licensing | Development Act |
| technology transfer | cross marketing | |
| brain drain | contract manufacturing | |

## Questions for Discussion

1. Of the quantitative and qualitative criteria that a firm has to satisfy to be considered a multinational corporation, which should be the major determinants?
2. Foreigners claim 5 percent of corporate earnings in the United States, yet there is concern about the selling off of corporate America. Is it justified?
3. Should every country have guidelines or a code of behavior for foreign companies to follow if they want to be viewed as good corporate citizens?
4. The Middle East is an attractive market for technology transfer. How would Saudi Arabia, Egypt, and Iran differ in the type of technology they seek?
5. Working conditions in subcontract factories have come under criticism for wages and working conditions. Using Nike's response (see **http://www.nike-workers.com**), assess the type of criticisms heard and the ability of a company to address them.
6. The rate of expropriation has been ten times greater for a joint venture with the host government than for a 100 percent U.S.–owned subsidiary, according to a study on expropriation since 1960. Is this not contrary to logic?
7. Comment on the observation that "a joint venture may be a combination of Leonardo da Vinci's brain and Carl Lewis's legs; one wants to fly, the other insists on running."
8. Why would an internationalizing company opt for a management contract over other modes of operation? Relate your answer especially to the case of hospitality companies such as Hyatt, Marriott, and Sheraton.

## Recommended Readings

Badaracoo, Joseph L. *The Knowledge Link: Competing Through Strategic Alliances.* Boston: Harvard Business School Press, 1991.

Barnet, Richard J., and John Cavanagh. *Global Dreams: Imperial Corporations and the New World Order:* New York: Simon & Schuster, 1994.

Bleeke, Joel, and David Ernst. *Using Strategic Alliances and Acquisitions in the Global Marketplace.* New York: John Wiley, 1993.

Culpan, Refik, ed. *Multinational Strategic Alliances.* Binghamton, N.Y.: International Business Press, 1993.

Dunning, John H. *Multinational Enterprises and the Global Economy.* Wokingham, England: Addison Wesley, 1994.

Dunning, John H., ed. *Theory of Transnational Corporations.* Boston, Mass.: Thomson Business Press, 1996.

Dunning, John H., ed. *The United Nations Library on Transnational Corporations.* Volumes 1–20. New York: Routledge, 1993.

Kotler, Philip, Somkid Jatusrupitak, and Suvit Maesincee. *The Marketing of Nations.* New York: Free Press, 1997.

Lewis, Jordan D. *Partnerships for Profit: Structuring and Managing Strategic Alliances.* New York: The Free Press, 1990.

Liu, Scott X. *Foreign Direct Investment and the Multinational Enterprise.* Westport, Conn.: Quorum Books, 1997.

Luostarinen, Reijo, and Lawrence Welch. *International Business Operations.* Helsinki, Finland: Kyriiri Oy, 1990.

Robinson, Richard D. *The International Transfer of Technology: Theory, Issues, and Practice.* Cambridge, Mass.: Ballinger, 1988.

## Notes

1. Mark Casson, *Alternatives to the Multinational Enterprise* (London: Macmillan, 1979), 1.
2. United Nations, *World Investment Report 1997* (New York: United Nations, 1997), xv.
3. "Perspective: The Heart of the New World Economy," *Financial Times,* October 1, 1997, 12 and United Nations, *Transnational Corporations in World Development* (New York: United Nations, 1988), 16.
4. United Nations, *Multinational Corporation in World Development* (New York: United Nations, 1973), 23.
5. Alan M. Rugman, *Inside the Multinationals* (London: Croom Helm, 1981), 31.
6. Raymond Vernon, *Sovereignty at Bay: The Multinational Spread of United States Enterprises* (New York: Basic Books, 1971), 11.
7. Alan M. Rugman, "Risk Reduction by International Diversification," *Journal of International Business Studies* 7 (Fall 1976): 75–80.
8. Donald Kircher, "Now the Transnational Enterprise," *Harvard Business Review* 42 (March-April 1964): 6–10, 172–176.
9. Howard V. Perlmutter, "The Tortuous Evolution of the Multinational Corporation," *Columbia Journal of World Business* 4 (January-February 1969): 9–18; Howard V. Perlmutter and David A. Heenan, "How Multinational Should Your Top Managers Be?" *Harvard Business Review* 52 (November-December 1974): 121–132; and Yoram Wind, Susan P. Douglas, and Howard V. Perlmutter, "Guidelines for Developing International Marketing Strategies," *Journal of Marketing* 37 (April 1973): 14–23.
10. John M. Stopford, *The World Directory of Multinational Enterprises* (London: Macmillan, 1982), xii.
11. "New Rivals Rush to Join the Fray," *Financial Times,* October 3, 1997, 11.
12. United Nations, *World Investment Report 1997* (New York: United Nations, 1997), table I.8.
13. Herbert E. Meyer, "Trudeau's War on U.S. Business," *Fortune,* (April 6, 1981): 74–82.
14. Jeffrey Arpan and David A. Ricks, "Foreign Direct Investments in the U.S. and Some Attendant Research Problems," *Journal of International Business Studies* 5 (Spring 1974): 1–7.
15. Harvey A. Poniachek, *Direct Foreign Investment in the United States* (Lexington, Mass.: Lexington Books, 1986), 2.
16. United Nations, *World Investment Report 1997* (New York: United Nations, 1997), xv.
17. U.S. Department of Commerce, Bureau of Economic Analysis, *Survey of Current Business,* August 1997. See also **http://www.bea.doc.gov**
18. Jaclyn Fierman, "The Selling Off of America," *Fortune* (December 22, 1986): 34–43. See also **http://www.laidlaw.com**
19. "The Global Deal Mill," *Business Week* (February 13,1995): 8.
20. "The Difference Japanese Management Makes," *Business Week* (July 14, 1986): 47–50.

21. Edward B. Flowers, "Oligopolistic Reactions in European and Canadian Direct Investment in the United States," *Journal of International Business Studies* 7 (Fall–Winter 1976): 43–55.

22. "Lowest Cost Isn't Always the Answer," *Financial Times,* October 15, 1997, 10–11.

23. Johny K. Johansson, Ilkka A. Ronkainen, and Michael R. Czinkota, "Negative Country-of-Origin Effects: The Case of the New Russia," *Journal of International Business Studies* 25 (first quarter 1994): 1–21.

24. Alan D. MacCormack, Lawrence J. Newman III, and Donald B. Rosenfeld, "The New Dynamics of Global Manufacturing Site Location," *Sloan Management Review* 36 (Summer 1994): 69–80.

25. Frank G. Vukmanic, Michael R. Czinkota, and David A. Ricks, "National and International Data Problems and Solutions in the Empirical Analysis of Intra-Industry Direct Foreign Investment," *Multinationals as Mutual Invaders: Intra-Industry Direct Foreign Investment* ed. A. Erdilek (Beckenham, Kent: Croom Helm Ltd., 1985), 160–184.

26. "Japan, U.S.A.," *Business Week* (July 14, 1986): 45–46.

27. Stephen Kobrin, "Assessing Political Risk Overseas," *The Wharton Magazine* 6, 2 (1981): 6–14.

28. Marie E. Wicks Kelly and George C. Philipatos, "Comparative Analysis of the Foreign Investment Evaluation Practices by U.S.–Based Manufacturing Multinational Companies," *Journal of International Business Studies* 13 (Winter 1982): 19–42.

29. Fierman, "The Selling Off of America," 35.

30. Casson, *Alternatives to the Multinational Enterprise,* 4.

31. Vivian Brownstein, "The Credit Crunch Myth," *Fortune* (December 17, 1990): 59–69.

32. Charles Albert Michalet and Therese Chevallier, "France," in *Multinational Enterprises, Economic Structure and International Competitiveness,* ed. John H. Dunning (Chichester, England: Wiley, 1985), 91–125.

33. Daniel van Den Bulcke, "Belgium," in *Multinational Enterprise, Economic Structure and International Competitiveness,* ed. John H. Dunning (Chichester, England: Wiley, 1985), 249–280.

34. "At Sanyo's Arkansas Plant the Magic Isn't Working," *Business Week* (July 14, 1986): 51–52.

35. Joseph S. Nye, "Multinational Corporations in World Politics," *Foreign Affairs* 53 (October 1974): 153–175.

36. Lawrence Franko, "Foreign Direct Investment in Less Developed Countries: Impact on Home Countries," *Journal of International Business Studies* 9 (Winter 1978): 55–65.

37. Paul S. Haar, "U.S. Government Political Risk Insurance Program" (Paper delivered at International Insurance and Political Risk Seminar, March 25, 1985, Washington, D.C.), 2.

38. Michael G. Harvey and Ilkka A. Ronkainen, "The Three Faces of the Foreign Corrupt Practices Act," *1984 AMA Educators' Proceedings* (Chicago: American Marketing Association, 1984), 230–235.

39. See http://www.oecd.org , and "IMF Hard Line On Corruption Should Help MNCs," *Crossborder Monitor* (August 20, 1997): 1.

40. Peter P. Gabriel, "MNCs in the Third World: Is Conflict Unavoidable?" *Harvard Business Review* 50 (July–August 1972): 91–102.

41. Victor H. Frank, "Living with Price Control Abroad," *Harvard Business Review* 62 (March–April 1984): 137–142.

42. Thomas W. Shreeve, "Be Prepared for Political Changes Abroad," *Harvard Business Review* 62 (July–August 1984): 111–118.

43. Jack N. Behrman, *Industrial Policies: International Restructuring and Transnationals* (Lexington, Mass.: Lexington Books, 1984), 114–115.

44. William C. Frederick, "The Moral Authority of Transnational Corporations," *Journal of Business Ethics* 10 (March 1991): 165–178; and United Nations, *World Investment Report: An Executive Summary* (New York: United Nations, 1993), 11–12.

45. John M. Kline, *International Codes and Multinational Business: Setting Guidelines for International Business Operations* (Westport Conn.: Quorum Books, 1985), Chapter 1. See also http://www.johnsonandjohnson.com for company's statement on social responsibility.

46. Oliver Williams, "Who Cast the First Stone?" *Harvard Business Review* 62 (September–October 1984): 151–160.

47. "Church Group Gnashes Colgate-Palmolive," *Advertising Age* (March 24, 1986): 46.

48. United Nations, *Draft International Code of Conduct on the Transfer of Technology* (New York: United Nations, 1981), 3.

49. Asim Erdilek, "International Technology Transfer in the Middle East," in *International Business with the Middle East,* ed. Erdener Kaynak (New York: Praeger, 1984), 85–99.

50. Dennis J. Encarnation and Sushil Vachani, "Foreign Ownership: When Hosts Change the Rules," *Harvard Business Review* 63 (September–October 1985): 152–160.

51. Richard H. Holton, "Making International Joint Ventures Work" (Paper presented at the seminar on the Management of Headquarters/Subsidiary

Relationships in Transnational Corporations, Stockholm School of Economics, June 2–4, 1980), 4.

52. Thomas Gross and John Neuman, "Strategic Alliances Vital in Global Marketing," *Marketing News* (June 19, 1989): 1–2.

53. Louis Kraar, "Your Rivals Can Be Your Allies," *Fortune* (March 27, 1989): 66–76.

54. "MD-90 Airliner Unveiled by McDonnell Douglas," *The Washington Post,* February 14, 1993, A4.

55. Jordan D. Lewis, *Partnerships for Profit: Structuring and Managing Strategic Alliances* (New York: The Free Press, 1990), 85–87.

56. "Video Warfare: How Toshiba Took the High Ground," *Business Week* (February 20, 1995): 64–65; and Nikhil Hutheesing, "Betamax Versus VHS All Over Again?" *Forbes* (January 3, 1994): 88–89.

57. Joel Bleeke and David Ernst. "Is Your Strategic Alliance Really a Sale?" *Harvard Business Review* 73 (January–February 1995): 97–105.

58. Gary Hamel, Yves L. Doz, and C. K. Prahalad, "Collaborate with Your Competitors— and Win," *Harvard Business Review* 67 (January–February 1989): 133–139.

59. Richard Gibson, "Cereal Venture Is Planning Honey of a Battle in Europe," *Wall Street Journal,* November 14, 1990, B1, B8.

60. Vern Terpstra and Chwo-Ming J. Yu, "Piggy-backing: A Quick Road to Internationalization," *International Marketing Review* 7, (1990): 52–63.

61. Lawrence S. Welch and Anubis Pacifico, "Management Contracts: A Role in Internationalization?" *International Marketing Review* 7, (1990): 64–74.

62. Richard Ellison, "An Alternative to Direct Investment Abroad," *International Management* 31 (June 1976): 25–27.

63. Michael Z. Brooke, *Selling Management Services Contracts in International Business* (London: Holt, Rinehart and Winston, 1985), 7.

64. Richard W. Wright and Colin S. Russel, "Joint Ventures in Developing Countries: Realities and Responses," *Columbia Journal of World Business* 10 (Spring 1975): 74–80.

65. "Saab and GM Prove a Good Match," *Business Week* (February 20, 1995): 48.

66. "Nokia ja Amerikkalainen Geoworks Laajentavat Yhteistyotaan," *Helsingin Sanomat,* July 24, 1997, A16. See also **http://www.geoworks.com.**

67. "Spain's Phone Giant has Latin America Buzzing," *Business Week* (September 12, 1994): 92.

68. Kathryn Rudie Harrigan, "Joint Ventures and Global Strategies," *Columbia Journal of World Business* 19 (Summer 1984): 7–16.

69. J. Peter Killing, *Strategies for Joint Venture Success* (New York: Praeger, 1983), 11–12.

70. Paul W. Beamish, "The Characteristics of Joint Ventures in Developed and Developing Countries," *Columbia Journal of World Business* 20 (Fall 1985), 13–19.

71. Charles Oman, *New Forms of International Investment in Developing Countries* (Paris: Organization for Economic Cooperation and Development, 1984), 79.

72. Yankelovich, Skelly and White, Inc., *Collaborative Ventures: A Pragmatic Approach to Business Expansion in the Eighties* (New York: Coopers and Lybrand, 1984), 10.

73. "What's the Word in the Lab? Collaborate," *Business Week* (June 27, 1994): 78–80.

74. Lee Smith, "Can Consortiums Defeat Japan?" *Fortune* (June 5, 1989): 245–254.

75. Jeremy Main, "Making Global Alliances Work," *Fortune* (December 17, 1990): 121–126.

76. United Nations, *Guidelines for Foreign Direct Investment* (New York: United Nations, 1975), 65–76.

77. Robert E. Spekman, Lynn A. Isabella, Thomas C. MacAvoy, and Theodore Forbes III, "Creating Strategic Alliances which Endure," *Long Range Planning* 29 3, 1996: 346–357.

78. "Airlines Urged to Link with Foreign Carriers," *The Washington Post,* November 2, 1994, F1, F3.

# Lakewood Forest Products

Since the 1970s the United States has had a merchandise trade deficit with the rest of the world. Up to 1982, this deficit mattered little because it was relatively small. As of 1983, however, the trade deficit increased rapidly and became, due to its size and future implications, an issue of major national concern. Suddenly, trade moved to the forefront of national debate. Concurrently, a debate ensued on the issue of the international competitiveness of U.S. firms. The onerous question here was whether U.S. firms could and would achieve sufficient improvements in areas such as productivity, quality, and price to remain long-term successful international marketing players.

U.S.–Japanese trade relations took on particular significance, because it was between those two countries that the largest bilateral trade deficit existed. In spite of trade negotiations, market-opening measures, trade legislation, and other governmental efforts, it was clear that the impetus for a reversal of the deficit through more U.S. exports to Japan had to come from the private sector. Therefore, the activities of any U.S. firm that appeared successful in penetrating the Japanese market were widely hailed. One company whose effort to market in Japan aroused particular interest was Lakewood Forest Products, of Hibbing, Minnesota.

## Company Background

In 1983, Ian J. Ward was an export merchant in difficulty. Throughout the 1970s his company, Ward, Bedas Canadian Ltd., had successfully sold Canadian lumber and salmon to countries in the Persian Gulf. Over time, the company had opened four offices worldwide. However, when the Iran–Iraq war erupted, most of Ward's long-term trading relationships disappeared within a matter of months. In addition, the international lumber market began to collapse. As a result, Ward, Bedas Canadian Ltd. went into a survivalist mode and sent employees all over

the world to look for new markets and business opportunities. Late that year, the company received an interesting order. A firm in Korea urgently needed to purchase lumber for the production of chopsticks.

### Learning about the Chopstick Market

In discussing the wood deal with the Koreans, Ward learned that in order to produce good chopsticks more than 60 percent of the wood fiber would be wasted. Given the high transportation cost involved, the large degree of wasted materials, and his need for new business, Ward decided to explore the Korean and Japanese chopstick industry in more detail.

He quickly determined that chopstick making in the Far East is a fragmented industry, working with old technology and suffering from a lack of natural resources. In Asia, chopsticks are produced in very small quantities, often by family organizations. Even the largest of the 450 chopstick factories in Japan turns out only 5 million chopsticks a month. This compares to an overall market size of 130 million pairs of disposable chopsticks a day. In addition, chopsticks represent a growing market. With increased wealth in Asia, people eat out more often and therefore have a greater demand for disposable chopsticks. The fear of communicable diseases has greatly reduced the use of reusable chopsticks. Renewable plastic chopsticks have been attacked by many groups as too newfangled and as causing future ecological problems.

From his research, Ward concluded that a competitive niche existed in the world chopstick market. He believed that, if he could use low-cost raw materials and ensure that the labor cost component would remain

SOURCE: This case was written by Michael R. Czinkota based on the following sources: Mark Clayton, "Minnesota Chopstick Maker Finds Japanese Eager to Import His Quality Waribashi," The Christian Science Monitor, October 16, 1987, 11; Roger Worthington, "Improbable Chopstick Capitol of the World," Chicago Tribune, June 5, 1988, 39; Mark Gill, "The Great American Chopstick Master," American Way, August 1, 1987, 34, 78–79; "Perpich of Croatia," The Economist, April 20, 1991, 27; and personal interview with Ian J. Ward, president, Lakewood Forest Products.

small, he could successfully compete in the world market.

### The Founding of Lakewood Forest Products

In exploring opportunities afforded by the newly identified international marketing niche for chopsticks, Ward set four criteria for plant location:

1. Access to suitable raw materials
2. Proximity of other wood product users who could make use of the 60 percent waste for their production purposes
3. Proximity to a port that would facilitate shipment to the Far East
4. Availability of labor

In addition, Ward was aware of the importance of product quality. People use chopsticks on a daily basis and are accustomed to products that are visually inspected one by one, so he would have to live up to high quality expectations to compete successfully. Chopsticks could not be bowed or misshapen, have blemishes in the wood, or splinter.

Ward needed financing to implement his plan. Private lenders were skeptical and slow to provide funds. The skepticism resulted from the unusual direction of Ward's proposal. Far Eastern companies have generally held the cost advantage in a variety of industries, especially those as labor intensive as chopstick manufacturing. U.S. companies rarely have an advantage in producing low-cost items. Further, only a very small domestic market exists for chopsticks.

However, Ward found that the state of Minnesota was willing to participate in his new venture. Since the decline of the mining industry, regional unemployment had been rising rapidly in the state. In 1983, unemployment in Minnesota's Iron Range peaked at 22 percent. Therefore, state and local officials were anxious to attract new industries that would be independent of mining activities. Of particular help was the enthusiasm of Governor Rudy Perpich. The governor had been boosting Minnesota business on the international scene by traveling abroad and receiving many foreign visitors. He was excited about Ward's plans, which called for the creation of more than 100 new jobs within a year.

Hibbing, Minnesota, turned out to be an ideal location for Ward's project. The area had an abundant supply of aspen wood, which, because it grows in clay soil, tends to be unmarred. The fact that Hibbing was the hometown of the governor also did not hurt. In addition, Hibbing

boasted an excellent labor pool, and both the city and the state were willing to make loans totaling $500,000. Further, the Iron Range Resources Rehabilitation Board was willing to sell $3.4 million in industrial revenue bonds for the project. Together with jobs and training wage subsidies, enterprise zone credits, and tax increment financing benefits, the initial public support of the project added up to about 30 percent of its start-up costs. The potential benefit of the new venture to the region was quite clear. When Lakewood Forest Products advertised its first 30 jobs, more than 3,000 people showed up to apply.

## The Production and Sale of Chopsticks

Ward insisted that to truly penetrate the international market, he would need to keep his labor cost low. As a result, he decided to automate as much of the production as possible. However, no equipment was readily available to produce chopsticks, because no one had automated the process before.

After much searching, Ward identified a European equipment manufacturer who produced machinery for making popsicle sticks. He purchased equipment from the Danish firm to better carry out the sorting and finishing processes. However, because aspen wood was quite different from the wood for which the machine was designed, as was the final product, substantial design adjustments had to be made. Sophisticated equipment was also purchased to strip the bark from the wood and peel it into long, thin sheets. Finally, a computer vision system was acquired to detect defects in the chopsticks. The system rejected more than 20 percent of the production, and yet some of the chopsticks that passed inspection were splintering. However, Ward firmly believed that further fine-tuning of the equipment and training of the new work force would gradually take care of the problem.

Given this fully automated process, Lakewood Forest Products was able to develop capacity for up to 7 million chopsticks a day. With a unit manufacturing cost of $0.03 and an anticipated unit selling price of $0.057, Ward expected to earn a pretax profit of $4.7 million in 1988.

Due to intense marketing efforts in Japan and the fact that Japanese customers were struggling to obtain sufficient supplies of disposable chopsticks, Ward was able to presell the first five years of production quite quickly. By late 1987, Lakewood Forest Products was ready to enter the international market. With an ample supply of raw materials and an almost totally automated plant, Lakewood was positioned as the world's largest and least labor-intensive manufacturer of chopsticks. The first shipment of six containers with a load of 12 million pairs of chopsticks to Japan was made in October 1987.

## Questions for Discussion

1. What are the future implications of continuing large U.S. trade deficits?
2. What are the important variables for the international marketing success of chopsticks?
3. Rank the variables in Question 2 according to the priority you believe they have for foreign customers.
4. What haven't Japanese firms thought of automating the chopstick production process?
5. How long will Lakewood Forest Products be able to maintain its competitive advantage?

# Damar International

Damar International, a fledgling firm importing handicrafts of chiefly Indonesian origin, was established in January 1984 in Burke, Virginia, a suburb of Washington, D.C. Organized as a general partnership, the firm is owned entirely by Dewi Soemantoro, its president, and Ronald I. Asche, its vice president. Their part-time, unsalaried efforts and those of Soemantoro's relatives in Indonesia constitute the entire labor base of the firm. Outside financing has been limited to borrowing from friends and relatives of the partners in Indonesia and the United States.

Damar International imported its first shipment of handicrafts in April 1984 and estimates that its current annual sales revenues are between $20,000 and $30,000. Although the firm has yet to reach the break-even point, its sales revenues and customer base have expanded more rapidly than anticipated in Damar's original business plan. The partners are generally satisfied with results to date and plan to continue to broaden their operations.

Damar International was established to capitalize on Soemantoro's international experience and contacts. The daughter of an Indonesian Foreign Service officer, Soemantoro spent most of her youth and early adulthood in western Europe and has for the past eighteen years resided in the United States. Her immediate family, including her mother, now resides in Indonesia. In addition

SOURCE: *This case was prepared by Michael R. Czinkota and Laura M. Gould.*

to English and Malay, Soemantoro speaks French, German, and Italian. Although she has spent the past four years working in information management in the Washington area, first for MCI and currently for Records Management Inc., her interest in importing derives from about six years she previously spent as a management consultant. In this capacity, she was frequently called on to advise clients about importing clothing, furniture, and decorative items from Indonesia. At the urging of family and friends, she decided to start her own business. While Soemantoro handles the purchasing and administrative aspects of the business, Asche is responsible for marketing and sales.

Damar International currently imports clothing, high-quality brassware, batik accessories, wood carvings, and furnishings from Indonesia. All of these items are handcrafted by village artisans working on a cottage-industry basis. Damar International estimates that 30 percent of its revenues from the sale of Indonesian imports are derived from clothing, 30 percent from batik accessories, and 30 percent from wood carvings, with the remainder divided equally between brassware and furnishings. In addition, Damar markets in the eastern United States comparable Thai and Philippine handcrafted items imported by a small California firm. This firm in turn markets some of Damar's Indonesian imports on the West Coast.

Most of Damar's buyers are small shops and boutiques. Damar does not supply large department stores or retail chain outlets. By participating in gift shows, trade fairs, and handicraft exhibitions, the firm has expanded its customer base from the Washington area to many locations in the eastern United States.

In supplying small retail outlets with handcrafted Indonesian artifacts, Damar is pursuing a niche strategy. Although numerous importers market similar mass-produced, manufactured Indonesian items chiefly to department stores and chain retailers, Damar knows of no competitors that supply handcrafted artifacts to boutiques. Small retailers find it difficult to purchase in sufficient volume to order directly from large-scale importers of mass-produced items. More important, it is difficult to organize Indonesian artisans to produce handcrafted goods in sufficient quantity to supply the needs of large retailers.

Damar's policy is to carry little if any inventory. Orders from buyers are transmitted by Soemantoro to her family in Indonesia, who contract production to artisans in the rural villages of Java and Bali. Within broad parameters, buyers can specify modifications of traditional Indonesian wares. Frequently, Soemantoro cooperates with her mother in creating designs that adapt traditional products to American tastes and to the specifications of U.S. buyers. Soemantoro is in contact with her family in Indonesia at least once a week by telex or phone to report new orders and check on the progress of previous orders. In addition, Soemantoro makes an annual visit to Indonesia to coordinate policy with her family and maintain contacts with artisans.

Damar also fills orders placed by Soemantoro's family in Indonesia. The firm therefore in essence acts as both an importer and an exporter despite its extremely limited personnel base. In this, as well as in its source of financing, Damar is highly atypical. The firm's great strength, which allows it to fill a virtually vacant market niche with extremely limited capital and labor resources, is clearly the Soemantoro family's nexus of personal connections. Without the use of middlemen, this single bicultural family is capable of linking U.S. retailers and Indonesian village artisans and supplying products which, while unique and nonstandardized, are specifically oriented to the U.S. market.

Damar's principal weakness is its financing structure. There are obvious limits to the amount of money that can be borrowed from family and friends for such an enterprise. Working capital is necessary because the Indonesian artisans must be paid before full payment is received from U.S. buyers. Although a 10 percent deposit is required from buyers when an order is placed, the remaining 90 percent is not due until 30 days from the date of shipment F.O.B. Washington, D.C. However, the simplicity of Damar's financing structure has advantages: To date, it has been able to operate without letters of credit and their concomitant paperwork burdens.

One major importing problem to date has been the paperwork and red tape involved in U.S. customs and quota regulations. Satisfying these regulations has occasionally delayed fulfillment of orders. Furthermore, because the Indonesian trade office in the United States is located in New York rather than Washington, assistance from the Indonesian government in expediting such problems has at times been difficult to obtain with Damar's limited personnel. For example, an order was once delayed in U.S. customs because of confusion between the U.S. Department of Commerce and Indonesian export authorities concerning import stamping and labeling. Several weeks were required to resolve the difficulty.

Although Damar received regulatory information directly from the U.S. Department of Commerce when it began importing, its routine contact with the government is minimal because regulatory paperwork is contracted to customs brokers.

One of the most important lessons that the firm has learned is the critical role of participating in gift shows, trade fairs, and craft exhibitions. Soemantoro believes that the firm's greatest mistake to date was not attending a trade show in New York. In connecting with potential buyers, both through trade shows and "walk-in scouting" of boutiques, Damar has benefited greatly from helpful references from existing customers. Buyers have been particularly helpful in identifying trade fairs that would be useful for Damar to attend. Here too, the importance of Damar's cultivation of personal contacts is apparent.

Similarly, personal contacts offer Damar the possibility of diversifying into new import lines. Through a contact established by a friend in France, Soemantoro is currently planning to import handmade French porcelain and silk blouses.

Damar is worried about sustained expansion of its Indonesian handicraft import business because the firm does not currently have the resources to organize large-scale cottage-industry production in Indonesia. Other major concerns are potential shipping delays and exchange rate fluctuations.

## Questions for Discussion

1. Evaluate alternative expansion strategies for Damar International in the United States.
2. Discuss Damar's expansion alternatives in Indonesia and France and their implications for the U.S. market.
3. How can Damar protect itself against exchange rate fluctuations?
4. What are the likely effects of shipment delays on Damar? How can these effects be overcome?

# Kadimi Group of Companies (India): Exports

Sitting in his comfortable office in New Delhi's busy commercial district, Rakesh Gupta, one of two partners at Kadimi, reflected on the meeting he had that morning with Rajiv Agarwal, partner and managing director. Of

*MBA Candidates Rahul Agarwal, Raphael Moreau, and Dixie Wang prepared this case under the supervision of Professor Michael Czinkota as the basis for class discussion rather than to illustrate either effective or ineffective handling of an administrative situation.*

late, the export department of the company had been receiving an unusually high number of complaints from its overseas customers. Previously, such complaints had been sporadic and infrequent and had been dealt with on a case-by-case basis by the two partners. However, the new spate of export-related complaints as well as growing consistency among worldwide complaints had put into question Kadimi's fluid policies and practices with regard to export complaint management. As he grappled with the ideas and concerns that were put forth in the meeting, Gupta wondered if Kadimi needed to adopt a complaint management system that would address the complaints in a consistent manner.

## The Firm's Activities

The Kadimi Group began operations in 1977 with the incorporation of its first division, Kadimi International. Functioning solely as a distributor, the division represented some of the leading Fastener-related International companies to serve India's growing Fastener and Electronic Component industries. Then, in 1984, Kadimi obtained technical collaboration with OSG Corporation, Japan to manufacture thread-rolling dies in India. In 1991, a new facility for manufacturing self-tapping screws was added.

By 1993, the company had developed a strong competence in manufacturing. The directors now desired to diversify the manufacturing activities by entering a new industry. At this time, the popularity of natural stones (slates, sandstones, and quartzites) was increasing in many parts of the World as an alternative to marble and granite for interior and exterior building facades and flooring. Kadimi decided to set up a new plant to process natural stone and create stone tiles and blocks. As opposed to their engineering products, however, the stone products were strictly intended for exports due to limited demand for natural stone in India.

Since then, the company has enjoyed phenomenal success, especially with exports of stone products. Exports have been growing steadily at approximately 15 percent per year and will soon become the main source of revenue for the company. Recently, the company acquired a third plant to add capacity for natural stone processing, as well as to set up new capabilities in marble and granite processing for both the domestic and foreign markets.

With offices in New Delhi, Madras, and Singapore, Kadimi International today supplies India's Fastener, and Electronic Component industries with nut/bolt making machinery, thread-rolling dies, cold heading quality steel, taps, endmills, and coil-winding machines imported from

manufacturers in Korea, Japan, Taiwan, Singapore, Italy, and the United States. The export department within the division is responsible for handling exports of products and components sourced externally (machinery, castor oil, and certain cutting tools), as well as manufactured in-house (self-tapping screws, thread-rolling dies, and stone products).

## Exports

Kadimi's exports could be broken down into two major product groups: engineering components and stone products. The engineering components that were exported included thread-rolling dies and self-tapping screws, both of which were manufactured at Kadimi's plant in New Delhi. High-quality steel was imported from Korea and Thailand to manufacture these components. Manufacturing assistance had been obtained from a Japanese firm and by 1996, multiple quality control mechanisms were in place to produce high quality components. As such, complaints from overseas OEMs were rare. Quality was far more important than price in the purchasing decision for industrial components, and Kadimi had priced their products at a slight premium with respect to domestic competitors and at par with foreign competitors. Nevertheless, sales were steady and customers were pressuring Kadimi to increase the scope of their operations to include more components.

Stone products, however, were a new addition to the Kadimi family and brought with them a whole new set of manufacturing processes and marketing issues. The stone tile industry, unlike the engineering component industry, was rife with competitors, all producing a relatively similar product. Competition was especially pronounced in the ceramic tile industry, where the major players were now attempting to woo the market with superior designs. Kadimi was facing intense pressure to compete on price or offer new and differentiated products.

Despite the difficulties it encountered in stone exports, Kadimi was heavily dependent on its exporting activities. In 1996, almost 50 percent of Kadimi's revenues and 60 percent of its profits came from the export division. Of the export revenues, almost 90 percent were from exports of stone products.

## Stone Industry

The natural stone industry was dominated by relatively few producers in select countries of Europe and Asia. This geographic concentration was a direct consequence of the availability of natural stone mines (slates, sandstones, and quartzites) that were scattered mainly in Southern Europe, India, and Indonesia. Success in this industry was dependent upon uninterrupted supply of natural stone from the mines. Not surprisingly, most producers owned mines themselves, or had exclusive arrangements with certain mine owners. However, along with stone availability, stone variability was also a success factor. Natural stone was mined straight from the earth and, very often, fluctuations in the earth's temperature and topography produced dramatic variations in stone colors and textures. Unusual stone colors and textures fetched a premium on world markets. Sometimes, however, the mined stone possessed faults such as spots or cracks that impaired the marketability of the finished product.

Kadimi sourced its stone from a number of quarries located in Northern and Southern India. For each stone variety, the company typically maintained a single supplier. Distances between the quarries and Kadimi's plant were significant. Road transportation was the most economical and practical option. It took from two to four days for the raw stone to be transported in trucks from the mines to the plant. The company had permanently stationed a company representative at each of the leading quarries to ensure monitoring of stone quality, timely ordering, and safe delivery to the plant. Kadimi also maintained limited stocks of the most popular stones, but due to storage and mining constraints, could not maintain stocks for very long.

Based upon its experience over a few years, Kadimi had developed an extensive nomenclature for its slate, sandstone, and quartzite varieties, despite the existence of variations within each variety. Stones that were mined in the same region or that possessed similar qualities (strength, color, recommended use, etc.) were grouped into families. For instance, the Peacock range of slates was multicolored and was obtained from the same mine in Northern India. Other groupings within slates, sandstones, and quartzites included the Spectra range, Everest range, and the Kanchan range. Several stones did not fit into any category and were marketed as unique stones. In all, Kadimi stocked thirty-six varieties of stones and was in constant search of new varieties to add to its stone repertoire. However, the addition of new stones was dependent on sufficient and regular availability of the stone, as well as favorable customer response to it. Therefore, Kadimi was very careful in selecting new stones and very often tested the response to a new stone at stone fairs before deciding to stock it.

The company marketed both its engineering and stone products at industrial and consumer fairs held worldwide at different times during the year. Engineering exports were primarily directed at key electronic and textile manufacturing facilities located in Asia. The company regularly participated in the annual industrial fairs held in Singapore, Japan, Korea, and Taiwan. By 1996, however, the company had developed a large base of regular customers for its engineering components and marketing was not as extensively required as before.

Stone products, on the other hand, required intensive and continuous marketing efforts. Kadimi was a regular participant in stone fairs held in Orlando, Nuremberg, Madrid, Verona, and Tokyo. Besides providing increased visibility for Kadimi products to worldwide customers, these fairs were strategically used by the company to introduce new products (such as new finishes, new stones, and new applications) and to perceive emerging trends in stone processing technology.

Kadimi's strategy in the stone business was to become the innovator and create new value for the commoditized industry. It did so by:

- Offering new and unusual stones to worldwide buyers
- Creating new stone textures and finishes (e.g. honed, polished, and calibrated)
- Developing customized stone applications (e.g. flooring and wall designs) for each client

As a result of these efforts, Kadimi soon became the leading stone exporter in India. With its unique product finishes and stone offerings, it also managed to raise the bar for all local stone exporters, most of whom were fly-by-night producers with low-key operations. The company's mission was to compete globally and create value-added services in the stone industry.

## The Export Process

The small number of engineering component exports was shipped directly to the OEM within few days of order placement. Lead times were short, and product specifications did not require extensive retooling. Billing and handling was managed entirely by the Singapore office. Bulk purchases made by the small number of regular clients had enabled the Singapore office to set up individual accounts with the largest buyers. Export-related complaints were also handled largely by the Singapore office that had developed long-standing relationships with the buyers in the Asia/Pacific region.

Stone exports presented a more complicated scenario. Unlike component exports, both distributors/retailers as well as individual customers demanded stone products. Due to economic efficiencies derived from bulk shipping, Kadimi was unable to directly serve individual customers and many small retailers, who all wanted small quantities. In the future, Kadimi anticipated having local distributors for its products in several countries. However, for the time being, only wholesaler orders were entertained.

Typically, a wholesaler placed an order with Kadimi at a stone fair or within a few months of a fair. In either case, orders were placed in terms of "containers."[1] Stone tiles were packed into wooden crates that were then loaded into containers at a port. Each container had capacity for sixteen crates, each of which held approximately 50–250 tiles, depending on the size and thickness of the tiles. Kadimi did not encourage orders for less than a full container unless the buyer was willing to bear the shipping cost for the entire container. (Bundling of several small orders into a single container was not allowed by the Indian port authorities.) Once the order was placed, the buyer then had to open a Letter of Credit (LC) with his bank that would guarantee payment to Kadimi. As opposed to some local competitors, Kadimi relied solely on the LC method of payment. There was no flexibility in this policy. Once the LC was opened, the order was executed with a forty-five-day lead time (not including the shipping time). All activities related to production and packaging were handled at the same plant. Once the crates were ready, they were transported by trucks to the Indian port city of Madras for shipment. The shipping agreement was always Free-On-Board, Madras.[2] Hamburg was the most frequent destination for Kadimi's large European customer base, and average shipping times were in excess of a month. In all, the company had about fifty worldwide customers, and the average transaction amount per container ranged from $4000–$15000, with a median around $6000.[3] Since 1994, the number of containers shipped annually had increased every year to reach 95 containers in 1996, and was expected to climb to 150 containers in 1997. The company enjoyed a very healthy 22 percent margin (average) on its stone exports, mainly as a result of its differentiation strategy.

## Export Complaints

Complaints, if any, were usually received by Kadimi upon receipt of the shipment by the customer (approximately forty-five days after shipment from India). Complaints were typically about product defects (70 percent) or shipping (30 percent). Almost all the product defect complaints were about the quality of the mined stone. Foreign customers were particularly conscious about spots or blemishes on the stone. Most of the times, these marks were created in the mining process. Shipping complaints were mainly about improper wooden crate packaging that had resulted in damage to certain tiles. Kadimi had not been able to develop packaging materials that were both safe and cost efficient. Recently, reinforced fiberglass crates were being explored as a packaging alternative, although it was uncertain whether the new packaging could be obtained quickly and in bulk from local suppliers.

Complaints were received from about 5 percent of all customers. Letters and faxes were the primary medium for communication, although Kadimi's recently developed Web site (**www.kadimi.com**) was becoming very popular as both a marketing and feedback channel.

Once a complaint was received, it was directed to the attention of either of the two partners. Depending upon the nature of the complaint (product vs. delivery), relationship to the customer (transaction vs. repeat), and shipment size, the complaint would be settled by either issuing a discount or replacing the product in a future shipment. In reaching a decision, the partners typically consulted with the export department manager. Kadimi's intention was to make instant reparation to the dissatisfied client, especially if he was perceived to be a repeat customer. Information about customer complaints circulated freely among the company's employees. However, only the relevant personnel (production/delivery/sales managers) were formally made aware of such shortcomings in their respective tasks.

Once the complaint was resolved, the matter was over for all practical purposes. Unless a particular complaint manifested itself again and again, past complaints were usually buried under the paperwork. There was no export complaint system in place to assimilate the complaint data and highlight existing problem areas or fore-

---

[1] *"Containers" were hollow rectangular metal boxes that safeguarded materials on ships.*

[2] *Kadimi was responsible for product delivery up to the port city of Madras, located approximately 1100 miles from New Delhi. Once the product was loaded into a container on the ship, responsibility over the product shifted to the buyer.*

[3] *With the addition of higher value-added stone processing techniques, these amounts were increasing every year and the median was expected to reach $10,000 by 1998.*

cast emerging ones. The company was inundated with orders and priority was given for order fulfillment rather than problem solving. In the past year alone, the company had achieved 50 percent export sales growth and was poised for even greater growth in 1997.

## The Decision

After refreshing his mind with all these facts, Gupta considered the decision at hand. The meeting that morning between the partners and functional managers had lasted two hours and two opposing viewpoints had emerged.

The production and delivery managers both agreed that corporate infrastructure was lacking to cater to the increased exporting requirements placed on the company. While the former wanted Kadimi to invest in additional machinery for the value-added finishes (polishing, honing, and calibrating), the delivery manager complained about the use of Madras as a shipping point. He argued that Bombay was much closer and that reduced transportation times would mean reduced lead times for customers. Both managers were of the view that a complaint management system would impair the current flexibility Kadimi enjoyed with respect to settling customer complaints. They added that increased capacity and better products would far better satisfy foreign clients than a consistent policy framework for complaint resolution.

The sales and export managers both agreed that enhancing capacity was important. However, they proposed that establishing trust and building relationships with foreign customers was more important to ensure continued growth. Inconsistency in dealing with customer complaints was creating confusion among foreign buyers regarding corporate policies for product or delivery shortcomings. This was undermining the credibility and reliability of Kadimi's managers in their dealings with foreign clients. A complaint management system, they argued, would be a first step in assuring their customers that the company's policies were fair and consistent. Later on, they added, a similar system could be instituted for the pricing function as well.

As he thought about the discussion, Gupta wondered how he would prioritize the company's problems. The whir of the fax machine broke his train of thought and he glanced over to look at the message he was receiving. It was from his representative at the Himachal quarries. A truckload of Kanchan red slates was on its way to New Delhi. However, the stones were slightly spotted.

Gupta sprang from his chair and made his way to Agarwal's office. He knew what had to be done.

## Questions for Discussion

1. How can Kadimi position itself better for global competitiveness?
2. How can a complaint management system help Kadimi improve its competitiveness?
3. What key issues would you consider in designing such a system for Kadimi?
4. How should Kadimi address the European situation?

# Aftermath of an Environmental Disaster: Union Carbide in Bhopal

On Sunday, December 3, 1984, the peaceful life of a city in India was joltingly disrupted. The Union Carbide plant at Bhopal, a city less than 400 miles from New Delhi, India, had leaked poisonous gas into the air. Within one week, over 2,000 people died, and more remained critically ill. Over 100,000 people were treated for nausea, blindness, and bronchial problems. It was one of history's worst industrial accidents, which continues to affect lives today. Through 1996, more than 4,000 people have died as a result of the accident and 500,000 have become ill. Families still live just outside the barbed wire fence of the abandoned Union Carbide facility, which is only now being dismantled for resale. Contamination of nearby water and soil is strongly suspected. Potable water flows each morning for only thirty minutes. Local farmlands have been abandoned due to sharp drops in crop yields in the years following the accident.

At the time, Union Carbide was America's thirty-seventh largest industrial corporation, with more than

SOURCES: *This case study was written by Michael R. Czinkota by adapting secondary source materials from Kenneth J. Cooper, "Slums Sprawl in Shadow of Bhopal Gas Leak,"* The Washington Post, *June 27, 1996, A19; "Bhopal Legacy Still Being Felt,"* Occupational Hazards *(February 1996): 28; Alan Hall, "The Bhopal Tragedy Has Union Carbide Reeling,"* Business Week *(December 17, 1984): 32; Clemens P. Work, "Inside Story of Union Carbide's India Nightmare,"* U.S. News World Report *(January 21, 1985): 51–52; Armin Rosencranz, "Bhopal, Transnational Corporations, and Hazardous Technologies,"* Ambio *17 (1988): 336–341; Sanjoy Hazarika, "Carbide Plant Closed by India Unrest,"* The New York Times, *Monday, May 13, 1991, D12; Scott McMurray, "India's High Court Upholds Settlement Paid by Carbide in Bhopal Gas Leak,"* The Wall Street Journal, *October 4, 1991, B8.*

100,000 employees and an annual sales volume of over $9 billion. The firm was active in petrochemicals, industrial gases, metals and carbon products, consumer products, and technology transfers.

Union Carbide operated fourteen plants in India. Total Indian operations accounted for less than 2 percent of corporate sales. In spite of a policy by the Indian government to restrict foreign majority ownership of plants, Union Carbide owned 50.9 percent of the Bhopal plant. This special arrangement was granted by the government because the plant served as a major technology transfer project. In order to achieve the goal of technology transfer, management of the plant was mostly carried out by Indian nationals. General corporate safety guidelines applied to the plant, but local regulatory agencies were charged with enforcing Indian environmental laws. Only three weeks before the accident, the plant had received an "environmental clearance certificate" from the Indian State Pollution Board.

The accident resulted in wide public awareness in the United States. A poll showed that 47 percent of those questioned linked Union Carbide's name to the Bhopal disaster. The direct impact of this awareness on Union Carbide's business remains uncertain. Most U.S. consumers do not connect the Union Carbide name to its line of consumer products, which consists of brands such as Energizer, Glad, and Presto. Industrial users, on the other hand, are highly aware of Union Carbide's products. One area that could be particularly affected is that of technology transfer, which in 1983 accounted for 24 percent of Union Carbide's revenues. The firm has concentrated increasingly on that sector, selling mainly its know-how in the fields of engineering, manufacturing, and personnel training.

## The Public Reaction

Internationally, the reaction was one of widespread consumer hostility. Environmentalists demonstrated at Union Carbide plants in West Germany and Australia. Some facilities were firebombed; most were spray painted. Plans for plants in Scotland had to be frozen. The operation of a plant in France was called into question by the French government.

Major financial repercussions occurred as well. Within a week of the accident, Union Carbide stock dropped by $10, a loss in market value of nearly $900 million. A $1.2 billion line of credit was frozen. Profits of Union Carbide India Ltd., which in 1984 had been about 8.2 million ru-

pees, or about $480,000, dropped by 1985 to 1.3 million rupees, or $78,000. By 1990, the company reported a loss of 132 million rupees, about $7.8 million.

In the ensuring debate of the Bhopal disaster, three basic issues were highlighted—responsible industrial planning, adequate industrial safety measures, and corporate accountability. In terms of industrial planning, both Union Carbide and the Indian government were said to have failed. The Indian subsidiary of Union Carbide did little to inform workers about the highly toxic methyl isocyanate (MIC) the plant was producing and the potential health threat to neighboring regions. When the accident occurred, the subsidiary's management team reportedly resisted the parent company's instructions to apply first aid to victims for fear of generating widespread panic within the corporation and the region. The Indian government, on the other hand, seemed to regard technology transfer as a higher priority than public safety. The local government approved construction of the plant with little medical and scientific investigation into its biological effects on the environment and on people.

The second issue was the absence of a "culture of safety" among Indian technicians, engineers, and management. From the very beginning, the project lacked a team of experienced maintenance personnel who would have recognized the need for higher safety measures and, more important, a different choice of technology. When the entire Indian government wholeheartedly approved the import of the most advanced chemical production facility in any developing country without qualified personnel to handle the material and without insight into appropriate precautionary measures in case of an accident, the seeds were sown for potential disaster.

The third area of interest in the Bhopal incident is that of corporate accountability. There are three general norms of international law concerning the jurisprudence of the home government over the foreign subsidiary:

1. Both state and nonstate entities are liable to pay compensation to the victims of environmental pollution and accidents.
2. The corporation is responsible for notifying and consulting the involved officials of actual and potential harm involved in the production and transport of hazardous technologies and materials.
3. The causer or originator of environmental damage is liable to pay compensation to the victims.

These and other developing norms of international law serve to make transnational corporations more responsible for their operation.

## Compensation to Victims

Five days after the incident, the first damage suit, asking for $15 billion, was filed in U.S. Federal District Court. Since then, more than 130 suits have been filed in the United States and more than 2,700 in India. Union Carbide offered to pay $300 million over a period of thirty years to settle the cases before the courts in the United States and India. The Indian government rejected the offer, claiming that the amount was far below its original request of $615 million. By 1986, most U.S. lawsuits had been consolidated in the New York Federal Court. In May 1986, however, the judge presiding over the collective Bhopal cases ruled that all suits arising out of the accident should be heard in the Indian judicial system, claiming that "India is where the accident occurred, and where the victims, witnesses, and documents are located." Although this decision appeared to benefit Union Carbide because of lower damage awards in India, the judge explicitly stated that (1) Union Carbide (USA) and its Indian affiliate must submit to the jurisdiction of the Indian court system, (2) Union Carbide must turn over all relevant documents to the plaintiffs' lawyers in India, as they would if in the United States, and (3) Union Carbide must agree to whatever judgment is rendered in India. This decision had a major effect on Union Carbide (USA) because (1) both Union Carbide (USA) and its Indian subsidiary now had to answer to the Indian court and (2) the entire company's assets had become involved.

In India, the class suit traveled from the Bhopal District court to the Madhya Pradesh High Court and finally to the Indian Supreme Court. Although a settlement agreement was reached between Union Carbide and the Indian government, the descendents of the 2,000 victims were not satisfied. Several victims' consumer groups and public interest lawyers filed petitions contesting the authority of the government to handle the lawsuit on behalf of the victims' descendents. The petitions claimed that the government had no right to represent the victims because governmental negligence had caused the accident in the first place and the government should be as much a target as Union Carbide in the suit itself. It was expected that if the Indian Supreme Court upheld this rationale, then the government would be unable to settle on the victims' behalf. In this case, the agreed-upon settlement amount would also be voided. As a result of the internal debate in India, the $421 million paid in settlement by Union Carbide was frozen. Instead, the Indian government itself disbursed 200 rupees, about $10, a month to all persons who lived in the neighborhoods affected by the gas leak.

On October 3, 1991, almost seven years after the incident, the Supreme Court of India rendered its decision. The total amount of $470 million, which had already been paid by Union Carbide, was upheld as settlement. Criminal charges against the Union Carbide corporation were reinstated, even though the court acknowledged that due to its lack of jurisdiction, it could not enforce any criminal fines in the United States.

Since the decision cannot be reviewed further, it freed up the frozen funds to be distributed to Bhopal victims and their families. Although many victims were delighted about that fact, Prashant Bhushan, a New Delhi attorney, had severe misgivings. He believed the upholding of the civil settlement to be a big blow to the development of law on the subject—particularly since he had argued that Carbide should be forced to pay "first-world" compensation rates to the victims rather than "third-world" rates. He is not alone in his fight. A consortium of twenty-five human rights and environmental organizations demanded in 1996 that Union Carbide stand trial in India on the charge of culpable homicide. The group, which includes Greenpeace and Friends of the Earth, have urged the New York State Attorney General to begin charter revocation proceedings against Union Carbide based on a state law that provides for dissolving corporations that cause great harm.

The lessons learned? As a result of Union Carbide's experience in Bhopal, several chemical companies have reduced the size of their storage tanks of toxic materials, while others have cut their inventories by as much as 50 percent. Many have provided information to the communities in which they manufacture. Some have even invested in risk assessment studies of their operations of hazardous materials. As to Union Carbide, the firm had 1996 revenues of $6.1 billion and 11,745 employees. The company was ranked 237th on the 1997 list of the Fortune 500.

### Questions for Discussion

1. Why did Union Carbide invest in India?
2. How could Union Carbide have planned for an event such as that in Bhopal?
3. How would such planning have improved corporate response to the disaster?
4. What are the future implications for the management of Union Carbide?
5. What are the future implications for the government of India?
6. What are your views on the delay of compensation paid to the victims?

# Water from Iceland

Stan Otis was in a contemplative mood. He had just hung up the phone after talking with Roger Morey, vice president of Citicorp. Morey had made him a job offer in the investment banking sector of the firm. The interviews had gone well, and Citicorp management was impressed with Stan's credentials from a major northeastern private university. "I think you can do well here, Stan. Let us know within a week whether you accept the job," Morey had said.

The three-month search had paid off well, Stan thought. However, an alternative plan complicated the decision to accept the position.

Stan had returned several months before from an extended trip throughout Europe, a delayed graduation

*SOURCE: This study was prepared by Michael R. Czinkota and Veronika Cveckova, using the following background material: International Bottled Water Association statistics: "Top 10 Bottled Water Companies: 1994," Beverage World (March 1995); "Water in Order," Beverage World (September 1996); Ann Arbor, "Consumers Reach for Bottled Water," Arroyo (March 1996).*

present from his parents. Among other places, he had visited Reykjavik, Iceland. Even though he could not communicate well, he found the island enchanting. What particularly fascinated him was the lack of industry and the purity of the natural landscape. In particular, he felt the water tasted extremely good. Returning home, he began to consider making this water available in the United States.

## The Water Market in the United States

In order to consider the possibilities of importing Icelandic water, Stan knew that he first had to learn more about the general water market in the United States. Fortunately, some former college friends were working in a market research firm. Owing Stan some favors, these friends furnished him with a consulting report on the water market.

### The Consulting Report

Bottled water has almost a 10 percent market share of total beverage consumption in the United States. The overall distribution of market share is shown in Figure 1. Primary types of water available for human consumption

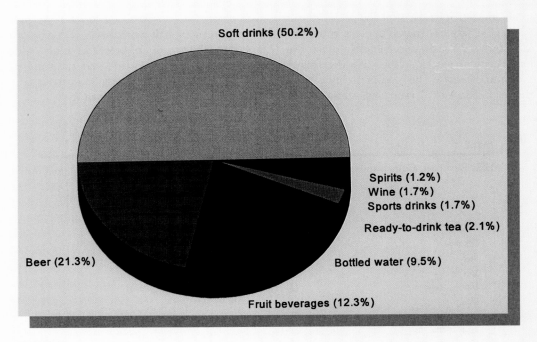

**FIGURE 1**

**Retail Market Shares of Beverage Products in 1995**
*Source:* Beverage World

in the United States are treated or processed water, mineral water, sparkling or effervescent water, spring well water, club soda, and tonic water.

Treated or processed water comes from a well stream or central reservoir supply. This water usually flows as tap water and has been purified and fluoridated.

Mineral water is spring water that contains a substantial amount of minerals, which may be injected or occur naturally. Natural mineral water is obtained from underground water strata or a natural spring. The composition of the water at its source is constant, and the source discharge and temperature remain stable. The natural content of the water at the source is not modified by an artificial process.

Sparkling or effervescent water is water with natural or artificial carbonation. Some mineral waters come to the surface naturally carbonated through underground gases but lose their fizz on the surface with normal pressure. Many of these waters are injected with carbon dioxide later on.

Club soda is obtained by adding artificial carbonation to distilled or regular tap water. Mineral content in this water depends on the water supply used and the purification process the water has undergone. Tonic water is derived from the same process as club soda, but has bitters added to it.

Minerals are important to the taste and quality of water. The type and variety of minerals present in the water can make it a very healthy and enjoyable drink. The combination of minerals present in the water determines its relative degree of acidity. The level of acidity is measured by the pH factor. A pH 7 rating indicates a neutral water. A higher rating indicates that the water contains more solids, such as manganese calcium, and is said to be "hard." Conversely, water with a lower rating is classified as "soft." Most tap water is soft, whereas the majority of commercially sold waters tend to be hard.

## Water Consumption in the United States

Tap water has generally been inexpensive, relatively pure, and plentiful in the United States. Traditionally, bottled water has been consumed in the United States by the very wealthy. In the past several years, however, bottled water has begun to appeal to a wider market. The four main reasons for this change are:

1. An increasing awareness among consumers of the impurity of city water supplies
2. Increasing dissatisfaction with the taste and odor of city tap water
3. Rising affluence in society
4. An increasing desire to avoid excess consumption of caffeine, sugar, and other substances present in coffee and soft drinks.

Bottled water consumers are found chiefly in the states of California, Florida, Texas, New York, and Illinois. Combined, these states represent 52 percent of nationwide bottled water sales. California alone represents over 29 percent of industry sales. Nationwide, bottled water is drunk by one out of every fifteen households. The per capita consumption in 1995 was estimated at 9.9 gallons. (For comparison of per capita consumption of bottled water and other beverages see Table 1).

**TABLE 1**

**U.S. Beverage Consumption in 1995**

| | Retail Receipts In Billions of Dollars | Per Capita Consumption in Gallons |
|---|---|---|
| Soft drinks | 52.1 | 52.1 |
| Beer | 51.6 | 22.1 |
| Spirits | 32.4 | 1.2 |
| Fruit beverages | 12.5 | 12.6 |
| Wine | 12.1 | 1.8 |
| Bottled water | 4.0 | 9.9 |
| Ready-to-drink tea | 2.8 | 2.2 |
| Sports drinks | 1.8 | 1.7 |

*Source: Beverage World.*

Before 1976, bottled water was considered primarily a gourmet specialty, a luxury item consumed by the rich. Today, there are over 700 brands of bottled water available on the U.S. market. Since the entry of Perrier Group into the U.S. market, bottled water consumption has shown exceptional growth. The volume of bottled water sold rose from 255 million gallons in 1976 to 2.7 billion gallons in 1995. Over the past decade, the U.S. consumption of bottled water increased by over 200 percent, taking market share from beverages such as coffee, tea, milk, juice, and alcoholic drinks.

In 1995, the industry's receipts totaled $2.9 billion in the wholesale and $4.1 billion at the retail level, an 8 percent increase from 1994. While bottled water gallonage increased by 8 percent between 1994 and 1995, nonsparkling bottled water volume was up by 9.7 percent for the same period. For more information on the growth of bottled water consumption in the United States, see Figures 2 and 3. Nonsparkling water accounts for over 90 percent of total bottled water gallonage.

As Figure 4 shows, in 1995, imported water held a 3.6 percent share of the domestic market in terms of volume but a 14.4 percent share in terms of wholesale prices (see Table 2). The leading country importing water to the

U.S. is France, with a 61.6 percent share of total bottled water imports. Canada is second with 25.5 percent and Italy third with 7 percent of the imported gallonage (see Figure 5).

Among producers, Perrier is a strong leader with a 25 percent market share. The Perrier Group's top three selling bottled water brands are Arrowhead, Poland Spring, and Ozarka. McKesson holds 8 percent of the market and Anjou International 5.2 percent.

Overall, a cursory analysis indicates good potential for success for a new importer of bottled water in the United States. This is especially true if the water is exceptionally pure and can be classified as mineral water.

## Additional Research

Further exploring his import idea, Stan Otis gathered information on various other marketing facets. One of his main concerns was government regulations.

### Bottled Water Regulations in the United States

The bottled water industry in the United States is regulated and controlled at two levels—by the federal government and by various state governments. Some states,

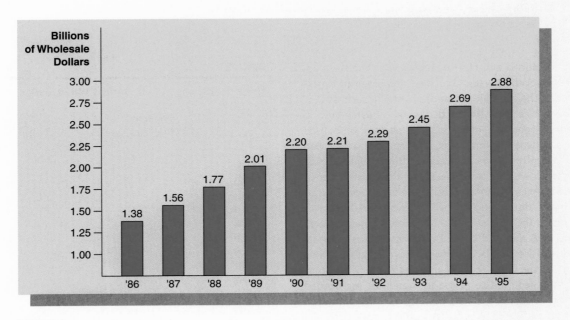

**FIGURE 2**

U.S. Bottled Water Sales in Billions of Wholesale Dollars
*Source:* Beverage Marketing Corporation

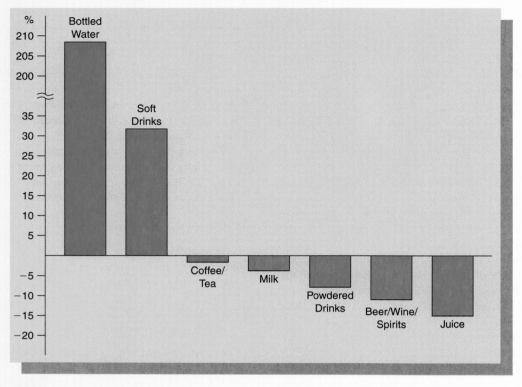

**FIGURE 3**

**U.S. Beverage Consumption: Growth Over the Past Ten Years**
*Source:* Norland International, Inc.

such as California and Florida, impose even stricter regulations on bottled water than they are required to follow under the federal regulations. Others, such as Arizona, do not regulate the bottled water industry beyond the federal requirements. About 75 percent of bottled water is obtained from springs, artesian wells, and drilled wells. The other 25 percent comes from municipal water systems, which are regulated by the Environmental Protection Agency (EPA). All bottled water is considered food and is thus regulated by the Food and Drug Administration (FDA). Under the 1974 Safe Drinking Water Act, the FDA adopted bottled water standards compatible with EPA's standards for water from public water systems. As the EPA revises its drinking water regulations, the FDA is required to revise its standards for bottled water or explain in the Federal Register why it decided not to do so. The FDA requires bottled water products to be clean and safe for human consumption, processed and distributed under sanitary conditions, and produced in compliance with FDA good manufacturing practices.

**TABLE 2**

**Share of Imports in U.S. Bottled Water Market**

|  | Estimated Wholesale Dollars | Gallonage |
|---|---|---|
| 1984 | 8% | 1.8% |
| 1985 | 11.7% | 2.8% |
| 1986 | 10% | 2.6% |
| 1987 | 11% | 2.7% |
| 1988 | 12.1% | 3.1% |
| 1989 | 11.9% | 3.1% |
| 1990 | 13% | 3.7% |
| 1991 | 11.2% | 3.5% |
| 1992 | 12.6% | 4.1% |
| 1993 | 15% | 4.1% |
| 1994 | 16.2% | 4.2% |
| 1995 | 14.4% | 3.6% |

*Source:* International Bottled Water Association

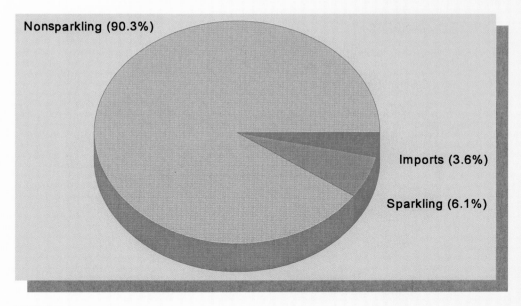

**FIGURE 4**

**Market Share of Bottled Water by Segment in 1995 (Based on Volume)**
*Source:* International Bottled Water Association

In addition, domestic bottled water producers engaged in interstate commerce are subject to periodic, unannounced FDA inspections.

In 1991, an investigation by the U.S. House Energy and Commerce Committee found that 25 percent of the higher-priced bottled water comes from the same sources as ordinary tap water, another 25 percent of producers were unable to document their sources of water, and 31 percent exceeded limits of microbiological contamination. The Committee faulted the FDA with negligent oversight. In response, the FDA established, in November of 1995, definitions for artesian water, groundwater, mineral water, purified water, sparkling bottled water, sterile water, and well water in order to ensure fair advertising by the industry. These results went into effect in May 1996. They include specification of the mineral content of water that can be sold as mineral water. Previously, mineral water was not regulated by the FDA, which resulted in varying standards for mineral water across states. In addition, under these rules, if bottled water comes from a municipal source, it must be labeled to indicate its origin.

**The Icelandic Scenario**

Iceland is highly import-dependent. In terms of products exported, it has little diversity and is dangerously depen-

dent on its fish crop and world fish prices. The government, troubled by high inflation rates and low financial reserves, is very interested in diversifying its export base. An Icelandic Export Board has been created and charged with developing new products for export and aggressively promoting them abroad.

The Ministry of Commerce, after consulting the Central Bank, has the ultimate responsibility in matters concerning import and export licensing. The Central Bank is responsible for the regulation of foreign exchange transactions and exchange controls, including capital controls. It is also responsible for ensuring that all foreign exchange due to residents is surrendered to authorized banks. All commercial exports require licenses. The shipping documents must be lodged with an authorized bank. Receipts exchanged for exports must be surrendered to the Central Bank.

All investments by nonresidents in Iceland are subject to individual approval. The participation of nonresidents in Icelandic joint venture companies may not exceed 49 percent. Nonresident-owned foreign capital entering in the form of foreign exchange must be surrendered.

Iceland is a member of the United Nations, the European Free Trade Association, and the World Trade Organization. Iceland enjoys "most favored nation" status

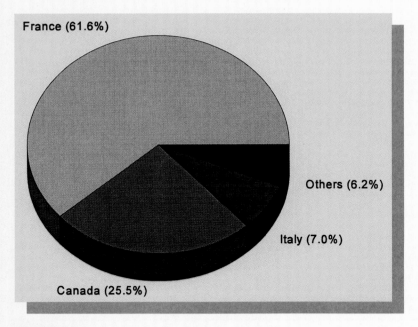

**FIGURE 5**

**Bottled Water Imports by Country in 1995 (Based on Volume)**
*Source:* Beverage Marketing Corporation

with the United States. Under this designation, mineral and carbonated water from Iceland is subject to a tariff of 0.33 cents per liter, and natural (still) water is tariff-free.

### Questions for Discussion

1. Is there sufficient information to determine whether importing water from Iceland would be a profitable business? If not, what additional information is needed to make a determination?
2. Is the market climate in the United States conducive to water imports from Iceland?
3. What are some possible reasons for the fluctuation in the market share held by imports over the past ten years?
4. Should the U.S. government be involved in regulating bottled water products?

# NIKE in Southeast Asia

"Good shoes are made in good factories. Good factories have good labor relations." These are the words from

Nike's chairman and CEO Phillip Knight responding to another attack on the company's labor relations. Over the past few years, Nike has had to answer a number of charges regarding its labor practices in its Southeast Asian plants.

Nike celebrated its 25th anniversary during the summer of 1997. Since its inception from the back of Chairman and CEO Philip Knight's car, Nike has grown into one of the most successful companies in the sports apparel industry. In 1972, the company began with seven models of shoes and collected $3 million in sales that first year. Sales of Nike athletic shoes have continued to grow over the past twenty-five years. Shoe sales reached $2.2 billion in 1990 and $9.2 billion at the end of 1997.

Nike's amazing growth is the result of an effective international marketing and promotion strategy. The company's sponsorship of Michael Jordan and other top

*SOURCE: This case study was written by William H. Heuer and Ilkka A. Ronkainen. The contribution of André Gamrasni is appreciated. For more information, see* **http://www.nike.com/faq/** *for the Nike point of view, and* **http://www.caa.org.au/campaigns/nike/index.html** *for an example of the criticism.*

athletes helped Nike become associated with high performance athletics. In addition, the company's motto "Just Do It!" is one of the most recognizable in the world and has become a part of popular culture. These are just a few examples of the shrewd moves that helped fuel Nike's rapid growth. Another essential factor of Nike's success is its ability to limit labor expenses. Since its inception over twenty-five years ago, the company has attempted to find the least expensive labor to manufacture its shoes, often finding Southeast Asia to offer the most attractive labor setting. Nike subcontracts production to a number of independent facilities throughout Asia for manufacturing of its shoes and its sportswear and concentrates itself in the design, marketing, and technology of footwear and apparel.

Traditionally, the company located in markets where labor unions were not very strong or were illegal. With the support of the governments in these countries, Nike limits its exposure to labor problems and keeps costs low. These facilities allow Nike to assemble and ship shoes for a cost of $22.50, then sell them in the United States for $90 (see Figure 1). In some cases, such as South Korea and Taiwan, Nike even moved production facilities after workers gained significant individual rights and labor costs began to rise. While these moves may have helped Nike's profitability, it opened the company up to increased criticism for creating sweatshop conditions in these plants. Nike began to face increased allegations of worker mistreatment in the early 1990s, forcing the company to develop some guidelines for their subcontractors to follow.

In 1992, Nike introduced its first Code of Conduct document. The Code was designed to illustrate the company's commitment to improving workers' rights in all respects. (A summary of the code's provisions are provided in Table 1.) In addition, the Code requires that management respect the individual worker's right to form a union and forbade management from harassing, abusing, or punishing employees. While the guidelines are in place, there are still many subcontractor plants that do not follow the code. Even after the Nike Code of Conduct was in place, the company faced continued criticism concerning their labor relations. Nike defended itself by saying that employing 500,000 people worldwide in contract manufacturing makes it very difficult to enforce the code, especially when Nike does not own the factories. Many people, however, still doubted Nike's desire to enforce their own Code of Conduct. Critics believed that strict enforcement of the Code would raise production costs for the company.

In September 1997, Nike terminated their contract with four subcontractors in Indonesia. The Company stated that the four factories did not comply with Nike standards in three important areas: overtime requirements, physical work environment, and meeting minimum wage requirements. According to the Company, the

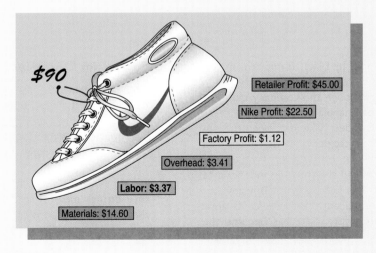

**FIGURE 1**

**Cost of a Pair of Nike Shoes**
*Source:* http://www.nike.com/faq/faq.html

**TABLE I**

**Excerpts from the Nike Code of Conduct**

NIKE designs, manufactures and markets products for sports and fitness consumers. At every step in that process, we are driven to do not only what is required, but what is expected of a leader. We expect our business partners to do the same. Specifically, NIKE seeks partners that share our commitment to the promotion of best practices and continuous improvement in:

1) Occupational health and safety, compensation, hours of work and benefits.
2) Minimizing our impact on the environment.
3) Management practices that recognize the dignity of the individual, the rights of free association and collective bargaining, and the right to a workplace free of harassment, abuse or corporal punishment.
4) The principle that decisions on hiring, salary, benefits, advancement, termination or retirement are based solely on the ability of an individual to do the job.

Wherever NIKE operates around the globe, we are guided by this Code of Conduct. We bind our business partners to these principles. While these principles establish the spirit of our partnerships, we also bind these partners to specific standards of conduct. These are set forth below:

**Forced Labor (Contractor)** certifies that it does not use any forced labor—prison, indentured, bonded or otherwise.

**Child Labor (Contractor)** certifies it does not employ any person under the minimum age established by local law, or the age at which compulsory schooling has ended, whichever is greater, but in no case under the age of 14.

**Compensation (Contractor)** certifies that it pays at least the minimum total compensation required by local law, including all mandated wages, allowances and benefits.

**Benefits (Contractor)** certifies that it complies with all provisions for legally mandated benefits, including but not limited to housing; meals; transportation and other allowances; health care; child care; sick leave; emergency leave; pregnancy and menstrual leave; vacation, religious, bereavement and holiday leave; and contributions for social security, life, health, worker's compensation and other insurance.

**Hours of Work/Overtime (Contractor)** certifies that it complies with legally mandated work hours; uses overtime only when employees are fully compensated according to local law; informs the employee at the time of hiring if mandatory overtime is a condition of employment; and, on a regularly scheduled basis, provides one day off in seven, and requires no more than 60 hours of work per week, or complies with local limits if they are lower.

**Health and Safety (Contractor)** certifies that it has written health and safety guidelines, including those applying to employee residential facilities, where applicable; and that it has agreed in writing to comply with NIKE's factory/vendor health and safety standards.

**Environment (Contractor)** certifies that it complies with applicable country environmental regulations; and that it has agreed in writing to comply with NIKE's specific vendor/factory environmental policies and procedures, which are based on the concept of continuous improvement in processes and programs to reduce the impact on the environment.

*Source:* **http://www.nikeworkers.com/code.html**

move represented an effort by Nike to improve the labor conditions in the subcontracted facilities. Nike did not name the factories, although the company did state that they were not shoe manufacturers. By not mentioning the production facilities, Nike kept open the option that it would use the factories once they were able to meet Nike standards.

While Nike acknowledged the move in Indonesia as a positive move, many critics felt that the Company was just attempting to counter recent criticism over its labor practices in Asia. In either case, Nike has become the most visible target for exploitation of labor by large multinational corporations. The company realizes the damage that these allegations cause to its reputation and its business, however, the company does not seem to have the answer to ending the problem.

**Questions for Discussion**

1. What recommendations would you offer Nike for dealing with the allegations of labor exploitation in Asia?
2. What value does the Code of Conduct offer to Nike? How can the Company ensure proper adherence to the Code?
3. Should Nike cancel contracts with these facilities if they do not meet Nike's requirements? What about the company's responsibility to the workers employed in these facilities? Does Nike have better options besides termination of the production contract?
4. Are there differences between Nike's responsibility to its shareholders and its responsibility to its stakeholders?

5. Do you think Nike should be responsible for the labor practices in subcontracted facilities? What should be their level of responsibility?

# ESPRIT

"Europe now has a position in technologies where we are no longer in danger of losing the pace." This statement by a European executive underlines the fact that Europe's experiment in cooperative research and development (R&D) is paying off. Since the mid-1980s, companies and research institutes from Denmark to Spain have pooled their resources in megaprojects ranging from genetic engineering to thermonuclear fusion. One of the most ambitious efforts is ESPRIT (European Strategic Programs for Research in Information Technologies). In the first period of ESPRIT (ESPRIT 1), 1984–1989, a total of 1.5 billion ECU ($2 billion) were spent; in the second period (ESPRIT 2), 1987–1991, an additional 3.2 billion ECU ($4.4 billion) was made available, and for ESPRIT 3, which ended in 1994, another 2.7 billion ECU ($3.7 billion) was allocated. ESPRIT 4, which started January 1, 1995, and will have a duration of four years, already has had 1.9 billion ($2.5 billion) proposed for its projects to "contribute toward the construction of a European information infrastructure in order to ensure the future competitive-

ness of all European industry and to improve the quality of life." ESPRIT is managed by the Directorate General (III) for Industry of the European Commission.

## Background

The history of intra-European cooperation had a shaky beginning at best. The rising costs of research in aerospace, electronics, and chemicals, as well as the substantial technological gap between European and U.S. firms in the 1960s, provided the impetus for greater intra-European collaboration. In April 1970, the European Commission proposed the creation of an EC office to coordinate development contracts in advanced technology. Although the number of mergers did rise in the 1970s, the decade was marked by a series of failures in intra-European cooperation. Most prominent was the failure of UNIDATA, a computing resource venture by Bull, Philips, and Siemens.

In 1980, Étienne Daignon, then Commissioner of Industry in the EC, invited twelve of Europe's largest information technology firms (Siemens, AEG, and Nixdorf of Germany; Plessey, GEC, and STC of the United Kingdom; CGE, Thomson, and Bull of France; Philips of the Netherlands; and Olivetti and Stet of Italy) to help create a cooperative work program for their industry to be called ESPRIT. The objectives of the effort were (1) to promote intra-European industrial cooperation, (2) to furnish European industry with the basic technologies that it would need to bolster its competitiveness over the next five to ten years, and (3) to develop European norms and standards. Five major themes were agreed upon: advanced micro electronics, software technology, advanced information processing, office systems, and computer integrated manufacture. The European Commission wanted to make clear from the beginning that ESPRIT was not meant as an industrial policy on a regional level, but rather a technology policy that had the task of identifying key areas of technology. ESPRIT launched a pilot program in 1983 and began full-scale operations a year later.

The involved parties and the influences in the decision-making process of European R&D projects are summarized in Figure 1. Industry specifies the subject areas and priorities, while the European Commission makes a coherent work plan, acts as a program director and contract manager, and makes the selection of projects and monitors their progress. The Commission is obligated to report to the Council of Ministers, the European Parliament, and the Economic and Social Committee.

*SOURCE: This case was complied by Ilkka A. Ronkainen. It is based on "Screened Out," The Economist (September 24, 1994): 66; Marc Van Wegberg, Arjen Van Witteloostuijn, and Michiel Roscam Abbing, "Multimarket and Multiproject Collusion," De Economist 142, 3 (1994): 253–285; Willem A. Ledeboer and Tjerk R. Gorter, "ESPRIT: Successful Industrial R&D Cooperation in Europe," International Journal of Technology Management 8, 6, 7, 8 (1993): 528–543; "Do Not adjust Your Set Yet," The Economist (February 27, 1993): 65–66: "Sematech Claims Major Advance by Halving Size of Chip Circuits," The Wall Street Journal, January 22, 1992, B5; Louis Kraar, "Your Rivals Can Be Your Allies," Fortune (March 27, 1989): 63–76; Les Smith, "Can Consortiums Defeat Japan?" Fortune (June 5, 1989): 215–254; Jonathan B. Levine, "Hanging Tough by Teaming Up," Business Week (October 22, 1990): 121; and Jeremy Main, "Making Global Alliances Work," Fortune (December 17, 1990): 121–126. Thanks to Boyd J. Miller for his assistance with an earlier version of this case. For more information, see* **http://www.cordis.lu/esprit/** *and* **http://europa.eu.int**

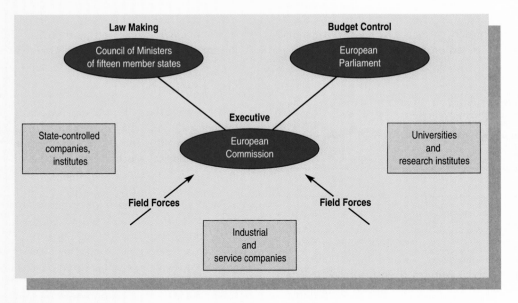

**FIGURE I**

**The Decision-Making Process of European R&D Programs**

*Source:* Willem A. Ledeboer and Tjerk R. Gorter, "ESPRIT: Successful Industrial R&D Cooperation in Europe," *International Journal of Technology Management* 8, 6, 7, 8 (1993): 530.

Today, roughly half of ESPRIT's budget is paid for by the EU. The other half is provided by the participating companies. Specific measures, such as actions to encourage standardization and measures to provide general service tools to research centers and universities, may qualify for an EU contribution of up to 100 percent of total costs. ESPRIT's project rules require that at least two firms located in two different EU countries be represented. This rule ensures that ESPRIT is an intercontinental program. Initially, the vast majority of programs included the Big-12 firms. Over time, smaller firms, research institutes, and universities have become significant contributors. With ESPRIT 4, approximately one-third are small and medium-sized enterprises, one-third large companies, and one-third research institutes and universities. Since a significant amount of financing comes from taxpayers, officials must disperse funds equitably rather than to the strongest competitors. This has allowed smaller firms, such as IMEC, to collaborate with multinational giants such as Philips. The results are discussed and exhibited annually during "ESPRIT Week" in Brussels.

ESPRIT plays different roles for the participating entities. For firms already engaged in alliances, ESPRIT has helped complement them. Commitment levels to R&D and to individual projects have also improved. For ex-

ample, European information technology companies increased their R&D and capital spending by 5 percent in the four years ended in 1990, to 19.2 percent of revenues from 14.5 percent, nearly matching the level of U.S. companies. Furthermore, ESPRIT has allowed participants to work together in the development of new European standards of technology to ensure, for example, that computer systems are able to work together.

By subsidizing the costs of R&D, facilitating the emergence of complementary technologies between firms, and promoting standardization, the ESPRIT program enhances interfirm cooperation without requiring explicit, formal, long-term contractual-arrangements. By 1997, a total of 1,027 projects have been started under ESPRIT's auspices: 241 with ESPRIT 1, 433 with ESPRIT 2, and 353 with ESPRIT 3 (many of which are still under execution). Fewer than 5 percent have been terminated because of poor results or trouble within the consortium.

## Industry Challenges

Both the computer and telecommunications industries suffer from rising R&D costs, relatively short product life cycles, rapid product obsolescence, and extensive capital requirements. As product development costs soar, small and medium-sized firms especially come under considerable financial pressure to keep up with technological developments.

It is estimated that it takes nearly $1 billion to develop a new telecommunications switching system or a new generation of semiconductor. For this investment to be profitable, markets of nearly $14 billion are needed. New production lines also require considerable capital investment. In semiconductors, for example, the minimum investment for a new microelectronics production line is approaching the total value of annual output for that plant.

With rising R&D costs and shortened product life cycles, competition has intensified, and firms see little future in becoming national monopolies. Securing access to foreign markets and reducing costs and risks are essential to long-term survival in the industry.

## Cooperative Efforts in Japan and the United States

The success of the Ministry of International Trade and Industry (MITI) in Japan in including the private sector in public planning decisions was the inspiration for ESPRIT. In the late 1970s, a consortium of six companies, including NTT, Mitsubishi, and Matsushita, that was designed to overtake the United States in producing very large scale integrated (VLSI) circuits—high-powered memories-on-a-chip—functioned so well that the U.S. government pressured the Japanese government to stop giving the consortium money. It was too late: by the mid-1980s, Japanese companies dominated the market. Since then, the Japanese have launched other consortia. One of them consists of nine companies (including Hitachi, Toshiba, and NEC) whose mission is to develop advanced computer technologies such as artificial intelligence and parallel processing.

Activities are organized under three headings: (1) underpinning technologies: software technologies, technologies for components and subsystems (e.g., semiconductors, microsystems, and peripherals), and multimedia; (2) long-term research to ensure potential for next-generation solutions; and (3) focused research on projects such as high-performance computing and networking and integration in manufacturing.

In the United States, well over 100 R&D consortia have registered with the Justice Department to pool their resources for research into technologies ranging from artificial intelligence to those needed to overtake the Japanese lead in semiconductor manufacturing. The major consortia are MCC (Microelectronics and Computer Technology Corp.) and Sematech, which boast as members the largest U.S. companies such as AT&T, GE, IBM, Motorola, and 3M. Sematech, founded in 1988, was formed to rescue an ailing U.S. computer chip industry. Funded jointly by the U.S. government and member companies, the consortium is credited with slowing the market-share drop of U.S. chip-equipment makers, who now control 53 percent of a $10 billion world market, up from less than 40 percent five years earlier. Although in theory most consortia have no real limitations on membership, barriers may exist. Sematech, for example, refuses to accept foreign firms, worrying that if Europeans were allowed to join, there would be no way to keep out the Japanese.

The race for developing the standard for high-definition television (HDTV) in the United States created interesting alliances. The government entity involved, the Federal Communications Commission (FCC), did not finance or participate actively in the choice of the standard; it formed a private sector advisory committee to pick the technically best system in an open contest. One team formed for this contest included the U.S. subsidiaries of France's Thomson and Holland's Philips (backed by the EU to develop Europe's standard) as well as NBC, one of the major U.S. broadcast networks. The other two teams included Zenith and AT&T in one and General Instrument (a maker of cable TV gear) and the Massachusetts Institute of Technology in the other one. In the spring of 1993, the FCC was encouraging all three teams to form a "grand alliance," combining all systems for a final round of testing. In late May of 1993, the three teams decided to join forces in a single approach, a move that was strongly supported by top federal officials. While many expected the agreement to hasten the introduction of HDTV (because it reduces the likelihood of protracted disputes and litigation and represents a broad technical consensus for the next generation of television sets), it has been delayed because of the reluctance of television networks to re-equip their studios and the forecast that consumers would not switch to HDTV until set prices would drop to around $500—an impossibility with today's technology.

## Management of Collaborative Efforts

Three factors have been shown to make collaborative efforts succeed: leaders who are inspired, angry, or even scared; goals that are limited and well defined; and a dependable source of revenue. Some never overcome inherent problems. As cooperative ventures, they are intrinsically anticompetitive, so they risk becoming sluggish and stifling.

The broader and more formal the collaborative effort, the greater the hazard that it will get bogged down in bureaucracy. Management by committee could be a problem if it results in a lack of responsiveness to the marketplace. Some also decry the participation of governments in these efforts, pointing to possible meddling in the choice of programs and the way they are run.

Culture clash can also threaten collaborative efforts, since the efforts are often staffed at least partly by people on the payrolls of their members. Mixing corporate cultures may result in conflict. "Consortia are the wave of the future, but they sure are hard to manage," said a former consortium chief operating officer. Furthermore, if dominant companies refuse to join in an effort, and those participating remain aloof and suspicious of each other, the effort will not succeed.

The bottom line is that entities participating in collaborative efforts have to be as attentive to executing and maintaining them as they are to initiating them. Since working with former competitors is frequently a new experience, it requires new ground rules: from domestic market to a global economic and cultural perspective, from blanket secrecy and suspicion to judicious trust and openness, and from win-lose to win-win relationships.

## Questions for Discussion

1. Can collaborative efforts, such as ESPRIT, really do things no single company could—or would—undertake?
2. What additional challenges are introduced when R&D collaboration is across national borders; that is, will ESPRIT prove to be more problematic than Sematech (which does not allow non-U.S. members)?
3. How will ESPRIT's development of pan-European standards help Europe and European companies?
4. Will small and medium-sized firms benefit more from their participation in projects such as ESPRIT than the large, multinational corporation?

# INTERNATIONAL BUSINESS STRATEGY AND OPERATIONS

## PART 5

Now that the firm has entered and established itself in international markets, it is important to devise and implement strategies which will help provide a competitively advantageous position. Part 5 starts with strategic planning and then focuses on important overarching dimensions such as services, logistics, and countertrade—as well as on the traditional functional areas of marketing, finance, accounting, taxation, human resources, and management.

Each one of the chapters in Part 5 is structured to differentiate between smaller firms and multinational corporations (MNCs). At the beginning of Part 5, low cost and low resource approaches are presented for firms with little international experience. Subsequent chapters assume a globally oriented perspective with a major focus on MNC. Part 5 concludes with a chapter covering the newest developments, knowledge, and speculations about international business as well as information about professional and employment options in the international business field.

# CHAPTER 13

# Strategic Planning in International Business

◆ *To outline the process of strategic planning in the context of the global marketplace*

◆ *To examine both the external and internal factors that determine the conditions for development of strategy and resource allocation*

◆ *To illustrate how best to utilize the environmental conditions within the competitive challenges and resources of the firm to develop effective programs*

◆ *To suggest how to achieve a balance between local and regional/global priorities and concerns in the implementation of strategy*

## Appliance Makers on a Global Quest

The $11 billion home appliance market is undergoing major consolidation and globalization. Many U.S.–based manufacturers are faced in their home markets with increased competition from foreign companies, such as the world's largest appliance maker, Electrolux. In addition, industry fundamentals in the United States are rather gloomy: stagnating sales, rising raw material prices, and price wars. On the other hand, markets abroad are full of opportunities. The European market, for example, is growing quite fast, and the breakdown of barriers within the European Union has made establishing business there even more attractive. Market potential is significant as well: While 65 percent of U.S. homes have dryers, only 18 percent of Europeans have them. Markets in Latin America and Asia are showing similar trends as well.

To take advantage of this growth, appliance makers have formed strategic alliances and made acquisitions. General Electric entered into a joint venture with Britain's General Electric PLC, and in its strategic shift to move the company's "center of gravity" from the industrialized world to Asia and Latin America, joint ventures were established in India with Godrej and in Mexico with Mabe. A strictly North American manufacturer before 1989, Whirlpool purchased the appliance business of Dutch giant N. V. Phillips. Whirlpool's move gave it ten plants on the European continent and some popular appliance lines, which is a major asset in a region characterized by loyalty to domestic brands. Today, Whirlpool is third in European market share after Electrolux and Bosch-Siemens. The company ranks first in the Americas, and while it only has a 1 percent market share in Asia, it is the region's largest Western appliance maker.

Product differences present global marketers with a considerable challenge. The British favor front-loading washing machines, while the French swear by top-loaders. The French prefer to cook their food at high temperatures, causing grease to splatter onto oven walls, which calls for self-cleaning ovens. This feature is in less demand in Germany, where lower temperatures are traditionally used. Manufacturers are hoping that European integration will bring about cost savings and product standardization. The danger to be avoided is the development of compromise products that in the end appeal to no one. Joint ventures present their share of challenges to the global marketers. For example, in Whirlpool's Shanghai facility teams of American, Italian, and Chinese technicians must work through three translators to set up production.

Although opportunities do exist, competition is keen. Margins have suffered as manufacturers (more than 300 in Europe alone) scrape for business. The major players have decided to compete in all the major markets of the world. "Becoming a global appliance player is clearly the best use of our management expertise and well-established brand line-up," Whirlpool executives have said. Whirlpool's long-term goal is to leverage its global manufacturing and brand assets strategically across the world.

Not everyone has succeeded, however. In its move toward globalization, Maytag acquired Chicago Pacific Corporation, best known for its Hoover appliances. The products have a strong presence in the United Kingdom and Australia but not on the European continent, where Maytag ended up essentially trying to introduce new products to new markets. After six years, Maytag sold its European operations to an Italian manufacturer at a loss of $135 million in 1995. ▨

*Sources:* "Did Whirlpool Spin too Far too Fast?" *Business Week* (June 24, 1996): 134–136; Regina Fazio Maruca, "The Right Way to Go Global: An Interview with Whirlpool CEO David Whitwam," *The Harvard Business Review* 72 (March–April 1994): 134–145; "Whirlpool Hangs Its Rivals Out to Dry," *USA Today,* December 10, 1993, 3B; "GE's Brave New World," *Business Week* (November 8, 1993): 64–69; and "Can Maytag Clean Up Around the World?" *Business Week* (January 30, 1989): 86–87.

## Globalization

The transformations in the world marketplace have been extensive and, in many cases, rapid. Local industries operating in protected national economies are challenged by integrated global markets contested by global players. National borders are becoming increasingly irrelevant as liberalization and privatization take place. This has then led to such phenomena as the growing scale and mobility of the world's capital markets and many companies' ability to leverage knowledge and talent across borders.[1] Even the biggest companies in the biggest home markets cannot survive on taking their situation as a given if they are in global industries such as automobiles, banking, consumer electronics, entertainment, pharmaceuticals, publishing, travel services, or washing machines. Rather than seeking to maximize their share of the pie in home markets, they have to seek to maximize the size of the pie by having a presence in all of the major markets of the world.[2] These changes and subsequent corporate action for the appliance industry are highlighted in the opening vignette for the chapter.

**Globalization** reflects a business orientation based on the belief that the world is becoming more homogeneous and that distinctions between national markets are not only fading but, for some products, will eventually disappear. As a result, companies need to globalize their international strategy by formulating it across markets to take advantage of underlying market, cost, environmental, and competitive factors.

As shown in Figure 13.1, globalization can be seen as a result of a process that culminates a process of international market entry and expansion. Before globalization, companies utilize to a great extent a country-by-country **multidomestic strategy**, with each country organization operated as a profit center.

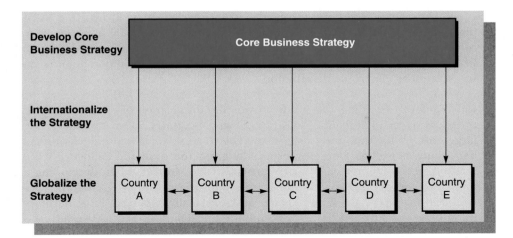

**FIGURE 13.1**

**Evolution of Global Strategy**
*Source:* Reprinted from "Global Strategy . . . In a World of Nations?" by George S. Yip, *Sloan Management Review* 31 (Fall 1989): 30, by permission of the publisher. Copyright 1989 by the Sloan Management Review Association. All rights reserved.

Each national entity markets a range of different products and services targeted to different customer segments, utilizing different strategies with little or no coordination of operations between countries.

However, with expanding operations, inefficiencies generated by the multidomestic approach, coupled with external forces integrating markets worldwide, start building pressure toward improved coordination across country markets.

Both external and internal factors will create the favorable conditions for development of strategy and resource allocation on a global basis. These factors can be divided into market, cost, environmental, and competitive factors.

## Globalization Drivers[3]

**Market Factors**   The world customer identified by Ernst Dichter more than thirty years ago has gained new meaning today.[4] For example, Kenichi Ohmae has identified a new group of consumers emerging in the triad of North America, Europe, and the Far East whom marketers can treat as a single market with the same spending habits.[5] Approximately 600 million in number, these consumers have similar educational backgrounds, income levels, lifestyles, use of leisure time, and aspirations. One reason given for the similarities in their demand is a level of purchasing power (ten times greater than that of LDCs or NICs) that translates into higher diffusion rates for certain products. Another reason is that developed infrastructures—ownership of telephones, faxes, and modems and an abundance of paved roads—lead to attractive markets for other products. Products can be designed to meet similar demand conditions throughout the triad. These similarities also enhance the transferability of other program elements.

At the same time, channels of distribution are becoming more global; that is, a growing number of retailers are now showing great flexibility in their strategies for entering new geographic markets.[6] Some are already world powers (e.g., Benetton and McDonald's), whereas others are pursuing aggressive growth (e.g., Toys 'Я' Us and IKEA). Also noteworthy are cross-border retail alliances, which expand the presence of retailers to new markets quite rapidly.

Technology is changing the landscape of markets as well. In the area of personal financial services, for instance, 95 percent of the $300 billion market is currently captured by nationally based competitors. By 2005, this market is likely to double in size and is going to be accessible to global competitors via transplants or electronic distribution.

**Cost Factors**   Avoiding cost inefficiencies and duplication of effort are two of the most powerful globalization drivers. A single-country approach may not be large enough for the local business to achieve all possible economies of scale and scope as well as synergies, especially given the dramatic changes in the marketplace. Take, for example, pharmaceuticals. In the 1970s, developing a new drug cost about $16 million and took four years. The drug could be produced in Britain or the United States and eventually exported. Now, developing a drug costs from $250 to $500 million and takes as long as twelve years, with competitive efforts close behind. Only a global product for a global market can support that much risk.[7] Size has become a major asset, which partly explains the many mergers and acquisitions (Bristol Myers and Squibb as well as Smith Kline and Beecham in the pharmaceutical industry, and Lockheed and Martin Marietta as well as Boeing and McDonnell Douglas in aerospace) of the past few years.[8] In the heavily contested consumer goods sectors, launching a new brand may cost as much as $100 million, meaning that companies such as Unilever and Procter & Gamble are not going to necessarily spend precious resources on one-country projects.

In many cases, expanded market participation and activity concentration can accelerate the accumulation of learning and experience. General Electric's philosophy is to be first or second in the world in a business or to get out. This can be seen, for example, in its global effort to develop premium computed tomography (CT), a diagnostic scanning system. In 1987, GE swapped its consumer electronics business with the French Thomson for Thomson's diagnostic imaging business. At the same time, GE established GE Medical Systems Asia in Tokyo, anchored on Yokogawa Medical Systems, which is 75 percent owned by GE.

**Environmental Factors**   As shown earlier in this text, government barriers have fallen dramatically in the last years to further facilitate the globalization of markets and the activities of companies within them. For example, the forces pushing toward a pan-European market are very powerful: The increasing wealth and mobility of European consumers (favored by the relaxed immigration controls), the accelerating flow of information across borders, the introduction of new products where local preferences are not well established, and the publicity surrounding the integration process itself all promote globalization.[9] Also, the resulting removal of physical, fiscal, and technical barriers is indicative of the changes that are taking place around the world on a greater scale.

At the same time, rapid technological evolution is contributing to the process. For example, Ford Motor Company is able to accomplish its globalization efforts by using new communications methods, such as teleconferencing and CAD/CAM links, as well as travel, to manage the complex task of meshing car companies on different continents. Newly emerging markets will benefit from advanced communications by being able to leapfrog stages of economic development. Places that until recently were incommunicado in China, Viet-

## BORN GLOBAL

**E**xports account for 95 percent of Cochlear's $40 million sales after a real annual compounded rate of 25 percent throughout the 1990s. Cochlear is a company specializing in the production of implants for the profoundly deaf. Based in Australia, it maintains a global technological lead through its strong links with hospitals and research units around the world and through its collaborative research with a network of institutions around the world.

Cochlear is a prime example of small to medium-sized firms that are remaking the global corporation of the 1990s. The term *mininational* has been coined to reflect their smaller size compared to the traditional multinationals. Sheer size is no longer a buffer against competition in markets where customers are demanding specialized and customized products. With the advent of electronic process technology, mininationals are able to compete on price and quality—often with greater flexibility. By taking advantage of today's more open trading regions, they can serve the world from a handful of manufacturing bases, sparing them from the necessity of building a plant in every country. Developments in information technology have enabled mininationals to both access data throughout most of the world and to run inexpensive and responsive sales and service operations across languages and time zones.

The smaller bureaucracies of the mininationals allow them to move swiftly in seizing new markets and developing new products, typically in focused markets. In many cases, these new markets have been developed by the mininationals themselves. For example, Symbol Technologies Inc. of Bohemia, New York, invented the field of handheld laser scanners and now dominates this field. In a field that did not even exist in 1988, Cisco Systems Inc. of Menlo Park, California, claims 50 percent of the world market for gear that connects networks of computers. The key, says Perkin-Elmer Corp. CEO Riccardo Pigliucci is to "do what you know how to do. Do it right. And do it everywhere." That helps companies grow without diversifying too far afield, which could make them vulnerable to the multinationals.

The lessons from these new generation global players are to (1) keep focused and concentrate on being number one or number two in a technology niche; (2) stay lean by having small headquarters to save on costs and to accelerate decision making; (3) take ideas and technologies to and from wherever they can be found; (4) take advantage of employees regardless of nationality to globalize thinking; and (5) solve customers' problems by involving them rather than pushing on them standardized solutions.

*Sources: Michael W. Rennie, "Born Global,"* The McKinsey Quarterly *(number 4, 1993): 45–52; and "Mininationals Are Making Maximum Impact,"* Business Week *(September 6, 1993): 66–69.*

nam, Hungary, or Brazil are rapidly acquiring state-of-the-art telecommunications that will let them foster both internal and external development.[10]

A new group of global players is taking advantage of today's more open trading regions and newer technologies. **Mininationals,** or newer companies with sales between $200 million and $1 billion, are able to serve the world from a handful of manufacturing bases, compared with having to build a plant in every country as the established multinational corporations once had to do. Their smaller bureaucracies have also allowed these mininationals to move swiftly to seize new markets and develop new products—a key to global success in the 1990s.[11] This phenomenon is highlighted in Global Perspective 13.1.

**Competitive Factors**   Many industries are already dominated by global competitors that are trying to take advantage of the three sets of factors mentioned earlier. To remain competitive, a company may have to be the first to do something or to be able to match or preempt competitors' moves. Products are now introduced, upgraded, and distributed at rates unimaginable a decade ago. Without a global network, carefully researched ideas may be picked off by other global players. This is what Procter & Gamble and Unilever did to Kao's Attack concentrated detergent, which they mimicked and introduced into the United States and Europe before Kao could react.

With the triad markets often both flat in terms of growth and fiercely competitive, many global marketers are looking for new markets and for new product categories for growth. Nestlé, for example, is setting its sights on consumer markets in fast-growing Asia, especially China, and has diversified into pharmaceuticals by acquiring Alcon and by becoming a major shareholder in the world's number one cosmetics company, the French L'Oreal.[12]

Market presence may be necessary to execute global strategies and to prevent others from having undue advantage in unchallenged markets. Caterpillar faced mounting global competition from Komatsu but found out that strengthening its products and operations was not enough to meet the challenge. Although Japan was a small part of the world market, as a secure home base (no serious competitors), it generated 80 percent of Komatsu's cash flow. To put a check on its major global competitor's market share and cash flow, Caterpillar formed a heavy-equipment joint venture with Matsushita to serve the Japanese market.[13] Similarly, when Unilever tried to acquire Richardson-Vicks in the United States, Procter & Gamble saw this as a threat to its home market position and outbid its archrival for the company.

**The Outcome**   The four globalization drivers have affected countries and sectors differently. While some industries are truly globally contested, such as paper and pulp and soft drinks, some sectors, such as government services, are still quite closed and will open up as a decades-long evolution. Commodities

| Global GDP, US$ trillion | **Industry** | | |
|---|---|---|---|
| | **Commodities and scale-driven goods** | **Consumer goods and locally delivered goods and services** | **Government services** |
| **Triad*** | Old arena $4 Globalized in 1980s | | |
| **Developing countries†** | Emerging arena $17 Globally contestable today | | |
| **Low-income countries ‡** | Closed arena $3 Still blocked or lacking significant opportunity | | |

Country (vertical axis label on left)
More globalized / Less globalized (vertical axis label on right)
Global ←————————————→ Local

\* 19 OECD countries from North America, Western Europe, and Asia; Japan and Australia included
† 68 countries with middle income per capita, plus China and India
‡ Countries of small absolute size and low income per capita

**FIGURE 13.2**

**The Global Landscape**

*Source:* Jane Fraser and Jeremy Oppenheim, "What's New About Globalization?" *The McKinsey Quarterly* 2 (1997), 173.

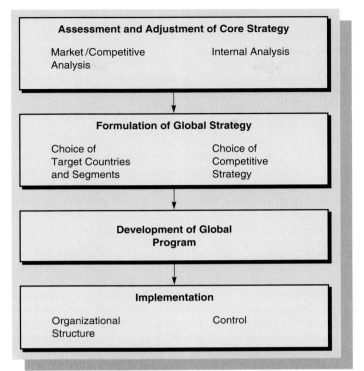

**FIGURE 13.3**

**Global Strategy Formulation**
The authors appreciate the contributions of Robert M. Grant in the preparation of this figure.

and manufactured goods are already in globalized state, while many consumer goods are accelerating towards more globalization. Similarly, the leading trading nations of the world display far more openness than low-income countries, thus advancing the state of globalization in general. The expansion of the global trade arena is summarized in Figure 13.2. The size of markets estimated to be global by the turn of the century is well over $21 billion, boosted by new sectors and markets becoming available.

It should also be noted that leading companies by their very actions drive the globalization process. There is no structural reason why soft drinks should be at a more advanced stage of globalization while beer and spirits remain more local except for the opportunistic behavior of Coca-Cola. Similarly, Nike and Reebok have driven their business in a global direction by creating global brands, a global customer segment, and a global supply chain.

## The Strategic Planning Process

Given the opportunities and challenges provided by the new realities of the marketplace, decision makers have to engage in strategic planning to match markets with products and other corporate resources more effectively and efficiently to strengthen the company's long-term competitive advantage. While the process has been summarized as a sequence of steps in Figure 13.3, many of the stages can occur in parallel. Furthermore, feedback as a result of evaluation and control may restart the process at any stage.

## Understanding and Adjusting the Core Strategy

The planning process has to start with a clear definition of the business for which strategy is to be developed. Generally, the strategic business unit (SBU) is the unit around which decisions are based. In practice, SBUs represent groupings based on product-market similarities based on (1) needs or wants to be met, (2) end-user customers to be targeted, or (3) the good or service used to meet the needs of specific customers. For a global company such as Black & Decker, the options may be to define the business to be analyzed as the home improvement business, the do-it-yourself business, or the power tool business. Ideally, each of these SBUs should have primary responsibility and authority in managing its basic business functions.

This phase of the planning process requires the participation of executives from different functions, especially marketing, production, finance, logistics, and procurement. Geographic representation should be from the major markets or regions as well as from the smaller, yet emerging, markets. With appropriate members, the committee can focus on product and markets as well as competitors whom they face in different markets, whether they are global, regional, or purely local. Heading this effort should be an executive with highest level experience in regional or global markets; for example, one global firm called on the president of its European operations to come back to headquarters to head the global planning effort. This effort calls for commitment by the company itself both in calling on the best talent to participate in the planning effort and later in implementing their proposals.

**Market and Competitive Analysis**   Planning on a country-by-country basis can result in spotty worldwide market performance. Processes that focus simultaneously across a broad range of markets provide tools to help balance risks, resource requirements, competitive economies of scale, and profitability to gain stronger long-term positions.[14] The usual approach is first to start with regions and further split the analysis by country. Many managers use multiple levels of regional groupings to follow the organizational structure of the company, e.g., splitting Europe into northern, central, and southern regions, which display similarities in demographic and behavioral traits. An important consideration is that data may be more readily available if existing structures and frameworks are used.[15]

Various **portfolio models** have been proposed as tools for this analysis. They typically involve two measures—internal strength and external attractiveness.[16] As indicators of internal strength, the following variables have been used: relative market share, product fit, contribution margin, and market presence, which would incorporate the level of support by constituents as well as resources allocated by the company itself. Country attractiveness has been measured using market size, market growth rate, number and type of competitors, governmental regulation, as well as economic and political stability. An example of such a matrix is provided in Figure 13.4.

The 3×3 matrix on country attractiveness and company strength is applied to the European markets. Markets in the invest/grow position will require con-

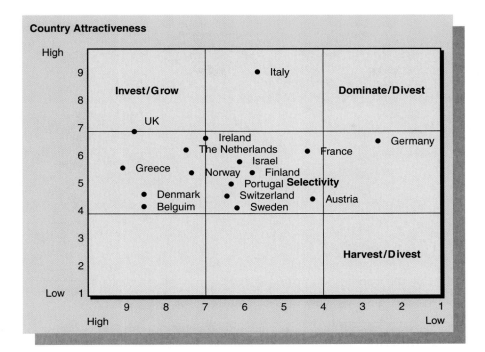

**Country Attractiveness**

**FIGURE 13.4**

**Example of a Market-Portfolio Matrix**

*Source:* Gilbert D. Harrell and Richard O. Kiefer, "Multinational Market Portfolios in Global Strategy Development," *International Marketing Review* 10, (1993): 60–72.

tinued commitment by management in research and development, investment in facilities, and the training of personnel and the country level. In cases of relative weakness in growing markets, the company's position may have to be strengthened (through acquisitions or strategic alliances) or a decision to divest may be necessary.[17] For example, Procter & Gamble decided to pull out of the disposable diaper markets in Australia and New Zealand due to well-entrenched competition, international currency fluctuations, and importation of products from distant production facilities into the markets.[18] Furthermore, it is critical that those involved in the planning endeavor consider potential competitors and their impact on the markets should they enter. In Europe, many industrial giants are entering the telecommunications market, most of them without any previous experience in the industry. Some of these newcomers are joining forces with foreign telecommunications entities thereby facilitating their new market development. For example, German steel maker Thyssen has teamed up with energy conglomerate Veba and U.S. BellSouth to build Germany's third digital cellular network.[19]

Portfolios should also be used to assess market, product, and business interlinkages. This effort should utilize increasing market similarities through corporate adjustments by setting up appropriate strategic business units and the coordination of programs. The presentation in Figure 13.5 shows a market-product-business portfolio for a global food company, such as Nestlé. The interconnections are formed by common target markets served, sharing of research and development objectives, use of similar technologies, and the benefits that can be drawn from sharing common marketing experience. The example suggests possibilities within regions and between regions: frozen food

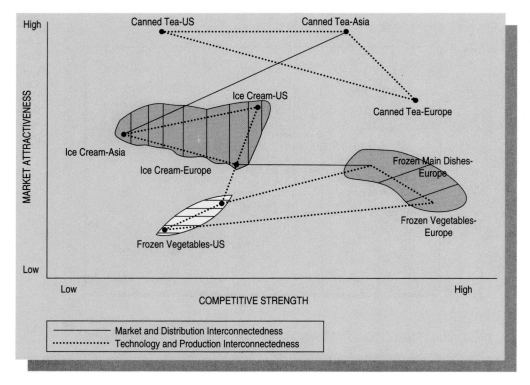

**FIGURE 13.5**

**Example of Strategic Interconnectedness Matrix**

*Source:* Adapted from Susan P. Douglas and C. Samuel Craig, "Global Portfolio Planning and Market Interconnectedness," *Journal of International Marketing* 4, 1 (1996): 93–110.

both in Europe and the United States, and ice cream throughout the three megamarkets.

**Internal Analysis**   Organizational resources have to be used as a reality check for any strategic choice. Industrial giants with deep pockets may be able to establish a presence in any market they wish, while more thinly capitalized companies may have to move cautiously. Human resources may also present a challenge for market expansion. A survey of multinational corporations revealed that good marketing managers, skilled technicians, and production managers were especially difficult to find. This difficulty is further compounded when the search is for people with cross-cultural experience to run future regional operations.[20]

At this stage it is imperative that the company assess its own readiness for the moves necessary. This means a rigorous assessment of organizational commitment to global or regional expansion, as well as an assessment of the good's readiness to face the competitive environment. In many cases this has meant painful decisions to focus on certain industries and leave others. For example, Nokia, the world's second largest manufacturer of cellular phones, started its rise in the industry when a decision was made at the company in 1992 to focus on digital cellular phones and to sell off dozens of other product lines. By focusing its efforts on this line, the company was able to bring new products to market quickly, build scale economies into its manufacturing, and concentrate on its customers thereby communicating a commitment to their needs.[21]

**Formulating Global Strategy**

The first step in the formulation of global strategy is the choice of markets to be entered or to be penetrated further. In each market's case, decisions need to be made on the extent of entry and the competitive strategy that should be employed.

**Country-Market Choice** In choosing country markets, a company must make decisions beyond those relating to market attractiveness and company position. A market expansion policy will determine the allocation of resources among various markets. The basic alternatives are concentration on a small number of markets and diversification, which is characterized by growth in a relatively large number of markets.

The conventional wisdom of globalization requires a presence in all of the major triad markets of the world. In some cases, markets may not be attractive in their own right but may have some other significance, such as being the home market of the most demanding customers, thereby aiding in product development, or being the home market of a significant competitor (a preemptive rationale). In its challenge of IBM, Fujitsu has acquired a substantial presence in both North America (through Amdahl Corp., the $2.2 billion-a-year Silicon Valley maker of IBM-compatible mainframes) and in Europe (through International Computers Ltd., Britain's largest manufacturer at $2.7 billion in annual sales).[22]

Therefore, for global companies three factors should determine country selection: (1) the stand-alone attractiveness of a market (e.g., China in consumer products due to its size), (2) global strategic importance (e.g., Finland in shipbuilding due to its lead in technological development in vessel design), and (3) due to possible synergies (e.g., entry into Latvia and Lithuania after success in the Estonian market given market similarities).

**Choice of Competitive Strategy** In dealing with the global markets, the manager has three general choices of strategies, as shown in Figure 13.6: (1) cost leadership, (2) differentiation, and (3) focus.[23] A focus strategy is defined by its emphasis on a single industry segment within which the orientation may be either toward low cost or differentiation. Any one of these strategies can be pursued on a global or regional basis, or the manager may decide to mix and match strategies as a function of market or product dimensions.

In pursuing **cost leadership,** the company offers an identical product or service at a lower cost than competition. This often means investment in scale economies and strict control of costs, such as overheads, research and development, and logistics. **Differentiation,** whether it is industry-wide or focused on a single segment, takes advantage of the manager's real or perceived uniqueness on elements such as design or after-sales service. It should be noted, however, that a low-price, low-cost strategy does not imply a commodity situation.[24] Although Japanese, U.S., and European technical standards differ, mobile phone manufacturers like Motorola and Nokia design their phones to be as

**FIGURE 13.6**

**Competitive Strategies**

*Source:* Michael Porter, *Competitive Advantage* (New York: The Free Press, 1987), ch. 1.

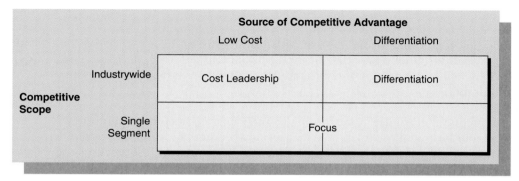

similar as possible to hold down manufacturing costs. As a result, they can all be made on the same production line, allowing the manufacturers to shift rapidly from one model to another to meet changes in demand and customer requirements. In the case of IKEA, the low-price approach is associated with clear positioning and a unique brand image focused on a clearly defined target audience of "young people of all ages." Similarly, companies who opt for high differentiation cannot forget the monitoring of costs. One common denominator of consumers around the world is their quest for value for their money. With the availability of information increasing and levels of education improving, customers are poised to demand even more of their suppliers.

Most global companies combine high differentiation with cost containment to enter markets and to expand their market shares. Flexible manufacturing systems using mostly standard components and total quality management reducing the occurrence of defects are allowing companies to customize an increasing amount of their production, while at the same time saving on costs. Global activities will in themselves permit the exploitation of scale economies not only in production but in marketing activities, such as advertising, as well.

**Segmentation**   Effective use of segmentation, that is, the recognition that groups within markets differ sufficiently to warrant individual approaches, allows global companies to take advantage of the benefits of standardization (such as economies of scale and consistency in positioning) while addressing the unique needs and expectations of a specific target group. This approach means looking at markets on a global or regional basis, thereby ignoring the political boundaries that define markets in many cases. The identification and cultivation of such intermarket segments is necessary for any standardization of programs to work.[25]

The emergence of segments that span across markets is already evident in the world marketplace. Global companies have successfully targeted the teenage segment, which is converging as a result of common tastes in sports and music fueled by their computer literacy, travels abroad, and, in many countries, financial independence.[26] Furthermore, a media revolution is creating a common fabric of attitudes and tastes among teenagers. Today satellite TV and global network concepts such as MTV are both helping create this segment and providing global companies an access to the teen audience around the world. For example, Reebok used a global ad campaign to launch its Instapump line of sneakers in the United States, Germany, Japan, and 137 other countries. Given that teenagers around the world are concerned with social issues, particularly environmentalism, Reebok has introduced a new ecological climbing shoe made from recycled and environmentally sensitive materials. Despite the convergence, global companies still have to make adjustments in some of the program elements for maximum impact. For example, while Levi's jeans are globally accepted by the teenage segment, European teens reacted negatively to the urban realism of Levi's U.S. ads. Levi's converted its ads in Europe, drawing on a mythical America.[27] Similarly, two other distinct segments have been detected to be ready for a panregional approach, especially in Europe.[28] These include trendsetters who are wealthier and better educated and tend to value independence, refuse consumer stereotypes, and appreciate exclusive products. The second one includes Europe's businesspeople who are well-to-do, regularly travel abroad, and have a taste for luxury goods.

The greatest challenge for the global company is the choice of an appropriate base for the segmentation effort. The objective is to arrive at a grouping or groupings that are substantial enough to merit the segmentation effort (for example, there are nearly 230 million teenagers in the Americas, Europe, and the Asia-Pacific with the teenagers of the Americas spending nearly $60 billion of their own money yearly) and are reachable as well by the marketing effort (for example, the majority of MTV's audience consists of teenagers).

The possible bases for segmentation are summarized in Figure 13.7. Managers have traditionally used environmental bases for segmentation. However, using geographic proximity, political system characteristics, economic standing, or cultural traits as stand-alone bases may not provide relevant data for decision making. Using a combination of them, however, may produce more meaningful results. One of the segments pursued by global companies around the world is the middle-class family. Defining the composition of this global middle class is tricky, given the varying levels of development among nations in Latin America and Asia. However, some experts estimate that 23 percent of the world population enjoy middle-class lives.[29] Using household income alone may be quite a poor gauge of class. Income figures ignore vast differences in international purchasing power. Chinese consumers, for example, spend less than 5 percent of their total outlays on rent, transportation, and health, while a typical U.S. household spends 45 to 50 percent. Additionally, income distinctions do not reflect education or values—two increasingly important barometers of middle-class status.

It has also been proposed that markets that reflect a high degree of homogeneity with respect to marketing mix variables could be grouped into segments and thereby targeted with a largely standardized strategy.[30] Whether bases related to product, promotion, pricing, or distribution are used, their influence should be related to environmentally based variables. Product-related bases include the degree to which products are culture-based, which stage of the life cycle they occupy, consumption patterns, attitudes toward product attributes (such as country of origin), as well as consumption infrastructure (for example, telephone lines for modems). The growth of microwave sales, for ex-

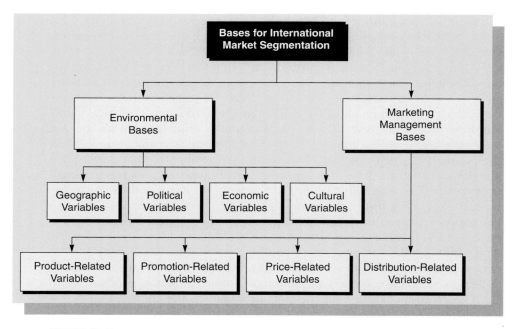

**FIGURE 13.7**

**Bases for Global Market Segmentation**

*Source:* Imad B. Baalbaki and Naresh K. Malhotra, "Marketing Management Bases for International Market Segmentation: An Alternate Look at the Standardization/Customization Debate," *International Marketing Review* 10, 1 (1993): 19–44.

ample, has been surprising in low-income countries; however, microwaves have become status symbols and buying them more of an emotional issue. Many consumers in these markets also want to make sure they get the same product as available in developed markets, thereby eliminating the need in many cases to develop market-specific products. Adjustments will have to be made, however. Noticing that for reasons of status and space, many Asian consumers put their refrigerators in their living rooms, Whirlpool makes refrigerators available in striking colors such as red and blue. The interaction of environmental and product variables can be seen in the segmentation effort of the Russian market reported in Global Perspective 13.2.

With promotional variables, the consumers' values and norms may necessitate local solutions rather than opting for a regional approach. Similar influences may be exerted by the availability, or lack, or media vehicles or government regulations affecting promotional campaigns. On the pricing side, dimensions such as customers' price sensitivity may lead the manager to go after segments that insist on high quality despite high price in markets where overall purchasing power may be low to ensure global or regional uniformity in the marketing approach. Affordability is a major issue for customers, whose buying power may fall short for at least the time being. Offering only one option may exclude potential customers of the future who are not yet part of a targeted segment. Companies like Procter & Gamble and Gillette offer an array of products at different price points to attract them and to keep them as they move up the income scale.[31] As distribution systems converge, for exam-

# SEGMENTING EMERGING MARKETS

Corporations who consider "Russia a dream that comes true only once in a lifetime" feel that it is none too soon to research the estimated 150 million consumers to assess how they will behave as consumers. The standard of living is rising on the average and a well-off middle class is rapidly expanding. More than half of the economy's output is being produced by the private sector. D'Arcy Masius Benton & Bowles, the twelfth largest advertising agency in the world, released a report on the emerging segments in the Russian market and identified five distinct groups and their likely preferences as outlined below.

| | Kuptsi, or Merchants | Cossacks | Students | Business Executives | Russian Souls |
|---|---|---|---|---|---|
| Men | 30% | 10% | 10% | 25% | 25% |
| Women | 45 | 10 | 5 | 10 | 30 |
| Dominant Traits | Reliant, nationalistic, practical, seeks value | Ambitious, independent, nationalistic, seeks status | Passive, scraping by, idealistic, practical | Ambitious, Western-oriented, busy, concerned with status | Passive, follows others, fears choices, hopeful |
| **Likely Preferences** | | | | | |
| Car | Volkswagen | BMW | Citroën 2CV | Mercedes | Lada |
| Cigarettes | Chesterfield | Dunhill | Marlboro | Winston | Marlboro |
| Liquor | Stolichnaya | Rémy Martin | Local vodka in Smirnoff bottles | Johnnie Walker | Smirnoff |

"The key is getting beyond the complex bureaucracies, logistics, and legal issues and going back to the psychology of people," said Nigel Clarke, strategic planning director at DMB&B Europe in London. "If we know how people think, feel, and act in their daily lives in buying things, we shall have a model that transcends the vagaries of current politics and economics." He sees Russia as ideal terrain for classic marketing techniques, as long as they are used in the context of the Russian psychology.

The *kuptsi* prefer Russian products in theory but disdain stamped-out, mass-produced goods. This segment, the largest among all five, admires some Western products, particularly well-engineered German and Northern European goods such as automobiles and consumer electronics. The cossacks, while aggressively nationalistic, still pursue Western products as status symbols from premium cigarettes such as Dunhill to expensive cognacs such as Rémy Martin.

Students are inclined toward a cosmopolitan view, open to the West. Although they covet Western brands, they usually have to make do with a cheaper version. Businessmen on the other hand are the yuppies of the market, and have the money to buy any product they desire. However, they buy only Western brands that are functional with some elements of Western imagery. Russian souls are too undermined by uncertainty to do much about anything. Because they are passive and choice is frightening for them, classic marketing techniques are difficult to apply. The best route is to have them witness the successful experience of others in buying and using a brand.

Talking about target marketing in present-day conditions may seem surreal, but if companies do not get in now, later may be more difficult. Marlboro, for example, has already managed to build itself into *the* cigarette in Russia, and now its competitors are going to have to think a lot harder and go for segments.

**Sources:** *"Russia's New Capitalism,"* **Business Week** *(October 10, 1994): 68–80; Stuart Elliott, "Figuring Out the Russian Consumer,"* **New York Times,** *April 1, 1992, D1, D19; Cyndee Miller, "From Kuptsi to Cossacks,"* **Marketing News** *(June 18, 1992): 18.*

ple, with the increase of global chains, markets can also be segmented by outlet types that reach environmentally defined groups. For example, toy manufacturers may look at markets not only in terms of numbers of children but by how effectively and efficiently they can be reached by global chains such as Toys 'Я' Us, as opposed to purely local outlets.

## Global Program Development

Decisions need to be made regarding how best to utilize the conditions set by globalization drivers within the framework of competitive challenges and the resources of the firm. Decisions will have to be made in four areas: (1) the degree of standardization in the product offering, (2) the marketing program beyond the product variable, (3) location and extent of value-adding activities, (4) and competitive moves to be made.

**Product Offering**    Globalization is not equal to standardization except in the case of the core product or the technology used to produce the product. The components used in a personal computer may to a large extent be standard, with the localization needed only in terms of the peripherals; for example, IBM produces twenty different keyboards for Europe alone. Product standardization may result in significant cost savings upstream. For example, Stanley Works' compromise between French preferences for handsaws with plastic handles and "soft teeth" and British preferences for wooden handles and "hard teeth"—to produce a plastic-handled saw with "hard teeth"—allowed consolidation for production and results in substantial economies of scale. At Whirlpool, use of common platforms allow European and American appliances to share technology and suppliers to lower cost and to streamline production. Many of the same components are procedures used for products that eventually are marketed to segments looking for top-of-the-line or no-frills versions.[32] Similar differences in customer expectations have CPC International Inc. selling fifteen versions of minestrone soup in Europe.

**Marketing Approach**    Nowhere is the need for the local touch as critical as in the execution of the marketing program. Uniformity is sought especially in elements that are strategic (e.g., positioning) in nature, whereas care is taken to localize necessary tactical elements (e.g., distribution). This approach has been called **glocalization.** For example, Unilever achieved great success with a fabric softener that used a common positioning, advertising theme, and symbol (a teddy bear) but differing brand names (e.g., Snuggle, Cajoline, Kuschelweich, Mimosin, and Yumos) and bottle sizes. Gillette Co. scored a huge success with its Sensor shaver when it was rolled out in the United States, Europe, and Japan with a common approach based on the premise that men everywhere want the same thing in a shave. Although the language of its TV commercials varied, the theme ("the best a man can get") and most of the footage were the same. A comparison of the marketing mix elements of two global marketers is given in Table 13.1. Notice that adaptation is present even at Coca-Cola, which is acknowledged to be one of the world's most global companies.

**Location of Value-Added Activities**    Globalization strives at cost reductions by pooling production or other activities or exploiting factor costs or capabilities within a system. Rather than duplicating activities in multiple, or even all, country organizations, a firm concentrates its activities. For example, Texas Instruments has designated a single design center and manufacturing organization for each type of memory chip. To reduce high costs and to be close to markets, it placed two of its four new $250-million memory chip plants in Taiwan and Japan. To reduce high R&D costs, it has entered into a strategic alliance with Hitachi. Many global companies have established R&D centers next to key production facilities so that concurrent engineering can take place every day

**TABLE 13.1**

**Globalization of the Marketing Mix**

| Marketing Mix Elements | Adaptation | | Standardization | |
|---|---|---|---|---|
| | Full | Partial | Partial | Full |
| Product design | | | N | C |
| Brand name | | | N | C |
| Product positioning | | N | | C |
| Packaging | | | C/N | |
| Advertising theme | | N | | C |
| Pricing | | N | C | |
| Advertising copy | N | | | C |
| Distribution | N | C | | |
| Sales promotion | N | C | | |
| Customer service | N | C | | |

Key: C = Coca-Cola; N = Nestlé.

*Source:* John A. Quelch and Edward J. Hoff, "Customizing Global Marketing," *Harvard Business Review*, May–June 1986 (Boston: Harvard Business School Publishing Division), 61. Reprinted by permission of Harvard Business Review. Copyright © 1986 by the President and Fellows of Harvard College; all rights reserved.

on the factory floor. To enhance the global exchange of ideas, the centers have joint projects and are in real-time contact with each other.

The quest for cost savings and improved transportation methods has allowed some companies to concentrate customer service activities rather than having them present in all country markets. For example, Sony used to have repair centers in all of the Scandinavian countries and Finland; today, all service and maintenance activities are actually performed in a regional center in Copenhagen, Denmark.

**Competitive Moves**   A company with regional or global presence will not have to respond to competitive moves only in the market where it is being attacked. A competitor may be attacked in its profit sanctuary to drain its resources, or its position in its home market may be challenged.[33] When Fuji began cutting into Kodak's market share in the United States in the mid-1980s, Kodak responded by drastically increasing its penetration in Japan and created a new subsidiary to deal strictly with that market.

**Cross-subsidization,** or the use of resources accumulated in one part of the world to fight a competitive battle in another, may be the competitive advantage needed for the long term.[34] One major market lost may mean losses in others, resulting in a domino effect. Jockeying for overall global leadership may result in competitive action in any part of the world. This has manifested itself in the form of "wars" between major global players in industries such as soft drinks, automotive tires, and computers. The opening of new markets often signals a new battle, as has happened in the 1990s in Russia, in Mexico after the signing of the North American Free Trade Agreement, and in Vietnam after the normalization of relations.[35] Given their multiple bases of operation, global companies may defend against a competitive attack in one country by countering in another country or, if the competitors operate in multiple businesses, countering in a different product category altogether.

The example of Nokia Mobile Phones, one of the leading manufacturers of cellular telephones in the world, highlights globalization as a strategy. The company's focus is on cellular mobile telephones (manufactured in Finland, Germany, and South Korea). The objective is to be a volume manufacturer, that is, to provide products for all major systems through a presence in all major markets. A global product range with customized variation for different distribution channels assures local acceptance.[36]

## Implementing Global Programs

The successful global companies of the 1990s will be those who can achieve a balance between the local and the regional/global concerns. Companies who have tried the global concept have often run into problems with local differences. Especially in the 1980s, global marketing was seen as a standardized marketing effort dictated to the country organizations by headquarters. Procter & Gamble stumbled badly in Japan when customers there spurned its Pampers in favor of rival brands. P&G's diapers were made and sold according to a formula imposed by Cincinnati headquarters. Japanese consumers found the company's hard-sell techniques alienating.[37]

**Challenges**    Pitfalls that handicap global programs and contribute to their suboptimal performance include market-related reasons, such as insufficient research and a tendency to overstandardize, as well as internal reasons, such as inflexibility in planning and implementation.

If a product is to be launched on a broader scale without formal research as to regional or local differences, the result may be failure. An example of this is Lego A/S, the Danish toy manufacturer, which decided to transfer sales promotional tactics successful in the U.S. market unaltered to other markets, such as Japan. This promotion included approaches such as "bonus packs" and gift promotions. However, Japanese consumers considered these promotions wasteful, expensive, and not very appealing.[38] Similarly, AT&T has had its problems abroad because its models are largely reworked U.S. models. Even after spending $100 million in adapting its most powerful switch for European markets, its success was limited because phone companies there prefer smaller switches.[39] Often, the necessary research is conducted only after a product or a program has failed.

Globalization by design requires a balance between sensitivity to local needs and deployment of technologies and concepts globally. This means that neither headquarters nor independent country managers can alone call the shots. If country organizations are not part of the planning process, or if adoption is forced on them by headquarters, local resistance in the form of the **not-invented-here syndrome (NIH)** may lead to the demise of the global program or, worse still, to an overall decline in morale. Subsidiary resistance may stem from resistance to any idea originating from the outside or from valid concerns about the applicability of a concept to that particular market. Without local commitment, no global program will survive.

## Localizing Global Moves

The successful global companies of the 1990s will be those who can achieve a balance between country managers and global product managers at headquarters. This balance may be achieved by a series of actions to improve a company's ability to develop and implement global strategy. These actions relate to management processes, organization structures, and overall corporate culture, all of which should ensure cross-fertilization within the firm.[40]

**Management Processes**   In the multidomestic approach, country organizations had very little need to exchange ideas. Globalization, however, requires transfer of information not only between headquarters and country organizations but also between the country organizations themselves. By facilitating the flow of information, ideas are exchanged and organizational values strengthened. Information exchange can be achieved through periodic meetings of marketing managers or through worldwide conferences to allow employees to discuss their issues and local approaches to solving them. IBM, for example, has a Worldwide Opportunity Council that sponsors fellowships for employees to listen to business cases from around the world and develop global platforms or solutions. IBM has found that some country organizations find it easier to accept input of other country organizations than that coming directly from headquarters. The approach used at Levi Strauss & Co. is described in Global Perspective 13.3.

Part of the preparation for becoming global has to be personnel interchange. Many companies encourage (or even require) midlevel managers to gain experience abroad during the early or middle stages of their careers. The more experience people have in working with others from different nationalities—getting to know other markets and surroundings—the better a company's global philosophy, strategy, and actions will be integrated locally.

The role of headquarters staff should be that of coordination and leveraging the resources of the corporation. For example, this may mean activities focused on combining good ideas that come from different parts of the company to be fed into global planning. Many global companies also employ world-class staffs whose role should be to consult subsidiaries by upgrading their technical skills and to focus their attention not only on local issues but also on those with global impact.

Globalization calls for the centralization of decision-making authority far beyond that of the multidomestic approach. Once a strategy has been jointly developed, headquarters may want to permit local managers to develop their own programs within specified parameters and subject to approval rather than forcing them to adhere strictly to the formulated strategy. For example, Colgate Palmolive allows local units to use their own approaches, but only if they can prove they can beat the global "benchmark" version. With a properly managed approval process, effective control can be exerted without unduly dampening a country manager's creativity.

Overall, the best approach against the emergence of the NIH syndrome is utilizing various motivational policies such as (1) ensuring that local managers participate in the development of strategies and programs, (2) encouraging local managers to generate ideas for possible regional or global use, (3) maintaining a product portfolio that includes local as well as regional and global brands, and (4) allowing local managers control over their budgets so that they can respond to local customer needs and counter global competition (rather than depleting budgets by forcing them to participate only in uniform campaigns).[41] Acknowledging this local potential, global companies can pick up successful brands in one country and make them cross-border stars. Since Nestlé acquired British candy maker Rowntree Mackintosh, it has increased its

## FINDING THE FIT OVERSEAS

Twice a year, Levi Strauss & Co. calls together managers from its worldwide operations for a meeting of the minds. In sessions that could be described as a cross between the United Nations general assembly and MTV, the participants brainstorm and exchange ideas on what seems to work in their respective markets, regionally, or globally. If a marketing manager finds an advertising campaign appealing, he or she is encouraged to take it back home to sell more Levi's blue jeans.

All told, Levi's approach epitomizes a slogan that is becoming popular among companies around the world: Think globally, act locally. Levi's has deftly capitalized on the Levi's name abroad by promoting it as an enshrined piece of Americana, and consumers have responded by paying top dollar for the product. An Indonesian commercial shows Levi's-clad teenagers cruising around Dubuque, Iowa, in 1960s convertibles. In Japan, James Dean serves as a centerpiece in virtually all Levi's advertising. Overseas, Levi's products have been positioned as upscale, which has meant highly satisfactory profit margins. To protect the image, Levi's has avoided the use of mass merchants and discounters in its distribution efforts.

Levi's success turns on its ability to fashion a global strategy that does not stifle local initiative. It is a delicate balancing act, one that often means giving foreign managers the freedom needed to adjust their tactics to meet the changing tastes of their home markets. In Brazil, Levi's prospers by letting local managers call the shots on distribution. For instance, Levi's penetrated the huge, fragmented Brazilian market by launching a

chain of 400 Levi's Only stores, some of them in tiny rural towns. Levi's is also sensitive to local tastes in Brazil, where it developed the Feminina line of jeans exclusively for women, who prefer ultratight jeans. What Levi's learns in one market can often be adopted in another. The Dockers line of chino pants and casual wear originated in the company's Argentine unit and was applied to loosely cut pants by Levi's Japanese subsidiary. The company's U.S. operation adopted both in 1986, and the line now generates $550 million in North American revenues.

Headquarters managers exercise control where necessary. To protect Levi's cherished brand identity and image of quality, the company has organized its foreign operations as subsidiaries rather than relying on a patchwork of licensees. "It is important for a brand like ours to have a single face," says Lee C. Smith, president of Levi Strauss International. "You cannot control that if you have twenty to twenty-five licensees around the world interpreting it in different ways." The company also keeps ahead of its competition by exporting its pioneering use of computers to track sales and manufacturing.

Ironically, it hasn't been that long since Levi's international efforts were mired in errors. In 1984 and 1985, international operations lost money. A strong dollar adversely affected sales, and the designer jeans craze made Levi's five-pocket model rather out of date. Furthermore, Levi's was losing its brand identity in jeans by getting into specialty apparel. Today, after a complete refocus on blue jeans, about 39 percent of the company's total revenues and 60 percent of its pretax profit before interest and corporate expenses come from abroad.

Levi's is now focusing on Central Europe and Russia. Marketing there will be full of challenges, especially because of currency and supply problems. However, given its persistence and marketing and production strength, Levi's is expected to repeat its success story in those markets as well.

*Source: "For Levi's a Flattering Fit Overseas," **Business Week** (November 5, 1990): 76–77.*

**WWW**

exports by 60 percent and made formerly local brands, such as After Eight Dinner mints, pan-European hits. Similarly, when Procter & Gamble gets its hands on an innovation or a product with global potential, rolling it out quickly worldwide is important. As a result of global reach, the sales of Pantene shampoo increased from $50 million in 1985 to over $700 million ten years later.

**Organization Structures**    Various organization structures have emerged to support the globalization effort. Some companies have established global or regional product managers and their support groups at headquarters. Their task is to develop long-term strategies for product categories on a worldwide basis and to act as the support system for the country organizations. This matrix structure focused on customers, which has replaced the traditional country-by-country approach, is considered more effective in today's global marketplace according to companies that have adopted it.

Whenever a product group has global potential, firms such as Procter & Gamble, 3M, and Henkel create strategic-planning units to work on the programs. These units, such as 3M's EMATs (European Marketing Action Teams) consist of members from the country organizations that market the products, managers from both global and regional headquarters, as well as technical specialists.

To deal with the globalization of customers, companies such as Hewlett-Packard and DHL are extending national account management programs across countries typically for the most important customers.[42] AT&T, for example, distinguishes between international and global customers and provides the global customers with special services including a single point of contact for domestic and international operations and consistent worldwide service. Executing **global account management** programs builds relationships not only with important customers but also allows for the development of internal systems and interaction.

**Corporate Culture**   In truly global companies, very little decision making occurs that does not support the goal of treating the world as a single market. Planning for and execution of programs take place on a worldwide basis.

Examples of manifestations of the global commitment are a global identity that favors no specific country (especially the "home country" of the company). The management features several nationalities, and whenever teams are assembled, people from various country organizations get represented. The management development system has to be transparent, allowing nonnational executives an equal chance for the fast track to top management.[43]

In determining the optimal combination of products and product lines to be marketed, a firm should consider choices for individual markets as well as transfer of products and brands from one region or market to another. This will often result in a particular country organization marketing product lines and goods that are a combination of global, regional, and national brands.

Decisions on specific targeting may result in the choice of a narrowly defined segment in the countries chosen. This is a likely strategy of specialized products to clearly definable markets, for example, ocean-capable sailing boats. Catering to multiple segments in various markets is typical of consumer-oriented companies that have sufficient resources for broad coverage.

## *Summary*

Globalization has become one of the most important strategy issues for managers in the 1990s. Many forces, both external and internal, are driving companies to globalize by expanding and coordinating their participation in foreign markets. The approach is not standardization, however. Managers may indeed occasionally be able to take identical concepts and approaches around the world, but most often, they must be customized to local tastes. Internally, companies must make sure that country organizations around the world are ready to launch global products and programs as if they had been developed only for their markets.

Managers need to engage in strategic planning to better adjust to the realities of the new marketplace. Understanding the firm's core strategy (i.e., what business they are really in) starts the process, and this assessment may lead to adjustments in what business the company may want to be in. In formulating global strategy for the chosen business, the decision makers have to assess and make choices about markets and competitive strategy to be used in penetrating them. This may result in the choice of one particular segment across markets or the exploitation of multiple segments in which the company has a competitive advantage. In manipulating and implementing programs for maximum effect in the chosen markets, the old adage, "think globally, act locally," becomes a critical guiding principle both as far as customers are concerned and in terms of country organization motivation.

## Key Terms and Concepts

| | | |
|---|---|---|
| globalization | portfolio models | cross-subsidization |
| multidomestic strategy | cost leadership | not-invented-here syndrome (NIH) |
| mininationals | differentiation | global account management |
| | glocalization | |

## Questions for Discussion

1. What is the danger in oversimplifying the globalization approach? Would you agree with the statement that "if something is working in a big way in one market, you better assume it will work in all markets"?
2. What are the critical ways in which globalization and standardization differ?
3. In addition to teenagers as a global segment, are there possibly other such groups with similar traits and behaviors that have emerged worldwide?
4. Why is the assessment of internal resources critical as early as possible in developing a global strategic plan?
5. What are the critical ways in which the multidomestic and global approaches differ in country-market selection?
6. Outline the basic reasons why a company does not necessarily have to be large and have years of experience to succeed in the global marketplace.
7. What are the basic reasons why country operations would not embrace a new regional or global plan (i.e., why the not-invented-here syndrome might emerge)?
8. Using the material available at their website (**http://www.unilever.com**), suggest ways in which Unilever's business groups can take advantage of global and regional strategies due to interconnections in production and marketing.

## Recommended Readings

Davidson, William H. *Global Strategic Management*. New York: Wiley, 1982.

The Economist Intelligence Unit. *151 Checklists for Global Management*. New York: The Economist Intelligence Unit, 1993.

Foster, Richard. *Innovation: The Attacker's Advantage*. New York: Summit Books, 1986.

Humes, Samuel. *Managing the Multinational: Confronting the Global-Local Dilemma*. London, England: Prentice-Hall International (U.K.) Ltd, 1993.

Kanter, Rosabeth Moss. *World Class*. New York: Simon & Schuster, 1995.

Kaynak, Erdener, ed. *The Global Business*. Binghamton, NY: Haworth Press, 1992.

Kotabe, Masaaki. *Global Sourcing Strategy: R&D, Manufacturing, and Marketing Interfaces*. Greenwich, CT: Greenwood Publishing Group, 1992.

Makridakis, Spyros G. *Forecasting, Planning, and Strategy for the 21st Century*. New York: Free Press, 1990.

Marton, Katherin. *Multinationals, Technology, and Industrialization*. Lexington, Mass.: Lexington Books, 1986.

Prahalad, C. K., and Yves L. Doz. *The Multinational Mission: Balancing Local and Global Vision*. New York: Free Press, 1987.

Yip, George. *Total Global Strategy*. Englewood Cliffs, NJ: Prentice Hall, 1992.

## Notes

1. "What's New About Globalization?" *The McKinsey Quarterly* 2. (1997): 168–179.

2. Jeremey Main, "How to Go Global—and Why," *Fortune* (August 28, 1989): 70–76.

3. The section draws heavily from George S. Yip, "Global Strategy . . . In a World of Nations?" *Sloan Management Review* 31 (Fall 1989): 29–41; Susan P. Douglas and C. Samuel Craig, "Evolution of Global Marketing Strategy: Scale, Scope, and Synergy," *Columbia Journal of World Business* 24 (Fall 1989): 47–58; and George S. Yip, Pierre M. Loewe, and Michael Y. Yoshino, "How to Take Your Company to the Global Market," *Columbia, Journal of World Business* 23 (Winter 1988): 28–40.

4. Ernst Dichter, "The World Customer,"*Harvard Business Review* 40 (July–August 1962): 113–122.

5. Kenichi Ohmae, *Triad Power—The Coming Shape of Global Competition* (New York: Free Press, 1985), 22–27.

6. Alan D. Treadgold, "The Developing Internationalisation of Retailing," *International Journal of Retail and Distribution Management* 18 (1990): 4–11.

7. "Vital Statistic: Disputed Cost of Creating a Drug," *The Wall Street Journal*, November 9, 1993, B1.

8. "The Stateless Corporation," *Business Week* (May 14, 1990): 98–106.

9. Gianluigi Guido, "Implementing a Pan-European Marketing Strategy," *Long Range Planning* 24 (1991): 23–33.

10. Pete Engardio, "Third World Leapfrog," *Business Week/The Information Leapfrog 1994*, 47–49.

11. "Mininationals Are Making Maximum Impact," *Business Week* (September 1993): 66–69.

12. Nestlé: A Giant in a Hurry," *Business Week* (March 22, 1993): 50–54; and http://www.nestle.com .

13. Jordan D. Lewis, *Partnerships for Profit* (New York: Free Press, 1990), 86.

14. Gilbert D. Harrell and Richard O. Kiefer, "Multinational Market Portfolios in Global Strategy Development," *International Marketing Review* 10, 1 (1993): 60–72.

15. George S. Yip, *Total Global Strategy: Managing for Worldwide Competitive Advantage* (Englewood Cliffs, NJ: Prentice-Hall, 1992), 242–246.

16. The models referred to are GE/McKinsey, Shell International, and A. D. Little portfolio models.

17. Yoram Wind and Susan P. Douglas, "International Portfolio Analysis and Strategy: Challenge of the '80s," *Journal of International Business Studies* 12 (Fall 1981): 69–82.

18. "P&G Puts Nappies to Rest in Australia," *Advertising Age* (September 19, 1994): I-31.

19. "A Feeding Frenzy in European Telecom," *Business Week* (November 21, 1994): 119–122.

20. Lori Ioannou, "It's a Small World After All," *International Business* (February 1994): 82–88.

21. "Grabbing Markets from the Giants," *Business Week/21st Century Capitalism* (1994), 156.

22. Brenton A. Schendler, "How Fujitsu Will Tackle the Giants," *Fortune* (July 1, 1991): 78–82.

23. Michael Porter, *Competitive Advantage* (New York: The Free Press, 1987), ch. 1.

24. Robert M. Grant, *Contemporary Strategy Analysis: Concepts, Techniques, Applications* (Oxford, England: Blackwell, 1995), 203–205.

25. Saeed Samiee and Kendall Roth, "The Influence of Global Marketing Standardization on Performance," *Journal of Marketing* 56 (April 1992): 1–17.

26. Shawn Tully, "Teens: The Most Global Market of All," *Fortune* (May 16, 1994): 90–97.

27. "The Euroteens (and How Not to Sell to Them)," *Business Week* (April 11, 1994): 84.

28. S. Vandermerwe and M. L'Huillier, "Euro-Consumers in 1992," *Business Horizons* 32 (January–February 1989): 34–40,

29. "Getting and Spending," *Business Week/21st Century Capitalism* (1994), 178–185.

30. Imad B. Baalbaki and Naresh K. Malhotra, "Marketing Management Bases for International Market Segmentation: An Alternate Look at the Standardization/Customization Debate," *International Marketing Review* 10, 1 (1993): 19–44.

31. Rahul Jacob, "The Big Rise," *Fortune* (May 30, 1994): 74–90.

32. "Call It Worldpool," *Business Week* (November 28, 1994): 98–99.

33. W. Chan Kim and R. A. Mauborgne, "Becoming an Effective Global Competitor," *Journal of Business Strategy* 8 (January–February 1988): 33–37.

34. Gary Hamel and C. K. Prahalad, "Do You Really Have a Global Strategy?" *Harvard Business Review* 63 (July–August 1985): 75–82.

35. "A Mexican War Heats up for Cola Giants," *The Wall Street Journal,* April 20, 1993. B1.

36. This example is courtesy of Jouko Hayrynen, vice president, exports, Nokia Mobile Phones Ltd.

37. "Marketing Globally, Thinking Locally," *Business Week* (May 13, 1991): 20–24.

38. Kamran Kashani, "Beware the Pitfalls of Global Marketing," *Harvard Business Review* 67 (September–October 1989): 91–98.

39. "AT&T Slowly Gets Its Global Wires Uncrossed," *Business Week* (February 11, 1991): 82–83.

40. John A. Quelch and Edward J. Hoff, "Customizing Global Marketing," *Harvard Business Review* 64 (May–June 1986): 59–68; Yip, Loewe, and Yoshino, "Take Your Company to the Global Market."

41. Quelch and Hoff, "Customizing Global Marketing."

42. George S. Yip and Tammy L. Madsen, "Global Account Management: The New Frontier in Relationship Marketing," *International Marketing Review* 13, 3 (1996): 24–42.

43. Globalization Starts with Company's Own View of Itself," *Business International* (June 10, 1991): 197–198.

# CHAPTER 14

# International Marketing

## LEARNING OBJECTIVES

- ◆ *To suggest how markets for international expansion can be selected, their demand assessed, and appropriate strategies for their development devised*

- ◆ *To describe how environmental differences generate new challenges for the international marketing manager*

- ◆ *To compare and contrast the merits of standardization versus localization strategies for country markets and of regional versus global marketing efforts*

- ◆ *To discuss market-specific and global challenges within each of the marketing functions: product, price, distribution, and promotion*

## Soup: Now It's M-M-Global

**B**y the year 2000, Campbell Soup wants half of company revenues to come from outside domestic markets. It is an ambitious goal, since only a quarter have come from foreign sales in the 1990s. Adding to the challenge is the fact that prepared food may be one of the toughest products to sell overseas. It is not as universal or easily marketed as soap or soft drinks, given regional taste preferences. Italians, not surprisingly, shy away from canned pasta, and while an average Pole consumes five bowls of soup a week, 98 percent of Polish soups are homemade.

Campbell has managed to overcome some cultural obstacles in selected countries. To shake the powdered-soup domination in Argentina, it markets its Sopa de Campbell as "The Real Soup," stressing its list of fresh ingredients on the label. In Poland, Campbell advertises to working Polish mothers looking for convenience. Says Lee Andrews, Campbell's new-product manager in Warsaw: "We can't shove a can in their faces and replace Mom."

However, in many regions, Campbell is trying to cook more like her. This means creating new products that appeal to distinctly regional tastes. The approach has been to use test kitchens and taste testing with consumers. Results have included fiery cream of chile poblano soup in Mexico as well as watercress and duck-gizzard soup for China. The cream of pumpkin has become Australia's top-selling canned soup.

Asia has traditionally accounted for only 2 percent of Campbell's worldwide sales, but the region—China, in particular—is being targeted as the area with the strongest growth potential. New markets are entered gingerly. Campbell typically launches a basic meat or chicken broth, which consumers can doctor with meats, vegetables, and spices. Later, more sophisticated soups are brought on line. In China, the real competition comes from homemade soup, which comprises over 99 percent of all consumption. With this in mind, Campbell's prices have been kept at an attractive level and the product promoted on convenience. While many of the products, such as corn-and-chicken soup have been developed in the company's Hong Kong kitchens, some U.S. standbys as cream of mushroom have been selling well, possibly to the segment of westernized Chinese.

Local ingredients may count, but Campbell draws the line on some Asian favorites. Dog soup is out, as is shark's fin, since most species are endangered. For most other options, including snake, for example, the company keeps an open mind.

Furthermore, Campbell is also finding that ethnic foods are growing in popularity around the world. With its emphasis on vegetables, Asian cuisine benefits from a healthy image in Europe and North America. This means that some new products being presently developed for the Asian consumer may become global favorites in no time. ◼

*Source:* "Souping Up Campbell's" *Business Week* (November 3, 1997): 70-72; Linda Grant, "Stirring It Up at Campbell," *Fortune* (May 13, 1996): 80-86; "Ethnic Food Whets Appetites in Europe, Enticing Producers to Add Foreign Fare," *The Wall Street Journal,* November 1, 1993, B5A; "Hmm. Could Use a Little More Snake," *Business Week* (March 15, 1993): 53; and "Canned and Delivered," *Business China* (November 16, 1992): 12. **http://www.campbellsoup.com**

Marketing is the process of planning and executing the conception, pricing, promotion, and distribution of ideas, goods, and services to create exchanges *markets* that satisfy individual and organizational objectives.[1] The concepts of satisfaction and exchange are at the core of marketing. For an exchange to take place, two or more parties have to come together physically, through the mails, or through technology, and they must communicate and deliver things of perceived value. Customers should be perceived as information seekers who evaluate marketers' offerings in terms of their own drives and needs. When the offering is consistent with their needs, they tend to choose the good or service; if it is not, other alternatives are chosen. A key task of the marketer is to recognize the ever-changing nature of needs and wants. Marketing techniques apply not only to goods but to ideas and services as well. Further, well over 50 percent of all marketing activities are business marketing—directed at other businesses, governmental entities, and various types of institutions.

The marketing manager's task is to plan and execute programs that will ensure a long-term competitive advantage for the company. This task has two integral parts: (1) the determining of specific target markets and (2) marketing management, which consists of manipulating marketing mix elements to best satisfy the needs of the individual target markets. Regardless of geographic markets, the basic tasks do not vary; they have been called the technical universals of marketing.[2]

This chapter will focus on the formulation of marketing strategy for international operations. The first section describes target market selection and how to identify pertinent characteristics of the various markets. The balance of the chapter is devoted to adjusting the elements of the marketing program to a particular market for maximum effectiveness and efficiency, while attempting to exploit global and regional similarities. The attempt to produce globally but market locally is described in the opening vignette.

## Target Market Selection

The process of target market selection involves narrowing down potential country markets to a feasible number of countries and market segments within them. Rather than try to appeal to everyone, firms best utilize their resources by (1) identifying potential markets for entry and (2) expanding selectively over time to those deemed attractive.

## Identification and Screening

A four-stage process for screening and analyzing foreign markets is presented in Figure 14.1. It begins with very general criteria and ends with product-specific market analyses. The data and the methods needed for decision making change from secondary to primary as the steps are taken in sequence. Although presented here as a screening process for choosing target markets, the process is also applicable to change of entry mode or even divestment.

If markets were similar in their characteristics, the international marketer could enter any one of the potential markets. However, differences among markets exist in three dimensions: physical, psychic, and economic.[3] Physical distance is the geographic distance between home and target countries; its impact has decreased as a result of recent technological developments. Psychic, or cultural, distance refers to differences in language, tradition, and customs between two countries. Economic distance is created by differences in the economic environments of the host country and the target market. Generally, the greater the overall distance—or difference—between the two countries, the less knowledge the marketer has about the target market. The amount of information that is available varies dramatically. For example, although the marketer can easily learn about the economic environment from secondary sources, invaluable interpretive information may not be available until the firm actually operates in the market. In the early stages of the assessment, international marketers can be assisted by numerous on-line and CD-ROM-based data sources as shown in Chapter 10.

The four stages in the screening process are: preliminary screening, estimation of market potential, estimation of sales potential, and identification of segments.[4] Each stage should be given careful attention. The first stage, for example, should not merely reduce the number of alternatives to a manageable few for the sake of reduction, even though the expense of analyzing markets in depth is great. Unless care is taken, attractive alternatives may be eliminated.

**Preliminary Screening** The preliminary screening process must rely chiefly on secondary data for country-specific factors as well as product- and industry-specific factors. Country-specific factors typically include those that would indicate the market's overall buying power; for example, population, gross national product in total and per capita, total exports and imports, and production of cement, electricity, and steel.[5] Product-specific factors narrow the analysis to the firm's specific areas of operation. A company such as Motorola, manufacturing for the automotive aftermarket, is interested in the number of passenger cars, trucks, and buses in use. The statistical analyses must be accompanied by qualitative assessments of the impact of cultural elements and the overall climate for foreign firms and products. A market that satisfies the levels set becomes a prospective target country.

**Estimating Market Potential** Total market potential is the sales, in physical or monetary units, that might be available to all firms in an industry during a given period under a given level of industry marketing effort and given environmental conditions.[6] The international marketer needs to assess the size of existing markets and forecast the size of future markets.

Because of the lack of resources, and frequently the lack of data, market potentials are often estimated using analytical techniques based on secondary

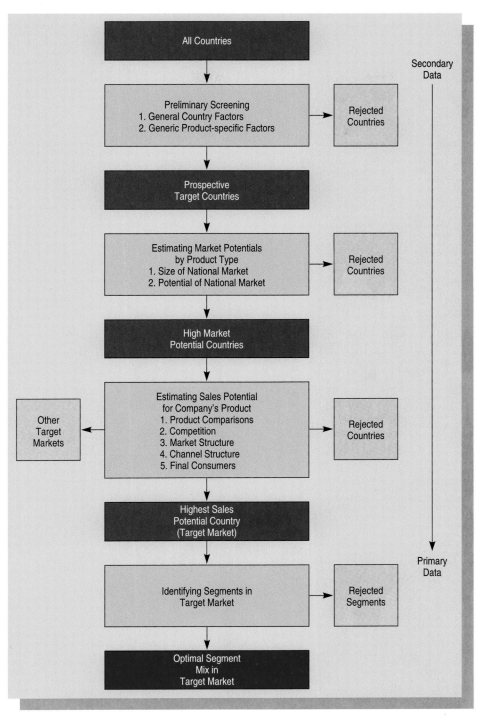

**FIGURE 14.1**

**The Screening Process in Target Market Choice**

*Source:* Reprinted by permission of the publisher from *Entry Strategies for International Markets,* p. 56, by Franklin R. Root (Lexington, Mass.: Lexington Books, D.C. Heath & Co., Copyright 1994, D. C. Heath & Co.).

data.[7] The techniques focus on or utilize demand patterns, income elasticity measurements, multiple-factor indexes, estimation by analogy, and input-output analysis.

## Income Distribution: A Factor in Evaluating Market Potential

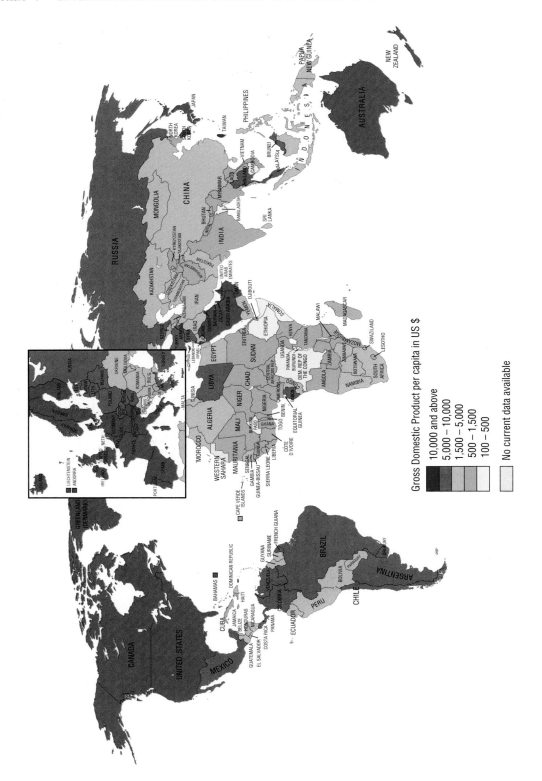

Gross Domestic Product per capita in US $

10,000 and above
5,000 – 10,000
1,500 – 5,000
500 – 1,500
100 – 500
No current data available

Source: *The World Factbook 1997–98*

**Demand pattern analysis** indicates typical patterns of growth and decline in manufacturing. At early stages of growth, for example, manufacturing is concentrated in food, beverage, and textile industries, and some light industry. An awareness of trends in manufacturing will enable the marketer to estimate potential markets for input, such as raw materials or machinery. **Income elasticity of demand** describes the relationship between demand and economic progress, as indicated by growth in income. The share of income spent on necessities will provide both an estimate of the market's level of development and an approximation of how much money is left for other purchases.

**Multiple-factor indexes** measure market potential indirectly by using proxy variables that have been shown (either through research or intuition) to correlate closely with the demand for the particular product. An index for consumer goods might involve population, disposable personal income, and retail sales in the market or area concerned. **Estimation by analogy** is used when data for a particular market do not exist. The market size for a product in country A is estimated by comparing a ratio for an available indicator (such as disposable income) for country A and country B, and using this ratio in conjunction with detailed market data available for country B. Few statistics serve as better indicators of future economic prospects or consumer demand than working-age population.

Finally, **input-output analysis** provides a method of estimating market potentials, especially in the industrial sector. Input-output tables provide a summary of the structure of an economy by showing the impact of changes in the demand for one industry's goods on other industries' goods. Using the tables and combining them with economic projections, the international marketer can estimate the volume demanded by the various sectors of the economy.

Despite the valuable insight generated through the techniques, caution should be used in interpreting the results. All of the quantitative techniques are based on historical data that may be obsolete or inapplicable because of differences in cultural and geographic traits of the market. Further, with today's technological developments, lags between markets are no longer at a level that would make all of the measurements valid. Moreover, the measurements look at a market as an aggregate; that is, no regional differences are taken into account. In industrialized countries, the richest 10 percent of the population consume 20 percent of all goods and services, whereas the respective figure for the developing countries may be as high as 47 percent.[8] Therefore, even in the developing countries with low GNP figures, segments exist with buying power rivaled only in the richest developed countries.

In addition to these quantitative techniques that rely on secondary data, international marketers can use various survey techniques. They are especially useful when marketing new technologies. A survey of end-user interest and responses may provide a relatively clear picture of the possibilities in a new market.

Comparing figures for market potential with actual sales will provide the international marketer with further understanding of his or her firm's chances in the market. If the difference between potential and reality is substantial, the reasons can be evaluated using **gap analysis.** The differences can be the result of usage, distribution, or product line gaps.[9] If the firm is already in the market, part of the difference between its sales and the market potential can be explained through the competitive gap. Usage gaps indicate that not all potential users are using the product or that those using it are not using as much as they could, which suggests mainly a promotional task. Distribution gaps indicate coverage problems, which may be vertical (not enough regions) or horizontal (if the product is not marketed as well as it could be). Product line gaps typically suggest latent demand. An emerging trend in which Japanese consumers want to acquire an American look will help drive sales for companies like Ralph Lauren, L. L. Bean, and Northeastern Log Homes.

**Estimating Sales Potential**   Even when the international marketer has gained an understanding of markets with the greatest overall promise, the firm's own possibilities in those markets are still not known. Sales potential is the share of the market potential that the firm can reasonably expect to get over the longer term. To arrive at an estimate, the marketer needs to collect product- and market-specific data. The data will have to do with:

1. Competition—strength, likely reaction to entry
2. Market—strength of barriers
3. Consumers—ability and willingness to buy
4. Product—degree of relative advantage, compatibility, complexity, trialability, and communicability
5. Channel structure—access to retail level

The marketer's questions can never be fully answered until the firm has made a commitment to enter the market and is operational. The mode of entry has special significance in determining the firm's sales potential.[10]

**Identifying Segments**   Within the markets selected, individuals and organizations will vary in their wants, resources, geographical locations, buying attitudes, and buying practices. Initially, the firm may cater to one or only a few segments and later expand to others, especially if the product is innovative. Segmentation is indicated when segments are indeed different enough to warrant individualized attention, are large enough for profit potential, and can be reached through the methods that the international marketer wants to use.

Once the process is complete for a market or group of markets, the international marketer may begin it again for another one. When growth potential is no longer in market development, the firm may opt for market penetration.

## Concentration versus Diversification

Choosing a market expansion policy involves the allocation of effort among various markets. The major alternatives are **concentration** on a small number of markets or **diversification,** which is characterized by growth in a relatively large number of markets in the early stages of international market expansion.[11]

**Expansion Alternatives**   Either concentration or diversification is applicable to market segments or to total markets, depending on the resource commitment the international marketer is willing and able to make. One option is a dual-concentration strategy, in which efforts are focused on a few segments in a limited number of countries. Another is a dual-diversification strategy, in which entry is to most segments in most available markets. The first is a likely strategy for small firms or firms that market specialized products to clearly definable markets, for example, ocean-capable sailing boats. The second is typical for large consumer-oriented companies that have sufficient resources for broad coverage. Market concentration/segment diversification opts for a limited number of markets but for wide coverage within them, putting emphasis on company acceptance. Market diversification/segment concentration usually involves the identification of a segment, possibly worldwide, to which the company can market without major changes in its marketing mix.

**Factors Affecting Expansion Strategy**   Expansion strategy is determined by the factors relating to market, mix, and company that are listed in Table 14.1. In most cases, the factors are interrelated as shown in Global Perspective 14.1.

*Market-Related Factors*   These factors are the ones that were influential in determining the attractiveness of the market in the first place. In the choice of expansion strategy, demand for the firm's products is a critical factor. With high and stable growth rates in certain markets, the firm will most likely opt for a concentration strategy. If the demand is strong worldwide, diversification may be attractive.

A forecast of the sales response function can be used to predict sales at various levels of marketing expenditure. Two general response functions exist: concave and S curve. When the function is concave, sales will increase at a decreasing rate because of competition and a lowering adoption rate. The function might involve a unique, innovative product or marketing program. An S-curve function assumes that a viable market share can be achieved only through sizable marketing efforts. This is typical for new entrants to well-established markets.

The uniqueness of the firm's offering with respect to competition is also a factor in the expansion strategy. If lead time over competition is consider-

**TABLE 14.1**

**Factors Affecting the Choice between Concentration and Diversification Strategies**

| Factor | Diversification | Concentration |
| --- | --- | --- |
| Market growth rate | Low | High |
| Sales stability | Low | High |
| Sales response function | Concave | S curve |
| Competitive lead time | Short | Long |
| Spillover effects | High | Low |
| Need for product adaptation | Low | High |
| Need for communication adaption | Low | High |
| Economics of scale in distribution | Low | High |
| Extent of constraints | Low | High |
| Program control requirements | Low | High |

*Source:* Igal Ayal and Jehiel Zif, "Marketing Expansion Strategies in Multinational Marketing." *Journal of Marketing* 43 (Spring 1979): 89.

# MAKING THE BIG PUSH OVERSEAS

**M**cDonald's is aggressively opening new resturants around the world, adding nearly five outlets per day. International operations are important on two accounts: McDonald's domestic operations lost market share in 1996, and international operations are now the largest sector, delivering 57 percent of the company's revenue and nearly 59 percent of the pretax profit.

McDonald's worldwide expansion is moving to a new phase. While it has entered 104 country markets, only a handful of countries account for 80 percent of its overseas earnings. Furthermore, the countries with a McDonald's franchise account for less than half of the world's total potential. "There are another 120 countries out there, but in terms of income levels they do not represent the same kind of opportunity," says James Cantalupo, president of McDonald's overseas operations. In 1997, new markets entered included Belarus, Paraguay, and Tahiti.

One of the countries with huge potential is Brazil, where McDonald's plans to spend $500 million to nearly double the number of its restaurants to more than 700 by the year 2000. Brazilians love Americana, and no symbol of it is better known than the Golden Arches. Yet millions of Brazilians have never tasted a Big Mac. For example, Salvador, a coastal city of nearly three million, has only 11 McDonald's restaurants, one-tenth as many as equally populous Chicago.

Brazil, a country where the developed and developing worlds meet, illustrates both the promise and challenges facing McDonald's. In 1995–1997, the company's revenue had doubled, to about $800 million. But that strength is largely due to Brazil's upper- and middle-class neighborhoods. The challenge is to sell milk shakes to the masses who are used to coconut milk sipped from the shell. Many people in poorer neighborhoods feel they work too hard for their money to experiment on American food. This attitude is not uncommon in a country where per-capita income is $3,500 per year.

McDonald's has also encountered some other cultural differences. The Brazilian custom of eating breakfast at home is so ingrained that McDonald's has not even tried to market Egg McMuffins. In many regions even lunch is a problem, in that people eat it at home and take a nap.

One big concern for McDonald's is the Brazilian government and its sometimes unpredictable policies. During the years of McDonald's operation in Brazil, the government has launched eight monetary stabilization plans, five currencies, and 54 changes in price controls. The government's current fixed-currency strategy is of concern because it resembles that of Mexico's before the peso collapsed in 1994. If Brazil's consumption boom is deflated by a currency bust, McDonald's expansion plans would be seriously undermined.

What is promising for McDonald's is the weakness of competition. For example, Pizza Hut has had its share of difficulties and some of its franchisees have closed restaurants. Also, while the developing markets may take longer to conquer, partly because many have not heard of a hamburger and fries, "once they come in and experience it, they just fall right into line," say Mr. Cantalupo.

**McDonald's Biggest Overseas Markets by Number of Restaurants**

| | | 1997 | 1996 |
|---|---|---|---|
| 1 | Japan | 2,241 | 1,823 |
| 2 | Canada | 1,030 | 959 |
| 3 | Germany | 802 | 698 |
| 4 | England | 702 | 619 |
| 5 | Australia | 633 | 572 |
| 6 | France | 613 | 500 |
| 7 | Brazil | 404 | 271 |
| 8 | Taiwan | 218 | 147 |
| 9 | Netherlands | 165 | 138 |
| 10 | Italy | 161 | 129 |
| 11 | China | 160 | 91 |

*Source: Company report*

*Source: "Why You Won't Find Any Egg McMuffins for Breakfast in Brazil," The Wall Street Journal, October 23, 1997, A1, A8.*
http://www.mcdonalds.com

WWW

able, the decision to diversify may not seem urgent. However, complacency can be a mistake in today's competitive environment; competitors can rush new products into the market in a matter of days.

In many product categories marketers will be, knowingly or unknowingly, affected by spillover effects. Consider, for example, the impact that satellite channels have had on advertising in Europe, where ads for a product now reach most of the European market. Where geographic (and psychic) distances are short, spillover is likely, and marketers are most likely to diversify.

Government constraints—or the threat of them—can be a powerful motivator in a firm's expansion. While government barriers may naturally prevent new-market entry, marketers may seek access through using new entry modes, adjusting marketing programs, or getting into a market before entry barriers are erected.

***Mix-Related Factors***  These factors relate to the degree to which marketing mix elements—primarily product, promotion, and distribution—can be standardized. The more that standardization is possible, the more diversification is indicated. Overall savings through economies of scale can then be utilized in marketing efforts.

Depending on the good, each market will have its own challenges. Whether constraints are apparent (such as tariffs) or hidden (such as tests or standards), they will complicate all of the other factors. Nevertheless, regional integration has allowed many marketers to diversify their efforts.

***Company-Related Factors***  These include the objectives set by the company for its international operations and the policies it adopts in those markets. As an example, the firm may require—either by stated policy or because of its goods—extensive interaction with intermediaries and clients. When this is the case, the firm's efforts will likely be concentrated because of resource constraints.

The opportunity to take advantage of diversification is available for all types of companies, not only the large ones. The identification of unique worldwide segments for which a customized marketing mix is provided has proven to be successful for many small and medium-sized companies. For example, Symbol Technologies invented the hand-held laser scanner and now dominates the field worldwide. Cisco Systems claims 50 percent of the world market for gear that connects networks of computers, a field not in existence ten years ago.[12]

## Marketing Management

After target markets are selected, the next step is the determination of marketing efforts at appropriate levels. A key question in international marketing concerns the extent to which the elements of the marketing mix—product, price, place, and distribution—should be standardized. The marketer also faces the specific challenges of adjusting each of the mix elements in the international marketplace.

The international marketer must first decide what modifications in the mix policy are needed or warranted. Three basic alternatives in approaching international markets are available:

**Standardization versus Adaptation**

1. Make no special provisions for the international marketplace but, rather, identify potential target markets and then choose products that can easily be marketed with little or no modification.

2. Adapt to local conditions in each and every target market (the multidomestic approach).
3. Incorporate differences into a regional or global strategy that will allow for
   local differences in implementation (globalization approach).

In today's environment, standardization usually means cross-national strategies
rather than a policy of viewing foreign markets as secondary and therefore not
important enough to have products adapted for them. Ideally, the international
marketer should think globally and act locally,[13] focusing on neither extreme:
full standardization or full localization. Global thinking requires flexibility in
exploiting good ideas and products on a worldwide basis.

The question of whether to standardize or to tailor marketing programs
in each country has continued to trouble practitioners and academics alike
and has produced many and varied opinions. In the 1960s, Robert Buzzell
stated that it depends on the strengths of the barriers to standardization, such
as national differences in consumer preferences and legal restrictions, and on
the potential payoffs of standardizing marketing strategy.[14] Studies on how
firms view standardization have found that arguments in favor of standardizing whenever possible fall into two categories: better marketing performance
and lower marketing cost.[15] Factors that encourage standardization or adaptation are summarized in Table 14.2.

**Factors Affecting Adaptation**    Even when marketing programs are based on
highly standardized ideas and strategies, they depend on three sets of variables:
(1) the market(s) targeted, (2) the product and its characteristics, and (3) company characteristics, including factors such as resources and policy.[16]

Questions of adaptation have no easy answers. Marketers in many firms
rely on decision-support systems to aid in program adaptation, while others
consider every situation independently. All goods must, of course, conform to
environmental conditions over which the marketer has no control. Further, the
international marketer may use adaptation to enhance its competitiveness in
the marketplace.

**Product Policy**    Goods or services form the core of the firm's international operations. Its success depends on how well goods satisfy needs and wants and how well they are
differentiated from those of the competition. This section focuses on product

**TABLE 14.2**

**Standardization versus Adaptation**

| Factors Encouraging Standardization | Factors Encouraging Adaptation |
|---|---|
| ■ Economies in product R & D | ■ Differing use conditions |
| ■ Economies of scale in production | ■ Government and regulatory influences |
| ■ Economies in marketing | ■ Differing buyer behavior patterns |
| ■ Control of marketing programs | ■ Local initiative and motivation in implementation |
| ■ "Shrinking" of the world marketplace | ■ Adherence to the marketing concept |

and product-line adaptation to foreign markets as well as product counterfeiting as a current problem facing international marketers.

**Factors in Product Adaptation** Factors affecting product adaptation to foreign market conditions are summarized in Figure 14.2. The changes vary from minor ones, such as translation of a user's manual, to major ones, such as a more economical version of the product. Many of the factors have an impact on product selection as well as product adaptation for a given market.

A detailed examination of 174 consumer packaged goods destined for developing countries showed that, on the average, 4.1 changes per product were made in terms of brand name, packaging, measurement units, labeling, constituents, product features, and usage instructions. Only one out of ten products was transferred without modification. Some of the changes were mandatory, some discretionary.[17]

*Regional, Country, or Local Characteristics* Typically, the market environment mandates the majority of product modifications. However, the most stringent requirements often result from government regulations. Some of the requirements may serve no purpose other than a political one (such as protection of domestic industry or response to political pressures). Because of the sovereignty of nations, individual firms must comply, but they can influence the situation either by lobbying directly or through industry associations to have the issue raised during trade negotiations. Government regulations may be spelled out, but firms need to be ever vigilant for changes and exceptions. The eighteen member countries of the European Economic Area are imposing standards in more than 10,000 product categories ranging from toys to tractor seats.

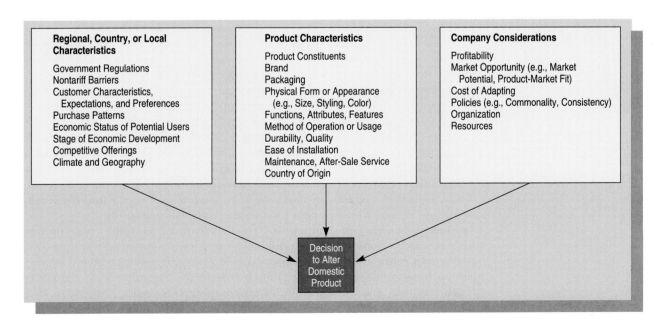

**FIGURE 14.2**

**Factors Affecting Product Adaptation Decisions**

*Source:* Adapted from V. Yorio, *Adapting Products for Export* (New York: The Conference Board, 1983), 7.

While companies such as Murray Manufacturing have had to change their products to comply with the standards (in Murray's case, making its lawnmowers quieter), they will be able to produce one European product in the future. Overall, U.S. producers may be forced to improve quality of all their products because some product rules require adoption of an overall system approved by the International Standards Organization (ISO).[18] By 1997, more than 127,000 ISO 9000 certificates (relating to product and process quality) had been issued worldwide, 12,000 of those in the United States.

Product decisions made by marketers of consumer products are especially affected by local behavior, tastes, attitudes, and traditions—all reflecting the marketer's need to gain the customer's approval. A knowledge of cultural and psychological differences may be the key to success. For example, Brazilians rarely eat breakfast or they eat it at home; therefore, Dunkin' Donuts markets doughnuts as snacks, as dessert, and for parties. To further appeal to Brazilians, doughnuts are made with local fruit fillings such as papaya and guava. Chinese and Western consumers share similar standards when it comes to evaluating brand names. Both appreciate a brand name that is catchy, memorable, distinct, and says something indicative of the product. But, because of cultural and linguistic factors, Chinese consumers expect more in terms of how the names are spelled, written, and styled, and whether they are considered lucky. PepsiCo, Inc., introduced Cheetos in the Chinese market under a Chinese name, *qi duo,* roughly pronounced "chee-do," that translates as "many surprises."[19]

Often no concrete product changes are needed, only a change in the product's **positioning.** Positioning is the perception by consumers of the firm's brand in relation to competitor's brands; that is, the mental image a brand, or the company as a whole, evokes. Coca-Cola took a risk in marketing Diet Coke in Japan because the population is not overweight by Western standards. Further, Japanese women do not like to drink anything clearly labeled as a diet product. The company changed the name to Coke Light and subtly shifted the promotional theme from "weight loss" to "figure maintenance."

Nontariff barriers include product standards, testing or approval procedures, subsidies for local products, and bureaucratic red tape. The nontariff barriers affecting product adjustments usually concern elements outside the core product. For example, France requires the use of the French language "in any offer, presentation, advertisement, written or spoken, instructions for use, specification or guarantee terms for goods or services, as well as for invoices and receipts." Because nontariff barriers are usually in place to keep foreign products out or to protect domestic producers, getting around them may be the single toughest problem for the international marketer.

The monitoring of competitors' product features, as well as determining what has to be done to meet and beat them, is critical to product-adaptation decisions. Competitive offerings may provide a baseline against which resources can be measured—for example, they may help to determine what it takes to reach a critical market share in a given competitive situation. American Hospital Supply, a Chicago-based producer of medical equipment, adjusts its product in a preemptive way by making products that are hard to duplicate. As a result, the firm increased sales and earnings in Japan about 40 percent a year over a ten-year period.

Management must take into account the stage of economic development of the overseas market. As a country's economy advances, buyers are in a better position to buy and to demand more sophisticated products and product versions. On the other hand, the situation in some developing markets may require **backward innovation;** that is, the market may require a drastically simplified version of the firm's product because of lack of purchasing power or of usage conditions. Economic conditions may affect packaging decisions. For example, Pillsbury packages its products in six- and eight-serving sizes for developing-country markets, while the most popular size in the North American market is two servings.[20]

The target market's physical separation from the host country and its climatic conditions will usually have an effect on the total product offering: the core product; tangible elements, mainly packaging; and the augmented features. The international marketer must consider two sometimes contradictory demands: on the one hand, the product itself has to be protected against longer transit times and possibly longer shelf life, but on the other hand, care has to be taken not to use proscribed preservatives.[21]

*Product Characteristics*   Product characteristics are the inherent features of the product offering, whether actual or perceived. The inherent characteristics of products, and the benefits they provide to consumers in the various markets in which they are marketed, make certain products good candidates for standardization—and others not.

The international marketer has to make sure that products do not contain ingredients that might violate legal requirements or religious or social customs. DEP Corporation, a Los Angeles manufacturer with $19 million in annual sales of hair and skin products, takes particular pains to make sure that no Japan-bound products contain formaldehyde, an ingredient commonly used in the United States, but illegal in Japan.[22] Where religion or custom determines consumption, ingredients may have to be replaced for the product to be acceptable. In Islamic countries, for example, vegetable shortening has to be substituted for animal fats.

Packaging is an area where firms generally do make modifications.[23] Due to the longer time that products spend in channels of distribution, international companies, especially those marketing food products, have used more expensive packaging materials and/or more expensive transportation modes for export shipments. Food processors have solved the problem by using airtight, reclosable containers that seal out moisture and other contaminants.

The promotional aspect of packaging relates primarily to labeling. The major adjustments concern legally required bilinguality, as in Canada (French and English), Belgium (French and Flemish), and Finland (Finnish and Swedish). Other governmental requirements include more informative labeling of products for consumer protection and education. Inadequate identification, failure to use the required languages, or inadequate or incorrect descriptions printed on the labels may all cause problems. Increasingly, environmental concerns are having an impact on packaging decisions. On the one hand, governments want to reduce the amount of packaging waste by encouraging marketers to adopt the four environmentally correct Rs: redesign, reduce, reuse, and recycle.[24] On the other hand, many markets have sizable segments of consumers who are concerned enough about protecting the environment to change their consumption patterns, which has resulted in product modifications such as the introduction of recyclable yogurt containers from marketers such as Dany and Danone in Europe.

Brand names convey the image of the good or service. Offhand, brands may seem to be one of the most standardizable items in the product offering. However, the establishment of worldwide brands is difficult; how can a marketer establish world brands when the firm sells 800 products in more than 200 countries, most of them under different names? This is the situation of Gillette. A typical example is Silkience hair conditioner, which is sold as Soyance in France, Sientel in Italy, and Silkience in Germany. Standardizing the name to reap promotional benefits is difficult because names have become established in each market, and the action would lead to objections from local managers or even government. Scott Paper is phasing out local brand names in favor of the Scott name in eighty foreign markets in the belief that the company's greatest asset is its name.[25]

Adjustments in product styling, color, size, and other appearance features are more common in consumer marketing than in industrial marketing. Color plays an important role in how consumers perceive a product, and marketers must be aware of what signal their product's color is sending. Color can be used for brand identification—for example, the yellow of Hertz or red of Avis. It can be used for feature reinforcement; for example, Rolls-Royce uses a dazzling silver paint that spells luxury. Colors communicate in a subtle way in developed societies, whereas they have direct meaning in more traditional societies.

The product offered in the dometic market may not be operable in the foreign market. One of the major differences faced by appliance manufacturers is electrical power systems. In some cases, variations may exist within a country, such as Brazil. Some companies have adjusted their products to operate in different systems; for example, VCR equipment can be adjusted to record and play back on different color systems.

When a product that is sold internationally requires repairs, parts, or service, the problems of obtaining, training, and holding a sophisticated engineering or repair staff are not easy to solve. If the product breaks down and the repair arrangements are not up to standard, the product image will suffer. In some cases, products abroad may not even be used for their intended purpose and thus may require not only modifications in product configuration but also in service frequency. For instance, snowplows exported from the United States are used to remove sand from driveways in Saudi Arabia.

The country of origin of a product, typically communicated by the phrase "made in (country)," has considerable influence on quality perceptions. The percention of products manufactured in certain countries is affected by a built-in positive or negative assumption about quality. One study of machine tool buyers found that the United States and Germany were rated higher than Japan, with Brazil rated below all three of them.[26] These types of findings indicate that steps must be taken by the international marketer to overcome or at least neutralize biases. The issue is especially important to developing countries that need to increase exports, and for importers who source products from countries different from where they are sold.[27]

***Company Considerations***   Company policy will often determine the presence and degree of adaptation. Discussions of product adaptation often end with the question, "Is it worth it?" The answer depends on the company's ability to control costs, to correctly estimate market potential, and, finally, to secure profitablity. The decision to adapt should be preceded by a thorough analysis of the market. Formal market research with primary data collection and/or testing is warranted. From the financial standpoint, some companies have specific return-on-investment levels (for example, 25 percent) to be satisfied before adaptation. Others let the requirement vary as a function of the market considered and also the time in the market—that is, profitability may be initially compromised for proper market entry.

Most companies aim for consistency in their market efforts. This means that all products must fit in terms of quality, price, and user perceptions. Consistency may be difficult to attain, for example, in the area of warranties. Warranties can be uniform only if use conditions do not vary drastically and if the company is able to deliver equally on its promise anywhere it has a presence.

**Product Line Management**   International marketers' product lines consist of local, regional, and global brands. In a given market, an exporter's product line, typically shorter than domestically, concentrates on the most profitable products. Product lines may vary dramatically from one market to another depending on the extent of the firm's operations. Some firms at first cater only to a particular market segment, then eventually expand to cover an entire market. For example, Japanese auto manufacturers moved into the highly profitable luxury car segment after establishing a strong position in the world small-car segment.[28]

The domestic market is not the only source of new-product ideas for the international marketer, nor is it the only place where they are developed.[29] Some products may be developed elsewhere for worldwide consumption because of an advantage in skills, for example. Mazda, which is 33.4 percent owned by Ford, has designed and engineered cars to be produced by others in the Ford empire. Ford Motor Co. of Australia Ltd. developed a two-seater, sports-style specialty car because of its expertise in low-volume production.[30] In fact, many firms have benefited greatly from subsidiaries' local or regional product lines when demand conditions changed in the domestic market to favor new product characteristics. U.S. car manufacturers, for example, have used products from their European operations to compete in the small-sized and sports-style segments.

Sensitivity to local tastes also has to be reflected in the company's product line. In Brazil, Levi Strauss developed a line of jeans exclusively for women there, who prefer ultratight jeans. However, what is learned in one market can often be adopted in another. Levi's line of chino pants and casual wear originated in the company's Argentine unit and was applied to loosely cut pants by its Japanese subsidiary. The company's U.S. operation adopted both in 1986, and the line became global in the 1990s.[31]

**Product Counterfeiting**   About $20 billion in domestic and export sales are estimated to be lost by U.S. companies annually because of product counterfeiting and trademark patent infringement of consumer and industrial products. The hardest hit are software, entertainment, and pharmaceutical sectors. Counterfeit goods are any goods bearing an unauthorized representation of a trademark, patented invention, or copyrighted work that is legally protected in the country where it is marketed.

The practice of product counterfeiting has spread to high technology and services from the traditionally counterfeited products: high-visibility, strong brand name consumer goods. In addition, a new dimension has emerged to complicate the situation. Previously, the only concern was whether a firm's product was being counterfeited; now, management has to worry about whether raw materials and components purchased for production are themselves real.[32]

Four types of action that can be taken against counterfeiting are legislative action, bilateral and multilateral negotiations, joint private sector action, and measures taken by individual firms. Governments have enacted special legislation and set country-specific negotiation objectives for reciprocity and retaliatory options for intellectual property protection.

In today's environment, firms are taking more aggressive steps to protect themselves. Victimized firms not only are losing sales but also goodwill in the longer term if customers, believing they are getting the real product, unknowingly end up with a copy of inferior quality. In addition to the normal measures of registering trademarks and copyrights, firms are taking steps in product development to prevent the copying of trademarked goods. For example, new authentication materials in labeling are virtually impossible to duplicate. Jointly, companies have formed organizations to lobby for legislation and to act as information clearinghouses.

## Pricing Policy

Pricing is the only element in the marketing mix that is revenue generating; all of the others are costs. It should therefore be used as an active instrument of strategy in the major areas of marketing decision making. Pricing in the international environment is more complicated than in the domestic market, however, because of such factors as government influence, different currencies, and additional costs. International pricing situations can be divided into three general categories: export pricing, foreign market pricing, and intracompany, or transfer, pricing.[33]

**Export Pricing**    Three general price-setting strategies in international marketing are a standard worldwide price; dual pricing, which differentiates between domestic and export prices; and market-differentiated pricing.[34] The first two are cost-oriented pricing methods that are relatively simple to establish, are easy to understand, and cover all of the necessary costs. **Standard worldwide pricing** is based on average unit costs of fixed, variable, and export-related costs.

In **dual pricing,** domestic and export prices are differentiated, and two approaches are available: the **cost-plus method** and the **marginal cost method.** The cost-plus strategy involves the actual costs, that is, a full allocation of domestic and foreign costs to the product. Although this type of pricing ensures margins, the final price may put the product beyond the reach of the customer. As a result, some exporters resort to flexible cost-plus strategy, wherein discounts are provided when necessary as a result of customer type, intensity of competition, or size of order. The marginal cost method considers the direct costs of producing and selling for export as the floor beneath which prices cannot be set. Fixed costs for plants, R&D, domestic overhead, and domestic marketing costs are disregarded. An exporter can thus lower export prices to be competitive in markets that otherwise might have been considered beyond access.

On the other hand, **market-differentiated pricing** is based on a demand-oriented strategy and is thus more consistent with the marketing concept. This method also allows consideration of competitive forces in setting export price. The major problem is the exporter's perennial dilemma: lack of information. Therefore, in most cases, marginal costs provide a basis for competitive comparisons, on which the export price is set.

In preparing a quotation, the exporter must be careful to take into account unique export-related costs and, if possible, include them. They are in addition to the normal costs shared with the domestic side. They include:

1. The cost incurred in modifying the good for foreign markets.
2. Operational costs of the export operation. Examples are personnel, market research, additional shipping and insurance costs, communications costs with foreign customers, and overseas promotional costs.
3. Costs incurred in entering foreign markets. These include tariffs and taxes; risks associated with a buyer in a different market (mainly commercial credit risks and political risks); and dealing in other than the exporter's domestic currency—that is, foreign exchange risk.

The combined effect of both clear-cut and hidden costs results in export prices far in excess of domestic prices. This is called **price escalation.** Dollar-based prices may also become expensive to local buyers in the case of currency devaluation. For example, during the 1997 Asian currency turmoil, many companies in Indonesia, Malaysia, South Korea, and Thailand scaled down their buying. The exporter has many alternatives under these circumstances, such as stretching out payment terms, cutting prices, or bringing scaled-down, more affordable products to the affected markets.[35]

Export credit and terms add another dimension to the profitability of an export transaction. Before the transaction, the exporter has in all likelihood formulated a credit policy that determines the degree of risk the firm is willing to assume and the preferred selling terms. The main objective is to meet the importer's requirements without jeopardizing the firm's financial goals. The exporter will be concerned about being paid for the goods shipped and will, therefore, consider the following factors in negotiating terms of payment: (1) the amount of payment and the need for protection, (2) terms offered by competitors, (3) practices in the industry, (4) capacity for financing international transactions, and (5) relative strength of the parties involved.[36] If the exporter is well established in the market with a unique product and accompanying service, price and terms of trade can be set according to the exporter's preferences. If, on the other hand, the exporter is breaking into a new market, or if competitive pressures exist, pricing and selling terms should be used as major competitive tools.

Inexpensive imports often trigger accusations of **dumping**—that is, selling goods overseas for less than in the exporter's home market, at a price below the cost of production, or both. Cases that have been reported include charges by Florida tomato growers that Mexican vegetables were being dumped across the border and the ruling of the Canadian Anti-Dumping Tribunal that U.S. firms were dumping radioactive diagnostic reagents in Canada.[37]

Dumping ranges from predatory to unintentional. Predatory dumping is the tactic of a foreign firm that intentionally sells at a loss in another country to increase its market share at the expense of domestic producers. This amounts to an international price war. Unintentional dumping is the result of time lags between the date of sales transactions, shipment, and arrival. Prices, including exchange rates, can change in such a way that the final sales price is below the cost of production or below the price prevailing in the exporter's home market.

In the United States, domestic producers may petition the government to impose antidumping duties on imports alleged to be dumped. The remedy is a duty equal to the dumping margin. International agreements and U.S. law provide for countervailing duties. They may be imposed on imports that are found to be subsidized by foreign governments. They are designed to offset the advantages imports would otherwise receive from the subsidy.

**Foreign Market Pricing**   Pricing within the individual markets in which the firm operates is determined by (1) corporate objectives, (2) costs, (3) customer behavior and market conditions, (4) market structure, and (5) environmental constraints. All of these factors vary from country to country, and pricing policies of the multinational corporation must vary as well. Despite arguments in favor of uniform pricing in multinational markets, price discrimination is an essential characteristic of the pricing policies of firms conducting business in differing markets. In a study of 42 U.S.-based multinational corporations, the major problem areas they reported in making pricing decisions were meeting competition, cost, lack of competitive information, distribution and channel factors, and governmental barriers.[38]

The issue of standard worldwide pricing may be mostly a theoretical one because of the influence of a variety of factors. However, coordination of the pricing function is necessary, especially in larger, regional markets such as the European Union. Standardization efforts usually address price levels and the use of pricing as a positioning tool.

Of great importance to multinational corporations is the control and co-ordination of pricing to intermediaries. When discrepancies in currency exchange rates widen, **gray markets** emerge. The term refers to brand-name imports that enter a country legally but outside regular, authorized distribution channels. The gray market is fueled by companies that sell goods in foreign markets at prices that are far lower than prices charged to, for example, U.S. distributors, and by one strong currency, such as the dollar or the yen. The gray market in the United States has flourished in cars, watches, and even baby powder, cameras, and chewing gum. The retail value of gray markets in the United States has been estimated at $6 billion to $10 billion. This phenomenon not only harms the company financially but also may harm its reputation, because authorized distributors often refuse to honor warranties on items bought through the gray market. Cars bought through the gray market in the United States, for example, may not pass EPA inspections and thus may cause major expense to the unsuspecting buyer.[39]

The proponents of gray marketing argue for their right to "free trade" by pointing to manufacturers who are both overproducing and overpricing in some markets. The main beneficiaries are consumers, who benefit from lower prices, and discount distributors, who now have access to the good.

**Transfer Pricing**    Transfer, or intracompany, pricing is the pricing of sales to members of the corporate family. The overall competitive and financial position of the firm forms the basis of any pricing policy. In this, transfer pricing plays a key role. Intracorporate sales can easily change consolidated global results because they often are one of the most important ongoing decision areas in a company. Transfer prices are usually set by the firm's major financial officer—the financial vice president or comptroller—and parent company executives are uniformly unwilling to allow much participation by other departments or subsidiary executives.[40]

Four main transfer-pricing possibilities have merged over time: (1) transfer at direct cost, (2) transfer at direct cost plus additional expenses, (3) transfer at a price derived from end-market prices, and (4) transfer at an **arm's length price,** or the price that unrelated parties would have reached on the same transaction. Doing business overseas requires coping with complexities of environmental peculiarities, the effect of which can be alleviated by manipulating transfer prices. Factors that call for adjustments include taxes, import duties, inflationary tendencies, unstable governments, and other regulations.[41] For example, high transfer prices on goods shipped to a subsidiary and low ones on goods imported from it will result in minimizing the tax liability of a subsidiary operating in a country with a high income tax. Tax liability thus results not only from the absolute tax rate but also from differences in how income is computed. On the other hand, a higher transfer price may have an effect on the import duty, especially if it is assessed on an ad valorem basis. Exceeding a certain threshold may boost the duty substantially and thus have a negative impact on the subsidiary's posture.

The main concerns with transfer pricing are both internal and external to the multinational corporation. Manipulating intracorporate prices complicates internal control measures and, without proper documentation, will cause major problems. If the firm operates on a profit-center basis, some consideration must be given to the effect of transfer pricing on the subsidiary's apparent profit and its actual performance. To judge a subsidiary's profit performance as not satisfactory when it was targeted to be a net source of funds can easily create morale problems. The situation may be further complicated by cultural differences among subsidiaries, especially if the need to subsidize less-efficient members of the corporate family is not made clear. An adjustment in the control mechanism is called for to give appropriate credit to the divisions for their actual contributions. The method called for may range from dual bookkeeping to compensation in budgets and profit plans. Regardless of the method, proper organizational communication is required to avoid unnecessary conflict between subsidiaries and headquarters.

Transfer prices will by definition involve tax and regulatory jurisdiction of the countries in which the company does business. Sales and transfers of tangible properties and transfers of intangibles such as patent rights and manufacturing know-how are subject to close review and to determinations about the adequacy of compensation received. Typically, authorities try to establish or approximate an arm's length level. Quite often the multinational corporation is put in a difficult position. U.S. authorities may think the transfer price is too low, whereas the foreign entity (especially a less-developed country) may perceive it to be too high. In a survey of 400 multinational companies, respondents facing transfer pricing disputes were able to defend their profit to local tax authorities in only half of the inquiries.[42]

In the host environments, the concern of the multinational corporation is to maintain its status as a good corporate citizen. Many corporations, in drafting multinational codes of conduct, have specified that intracorporate pricing will follow the arm's length principle. Multinationals have also been found to closely abide by tax regulations governing transfer pricing.[43] The OECD has issued transfer pricing guidelines including methodology and documentation scenarios to assist in the compliance process.

## Distribution Policy

Channels of distribution provide the essential linkages that connect producers and customers. The channel decision is the longest term of the marketing mix decisions in that it cannot be readily changed. In addition, it involves relinquishing some of the control the firm has over the marketing of its products. The two factors make choosing the right channel structure a crucial decision. Properly structured and staffed, the distribution system will function more as one rather than as a collection of often quite different units.

**Channel Design** The term *channel design* refers to the length and width of the channel employed. **Channel design** is determined by factors that can be summarized as the 11 Cs: customer, culture, competition, company, character, capital, cost, coverage, control, continuity, and communication. While there are no standard answers to channel design, as shown in Global Perspective 14.2, the international marketer can use the 11 Cs as a checklist to determine the proper approach to reach target audiences before selecting channel members to fill the roles. The first three factors are givens in that the company must adjust its approach to the existing structures. The other eight are controllable to a certain extent by the marketer.

The demographic and psychographic characteristics of targeted *customers* will form the basis for channel-design decisions. Answers to questions such as what customers need as well as why, when, and how they buy are used to determine ways in which products should be made available to generate a competitive advantage. Anheuser-Busch's success in Japan began, for example, when Suntory, one of the country's largest liquor distillers, acquired the importing rights. One important aspect of Suntory's marketing plan was to stress distribution of Budweiser in discos, pubs, and other night spots where Japan's affluent, well-traveled youth gather. Young people in Japan are influenced by American culture and adapt more readily to new products than do older Japanese. Taking advantage of this fact, Suntory concentrated its efforts on one generation. The result was that on-premise sales led to major off-premise (retail outlet) sales as well.

Customer characteristics may cause one product to be distributed through two different types of channels. All sales of Caterpillar's earthmoving equipment are handled by independent dealers, except for sales to the U.S. government and the People's Republic of China, which are direct.

The marketer must analyze existing channel structures, or what might be called the distribution *culture* of a market. For example, the general nature of

## CHOOSING THE SYSTEM THAT WORKS IN LATIN AMERICA

Changing market conditions from the Rio Grande to Tierra del Fuego are making U.S., European, and Japanese companies reassess their distribution strategies in South and Central America. Regional trade pacts and free trade are enabling companies to both consider entry and reformulate their strategies in the region. In the past, the infrastructure for effective and efficient distribution was largely missing. For example, underdeveloped and monopolistic distributor networks saw their primary job as distributing sales literature, cutting through red tape, and charging invariably high fees.

Times are changing for these intermediaries, however. The agent of that change is competition. Outside competition has forced distributors to add value to what they do, either by carrying inventory, providing specialized packaging, participating in the logistics infrastructure, or otherwise serving the customers' needs. And if locals do not measure up, companies are willing to look for other solutions, such as using outside captive distribution systems or putting their own people in place.

There are no standard answers to the problems of distribution system design. In many cases, companies have found that a mix of techniques yields the best results and allows greater responsiveness to customer requests, as shown by the following three examples.

### Motorola in Brazil

Motorola's subsidiary combines in-house systems with an independent distributor network. It uses an in-house sales force to service large manufacturing clients and major end users of its line of imported and domestic semiconductors, portable radios, and cellular telephones. Other customers are served through four large distribution firms. Subrepresentatives are contracted by distributors to provide coverage in areas where they do not have a direct presence. The company has determined that sales made via a distributor at this level are cheaper than direct sales. Distributors can offer fast delivery because in-house inventories are maintained.

### ICI in Mexico

ICI markets agrochemicals, explosives, paints, and specialty chemicals, as well as dyes, and chooses a distribution approach based on the size of sales and the need for technical assistance. The company prefers to sell industrial products directly when possible due to the technical service they require. For example, the firm trains mining clients in explosives and provides on-site studies to determine appropriate blasting methods. The paint business in Mexico City is handled by in-house sales representatives that sell directly to retail stores. ICI products are oriented towards the high-quality, high-price market. Management take pains to ensure the quality of retail service, with sales representatives monitoring outlets. Even when independents handle products, the company's sales department continuously assesses the performance of the distribution chain.

### Eveready in Argentina

Battery makers sell a large share of their production through small retailers. In Argentina, where kiosks are one of the most important outlets and product turnover is high, Eveready reaches thousands of kiosks by selling to some 600 independent distributors throughout the country. Distributors are attracted to the firm because of the high product turnover rate and its strong name recognition. Eveready reaches distributors through a national shipping company that carries products to remote markets.

*Source: Erika Morphy, "Pan-American Byways,"* Export Today *(December 1996): 20–28; Joseph V. Barks, "Penetrating Latin America,"* International Business *(February 1994): 76–80; "Choosing the Right System: Direct Sales vs. Independents,"* Business International *(January 13, 1992): 12; and "Winning Approaches to Distribution in LA,"* Business International *(January 13, 1992): 12–13.* http://www.mot.com; http://www.demon.co.uk/ici/; http://www.everyready.com

the Japanese distribution system presents one of the major reasons for the apparent failure of foreign companies to penetrate the market.[44] In most cases, the international marketer must adjust to existing structures. In Finland, for example, 92 percent of all distribution of nondurable consumer goods is through four wholesale chains. In the United Kingdom, major retail chains control markets. Without their support, no significant penetration of the market is possible.

**WWW**

Foreign legislation affecting distributors and agents is an essential part of the distribution culture of a market. For example, legislation may require foreign companies to be represented only by firms that are 100 percent locally owned. Some countries have prohibited the use of dealers so as to protect consumers from abuses in which intermediaries have engaged.

Channels used by *competitors* form another basis for plans. First, channels utilized by the competition may make up the only distribution system that is accepted both by the trade and by consumers. In this case, the international marketer's task is to use the structure more effectively and efficiently. An alternate strategy is to use a totally different distribution approach from the competition and hope to develop a competitive advantage in that manner. A new approach will have to be carefully analyzed and tested against the cultural, political, and legal environments in which it is to be introduced. In some cases, all feasible channels may be blocked by domestic competitors through contractual agreements or other means.

No channel of distribution can be properly selected unless it meets the requirements set by overall *company objectives* for market share and profitability. Sometimes management may simply want to use a particular channel of distribution, even though no sound business basis exists for the decision. Some management goals may have conflicting results. When investment in the restaurant business in Japan was liberalized, a number of U.S. fast-food chains rushed in to capitalize on the development. The companies attempted to establish mass sales as soon as possible by opening numerous restaurants in the busiest sections of several Japanese cities. Unfortunately, control proved to be quite difficult because of the sheer number of openings over a relatively short period of time. The individual stores changed the product as they grew, ruining the major asset—standardization—that the U.S. companies were advocating.[45]

The *character* of the good will have an impact on the design of the channel. Generally, the more specialized, expensive, bulky, or perishable the product and the more it may require after-sale service, the more likely the channel is to be relatively short. Staple items, such as soap, tend to have longer channels, while services have short channels. The type of channel chosen has to match the overall positioning of the product in the market. Changes in overall market conditions, such as currency fluctuations, may require changes in distribution as well. An increase in the value of the dollar may cause a repositioning of the marketed product as a luxury item, necessitating an appropriate channel (such as an upscale department store) for its distribution.

The term *capital* is used to describe the financial requirements in setting up a channel system. The international marketer's financial strength will determine the type of channel and the basis on which channel relationships will be built. The stronger the marketer's finances, the more able the firm is to establish channels it either owns or controls. Intermediaries' requirements for beginning inventories, selling on a consignment basis, preferential loans, and need for training will all have an impact on the type of approach chosen by the international marketer.

Closely related to the capital dimension is *cost*—that is, the expenditure incurred in maintaining a channel once it is established. Costs will naturally vary over the life cycle of the relationship as well as over the life cycle of the product marketed. An example of the costs involved is promotional monies spent by a distributor for the marketer's product. Costs may also be incurred in protecting the company's distributors against adverse market conditions. A number of U.S. manufacturers helped their distributors maintain competitive prices through subsidies when the exchange rate for the U.S. dollar caused pricing problems.

The term *coverage* is used to describe both the number of areas in which the marketer's products are represented and the quality of that representation. Coverage, therefore, is two dimensional in that both horizontal and vertical coverage need to be considered in channel design. The number of areas to be covered depends on the dispersion of demand in the market and also the time elapsed since the product's introduction to the market. A company typically enters a market with one local distributor, but, as volume expands, the distribution base often has to be adjusted.

The use of intermediaries will automatically lead to loss of some *control* over the marketing of the firm's products. The looser the relationship is between the marketer and the intermediaries, the less control can be exerted. The longer the channel, the more difficult it becomes for the marketer to have a final say over pricing, promotion, and the types of outlets in which the product will be made available.

Nurturing *continuity* rests heavily on the marketer because foreign distributors may have a more short-term view of the relationship. For example, Japanese wholesalers believe that it is important for manufacturers to follow up initial success with continuous improvement of the product. If such improvements are not forthcoming, competitors are likely to enter the market with similar, but lower-priced, products and the wholesalers of the imported product will turn to the Japanese suppliers.[46]

*Communication* provides the exchange of information that is essential to the functioning of the channel. Proper communication will perform important roles for the international marketer. It will help convey the marketer's goals to the distributors, help solve conflict situations, and aid in the overall marketing of the product. Communication is a two-way process that does not permit the marketer to dictate to intermediaries. Sometimes the planned program may not work because of a lack of communication. Prices may not be competitive; promotional materials may be obsolete or inaccurate and not well received overall.

**Selection and Screening of Intermediaries**   Once the basic design of the channel has been determined, the international marketer must begin a search to fill the defined roles with the best available candidates. Choices will have to be made within the framework of the company's overall philosophy on distributors versus agents, as well as whether the company will use an indirect or direct approach to foreign markets.

Firms that have successful international distribution attest to the importance of finding top representatives. The undertaking should be held in the same regard as recruiting and hiring within the company because "an ineffective foreign distributor can set you back years; it is almost better to have no distributor than a bad one in a major market."[47]

Various sources exist to assist the marketer in locating intermediary candidates. One of the easiest and most economical ways is to use the services of governmental agencies. The U.S. Department of Commerce has various services that can assist firms in identifying suitable representatives abroad; some have been designed specifically for that purpose. A number of private sources are also available to the international marketer. Trade directories, many of them published by Dun & Bradstreet, usually list foreign representatives geographically and by product classification. Telephone directories, especially the yellow page sections or editions, can provide distributor lists. Although not detailed, the listings will give addresses and an indication of the products sold. The firm can solicit the support of some of its facilitating agencies, such as banks, advertising agencies, shipping lines, and airlines. The marketer can take an even more direct approach by buying advertising space to solicit representation. The advertisements typically indicate the type of support the marketer will be able to give to its distributor.

Intermediaries can be screened on their performance and professionalism. An intermediary's performance can be evaluated on the basis of financial standing and sales as well as the likely fit it would provide in terms of its existing product lines and coverage. Professionalism can be assessed through reputation and overall standing in the business community.

**Managing the Channel Relationship**   A channel relationship can be likened to a marriage in that it brings together two independent entities that have shared goals. For the relationship to work, each party has to be open about its expectations and openly communicate changes perceived in the other's behavior that might be contrary to the agreement. An excellent framework for managing channel relationships is provided in Table 14.3.

**TABLE 14.3**

**Managing Relations with Overseas Distributors**

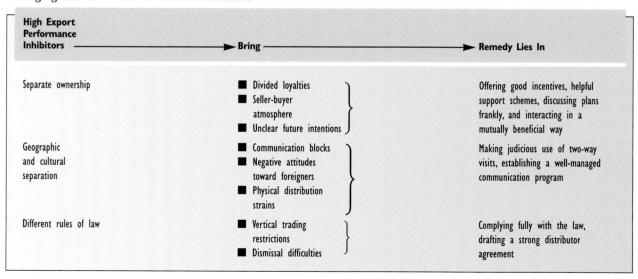

| High Export Performance Inhibitors ⟶ | Bring ⟶ | Remedy Lies In |
| --- | --- | --- |
| Separate ownership | ■ Divided loyalties<br>■ Seller-buyer atmosphere<br>■ Unclear future intentions | Offering good incentives, helpful support schemes, discussing plans frankly, and interacting in a mutually beneficial way |
| Geographic and cultural separation | ■ Communication blocks<br>■ Negative attitudes toward foreigners<br>■ Physical distribution strains | Making judicious use of two-way visits, establishing a well-managed communication program |
| Different rules of law | ■ Vertical trading restrictions<br>■ Dismissal difficulties | Complying fully with the law, drafting a strong distributor agreement |

*Source:* Philip J. Rosson, "Source Factors in Manufacture—Overseas Distributor Relationships in International Marketing," in *International Marketing Management,* ed. Erdener Kaynak (New York: Praeger, 1984), 95.

The complicating factors that separate the two parties fall into three categories: ownership, geographic and cultural distance, and different rules of law. Rather than lament their existence, both parties must take strong action to remedy them. Often the first major step is for both parties to acknowledge that differences exist.

**Promotional Policy**

The international marketer must choose a proper combination of the various promotional tools—advertising, personal selling, sales promotion, and publicity—to create images among the intended target audience. The choice will depend on the target audience, company objectives, the product or service marketed, the resources available for the endeavor, and the availability of promotional tools in a particular market. Increasingly, the focus is not a product or service but the company's image, as shown in Global Perspective 14.3.

**Advertising** The key decision-making areas in advertising are (1) media strategy, (2) the promotional message, and (3) the organization of the promotional program.

**Media strategy** is applied to the selection of media vehicles and the development of a media schedule. Worldwide media spending, which totaled $300 billion in 1996, varies dramatically around the world. In absolute terms, the United States spends the most, followed by Japan, the United Kingdom, Germany, Canada, and France. The mature U.S. market anticipates slower growth in the future, but European integration and the development of the Pacific Rim's consumer markets are likely to fuel major growth.[48] The major spenders were Procter & Gamble ($2.4 billion), Unilever ($2.3 billion), and Nestlé ($1.5 billion). While P&G spent 52 percent of its budget in the United States, Unilever's spending there was only 28 percent.[49]

Media spending varies also by market. Countries devoting the highest percentage to television were Peru (84 percent) and Mexico (73 percent). In some countries, the highest percentage is devoted to print: Kuwait (91) and Norway (77). Radio accounts for more than 20 percent in only a few countries, such as Trinidad and Tobago, and Nepal. Outdoor advertising accounted for 48 percent of Bolivia's media spending but only 3 percent in Germany. Cinema advertising is important in India and Nigeria.[50]

Media regulations will also vary. Some regulations include limits on the amount of time available for advertisements; in Italy, for example, the state channels allow a maximum of 12 percent of advertising per hour and 4 percent over a week, and commercial stations allow 18 percent per hour and 15 percent per week. Furthermore, the leading Italian stations do not guarantee audience delivery when spots are bought. Strict separation between programs and commercials is almost a universal requirement, preventing U.S.–style sponsored programs. Restrictions on items such as comparative claims and gender stereotypes are prevalent; for example, Germany prohibits the use of superlatives such as "best."

Global media vehicles have been developed that have target audiences on at least three continents and for which the media buying takes place through a centralized office. These media have traditionally been publications that, in addition to the worldwide edition, have provided advertisers the option of using regional editions. For example, *Time* provides 133 editions, enabling ad-

## NURTURING A GLOBAL IMAGE

**C**orporate advertising can play a vital role in providing constituents with reassurances of quality and promises of trusted service. It is typically focused to support the company in several areas, such as product support, employment recommendation, crisis support, joint venture consideration, and stock purchase.

Several global marketers have used global image advertising to achieve particular objectives. Nokia is the world's second largest company in the cellular business. However, many customers are not aware of Nokia to the extent that they are of its competitors such as Motorola. Nokia has, therefore, engaged in a number of corporate efforts, one of which is the title sponsorship of the Sugar Bowl for 1995–1998 (see below). The sponsorship costs Nokia approximately $2.5 million annually. Similarly, the German chemical company BASF has wanted to increase constituent awareness of its far-flung operations: It has 100 companies under its umbrella producing in 39 countries and markets these goods in over 170. Its campaign theme, "We do not make many of the products you use, but we make many of the products you use better," is intended to increase its brand equity and subsequently the behavior of important stakeholders.

In some cases corporations may look to reposition themselves. As a bloated, government-owned company, British Airways was generally regarded as "Bloody Awful." Upon privatization, the company needed to quickly change its image amongst stakeholders to a more positive perception. A series of corporate image campaigns since 1983 have helped change the airline into one of the most positively regarded in the industry.

Some consider crises to be as sure as death and taxes. A solid corporate image and the ability of customers to get the company's point of view are tasks for image campaigns. Companies such as Mobil Corporation have regularly engaged in extending the corporate view to dispel myths or misconceptions. In 1998, for example, one of Mobil's campaigns focused on its investments in developing countries, especially ones in the public eye (e.g., Indonesia). Mobil argued that rather than cut and run from them, it would work to change them.

Some marketers have elected to engage in promoting social causes as part of their image advertising. Probably the most controversial in this category are advertisements from Benetton, which have focused on promoting harmony and understanding among peoples but have created discussion about the appropriateness of the message delivery.

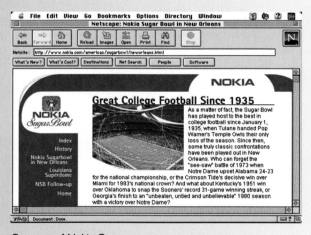

Courtesy of Nokia Group

*Source: "Growing from the Top," **Marketing Management** (Winter/Spring 1996): 10–19; and Rahul Jacob, "Nokia Fumbles, But Don't Count It Out," Fortune (February 19, 1996): 86–88.* **http://www.nokia.com, www.basf.com, www.british-airways.com, www.mobil.com, and www.benetton.com.**

vertising to reach a particular country, a continent, or the world. Other global publications include *The International Herald Tribune, The Wall Street Journal,* and *National Geographic.*

In broadcast media, panregional radio stations have been joined in Europe by television as a result of satellite technology. By the end of the 1990s, approximately half of the households in Europe will have access to additional television broadcasts either through cable or direct satellite, and television will no longer be restricted by national boundaries. As a result, marketers need to make sure that advertising works not only within markets but across countries as well. The launch of STAR TV has increased the use of regional advertising in Asia.

Developing the **promotional message** is referred to as creative strategy. The marketer must determine what the consumer is really buying—that is, the consumer's motivations. They will vary, depending on:

1. The diffusion of the product into the market. For example, to penetrate Third World markets with business computers is difficult when potential customers may not be able to type.
2. The criteria on which the consumer will evaluate the product. For example, in traditional societies, the time-saving qualities of a product may not be the best ones to feature, as Campbell Soup learned in Italy and in Brazil, where housewives felt inadequate as homemakers if they did not make soups from scratch.
3. The product's positioning. For example, Parker Pen's upscale image around the world may not be profitable enough in a market that is more or less a commodity business. The solution is to create an image for a commodity product and make the public pay for it—for example, the positioning of Perrier in the United States as a premium mineral water.

The ideal situation in developing message strategy is to have a world brand—a product that is manufactured, packaged, and positioned the same around the world. However, a number of factors will force companies to abandon identical campaigns in favor of recognizable campaigns. The factors are culture, of which language is the main manifestation, economic development, and lifestyles. Consider, for example, the campaign for Marriott International presented in Figure 14.3. While the ads share common graphic elements, two distinct approaches are evident. The top set of advertisements from the United States and Saudi Arabia are an example of a relatively standard approach, given the similarity in target audiences (i.e., the business traveler) and in the competitive conditions in the markets. The second set features ads for Latin American and German-speaking Europe. While the Latin advertisement stresses comfort, the German version focuses on results. While most of Marriott's ads have the theme ("When you're comfortable you can do anything") translated, the German version keeps the original English-language theme.

Many multinational corporations are staffed and equipped to perform the full range of promotional activities. In most cases, however, they rely on the outside expertise of advertising agencies and other promotions-related companies such as media-buying companies and specialty marketing firms. According to a Grey Advertising survey of fifty multinational marketers, 76 percent believe the ideal situation is to use the same agency worldwide, with some local deviation as necessary. The same percentage believes an ad agency should be centrally run, and 72 percent believe in using the same advertising strategy worldwide.[51] Local agencies will survive, however, because of governmental regulations. In Peru, for example, a law mandates that any commercial aired on Peruvian television must be 100 percent nationally produced. Local agencies tend to forge ties with foreign ad agencies for better coverage and customer service, and thus become part of the general globalization effort.

Room 324.
Wants to
cut the
oil deal
of his life.

We have just the right environment and services that allow your clients to conduct their business in peace. So whether they're working on that important speech, finishing a project, making a conference call or just relaxing, we'll help them do it with absolute ease and comfort. Because at Marriott, we believe:

When you're comfortable you can do anything.℠

**Marriott**
HOTELS · RESORTS · SUITES

Habitación 639.
Quiere
trabajar
sin
corbata.

Usted puede contar con los Hoteles Marriot, ya que le proveen los servicios más confiables y eficientes y el staff necesario para hacer el trabajo de manera que usted pueda llevarse todo el crédito.

Cuando usted está cómodo puede lograr lo que quiera.℠

**Marriott**
HOTELS · RESORTS · SUITES

Zimmer 412.
will heute noch
den Deal seines
Lebens machen.

Legen Sie ganz entspannt die Füße hoch. Schließlich haben Sie alles, was man für einen erfolgreichen Deal braucht: die nötige Ruhe, die richtige Umgebung – und den Business-Service. Wir stellen Ihnen unser gesamtes Equipment zur Verfügung. Und tun für Sie, was wir können. Damit Sie tun können, was Ihnen wirklich wichtig ist. Reservierungen in über 300 Marriott Hotels, Resorts & Suites weltweit unter 0130/85 44 22.

When you're comfortable you can do anything.

**Marriott**
HOTELS · RESORTS · SUITES

**FIGURE 14.3**

**Global Advertising Campaign Approaches**

Courtesy: Marriott International **http://www.marriott.com**

**Internet**   Increasing numbers of companies worldwide are committing to the Internet's World Wide Web.[52] Information technology and marketing and sales, as well as public relations, are driving the decision to build a Web site. With the increase in personal computer ownership today and the future Web TV (Web access through new generation TVs) and network computers, ready access to the mass market will be a reality.

Due to the rapid growth of the Internet, the actual number of users has been estimated at 30 million and projected to reach 100 million by the year 2000. The use is dominated by business-to-business use, and individual use is skewed toward the United States, more men than women, and above-average income levels. However, with rapid growth, these differences are evening out.

Having a Web site is seen necessary if not for anything else than for image reasons; lack of one may convey a negative image. The most important reason for most is twenty-four-hour access to international customers and prospects, followed by the wish to advertise on the Web. Many see the Web as a new sales channel and a way to strengthen brand loyalty. The Web also provides a way to generate sales leads by attracting those who are interested in the company and its products. The Web provides continuous access for customers and other constituents to company information.

Those companies that are not planning to have a Web site state no perceived benefit, concerns about safety, and a willingness to wait for the concept to mature before using it for marketing purposes. For some, the mere presence is not enough; they want to have effective methods of interaction and of measuring the return on their investment in the site.

Dell Computer Corp., the world's largest computer maker, established a major transactional Web site with the help of Grey's Interactive[53] to make it easier for business computer users to do business with Dell—to get product information, buy a computer or get order status, and to get tech support or news. Dell's sales reach the entire globe and the products it sells in the United States are not always the same as those available elsewhere. Therefore, its on-line store uses transaction and targeting technology to deliver the content applicable to each market.[54]

Although the volume of electronic commerce was only $2 to $3 billion in 1997, revenues generated from commercial Web sites are expected to exceed $300 billion by 2001.[55] Concerns about security and privacy will have to be solved and calmed before that will happen.

While most of the users today are in the United States and are English speaking, marketers have to have more than translations of their sites. To be successful, they must provide fully local versions of their sites. One such story is Yahoo!, a California-based Internet index service. After witnessing the appeal of its localized service in the United Kingdom and Ireland, Yahoo! has created sites in Germany and France as well. Marketers using the Web as an advertising medium will have to be concerned about regional and local regulations. For example, Germany sued Benetton for exploiting "feelings of pity" with one of its advertising campaigns.[56]

**Personal Selling**   Although advertising is often equated with the promotional effort, in many cases promotional efforts consist of personal selling. In the early stages of internationalization, exporters rely heavily on personal contact. The marketing of industrial goods, especially of high-priced items, requires strong personal selling efforts. In some cases, personal selling may be truly international; for example, Boeing or Northrop Grumman salespeople engage in sales efforts around the world. However, in most cases, personal selling takes place at the local level. The best interests of any company in the industrial area lie in establishing a solid base of dealerships staffed by local people. Personal selling efforts can be developed in the same fashion as advertising. For the multinational company, the primary goal again is the enhancement and standardization of personal selling efforts, especially if the product offering is standardized.

As an example, Eastman Kodak has developed a line-of-business approach to allow for standardized strategy throughout a region.[57] In Europe, one person is placed in charge of the entire copier-duplicator program in each country. That person is responsible for all sales and service teams within the country. Typically, each customer is served by three representatives, each with a different responsibility. Sales representatives maintain ultimate responsibility for the account; they conduct demonstrations, analyze customer requirements, determine the right type of equipment for each installation, and obtain orders. Service representatives install and maintain the equipment and retrofit new-product improvements to existing equipment. Customer service representatives are the liaison between sales and service. They provide operator training on a continuing basis and handle routine questions and complaints. Each team is positioned to respond to any European customer within four hours.

**Sales Promotion**   Sales promotion has been used as the catchall term for promotion that is not advertising, personal selling, or publicity. Sales promotion directed at consumers involves such activities as couponing, sampling, premiums, consumer education and demonstration activities, cents-off packages, point-of-purchase materials, and direct mail. The success in Latin America of Tang, General Foods's presweetened powder juice substitute, is for the most part traceable to successful sales promotion efforts. One promotion involved trading Tang pouches for free popsicles from Kibon (General Foods's Brazilian subsidiary). Kibon also placed coupons for free groceries in Tang pouches. In Puerto Rico, General Foods ran Tang sweepstakes. In Argentina, in-store sampling featured Tang poured from Tang pitchers by girls in orange Tang dresses. Decorative Tang pitchers were a hit throughout Latin America.

For sales promotion to work, the campaigns planned by manufacturers or their agencies have to gain the support of the local retailer population. As an example, retailers must redeem coupons presented by consumers and forward them to the manufacturer or to the company handling the promotion. A. C. Nielsen tried to introduce cents-off coupons in Chile and ran into trouble with the nation's supermarket union, which notified its members that it opposed the project and recommended that coupons not be accepted. The main complaint was that an intermediary, such as Nielsen, would unnecessarily raise costs and thus the prices to be charged to consumers. Also, some critics felt that coupons would limit individual negotiations, because Chileans often bargain for their purchases.

Sales promotion directed at intermediaries, also known as trade promotion, includes activities such as trade shows and exhibits, trade discounts, and cooperative advertising. For example, attendance at an appropriate trade show is one of the best ways to make contacts with government officials and decision makers, work with present intermediaries, or attract new ones.

**Public Relations**   Public relations is the marketing communications function charged with executing programs to earn public understanding and acceptance, which means both internal and external communication. Internal communication is important, especially in multinational companies, to create an appropriate corporate culture. External campaigns can be achieved through the use of corporate symbols, corporate advertising, customer relations programs, and the generation of publicity. Some material on the firm is produced for special audiences to assist in personal selling.

A significant part of public relations activity focuses on portraying multinational corporations as good citizens of their host markets. IBM's policy of good corporate citizenship means accepting responsibility as a participant in community and national affairs and striving to be among the most admired companies in host countries. In Thailand, for example, IBM provides equipment and personnel to universities and donates money to the nation's wildlife fund and environmental protection agency.[58]

Public relations activity includes anticipating and countering criticism. The criticisms range from general ones against all multinational corporations to specific complaints. They may be based on a market, for example, a company's presence in China. They may concern a product, for example, Nestlé's practices in advertising and promoting infant formula in developing countries where infant mortality is unacceptably high. They may center on the company's conduct in a given situation, for example, Union Carbide's perceived lack of response in the Bhopal diaster. If not addressed, such criticisms can lead to more significant problems, such as an internationally orchestrated boycott of products. The six-year boycott of Nestlé did not so much harm earnings as it harmed image and employee morale.

## Summary

The task of the international marketer is to seek new opportunities in the world marketplace and satisfy emerging needs through creative management of the firm's good, pricing, distribution, and promotional policies. By its very nature, marketing is the most sensitive of business functions to environmental effects and influences.

The analysis of target markets is the first of the international marketer's challenges. Potential and existing markets need to be evaluated and priorities established for each, ranging from rejection to a temporary holding position to entry. Decisions at the level of the overall marketing effort must be made with respect to the selected markets, and a plan for future expansion must be formulated. The closer that potential target markets are in terms of their geographical, cultural, and economic distance, the more attractive they typically are to the international marketer.

A critical decision in international marketing concerns the degree to which the overall marketing program should be standardized or localized. The ideal is to standardize as much as possible without compromising the basic task of marketing: satisfying the needs and wants of the target market. Many multinational marketers are adopting globalization strategies that involve the standardization of good ideas, while leaving the implementation to local entities.

The technical side of marketing management is universal, but environments require adaptation within all of the mix elements. The degree of adaptation will vary by market, good, or service marketed, and overall company objects.

## Key Terms and Concepts

| | | |
|---|---|---|
| demand pattern analysis | positioning | price escalation |
| income elasticity of demand | backward innovation | dumping |
| multiple-factor indexes | standard worldwide pricing | gray markets |
| estimation by analogy | dual pricing | arm's length price |
| input-output analysis | cost-plus method | channel design |
| gap analysis | marginal cost method | media strategy |
| concentration | market-differentiated | promotional message |
| diversification | pricing | |

## Questions for Discussion

1. Many rational reasons exist for rejecting a particular market in the early stages of screening. Such decisions are made by humans, thus some irrational reasons must exist as well. Suggest some.
2. If, indeed, the three dimensions of distance are valid, to which countries would U.S. companies initially expand? Consider the interrelationships of the distance concepts.
3. Is globalization ever a serious possibility, or is the regional approach the closest the international marketer can ever hope to get to standardization?
4. What are the possible exporter reactions to extreme foreign exchange rate fluctuations?
5. Argue for and against gray marketing.
6. What courses of action are open to an international marketer who finds all attractive intermediaries already under contract to competitors?
7. You are planning a pan-European advertising campaign with a back-to-school theme for calculators. The guideline specifies illustrating the various models sold in the market along the margins of the advertisement and using a title that suggests calculators help students to do better in school and college. What type of local adjustments do you expect to make to the campaign?
8. Benetton, the Italian manufacturer of sportswear, has been in the center of controversy ever since its "United Colors of Benetton" campaigns were launched to symbolize its commitment to "racial and multicultural harmony." Using Benetton's Web site and its gallery of advertising (**http://www.benetton.com**), assess whether shock and publicity value fit with a global image campaign.

WWW

## Recommended Readings

Czinkota, Michael R., and Ilkka A. Ronkainen. *Global Marketing Imperative: Positioning Your Company for the New World of Business.* Lincolnwood, Ill.: NTC, 1995.

Czinkota, Michael R., and Ilkka A. Ronkainen. *International Marketing.* Ft. Worth, Texas: Dryden, 1998.

Czinkota, Michael R., and Jon Woronoff. *Unlocking Japan's Market.* Chicago: Probus Publishers, 1991.

Douglas, Susan P., and C. Samuel Craig. *International Marketing Research.* Englewood Cliffs, N.J.: Prentice-Hall, 1983.

Leo Burnett. *Worldwide Advertising and Media Fact Book.* Chicago, IL: Triumph Books, 1994.

Ohmae, Kenichi. *Triad Power: The Coming Shape of Global Competition.* New York: The Free Press, 1985.

Root, Franklin. *Entry Strategies for International Markets.* Lexington, Mass.: Lexington Books, 1990.

Smith, N. Craig, and John A. Quelch. *Ethics in Marketing.* Homewood, Ill.: Irwin, 1993.

U.S. Department of Commerce. *A Basic Guide to Exporting.* Washington, D.C.: U.S. Government Printing Office, 1992

Walmsley, James. *The Development of International Markets.* Hingham, Mass.: Graham & Trotman, 1990.

Yip, George S. *Total Global Strategy.* Englewood Cliffs, N.J.: Prentice-Hall, 1992.

## Notes

1. "AMA Board Approves New Marketing Definition," *Marketing News* (March 1, 1985): 1.

2. Robert Bartels, "Are Domestic and International Marketing Dissimilar?" *Journal of Marketing* 36 (July 1968): 56–61.

3. Reijo Luostarinen, *Internationalization of the Firm* (Helsinki, Finland: The Helsinki School of Economics, 1979), 124–133.

4. Franklin R. Root, *Entry Strategies for Foreign Markets: From Domestic to International Business* (Lexington, Mass.: Lexington Books, 1990), 15–20.

5. For one of the best summaries, see Business International, *Indicators of Market Size for 117 Countries* (New York: Business International, 1992).

6. Philip Kotler, *Marketing Management: Analysis, Planning and Control* (Englewood Cliffs, N.J.: Prentice-Hall, 1984), 234.

7. Reed Moyer, "International Market Analysis," *Journal of Marketing Research* 16 (November 1968): 353–360.

8. The World Bank, *World Development Report 1993* (New York: Oxford University Press, 1993), 296.

9. J. A. Weber, "Comparing Growth Opportunities in the International Marketplace," *Management International Review* 19 (Winter 1979): 47–54.

10. Root, *Entry Strategies for Foreign Markets,* 19.

11. Igal Ayal and Jehiel Zif, "Marketing Expansion Strategies in Multinational Marketing," *Journal of Marketing* 43 (Spring 1979): 84–94.

12. Michael Rennie, "Born Global," *The McKinsey Quarterly* 4 (1993): 45–52.

13. Alice Rudolph, "Standardization Not Standard for Global Marketers," *Marketing News* (September 27, 1985): 3–4.

14. Robert Buzzell, "Can You Standardize Multinational Marketing?" *Journal of Marketing* 46 (November–December 1968): 98–104.

15. Ralph Z. Sorenson and Ulrich E. Wiechmann, "How Multinationals View Marketing Standardization," *Harvard Business Review* 53 (May–June 1975): 38–56.

16. V. Yorio, *Adapting Products for Export* (New York: The Conference Board, 1983), 1.

17. John S. Hill and Richard R. Still, "Adapting Products to LDC Tastes," *Harvard Business Review* 62 (March–April 1984): 92–101.

18. Mark Morrow, "ISO as SOP," *Export Today,* December 1996, 62–64.

19. "The Puff, the Magic, the Dragon," *The Washington Post,* September 2, 1994, B1, B3; and "Big Names Draw Fine Line on Logo Imagery," *South China Morning Post,* July 7, 1994, 3.

20. Hill and Still, "Adapting Products to LDC Tastes," 92–101.

21. "Brazilian Sweets Marketer Tastes Success in Exporting," *Advertising Age International* (September 1997): i40.

22. "Going through Customs," *Inc.* (December 1984): 180–184.

23. Bruce Seifert and John Ford, "Are Exporting Firms Modifying Their Product, Pricing and Promotion Policies?" *International Marketing Review* 6, 6 (1989): 53–68.

24. Barry Lynn, "Germany: the Packaging Environment," *Export Today* 11 (July, 1995): 58–64.

25. "Marketing Scott Rolls Out a Risky Strategy," *Business Week* (May 22, 1995): 88–89.

26. Phillip D. White and Edward W. Cundiff, "Assessing the Quality of Industrial Products," *Journal of Marketing* 42 (January 1978): 80–86.

27. Johny K. Johansson, Ilkka A. Ronkainen, and Michael R. Czinkota, "Negative Country-of-Origin Effects: The Case of the New Russia," *Journal of International Studies* 25, 1 (1994): 1–21.

28. "Detroit Beware: Japan Is Ready to Sell Luxury," *Business Week,* December 9, 1985, 114–118.

29. Ilkka A. Ronkainen, "Product Development in the Multinational Firm," *International Marketing Review* 1 (Winter 1983): 24–30.

30. "Can Ford Stay on Top?" *Business Week,* September 28, 1987, 78–88.

31. "For Levi's, a Flattering Fit Overseas," *Business Week* (November 5, 1990): 76–77.

32. Michael G. Harvey and Ilkka A. Ronkainen, "International Counterfeiters: Marketing Success without the Cost or Risk," *Columbia Journal of World Business* 20 (Fall 1985): 37–46. For worldwide piracy information, see **http://www.iipa.com** .

33. Helmut Becker, "Pricing: An International Marketing Challenge," in *International Marketing Strategy,* ed. Hans Thorelli and Helmut Becker (New York: Pergamon Press, 1980), 201–215.

34. S. Tamer Cavusgil, "Unraveling the Mystique of Export Pricing," *Business Horizons* 31 (May–June 1988): 54–63.

35. "Asian Flu Gives Medical-Equipment Firms a Headache," *The Wall Street Journal,* December 15, 1997, B4.

36. Chase Manhattan Bank, *Dynamics of Trade Finance* (New York: Chase Manhattan Bank, 1984), 10–11.

37. Steven Plaut, "Why Dumping Is Good for Us," *Fortune* (May 5, 1980): 212–222.

38. James C. Baker and John K. Ryans, "Some Aspects of International Pricing: A Neglected Area of Management Policy," *Management Decisions* (Summer 1973): 177–182.

39. Ilkka A. Ronkainen and Linda Van de Gucht, "Making a Case for Gray Markets," *Journal of Commerce,* January 6, 1987, 13A.

40. Jeffrey Arpan, "Multinational Firm Pricing in International Markets," *Sloan Management Review* 15 (Winter 1973): 1–9.

41. James Shulman, "When the Price is Wrong—By Design," *Columbia Journal of World Business* 4 (May–June 1967): 69–76.

42. "Multinationals Lose Half of Transfer Price Spats," *The Journal of Commerce* (September 4, 1997): 2a.

43. Mohammad F. Al-Eryani, Pervaiz Alam, and Syed H. Akhter, "Transfer Pricing Determinants of U.S. Multinationals," *Journal of International Business Studies* 21 (Fall 1990): 409–425.

44. Gregory L. Miles, "Unmasking Japan's Distributors," *International Business* (April 1994): 38–42.

45. Robert H. Luke, "Successful Marketing in Japan: Guidelines and Recommendations," in *Contemporary Perspectives in International Business,* ed. Harold W. Berkman and Ivan R. Vernon (Chicago, Ill.: Rand McNally, 1979), 307–315.

46. Michael R. Czinkota, "Distribution of Consumer Products in Japan," *International Marketing Review* 2 (Autumn 1985): 39–51.

47. "How to Evaluate Foreign Distributors: A *BI* Checklist," *Business International* (May 10, 1985: 145–149.

48. Julie S. Hill, "Euro, Pacific Spending Spree, *Advertising Age* (April 10, 1989): 4, 55. See also the following Web site: **http://www.zenithmedia.com** .

49. "Top Global Marketers," *Advertising Age International* (November 1997): 9.

50. Compiled from Leo Burnett, *Worldwide Advertising and Media Fact Book* (Chicago: Triumph Books, 1994).

51. Dennis Chase, "Global Marketing: The New Wave," *Advertising Age* (June 25, 1984): 49, 74.

52. The WebSite Consultancy through **http://www.twsc.co.uk** .

53. For additional information, refer to **http://www.dell.com** .

54. "Grey Interactive Shines in Light of P&G Deal," *Advertising Age* (November 11, 1996): 42–46.

55. Lou Gerstner, "Open for Business," *Leadership* 2, 2 (1997): 2–3.

56. Lewis Rose, "Before You Advertise on the Net— Check the International Marketing Laws," *Bank Marketing* (May 1996): 40–42.

57. Joseph A. Lawton, "Kodak Penetrates the European Copier Market with Customized Marketing Strategy and Product Changes," *Marketing News* (August 3, 1984): 1, 6.

58. "IBM Promotes Education," *Business Latin America* (May 24, 1993): 6–7.

# CHAPTER 15

# International Services

## LEARNING OBJECTIVES

◆ *To examine the increasingly important role of services in international business*

◆ *To understand why international trade in services is more complex than international trade in goods*

◆ *To appreciate the heightened sensitivity required for international service success*

◆ *To learn that stand-alone services are becoming more important to world trade*

◆ *To examine the competitive advantage of firms in the service sector*

## White-Collar Jobs Go Overseas

For years, workers in industrialized countries have complained about losing manufacturing jobs overseas to countries that pay lower wages than in the United States or Europe. Now Americans are discovering that U.S. companies are also taking advantage of lower wage white-collar workers abroad for service jobs that used to be done in their offices. Instead of paying someone down the hall for jobs like data entry, some U.S. firms are hiring workers in Barbados or India.

With the advent of high-speed modems and low-cost satellite and fiber-optic communications, service workers in foreign countries can sometimes deliver faster results than their American counterparts. In the field of medical records transcription, the quick turnaround can mean shorter hospital stays. For example, a doctor in a Virginia hospital can dictate a medical summary on a patient at 7:00 A.M. and have a clerk send the recorded words over high-speed data lines to a medical transcriptionist in Bangalore, India. The Indian worker then types up a transcript and sends it back to a proofreader in Virginia. By 11:00 A.M. the doctor has the paperwork back and can discharge the patient the same day. For comparison, discharge summaries processed in the hospital typically have a 72-hour turnaround time.

The quality of the work sent overseas also compares favorably with the services available in the United States. The transcriptionists in Bangalore usually have a college degree in the medical sciences, although they are paid roughly one-tenth the salary of full-time medical transcriptionists in the United States, who usually only have high school degrees. Whereas most U.S. transcription services still use 1980s-vintage word-processing programs or even sometimes typewriters to prepare paper transcripts, the Indian workers are quick to point out their Pentium-equipped computers.

As the U.S. Bureau of Labor Statistics has noted, overseas workers are performing jobs for which there is not a large enough qualified labor supply in the United States. Overseas information services jobs originally were mostly low-skilled data entry positions—processing insurance claims, credit card applications, and direct-mail responses. But today those overseas jobs are increasingly found in areas requiring more skills and education. Bangalore's boom in offshore software development is a prime example. Fortune 500 companies are hiring Indian PhDs in computer science to write software code for $9,000 a year or less.

Although the number of service sector jobs sent overseas still remains relatively small, the practice has sparked governments in several countries to form special development corporations to help attract U.S. service jobs. Barbados,

Ireland, Jamaica, the Philippines, St. Kitts, and St. Lucia have all entered the business. For many of these countries, the payoff is substantial: Barbados's largest single private employer is American Airlines' Caribbean Data Services, which has hired 1,100 people there to enter data about airline tickets.

*Source:* Mike Mills, "In the Modem World, White-Collar Jobs Go Overseas," *The Washington Post,* September 17, 1996: A1, A7.

International services are a major component of world trade. This chapter will highlight international business dimensions that are specific to services. A definition of services will be provided, and trade in services and in goods will be differentiated. The role of services in the world economy will then be explained. The chapter will discuss the opportunities and new problems that have arisen because of increasing service trade, with particular focus on the worldwide transformations of industries as a result of profound changes in the environment and in technology. The strategic responses to the transformations by both governments and firms will be explained. Finally, the chapter will outline the initial steps that firms need to undertake to offer services internationally and will look at the future of international service trade.

## Differences between Services and Products

We rarely contemplate or analyze the precise role of services in our lives. Services often accompany goods, but they are also, by themselves, an increasingly important part of the economy. One author has contrasted services and products by stating that "a good is an object, a device, a thing; a service is a deed, a performance, an effort."[1] That definition, although quite general, captures the essence of the difference between goods and services. Services tend to be more intangible, personalized, and custom-made than goods. In addition, services are the fastest growing sector in world trade and as this chapter's opening vignette shows, employment in the services sector is becoming increasingly global. These major differences add dimensions to services that are not present in goods.

**Linkage between Services and Goods**

Services may complement goods; at other times, goods may complement services. The offering of goods that are in need of substantial technological support and maintenance may be useless if no proper assurance for service can be provided. For this reason, the initial contract of sale often includes the service dimension. This practice is frequent in aircraft sales. When an aircraft is purchased, the buyer contracts not only for the physical good—namely, the plane—but often for the training of personnel, maintenance service, and the promise of continuous technological updates. Similarly, the sale of computer hardware depends on the availability of proper servicing and software. In an international setting, the proper service support can often be crucial. Particularly for newly opening markets or for goods new to market, the provision of the good alone may be insufficient. The buyer wants to be convinced that proper service backup will be provided for the good before making a commitment. In addition, communication services need to be used to inform the new market about the availability and performance of the good.

The linkage between goods and services often brings a new dimension to international business efforts. A foreign buyer, for example, may want to purchase helicopters and contract for service support over a period of ten years. If the sale involves a U.S. firm, both the helicopter and the service sale will require an export license. Such licenses, however, are issued only for an immediate sale. Therefore, over the ten years, the seller will have to apply for an export license each time service is to be provided. The issuance of a license is often dependent on the political climate, therefore, the buyer and the seller are haunted by uncertainty. As a result, sales may be lost to firms in countries that can unconditionally guarantee the long-term supply of support services.

Services can be just as dependent on goods. For example, an airline that prides itself on providing an efficient reservation system and excellent linkups with rental cars and hotel reservations could not survive if it were not for its airplanes. As a result, many offerings in the marketplace consist of a combination of goods and services. A graphic illustration of the tangible and intangible elements in the market offering of an airline is provided in Figure 15.1.

The simple knowledge that services and goods interact, however, is not enough. Successful managers must recognize that different customer groups will frequently view the service-good combination differently. The type of use and the usage conditions will affect evaluations of the market offering. For example, the intangible dimension of "on-time arrival" by airlines may be valued differently by college students than by business executives. Similarly, a twenty-minute delay will be judged differently by a passenger arriving at his or her final destination than by one who has just missed an overseas connection. As a result, adjustment possibilities in both the service and the goods areas emerge that can be used as a strategic tool to stimulate demand and increase profitability. As Figure 15.2 shows, service and goods elements may vary substantially in any market offering. The manager must identify the role of each and adjust all of them to meet the desires of the target customer group. By rating the offerings on a scale ranging from dominant tangibility to dominant intangibility, the manager can compare offerings and also generate information for subsequent market positioning strategies.

## Stand-Alone Services

Services do not have to come in unison with goods. They can compete against goods and become an alternative offering. For example, rather than buy an in-house computer, the business executive can contract computing work to a local or foreign service firm. Similarly, the purchase of a car (a good) can be converted into the purchase of a service by leasing the car from an agency.

Services by themselves can satisfy needs and wants of customers. Entertainment services such as movies or music offer leisure time enjoyment. Insurance services can protect people from financial ruin in case of a calamity.

Services may also compete against one another. As an example, a store may have the option of offering full service to customers or of converting to the

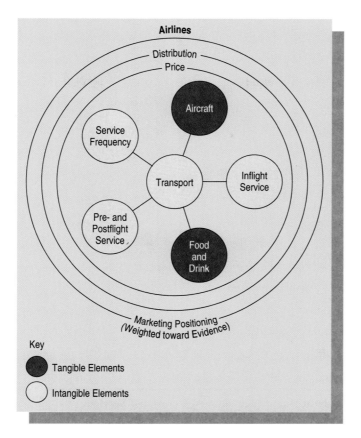

**Airlines**

Distribution
Price

Aircraft

Service Frequency

Transport

Inflight Service

Pre- and Postflight Service

Food and Drink

Marketing Positioning
(Weighted toward Evidence)

Key

● Tangible Elements

○ Intangible Elements

**FIGURE 15.1**

**Tangible and Intangible Offerings of Airlines**
*Source:* G. Lynn Shostack, "Breaking Free from Product Marketing," in *Services Marketing: Text, Cases, and Readings,* ed. Christopher H. Lovelock (Englewood Cliffs, N.J.: Prentice-Hall, Inc., 1984), 40.

self-service format. The store may provide only checkout services, with customers engaging in other activities such as selection, transportation, and sometimes even packaging and pricing.

Services differ from goods most strongly in their **intangibility:** They are frequently consumed rather than possessed. Though the intangibility of services is a primary differentiating criterion, it is not always present. For example, publishing services ultimately result in a tangible good—namely, a book or a computer disk. Similarly, construction services eventually result in a building, a subway, or a bridge. Even in those instances, however, the intangible component that leads to the final good is of major concern to both the producer of the service and the recipient of the ultimate output, because it brings with it major considerations that are non-traditional to goods.

Another major difference concerns the storing of services. Due to their nature, services are difficult to inventory. If they are not used, the "brown around the edges" syndrome tends to result in high **perishability.** Unused capacity in the form of an empty seat on an airplane, for example, becomes nonsalable quickly. Once the plane has taken off, selling an empty seat is virtually impossible—except for an in-flight upgrade from coach to first class—and the capacity cannot be stored for future use. The difficulty of inventorying services makes it troublesome to provide service back-up for peak demand. To main-

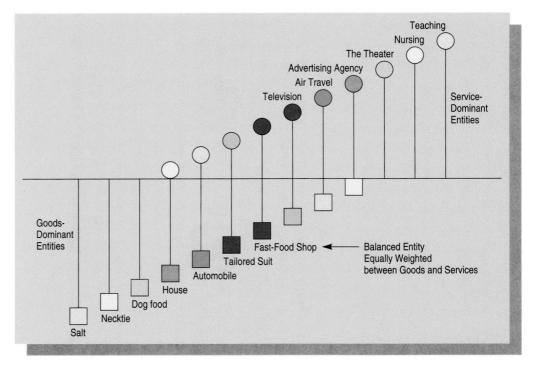

**FIGURE 15.2**

**Scale of Dominance between Goods and Services**

*Source:* Reprinted with permission from *Marketing of Services*, eds. J. Donnelly and W. George; G. Lynn Shostack, "How to Design a Service," 1981, p. 222, published by the American Marketing Association, Chicago, IL 60606.

tain **service capacity** constantly at levels necessary to satisfy peak demand would be very expensive. The business manager must therefore attempt to smooth out demand levels in order to optimize overall use of capacity.

For the services offering, the time of production is usually very close to or even simultaneous with the time of consumption. This often means close **customer involvement** in the production of services. Customers frequently either service themselves or cooperate in the delivery of services. As a result, the service provider may need to be physically present when the service is delivered. This physical presence creates both problems and opportunities, and introduces a new constraint that is seldom present in the marketing of goods. For example, close interaction with the customer requires a much greater understanding of and emphasis on the cultural dimension of each market. A good service delivered in a culturally unacceptable fashion is doomed to failure as Figure 15.3 explains. A common pattern of internationalization for service businesses is therefore to develop stand-alone business systems in each country.[2]

The close interaction with customers also points to the fact that services often are custom-made. This contradicts the desire of the firm to standardize its offering; yet at the same time, it offers the service provider an opportunity to differentiate the service. The concomitant problem is that, in order to fulfill customer expectations, **service consistency** is required. For anything offered on-line, however, consistency is difficult to maintain over the long run. Therefore, the human element in the service offering takes on a much greater role than in the offering of goods. Errors may enter the system, and unpredictable individual influences may affect the outcome of the service delivery. The issue of quality control affects the provider as well as the recipient of services because efforts to increase control through uniform service may sometimes be perceived by customers as the limiting of options. It may therefore have a negative market effect.[3]

Buyers have more difficulty observing and evaluating services than goods. This is particularly true when the shopper tries to choose intelligently among service providers. Even when sellers of services are willing and able to provide more **market transparency,** the buyer's problem is complicated: Customers receiving the same service may use it differently. This aspect of service heterogeneity results in services that may never be the same from one delivery to another. For example, the counseling by a teacher, even if it is provided on the same day by the same person, may vary substantially depending on the student. But over time, even for the same student, the counseling may change. As a result, service offerings are not directly comparable, which makes quality measurements quite challenging. Therefore, service quality may vary for each delivery. Nonetheless, maintaining service quality is vitally important, since the reputation of the service provider plays an overwhelming role in the customer's choice process.

Services often require entirely new forms of distribution. Traditional channels frequently are multitiered and long and therefore slow. They often cannot be used at all because of the perishability of services. A weather news service, for example, either reaches its audience quickly or rapidly loses value. As a result, direct delivery and short distribution channels are required for international services. When they do not exist, service providers need to be distribution innovators to reach their market.

Increasingly, many services are "footloose," in that they are not tied to any specific location. Advances in technology make it possible for firms to separate production and consumption of services. As a result, labor-intensive service performance can be moved anywhere around the world where qualified, low-cost labor is plentiful. As communication technology further improves, services such as teaching, medical diagnosis, or bank account management can originate from any point in the world and reach customers around the globe.

The unique dimensions of services exist in both international and domestic settings, but their impact has greater importance for the international manager. For example, the perishability of a service, which may be a mere obstacle in domestic business, may become a major barrier internationally because of the longer distances involved. Similarly, quality control for international services may be much more difficult because of different service uses, changing expectations, and varying national regulations.

Services are delivered directly to the user and are therefore frequently much more sensitive to cultural factors than are products. Their influence on the individual abroad may be welcomed or greeted with hostility. For example, countries that place a strong emphasis on cultural identity have set barriers inhibiting market penetration by foreign films. France is leading a major effort within the European Union, for instance, to cap the volume of U.S.-produced films to obtain more playing time for French movies.

## The Role of Services in the U.S. Economy

Since the Industrial Revolution, the United States has seen itself as a primary international competitor in the production of goods. In the past few decades, however, the U.S. economy has increasingly become a service economy, as Figure 15.4 shows. The service sector now produces 75 percent of the GNP and employs 79 percent of the workforce. The major segments that comprise the

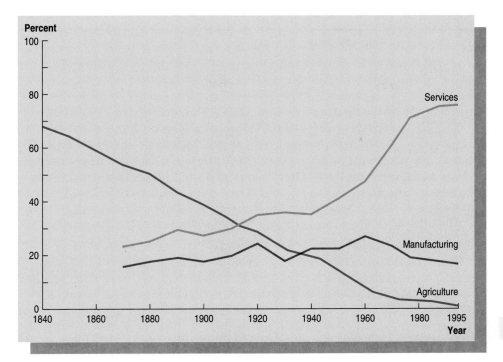

**FIGURE 15.4**

**Employment in Industrial Sectors as a Percentage of the Total Labor Force**
*Sources:* Quarterly Labor Force Statistics, Paris, Organization for Economic Cooperation and Development, 1996, No. 2; J. B. Quinn, "The Impacts of Technology on the Service Sector," *Technology and Global Industry: Companies and Nations in the World Economy* (Washington, D.C.: National Academy of Sciences, 1987).

service sector are communications, transportation, public utilities, finance, insurance and real estate, wholesale and retail businesses, government, and "services" (a diverse category including business services, personal services, and professional and health services). The service sector accounts for most of the growth in total nonfarm employment.

Only a limited segment of the total range of U.S. services is sold internationally. Federal, state, and local government employees, for example, sell few of their services to foreigners. U.S. laundries and restaurants only occasionally service foreign tourists. Many service industries that do sell abroad often have at their disposal large organizations, specialized technology, or advanced professional expertise. Strength in these characteristics has enabled the United States to become the world's largest exporter of services. Total U.S. services exported grew from $14 billion in 1970 to more than $253 billion in 1997.

Global service trade has had very beneficial results for many U.S. firms. Citibank, for example, receives 65 percent of its total revenues from foreign operations. Most of the large management consulting firms derive more than half of their revenue from international sources. The largest advertising agencies serve customers around the globe, some of them in 107 countries. Table 15.1 shows how many countries are served by these agencies and how many accounts they service in ten or more countries. Interesting is the fact that six of the firms have the term *worldwide* in their name. After many years of increasing activity by foreign insurance companies in the United States, U.S. firms are now aggressively beginning to enter the $1.4 trillion world insurance market. These facts demonstrate that many service firms have become truly international and formidable in size.

**TABLE 15.1**

**The Globalization of Advertising Agencies**

| Agency | Countries Served | Single Accounts in 10+ Countries |
|---|---|---|
| Ammirati Puris Lintas | 58 | 12 |
| Worldwide | 68 | 23 |
| Bates Worldwide | 69 | 17 |
| DDB Needham Worldwide | 86 | 21 |
| D'Arcy Masius Benton & Bowles | 98 | 15 |
| Grey Advertising | 78 | 43 |
| J. Walter Thompson Co. | 67 | 25 |
| Leo Burnett Co. | 65 | 14 |
| McCann Erickson Worldwide | 107 | 49 |
| Ogilvy & Mather Worldwide | 79 | 26 |
| Saatchi & Saatchi Advertising Worldwide | 93 | 21 |
| Young & Rubicam Advertising | 64 | 24 |

*Source:* Laurel Wentz and Sasha Emmons, "'AAI' Charts Show Yearly Growth, Consolidation," *Advertising Age International* (September, 1996) 133.

However, dramatic global growth is not confined to U.S. firms. The import of services into the United States is also increasing dramatically. In 1997, the United States imported almost $168 billion worth of services. Competition in global services is rising rapidly at all levels. Hong Kong, Singapore, and Western Europe are increasingly active in service industries such as banking, insurance, and advertising. Years ago, U.S. construction firms could count on a virtual monopoly on large-scale construction projects. Today, firms from South Korea, Italy, and other countries are taking a major share of the international construction business. The United States has also long been recognized as the leader in software development; yet, as Global Perspective 15.1 indicates, this lead may be challenged soon. The overall result of these developments is that the U.S. share of global service trade is estimated to have declined in relative terms—from 25 to 20 percent of the world market—within a decade.

## The Role of Global Services in the World Economy

The United States is not unique in its conversion to a service economy. Similar changes have taken place globally, and several developing countries have service sectors that produce more than 50 percent of their gross domestic products. At the present time, services trade is taking place mainly among the industrialized countries. However, this trend appears to be changing

The economies of developing countries have traditionally first established a strong agricultural and then a manufacturing sector to meet basic needs such

**INDIAN EXPORTS: NOT JUST CARPETS BUT SOFTWARE**

Tata Consultancy Services, the leading software maker in India, sold in just one year 11,000 copies of a $140 accounting program for personal computers. That is remarkable, because it shows that the world's second most populous nation is developing a viable domestic software market. Such a development is putting India in a position to compete in global software markets.

India's domestic software market grew by 49 percent from 1996 to 1997. This growth is helping the hundreds of local software houses to hone their development and marketing skills at home so they can sell abroad. India's annual software exports are now running at $1.1 billion, up from just $100 million at the beginning of the 1990s. Although it is only a fraction of the $250 billion global software market, the exports are growing about 50 percent per year. With such growth figures, India's over 2.5 million computer and software professionals are finding opportunities to advance their careers without relocating abroad.

When the World Bank surveyed 150 prominent U.S. and European hardware and software manufacturers, India's programmers were ranked first out of eight countries for both on-site and offshore software development, ahead of Ireland, Israel, Mexico, and Singapore. In fact, one in four software engineers in the world is of Indian origin. With average annual programmer salaries of about $3,000, quality software production in India costs much less than what it would cost in the United States. No wonder multinationals like IBM, Motorola, and Honeywell have moved into the country's technology parks, attracted to the highly skilled, but low-wage labor force.

*Sources: John Zubrzycki, "Mastering Software Helps India Youths Snag Foreign Jobs,"* The Christian Science Monitor, *November 13, 1997, p. 1; "Country Buzz,"* Computers Today *(May 1, 1997): 14–33; Sunita Wadekar Bhargava, "Software from India? Yes, it's for Real,"* Business Week *(January 18, 1993): 77.*

as food and shelter before venturing into the services sector. Some developing countries, such as Mexico, Singapore, Hong Kong, Bermuda, and the Bahamas, are steering away from the traditional economic development pattern and are concentrating on developing strong service sectors.[4] The reasons vary from a lack of natural resources with which to develop agricultural and/or manufacturing sectors to recognition of the strong demand for services and the ability to provide them through tourism and a willing, skilled, and inexpensive labor force. As a result, it is anticipated that services trade will continue to grow. However, as more countries enter the sector, the global services business will become more competitive.

## Global Transformations in the Services Sector

Two major factors, environmental and technological change, account for the dramatic rise in services trade. One key environmental change has been the reduction of government regulation of service industries. In the early 1980s, many governments adopted the view that reduced government interference in the marketplace would enhance competition. As a result, new players have entered the marketplace. Some service sectors have benefited and others have suffered from this withdrawal of government intervention. Regulatory changes were initially thought to have primarily domestic effects, but they have rapidly

Istanbul, Turkey, at the crossroads of Europe and Asia, is served by a Motorola digital cellular telephone system. Motorola has contracts worldwide for GSM systems. (Global System for Mobile Communications).

*Source:* Courtesy of Motorola, Inc.

spread internationally. For example, the 1984 **deregulation** of the U.S. telecommunication giant AT&T has given rise to competition not only in the United States. Japan's telecommunication monopoly, NT&T, was deregulated in 1985 and European deregulation followed in the mid-1990s.

Similarly, deregulatory efforts in the transportation sector have had international repercussions. New air carriers have entered the market to compete against established trunk carriers and have done so successfully by pricing their services differently, both nationally and internationally. Obviously, a British airline can count only to a limited extent on government support to remain competitive with new, low-priced fares offered by other carriers also serving the British market. The deregulatory movement has fostered new competition and new competitive practices. Many of these changes resulted in lower prices, stimulating demand and leading to a rise in the volume of international services trade.

Another major environmental change has been the decreased regulation of service industries by their service groups. For example, business practices in fields such as health care, law, and accounting are becoming increasingly competitive and aggressive. New economic realities require firms in these industries to search for new ways to attract market share and expand their markets. International markets are one frequently untapped possibility for market expansion and have therefore become a prime target for such firms.

Technological advancement is the second major change that has taken place. Increasingly, progress in technology is offering new ways of doing business and is permitting businesses to expand their horizons internationally. Through computerization, for instance, service exchanges that previously would have been prohibitively expensive are now feasible. As an example, Ford Motor Company uses one major computer system to carry out new car designs simultaneously in the United States and in Europe. This practice not only lowers expenditures on hardware and permits better utilization of existing equipment but also allows design teams based in different countries to interact closely and produce a car that can be successful in multiple markets. Of course, this development could take place only after advances in data transmission procedures. Technology has also sharply reduced the **cost of communication.** Fiberoptic cables have made the cost of international links trivial. A minute on a transatlantic cable laid forty years ago cost $2.44, but now the same amount of time costs barely more than one cent. Although that figure does not allow for billing, marketing, and local network access costs, it does illustrate the revolution in the economics of international calls.[5]

Another result of technological advancement is that service industry expansion is not confined to those services that are labor intensive and therefore better performed in areas of the world where labor possesses a comparative advantage. Rather, technology-intensive services are becoming the sunrise industries of the next century. Increasingly, firms in a variety of industries can reconfigure their service delivery in order to escape the location-bound dimension. Banks, for example, can offer their services through automatic teller machines or telephone banking. Consultants can advise via videoconferences and teachers can teach the world through multimedia classrooms. Physicians can perform operations in a distant country if proper computer linkages can drive roboticized medical equipment.

As a result, many service providers have the opportunity to become truly global players. To them, the traditional international market barrier of distance no longer matters. Knowledge, the core of many service activities, can offer a global reach without requiring a local presence. Service providers therefore may have only a minor need for local establishment, since they can operate without premises. You don't have to be there to do business! The effect of such a shift in service activities will be major. Insurance and bank palaces in the downtowns of the world may soon become obsolete. Talented service providers will see the demand for their performance increase, while less capable ones will suffer from increased competition. Most importantly, consumers and society will have a much broader range and quality of service choices available, often at a lower cost.

## Problems in International Service Trade

Together with the increase in the importance of service trade, new problems have emerged in the service sector. Many of these problems have been characterized as affecting mainly the negotiations between nations, but they are of sufficient importance to firms engaged in international activities to merit a brief review.

### Data Collection Problems

The data collected on service trade are often sketchy. Service transactions are often invisible statistically as well as physically. For example, the trip abroad of a consultant for business purposes may be hard to track and measure. The interaction between variables such as citizenship, residency, location of the trans-

## Services as a Portion of Gross Domestic Product

Services as a percent of GDP

- 60% to 85%
- 40% to 60%
- 20% to 40%
- 0% to 20%
- No current data available

Source: *The World Factbook 1997–98*

action, and who or what (if anything) crosses national boundaries further contribute to the complexity of services transactions. Imagine that an Irish citizen working for a Canadian financial consulting firm headquartered in Sweden advises an Israeli citizen living in India on the management of funds deposited in a Swiss bank. Determining the export and import dimensions of such a services transaction is not easy.[6]

The fact that governments have precise data on the number of trucks exported down to the last bolt but little information on reinsurance flows reflects past governmental inattention to services. Only recently has it been recognized that the income generated and the jobs created through the sale of services abroad are just as important as income and jobs resulting from the production and exportation of goods. Consequently, estimates of services trade vary widely. Total actual volume of services trade may actually be much larger than the amount shown by official statistics.

When considering the dimension of the problem of data collection on services in industrialized countries, with their sophisticated data gathering and information systems, it is easy to imagine how many more problems are encountered in countries lacking such elaborate systems and unwilling to allocate funds for them. Insufficient knowledge and information have led to a lack of transparency, making it difficult for nations either to gauge or to influence services trade. As a result, regulations are often put into place without precise information as to their repercussions on actual trade performance.

## U.S. Disincentives to the Offering of International Services

Despite its commitment to free trade, the United States has erected and maintained major barriers to international services. These disincentives affect both inbound and outbound services. Barriers to services destined for the U.S. market result mainly from regulatory practices. The fields of banking, insurance, and accounting provide some examples. These industries are regulated at both federal and state levels, and the regulations often pose a formidable barrier to potential entrants from abroad.

The chief complaint of foreign countries is not that the United States discriminates against foreign service providers, but rather that the United States places more severe restrictions on them than do foreign countries. The barriers are, of course, a reflection of the decision-making process within the U.S. domestic economy and are unlikely to change in the near future. A coherent approach toward international commerce in services is hardly likely to emerge from the disparate decisions of agencies such as the Interstate Commerce Commission (ICC), the Federal Communications Commission (FCC), the Securities and Exchange Commission (SEC), and the many licensing agencies at the state level.

## Global Regulations of Services

Global obstacles to service trade can be categorized into two major types: barriers to entry and problems in performing services abroad.

Barriers to entry are often explained by reference to "national security" and "economic security." For example, the impact of banking on domestic economic activity is given as a reason why banking should be carried out only by nationals or indeed should be operated entirely under government control.

Sometimes the protection of service users is cited, particularly of bank depositors and insurance policyholders. Another justification used for barriers is the infant-industry argument: "With sufficient time to develop on our own, we can compete in world markets." Often, however, this argument is used simply to prolong the ample licensing profits generated by restricted entry. Yet, defining a barrier to services is not always easy. For example, Taiwan gives an extensive written examination to prospective accountants (as do most countries) to ensure that licensed accountants are qualified to practice. Naturally, the examination is given in Chinese. The fact that few German accountants, for example, read and write Chinese and hence are unable to pass the examination does not necessarily constitute a barrier to trade in accountancy services.[7]

Service companies also encounter difficulties once they have achieved access to the local market. One reason is that rules and regulations based on tradition may inhibit innovation. A more important reason is that governments pursue social objectives through national regulations. The distinction between **discriminatory** and **nondiscriminatory regulations** is of primary importance here. Regulations that impose larger operating costs on foreign service providers than on the local competitors, that provide subsidies to local firms only, or that deny competitive opportunities to foreign suppliers are a proper cause for international concern. The problem of discrimination becomes even more acute when foreign firms face competition from government-owned or government-controlled enterprises. On the other hand, nondiscriminatory regulations may be inconvenient and may hamper business operations, but they offer less cause for international criticism. Yet, such national regulations can be key inhibitors for service innovations. For example, in Japan, pharmaceuticals cannot be sold outside of a licensed pharmacy. Similarly, travel arrangements can only be made within a registered travel office and banking can only be done during banking hours. As a result, innovations offered by today's communications technology cannot be brought to bear in these industries.[8]

All of these regulations make it difficult for international services to penetrate world markets. At the governmental level, services frequently are not recognized as a major facet of world trade or are viewed with suspicion because of a lack of understanding, and barriers to entry often result. To make progress in tearing them down, much educational work needs to be done.

In a major breakthrough in the Uruguay Round, the major GATT participants agreed to conduct services trade negotiations parallel with goods negotiations. The negotiations resulted in 1995 in the forging of a **General Agreement on Trade in Services (GATS)** as part of the World Trade Organization, the first multilateral, legally enforceable agreement covering trade and investment in the services sector. Similar to earlier agreements in the goods sector, GATS provides for most-favored-nation treatment, national treatment, transparency in rule making, and the free flow of payments and transfers. Market-access provisions restrict the ability of governments to limit competition and new-market entry. In addition, sectoral agreements were made for the movement of personnel, telecommunications, and aviation. However, in several sectors, such as entertainment, no agreement was obtained. In addition, many provisions, due to their newness, are very narrow. Therefore, future negotiations have been agreed upon, which, at five-year intervals, will attempt to improve free trade in services.[9]

## Corporate Involvement in International Service Trade

Although many firms are active in the international service arena, others do not perceive their existing competitive advantage. Numerous services that are efficiently performed in the home market may have great potential for internationalization.

Financial institutions can offer some functions very competitively internationally in the field of banking services. U.S. banks possess advantages in fields such as mergers and acquisitions, securities sales, and asset management. Banks in Europe and Japan are boosting their leadership through large assets and capital bases.

Construction, design, and **engineering services** also have great international potential. Providers of these services can achieve economies of scale not only for machinery and material but also in areas such as personnel management and the overall management of projects. Particularly for international projects that are large scale and long term, the experience advantage weighs heavily in favor of international firms.

**Insurance services** can be sold internationally by firms knowledgeable about underwriting, risk evaluation, and operations. Firms offering legal and accounting services can aid their clients abroad through support activities; they can also help foreign firms and countries improve business and governmental operations. Knowledge of computer operations, data manipulations, data transmission, and data analysis is insufficiently exploited internationally by many small and medium-sized firms.

Similarly, **communication services** have substantial future international opportunities. For example, firms experienced in the areas of videotext, home banking, and home shopping can find international success, particularly where geographic obstacles make the establishment of retail outlets cumbersome and expensive. Alternatively, global communication services, as shown in Figure 15.5, can greatly expand the reach of corporations.

Many institutions in the educational and the corporate sectors have developed expertise in **teaching services.** They are very knowledgeable in training and motivation as well as in the teaching of operational, managerial, and theoretical issues, yet have largely concentrated their work in their domestic markets. It is time to take education global! Too much good and important knowledge is not made available to broad audiences. More knowledge must be communicated, be it through distance learning, study and teaching abroad, or attracting foreign students into the domestic market. The latter option can spur a service industry in itself, as Global Perspective 15.2 shows.

Management **consulting services** can be provided by firms and individuals to the many countries and corporations in need of them. Of particular value is management expertise in areas where many developing economies need most help, such as transportation and logistics. Major opportunities also exist for industries that deal with societal problems. For example, firms that develop environmentally safe products or produce pollution-control equipment can find new markets, as nations around the world increase their awareness of and concern about the environment and tighten their laws. Similarly, advances in health

**Typical International Services**

**FIGURE 15.5**

**An Advertisement for an International Communications Service**
Source: Courtesy of AT&T.

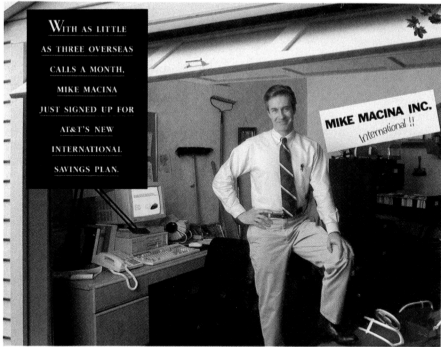

WITH AS LITTLE
AS THREE OVERSEAS
CALLS A MONTH,
MIKE MACINA
JUST SIGNED UP FOR
AT&T'S NEW
INTERNATIONAL
SAVINGS PLAN.

MIKE MACINA INC.
International !!

**AT&T INTRODUCES THE INTERNATIONAL BUSINESS ALTERNATIVE, A SAVINGS PLAN THAT'S SPECIFICALLY DESIGNED FOR SMALL BUSINESS.** There's no other overseas calling plan like it. With the AT&T International Business Alternative, businesses that make as little as three international calls a month will get the kind of discounts bigger companies get.

That means even start-up companies like Mike Macina Inc. can enjoy savings of up to 10% whenever they dash off faxes or make quick calls around the world.

So they can make more of the kinds of calls needed to secure orders and solidify overseas business relationships.

The plan also lets you save when you call the most: during your business hours. And includes just two calling periods: prime and non-prime.

We're so sure this new alternative stacks up against anything the competition has to offer, we invite you to call **1 800 222-0900, ext. 2736** now and discover just how your business can start saving on overseas calls today.* The new International Business Alternative.

**A World of Help™ from AT&T.**

*Standby charges will apply. IBA includes your subscription to applicable Small Business Options Plan for domestic and international calling. Pending tariff effectiveness. © 1992 AT&T

care or new knowledge in combating AIDS offer major opportunities for global service success.

**Tourism** also represents a major service export. Every time foreign citizens come to a country and spend their funds, the current account effect is that of an export. Measured in current dollars, worldwide tourism receipts have tripled in the past ten years to $450 billion, making this particular service one of the most important ones in the world.[10] Global Perspective 15.3 demonstrates the significance of tourism.

An attractive international service mix might also be achieved by pairing the strengths of different partners. For example, information technology from one country can be combined with the financial resources of other countries. The strengths of the partners can then be used to offer maximum benefits to the international community.

Combining international advantages in services may ultimately result in the development of an even more drastic comparative lead. For example, the

## A New Services Industry: Finding Basketball Players

**T**all kids in countries around the world are finding golden opportunities on American basketball courts. The number of foreign players on U.S. college and professional basketball teams has recently jumped from 144 to 243 in a four-year period, and American recruiters can't seem to get enough of the foreign imports. Hakeem Olajuwon, an NBA star from Nigeria, has achieved the status of folk hero among many fans around the globe. Many credit his success with the current rush to recruit players from abroad.

Stiff competition for the tallest players has even led to recruiting foreign players at younger levels of the sport; high schools commonly use foreign exchange programs to fortify their teams with international talent. High school coaches are linked with foreign players through middlemen, like the Nigerian lawyer, Toyin Sonoiki, who spent $500,000 to send nine players to U.S. schools.

The role of middlemen is crucial in obtaining visas for the students. Another Nigerian lawyer, Lloyd Ukwu, lives in Washington, D.C., and recruits on business trips back home. He started helping young Nigerians obtain U.S. visas in 1988. After meeting some players on a trip to Nigeria, he asked an assistant basketball coach at American University to write invitations for eight Nigerian players to visit the United States, and these letters were influential in helping them win visas. Word spread about Ukwu's recruiting efforts, and soon other universities were using his services.

The internationalization of the sport has changed the jobs of many American coaches and recruiters. For years, college recruiting has used tip sheets to describe U.S. high school players, but now there is one recruiting service that gives the scoop on foreign players as well. Dale Mock, a Georgia elementary-school physical-education teacher, runs International Scouting Service, a five-year-old enterprise. His tip sheets give subscribers the details about foreign players and contact information for $300 a year. Although he hasn't yet quit his day job, his subscriber list is up to 100, from a start of only 20 his first year. Dale Brown, Louisiana State's former coach, described the internationalization of the recruiting scene: "In the 1960s, I would go to the European championships, to the Asian games and all the rest—and I was the only American. Now, so many Americans are there it's like being in Grand Central Station."

*Source: Marc Fisher and Ken Denlinger, "The Market for Imports is Booming," The Washington Post, March 28, 1997, C1.*

United States has an international head start in such areas as high technology, information gathering, information processing, information analysis, and teaching. Ultimately, the major thrust of U.S. international services might not be to provide these service components individually but rather to ensure that, based on a combination of competitive resources, better decisions are made. If better decision making is transferable to a wide variety of international situations, this in itself might become the overriding future comparative advantage of the United States in the international market.

Management consulting services can be provided by firms to institutions and corporations around the globe. Of particular value is management expertise in areas where firms possess global leadership, be it in manufacturing or process activities. For example, companies with highly refined transportation or logistics activities can sell their management experience abroad.

## Starting to Offer Services Internationally

For services that are delivered mainly in support of or in conjunction with goods, the most sensible approach for the international novice is to follow the path of the good. For years, many large accounting and banking firms have done this by determining where their major multinational clients have set up new operations and then following them. Smaller service providers who sup-

## TOURISM DOWN UNDER

**A**ustralia is selling itself as a "country of surprises" in its bid to become the most popular vacation spot for Japanese tourists. In attracting nearly a million Japanese tourists a year, Australia has come a long way from the rift World War II created between the two countries. Although veteran's groups in Australia are still embittered by memories of mistreatment of Australian prisoners of war captured by the Japanese, today's Japanese and Australian officials see the countries developing a new partnership based on trade.

Hawaii frowns on this trend; starting in the early 1990s, it enjoyed a yearly expansion of Japanese tourism, but the pace has started to level off as Japanese tourists discover Australia. Hawaii reports that Japanese visitors spend more than $11 billion a year and add nearly $850 million in tax revenues to state coffers, accounting for nearly 35 percent of the total. But for the Japanese, the two destinations have competing attractions. It takes the same eight hours to fly from Tokyo to Honolulu or to the northern Australian beach resorts.

Price can play a major role for attracting tourists to one destination over the other. Australia's government is working with Japan to reduce high air fares between the two countries. In fact, the role of government in strengthening the trade is significant; both countries want to solidify their new partnership by encouraging the tourism business. Current trade between Australia and Japan consists mostly of Australian natural resource exports such as coal, minerals, and wheat and Japanese exports of finished products like laptops and cars. These two countries, serving as the north and south anchors of the western Pacific, are discovering that they rely on each other more as major parts of the world are swallowed up in trading blocs like the European Union and the North American Free Trade Association.

The increase in Japanese tourism to Australia has certainly been dramatic. In 1980, only one in 125 Japanese tourists ventured to Australia, whereas by 1996 the number had risen to one out of twenty Japanese visitors abroad. Australians are devising clever tour packages to entice Japanese visitors, ranging from honeymoon packages to tours of ocean farms that cultivate bluefin tuna, a popular export to Japan. South Australia and other states also fly in Japanese travel executives and journalists with the hope that they will spread the word about Australia's relaxation spots.

*Source: Clyde H. Farnsworth, "Can You Say 'G'day, Mate' In Japanese?"* **The New York Times,** *April 19, 1997, Business pp 1, 25.*

ply manufacturing firms can determine where the manufacturing firms are operating internationally. Ideally, of course, it would be possible to follow clusters of manufacturers abroad to obtain economies of scale internationally while simultaneously looking for entirely new client groups.

Service providers whose activities are independent from goods need a different strategy. These individuals and firms must search for market situations abroad that are similar to the domestic market. Such a search should be concentrated in their area of expertise. For example, a design firm learning about construction projects abroad can investigate the possibility of rendering its design services. Similarly, a management consultant learning about the plans of a country or firm to computerize its operations can explore the possibility of overseeing a smooth transition from manual to computerized activities. What is required is the understanding that similar problems are likely to occur in similar situations.

Another opportunity consists of identifying and understanding points of transition abroad. If, for example, new transportation services are introduced in a country, an expert in containerization may wish to consider whether to offer his or her service to improve the efficiency of the new system.

Leads for international service opportunities can also be gained by keeping informed about international projects sponsored by domestic organizations

such as the U.S. Agency for International Development or the Trade and Development Agency, as well as international organizations such as the United Nations, the International Finance Corporation, or the World Bank. Frequently, such projects are in need of support through services. Overall, the international service provider needs to search for similar situations, similar problems, or scenarios requiring similar solutions to formulate an effective international expansion strategy.

## Strategic Indications

To be successful in the international service offering, the manager must first determine the nature and the aim of the services-offering core—that is, whether the service will be aimed at people or at things and whether the service act in itself will result in tangible or intangible actions. Table 15.2 provides examples of such a classification strategy that will help the manager to better determine the position of the services effort.

During this determination, the manager must consider other tactical variables that have an impact on the preparation of the service offering. For example, in conducting research for services, the measurement of capacity and delivery efficiency often remains highly qualitative rather than quantitative. In communication and promotional efforts, the intangibility of the service reduces the manager's ability to provide samples. This makes communicating the service offered much more difficult than communicating an offer for a good. Brochures or catalogs explaining services often must show a proxy for the service to provide the prospective customer with tangible clues. A cleaning service, for instance, can show a picture of an individual removing trash or clean-

**TABLE 15.2**

### Understanding the Nature of the Service Act

| Nature of the Service Act | Direct Recipient of the Service | |
|---|---|---|
| | **People** | **Things** |
| **Tangible Actions** | **Services directed at people's bodies:**<br>Health care<br>Passenger transportation<br>Beauty salons<br>Exercise clinics<br>Restaurants<br>Haircutting | **Services directed at goods and other physical possessions:**<br>Freight transportation<br>Industrial equipment repair and maintenance<br>Janitorial services<br>Laundry and dry cleaning services<br>Landscaping/lawn care<br>Veterinary care |
| **Intangible Actions** | **Services directed at people's minds:**<br>Education<br>Broadcasting<br>Information services<br>Theaters<br>Museums | **Services directed at intangible assets:**<br>Banking<br>Legal services<br>Accounting<br>Securities<br>Insurance |

*Source:* Christopher H. Lovelock, *Services Marketing,* 3d ed. (Upper Saddle River, N.J.: Prentice-Hall, Inc., 1996), 29.

ing a window. However, the picture will not fully communicate the performance of the service. Service exporters have three ways to gain credibility abroad: providing objective verification of their capabilities—perhaps through focusing on the company's professional license or certification by international organizations; providing personal guarantees of performance, including referrals and testimonials by satisfied customers; and cultivating a professional image through public appearances at international trade events or conferences and promotional materials such as a Web site.[11] Due to the different needs and requirements of individual consumers, the manager must also pay attention to the two-way flow of communication. In the service area, mass communication often must be supported by intimate one-on-one follow-up.

The role of personnel deserves special consideration in international service delivery. The customer interface is intense, therefore, proper provisions need to be made for training of personnel both domestically and internationally. Major emphasis must be placed on appearance. Most of the time the person delivering the service—rather than the service itself—will communicate the spirit, value, and attitudes of the service corporation. Since the service person is both the producer as well as the marketer of the service, recruitment and training techniques must focus on dimensions such as customer relationship management and image projection as well as competence in the design and delivery of the service.[12]

This close interaction with the consumer will also have organizational implications. While tight control over personnel may be desired, the individual interaction that is required points toward the need for an international decentralization of service delivery. This, in turn, requires delegation of large amounts of responsibility to individuals and service "subsidiaries" and requires a great deal of trust in all organizational units. This trust, of course, can be greatly enhanced through proper methods of training and supervision. Sole ownership also helps strengthen this trust. Research has shown that service firms, in their international expansion, tend to greatly prefer the establishment of full-control ventures. Only when costs escalate and the company-specific advantage diminishes will service firms seek out shared-control ventures.[13]

The areas of pricing and financing require special attention. Because services cannot be stored, much greater responsiveness to demand fluctuation must exist, and therefore greater pricing flexibility must be maintained. At the same time, flexibility is countered by the desire to provide transparency for both the seller and the buyer of services in order to foster an ongoing relationship. The intangibility of services also makes financing more difficult. Frequently, even financial institutions with large amounts of international experience are less willing to provide financial support for international services than for products. The reasons are that the value of services is more difficult to assess, service performance is more difficult to monitor, and services are difficult to repossess. Therefore, customer complaints and difficulties in receiving payments are much more troublesome for a lender to evaluate in the area of services than for goods.

Finally, the distribution implications of international services must be considered. Usually, short and direct channels are required. Within these channels, closeness to the customer is of overriding importance to understand what the customer really wants, to trace the use of the service, and to aid the customer in obtaining a truly tailor-made service.

## Summary

Services are taking on an increasing importance in international trade. They need to be considered separately from trade in merchandise because they no longer simply complement goods. Often, goods complement services or are in competition with them. Service attributes such as their intangibility, their perishability, their custom design, and their cultural sensitivity frequently make international trade in services more complex than trade in goods.

Services play an increasing role in the global economy. International growth and competition in this sector have begun to outstrip that of merchandise trade and are likely to intensify in the future. Even though services are unlikely to replace production, the sector will account for the shaping of new competitive advantages internationally.

The many service firms now operating only domestically need to investigate the possibility of going global. Historical patterns of service providers following manufacturers abroad have become partially obsolete as stand-alone services become more important to world trade. Management must therefore assess its vulnerability to service competition from abroad and explore opportunities to provide its services internationally.

## Key Terms and Concepts

intangibility

perishability

service capacity

customer involvement

service consistency

market transparency

cost of communication

deregulation

discriminatory and
  nondiscriminatory
  regulations

General Agreement on
  Trade in Services
  (GATS)

engineering services

insurance services

communication
  services

teaching services

consulting services

## Questions for Discussion

1. Discuss the major reasons for the growth of international services.
2. How does the international sale of services differ from the sale of goods?
3. What are some of the international business implications of service intangibility?
4. What are some ways for a firm to expand its services internationally?
5. Some predict that "the main future U.S. international service will be to offer better decisions." Do you agree? Why or why not?
6. How can a firm in a developing country participate in the international services boom?
7. Which services would you expect to migrate abroad in the next decade? Why?
8. Determine the ten leading exporters and importers of commercial services and their world market share (use the WTO international trade data found on their Web site, **www.wto.org**).
9. What are the underlying principles of the General Agreement on Trade in Services (use the WTO Web site's section on services, **www.wto.org**)?
10. Using data from the Department of Commerce's Bureau of Economic Analysis (**www.bea.doc.gov**), determine the top ten types of services exports and imports for the United States.

## Recommended Readings

Aharoni, Yair. *Coalitions and Competition: The Globalization of Professional Business Services.* London and New York: Routledge, 1993.

Bateson, John E. G. *Managing Services Marketing.* 3d ed. Fort Worth, Tex.: Dryden Press, 1995.

Hoekman, Bernard M. *Liberalizing Trade in Services.* Washington, D.C.: The World Bank, 1994.

Kostecki, Michel, and András Fehérváry, eds. *Services in Transition Economies: Business Options for Trade and Investment.* Oxford: Pergamon, 1996.

Lovelock, Christopher H. *Services Marketing.* 3d ed. Upper Saddle River, N.J.: Prentice-Hall, 1996.

McKee, David L., and Don E. Garner. *Accounting Services, The International Economy and Third World Development.* New York: Praeger, 1992.

Organization for Economic Co-operation and Development. *International Trade in Professional Services: Advancing Liberalisation Through Regulatory Reform.* Paris: OECD, 1997.

## Note

1. Leonard L. Berry, "Services Marketing Is Different," in *Services Marketing,* ed. Christopher H. Lovelock (Englewood Cliffs, N.J.: Prentice-Hall, 1984), 30.

2. *Winning in the World Market* (Washington, D.C.: American Business Conference, November 1987), 17.

3. G. Lynn Shostack, "Service Positioning through Structural Change," *Journal of Marketing* 51 (January 1987): 38.

4. Allen Sinai and Zaharo Sofianou, "Service Sectors in Developing Countries: Some Exceptions to the Rule," *The Service Economy,* July 1990, 13.

5. "Down with Distance," *The Economist* (September 13, 1997): p. 21.

6. Terry Clark, Daniel Rajaratnam, and Timothy Smith, "Toward a Theory of International Services: Marketing Intangibles in a World of Nations," *Journal of International Marketing* 4, 2 (1996): 9–28.

7. Dorothy I. Riddle, *Key LDCs: Trade in Services,* American Graduate School of International Studies, Glendale, Ariz., March 1987, 346–347.

8. Masao Yukawa, *The Information Superhighway and Multimedia: Dreams and Realities in Japan,* American Chamber of Commerce in Japan, Tokyo, October 12, 1994.

9. Letter from President Clinton to Speaker of the House Tom Foley, Washington, D.C., December 15, 1993.

10. Global Tourist Arrivals and Receipts, World Tourism Organization, Internet Document, January 20, 1998.

11. Dorothy I. Riddle, "Gaining Credibility Abroad as a Service Exporter," *International Trade Forum* 1 (1997): 4–7.

12. Paul G. Patterson and Muris Cicic, "A Typology of Service Firms in International Markets: An Empirical Investigation," *Journal of International Marketing* 3, 4 (1995): 57–83.

13. M. Krishna Erramilli and C. P. Rao, "Service Firms' International Entry-Mode Choice: A Modified Transaction-Cost Analysis Approach," *Journal of Marketing* 57 (July 1993): 19–38.

# CHAPTER 16

# International Logistics and Supply-Chain Management

## LEARNING OBJECTIVES

◆ *To understand the escalating importance of international logistics and supply-chain management as crucial tools for competitiveness*

◆ *To learn about materials management and physical distribution*

◆ *To learn why international logistics is more complex than domestic logistics*

◆ *To see how the transportation infrastructure in host countries often dictates the options open to the international manager*

◆ *To learn why inventory management is crucial for international success*

## Supply-Chain Management Reduces Capacity Requirements

U.S. chemical companies are redesigning their supply-chain strategies to meet new industry challenges, according to a study by the international consulting firm A.T. Kearney. Increasing competition in Asia and consolidation among chemical companies' customers are fueling supply-chain reconfigurations. Changing supply-chain management will reap big savings for chemical companies—60 to 80 percent of their cost structure is tied up in the supply chain. In other words, a 10 percent reduction in supply-chain expenses can lead to a 40 to 50 percent improvement in before-tax profits.

The U.S. chemical industry is particularly sensitive to the economics of supply chains; two-thirds of all U.S. chemical exports are sent to the foreign affiliates of U.S. companies. Chemicals are the largest single U.S. export group, ranging from fertilizers to plastics. But U.S. chemical exports are facing increasing competition from new operations in Malaysia, Singapore, South Korea, and Taiwan.

One U.S. firm, ARCO Chemical Co., decided to reorganize its supply chain in order to meet the challenges of global competition. Separate units in the nine countries where it operated had previously controlled different functions of its global supply chain. Adopting a new strategy, ARCO consolidated control of the supply chain under one organization responsible for purchasing raw materials, customer support, and logistics. The company's spokeswoman, Sallie Anderson, stated that "by putting these activities into one organization and redesigning the processes we will achieve significant working capital savings and more efficiency." In fact, the streamlined supply-chain management is part of a cost-cutting program that plans to cut $150 million from the annual $750 million budget for structural costs.

The A.T. Kearney study confirmed the importance of supply-chain management in producing high earnings in the chemical industry; the four companies given the highest marks for supply-chain management also had earnings that were 5 to 7 percent higher than the other companies reviewed. Besides a clear supply-chain strategy, the study cited other important factors contributing to industry success, including smooth integration of suppliers and customers and the successful use of information technology. U.S. chemical companies that want to thrive in a globalized market will have to develop well-run supply chains to avoid prematurely expanding production capacity, a practice that contributes to boom and bust cycles. A.T. Kearney's vice president for chemical practice, Michael Eckstut, offered some advice for firms trying to reduce costs and stay competitive: "If you have a very efficient supply chain with good forecasting, tight scheduling and distribution, you can get by with less capacity."

*Source:* Arthur Gottschalk, "Chemical Firms Redesigning Supply-Chain Strategies," *The Journal of Commerce* (July 8, 1997): 1A, 6A.

For the international firm, customer locations and sourcing opportunities are widely dispersed. The firm can attain a strategically advantageous position only if it is able to successfully manage complex international networks, consisting of its vendors, suppliers, other third parties, and its customers. Neglect of linkages within and outside of the firm brings not only higher costs but also the risk of eventual noncompetitiveness, due to diminished market share, more expensive supplies, or lower profits. As discussed in the opening vignette, effective international logistics and supply-chain management can produce higher earnings and greater corporate efficiency, which are the cornerstones to corporate competitiveness.

This chapter will focus on international logistics and supply-chain management. Primary areas of concentration will be the linkages between the firm, its suppliers, and its customers, as well as transportation, inventory, packaging, and storage issues. The logistics management problems and opportunities that are peculiar to international business will also be highlighted.

## A Definition of International Logistics

International logistics is design and management of a system that controls the flow of materials into, through, and out of the international corporation. It encompasses the total movement concept by covering the entire range of operations concerned with goods movement, including therefore both exports and imports simultaneously. By taking a systems approach, the firm explicitly recognizes the linkages among the traditionally separate logistics components within and outside of corporation. By incorporating the interaction with outside organizations and individuals such as suppliers and customers, the firm is enabled to build on jointness of purpose by all partners in the areas of performance, quality, and timing. As a result of implementing these systems considerations successfully, the firm can develop just-in-time (JIT) delivery for lower inventory cost, electronic data interchange (EDI) for more efficient order processing, and early supplier involvement (ESI) for better planning of goods development and movement. In addition, the use of such a systems approach allows a firm to concentrate on its core competencies and to form outsourcing alliances with other companies. For example, a firm can choose to focus on manufacturing and leave all aspects of order filling and delivery to an outside provider. By working closely with customers such as retailers, firms can also develop efficient customer response (ECR) systems, which can track sales activity on the retail level. As a result, manufacturers can precisely coordinate production in response to actual shelf replenishment needs, rather than based on forecasts.

Two major phases in the movement of materials are of logistical importance. The first phase is **materials management,** or the timely movement of raw materials, parts, and supplies into and through the firm. The second phase is **physical distribution,** which involves the movement of the firm's finished product to its customers. In both phases, movement is seen within the context of the entire process. Stationary periods (storage and inventory) are therefore included. The basic goal of logistics management is the effective coordination of both phases and their various components to result in maximum cost effectiveness while maintaining service goals and requirements.

The growth of logistics as a field has brought to the forefront three major new concepts: the systems concept, the total cost concept, and the trade-off concept. The **systems concept** is based on the notion that materials-flow activities within and outside of the firm are so extensive and complex that they can be considered only in the context of their interaction. Instead of each corporate function, supplier, and customer operating with the goal of individual optimization, the systems concept stipulates that some components may have to work suboptimally to maximize the benefits of the system as a whole. The systems concept intends to provide the firm, its suppliers, and its customers, both domestic and foreign, with the benefits of synergism expected from the coordinated application of size.

In order for the systems concept to work, information flows and partnership trust are instrumental. Logistics capability is highly information dependent, since information availability influences not only the network planning process but also the day-to-day decisions that affect performance.[1] Long-term partnership and trust are required in order to forge closer links between firms and managers. An abuse of power is the fastest way to build barriers to such linkages.[2]

A logical outgrowth of the systems concept is the development of the **total cost concept.** To evaluate and optimize logistical activities, cost is used as a basis for measurement. The purpose of the total cost concept is to minimize the firm's overall logistics cost by implementing the systems concept appropriately.

Implementation of the total cost concept requires that the members of the system understand the sources of costs. To develop such understanding, a system of activity-based costing has been developed, which is a technique designed to more accurately assign the indirect and direct resources of an organization to the activities performed based on consumption.[3] In the international arena, the total cost concept must also incorporate the consideration of total after-tax profit, by taking the impact of national tax policies on the logistics function into account. The objective is to maximize after-tax profits rather than minimizing total cost. Tax variations in the international arena often have major consequences, therefore, the focus can be quite important.[4]

The **trade-off concept,** finally, recognizes the linkages within logistics systems that result from the interaction of their components. For example, locating a warehouse near the customer may reduce the cost of transportation. However, additional costs are associated with new warehouses. Similarly, a reduction of inventories will save money but may increase the need for costly emergency shipments. Managers can maximize performance of logistics systems only by formulating decisions based on the recognition and analysis of such trade-offs. A trade-off of costs may go against one's immediate interests. Consider a manufacturer building several different goods. The goods all use one or both of two parts, A and B, which the manufacturer buys in roughly equal amounts. Most of the goods produced use both parts. The unit cost of part A is $7, of part B, $10. Part B has more capabilities than part A; in fact, B can replace A. If the manufacturer doubles its purchases of part B, it qualifies for a discounted $8 unit price. For products that incorporate both parts, substituting B for A makes sense to qualify for the discount, since the total parts cost is $17 using A and B, but only $16 using Bs only. Part B should therefore become a standard part for the manufacturer. But departments building products that only use part A may be reluctant to accept the substitute part B because, even discounted, the cost of B exceeds that of A. Use of the trade-off concept will solve the problem.[5]

## Supply-Chain Management

The integration of these three concepts has resulted in the new paradigm of **supply-chain management,** where a series of value-adding activities connect a company's supply side with its demand side. This approach views the supply chain of the entire extended enterprise, beginning with the supplier's suppliers and ending with consumers or end users. The perspective encompasses the entire product and information and funds flow that form one cohesive link to acquire, purchase, convert/manufacture, assemble, and distribute goods and services to the ultimate consumers. The implementation effects of such supply-chain management systems can be major. Efficient supply-chain design can increase customer satisfaction and save money at the same time.[6] For example, it has permitted Wal-Mart, the largest U.S. retailer, to reduce inventories by 90 percent, has saved the company hundreds of millions of dollars in inventory holding costs, and allows it to offer low prices to its customers.[7] On an industry-wide basis, research by Coopers and Lybrand has indicated that the use of such tools in the structuring of supplier relations could reduce operating costs of the European grocery industry by $27 billion per year, with savings equivalent to a 5.7 percent reduction in price.[8] Clearly, the use of such strategic tools will be crucial for international managers to develop and maintain key competitive advantages. An overview of the international supply chain is shown in Figure 16.1.

## The Impact of International Logistics

Logistics costs comprise between 10 and 30 percent of the total landed cost of an international order.[9] International firms already have achieved many of the cost reductions that are possible in financing and production, and are now beginning to look at international logistics as a competitive tool. Research shows that the environment facing logistics managers in the next ten years will be dynamic and explosive. Technological advances and progress in communication systems and information-processing capabilities will be particularly significant in the design and management of logistics systems.

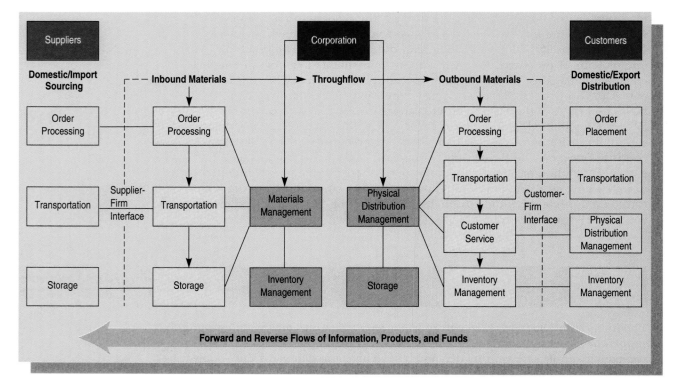

**FIGURE 16.1**

**The International Supply Chain**

For example, close collaboration with suppliers is required to develop a just-in-time inventory system, which in turn may be crucial to maintaining manufacturing costs at globally competitive levels. Yet, without electronic data interchange, such collaborations or alliances are severely handicapped. While most industrialized countries can offer the technological infrastructure for such computer-to-computer exchange of business information, the application of such a system in the global environment may be severely restricted. It may not be just the lack of technology that forms the key obstacle to modern logistics management, but rather the entire business infrastructure, ranging from ways of doing business in fields such as accounting and inventory tracking, to the willingness of businesses to collaborate with each other. A contrast between the United States and Russia is useful here.

In the United States, 40 percent of shipments are under a just-in-time/quick response regime. For the U.S. economy, the total cost of distribution is close to 10 percent of GNP.[10] By contrast, Russia only now is beginning to learn about the rhythm of demand and the need to bring supply in line. The country is battling space constraints, poor lines of supply, nonexistent distribution and service centers, limited rolling stock, and inadequate transportation systems. Producers are uninformed about issues such as inventory carrying costs, store assortment efficiencies, and replenishment techniques.

The need for information development and exchange systems, for integrated supplier–distributor alliances, and for efficient communication systems is only poorly understood. As a result, distribution costs remain at well above 30 percent of GNP, holding back the domestic economy and severely restricting its international competitiveness. Unless substantial improvements are made, major participation by Russian producers in world trade will be severely handicapped,[11] since the high logistics and transaction costs let Western buyers encounter high "frictional resistance" in their procurement process.[12]

Logistics and supply-chain management increasingly are the key dimensions by which firms distinguish themselves internationally. Given the speed of technological change and the efficiency demands placed on business, competitiveness, international sales growth, and international business success increasingly will depend on the logistics function.[13]

## Differences between Domestic and International Logistics

In domestic operations, logistics decisions are guided by the experience of the manager, possible industry comparisons, an intimate knowledge of trends, and discovered heuristics—or rules of thumb. The logistics manager in the international firm, on the other hand, frequently has to depend on educated guesses to determine the steps required to obtain a desired service level. Variations in locale mean variations in environment. Lack of familiarity with such variations leads to uncertainty in the decision-making process. By applying decision rules based only on the environment encountered at home, the firm will be unable to adapt well to new circumstances, and the result will be inadequate profit performance. The long-term survival of international activities depends on an understanding of the differences inherent in the international logistics field. The variations can be classified as basic differences and country-specific differences.[14]

**Basic Differences**   Basic differences in international logistics emerge because the corporation is active in more than one country. One example of a basic difference is distance. International business activities frequently require goods to be shipped farther to reach final customers. These distances in turn result in longer lead times, more opportunities for things to go wrong, more inventories—in short, greater complexity. Currency variation is a second basic difference in international logistics. The corporation must adjust its planning to incorporate different currencies and changes in exchange rates. The border-crossing process brings with it the need for conformity with national regulations, an inspection at customs, and proper documentation. As a result, additional intermediaries participate in the international logistics process. They include freight forwarders, customs agents, customs brokers, banks, and other financial intermediaries. Finally, the **transportation modes** may also be different. Most domestic transportation is either by truck or by rail, whereas the multinational corporation quite frequently ships its products by air or by sea. Airfreight and ocean freight have their own stipulations and rules that require new knowledge and skills.

**Country-Specific Differences**   Within each country, the firm faces specific logistical attributes that may be quite different from those experienced at home. Differences and barriers in the areas of infrastructure, transportation services, inventory control, and warehousing services often mean long transit times, high transportation costs, and high inventory levels.[15] Transportation systems and intermediaries may vary. The computation of freight rates may be unfamiliar. Packaging and labeling requirements differ from country to country. Management must consider all of these factors to develop an efficient international logistics operation.

## International Transportation Issues

International transportation is of major concern to the international firm because transportation determines how and when goods will be received. Global Perspective 16.1 details some of the problems that can be encountered in the transportation process. The transportation issue can be divided into three components: infrastructure, the availability of modes, and the choice of modes among the given alternatives.

### Transportation Infrastructure

In industrialized countries, firms can count on an established transportation network. Around the globe, however, major infrastructural variations will be encountered. Some countries may have excellent inbound and outbound transportation systems but weak internal transportation links. This is particularly true in former colonies, where the original transportation systems were designed to maximize the extractive potential of the countries. In such instances, shipping to the market may be easy, but distribution within the market may represent a very difficult and time-consuming task. Infrastructure problems can also be found in countries where most transportation networks were established between major ports and cities in past centuries. The areas lying outside the major transportation networks will encounter problems in bringing their goods to market.

Due to the political changes that have occurred in the recent past, new routes of commerce have also opened up, particularly between the former East and West political blocs. Yet, without the proper infrastructure the opening of markets is mainly accompanied by major new bottlenecks. On the part of the firm, it is crucial to have wide market access to be able to appeal to sufficient customers. The firm's **logistics platform,** which is determined by a location's ease and convenience of market reach under favorable cost circumstances, is a key component of a firm's competitive position. Since different countries and regions may offer alternative logistics platforms, the firm must recognize that such alternatives can be the difference between success and failure.

The logistics manager must therefore learn about existing and planned infrastructures abroad and at home and factor them into the firm's strategy. In some countries, for example, railroads may be an excellent transportation mode, far surpassing the performance of trucking, while in others the use of railroads for freight distribution may be a gamble at best. The future routing of pipelines must be determined before any major commitments are made to a particular location if the product is amenable to pipeline transportation. The transportation methods used to carry cargo to seaports or airports must be investigated. Mistakes in the evaluation of transportation options can prove to

## LATE, LOST, AND DAMAGED GOODS

**N**o shipper would want to win Roberts Express "Shipments from Hell" contest. "Winners" have nightmare tales of late, lost, broken, or even burned shipments, demonstrating just about everything that could possibly go wrong in transit. Judges from *Industry Week* and *Transportation and Distribution* magazines gave the top award to a shipment of auto parts that needed to be at an assembly plant in a few hours, since the factory operated on a just-in-time basis. But a misunderstanding over the chartered plane's arrival time and the time the parts needed to arrive kept the freight on the ground for hours. The entire production line was forced to shut down, costing thousands of dollars a minute. Then a thunderstorm delayed the plane's takeoff by another half-hour, adding more dollars to the cost of the late shipment.

In another "Shipment from Hell," attention to detail could have averted a sticky disaster. A Danish company arranged to send a shipment by rail from New York to Washington State, but forgot to mention that the cargo needed refrigeration. After a week's journey in a railcar, the shipment of imported margarine was a gooey yellow mess. Instances of damaged or destroyed goods abound in the contest. One "winner" found its custom-made products at the bottom of Houston Harbor. Another company's million-dollar computer system was smashed as it rolled off the delivery truck. In an ironic twist on the damaged goods problem, one shipment was found burned and melted inside a forty-foot ocean container. It turned out the goods were firefighting equipment, sprinklers, and valves.

One contest "winner" had to bring in the police to retrieve a lost shipment. A medical supply house handed over a $90,000 surgical kit to a courier who signed for it and then lost it. The company eventually reported the kit stolen so that police could search the courier's offices. They found that the kit had been there all along.

The stories behind the "Shipments from Hell" illustrate that a host of bizarre circumstances can turn an ordinary shipment into a comedy of errors. Other notable shipping calamities included a shipment held hostage, another sent with stowaway black widow spiders, and several that were frozen or melted along the way.

*Source: Gregory S. Johnson, "Damaged Goods: Hard-luck Tales of '97," **The Journal of Commerce** (January 9, 1998): 1A.*

be very costly. One researcher reported the case of a food processing firm that built a pineapple cannery at the delta of a river in Mexico. Since the pineapple plantation was located upstream, the company planned to float the ripe fruit down to the cannery on barges. To its dismay, however, the firm soon discovered that at harvest time the river current was far too strong for barge traffic. Since no other feasible alternative method of transportation existed, the plant was closed and the new equipment was sold for a fraction of its original cost.[16]

Extreme variations also exist in the frequency of transportation services. For example, a particular port may not be visited by a ship for weeks or even months. Sometimes only carriers with particular characteristics, such as small size, will serve a given location.

All of these infrastructural concerns must be taken into account in the planning of the firm's location and transportation framework. The opportunity of a highly competitive logistics platform may be decisive for the firm's investment decision, since it forms a key component of the cost advantages sought by multinational corporations, as was explained in Chapter 12. If a location loses its logistics benefits, due to, for example, a deterioration of the railroad system, a firm may well decide to move on to another, more favorable locale. Business strategist Michael Porter addressed the importance of infrastructure as a determinant of national competitive advantage and highlighted the capability of governmental efforts to influence this critical issue.[17] Governments must keep the transportation dimension in mind when attempting to attract new industries or trying to retain existing firms.

## Availability of Modes

International transportation frequently requires ocean or airfreight modes, which many corporations only rarely use domestically. In addition, combinations such as **land bridges** or **sea bridges** may permit the transfer of freight among various modes of transportation, resulting in **intermodal movements.** The international logistics manager must understand the specific properties of the different modes to be able to use them intelligently.

**Ocean Shipping**   Water transportation is a key mode for international freight movement.[18] Three types of vessels operating in **ocean shipping** can be distinguished by their service: liner service, bulk service, and tramp or charter service. **Liner service** offers regularly scheduled passage on established routes. **Bulk service** mainly provides contractual services for individual voyages or for prolonged periods of time. **Tramp service** is available for irregular routes and scheduled only on demand.

In addition to the services offered by ocean carriers, the type of cargo a vessel can carry is also important. Most common are conventional (break bulk) cargo vessels, container ships, and roll-on-roll-off vessels. Conventional cargo vessels are useful for oversized and unusual cargoes but may be less efficient in their port operations. **Container ships** carry standardized containers that greatly facilitate the loading and unloading of cargo and intermodal transfers. As a result, the time the ship has to spend in port is reduced as are the port charges. **Roll-on-roll-off (RORO)** vessels are essentially oceangoing ferries. Trucks can drive onto built-in ramps and roll off at the destination. Another vessel similar to the RORO vessel is the LASH (lighter aboard ship) vessel. LASH vessels consist of barges stored on the ship and lowered at the point of destination. The individual barges can then operate on inland waterways, a feature that is particularly useful in shallow water.

The availability of a certain type of vessel, however, does not automatically mean that it can be used. The greatest constraint in international ocean shipping is the lack of ports and port services. For example, modern container ships cannot serve some ports because the local equipment cannot handle the resulting traffic. The problem is often found in developing countries, where local authorities lack the funds to develop facilities. In some instances, nations may purposely limit the development of **ports** to impede the inflow of imports. Increasingly, however, governments have begun to recognize the importance of an appropriate port facility structure and are developing such facilities in spite of the large investments necessary.

**Air Shipping**   **Airfreight** is available to and from most countries. This includes the developing world, where it is often a matter of national prestige to operate a national airline. The tremendous growth in international airfreight over past decades is shown in Figure 16.2. The total volume of airfreight in relation to total shipping volume in international business remains quite small. It accounts for less than 1 percent of the total volume of international shipments, although it often represents more than 20 percent of the value shipped by in-

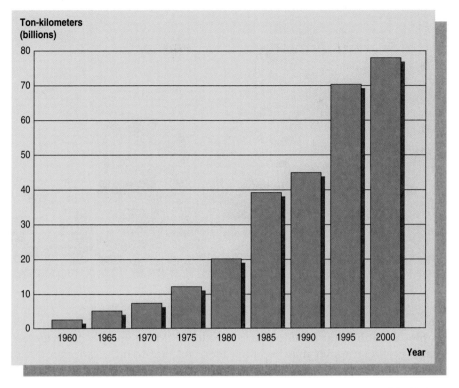

Based on data supplied by member states of the International Civil Aviation Organization (ICAO). As the number of member states increased from 116 in 1970 to 150 in 1983, there is some upward bias in the data, particularly from 1970 on, when data for the USSR were included for the first time.

**FIGURE 16.2**

**International Airfreight, 1960–2000**

*Sources: Civil Aviation Statistics of the World* (Montreal: ICAO, 1996), and **www.icao.org**. Michael Kayal, "World Air Cargo Seen Growing 7.5% a Year to 2001," *The Journal of Commerce* (December 30, 1997): 10A.

dustrialized countries.[19] Clearly, high-value items are more likely to be shipped by air, particularly if they have a high **density,** that is, a high weight-to-volume ratio.

Over the years, airlines have made major efforts to increase the volume of airfreight. Many of these activities have concentrated on developing better, more efficient ground facilities, automating air waybills, introducing airfreight containers, and providing and marketing a wide variety of special services to shippers. In addition, some airfreight companies and ports have specialized and become partners in the international logistics effort.

Changes have also taken place within the aircraft. As an example, 30 years ago, the holds of large propeller aircraft could take only about 10 tons of cargo. Today's jumbo jets can hold more than 92 tons and can therefore transport bulky products, as Figure 16.3 shows. In addition, aircraft manufacturers have responded to industry demands by developing both jumbo cargo planes and combination passenger and cargo aircraft. The latter carry passengers in one section of the main deck and freight in another. These hybrids can be used by carriers on routes that would be uneconomical for passengers or freight alone.

From the shipper's perspective, the products involved must be appropriate for air shipment in terms of their size. In addition, the market situation for any given product must be evaluated. Airfreight may be needed if a product is perishable or if, for other reasons, it requires a short transit time. The level of

**FIGURE 16.3**

**Loading a Train on a Plane**
Shipping by air freight has really taken off in the past 20 years. Even large and heavy items, such as this locomotive, are shipped to their destination by air.
*Source:* Printed in the *Journal of Commerce*, August 29, 1994.

customer service needs and expectations can also play a decisive role. For example, the shipment of an industrial product that is vital to the ongoing operations of a customer may be much more urgent than the shipment of packaged consumer products.

**Choice of Modes**

The international logistics manager must make the appropriate selection from the available modes of transportation. The decision will be heavily influenced by the needs of the firm and its customers. The manager must consider the performance of each mode on four dimensions: transit time, predictability, cost, and noneconomic factors.

**Transit Time**   The period between departure and arrival of the carrier varies significantly between ocean freight and airfreight. For example, the 45-day **transit time** of an ocean shipment can be reduced to 24 hours if the firm chooses airfreight. The length of transit time can have a major impact on the overall operations of the firm. As an example, a short transit time may reduce or even eliminate the need for an overseas depot. Also, inventories can be significantly reduced if they are replenished frequently. As a result, capital can be freed up and used to finance other corporate opportunities. Transit time can also play a major role in emergency situations. For example, if the shipper is about to miss an important delivery date because of production delays, a shipment normally made by ocean freight can be made by air.

Perishable products require shorter transit times. Transporting them rapidly prolongs the shelf life in the foreign market. As shown in Figure 16.4, air delivery may be the only way to enter foreign markets successfully with products that have a short life span. International sales of cut flowers have reached their current volume only as a result of airfreight.

The interaction among selling price, market distance, and form of transportation is not new. Centuries ago, Johann von Thünen, a noted German economist, developed models for the market reach of agricultural products that incorporated these factors. Yet, given the forms of transportation available today, the factors no longer pose the rigid constraints postulated by von Thünen, but rather offer new opportunities in international business.

**Predictability**   Providers of both ocean freight and airfreight service wrestle with the issue of reliability. Both modes are subject to the vagaries of nature, which may impose delays. Yet, because **reliability** is a relative measure, the delay of one day for airfreight tends to be seen as much more severe and "unreliable" than the same delay for ocean freight. However, delays tend to be shorter in absolute time for air shipments. As a result, arrival time via air is more predictable. This attribute has a major influence on corporate strategy. For example, because of the higher predictability of airfreight, inventory safety

**FIGURE 16.4**

**An Advertisement for Cut Flowers**

*Source:* Courtesy of Customer and Marketing Services Division, Aviation Department, Port Authority of New York and New Jersey.

shock can be kept at lower levels. Greater predictability also can serve as a useful sales tool, since it permits more precise delivery promises to customers. If inadequate port facilities exist, airfreight may again be the better alternative. Unloading operations for oceangoing vessels are more cumbersome and time consuming than for planes. Merchandise shipped via air is likely to suffer less loss and damage from exposure of the cargo to movement. Therefore, once the merchandise arrives, it is more likely to be ready for immediate delivery—a fact that also enhances predictability.

An important aspect of predictability is also the capability of a shipper to track goods at any point during the shipment. **Tracking** becomes particularly important as corporations increasingly obtain products from and send them to multiple locations around the world. Being able to coordinate the smooth flow of a multitude of interdependent shipments can make a vast difference in a corporation's performance.[20] Tracking allows the shipper to check on the functioning of the supply chain and to take remedial action if problems occur. Cargo also can be redirected if sudden demand surges so require. However, such enhanced corporate response to the predictability issue is only possible if an appropriate information system is developed by the shipper and the carrier.

**Cost of Transportation**    International transportation services are usually priced on the basis of both cost of the service provided and value of the service to the shipper. Due to the high value of the products shipped by air, airfreight is often priced according to the value of the service. In this instance, of course, price becomes a function of market demand and the monopolistic power of the carrier.

The manager must decide whether the clearly higher cost of airfreight can be justified. In part, this will depend on the cargo's properties. The physical density and the value of the cargo will affect the decision. Bulky products may be too expensive to ship by air, whereas very compact products may be more appropriate for airfreight transportation. High-priced items can absorb transportation costs more easily than low-priced goods because the cost of transportation as a percentage of total product cost will be lower. As a result, sending diamonds by airfreight is easier to justify than sending coal. Alternatively, a shipper can decide to mix modes of transportation in order to reduce overall cost and time delays. For example, part of the shipment route can be covered by air, while another portion can be covered by truck or ship.

Most important, however, are the supply-chain considerations of the firm. The manager must determine how important it is for merchandise to arrive on time. The need to reduce or increase international inventory must be carefully measured. Related to these considerations are the effect of transportation cost on price and the need for product availability abroad. For example, some firms may want to use airfreight as a new tool for aggressive market expansion. Airfreight may also be considered a good way to begin operations in new markets without making sizable investments for warehouses and distribution centers. Simply comparing transportation modes on the basis of price alone is insufficient. The manager must factor in all corporate, supplier, and customer activities that are affected by the modal choice and explore the full implications of each alternative.

**Noneconomic Factors**   The transportation sector, nationally and internationally, both benefits and suffers from government involvement. Even though transportation carriers are one prime target in the sweep of privatization around the globe, many carriers are still owned or heavily subsidized by governments. As a result, governmental pressure is exerted on shippers to use national carriers, even if more economical alternatives exist. Such **preferential policies** are most often enforced when government cargo is being transported. Restrictions are not limited to developing countries. For example, in the United States, the federal government requires that all travelers on government business use national flag carriers when available.

For balance of payments reasons, international quota systems of transportation have been proposed. The United Nations Conference on Trade and Development (UNCTAD), for example, has recommended that 40 percent of the traffic between two nations be allocated to vessels of the exporting country, 40 percent to vessels of the importing country, and 20 percent to third-country vessels. However, stiff international competition among carriers and the price sensitivity of customers frequently render such proposals ineffective, particularly for trade between industrialized countries.

Although many justifications are possible for such national policies, ranging from prestige to national security, they distort the economic choices of the international corporation. Yet, these policies are a reflection of the international environment within which the firm must operate. Proper adaptation is necessary.

A firm must deal with numerous forms and documents when exporting to ensure that all goods meet local and foreign laws and regulations.

A **bill of lading** is a contract between the exporter and the carrier indicating that the carrier has accepted responsibility for the goods and will provide transportation in return for payment. The bill of lading can also be used as a receipt and to prove ownership of the merchandise. There are two types of bills, negotiable and nonnegotiable. **Straight bills of lading** are nonnegotiable and are typically used in prepaid transactions. The goods are delivered to a specific individual or company. **Shipper's order** bills of lading are negotiable; they can be bought, sold, or traded while the goods are still in transit and are used for letter of credit transactions. The customer usually needs the original or a copy of the bill of lading as proof of ownership to take possession of the goods.

A **commercial invoice** is a bill for the goods stating basic information about the transaction, including a description of the merchandise, total cost of the goods sold, addresses of the shipper and seller, and delivery and payment terms. The buyer needs the invoice to prove ownership and to arrange payment. Some governments use the commercial invoice to assess customs duties.

Other export documents that may be required include export licenses, consular invoices (used to control and identify goods, they are obtained from the country to which the goods are being shipped), certificates of origin, inspection certification, dock and/or warehouse receipts, destination control statements (serve to notify the carrier and all foreign parties that the item may only be exported to certain destinations), insurance certificates, shipper's ex-

**Export Documentation and Terms**

port declarations (used to control exports and compile trade statistics), and export packaging lists.[21]

The documentation required depends on the merchandise in the shipment and its destination. The number of documents required can be quite cumbersome and costly, creating a deterrent to trade. For example, before the introduction of document simplification, it was estimated that the border-related red tape and controls within the then-European Community cost European companies $9.2 billion in extra administrative costs and delays annually.[22] To eliminate the barriers posed by all this required documentation, the EC introduced the Single Administrative Document (SAD) in 1988. The SAD led to the elimination of nearly 200 customs forms required of truckers throughout the EC when traveling from one member country to another.

To ensure that all documentation required is accurately completed and to minimize potential problems, firms just entering the international market should consider using **freight forwarders,** who specialize in handling export documentation. Freight forwarders increasingly choose to differentiate themselves through the development of sophisticated information management systems, particularly with electronic data interchange (EDI). In fact, over half of freight forwarders currently use EDI.[23] Adoption of new technology by such intermediaries will be quite rapid, in light of the growing competitive pressures explained in Global Perspective 16.2.

**Terms of Shipment and Sale** The responsibilities of the buyer and the seller should be spelled out as they relate to what is and what is not included in the price quotation and when ownership of goods passes from seller to buyer. **Incoterms** are the internationally accepted standard definitions for terms of sale by the International Chamber of Commerce (ICC). Although the same terms may be used in domestic transactions, they gain new meaning in the international arena. The most common Incoterms used in international business are summarized in Figure 16.5.

Prices quoted **ex-works (EXW)** apply only at the point of origin, and the seller agrees to place the goods at the disposal of the buyer at the specified place on the date or within the fixed period. All other charges are for the account of the buyer.

**Free carrier (FCA)** applies only at a designated inland shipping point. The seller is responsible for loading goods into the means of transportation; the buyer is responsible for all subsequent expenses. If a port of exportation is named, the costs of transporting the goods to the named port are included in the price.

**Free alongside ship (FAS)** at a named port of export means that the exporter quotes a price for the goods, including charges for delivery of the goods alongside a vessel at the port. The seller handles the cost of unloading and wharfage; loading, ocean transportation, and insurance are left to the buyer.

**Free on board (FOB)** applies only to vessel shipments. The seller quotes a price covering all expenses up to and including delivery of goods on an overseas vessel provided by or for the buyer.

Under **cost and freight (CFR)** to a named overseas port of import, the seller quotes a price for the goods, including the cost of transportation to the named port of debarkation. The cost of insurance and the choice of insurer are left to the buyer.

## FREIGHT FORWARDING SERVICES AND THE INTERNET

**A** variety of players who were formerly vital to international shipping, including freight forwarders, wholesale warehousers, and other middlemen, are threatened by the Internet's ability to link customers and merchandise directly. Customers around the world no longer have to go into shops and browse the aisles to find products; they can simply check out a virtual store on the World Wide Web, browse through its catalog, and order instantly. Merchandise then arrives as soon as the next day, via express mail services like United Parcel Service or Federal Express.

Although manufacturers have always had catalogs, the Internet has radically changed the whole process of shopping by catalog. Using search engines on electronic catalogs has proven much less time consuming for customers seeking the right part among the tens of thousands of items in some catalogs. The customer simply enters the technical specifications of the part needed and then the search engine finds which product fits the customer's needs. The next step in the process also offers time and cost savings that eliminate middlemen. FedEx, UPS, and others have set up Web pages that link to these electronic catalogs. Then customers enter their own air bill tracking numbers, eliminating a task once performed by the shipping companies themselves.

While freight forwarders bemoan the arrival of Internet catalogs, software companies are taking advantage of the international demand for electronic commerce by exporting abroad. One Seattle-based company, iCat Corporation, specializes in electronic commerce software that allows businesses to create electronic catalogs. The company now has operations in Japan, the United Kingdom, France, and Germany. Web catalogs are gaining popularity worldwide as businesses discover their ability to reach a geographically dispersed audience with extensive product information.

So, is there any place left for the middlemen left out in the cold by the Internet revolution? Perhaps, if the freight forwarders can exploit the lack of alternatives in carriers. When customers use Web catalogs they cannot choose which cargo carrier they prefer, so perhaps forwarders can create a niche that provides universal on-line booking and tracking.

*Sources: Alan Abrams, "The Threat of the Net," AirCommerce (March 31, 1997): 11; iCat Corporation:* **www.icat.com**.

With **cost, insurance, and freight (CIF)** to a named overseas port of import, the seller quotes a price including insurance, all transportation, and miscellaneous charges to the point of debarkation from the vessel or aircraft. Items that may enter into the calculation of the CIF cost are (1) port charges: unloading, wharfage (terminal use) handling, storage, cartage, heavy lift, and demurrage; (2) documentation charges: certification of invoice, certificate of origin, weight certificate, and consular forms; and (3) other charges, such as fees of the freight forwarder and freight (inland and ocean) insurance premiums (marine, war, credit).

With **delivery duty paid (DDP),** the seller delivers the goods, with import duties paid, including inland transportation from import point to the buyer's premises. With **delivered duty unpaid (DDU),** only the destination customs duty and taxes are paid by the consignee. When comparing the different terms it becomes evident that ex-works signifies the maximum obligation for the buyer; delivered duty paid puts the maximum burden on the seller.

The careful determination and clear understanding of terms used and their acceptance by the parties involved are vital if subsequent misunderstandings and disputes are to be avoided. The terms are also powerful competitive tools. The exporter should therefore learn what importers usually prefer in the particular market and what the specific transaction may require. An exporter should quote CIF whenever possible because it clearly shows the buyer the cost

**FIGURE 16.5**

**Selected Trade Terms**

*Source: Foreign Commerce Handbook,* 1994.

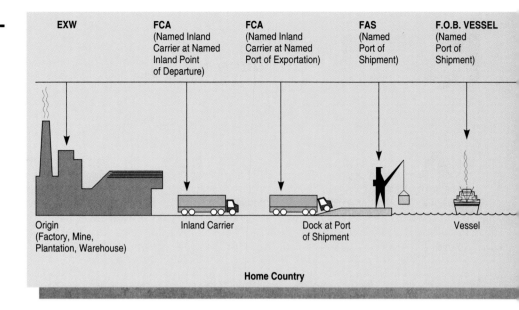

to get the product to a nearby port. An inexperienced importer might be discouraged from further action by a quote such as ex-plant Jessup, Maryland, whereas CIF Kotka will enable the Finnish importer to handle the remaining costs because they are incurred at home.

## International Inventory Issues

Inventories tie up a major portion of corporate funds. Capital used for inventory is not available for other corporate opportunities. Annual **inventory carrying costs** (the expense of maintaining inventories) can easily account for 25 percent or more of the value of the inventories themselves.[24] Therefore, proper inventory policies should be of major concern to the international logistician. In addition, **just-in-time inventory** policies, which minimize the volume of inventory by making it available only when it is needed, are increasingly required by multinational manufacturers and distributors engaging in supply-chain management. They choose suppliers on the basis of their delivery and inventory performance and their ability to integrate themselves into the supply chain. Proper inventory management may therefore become a determining variable in obtaining a sale.

The purpose of establishing **inventory** systems—to maintain product movement in the delivery pipeline and to have a cushion to absorb demand fluctuations—is the same for domestic and international operations. The international environment, however, includes unique factors such as currency exchange rates, greater distances, and duties. At the same time, international operations provide the corporation with an opportunity to explore alternatives not available in a domestic setting, such as new sourcing or location alterna-

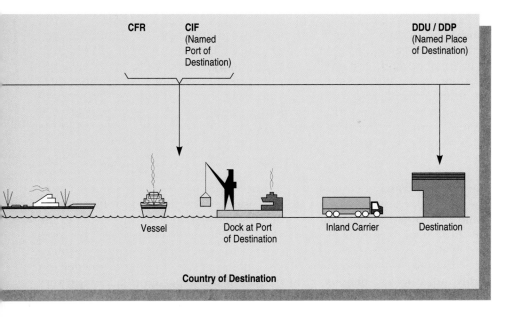

tives. In international operations, the firm can make use of currency fluctuations by placing varying degrees of emphasis on inventory operations, depending on the stability of the currency of a specific country. Entire operations can be shifted to different nations to take advantage of new opportunities. International inventory management can therefore be much more flexible in its response to environmental changes.

In deciding the level of inventory to be maintained, the international manager must consider three factors: the order cycle time, desired customer service levels, and use of inventories as a strategic tool.

## Order Cycle Time

The total time that passes between the placement of an order and the receipt of the merchandise is referred to as **order cycle time.** Two dimensions are of major importance to inventory management: the length of the total order cycle and its consistency. In international business, the order cycle is frequently longer than in domestic business. It comprises the time involved in order transmission, order filling, packing and preparation for shipment, and transportation. Order transmission time varies greatly internationally depending on the method of communication. Supply-chain driven firms use electronic data interchange (EDI) rather than facsimile, telex, telephone, or mail.

EDI is the direct transfer of information technology between computers of trading partners.[25] The usual paperwork the partners send each other, such as purchase orders and confirmations, bills of lading, invoices, and shipment notices, are formatted into standard messages and transmitted via a direct link network or a third party network. EDI saves a large part of the 15 percent in processing and administrative costs associated with traditional ways of exchanging information.[26]

The order-filling time may also increase because lack of familiarity with a foreign market makes the anticipation of new orders more difficult. Packing and shipment preparation require more detailed attention. Finally, of course, transportation time increases with the distances involved. As a result, total order cycle time can approach 100 days or more. Larger inventories may have to be maintained both domestically and internationally to bridge the time gaps.

Consistency, the second dimension of order cycle time, is also more difficult to maintain in international business. Depending on the choice of transportation mode, delivery times may vary considerably from shipment to shipment. The variation requires the maintenance of larger safety stocks to be able to fill demand in periods when delays occur.

## Customer Service Levels

The level of **customer service** denotes the responsiveness that inventory policies permit for any given situation. A customer service level of 100 percent would be defined as the ability to fill all orders within a set time—for example, three days. If, within the same three days, only 70 percent of the orders can be filled, the customer service level is 70 percent. The choice of customer service level for the firm has a major impact on the inventories needed. In highly industrialized nations, firms frequently are expected to adhere to very high levels of customer service. For example, in the European Union, actual performance measures for on-time delivery are 92 percent, for order accuracy 93 percent, and for damage-free delivery 95 percent.[27] Corporations are often tempted to design international customer service standards to similar levels.

Many managers do not realize that standards determined heuristically and based on competitive activity in the home market may be inappropriate abroad. Different locales have country-specific customer service needs and requirements. Service levels should not be oriented primarily around cost or customary domestic standards. Rather, the level chosen for use internationally should be based on expectations encountered in each market. The expectations are dependent on past performance, product desirability, customer sophistication, and the competitive status of the firm.

Because high customer service levels are costly, the goal should not be the highest customer service level possible, but rather an acceptable level. Different customers have different priorities. Some will be prepared to pay a premium for speed, some may put a higher value on flexibility, and another group may see low cost as the most important issue. Flexibility and speed are expensive, so it is wasteful to supply them to customers who do not value them highly.[28] If, for example, foreign customers expect to receive their merchandise within 30 days, for the international corporation to promise delivery within 10 or 15 days does not make sense. Indeed, such delivery may result in storage problems. In addition, the higher prices associated with higher customer service levels may reduce the competitiveness of a firm's product.

## Inventory as a Strategic Tool

Inventories can be used by the international corporation as a strategic tool in dealing with currency valuation changes or to hedge against inflation. By increasing inventories before an imminent devaluation of a currency instead of holding cash, the corporation may reduce its exposure to devaluation losses. Similarly, in the case of high inflation, large inventories can provide an important inflation hedge. In such circumstances, the international inventory manager must balance the cost of maintaining high levels of inventories with the benefits accruing from hedging against inflation or devaluation. Many countries, for example, charge a property tax on stored goods. If the increase in tax payments outweighs the hedging benefits to the corporation, it would be unwise to increase inventories before a devaluation.

## International Packaging Issues

Packaging is of particular importance in international logistics because it is instrumental in getting the merchandise to the ultimate destination in a safe, maintainable, and presentable condition. Packaging that is adequate for domestic shipping may be inadequate for international transportation because the shipment will be subject to the motions of the vessel on which it is carried. Added stress in international shipping also arises from the transfer of goods among different modes of transportation. Figure 16.6 provides examples of some sources of stress in intermodal movement that are most frequently found in international transportation.

The responsibility for appropriate packaging rests with the shipper of goods. The U.S. Carriage of Goods by Sea Act of 1936 states: "Neither the carrier nor the ship shall be responsible for loss or damage arising or resulting from insufficiency of packing." The shipper must therefore ensure that the goods are prepared appropriately for international shipping. This is important because it has been found that "the losses that occur as a result of breakage, pilferage, and theft exceed the losses caused by major maritime casualties, which include fires, sinkings, and collision of vessels. Thus the largest of these losses is a preventable loss."[29]

Packaging decisions must also take into account differences in environmental conditions—for example, climate. When the ultimate destination is very

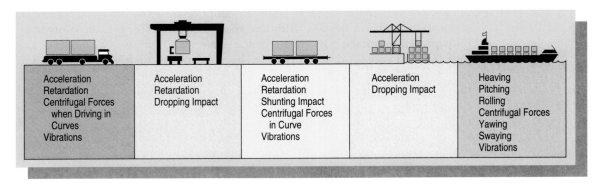

**FIGURE 16.6**

**Stresses in Intermodal Movement**

*Note:* Each transportation mode exerts a different set of stresses and strains on containerized cargoes. The most commonly overlooked are those associated with ocean transport.

*Source:* David Greenfield, "Perfect Packing for Export," from *Handling and Shipping Management,* September 1980 (Cleveland, Ohio: Penton Publishing), 47.

humid or particularly cold, special provisions must be made to prevent damage to the product. The task becomes even more challenging when one considers that, in the course of long-distance transportation, dramatic changes in climate can take place. Still famous is the case of a firm in Taiwan that shipped drinking glasses to the Middle East. The company used wooden crates and padded the glasses with hay. Most of the glasses, however, were broken by the time they reached their destination. As the crates traveled into the drier Middle East, the moisture content of the hay dropped. By the time the crates were delivered, the thin straw offered almost no protection.[30]

The weight of packaging must also be considered, particularly when airfreight is used, as the cost of shipping is often based on weight. At the same time, packaging material must be sufficiently strong to permit stacking in international transportation. Another consideration is that, in some countries, duties are assessed according to the gross weight of shipments, which includes the weight of packaging. Obviously, the heavier the packaging, the higher the duty will be.

The shipper must pay sufficient attention to instructions provided by the customer for packaging. For example, requests by the customer that the weight of any one package should not exceed a certain limit or that specific package dimensions should be adhered to, usually are made for a reason. Often they reflect limitations in transportation or handling facilities at the point of destination.

Although the packaging of a product is often used as a form of display abroad, international packaging can rarely serve the dual purpose of protection and display. Therefore double packaging may be necessary. The display package is for future use at the point of destination; another package surrounds it for protective purposes.

One solution to the packaging problem in international logistics has been the development of intermodal containers—large metal boxes that fit on trucks, ships, railroad cars, and airplanes and ease the frequent transfer of goods in international shipments. Developed in different forms for both sea and air transportation, containers also offer better utilization of carrier space because of standardization of size. The shipper therefore may benefit from lower transportation rates. In addition, containers can offer greater safety from pilferage and damage. Of course, at the same time, the use of containers allows thieves to abscond with an entire shipment rather than just parts of it. On some routes in Russia, for example, theft and pilferage of cargo are so common that liability insurers will not insure container haulers in the region.[31] Container technology has greatly improved over the years. As Global Perspective 16.3 shows, specialized containers can greatly expand the trading range of products.

Container traffic is heavily dependent on the existence of appropriate handling facilities, both domestically and internationally. In addition, the quality of inland transportation must be considered. If transportation for containers is not available and the merchandise must be removed, the expected cost reductions may not materialize.

In some countries, rules for the handling of containers may be designed to maintain employment. For example, U.S. union rules obligate shippers to withhold containers from firms that do not employ members of the International Longshoremen's Association for the loading or unloading of containers

## KEEPING EXPORTED PRODUCE FRESH

**F**rom the outside, the intermodal steel container may not appear to be a very exciting piece of transportation equipment, but inside, some of them incorporate advanced technology that maintain the condition and value of the cargo. Such is the case of Sea-Land Service's "Fresh Mist" humidity-controlled refrigerated containers, designed to prevent dehydration of fresh produce during long ocean voyages. It does this by maintaining the moisture inside a refrigerated container at optimal levels, which keeps the produce fresh longer. The fresh produce arrives heavier and better looking, with a longer shelf-life and commands a higher price in overseas markets.

Inside the container, sophisticated microprocessor technology atomizes water into minute particles and injects them into the air stream—maintaining optimal humidity levels without damage to the product packaging.

**Temperature and Humidity Requirements for Selected Fruits and Vegetables**

| Fresh Fruits and Vegetables | Percent Water Content | Expected Shelf Life | Optimum Temperature | Optimum Humidity |
|---|---|---|---|---|
| Artichoke | 83.7 | 2–3 weeks | 32–33 | 90–95% |
| Asparagus | 93.0 | 2–3 weeks | 32–35 | 90–95% |
| Broccoli | 89.9 | 10–14 days | 32–33 | 90–95% |
| Cabbage (early) | 92.4 | 3–6 weeks | 32–33 | 95–100% |
| Celery | 93.7 | 2–3 months | 32–33 | 90–95% |
| Grapes | 81.9 | 8–26 weeks | 32–33 | 90–95% |
| Green onions | 89.4 | 2–3 weeks | 32–33 | 95–100% |
| Leeks | 85.4 | 2–3 months | 32–33 | 95–100% |
| Lettuce | 94.8 | 2–3 weeks | 32–33 | 90–95% |

*Source: Sea-Land Service, Inc., (July 1997).*

within a fifty-mile radius of Atlantic or Gulf ports. Such restrictions can result in an onerous cost burden.

Overall, cost attention must be paid to international packaging. The customer who ordered and paid for the merchandise expects it to arrive on time and in good condition. Even with replacements and insurance, the customer will not be satisfied if there are delays. Dissatisfaction will usually translate directly into lost sales.

## International Storage Issues

Although international logistics is discussed as a movement or flow of goods, a stationary period is involved when merchandise becomes inventory stored in warehouses. Heated arguments can arise within a firm over the need for and utility of warehousing internationally. On the one hand, customers expect quick responses to orders and rapid delivery. Accommodating the customer's expectations would require locating many distribution centers around the world. On the other hand, warehouse space is expensive. In addition, the larger volume of inventory increases the inventory carrying cost. Fewer warehouses allow for consolidation of transportation and therefore lower transportation rates to the warehouse. However, if the warehouses are located far from customers, the cost of outgoing transportation increases. The international logistician must consider the tradeoffs between service and cost to the supply chain in order to determine the appropriate levels of warehousing.

## Trade and Travel Networks

Civilization depends on trade for growth and travel makes this possible. Shipping is the most important method of world transport but economic progress and mobility are constantly being improved by the development of new routes and new methods of transport.

### Road and Rail

Integrated road and rail networks are the basis of industrial society. Containerization and the extension of modern highway systems have increased flexibility and reduced the emphasis on railways transporting freight.

### Roads

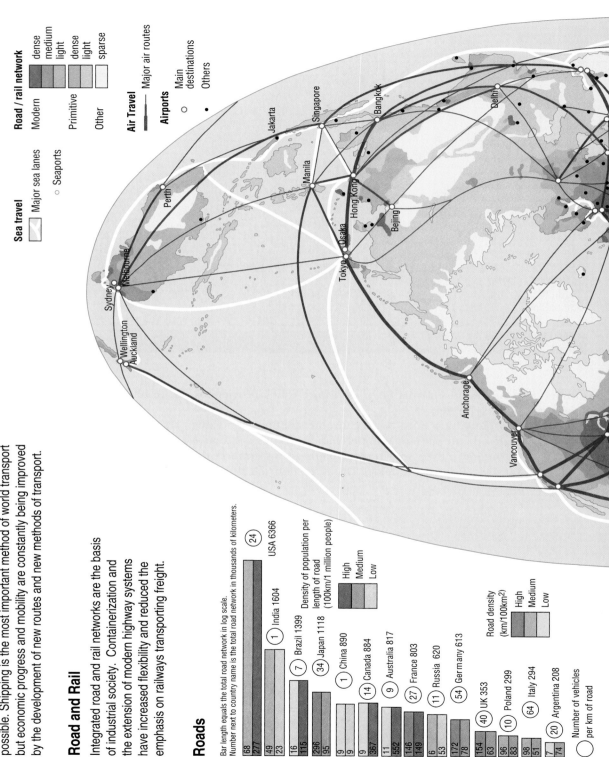

Bar length equals the total road network in log scale.
Number next to country name is the total road network in thousands of kilometers.

**Sea travel**
Major sea lanes
○ Seaports

**Road / rail network**

| Modern | dense / medium / light |
| Primitive | dense / light |
| Other | sparse |

**Air Travel**
Major air routes
**Airports**
○ Main destinations
• Others

USA 6366
① India 1604
⑦ Brazil 1399
㉞ Japan 1118
① China 890
⑭ Canada 884
⑨ Australia 817
㉗ France 803
⑪ Russia 620
㊴ Germany 613
㊵ UK 353
⑩ Poland 299
㉚ Italy 294
⑳ Argentina 208

Density of population per length of road
(100km/1 million people)
High / Medium / Low

Road density
(km/100km²)
High / Medium / Low

○ Number of vehicles per km of road

68 / 277
49 / 23
16 / 115
296 / 95
9 / 9
9 / 367
11 / 552
146 / 149
6 / 53
172 / 78
154 / 63
96 / 83
98 / 51
7 / 74

Jakarta
Singapore
Bangkok
Delhi
Perth
Manila
Hong Kong
Osaka
Beijing
Sydney
Melbourne
Tokyo
Wellington
Auckland
Anchorage
Vancouver

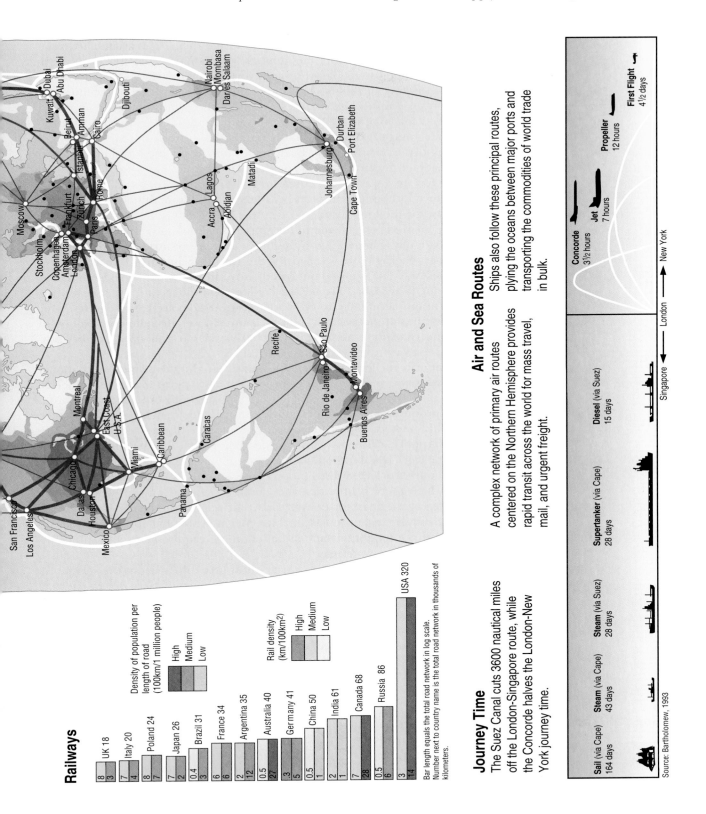

**Railways**

Density of population per
length of road
(100km/1 million people)

High
Medium
Low

| | |
|---|---|
| 8 / 3 | UK 18 |
| 7 / 4 | Italy 20 |
| 8 / 7 | Poland 24 |
| 7 / 2 | Japan 26 |
| 0.4 / 3 | Brazil 31 |
| 6 / 6 | France 34 |
| 2 / 12 | Argentina 35 |
| 0.5 / 27 | Australia 40 |
| .3 / 5 | Germany 41 |
| 0.5 / 1 | China 50 |
| 2 / 1 | India 61 |
| 7 / 28 | Canada 68 |
| 0.5 / 6 | Russia 86 |
| 3 / 14 | USA 320 |

Rail density
(km/100km²)

High
Medium
Low

Bar length equals the total road network in log scale.
Number next to country name is the total road network in thousands of
kilometers.

## Journey Time
The Suez Canal cuts 3600 nautical miles
off the London-Singapore route, while
the Concorde halves the London-New
York journey time.

## Air and Sea Routes
A complex network of primary air routes
centered on the Northern Hemisphere provides
rapid transit across the world for mass travel,
mail, and urgent freight.

Ships also follow these principal routes,
plying the oceans between major ports and
transporting the commodities of world trade
in bulk.

**Concorde**
3½ hours

**Jet**
7 hours

**Propeller**
12 hours

**First Flight**
4½ days

Singapore ⟶ London ⟶ New York

**Sail** (via Cape)
164 days

**Steam** (via Cape)
43 days

**Steam** (via Suez)
28 days

**Supertanker** (via Cape)
28 days

**Diesel** (via Suez)
15 days

Source: Bartholomew, 1993

## Storage Facilities

The international logistician is faced with the **location decision** of how many distribution centers to have and where to locate them. The availability of facilities abroad will differ from the domestic situation. For example, while public storage is widely available in some countries, such facilities may be scarce or entirely lacking in others. Also, the standards and quality of facilities can vary widely. As a result, the storage decision of the firm is often accompanied by the need for large-scale, long-term investments. Despite the high cost, international storage facilities should be established if they support the overall logistics effort. In many markets, adequate storage facilities are imperative to satisfy customer demands and to compete successfully. For example, since the establishment of a warehouse connotes a visible presence, in doing so a firm can convince local distributors and customers of its commitment to remain in the market for the long term.

Once the decision is made to use storage facilities abroad, the warehouses must be carefully analyzed. As an example, in some countries warehouses have low ceilings. Packaging developed for the high stacking of products is therefore unnecessary or even counterproductive. In other countries, automated warehousing is available. Proper bar coding of products and the use of package dimensions acceptable to the warehousing system are basic requirements. In contrast, in warehouses still stocked manually, weight limitations will be of major concern. And, if no forklift trucks are available, palletized delivery is of little use.

To optimize the logistics system, the logistician should analyze international product sales and then rank order products according to warehousing needs. Products that are most sensitive to delivery time might be classified as "A" products. "A" products would be stocked in all distribution centers, and safety stock levels would be kept high. Alternatively, the storage of products can be more selective, if quick delivery by air can be guaranteed. Products for which immediate delivery is not urgent could be classified as "B" products. They would be stored only at selected distribution centers around the world. Finally, products for which there is little demand would be stocked only at headquarters. Should an urgent need for delivery arise, airfreight could again assure rapid shipment. Classifying products enables the international logistician to substantially reduce total international warehousing requirements and still maintain acceptable service levels.

However, at all times the logistician must take into account the service requirements and sensitivities of the customer. When equipment downtime runs $100,000 an hour, delivery of a part within 24 or 48 hours is simply not acceptable. In such instances, strategically placed depots in a region must ensure that instantaneous response becomes possible. For example, Storage Technologies, a maker of storage devices for mainframe computers, keeps parts at seven of its European subsidiary offices so that in an emergency it can reach any continental customer within four hours.[32]

## Special Trade Zones

Areas where foreign goods may be held or processed and then reexported without incurring duties are called **foreign trade zones.** The zones can be found at major ports of entry and also at inland locations near major production facilities. For example, Kansas City, Missouri, has one of the largest foreign trade zones in the United States.

The existence of trade zones can be quite useful to the international firm. For example, in a particular country, the benefits derived from lower labor costs may be offset by high duties and tariffs. As a result, location of manufacturing and storage facilities in that country may prove uneconomical. Foreign trade zones are designed to exclude the impact of duties from the location decision. This is done by exempting merchandise in the foreign trade zone from duty payment. The international firm can therefore import merchandise; store it in the foreign trade zone; and process, alter, test, or demonstrate it—all without paying duties. If the merchandise is subsequently shipped abroad (that is, reexported), no duty payments are ever due. Duty payments become due only if the merchandise is shipped into the country from the foreign trade zone.

Trade zones can also be useful as transshipment points to reduce logistics cost and redesign marketing approaches. For example, Audiovox was shipping small quantities of car alarms from a Taiwanese contract manufacturer directly to distributors in Chile. The shipments were costly and the marketing strategy of requiring high minimum orders stopped distributors from buying. The firm resolved the dilemma by using a Miami trade zone to ship the alarms from Taiwan and consolidate the goods with other shipments to Chile. The savings in freight costs allowed the Chilean distributors to order whatever quantity they wanted and allowed the company to quote lower prices. As a result, sales improved markedly.[33]

All parties to the arrangement benefit from foreign trade zones. The government maintaining the trade zone achieves increased employment and investment. The firm using the trade zone obtains a spearhead in the foreign market without incurring all of the costs customarily associated with such an activity. As a result, goods can be reassembled, and large shipments can be broken down into smaller units. Also, goods can be repackaged when packaging weight becomes part of the duty assessment. Finally, goods can be given domestic "made-in" status if assembled in the foreign trade zone. Thus, duties may be payable only on the imported materials and component parts rather than on the labor that is used to finish the product.

In addition to foreign trade zones, governments also have established export processing zones and special economic areas. The common dimensions for all the zones are that special rules apply to them when compared with other regions of the country, and that the purpose of these special rules lies in the government's desire to stimulate the economy, particularly the export side of international trade.

Export processing zones usually provide tax- and duty-free treatment for production facilities whose output is destined abroad. The **maquiladoras** of Mexico are one example of a program that permits firms to take advantage of sharp differentials in labor costs. Firms can carry out the labor-intensive part of their operations in Mexico, while sourcing raw materials or component parts from other nations.

One country that has used trade zones very successfully for its own economic development is China. Through the creation of *special economic zones,* in which there are no tariffs, substantial tax incentives, and low prices for land and labor, the government has attracted many foreign investors bringing in billions of dollars. The investors have brought new equipment, technology, and managerial know-how and have increased local economic prosperity substan-

WWW

tially. For example, the job generation effect has been so strong that the central Chinese government has expressed concern about the overheating of the economy and the inequities between regions with and without trade zones.[34]

For the logistician, the decision whether to use such zones mainly is framed by the overall benefit for the supply-chain system. Clearly, additional transport and retransport are required, warehousing facilities need to be constructed, and material handling frequency will increase. However, the costs may well be balanced by the preferential government treatment or by lower labor costs.

## Management of International Logistics

The very purpose of a multinational firm is to benefit from system synergism and a persuasive argument can be made for the coordination of international logistics at corporate headquarters. Without coordination, subsidiaries will tend to optimize their individual efficiency but jeopardize the efficiency of the overall performance of the supply chain.

### Centralized Logistics Management

A significant characteristic of the centralized approach to international logistics is the existence of headquarters staff that retains decision-making power over logistics activities affecting international subsidiaries. If headquarters exerts control, it must also take the primary responsibility for its decisions. Clearly, ill will may arise if local managers are appraised and rewarded on the basis of a performance they do not control. This may be particularly problematic if headquarters staff suffers from a lack of information or expertise.

To avoid internal problems, both headquarters staff and local management should report to one person. This person, whether the vice president for international logistics or the president of the firm, can then become the final arbiter to decide the firm's priorities. Of course, the individual should also be in charge of determining appropriate rewards for managers, both at headquarters and abroad, so that corporate decisions that alter a manager's performance level will not affect the manager's appraisal and evaluation. Further, the individual can contribute an objective view when inevitable conflicts arise in international logistics coordination. The internationally centralized decision-making process leads to an overall supply-chain management perspective that can dramatically improve profitability.

### Decentralized Logistics Management

An alternative to the centralized international logistics system is decentralization. The main rationale for such decentralization is the fact that dealing with markets on a global sale can quickly lead to problems of coordination. Particularly when the firm serves many international markets that are diverse in nature, total centralization might leave the firm unresponsive to local adaptation needs.

If each subsidiary is made a profit center in itself, each one carries the full responsibility for its performance, which can lead to greater local management satisfaction and to better adaptation to local market conditions. Yet often such decentralization deprives the logistics function of the benefits of coordination.

For example, while headquarters, referring to its large volume of overall international shipments, may be able to extract bottom rates from transportation firms, individual subsidiaries by themselves may not have similar bargaining power. The same argument applies also to the sourcing situation, where the coordination of shipments by the purchasing firm may be much more cost-effective than individual shipments from many small suppliers around the world.

Once products are within a specific market, however, increased input from local logistics operations should be expected and encouraged. At the very least, local managers should be able to provide input into the logistics decisions generated by headquarters. Ideally, within a frequent planning cycle, local managers can identify the logistics benefits and constraints existing in their particular market and communicate them to headquarters. Headquarters can then either adjust its international logistics strategy accordingly or explain to the manager why system optimization requires actions different from the ones recommended. Such a justification process will help greatly in reducing the potential for animosity between local and headquarters operations.

## Outsourcing Logistics Services

A third option, used by some corporations, is the systematic outsourcing of logistics capabilities. By collaborating with transportation firms, private warehouses, or other specialists, corporate resources can be concentrated on the firm's core product. Global Perspective 16.4 provides an example.

Many firms whose core competency does not include logistics find it more efficient to use the services of companies specializing in international shipping. This is usually true for smaller shipping volumes, for example in cases when smaller import-export firms or smaller shipments are involved. Such firms prefer to outsource at least some of the international logistics functions, rather than detracting from staff resources and time. Some logistical services providers carve specific niches in the transnational shipping market, specializing for example in consumer goods forwarding. The resulting lower costs and better service make such third parties the preferred choice for many firms. On the other hand, when hazardous or other strictly regulated materials are involved, some firms may choose to retain control over handling and storing activities, in view of possible liability issues.[35]

Going even further, **one-stop logistics** allows shippers to buy all the transportation modes and functional services from a single carrier,[36] instead of going through the pain of choosing different third parties for each service. One-stop logistics ensures a more efficient global movement of goods via different transportation modes. Specialized companies provide EDI tracking services and take care of cumbersome customs procedures; they also offer distribution services, such as warehousing and inventory management. Finally, third parties may even take some of the international shipper's logistical functions. This rapidly growing trend provides benefits to both carriers and shippers.[37] The latter enjoy better service and simplified control procedures, and claims settlement. On the other hand, one-stop logistics can help carriers achieve economies of scale and remain competitive in a very dynamic market. The proliferation of one-stop logistics practices is facilitated by the wider acceptance of EDI and the growing importance of quality criteria versus cost criteria in shipping decision.

## CUTTING DELIVERY FROM TWO WEEKS TO TWO DAYS

**T**oday information moves around the world in the blink of an eye. Semiconductors are instrumental in making this happen. Increasingly producers of semiconductors recognize that their products need to move from producer to customer nearly as fast.

One company that attempts to do just that is National Semiconductor Corporation (NSC) located in California. The firm realized that to allow greater speed of delivery, it needed to overhaul its global supply network. The old logistical network of decentralized control was a tangle of unnecessary interchanges, propped up by 44 different international freight forwarders and 18 different air carriers. "The complexity of it all wasn't allowing consistent service," commented Kelvin Phillips, NSC director of worldwide logistics.

National Semiconductor wanted to change its 5- to 18-day delivery and offer a 2-day delivery guarantee. The key factor in the strategy was the recruitment of a third party logistics firm to provide valuable expertise as well as needed infrastructure.

NSC turned to Federal Express's Business Logistics Services (BLS) as a partner. Explained Phillips, "Our company competes on technology; we cannot compete on logistics. Federal's core competency is delivery. It can do what we can't." BLS was able to provide National Semiconductor with a formidable logistics network by granting access to 420 aircraft, 1,869 worldwide facilities, more than 100,000 computer terminals, 31,211 surface vehicles, and an infrastructure with more than 90,000 employees. Phillips views Federal as "using the experts who spend billions on logistics."

Five Asian NSC plants produce 95 percent of its product. In the past, an unconsolidated system of distribution existed where each plant optimized its own business performance by individually holding an inventory, performing pick and pack, and directing shipments to the main distribution centers in Scotland and California. With the help of BLS, product pickups are now made at each of the plants and funneled to a centralized distribution center in Singapore. At this point, orders are consolidated for more cost-effective routing and deliveries are made directly from Singapore within two business days. An additional advantage of using BLS is the availability of dedicated freighter capacity, something in short supply in this market during certain seasons.

The undertaking was of no small scale and as Phillips noted, "When people have been doing things one way for 20 years, the switch is difficult." However, the cost of change is worth the savings gained from a more efficient and sensible global delivery system.

*Source: "Macro Logistics for Microprocessors," Distribution (April 1993): 66–72.*

While the cost savings and specialization benefits of such a strategy seem clear, one must also consider the loss of control for the firm, its suppliers, and its customers that may result from such outsourcing. Yet, contract logistics does not and should not require the handing over of control. Rather, it offers concentration on one's specialization—a division of labor. The control and responsibility toward the supply chain remain with the firm, even though operations may move to a highly trained outside organization.

## Logistics and the Environment

The logistician plays an increasingly important role in allowing the firm to operate in an environmentally conscious way. Environmental laws, expectations, and self-imposed goals set by firms are difficult to adhere to without a logistics orientation that systematically takes such concerns into account. Since laws and regulations differ across the world, the firm's efforts need to be responsive to a wide variety of requirements. One new logistics orientation that has grown in importance due to environmental concerns is the development of **reverse distribution** systems. Such systems are instrumental in ensuring that the firm not only delivers the product to the market, but also can retrieve it from the market for subsequent use, recycling, or disposal. To a growing degree the ability to develop such reverse logistics is a key determinant for market acceptance and profitability.

Society is also beginning to recognize that retrieval should not be restricted to short-term consumer goods, such as bottles. Rather, it may be even more important to devise systems that enable the retrieval and disposal of long-term capital goods, such as cars, refrigerators, air conditioners, and industrial goods, with the least possible burden on the environment. In Germany, for example, car manufacturers are required to take back their used vehicles for dismantling and recycling purposes.

Managers are often faced with the trade-offs between environmental concerns and logistical efficiency. Companies increasingly need to learn how to simultaneously achieve environmental and economic goals. Esprit, the apparel maker, and The Body Shop, the well-known British cosmetics producer, screen their suppliers for environmental and social responsibility practices. The significance of this trend is reaffirmed in the new set of rules issued by the International Organization of Standardization. ISO-14000 specifically targets international environmental practices by evaluating companies both at the organization level (management systems, environmental performance, and environmental auditing) and product level (life-cycle assessment, labeling, and product standards).[38]

From the perspective of materials management and physical distribution, environmental practices are those that bring about fewer shipments, less handling, and more direct movement. Such practices are to be weighted against optimal efficiency routines, including just-in-time inventory and quantity discount purchasing.

On the transportation side, logistics managers will need to expand their involvement in carrier and routing selection. For example, as Global Perspective 16.5 describes, shippers of oil or other potentially hazardous materials increasingly will need to ensure that the carriers used have excellent safety records and use only double-hulled ships. Society may even expect corporate involvement in choosing the route that the shipment will travel, preferring routes that are far from ecologically important and sensitive zones. Firms will need to assert leadership in such consideration of the environment to provide society with a better quality of life.

## Summary

As competitiveness is becoming increasingly dependent on efficiency, international logistics and supply-chain management are becoming of major importance.

International logistics is concerned with the flow of materials into, through, and out of the international corporation and therefore includes materials management as well as physical distribution. The logistician must recognize the to-

## MOBIL AIMS FOR SAFETY

**M**obil Corporation's fleet of oil tankers navigates the world's oceans, delivering about 2 million barrels of crude oil and refined petroleum products each day to ports around the globe. That amounts to about 5 percent of the petroleum products transported worldwide by sea—or enough oil to power 30 million cars for a day. Gerhard Kurz, president of Mobil's shipping subsidiary, says that not a day goes by that he doesn't ponder lessons learned from *Exxon Valdez*. Amazingly, Mobil's ships spilled a mere eight barrels of oil in 1995.

Kurz and other industry executives say that the improving numbers on spills reflect a new emphasis on safety that has sharply reduced the risk of major oil spills, at least within U.S. waters. A key is to focus on prevention, they say, requiring modernized tankers, constant inspections, and a well-trained crew. Like any corporate executive, Mobil is also striving for profitability—and this can create tough decisions.

In Kurz's view, the high costs of new safety measures and building expensive but safer tankers are dwarfed by the potentially larger costs of oil spill cleanups and punitive lawsuits. "We do our shipping for safety and environmental reasons," said Kurz. "Our goal is to have a high quality operation that sets a benchmark . . . but we also want to provide safe, cost-effective transportation for the corporation."

So, can Mobil provide safety and a sizable profit? Kurz believes that over the long run, Mobil's decision to spend heavily on more expensive, double-hull tankers may pay off in profits, partly because the ships are vastly more efficient than cheaper ones and require much less maintenance. Even the simplest of these large tankers will cost at least $80 million to build. This means that a shipowner must earn about $38,000 a day throughout the ship's life span simply to break even. This compares to about $20,000 a day for cheaper single-hull ships.

Kurz foresees a time not too far off when shipowners will have to scrap many of their old tankers and rush to build new double-hull ones. (Under international rules, twenty-five-year-old ships must be retired or replaced with double-hull ships.) At that point, the price of the ships will probably go up as a limited number of shipyards try to meet demand. Tanker scrappings will exceed new ship deliveries and the world's demand for oil will expand. Then Mobil, with four double-hull ships already under construction or in service, will have an edge. Kurz believes, at this point, Mobil will have it all—safety and profit.

*Source: Daniel Sutherland, "Mobilizing the Fleet," The Washington Post, June 23, 1996, H1.*

tal systems demands on the firm, its suppliers, and customers to develop trade-offs between various logistics components. By taking a supply-chain perspective, the manager can develop logistics systems that are supplier and customer focused and highly efficient. Implementation of such a system requires close collaboration between all members of the supply chain.

International logistics differs from domestic activities in that it deals with greater distances, new variables, and greater complexity because of national differences. One major factor to consider is transportation. The international manager needs to understand transportation infrastructures in other countries and modes of transportation such as ocean shipping and airfreight. The choice among these modes will depend on the customer's demands and the firm's transit time, predictability, and cost requirements. In addition, noneconomic factors such as government regulations weigh heavily in this decision.

Inventory management is another major consideration. Inventories abroad are expensive to maintain yet often crucial for international success. The logistician must evaluate requirements for order cycle times and customer service levels to develop an international inventory policy that can also serve as a strategic management tool.

International packaging is important because it ensures arrival of the merchandise at the ultimate destination in safe condition. In developing packaging, environmental conditions such as climate and handling conditions must be considered.

The logistics manager must also deal with international storage issues and determine where to locate inventories. International warehouse space will have to be leased or purchased and decisions will have to be made about utilizing foreign trade zones.

International logistics management is increasing in importance. Implementing the logistics function with an overall supply-chain perspective that is responsive to environmental demands will increasingly be a requirement for successful global competitiveness.

## Key Terms and Concepts

| | | |
|---|---|---|
| materials management | roll-on-roll-off (RORO) | free on board (FOB) |
| physical distribution | ports | cost and freight (CFR) |
| systems concept | airfreight | cost, insurance, and |
| total cost concept | density | freight (CIF) |
| trade-off concept | transit time | delivery duty paid (DDP) |
| supply-chain | reliability | delivery duty unpaid |
| management | tracking | (DDU) |
| transportation modes | preferential policies | inventory carrying costs |
| logistics platform | bill of lading | just-in-time inventory |
| land bridges | straight bill of lading | inventory |
| sea bridges | shipper's order | order cycle time |
| intermodal movements | commercial invoice | customer service |
| ocean shipping | freight forwarders | location decision |
| liner service | Incoterms | foreign trade zones |
| bulk service | ex-works (EXW) | maquiladora |
| tramp service | free carrier (FCA) | reverse distribution |
| container ships | free alongside ship (FAS) | one-stop logistics |

## Questions for Discussion

1. Explain the key aspects of supply-chain management.
2. Contrast the use of ocean shipping and airfreight.
3. Explain the meaning and impact of transit time in international logistics.
4. How and why do governments interfere in "rational" freight carrier selection?
5. How can an international firm reduce its order cycle time?
6. Why should customer service levels differ internationally? Is it, for example, ethical to offer a lower customer service level in developing countries than in industrialized countries?
7. What role can the international logistician play in improving the environmental friendliness of the firm?
8. How would a company use an online database to select a freight forwarder? (Refer to **www.freightnet.com** or **http://forwarders.com**, directories of freight forwarders, and give examples of company information you find there.)

9. What types of information are available to the exporter on The Transport Web? Go to the site, **www.transportweb.com**, and give examples of transportation links that an exporter would find helpful and explain why.

## Recommended Readings

Coyle, John J., Edward J. Bardi, and C. John Langley, Jr. *The Management of Business Logistics*. 6th ed. Minneapolis: West Publishing Company, 1996.

Kotabe, Masaaki. *Global Sourcing Strategy: R&D, Manufacturing and Marketing Interfaces*. New York: Quorum Books, 1992.

LaLonde, Bernard J., and James L. Gitner, *Supply Chain Management Bibliography*. Columbus, Ohio: The Supply Chain Management Research Group, Spring 1996.

McConville, J. *Shipping Business and Maritime Economics: An Annotated International Bibliography*. London: Mansell, 1995.

Poirier, Charles C., and Stephen E. Reiter. *Supply Chain Optimization: Building the Strongest Total Business Network*. San Francisco: Berrett-Koehler Publishers, 1996.

Pollock, Daniel. *Precipice*. Oak Brook, Il.: Council of Logistics Management, 1997.

Ross, Frederick David. *Distribution Planning and Control*. New York: Chapman & Hall, 1996.

Schary, Philip B., and Tage Skjott-Larsen. *Managing the Global Supply Chain*. Copenhagen: Copenhagen Studies in Economics and Management, 1995.

Vos, Bart. *Restructuring Manufacturing and Logistics in Multinationals: Application of a Design Method in Five Case Studies*. Aldershot, England: Avebury, 1997.

Wood, Donald E., ed. *International Logistics*. New York: Chapman & Hall, 1995.

## Notes

1. Stanley E. Fawcett, Linda L. Stanley, and Sheldon R. Smith, "Developing a Logistics Capability to Improve the Performance of International Operations," *Journal of Business Logistics*, 18, 2 (1997): 101–127.

2. Patrick M. Byrne and Stephen V. Young, "UK Companies Look at Supply Chain Issues," *Transportation and Distribution* (February 1995): 50–56.

3. Bernard LaLonde and James Gitner, "Activity-Based Costing: Best Practices," *Paper # 606*, The Supply Chain Management Research Group, The Ohio State University, September 1996.

4. Paul T. Nelson and Gadi Toledano, "Challenges for International Logistics Management," *Journal of Business Logistics* 1, 2 (1979): 7.

5. Toshiro Hiromoto, "Another Hidden Edge: Japanese Management Accounting, "in *Trends in International Business: Critical Perspectives* ed. M. Czinkota and M. Kotabe (Oxford, Blackwell Publishers, 1998, 217–222.

6. Tom Davis, "Effective Supply Chain Management," *Sloan Management Review* (Summer 1993): 35–45.

7. Perry A. Trunick, "CLM: Breakthrough of Champions, Council of Logistics Management's 1994 Conference," *Transportation and Distribution* (December 1994).

8. Coopers and Lybrand, "The Value Chain Analysis," *Efficient Consumer Response Europe* (London, 1995).

9. Richard T. Hise, "The Implications of Time-Based Competition on International Logistics Strategies," *Business Horizons* (September/October 1995): 39–45.

10. Charles C. Poirier and Stephen E. Reiter, *Supply Chain Optimization: Building the Strongest Total Business Network* (San Francisco: Berrett-Koehler Publishers, 1996).

11. Michael R. Czinkota, "Global Neighbors, Poor Relations," *Marketing Management* 3, 1 (1994): 46–52.

12. Hans-Christian Pfohl and Rudolf Lange, "Sourcing from Central and Eastern Europe: Conditions and Implementation," *International Journal of Physical Distribution and Logistics Management* 23, 8 (1993): 5–15.

13. James H. Perry, "Emerging Economic and Technological Futures: Implications for Design and Management of Logistics Systems in the 1990's," *Journal of Business Logistics* 12 (1991): 1–16.

14. Nelson and Toledano, "Challenges for International Logistics Management," 2.

15. Joseph R. Carter, John N. Pearson, and Li Peng, "Logistics Barriers to International Operations: The Case of the People's Republic of China," *Journal of Business Logistics*, 18, 2 (1997): 129–144.

16. David A. Ricks, *Blunders in International Business* (Cambridge: Blackwell Publishers, 1993), 16.

17. Michael E. Porter, *The Competitive Advantage of Nations* (New York: The Free Press, 1990).

18. Paul R. Murphy, Douglas R. Dalenberg, and James M. Daley, "Analyzing International Water Transportation: The Perspectives of Large U.S. Industrial Corporations," *Journal of Business Logistics* 12 (1991): 169–190.

19. Gunnar K. Sletmo and Jacques Picard, "International Distribution Policies and the Role of Air Freight," *Journal of Business Logistics* 6, 1 (1984): 35–52.

20. Peter Buxbaum, "Timberland's New Spin on Global Logistics," *Distribution* (May 1994): 32–36.

21. U.S. Department of Commerce, *A Basic Guide to Exporting* (Washington, D.C.: U.S. Government Printing Office, 1992).

22. Julie Wolf, "Help for Distribution in Europe," *Northeast International Business,* January 1989, 52.

23. Paul R. Murphy and James M. Daley, "International Freight Forwarder Perspectives on Electronic Data Interchange and Information Management Issues," *Journal of Business Logistics* 17, 1 (1996): 65, 77.

24. Bernard J. LaLonde and Paul H. Zinszer, *Customer Service: Meaning and Measurement* (Chicago: National Council of Physical Distribution Management, 1976).

25. Huan Neng Chiu, "The Integrated Logistics Management System: A Framework and Case Study," *International Journal of Physical Distribution and Logistics Management* 6 (1995): 4–22.

26. L. Solis, "Is It Time for EDI?" *Global Trade and Transportation* 5 (1993): 30.

27. Patrick M. Byrne, Johan C. Aurik, and Jan Van der Oord, "New Priorities for Logistics Services in Europe," *Transportation and Distribution* (February 1994): 43–48.

28. Bernard LaLonde, Kee-Hian Tan, and Michael Standing, "Forget Supply Chains, Think of Value Flows," *Transformation,* Gemini Consulting, 3 (Summer 1994): 24–31.

29. Charles A. Taft, *Management of Physical Distribution and Transportation,* 7th ed. (Homewood, Ill.: Irwin, 1984), 324.

30. Ricks, *Blunders in International Business,* 27.

31. Elizabeth Canna, "Russian Supply Chains," *American Shipper* (June 1994): 49–53.

32. Gregory L. Miles, "Have Spares, Will Travel," *International Business* (December 1994): 26–27.

33. Marita von Oldenborgh, "Power Logistics," *International Business* (October 1994): 32–34.

34. Li Rongxia, "Free Trade Zones in China," *Beijing Review* (August 2–8, 1993): 14–21.

35. Kant Rao and Richard R. Young, "Factors Influencing Outsourcing of Logistics Functions," *International Journal of Physical Distribution and Logistics Management* 6 (1994): 11–19.

36. B.J. LaLonde, "Whatever Happened to One-Stop Transportation Shopping?" *Transport Topics* 13 (1991): 1.

37. Janjaap Semeijn and David B. Vellenga, "International Logistics and One-Stop Shopping," *International Journal of Physical Distribution and Logistics Management* 10 (1995): 26–44.

38. Haw-Jan Wu and Steven C. Dunn, "Environmentally Responsible Logistics Systems," *International Journal of Physical Distribution and Logistics Management* 2 (1995): 20–38.

# CHAPTER 17

# Multinational Financial Management

## LEARNING OBJECTIVES

◆ *To understand how value is measured and managed across the multiple units of the multinational firm*

◆ *To understand how international business and investment activity alters and adds to the traditional financial management activities of the firm*

◆ *To understand the three primary currency exposures that confront the multinational firm*

◆ *To examine how exchange rate changes alter the value of the firm, and how management can manage or hedge these exposures*

## Changing Values: Satisfying Shareholders

**U**lrich Hartmann, the chief executive of industrial giant Veba AG, is doing something unheard of in Germany: He's worrying about shareholder value. He has laid off thousands of workers, fired longtime managers and closed divisions that date back to Veba's beginnings—all in the name of investors. "Our commitment," he said in last year's annual report, "is to create value for you, our shareholders."

The developments at Veba, Germany's fourth-largest company in revenue terms, underscore a trend catching hold in German boardrooms. Mr. Hartmann believes the trend will pick up in Germany if only, he says, because the pursuit of shareholder value is in everyone's interest. "Satisfying the shareholders is the best way to make sure that other stakeholders are served as well," he says. "It does no good when all the jobs are at sick companies."

But the German public—used to a fabled "German model" of management that advocates describe as "capitalism with a human face"—remains deeply suspicious of the alternative way of doing business." A number of people are left behind," says Norbert Wieczorek, a member of Germany's lower house of parliament and an economic expert with the opposition Social Democratic Party. "That's not the German way."

Mr. Hartmann is one of a new breed of German managers who are enthusiastically embracing the shareholder-value concept. Others are Juergen Dormann at Hoescht AG and Juergen Schrempp at Daimler-Benz AG. During a recent interview, a secretary interrupted the conversation to notify Mr. Schrempp of Daimler's opening stock price. "A year ago, no one in the company knew what the stock price was," he says. Now, he adds, the company keeps stockholders in mind with everything it does.

Driving companies to change are ever-growing capital requirements. Unable to raise enough money in Germany, companies are turning to foreigners. Nearly half the shares of drug companies Hoechst, Bayer AG and Schering AG are owned by non-Germans, who want more than just a dividend check. "There is no German or French or American capital market anymore," says Veba's Mr. Hartmann. "It is a global capital market, and we all have to play by the same rules." ▦

*Source:* "Changing Values: Satisfying Shareholders Is a Hot New Concept At Some German Firms," Greg Steinmetz, *The Wall Street Journal*, Wednesday March 6, 1996, A1, A10.

What exactly is *management* of the multinational firm attempting to achieve? The **maximization of shareholder value** is, of course, the ultimate goal, and given the good graces of the marketplace, that is indeed what is eventually achieved. But internally, within the virtual walls of the multinational firm, what exactly is management trying to maximize or minimize in pursuit of this goal? This chapter discusses first how the global firm trades off complex goals in order to preserve and create shareholder value, and secondly, how the financial management activities of the firm are expanded and differ from domestic management.

## Global Financial Goals

The multinational firm, because it is a conglomeration of many firms operating in a multitude of economic environments, must determine for itself the proper balance between three primary financial objectives:

1. Maximization of consolidated, after-tax, income
2. Minimization of the firm's effective global tax burden
3. Correct positioning of the firm's income, cash flows, and available funds

These goals are frequently inconsistent, in that the pursuit of one goal may result in a less desirable outcome in regard to another goal. Management must make decisions about the proper trade-offs between goals about the future (which is why people are employed as managers, not computers).

**Genus Corporation**  A sample firm aids in illustrating how the various components of the multinational firm fit together, and how financial management must make decisions regarding tradeoffs. Genus Corporation is a U.S.-based manufacturer and distributor of extremity-stimulus medical supplies.[1] The firm's corporate headquarters and original manufacturing plant are in New Orleans, Louisiana.

Genus currently has three wholly owned foreign subsidiaries located in Brazil, Germany, and China. In addition to the parent company selling goods in the domestic (U.S.) market and exporting goods to Mexico and Canada, each of the foreign subsidiaries purchases subassemblies (transfers) from the parent company. The subsidiaries then add value in the form of specific attributes and requirements for the local-country market, and distribute and sell the goods in the local market (Brazil, Germany, and China).

The three countries where Genus has incorporated subsidiaries pose very different challenges for the financial management of the firm. These challenges are outlined in Figure 17.1.

**Tax Management**  Genus, like all firms in all countries, would prefer to pay less taxes rather than more. Whereas profits are taxed at relatively low to moderate rates in China and Brazil, Germany's income tax rate is relatively high (though currently equal to that in the United States). If Genus could "rearrange" its profits among its units, it would prefer to make more of its profits in China and Brazil, given the lower tax burden placed upon profits in those countries.

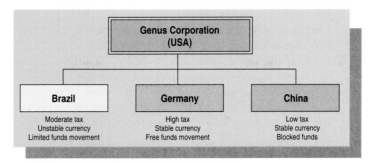

**FIGURE 17.1**

**Genus Corporation &
Foreign Subsidiaries**

**Currency Management**   Ultimately, for valuation purposes, the most important attribute of any of the three country currencies is its ability to maintain its value versus the U.S. dollar, the reporting currency of the parent company. The German mark (Deutschemark) is considered one of the world's three primary currencies, and although it occasionally suffers wide swings in value versus the dollar, has maintained its value well over time. The Chinese renminbi (or yuan as it is sometimes called) is not freely convertible into other currencies without governmental approval, and its value is therefore highly controlled and maintained. The Brazilian real, however, is of particular worry. In previous years the value of the Brazilian currency has been known to fall dramatically, wiping out the value of profits generated in Brazil when converted to any other currency, like the dollar. As opposed to what tax management would recommend, Genus would prefer to "rearrange" its profits into Germany and Deutschemarks for currency management purposes.

**Funds Flow Management**   The ability to move funds with relative ease and timeliness in a multinational firm is extremely important. For Genus, the German subsidiary experiences no problems with funds movements, as the German financial system is highly developed and open. Although Brazil possesses a number of bureaucratic requirements for justifying the movement of funds in and out of the country, it is still relatively open for moving funds cross-border. Genus's problems lie in China. The Chinese government makes it nearly impossible for foreign corporations to move funds out of China with any frequency, although bringing capital into China is not a problem. For funds management purposes, Genus would like to "rearrange its profits and cash flows to minimize having funds blocked up in China.

The challenge to financial management of the global firm is management's ability to find the right trade-off between these often conflicting goals and risks.

A number of helpful reminders about multinational companies aid in describing the financial management issues confronting Genus:

## Multinational Management

- The primary goal of the firm, domestic or multinational, is the maximization of consolidated profits, after tax.
- *Consolidated profits* are the profits of all the individual units of the firm originating in many different currencies as expressed in the currency of the parent company, in this case, the U.S. dollar. Consolidated profits are *not*

limited to those earnings that have been brought back to the parent company (repatriated), and in fact these profits may never be removed from the country in which they were earned.

■ Each of the incorporated units of the firm (the U.S. parent company and the three foreign subsidiaries) has its own set of traditional financial statements: statement of income, balance sheet, and statement of cash flows. These financial statements are expressed in the local currency of the unit for tax and reporting purposes to the local government.

Table 17.1 provides an overview of the current year's profits before and after tax on both the individual unit level and on the consolidated level, in both local currency and U.S. dollar value.

■ The owners of Genus, its shareholders, track the firm's financial performance on the basis of its earnings per share (EPS). EPS is simply the consolidated profits of the firm, in U.S. dollars, divided by the total number of shares outstanding:

$$\text{EPS} = \frac{\text{Consolidated profits after tax}}{\text{Shares outstanding}} = \frac{\text{US\$8,928,000}}{10,000,000} = \text{US\$0.89/share}$$

■ Each affiliate is located within a country's borders and is therefore subject to all laws and regulations applying to business activities within that country. These laws and regulations include specific practices as they apply to corporate income and tax rates, currency of denomination of operating and financial cash flows, and conditions under which capital and cash flows may move into and out of the country.

**TABLE 17.1**

**Genus Corporation's Consolidated Gross Profits (in 000s)**

| Unit (currency symbol) | Gross Profit (local currency) | Income Tax Rate (percent) | Taxes Payable (local currency) | Profit After tax (local currency) | Exchange Rate (fc/US$) | Gross Profit (US$) |
|---|---|---|---|---|---|---|
| U.S. Parent company (US$) | 4,500 | 35% | 1,575 | 2,925 | ——— | $2,925 |
| Brazilian subsidiary (R$) | 6,250 | 25% | 1,563 | 4,688 | 1.1500 | $4,076 |
| German subsidiary (DEM) | 4,500 | 35% | 1,575 | 2,925 | 1.7000 | $1,721 |
| Chinese subsidiary (RMB) | 2,500 | 30% | 750 | 1,750 | 8.5000 | $ 206 |
| **Consolidated** | | | | | | |
| Profits after tax (000s) | | | | | | $8,928 |
| Shares outstanding | | | | | | 10,000,000 |
| Earnings per share (EPS) | | | | | | $ 0.89 |

Notes:
1. Each individual unit of the company maintains its books in local currency as required by host governments.
2. fc is foreign currency.
3. Each individual unit's profits are translated into U.S. dollars using the average exchange rate for the period (year).
4. U.S. parent company's sales are derived from both sales to unrelated parties in the United States, Mexico (exports), and Canada (exports), as well as intra-firm sales (transfers) to the three individual foreign subsidiaries.
5. Tax calculations assume all profits are derived from the active conduct of merchandise trade, and all profits are retained in the individual units (no dividend distributions from subsidiaries to parent).

Multinational financial management is not a separate set of issues from domestic or traditional financial management, but the additional levels of risk and complexity introduced by the conduct of business across borders. Business across borders introduces different laws, different methods, different markets, different interest rates, and most of all, different currencies.

The many dimensions of multinational financial management are most easily explained in the context of a firm's financial decision-making process in evaluating a potential foreign investment. Such an evaluation includes:

■ Capital budgeting, which is the process of evaluating the financial feasibility of an individual investment, whether it be the purchase of a stock, real estate, or a firm

■ Capital structure, which is the determination of the relative quantities of debt capital and equity capital that will constitute the funding of the investment

■ Raising long-term capital, which is the acquisition of equity or debt for the investment; it requires the selection of the exact form of capital, its maturity, its reward or repayment structure, its currency of denomination, and its source

■ Working capital and cash flow management, which is the management of operating and financial cash flows passing in and out of a specific investment project

Multinational financial management means that all the above financial activities will be complicated by the differences in markets, laws, and especially currencies. This is the field of financial risk management. Firms may intentionally borrow foreign currencies, buy forward contracts, or price their products in different currencies to manage their cash flows that are denominated in foreign currencies.

Changes in interest and exchange rates will affect each of the above steps in the international investment process. All firms, no matter how "domestic" they may seem in structure, are influenced by exchange rate changes. The financial managers of a firm that has any dimension of international activity, imports or exports, foreign subsidiaries or affiliates, must pay special attention to these issues if the firm is to succeed in its international endeavors. The discussion begins with the difficulties of simply getting paid for international sales, import/export financing.

## Import/Export Trade Financing

Unlike most domestic business, international business often occurs between two parties that do not know each other very well. Yet, in order to conduct business, a large degree of financial trust must exist. This financial trust is basically the trust that the buyer of a product will actually pay for it on or after delivery. For example, if a furniture manufacturer in South Carolina receives an order from a distributor located in Cleveland, Ohio, the furniture maker will ordinarily fill the order, ship the furniture, and await payment. Payment terms are usually 30 to 60 days. This is trade on an "open account basis." The furniture manufacturer has placed a considerable amount of financial trust in the buyer but normally is paid with little problem.

Internationally, however, financial trust is pushed to its limit. An order from a foreign buyer may constitute a degree of credit risk (the risk of not being re-paid) that the producer (the exporter) cannot afford to take. The exporter needs some guarantee that the importer will pay for the goods. Other factors that tend to intensify this problem include the increased lag times necessary for international shipments and the potential risks of payments in different currencies. For this reason, arrangements that provide guarantees for exports are important to countries and companies wanting to expand international sales. This can be accomplished through a sequence of documents surround-ing the letter of credit.

## Trade Financing Using a Letter of Credit (L/C)

A lumber manufacturer in the Pacific Northwest of the United States, Vanport, receives a large order from a Japanese construction company, Endaka, for a shipment of old-growth pine lumber. Vanport has not worked with Endaka be-fore and therefore seeks some assurance that payment for the lumber will ac-tually be made. Vanport ordinarily does not require any assurance of the buyer's ability to pay (sometimes a small down payment or deposit is made as a sign of good faith), but an international sale of this size is too large a risk. If En-daka could not or would not pay, the cost of returning the lumber products to the United States would be prohibitive. Figure 17.2 illustrates the following se-quence of events that will complete the transaction.

1. Endaka Construction (JAP) requests a letter of credit (L/C) to be issued by its bank, Yokohama Bank.
2. Yokohama Bank will determine whether Endaka is financially sound and ca-pable of making the payments as required. This is a very important step be-cause Yokohama Bank simply wants to guarantee the payment, not make the payment.

**FIGURE 17.2**

**Trade Financing with a Letter of Credit (L/C)**

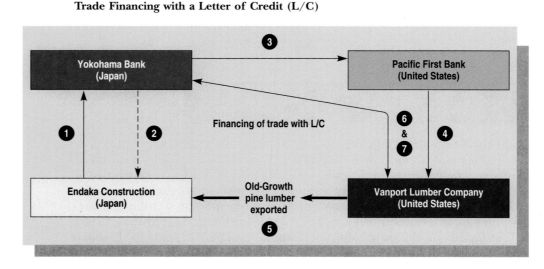

3. Yokohama Bank, once satisfied with Endaka's application, issues the L/C to a representative in the United States or to the exporter's bank, Pacific First Bank. The L/C guarantees payment for the merchandise if the goods are shipped as stipulated in accompanying documents. Customary documents include the commercial invoice, customs clearance and invoice, the packing list, certification of insurance, and a bill of lading.

4. The exporter's bank, Pacific First, assures Vanport that payment will be made after evaluating the letter of credit. At this point the credit standing of Yokohama Bank has been substituted for the credit standing of the importer itself, Endaka Construction.

5. When the lumber order is ready, it is loaded onboard the shipper (called a common carrier). When the exporter signs a contract with a shipper, the signed contract serves as the receipt that the common carrier has received the goods, and it is termed the **bill of lading.**

6. Vanport draws a **draft** against Yokohama Bank for payment. The draft is the document used in international trade to effect payment and explicitly requests payment for the merchandise, which is now shown to be shipped and insured consistent with all requirements of the previously issued L/C. (If the draft is issued to the bank issuing the L/C, Yokohama Bank, it is termed a **bank draft.** If the draft is issued against the importer, Endaka Construction, it is a **trade draft.**) The draft, L/C, and other appropriate documents are presented to Pacific First Bank for payment.

7. If Pacific First Bank (US) had **confirmed** the letter of credit from Yokohama Bank, it would immediately pay Vanport for the lumber and then collect from the issuing bank, Yokohama. If Pacific First Bank had not confirmed the letter of credit, it only passes the documents to Yokohama Bank for payment (to Vanport). The confirmed, as opposed to unconfirmed, letter of credit obviously speeds up payment to the exporter.

Regardless, with the letter of credit as the financial assurance, the exporter or the exporter's bank is collecting payment from the importer's bank, not from the importer itself. It is up to the specific arrangements between the importer (Endaka) and the importer's bank (Yokohama) to arrange the final settlement at that end of the purchase.

If the trade relationship continues over time, both parties will gain faith and confidence in the other. With this strengthening of financial trust, the trade financing relationship will loosen. Sustained buyer-seller relations across borders eventually end up operating on an open account basis similar to domestic commerce.

## International Capital Budgeting

Any investment, whether it be the purchase of stock, the acquisition of real estate, or the construction of a manufacturing facility in another country, is financially justified if the present value of expected cash inflows is greater than the present value of expected cash outflows, in other words, if it has a positive **net present value (NPV).** The construction of a **capital budget** is the process of projecting the net operating cash flows of the potential investment to determine if it is indeed a good investment.

## Capital Budget Components and Decision Criteria

All capital budgets are only as good as the accuracy of the cost and revenue assumptions. Adequately anticipating all of the incremental expenses that the individual project imposes on the firm is critical to a proper analysis.

A capital budget is composed of three primary cash flow components:

1. **Initial Expenses and Capital Outlays.** The initial capital outlays are normally the largest net cash outflow occurring over the life of a proposed investment. Because the cash flows occur up front, they have a substantial impact on the net present value of the project.
2. **Operating Cash Flows.** The operating cash flows are the net cash flows the project is expected to yield once production is under way. The primary positive net cash flows of the project are realized in this stage; net operating cash flows will determine the success or failure of the proposed investment.
3. **Terminal Cash Flows.** The final component of the capital budget is composed of the salvage value or resale value of the project at its end. The terminal value will include whatever working capital balances can be recaptured once the project is no longer in operation (at least by this owner).

The financial decision criterion for an individual investment is whether the net present value of the project is positive or negative.[2] The net cash flows in the future are discounted by the average cost of capital for the firm (the average of debt and equity costs). The purpose of discounting is to capture the fact that the firm has acquired investment capital at a cost (interest). The same capital could have been used for other projects of other investments. It is therefore necessary to discount the future cash flows to account for this foregone income of the capital, its opportunity cost. If NPV is positive, then the project is an acceptable investment. If the project's NPV is negative, then the cash flows expected to result from the investment are insufficient to provide an acceptable rate of return, and the project should be rejected.

## A Proposed Project Evaluation

The capital budget for a manufacturing plant in Singapore serves as a basic example. ACME, a U.S. manufacturer of household consumer products, is considering the construction of a plant in Singapore in 1999. It would cost US$1,660,000 to build and would be ready for operation on January 1, 2000. ACME would operate the plant for three years and then would sell the plant to the Singapore government.

To analyze the proposed investment, ACME must estimate what the sales revenues would be per year, the costs of production, the overhead expenses of operating the plant per year, the depreciation allowances for the new plant and equipment, and the Singapore tax rate on corporate income. The estimation of all net operating cash flows is very important to the analysis of the project. Often the entire acceptability of a foreign investment may depend on the sales forecast for the foreign project.

But ACME needs U.S. dollars, not Singapore dollars. The only way the stockholders of ACME would be willing to undertake the investment is if it would be profitable in terms of their own currency, the U.S. dollar. This is the primary theoretical distinction between a domestic capital budget and a multinational capital budget. The evaluation of the project in the viewpoint of the parent will focus on whatever cash flows, either operational or financial, will find their way back to the parent firm in U.S. dollars.

**TABLE 17.2**

**Multinational Capital Budget: Singapore Manufacturing Facility**

| Line # | Description | 1999 | 2000 | 2001 | 2002 |
|--------|-------------|------|------|------|------|
| 1 | Net cash flow in S$ | (1,660,000) | 300,000 | 600,000 | 1,500,000 |
| 2 | Exchange rate, S$/US$ | 1.6600 | 1.7430 | 1.8302 | 1.9217 |
| 3 | Net cash flow in US$ | (1,000,000) | 172,117 | 327,833 | 780,559 |
| 4 | Present value factor | 1.0000 | 0.8621 | 0.7432 | 0.6407 |
| 5 | Present value in US$ | (1,000,000) | 148,377 | 243,633 | 500,071 |
| 6 | Net present value in US$ | (107,919) | | | |
| 7 | Net present value in S$ | 5,505 | | | |

Notes:
a. The spot exchange rate of S$1.6600/US$ is assumed to change by 5 percent per year, $1.6600 \times 1.05 = 1.7430$.
b. The present value factor assumes a weighted average cost of capital, the discount rate, of 16 percent. The present value factor then is found using the standard formula of $1/(1 + .16)^t$, where t is the number of years in the future (1, 2, or 3).

ACME must therefore forecast the movement of the Singapore dollar (S$) over the four-year period as well. The spot rate on January 1, 1999 is S$1.6600/US$. ACME concludes that the rate of inflation will be roughly 5 percent higher per year in Singapore than in the United States. If the theory of purchasing power parity holds, as described in Chapter 7, it should take roughly 5 percent more Singapore dollars to buy a U.S. dollar per year. Using this assumption, ACME forecasts the exchange rate from 1999 to 2002.

After considerable study and analysis, ACME estimates that the net cash flows of the Singapore project, in Singapore dollars, would be those on line 1 in Table 17.2. Line 2 lists the expected exchange rate between Singapore dollars and U.S. dollars over the four-year period, assuming it takes 5 percent more Singapore dollars per U.S. dollar each year (the Singapore dollar is therefore expected to depreciate versus the U.S. dollar). Combining the net cash flow forecast in Singapore dollars with the expected exchange rates, ACME can now calculate the net cash flow per year in U.S. dollars. ACME notes that although the initial expense is sizable, S$1,660,000 or US$1,000,000, the project produces positive net cash flows in its very first year of operations (2000) of US$172,117, and remains positive every year after.

ACME estimates that its cost of capital, both debt and equity combined (the weighted average cost of capital), is about 16 percent per year. Using this as the rate of discount, the discount factor for each of the future years is found. Finally, the net cash flow in U.S. dollars multiplied by the present value factor yields the present values of each net cash flow. The net present value of the Singapore project is a negative US$107,919; ACME may now decide not to proceed with the project since it is financially unacceptable.

**Risks in International Investments**

How is the ACME capital budget different from a similar project constructed in Bangor, Maine? It is riskier, at least from the standpoint of cross-border risk. The higher risk of an international investment arises from the different countries, their laws, regulations, potential for interference with the normal operations of the investment project, and obviously currencies, all of which are unique to international investment.

## Inflation Rates and Interest Rates Around the World

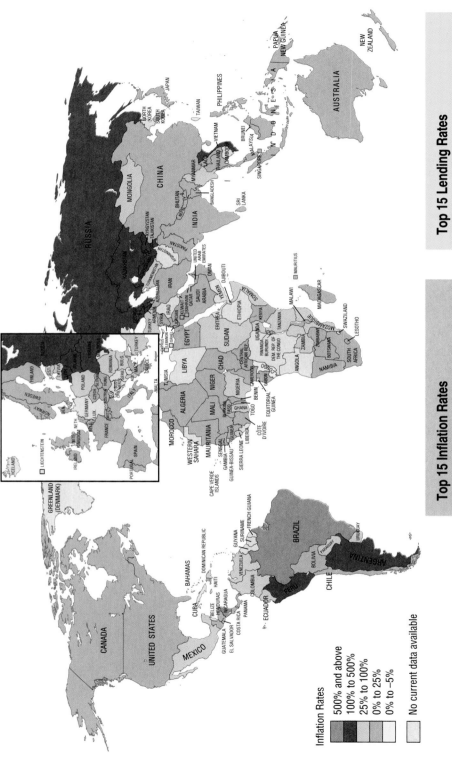

**Inflation Rates**

- 500% and above
- 100% to 500%
- 25% to 100%
- 0% to 25%
- 0% to –5%
- No current data available

**Top 15 Inflation Rates**

| | | | |
|---|---|---|---|
| Nicaragua | 1311.2 | Belarus | 136.7 |
| Brazil | 900.3 | Azerbaijan | 122.8 |
| Peru | 492.2 | Uzbekistan | 109.1 |
| Argentina | 317.2 | Tajikistan | 104.3 |
| Ukraine | 297.0 | Vietnam | 102.6 |
| Georgia | 228.3 | Lithuania | 102.3 |
| Kazakhstan | 150.2 | Kyrgyzstan | 100.9 |
| Armenia | 138.6 | | |

**Top 15 Lending Rates**

| | | | |
|---|---|---|---|
| Ukraine | 250.3 | Peru | 53.6 |
| Mongolia | 233.6 | Jamaica | 49.5 |
| Zambia | 113.3 | Venezuela | 46.6 |
| Uruguay | 95.1 | Ecuador | 44.0 |
| Bulgaria | 64.1 | Colombia | 40.5 |
| Lithuania | 62.3 | Slovenia | 39.4 |
| Latvia | 55.9 | Ethiopia | 39.0 |
| Bolivia | 55.6 | | |

Source: *World Development Report 1996*

The risk of international investment is considered greater because the proposed investment will be within the jurisdiction of a different government. Governments have the ability to pass new laws, including the potential nationalization of the entire project. The typical problems that may arise from operating in a different country are changes in foreign tax laws, restrictions placed on when or how much in profits may be repatriated to the parent company, and other types of restrictions that hinder the free movement of merchandise and capital among the proposed project, the parent, and any other country relevant to its material inputs or sales.

The other major distinction between a domestic investment and a foreign investment is that the viewpoint or perspective of the parent and the project are no longer the same. The two perspectives differ because the parent only values cash flows it derives from the project. So, for example, in Table 17.2 the project generates sufficient net cash flows in Singapore dollars that the project is acceptable from the project's viewpoint, but not from the parent's viewpoint. Assuming the same 16 percent discount rate, the NPV in Singapore dollars is +S$5,505, while the NPV to the U.S. parent was −US$107,919 as noted previously. But what if the exchange rate were not to change at all—remain *fixed* for the 1999–2002 period? The NPV would then be positive from both viewpoints (project NPV remains +S$5,505, parent's NPV is now US$3,316). Or what if the Singapore government were to restrict the payment of dividends back to the U.S. parent firm, or somehow prohibit the Singapore subsidiary

Although projects may be similar, the capital budgeting process must include an assessment of the higher risks associated with international projects, such as Mobil Corporation's expanded oil production platforms in the British sector of the North Sea. *Source:* © Larry Lee 1992.

from exchanging Singapore dollars for U.S. dollars (capital controls)? Without cash flows in U.S. dollars, the parent would have no way of justifying the investment. And all of this could occur while the project itself is sufficiently profitable when measured in local currency (Singapore dollars). This split between project and parent viewpoint is a critical difference in international investment analysis.

## Capital Structure: International Dimensions

The choice of how to fund the firm is called capital structure. Capital is needed to open a factory, build an amusement park, or even start a hot dog stand. If capital is provided by owners of the firm, it is called equity. If capital is obtained by borrowing from others, such as commercial banking institutions, it is termed debt. Debt must be repaid with interest over some specified schedule. Equity capital, however, is kept in the firm. Owners are risking their own capital in the enterprise; they are entitled to a proportion of the profits.

### The Capital Structure of the Firm

The trade-offs between debt and equity are easily seen by looking at extreme examples of capital structures. If a firm had no debt, all capital would have to come from the owners. This may limit the size of the firm, as the owners do not have bottomless pockets. The primary benefit is that all net operating revenues are kept. There are no principal or interest payments to make. A firm with a large debt (highly leveraged), however, would have the capital of others with which to work. The scale of the firm could be larger, and all net profits would still accrue to the equity holders alone. The primary disadvantage of debt is the increasing expense of making principal and interest payments. At the extreme, this could prove to be an ever-increasing proportion of net cash flows.

Any firm's ability to grow and expand is dependent on its ability to acquire additional capital as it grows. The net profits generated over previous periods may be valuable but are rarely enough to provide needed capital expansion. Firms therefore need access to capital markets, both debt and equity. Chapter 7 provided an overview of the major debt and equity markets available internationally, but it is important to remember that the firm must have *access* to the markets to enjoy their fruits.

### The Capital Structure of Foreign Subsidiaries

The choice of what proportions of debt and equity to use in international investments is usually dictated by either the debt-equity structure of the parent or the debt-equity structure of competitive firms in the host country. The parent firm sees equity investment as capital at risk; therefore, it would usually prefer to provide as little equity capital as possible. Although funding the foreign subsidiary primarily with debt would still put the parent's capital at risk, debt service provides a strict schedule for cash flow repatriation to the lender. Equity capital's return, dividends from profits, depends on managerial discretion. It is this discretion, the proportion of profits returned to the parent versus profits retained and reinvested in the project or firm, that often leads to conflict between host-country authorities and the multinational firm.

**TABLE 17.3**

**Financing Alternatives for Foreign Affiliates**

| Foreign Affiliate Can Raise Equity Capital: | Foreign Affiliate Can Raise Debt Capital: |
|---|---|
| 1. From the parent | 1. From the parent |
| 2. From a joint-venture partner in the parent's country, a joint-venture partner in the host country, or a share issue in the host country | 2. From a bank loan or bond issue in the host country or the parent firm's home country |
| 3. From a third-country market such as a share issue in the Euro-equity market | 3. From a third-country bank loan, bond issue, Euro-syndicated credit, or Euro-bond issue |

The sources of debt for a foreign subsidiary theoretically are quite large, but in reality they often are quite limited. The alternatives listed in Table 17.3 are often radically reduced in practice because many countries have relatively small capital markets. These countries often either officially restrict the borrowing by foreign-owned firms in their countries or simply do not have affordable capital available for the foreign firm's use. The parent firm is then often forced to provide not only the equity but also a large proportion of the debt to its foreign subsidiaries.

The larger firms internationally will often have their own financial subsidiaries, companies purely for the purpose of acquiring the capital needed for the entire company's continuing growth needs. These financial subsidiaries will often be the actual unit extending the debt or equity capital to the foreign project or subsidiary. The hope is that, with time and success, the foreign investment will grow sufficiently to establish its own credit standing and acquire more and more of its capital needs from the local markets in which it operates.

# International Working Capital and Cash Flow Management

**Working capital management** is the financing of short-term or current assets, but the term is used here to describe all short-term financing and financial management of the firm. Even a small multinational firm will have a number of different cash flows moving throughout its system at one time. The maintenance of proper liquidity, the monitoring of payments, and the acquisition of additional capital when needed—all of these require a great degree of organization and planning in international operations.

Firms possess both operating cash flows and financing cash flows. **Operating cash flows** arise from the everyday business activities of the firm such as paying for materials or resources (accounts payable) or receiving payments for items sold (accounts receivable). In addition to the direct cost and revenue cash flows from operations, there are a number of indirect cash flows. The indirect cash flows are primarily license fees paid to the owners of particular technological processes and royalties to the holders of patents of copyrights.

**Operating Cash Flows and Financing Cash Flows**

**Financing cash flows** arise from the funding activities of the firm. The servicing of existing funding sources, interest on existing debt, and dividend payments to shareholders constitute potentially large and frequent cash flows. Periodic additions to debt or equity through new bank loans, new bond issuances, or supplemental stock sales may also add to the volume of financing cash flows in the multinational firm.

## A Sample Cash Flow Mapping

Figure 17.3 provides an overview of how operational and financial cash flows may appear for a U.S.–based multinational firm. In addition to having some export sales in Canada, it may import some materials from Mexico. The firm has gained access to several different European markets by first selling its product to its German subsidiary, which then provides the final touches necessary for sales in Germany, France, and Switzerland. Sales and purchases by the parent with Canada and Mexico give rise to a continuing series of accounts receivables and accounts payable, which may be denominated in Canadian dollars, Mexican pesos, or U.S. dollars.

## Intrafirm Cash Flows and Transfer Prices

Cash flows between the U.S. parent and the German subsidiary will be both operational and financial in nature. The sale of the major product line to the German subsidiary creates intrafirm account receivables and payables. The payments may be denominated in either U.S. dollars or German marks. The intrafirm sales may, in fact, be two way if the German subsidiary is actually producing a form of the product not made in the United States but needed there.

One of the most difficult pricing decisions many multinational firms must make concerns the price at which they sell their products to their own subsidiaries and affiliates. These prices, called **transfer prices,** theoretically are equivalent to what the same product would cost if purchased on the open market. However, it is often impossible to find such a product on the open market; it may be unique to the firm and its product line. The result is a price that is set internally and may result in the subsidiary being more or less profitable. This, in turn, has im-

**FIGURE 17.3**

**Operating and Financing Cash Flows of a U.S.–Based Multinational Firm**

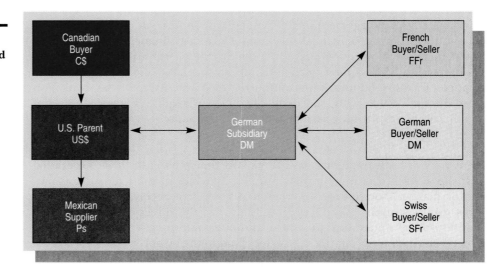

pacts on taxes paid in host countries. Global Perspective 17.1 illustrates what happens when governments and firms do not agree on transfer prices. (See Chapter 15 for a more detailed discussion of transfer pricing.)

The foreign subsidiary may also be using techniques, machinery, or processes that are owned or patented by the parent firm and so must pay royalties and license fees. The cash flows are usually calculated as a percentage of the sales price in Germany. Many multinational firms also spread the overhead and management expenses incurred at the parent over their foreign affiliates and subsidiaries that are using the parent's administrative services.

There are also a number of financing cash flows between the U.S. parent and the German subsidiary. If the subsidiary is partially financed by loans extended by the parent, the subsidiary needs to make regular payments to the parent. If the German subsidiary is successful in its operations and generates a profit, then dividends will be paid back to the parent. If, at some point, the German subsidiary needs more capital than what it can retain from its own profits, it may need additional debt or equity capital (from any of the potential sources listed in Table 17.3). These obviously would add to the potential financial cash flow volume.

The subsidiary, in turn, is dependent on its sales in Germany (German mark revenues), France (French franc revenues), and Switzerland (Swiss franc revenues) to generate the needed cash flows for paying everyone else. This "map" of operating and financing cash flows does not even attempt to describe the frequency of the various foreign currency cash flows, or to assign the responsibility for managing the currency risks. The management of cash flows in a larger multinational firm, one with possibly ten or twenty subsidiaries, is obviously complex. The proper management of the cash flows is, however, critical to the success of the multinational business.

## Cash Flow Management

The structure of the firm dictates how cash flows and financial resources can be managed. The trend in the past decade has been for the increasing centralization of most financial and treasury operations. The centralized treasury

---

**GLOBAL PERSPECTIVE 17.1**

## SWISS UNIT PAYS PENALTY FOR TRANSFER PRICING ABUSE

**T**ax authorities believe that Nippon Roche K.K. failed to declare taxable income totaling ¥14billion between 1992 and 1995, according to sources familiar with the case. The income in question was allegedly transferred to the company's Swiss parent firm, Roche Holding Ltd., through a practice known as transfer pricing, in which a subsidiary pays artificially inflated prices for goods purchased from its overseas parent to cut taxable income in the host country, they said.

The sources said Nippon Roche allegedly manipulated prices of raw materials for cancer drugs and other medicine purchased from F. Hoffman-La Roche Ltd., a drug company under Roche Holding. Nippon Roche could be ordered to pay an additional ¥3.8billion in taxes for failing to declare ¥4.5billion in taxable income between 1989 and 1991. Under an agreement with Swiss tax authorities earlier this year, Japanese tax authorities settled on a figure of some ¥5.5billion for the amount of undeclared income transferred to the parent firm to avoid double taxation.

*Source: "Swiss Unit Faces Hefty Penalty for Tax Evasion,"* **Japan Times**, *November 10, 1996.*

often is responsible for both funding operations and cash flow management. The centralized treasury often may enjoy significant economies of scale, offering more services and expertise to the various units of the firm worldwide than the individual units themselves could support. However, regardless of whether the firm follows a centralized or decentralized approach, there are a number of operating structures that help the multinational firm manage its cash flows.

**Netting**   Figure 17.4 expands our firm to two European subsidiaries, one in Germany and one in France. The figure illustrates how many of the cash flows between units of a multinational firm are two way and may result in unneeded transfer costs and transaction expenses. Coordination between units simply requires planning and budgeting of intrafirm cash flows so that two-way flows are "netted" against one another, with only one smaller cash flow as opposed to two having to be undertaken.

   **Netting** can occur between each subsidiary and the parent, and between the subsidiaries themselves (it is often forgotten that many of the activities in a multinational firm occur between subsidiaries, and not just between individual subsidiaries and the parent). Netting is particularly helpful if the two-way flow is in two different currencies, as each would be suffering currency exchange charges for intrafirm transfers.

**Cash Pooling**   A large firm with a number of units operating both within an individual country and across countries may be able to economize on the amount of firm assets needed in cash if one central pool is used for **cash pooling.** With one pool of capital and up-to-date information on the cash flows in and out of the various units, the firm spends much less in terms of foregone interest on cash balances, which are held in safekeeping against unforeseen cash flow shortfalls.

   For example, for the firm described in Figure 17.4, the parent and German and French subsidiaries may be able to consolidate all cash management and resources in one place—for example, New York (associated with the U.S. parent). One cash manager for all units would be in a better position for planning intercompany payments, including controlling the currency exposures of the individual units. A single large pool also may allow the firm to negotiate better financial service rates with banking institutions for cash-clearing pur-

**FIGURE 17.4**

**Netting and Cash Pooling of Cash Flows in the Multinational Firm**

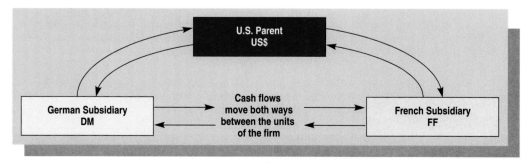

poses. In the event that the cash manager would need to be closer to the individual units (both proximity and time zone), the two European units could combine to run cash from one or the other for both.

**Leads and Lags**  The timing of payments between units of a multinational is somewhat flexible. Again, this allows the management of payments between the French and German subsidiaries and between the parent and the subsidiaries to be much more flexible, allowing the firm not only to position cash flows where they are needed most, but also to help manage currency risk. A foreign subsidiary that is expecting its local currency to fall in value relative to the U.S. dollar may try to speed up or **lead** its payments to the parent. Similarly, if the local currency is expected to rise versus the dollar, the subsidiary may want to wait, or **lag,** payments until exchange rates are more favorable.

**Reinvoicing**  Multinational firms with a variety of manufacturing and distribution subsidiaries scattered over a number of countries within a region may often find it more economical to have one office or subsidiary taking ownership of all invoices and payments between units.

For example, Figure 17.5 illustrates how our sample firm could be restructured to incorporate a **reinvoicing** center. The site for the reinvoicing center in this case is Luxembourg, a country that is known to have low taxes and few restrictions on income earned from international business operations. The Luxembourg subsidiary buys from one unit and sells to a second unit, therefore taking ownership of the goods and reinvoicing the sale to the next unit. Once ownership is taken, the sale/purchase can be redenominated in a different currency, netted against other payments, hedged against specific currency exposures, or repriced in accordance with potential tax benefits of the reinvoicing center's host country.

**Internal Banks**  Some multinational firms have found that their financial resources and needs are becoming either too large or too sophisticated for the financial services that are available in many of their local subsidiary markets.

**FIGURE 17.5**

**Establishing a Reinvoicing Center in the Multinational Firm**

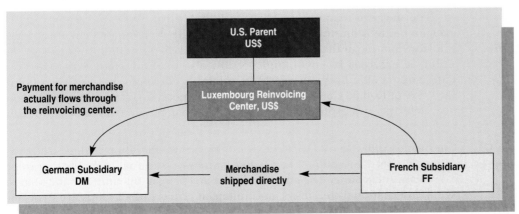

One solution to this has been the establishment of an **internal bank** within the firm. The internal bank actually buys and sells payables and receivables from the various units, which frees the units of the firm from struggling for continual working capital financing and lets them focus on their primary business activities.

All of these structures and management techniques often are combined in different ways to fit the needs of the individual multinational firm. Some techniques are encouraged or prohibited by laws and regulations (for example, many countries limit the ability to lead and lag payments), depending on the host-country's government and stage of capital market liberalization. Multinational cash flow management requires flexibility in thinking—artistry in some cases—as much as technique on the part of managers.

## Financial Risk Management

All firms are in some way influenced by three financial prices; exchange rates, interest rates, and commodity prices. The management of these prices—these risks—is termed **financial risk management.** Interest rates have always received, deservedly, much of management's attention in business; it is only recently that many firms have chosen to acknowledge their financial health is also affected by exchange rates and commodity prices. The following analysis focuses on the exchange rate risks suffered by firms operating internationally.

### Financial Price Risk and Firm Value

*Risk* is a word that deserves more respect than it is commonly afforded. Most dictionaries will refer to risk as the possibility of suffering harm or loss; danger; or a factor or element involving uncertain hazards. These definitions are negative. Yet in the field of finance, the word *risk* has a neutral definition: a value or result that is at present unknown.

There are three categories of financial price risk: interest rate risk, exchange rate risk, and commodity price risk. Each can have potentially positive or negative impacts on the profitability and value of the firm. For example, a U.S. exporter such as Eastman Kodak pays specific attention to the value of the U.S. dollar. If the dollar were to appreciate against other major currencies such as the Japanese yen, Kodak's products would be more expensive to foreign buyers, and it could lose market share to foreign competitors (like Fuji).

The negative relationship between Kodak's firm value and the yen-dollar exchange rate is illustrated in Figure 17.6. As the dollar appreciates versus the yen (for example, if the spot rate moved from ¥125/$ to ¥140/$), Kodak would suffer falling sales in Japan, and possibly also in the United States, because Fuji's comparable products would be relatively cheaper. The result is a fall in the value of Kodak. Corporate management expects financial managers to control such risks and protect the firm against exchange rate risks as best they can.

### Classification of Foreign Currency Exposures

Companies today know the risks of international operations. They are aware of the substantial risks to balance sheet values and annual earnings that interest rates and exchange rates may inflict on any firm at any time. Financial managers, international treasurers, and financial officers of all kinds are expected

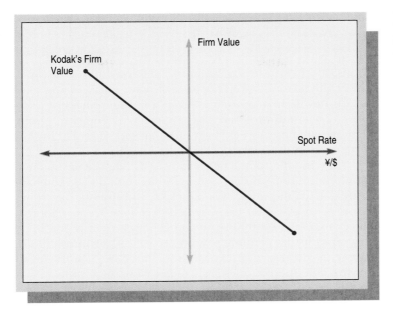

**FIGURE 17.6**

**Financial Price Risks and the Value of the Firm**

to protect the firm from such risks. Firms have, in varying degrees, three types of foreign currency exposure:

1. **Transaction exposure.** This is the risk associated with a contractual payment of foreign currency. For example, a U.S. firm that exports products to France will receive a guaranteed (by contract) payment in French francs in the future. Firms that buy or sell internationally have **transaction exposure** if any of the cash flows are denominated in foreign currency.
2. **Economic exposure.** This is the risk to the firm that its long-term cash flows will be affected, positively or negatively, by unexpected future exchange rate changes. Although many firms that consider themselves to be purely domestic may not realize it, all firms have some degree of **economic exposure.**
3. **Translation exposure.** This risk arises from the legal requirement that all firms consolidate their financial statements (balance sheets and income statements) of all worldwide operations annually. Therefore, any firm with operations outside its home country, operations that will be either earning foreign currency or valued in foreign currency, has **translation exposure.**

Transaction exposure and economic exposure are "true exposures" in the financial sense. This means they both present potential threats to the value of a firm's cash flows over time. The third exposure, translation, is a problem that arises from accounting. Under the present accounting principles in practice across most of the world's industrialized countries, translation exposure is not the problem it once was. For the most part, few real cash resources should be devoted to a purely accounting-based event.

## Transaction Exposure

Transaction exposure is the most commonly observed type of exchange rate risk. Only two conditions are necessary for a transaction exposure to exist: (1) a cash flow that is denominated in a foreign currency and (2) the cash flow will occur at a future date. Any contract, agreement, purchase, or sale that is denominated in a foreign currency that will be settled in the future constitutes a transaction exposure.

The risk of a transaction exposure is that the exchange rate might change between the present date and the settlement date. The change may be for the better or for the worse. For example, suppose that an American firm signs a contract to purchase heavy rolled-steel pipe from a South Korean steel producer for 21,000,000 Korean won. The payment is due in 30 days upon delivery. The 30-day account payable, so typical of international trade and commerce, is a transaction exposure for the U.S. firm. If the spot exchange rate on the date the contract is signed is Won 700/$, the U.S. firm would expect to pay

$$\frac{\text{Won } 21,000,000}{\text{Won } 700/\$} = \$30,000$$

But the firm is not assured of what the exchange rate will be in 30 days. If the spot rate at the end of 30 days is Won 720/$, the U.S. firm would actually pay less. The payment would then be $29,167. If, however, the exchange rate changed in the opposite direction, for example to Won 650/$, the payment could just as easily increase to $32,308. This type of price risk, transaction exposure, is a major problem for international commerce.

**Transaction Exposure Management**

Management of transaction exposures usually is accomplished by either **natural hedging** or **contractual hedging.** Natural hedging is the term used to describe how a firm might arrange to have foreign currency cash flows coming in and going out at roughly the same times and same amounts. This is referred to as natural hedging because the management or hedging of the exposure is accomplished by matching offsetting foreign currency cash flows and, therefore, does not require the firm to undertake unusual financial contracts or activities to manage the exposure. For example, a Canadian firm that generates a significant portion of its total sales in U.S. dollars may acquire U.S. dollar debt. The U.S. dollar earnings from sales could then be used to service the dollar debt as needed. In this way, regardless of whether the C$/US$ exchange rate goes up or down, the firm would be naturally hedged against the movement. If the U.S. dollar went up in value against the Canadian dollar, the U.S. dollars needed for debt service would be generated automatically by the export sales to the United States. U.S. dollar inflows would match U.S. dollar cash outflows.

Contractual hedging is when the firm uses financial contracts to hedge the transaction exposure. The most common foreign currency contractual hedge is the **forward contract,** although other financial instruments and derivatives, such as currency futures and options, are also used. The forward contract (see

Chapter 7) would allow the firm to be assured a fixed rate of exchange between the desired two currencies at the precise future date. The forward contract would also be for the exact amount of the exposure. Both natural hedging and contractual hedging are discussed in Global Perspective 17.2.

A **hedge** is an asset or a position whose value moves in the equal but opposite direction of the exposure. This means that if an exposure experienced a loss in value of $50, the hedge asset would offset the loss with a gain in value of $50. The total value of the position would not change. This would be termed a perfect hedge.

But perfect hedges are hard to find, and many people would not use them if they were readily available. Why? The presence of a perfect hedge eliminates all downside risk, but also eliminates all upside potential. Many businesses accept this two-sided risk as part of doing business. However, it is generally best to accept risk in the line of business, not in the cash-payment process of settling the business.

GLOBAL
PERSPECTIVE 17.2

## "LOST IN A MAZE OF HEDGES"

**V**olatile exchange rates in recent weeks have sent many a nervous boss scurrying to his finance department to check up on its currency hedging strategy. Few of them will emerge much the wiser, for the typical multinational's strategy can seem impenetrable.

Hedging is simple enough in theory. Just doing business exposes many firms to foreign exchange risk: if an exchange rate moves the wrong way, profit or the balance sheet suffers. Suppose a British exporter sells goods that will be paid for in dollars three months later. If the dollar weakens against the pound, the exporter will get less in sterling than it expected. Hedging lets firms reduce or eliminate this risk by using a financial instrument that moves in the opposite way when exchange rates change. For the British exporter, that means one that is worth more pounds as the dollar falls.

The best way to hedge is to do it "naturally." Firms can design their trading, borrowing, and investment strategies to match their sales and assets in a particular currency with their purchases and liabilities in it. If, say, a British firm owns an asset valued in dollars, it can hedge by borrowing in dollars. No matter what happens to the pound–dollar exchange rate, there will be no net effect on the firm's balance sheet.

Few firms can hedge all, or even most, of their risk natu-

rally. So many hedge actively in the financial markets, mainly using forward contracts and options. Forward contracts, agreements to buy or sell a given amount of a currency at an agreed exchange rate on a particular date, get rid of all exchange rate risk, and are often thought of as the perfect hedge. If the British exporter is going to be paid $1m in three months, it can make a forward contract to sell the $1m on that date and know exactly how many pounds it will get in return even if exchange rates fluctuate in the spot market.

The trouble with forward contracts is that they are irrevocable. If the dollar strengthens against sterling, the British exporter with a forward contract is worse off than it would have been with no hedge at all. Options, which give firms the right, but not the obligation, to use a particular forward contract, are more flexible. Imagine that the British exporter buys an option to sell dollars in three months at the forward rate. If the exchange rate moves against the firm, it can use its option and limit the damage; if the rate goes in its favor, it can let the option lapse and enjoy the windfall.

Firms seem to use forward contracts at least twice as often as options. One reason is cost. Forward contracts are no dearer than an ordinary trade in the spot market. Options, by contrast, are expensive and must be paid for whether or not they are used. Option prices can jump about wildly, depending on which currencies are involved and how volatile the market is. Prices have gone through the roof recently: on September 29 Swiss Bank Corporation priced a three-month option to sell dollars at 2.7 percent of the contract, a hefty $27,000 for a British exporter wanting to hedge $1 million.

*Source: Abstracted from "Lost in a Maze of Hedges," The Economist, October 3, 1992, p. 84. Copyright © 1992, The Economist, Ltd. Distributed by The New York Times/Special Features.*

**Risk Management versus Speculation**

The distinction between managing currency cash flows and speculating with currency cash flows is sometimes lost among those responsible for the safe-keeping of the firm's treasury. If the previous description of currency hedging is followed closely (the selection of assets or positions only to counteract potential losses on existing exposures), few problems should arise. Problems arise when currency positions or financial instruments are purchased (or sold) with the expectation that a specific currency movement will result in a profit, termed speculation.

There are a number of major multinational firms that treat their international treasury centers as "service centers," but rarely do they consider financial management a "profit center." One of the most visible examples of what can go wrong when currency speculation is undertaken for corporate profit occurred in Great Britain in 1991. A large British food conglomerate, Allied-Lyons, suffered losses of £158 million ($268 million) on currency speculation after members of its international treasury staff suffered losses on currency positions at the start of the Persian Gulf War and then doubled-up on their positions in the following weeks in an attempt to recover previous losses. They lost even more.[3]

**Transaction Exposure Case: Lufthansa (1985)**

In January 1985, the German airline Lufthansa purchased 20 Boeing 737 jet aircraft. The jets would be delivered to Lufthansa in one year, in January 1986. Upon delivery of the aircraft, Lufthansa would pay Boeing (U.S.) $500 million. This constituted a huge transaction exposure for Lufthansa. (Note that the exposure falls on Lufthansa not Boeing. If the purchase agreement had been stated in deutschemarks, the transaction exposure would have been transferred to Boeing.)

**The Exposure**   The spot exchange rate in January 1985, when Lufthansa signed the agreement, was DM 3.2/$. The expected cost of the aircraft to Lufthansa was then

$$\$500,000,000 \times \text{DM}3.2/\$ = \text{DM}1,600,000,000.$$

Figure 17.7 illustrates how the expected total cost of $500 million changes to Lufthansa with the spot exchange rate. If the deutschemark continued to fall against the U.S. dollar as it had been doing for more than four years, the cost to Lufthansa of the Boeing jets could skyrocket easily to more than DM 2 billion.

But the most important word here is expected. There was no guarantee that the spot exchange rate in effect in January of the following year would be DM 3.2/$. The U.S. dollar had been appreciating against the deutschemark for more than four years at this point. Senior management of Lufthansa was afraid the appreciating dollar trend might continue. For example, if the U.S. dollar appreciated over the coming year from DM 3.2/$ to DM 3.4/$, the cost of the aircraft purchased from Boeing would rise by DM 100 million. Figure 17.8 shows how the DM/$ exchange rate had continued to trend upward for several years. By looking at graphics such as this, it was hard to believe that the U.S. dollar would do anything but continue to rise. It takes the truly brave to buck the trend.

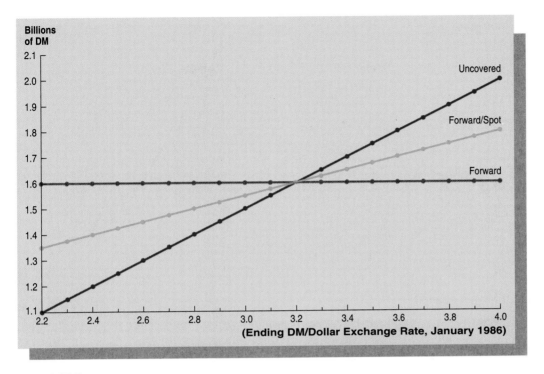

**FIGURE 17.7**

**Lufthansa's Transaction Exposure: Alternatives for Managing the Purchase of $500 Million in Boeing 737s**

But at the same time many senior members of Lufthansa's management believed that the U.S. dollar had risen as far as it would go. They argued that the dollar would fall over the coming year against the deutschemark (see Figure 17.8). If, for example, the spot rate fell to DM 3.0/$ by January 1986, Lufthansa would pay only DM 1,500 million, a savings of DM 100 million. This was true currency risk in every sense of the word.

**The Management Strategy**  After much debate, Lufthansa's management decided to use forward contracts to hedge one-half of the $500 million exposure. This was obviously a compromise. First, because the exposure was a single large foreign currency payment, to occur one time only, natural hedging was not a realistic alternative. Second, although management believed the dollar would fall, the risk was too large to ignore. It was thought that by covering one-half of the exposure, Lufthansa would be protected against the U.S. dollar appreciating, yet still allow Lufthansa some opportunity to benefit from a fall in the dollar. Lufthansa signed a one-year forward contract (sold $250 million forward) at a forward rate of DM 3.2/$. The remaining $250 million owed Boeing was left unhedged.

**The Outcome**  By January 1986, the U.S. dollar not only fell, it plummeted versus the deutschemark. The spot rate fell from DM 3.2/$ in January 1985 to

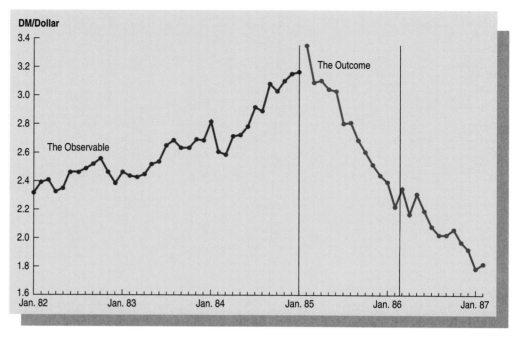

**FIGURE 17.8**

**The DM/$ Spot Exchange Rate: Where Was It Headed?**

DM 2.3/$ in January 1986. Lufthansa had therefore benefited from leaving half the transaction exposure uncovered. But this meant that the half that was covered with forward contracts "cost" the firm DM 225 million!

The total cost to Lufthansa of delivering $250 million at the forward rate of DM 3.2/$ and $250 million at the ending spot rate of DM 2.3/$ was

$$[\$250,000,000 \times DM3.2/\$] + [\$250,000,000 \times DM2.3/\$] = DM\ 1,375,000,000.$$

Although this was DM 225 million less than the expected purchase price when the contract was signed in January 1985, Lufthansa's management was heavily criticized for covering any of the exposure. If the entire transaction exposure had been left uncovered, the final cost would have been only DM 1,150 million. The critics, of course, had perfect hindsight.

## Currency Risk Sharing

Firms that import and export on a continuing basis have constant transaction exposures. If a firm is interested in maintaining a good business relationship with one of its suppliers, it must work with that supplier to assure it that it will not force all currency risk or exposure off on the other party on a continual basis. Exchange rate movements are inherently random; therefore some type of risk-sharing arrangement may prove useful.

If Ford (U.S.) imports automotive parts from Mazda (Japan) every month, year after year, major swings in exchange rates can benefit one party at the expense of the other. One solution would be for Ford and Mazda to agree that all purchases by Ford will be made in Japanese yen as long as the spot rate on the payment date is between ¥120/$ and ¥130/$. If the exchange rate is between these values on the payment dates, Ford agrees to accept whatever transaction exposure exists (because it is paying in a foreign currency). If, however, the exchange rate falls outside of this range on the payment date, Ford and Mazda will "share" the difference. If the spot rate on settlement date is ¥110/$, the Japanese yen would have appreciated versus the dollar, causing Ford's costs of purchasing automotive parts to rise. Since this rate falls outside the contractual range, Mazda would agree to accept a total payment in Japanese yen that would result from a "shared" difference of ¥10. Thus, Ford's total payment in Japanese yen would be calculated using an exchange rate of ¥115/$.

Risk-sharing agreements like these have been in use for nearly fifty years on world markets. They became something of a rarity during the 1950s and 1960s, when exchange rates were relatively stable (under the Bretton Woods Agreement). But with the return to floating exchange rates in the 1970s, firms with long-term customer-supplier relationships across borders returned to some old ways of keeping old friends. And sometimes old ways work very well.

## Economic Exposure

Economic exposure, also called operating exposure, is the change in the value of a firm arising from unexpected changes in exchange rates. Economic exposure emphasizes that there is a limit to a firm's ability to predict either cash flows or exchange rate changes in the medium to long term. All firms, either directly or indirectly, have economic exposure.

It is customary to think of only firms that actively trade internationally as having any type of currency exposure (such as Lufthansa or Eastman Kodak described previously). But actually all firms that operate in economies affected by international financial events, such as exchange rate changes, are affected. A barber in Ottumwa, Iowa, seemingly isolated from exchange rate chaos, still is affected when the dollar rises as it did in the early 1980s. U.S. products become increasingly expensive to foreign buyers, American manufacturers such as John Deere & Co. in Iowa are forced to cut back production and lay off workers, and businesses of all types decline. Even the business of barbers. The impacts are real, and they affect all firms, domestic and international alike.

How exposed is an individual firm in terms of economic exposure? It is impossible to say. Measuring economic exposure is subjective, and for the most part it is dependent on the degree of internationalization present in the firm's cost and revenue structure, as well as potential changes over the long run. But simply because it is difficult to measure does not mean that management cannot take some steps to prepare the firm for the unexpected.

## Impact of Economic Exposure

The impacts of economic exposure are as diverse as are firms in their international structure. Take the case of a U.S. corporation with a successful British subsidiary. The British subsidiary manufactured and then distributed the firm's products in Great Britain, Germany, and France. The profits of the British subsidiary are paid out annually to the American parent corporation. What would be the impact on the profitability of the British subsidiary and the entire U.S.

Companies are establishing manufacturing operations in countries around the world. As part of its global strategy, Corning Incorporated aims to be insulated against market fluctuations in any one particular country. This is a Japanese worker at the Corning Japan K.K. plant in Shizuoka, Japan.
*Source:* Courtesy of Corning Inc.

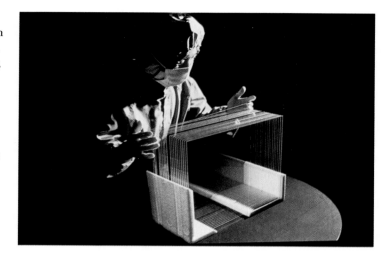

firm if the British pound suddenly fell in value against all other major currencies (as it did in September and October 1992)?

If the British firm had been facing competition in Germany, France, and its own home market from firms from those other two continental countries, it would now be more competitive. If the British pound is cheaper, so are the products sold internationally by British-based firms. The British subsidiary of the American firm would, in all likelihood, see rising profits from increased sales.

But what of the value of the British subsidiary to the U.S. parent corporation? The same fall in the British pound that allowed the British subsidiary to gain profits would also result in substantially fewer U.S. dollars when the British pound earnings are converted to U.S. dollars at the end of the year. It seems that it is nearly impossible to win in this situation. Actually, from the perspective of economic exposure management, the fact that the firm's total value, subsidiary and parent together, is roughly a wash as a result of the exchange rate change is desirable. Sound financial management assumes that a firm will profit and bear risk in its line of business, not in the process of settling payments on business already completed.

## Economic Exposure Management

Management of economic exposure is being prepared for the unexpected. A firm such as Hewlett Packard (HP), which is highly dependent on its ability to remain cost competitive in markets both at home and abroad, may choose to take actions now that would allow it to passively withstand any sudden unexpected rise of the dollar. This could be accomplished through diversification: diversification of operations and diversification of financing.

Diversification of operations would allow the firm to be desensitized to the impacts of any one pair of exchange rate changes. For example, a multinational firm such as Hewlett Packard may produce the same product in manufacturing facilities in Singapore, the United States, Puerto Rico, and Europe. If a sudden and prolonged rise in the dollar made production in the United States prohibitively expensive and uncompetitive, HP is already positioned to shift production to a relatively cheaper currency environment. Although firms rarely diversify production location for the sole purpose of currency diversification, it is a substantial additional benefit from such global expansion.

Diversification of financing serves to hedge economic exposure much in the same way as it did with transaction exposures. A firm with debt denominated in many different currencies is sensitive to many different interest rates. If one country or currency experiences rapidly rising inflation rates and interest rates, a firm with diversified debt will not be subject to the full impact of such movements. Purely domestic firms, however, are actually somewhat captive to the local conditions and are unable to ride out such interest rate storms as easily.

It should be noted that, in both cases, diversification is a passive solution to the exposure problem. This means that without knowing when or where or what the problem may be, the firm that simply spreads its operations and financial structure out over a variety of countries and currencies is prepared. For example, the Asian financial crisis caught many firms by surprise. As illustrated in Global Perspective 17.3, among Thai firms, some were hit much harder than others.

## Translation Exposure

Translation or accounting exposure results from the conversion or translation of foreign currency denominated financial statements of foreign subsidiaries and affiliates into the home currency of the parent. This is necessary to prepare consolidated financial statements for all firms as country-law requires. The purpose is to have all operations worldwide stated in the same currency terms for comparison purposes. Management often uses the translated statements to judge the performance of foreign affiliates and their personnel on the same currency terms as the parent itself.

The problem, however, arises from the translation of balance sheets in foreign currencies into the domestic currency. Which assets and liabilities are to be translated at current exchange rates (at the current balance sheet date) versus historical rates (those in effect on the date of the initial investment)? Or should all assets and liabilities be translated at the same rate? The answer is somewhere in between, and the process of translation is dictated by financial accounting standards.

### The Current Rate Method

At present in the United States, the proper method for translating foreign financial statements is given in Financial Accounting Standards Board statement No. 52 (FASB 52). According to FASB 52, if a foreign subsidiary is operating in a foreign currency functional environment,[4] most assets, liabilities, and income statement items of foreign affiliates are translated using current exchange rates (the exchange rate in effect on the balance sheet date). For this reason, it is often referred to as the current rate method. Table 17.4 provides an example of how this translation process might work.

A U.S. firm, Moab, established a Canadian subsidiary two years ago. The subsidiary, Moab-Can, is wholly owned and operated by Moab. The balance sheet of Moab-Can on December 31, 1998, is shown in Canadian dollars in Column (1) of Table 17.4. To construct a consolidated financial statement, all Moab-Can's assets and liabilities must be translated into U.S. dollars at the end-of-year exchange rate. This rate is C$1.20/$. All assets and liabilities are trans-

## BAHT BASED BRUISES: THE IMPACT OF FOREIGN EXCHANGE LOSSES ON THAI FIRMS

**O**ne research report by Capital Nomura Securities analyzed the effects of foreign-exchange losses on net profits for 45 nonfinancial firms on the Stock Exchange of Thailand, with a capitalization worth 42 percent of the total market. Although some portion of the losses stemmed from the economic slowdown, the majority came from foreign currency losses because of the depreciating baht. More than 20 companies already face delisting from the SET [Stock Exchange of Thailand] because of weakened financial standing or low trading liquidity.

### Payback time

Impact of foreign exchange losses on corporate earnings for selected SET companies

| Company | 3Q, 1997F | | | 1997F | | |
|---|---|---|---|---|---|---|
| | Excluding forex (bt m) | Including forex (bt m) | EPS (bt) | Excluding forex (bt m) | Including forex (bt m) | EPS (bt) |
| **Building** | | | | | | |
| Siam Cement | 1,463.00 | -18,512.00 | -154.30 | 6,683.20 | -20,191.80 | -168.30 |
| Siam City Cement | 130.00 | -8,225.00 | -53.20 | 750.00 | -5,605.00 | -47.90 |
| Sahaviriya Steel | 315.70 | -4,149.00 | -8.12 | -1,246.00 | -5,079.50 | -9.95 |
| Tipco Asphalt | 210.00 | -333.26 | -2.95 | 696.00 | 327.00 | 2.90 |
| TPI Polene | 155.00 | -9,070.00 | -17.90 | 664.00 | -8,681.00 | -18.86 |
| **Chemical** | | | | | | |
| Aromatics Thailand | -318.92 | -5,010.36 | -12.53 | -162.20 | -5,172.62 | -12.96 |
| National Fertiliser | 282.41 | -1,203.59 | -3.88 | 1,045.44 | -158.15 | -0.51 |
| Thai Plastic | 193.24 | -301.12 | -3.44 | 777.17 | 282.82 | 3.23 |
| TPI | -337.62 | -21,248.96 | -13.08 | 2,196.35 | -19,052.61 | -4.27 |
| Vinythai | 35.88 | -2,596.74 | -4.31 | 58.83 | -2,573.78 | -11.72 |
| **Communications** | | | | | | |
| Advanced Info | 843.00 | 697.20 | 2.98 | 3,535.70 | 3,392.00 | 14.50 |
| Shinawatra Sat | 100.00 | -1,804.40 | -5.18 | 74.50 | -1,829.90 | -5.23 |
| Shinawatra | 609.00 | 191.50 | 13.88 | 2,162.00 | 1,544.60 | 13.37 |
| Telecom Asia | -1,470.00 | -10,992.00 | -4.94 | -4,255.90 | -13,777.90 | -6.20 |
| TT&T | -410.00 | -2,631.80 | -2.63 | -596.00 | -2,818.80 | -2.82 |
| UCOM | 588.00 | 296.00 | 1.26 | 2,020.50 | 1,754.50 | 7.50 |
| **Electronics** | | | | | | |
| Delta | 378.00 | 378.00 | 8.30 | 987.00 | 1,433.00 | 23.88 |
| Kuang Charoen | 61.00 | -90.00 | -4.29 | 249.00 | 154.00 | 7.33 |
| KR Precision | 70.00 | -181.50 | -6.85 | 409.00 | 135.30 | 5.11 |
| Hana | 75.00 | -848.50 | -23.04 | 366.00 | -633.90 | -14.55 |
| **Energy** | | | | | | |
| Ban Pu Coal | 205.77 | -2,226.36 | -42.84 | 823.07 | -1,219.29 | -23.87 |
| Bang Chak | -40.37 | -1,496.32 | -2.87 | -101.73 | -1,557.69 | -2.98 |
| The Cogeneration | 263.54 | 153.91 | 0.88 | 1,064.15 | 994.52 | 3.62 |
| Electicity Generation | 288.10 | -4,548.53 | -8.90 | 1,772.01 | -2,910.08 | -5.73 |
| Lanna Lignite | 107.55 | -66.87 | -1.01 | 405.76 | 231.34 | 6.61 |
| PTT Exp & Prod | 380.03 | -3,258.64 | -10.51 | 1,357.57 | -903.52 | -2.91 |
| **Entertainment** | | | | | | |
| BEC World | 494.00 | 494.00 | 2.47 | 2,100.00 | 2,100.00 | 10.50 |
| Grammy | 154.55 | 134.55 | 2.69 | 602.25 | 602.25 | 12.05 |
| Media of Medias | 22.63 | 22.66 | 0.87 | 103.33 | 103.03 | 3.97 |
| ONPA International | 60.12 | 60.12 | 1.05 | 354.49 | 354.49 | 6.22 |
| **Property** | | | | | | |
| Ch Karnchang | 67.30 | -199.70 | -1.90 | 482.30 | 282.00 | 2.88 |
| Central Pattana | 171.80 | -37.40 | -0.37 | 836.41 | 285.61 | 2.68 |
| Italian Thai | 189.00 | -2,169.00 | -8.70 | 1,174.80 | -1,182.70 | -4.70 |
| Land and House | 387.50 | -1,802.40 | -8.24 | 317.40 | -1,911.10 | -8.74 |
| Property Perfect | 44.60 | -585.70 | -9.01 | 203.80 | -428.30 | -8.59 |
| Quality Houses | 74.20 | -863.70 | -5.01 | 104.30 | -770.05 | -2.80 |
| Supalai | 88.70 | -181.30 | -3.58 | 112.50 | -102.40 | -2.02 |
| **Transportation** | | | | | | |
| Bangkok Expressway | -8.65 | -136.65 | -0.18 | 240.65 | 20.65 | 0.03 |
| **Others** | | | | | | |
| Padaeng Industry | 9.52 | -938.6 | -8.18 | 129.56 | -767.2 | -5.05 |
| Thai Stanley | 50 | 50 | 1.3 | 241.6 | 156.6 | 4.1 |
| Saha Union | 158.31 | -141.22 | -0.47 | 754.79 | 156.3 | 4.1 |
| Pizza Company | 72.5 | 35.47 | 1.18 | 257.11 | 222.11 | 7.4 |
| Malee Sampran | 67.62 | 67.62 | 1.37 | 255.22 | 255.22 | 5.1 |

Source: Capital Nomura         POSTgraphics

**Source: Adapted from "Baht Heads toward 40, Earnings in Jeopardy," Bangkok Post, Friday October 24, 1997.**

**TABLE 17.4**

**Translation of Foreign Affiliate's Balance Sheet: Canadian Subsidiary of a U.S. Firm**

| | (1)<br>Canadian<br>Dollars<br>(thousands) | (2)<br>Current<br>Rate<br>C$/$ | (3)<br>U.S.<br>Dollars<br>(thousands) |
|---|---|---|---|
| **Assets** | | | |
| Cash | 120 | 1.20 | 100 |
| Accounts payable | 240 | 1.20 | 200 |
| Inventory | 120 | 1.20 | 100 |
| Net plant and equipment | 480 | 1.20 | 400 |
| Total | C$ 960 | | $ 800 |
| **Liabilities and Net Worth** | | | |
| Accounts payable | 120 | 1.20 | 100 |
| Short-term debt | 120 | 1.20 | 100 |
| Long-term debt | 240 | 1.20 | 200 |
| Equity capital | 480 | 1.10 | 436 |
| Cumulative Translation Adjustment | | | (36) |
| Total | C$ 960 | | $ 800 |

lated at the current rate except for equity capital, which is translated at the exchange rate in effect at the time of the Canadian subsidiary's establishment, C$1.10/$. The exchange rates used to translate each individual asset and liability of the Canadian subsidiary are listed in Column (2).

The U.S.–dollar value of all translated assets and liabilities is shown in Column (3). An imbalance results because all assets and liabilities, except equity capital, were translated at the current rate. A new account must be created for the translated balance sheet to balance. The new account, the **cumulative translation adjustment (CTA)** takes on a gain or loss value necessary to maintain a balanced translation. Moab-Can in this case suffers a CTA loss of US$36,000.

What does this translation loss mean to the company? The CTA account is an accounting construction. It is created to produce a consolidated balance sheet. Neither the Canadian subsidiary nor the U.S. parent experiences any cash flow impact as a result of the translation gain or loss.

The CTA account remains a "paper fiction" until the time the Canadian subsidiary is either sold or liquidated. On the sale or liquidation of the Canadian subsidiary, the CTA gains or losses attributed to Moab-Can must be realized by the parent company.[5]

**Translation Exposure Management**

Translation exposure under FASB 52 results in no cash flow impacts under normal circumstances. Although consolidated accounting does result in CTA translation losses or gains on the parent's consolidated balance sheet, the accounting entries are not ordinarily realized. Unless liquidation or sale of the subsidiary is anticipated, neither the subsidiary nor the parent firm should expend real resources on the management of an accounting convention. Global

## MANAGEMENT'S ANALYSIS

In 1995, Mexico was an extreme example of how movements in currency exchange rates impact operating results. In Mexico, PepsiCo's largest international market in 1994, operations were adversely impacted by the effects of the approximately 50 percent devaluation of the Mexican peso which triggered an extremely high level of inflation. Consumer demand shrank dramatically for most goods and services in response to declining real incomes and increased unemployment. Price increases taken to offset rising operating and product cost further dampened weak consumer demand. Actions taken by PepsiCo to mitigate these adverse effects, such as introducing various volume building programs to stimulate demand and reducing costs and capital spending, resulted in only a modest decline in local currency segment operating profit for Mexico. However, on a U.S. dollar basis, combined segment operating profit and identifiable assets in Mexico declined dramatically, reflecting the unfavorable translation effect of the much weaker peso in 1995.

*Source: Excerpts taken from PepsiCo, Inc., Form 10-K, Annual Report, Securities and Exchange Commission filing, for the fiscal year ended December 30, 1995, p. 7.*

Perspective 17.4 illustrates how translation exposure is reflected in the firm's—in this case PepsiCo—annual review of activities.

## Interest Rate and Currency Swaps

One of the most significant developments in international finance in the past twenty years was the development of the interest rate and currency swap market. Although markets of all kinds (goods, services, labor, and capital) have continued to open up across the world in the past two decades, there are still "paper walls" between many capital markets. Firms operating in their home markets are both helped and hindered; they are well known in their own capital markets but still may not be recognized in other potentially larger capital markets. The interest rate and currency swap markets have allowed firms to arbitrage the differences between markets, using their comparative advantage of borrowing in their home market and swapping for interest rates or currencies that are not as readily accessible.

**Interest Rate Swaps**   Firms that are considered to be better borrowers in financial markets borrow at lower rates. The lower rates may be lower fixed rates or lower spreads over floating rate bases. In fact, lower quality borrowers often are limited in their choices to floating rates in many markets. The **interest rate swap,** often called the "plain vanilla swap," allows one firm to use its good credit standing to borrow capital at low fixed rates and exchange its interest payments with a slightly lower credit-rated borrower who has debt service payments at floating rates. Each borrower ends up making net interest payments at rates below those it could have achieved on its own.

If Firm Alpha is considered an extremely sound borrower, it can borrow capital at lower interest rates, probably fixed rates, than a second firm, Zeta. Zeta, although profitable and sound, is simply not rated as highly as a borrower in the eyes of the financial markets, and it must borrow at higher rates, often only at floating rates. If each firm were to borrow where it is "well received," using its comparative advantages, they may then swap or exchange their debt service payments. Alpha, which has taken on fixed rate debt service payments, will exchange these payments for Zeta's floating rate payments. Both companies end up paying less interest in the form that they desired by negotiating rates between themselves that are better than what the markets had offered directly.

## Currency Swaps

The **currency swap** is the equivalent of the interest rate swap, only the currency of denomination of the debt is different. Many international and multinational firms need capital denominated in different currencies for international investments or even for the purpose of risk management (for natural hedging, as described previously). Foreign firms often find themselves at a disadvantage, however, when trying to enter new markets. The interest rates available to them in the necessary currencies simply may not be affordable.

Figure 17.9 illustrates how a currency swap arrangement would work for a Swedish firm desiring U.S. dollar debt, and a U.S. firm desiring Swedish krona debt. The mechanics of the swap are actually quite simple. The Swedish firm, Ericcsson, borrows capital in its home market, where it is well known and can obtain capital at attractive interest rates. The U.S. firm, Sioux, also acquires local debt in its own advantaged-access market. Then, working through a swap dealer, each firm exchanges the debt service payment schedule on its own debt for the debt service payment schedule of the other firm's debt. The principal amounts borrowed must be equal at current exchange rates for the swap to be made. The U.S. firm, Sioux, now agrees to make interest payments in Swedish

**FIGURE 17.9**

Sample Currency Swap: Arbitrage between the U.S. Dollar and Swedish Krona Debt Markets

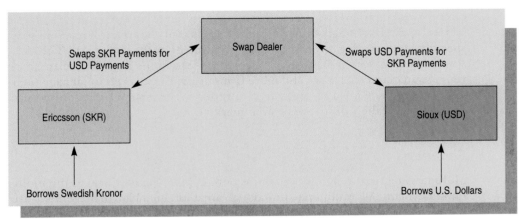

# THE INTERNATIONAL SWAPS AND DERIVATIVES ASSOCIATION (ISDA) MARKET SURVEY RESULTS

## 1997 FIRST HALF ACTIVITY DATA

### Currency Swaps[3]

| Currency[1] | 6-Month Period Ended June 30, 1996 | 6-Month Period Ended June 30, 1997 | % Change | June 30, 1997 As % of Total |
|---|---|---|---|---|
| Deutschemark (DEM) | 35,342 | 27,041 | −23.5% | 5.8% |
| French Franc (FRF) | 13,482 | 20,344 | 50.9% | 4.4% |
| British Sterling (GBP) | 19,684 | 19,586 | −0.5% | 4.2% |
| Japanese Yen (JPY) | 71,866 | 77,653 | 8.1% | 16.8% |
| US Dollar (USD) | 118,428 | 185,064 | 56.3% | 40.0% |
| Other Currencies (OTH) | 115,224 | 133,400 | 15.8% | 28.8% |
| TOTALS[2] | $374,026 | $463,088 | 23.8% | 100.00% |

1. All Amounts in US $ whole millions
2. Immaterial footing differences may exist due to rounding.
3. Totals have been adjusted to account for both sides of currency swaps.

### Interest Rate Swaps

| Currency[1] | 6-Month Period Ended June 30, 1996 | 6-Month Period Ended June 30, 1997 | % Change | June 30, 1997 As % of Total |
|---|---|---|---|---|
| Deutschemark (DEM) | 967,493 | 1,298,393 | 34.2% | 12.0% |
| French Franc (FRF) | 774,978 | 1,320,529 | 70.4% | 12.2% |
| British Sterling (GBP) | 323,547 | 705,462 | 118.0% | 6.5% |
| Japanese Yen (JPY) | 1,564,192 | 1,968,671 | 25.9% | 18.2% |
| US Dollar (USD) | 1,844,854 | 3,032,504 | 64.4% | 28.1% |
| Other Currencies (OTH) | 1,045,283 | 2,466,649 | 136.0% | 22.9% |
| TOTALS[2] | $6,520,347 | $10,792,208 | 65.5% | 100.00% |

1. All Amounts in US $ whole millions
2. Immaterial footing differences may exist due to rounding.

*Source:* **http://www.isda.org/d16.html** *(January 1998)*

kronor, and the Swedish firm, Ericcsson, agrees to make U.S. dollar interest payments. The two firms have swapped payment schedules.

But what of the risk of nonpayment? If one of the swap parties does not make its agreed-upon payments, who is responsible for meeting the obligations of the original debt agreement? The answer is that the initial borrower is responsible for covering any shortfall or nonpayment by the swap party. This risk, termed counterparty risk, is an increasing concern in the interest rate and currency swap markets as more and more firms utilize the markets to manage their debt structures. Global Perspective 17.5 reports recent survey data on the size and activity of the international swap markets.

## Summary

Multinational financial management is both complex and critical to the multinational firm. All traditional functional areas of financial management are affected by the internationalization of the firm. Capital budgeting, firm financing, capital structure, and working capital and cash flow management, all traditional functions, are made more difficult by business activities that cross borders and oceans, not to mention currencies and markets.

In addition to the traditional areas of financial management, international financial management must deal with the three types of currency exposure: (1) transaction exposure, (2) economic exposure, and (3) translation exposure. Each type of currency risk confronts a firm with serious choices regarding its exposure analysis and its degree of willingness to manage the inherent risks.

This chapter described not only the basic types of risk, but also outlined a number of the basic strategies employed in the management of the exposures. Some of the solutions available today have only arisen with the development of new types of international financial markets and instruments, such as the currency swap. Others, such as currency risk-sharing agreements, are as old as exchange rates themselves.

## Key Terms and Concepts

| | | |
|---|---|---|
| maximization of shareholder value | financing cash flows | transaction exposure |
| net present value (NPV) | transfer prices | economic exposure |
| capital budget | netting | translation exposure |
| bill of lading | cash pooling | natural hedging |
| bank draft | leads | contractual hedging |
| trade draft | lags | forward contract |
| working capital management | reinvoicing | hedge |
| operating cash flows | internal bank | interest rate swap |
| | financial risk management | currency swap |

## Questions for Discussion

1. Why is it important to identify the cash flows of a foreign investment from the perspective of the parent rather than from just the project?
2. Is currency risk unique to international firms? Is currency risk good or bad for the potential profitability of the multinational?
3. Which type of currency risk is the least important to the multinational firm? Should resources be spent to manage this risk?
4. Are firms with no direct international business (imports and exports) subject to economic exposure?
5. What would you have recommended that Lufthansa do to manage its transaction exposure if you had been the airline's chief financial officer in January 1985?
6. Why do you think Lufthansa and Boeing did not use some form of "currency risk sharing" in their 1985–1986 transaction?
7. Which type of firm do you believe is more "naturally hedged" against exchange rate exposure, the purely domestic firm (the barber) or the multinational firm (subsidiaries all over the world)?
8. Why have the currency and interest rate swap markets grown so rapidly in the past decade?

9. Although major currencies like the U.S. dollar and the Japanese yen dominate the headlines, there are nearly as many currencies as countries in the world. Many of these currencies are traded in extremely thin and highly regulated markets, making their convertibility suspect. Finding quotations for these currencies is sometimes very difficult. Using some of the Web pages listed below, see how many African currency quotes you can find. See Emerging Markets at **http://emgmkts.com/**

10. JP Morgan calculates and maintains indices of many of the world's major currencies' values relative to baskets of other major currencies. Like those published by the International Monetary Fund, these indices serve as more fundamental and general indicators of relative currency value. Look at JP Morgan Currency Indices at **http//jpmorgan.com/MarketDataInd/ Forex/CurrIndex.html**

11. The single unobservable variable in currency option pricing is the volatility, since volatility inputs are expected standard deviation of the daily spot rate for the coming period of the option's maturity. Using the following Web sites, pick one currency volatility and research how its value has changed in recent periods over historical periods. See Philadelphia Stock Exchange at **http://www.phlx.com/**

12. Using the following major periodicals as starting points, find a current example of a firm with a substantial operating exposure problem. To aid in your search, you might focus on businesses having major operations in countries with recent currency crises, either through devaluation or major home currency appreciation. Sources are *Financial Times* at **http:// www.ft.com/**; *The Economist* at **http://www.economist.com/**; *The Wall Street Journal* at **http://www.wsj.com/**

## Recommended Readings

Brealey, Richard A., and Stewart C. Myers. *Principles of Corporate Finance.* 5th ed. New York: McGraw-Hill, 1996.

Eaker, Mark R., Frank J. Fabozzi, and Dwight Grant. *International Corporate Finance.* Fort Worth, Tex.: The Dryden Press, 1996.

Eiteman, David K., Arthur I. Stonehill, and Michael H. Moffett. *Multinational Business Finance.* 8th ed. Reading, Mass.: Addison-Wesley Longman, 1998.

Eun, Cheol S., and Bruce G. Resnick. *International Financial Management.* Boston, Mass.: Irwin McGraw-Hill, 1998.

Giddy, Ian H., *Global Financial Markets.* Lexington, Mass.: Elsevier, 1994.

Jacque, Laurent L. *Management and Control of Foreign Exchange Risk.* Boston, Mass.: Kluwer Academic Publishers, 1996.

Madura, Jeff. *International Financial Management.* 5th ed. Cincinnati, Ohio: South-western Publishing, 1998.

Shapiro, Alan C. *Foundations of Multinational Financial Management.* 3d ed. Upper Saddle River, N.J.: Prentice Hall, 1998.

Smith, Clifford W., Charles W. Smithson, and D. Sykes Wilford. *Managing Financial Risk.* The Institutional Investor Series in Finance. New York: Harper Business, 1990.

## Notes

1. Extremity-stimulus medical appliances are electrically charged sheaths that are fit over the hands, feet, or other extremities of the human subject where increased blood flow and nerve tissue regeneration is desired. This is a fictional product.

2. There are, of course, other traditional decision criteria used in capital budgeting, such as the internal rate of return, modified internal rate of return, payback period, and so forth. For the sake of simplicity, NPV is used throughout the analysis in this chapter.

Under most conditions, NPV is also the most consistent criterion for selecting good projects, as well as selecting among projects.

3. A note of particular irony in this case was that the chief currency trader for Allied-Lyons had authored an article in the British trade journal *The Treasurer* only a few months before. The article had described the proper methods and strategies for careful corporate foreign currency risk management. He had concluded with the caution to never confuse "good luck with skillful trading."

4. The distinction as to what the "functional currency" of a foreign subsidiary or affiliate operation is depends on a number of factors, including the currency that dominates expenses and revenues. If the foreign subsidiary's dominant currency is the local currency, the current rate method of translation is used. If, however, the functional currency of the foreign subsidiary is identified as the currency of the parent, the U.S. dollar in the example, the temporal method of translation is used. The temporal method is the procedure that was used in the United States from 1975 to 1981 under FASB 8.

5. Prior to the passage of FASB 52, FASB 8 had been the primary directive on translation in the United States. FASB 8, often termed the monetary/nonmonetary method, differed from FASB 52 in two important ways. First, it applied historical exchange rates to several of the long-term asset categories, usually resulting in a lower net exposed asset position. Second, all translation gains and losses were passed through the parent's consolidated income for the current period. This resulted in volatile swings in the critical earnings per share (EPS) reported by multinational firms. Although this was still only an accounting convention, the volatility introduced to EPS caused much concern among firms.

# CHAPTER 18

# Countertrade

## LEARNING OBJECTIVES

◆ *To understand why countertrade transactions are becoming increasingly common*

◆ *To see how countertrade transactions are becoming more sophisticated and creative*

◆ *To discover some of the problems and dislocations caused by countertrade*

◆ *To understand that corporations increasingly use countertrade as a competitive tool to maintain or increase market share*

◆ *To learn about the new intermediaries that have emerged to facilitate countertrade transactions*

## The Booming Business of Countertrade

**M**any Fortune 500 companies are now turning to barter or counter-trade arrangements to clear their warehouses of everything from corporate jets to boxer shorts and dinner mints. With today's faster product cycles, increasingly rapid introduction of new technologies, and shorter business cycles, companies are anxious to get rid of older or obsolete merchandise without flooding established markets. Fueled by these developments in the business world, the practice of barter has grown tenfold over the past twenty years.

Barter allows companies to become more flexible and quicker in the face of international competition. Rather than selling old inventory for only twenty cents on the dollar in cash, firms can gain eighty cents or more by bartering. Big deals are increasingly found in corporate barter. In fact, North American companies traded $7.6 billion in goods and services in 1996, up from $980 million two decades ago, according to the Corporate Barter Council.

The deals have become increasingly complex and geographically dispersed. Some examples of recent countertrade arrangements include the following:

- IBM's Mexico subsidiary exchanged 2,600 outmoded computers worth $1.7 million for $1 million worth of Volkswagen vehicles, plus $250,000 in trucking services and a quarter million worth of express-mail shipments.
- A cruise line used a barter company to trade $1 million worth of empty cabins for $1 million in trade credits. The cruise company used the credits, along with $3 million in cash, for a $4 million advertising campaign.
- A dental-care manufacturer exchanged 200,000 extra toothbrushes packaged in bulk for advertising worth twice the amount of the toothbrushes. A barter company repackaged the toothbrushes to be sold as a travel kit through a regional chain store.
- Volvo Cars of North America sold autos to the Siberian police force when it had no currency for the deal. A barter company accepted oil as payment for the vehicles, and used the gains from its sale to provide Volvo with advertising credits equal to the value of the cars.

*Source:* Paula L. Green, "The Booming Barter Business," *The Journal of Commerce* (April 1, 1997): 1A, 5A.

General Motors exchanged automobiles for a trainload of strawberries. Control Data swapped a computer for a package of Polish furniture, Hungarian carpet backing, and Russian greeting cards. Uzbekistan, one of the new countries of the former Soviet Union, is offering crude venom of vipers, toads, scorpions, black widows, and tarantulas, as well as growth-controlling substances from snakes and lizards, in countertrade.[1] These are all examples of counter-trade activities carried out around the world. As noted in the chapter's opening vignette, countertrade is growing in volume as well as in complexity.

This chapter will focus on the ancient, yet new, forms of barter and countertrade. The types of countertrade that currently exist and the reasons why these types of transactions are reemerging will be discussed. Policy issues associated with countertrade will be explored by examining the attitudes held toward countertrade by both national governments and international bodies such as the WTO, the OECD, and the U.N. Corporate countertrade practices will be reviewed as we examine what firms do and why they do it. Finally, information will be provided on how to organize for countertrade, how to cope with potential problems, and how countertrade can be used as an effective international business tool.

## A Definition of Countertrade

Countertrade is a sale that encompasses more than an exchange of goods, services, or ideas for money. In the international market, countertrade transactions "are those transactions that have as a basic characteristic a linkage, legal or otherwise, between exports and imports of goods or services in addition to, or in place of, financial settlements."[2] Historically, countertrade was mainly conducted in the form of **barter,** which is a direct exchange of goods of approximately equal value between parties, with no money involved. Such transactions were the very essence of business at times during which no money—that is, no common medium of exchange—existed or was available. Over time, money emerged as a convenient medium that unlinked transactions from individual parties and their joint timing and therefore permitted greater flexibility in trading activities. Repeatedly, however, we can see returns to the barter system as a result of environmental circumstances. For example, because of the tight financial constraints of both students and the institution, Georgetown University during its initial years of operation after 1789 charged part of its tuition in foodstuffs and required students to participate in the construction of university buildings. During periods of high inflation in Europe in the 1920s, goods such as bread, meat, and gold were seen as much more useful and secure than paper money, which decreased in real value by the minute. In the late 1940s, American cigarettes were an acceptable medium of exchange in most European countries, much more so than any particular currency except for the dollar.

Countertrade transactions have therefore always arisen when economic circumstances made it more acceptable to exchange goods directly rather than to use money as an intermediary. Conditions that encourage such business activities are lack of money, lack of value of or faith in money, lack of acceptability of money as an exchange medium, or greater ease of transaction by using goods.

The same reasons prevail in today's resurgence of countertrade. Beginning in the 1950s, countertrade and barter transactions were mainly carried out with Eastern bloc countries. The currencies of these countries were not acceptable elsewhere, because they were not freely convertible. At the same time, the countries did not want their currencies distributed outside of their economic bloc. They did not possess sufficient foreign "hard" currency to make purchases of crucial goods that were not available within COMECON countries. Therefore, many Eastern bloc countries insisted in their dealings with Western nations that the goods they produced be taken in exchange for imports so as to reduce their need for foreign currencies.

Throughout the decades, the use of countertrade has steadily increased. In 1972, countertrade was in regular use by only 15 countries. By 1983, the countries conducting countertrade transactions numbered 88, and by 1997 the number was more than 100. Estimates of the total volume of global countertrade vary. The American Countertrade Association estimates that 25 percent of world exports are now linked to countertrade transactions. Some researchers anticipate that by the year 2000, one-half of all international trade will be linked to countertrade.[3] A consensus of experts has put the percentage of world trade financed through countertrade transactions of between 15 and 20 percent.[4] Such an estimate conflicts with IMF figures, which attribute only a very small percentage of world trade to countertrade. Yet, if all business transactions in which countertrade plays some kind of role are considered, the estimate could be reasonable.

Increasingly, countries and companies are deciding that countertrade transactions are more beneficial to them than transactions based on financial exchange alone. One reason is that the world debt crisis has made ordinary trade financing very risky. Many countries, particularly in the developing world, simply cannot obtain the trade credit or financial assistance necessary to pay for desired imports. Heavily indebted countries, faced with the possibility of not being able to afford imports at all, hasten to use countertrade to maintain at least some product inflow. However, it should be recognized that countertrade does not reduce commercial risk. Countertrade transactions will therefore be encouraged by stability and economic progress. Research has shown that countertrade appears to increase with a country's creditworthiness, since good credit encourages traders to participate in unconventional trading practices.[5]

The use of countertrade permits the covert reduction of prices and therefore allows the circumvention of price and exchange controls.[6] Particularly in commodity markets with cartel arrangements, such as oil or agriculture, this benefit may be very useful to a producer. For example, by using oil as a countertraded product for industrial equipment, a surreptitious discount (by using a higher price for the acquired products) may expand market share.

Another reason for the increase in countertrade is that many countries are again responding favorably to the notion of bilateralism. Thinking along the lines of "you scratch my back and I'll scratch yours," they prefer to exchange goods with countries that are their major business partners.

Countertrade is also often viewed by firms and nations alike as an excellent mechanism to gain entry into new markets. When a producer believes that marketing is not its strong suit, the producer often hopes that the party receiving the goods will serve as a new distributor, opening up new international marketing channels and ultimately expanding the original market. For example, countertrade transactions agreed to between the Japanese firm NEC and the government of Egypt have resulted in a major increase of Japanese tourism to Egypt.[7]

Because countertrade is highly sought after in many large markets such as China, the former Eastern bloc countries, as well as South America, engaging in such transactions can provide major growth opportunities for firms. In increasingly competitive world markets, countertrade can be a good way to attract new buyers. By providing countertrade services, the seller is in effect differentiating its product from those of its competitors.[8]

Countertrade also can provide stability for long-term sales. For example, if a firm is tied to a countertrade agreement, it will need to source the product from a particular supplier, whether or not it wants to do so. This stability is often valued very highly because it eliminates, or at least reduces, vast swings in demand and thus allows for better planning. Countertrade, therefore, can serve as a major mechanism to shift risk from the producer to another party. In that sense, one can argue that countertrade offers a substitute for missing forward markets.[9] Finally, under certain conditions, countertrade can ensure the quality of an international transaction. In instances where the seller of technology is paid in output produced by the technology delivered, the seller's revenue depends on the success of the technology transfer and maintenance services in production. Therefore, the seller is more likely to be concerned about providing services, maintenance, and general technology transfer.[10]

In spite of all the apparent benefits of countertrade, there are strong economic arguments against the activity. The arguments are based mainly on efficiency grounds. As Samuelson stated, "Instead of there being a double coincidence of wants, there is likely to be a want of coincidence; so that, unless a hungry tailor happens to find an undraped farmer, who has both food and a desire for a pair of pants, neither can make a trade."[11] Clearly, countertrade ensures that instead of balances being settled on a multilateral basis, with surpluses from one country being balanced by deficits with another, accounts must now be settled on a country-by-country or even transaction-by-transaction basis. Trade then results only from the ability of two parties or countries to purchase specified goods from one another rather than from competition. As a result, uncompetitive goods may be traded. In consequence, the ability of countries and their industries to adjust structurally to more efficient production may be restricted. Countertrade can therefore be seen as eroding the quality and efficiency of production and as lowering world consumption.

These economic arguments notwithstanding, however, countries and companies increasingly see countertrade as an alternative that may be flawed but worthwhile to undertake, since some trade is preferable to no trade. As the accompanying map shows, both industrialized and developing countries exchange a wide variety of goods via countertrade.

## Types of Countertrade

In barter arrangements, goods are exchanged directly for other goods of approximately equal value. As Table 18.1 shows, such transactions can encompass the exchange of a wide variety of goods—for example, an airplane for mango juice—and are carried out both in developing and industrialized countries. However, such straightforward barter transactions, which were quite frequent in the 1950s, are used less often today "because it is difficult to find two par-

**TABLE 18.1**

**A Sample of Barter Agreements**

| Country | | Exported Commodity | |
| --- | --- | --- | --- |
| **A** | **B** | **A** | **B** |
| Hungary | Ukraine | ■ Foodstuffs<br>■ Canned foods<br>■ Pharmaceuticals | ■ Timber |
| Austria | Ukraine | ■ Power station emissions control equipment | ■ 800 megakilowatts/year for 15 years |
| U.S. (Chrysler) | Jamaica | ■ 200 pickup trucks | ■ Equivalent value in iron ore |
| Ukraine | Czech Republic | ■ Iron ore | ■ Mining equipment |
| U.S. (Pierre Cardin) | China | ■ Technical advice | ■ Silks and cashmeres |
| U.K. (Raleigh Bicycle) | CIS | ■ Training CIS scientists in mountain bike production | ■ Titanium for 30,000 bike frames per year |
| Indonesia | Uzbekistan | ■ Indian tea<br><br>■ Vietnamese rice<br>■ Miscellaneous Indonesian products | ■ 50,000 tons of cotton/year for three years |
| Zaire | Italy | ■ Scrap iron | ■ 12 locomotives |
| China | Russia | ■ 212 railway trucks of mango juice | ■ Passenger jet |
| Morocco | Romania | ■ Citrus products | ■ Several large ports/ small harbors |

*Sources:* American Countertrade Association: December 1996; Aspy P. Palia and Oded Shenkar, "Countertrade Practices in China," *Industrial Marketing Management,* 1991, 58.
**http://www.i-trade.com**

ties prepared to make a simultaneous or near-simultaneous exchange of goods of equivalent value."[12]

Increasingly, participants in countertrade have resorted to more sophisticated versions of exchanging goods that often also include some use of money. Figure 18.1 provides an overview of the different forms of countertrade. One such refinement of simple barter is the **counterpurchase,** or **parallel barter,** agreement. To unlink the timing of contract performance, the participating parties sign two separate contracts that specify the goods and services to be exchanged. In this way, one transaction can go forward even though the second transaction needs more time. Such an arrangement can be particularly advantageous if delivery performance is dependent on a future event—for example, the harvest. Frequently, the exchange is not of precisely equal value; therefore some amount of cash will be involved. A special case of parallel barter is that of reverse reciprocity, "whereby parallel contracts are signed, granting each party access to needed resources (for example, oil in exchange for nuclear power plants)."[13] Such contracts are useful when long-term exchange relationships are desired.

Another common form of countertrade is the **buy-back,** or **compensation arrangement.** One party agrees to supply technology or equipment that en-

# Preferred Items for Export in Countertrade Transactions

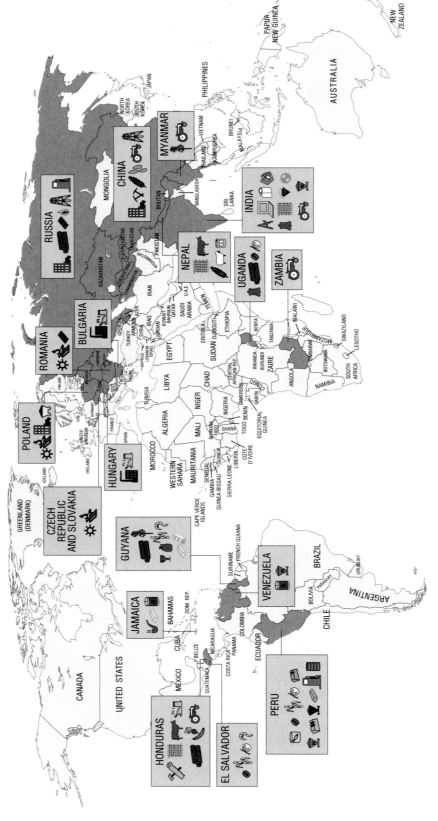

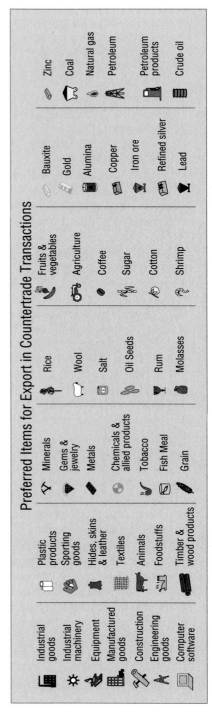

## Preferred Items for Export in Countertrade Transactions

| | | | | |
|---|---|---|---|---|
| Industrial goods | Plastic products | Minerals | Rice | Fruits & vegetables | Bauxite | Zinc |
| Industrial machinery | Sporting goods | Gems & jewelry | Wool | Agriculture | Gold | Coal |
| Equipment | Hides, skins & leather | Metals | Salt | Coffee | Alumina | Natural gas |
| Manufactured goods | Textiles | Chemicals & allied products | Oil Seeds | Sugar | Copper | Petroleum |
| Construction | Animals | Tobacco | Rum | Cotton | Iron ore | Petroleum products |
| Engineering goods | Foodstuffs | Fish Meal | Molasses | Shrimp | Refined silver | Crude oil |
| Computer software | Timber & wood products | Grain | | | Lead | |

614

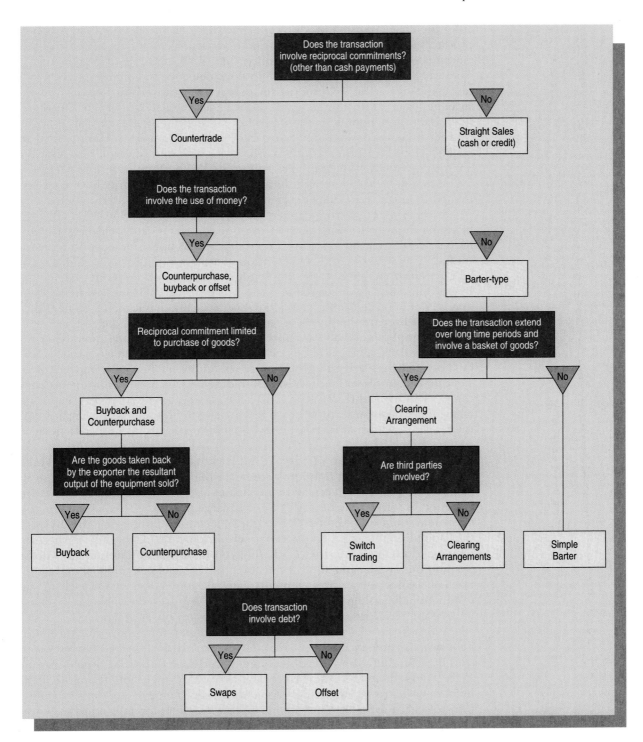

**FIGURE 18.1**

**Classification of Forms of Countertrade**

*Source:* Adapted from Jean-François Hennart, "Some Empirical Dimensions of Countertrade," *Journal of International Business Studies* 21, 2 (1990): 245.

ables the other party to produce goods with which the price of the supplied products or technology is repaid. These arrangements often "include larger amounts of time, money, and products than straight barter arrangements."[14] They originally evolved in response to the reluctance of communist countries to permit ownership of productive resources by the private sector, thus restricting foreign direct investment.[15] One example of such a buy-back arrangement is an agreement entered into by Levi Strauss and Hungary. The company transferred know-how and the Levi's trademark to Hungary. A Hungarian firm began to produce Levi's products. Some of the output was sold domestically and the rest was marketed in western Europe by Levi Strauss, in compensation for the know-how. In the past decade, buy-back arrangements have been extended to encompass many developing and newly industrialized nations.

Another form of more refined barter, which tries to reduce the effect of bilateralism and the immediacy of the transaction, is called **clearing account barter.** Here, clearing accounts are established to track debits and credits of trades. The entries merely represent purchasing power, however, and are not directly withdrawable in cash. As a result, each party can agree in a single contract to purchase goods or services of a specified value. Although the account may be out of balance on a transaction-by-transaction basis, the agreement stipulates that over the long term a balance in the account will be restored. Frequently, the goods available for purchase with clearing account funds are tightly defined. In fact, funds have on occasion been labeled "apple clearing dollars" or "horseradish clearing funds." Sometimes, additional flexibility is given to the clearing account by permitting **switch-trading,** in which credits in the account can be sold or transferred to a third party. Doing so can provide creative intermediaries with opportunities for deal making by identifying clearing account relationships with major imbalances and structuring business transactions to reduce them.

Another major form of countertrade arrangement is called **offset.** These arrangements are most frequently found in the defense-related sector and in sales of large-scale, high-priced items such as aircraft. Offset arrangements are designed to "offset" the negative effects of large purchases from abroad on the current account of a country. For example, a country purchasing aircraft from the United States might require that certain portions of the aircraft be produced and assembled in the purchasing country. Such a requirement is often a condition for awarding the contract or is used as a determining factor in contract decisions. Offset arrangements can take on many forms, such as coproduction, licensing, subcontracting, or joint ventures; they typically are long term. Table 18.2 provides an overview of some key offset practices.

A final form of countertrade, chiefly used as a financial tool, consists of **debt swaps.** These swaps are carried out particularly with less-developed countries in which both the government and the private sector face large debt burdens. The debtors are unable to repay the debt anytime soon, therefore, debt holders have grown increasingly amenable to exchange of the debt for something else. Five types of swaps are most prevalent: debt-for-debt swaps, debt-for-equity swaps, debt-for-product swaps, debt-for-nature swaps, and debt-for-education swaps.

A **debt-for-debt swap** takes place when a loan held by one creditor is simply exchanged for a loan held by another creditor. For example, a U.S. bank may swap Argentine debt for Chilean debt with a German bank. Through this

**TABLE 18.2**

A Sample of Direct and Indirect Offset Practices

| Type | Description |
|---|---|
| **Direct Offsets** | |
| Coproduction | Overseas production based on government-to-government or producer agreements that permit a foreign government to acquire the technical information and tooling to manufacture all or part of a defense article. |
| Directed Subcontracting | The procurement of domestic-made components for incorporation or installation in the items sold to that same nation under direct commercial contracts. |
| Concessions | Commercial compensation practices whereby capabilities and items are given free of charge to the buyer. |
| Technology transfers/ Licensed production | Helping countries establish defense industry capabilities by providing valuable technology and manufacturing know-how. |
| Investments in defense firms | Capital invested to establish or expand a company in the purchasing country. |
| **Indirect Offsets** | |
| Procurements | Purchases of parts/components from the purchasing country that are unrelated to the military system being acquired. |
| Investments in nondefense firms | Establishing corporations in the purchasing countries to invest capital in the nations' companies. |
| Trading of commodities | Using brokers to link buyers with commodities sellers in the purchasing country. |
| Foreign defense-related projects | Assisting the recipient country's military services. |

*Source:* United States General Accounting Office, *Report to Congressional Requesters, Military Exports: Concerns Over Offsets Generated With U.S. Foreign Military Financing Program Funds,* June 1994: 18–19.

mechanism, debt holders are able to consolidate their outstanding loans and concentrate on particular countries or regions.

**Debt-for-equity swaps** arise when debt is converted into foreign eqity in a domestic firm. The swap therefore serves as the vehicle for foreign direct investment. Although the equity itself is denominated in local currency, the terms of the conversion may allow the investor future access to foreign exchange for dividend remittances and capital repatriation.[16] In some countries, the debt-for-equity swaps have been very successful. For example, within a few years, investments in Chile retired about $13 billion of the country's external debt.[17]

A third form of debt swap consists of **debt-for-product swaps.** Here, debt is exchanged for products. Usually, the transactions require that an additional cash payment be made for the product. For example, First Interstate Bank of California concluded an arrangement with Peruvian authorities whereby a commitment was made to purchase $3 worth of Peruvian products for every $1 of products supplied by Peru against debt.[18]

One form of debt swap with major environmental implications is that of the **debt-for-nature swap.** Firms or entities buy what are otherwise considered to be nonperforming loans at substantial discounts and return the debt to the country in exchange for the preservation of natural resources. The banks like these deals because they recoup some of the money they had written off; some countries like them, as they are able to retire debt, but others do not because they believe they are selling their natural resources. However, pressing environmental concerns can be addressed by applying debt-for-nature swaps. As an example, Conservation International, an American environmental group, paid Citicorp $100,000 for $650,000 of Bolivian debt, then returned the debt to Bolivia in exchange for an agreement to turn a 4-million-acre stretch of the Amazon Basin into a wildlife sanctuary and pay for its upkeep.[19] Growing environmental concerns combined with ongoing difficulties of debt repayment are likely to increase the swaps of debt for social causes.

**Debt-for-education swaps** have been suggested in the U.S. government by one of the authors as a means to reduce debt burdens and to enable more students to study abroad. This approach can greatly enhance the international orientation, foreign language training, and cultural sensitivity of an educational system.[20] As Global Perspective 18.1 shows, some universities are taking advantage of this form of countertrade.

With the increasing sophistication of countertrade, the original form of straight barter is less used today. Most frequently used is the counterpurchase agreement. Figure 18.2 presents the results of a survey that showed the relatively low use of barter, findings confirmed by other research.[21] Investigations in other countries have shown that compensation or buy-back arrangements are on the rise.[22]

### DEBT FUNDS STUDY ABROAD

**H**arvard University recently agreed to extend a helping hand to the debt-burdened government of Ecuador in South America. In an unprecedented agreement, the university will help convert a portion of Ecuador's $11 billion debt into scholarships for Ecuadorean students to attend Harvard.

The debt-for-scholarship agreement exchanges foreign debt for educational opportunities. Ecuador has passed special legislation making the agreement possible. "Harvard is putting up the original money to purchase the debt, and then the Ecuadorean government is basically financing the rest through the debt swap," said Ned Strong, area director of the Harvard-based Latin American Scholarship Program of American Universities (LASPAU). Harvard will buy $5 million in Ecuadorean debt at the market price. The current rate is 15 percent of face value; therefore, the school will invest $750,000.

That debt will be given to the Fundacion Capacitar, an educational foundation in Ecuador that will exchange the debt for Ecuadorean government bonds worth 50 percent of the debt's face value, or $2.5 million.

"The national government obviously much prefers to have half as much debt outstanding," says Robert Scott, vice president for finance at Harvard.

The government bonds, issued in *sucres,* the local currency, will be sold in Ecuador by the foundation. Income from the sale will be converted to dollars and invested in the United States to create an endowment providing scholarship funds for the Ecuadorean students.

The arrangement also provides funds for Harvard students and professors to conduct research and internships in Ecuador. For the Ecuadoreans, the debt-reduction agreement is simply a mechanism to bring educational opportunities to their citizens. "The main purpose is the capacity for studying at Harvard," said Miguel Falconi, president of Fundacion Capacitar.

"It's definitely a two-way street," said Strong of LASPAU. The foreign student gets advanced training and enriches the university community, he says.

*Source: Laurel Shaper Walters, "Debts Fund Scholars," **The Christian Science Monitor**, July 30, 1990, 14. Reprinted by permission from* **The Christian Science Monitor.** *© 1990 The Christian Science Publishing Society. All rights reserved.*

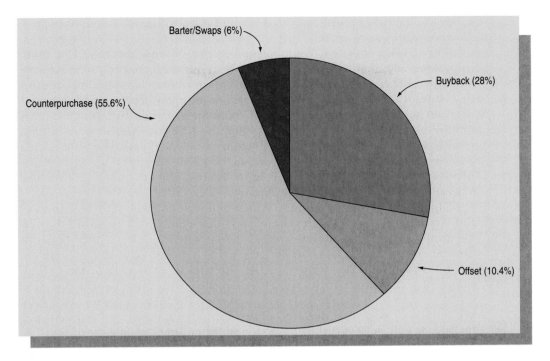

**FIGURE 18.2**

**Countertrade Usage—By Types**

*Source:* Richard Fletcher, "Australian Countertrade in the Global Economy," *Working Paper Series,* January 1996, University of Technology, Sydney, 1996.

## *Official Attitudes Toward Countertrade*

When trying to ascertain government policy, one must investigate the various departments within the executive, legislative, and judicial branches. On occasion, a coherent policy view can be identified. More often than not, discrepancies among the different groups become visible because they have different outlooks and serve different constituencies. Such discrepancies are particularly obvious when looking at the issue of countertrade.

**A U.S. Policy Perspective**

A government report on U.S. competitiveness made a strong statement against countertrade by concluding "that the transactions are purely bilateral in nature and are not competitive since they squeeze out competition from a third market or specify the export market. Trade is formulated on the basis of the willingness to countertrade and not on economic considerations."[23]

The Department of the Treasury stated that "offset and coproduction agreements mandated by governments [do not] promote . . . economic . . . efficiency. They may constitute implicit subsidies to the industry of the purchasing countries. They may result in diversion of business away from efficient U.S. producers . . . thus causing economic inefficiency and dislocations . . . . Since these practices appear to involve spillover effects on nondefense production and trade, they may have adverse effects on future U.S. production, trade, employment, and tax revenue."[24]

The Office of the U.S. Trade Representative, which is the chief U.S. trade negotiator, is somewhat more flexible. "Our position is that countertrade is a second-best option for international trade transactions. It represents a distortion of international trade and is contrary to an open, free trading system. It is not in the long-run interest of the United States or the U.S. business community. Nevertheless, as a matter of policy, the U.S. government does not oppose U.S. companies' participating in countertrade arrangements unless such actions could have a negative impact on national security. If a company believes a countertrade transaction is in its interest, the company is in a better position than we are to make that business decision."[25]

The Department of Defense is concerned with enhancing its principles of RSI—rationalization, standardization, and interoperability. This means that the department strongly encourages other nations allied with the United States to use similar equipment that can be interchanged in case of an armed conflict. For this reason, the Department of Defense tries to encourage foreign acquisitions of U.S. military hardware. However, such acquisition is likely to come about only through promises of offsets and coproduction. Hampered by a 1990 White House policy that declared offsets for military exports as economically inefficient and market distorting and established that "no agency of the U.S. government shall encourage or commit U.S. firms to any offset arrangements,"[26] the department tends to display a policy of "positive neutrality" toward the countertrade methods.

This attitude makes sense from the perspective of production cost. Given the economies of scale and the learning curve effects inherent in the manufacture of arms, more international sales result in longer production runs, which in turn permit weapons manufacturers to offer their products at a lower price. If the Department of Defense can encourage more international sales, it can either buy a given number of products for less money or purchase more products with a given budget. From that perspective, one could argue that countertrade transactions contribute to U.S. national security.

The Department of Commerce displays the most supportive view of countertrade in the official community. Given its mandate to help U.S. firms compete internationally, the department has its own Office of Barter and Countertrade, which provides advice to firms interested in such transactions. However, this office was established only after significant congressional pressure.

While all these different views exist within the departments of the administration, Congress repeatedly has passed bills that permit or even encourage countertrade transactions. The legislation primarily has focused on barter possibilities for U.S. agricultural commodities or stockpiling purposes. As a result, the Commodities Credit Corporation and the General Services Administration have been carrying out countertrade transactions for years. An example is the swap of U.S. agricultural commodities for Jamaican bauxite. This large-scale transaction was designed to reduce the U.S. surplus of agricultural products while increasing national stockpiles of a strategic material.

In the judicial branch, countertrade involvement stems mostly from the enforcement activities of the Internal Revenue Service. The IRS is, of course, primarily concerned with the accounting and taxation issues presented in the next chapter. In the countertrade context, this concern refers to the valuation

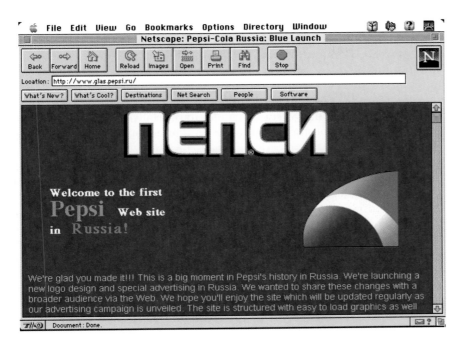

Pepsi Co. ia a longtime participant in countertrade options. Pepsi brand cola is shipped to Russia and Stoli brand vodka is shipped to the United States in return. © Pepsi Co., Inc. 1996. Used with permission. Pepsi and Globe design are registered trademarks of Pepsi Co. Inc.

of countertrade transactions and with ensuring that appropriate tax payments are made. A proper **assessment of taxes,** however, usually requires a painstaking determination of all facets of the transaction. Difficulties are often encountered in ascertaining the exact value of the countertraded goods, the time when the income has been received, and the profitability of the entire transaction. As a result of these problems, tax authorities are not in favor of countertrade. Other judicial activities are mainly concerned with valuation issues for import purposes. One major concern is that countertrade activities can be used to mask dumping,[27] whereby goods obtained through countertrade transactions may be disposed of cheaply in the domestic market and therefore harm domestic competitors, who do not benefit from the sales end of a countertrade transaction.

The differing views within the administration and in the legislative and the judicial branches indicate that countertrade is partially encouraged, as long as no major negative effects on nonparticipants are visible within the domestic economy.

## Other Government Views

Most industrialized countries, including western European countries, Japan, New Zealand, and Australia, have participated actively in the growing countertrade phenomenon. Frequently, they are catalysts for countertrade transactions. The emerging market economies have continued to favor countertrade. Countries in the developing world have taken varied positions. Indonesia, for example, cited two choices it faced as its export revenues declined dramatically: One was to drastically limit its imports, the other was to liberalize its trade with alternative measures such as countertrade. As a result, the government officially instituted a mandatory countertrade requirement for any transaction exceeding a value of $500,000.

Other developing countries have more subtle policies but are implementing and supporting countertrade nonetheless. Brazil, for example, keeps quite a low profile. Although the country "has issued no countertrade regulations and does not officially sanction its practice, . . . awards of import licenses and export performance are linked at the level of the firm."[28] This is a position taken more and more frequently by less-developed countries. Although officially they abhor the use of countertrade, unofficially they have made it clear that, in order to do business, countertrade transactions are mandatory.

## Attitudes of International Organizations

**WWW**

International organizations almost uniformly condemn countertrade. Public statements by both the IMF and the WTO indicate that their opposition is based on broad considerations of macroeconomic efficiency. These authorities complain that instead of a rational system of exchange, based on product quality and price, countertrade introduces extraneous elements into the sales equation. Countertrade is viewed as being inconsistent with an open, free trading system and not in the best long-term interest of the contracting parties.[29] The WTO, for example, sees dangers to the principle of nondiscrimination and warns of the politicization of international trade.

Officials from the OECD (Organization for Economic Cooperation and Development) also deplore countertrade arrangements. They think that such arrangements would lead to an increase in trade conflicts as competitive suppliers, unwilling to undertake countertrade arrangements, are displaced by less competitive suppliers who are willing to do so.[30]

The international organization most neutral toward countertrade is the United Nations. A report of the secretary general stated only that there appeared to be some economic and financial problems with countertrade transactions and that any global, uniform regulation of countertrade might be difficult to implement because of the complexity and variety of transactions. The report lacks any kind of general conclusion, because such conclusions "may be somewhat hazardous in the absence of a sufficient volume of contracts that are easily available."[31]

The United Nations statement highlights one of the major problems faced by policymakers interested in countertrade. Corporations and executives consider the subject of countertrade to be sensitive, because public discussion of such practices could imply that a product line may be difficult to sell or indicate that the corporation is willing to conduct countertrade. Since such knowledge would result in a weakening of the corporation's international negotiation position, executives are usually tight-lipped about their firm's countertrade transactions.[32] At the same time, rumors about countertrade deals are often rampant, even thought many of the transactions gossiped about may never materialize. To some extent, therefore, the public view of countertrade may represent an inverted iceberg: Much more is on the surface than below. Policymakers therefore are uncertain about the precise volume and impact of countertrade, a fact that makes taking proper policy actions all the more difficult.

Countertrade does appear to be on the increase. The main reason for that conclusion is the fact that countertrade may perhaps be the only practical solution to the fundamental difficulties in the world economy, of which it is a symptom. Access to developed markets for the less-developed countries has become increasingly limited. Balance of payment crises, debt problems, and other financial difficulties have hurt their ability to import needed products. In the face of limited trade and investment opportunities, both less-developed countries and industrialized nations appear to regard countertrade as an acceptable alternative solution to no trade at all.[33]

## The Corporate Situation

A few years ago, most executives claimed both in public and in private that countertrade was a hindrance to international business and was avoided by their firms. More recently, however, changes in corporate thinking have taken place. Even though companies may not like countertrade transactions, a refusal may mean business lost to foreign rivals who are willing to participate in countertrade. Increasingly, companies are altering their perspective from a reactive to a proactive one. In the past, corporations frequently resorted to countertrade only because they were compelled by circumstances to do so. Today, however, companies have begun to use countertrade as a tool to improve their market position. For example Daimler-Benz has established a countertrade subsidiary that swaps warning triangles, screwdrivers, jacks, and even bananas for Mercedes trucks.

Increasingly, companies are formulating international business strategies and are planning to acquire market share from their competition by seeking out countertrade opportunities, provided they lead to an expansion of their own product sales. They are using countertrade systematically as a strategic tool that brings with it favorable government consideration and greater pricing flexibility. Yet, as Global Perspective 18.2 shows, the development of such a new corporate direction is not without its problems.

Human nature and the structure of corporate compensation systems also contribute to the increase in countertrade. Particularly for longer range countertrade transactions, executives may not be as risk averse as for shorter range transactions. By the time the countertrade requirements fall due, which may be five to ten years in the future, they may not be around to take the blame if problems arise because they may have been promoted, changed positions, or retired. On the other hand, the rewards for deals done come today.

Companies and countries imposing countertrade requirements believe that there are more merits to the transactions than purely conserving foreign currency. For example, the countertrade partner can be used as a marketing arm to explore new markets. Long-term countertrade requirements can ensure markets for future output; these are particularly important to producers in industries that are highly sensitive to capacity utilization. Security and stability of purchasing and sales arrangements can also play a major role. Some countries also see counterpurchases as a major way of ensuring that technology transfer is carried out as promised, because the transferor will have to take back the product produced and will therefore ensure that the repayment will be of high quality.

Other reasons for engaging in countertrade can be more effective introduction of new products, the desire to more easily enter new markets, and the

## COPING WITH OFFSETS

**M**any governments of countries that experience trade deficits view imports as a problem. As a result, they may limit imports through the use of tariffs, quotas, or other nontariff barriers. A small but growing number of governments restrict imports, and simultaneously encourage exports, by requiring firms to offset import sales with export spending. The rationale behind such actions is to restrict imports, increase exports, and create jobs.

One way governments offset a negative impact on the trade or current account is through offset purchasing. This means that a company that desires to import products must prove to the government that it is purchasing an agreed-upon percentage of the imports in local goods or services, which in turn are exported. The thought is that if the importer purchases local products for export, local companies will be strengthened and export volume will grow.

The Business Development Group at a U.S. computer firm faces offset regulations every day. In its drive to open new markets around the globe, the firm is increasingly confronted with government demands to offset the trade balance effect of its computer imports. The Business Development Group works with the Procurement Group, third-party suppliers, and governments to comply with offset regulations. For example, the Business Development Group will attempt to source components that are required to build computers, printers, and peripherals from firms in those countries to which computers are exported. Often, the goals of the Business Development Group and the procurement organization within the firm tend to clash. Procurement favors suppliers that offer the best combination of cost, quality, and delivery. Business Development, in turn, prefers sourcing from those suppliers that enable the company to fulfill offset requirements, since doing so will increase sales volume abroad. Unfortunately, the suppliers often do not offer lowest cost, highest quality, or fastest delivery. To reduce the intraorganizational conflict, Business Development has begun to work with foreign suppliers to give them the tools necessary to compete with other suppliers. As a result, technology transfer, training, and quality instructions are often provided abroad.

One concurrent problem faced by the Business Development Group is the fact that it is very difficult to count the dollar volume of purchases from countries. Today, international trade is so complex that it is difficult to tell from which country a good or service originated. Goods are often transshipped before arriving at their final destination. Distributors often do not know from where a certain shipment came. Goods and services often have component parts from a number of countries. In consequence, the Business Development Group is in the process of revamping the firm's entire sourcing system in order to track country of origin more carefully.

*Source: Scott Ciener, Georgetown University.*

goal of expanding the company's market share. Countertrade has been found to provide "outlets for integrative growth in addition to market penetration and development.[34] Finally, countertrade can provide markets and open up new trade channels for surplus products that could not be sold otherwise.[35] Particularly in instances when a world market glut exists for commodities that are in ample supply in some countries yet scarce in others, countertrade transactions may be an appealing trade mechanism.

## The Emergence of New Intermediaries

The rise in countertrade transactions has resulted in the emergence of new specialists to handle such transactions. The intermediaries can be either in-house or outside the corporation. Some companies have been founded to facilitate countertrade transactions for other firms. By purchasing unwanted inventories from companies at a steep discount, sometimes very high profit margins can be obtained.

Intermediaries that have benefited from the rise of countertrade are trading companies or trading houses. Some of them are subsidiaries of large corporations that seek to supplement the trading volume generated by their corporation with business from other firms. An example of such multinational activity is provided in Figure 18.3. Due to their widespread connections around the world, trading companies can dispose of countertraded goods more easily than can corporations that only infrequently consummate countertrade transactions. They are also more capable of evaluating the risks of such transactions and can benefit from both the discount and the markup portion of the exchange.

Firms that deal with trading houses to receive assistance in their countertrade transactions need to be aware that the fees charged are often quite steep and may increase cumulatively. For example, there may be an initial consulting fee when the transaction is contemplated, a fee for the consummation of the acquisition, and a subsequent steep discount for the disposal of the acquired products. Also, the trading houses frequently refuse to take countertraded goods on a nonrecourse basis, which means that the company that has obtained countertraded goods still shares some of the risks inherent in their disposal.

**FIGURE 18.3**

**Advertisement Offering Countertrade Services**

**FIGURE 18.4**

**An Advertisement for a Countertrade Database**

*Source:* Courtesy of DP Publications Company.

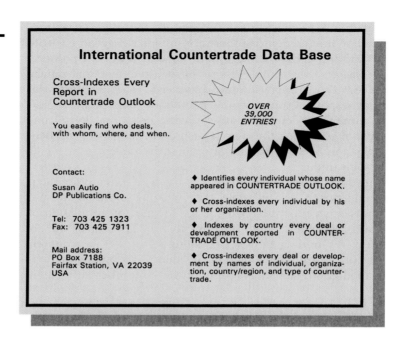

International banks also have some involvement in countertrade to serve their clients better and to increase their own profitability. Banks may be able to use their experience in international trade finance and apply it to the financial aspects of countertrade transactions. Some banks may also have a comparative advantage over trading firms by having more knowledge and expertise about financial risk management and more information about and contacts with the global market.

Countertrade intermediaries need not be large. Smaller firms can successfully compete with a niche strategy. By exploiting specialized geographic or product knowledge and developing countertrade transactions that may be too small for the multinational firm, an entrepreneur can conduct trades with little capital, yet receive sound profit margins.

Another type of intermediary, mostly smaller, is represented by countertrade information service providers. They provide databases on countertrade products and countertrade regulations in various countries, which subscribers may tap. They can also provide computerized matchmaking services between companies in debit to some country's counterpurchase system and those in credit, or those willing to buy counterpurchase items.[36] Figure 18.4 provides an example of such a database service.

## Preparing for Countertrade

The majority of countertrade transactions are consummated by countertrade specialists who are outside the corporation. However, increasingly companies consider carrying out countertrade transactions in-house. If this can be done, the need for steep discounts may decrease and the profitability of countertrade may improve.

Developing an in-house capability for handling countertrade should be done with great caution. First, the company should determine the import priorities of its products to the country or firm to which it is trying to sell. Goods that are highly desirable and/or necessary for a country mandating countertrade are less likely to be subject to countertrade requirements or may be subject to less stringent requirements than goods considered luxurious and unnecessary. Next, the firm needs to identify the countertrade arrangements and regulations that exist in the country to which it exports. An awareness of the alternatives available and of the various countertrade percentages demanded will strengthen the company's bargaining position at the precontract stage. Obtaining this information is also important to incorporate possible countertrade costs early into the pricing scheme. Once a "cash deal" price has been quoted, increasing the price is difficult if a subsequent countertrade demand is made.

At this stage, the most favored countertrade arrangement from the buyer's perspective should be identified. The company should find out why this particular arrangement is the most favored one and explore whether other forms of transactions would similarly meet the objectives of the countertrading partner. To do this, the goals and objectives of the countertrading parties need to be determined. As discussed earlier, they can consist of investment or import substitution, a preservation of hard currency, export promotion, and so on.

The next step is to match the strengths of the firm with current and potential countertrade situations. This requires an assessment of corporate capabilities and resources. Any internal sourcing needs that might be used to fulfill a countertrade contract should be determined—that is, raw materials or intermediate products that could be obtained from the countertrade partner rather than current suppliers. However, this assessment should not be restricted to the internal corporate use of a countertraded product. The company should also determine whether it can use, for example, its distribution capabilities or its contacts with other customers and suppliers to help in its countertrade transactions. Global Perspective 18.3 recounts some of the creative countertrade approaches employed by Pepsi-Cola.

At this point, the company can decide whether it should engage in countertrade transactions. The accounting and taxation aspects of the countertrade transactions should be considered, because they are often quite different from usual procedures. The use of an accounting or tax professional is essential to compliance with difficult and obscure tax regulations in this area.

Next, all of the risks involved in countertrade must be considered. This means that the goods to be obtained need to be specified, that the delivery time for the goods needs to be determined, and that the reliability of the supplier and the quality and consistency of the goods need to be assessed. It is also useful to explore the impact of countertrade on future prices, both for the specific goods obtained and for the world market price for the category of goods. For example, a countertrade transaction may appear to be quite profitable at the time of agreement. Several months or even years may pass before the transaction is actually consummated. A change in world market prices may severely affect the transaction's profitability. The effect of a countertrade transaction on the world market price should also be considered. In cases of large-volume transactions, the established price may be affected because of a glut of supply. Such a situation may not only affect the profitability of a transaction but can also result in possible legal actions by other suppliers of similar products.

## COUNTERTRADE IN EMERGING MARKETS

**P**epsi-Cola is one of many exporters using creative countertrade to exploit new business opportunities in emerging markets. When doing business with the cash-strapped former Soviet Union, Pepsi accepted payments in the form of products rather than currency. In a historic case, Pepsi took Stolichnaya vodka as payment for installing soda machines in the former Soviet Union. Then Pepsi's wine and spirits division took the Stolichnaya name global in a well-known marketing campaign.

In an even more startling case, Pepsi accepted hardware as payment, including seventeen submarines, a cruiser, a frigate, and a destroyer. Pepsi didn't plan on forming its own navy; it sold the vessels for scrap at a profit. Although companies using countertrade rarely acquire their own naval squadron, many are finding countertrade to be a valuable marketing tool in a wide range of transactions. Across Eastern Europe, Latin Amer-

ica, and Southeast Asia, exporters are finding that countertrade provides a viable option to help expand their markets, increase competitiveness, or get around these countries' cash-flow problems.

The practice is not without risks. Pepsi actually was left with excess Stolichnaya after its vodka deal flooded the market. It had calculated the exchange based on current market prices for vodka in the U.S., not figuring that importing such high volumes would sink prices.

One way for companies to deal with the risk of countertrade is to arrange for a third party to accept the customer's goods for cash. For example, one medical supply company that wanted to sell its products to Burma was offered twenty metric tons of rice in exchange for $3.8 million in supplies. At first the company didn't know where to turn with the rice offer, and a manager actually contacted Uncle Ben's after reading their toll-free number on a rice box. Uncle Ben's couldn't help them, but the rice seller did point them in the direction of a supplier that eventually took on the rice as part of a deal. The medical supply company sold its product in a new market without ever touching the rice or risking a change in commodity prices.

*Source: Daniel S. Levine, "Got a Spare Destroyer Around? Make a Trade," World Trade (June 1997): 34–35.*

In conjunction with the evaluation of the countertraded products, which should be specified in as much detail as possible rather than left open, the corporation needs to explore the market for the products. This includes forecasting future market developments, paying particular attention to competitive reaction and price fluctuations. It is also useful at this stage to determine the impact of the countertraded products on the sales and profits of other complementary product lines currently marketed by the firm. Possible repercussions from outside groups should be investigated. Such repercussions may consist of reactions from totally unsuspected quarters. For example, McDonnell-Douglas ran into strong opposition when it used bartered Yugoslavian ham in its employees' cafeteria and as Christmas gifts. The local meatpackers' union complained vociferously that McDonnell-Douglas was threatening the jobs of its members.

One should also evaluate the length of the intended relationship with the countertrading partner and the importance of the relationship for future plans and goals. Such parameters may be decisive, because they may override short-term economic effects. Management can then make the final decision as to whether the transaction should be handled within or outside of the firm. Table 18.3 summarizes the advantages and disadvantages of such organizational alternatives. Overall, management needs to remember that, in most instances, a countertrade transaction should remain a means for successful international business and not become an end in itself.

**TABLE 18.3**

**Organizing for Countertrade: In-House versus Third Parties**

| Advantages | Disadvantages |
|---|---|
| **In-House** | |
| ■ Lower costs | ■ Less expertise |
| ■ Customer contact | ■ Reselling problems |
| ■ More control | ■ Recruitment and training costs |
| ■ More flexibility | ■ Less objectivity |
| ■ More learning | ■ Problems coordinating interfunctional staff |
| ■ More confidentiality | |
| **Third Parties** | |
| ■ Expert specialists | ■ May be costly |
| ■ Customer contacts | ■ Distanced from customer |
| ■ Reselling contacts | ■ Less flexibility |
| ■ Legal acumen | ■ Less confidentiality |
| ■ More objectivity | ■ Less learning |

*Source:* Charles W. Neale, David D. Shipley, and J. Colin Dodds, "The Countertrading Experience of British and Canadian Firms," *Management International Review* 31 no. 1 (1991): 33.

## Summary

Countertrades are business transactions in which the sale of goods is linked to other goods or performance rather than only to money. In spite of their economic inefficiency, such transactions are emerging with increasing frequency in many nations around the world.

Concurrent with their increased use, countertrade transactions also have become more sophisticated. Rather than exchange goods for goods in a straight barter deal, companies and countries now structure counterpurchase agreements, compensation arrangements, clearing accounts, offset agreements, and debt swaps to promote their industrial policies and encourage development.

Governments and international organizations are concerned about the trend toward countertrade, yet in light of existing competition and the need to find creative ways of financing trade, they exercise very little interference with countertrade.

Corporations are increasingly using countertrade as a competitive tool to maintain or increase market share. The complexity of the transactions requires careful planning in order to avoid major corporate losses. Management must consider how the acquired merchandise will be disposed of, what the potential for market disruptions is, and to what extent countertraded goods fit in with the corporate mission.

New intermediaries have emerged to facilitate countertrade transactions, yet their services can be very expensive. However, they can enable firms without countertrade experience to participate in this growing business practice. In addition, the development of intermediary skills may offer profitable opportunities for small business entrepreneurs.

## Key Terms and Concepts

| | | |
|---|---|---|
| barter | clearing account barter | debt-for-equity swap |
| counterpurchase | switch-trading | debt-for-product swap |
| parallel barter | offset | debt-for-nature swap |
| buy-back | debt swaps | debt-for-education swap |
| compensation arrangement | debt-for-debt swap | assessment of taxes |

## Questions for Discussion

1. What are some of the major causes for the resurgence of countertrade?
2. What forms of countertrade exist and how do they differ?
3. Discuss the advantages and drawbacks of countertrade.
4. How would you characterize the government's position toward countertrade?
5. How consistent is countertrade with the international trade framework?
6. Why would firm take goods rather than cash?
7. Why would a buyer insist on countertrade transactions?
8. What particular benefits can an outside countertrade intermediary offer to a firm engaged in such transactions?
9. How would you prepare your firm for countertrade?
10. Develop a corporate goals statement that uses countertrade as a proactive tool for international expansion.
11. Explain why countertrade may be encouraged by the increasing technology transfer taking place.
12. What are some of the dangers of using countertraded goods in-house?
13. In the World Trade Organization's Agreement on Government Procurement, how are offsets defined and what stance is taken toward them (refer to the government procurement page on the Web site **www.wto.org**)?

## Recommended Readings

*Countertrade and Offsets.* A newsletter published by DP Publications Co., Fairfax Station, Virginia.

*Directory of Organizations Providing Countertrade Services 1996–97.* 7th ed. Fairfax Station, VA: DP Publications Co., 1996.

*International Buy-Back Contracts.* New York: United Nations, 1991.

Martin, Stephen, ed. *The Economics of Offsets: Defence Procurement and Countertrade.* Amsterdam: Harwood Academic Publishers, 1996.

Mohring, Wolfgang. *Gegengeschaefte: Analyse einer Handelsform.* Frankfurt: M.P. Lang, 1991.

"Offsets," *Business America* 117, 9. Washington D.C.: U.S. Department of Commerce, September, 1996.

*Offsets in Defense Trade.* Bureau of Export Administration, U.S. Department of Commerce, Washington D.C., May 1996.

*UNCITRAL Legal Guide on International Countertrade Transactions.* New York: United Nations, 1993.

Verzariu, Pompiliu, and Paula Mitchell, *A Guide on Countertrade Practices in the Newly Independent States of the Former Soviet Union,* Washington D.C.: U.S. Department of Commerce, 1995.

## Notes

1. *Trade Finance,* May 1992, 13.
2. "Current Activities of International Organizations in the Field of Barter and Barter-Like Transactions," *Report of the Secretary General,* United Nations, General Assembly, 1984, 4.
3. Kreuze, Jerry G. "International Countertrade," *Internal Auditor* 54, 2 (April 1997): 42–47.
4. Jean-François Hennart and Erin Anderson, "Countertrade and the Minimization of Transaction Costs: An Empirical Examination," *The Journal of*

*Law, Economics, and Organization*, September 2, 1993, 290–313.

5. Ibid., 307.

6. Jean-François Hennart, "Some Empirical Dimensions of Countertrade," *Journal of International Business Studies* 21, 2 (Second Quarter, 1990): 243–270.

7. Abla M. Abdel-Latif and Jeffrey B. Nugent, "Countertrade as Trade Creation and Trade Diversion," *Contemporary Economic Policy* 12 (January 1994): 1–10.

8. Jong H. Park, "Is Countertrade Merely a Passing Phenomenon? Some Public Policy Implications," in *Proceedings of the 1988 Conference,* ed. R. King (Charleston, S.C.: Academy of International Business, Southeast Region, 1988), 67–71.

9. Hennart, "Some Empirical Dimensions of Countertrade."

10. Rolf Mirus and Bernard Yeung, "Why Countertrade? An Economic Perspective," *The International Trade Journal* 7, 4 (1993): 409–433.

11. Paul Samuelson, *Economics,* 11th ed. (New York: McGraw Hill, 1980), 260.

12. "Current Activities of International Organizations," 4.

13. Christopher M. Korth, "The Promotion of Exports with Barter," in *Export Promotion,* ed. M. Czinkota (New York: Praeger, 1983), 42.

14. Donna U. Vogt, *U.S. Government International Barter;* Congressional Research Service, Report No. 83-211ENR (Washington, D.C.: Government Printing Office, 1983), 65.

15. Korth, "The Promotion of Exports with Barter," 42.

16. Richard A. Debts, David L. Roberts, and Eli M. Remolona, *Finance for Developing Countries* (New York: Group of 30, 1987), 18.

17. Rudolph Mye, U.S. Department of Commerce, Chilean Desk, October 1991.

18. Pompiliu Verzariu, "An Overview of Nontraditional Finance Techniques in International Commerce," in *Trade Finance: Current Issues and Developments* (Washington, D.C.: Government Printing Office, 1988), 50.

19. "Greensback-Debt," *The Economist* (August 6, 1988): 62–63.

20. Michael R. Czinkota and Martin J. Kohn, *A Report to the Secretary of Commerce: Improving U.S. Competitiveness—Swapping Debt for Education* (Washington, D.C.: Government Printing Office, 1988).

21. Donald J. Lecraw, "The Management of Countertrade: Factors Influencing Success," *Journal of International Business Studies* 20 (Spring 1989): 41–59.

22. Aspy P. Palia and Oded Shenkar, "Countertrade Practices in China," *Industrial Marketing Management* 20 (1991): 57–65.

23. *Report of the President on U.S. Competitiveness* (transmitted to Congress in September, 1980), V-45.

24. John D. Lange, Jr., Director, Office of Trade Finance, U.S. Department of the Treasury, testimony before the House Economic Stabilization Subcommittee, Committee on Banking, Finance, and Urban Affairs, 97th Congress, 1st session, September 24, 1981.

25. Donald W. Eiss, statement before the Subcommittee on Arms Control, International Security and Science and the Subcommittee on International Economic Policy and Trade, Committee on Foreign Affairs, U.S. House of Representatives, July 1, 1987, 4–5.

26. Public Law 102-558, Title I §124,106 Stat.4207, 1990.

27. Dorothy A. Paun, Larry D. Compeau, and Dhruv Grewal, "A Model of the Influence of Marketing Objectives on Pricing Strategies in International Countertrade," *Journal of Public Policy and Marketing* 16, 1 (Spring 1997): 69–82.

28. Steven M. Rubin, "Countertrade Controversies Stirring Global Economy," *The Journal of Commerce* (September 24, 1984): 14.

29. Patricia Daily and S. M. Ghazanfar, "Countertrade: Help or Hindrance to Less-Developed Countries," *The Journal of Social, Political and Economic Studies* 18, 1 (1993): 61–76.

30. Jacques de Miramon, "Countertrade: A Modern Form of Barter," *OECD Observer* (January 1982): 12.

31. "Current Activities of International Organizations," 5.

32. Michael R. Czinkota, "New Challenges in U.S.–Soviet Trade," *Journal of the Academy of Marketing Science* 5 (Special Issue, Summer 1977): 17–20.

33. Michael R. Czinkota and Anne Talbot, "Countertrade and GATT: Prospects for Regulation," *International Trade Journal* 1 (Fall 1986): 173.

34. Sandra M. Huszagh and Hiram C. Barksdale, "International Barter and Countertrade: An Exploratory Study," *Journal of the Academy of Marketing Science* 14 (Spring 1986): 21–28.

35. Lynn G. Reiling, "Countertrade Revives 'Dead Goods,'" *Marketing News* (August 29, 1986): 1, 22.

36. Kate Mortimer, "Countertrade in Western Europe," in *International Countertrade,* ed. Christopher M. Korth (Westport, Conn.: Quorum Books, 1987), 41.

# CHAPTER 19

# International Accounting and Taxation

## LEARNING OBJECTIVES

◆ *To understand how accounting practices differ across countries, and how these differences may alter the competitiveness of firms in international markets*

◆ *To isolate which accounting practices are likely to constitute much of the competitiveness debate in the coming decade*

◆ *To examine the two basic philosophies of international taxation as practiced by governments, and how they in turn deal with foreign firms in their home markets and domestic firms in foreign markets*

◆ *To understand how the degree of ownership and control of a foreign enterprise alters the taxable income of a foreign enterprise in the eyes of U.S. tax authorities*

◆ *To understand the problems faced by many U.S.-based multinational firms in paying taxes both in foreign countries and in the United States*

## The Tax Man & Transfer Prices

Tokyo—Foreign companies in Japan are getting more frequent visits from the Tokyo tax man these days. Tax authorities are clamping down on what they say is a propensity by multinationals to avoid the nation's high corporate taxes by illegally shifting profits of their books in Japan. Japan's National Tax Administration says it has stepped up its hunt for Japanese units of multinational companies that engage in "transfer-pricing," an accounting trick in which a company artificially depresses the profits it reports on its books in one country by moving those profits onto books in another.

Companies caught engaging in transfer-pricing often face a whopping bill. In 1994 Coca-Cola Co.'s Japan unit announced it would contest a big claim for back taxes, which this newspaper reported to be for $140 million. The Japanese unit of Goodyear Tire & Rubber Co. was hit for roughly 600 million yen in 1994. Tax officials claimed 800 million yen from the Japanese unit of Procter & Gamble Co. in the same year, according to Japanese press reports that P&G faxes to a reporter; P&G wouldn't comment on the report.

Calculating proper payments for something like a trademark is difficult. Because trademarks aren't traded in the open market, their value is unclear. Mr. Shimamura, the tax official, says his department sets a figure by examining both the company that's being audited and similar transactions at unrelated companies. That, he says, gives auditors a clear idea of what a trademark or an import might be worth in the market and how much a Japanese unit might have overpaid. ■

*Source:* Adapted from "Japan's Tax Man Leans on Foreign Firms," Robert Steiner, *The Wall Street Journal,* November 25, 1996, p. A15.

The methods used in the measurement of company operations, accounting principles, and practices, vary across countries. The methods have a very large impact on how firms operate, how they compare against domestic and international competitors, and how governments view their respective place in society. Accounting principles are, however, moving toward more standardization across countries.

Taxation and accounting are fundamentally related. The principles by which a firm measures its sales and expenses, its assets and liabilities, all go into the formulation of profits, which are subject to taxation. The tax policies of more and more governments, in conjunction with accounting principles, are also becoming increasingly similar. Many of the tax issues of specific interest to officials, such as the avoidance of taxes in high-tax countries or the shielding of income from taxation by holding profits in so-called tax havens, are slowly being eliminated by increasing cooperation between governments.

Like the old expression of "death and taxes," they are today, more than ever, inevitable.

This chapter provides an overview of the major differences between accounting practices and corporate taxation philosophies among major industrial countries. Although the average business manager cannot be expected to have a detailed understanding (or recall) of the multitudes of tax laws and accounting principles across countries, a basic understanding of many of these issues aids in the understanding of why "certain things are done certain ways" in international business.

## Accounting Diversity

The fact that accounting principles differ a cross countries is not, by itself, a problem. The primary problem is that real economic decisions by lenders, investors, or government policymakers may be distorted by the differences. Table 19.1 provides a simple example of the potential problems that may arise if two identical firms were operating in similar or dissimilar economic and accounting environments.

First, if two identical firms (in terms of structure, products, and strategies) are operating in similar economic situations and are subject to similar accounting treatment (cell A), a comparison of their performance will be logical in practice and easily interpreted. The results of a competitive comparison or even an accounting audit (measurement and monitoring of their accounting practices) will lead to results that make sense. The two same firms operating in dissimilar economic situations will, when subject to the same accounting treatment, potentially look very different. And it may be that they should appear different if they are operating in totally different environments.

For example, one airline may depreciate its aircraft over five years, while another airline may depreciate over ten years. Is this justified? It is if the two identical air carriers are in fundamentally different economic situations. If the first airline flies predominantly short commuter routes, which require thousands of takeoffs and landings, and the second airline flies only long inter-

**TABLE 19.1**

**Accounting Diversity and Economic Environments**

| Accounting Treatment | Economic Situation of Two Identical Firms | |
| | Similar | Dissimilar |
| --- | --- | --- |
| **Similar** | Logical practice          A<br>Results are comparable | May/may not be logical       B<br>Results may/may not be comparable |
| **Dissimilar** | Illogical practice        C<br>Results are not comparable | Logical practice             D<br>Results may not be comparable |

*Source:* "International Accounting Diversity and Capital Market Decisions," Frederick D.S. Choi and Richard Levich, in *The Handbook of International Accounting,* Frederick D.S. Choi, ed., 1992.

continental flights, which require far fewer takeoffs and landings, the first may be justified in depreciating its fixed assets much faster. The airline with more frequent takeoffs and landings will wear out its aircraft more quickly, which is what the accounting principle of depreciation is attempting to capture.[1] The economic situations are different.

The most blatantly obvious mismatch of economic environments and accounting treatments is probably that of cell C. Two identical firms operating within the same economic environment that receive different accounting treatment are not comparable. The same firms, if placed in the same environment, would appear differently, with one potentially gaining competitive advantage over the other simply because of accounting treatment. This is inconsistent with most of the private and public goals of accounting in all countries.

Finally, cell D offers the mismatch of different environments and different accounting treatments. Although logical in premise, the results are most likely incomparable in outcome. Identical firms in differing economic environments require differing approaches to financial measurement. But the fact that the results of financial comparison may not be usable is not an error; it is simply a fact of the differing markets in which the firms operate. As firms expand internationally, as markets expand across borders, as businesses diversify across currencies, cultures, and economies, the movement toward cell A continues from market forces rather than from government intention.

## Principal Accounting Differences Across Countries

International **accounting diversity** can lead to any of the following problems in international business conducted with the use of financial statements: (1) poor or improper business decision making; (2) hinder the ability of a firm or enterprise to raise capital in different or foreign markets; and (3) hinder or prevent a firm from monitoring competitive factors across firms, industries, and countries. Examples of these problems abound in international business literature. For example, it is widely believed that much of the recent trend of British firms acquiring U.S. companies is primarily a result of their ability to completely expense "goodwill" (the added cost of a firm purchased over and above the fair market value of its constituent components).

**Origins of Differences**

Accounting standards and practices are in many ways no different from any other legislative or regulatory statuses in their origins. Laws reflect the people, places, and events of their time (see Global Perspective 19.1). Most accounting practices and laws are linked to the objectives of the parties who will use the financial information, including investors, lenders, and governments.

National accounting principles are also frequently affected by other environmental factors, such as the dominance of one country's trade and financial activity over the trade and financial activity of another country. Although there are substantial differences between U.S. and Canadian accounting practices, many of the recent changes forced on Canadian firms have their origins in U.S. practice.

## THE FATHER OF ACCOUNTING: LUCA PACIOLI WHO?

**D**octors have Hippocrates and philosophers have Plato. But who is the father of accounting? Knowing that accountants have long had inferiority complexes, two Seattle University professors have decided that the profession should have a father and that he should be Luca Pacioli.

But their anointing of the Renaissance scholar occasions an identity crisis. Hardly anyone—accountants included—has ever heard of Pacioli (pronounced pot-CHEE-oh-lee).

Five centuries ago, Pacioli published "*Summa de Arithmetica, Geometria, Proportioni et Proportionalita.*" It contained a slender tract for merchants on double-entry bookkeeping, which had been in wide use in Venice for years. Due to that, some accounting historians including Professors Weis and Tinius credit Pacioli with codifying accounting principles for the first time. That would seem to establish paternity.

Professor Vangermeersch, of the University of Rhode Island, says the origins of double-entry bookkeeping are open to question. "If you're crediting people of past centuries for contributions to accounting, you should include Leonardo of Pisa, who brought Arabic numerals to the West; James Pelle, who initiated journal-entry systems; and Emile Garcke and J.M. Fells, who applied accounting to factory use," he said. All the men have another thing in common, he added: They are just as obscure as Luca Pacioli.

Even in literature, says Vangermeersch, the only famous accountant was Daniel Defoe, who wrote *Robinson Crusoe.* Unfortunately, Defoe was a terrible businessman and failed in a series of ventures, the professor observed. "Even as a dissenter and pamphleteer, he was tarred and feathered by the public."

*Source: Abstracted from "Father of Accounting Is a Bit of a Stranger To His Own Progeny," The Wall Street Journal, January 29, 1993, A1, A6. Reprinted by permission of The Wall Street Journal, © 1993 Dow Jones & Company, Inc. All Rights Reserved Worldwide.*

## Classification Systems

There are several ways to classify and group national accounting systems and practices. Figure 19.1 illustrates one such classification based on a statistically based clustering of practices across countries by C. W. Nobes. The systems are first subdivided into microbased (characteristics of the firms and industries) and macro-uniform (following fundamental government or economic factors per country). The microbased national accounting systems are then broken down into those that follow a theoretical principle or pragmatic concerns. The latter category includes the national accounting systems of countries as diverse as the United States, Canada, Japan, the United Kingdom, and Mexico.

The macro-uniform systems, according to Nobes, are primarily used in European countries. The continental Europeans are typified by accounting systems that are formulated in secondary importance to legal organizational forms (Germany), for the apportionment and application of national tax laws (France, Spain, Italy), or the more pure forms of government and economic models (Sweden). An alternative approach to those in the European classification would be those such as Sweden and Germany, which have pushed their firms to adopt more widespread uniform standards. However, as with all classification systems, the subtle differences across countries can quickly make such classifications useless in practice. As the following sections will illustrate, slight differences can also yield significant competitive advantages or disadvantages to companies organized and measured under different financial reporting systems.

## Principal Differences: The Issues

The resulting impact of accounting differences is to separate or segment international markets for investors and firms alike. Communicating the financial results of a foreign company operating in a foreign country and foreign currency is often a task that must be undertaken completely separately from the

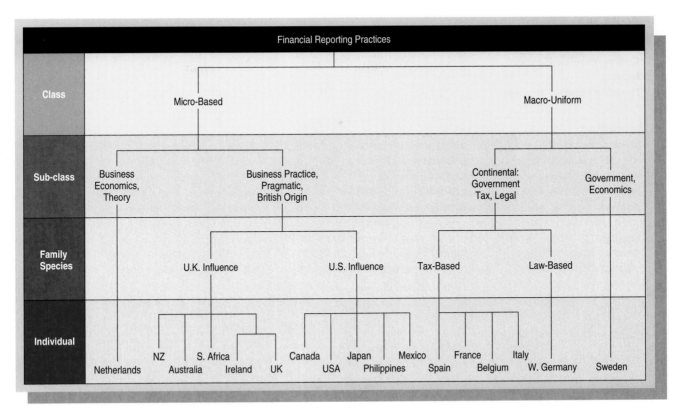

**FIGURE 19.1**

**Nobes Classification of National Accounting Systems**

*Source:* C.W. Nobes, "International Classification of Accounting Systems," unpublished paper, April 1980. Table C, as cited in *International Accounting,* 2d ed., Frederick D.S. Choi and Gerhard G. Mueller, Englewood Cliffs, N.J.: Prentice-Hall, 1992, p. 34.

accounting duties of the firm. Actually, financial results must often be reinterpreted and presented in other markets as illustrated in Figure 19.2, in which Cathay Pacific, a Hong Kong–based firm, must have its financial results presented in terms that are known to the larger U.S. dollar markets through a marketing presentation. As long as significant accounting practices differ across countries, markets will continue to be segmented (and accountants may be required to be interpreters and marketers as much as bookkeepers).

Table 19.2 provides an overview of nine major areas of significant differences in accounting practices across countries.[2] There are, of course, many more hundreds of differences, but the nine serve to highlight some of the fundamental philosophical differences across countries. Accounting differences are real and persistent, and there is still substantial question of competitive advantages and informational deficiencies that may result from these continuing differences across countries.

**Accounting for Research and Development Expenses**   Are research and development expenses capitalized or expensed as costs are incurred? Those who argue that there is no certainty that the R&D expenditures will lead to bene-

**FIGURE 19.2**

**Cathay Pacific Airways: Communicating Financial Results**

*Source: The Economist,* September 5, 1992, 22.

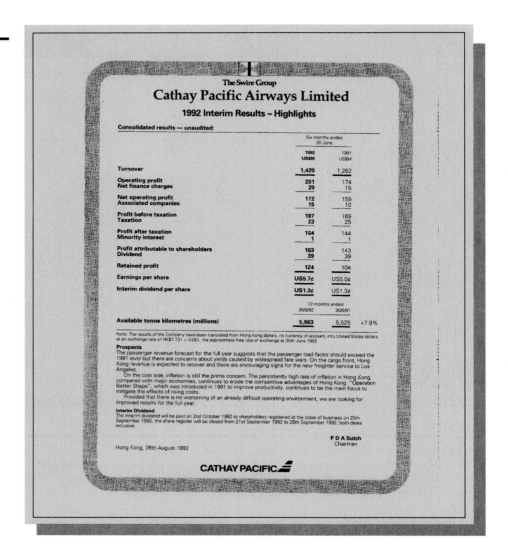

fits in future periods would require immediate recognition of all expenses as in typical conservative practice. Alternatively, if R&D expenditures do lead to future benefits and revenues, the matching of expenses and revenues would be better served if the R&D expenditures were capitalized, and expenses therefore spread out over the future benefit periods.

**Accounting for Fixed Assets**   How are fixed assets (land, buildings, machinery, equipment) to be expensed and carried? The assets constitute large outlays of capital, result in assets that are held by the firm for many years, and yield benefits for many future years. All countries require companies to capitalize these fixed assets, so that they are depreciated over their future economic lives (once again spreading the costs out over periods roughly matching the revenue-earning useful life). There are, however, significant differences in depreciation methods used (straight-line, sum-of-years-digits, accelerated meth-

**TABLE 19.2**

**Summary of Principal Accounting Differences around the World**

| Accounting Principle | United States | Japan | United Kingdom | France | Germany | Netherlands | Switzerland | Canada | Italy | Brazil |
|---|---|---|---|---|---|---|---|---|---|---|
| 1. Capitalization of R&D costs | Not allowed | Allowed in certain cases | Allowed in certain cases | Allowed in certain cases | Not allowed | Allowed in certain cases | Allowed in certain cases | Allowed in certain cases | Allowed in certain cases | Allowed in certain cases |
| 2. Fixed asset revaluations stated at amount in excess of cost | Not allowed | Not allowed | Allowed | Allowed | Not allowed | Allowed in certain cases | Not allowed | Not allowed | Allowed in certain cases | Allowed |
| 3. Inventory valuation using LIFO | Allowed | Allowed | Allowed but rarely done | Not allowed | Allowed in certain cases | Allowed | Allowed | Allowed | Allowed | Allowed but rarely done |
| 4. Finance leases capitalized | Required | Allowed in certain cases | Required | Not allowed | Allowed in certain cases | Required | Allowed | Required | Not allowed | Not allowed |
| 5. Pension expense accrued during period of service | Required | Allowed | Required | Allowed | Required | Required | Allowed | Required | Allowed | Allowed |
| 6. Book and tax timing differences on balance sheet as deferred tax | Required | Allowed in certain cases | Allowed | Allowed in certain cases | Allowed but rarely done | Required | Allowed | Allowed | Allowed but rarely done | Allowed |
| 7. Current rate method of currency translation | Required | Allowed in certain cases | Required | Allowed | Allowed | Required | Required | Allowed in certain cases | Required | Required |
| 8. Pooling method used for mergers | Required in certain cases | Allowed in certain cases | Allowed in certain cases | Not allowed | Allowed in certain cases | Allowed but rarely done | Allowed but rarely done | Allowed but rarely done | Not allowed | Allowed but rarely done |
| 9. Equity method used for 20–50% ownership | Required | Required | Required | Allowed in certain cases | Allowed | Required | Required | Required | Allowed | Required |

*Source:* Adapted from "A Summary of Accounting Principle Differences Around the World," Phillip R. Peller and Frank J. Schwitter, 1991, p. 4.3.

ods of cost recovery, and so forth), resulting in very different expensing schedules across countries.

The primary issue related to the accounting of fixed assets is whether they are to be carried on company financial statements at historical cost or current value. The conservative approach, used, for example, in the United States, is to carry the fixed assets at historical cost and to allow analysts to use their own methods and additional financial statement notes to ascertain current values of individual fixed assets. The alternative is to allow the values of fixed assets to be periodically revalued up or down, depending on the latest appraised value. Countries such as the Netherlands argue that this is more appropriate, given that the balance sheet of a firm should present the present fair market value of all assets. There is no doubt, however, that with more flexibility in the valuation of fixed assets there is also more opportunity for abuse of the valuation methods, potentially giving firms the ability to manipulate the values of fixed assets carried on the balance sheet.

**Inventory Accounting Treatment**   How are inventories to be valued? For many companies inventories are their single largest asset. Therefore, the reconciliation of how goods are valued as sold (on the income statement) and valued as carried in inventory unsold (on the balance sheet) is important. The three typical inventory-valuation principles are last-in-first-out, **LIFO,** the **average cost method,** and first-in-first-out, **FIFO.**

The LIFO method assumes that the last goods purchased by the firm (last-in) are the first ones sold (first-out). This is considered conservative by accounting standards in that the remaining inventory goods were the first ones purchased. The resulting expenses of cost of goods sold is therefore higher. The only country listed in Table 19.2 that does not allow the use of LIFO is France, although Germany only allows its use in specific cases, making it rarely used. The use of FIFO is thought to be more consistent theoretically with the matching of costs and revenues of actual inventory flows. The use of FIFO is generally regarded as creating a more accurately measured balance sheet, as inventory is stated at the most recent prices.

**Capitalizing or Expensing Leases**   Are financing leases to be capitalized? The recent growth in popularity of leasing for its financial and tax flexibility has created a substantial amount of accounting discussion across countries. The

Differences in depreciation methods used in accounting for fixed assets result in different expensing schedules across countries. The issue is quite complex for the many international firms participating in the Three Georges project, which proposes to build the largest hydroelectric project in the history of the world on China's Yangtze River.
*Source:* © Photographers Photos Co. Bejing/Gamma-Liaison

primary question is whether a leased item should actually be carried on the balance sheet of the firm at all, since a lease is essentially the purchase of an asset only for a specified period of time. If not carried on the books, should the lease payments be expenses paid as if they were a rent payment?

Some argue that the lease results in the transfer of all risks and benefits of ownership to the firm (from the lessor to the lessee) and the lease contract should be accounted for as the purchase of an asset. This would be a capital lease, and if the lessee borrowed money in order to acquire the asset, the lease payments of principal and interest should be accounted for in the same manner as the purchase of any other capital asset. The Netherlands, the United Kingdom, Switzerland, the United States, and other countries require capital lease payment if certain criteria are met.

The alternative is that the lessee has simply acquired the rental use of the services of the asset for a specified period of time, and payments on this **operating lease** should be treated only as rent. In this case the asset would remain on the books of the lessor. France, Italy, and Brazil require all leases to be treated as operating leases.

**Pension Plan Accounting**   The accounting treatment of private pension plans is one of the most recent and significant accounting developments. A private pension plan is the promise by an employer to provide a continuing income stream to employees after their retirement from the firm. The critical accounting question is whether the pension promise should be expensed and carried at the time the employee is working for the firm (providing a service to the firm that will not be fully paid for by the firm until all pension payments are completed) or expensed only as pension payments are made after retirement.

The primary problem with expensing the pension as the services are provided is that the firm does not know the exact amount or timing of the eventual pension payments. If it is assumed that these eventual pension payments can be reasonably approximated, the conservative approach is to account for the expenses as employee services are provided and to carry the **pension liabilities** on the books of the firm. In some countries if it is believed that these pension liabilities cannot be accurately estimated, they will be expensed only as they are incurred on payment.

**Accounting for Income Taxes**   All countries require the payment of income taxes on earnings, however, the definition and timing of earnings can constitute a problem. In many countries the definition of earnings for financial accounting purposes differs from earnings for tax purposes. The question then focuses on whether the tax effect should be recognized during the period in which the item appears on the income statement or during the period in which the item appears on the tax return.

If the expense is recognized during the period in which the item appears on the income statement, the tax gives rise to an associated asset or liability referred to as deferred tax. Some countries do not suffer the debate of whether the deferred tax should actually appear on the balance sheet of the firm by having all financial reporting follow tax rules. Examples include Germany, France, and Japan. However, most countries must deal with the timing mismatch of the deferred tax.

**Foreign Currency Translation**   As discussed in Chapter 17, corporations that operate in more than one country and one currency must periodically *translate* and *consolidate* all financial statements for home-country reporting purposes. The primary issues in foreign currency translation are which exchange rates should be used in the translation of currencies (historical or current rates) and how gains or losses resulting from the translation should be handled in the consolidation. The critical handling issue is whether the gains or losses are recognized in current income or carried on the consolidated balance sheet as an item under equity capital.

Figure 19.3 provides a simple decision tree approach to translation of foreign affiliates for U.S. corporations. The mechanical details of the translation of foreign affiliate balance sheets are covered in Chapter 17.

**FIGURE 19.3**

**United States Translation Procedure Flow Chart**

*The term *remeasure* means to translate so as to change the unit of measure from a foreign currency to the functional currency.

*Source:* Frederick D.S. Choi and Gerhard G. Mueller, *International Accounting*, 2d ed. (Englewood Cliffs, N.J.: Prentice-Hall, 1992) p. 169.

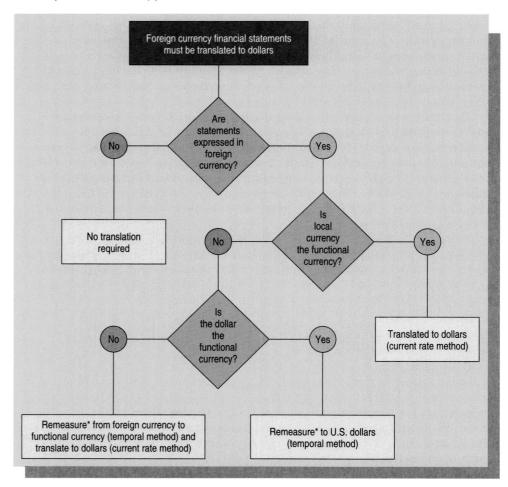

**Accounting for Mergers and Acquisitions** This is a relatively new issue in international accounting, given the sudden and rapid growth of merger and acquisition activity beginning in the United States and the United Kingdom in the 1980s. The primary accounting question is whether the assets and liabilities acquired should be carried at their original historic value or at the value at acquisition. In certain cases, however, it is believed that the shareholders of the acquired company end up owning shares of the acquirer, and accountants argue that their assets and liabilities should not be revalued, but simply merged or pooled. Accounting principles in the countries experiencing most mergers and acquisitions, the United States, the United Kingdom, Germany, and Japan, allow the use of pooling or merger accounting when certain criteria are met.

A second accounting issue of some concern is that often in the case of acquisitions, the price paid exceeds the fair value of the assets acquired. This is termed "goodwill" and constitutes a significant accounting problem. Many accountants argue that this is a true value that is purchased, and would not have been paid for if it did not exist. Even if goodwill is accepted as a legitimate economic value, the question remains as to how it is to be carried on the firm's balance sheet, as shown in the chapter's opening vignette. The United States, Japan, France, Canada, and Brazil all require that goodwill be accounted for as an asset, with amortization occurring over a maximum of anywhere from five to forty years.

In other countries, accountants do not believe that goodwill is a real asset and therefore should not be carried on the books of the firm. In this case, such as in the United Kingdom, the firm is allowed to write off the entire amount against equity in the year of acquisition. It is also argued that this gives British firms a distinct advantage in their ability to make acquisitions and not suffer income statement dilution impacts in the years following as the asset is amortized in the countries that capitalize goodwill. This is a classic example of the potential competitive benefits of a similar activity receiving dissimilar accounting treatment discussed at the beginning of this chapter and presented in Table 19.1. As international accounting standards, firms (as illustrated by Global Perspective 19.2), and practitioners expand globally, these competitive differences will be forced to harmonize.

**Consolidation of Equity Securities Holdings** When one company purchases and holds an investment in another company, the question arises as to how to account for the holdings. There are two major methods of consolidation of equity holdings, the equity method and the consolidation method. The equity method requires that the holder list the security holdings as a line item on the firm's balance sheet. This is generally required when the firm holds substantial interest in the other firm, typically 20 to 50 percent of outstanding voting shares, such that it can exert substantial influence over the other firm but not necessarily dictate management or policy. The equity method is required in many countries, including the United States, Japan, Switzerland, Canada, and Brazil.

The second method of equity holdings, the consolidation method, requires the addition of all of the investee's individual assets and liabilities to the company's assets and liabilities. A minority interest is then subtracted out for all assets for the percentage of the net asset not owned. When an investor has controlling interest in the other firm, most countries require the use of the consolidation method. The remaining accounting debates focus on whether

## COOPERS & LYBRAND EXPAND TO CHINA

**N**ew York (Dec. 23) Business Wire—Coopers & Lybrand, one of the world's leading international accounting and business consulting organizations, has expanded its network in China by signing an agreement with Yangcheng CPAs, the largest and most prestigious CPA firm in Guangzhou, Guangdong Province. With the addition of Yangcheng, Coopers & Lybrand now has over 1,500 personnel able to provide professional business services to clients on China related matters, with 625

based in the People's Republic of China and over 900 in Hong Kong SAR.

Coopers & Lybrand was the first of the international accounting firms to open a legally established representative office in the People's Republic of China in January 1981. Yangcheng CPAs was founded in 1984 and is the largest and most prestigious firm in Guangzhou, the capital of Guangdong Province. This province benefited earliest from the "Open Door Policy," which was started in China in 1979, because of its proximity to Hong Kong. Coopers & Lybrand has enjoyed a close working relationship with Yangcheng since the mid 1980s, including working together on joint audits of foreign investment enterprises and state owned enterprises listed in Hong Kong, training of Yangcheng staff and secondments of partners and staff to Hong Kong.

*Source: Abstracted from "Coopers & Lybrand Expands Network in China," http://www.pathfinder.com/money/latest/press/BU/1997Dec23/1121.html*

the individual assets and liabilities should be consolidated when the subsidiaries are very dissimilar, even if controlling interest is held. Countries such as Italy and the United Kingdom believe that consolidation of dissimilar firms results in misleading information regarding the true financial status of the firms.

## The Process of Accounting Standardization

One of the best indications as to the degree of success that has been achieved in international accounting standards is that there is still some conflict over the terminology of harmonization, standardization, or promulgation of uniform standards. As early as 1966, an Accountants International Study Group was formed by professional institutes in Canada, the United States, and the United Kingdom to begin the study of significant accounting differences across countries. They were primarily only to aid in the understanding of foreign practices, not to form guidelines for more consistent or harmonious policies.

The establishment of the International Accounting Standards Committee (IASC) in 1973 was the first strong movement toward the establishment of international accounting standards. In the latter half of the 1970s, other international institutions such as the United Nations, the Organization for Economic Cooperation and Development (OECD), and the European Union also began forming study groups and analyzing specific issues of confusion, such as corporate organization and varying degrees of disclosure required across countries.[3] The efforts of the European Union to harmonize standards between countries, not standardize, is particularly important in understanding how accounting principles and practices may be reformed to allow individual country differences but at the same time minimize the economic distortions. The recent completion of much of the Internal Financial Market of the Single Eu-

## HOW GREEN IS MY BALANCE SHEET?

**W**hen it comes to environmental accounting, many companies have yet to come clean. Those that publish green accounts usually offer a few charts (printed, of course, on recycled and unbleached paper) showing trends in their output of waste. But the gases and gunk are measured in kilos or tonnes, not pounds or dollars. Few companies convert such data into figures that can appear in financial accounts (which are usually printed on recycled, chlorine-bleached paper).

The task is easier in America than elsewhere, if only because U.S. accounting rules force companies to include detailed data on known environmental liabilities in their accounts. But in Europe, where no such rules exist, information is much more patchy. Some firms, such as British Coal and Thorn EMI, publish figures on environmental liabilities. But Roger Adams, of Britain's Chartered Association of Certified Accountants,

wishes that more would follow their lead. For the past four years, his institute has run a competition for the best corporate environmental accounts in Britain; this year, it is inviting entries from companies in other parts of Europe, too.

It might help if companies had a blueprint to follow. In fact, there are several different guidelines on corporate environmental reporting, including ones from the International Chamber of Commerce and from Japan's employers' association. Most favor reporting a firm's energy consumption and impact on the environment, but none tell green bean-counters how to translate this into monetary values in firms' accounts.

A few have tried anyway. One is BSO/Origin, a Dutch information-technology firm in which Philips, an electronics firm, has a 40 percent stake. It has recently published its fourth annual attempt to value the natural resources it uses and the environmental damage it does. In 1993, its environmental costs totalled 3.7m guilders ($2m), from which the company subtracted 450,000 guilders of "environmental expenditure"—taxes on fuel and waste collection—to arrive at a total of 3.3m guilders of "net value extracted." Eckhart Wintzen, BSO's president, wishes that companies were taxed on this figure. BSO/Origin's big shareholders, a less environmentally sensitive bunch, disagree.

*Source: Abstracted from "How Green Is My Balance Sheet?" **The Economist**, September 3, 1994, 75.*

ropean Program known as 1992 Europe has seen much progress along this harmonization front.

Two other recent developments concerning international standardization merit special note. In 1985, the General Electric Company became the first major U.S. corporation to acknowledge that the accounting principles underlying its 1984 financial statements "are generally accepted in the United States and are consistent with standards issued by the International Accounting Standards Committee."[4] Second, the Financial Accounting Standards Board (FASB), the organization in the United States charged with setting most standards for corporate accounting practices, committed itself to the full consideration of "an international perspective" to all its work in the future. And as other issues of international consequence arise—even environmentalism—accounting questions arise, as shown in Global Perspective 19.3.

## International Taxation

Governments alone have the power to tax. Each government wants to tax all companies within its jurisdiction without placing burdens on domestic or foreign companies that would restrain trade. Each country will state its jurisdictional approach formally in the tax treaties that it signs with other countries.

## OFFSHORE CENTRES' REGULATION UNDER FIRE

**T**he European Commission's chief fraud-fighter yesterday accused the Channel Islands and the Isle of Man of having "lax regulation even by offshore standards," making them an ideal location for hiding illegal activities. The secrecy afforded by Switzerland was also a problem for its European Union neighbors and a "boon to fraudsters," Mr. Per Brix Knudesen, director of the Commission's antifraud coordination unit, told an International Financial Fraud Convention in London. His remarks were publicly challenged by Ms. Jannine Birtwistle, head of compliance at Credit Suisse (Guernsey) and a former regulator on the island. She said Guernsey's regulation had been favourably assessed by the Financial Action Task Force set up by the G7.

But Mr. Knudsen's attack on offshore centres was echoed by Mr. John Moscow, deputy chief of investigations for the New York district attorney's office. After outlining a case involving the Cook Islands, a New Zealand protectorate, Mr. Moscow said: "There are jurisdictions which wish to earn their living protecting crooks." Mr. Knudsen a Dane, said illicit entry of goods into the EU was alone costing member countries' treasuries Ecu5bn–Ecu6bn ($6.3bn–$7.6bn) in lost revenue each year. Smugglers' potential profit per lorry or container-load ranged from Ecu1m for cigarettes to Ecu100,000 for agricultural produce. The Commission unit was also focusing on fraud in the public sector.

He said: "None of this is exclusive to the European Union. This is a truly worldwide phenomenon." Money acquired illicitly was then hidden in "phantom entities in safe havens and offshore centres." Existing arrangements for international judicial co-operation were "old-fashioned and bureaucratic," Mr. Knudsen said. These needed to be simplified and streamlined, and national law enforcement agencies should integrate their efforts and introduce more specialisation.

*Source: Adapted from "Offshore Centres' Regulation Under Fire,"* Financial Times, *Wednesday December 4, 1996, p. 2.*

One of the primary purposes of tax treaties is to establish the bounds of each country's jurisdiction to prevent double taxation of international income. Global Perspective 19.4 shows the effect of taxes on one firm by its own government.

## Tax Jurisdictions

Nations usually follow one of two basic approaches to international taxation: a residential approach or a territorial or source approach. The residential approach to international taxation taxes the international income of its residents without regard to where the income is earned. The territorial approach to transnational income taxes all parties, regardless of country of residency, within its territorial jurisdiction.

Most countries in practice must combine the two approaches to tax foreign and domestic firms equally. For example, the United States and Japan both apply the residential approach to their own resident corporations and the territorial approach to income earned by nonresidents within their territorial jurisdictions. Other countries, such as Germany, apply the territorial approach to dividends paid to domestic firms from their foreign subsidiaries; such dividends are assumed taxed abroad and are exempt from further taxation.

Within the territorial jurisdiction of tax authorities, a foreign corporation is typically defined as any business that earns income within the host country's borders but is incorporated under the laws of another country. The foreign corporation usually must surpass some minimum level of activity (gross income) before the host country assumes primary tax jurisdiction. However, if the for-

Accounting practices for the costs of environmental contamination treatment and restoration, such as Amoco Corporation's reclamation of the dunes of Coatham Sands, Great Britain, is an evolving issue in international business.
*Source:* Courtesy of Amoco Corporation

eign corporation owns income-producing assets or a permanent establishment, the threshold is automatically surpassed. As illustrated by Global Perspective 19.4, it is not always easy to capture income.

## Tax Types

Taxes are generally classified as direct and indirect. **Direct taxes** are calculated on actual income, either individual or firm income. **Indirect taxes,** such as sales taxes, severance taxes, tariffs, and value-added taxes, are applied to purchase prices, material costs, quantities of natural resources mined, and so forth. Although most countries still rely on income taxes as the primary method of raising revenue, tax structures vary widely across countries.

The **value-added tax (VAT)** is the primary revenue source for the European Union. A value-added tax is applied to the amount of product value added by the production process. The tax is calculated as a percentage of the product price less the cost of materials and inputs used in its manufacture, which have been taxed previously. Through this process, tax revenues are collected literally on the value added by that specific stage of the production process. Under the existing General Agreement on Tariffs and Trade (GATT), the legal framework under which international trade operates, value-added taxes may be levied on imports into a country or group of countries (such as the European Union) in order to treat foreign producers entering the domestic markets equally with firms within the country paying the VAT. Similarly, the VAT may be refunded on export sales or sales to tourists who purchase products for consumption outside the country or community. For example, an American tourist leaving London may collect a refund on all value-added taxes paid on goods purchased within the United Kingdom. The refunding usually requires documentation of the actual purchase price and the amount of tax paid.

## Income Categories and Taxation

There are three primary methods used for the transfer of funds across tax jurisdictions: royalties, interest, and dividends. Royalties are under license for the use of intangible assets such as patents, designs, trademarks, techniques, or copyrights. Interest is the payment for the use of capital lent for the financing of normal business activity. Dividends are income paid or deemed paid to the shareholders of the corporation from the residual earnings of operations. When a corporation declares the percentage of residual earnings that is to go to shareholders, the dividend is declared and distributed.

Taxation of corporate income differs substantially across countries. Table 19.3 provides a summary comparison for Japan, Germany, and the United States. In some countries, for example the United States and Japan, there is one **corporate income tax** rate applied to all residual earnings, regardless of what is retained versus what is distributed as dividends. In other countries, for example Germany, separate tax rates apply to **distributed** and **undistributed earnings.** (Note that Germany lists a specific corporate income tax rate for the branches of foreign corporations operating within Germany.)

Royalty and interest payments to nonresidents are normally subject to **withholding taxes.** Corporate profits are typically double taxed in most countries, through corporate and personal taxes. Corporate income is first taxed at the business level with corporate taxes, then a second time when the income of distributed earnings is taxed through personal income taxes. Withholding tax rates also differ by the degree of ownership that the corporation possesses in the foreign corporation. Minor ownership is termed portfolio, while major or controlling influence is categorized as substantial holdings. In the case of dividends, interest, or royalties paid to nonresidents, governments routinely apply withholding taxes to their payment in the reasonable expectation that the nonresidents will not report and declare such income with the host-country tax authorities. Withholding taxes are specified by income category in all bilateral tax treaties. Notice in Table 19.3 the differentials in withholding taxes across countries by bilateral tax treaties. The U.S. tax treaty with Germany results in a 0 percent withholding of interest or royalty payments earned by German corporations operating in the United States.

## U.S. Taxation of Foreign Operations

The United States exercises its rights to tax U.S. residents' incomes regardless of where the income is earned. The two major categories for U.S. taxation of foreign-source income are foreign branches of U.S. corporations and foreign subsidiaries of U.S. corporations.

**Taxation of Foreign Branches of U.S. Corporations**

The income of a foreign branch of a U.S. corporation is treated the same as if the income was derived from sources within the United States. Since a foreign branch is an extension of the U.S. corporation and not independently capitalized and established, its profits are taxed with those of the parent whether actually remitted to the parent or not. Similarly, losses suffered by foreign branches of U.S. corporations are also fully and immediately deductible against U.S. taxable income.

As always, however, the U.S. tax authorities want to prevent double taxation. The United States grants primary tax authority to the country in which the income is derived. If taxes are paid by the foreign branch to host-country tax authorities, the tax payments may be claimed as a tax credit toward U.S. tax liabilities on the same income.

**TABLE 19.3**

**Comparison of Corporate Tax Rates: Japan, Germany, and the United States**

| Taxable Income Category | Japan | Germany | United States |
|---|---|---|---|
| Corporate income tax rates: | | | |
|   Profits distributed to stockholders | 37.5% | 30% | 35% |
|   Undistributed profits | 37.5% | 45% | 35% |
|   Branches of foreign corporations | 37.5% | 42% | 35% |
| Withholding taxes on dividends (portfolio): | | | |
|   with Japan | — | 15% | 15% |
|   with Germany | 15% | — | 15% |
|   with United States | 15% | 5% | — |
| Withholding taxes on dividends (substantial holdings):[a] | | | |
|   with Japan | — | 25% | 10% |
|   with Germany | 10% | — | 5% |
|   with United States | 10% | 10% | — |
| Withholding taxes on interest: | | | |
|   with Japan | — | 10% | 10% |
|   with Germany | 10% | — | 0% |
|   with United States | 10% | 0% | — |
| Withholding taxes on royalties: | | | |
|   with Japan | — | 10% | 10% |
|   with Germany | 10% | — | 0% |
|   with United States | 10% | 0% | — |

[a]"Substantial holdings" for the United States apply only to intercorporate dividends. In Germany and Japan, "substantial holdings" apply to corporate shareholders of greater than 25 percent.

Source: *Corporate Taxes: A Worldwide Summary,* Price Waterhouse, 1996.

Just as the United States taxes corporations from other countries operating within its borders, foreign countries tax the operations of U.S. corporations within their jurisdiction. Corporations operating in more than one country are therefore subject to double taxation. Double taxation could hinder the ability of U.S. corporations to operate and compete effectively abroad. The U.S. tax code removes the burden by reducing the U.S. taxes due on the foreign-source income by the amount of foreign taxes deemed paid.

The calculation of the foreign income taxes deemed paid and the additional U.S. taxes due, if any, involves the interaction of the following four components.

- **Degree of Ownership and Control.** The degree of ownership and control of the foreign corporation has a significant impact on the calculation of U.S. taxes payable on the foreign-source income. There are three basic ownership ranges applicable to taxation: (1) less than 10 percent; (2) 10 to 50 percent; and (3) more than 50 percent. Figure 19.4 illustrates the three ownership classes under U.S. tax law. If the U.S. corporation owns more than 50 percent of the voting shares in the foreign corporation, the foreign corporation is classified as a Controlled Foreign Corporation (CFC).[5]

**Taxation of Foreign Subsidiaries of U.S. Corporations**

# Corporate Tax Rates Around the World

Source: *1993 International Tax Summaries: A Guide for Planning and Decisions*
Note: Tax rates listed are statutory rates for general manufacturing firms incorporated in the host country listed. Rates may not apply to firms operating in industries or areas under specific provisions or development programs of the host country.

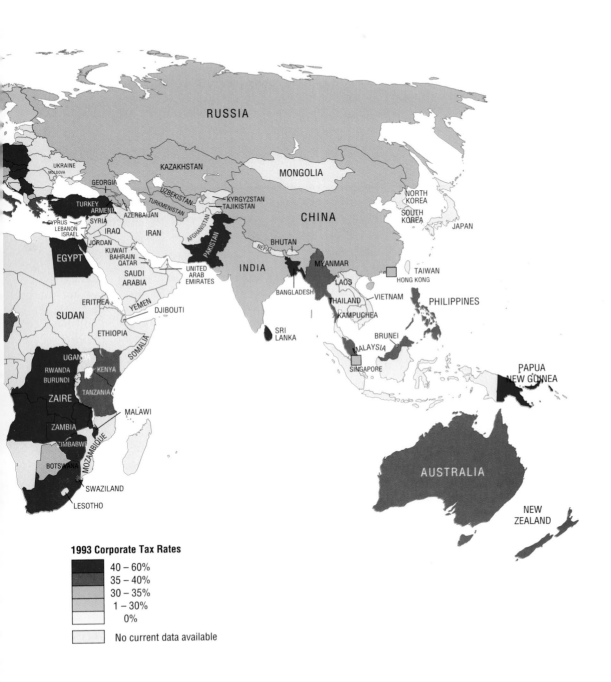

**1993 Corporate Tax Rates**

- 40 – 60%
- 35 – 40%
- 30 – 35%
- 1 – 30%
- 0%
- No current data available

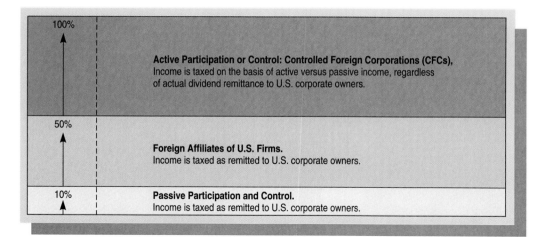

**FIGURE 19.4**

**Classification of U.S. Ownership of Foreign Corporations for Tax Uses**

*Source:* Adapted from Eiteman, Stonehill, and Moffett, *Multinational Business Finance,* 8th ed. (Reading, Mass.: Addison-Wesley, 1998), Chapter 17.

■ **Proportion of Income Distributed.** The proportion of after-tax income that is distributed as profits to stockholders as dividends is also important to the calculation of U.S. tax liability. Income that is retained by the foreign corporation and not distributed to shareholders, U.S. or other, will have the result, in certain cases, of reducing the U.S. tax liability on the foreign corporation's income.

■ **Active versus Passive Income.** If a foreign subsidiary generates income through its own actions or activities (e.g., producing a product, selling a product, providing a service), the income is classified as *active.* If, however, the foreign subsidiary or affiliate earns income through its ownership in another firm, or by acting as a creditor to another firm and earning interest income, the income is classified as *passive.* It is quite common for a foreign subsidiary to have both active and passive income. Each is then treated separately for tax purposes.

■ **Relative Corporate Income Taxes.** Whether foreign corporate income taxes are higher or lower than similar U.S. corporate income taxes will largely determine whether the U.S. shareholders will owe additional taxes in the United States on the foreign-source income, or whether the foreign tax credit will completely cover U.S. tax liabilities. If withholding taxes were applied to dividends paid to nonresidents (the U.S. corporation owner), this also would affect the U.S. tax liability.

**Calculation of U.S. Taxes on Foreign-Source Earnings**

Table 19.4 illustrates the complete calculation of foreign taxes, U.S. tax credits, additional U.S. taxes due on foreign income, and total worldwide tax burdens for four different potential cases. Each of the four cases is structured to highlight the different combinations of the three components, relative corporate income taxes (lines a, b, and c), degree of control or ownership of the

**TABLE 19.4**

U.S. Taxation of Foreign-Source Income (thousands of U.S. dollars)

| | Case 1 | Case 2 | Case 3 | Case 4 |
|---|---|---|---|---|
| **Baseline Values** | | | | |
| a. Foreign corporate income tax rate | 40% | 20% | 20% | 20% |
| b. U.S. corporate income tax rate | 35% | 35% | 35% | 35% |
| c. Foreign dividend withholding tax rate | 10% | 10% | 10% | 10% |
| d. Proportional ownership held by U.S. corporation in foreign corporation | 30% | 30% | 30% | 100% |
| e. Payout rate (proportion of after-tax income declared as dividends) | 100% | 100% | 50% | 100% |
| **Foreign Affiliate Tax Computation** | | | | |
| 1. Taxable income of foreign affiliate | $2,000 | $2,000 | $2,000 | $2,000 |
| 2. Foreign corporate income taxes (@ rate a above) | (800) | (400) | (400) | (400) |
| 3. Net income available for profit distribution | $1,200 | $1,600 | $1,600 | $1,600 |
| 4. Retained earnings (1 − rate e above × line 3) | — | — | 800 | — |
| 5. Distributed earnings (rate e above × line 3) | $1,200 | $1,600 | $800 | $1,600 |
| 6. Distributed earnings to U.S. corporation (rate d × line 5) | $360 | $480 | $240 | $1,600 |
| 7. Withholding taxes on dividends to nonresidents (rate c × line 6) | (36) | (48) | (24) | (160) |
| 8. Remittance of foreign income to U.S. corporation | $324 | $432 | $216 | $1,440 |
| **U.S. Corporate Tax Computation on Foreign-Source Income** | | | | |
| 9. Grossed-up U.S. income (rate d × rate e × line 1) | $600 | $600 | $300 | $2,000 |
| 10. Tentative (theoretical) U.S. tax liability (rate b × line 9) | −210 | −210 | −105 | −700 |
| 11. Foreign tax credit (rate d × rate e × line 2 + line 7) | 276 | 168 | 84 | 560 |
| 12. Additional U.S. taxes due on foreign-source income (line 10 + line 11; if 11 > 10, U.S. tax liability is 0) | 0 | −42 | −21 | −140 |
| 13. After-tax dividends received by U.S. corporation (line 8 + line 12) | $324 | $390 | $195 | $1,300 |
| **Worldwide Tax Burden** | | | | |
| 14. Total worldwide taxes paid (line 10 or line 11, whichever is greater) | 276 | 210 | 105 | 700 |
| 15. Effective tax rate on foreign income (line 14/line 9) | 46.0% | 35.0% | 35.0% | 35.0% |

*Note:* When proportional ownership of the foreign corporation exceeds 50 percent, U.S. tax authorities classify it as a Controlled Foreign Corporation (CFC) and all passive income earned is taxed regardless of the payout rate or actual remittance to the U.S. corporation.

U.S. corporation in the foreign corporation (line d), and the proportion of available income distributed to stockholders as dividends (line e).

**Case 1: Foreign Affiliate of a U.S. Corporation in a High-Tax Environment**
This is a very common case. A U.S. corporation earns income in the form of distributed earnings (100 percent payout of available earnings to stockholders) from a foreign corporation in which it holds substantial interest (more than 10 percent) but does not control (less than 50 percent). The foreign corporate income tax rate (40 percent) is higher than the U.S. rate (35 percent). The foreign corporation has total taxable income of $2,000 (thousands of dollars), pays a 40 percent corporate income tax in the host country of $800, and distributes the entire after-tax income to stockholders. Total distributed earnings are therefore $1,200.

The foreign country imposes a 10 percent withholding tax on dividends paid to nonresidents. The U.S. corporation therefore receives its proportion of earnings (its 30 percent ownership entitles it to 30 percent of all dividends paid out) less the amount of the withholding taxes, $360 − $36, or $324. This is the net cash remittance actually received by the U.S. corporation on foreign earnings.

The calculation of U.S. taxes on foreign-source income requires first that the income be "grossed up," or reinflated to the amount of income the U.S. corporation has rights to prior to taxation by the foreign government. This is simply the percentage of ownership (30 percent) times the payout rate (100 percent) times the gross taxable income of the foreign affiliate ($2,000), or $600. A theoretical or **"tentative U.S. tax"** is calculated on this income to estimate U.S. tax payments that would be due on this income if it had been earned in the United States (or simply not taxed at all in the foreign country). U.S. taxes of 35 percent yield a tentative tax liability of $210.

Since taxes were paid abroad, however, U.S. tax law allows U.S. tax liabilities to be reduced by the amount of the **foreign tax credit.** The foreign tax credit is the proportion of foreign taxes deemed paid attributable to its ownership (30 percent ownership times the 100 percent payout rate of the foreign taxes paid, $800, plus the amount of withholding taxes imposed on the distributed dividends to the U.S. corporation, $36). The total foreign tax credit is then $240 + $36, or $276. Since the foreign tax credit exceeds the total tentative U.S. tax liability, no additional taxes are due the U.S. tax authorities on this foreign-source income. Special note should be made that the foreign tax credit may exceed the U.S. tax liabilities, but any excess cannot be applied toward other U.S. tax liabilities in the current period (it can be carried forward or back against this foreign-source income, however).

Finally, an additional calculation allows the estimation of the total taxes paid, both abroad and in the United States, on this income. In this first case, the $276 of total tax on gross income of $600 is an **effective tax rate** of 46 percent.

**Case 2: Foreign Affiliate of a U.S. Corporation in a Low-Tax Environment**
This case is exactly the same as the previous example, with the sole exception that the foreign tax rate (20 percent) is lower than the U.S. corporate tax rate (35 percent). All earnings, tax calculations, and dividends distributions are the same as before.

With lower foreign corporate income taxes, there is obviously more profit to be distributed, more income to the U.S. corporation's 30 percent share, and more withholding taxes to be paid on the larger dividends distributed. Yet the grossed-up income of the foreign-source income is the same as in the previous case, because grossed-up income is proportional ownership and distribution in the absence of taxes.

With lower foreign taxes, the foreign tax credit is significantly lower and is no longer sufficient to cover fully the tentative U.S. tax liability. The U.S. corporation will have an additional $42 due in taxes on the foreign-source income. After-tax dividends in total are still higher, however, rising to $390 from $324. Total worldwide taxes paid are now significantly less, $210 rather than $276.

Cases 1 and 2 point out the single most significant feature of the U.S. tax code's impact on foreign operations of U.S. corporations: The effective tax rate may be higher on foreign-source income but will never drop lower than the basic corporate income tax rate in effect in the United States (35 percent).

**Case 3: Foreign Affiliate of a U.S. Corporation in a Low-Tax Environment, 50 Percent Payout** The third case changes only one of the baseline values of the previous case, the proportion of income available for dividends that is paid out to stockholders. All distributed earnings and withholding taxes are therefore half what they were previously, as is grossed-up income and the additional U.S. tax liability (because the foreign tax credit has also been cut in half).

This third case illustrates that a reduced income distribution by the foreign subsidiary does reduce income received and taxes due in the United States on the foreign income. The effective tax rate is again at the minimum achievable, the rate of taxation that would be in effect if the income had been earned within the United States. As will be shown in the fourth and final case, this third case's results rely partially on the fact that the foreign corporation is only an affiliate (less than 50 percent ownership) of the U.S. corporation and is not controlled by the U.S. corporation.

**Case 4: Foreign Subsidiary of a U.S. Corporation Is a CFC in a Low-Tax Environment** This final case highlights one of the critical components of U.S. taxation of foreign subsidiary earnings. If the foreign corporation is effectively controlled by the U.S. corporation, as indicated by its greater than 50 percent ownership, and all income is passive income, U.S. tax authorities calculate U.S. tax liabilities on the foreign income as if the entire income available for distribution to shareholders were remitted to the U.S. parent, regardless of what the actual payout rate is.

This tax policy, a result of the 1962 tax reform act, is referred to as Subpart F income. Subpart F income taxation is a reflection of the control component; it is assumed that the U.S. corporation exercises sufficient control over the management of the foreign subsidiary to determine the payout rate. If the subsidiary has chosen not to pay out all passive earnings, it is taken as a choice of the U.S. corporation and is deemed to be an effort at postponing U.S. tax liabilities on the income.

The 1962 tax act was largely aimed at eliminating the abuses of foreign affiliates of U.S. corporations paying dividends and other passive income flows out to subsidiaries in various tax havens (such as Bermuda, the Bahamas, Panama, Luxembourg, and the Cayman Islands), and not remitting the income back to the U.S. corporation. By placing the passive income in the tax havens, they effectively were postponing and evading taxation by the U.S. government.

## Concluding Remarks Regarding U.S. Taxation of Foreign Income

The previous series of sample tax calculations highlights the interplay of ownership, distribution, and relative tax rates between countries in determining the tax liabilities of income earned by U.S. interests abroad. In many ways, the case with the most long-term strategic significance was the first, the high-tax foreign environment. U.S. corporate income tax rates are among the lowest in the world. The usual result is the accumulation of substantial foreign tax credits by U.S. corporate interests, credits that increasingly cannot be applied to U.S. tax liabilities. The result is, as in Case 1, an effective tax rate that is significantly higher than if the income had been generated in the United States.

Recent accounting and tax rule changes may actually result in worsening this effective tax rate and excess foreign tax credit problem for U.S. corporations. Recent rule changes now require U.S. corporations to spread increasing amounts of parent-supplied overhead expenses to their foreign affiliates and subsidiaries, charging them for services provided. This results in increased costs for the foreign subsidiaries, reducing their profitability, reducing their taxable gross income, and subsequently reducing the foreign taxes, and tax credits, deemed paid. This is likely to increase the proportion of total taxes that are paid in the United States on the foreign-source income. Unfortunately, many of the overhead distributions are not recognized as a legitimate expense by many other governments (differing accounting practices in action), and the foreign units are paying a charge to the U.S. corporation that they are unable to expense against their local earnings. Recent concerns over the use of intrafirm sales (so-called transfer prices; see Chapter 15) to manipulate the profitability of foreign firms operating in the United States also has added fuel to the fires of governments and their individual shares of the world "tax pie." With that, the subject of accounting and taxation of international operations has completed a full circle.

## Summary

Accounting practices differ substantially across countries. The efforts of a number of international associates and agencies in the past two decades have, however, led to increasing cooperation and agreement among national accounting authorities. Real accounting differences remain, and many of these differences still contribute to the advantaged competitive position of some countries' firms over international competitors.

International taxation is a subject close to the pocketbook of every multinational firm. Although the tax policies of most countries are theoretically designed to not change or influence financial and business decision making by firms, they often do.

The taxation of the foreign operations of U.S. multinational firms involves the elaborate process of crediting U.S. corporations for taxes paid to foreign governments. The combined influence of different corporate tax rates across countries, the degree of ownership and control a multinational may have or exercise in a foreign affiliate, and the proportion of profits distributed to stockholders at home and abroad combine to determine the size of the parent's tax bill. As governments worldwide search for new ways to close their fiscal deficits and tax shortfalls, the pressures on international taxation and the reporting of foreign-source income will only increase.

## Key Terms and Concepts

| | | |
|---|---|---|
| accounting diversity | direct taxes | undistributed earnings |
| LIFO | indirect taxes | withholding taxes |
| average cost method | value-added tax (VAT) | "tentative U.S. tax" |
| FIFO | corporate income tax | foreign tax credit |
| operating or service lease | distributed earnings | effective tax rate |
| pension liabilities | | |

## Questions for Discussion

1. Do you think all firms, in all economic environments, should operate under the same set of accounting principles?

2. What is the nature of the purported benefit that accounting principles provide British firms over American firms in the competition for mergers and acquisitions?
3. Why do most U.S. corporations prefer the current rate method of translation over the temporal method? How does each method affect reported earnings per share per period?
4. Name two major indications that progress is being made toward standardizing accounting principles across countries.
5. What is the distinction between harmonizing accounting rules and standardizing accounting procedures and practices across countries?
6. Why are foreign subsidiaries in which U.S. corporations hold more than 50 percent voting power classified and treated differently for U.S. tax purposes?
7. Why do the U.S. tax authorities want U.S. corporations to charge their foreign subsidiaries for general and administrative services? What does this mean for the creation of excess foreign tax credits by U.S. corporations with foreign operations?
8. What would be the tax implications of combining Cases 1 and 4 in the U.S. taxation of foreign-source income, a U.S. Controlled Foreign Corporation (CFC) that is operating in a high-tax environment?
9. Why does countertrade pose special problems for accountants?
10. In order to analyze an individual firm's operating exposure more carefully, it is necessary to have more detailed information available than is in the normal annual report. Choose a specific firm with substantial international operations, for example Coca-Cola or PepsiCo, and search the Security and Exchange Commission's Edgar Files for more detailed financial reports of their international operations. Search SEC EDGAR Archives at **http://www.sec.gov/cgi-bin/srch-edgar**
11. The Financial Accounting Standards Board promulgates standard practices for the reporting of financial results by companies in the United States. It also, however, often leads the way in the development of new practices and emerging issues around the world. One major such issue today is the valuation and reporting of financial derivatives and derivative agreements by firms. Use the FASB's home page and the Web pages of several of the major accounting firms and other interest groups around the world to see current proposed accounting standards and the current state of reaction to the proposed standards. Use the Web sites of FASB home page at **http://raw.rutgers.edu/raw/fasb/** and Treasury Management Association at **http://www.tma.org/**
12. Using Nestlé's Web page, check Current Press Releases for more recent financial results, including what the company reports as the primary currencies and average exchange rates used for translation of international financial results during the most recent period. See Nestlé: The World Food Company at **http://www.nestle.com/press/current/**

## Recommended Readings

Alhashim, Dhia D., and Jeffrey S. Arpan. *International Dimensions of Accounting.* 3d ed. Boston: PWS-Kent Publishing Company, 1992.

Arpan, Jeffrey S., and Lee H. Radebaugh. *International Accounting and Multinational Enterprises.* New York: John Wiley & Sons, 1985.

BenDaniel, David J., and Arthur H. Rosenbloom. *The Handbook of International Mergers and Acquisitions*. Englewood Cliffs, NJ: Prentice-Hall, 1990.

Bodner, Paul M. "International Taxation." In *The Handbook of International Accounting*, ed. Frederick D.S. Choi. New York: John Wiley & Sons, 1992.

Choi, Frederick D.S., ed. *The Handbook of International Accounting*. 2d ed. New York: John Wiley & Sons, 1997.

Choi, Frederick D.S., and Richard Levich. "International Accounting Diversity and Capital Market Decisions." In *The Handbook of International Accounting*, ed. Frederick D.S. Choi. New York: John Wiley & Sons, 1992.

Choi, Frederick D.S., and Gerhard G. Mueller. *International Accounting*. 2d ed. Englewood Cliffs, N.J. Prentice-Hall, 1992.

Coopers & Lybrand, *International Accounting Summaries*. 2d ed. New York: John Wiley & Sons, 1993.

Eiteman, David K., Arthur I. Stonehill, and Michael H. Moffett. *Multinational Business Finance*. 8th ed. Reading, Mass.: Addison-Wesley Publishing, 1998.

Goeltz, Richard K. "International Accounting Harmonization: The Impossible (and Unnecessary?) Dream," *Accounting Horizons* (March 1991): 85–88.

Haskins, M., K. Ferris, and T. Selling. *International Financial Reporting and Analysis*. Burr Ridge, Ill.: R. D. Irwin, 1995.

Hosseini, Ahmad, and Raj Aggarwal. "Evaluating Foreign Affiliates: The Impact of Alternative Foreign Currency Translation Methods." *International Journal of Accounting* (Fall (1983): 65–87.

Neuhausen, Benjamin. "Consolidated Financial Statements and Joint Venture Accounting." In *The Handbook of International Accounting*, ed., Frederick D.S. Choi. New York: John Wiley & Sons, 1992.

Nobes, Christopher, and Robert Parker. *Comparative International Accounting*. 3d ed. London: Prentice Hall International, Ltd., 1991.

Price Waterhouse. *Corporate Taxes: A Worldwide Summary*. 1997 International edition. New York, 1997.

## Notes

1. This example is borrowed from "International Accounting Diversity and Capital Market Decisions," by Choi and Levich, 1992.

2. This table and the following associated discussion draws heavily on the recent excellent study of this subject by Philip R. Peller and Frank J. Schwitter of Arthur Andersen & Company, "A Summary of Accounting Principle Differences Around the World," in *The Handbook of International Accounting*, ed. Frederick D.S. Choi, 1992, Chapter 4.

3. Disclosure has continued to be one of the largest sources of frustration between countries. The disclosure requirements of the Securities and Exchange Commission (SEC) in the United States for firms—foreign or domestic—in order to issue publicly traded securities are some of the strictest in the world. Many experts in the field have long been convinced that the depth of U.S. disclosure requirements has prevented many foreign firms from issuing securities in the United States. The SEC's approval of Rule 144A, selective secondary market trading of private placements, is an attempt to alleviate some of the pressure on foreign firms from U.S. disclosure.

4. Frederick D.S. Choi and Gerhard G. Mueller, *International Accounting*, 2d ed. (Englewood Cliffs, N.J.: Prentice-Hall, 1992), 262.

5. A U.S. shareholder is a U.S. person (a citizen or resident of the United States, domestic partnership, domestic corporation, or any nonforeign trust or estate) owning 10 percent or more of the voting power of a controlled foreign corporation. A controlled foreign corporation (CFC) is any foreign corporation in which U.S. shareholders, including corporate parents, own more than 50 percent of the combined voting power or total value. The percentages are calculated on a constructive ownership basis, in which an individual is considered to own shares registered in the name of other family members, members of a trust, or any other related group.

# CHAPTER 20

# International Human Resource Management*

### LEARNING OBJECTIVES

◆ To describe the challenges of managing managers and labor personnel both in individual international markets and in worldwide operations

◆ To examine the sources, qualifications, and compensation of international managers

◆ To assess the effects of culture on managers and management policies

◆ To illustrate the different roles of labor in international markets, especially that of labor participation in management

*This chapter was contributed by Susan C. Ronkainen.

## The Hunt for The Global Manager

**M**any corporate decision makers have realized that human resources play at least as significant a role as advanced technology and economies of scale do when it comes to competing successfully in the new global world order.

According to a survey of 1,200 midsize U.S. multinationals with annual sales of $1 billion or less conducted by *International Business* magazine, senior executives seek managers who are culturally diverse but responsive to the direction of headquarters. Most U.S.–based companies try to fill senior positions abroad with locals (see chart below), using expatriates only for such specific projects as technology transfer. However, the same companies send their U.S. middle managers the clear message that overseas operations are so important to corporate welfare that solid international experience is needed for advancement.

While major markets in Europe and Asia possess deeper pools of managerial talent than ever before, many of these nationals prefer to work for domestic rather than foreign firms. In particular short supply are marketing managers—49 percent of the surveyed companies say marketing is the hardest slot to fill (see chart below). It is especially hard to find people who have the cross-cultural experience to make good regional managers.

Very few global leaders are born that way, that is, with an international childhood, a command of several languages, and an education from an institution with an international focus. In most cases, they have to be trained and nurtured carefully. To achieve this goal, companies are using various approaches.

Gaynor Kelley, chairman, and Riccardo Pigliucci, president and COO, of Perkin-Elmer Corp. (makers of analytical instruments) frequently attend monthly meetings of senior executives held at production and sales locations around the world. These meetings permit the two men to assess the performance of company managers—be they nationals or expatriates. Mr. Pigliucci is a prime example of Perkin-Elmer's desire to breed global managers. He joined the company as a chemist from the University of Milan and served stints in product development, sales, and marketing both in Europe and North America.

NetFRAME Systems Inc., a maker of networking computers, gathers its expatriate and non–U.S. managers at its California headquarters every quarter. The idea is to encourage joint planning and problem solving on a global basis.

Some companies take what can be called the "Dutch uncle" approach. They pair a key overseas manager with one at headquarters. This helps top management to keep tabs on the manager's progress and helps the manager stay in tune with what is going on back at the source of power. Such mentoring can also provide vital input into management succession strategizing.

Companies that spend time and money creating and training global talent naturally want to retain it as long as possible. Loctite Corp., maker of industrial adhesives, offers global opportunity, professional challenge, and a competitive compensation package to keep its rising stars. Of the three approaches, claims the company, compensation is the least important to the managers.

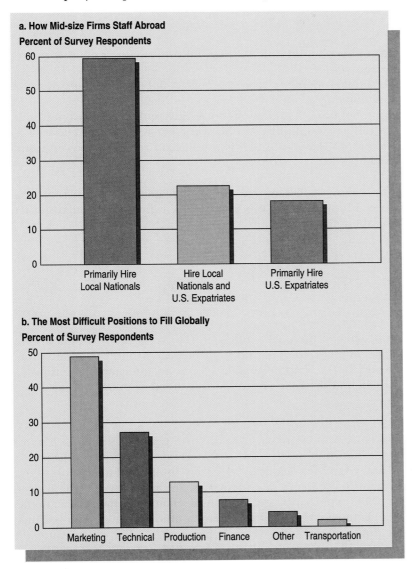

**a. How Mid-size Firms Staff Abroad**
Percent of Survey Respondents

(Bar chart with vertical axis from 0 to 60)
- Primarily Hire Local Nationals: ~60
- Hire Local Nationals and U.S. Expatriates: ~23
- Primarily Hire U.S. Expatriates: ~19

**b. The Most Difficult Positions to Fill Globally**
Percent of Survey Respondents

(Bar chart with vertical axis from 0 to 50)
- Marketing: ~49
- Technical: ~27
- Production: ~13
- Finance: ~8
- Other: ~5
- Transportation: ~2

*Source:* "Globe Trotter: If It's 5:30, This Must Be Tel-Aviv," *Business Week* (October 17, 1994); Lori Ioannou, "It's a Small World After All," *International Business* (February 1994): 82–88; Shawn Tully, "The Hunt for the Global Manager," *Fortune* (May 21, 1990): 140–144.
**http://www.perkin-elmer.com   http://www.netframe.com   http://www.loctite.com**

Organizations have two general human resource objectives.[1] The first is the recruitment and retention of a workforce made up of the best people available for the jobs to be done. The recruiter in international operations will need to keep in mind both cross-cultural and cross-national differences in productivity

**WWW**

and expectations when selecting employees. Once they are hired, the firm's best interest lies in maintaining a stable and experienced workforce.

The second objective is to increase the effectiveness of the workforce. This depends to a great extent on achieving the first objective. Competent managers or workers are likely to perform at a more effective level if proper attention is given to factors that motivate them.

To attain the two major objectives, the activities and skills needed include:

1. Personnel planning and staffing, the assessment of personnel needs, and recruitment
2. Personnel training to achieve a perfect fit between the employee and the assignment
3. Compensation of employees according to their effectiveness
4. An understanding of labor-management relations in terms of how the two groups view each other and how their respective power positions are established

This chapter will examine the management of human resources in international business from two points of view, first that of manages and then that of labor.

## Managing Managers

The importance of the quality of the workforce in international business cannot be overemphasized, regardless of the stage of internationalization of the firm. As seen in the chapter's opening vignette, international business systems are complex and dynamic and require competent people to develop and direct them.

### Early Stages of Internationalization

The marketing or sales manager of the firm typically is responsible for beginning export activities. As foreign sales increase, an export manager will be appointed and given the responsibility for developing and maintaining customers, interacting with the firm's intermediaries, and planning for overall market expansion. The export manager also must champion the international effort within the company because the general attitude among employees may be to view the domestic market as more important. Another critical function is the supervision of export transactions, particularly documentation. The requirements are quite different for international transactions than for domestic ones, and sales or profits may be lost if documentation is not properly handled. The first task of the new export manager, in fact, often is to hire a staff to handle paperwork that typically had previously been done by a facilitating agent, such as a freight forwarder.

The firm starting international operations will usually hire an export manager from outside rather than promote from within. The reason is that knowledge of the product or industry is less important than international experience. The cost of learning through experience to manage an export department is simply too great from the firm's standpoint. Further, the inexperienced manager would be put in the position of having to demonstrate his or her effectiveness almost at once.

The manager who is hired will have obtained experience through Foreign Service duty or with another corporation. In the early stages, a highly entrepreneurial spirit with a heavy dose of trader mentality is required. Even then, management should not expect the new export department to earn a profit for the first few years.

## Advanced Stages of Internationalization

As the firm progresses from exporting to an international division to foreign direct involvement, manpower-planning activities will initially focus on need vis-à-vis various markets and functions. Existing personnel can be assessed and plans made to recruit, select, and train employees for positions that cannot be filled internally. The four major categories of overseas assignments are: (1) CEO, to oversee and direct the entire operation; (2) functional head, to establish and maintain departments and ensure their proper performance; (3) troubleshooters, who are utilized for their special expertise in analyzing, and thereby preventing or solving, particular problems; and (4) white- or blue-collar workers.[2] International oil companies typically assign many employees overseas when the available pool is small, such as in Saudi Arabia.

One of the major sources of competitive advantage of global corporations is their ability to attract talent around the world. The corporations need systematic management-development systems, with the objective of creating and carefully allocating management personnel. An example of this is provided in Figure 20.1. Increasingly, plans call for international experience as a prerequisite for advancement; for example, at Ford, the goal is to have 100 percent of the top managers with international work experience with the company.[3]

**FIGURE 20.1**

**An Example of an International Management Development System**
*Source:* Ingo Theuerkauf, "Reshaping the Global Organization," *McKinsey Quarterly* 3 (1991): 103–119.

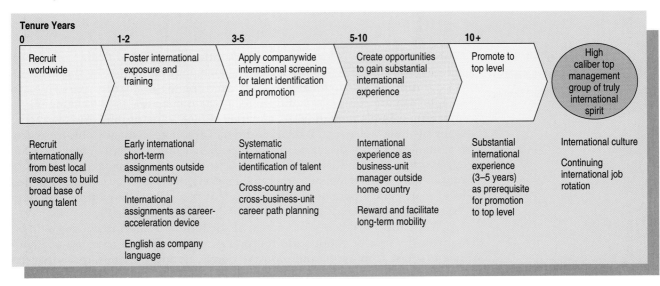

In global corporations, there is no such thing as a universal global manager, but a network of global specialists in four general groups of managers has to work together.[4] Global business (product) managers have the task to further the company's global-scale efficiency and competitiveness. Country managers have to be sensitive and responsive to local market needs and demands but, at the same time, be aware of global implications. Functional managers have to make sure that the corporation's capabilities in technical, manufacturing, marketing, human resource, and financial expertise are linked and can benefit from each other. Corporate executives at headquarters have to manage interactions among the three groups of managers as well as to identify and develop the talent to fill the positions.

As an example of this planning, a management review of human resources is conducted twice a year with each general manager of Heineken operating companies, which are located in such countries as Canada, France, Ireland, and Spain. The meeting is attended by the general manager, the personnel manager, the regional coordinating director in whose region the operating company is located, and the corporate director of management development. Special attention is given to managers "in the fast lane," the extent to which they are mobile, what might be done to foster their development, and where they fit into succession planning.[5] Of course, any gaps must be filled by recruitment efforts.

International companies should show clear career paths for managers assigned overseas and develop the systems and the organization for promotion. This approach serves to eliminate many of the perceived problems and thus motivates managers to seek out foreign assignments. Foreign assignments can occur at various stages of the manager's tenure. In the early stages, assignments may be short-term, such as a membership in an international task force or six to twelve months at headquarters in a staff function. Later, an individual may serve as a business-unit manager overseas. Many companies use cross-postings to other countries or across product lines to further an individual's acculturation to the corporation.[6] A period in a head office department or a subsidiary will not only provide an understanding of different national cultures and attitudes but also improve an individual's "know-who" and therefore establish unity and common sense of purpose necessary for the proper implementation of global programs.

## Interfirm Cooperative Ventures

Global competition is forging new cooperative ties between firms from different countries, thereby adding a new management challenge for the firms involved. Although many of the reasons cited for these alliances (described in Chapter 12) are competitive and strategic, the human resource function is critical to their implementation. As a matter of fact, some of the basic reasons so many of these ventures fail relate to human resource management; for example, managers from disparate venture partners cannot work together, or managers within the venture cannot work with the owners' managers.[7] As more ventures are created in newly emerging markets, the challenge of finding skilled local managers is paramount. If such talent is secured, developing loyalty to the company may be difficult.[8]

While the ingredients for success of the human resource function will differ with the type of cooperative venture, two basic types of tasks are needed.[9] The first task is to assign and motivate people in appropriate ways so that the venture will fulfill its set strategic tasks. This requires particular attention to such issues as job skills and compatibility of communication and other work styles. For example, some cooperative ventures have failed due to one of the partners' assigning relatively weak management resources to the venture or due to managers' finding themselves with conflicting loyalties to the parent organization and the cooperative venture organization. The second task is the strategic management of the human resources, that is, the appropriate use of managerial capabilities not only in the cooperative venture but in other later contexts, possibly back in the parent organization. An individual manager needs to see that an assignment in a cooperative venture is part of his or her overall career development.

The location and the nationality of candidates for a particular job are the key issues in recruitment. A decision will have to be made to recruit from within the company or, in the case of larger corporations, within other product or regional groups, or to rely on external talent. Similarly, decisions will have to be made whether to hire or promote locally or use **expatriates;** that is, home-country nationals or third-country nationals (citizens of countries other than the home or host country). Typically, three-fourths of expatriates are posted in subsidiaries, while the remaining one-fourth have assignments in their company's headquarter's country (i.e., they are inpatriates).[10] The factors that influence this choice process are summarized in Table 20.1. They fall into three general categories: (1) the availability and quality of the talent pool, (2) corporate policies and their cost, and (3) environmental constraints.

The recruitment approach changes over the internationalization process of the firm. During the export stage, outside expertise is sought at first, but the firm then begins to develop its own personnel for international operations. With expanded and more involved foreign operations, the firm's reliance on home-country personnel will be reduced as host-country nationals are prepared for management positions. The use of home-country and third-country nationals may be directed at special assignments, such as transfer of technology or expertise. The use of expatriates will continue as a matter of corporate policy to internationalize management and to foster the infusion of particular corporate culture into operations around the world.

When international operations are expanded, a management development dilemma may result. Through internal recruitment, young managers will be offered interesting new opportunities. However, some senior managers may object to the constant drain of young talent from their units. Selective recruit-

## Sources for Management Recruitment

**TABLE 20.1**

**Factors Determining the Choice between Local and Expatriate Managers**

| ■ Availability of Managers | ■ Corporate objectives | ■ Cost |
| ■ Competence | Control | ■ Environment |
| Market | Management development | Legal |
| Technical | Corporate citizenship | Cultural |
| | | Economic |

ment from the outside will help to maintain a desirable combination of inside talent and fresh blood. Furthermore, with dynamic market changes or new markets and new business development, outside recruitment may be the only available approach. Even in Japan, the taboo against hiring executives from other companies is breaking down. The practice of hiring from the top universities can no longer be depended on to provide the right people in all circumstances.[11]

Currently, most managers in subsidiaries are host-country nationals. The reasons include an increase in availability of local talent, corporate relations in the particular market, and the economies realized by not having to maintain a corps of managers overseas. Local managers are generally more familiar with environmental conditions and how they should be interpreted. By employing local management, the multinational is responding to host-country demands for increased localization and providing advancement as an incentive to local managers. In this respect, however, localization can be carried too far. If the firm does not subscribe to a global philosophy, the manager's development is tied to the local operation or to a particular level of management in that operation. This has been an issue of contention, especially with Japanese employers in the United States. As a result, managers who outgrow the local operation may have nowhere to go except to another company.[12] Although the Japanese continue to express frustration in what they perceive to be disloyalty and opportunism on the part of U.S. employees, they are starting to change their practices so that they can retain talented U.S. nationals.[13]

Local managers, if not properly trained and indoctrinated, may see things differently from the way they are viewed at headquarters. As a result, both control and the overall coordination of programs may be jeopardized. For the corporation to work effectively, of course, employees must first of all understand each other. Most corporations have adopted a common corporate language, with English as the **lingua franca;** that is, the language habitually used among people of diverse speech to facilitate communication. At Olivetti, all top-level meetings are conducted in English.[14] In some companies, two languages are officially in use; for example, at Nestlé both English and French are corporate languages. A second goal is to avoid overemphasis on localization, which would prevent the development of an internationalized group of managers with a proper understanding of the impact of the environment on operations. To develop language skills and promote an international outlook in their management pools, multinational corporations are increasingly recruiting among foreign students at business schools in the United States, western Europe, and the Far East. When these young managers return home, following an initial assignment at corporate headquarters, they will have a command of the basic philosophies of multinational operations.

Cultural differences that shape managerial attitudes must be considered when developing multinational management programs. For example, British managers place more emphasis than most other nationals on individual achievement and autonomy. French managers, however, value competent supervision, sound company policies, fringe benefits, security, and comfortable working conditions.[15]

The decision as to whether to use home-country nationals in a particlar operation depends on such factors as the type of industry, the life-cycle stage of the product, the availability of managers from other sources, and the func-

In Tokyo, Merck representative Satomi Tomihari confers with Yasumasa Nakamura, M.D. Tomihari is one of twenty-five women recruited by Merck affiliate, Banyu Pharmaceutical, Ltd.
*Source:* Griffiths, photographer for Magnum Photo, Courtesy of Merck & Co., Inc.

tional areas involved. The number of home-country managers is typically higher in the service sector than in the industrial sector, and overseas assignments may be quite short term. For example, many international hotel chains have established management contracts in the People's Republic of China with the understanding that home-country managers will train local successors within three to five years. In the start-up phase of an endeavor, headquarters involvement is generally substantial. This applies to all functions, including personnel. Especially if no significant pool of local managers is available or their competence levels are not satisfactory, home-country nationals may be used. For control and communication reasons, some companies always maintain a home-country national as manager in certain functional areas, such as accounting or finance.

The number of home-country nationals in an overseas operation rarely rises above 10 percent of the work force and is typically only 1 percent. The reasons are both internal and external. In addition to the substantial cost of transfer, a manager may not fully adjust to foreign working and living conditions. Good corporate citizenship today requires multinational companies to develop the host country's workforce at the management level. Legal impediments to manager transfers may exist, or other difficulties may be encountered. Many U.S.–based hotel corporations, for example, have complained about delays in obtaining visas to the United States not only for managers but also for management trainees.

The use of third-country nationals is most often seen in large multinational companies that have adopted a global philosophy. The practice of some companies, such as the Dutch electronics giant N. V. Philips, is to employ third-country nationals as managing directors in subsidiaries. An advantage is that third-country nationals may contribute to the firm's overall international expertise. However, many third-country nationals are career international managers, and they may become targets for raids by competitors looking for high levels of talent. They may be a considerable asset in regional expansion; for example, established subsidiary managers in Singapore might be used to start up a subsidiary in Malaysia. On the other hand, some transfers may be inadvisable for cultural or historical reasons, with transfers between Turkey and Greece as an example.

The ability to recruit for international assignments is determined by the value an individual company places on international operations and the experience gained in working in them. Based on a survey of 1,500 senior executives around the world, U.S. executives still place less emphasis on international dimensions than their Japanese, western European, and Latin American counterparts. While most executives agree that an international outlook is essential for future executives, 70 percent of foreign executives think that experience outside one's home country is important, compared with only 35 percent of U.S. executives, and foreign language capability was seen as important by only 19 percent of U.S. respondents, compared with 64 percent of non–U.S. executives.[16]

In an era of regional integration, many companies are facing a severe shortage of managers who can think and operate regionally or even globally. Very few companies—even those characterizing themselves as global—have systematically developed international managers by rotating young executives through a series of assignments in different parts of the world.[17] To help find the best cross-border talent executive search firms, such as A. T. Kearney and Heidrick & Struggles, can be used.

## Selection Criteria for Overseas Assignments

The traits that have been suggested as necessary for the international manager range from the ideal to the real. One characterization describes "a flexible personality, with broad intellectual horizons, attitudinal values of cultural empathy, general friendliness, patience and prudence, impeccable educational and professional (or technical) credentials—all topped off with immaculate health, creative resourcefulness, and respect of peers. If the family is equally well endowed, all the better."[18] Although this would seem to describe a supermanager, a number of companies believe that the qualities that make a successful international manager are increasingly the traits needed at headquarters.[19] Traits typically mentioned in the choosing of managers for overseas assignments are listed in Table 20.2. Their relative importance may vary dramatically, of course, depending on the firm and the situation.

**Competence Factors**   An expatriate manager usually has far more responsibility than a manager in a comparable domestic position and must be far more self-sufficient in making decisions and conducting daily business. To be selected in the first place, the manager's technical competence level has to be superior

**TABLE 20.2**

**Criteria for Selecting Managers for Overseas Assignment**

| Competence | Adaptability | Personal Characteristics |
|---|---|---|
| Technical knowledge | Interest in overseas work | Age |
| Leadership ability | Relational abilities | Education |
| Experience, past performance | Cultural empathy | Sex |
| Area expertise | Appreciation of new management styles | Health |
| Language | Appreciation of environmental constraints | Marital relations |
| | Adaptability of family | Social acceptability |

to that of local candidates'; otherwise, the firm would in most cases have chosen a local person. The manager's ability to do the job in the technical sense is one of the main determinants of ultimate success or failure in an overseas assignment.[20] However, management skills will not transfer from one culture to another without some degree of adaptation. This means that, regardless of the level of technical skills, the new environment still requires the ability to adapt the skills to local conditions. Technical competence must also be accompanied by the ability to lead subordinates in any situation or under any conditions.

Especially in global-minded enterprises, managers are selected for overseas assignments on the basis of solid experience and past performance. Many firms use the foreign tour as a step toward top management. By sending abroad internally recruited, experienced managers, the firm also ensures the continuation of corporate culture—a set of shared values, norms, and beliefs and an emphasis on a particular facet of performance. Two examples are IBM's concern with customer service and 3M's concentration on innovation.[21]

The role of **factual cultural knowledge** in the selection process has been widely debated. **Area expertise** includes a knowledge of the basic systems in the region or market for which the manager will be responsible—such as the roles of various ministries in international business, the significance of holidays, and the general way of doing business. None of these variables is as important as language, although language skill is not always highly ranked by firms themselves.[22] A manager who does not know the language of the country may get by with the help of associates and interpreters but is not in a position to assess the situation fully. Of the Japanese representing their companies in the United States, for example, almost all speak English. As a matter of fact, some Japanese companies, such as Honda, have deployed some of their most talented executives to U.S. operations.[23] Of the Americans representing U.S. companies in Japan, however, few speak Japanese well.[24] Some companies place language skills or aptitude in a larger context; they see a strong correlation between language skill and adaptability. Another reason to look for language competence in managers considered for assignments overseas is that all managers spend most of their time communicating.

**Adaptability Factors** The manager's own motivation to a great extent determines the viability of an overseas assignment and consequently its success. The manager's interest in the foreign culture must go well beyond that of the average tourist if he or she is to understand what an assignment abroad involves. In most cases, the manager will need counseling and training to comprehend the true nature of the undertaking.

Adaptability means a positive and flexible attitude toward change. The manager assigned overseas must progress from factual knowledge of culture to **interpretive cultural knowledge,** trying as much as possible to become part of the new scene, which may be quite different from the one at home. The work habits of middle-level managers may be more lax, productivity and attention to detail less, and overall environmental restrictions far greater. The manager on a foreign assignment is part of a multicultural team, in which both internal and external interactions determine the future of the firm's operations. For example, a manager from the United States may be used to an informal, democratic type of leadership that may not be applicable in countries such as Mexico or Japan, where employees expect more authoritarian leadership.[25]

Adaptability does not depend solely on the manager. Firms look carefully at the family situation because a foreign assignment often puts more strain on other family members than on the manager. As an example, a U.S. engineering firm had problems in Italy that were traced to the inability of one executive's wife to adapt. She complained to other wives, who began to feel that they too suffered hardships and then complained to their husbands. Morale became so low that the company, after missing important deadlines, replaced most of the Americans on the job.[26] This extreme case shows that spouses need to participate throughout the decision process.

The characteristics of the family as a whole are important. Screeners look for family cohesiveness and check for marital instability or for behavioral difficulties in children. Abroad, the need to work together as a family often makes strong marriages stronger and causes the downfall of weak ones. Further, commitments or interests beyond the nuclear family affect the adjustment of family members to a new environment. Some firms use earlier transfers within the home country as an indicator of how a family will handle transfer abroad. With the dramatic increase in two-career households, foreign assignments may call for one of the spouses to sacrifice a career or, at best, to put it on hold. Increasingly transferees are requesting for spouse re-employment assistance.[27] As a result, corporations are forming a consortia to try to tackle this problem. Members of the group interview accompanying spouses and try to find them positions with other member companies.[28]

**Personal Characteristics**   Despite all of the efforts made by multinational companies to recruit the best person available, demographics still play a role in the selection process. Due to either a minimum age requirement or the level of experience needed, many foreign assignments go to managers in their mid-30s or older. Normally, companies do not recruit candidates from graduating classes for immediate assignment overseas. They want their international people first to become experienced and familiar with the corporate culture, and this can best be done at the headquarters location.

Although the number of women in overseas assignments is only 12 percent according to one count, women are as interested as men are in the assignments.[29] Corporate hiring practices may be based on the myth that women will not be accepted in the host countries. Many of the relatively few women managers report being treated as foreign business people and not singled out as women.[30] These issues are highlighted in Global Perspective 20.1.

In the selection process, firms are concerned about the health of the people they may send abroad. Some assignments are in host countries with dramatically different environmental conditions from the home country, and they may aggravate existing health problems. Moreover, if the candidate selected is not properly prepared, foreign assignments may increase stress levels and contribute to the development of peptic ulcers, colitis, or other problems.

When candidates are screened, being married is usually considered a plus. Marriage brings stability and an inherent support system, provided family relations are in order. It may also facilitate adaptation to the local culture by increasing the number of social functions to which the manager is invited.

Social acceptability varies from one culture to another and can be a function of any of the other personal characteristics. Background, religion, race, and sex usually become critical only in extreme cases in which a host environment would clearly reject a candidate based on one or more of these vari-

## WOMEN'S GLOBAL CAREER LADDER

There is growing evidence to suggest that women are making greater strides on the international front than ever before. The 1996 Global Relocation Survey, conducted by Windham International and the National Foreign Trade Council, provides various measures of this trend. A full 14 percent of American corporate expatriates are women, up from 5 percent in 1992. The figure is expected to reach 20 percent by the year 2000. *Fortune* magazine summarized it by stating, "The best reason for believing that more women will be in charge before long is that in a ferociously competitive global economy, no company can afford to waste valuable brainpower simply because it's wearing a skirt."

Some argue that the numbers are relatively small due to commonly held myths about women in international business. The first is that women do not want to be international managers, and the second is that foreigners' prejudice against them renders them ineffective, whether they are nationals or not.

In a study of more than 1,000 graduating MBAs from schools in North America and Europe, females and males displayed equal interest in pursuing international careers. They did also agree that firms offer fewer opportunities to women pursuing international careers than to those pursuing domestic ones. Women expatriate managers agree that convincing superiors to let them go called for patience and persistence.

Expatriate women have generally reported numerous professional advantages to being female. Being highly visible (both internally and externally) has often been quoted as an advantage given that many women expatriates are "firsts" for their companies. Foreign clients are curious about them, want to meet them, and remember them after the first encounter. Emanuel Monogenis, a managing partner at the international search firm of Heidrick & Struggles, observed, "My clients now see women as equals in top global searches. In fact, more and more executives are saying they prefer women because they feel they are willing to work harder and take less for granted than male counterparts. Many also believe women have more of a sensibility and insight into human behavior and relationships than their male counterparts, and this is highly valued in culturally diverse workforces."

No person will be chosen for an assignment abroad without having the necessary technical and professional qualifications. The most successful approach for female managers is to be gently persistent in "educating" one's employer and constituents around the world to be open to the possibility of sending women abroad and granting them the same status and support accorded to male peers. One female expatriate summarized her experiences in this way, "Although I am viewed as a foreigner, I still have to cope with some chauvinism, but after I prove I have a brain, it is business as usual."

*Sources:* **1996 Global Relocation Trends Survey Report,** *New York: Windham International, 1997; Lori Ioannou,* "Women's Global Career Ladder," **International Business** *(December 1994); 57–60; Nancy J. Adler and Dafna N. Izraeli, eds.,* **Competitive Frontiers: Women Managers in a Global Economy** *(Cambridge, Mass.: Blackwell Business, 1994): Chapters 1 and 2; Diana Kunde,* "Management Opportunities for Women Brighten," *The Washington Post, December 19, 1993, H2; and Anne B. Fisher,* "When Will Women Get to the Top?" *Fortune (September 21, 1992): 44–56.*

http://www.windhamint.com

ables. The Arab boycott of the state of Israel, for example, puts constraints on the use of managers of Jewish and Arab origin. Women cannot negotiate contracts in many Middle Eastern countries. This would hold true even if the woman were president of the company.

**The Selection and Orientation Challenge** Due to the cost of transferring a manager overseas, many firms go beyond standard selection procedures and use **adaptability screening** as an integral part of the process. During the screening phase, the method most often used involves interviewing the candidate and the family. The interviews are conducted by senior executives, human relations specialists within the firm, or outside firms. Interviewers ask the candidate and the family to consider the personal issues involved in the transfer; for example, what each will miss the most. In some cases, candidates themselves will refuse an assignment. In others, the firm will withhold the assignment on the basis of interviews that clearly show a degree of risk.

The candidate selected will participate in an **orientation program** on internal and external aspects of the assignment. Internal aspects include issues such as compensation and reporting. External aspects are concerned with what to expect at the destination in terms of customs and culture. The extent and level of the programs will vary; for example, in a survey of 120 U.S. companies, 42 percent reported having no cultural preparation training for their executives. As shown in Figure 20.2, most programs offered extend the orientation to the spouse or the entire family. If the company is still in the export stage, the emphasis in this training will be on interpersonal skills and local culture. With expatriates, the focus will be on both training and interacting with host-country nationals. Actual methods vary from area studies to sensitivity training. For a discussion of these methods, see Chapter 2.

The attrition rate in overseas assignments averages 40 percent among companies with neither adaptability screening nor orientation programs, 25 percent among companies with cultural orientation programs, and 5 to 10 percent among companies that use both kinds of programs. Considering the cost of a transfer, catching even one potentially disastrous situation pays for the program for a full year. Most companies have no program at all, however, and others provide them for higher level management positions only. Companies that have the lowest failure rates typically employ a four-tiered approach to expatriate use: (1) clearly stated criteria, (2) rigorous procedures to determine the suitability of an individual across the criteria, (3) appropriate orientation, and (4) constant evaluation of the effectiveness of the procedures.[31]

It is important that the expatriate and his or her family feel the support continuing during their tour. A significant share of the dissatisfaction expressed pertains to perceived lack of support during the international experience, especially in cases of dual-career households.[32]

## Culture Shock

The effectiveness of orientation procedures can be measured only after managers are overseas. A unique phenomenon they face is **culture shock.** Although they all feel it, individuals differ widely in how they allow themselves to be affected by it.

**FIGURE 20.2**

**Companies Offering Cultural Training**

*Source:* Lori Ioannou, "Cultivating the New Expatriate Executive," *International Business* (July 1994): 46.

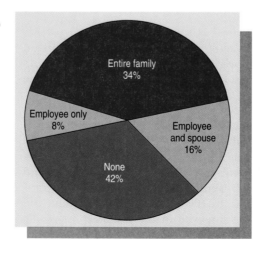

Entire family
34%

Employee only
8%

Employee and spouse
16%

None
42%

**Causes and Remedies**   Culture shock is the term used for the more pronounced reactions to the psychological disorientation that most people experience when they move for an extended period of time into a culture markedly different from their own.[33] Culture shock and its severity may be a function of the individual's lack of adaptability but may equally be a result of the firm's lack of understanding of the situation into which the manager was sent. Often goals set for a subsidiary or a project may be unrealistic or the means by which they are to be reached may be totally inadequate. All of these lead to external manifestations of culture shock, such as bitterness and even physical illness. In extreme cases, they can lead to hostility toward anything in the host environment.

The culture-shock cycle for an overseas assignment is presented in Figure 20.3. Four distinct stages of adjustment exist during a foreign assignment. The length of the stages is highly individual. The four stages are:

1. **Initial Euphoria:** Enjoying the novelty, largely from the perspective of a spectator
2. **Irritation and Hostility:** Experiencing cultural differences, such as the concept of time, through increased participation
3. **Adjustment:** Adapting to the situation, which in some cases leads to biculturalism and even accusations from corporate headquarters of "going native"
4. **Reentry:** Returning home to face a possibly changed home environment

The manager may fare better at the second stage than other members of the family, especially if their opportunities for work and other activities are severely restricted. The fourth stage may actually cause a reverse culture shock when the adjustment phase has been highly successful and the return home is not desired.

**FIGURE 20.3**

**Culture Shock Cycle for an Overseas Assignment**

*Note:* Lines indicate the extreme severity with which culture shock may attack.

*Source:* L. Robert Kohls, *Survival Kit for Overseas Living* (Yarmouth, Maine: Intercultural Press, 1984), 68.

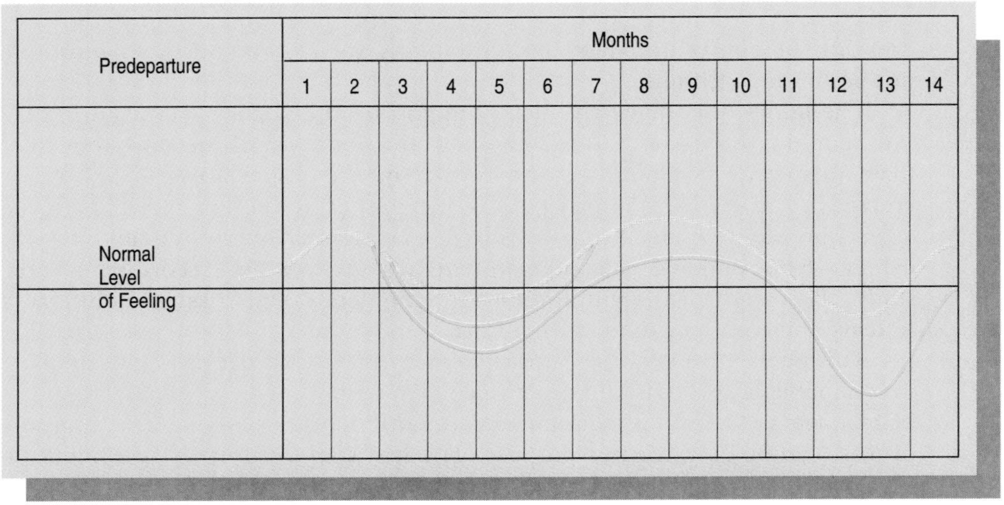

| Predeparture | Months | | | | | | | | | | | | | |
|---|---|---|---|---|---|---|---|---|---|---|---|---|---|---|
| | 1 | 2 | 3 | 4 | 5 | 6 | 7 | 8 | 9 | 10 | 11 | 12 | 13 | 14 |
| Normal Level of Feeling | | | | | | | | | | | | | | |

Firms themselves must take responsibility for easing one of the causes of culture shock: isolation. By maintaining contact with the manager beyond business-related communication, some of the shock may be alleviated. Exxon, for example, assigns each expatriate a contact person at headquarters to share general information.

**Terrorism: Tangible Culture Shock**  International terrorists have frequently targeted corporate facilities, operations, and personnel for attack.[34] In 1996, a total of 3,638 acts of terrorism were committed, with businesses targeted in 1,178 of them. Of the 75 incidents against U.S. interests abroad in 1996, 25 were attacks on businesses.[35] Corporate reactions have ranged from letting terrorism have little effect on operations to abandoning certain markets. Some companies try to protect their managers in various ways by fortifying their homes and using local-sounding names to do business in troubled parts of the world.[36] Of course, insurance is available to cover key executives; the cost ranges from a few thousand dollars to hundreds of thousands a year depending on the extent and location of the company's operations. Leading insurers include American International Underwriters, Chubb & Son, and Lloyd's of London.[37] The threat of terrorist activity may have an effect on the company's operations beyond the immediate geographic area of concern. Travel may be banned or restricted in times or areas threatened.

**Repatriation**

Returning home may evoke mixed feelings on the part of the expatriate and the family. Their concerns are both professional and personal. Even in two years, dramatic changes may have occurred not only at home but also in the way the individual and the family perceive the foreign environment. At worst, reverse culture shock may emerge.

The most important professional issue is finding a proper place in the corporate hierarchy. If no provisions have been made, a returning manager may be caught in a holding pattern for an intolerable length of time. For this reason, Dow Chemical, for example, provides each manager embarking on an overseas assignment with a letter that promises a job at least equal in responsibility upon return. Furthermore, because of their isolation, assignments abroad mean greater autonomy and authority than similar domestic positions. Both financially and psychologically, many expatriates find the overseas position difficult to give up. Many executive perks, such as club memberships, will not be funded at home.

The family, too, may be reluctant to give up their special status. In India, for example, expatriate families have servants for most of the tasks they perform themselves at home. Many longer-term expatriates are shocked by increases in the prices of housing and education at home. For the many managers who want to stay abroad, this may mean a change of company or even career—from employee to independent business person. According to one study, 20 percent of the employees who complete overseas assignments want to leave the company upon their return.[38]

This alternative is not an attractive one for the company, which stands to lose valuable individuals who could become members of an international corps of managers. Therefore, planning for repatriation is necessary.[39] A four-step process can be used for this purpose. The first step involves an assessment of foreign assignments in terms of environmental constraints and corporate objectives, making sure that the latter are realistically defined. The second stage is preparation of the individual for an overseas assignment, which should include a clear understanding of when and how repatriation takes place. During the actual tour, the manager should be kept abreast of developments at headquarters, especially in terms of career paths. Finally, during the actual reentry, the manager should receive intensive organizational reorientation, reasonable professional adjustment time, and counseling for the entire family on matters of, for example, finance. A program of this type allows the expatriate to feel a close bond with headquarters regardless of geographical distance.

## Compensation

A Japanese executive's salary in cash is quite modest by U.S. standards, but he is comfortable in the knowledge that the company will take care of him. Compensation is paternalistic; for example, a manager with two children in college and a sizable mortgage would be paid more than a childless manager in a comparable job. As this example suggests, Japanese compensation issues go beyond salary comparisons. They include exchange rates, local taxes, and what the money will buy in different countries. Many compensation packages include elements other than cash.[40]

A firm's international compensation program has to be effective in (1) providing an incentive to leave the home country on a foreign assignment, (2) maintaining a given standard of living, (3) taking into consideration career and family needs, and (4) facilitating reentry into the home country.[41] To achieve these objectives, firms pay a high premium beyond base salaries to induce managers to accept overseas assignments. The costs to the firm are 2 to 2.5 times the cost of maintaining a manager in a comparable position at home. For example, the average compensation package of a U.S. manager in Hong Kong is $225,500 (base salary is 47 percent of this figure) and for the British manager $170,500 (57 percent). U.S. firms traditionally offer their employees more high-value perks, such as bigger apartments.[42]

The compensation of the manager overseas can be divided into two general categories: (1) base salary and salary-related allowances and (2) nonsalary-related allowances. Although incentives to leave home are justifiable in both categories, they create administrative complications for the personnel department in tying them to packages at home and elsewhere. As the number of transfers increases, firms develop general policies for compensating the manager rather than negotiate individually on every aspect of the arrangement.

**Base Salary and Salary-Related Allowances**   A manager's **base salary** depends on qualifications, responsibilities, and duties, just as it would for a domestic position. Furthermore, criteria applying to merit increases, promotions, and other increases are administered as they are domestically. Equity and comparability with domestic positions are important, especially in ensuring that repatriation will not cause cuts in base pay.[43] For administrative and control purposes, the compensation and benefits function in multinational corporations is most often centralized.[44]

The cost of living varies considerably around the world, as can be seen in Global Perspective 20.2. The purpose of the **cost of living allowance (COLA)** is to enable the manager to maintain as closely as possible the same standard

# HOW FAR WILL YOUR SALARY GO?

**L**iving cost comparisons for Americans residing in foreign areas are developed four times a year by the U.S. Department of State Allowances Staff. For each post, two measures are computed: (1) a government index to establish post allowances for U.S. government employees and (2) a local index for use by private organizations. The government index takes into consideration prices of goods imported to posts and price advantages available only to U.S. government employees.

The local index is used by many business firms and private organizations to determine the cost of living allowance for their American employees assigned abroad. Local index measures for 12 key areas around the world are shown in the accompanying table. Maximum housing allowances, calculated separately, are also given.

The reports are issued four times annually under the title *U.S. Department of State Indexes of Living Costs Abroad, Quarters Allowances, and Hardship Differentials* by the U.S. Department of Labor.

| Location | Cost of Living Index[a] (Washington, D.C. = 100) | | Maximum Annual Housing Allowance[b] | | |
|---|---|---|---|---|---|
| | Survey Date | Index | Effective Date | Family of 2 | Family of 3–4 |
| Buenos Aires, Argentina | Nov. 1996 | 155 | NA | NA | NA |
| Canberra, Australia | Jan. 1997 | 112 | NA | NA | NA |
| Brussels, Belgium | Jul. 1995 | 166 | July 1997 | $28,500 | $31,350 |
| Rio de Janeiro, Brazil | Nov. 1996 | 112 | NA | NA | NA |
| Paris, France | May 1996 | 161 | July 1997 | $32,300 | $35,530 |
| Frankfurt, Germany | Jul. 1996 | 156 | July 1997 | $23,200 | $25,520 |
| Hong Kong | Aug. 1996 | 130 | NA | NA | NA |
| Tokyo, Japan | Mar. 1997 | 205 | July 1997 | $70,400 | $77,440 |
| Mexico City | May 1995 | 112 | June 1995 | $37,500 | $41,250 |
| The Hague, Netherlands | Feb. 1996 | 138 | July 1997 | $32,100 | $35,310 |
| Geneva, Switzerland | Jun. 1996 | 165 | July 1997 | $45,900 | $50,490 |
| London, U.K. | Jun. 1996 | 139 | July 1997 | $40,700 | $44,770 |

[a]*Excluding housing and education.*
[b]*For a family of three to four members with an annual income of $62,000 and over. Allowances are computed and paid in U.S. dollars.*
*NA = not available.*
**http://www.state.gov**

**WWW**

of living that he or she would have at home. COLA is calculated by determining a percentage of base salary that would be spent on goods and services at the foreign location. (Figures around 50 percent are typical.) The ratios will naturally vary as a function of income and family size. COLA tables for various U.S. cities (of which Washington, D.C., is the most often used) and locations worldwide are available through the U.S. State Department Allowances Staff and various consulting firms, such as Business International Corporation. Fluctuating exchange rates will of course have an effect on the COLA as well, and changes will call for reviews of the allowance. As an example, assume that living in Helsinki costs the manager 71 percent more than living in Washington, D.C. The manager's monthly pay is $4,000, and for his family of four, the disposable income is $2,150 (53.75 percent). Further assume that the dollar weakens from 5.5 Fmks to 4.7 Fmks. The COLA would be:

$$\$2,150 \times 171/100 \times 5.5/4.7 = \$4,302.$$

Similarly, if the local currency depreciated, the COLA would be less. When the cost of living is less than in the United States, no COLA is determined.

The **foreign service premium** is actually a bribe to encourage a manager to leave familiar conditions and adapt to new surroundings. Although the methods of paying the premium vary, as do its percentages, most firms pay it as a percentage of the base salary. The percentages range from 10 to 25 percent of base salary. One variation of the straightforward percentage is a sliding scale by amount—15 percent of the first $20,000, then 10 percent, and sometimes a ceiling beyond which a premium is not paid. Another variation is by duration, with the percentages decreasing with every year the manager spends abroad. Despite the controversial nature of foreign service premiums paid at some locations, they are a generally accepted competitive practice.

The environments in which a manager will work and the family will live vary dramatically. For example, consider being assigned to London or Brisbane versus Dar es Salaam or Port Moresby or even Bogota or Buenos Aires. Some locations may require little, if any, adjustment. Some call for major adaptation because of climatic differences; political instability; inadequacies in housing, education, shopping, or recreation; or overall isolation. For example, a family assigned to Beijing may find that schooling is difficult to arrange, with the result that younger children go to school in Tokyo and the older ones in the United States. To compensate for this type of expense and adjustment, firms pay **hardship allowances.** The allowances are based on U.S. State Department Foreign Post Differentials. The percentages vary from zero (for example, the manager in Helsinki) to 50 percent (as in Monrovia). The higher allowances typically include a danger pay extra added to any hardship allowance.[45]

Housing costs and related expenses are typically the largest expenditure in the expatriate manager's budget. Firms usually provide a **housing allowance** commensurate with the manager's salary level and position. When the expatriate is the country manager for the firm, the housing allowance will provide for suitable quarters in which to receive business associates. In most cases, firms set a range within which the manager must find housing. For common utilities, firms either provide an allowance or pay the costs outright.

One of the major determinants of the manager's lifestyle abroad is taxes. A U.S. manager earning $100,000 in Canada would pay nearly $40,000 in taxes—in excess of $10,000 more than in the United States. For this reason, 90 percent of U.S. multinational corporations have **tax-equalization** plans. When a manager's overseas taxes are higher than at home, the firm will make up the difference. However, in countries with a lower rate of taxation, the company simply keeps the difference. The firms' rationalization is that "it does not make any sense for the manager in Hong Kong to make more money than the guy who happened to land in Singapore."[46] Tax equalization is usually handled by accounting firms that make the needed calculations and prepare the proper forms. Managers can exclude a portion of their expatriate salary from

U.S. tax; in 1998 the amount was $72,000, with the figure increasing annually by $2,000.[47]

**Nonsalary-Related Allowances**   Other types of allowances are made available to ease the transition into the period of service abroad.[48] Typical allowances during the transition stage include (1) a relocation allowance to compensate for the additional expense of a move, such as purchase of electric converters; (2) a mobility allowance as an incentive to managers to go overseas, usually paid in a lump sum and as a substitute for the foreign service premium (some companies pay 50 percent at transfer, 50 percent at repatriation); (3) allowances related to housing, such as home sale or rental protection, shipment and storage of household goods, or provision of household furnishings in overseas locations; (4) automobile protection in terms of covering possible losses on the sale of a car or cars at transfer and having to buy others overseas, usually at a higher cost; (5) travel expenses, using economy-class transportation except for long flights (for example, from Washington to Taipei); and (6) temporary living expenses, which may become substantial if housing is not immediately available—as for the expatriate family that had to spend a year at a hotel in Beijing, for example. Companies are also increasingly providing support to make up for income lost by the accompanying spouse.

Education for children is one of the major concerns of expatriate families. Free public schooling may not be available and the private alternatives expensive. In many cases, children may have to go to school in a different country. Firms will typically reimburse for such expenses in the form of an **education allowance.** In the case of college education, firms reimburse for one round-trip airfare every year, leaving tuition expenses to the family.

Finally, firms provide support for medical expenses, especially to provide medical services at a level comparable to the expatriate's home country. In some cases, this means traveling to another country for care; for example, from Malaysia to Singapore, where the medical system is the most advanced in southeast Asia.

Other issues should be covered by a clearly stated policy. Home leave is provided every year, typically after 11 months overseas, although some companies require a longer period. Home leaves are usually accompanied by consultation and training sessions at headquarters. Some hardship posts, such as Port Moresby, include rest and relaxation leaves to maintain morale. At some posts, club memberships are necessary because (1) the status of the manager requires them and (2) they provide family members with access to the type of recreation they are used to in the home environment. Because they are extremely expensive—for example, a "mandatory" golf club membership in Tokyo might cost thousands of dollars—the firm's assistance is needed.

**Method of Payment**   The method of payment, especially in terms of currency, is determined by a number of factors. The most common method is to pay part of the salary in the local currency and part in the currency of the manager's home country. Host-country regulations, ranging for taxation to the availability of foreign currency, will influence the decision. Firms themselves look at the situation from the accounting and administrative point of view and would like, in most cases, to pay in local currencies to avoid burdening the subsidiary. The expatriate naturally will want to have some of the compensation in his or her own currency for various reasons; for example, if exchange controls are in effect, to get savings out of the country upon repatriation may be very difficult.

**Compensation of Host-Country Nationals**   The compensation packages paid to local managers—cash, benefits, and privileges—are largely determined as a function of internal equity and external competitiveness. Internal equity may be complicated because of cultural differences in compensation; for example, in Japan a year-end bonus of an additional month's salary is common. On the other hand, some incentive programs to increase productivity may be unknown to some nationals. Furthermore, in many countries, the state provides benefits that may be provided by the firm elsewhere. Since the firm and its employees contribute to the programs by law, the services need not be duplicated.

External competitiveness depends on the market price of trained individuals and their attraction to the firm. External competitiveness is best assessed through surveys of compensation and benefits levels for a particular market. The firm must keep its local managers informed of the survey results to help them realize the value of their compensation packages.

## Managing Labor Personnel

None of the firm's objectives can be realized without a labor force, which can become one of the firm's major assets or one of its major problems depending on the relationship that is established. Because of local patterns and legislation, headquarters' role in shaping the relations is mainly advisory, limited to setting the overall tone for the interaction. However, many of the practices adopted in one market or region may easily come under discussion in another, making it necessary for multinational corporations to set general policies concerning labor relations. Often multinational corporations have been instrumental in bringing about changes in the overall work environment in a coun-

UPS, the world's largest package distribution company, transports more then 3.1 billion parcels and documents annually. To transport packages most efficiently, UPS has developed an elaborate network of "hubs" or central sorting facilities located throughout the world.
Photo courtesy of United Parcel Service

try. And as decisions are made where to locate and how to streamline operations, education and training become important criteria for both countries and companies.

At many companies, educational programs are a means of leveraging valuable company resources. Eastman Kodak has established eight training centers of excellence with functional specializations (for example, technical training and general business education). In China, AT&T has provided customized technical training to the government workers who will run the AT&T–supplied telecommunications networks.[49]

Labor strategy can be viewed from three perspectives: (1) the participation of labor in the affairs of the firm, especially as it affects performance and well-being; (2) the role and impact of unions in the relationship; and (3) specific human resource policies in terms of recruitment, training, and compensation.

## Labor Participation in Management

Over the past quarter century, many changes have occurred in the traditional labor-management relationship as a result of dramatic changes in the economic environment and the actions of both firms and the labor force. The role of the worker is changing both at the level of the job performed and in terms of participation in the decision-making process. To enhance workers' role in decision making, various techniques have emerged: self-management, codetermination, minority board membership, and works councils. In striving for improvements in quality of work life, programs that have been initiated include flextime, quality circles, and work-flow reorganization. Furthermore, employee ownership has moved into the mainstream.

### Labor Participation in Decision Making

The degree to which workers around the world can participate in corporate decision making varies considerably. Rights of information, consultation, and codetermination develop on three levels:

1. The shop-floor level, or direct involvement; for example, the right to be consulted in advance concerning transfers.
2. The management level, or through representative bodies; for example, works council participation in setting of new policies or changing of existing ones.
3. The board level: for example, labor membership on the board of directors.[50]

The extent of worker participation in decision making in eleven countries is summarized in Table 20.3. Yugoslavia, before its breakup, used to have the highest amount of worker participation in any country; **self-management** was standard through workers' councils, which decided all major issues including the choice of managing director and supervisory board.[51]

In some countries, employees are represented on the supervisory boards to facilitate communication between management and labor by giving labor a clearer picture of the financial limits of management and by providing management with a new awareness of labor's point of view. The process is called **codetermination.** In Germany, companies have a two-tiered management system with a supervisory board and the board of managers, which actually runs

# Organized Labor as a Percentage of the Labor Force

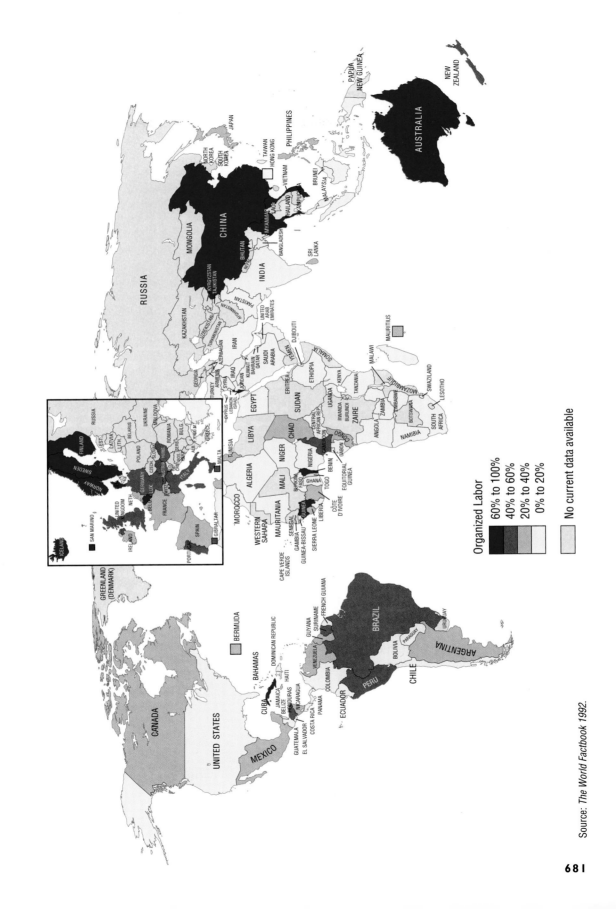

Organized Labor

- 60% to 100%
- 40% to 60%
- 20% to 40%
- 0% to 20%
- No current data available

Source: *The World Factbook 1992.*

**TABLE 20.3**

**Degree of Worker Involvement in Decision Making of Firms**

| | Direct Involvement of Workers[a] | Involvement of Representative Bodies[a] | Board Representation Standing[b] | Overall Standing[c] |
|---|---|---|---|---|
| Germany | 3 | 1 | 1 | A |
| Sweden | 4 | 2 | 1 | A |
| Norway | 1 | 10 | 1 | B |
| Netherlands | 9 | 4 | 2 | C |
| France | 7 | 3 | 2 | C |
| Belgium | 5 | 6 | 3 | D |
| Finland | 2 | 9 | 3 | D |
| Denmark | 8 | 7 | 1 | D |
| Israel | 11 | 5 | 3 | D |
| Italy | 6 | 8 | 3 | E |
| Great Britain | 10 | 11 | 3 | E |

[a]Involvement is rated on an 11-point scale, where 1 stands for the greatest degree of involvement and 11 for almost no involvement.
[b]All cases without any kind of board participation are coded 3; the right to appoint two or more members, 1; the in-between category, 2.
[c]Rankings are from high (A) to low (E).

*Source:* Industrial Democracy in Europe International Research Group, *Industrial Democracy in Europe* (Oxford, England: Clarendon Press, 1981), 291.

the firm. In a firm with 20,000 employees, for example, labor would have ten of the twenty supervisory board slots divided in the following way: three places for union officials and the balance to be elected from the workforce. At least one member must be a white-collar employee and one a managerial employee.[52] The supervisory board is legally responsible for the managing board. Reactions to codetermination vary. Six European nations—Sweden, the Netherlands, Norway, Luxembourg, Denmark, and France—have introduced their own versions and report lower levels of labor strife.[53] In some countries, labor has **minority participation.** In the Netherlands, for example, works councils can nominate (not appoint) board members and can veto the appointment of new members appointed by others. In other countries, such as the United States, codetermination has been opposed by unions as an undesirable means of cooperation, especially when management–labor relations are confrontational.

A tradition in labor relations, especially in Britain, is **works councils.** They provide labor a say in corporate decision making through a representative body, which may consist entirely of workers or of a combination of managers and workers. The councils participate in decisions on overall working conditions, training, transfers, work allocation, and compensation. In some countries, such as Finland and Belgium, workers' rights to direct involvement, especially as it involves their positions, are quite strong. The European Union's works council directive will ultimately require over 1,000 multinational companies, both European and non-European, to negotiate works council agreements. The agreements will provide for at least one meeting per year to improving dialogue between workers and management.[54]

The countries described are unique in the world. In many countries and regions, workers have few, if any, of these rights. The result is long-term potential for labor strife in those countries and possible negative publicity elsewhere. In addition to labor groups and the media, investors and shareholders also are scrutinizing multinationals' track records on labor practices. As a result, a company investing in foreign countries should hold to international standards of safety and health, not simply local standards. This can be achieved, for example, through the use of modern equipment and training. Local labor also should be paid adequately. This increases the price of labor, yet ensures the best available talent and helps avoid charges of exploitation.[55] Companies subcontracting work to local or joint-venture factories need to evaluate industrial relations throughout the system not only to avoid lost production due to disruptions such as strikes, but to ensure that no exploitation exists at the facilities. Several large firms, such as Nike and Reebok, require subcontractors to sign agreements saying they will abide by minimum wage standards.[56]

**Improvement of Quality of Work Life**   The term **quality of work life** has come to encompass various efforts in the areas of personal and professional development. Its two clear objectives are to increase productivity and to increase the satisfaction of employees. Of course, programs leading to increased participation in corporate decision making are part of the programs; however, this section concentrates on individual job-related programs: work redesign, team building, and work scheduling.[57]

By adding both horizontal and vertical dimensions to the work, **work redesign programs** attack undesirable features of jobs. Horizontally, task complexity is added by incorporating work stages normally done before and after the stage being redesigned. Vertically, each employee is given more responsibility for making the decisions that affect how the work is done.[58] Japanese car manufacturers have changed some of the work routines in their plants in the United States. For example, at Honda's unit in Marysville, Ohio, workers have reacted favorably to the responsibilities they have been given, such as inspecting their own work and instructing others.[59] On the other hand, work redesign may have significant costs attached, including wage increases, facility change costs, and training costs.

Closely related to work redesign are efforts aimed at **team building.** For example, at Volvo's Kalmar plant in Sweden, work is organized so that groups are responsible for a particular, identifiable portion of the car, such as interiors. Each group has its own areas in which to pace itself and to organize the work. The group must take responsibility for the work, including inspections, whether it is performed individually or in groups. The group is informed about its performance through a computer system.[60] The team-building effort includes job rotation to enable workers to understand all facets of their jobs. Visiting American autoworkers were impressed with Volvo's physical working conditions, but they believed that teamwork would become tedious. Despite claims for increased worker participation, Americans expressed a preference for the more grassroots unionism of the United States and its well-tested grievance procedure.[61] Another approach to team building makes use of **quality circles,** in which groups of workers regularly meet to discuss issues relating to their productivity. Pioneered in Japan, quality circles began to appear in U.S. industry in the mid-1970s.

Flexibility in **work scheduling** has led to changes in when and how long workers are at the workplace. **Flextime** allows workers to determine their starting and ending hours in a given workday; for example, they might arrive between 7:00 and 9:30 A.M. and leave between 3:00 and 5:30 P.M. The idea spread from Germany, to the European Union and to other countries such as Switzerland, Japan, New Zealand, and the United States. Despite its advantages in reducing absenteeism, flextime is not applicable to industries using assembly lines. Flexible work scheduling has also led to compressed workweeks—for example, the four-day week—and job sharing, which allows a position to be filled by more than one person.

Firms around the world also have other programs for personal and professional development, such as career counseling and health counseling. All of them are dependent on various factors external and internal to the firm. Of the external factors, the most important are the overall characteristics of the economy and the labor force. Internally, either the programs must fit into existing organizational structures or management must be inclined toward change. In many cases, labor unions have been one of the major resisting forces. Their view is that firms are trying to prevent workers from organizing by allowing them to participate in decision making and management.

## The Role of Labor Unions

When two of the world's largest producers of electrotechnology, Swedish Asea and Switzerland's Brown Boveri, merged to remain internationally competitive in a market dominated by a few companies such as General Electric, Siemens, Hitachi, and Toshiba, not everyone reacted positively to the alliance. For tax reasons, headquarters would not be located in Sweden, and this caused the four main Swedish labor unions to oppose the merger. They demanded that the Swedish government exercise its right to veto the undertaking because Swedish workers would no longer have a say in their company's affairs if it were headquartered elsewhere. Furthermore, Swedes objected to Brown Boveri's four subsidiaries in South Africa.[62]

The incident is an example of the role labor unions play in the operation of a multinational corporation. It also points up the concerns of local labor unions when they must deal with organizations directed from outside their national borders.

The role of labor unions varies from country to country, often because of local traditions in management–labor relations. The variations include the extent of union power in negotiations and the activities of unions in general. In Europe, especially in the northern European countries, collective bargaining takes place between an employers' association and an umbrella organization of unions, on either a national or a regional basis, establishing the conditions for an entire industry. On the other end of the spectrum, negotiations in Japan are on the company level, and the role of larger-scale unions is usually consultative. Another striking difference emerges in terms of the objectives of unions and the means by which they attempt to attain them. In the United Kingdom, for example, union activity tends to be politically motivated and identified with political ideology. In the United States, the emphasis has always been on improving workers' overall quality of life.

Internationalization of business has created a number of challenges for labor unions. The main concerns that have been voiced are: (1) the power of the firm to move production from one country to another if attractive terms are not reached in a particular market; (2) the availability of data, especially financial information, to support unions' bargaining positions; (3) insufficient attention to local issues and problems while focusing on global optimization; and (4) difficulty in being heard by those who eventually make the decisions.[63]

Although the concerns are valid, all of the problems anticipated may not develop. For example, transferring production from one country to another in the short term may be impossible, and labor strife in the long term may well influence such moves. To maintain participation in corporate decision making, unions are taking action individually and across national boundaries as seen in Global Perspective 20.3. Individual unions refer to contracts signed elsewhere when setting the agenda for their own negotiations. Supranational organizations such as the International Trade Secretariats and industry-specific organizations such as the International Metal Workers' Federation exchange information and discuss bargaining tactics. The goal is also to coordinate bar-

## GLOBAL UNIONS VS. GLOBAL COMPANIES

**T**he United States is perceived by European companies from the labor point of view as more flexible and less costly. However, when these companies attempt to challenge U.S. unions by downsizing the workforce to increase profitability, they meet resistance not only from the U.S. unions but from the international federations of trade unions. Conflict arises when there are different understandings of the role of labor unions.

Trelleborg, a Swedish metal and mining conglomerate with operations in eight European countries, expanded into the United States with the purchase of a plant in Copperhill, Tennessee, in 1991 after the owner went bankrupt. The plant was managed under Trelleborg's subsidiary, Boliden Intertrade Inc. The unions at Copperhill deferred over $5 million in wages to help keep the plant alive in the early 1990s. But labor-management relations deteriorated during contract negotiations in 1996, when Trelleborg insisted on sweeping changes in work rules. Boliden executives recognized that there would be a considerable loss of jobs, but saw no other way to regain competitiveness.

The workers saw the changes as a direct assault on their seniority system and a threat to worker safety, and went to strike after their contract expired. The company responded by hiring replacement workers and a squad of security guards. Two weeks later, the company said it had received a petition from its new employees indicating they did not want a union. Unions, on their part, demanded that Boliden withdraw its letter of derecognition and remove the replacement workers.

U.S. unions represent 16 percent of the public- and private-sector workforce, but in Sweden the unionization rate is over 80 percent. Although strikes are relatively rare in Sweden, replacing workers during a walkout is virtually unheard of. Swedish workers also have the right to shut down a company during a strike by stopping delivery trucks and other services, all actions that are banned in the United States.

Union activity was not limited to local moves in Tennessee. Metal, the powerful Swedish labor union representing Swedish workers in the industry, was recruited to pressure the parent company in Sweden. The International Federation of Chemical, Energy, Mine, and General Workers' Unions launched a campaign to pressure Trelleborg to rehire the Copperhill strikers. U.S. and Canadian unions warned institutional investors and pension fund managers that an investment in Boliden could be risky. They made their warnings as Trelleborg executives were visiting North America to raise $900 million in an initial public offering on the Toronto Stock Exchange.

Two months into the crisis, Trelleborg announced it would sell its U.S. subsidiary.

*Source: Tim Schorrock, "Firm to Sell U.S. Unit at Center of Labor Flap,"* The Journal of Commerce *( June 3, 1997); 3A: Joan Campbell,* The European Labor Unions *(Greenwood, Conn.: Greenwood Press, 1994), 429; and Tom DeVos,* U.S. Multinationals and Worker Participation in Management *(Westport, Conn.: Quorum Books, 1981), 195;* **http://www.trellgroup.se**

gaining with multinational corporations across national boundaries. The International Labor Organization, a specialized agency of the United Nations, has an information bank on multinational corporations' policies concerning wage structures, benefits packages, and overall working conditions.

The relations between companies and unions can be cooperative as well. Alliances between labor and management have emerged to continue providing well-paying factory jobs in the United States in face of global competition. For example, the Amalgamated Clothing and Textile Workers Union of America and Xerox have worked jointly to boost quality and cut costs to keep their jobs from going to Mexico, where wage rates are less than $1 an hour.[64]

## Human Resource Policies

The objectives of a human resource policy pertaining to workers are the same as for management: to anticipate the demand for various skills and to have in place programs that will ensure the availability of employees when needed. For workers, however, the firm faces the problem on a larger scale and does not have, in most cases, an expatriate alternative. This means that, among other things, when technology is transferred for a plant, it has to be adapted to the local workforce.

Although most countries have legislation and restrictions concerning the hiring of expatriates, many of them—for example some of the EU countries and some oil-rich Middle Eastern countries—have offset labor shortages by importing large numbers of workers from countries such as Turkey and Jordan. The EU by design allows free movement of labor. A mixture of backgrounds in the available labor pool can put a strain on personnel development. As an example, the firm may incur considerable expense to provide language training to employees. In Sweden, a certain minimum amount of language training must be provided for all "guest workers" at the firm's expense.

Bringing a local labor force to the level of competency desired by the firm may also call for changes. As an example, managers at Honda's plant in Ohio encountered a number of problems: Labor costs were 50 percent higher and productivity 10 percent lower than in Japan. Automobiles produced there cost $500 more than the same models made in Japan and then delivered to the United States. Before Honda began to produce the Accord in the United States, it flew 200 workers representing all areas of the factory to Japan to learn to build Hondas the Sayama way and then to teach their coworkers the skills.[65]

Compensation of the work force is a controversial issue. Payroll expenses must be controlled for the firm to remain competitive; on the other hand, the firm must attract in appropriate numbers the type of workers it needs. The compensation packages of U.S.–based multinational companies have come under criticism, especially when their level of compensation is lower in developing countries than in the United States. Criticism has occurred even when the salaries or wages paid were substantially higher than the local average.[66]

Comparisons of compensation packages are difficult because of differences in the packages that are shaped by culture, legislation, collective bargaining, taxation, and individual characteristics of the job. In northern Europe, for example, new fathers can accompany their wives on a two-week paternity leave at the employer's expense.

## Summary

A business organization is the sum of its human resources. To recruit and retain a pool of effective people for each of its operations requires (1) personnel planning and staffing, (2) training activities, (3) compensation decisions, and (4) attention to labor–management relations.

Firms attract international managers from a number of sources, both internal and external. In the earlier stages of internationalization, recruitment must be external. Later, an internal pool often provides candidates for transfer. The decision then becomes whether to use home-country, host-country, or third-country nationals. If expatriate managers are used, selection policies should focus on competence, adaptability, and personal traits. Policies should also be set for the compensation and career progression of candidates selected for out-of-country assignments. At the same time, the firm must be attentive to the needs of local managers for training and development.

Labor can no longer be considered as simply services to be bought. Increasingly, workers are taking an active role in the decision making of the firm and in issues related to their own welfare. Various programs are causing dramatic organizational change, not only by enhancing the position of workers but by increasing the productivity of the work force as well. Workers employed by the firm usually are local, as are the unions that represent them. Their primary concerns in working for a multinational firm are job security and benefits. Unions therefore are cooperating across national boundaries to equalize benefits for workers employed by the same firm in different countries.

## Key Terms and Concepts

| | | |
|---|---|---|
| lingua franca | base salary | codetermination |
| factual cultural knowledge | cost of living allowance (COLA) | minority participation |
| area expertise | foreign service premium | works councils |
| interpretive cultural knowledge | hardship allowance | quality of work life |
| adaptability screening | housing allowance | work redesign programs |
| orientation program | tax equalization | team building |
| culture shock | education allowance | quality circles |
| expatriate | self-management | work scheduling |
| | | flextime |

## Questions for Discussion

1. Is a "supranational executive corps," consisting of cosmopolitan individuals of multiple nationalities who would be an asset wherever utilized, a possibility for any corporation?

2. Comment on this statement by Lee Iacocca: "If a guy wants to be a chief executive 25 or 50 years from now, he will have to be well rounded. There will be no more of 'Is he a good lawyer, is he a good marketing guy, is he a good finance guy?' His education and his experience will make him a total entrepreneur in a world that has really turned into one huge market. He bet-

ter speak Japanese or German, he better understand the history of both of those countries and how they got to where they are, and he better know their economics pretty cold."

3. What additional benefit is brought into the expatriate selection and training process by adaptability screening?

4. Develop general principles that firms could use in dealing with terrorism, apart from pulling out of a given market.

5. A manager with a current base salary of $100,000 is being assigned to Lagos, Nigeria. Assuming that you are that manager, develop a compensation and benefits package for yourself in terms of both salary-related and nonsalary-related items.

6. Using the Homebuyer's Fair Web site (**http://www.homefair.com**), compare the cost of living in your home city vs. Vienna, Austria; Brussels, Belgium; Shanghai, China; Bogota, Colombia; and New Delhi, India. What accounts for the differences present?

7. What accounts for the success of Japanese companies with both American unions and the more ferocious British unions? In terms of the changes that have come about, are there winners or losers among management and workers? Could both have gained?

8. Develop general policies that the multinational corporation should follow in dealing (or choosing not to deal) with a local labor union.

## Recommended Readings

Adler, Nancy J., and Dafna N. Izraeli, eds. *Competitive Frontiers: Women Managers in a Global Economy.* Cambridge, Mass.: Blackwell Business, 1994.

Austin, James. *Managing in Developing Countries.* New York: Free Press, 1990.

Bamber, Greg J., and Russell D. Lansbury, eds. *International and Comparative Industrial Relations.* London, England: Allen & Unwin, 1989.

Black, J. Stewart, Hal B. Gregsen, and Mark E. Mendenhall. *Global Assignments.* San Francisco, Calif.: Jossey-Bass Publishers, 1992.

Casse, Pierre. *Training for the Multicultural Manager.* Washington, D.C.: SIETAR, 1987.

Deresky, Helen. *International Management: Managing Across Borders and Cultures.* Reading, Mass.: Addison-Wesley, 1997.

Harris, Philip, and Robert T. Moran. *Managing Cultural Differences.* Houston, Tex.: Gulf, 1990.

Hodgetts, Richard, and Fred Luthans. *International Management.* New York: McGraw-Hill, 1994.

Holley, William H., and Kenneth M. Jennings. *The Labor Relations Process.* Fort Worth, Tex.: Dryden Press, 1994.

Lane, Henry W., Joseph J. DiStephano, and Martha L. Maznevski. *International Management Behavior.* Cambridge, Mass.: Blackwell Publishers, 1997.

Lewis, Tom, and Robert Jungman, eds. *On Being Foreign: Culture Shock in Short Fiction.* Yarmouth, Maine: Intercultural Press, 1986.

Marquardt, Michael J., and Dean W. Engel. *Global Resource Development.* Englewood Cliffs, N.J.: Prentice-Hall, 1993.

Mendenhall, Mark, and Gary Oddou. *International Human Resource Management.* Boston: PWS–Kent, 1991.

Pucik, Vladimir, Noel M. Tichy, and Carole K. Barnett. *Globalizing Management: Creating and Leading the Competitive Organization.* New York: John Wiley, 1992.

Slomp, Hans. *Between Bargaining and Politics.* Westport, Conn.: Praeger, 1996.

## Notes

1. Herbert G. Heneman and Donald P. Schwab, "Overview of the Personnel/Human Resource Function," in *Perspectives on Personnel/Human Resource Management,* ed. Herbert G. Heneman and Donald P. Schwab (Homewood, Ill.: Irwin, 1986), 3–11.

2. Richard D. Hays, "Expatriate Selection: Insuring Success and Avoiding Failure," *Journal of Interna-*

*tional Business Studies* 5 (Summer 1974): 25–37.

3. "Ford's Brave New World," *The Washington Post,* October 16, 1994, H1, H4.

4. Christopher A. Bartlett and Sumantra Ghoshal, "What Is a Global Manager?" *Harvard Business Review* 70 (September–October 1992): 124–132.

5. Jan van Rosmalen, "Internationalising Heineken: Human Resource Policy in a Growing International Company," *International Management Development* (Summer 1985): 11–13.

6. Floris Majlers, "Inside Unilever: The Evolving Transnational Company," *Harvard Business Review* 70 (September–October 1992): 46–52.

7. Randall S. Schuler, Susan E. Jackson, Peter J. Dowling, and Denice E. Welch, "The Formation of an International Joint Venture: Davidson Instrument Panel," in *International Human Resource Management,* ed. Mark Mendenhall and Gary Oddou (Boston: PWS–Kent, 1991), 83–96.

8. "Company & Industry: Ukraine," *Crossborder Monitor* (October 23, 1996): 4; and "Middle Managers In Vietnam," *Business Asia* (May 8, 1995): 3–4.

9. Peter Lorange, "Human Resource Management in Multinational Cooperative Ventures," *Human Resources Management* 25 (Winter 1986): 133–148.

10. *1996 Global Relocation Trends Survey Report* (New York: Windham International, 1997); available on http://www.windhamworld.com/surv_96.hmtl .

11. Carla Rapoport, "The Switch Is On in Japan," *Fortune* (May 21, 1990): 144.

12. Anders Edström and Peter Lorange, "Matching Strategy and Human Resources in Multinational Corporations," *Journal of International Business Studies* 16 (Fall 1985): 125–137.

13. Elizabeth Klein, "The U.S./Japanese HR Culture Clash," *Personnel Journal* 71 (November 1992): 30–38.

14. "How Business Is Creating Europe Inc.," *Business Week* (September 7, 1987): 40–41.

15. Rabindra Kanungo and Richard W. Wright, "A Cross-Cultural Comparative Study of Managerial Job Attitudes," *Journal of International Business Studies* 14 (Fall 1983): 115–129.

16. Lester B. Korn, "How the Next CEO Will Be Different," *Fortune* (May 22, 1990): 157–161.

17. "The Elusive Euromanager," *The Economist* (November 7, 1993): 83.

18. Jean E. Heller, "Criteria for Selecting an International Manager," *Personnel* (May–June 1980): 18–22.

19. Walter Kiechel, "Our Person in Pomparippu," *Fortune* (October 17, 1983): 213–218.

20. Richard D. Hays, "Ascribed Behavioral Determinants of Success-Failure among U.S. Expatriate Managers," *Journal of International Business Studies* 2 (Summer 1971): 40–46.

21. Richard Pascale, "Fitting New Employees into the Corporate Culture," *Fortune* (May 28, 1984): 28–40.

22. *Compensating International Executives* (New York: Business International, 1970), 35.

23. Joel Bleeke and David Ernst, *Collaborating to Compete* (New York: John Wiley & Sons, 1993), 179.

24. Lennie Copeland, "Training Americans to Do Business Overseas," *Training* (July 1984): 22–33.

25. Lee Smith, "Japan's Autocratic Managers," *Fortune* (January 7, 1985): 14–23.

26. "Gauging a Family's Suitability for a Stint Overseas," *Business Week* (April 16, 1979): 127–130.

27. *Runzheimer Reports on Relocation,* Rochester, Wis.: Runzheimer International, 1997, available on http://www.runzheimer.com .

28. "Global Managing," *The Wall Street Journal Europe,* January 10–11, 1992, 1, 20.

29. Nancy J. Adler, "Expecting International Success: Female Managers Overseas," *Columbia Journal of World Business* 19 (Fall 1984): 79–85.

30. Nancy J. Adler, "Pacific Basin Managers: A Gaijin, Not a Woman," *Human Resource Management* 26 (Summer 1987): 169–191.

31. Rosalie Tung, "Selection and Training of Personnel for Overseas Assignments," *Columbia Journal of World Business* 16 (Spring 1981): 68–78.

32. Michael G. Harvey, "Dual-Career Expatriates: Expectations, Adjustment and Satisfaction with International Relocation," *Journal of International Business Studies* 28, 3 (1997): 627–658.

33. L. Robert Kohls, *Survival Kit for Overseas Living* (Yarmouth, Maine: Intercultural Press, 1979), 62–68.

34. Harvey Iglarsh, "Terrorism and Corporate Costs," *Terrorism* 10 (Fall 1987): 22–25.

35. Data provided by Pinkerton Risk Assessment Services, December 10, 1997.

36. Michael G. Harvey, "A Survey of Corporate Programs for Managing Terrorist Threats," *Journal of International Business Studies* 24, 3 (1993): 465–478.

37. Mary Helen Frederick, "Keeping Safe," *International Business* (October, 1992): 68–69.

38. Nancy J. Adler, *International Dimensions of Organizational Behavior* (Boston: PWS–Kent, 1990), Chapter 4.

39. Michael G. Harvey, "The Other Side of Foreign Assignments: Dealing with the Repatriation Dilemma," *Columbia Journal of World Business* 16 (Spring 1981): 79–85.

40. Lisa Miller Mesdag, "Are You Underpaid?" *Fortune* (March 19, 1984): 20–25.

41. Raymond J. Stone, "Compensation: Pay and Perks

for Overseas Executives," *Personnel Journal* (January 1986): 64–69.

42. "Americans Lead the HK Perks Race," *Sunday Morning Post*, July 12, 1992, 14.

43. *1987 Professional Development Seminar: International Compensation* (Phoenix, Ariz.: American Compensation Association, 1987), module 1.

44. Brian Toyne and Robert J. Kuhne, "The Management of the International Executive Compensation and Benefits Process," *Journal of International Business Studies* 14 (Winter 1983): 37–49.

45. U.S. Department of State, *Indexes of Living Costs Abroad, Quarters Allowances, and Hardship Differentials*, January 1995, Table 1.

46. "How to Make a Foreign Job Pay," *Business Week* (December 23, 1985): 84–85.

47. Courtesy of Thomas B. Cooke, Esq.

48. *1987 Professional Development Seminar: International Compensation*, modules 4 and 5.

49. "The Winds of Change Blow Everywhere," *Business Week* (October 17, 1994): 87–88; and "School Days at Work: Firms See Training as Key to Empowerment," *Crossborder Monitor* (August 3, 1994): 1, 7.

50. Industrial Democracy in Europe International Research Group, *Industrial Democracy in Europe* (Oxford, England: Clarendon Press, 1981), Chapter 14.

51. Osmo A. Wiio, *Yritysdemokratia ja Muuttuva Yhteiskunta* (Tapiola, Finland: Weilin + Goos, 1970), Chapter 13.

52. E. B. Hoffman, "The German Way of Industrial Relations—Could We, Should We, Import It?" *Across the Board* (October 1977): 38–47.

53. Richard D. Robinson, *Internationalization of Business*

(Hinsdale, Ill.: Dryden, 1986), Chapter 3.

54. "EU Works Councils Get Underway," *Crossborder Monitor* (October 16, 1996): 4.

55. "MNCs Under Fire to Link Trade with Global Labor Rights," *Crossborder Monitor* (May 25, 1994): 1.

56. "Labor Strife in Indonesia Spotlights Development Challenge," *Crossborder Monitor* (May 25, 1994): 7.

57. Herman Gadon, "Making Sense of Quality of Work Life Programs," *Business Horizons* 27 (January–February 1984): 42–46.

58. Antone Alber, "The Costs of Job Enrichment," *Business Horizons* 22 (February 1984): 60–72.

59. Faye Rice, "America's New No. 4 Automaker—Honda," *Fortune* (October 28, 1985): 26–29.

60. Pehr G. Gyllenhammar, "How Volvo Adapts Work to People," *Harvard Business Review* 55 (July–August 1977): 24–28.

61. Joe Kelly and Kamran Khozan, "Participative Management: Can It Work?" *Business Horizons* 23 (August 1980): 74–79.

62. "Asean Ammattiliitot Vaativat Suuryhtyman Paapaikkaa Ruotsiin," *Helsingin Sanomat*, September 16, 1987, 34.

63. S. B. Prasad and Y. Kirshna Shetty, *An Introduction to Multinational Management* (Englewood Cliffs, N.J.: Prentice-Hall, 1976), Appendix 8–A.

64. "Cooperation Worth Copying?" *The Washington Post*, December 13, 1992, H1, H6.

65. Rice, "America's New No. 4 Automaker—Honda."

66. Oliver Williams, "Who Cast the First Stone?" *Harvard Business Review* 62 (September–October 1984): 151–160.

# CHAPTER 21

# Organization, Implementation, and Control of International Operations

## LEARNING OBJECTIVES

◆ *To describe alternative organizational structures for international operations*

◆ *To highlight factors affecting decisions about the structure of international organizations*

◆ *To indicate roles for country organizations in the development of strategy and implementation of programs*

◆ *To outline the need for and challenges of controls in international operations*

## Recasting the Corporate Mind

Ford Motor Co. has been an international enterprise from the days of Henry Ford selling the Model A. Five years after its founding in 1903, it set up its first overseas sales branch in France and by 1911 it was making cars in Britain. But more than eighty years and dozens of overseas endeavors later, Ford is still making adjustments to leverage its resources across borders.

The latest reorganization at Ford in April of 1994 was dramatic: Ford merged its large and culturally distinct European and North American auto operations and plans to fold in Latin America and the Asia-Pacific operations later. The rationale according to Ford's chairman Alexander J. Trotman is make more efficient use of its engineering and product development resources against rapidly globalizing rivals in the "all out global car race." The potential advantages are considerable. If resources can be pooled and turf wars between national entities eliminated, Ford estimates that its savings can reach $3 billion a year. Planning and implementation have to work, however. When a company like Ford centralizes all product development, a mistake that would have been confined to one country in the former organizational structure could become a global disaster. "If you misjudge the market, you are wrong in fifteen countries rather than only one," says one European executive.

Ford's move makes one thing clear: with world markets rapidly merging and converging, companies that have been slow to globalize their operations will now have to scramble to play catch-up. In May 1994, IBM reorganized its marketing and sales organizations into fourteen worldwide industry groups, such as banking, retail, and insurance. In moving away from an organization based on geography, IBM hopes to enhance its responsiveness to customers, many of which are themselves global operators. Soon after IBM's announcement, drug giant Bristol-Myers Squibb Co. revamped its consumer business by installing a new chief responsible for its worldwide consumer medicines business such as Excedrin and Bufferin. A new unit was also formed to have worldwide responsibility for its Clairol and other hair-care products.

Globalization is not taking any one form. Indeed, most companies have adopted mixed organizational formats. Unilever plc uses a classic regional structure with local managers in three areas of the world: Africa/Middle East, Latin America, and East Asia/Pacific. But in Europe and North America, where consumer preferences are more similar, the structure is different. The president of Lever Brothers Co. in New York, for example, reports to the Unilever worldwide detergents-products coordinator in London.

Simply redrawing lines on an organization chart will not make a company global. Building trust and creating a common vision among the entities that will now cooperate rather than work independently is the critical task. This effort will focus on eliminating headquarters myopia and use of cross-cultural teams to foster a one-company culture. ▪

*Source:* "Big Blue Bounces Back," *The Washington Post,* December 15, 1996, H1-4; "Red Alert at Ford," *Business Week* (December 2, 1996): 38–39; "Borderless Management: Companies Strive to Become Truly Stateless," *Business Week* (May 23, 1994): 24–25; "IBM Revamps Sales Teams," *Advertising Age* (May 9, 1994): 2; Regina Fazio Maruca, "The Right Way to Go Global: An Interview with Whirlpool CEO David Whitwam," *Harvard Business Review* 72 (March–April 1994): 134–145; and "The Global Firm: R.I.P.," *The Economist* (February 6, 1993): 69.
**http://www.ford.com   http://www.ibm.com   http://www.bms.com   http://www.unilever.com**

**WWW**

As companies evolve from purely domestic to multinational, their organizational structure and control systems must change to reflect new strategies. With growth comes diversity in terms of products and services, geographic markets, and people in the company itself, bringing along a set of challenges for the company. Two critical issues are basic to all of these challenges: (1) the type of organization that provides the best framework for developing worldwide strategies and maintaining flexibility in implementation with respect to individual markets and operations, and (2) the type and degree of control to be exercised from headquarters to maximize total effort. Organizational structures and control systems have to be adjusted as market conditions change, as seen in the chapter's opening vignette.

This chapter will focus on the advantages and disadvantages of various organizational structures, as well as their appropriateness at different stages of internationalization. A determining factor is where decision-making authority within the organizational structure will be placed. Also, the roles of the different entities that make up the organization need to be defined. The chapter will also outline the need for devising a control system to oversee the international operations of the company, emphasizing the additional control instruments needed beyond those used in domestic business and the control strategies of multinational corporations. The appropriateness and eventual cost of the various control approaches will vary as the firm expands its international operations. The overall objective of the chapter is to study the intraorganizational relationships critical to the firm's attempt to optimize its competitiveness.

## Organizational Structure

The basic functions of an organization are to provide (1) a route and locus of decision making and coordination and (2) a system for reporting and communications. Authority and communication networks are typically depicted in the organizational chart.

### Organizational Designs

The basic configurations of international organizations correspond to those of purely domestic ones; the greater the degree of internalization, the more complex the structures can become. The types of structures that companies use to manage foreign activities can be divided into three categories, based on the degree of internationalization:

1. Little or no formal organizational recognition of international activities of the firm. This category ranges from domestic operations handling an occasional international transaction on an ad hoc basis to firms with separate export departments.
2. International division. Firms in this category recognize the ever-growing importance of the international involvement.
3. Global organizations. These can be structured by product, area, function, process, or customer, but ignore the traditional domestic-international split.

Hybrid structures may exist as well, in which one market may be structured by product, another by areas. Matrix organizations have merged in large multinational corporations to combine product-specific, regional, and functional expertise. As worldwide competition has increased dramatically in many industries, the latest organizational response is networked global organizations in which heavy flows of hardware, software, and personnel take place between strategically interdependent units to establish greater global integration.

**Little or No Formal Organization**  In the very early stages of international involvement, domestic operations assume responsibility for international activities. The role of international activities in the sales and profits of the corporation is initially so minor that no organizational adjustment takes place. No consolidation of information or authority over international sales is undertaken or is necessary. Transactions are conducted on a case-by-case basis, either by the resident expert or quite often with the help of facilitating agents, such as freight forwarders.

As demand from the international marketplace grows and interest within the firm expands, the organizational structure will reflect it. As shown in Figure 21.1, an export department appears as a separate entity. This may be an outside export management company—that is, an independent company that becomes the de facto export department of the firm. This is an indirect approach to international involvement in that very little experience is accumulated within the firm itself. Alternatively, a firm may establish its own export department, hiring a few seasoned individuals to take responsibility for international activities. Organizationally, the department may be a subdepartment of marketing (alternative b in Figure 21.1) or may have equal ranking with the various functional departments (alternative a). The choice will depend on the importance assigned to overseas activities by the firm. The export department is the first real step toward internationalizing the organizational structures; it should be a full-fledged marketing organization and not merely a sales organization.

Licensing as an international entry mode may be assigned to the R&D function despite its importance to the overall international strategy of the firm. A formal liaison among the export, marketing, production, and R&D functions has to be formed for the maximum utilization of licensing.[1] If licensing indeed becomes a major activity for the firm, a separate manager should be appointed.

The more the firm becomes involved in foreign markets, the more quickly the export department structure will become obsolete. For example, the firm may undertake joint ventures or direct foreign investment, which require those

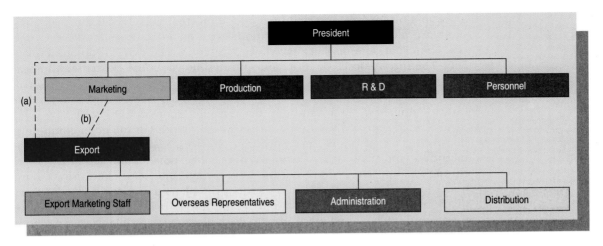

**FIGURE 21.1**

**The Export Department Structure**

involved to have functional experience. The firm therefore typically establishes an international division.

Some firms that acquire foreign production facilities pass through an additional stage in which foreign subsidiaries report directly to the president or to a manager specifically assigned the duty.[2] However, the amount of coordination and control that are required quickly establish the need for a more formal international organization in the firm.

**The International Division** The international division centralizes in one entity, with or without separate incorporation, all of the responsibility for international activities, as illustrated in Figure 21.2. The approach aims to eliminate

**FIGURE 21.2**

**The International Division Structure**

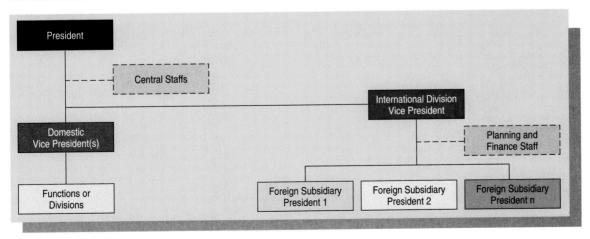

a possible bias against international operations that may exist if domestic divisions are allowed to serve international customers independently. In some cases, international markets have been treated as secondary to domestic markets. The international division concentrates international expertise, information flows concerning foreign market opportunities, and authority over international activities. However, manufacturing and other related functions remain with the domestic divisions to take advantage of economies of scale.

To avoid putting the international division at a disadvantage in competing for products, personnel, and corporate services, coordination between domestic and international operations is necessary. Coordination can be achieved through a joint staff or by requiring domestic and international divisions to interact in strategic planning and to submit the plans to headquarters. Further, many corporations require and encourage frequent interaction between domestic and international personnel to discuss common problems in areas such as product planning. At Loctite Corporation, for example, coordination is also important because domestic operations are typically organized along product or functional lines, whereas international divisions are geographically oriented.

International divisions best serve firms with few products that do not vary significantly in terms of their environmental sensitivity and with international sales and profits that are still quite insignificant compared with those of the domestic divisions.[3] Companies may outgrow their international divisions as their international sales grow in significance, diversity, and complexity. A number of U.S.–based companies in the 1970s started the shift from a traditional organizational structure with an independent international division to entities built around worldwide or global structures with no differentiation between "domestic" and "international" operations.[4]

Size in itself is not a limitation on the use of the international division structure. Some of the world's largest corporations rely on international divisions.[5] The management of these companies believes that specialization is needed, primarily in terms of the environment.

**Global Organizational Structures**   Global structures have grown out of competitive necessity. In many industries, competition is on a global basis, with a result that companies must have a high degree of reactive capability. European firms have traditionally had a global structure because of the relatively small size of their domestic markets. Philips, Nestlé, or Nokia, for example, never could have grown to their current status by relying only on their home markets.

Six basic types of global structures are available:

1. Global product structure, in which product divisions are responsible for all manufacture and marketing worldwide
2. Global area structure, in which geographic divisions are responsible for all manufacture and marketing in their respective areas
3. Global functional structures, in which functional areas (such as production, marketing, finance, and personnel) are responsible for the worldwide operations of their own functional area
4. Global customer structures, in which operations are structured based on distinct worldwide customer groups
5. Mixed—or hybrid—structures, which may combine the other alternatives

**6.** Matrix structures, in which operations have reporting responsibility to more than one group (typically, product, functions, or area)

*Product Structure*   The **product structure** is the form most often used by multinational corporations.[6] The approach gives worldwide responsibility to strategic business units for the marketing of their product lines, as shown in Figure 21.3. Most consumer-product firms use some form of this approach, mainly because of the diversity of their products. One of the major benefits of the approach is improved cost efficiency through centralization of manufacturing facilities. This is crucial in industries in which competitive position is determined by world market share, which in turn is often determined by the degree to which manufacturing is rationalized.[7] Adaptation to this approach may cause problems because it is usually accompanied by consolidation of operations and plant closings. A good example is Black & Decker, which rationalized many of its operations in its worldwide competitive effort against Makita, the Japanese power tool manufacturer. Similarly, Goodyear reorganized itself into a single global organization with a complete business-team approach for tires and general products. The move was largely prompted by tightening worldwide competition.[8]

Other benefits of the product structure are the ability to balance the functional inputs needed for a product and the ability to react quickly to product-specific problems in the marketplace. Even smaller brands receive individual attention. Product-specific attention is important because products vary in

**FIGURE 21.3**

**The Global Product Structure**

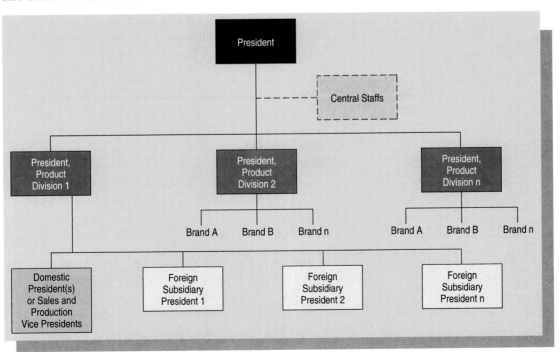

terms of the adaptation they need for different foreign markets. All in all, the product approach is ideally suited to the development of a global strategic focus in response to global competition.

At the same time, the product structure fragments international expertise within the firm because a central pool of international experience no longer exists. The structure assumes that managers will have adequate regional experience or advice to allow them to make balanced decisions. Coordination of activities among the various product groups operating in the same markets is crucial to avoid unnecessary duplication of basic tasks. For some of these tasks, such as market research, special staff functions may be created and then filled by the product divisions when needed. If they lack an appreciation for the international dimension, product managers may focus their attention only on the larger markets or only on the domestic, and fail to take the long-term view.

*Area Structure*   The second most used approach is the **area structure,** illustrated in Figure 21.4. Such firms are organized on the basis of geographical areas; for example, operations may be divided into those dealing with North America, the Far East, Latin America, and Europe. Ideally, no special preference is given to the region in which the headquarters is located—for example, North America or Europe. Central staffs are responsible for providing coordination support for worldwide planning and control activities performed at headquarters.

Regional integration is playing a major role in area structuring; for example, many multinational corporations have located their European headquarters in Brussels, where the EU has its headquarters. Procter & Gamble's Latin American subsidiaries report to the Latin American headquarters in Caracas, Venezuela, rather than to Cincinnati, where headquarters for the operations used to exist.[9] Organizational changes made at 3M Company as a result of economic integration are recounted in Global Perspective 21.1. Ideally, no special preference is given to the region in which headquarters is located. Central

**FIGURE 21.4**

**The Global Area Structure**

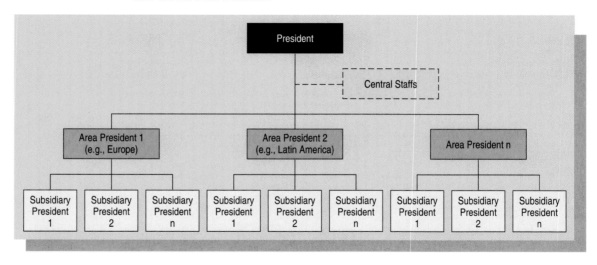

## RESTRUCTURING FOR ECONOMIC INTEGRATION

**A**s regions continue their drive toward single economic markets, companies are positioning themselves to capitalize on the opportunities such developments are providing. 3M is responding in two of its key markets, Europe and the Americas, by bold organizational moves. In Europe, the formation of European Business Centers (EBCs) is focused on reaching the pan-European marketplace more efficiently. Each of the EBCs (e.g., Malakoff in France for dental products or Diegem, Belgium, for electro products) operates along product rather than geographic lines, and each is responsible for the business functions throughout Europe.

3M's North American Operational Plan centers on organizational restructuring based on three concepts: simplification, linkage, and empowerment. The plan was fully implemented in the United States and Canada in 1992 with Mexico added in 1994. Before the restructuring, Mexico was treated "as a far-off, foreign country." Now 3M manages by area rather than by country. Key goals of the operational plan are:

■ Eliminate the role of 3M International Operations in cross-border activities within North America. All business units in Canada and Mexico will deal directly with 3M's divisions in the United States.

■ Redefine management functions. General sales and marketing managers in Canada and Mexico will have a new title—business manager—and will serve as the key link between local customers and the corresponding U.S. general managers. The business managers will also be members of 3M US's planning, pricing, and operating committees; participate in the early stages of the global business planning; and execute the global strategy in Canada and Mexico.

■ Coordinate functions and share resources among the

three countries, especially in marketing, advertising, and sales. New-product launches will be synchronized throughout North America, with standardized sizing and part numbers wherever possible. Distribution strategies and agreements will be coordinated. Sales literature, packaging, and labeling will be uniform and written in the appropriate local language.

■ Establish North American tactical teams. Members from these groups, drawn from all three countries, will work on projects such as market research, new-product development, and competitor monitoring.

■ Set up centers of excellence. To maximize efficiency and to avoid duplication of effort, each country will specialize in the function or process that it does best and eliminate those that can be performed better elsewhere. These centers may be built around manufacturing of a product or product line, market niches, customer service, or technical skills.

■ Modify performance-measurement criteria. North American performance will be gauged by North American—not U.S., Canadian, or Mexican—market share, earnings growth, and income.

At 3M Canada, major changes have taken place. Layers of management have been trimmed, communication and coordination greatly enhanced, and the requirement to go through the international division removed. Incorporating Mexico into the plan presents some unique challenges, however. For 3M U.S. headquarters, meeting or communicating electronically with Canadian counterparts is far easier than doing the same with Mexico. Language and cultural barriers also present potential challenges. Given that only products are free to cross borders—not people—sales personnel cannot solicit business across borders, and direct cross-border reporting may not be possible.

Latin America and the Caribbean are managed separately from North America at this time, but the advancement of regional economic integration may cause them to be incorporated into an Americas organization in the future.

*Source: "3M Restructuring for NAFTA," Business Latin America (July 19, 1993): 6–7.* **http://www.mmm.com**

staffs are responsible for providing coordination support for worldwide planning and control activities performed at headquarters.

The area approach follows the marketing concept most closely because individual areas and markets are given concentrated attention. If market conditions with respect to product acceptance and operating conditions vary dramatically, the area approach is the one to choose. Companies opting for this alternative typically have relatively narrow product lines with similar end uses and end users. However, expertise is needed in adapting the product and its marketing to local market conditions. Once again, to avoid duplication of effort in product management and in functional areas, staff specialists—for product categories, for example—may be used.

Without appropriate coordination from the staff, essential information and experience may not be transferred from one regional entity to another. Also, if the company expands its product lines and if end markets begin to diversify, the area structure may become inappropriate.

*Functional Structure*   Of all the approaches, the **functional structure** is the simplest from the administrative viewpoint because it emphasizes the basic tasks of the firm—for example, manufacturing, sales, and research and development. The approach, illustrated in Figure 21.5, works best when both products and customers are relatively few and similar in nature. Coordination is typically the key problem, therefore, staff functions have been created to interact between the functional areas. Otherwise, the company's marketing and regional expertise may not be exploited to the fullest extent possible.

A variation of the functional approach is one that uses processes as a basis for structure. The **process structure** is common in the energy and mining industries, where one corporate entity may be in charge of exploration worldwide and another may be responsible for the actual mining operations.

*Customer Structure*   Firms may also organize their operations using the **customer structure,** especially if the customer groups they serve are dramatically different—for example, consumers and businesses and governments. Catering to such diverse groups may require concentrating specialists in particular divisions. The product may be the same, but the buying processes of the various

**FIGURE 21.5**

**The Global Function Structure**

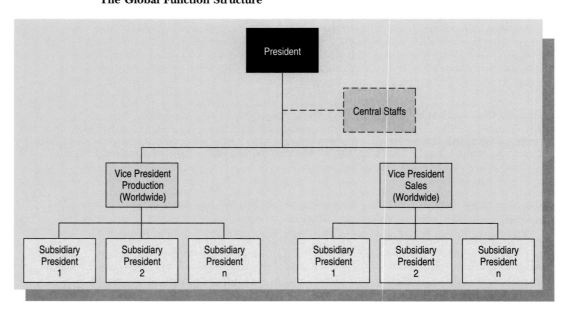

customer groups may differ. Governmental buying is characterized by bidding, in which price plays a larger role than when businesses are the buyers.

*Mixed Structure*   In some cases, mixed, or hybrid, organizations exist. A **mixed structure** combines two or more organizational dimensions simultaneously. It permits adequate attention to product, area, or functional needs as is needed by the company. The approach may only be a result of a transitional period after a merger or an acquisition, or it may come about due to unique market characteristics or product line. It may also provide a useful structure before the implementation of a worldwide matrix structure.[10] At Procter & Gamble, for example, U.S.–based operations are organized along product lines, whereas international operations are by area through four continental groups. The area organizations are divided further, for example, European operations into Northern Europe, Central Europe, Southern Europe, and Africa/Middle East. For Disposables and Beverages, the profit-and-loss responsibility has been established on a pan-European basis. As a consequence of the Richardson-Vicks acquisition, there still are two separate sets of European operations. Given environmental trends, P&G eventually may move from an area emphasis to more of a product focus.[11]

Naturally, organizational structures are never as clear-cut and simple as presented here. Whatever the basic format, product, functional, and area inputs are needed. Alternatives could include an initial product structure that would subsequently have regional groupings or an initial regional structure with subsequent product groupings. However, in the long term, coordination and control across such structures become tedious.

*Matrix Structure*   Many multinational corporations, in an attempt to facilitate planning for, organizing, and controlling interdependent businesses, critical resources, strategies, and geographic regions, have adopted the **matrix structure**.[12] Eastman Kodak shifted from a functional organization to a matrix system based on business units. Business is driven by a worldwide business unit (for example, photographic products or commercial and information systems) and implemented by a geographic unit (for example, Europe or Latin America). The geographical units, as well as their country subsidiaries, serve as the "glue" between autonomous product operations.[13]

Organizational matrices integrate the various approaches already discussed, as the Philips example in Figure 21.6 illustrates. The eight product divisions (which are then divided into sixty product groups) have rationalized manufacturing to provide products for continentwide markets rather than lines of products for individual markets. Philips has three general types of country organizations. In "key" markets, such as the United States, France, and Japan, product divisions manage their own marketing as well as manufacturing. In "local business" countries, such as Nigeria and Peru, the organizations function as importers from product divisions, and if manufacturing occurs, it is purely for the local market. In "large" markets, such as Brazil, Spain, and Taiwan, a hybrid arrangement is used, depending on the size and situation. The product divisions and the national subsidiaries interact in a matrixlike configuration, with the product divisions responsible for the globalization dimension and the national subsidiaries responsible for local representation and coordination of common areas of interest, such as recruiting.

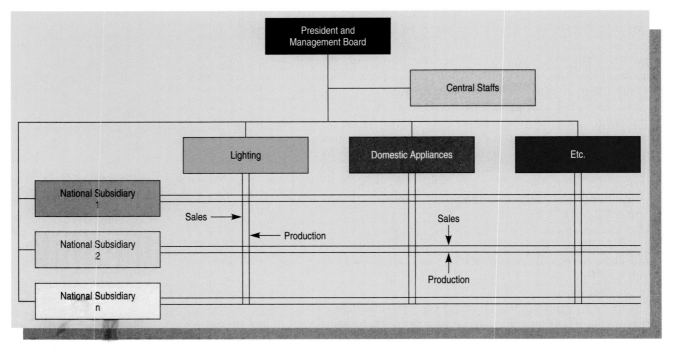

**FIGURE 21.6**

**The Global Matrix Structure at Philips**

Matrices vary in terms of their number of dimensions. For example, Dow Chemical's three-dimensional matrix consists of five geographic areas, three major functions (marketing, manufacturing, and research), and more than seventy products. The matrix approach helps cut through enormous organizational complexities in making business managers, functional managers, and strategy managers cooperate. However, the matrix requires sensitive, well-trained middle managers who can cope with problems that arise from reporting to two bosses—for example, a product-line manager and an area manager. At 3M, for example, every management unit has a multidimensional reporting relationship, which may cross functional, regional, or operational lines. For example, on a regional basis, group managers in Europe report administratively to a vice president of operations for Europe, but report functionally to group vice presidents at headquarters in Minneapolis-St. Paul.[14]

Most companies have found the matrix arrangement problematic.[15] The dual reporting channel easily causes conflict, complex issues are forced into a two-dimensional decision framework, and even minor issues may have to be solved through committee discussion. Ideally, managers should solve the problems themselves through formal and informal communication; however, physical and psychic distance often make that impossible. The matrix structure, with its inherent complexity, may actually increase the reaction time of a company, a potentially serious problem when competitive conditions require quick responses. As a result, the authority has started to shift in many organizations from area to product, although the matrix still may officially be used.

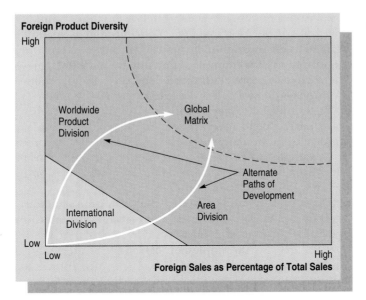

**Foreign Product Diversity**

**Foreign Sales as Percentage of Total Sales**

**FIGURE 21.7**

**Evolution of International Structures**

*Source:* From Christopher A. Bartlett, "Building and Managing the Transnational: The New Organizational Challenge," in *Competition in Global Industries,* ed. Michael E. Porter (Boston: Harvard Business School Press, 1986), 368.

**Evolution of Organizational Structures**   Companies have been shown to develop new structures in a pattern of stages as their products diversify and share of foreign sales increases.[16] At the first stage of autonomous subsidiaries reporting directly to top management; the establishment of an international division follows. As product diversity and the importance of the foreign marketplace increase, companies develop global structures to coordinate subsidiary operations and to rationalize worldwide production. As multinational corporations have been faced with simultaneous pressures to adapt to local market conditions and to rationalize production and globalize competitive reactions, many have opted for the matrix structure.[17] The matrix structure probably allows a corporation to best meet the challenges of global markets (to be global and local, big and small, decentralized with centralized reporting) by allowing the optimizing of businesses globally and maximizing performance in every country of operation.[18] The evolutionary process is summarized in Figure 21.7.

## Implementation

Organizational structures provide the frameworks for carrying out decision-making processes. However, for that decision making to be effective, a series of organizational initiatives are needed to develop strategy to its full potential, that is, to secure implementation both at the national level and across markets.[19]

Organizational structures themselves do not indicate where the authority for decision making and control rests within the organization. If subsidiaries are granted a high degree of autonomy, the system is called **decentralization.** In decentralized systems, controls are relatively loose and simple, and the flows between headquarters and subsidiaries are mainly financial; that is, each sub-

**Locus of Decision Making**

sidiary operates as a profit center. On the other hand, if controls are tight and the strategic decision making is concentrated at headquarters, the system is described as **centralization.** Firms are typically neither completely centralized nor decentralized; for example, some functions of the firm—such as finance—lend themselves to more centralized decision making; others—such as promotional decisions—do so far less. Research and development in organizations is typically centralized, especially in cases of basic research work. Some companies have, partly due to governmental pressures, added R&D functions on a regional or local basis. In many cases, however, variations are product and market based; for example, Corning Incorporated's TV tube marketing strategy requires global decision making for pricing and local decision making for service and delivery.

The basic advantage of allowing maximum flexibility at the subsidiary level is that subsidiary management knows its market and can react to changes more quickly. Problems of motivation and acceptance are avoided when decision makers are also the implementors of the strategy. On the other hand, many multinationals faced with global competitive threats and opportunities have adopted global strategy formulation, which by definition requires a higher degree of centralization. What has emerged as a result can be called **coordinated decentralization.** This means that overall corporate strategy is provided from headquarters, while subsidiaries are free to implement it within the range agreed on in consultation with headquarters.

Organizationally, the forces of globalization are changing the country manager's role significantly. With profit-and-loss responsibility, oversight of multiple functions, and the benefit of distance from headquarters, country managers enjoyed considerable decision-making autonomy as well as entrepreneurial initiative when country operations were largely stand-alone. Today, however, many companies have to emphasize global and regional priorities, which means that the power has to shift at least to some extent from the country manager to worldwide strategic business unit and product-line managers. Many of the local decisions are now subordinated to global strategic moves. Therefore, the future country manager will have to wear many hats in balancing the needs of the operation for which the manager is directly responsible with those of the entire region or strategic business unit.[20]

## Factors Affecting Structure and Decision Making

The organizational structure and locus of decision making in a multinational corporation are determined by a number of factors, such as (1) its degree of involvement in international operations, (2) the products the firm markets, (3) the size and importance of the firm's markets, and (4) the human resource capability of the firm.[21]

The effect of the degree of involvement on structure and decision making was discussed earlier in the chapter. With low degrees of involvement, subsidiaries can enjoy high degrees of autonomy as long as they meet their profit targets. The same situation can occur even with the most globally oriented companies, but within a different framework. Consider, for example, the North American Philips Corporation, a separate entity from the Dutch Philips, which enjoys independent status in terms of local policy setting and managerial practices but is still, nevertheless, within the parent company's planning and control system.

The firm's country of origin and the political history of the area can also affect organizational structure and decision making. For example, Swiss-based Nestlé, with only 3 to 4 percent of its sales from its small domestic market, has traditionally had a highly decentralized organization. Moreover, European history for the past eighty years—particularly the two world wars—has often forced subsidiaries of European-based companies to act independently to survive.

The type and variety of products marketed will affect organizational decisions. Companies that market consumer products typically have product organizations with high degrees of decentralization, allowing for maximum local flexibility. On the other hand, companies that market technologically sophisticated products—such as GE, which markets turbines—display centralized organizations with worldwide product responsibilities. Even within matrix organizations, one of the dimensions may be granted more say in decisions; for example, at Dow Chemical, geographical managers have been granted more authority than other managers.

Going global has recently meant transferring world headquarters of important business units abroad. For example, Hyundai Electronics Industries moved its personal computer division to San Jose, California, from Seoul, South Korea, to better compete in that industry's biggest market.[22]

## The Networked Global Organization

No international structure is ideal and some have challenged the wisdom of even looking for one. They have recommended attention to new processes that would, in a given structure, help to develop new perspectives and attitudes that reflect and respond to the complex, opposing demands of global integration and local responsiveness.[23] The question thus changes from which structural alternative is best to how the different perspectives of various corporate entities can better be taken into account when making decisions. In structural terms, nothing may change. As a matter of fact, Philips has not changed its basic matrix structure, yet major changes have occurred in internal relations.[24] The basic change was from a decentralized federation model to a networked global organization, the effects of which are depicted in Figure 21.8. The term **glocal** has been coined to describe this approach.[25]

Companies that have adopted the approach have incorporated the following three dimensions into their organizations: (1) the development and communication of a clear corporate vision, (2) the effective management of human resource tools to broaden individual perspectives and develop identification with corporate goals, and (3) the integration of individual thinking and activities into the broad corporate agenda.[26] The first dimension relates to a clear and consistent long-term corporate mission that guides individuals wherever they work in the organization. Examples of this are Johnson & Johnson's corporate credo of customer focus and NEC's C&C (computers and communications). The second relates both to the development of global managers who can find opportunities in spite of environmental challenges as well as creating a global perspective among country managers. The last dimension relates to the development of a cooperative mind-set among country organizations to ensure effective implementation of global strategies. Managers may believe that global strategies are intrusions on their operations if they do not have an understanding of the corporate vision, if they have not contributed to the global corporate agenda, or if they are not given direct responsibility for its imple-

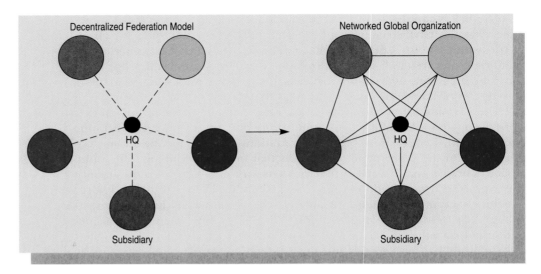

**FIGURE 21.8**

**The Networked Global Organization**

*Source:* Thomas Gross, Ernie Turner, and Lars Cederholm, "Building Teams for Global Operations," *Management Review,* June 1987 (New York: American Management Association), 34.

mentation. Defensive, territorial attitudes can lead to the emergence of the **"not-invented-here" syndrome,** that is, country organizations objecting to or rejecting an otherwise sound strategy.

The network avoids the problems of effort duplication, inefficiency and resistance to ideas developed elsewhere by giving subsidiaries the latitude, encouragement, and tools to pursue local business development within the framework of the global strategy. Headquarters considers each unit a source of ideas, skills, capabilities, and knowledge that can be utilized for the benefit of the entire organization. This means that subsidiaries must be upgraded from mere implementors and adaptors to contributors and partners in the development and execution of worldwide strategies. Efficient plants may be converted into international production centers, innovative R&D units converted into centers of excellence (and thus role models), and leading subsidiary groups given the leadership role in developing new strategies for the entire corporation. At Ford Motor Company, development of a specific car or component is centralized in whichever Ford technical center worldwide has the greatest expertise in that product.

One tool for implementing this approach is international teams of managers who meet regularly to develop strategy. While final direction may come from headquarters, it has been informed of local conditions, and implementation of the strategy is enhanced since local-country managers were involved in its development. The approach has worked even in cases involving seemingly impossible market differences. Both Procter & Gamble and Henkel have successfully introduced pan-European brands for which strategy was developed by European teams. These teams consisted of country managers and staff personnel to smooth eventual implementation and to avoid unnecessarily long and disruptive discussions about the fit of a new product to individual markets.

The term *network* also implies two-way communications between head-quarters and subsidiaries and between subsidiaries themselves. While this communication can take the form of newsletters or regular and periodic meetings of appropriate personnel, new technologies are allowing businesses to link far-flung entities and eliminate the traditional barriers of time and distance. **Intranets** integrate a company's information assets into a single accessible system using Internet-based technologies such as e-mail, news groups, and the World Wide Web. In effect, the formation of **virtual teams** becomes a reality. For example, employees at Levi Strauss & Co. can join an electronic discussion group with colleagues around the world, watch the latest Levi's commercials, or comment on latest business programs or plans.[27] The benefits of Intranet are (1) increased productivity in that there is no longer a time lag between an idea and the information needed to assess and implement it; (2) enhanced knowledge capital, which is constantly updated and upgraded; (3) facilitated teamwork enabling on-line communication at insignificant expense; and (4) incorporation of best practice at a moment's notice by allowing managers and functional-area personnel to make to-the-minute decisions anywhere in the world.

As can be seen from the discussion, the networked approach is not a structural adaptation but a procedural one, calling for a change in management mentality. It requires adjustment mainly in the coordination and control functions of the firm. And while there is still considerable disagreement as to which of the approaches work, some measures have been shown to correlate with success as seen in Global Perspective 21.2. Of the many initiatives developed to enhance the workings of a networked global organization, such as cross-border task forces and establishment of centers of excellence, the most significant was the use of electronic networking capabilities.[28]

## The Role of Country Organizations

Country organizations should be treated as a source of supply as much as a source of demand. Quite often, however, headquarters managers see their role as the coordinators of key decisions and controllers of resources and perceive subsidiaries as implementors and adaptors of global strategy in their respective local markets. Furthermore, they may see all country organizations as the same. This view severely limits utilization of the firm's resources and deprives country managers of the opportunity to exercise their creativity.[29]

The role that a particular country organization can play naturally depends on that market's overall strategic importance as well as its organizational competence. Using these criteria, four different roles emerge, as shown in Figure 21.9.

The role of a **strategic leader** can be played by a highly competent national subsidiary located in a strategically critical market. Such a country organization serves as a partner of headquarters in developing and implementing strategy. Procter & Gamble's Eurobrand teams, which analyze opportunities for greater product and marketing program standardization, are chaired by a brand manager from a "lead country."[30]

A **contributor** is a country organization with a distinctive competence, such as product development. Increasingly, country organizations are the source of new products. These range from IBM's recent breakthrough in superconductivity research, generated in its Zurich lab, to low-end innovations such as Proc-

**FIGURE 21.9**

**Roles for Country Organizations**

*Source:* Christopher Bartlett and Sumantra Ghoshal, "Tap Your Subsidiaries for Global Reach," *Harvard Business Review* 64, November–December 1986 (Boston: Harvard Business School Publishing Division), 87–94.

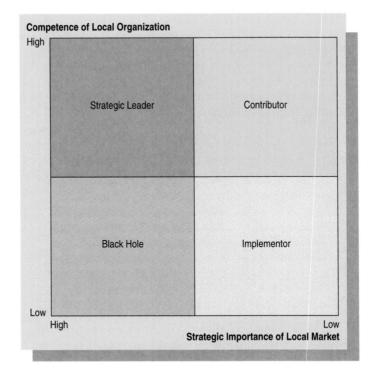

ter & Gamble's liquid Tide, made with a fabric-softening compound developed in Europe.[31] Similarly, country organizations may be designated as worldwide centers of excellence for a particular product category, such as ABB Strömberg in Finland for electric drives, a category for which it is a recognized world leader.[32]

**Implementors** provide the critical mass for the international marketing effort. These country organizations may exist in smaller, less-developed countries in which there is less corporate commitment for market development. Although most entities are given this role, it should not be slighted, since the implementors provide the opportunity to capture economies of scale and scope that are the basis of a global strategy.

The **black hole** situation is one in which the international marketer has a low-competence country organization—or no organization at all—in a highly strategic market. In strategically important markets such as the European Union, a local presence is necessary to maintain the company's global position and, in some cases, to protect others. One of the major ways of remedying the black hole situation is to enter into strategic alliances. For example, AT&T, which had long restricted itself to its domestic market, needed to go global fast. Some of the alliances it formed were with Philips in telecommunications and Olivetti in computers and office automation.[33] In some cases, firms may use their presence in a major market as an observation post to keep up with developments before a major thrust for entry is executed.

Depending on the role of the country organization, its relationship with headquarters will vary from loose control based mostly on support to tighter control to ensure that strategies get implemented appropriately. Yet, in each of these cases, it is imperative that country organizations have enough oper-

# CHARACTERISTICS OF SUCCESS

**A** survey of chief executive officers of forty-three leading U.S. consumer companies by McKinsey & Co. sheds light on organizational features that distinguish internationally successful companies. Companies were classified as more or less successful compared to their specific industry average, using international sales and profit growth over a five-year period as the most important indicators of success.

The survey results indicate eleven distinctive traits that are correlated with high performance in international markets. The following are moves that companies can make to enhance prospects for international success:

- Take a different approach to international decision making.
- Differentiate treatment of international subsidiaries.

- Let product managers in subsidiaries report to the country general manager.
- Have a worldwide management development program.
- Make international experience a condition for promotion to top management.
- Have a more multinational management group.
- Support international managers with global electronic networking capabilities.
- Manage cross-border acquisitions particularly well.
- Have overseas R & D centers.
- Focus on international.
- Remain open to organizational change and continuous self-renewal.

In general, successful companies coordinate their international decision making globally, with more central direction than less successful competitors, as seen in the accompanying exhibit. The difference is most marked in brand positioning, designing packaging, and setting prices. The one notable exception is an increasing tendency to decentralize product development.

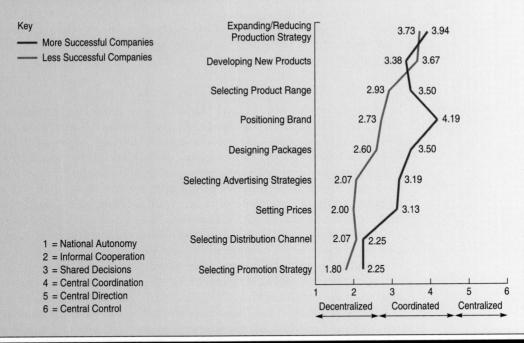

Key
— More Successful Companies
— Less Successful Companies

1 = National Autonomy
2 = Informal Cooperation
3 = Shared Decisions
4 = Central Coordination
5 = Central Direction
6 = Central Control

| Strategy | More | Less |
|---|---|---|
| Expanding/Reducing Production Strategy | 3.73 | 3.94 |
| Developing New Products | 3.38 | 3.67 |
| Selecting Product Range | 2.93 | 3.50 |
| Positioning Brand | 2.73 | 4.19 |
| Designing Packages | 2.60 | 3.50 |
| Selecting Advertising Strategies | 2.07 | 3.19 |
| Setting Prices | 2.00 | 3.13 |
| Selecting Distribution Channel | 2.07 | 2.25 |
| Selecting Promotion Strategy | 1.80 | 2.25 |

1 — 2 (Decentralized) — 3 — 4 (Coordinated) — 5 — 6 (Centralized)

*Source: Ingo Theuerkauf, David Ernst, and Amir Mahini, "Think Local, Organize . . . ?* **International Marketing Review 13, (1996):** 7–12.

ating independence to cater to local needs and to provide motivation to country managers. For example, an implementor's ideas concerning the development of a regional or global strategy or program should be heard. Strategy formulators should make sure that appropriate implementation can be achieved at the country level.

# Controls

The function of the organizational structure is to provide a framework in which objectives can be met. A set of instruments and processes is needed, however, to influence the performance of organizational members so as to meet the goals. Controls focus on means to verify and correct actions that differ from established plans. Compliance needs to be secured from subordinates through different means of coordinating specialized and interdependent parts of the organization.[34] Within an organization, control serves as an integrating mechanism. Controls are designed to reduce uncertainty, increase predictability, and ensure that behaviors originating in separate parts of the organization are compatible and in support of common organizational goals despite physical, psychic, and temporal distances.[35]

The critical issue here is the same as with organizational structure: What is the ideal amount of control? On the one hand, headquarters needs controls to ensure that international activities contribute the greatest benefit to the overall organization. On the other hand, they should not be construed as a code of laws and subsequently allowed to stifle local initiative.

This section will focus on the design and functions of control instruments available for international business operations, along with an assessment of their appropriateness. Emphasis will be placed on the degree of formality of controls used by firms.

## Types of Controls

Most organizations display some administrative flexibility, as demonstrated by variations in how they apply management directives, corporate objectives, or measurement systems. A distinction should be made, however, between variations that have emerged by design and those that are the result of autonomy. The first are the result of a management decision, whereas the second typically have grown without central direction and are based on emerging practices. In both instances, some type of control will be exercised. Controls that result from headquarters initiative rather than those that are the consequences of tolerated practices will be discussed here. Firms that wait for self-emerging controls often experience rapid international growth but subsequent problems in product-line performance, program coordination, and strategic planning.[36]

Whatever the system, it is important in today's competitive environment to have internal benchmarking. This relates to organizational learning and sharing of best practices throughout the corporate system to avoid the costs of reinventing solutions that have already been discovered. A description of the knowledge transfer is provided in Global Perspective 21.3. Three critical features are necessary in sharing best practice. First, there needs to be a device for organizational memory. For example, at Xerox, contributors to solutions can send their ideas to an electronic library where they are indexed and provided to potential adopters in the corporate family. Second, best practice must be updated and adjusted to new situations. For example, best practice adopted by a company's China office will be modified and customized, and this learning should then become part of the database. Finally, best practice must be legitimized. This calls for a shared understanding that exchanging knowledge across units

## INTERNATIONAL BEST PRACTICE EXCHANGE

**A**s growing competitive pressures challenge many global firms, strategies to improve the transfer of best practice across geographically dispersed units and time zones becomes critical. The premise is that a company with the same product range targeting the same markets panregionally should be able to use knowledge gained in one market throughout the organization. The fact is, however, that companies use only 20 percent of their most precious resources—knowledge, in the form of technical information, market data, internal know-how, and processes and procedures. Trying to transfer best practices internationally amplifies the problem even more.

U.K.–based copier maker Rank Xerox, with its thirty eight operating companies, is working hard to make better use of the knowledge that resides within those companies. A thirty five-person group identified nine practices that could be applicable throughout the group. These ranged from the way the Australian subsidiary retains customers to Italy's method of gathering competitive intelligence to a procedure for handling new major accounts in Spain. These practices were thought to

be easier to "sell" to other operating companies, easy to implement, and would provide a good return on investment.

Three countries were much quicker in introducing new products successfully than others. In the case of France, this was related to the training given to employees. The subsidiary gave its sales staff three days of hands-on practice, including competitive benchmarking. Before they attended the course, salespeople were given reading materials and were tested when they arrived. Those remaining were evaluated again at the end of the course, and performance reports were sent to their managers.

The difficult task is to achieve buy-in from the other country organizations. Six months might be spent in making detailed presentations of the best practices to all the companies and an additional three years helping them implement the needed changes. It is imperative that the country manager is behind the proposal in each subsidiary's case. However, implementation cannot be left to the country organizations after the concept has been presented. This may result in the dilution of both time and urgency and with possible country-specific customization that negate comparisons and jeopardize the success of the change.

While only half of the recommendations have been adopted by half of the organization, senior executives at Rank Xerox are pleased with the $400 million savings that are attributed to the changes so far.

*Source: Michael McGann, "Chase Harnesses Data with Lotus Notes,"* Bank Systems and Technology 34 *(May, 1997): 38; "Rank Xerox Aims at Sharing Knowledge,"* Crossborder Monitor *(September 18, 1996): 8; "World-wise: Effective Networking Distinguishes These 25 Global Companies,"* Computerworld *(August 26, 1996): 7.* **http://www.rankxerox.co.uk**

is organizationally valued and that these systems are important mechanisms for knowledge exchange. Use can be encouraged by including an assessment in employee performance evaluations of how effectively employees share information with colleagues.

**WWW**

In the design of the control systems, a major decision concerns the object of control. Two major objects are typically identified: output and behavior.[37] Output controls include balance sheets, sales data, production data, product-line growth, and performance reviews of personnel. Measures of output are accumulated at regular intervals and forwarded from the foreign locale to headquarters, where they are evaluated and critiqued based on comparisons to the plan or budget. Behavioral controls require the exertion of influence over behavior after—or, ideally, before—it leads to action. Behavioral controls can be achieved through the preparation of manuals on such topics as sales techniques to be made available to subsidiary personnel or through efforts to fit new employees into the corporate culture.

To institute either of these measures, instruments of control have to be decided upon. The general alternatives are either bureaucratic/formalized control or cultural control.[38] Bureaucratic controls consist of a limited and explicit set of regulations and rules that outline the desired levels of performance. Cultural controls, on the other hand, are much less formal and are the result of shared beliefs and expectations among the members of an organization. Table 21.1 provides a schematic explanation of the types of controls and their objectives.

**Bureaucratic/Formalized Control**  The elements of a bureaucratic/formalized control system are (1) an international budget and planning system, (2) the functional reporting system, and (3) policy manuals used to direct functional performance.

*Budgets* refers to shorter term guidelines regarding investment, cash, and personnel policies, while *plans* refers to formalized plans with more than a one-year horizon. The budget and planning process is the major control instrument in headquarters-subsidiary relationships. Although systems and their execution vary, the objective is to achieve as good a fit as possible with the objectives and characteristics of the firm and its environment.

The budgetary period is typically one year, since it is tied to the accounting systems of the multinational. The budget system is used for four main purposes: (1) allocation of funds among subsidiaries, (2) planning and coordination of global production capacity and supplies, (3) evaluation of subsidiary performance, and (4) communication and information exchange among subsidiaries, product organizations, and corporate headquarters,[39] Long-range plans vary dramatically, ranging from two years to ten years in length, and are more qualitative and judgmental in nature. However, shorter periods such as two years are the norm, considering the added uncertainty of diverse foreign environments.

Although firms strive for uniformity, achieving it may be as difficult as trying to design a suit to fit the average person. The processes themselves are very formalized in terms of the schedules to be followed.

Functional reports are another control instrument used by headquarters in managing subsidiary relations. These vary in number, complexity, and frequency. Table 21.2 summarizes the various types of functional reports used in a total of 117 multinational corporations in the United States, Germany, and Japan. The structure and elements of the reports are typically highly standardized to allow for consolidation in the headquarters level.

Since the frequency of reports required from subsidiaries is likely to increase due to globalization, it is essential that subsidiaries see the rationale for the often time-consuming exercise. Two approaches, used in tandem, can fa-

**TABLE 21.1**

**Comparison of Bureaucratic and Cultural Control Mechanisms**

| | Type of Control | |
|---|---|---|
| **Object of Control** | **Pure Bureaucratic/Formalized Control** | **Pure Cultural Control** |
| Output | Formal performance reports | Shared norms of performance |
| Behavior | Company policies, manuals | Shared philosophy of management |

*Source:* B.R. Baliga and Alfred M. Jaeger, "Multinational Corporations: Control Systems and Delegation Issues," *Journal of International Business Studies* 15 (Fall 1984): 25–40.

**TABLE 21.2**

**Types of Functional Reports in Multinational Corporations**

| Type of Report | U.S. MNCs (33) | German MNCs (44) | Japanese MNCs (40) |
|---|---|---|---|
| Balance sheet | 97 | 49 | 42 |
| Profit and loss statements | 91 | 49 | 42 |
| Production output | 94 | 50 | 47 |
| Market share | 70 | 48 | 31 |
| Cash and credit statement | 100 | 41 | 39 |
| Inventory levels | 88 | 46 | 38 |
| Sales per product | 88 | 37 | 44 |
| Performance review of personnel | 9 | 15 | 2 |
| Report on local economic and political conditions | 33 | 32 | 12 |

*Source:* Anant R. Negandhi and Martin Welge, *Beyond Theory Z* (Greenwich, Conn.: JAI, 1984): 18.

cilitate the process: participation and feedback. The first refers to avoiding the perception at subsidiary levels that reports are "art for art's sake" by involving the preparers in the actual use of the reports. When this is not possible, feedback about their consequences is warranted. Through this process, communication is enhanced as well.

On the behavioral front, headquarters may want to guide the way in which subsidiaries make decisions and implement agreed-upon strategies. U.S.–based multinationals tend to be far more formalized than their Japanese and European counterparts, with a heavy reliance on manuals for all major functions.[40] The manuals discuss such items as recruitment, training, motivation, and dismissal policies. The use of manuals is in direct correlation with the required level of reports from subsidiaries, discussed in the previous section.

**Cultural Control**   As seen from the country comparisons, less emphasis is placed outside the United States on formal controls, as they are viewed as too rigid and too quantitatively oriented. Rather, MNCs in other countries emphasize corporate values and culture, and evaluations are based on the extent to which an individual or entity fits in with the norms. Cultural controls require an extensive socialization process to which informal, personal interaction is central. Substantial resources have to be spent to train the individual to share the corporate cultures, or "the way things are done at the company."[41] To build common vision and values, managers spend a substantial share of their first months at Matsushita in what the company calls "cultural and spiritual training." They study the company credo, the "Seven Spirits of Matsushita," and the philosophy of the founder, Konosuke Matsushita and learn how to translate the internalized lessons into daily behavior and operational decisions. Although more prevalent in Japanese organizations, many Western entities have similar programs, such as Philips's "organization cohesion training" and Unilever's "indoctrination."[42] This corporate acculturation will be critical to achieve the acceptance of possible transfers of best practice within the organization.[43]

The primary instruments of cultural control are the careful selection and training of corporate personnel and the institution of self-control. The choice of cultural controls can be justified if the company enjoys a low turnover rate; they are thus applied when companies can offer and expect lifetime or long-term employment, as many firms do in Japan.

In selecting home-country nationals and, to some extent, third-country nationals, MNCs are exercising cultural control. The assumption is that the managers have already internalized the norms and values of the company. For example, only four of 3M's fifty-three managing directors of overseas subsidiaries are local nationals. The company's experience is that nonnationals tend to run a country organization with a more global view. In some cases, the use of headquarters personnel to ensure uniformity in decision making may be advisable; for example, Volvo uses a home-country national for the position of chief financial officer. Expatriates are used in subsidiaries not only for control purposes but also to effect change processes. Companies control the efforts of management specifically through compensation and promotion policies, as well as through policies concerning replacement.

When the expatriate corps is small, headquarters can still exercise its control through other means. Management training programs for overseas managers as well as time at headquarters will indoctrinate individuals to the company's ways of doing things. For instance, a Chinese executive selected to run Loctite's new operation in China spent two years at the company's headquarters before taking over in Beijing.[44] Similarly, formal visits by headquarters teams (for example, for a strategy audit) or informal visits (perhaps to launch a new product) will enhance the feeling of belonging to the same corporate family.

Corporations rarely use one pure control mechanism. Rather, most use both quantitative and qualitative measures. Corporations are likely, however, to place different levels of emphasis on different types of performance measures and on how they are derived.

## Exercising Controls

Within most corporations, different functional areas are subject to different guidelines because they are subject to different constraints. For example, the marketing function has traditionally been seen as incorporating many more behavioral dimensions than manufacturing or finance. As a result, many multinational corporations employ control systems that are responsive to the needs of the function. Yet such differentiation is sometimes based less on appropriateness than on personalities. It has been hypothesized that manufacturing subsidiaries are controlled more intensively than sales subsidiaries because production more readily lends itself to centralized direction, and technicians and engineers adhere more firmly to standards and regulations than do salespeople.[45]

In their international operations, U.S.–based multinationals place major emphasis on obtaining quantitative data. Although this allows for good centralized comparisons against standards and benchmarks or cross-comparisons among different corporate units, it entails several drawbacks. In the international environment, new dimensions—such as inflation, differing rates of taxation, and exchange rate fluctuations—may distort the performance evaluation of any given individual or organizational unit. For the global corporation, measurement of whether a business unit in a particular country is earning a superior return on investment relative to risk may be irrelevant to the contribution an investment may make worldwide or to the long-term results of the firm. In the short term, the return may even be negative.[46] Therefore, the control mechanism may quite inappropriately indicate reward or punishment. Standardizing the information received may be difficult if the various environments involved fluctuate and require frequent and major adaptations. Further complicating the issue is the fact that although quantitative information may be collected monthly, or at least quarterly, environmental data may be acquired annually or "now and then," especially when a crisis seems to loom on the horizon. To design a control system that is acceptable not only to headquarters but also to the organization and individuals abroad, great care must be taken to use only relevant data. Major concerns, therefore, are the data collection process and the analysis and utilization of data. Evaluators need management information systems that provide for greater comparability and equity in administering controls. The more behaviorally based and culture-oriented controls are, the more care needs to be taken.[47]

In designing a control system, management must consider the costs of establishing and maintaining it versus the benefits to be gained. Any control system will require investment in a management structure and in systems design. Consider, for example, costs associated with cultural controls: personal interaction, use of expatriates, and training programs are all quite expensive. Yet these expenses may be justified by cost savings through lower employee turnover, an extensive worldwide information system, and an improved control system.[48] Moreover, the impact goes beyond the administrative component. If controls are misguided or too time-consuming, they can slow or undermine the strategy implementation process and thus the overall capability of the firm. The result will be lost opportunities or, worse yet, increased threats. In addition, time spent on reporting takes time from everything else, and if the exercise is seen as mundane, it results in lowered motivation. A parsimonious design is therefore imperative. The control system should collect all the information required and trigger all the intervention necessary; however, it should not lead to the pulling of strings by a puppeteer.

The impact of the environment has to be taken into account, as well, in two ways. First, the control system must measure only those dimensions over which the organization has actual control. Rewards or sanctions make little sense if they are based on dimensions that may be relevant to overall corporate performance but over which no influence can be exerted, such as price controls. Neglecting the factor of individual performance capability would send wrong signals and severely harm motivation. Second, control systems have to be in harmony with local regulations and customs. In some cases, however, corporate behavioral controls have to be exercised against local customs even though overall operations may be affected negatively. This type of situation occurs, for example, when a subsidiary operates in markets in which unauthorized facilitating payments are a common business practice.

Corporations are faced with major challenges in appropriate and adequate control systems in today's business environment. Given increased local government demands for a share in companies established, controls can become tedious, especially if the MNC is a minority partner. Even if the new entity is a result of two companies' joining forces through a merger—such as the one between Ciba and Sandoz to create Novartis—or two companies joining forces to form a new entity—such as Siecor established by Siemens AG and Corning

Incorporated—the backgrounds of the partners may be different enough to cause problems in devising the required controls.

## Summary

This chapter discussed the structures and control mechanisms needed to operate in the international business field. The elements define relationships between the entities of the firm and provide the channels through which the relationships develop.

International firms can choose from a variety of organizational structures, ranging from a domestic organization that handles ad hoc export orders to a full-fledged global organization. The choice will depend heavily on the degree of internationalization of the firm, the diversity of international activities, and the relative importance of product, area, function, and customer variables in the process. A determining factor is also the degree to which headquarters wants to decide important issues concerning the whole corporation and the individual subsidiaries. Organizations that function effectively still need to be revisited periodically to ensure that they remain responsive to a changing environment. Some of the responsiveness is showing up not as structural changes, but rather in how the entities conduct their internal business.

In addition to organization, the control function takes on major importance for multinationals, due to the high variability in performance resulting from divergent local environments and the need to reconcile local objectives with the corporate goal of synergism. While it is important to grant autonomy to country organizations so that they can be responsive to local market needs, it is of equal importance to ensure close cooperation among units to optimize corporate effectiveness.

Control can be exercised through bureaucratic means, which emphasize formal reporting and evaluation of benchmark data or through cultural means, in which norms and values are understood by the individuals and entities that make up the corporation. U.S. firms typically rely more on bureaucratic controls, while MNCs from other countries frequently run operations abroad through informal means and rely less on stringent measures.

The implementation of controls requires great sensitivity to behavioral dimensions and the environment. The measurements used must be appropriate and reflective of actual performance rather than marketplace vagaries. Similarly, entities should be judged only on factors over which they have some degree of control.

Table 21.3 shows how some of the world's most successful multinational corporations deal with the organizational and control issues discussed in this chapter. As can be seen in the table, they use widely varying approaches to achieve an overall balance between control and attention to local conditions.

## Key Terms and Concepts

| | | |
|---|---|---|
| product structure | matrix structure | Intranet |
| area structure | decentralization | virtual team |
| functional structure | centralization | strategic leader |
| process structure | coordinated decentralization | contributor |
| customer structure | glocal | implementor |
| mixed structure | not-invented-here syndrome | black hole |

## Questions for Discussion

1. Firms differ, often substantially, in their organizational structures even within the same industry. What accounts for the differences in their approaches?
2. Discuss the benefits gained by adopting a matrix form of organizational structure.
3. What changes in the firm and/or in the environment might cause a firm to abandon the functional approach?
4. Is there more to the not-invented-here syndrome than simply hurt feelings on the part of those who believe they are being dictated to by headquarters?
5. "Implementors are the most imporant country organizations in terms of buy-in for a global strategy." Comment.
6. Improving internal communications is an objective for networked global organizations. Using the Web site of the Lotus Development Corporation **(http://www.lotus.com)** and their section on solutions and success stories, outline how companies have used Lotus Notes to help companies interactively share information.

7. Why do European-based multinational corporations differ from U.S.–based corporations in the instruments they choose for exerting control?
8. One of the most efficient means of control is self-control. What type of program would you prepare for an incoming employee?

## Recommended Readings

Bartlett, Christopher, and Sumantra Ghoshal. *Managing Across Borders*. Cambridge, Mass.: Harvard Business Press, 1989.

Davidson, William H., and José de la Torre. *Managing the Global Corporation*. New York: McGraw-Hill, 1989.

Hedlung, Gunar, and Per Aman. *Managing Relationships with Foreign Subsidiaries*. Stockholm, Sweden: Mekan, 1984.

Humes, Samuel. *Managing the Multinational: Confronting the Global-Local Dilemma*. London, England: Prentice-Hall, 1993.

Moran, Robert T., Philip R. Harris, and William G.

Strip. *Developing the Global Organization*. Houston, TX: Gulf Publishing Co., 1993.

Negandhi, Anant, and Martin Welge. *Beyond Theory Z*. Greenwich, Conn.: JAI Press, 1984.

Otterback, Lars, ed. *The Management of Headquarters-Subsidiary Relationships in Multinational Corporations*. Aldershot, England: Gower Publishing Company, 1981.

Porter, Michael E., ed. *Competition in Global Industries*. Boston: Harvard Business School Press, 1986.

*Transforming the Global Corporation*. New York: The Economist Intelligence Unit, 1994.

## Notes

1. Michael Z. Brooke, *International Management: A Review of Strategies and Operations* (London: Hutchinson, 1986); 173–174.
2. Stefan Robock and Kenneth Simmonds, *International Business and Multinational Enterprises* (Homewood, Ill.: Richard D. Irwin, 1973), 429.
3. Richard D. Robinson, *Internationalization of Business: An Introduction* (Hinsdale, Ill.: The Dryden Press, 1984).
4. William H. Davidson and Philippe Haspeslagh, "Shaping a Global Product Organization," *Harvard Business Review* 59 (March/April 1982): 69–76.

5. L. S. Walsh, *International Marketing* (Plymouth, England: MacDonald and Evans, 1981), 161.
6. See Joan P. Curhan, William H. Davidson, and Suri Rajan, *Tracing the Multinationals* (Cambridge, Mass.: Ballinger, 1977); M.E. Wicks, *A Comparative Analysis of the Foreign Investment Evaluation Practices of U.S.–based Multinational Corporations* (New York: McKinsey & Co., 1980); and Lawrence G. Franko, "Organizational Structures and Multinational Strategies of Continental European Enterprises," in *European Research in International Business,* ed. Michel Ghertman and James Leontiades (Amster-

**TABLE 21.3**

**Organizational and Control Characteristics of Selected Multinational Corporations**

| Company | Dominant Organizational Concept | Planning and Control | Research and/or Product Development | Handling of U.S. Business |
|---|---|---|---|---|
| Novartis (Switzerland) | Product divisions with global responsibility. | Moderate reliance on strategic planning by global product divisions: gradual buildup of the role of key regional companies in the planning process; operational plans and capital budgets by country organizations and their product divisions, with the latter playing the more active role. | Research and product development activities carried out by domestic product divisions and certain product divisions by key geographic areas. | Dual-reporting relationship with U.S. company reporting directly to headquarters and its local divisions also reporting to their counterpart domestic divisions. |
| Imperial Chemical Industries (U.K.) | Strategic business units with global responsibility supported by limited regional organization, especially in developing markets. | Strategic and operational planning at the strategic business level with portfolio, financial, and other performance monitoring tightly controlled by headquarters. | Research and product/process development driven by the business units sometimes using shared regional facilities. A network of technical staff provides custodianship of identified technological areas of core competence. | U.S. board sets local policies and standards for U.S. units, which operate within the strategies agreed on for the international strategic business. |
| Philips Electronics N.V (The Netherlands) | Product divisions with global responsibility. | Moderate to heavy reliance on strategic planning by product divisions, selected national organizations, and Central Planning Department; operational plans by division and national organizations, with initiative from the former; monthly review of performance. | Highly centralized research, but with product development by product divisions; research centers located in U.S. plus other key countries. | Philips Electronics North America Corporation, New York, reports to parent and coordinates corporate services for domestic product divisions. Certain U.S. product divisions operate research, design, and manufacturing centers abroad. U.S. divisions also export, particularly components. |

dam, Holland: North Holland Publishing Co., 1977).

7. Davidson and Haspeslagh, "Shaping a Global Product Organization."

8. "How Goodyear Sharpened Organization and Production for a Tough World Market," *Business International* (January 16, 1989): 11–14.

9. "Integration for Profit," *Business Latin America* (July 5, 1993): 6–7.

10. Daniel Robey, *Designing Organizations: A Macro Per-* spective (Homewood, Ill.: Richard D. Irwin, 1982), 327.

11. Samuel Humes, *Managing the Multinational* (London, England: Prentice-Hall, 1993), 143.

12. Thomas H. Naylor, "International Strategy Matrix," *Columbia Journal of World Business* 20 (Summer 1985): 11–19.

13. "Kodak's Matrix System Focuses on Product Business Units," *Business International* (July 18, 1988): 221–223.

**TABLE 21.3 (CONTINUED)**

| Company | Dominant Organizational Concept | Planning and Control | Research and/or Product Development | Handling of U.S. Business |
|---|---|---|---|---|
| Rhône-Poulenc S.A. (France) | Product divisions with global responsibility, but special status business enterprises responsible for operations in geographical zones: North America, Europe, Latin America, and Asia/Pacific. | Strategic planning responsibility resides with business leaders. Each business has leader in one of the four zones designated to provide strategic leadership to worldwide business | Research and product development activities carried out by product divisions, several large centers, each focusing on different specializations. | Special reporting relationship directly to headquarters. U.S. Company coordinates activities with product divisions at headquarters. |
| Solvay S.A. (Belgium) | Management of product sectors have primary responsibility for strategic direction of business activities (with functional support from regional organizations). Delegation of authority and responsibility as much as possible to create a lean, participative, and entrepreneurial organization that is highly responsive to the market. | Overall strategy and budgets are defined by sector by the senior management of the parent company, in consultation with regional organizations. | A central research and product development activity, with major national organizations also carrying out product development (main research centers: USA—Houston, Tex.; Minneapolis, Minn.; Atlanta, Ga.; Elkhart, Ind.; Europe—Belgium, the Netherlands, Germany, France, Italy, the United Kingdom; Asia—Tokyo; South America—Brazil) | U.S. holding company and its subsidiaries are legal entities. Holding company oversees activities of subsidiaries, which are responsible for conducting operations within strategic guidelines set by sector management at European parent. |

*Source:* Company data collected by interview, January 1995. Original chart appears in Drake Rodman and Lee M. Caudill, "Management of the Large Multinational: Trends and Future Challenges," *Business Horizons* 24 (May–June 1981): 88–90.

14. "How 3M Develops Managers to Meet Global Strategic Objectives," *Business International* (March 21, 1988): 81–82.
15. Thomas J. Peters, "Beyond the Matrix Organization," *Business Horizons* 22 (October 1979): 15–27.
16. See John M. Stopford and Louis T. Wells, *Managing the Multinational Enterprise* (New York: Basic Books, 1972); also A. D. Chandler, *Strategy and Structure* (Cambridge, Mass.: MIT Press, 1962); and B. R. Scott, *Stages of Corporate Development* (Boston: ICCH, 1971).
17. Stanley M. Davis, "Trends in the Organization of Multinational Corporations," *Columbia Journal of World Business* 11 (Summer 1976): 59–71.
18. William Taylor, "The Logic of Global Business," *Harvard Business Review* 68 (March–April 1990): 91–105.
19. Ilkka A. Ronkainen, "Thinking Globally, Implementing Successfuly," *International Marketing Review* 13, 3 (1996): 4–6.
20. John A. Quelch and Helen Bloom, "The Return of the Country Manager," *International Marketing Review* 13, 3 (1996): 31–43.
21. Rodman Drake and Lee M. Caudill, "Management of the Large Multinational: Trends and Future Challenges," *Business Horizons* 24 (May–June 1981): 83–91.
22. "So Big," *Across the Board,* 30 (January/February 1993): 16–21.
23. Christopher Bartlett, "MNCs: Get off the Reorganization Merry-Go-Round," *Harvard Business Review* 60 (March/April 1983): 138–146.
24. Cheryll Barron, "Format Fears at Philips," *Management Today* (August 1978): 35–41, 101–102.

25. Thomas Gross, Ernie Turner, and Lars Cederholm, "Building Teams for Global Operations" *Management Review* (June 1987): 32–36.

26. Christopher A. Bartlett and Sumantra Ghoshal, "Matrix Management: Not a Structure, a Frame of Mind," *Harvard Business Review* 68 (July–August 1990): 138–145.

27. "Internet Software Poses Big Threat to Notes, IBM's Stake in Lotus," *The Wall Street Journal,* November 7, 1995, A1–5.

28. Ingo Theuerkauf, David Ernst, and Amir Mahini, "Think Local, Organize . . . ." *International Marketing Review* 13, 3 (1996): 7–12.

29. Christopher A. Bartlett and Sumantra Ghoshal, "Tap Your Subsidiaries for Global Reach," *Harvard Business Review* 64 (November–December 1986): 87–94.

30. John A. Quelch and Edward J. Hoff, "Customizing Global Marketing," *Harvard Business Review* 64 (May–June 1986): 59–68.

31. Richard I. Kirkland, Jr., "Entering a New World of Boundless Competition," *Fortune* (March 14, 1988): 18–22.

32. "Percy Barnevik's Global Crusade," *Business Week Enterprise 1993,* 204–211.

33. Louis Kraar, "Your Rivals Can Be Your Allies," *Fortune* (March 27, 1989): 66–76.

34. Amitai Etzioni, *A Comparative Analysis of Complex Organizations* (Glencoe, England: Free Press, 1961).

35. William G. Egelhoff, "Patterns of Control in U.S., U.K., and European Multinational Corporations," *Journal of International Business Studies* 15 (Fall 1984): 73–83.

36. William H. Davidson, "Administrative Orientation and International Performance," *Journal of International Business Studies* 15 (Fall 1984): 11–23.

37. William G. Ouchi, "The Relationship between Organizational Structure and Organizational Control," *Administrative Science Quarterly* 22 (March 1977): 95–112.

38. B. R. Baliga and Alfred M. Jaeger, "Multinational Corporations: Control Systems and Delegation Issues," *Journal of International Business Studies* 15 (Fall 1984): 25–40.

39. Laurent Leksell, *Headquarters-Subsidiary Relationships in Multinational Corporations* (Stockholm, Sweden: Stockholm School of Economics, 1981), Chapter 5.

40. Anant R. Negandhi and Martin Welge, *Beyond Theory Z* (Greenwich, Conn.: JAI Press, 1984), 16.

41. Richard Pascale, "Fitting New Employees into the Company Culture," *Fortune* (May 28, 1984): 28–40.

42. Bartlett and Ghoshal, "Matrix Management: Not a Structure, a Frame of Mind."

43. Michael R. Czinkota and Ilkka A. Ronkainen, "International Business and Trade in the Next Decade: Report from a Delphi Study," *Journal of International Business Studies* 28, 4 (1997): 676–694.

44. Nathaniel Gilbert, "How Middle-Sized Corporations Manage Global Operations," *Management Review* (October 1988): 46–50.

45. R. J. Alsegg, *Control Relationships between American Corporations and Their European Subsidiaries,* AMA Research Study No. 107 (New York: American Management Association, 1971), 7.

46. John J. Dyment, "Strategies and Management Controls for Global Corporations," *Journal of Business Strategy* 7 (Spring 1987): 20–26.

47. Hans Schoellhammer, "Decision-Making and Intra-organizational Conflicts in Multinational Companies," presentation at the Symposium on Management of Headquarter-Subsidiary Relationships in Transnational Corporations, Stockholm School of Economics, June 2–4, 1980.

48. Alfred M. Jaeger, "The Transfer of Organizational Culture Overseas: An Approach to Control in the Multinational Corporation," *Journal of International Business Studies* 14 (Fall 1983): 91–106.

# CHAPTER 22

# The Future

## LEARNING OBJECTIVES

- ◆ *To understand the many changing dimensions that shape international business*

- ◆ *To learn about and evaluate the international business forecasts made by a panel of experts*

- ◆ *To be informed about different career opportunities in international business*

## Riding the Global Wave to the Top

Although E.V. Goings, president of Tupperware, recently finished a total-immersion program in Spanish—his third language—he hardly stands out on his company's executive committee. The eight other members of the group speak two to four languages each, and all can boast of international work experience. International exposure has long been trumpeted as essential for middle managers in multinationals, but these days, even chief executives are going global. To keep up with the growing importance of foreign markets, more companies are requiring candidates for top management positions to have strong international resumes.

Executives who climbed the corporate ladder in the past typically ran successively bigger operations of a single product line or specialized in one discipline like finance. Leaving the United States for an overseas post was often perceived as dangerous, taking executives far from the center of power. Today, however, international experience is often a top priority for executive headhunters. Executive-search firms report that major corporations required candidates with international experience in 28 percent of senior-level searches last year, up from 4 percent in 1990.

"It sends the most powerful signal you can send [to the employees] if the CEO has international experience or has been selected for that reason," says Jean-Pierre Rosso, the president and CEO of Chase Corp. Rosso spent twelve years at Honeywell Inc. in France and Belgium. Dana Mead, the CEO of Tenneco Inc. and the person responsible for picking Rosso for the job, says that he "showed he could operate in both [American and French] cultures."

Combining high-profile roles abroad and at home seems to be the formula of success for many top management candidates. The Egyptian-born CEO of Goodyear Tire and Rubber, Samir Gibara, caught the eye of his predecessor Stanley Gault by turning around Goodyear's losses in its European operation in the early 1990s. Then Gibara took on several key U.S. jobs at the tire maker's Akron, Ohio, headquarters before becoming CEO.

Other types of foreign exposure can also offer executives the opportunity for great upward mobility. Expertise in the bigger and more challenging emerging markets such as Brazil, China, and India can often pave the way to success. Alfredo Cuello, president of Avon Products Inc.'s continental European operation, gained his position after having successfully managed operations in Venezuela and some other emerging markets in Latin America. Likewise, GE's Mr. McNerney helped to negotiate several major deals with China and Indonesia while he was in Asia, the company's fastest growing market.

*Source:* Joann S. Lublin, "An Overseas Stint Can Be a Ticket to the Top," *The Wall Street Journal,* Jan 29, 1996, B1.

All international businesses face constantly changing world economic conditions. This is not a new situation nor one to be feared, because change provides the opportunity for new market positions to emerge and for managerial talent to improve the competitive position of the firm. Recognizing change and adapting creatively to new situations are the most important tasks of the international business executive. Therefore, international exposure and experience increasingly becomes a prerequisite for upward career mobility, as this chapter's opening vignette shows.

Recently, changes are occurring more frequently, more rapidly, and have a more severe impact. The past has lost much of its value as a predictor of the future. What occurs today may not only be altered in short order but be completely overturned or reversed. For example, political stability in a country can be completely disrupted over the course of a few months. A major, sudden decline in world stock markets leaves corporations, investors, and consumers with strong feelings of uncertainty. Overnight currency declines result in an entirely new business climate for international suppliers and their customers. In all, international business managers today face complex and rapidly changing economic and political conditions.

This chapter will discuss possible future developments in the international business environment, highlight the implications of the changes for international business management, and offer suggestions for a creative response to the changes. The chapter also will explore the meaning of strategic changes as they relate to career choice and career path alternatives in international business.

## The International Business Environment

This section analyzes the international business environment by looking at political, financial, societal, and technological conditions of change and providing a glimpse of possible future developments as envisioned by an international panel of experts.[1] The impact of these factors on doing business abroad, on international trade relations, and on government policy is of particular interest to the international manager.

### The Political Environment

The international political environment is undergoing a substantial transformation characterized by the reshaping of existing political blocks, the formation of new groupings, and the breakup of old coalitions.

**The East-West Relationship**   From 1945 to 1985, the adverse relationship between the dominant powers in the East and West changed little. Within a few years, however, the relationship was transformed. The Communist empire briefly reshaped itself into a socialist league, only to emerge shortly thereafter as individual, distinct entities. The former eastern European satellite nations of the Soviet Union reasserted their independence and implemented market-oriented economies. The Soviet Union itself has been replaced by a loose confederation of independent states. Politically and economically, the repercussions of the changes have been far reaching. The key collaborative military mechanism in the East—the Warsaw Pact—ceased to exist. The economic agreement among the socialist countries—the Council for Mutual Economic Assistance (CMEA or COMECON)—has been disbanded.

The raising of the Iron Curtain has brought two separate economic and business systems closer together. A reduction of export controls, direct linkages with economic blocks, and the West's desire to help are transforming the business relations of the past.

As a result of easing political tensions, firms are presented with new opportunities. Demand—particularly for consumer products, which had been repressed in the past—now can be met with goods from the West.

Over the next five years the countries of Eastern and Central Europe will continue to be attractive for international investment due to relatively low labor cost, low-priced input factors, and large unused production capacities. This attractiveness, however, will translate mainly into growing investment from Western Europe for reasons of geographic proximity and attractive outsourcing opportunities.[2] Even these investment flows, however, are likely to take place only selectively, resulting in very unbalanced economic conditions in the region. Furthermore, they are likely to be restricted by the erection of trade barriers on the part of the European Union, designed to prevent major economic displacements due to the onslaught of narrowly targeted competition from the region. Firms and governments outside of Western Europe are likely to be much more reluctant to invest in Eastern Europe. This aversion is not so much driven by caution about a potential resurgence of Communism or fear of economic and political instability, but mainly due to attractive investment alternatives elsewhere.

Russia and the other nations of the former Soviet Union are seen as facing great difficulty. Economic recovery and participation in world trade are likely to be very gradual. In part, the slowness is a function of self-imposed constraints due to domestic fears of outsiders. For political reasons, financial inflows into the region will continue in the near future, yet, if these flows are to make a difference, governments need to find market-oriented ways to reduce the flight of capital abroad.

Overall, many business activities will be subject to regional economic and political instability, increasing the risk of foreign business partners. Progress toward the institution of market-based economies may be halted or even reversed as large population segments are exposed to growing hardship during the transformation process.

**The North-South Relationship**   The distinction between developed and less-developed countries (LDCs) is unlikely to change. The ongoing disparity between developed and developing nations is likely to be based, in part, on continuing debt burdens and problems with satisfying basic needs. As a result, political uncertainty may well result in increased polarization between the haves and have-nots, with growing potential for political and economic conflict. Demands for political solutions to economic and financial problems are likely to increase. Some countries may consider migration as a key solution to population-growth problems, yet many emigrants may encounter government barriers to their migration. As a result, there may well be more investment flows by firms bringing their labor and skill-intensive manufacturing operations to these countries.[3] In addition, new approaches to international development taken by multilateral institutions may be effective in strengthening the grass roots of developing economies. Global Perspective 22.1 provides an example.

## LENDERS TARGET WOMEN IN THE DEVELOPING WORLD

The developing world's women are gaining a measure of economic autonomy as perceptions of them and their role in developing economies change. Even the big development agencies and multilateral banks are increasingly funding women-led small businesses and farming projects based on an assumption that women, more than men, are the critical players in the fight to relieve poverty. Agencies such as the World Bank, Agency for International Development, and Inter-American Development Bank say women are usually better at repaying their loans and less prone to waste or loot development money.

The motivation to target women has less to do with sexual politics than with the economic reality that women do much of the work in developing countries. "All over the developing world, in rural areas, the women are the mainstay of the local economy," said Gustave Speth, administrator of the United Nations Development Programme. A recent World Bank study found that women head half the households in sub-Saharan Africa. A study of village life in Cameroon found that women work an average of 64 hours a week, compared with 32 for men. And women's earnings are more likely to be used for the health and education of the next generation.

The focus on women's economic activities coincides with a growing interest in financing the thousands of tiny businesses that make up the developing world's vast "informal sector."

Many of these so-called microenterprises, ranging from food sellers on street corners to one-person apparel makers, are run by women. Though statistics are shaky, it is estimated that informal-sector businesses make up as much as half of all economic activity in many developing countries. Yet, until recently, the international institutions have funneled nearly all development funds to governments and state enterprises for projects that often did little for the poorest population segments.

In the Dominican Republic, the marriage between the large international agencies and grassroots groups is helping to get money into the hands of more poor women running businesses. To some extent, the small Caribbean state is seen as a model for others working on programs to lend to the poor. Within a year, development experts from Botswana, Brazil, Colombia, Jamaica, Mexico, and Senegal visited and studied how Dominican lenders extend credit to the poorest segments of society but still cover costs and stay afloat. Pedro Jimenez, the executive director of the largest small-enterprise lender in the Dominican Republic, argued that bankers to the poor have to avoid a "charity window" mentality. To stay in business, he says, lenders must charge real interest rates, usually about 30 percent, that cover the lenders' costs plus any inflation risk. Jimenez's bank grants loans for an average amount of $800 and has a 98.6 percent repayment rate.

In Niger, CARE is helping establish women's savings groups in about 45 villages. "They haven't had access to banking systems anywhere," said Ann Duval, the program's overseer. About 35 women contribute 50 cents per week. Two-week loans are made, with an interest rate of about 10 percent. Periodically the women liquidate their banks and distribute the money for certain needs. But the banks always start up again. Once they have had a bank, the women don't want to go without one.

*Source: Tim Carrington, "Gender Economics: In Developing World, International Lenders Are Targeting Women," The Wall Street Journal, June 22, 1994, A1.*

Throughout the late 1990s, firms see the developing countries of Africa as a relatively cool region for international business purposes. Continuing political instability and the resulting inability of many African firms to be consistent trading partners are the key reasons for such a pessimistic view. In light of increasing competition for scarce investment capital, these drawbacks are instrumental in holding both investment and trade down to a trickle. This starvation for funds is unlikely to be addressed by corporations. Periodic surges in the social conscience of industrialized nations may result in targeted investments by governments, multilateral institutions, and non-governmental organizations (NGOs), but these funds are likely to be insufficient for a transformation of the economic future of the region, unless accompanied by internal reform. Nevertheless, global trade liberalization may offer some hope to the region by permitting easier exports.

The issue of **environmental protection** will also be a major force shaping the relationship between the developed and the developing world. In light of the need and desire to grow their economies, however, there may be much disagreement on the part of the industrializing nations as to what approaches to take. Three possible scenarios emerge.

One scenario is that of continued international cooperation. The developed countries could relinquish part of their economic power to less-developed ones, thus contributing actively to their economic growth through a sharing of resources and technology. Although such cross-subsidization will be useful and necessary for the development of LDCs, it may reduce the rate of growth of the standard of living in the more developed countries. It would, however, increase trade flows between developed and less developed countries and precipitate the emergence of new international business opportunities.

A second scenario is that of confrontation. Due to an unwillingness to share resources and technology sufficiently (or excessively, depending on the point of view), the developing and the developed areas of the world may become increasingly hostile toward one another. As a result, the volume of international business, both by mandate of governments and by choice of the private sector, could be severely reduced.

A third scenario is that of isolation. Although there may be some cooperation between them, both groups, in order to achieve their domestic and international goals, may choose to remain economically isolated. This alternative may be particularly attractive if each region believes that it faces unique problems and therefore must seek their own solutions.

**Emerging Markets**    Much of the growth of the global economy will be fueled by the emerging markets of Latin America and the Asia Pacific region. In Latin America, the international business climate will improve due to economic integration, market liberalization, and privatization. In spite of some inefficiencies, Mercosur continues to bring countries closer together and encourages their collaboration. Due to substantial natural resources and relatively low cost of production, an increased flow of foreign direct investment and trade activity is forecast, emanating not only from the United States, but also from Europe and Japan.

The Asia Pacific region is likely to regain its growth in the next decade. For the industrialized nations, this development will offer a significant opportunity for exports and investment, but it will also diminish, in the longer term, the basis for their status and influence in the world economy. While the nations in the region are likely to collaborate, they are not expected to form a bloc of the same type as the European Union or NAFTA. Rather, their relationship is likely to be defined in terms of trade and investment flows (e.g., Japan) and social contacts (e.g., the Chinese business community). A cohesive bloc may only emerge as a reaction to a perceived threat by other major blocs.

China's emergence is likely to be the economic event of the decade. Despite innumerable risks, experts see Chinese pragmatism prevailing. Companies already present in the market and those willing to make significant investments are likely to be the main beneficiaries of growth. Long-term commitment, willingness to transfer technology, and an ability to partner either with local firms through joint ventures or with overseas Chinese-run firms are considered crucial for success.

Among the other promising emerging markets are Korea and India. Korea could emerge as a participant in worldwide competition, while India is considered more important for the size of its potential market. Korean firms must still improve their ability to adopt a global mindset and improve the quality of their products beyond the current level. Some experts are also concerned about the chaebols status as the Korean economy becomes democratized. In addition, the possible impact of the reunification of the Korean peninsula on the country's globalization efforts must be taken into account.

With the considerable liberalization that has taken place in India during the 1990s, many expect it to offer major international marketing opportunities due to its size, its significant natural wealth, and its large, highly educated middle class. While many experts believe that political conflict both domestic and regional, nationalism, and class structure may temper the ability of Indian companies to emerge as a worldwide competitive force, there is strong agreement that India's disproportionately large and specialized workforce in engineering and computer sciences make the nation a power to be reckoned with.

Overall, the growth potential by these emerging economies may be threatened by uncertainty in terms of international relations, and domestic policies, as well as social and political dimensions, particularly those pertaining to income distribution. Concerns also exist about infrastructural inadequacies, both physical—such as transportation—and societal—such as legal systems. The consensus of experts is, however, that growth in these countries will be significant.

**A Divergence of Values**   It might well be that different nations or cultures become increasingly disparate in terms of values and priorities. For example, in some countries, the aim for financial progress and an improved quantitative standard of living may well give way to priorities based on religion or the environment. Even if nations share similar values, their priorities among these values may differ strongly. For example, within a market-oriented system, some countries may prioritize profits and efficiency, while others may place social harmony first, even at the cost of maintaining inefficient industries.

Such a divergence of values will require a major readjustment of the activities of the international corporation. A continuous scanning of newly emerging national values thus becomes imperative for the international executive.

## The International Financial Environment

The international debt problem of nations will remain a major international trade and business issue into the 2000s. Debt constraints and low commodity prices create slow growth prospects for many developing countries. They will be forced to reduce their levels of imports and to exert more pressure on industrialized nations to open up their markets. Even if the markets are opened, however, demand for most primary products will be far lower than supply. Ensuing competition for market share will therefore continue to depress prices.

Developed nations have a strong incentive to help the debtor nations. The incentive consists of the market opportunities that economically healthy developing countries can offer and of national security concerns. As a result, industrialized nations may very well find that funds transfers to debtor nations, accompanied by debt-relief measures such as debt forgiveness, are necessary to achieve economic stimulation at home.

The dollar will remain one of the major international currencies with little probability of gold returning to its former status in the near future. However, international transactions in both trade and finance are increasingly likely to be denominated in nondollar terms, using regional currencies such as the Euro. The system of floating currencies will likely continue, with occasional attempts by nations to manage exchange rate relationships or at least reduce the volatility of swings in currency values. However, given the vast flows of financial resources across borders, it would appear that market forces rather than government action will be the key determinant of a currency's value. Factors such as investor trust, economic conditions, earnings perceptions, and political stability are therefore likely to have a much greater effect on the international value of currencies than domestic monetary and fiscal experimentation.

Given the close linkages among financial markets, shocks in one market will quickly translate into rapid shifts in others and easily overpower the financial resources of individual governments. Even if there should be a decision by governments to pursue closely coordinated fiscal and monetary policies, they are unlikely to be able to negate long-term market effects in response to changes in economic fundamentals.

A looming concern in the international financial environment will be the **international debt load** of the United States. Both domestically and internationally, the United States is incurring debt that would have been inconceivable only a few decades ago. For example, in the 1970s the accumulation of financial resources by the Arab nations was of major concern in the United States. Congressional hearings focused on whether Arab money was "buying out America." At that time, however, Arab holdings in the United States were $10 billion to $20 billion. Today the accumulation of dollar holding inside and outside of the United States has led to much more significant shifts in foreign holdings.

In 1985, the United States became a net negative investor internationally. The United States entered the late 1990s with an international debt burden of more than $870 billion, making it the largest debtor nation in the world, owing more to other nations than all the developing countries combined. Mitigating this burden are the facts that most of the debts are denominated in U.S. dollars and that, even at such a large debt volume, U.S. debt-service requirements are only a small portion of GNP. Yet this accumulation of foreign debt may very well introduce entirely new dimensions into the international business relationships of individuals and nations. Once debt has reached a certain level, the creditor as well as the debtor is hostage to the loans.

Since foreign creditors expect a return on their investment, a substantial portion of future U.S. international trade activity will have to be devoted to generating sufficient funds for such repayment. For example, at an assumed interest rate or rate of return of 10 percent, the international U.S. debt level—without any growth—would require the annual payment of $87 billion, which amounts to about 10 percent of current U.S. exports. Therefore, it seems highly likely that international business will become a greater priority than it is today and will serve as a source of major economic growth for firms in the United States.

To some degree, foreign holders of dollars may also choose to convert their financial holdings into real property and investments in the United States. This will result in an entirely new pluralism in U.S. society. It will become increasingly difficult and, perhaps, even unnecessary to distinguish between domestic and foreign products—as is already the case with Hondas made in Ohio.

Senators and members of Congress, governors, municipalities, and unions will gradually be faced with conflicting concerns in trying to develop a national consensus on international trade and investment. National security issues may also be raised as major industries become majority owned by foreign firms.

U.S. financial absorption combined with the financial demands of the emerging growth markets, the requirement of the central and eastern European economies, and the needs of many developing nations are likely to lead to heated global competition for capital and relatively high real interest rates. U.S. international debt will also contribute to an increasingly tight money supply around the world. Industrialized countries are likely to attempt to narrow the domestic gap between savings and investments through fiscal policies. Without concurrent restrictions on international capital flows, such policies are likely to meet with only limited success. Lending institutions can be expected to become more conservative in their financing, a move that may hit smaller firms and developing countries the hardest. At the same time, the entire financial sector is likely to face continuous integration, ongoing bank acquisitions, and a reduction in financial intermediaries. Customers will be able to assert their independence by increasingly being able to present their financial needs globally and directly to financial markets, and thus obtaining better access to financial products and providers.

## The Effects of Population Shifts

The population discrepancy between less-developed nations and the industrialized countries will continue to increase. In the industrialized world, a **population increase** will become a national priority, given the fact that in many countries, particularly in Western Europe, the population is shrinking. The shrinkage may lead to labor shortages and to major societal difficulties in providing for a growing elderly population.

In the developing world, **population stabilization** will continue to be one of the major challenges of governmental policy. In spite of well-intentioned economic planning, continued rapid increases in population will make it more difficult to ensure that the pace of economic development exceeds population growth. If the standard of living of a nation is determined by dividing the GNP by its population, any increase in the denominator will require equal increases in the numerator to maintain the standard of living. With an annual increase in the world population of 100 million people, the task is daunting. It becomes even more complex when one considers that within countries with high population increases, large migration flows take place from rural to urban areas. As a result, by the end of this decade, most of the world's ten largest metropolitan areas will be in the developing world.[4]

## The Technological Environment

The concept of the global village is commonly accepted today and indicates the importance of communication in the technological environment. The rapidly expanding use of fax machines, portable telephones, and personal communication devices points to the evolution of unrestricted information flows. U.S. society has already reached a watershed in terms of individual technology orientation. Just consider: 35 percent of American families and 50 percent of American teenagers have a personal computer at home; 30 million people are estimated to be on the Internet: Web sites are doubling every fifty days; a new home page comes on-line every four seconds.[5] Other countries also will soon experience this exponential growth in technology use. As a result, vast amounts of data and communication opportunities are becoming available globally. These new technologies, in turn, offer exciting new opportunities to conduct international business, as Global Perspective 22.2 shows.

Changes in other technologies will be equally rapid and will have a major effect on business in general. For example, the appearance of superconductive materials and composite materials has made possible the development of new systems in fields such as transportation and electric power, pushing the frontiers of human activity into as yet unexplored areas such as outer space and the depths of the oceans. The development of biotechnology is already leading to revolutionary progress not only in agriculture, medicine, and chemistry but also in manufacturing systems within industry.[6]

High technology is expected to become one of the more volatile areas of economic activity. Order of magnitude changes in technology can totally wipe out private and public national investment in a high-technology sector. In the hard-hitting race toward technological primacy, some nations will inevitably fall behind and others will be able to catch up only with extreme difficulty.

## GLOBAL SHOPPING AT THE CYBERMALL

Can't find a U.S.–made snowboard at your local department store in Japan? Try the new mall on the Internet. A Portland, Oregon, a firm is creating what could be described as a Japanese cybermall, an on-line shopping service that enables U.S. manufacturers and retailers to advertise and sell their products directly to consumers—in Japanese. The Japanese Internet service also teaches customers in Japan how to order products and services directly from the United States. While dollar sales so far are small, the potential for future sales in Japan and elsewhere seems enormous.

By setting up shop in local language cybermalls, U.S. firms could target potential customers around the globe without the costly headaches that often scare them away from the international marketplace. TK Associates International calls the electronic service it created the "World Wide Web's Do-it-Yourself Import Center." It has been in existence since July 1995 and had about forty U.S. participants by mid-1996, said owner Tim Clark. "We're helping companies enter the Japanese market, companies that want to take a crack without paying for major magazine ads or huge marketing campaigns," he said. The service is for companies "interested in dealing directly with customers in Japan," through catalog sales, for example, he said.

Here's how it works: A U.S. manufacturer or retailer pays TK Associates a fee for a display on the Import Center site. The fee varies according to the size and complexity of the display, but runs $350 and up. TK Associates, whose staff includes fluent Japanese speakers, translates the copy into Japanese. For the Japanese consumer, the Web site is an information resource for customers who want to buy products or services "without going through middlemen or trading companies," said Mr. Clark. Access is free of charge in Japan. The site has two features: One provides general information on importing, such as tariff and shipping procedures, to help people get started. The other is the menu of companies ready to offer products such as software, clothes, sporting goods, and household goods.

Mickey Kerbel, president of Xtreme Inc., which makes snowboards, said he paid $345 for a one-year listing with TK and has sold about $2,000 worth of merchandise in only a couple of months since going on-line. The site provides a low-cost way to gain access to some of the world's most affluent customers, said Tim Clark. And while the number of Internet users in Japan is small, the growth rate in Japan is outstripping that of the United States, he said. "We're happy with the service and the list-building it has helped us with in the Japan market," said Mike Delph, management information systems manager at U.S. Cavalry, a Kentucky retailer of outdoor equipment and survival gear. He said he's amassed a large list of names through electronic mail. "We've had more responses from the (Import Center) than we have on our own English language site," said Matthew Sandoz, system administrator for Blue Tech, a computer products retailer based in La Jolla, California.

*Source: William DiBenedetto, "Home Shopping Internetwork: Buyers Find U.S. Goods at Japanese Cybermall,"* **The Journal of Commerce** *(January 8, 1996): 1A. (TK Associates' Internet address is* **http://www.webcom.com/kyc)**

Even firms and countries that are at the leading edge of technology will find it increasingly difficult to marshal the funds necessary for further advancements. For example, investments in semiconductor technology are measured in billions rather than millions of dollars and do not bring any assurance of success. Not to engage in the race, however, will mean falling behind quickly in all areas of manufacturing when virtually every industrial and consumer product is "smart" due to its chip technology.

## Changes in Trade Relations

The formation of the World Trade Organization (WTO) has brought to conclusion a lengthy and sometimes acrimonious round of global trade negotiations. However, key disagreements among major trading partners are likely to persist. Ongoing major imbalances in trade flows will tempt nations to apply their own national trade remedies, particularly in the antidumping field. Even though WTO rules permit for a retaliation against unfair trade practices, such actions would only result in an ever-increasing spiral of adverse trade relations.

A key question will be whether nations are willing to abrogate some of their sovereignty even during difficult economic times. An affirmative answer will strengthen the multilateral trade system and enhance the flow of trade. However, if key trading nations resort to the development of insidious nontariff barriers, unilateral actions, and bilateral negotiations, protectionism will increase on a global scale and the volume of international trade is likely to decline.

International trade relations also will be shaped by new participants whose market entry will restructure the composition of global trade. For example, new players with exceptionally large productive potential, such as the People's Republic of China and Central Europe will substantially alter world trade flows. And while both governments and firms will be required to change many trading policies and practices as a result, they will also benefit in terms of market opportunities and sourcing alternatives.

Finally, the efforts of governments to achieve self-sufficiency in economic sectors, particularly in agriculture and heavy industries, have ensured the creation of long-term, worldwide oversupply of some commodities and products, many of which historically had been traded widely. As a result, after some period of intense market share competition aided by subsidies and governmental support, a gradual and painful restructuring of these economic sectors will have to take place. This will be particularly true for agricultural cash crops such as wheat, corn, and dairy products and industrial products such as steel, chemicals, and automobiles.

## Governmental Policy

International trade activity now affects domestic policy more than ever. For example, trade flows can cause major structural shifts in employment. Linkages between industries spread these effects throughout the economy. Fewer domestically produced automobiles will affect the activities of the steel industry. Shifts in the sourcing of textiles will affect the cotton industry. Global productivity gains and competitive pressures will force many industries to restructure their activities. In such circumstances, industries are likely to ask their governments to help in their restructuring efforts. Often, such assistance includes a built-in tendency toward protectionist action.

Such restructuring is not necessarily negative. For example, since the turn of the century, farm employment in the United States has dropped from more than 40 percent of the population to less than 3 percent.[7] Yet today, the farm industry feeds 270 million people in the United States and still produces large surpluses. A restructuring of industries can greatly increase productivity and provide the opportunity for resource allocation to emerging sectors of an economy.

Governments cannot be expected, for the sake of the theoretical ideal of "free trade," to sit back and watch the effects of deindustrialization on their countries. The most that can be expected is that they will permit an open-market orientation subject to the needs of domestic policy. Even an open-market orientation is maintainable only if governments can provide reasonable assurances to their own firms and citizens that the openness applies to foreign markets as well. Therefore, unfair trade practices such as governmental subsidization, dumping, and industrial targeting will be examined more closely, and retaliation for such activities is likely to be swift and harsh.

Increasingly, governments will need to coordinate policies that affect the international business environment. The development of international indexes and **trigger mechanisms,** which precipitate government action at predetermined intervention points, will be a useful step in that direction. Yet, for them to be effective, governments will need to muster the political fortitude to implement the policies necessary for cooperation. For example, international monetary cooperation will work in the long term only if domestic fiscal policies are responsive to the achievement of the coordinated goals.

At the same time as the need for collaboration among governments grows, it will become more difficult to achieve a consensus. In the Western world, the time from 1945 through 1990 was characterized by a commonality of purpose. The common defense against the Communist enemy remanded trade relations to second place, and provided a bond that encouraged collaboration. With the common threat gone, however, the bonds have been diminished—if not dissolved—and the priority of economic performance has increased. Unless a new key jointness of purpose can be found by governments, collaborative approaches will become increasingly difficult.[8]

Governmental policymakers must take into account the international repercussions of domestic legislation. For example, in imposing a special surcharge tax on the chemical industry designed to provide for the cleanup of toxic waste products, they need to consider its repercussions on the international competitiveness of the chemical industry. Similarly, current laws such as antitrust legislation need to be reviewed if the laws hinder the international competitiveness of domestic firms.

Policymakers also need a better understanding of the nature of the international trade issues confronting them. Most countries today face both short-term and long-term trade problems. Trade balance issues, for example, are short term in nature, while competitiveness issues are much more long term. All too often, however, short-term issues are attacked with long-term **trade policy measures,** and vice versa. In the United States, for example, the desire to "level the international playing field" with mechanisms such as vigorous implementation of import restrictions or voluntary restraint agreements may serve long-term competitiveness well, but it does little to alleviate the publicly perceived problem of the trade deficit. Similarly, a further opening of Japan's market to foreign corporations will have only a minor immediate effect on that country's trade surplus or the trading partners' deficit. Yet it is the expectation and hope of many in both the public and the private sectors that such instant changes will occur. For the sake of the credibility of policymakers, it therefore becomes imperative to precisely identify the nature of the problem and to design and use policy measures that are appropriate for its resolution.

In the years to come, governments will be faced with an accelerating technological race and with emerging problems that seem insurmountable by individual firms alone, such as pollution of the environment and global warming. As market gaps emerge and time becomes crucial, both governments and the private sector will find that even if the private sector knows that a lighthouse is needed, it may still be difficult, time-consuming, and maybe even impossible to build one with private funds alone. As a result, it seems likely that the concepts of administrative guidance and government-corporate collaboration will increasingly become part of the policy behavior of governments. The international manager in turn will have to spend more time and effort dealing with governments and with macro rather than micro issues.

## The Future of International Business Management

Global change results in an increase in risk. One shortsighted alternative for risk-averse managers would be the termination of international activities altogether. However, businesses will not achieve long-run success by engaging only in risk-free actions. Further, other factors make the pursuit of international business mandatory.

International markets remain a source of high profits, as a quick look at a list of multinational firms would show.[9] International activities help cushion slack in domestic sales resulting from recessionary or adverse domestic conditions and may be crucial to the very survival of the firm. International markets also provide firms with foreign experience that helps them compete more successfully with foreign firms in the domestic market.

**International Planning and Research**

Firms must continue to serve customers well to be active participants in the international marketplace. One major change that will come about is that the international manager will need to respond to general governmental concerns to a greater degree when planning a business strategy. Further, societal concern about macro problems needs to be taken into account directly and quickly because societies have come to expect more social responsibility from corporations. Taking on a leadership role regarding social causes may also benefit corporations' bottom lines, since consumers appear more willing than ever to act as significant pressure points for policy changes and to pay for their social concerns.

Increased competition in international markets will create a need for more niches in which firms can create a distinct international competence. As a result, increased specialization and segmentation will let firms fill very narrow and specific demands or resolve very specific problems for their international customers. Identifying and filling the niches will be easier in the future because of the greater availability of international research tools and information. The key challenge to global firms will be to build and manage decision-making processes that allow quick responses to multiple changing environmental demands. This capability is important since firms face a growing need for worldwide coordination and integration of internal activities, such as logistics and operations, while being confronted with the need for greater national differentiation and responsiveness at the customer level.[10]

In spite of the frequent short-term orientation by corporations and investors, companies will need to learn to prepare for long-term horizons. Particularly in an environment of heated competition and technological battles, of large projects and slow payoffs, companies, their stakeholders, and governments will need to find avenues that not only permit but encourage the development of strategic perspectives. Figure 22.1 provides an example of such a long-term view.

Governments both at home and abroad will demand that private business practices not increase public costs and that businesses serve customers equally and nondiscriminately. The concept directly counters the desire to serve first the markets that are most profitable and least costly. International executives will therefore be torn in two directions and, to provide results that are acceptable both to customers and to the societies they serve, they must walk a fine line, balancing the public and the private good.

## International Product Policy

One key issue affecting product planning will be environmental concern. Major growth in public attention paid to the natural environment, environmental pollution, and global warming will provide many new product opportunities and affect existing products to a large degree. For example, manufacturers will increasingly be expected to take responsibility for their products from cradle to grave, and be intimately involved in product disposal and recycling.

Firms will therefore have to plan for a final stage in the product life cycle, the "post-mortem" stage, during which a firm continues to expend further corporate investment and management attention, even though the product may have been terminated some time ago.[11]

Although some consumers show a growing interest in truly "natural" products, even if they are less convenient, consumers in most industrialized nations will require products that are environmentally friendly but at the same time do not require too much compromise on performance and value. Management is likely to resist the additional business cost and taxes required for environmental protection, at least until investors and other constituent groups assure executives that environmental concern is acceptable even if it cuts into profit.

Worldwide introduction of products will occur much more rapidly in the future. Already, international product life cycles have accelerated substantially. Whereas product introduction could previously be spread out over several years, firms now must prepare for product life cycles that can be measured in months

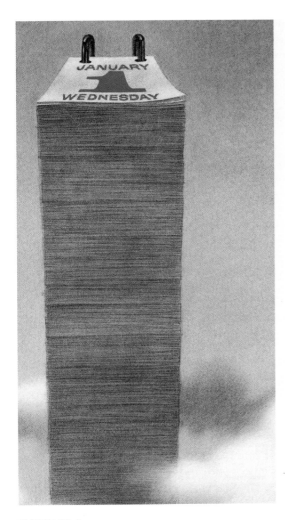

**In our business, it's important to keep an eye on the next quarter. The one that ends midnight, December 31, 2025.**

With a lot of hard work and several billion dollars, our 777 jetliner will be delivered, service-ready, in mid-1995.

And, if the market accepts our new airplane as well as it has previous Boeing jetliners, it's reasonable to expect the 777 will be part of the world air transportation system for at least the first half of the next century.

And Boeing will offer service and support for 777s as long as they're in service.

Such long-term expectations and responsibilities are at the very heart of our Company, from jetliners to spacecraft. They are the source of our most important challenges and successes.

And, they're reasons for our continuous investments in research and development, in new plants and equipment, and in talented people capable of mastering rapidly advancing technologies.

Like all businesses, we're subject to the disciplines of financial performance measurements.

But in aviation and aerospace, we have a long horizon.

After 75 years, we've learned that if you aren't in this business for the long term, you aren't likely to be in it for long.

*BOEING*

**FIGURE 22.1**

**Long-Term Planning**
*Source: The Economist,* October 24, 1992, 29.

or even weeks.[12] As a result, firms must design products and plan even their domestic marketing strategies with the international product cycle in mind. Product introduction will grow more complex, more expensive, and more risky, yet the rewards to be reaped from a successful product will have to be accumulated more quickly.

Early incorporation of the global dimension into product planning, however, does not point toward increased standardization. On the contrary, companies will have to be ready to deliver more mass customization. Customers are no longer satisfied with simply having a product: They want it to precisely meet their needs and preferences. Mass customization requires working with existing product technology, often in modular form, to create specific product bundles for a particular customer. For example, Toyota is developing an information and production system that will make it possible for an individual customer to specify a car with all its options, and for the car to be delivered to the home within a few days of ordering.[13]

Factor endowment advantages have a significant impact on the decisions of international executives. Nations with low production costs will be able to replicate products more quickly and cheaply. Countries such as India, Israel, and the Philippines offer large pools of skilled people at labor rates much lower than in Europe, Japan, or the United States. All this talent also results in a much wider dissemination of technological creativity, a factor that will affect the innovative capability of firms. For example, in 1997, nearly half of all the patents in the United States were granted to foreign entities. Table 22.1 provides an overview of the patents granted to foreign inventors.

This indicates that firms need to make nondomestic know-how part of their production strategies, or they need to develop consistent comparative advantages in production technology in order to stay ahead of the game. Similarly, workers engaged in the productive process must attempt, through training and skill enhancement, to stay ahead of foreign workers who are willing to charge less for their time.

An increase will occur in the trend toward strategic alliances, or partnerings, permitting the formation of collaborative arrangements between firms. These alliances will enable firms to take risks that they could not afford to take alone, facilitate technological advancement, and ensure continued international market access. These partners do not need to be large in order to make a major contribution. Depending on the type of product, even small firms can serve as coordinating subcontractors and collaborate in product and service development, production, and distribution.

## International Communications

The advances made in international communications will also have a profound impact on international management. Entire industries are becoming more footloose in their operations; that is, they are less tied to their current location in their interaction with markets. Most affected by communications advances will be members of the services sector. For example, Best Western Hotels in the United States has channeled its entire reservation system through a toll-free number that is being serviced out of the prison system in Utah. Companies could even concentrate their communications activities in other countries. Communications for worldwide operations, for example, could easily be located in Africa or Asia without impairing international corporate activities.

For manufacturers, staff in different countries can not only talk together but can also share pictures and data on their computer screens. These simultaneous interactions with different parts of the world will strengthen research and development efforts. Faster knowledge transfer will allow for the concentration of product expertise, increased division of labor, and a proliferation of global operations.

## Distribution Strategies

Innovative distribution approaches will determine new ways of serving markets. For example, television, through QVC, has already created a $2.2 billion shopping mall available in more than 60 million homes in the United States and 4 million in the United Kingdom. The use of the Internet will offer new distribution alternatives. Over time, it can easily be envisioned that self-sustaining

**TABLE 22.1**

## U.S. Patents Granted to Foreign Inventors in 1997

| State/Country | Totals | State/Country | Totals |
|---|---|---|---|
| Argentina | 41 | Liechtenstein | 10 |
| Aruba | 2 | Lithuania | 2 |
| Australia | 592 | Luxembourg | 28 |
| Austria | 391 | Malaysia | 26 |
| The Bahamas | 5 | Malta | 1 |
| Bahrain | 1 | Mexico | 48 |
| Belarus | 4 | Monaco | 7 |
| Belgium | 559 | Netherlands | 878 |
| Bermuda | 1 | New Zealand | 95 |
| Brazil | 72 | Nigeria | 2 |
| Bulgaria | 4 | Norway | 156 |
| Canada | 2803 | Pakistan | 1 |
| Cayman Islands | 5 | Panama | 1 |
| Chile | 4 | Peru | 2 |
| China P. Rep. | 59 | Philippines | 15 |
| Colombia | 8 | Poland | 15 |
| Costa Rica | 7 | Portugal | 6 |
| Croatia | 8 | Romania | 1 |
| Cuba | 4 | Russian Federation | 113 |
| Cyprus | 2 | S. Africa | 112 |
| Czech Republic | 13 | Saudi Arabia | 16 |
| Czechoslovakia | 9 | Singapore | 111 |
| Denmark | 362 | Slovakia | 2 |
| Egypt | 2 | Slovenia | 9 |
| El Salvador | 1 | South Korea | 1828 |
| Finland | 482 | Spain | 176 |
| France | 3121 | Sri Lanka | 1 |
| Georgia | 1 | Sweden | 996 |
| Germany | 7180 | Switzerland | 1176 |
| Greece | 14 | Taiwan | 2490 |
| Guatemala | 1 | Thailand | 16 |
| Haiti | 1 | Turkey | 5 |
| Honduras | 1 | Turks and Caicos | 1 |
| Hong Kong | 255 | United Arab Emirates | 1 |
| Hungary | 32 | U.S.S.R. | 7 |
| Iceland | 4 | Ukraine | 11 |
| India | 43 | United Kingdom | 2784 |
| Indonesia | 12 | Uruguay | 4 |
| Ireland | 77 | Venezuela | 20 |
| Israel | 573 | Virgin Islands (Br.) | 3 |
| Italy | 1422 | Yugoslavia | 4 |
| Jamaica | 1 | Zaire | 1 |
| Japan | 24314 | Total patents issued in U.S. 1997 | 122,977 |
| Jordan | 5 | Total patents issued to U.S. inventors | 69,294 |
| Kenya | 1 | Total patents issued to foreign inventors | 53,683 |
| Kuwait | 1 | Foreign patents as percentage of total | 43.7% |
| Kyrgyzstan | 1 | | |
| Lebanon | 1 | | |

*Source:* U.S. Patent and Trademark Office/TAF Database, January 22, 1998.

consumer distributor relationships emerge through, say, refrigerators that report directly to grocery store computers that they are running low on supplies and require a home delivery billed to the customer's account.[14] Firms that are not part of such a system will simply not be able to have their offer considered for the transaction.

The link to distribution systems will also be crucial to international firms on the business-to-business level. As large retailers develop sophisticated inventory tracking and reordering systems, only the firms able to interact with such systems will remain eligible suppliers. Therefore, firms need to create their own distribution systems that are able to respond to just-in-time (JIT) and direct-order entry requirements around the globe.

More sophisticated distribution systems will, at the same time, introduce new uncertainties and fragilities into corporate planning. For example, the development of just-in-time delivery systems makes firms more efficient yet, on an international basis, also exposes them to more risk due to distribution interruptions. A strike in a faraway country may therefore be newly significant for a company that depends on the timely delivery of supplies.

## International Pricing

International price competition will become increasingly heated. As their distribution spreads throughout the world, many products will take on commodity characteristics, as semiconductors did in the 1980s. Therefore, price differentials of one cent per unit may become crucial in making an international sale. However, since many new products and technologies will address completely new needs, forward pricing will become increasingly difficult and controversial as demand levels are impossible to predict with any kind of accuracy.

Even for consumer products, price competition will be substantial. Because of the increased dissemination of technology, the firm that introduces a product will no longer be able to justify higher prices for long; domestically produced products will soon be of similar quality. As a result, exchange rate move-

Advances in telecommunications allow staff in different countries to talk together and share pictures and data on their computer screens. In the state-of-the-art video conference center at Hoffmann-LaRoche's U.S. headquarters in Nutley, N.J., scientists discuss research goals and results with Roche colleagues in Basel, Switzerland.
*Source:* Courtesy of Hoffmann-LaRoche, Inc.

ments may play more significant roles in maintaining the competitiveness of the international firm. Firms can be expected to prevail on their government to manage the country's currency to maintain a favorable exchange rate.

Through subsidization, targeting, government contracts, or other hidden forms of support, nations will attempt to stimulate their international competitiveness. Due to the price sensitivity of many products, the international manager will be forced to identify such unfair practices quickly, communicate them to his or her government, and insist on either similar benefits or government action to create an internationally level playing field.

At the same time, many firms will work hard to reduce the price sensitivity of their customers. By developing relationships with their markets rather than just carrying out transactions, other dimensions such as loyalty, consistency, the cost of shifting suppliers, and responsiveness to client needs may become much more important than price in future competition.

## Careers in International Business

By studying this book you have learned about the intricacies, complexities, and thrills of international business. Of course, a career in international business is more than jet-set travel between New Delhi, Tokyo, Frankfurt, and New York. It is hard work and requires knowledge and expertise. Yet, in spite of the difficulties, international business allows an individual to break away from set patterns and offers new horizons, new experiences, and new opportunities for growth, as Global Perspective 22.3 shows.

To prepare, you should be well versed in a specific functional business area and take summer internships abroad. You should take language courses and travel, not simply for pleasure but to observe business operations abroad and gain a greater appreciation of different peoples and cultures. The following pages provide an overview of key further training and employment opportunities in the international business field.

### Further Training

One option for the student on the road to more international involvement is to obtain further in-depth training by enrolling in graduate business school programs that specialize in international business education. A substantial number of universities in the United States and around the world specialize in training international managers. According to the Institute of International Education, the number of U.S. students studying for a degree at universities abroad rose 6 percent to 90,000 students in 1995–96, on top of an 11 percent increase the year before. Furthermore, American students increasingly go abroad for business and economics degrees, not just for a semester or two. At the same time, business and management are the most popular fields of study for international students at American universities.[15] A review of college catalogues and of materials from groups such as the Academy of International Business will be useful here.

In addition, as the world becomes more global, more organizations are able to assist students interested in studying abroad or in gathering foreign

WWW

## LOOKING FOR WORK? TRY THE WORLD

**I**n growing numbers, students in U.S. colleges and professional schools are looking to go abroad. Traveling and working abroad traditionally has been a way to let off steam after school and gain experience before going home to the serious business of life. The difference today is that younger people are leaving the United States not for pleasure but for the "serious business of life."

U.S. business schools have noticed a quiet brain drain as of late. Fourteen percent of Stanford's class of 1994 elected to work abroad, compared to 6 percent in 1989. Business schools across the country—from UCLA to the University of Chicago to Harvard—report similar numbers. At New York University's Stern School of Business, the number of American graduates taking jobs overseas jumped 20 percent in 1994 compared to a year earlier.

Undergraduates are likewise increasing their international interests. Student applications for the University of Michigan's overseas study programs in 20 countries have shot up 70 percent during 1993 and 1994. At Duke, 9.2 percent of 1993's graduating seniors said they planned to work abroad, in contrast to 3.2 percent a year earlier.

In Buenos Aires, Martin Porcel, spokesman for the American Chamber of Commerce in Argentina, receives between 8 and 10 resumes per month. Some 19 Americans arrive in Hong Kong each day to take up jobs. In 1994, the Japanese government's Japan Exchange and Teaching Program, which offers one-year contracts to foreigners to work with local municipalities or as assistant language teachers, attracted 4,100 U.S. applicants, up fourfold since 1989. This whole phenomenon even has its own magazine, *Transitions Abroad,* targeted at American college students who want to work overseas.

Are young people venturing abroad completely out of entrepreneurial zeal, or does it also have something to do with the squeezed and stymied U.S. job market? One observer says the twentysomethings she listens to express frustration at the "logjam caused by baby boomers, so many of whom are ahead of them in management jobs and won't retire for another 20 years."

Michael Kahan is a political science professor at Brooklyn College of the City University of New York. He tells his students, all within a subway ride of Wall Street, to think globally if they can't find work at home. "Their skills could be put to better use in less developed places like Mexico and the former Soviet Union. If my students ask me where they should look for jobs, I say, 'Learn Spanish and go to Mexico. Try the unconventional. Don't just look in the *New York Times* for a job; look in *The Economist.'*" Kahan thinks worldwide career searches are likely to be commonplace in the future. "It is going to be a life choice, not a vacation or a lark like the Peace Corps, where the purpose was always to come back."

Three areas are attracting the majority of U.S. graduates: the Pacific Rim, including Tokyo and Hong Kong, but also places such as China, Vietnam, and Cambodia; Latin America, especially Mexico; and Eastern Europe and countries of the former U.S.S.R., where capitalism is breaking out all over.

Should this temporary or permanent loss of such ambitious and energetic talents be a cause of concern? William Glavin, former vice chairman of Xerox and now the president of Babson College, says, "It is not a brain drain but an enhancement of the brain power of the U.S." Glavin believes the new expatriates are receiving—and will return with—invaluable training they cannot now get at home: "A major problem in corporate America is a lack of global management knowledge. They are not going to learn much from managers in the U.S."

The dean of the Haas School of Business at the University of California, Berkeley, William Hasler, finds the current outflux of young business people "very positive, because most of these people will end up working for American companies and will be able to make those companies more successful and globalized." Even those who don't return, Hasler argues, will benefit American businesses by providing advice to their foreign employers on how to deal most productively and profitably in the United States.

Jameson Firestone is 27 and works in Moscow. He says, "Here the work is like being a doctor in an emergency room—everything is critical." What could be next for Firestone? "Jakarta, maybe. I hear that's a pretty interesting place."

*Source: Paul Gray, "Looking for Work? Try the World," Time, September 19, 1994: 44*

work experience. Over time, an increasing number of scholarships and exchange programs have become available. Table 22.2 lists some key international exchange and training programs and the eligible participants.

For those ready to enter or rejoin the "real world," different employment opportunities need to be evaluated.

**TABLE 22.2**

## U.S.-Funded International Exchange and Training Programs

| Agency and Name of Program | Under-graduate Students | Graduate Students | Other Students | Teachers | Professors | Researchers | Post doctorate Scholars |
|---|---|---|---|---|---|---|---|
| **Agency for International Development** | | | | | | | |
| Thomas Jefferson Fellowship Program | X | X | | X | X | X | X |
| Participant Training Program Europe | X | X | | X | X | X | X |
| Regional Human Resources Program | X | X | | X | | | |
| **Department of Agriculture** | | | | | | | |
| Research and Scientific Exchange Program | | X | | X | X | X | X |
| **Department of Commerce** | | | | | | | |
| Exchange Visitor Program | | | | | | X | |
| Special American Business Internship Training Program | | | | | | | |
| **Department of Defense** | | | | | | | |
| International Military Education and Training Program | | X | | X | X | | |
| National Security Education Program | X | X | | | | | X |
| Navy Exchange Scientist Program | | | | | | | |
| Professional Military Education Exchanges | | | | | | | |
| U.S. Military Academies Exchanges | X | | | | | | |
| **Department of Education** | | | | | | | |
| Foreign Language and Area Studies Fellowship Program | | X | | | | | |
| Fulbright-Hays Group Projects Abroad | X | X | | X | X | | |
| Fulbright-Hays Doctoral Dissertation Research Abroad | | X | | | | | |
| Fulbright-Hays Faculty Research Abroad | | | | | X | X | X |
| Fulbright-Hays Seminars Abroad | | | | X | X | | |
| **Department of Health and Human Services** | | | | | | | |
| International Research Fellowships | | | | | | X | |
| Senior International Fellowships | | | | | X | X | |
| Scholars in Residence | | | | | X | X | |
| National Research Service Awards | | | | | | | |
| Visitor and Training Program | | | | | | | |
| Individual Health Scientist Exchanges and Biomedical Research Exchange Programs | | | | | X | X | |
| Visiting Program | | | | | | X | |
| National Institutes of Health-French Postdoctoral Fellowship | | | | | X | X | |
| **Inter-American Foundation** | | | | | | | |
| Academic Fellowship Program | | X | | | | | |
| **Department of the Interior** | | | | | | | |
| U.S.–Russia Environmental Agreement | | | | | | X | |
| U.S.–China Nature Conservation Protocol | | | | | | X | |
| **Japan–U.S. Friendship Commission** | | | | | | | |
| Japan–U.S. Friendship Commission Grants | | X | | X | X | X | |
| **Department of Labor** | | | | | | | |
| International Visitors Labor Studies | | | | | | | |
| **National Endowment for the Arts** | | | | | | | |
| U.S. Artists at International Festivals and Exhibitions | | | | | | | |
| U.S.–Japan Artist Exchanges | | | | | | | |
| International Projects Initiative | | | | | | | |
| Travel Grants Program | | | | | | | |
| U.S.–Mexico Artist Residencies | | | | | | | |
| British America Arts Association Fellowships | | | | | | | |

TABLE 22.2   (continued)

## U.S.-Funded International Exchange and Training Programs

| Agency and Name of Program | Under-graduate Students | Graduate Students | Other Students | Teachers | Professors | Researchers | Post doctorate Scholars |
|---|---|---|---|---|---|---|---|
| **National Endowment for the Humanities** | | | | | | | |
| Elementary and Secondary Education in the Humanities | | | | X | | | |
| Higher Education in the Humanities | | | | | X | | |
| NEH Teachers-Scholars | | | | X | X | | |
| Foreign Language Education | | | | X | X | | |
| Travel to Collections | | | | | X | | X |
| Interpretive Research | | | | | X | X | X |
| Summer Seminars for School Teachers | | | | X | | | |
| International Research | | | | | | | X |
| Summer Stipends | | | | X | X | | X |
| Humanities Projects in Museums and Historical Organizations | | | | | | X | |
| Summer Seminars for College Teachers | | | | | X | X | X |
| Fellowship for College Teachers and Independent Scholars | | | | X | X | X | X |
| Humanities Projects in Media | | | | | X | X | |
| Public Humanities Projects | | | | | X | X | |
| Centers for Advanced Study | | | | | | | X |
| Fellowship for University Teachers | | | | X | X | | X |
| Humanities Projects in Libraries and Archives | | | | | | X | |
| **National Science Foundation** | | | | | | | |
| Summer Institute in Japan | | X | | | | | |
| U.S.—India Exchange of Scientists | | | | | X | X | X |
| **Smithsonian Institution** | | | | | | | |
| Bureau Appointments | X | X | | | | | X |
| Wildlife Conservation and Management Training | X | X | | X | X | X | X |
| **Department of State** | | | | | | | |
| Russian, Eurasian, and Eastern European Studies Program | | X | | | X | X | X |
| **U.S. Information Agency** | | | | | | | |
| Fulbright Academic Program | X | X | | X | X | X | X |
| International Visitors Program | | | | | X | | |
| Citizens Exchanges | X | X | | X | X | | |
| Hubert H. Humphrey Fellowship | | | | | | | |
| Youth Programs | X | | X | | | | |
| University Affiliations Program | | | | | X | X | X |
| Performing Arts Exchanges | | | | | | | |
| Study of the United States | | | | X | X | | |
| Academic Specialist Program | | | | | X | | |
| U.S. Speakers | | | | | X | X | |
| Media Training Program | | | | | | | |
| Arts America Program | | | | | | | |
| Fulbright Teacher Exchange | | | | X | | | |
| Library Fellows Program | | | | | | | |
| English Teaching Fellow | | | | X | | | |
| American Cultural Specialists | | | | | | | |
| Artistic Ambassadors | | | | | | | |
| Arts America Speakers | | | | | | | |

*Source:* U.S. General Accounting Office, *Exchange Programs: Inventory of International Educational, Cultural and Training Programs,* Washington, D.C., June 1993.

One career alternative in international business is to work for a large multi-national corporation. These firms constantly search for personnel to help them in their international operations. For example, a Procter & Gamble recruiting advertisement published in a university's student newspaper is reproduced in Figure 22.2

Many multinational firms, while seeking specialized knowledge such as languages, expect employees to be firmly grounded in the practice and management of business. Rarely, if ever, will a firm hire a new employee at the starting level and immediately place him or her in a position of international responsibility. Usually, a new employee is expected to become thoroughly familiar with the company's internal operations before being considered for an international position. Reasons a manager is sent abroad include that the company expects him or her to reflect the corporate spirit, to be tightly wed to the corporate culture, and to be able to communicate well with both local and corporate management personnel. In this liaison position, the manager will have to be exceptionally sensitive to both headquarters and local operations. As an intermediary, the expatriate must be empathetic, understanding, and yet fully prepared to implement the goals set by headquarters.

It is very expensive for companies to send an employee overseas. As this chapter's map shows, the annual cost of maintaining a manager overseas is often a multiple of the cost of hiring a local manager. Companies want to be sure that the expenditure is worth the benefit they will receive. Failure not only affects individual careers, but also sets back the business operations of the firm. Therefore, firms increasingly develop training programs for employees destined to go abroad.

Even if a position opens up in international operations, there is some truth in the saying that the best place to be in international business is on the same floor as the chief executive at headquarters. Employees of firms that have taken the international route often come back to headquarters to find only a few positions available for them. After spending time in foreign operations, where independence is often high and authority significant, a return to a regular job at home, which sometimes may not even call on the many skills acquired abroad, may turn out to be a difficult and deflating experience. Such encounters lead to some disenchantment with international activities as well as to financial pressures and family problems, all of which may add up to significant executive stress during reentry.[16] Although many firms depend on their international operations for a substantial amount of sales volume and profits, reentry programs are often viewed as an unnecessary expense. The decision is difficult for the internationalist who wants to go abroad, make his or her mark, and return home to an equivalent or even better position. However, as firms begin to recognize the importance of international operations, more efforts to make use of international expertise are likely.

A second alternative is to begin work in a small or medium-sized firm. Very often, such firms have only recently developed an international outlook, and the new employee will arrive on the "ground floor." Initial involvement will normally be in the export field—evaluating potential foreign customers, preparing quotes, and dealing with activities such as shipping and transportation. With a very limited budget, the export manager will only occasionally visit in-

## Employment with a Large Firm

## Employment with a Small or Medium-Sized Firm

## EN BUSCA DE SU TALENTO

### Procter & Gamble
### División de Peru/Latino America

¤ Más de 40 productos de consumo en Latino America como Pampers, Ace, Ariel, Crest, Head & Shoulders, Camay  y Vicks.

¤El area tiene el mayor volumen de ventas entre todas las divisiones Internacionales de P&G.

¤Oportunidades de desarrollar una carrera profesional en areas como Mercadeo, Finanzas, Computación, Ventas, etc.

Buscamos individuos con Talento, Empuje, Liderazgo, y continuo afán de superación para posiciones permanentes o practicas de verano en Peru, Puerto Rico, México, Colombia, Venezuela, Brazil, Chile, etc.

Es muy importante que envies tu RESUME pronto
ya que estaremos visitando tu Universidad
en la primera semana de Noviembre.

### ¿QUE DEBES HACER?
Envia tu resume tan pronto como sea posible a la atencion de Ms. Cynthia Huddleston (MBA Career Services) antes del 18 de Octubre.

**FIGURE 22.2**

**An Advertisement Recruiting New Graduates for Employment in International Operations**

*Source: The Hoya*, Georgetown University.

# The Cost of Living in the World's Major Business Cities
(in U.S. dollars)

Legend:
- Public transportation
- Food prices
- Prices including rent by city
- Apartment rents

Hong Kong — $2,390 / 95.2 / $354 / $1.07

Sydney — $640 / 79.2 / $349 / $1.89

Singapore — $2,140 / 109.3 / $440 / $1.04

Johannesburg — $550 / 51.4 / $242 / $1.00

Tokyo — $1,910 / 136.2 / $754 / $1.62

Geneva — $860 / 93.8 / $539 / $1.51

Frankfurt — $1150 / 86.4 / $402 / $1.67

Rio de Janeiro — $1,450 / 88.6 / $325 / $0.73

Buenos Aires — $900 / 72.4 / $280 / $0.85

London — $2,560 / 101.4 / $364 / $1.97

Chicago — $1200 / 84.4 / $396 / $1.50

Mexico City — $1,510 / 62.1 / $244 / $0.16

Source: *Prices and Earnings Around the Globe, 1997 edition*, Union Bank of Switzerland.

Note: Prices including rent by city are indexed, with Zurich = 100. The cost of a basket of 108 goods and services, including 3 rent categories, based on European consumer habits is between 30 and 64% higher in Oslo, Zurich, Geneva, Copenhagen, Stockholm, Singapore, and Tokyo. The indexed average for all cities surveyed was 74.3 points. Food prices are based on a basket consisting of 39 food and beverage items. Apartment rents reflect medium local monthly rent for unfurnished 3-room apartment. Public transportation based on single ticket for bus, streetcar, or subway for a 10-kilometer (6-mile) trip.

ternational markets to discuss business strategies with distributors abroad. Most of the work will be done by mail, via telex, by fax, or by telephone. The hours are often long because of the need, for example, to reach a contact during business hours in Hong Kong. Yet the possibilities for implementing creative business transactions are virtually limitless. It is also gratifying and often rewarding that one's successful contribution will be visible directly through the firm's growing export volume.

Alternatively, international work in a small firm may involve importing; that is, finding low-cost sources that can be substituted for domestically sourced products. Decisions often must be based on limited information, and the manager is faced with many uncertainties. Often things do not work out as planned. Shipments are delayed, letters of credit are canceled, and products almost never arrive in exactly the form and shape anticipated. Yet the problems are always new and offer an ongoing challenge.

As a training ground for international activities, there probably is no better starting place than a small or medium-sized firm. Later on, the person with some experience may find work with a trading or export management company, resolving other people's problems and concentrating almost exclusively on the international arena.

## Self-Employment

A third alternative is to hang up a consultant's shingle or to establish a trading firm. Many companies are in need of help for their international business efforts and are prepared to part with a portion of their profits in order to receive it. Yet it requires in-depth knowledge and broad experience to make a major contribution from the outside or to successfully run a trading firm.

Specialized services that might be offered by a consultant include international market research, international strategic planning, or, particularly desirable, beginning-to-end assistance for international entry or international negotiations. For an international business expert, the hourly billable rate typically is as high as $250 for principals and $100 for staff. Whenever international travel is required, overseas activities are often billed at the daily rate of $2,000 plus expenses. Even at such high rates, solid groundwork must be completed before all the overhead is paid. The advantage of this career option is the opportunity to become a true international entrepreneur. Consultants and those who conduct their own export-import or foreign direct investment activities work at a higher degree of risk than those who are not self-employed, but they have an opportunity for higher rewards.

## Opportunities for Women in Global Management

As firms become more and more involved in global business activities, the need for skilled global managers is growing. Concurrent with this increase in business activity is the ever growing presence and managerial role of women in international business.

Research conducted during the mid-1980s[17] indicated that women held 3.3 percent of the overseas positions in U.S. business firms. Five years prior to that time, almost no women were global managers in either expatriate or professional travel status. Thus, the 3.3 percent figure represents a significant increase. The reason for the past low participation of women in global management roles seems to have been the assumption that because of the subservient roles of women in Japan, Latin America, and the Middle East, neither local nor expatriate women would be allowed to succeed as managers. The error is that expatriates are not seen as local women, but rather as "foreigners who happen to be women," thus solving many of the problems that would be encountered by a local woman manager.

There appear to be some distinct advantages for a woman in a management position overseas. Among them are the advantages of added visibility and increased access to clients. Foreign clients tend to assume that "expatriate women must be excellent, or else their companies would not have sent them."

It also appears that companies that are larger in terms of sales, assets, income, and employees send more women overseas than smaller organizations. Further, the number of women expatriates are not evenly distributed among industry groups. Industry groups that utilize greater numbers or percentages of women expatriates include banking, electronics, petroleum, publishing, diversified corporations, pharmaceuticals, and retailing and apparel.

For the future, it is anticipated that the upward trend previously cited reflects increased participation of women in global management roles in the future.

## Summary

This final chapter has provided an overview of the environmental changes facing international managers and alternative managerial response to the changes. International business is a complex and difficult activity, yet it affords many opportunities and challenges. Observing changes and analyzing how to best incorporate them in the international business mission is the most important task of the international manager. If the international environment were constant, there would be little challenge to international business. The frequent changes are precisely what make international business so fascinating and often highly profitable for those who are active in the field.

## Key Terms and Concepts

| | | |
|---|---|---|
| **international debt load** | **population stabilization** | **trade policy measures** |
| **population increase** | **trigger mechanisms** | |

## Questions for Discussion

1. For many developing countries, debt repayment and trade are closely linked. What does protectionism mean to them?
2. Should one worry about the fact that the United States is a debtor nation?
3. How can a firm in a developed country compete in light of low wages paid to workers abroad?
4. Is international segmentation ethical if it deprives poor countries of products?
5. How would our lives and our society change if imports were banned?
6. What international business, trade, and economics educational exchange programs are sponsored by the Institute for International Education (see the Web site, **www.iie.org**)?

## Recommended Readings

Adler, Nancy J., and Dafna N. Izraeli, eds. *Competitive Frontiers: Women Managers in a Global Economy.* Cambridge, Mass.: Blackwell, 1994.

Czinkota, Michael R., and Masaaki Kotable. *Trends in International Business: Critical Perspectives.* Oxford: Blackwell Publishers, 1998.

Czinkota, Michael R., and Ilkka Ronkainen. "International Business and Trade in the Next Decade: Report from a Delphi Study," *Journal of International Business Studies* 4 (Winter 1997): 827–844.

Fatemi, Khosrow, ed. *International Trade in the Twenty-First Century.* Oxford: Pergamon, 1997.

Organisation for Economic Co-operation and Development. *The World in 2020: Towards a New Global Age.* Paris: OECD, 1997.

Osland, Joyce Sautters. *The Adventure of Working Abroad: Hero Tales from the Global Frontier.* San Francisco: Jossey-Bass, 1995.

Pinto Carland, Maria, and Michael Trucano, eds. *Careers in International Affairs.* 6th ed. Washington D.C.: Georgetown University Press, 1997.

Rhinesmith, Stephen H. *A Manager's Guide to Globalization: Six Skills for Success in a Changing World.* 2d ed. Alexandria, Virginia: American Society for Training and Development, 1996.

## Notes

1. The information presented here is based largely on an original Delphi study by Michael R. Czinkota and Ilkka A. Ronkainen utilizing an international panel of experts. More details can be found in: M.R. Czinkota and I. A. Ronkainen, "International Business and Trade in the Next Decade: Report from a Delphi Study," *Journal of International Business Studies* 28, 4 (Fourth Quarter 1997): 827–844.

2. Michael R. Czinkota, Helmut Gaisbauer, and Reiner Springer, "A Perspective of Marketing in Central and Eastern Europe," *The International Executive* 39, 6 (1997): 831–848.

3. William B. Johnston, "Global Workforce 2000: The New World Labor Market," *Harvard Business Review* (March–April 1991): 115–127.

4. *State of World Population* London: United Nations Population Fund, 1993.

5. Nicholas Negroponte, *Being Digital* (New York: Vintage Books, 1996, 5, 233.

6. Shinji Fukukawa, *The Future of U.S.–Japan Relationship and Its Contribution to New Globalism* (Tokyo: Ministry of International Trade and Industry, 1989), 10–11.

7. Labour Force Statistics, 1976–1996, Paris, OECD, 1997: 42.

8. Michael R. Czinkota, "Rich Neighbors, Poor Relations," *Marketing Management* (Spring 1994): 46–52.

9. *U.S. Manufacturers in the Global Marketplace* (New York: The Conference Board, 1994).

10. Benn R. Konsynski and Jahangir Karimi, "On the Design of Global Information Systems," in *Globalization, Technology, and Competition: The Fusion of Computers and Telecommunications in the 1990s,* ed. S. Bradley, J. Hausman, and R. Nolan (Boston: 1993): 81–108.

11. Michael R. Czinkota, Masaaki Kotabe, and David Mercer, *Marketing Management: Text and Cases* (Cambridge, Mass.: Blackwell Publishers, 1997, 252–253.

12. Michael R. Czinkota and Masaaki Kotabe, "Product Development the Japanese Way," in *Trends in International Business: Critical Perspectives,* ed. M. Czinkota and M. Kotabe (Oxford: Blackwell Publishing 1998), 153–158.

13. Frederick E. Webster, Jr., "Defining the New Marketing Concept," *Marketing Management* 2 (4, 1994): 22–31.

14. Vic Sussman and Kenan Pollack, "Goldrush in Cyberspace," *U.S. News and World Report,* November 13, 1995, 77.

15. Institute of International Education, *Open Doors 1996–97,* Internet Document, December 1997, **www.iie.org.**

16. Michael G. Harvey, "Repatriation of Corporate Executives: An Empirical Study," *Journal of International Business Studies* 20 (Spring 1989): 131–144.

17. Nancy J. Adler, "Women in International Management: Where are They?" *California Management Review* 26, 4 (1984): 78–89.

# The Culture of Commerce

The world has always been a diverse place. So it's no surprise that each country has its own way of doing business. That's particularly true of the capitalistic global giants Germany, Japan, and the United States.

In the Japanese culture, employees enter what has customarily been regarded as a lifetime agreement. They pledge their best efforts and are loyal to the companies almost as though a familial bond existed. This sentiment endures because company objectives are regarded as morally correct. Often, ceremonies play an important part in reinforcing these ties. The company's side of the bargain is fulfilled by a de facto guarantee of lifetime employment. Recently, this implied contract has been tested. Difficult economic times have made employee cutbacks unavoidable. But most workers who were laid off saw their companies honor the spirit of this agreement. Instead of offering severance pay or job counseling, many companies actually found their workers new positions.

Hard economic times have also come to Germany. But in Germany's capitalistic system, government and private industries work in close cooperation. The law requires companies to come up with written plans detailing how layoffs can be minimized, if not avoided completely. And within the companies themselves, labor and management also closely coordinate activities. Generally, all parties—government, industry, and labor—give input on how best to keep workers employed.

The approach of U.S. companies to layoffs is quite different. Workers are often given only two weeks notice—some are shown the door without even being allowed to clean out their desks—once the company no longer needs them. Retraining and job placement help is spotty. Management focuses instead on daily stock prices and quarterly profits.

Three cultures, all capitalistic, but with very different value systems and approaches to dealing with employees. A closer look inside some actual companies can shed even more light on the issue.

The midsized German steelmaker, VSG, is a recent example of the cooperation between the government and private industry. The company had to cut costs to stay competitive. But simply turning the workers out on the street was not considered an option. Instead, a joint group of company managers and state officials retrained the workers who would have been laid off. In Germany, this is viewed as managing structural changes in the economy.

The German approach contrasts sharply with how things are done in the U.S. steel industry. Take the Monongahela Valley Works Steel Co. in Pittsburgh. It spent $250 million in capital improvements for the specific purpose of cutting labor costs. US Steel put off similar reinvestment in automation so long that it was forced to lay off huge numbers of workers when the plan was finally implemented. Many steelworkers have been unemployed as long as two years, and it's estimated that as many as 80 percent have left the region for good. Those who remain have often had to take a two-thirds cut in pay for the work they can find.

US Steel CEO Tom Usher's view of the company's responsibilities to terminated workers offers insight into the U.S. mentality. Essentially, he thinks economic fluctuations that put people out of work are simply the reality of capitalism. Finding another job is the worker's own problem. And if they require retraining, the company has no obligation to offer assistance. According to Usher, management's primary responsibility is to maximize returns to shareholders.

## Questions for Discussion

1. Would the German model of cooperation between government and industry work in the United States? Why or why not?
2. What long-term repercussions, if any, do U.S. companies face as a result of their hard-line approach to layoffs?
3. Who should management feel primarily responsible to: the workforce or the stockholders?

The way things work at Daimler Benz in Germany would probably give a U.S. executive like Usher heartburn. The automaker's board is divided evenly between owners and representatives for the company's 360,000 employees. The workforce is the nation's highest paid, and it also has the most benefits. Cooperation between labor and management is smooth and fluid. Work councils determine the best and most efficient method of getting work done. Strikes are extremely rare. The system is known as codetermination.

The actual way power is shared at Daimler Benz might well give Usher a heart attack. Labor can veto the appointment of any top executive, including the CEO. Not surprisingly, this setup has led to fair and evenhanded dealings between the company's top brass and the rank and file. Power sharing also has led to strong alliances between executives and labor representatives. It helps that most German companies, including Daimler Benz, don't focus on the short term, but instead have business plans that stretch as long as seven years.

Again, things are different in the United States, and a couple of companies graphically illustrate this fact. Probably nowhere else in the world are labor-management relations as poisoned as at Caterpillar. In 1992, CEO Don Fites, arguing that labor costs had to be reduced or the company could not compete in the world market, effectively declared war on labor. The bitterness that ensued is unmatched in anything seen since the early 1900s. Many union workers are back on the job, but they are resentful of the company and most put forth only the minimum level of effort.

Recent problems at General Motors can be attributed in large part to a compliant board of directors. This handpicked group of cronies failed in their function as overseers under the assumption that CEO Roger Smith knew how to run the business. But Smith spent $77 billion in capital improvements that made the automaker inflexible and inefficient because of overcapacity. As for employees, GM management doesn't have any labor representatives on the board. Most executives never even see actual workers.

The Mitsubishi company is a good example of why multinationals from anywhere else in the world find it tough to crack the Japanese market. Mitsubishi literally has millions of products and processes. But the major difference between Mitsubishi and its overseas competitors is this: its executives will seldom do business with any company not underneath their corporate umbrella. These groups, called keiretsus, work together and provide complimentary services, including manufacturing processes, marketing, distribution, and the like. Often, banks are part

of the process as well. And when governmental assistance is also thrown in, a formidable entity is created. Few outside companies can effectively compete.

Capitalistic purists may scream foul, but the governments of many countries now actively support their private industries. A while back, and much to the chagrin of the Boeing Corporation and other U.S. aircraft manufacturers, the governments of France, Germany, Britain, and Spain cooperated on the development of the Airbus. They soon captured nearly a third of the world market. They eclipsed McDonnell Douglas and were closing in on Boeing, both of which were still smarting from Defense Department contract cutbacks.

Boeing counterpunched with its 777 aircraft. The plane represented a leap forward for the company. The old-line approach was scrapped, and the plane was largely designed by computer. Teams of engineers, factory hands, marketing personnel, and even financial people all assisted. And in the biggest break with tradition, Boeing permitted eight other airline manufacturers to offer input on how best to create the jet.

Top executives came away from the experience convinced that a cooperative effort between government and industry is the only way to keep the playing field level and to give the United States a chance to be competitive in world markets.

Even a quick overview of various economies and companies leaves little doubt that capitalistic systems differ greatly. Culture and customs are huge factors in how capitalism evolves. But some fundamentals can be pinned down. Just as companies must stay close to their customer base, so too must they stay close to their employees. U.S. management and labor may never develop the rapport that exists in Japan or Germany, but it certainly would appear they could benefit from a closer relationship than now exists.

## Questions for Discussion

4. List what you think are the three primary strengths of the Japanese and German systems. What are the principal shortcomings?

5. If you were a U.S. executive, what approach would you take to outmaneuver the keiretsu groups and crack the Japanese market?

6. What are the biggest differences in the way Boeing designed and built the 777 from the traditional design and manufacturing process?

# Charting a Course in a Global Economy

The goal in the world of private, for-profit industry is simple: maximizing shareholder wealth. But some believe private businesses have other responsibilities as well, including the duty to be a good corporate citizen. After all, businesses do not exist in a vacuum, some argue. They are part of a larger community and draw from the resources of that community to exist and succeed. Therefore, they should act responsibly.

Assume that your organization decides to adopt an ethical approach to business, what then? Who is to say what is ethical in any given situation? Whose ethics? The dilemma becomes more complicated if your business is global in nature. What if your foreign customers and competitors have a different set of moral bearings? Consider the case of human resource management in an international setting where cultural differences can complicate decision making.

A group from the Columbia University Business School was asked the following: What would you do if you were responsible for appointing a new director for your company's Asian office? The position is a key step on the fast track, and the most qualified candidate is a woman. However, you know that several important customers in the region will refuse to deal with a woman. You also expect some friction from the local staff. Do you go ahead with the appointment anyway?

Jennifer McVea is a manager in the international advertising group at AT&T. She is in Columbia's MBA program for midcareer executives. "I can speak from personal experience on this, having done business in the Far East," she said. "I think it would be difficult, especially in some countries perhaps more than others, to be in a leadership role as a woman. Some other cultures, and especially some Asian cultures, have not necessarily accepted women in that role yet. And while we Americans have, and perhaps as an American company operating in an Asian country, I don't believe that we can necessarily force our values on another culture."

SOURCE: *This case was drawn from the Public Broadcasting System's television program "Adam Smith," which aired on Oct. 5, 1990. Producer: Alvin H. Perlmutter, Inc.*

McVea was then asked how she would respond if her company appointed her director of Asian affairs.

"I think if a company made the decision that it was going to offer the job to a woman, I would just hope that it would have taken into account, first of all, the cultural shock for the woman in terms that she may not get the same level of acceptance that a man would," McVea said. "But also the possible business repercussions, in terms of other people either in that office, if they are nationals, who may not even be used to working for an American, let alone an American woman."

But given that condition, perhaps American companies should consider whether they have a role in influencing change in that condition, McVea was told.

Steve Markscheid, a vice president at First Chicago Bank and also a student in Columbia's executive MBA program, has some dealings with China through his work. Markscheid disagreed with McVea.

"I think we're working for American companies, and we have American values. And we don't let those fall by the wayside when we do our business overseas," recognizing, of course, that there could be a cost involved, he said.

The panel was asked what would happen if a woman who got the Asian appointment didn't do well on the job because she could not hurdle the cultural barriers.

Eric Guthrie, a law student who is studying ethics at the business school, replied. "I think Asian companies have to realize that the women in the corporations today are playing a major role. If they want to expand to the [West] and all around the globe, they have to consider that the woman is going to play a major part in the corporation," he said.

The panel was asked to consider the fact that competitors to the company might not have women in such roles and might thus find it easier to conduct business.

James Kuhn is a professor at Columbia who runs the school's teaching program in business ethics. "If you stop at women, where do we stop?" he asked. "Because we have blacks, we have Hispanics, we have Flipinos. I don't think this country can afford to give up on that kind of value."

Markscheid added: "What sort of message are we sending to the people who work in our company back home, as well as to our customers? That we discriminate internally to take advantage of transient commercial opportunities overseas?"

Boors Yavitz, a former dean, also teaches in the Columbia business school. "I think that's an easy one," he said. "Assuming that the company has thought through and said, 'This is the right person,' and I assume they're not novices and they know the difficulties a woman will have, I think you clearly have to stick to your guns. Not only is it the right thing, but I think this is an interesting reversal of the Europeans and the Asians always preaching to us to be sensitive to their cultural differences. We have to make it clear to our Asian customers that we operate in an American environment where this is not acceptable."

What do you do after a year if your company is losing ground, the panel was asked.

"Well, there is the short term and the long term," replied Guthrie. "And maybe in the short term you will lose some ground, but the adversity in the long term is very profitable. It will pay off in the long run, and the corporations that do practice those stringent procedures will eventually turn around—at least I would hope so," he said.

"We've got to be true to whatever our culture is, and its basic values—and we're talking about a very basic value here—and on this, I think we may be leaders in the world," said Kuhn. "If we pay a cost for that, then I think it is a short-term cost that will have a very high payoff in the long term."

Global standards are changing, are beginning to become more homogenized, said Yavitz. "I think they're moving to the more enlightened, liberal kind of view of life. Part of that is simply the sunlight, the fact that more and more is known, more and more is publicized. And my sense is that if we as American companies push our set of values and keep emphasizing those, that they do rub off, that you do get a change in the way global business is done."

### Questions for Discussion

1. If U.S. companies can transmit their values abroad, should foreign firms be allowed to apply theirs in the United States?
2. Should personal characteristics, such as gender, nationality, or age, for example, be taken into consideration when selecting managers for overseas assignments? Why or why not? What could be the outcome of considering, or not considering, personal characteristics?
3. Other than personal characteristics, what are other selection criteria for overseas managers? Provide examples of each. What are the most important criteria? Why?

4. Define culture shock. What are its four stages? What can be done to alleviate it?

# Corporate Crisis Management: The Audi 5000

In July 1989, Audi of America published multiple advertisements in business publications, newspapers, and journals across the United States declaring the "case closed" on the issue of sudden acceleration that had severely hampered its sales, stock values, and public relations during the preceding three years.

## Company Background

Audi AG traces its history to 1909 when August Horch left his own company, A. Horch & Cie., to form a new firm called August Horch Automobilwerke GmbH. By 1914, the plant, in Ingolstadt, Germany, was manufacturing a range of models. In 1925, total production climbed to 1,116 vehicles. From 1912 through 1928, Audi was also involved in the production of military vehicles for the German army.

In 1932, because of the depression, Audi merged with Horch, Zschopauer Maschinenfabrik J. S. Rasmussen (DKW), and the car division of Wanderer Werke to form the Auto Union AG, with Daimler-Benz holding the majority of shares. Total production of the new company quickly rose to approximately 62,100 cars and 63,500 motorcycles.

Another year of transition was 1969, when Volkswagenwerk AG purchased Auto Union's stock from Daimler-Benz and merged the firm with the Neckarsulmer Strickmaschinenfabrik (NSU). This action brought together a conglomeration of expertise in the manufacturing of bicycles, motorcycles, typewriters, automobiles, aircraft, and submarine parts. The newly formed Audi NSU Auto Union AG experienced an explosive rate of expansion throughout the 1970s.

SOURCE: This case was written by Michael R. Czinkota and Bao-Nga Tran based on public sources such as Automotive News and Automotive Litigation Reporter; the videotape "Unintended Acceleration: The Myth and the Reality," Audi of America, Troy, Michigan, 1989; History of Progress 1988, Audi AG, Ingolstadt, Germany, 1988; interviews with executives of Audi of America and Volkswagen of America.

Throughout the history of the company, Audi cars were known for their performance, durability, and quality. Awards won by Audi cars include the U.S. Sports Car Club of America PRO Rally Manufacturers' Championship and the championships in the Pikes Peak Hill Climb.

## Entry in the United States

Auto Union GmbH had exported to the United States as early as 1940. From 1949 through 1960, Auto Union exported to the United States a total of 5,801 vehicles. Exports climbed slowly, and by the end of 1970, the newly formed Audi sold just under 7,700 cars through 138 dealers in the United States. A wholly owned subsidiary, Audi of America Inc., was established on September 1, 1985, and assumed from the American subsidiary of Volkswagan AG the functions of sales, service, advertising, merchandising, and public relations for Audi operations. By 1985, Audi of America's sales reached 74,061, capturing over 35 percent of Volkswagen of America's total sales in the United States. Vice President Peter Fischer of Audi of America estimated in 1985 that Audi's "5000 series will be the backbone' of Audi's lineup and will represent 64 percent of Audi's U.S. sales in 1986."

## Adverse Media Coverage

In March 1986, the Center for Auto Safety submitted a petition to Audi of America, requesting the recall of all 1978 through 1986 Audi 5000 models because of repeated cases of dangerous malfunction. At the beginning of November 1986, New York's attorney general Robert Abrams publicly asked Audi of America to stop selling Audi 5000 automobiles with automatic transmissions. Both parties claimed that hundreds of accidents had been caused by the improper acceleration of Audi 5000s. Then, on the evening of November 23, 1986, CBS broadcast a *60 Minutes* episode with the Audi 5000 featured as one of its segments.

During this broadcast, Audi was accused before 65 million viewers of manufacturing and distributing the Audi 5000 series without warning the public of the possible danger of a phenomenon known as "sudden acceleration." Sudden acceleration was hypothesized to occur when "the driver starts the engine and moves the shift lever from 'park' into reverse or drive. The car [at times suddenly] hurtles forward or backward at great speed, with the driver unable to stop."

During the segment, CBS interviewed several drivers who claimed to have experienced the problem of unintended sudden acceleration. One man claimed he suffered shin splints because he pressed his foot too hard on the brake petal. Another witness broke the car seat while fighting to brake her uncontrollable Audi. The most dramatic account of all came from Mrs. Brodosky, whose car killed her own son when it suddenly accelerated and pinned his body against the wall. These interviews quickly placed Audi on the defensive because the drivers were seen as helpless victims while operating a luxury automobile promised by Audi to be reliable and safe.

The *60 Minutes* broadcast included professional input from an automobile engineer and a representative of the American Standard Testing Bureau, who speculated on the case of sudden acceleration. These professional opinions were both the same: "The idle stabilizer which keeps gas flowing to the engine may be fooled into sending too much. This transient malfunction would totally bypass the accelerator system, leaving the driver helpless, and would not leave any internal engine damage." To test this hypothesis, CBS had an engineer demonstrate how sudden acceleration could occur. The demonstrating driver shifted into drive with no foot on the brake or the accelerator pedals, and the car lurched forward.

## Audi's Response

Following the CBS broadcast, Audi AG and Volkswagen of America denied the allegations, stating that sudden acceleration results from the negligence of the drivers. Through letters to Audi dealers and owners, both Audi and Volkswagen attempted "not only to counteract the *(60 Minutes)* report, but really more to educate (consumers) as to the issue and assure them [they] are building safe cars." Audi, in addition, spent over $1 million in December 1986 placing ads in *The Wall Street Journal, USA Today,* and over 100 newspapers in thirty-three major cities, highlighting the fact that other manufacturers such as Nissan, Mercedes-Benz, and Volvo had received similar complaints.

By January 1987, Audi was forced to take more decisive action and recalled 25,000 of the 5000 series to install an idle stabilizer that required the driver to place a foot on the brake pedal before shifting gears. Further, Audi publicly denounced the CBS *60 Minutes* news team for news manipulation. In their opinion, CBS was unethical in not revealing to the public that the engineer interviewed on the program had to "dismantle three internal pressure relief valves, drill a hole into the transmission housing, and introduce artificial pressure from outside, pressure far greater than could ever occur in normal operaton of the vehicle" in order to accelerate without pressing on the gas pedal. Audi executives believed that, had this been revealed, the impact of the CBS theory would have been lessened.

## The Market Response

Within a year and a half following the CBS broadcast, Audi was beset with huge financial losses and faced hundres of court cases from its customers and dealers.

In the four-year period from 1985 to 1988, the company's sales dropped from 74,061 to 22,943, as shown in Table 1. According to Audi AG Chairman Ferdinand Piech, the impact of falling sales resulted in a loss of $120 million in 1987 alone. In addition, Volkswagen's stocks, which closed on July 30, 1986, at 454.0, plummeted to a low of 248.5 by the close of July 29, 1988. A loss of public faith and interest is reflected in decreasing resale values of Audi 5000s in comparison to the Volvo 740 GLE and the BMW 325i 6, as highlighted in Table 2.

Along with the financial losses, Audi of America and Volkswagen of America faced court suits for injuries suffered due to sudden acceleration and the loss of resale car value. For example, in the class action suit of *Paul Perona et al.* v. *Audi AG et al.,* the plaintiffs list the following points of redress:[1]

- Breach of implied warranty of merchantability under the Uniform Commercial Code
- Violation of Consumer Fraud and Deceptive Trade Business Practice Act
- Breach of express warranties under the Uniform Commercial Code
- Breach of implied covenant of good faith and fair dealing

---

[1]*American Litigation Reporter, 8 (April 7, 1987):449–457.*

## TABLE 1

### Audi Sales in the United States, 1985–1988

| Year | Number of Sales | Percent of Sales Total Import Sales | Loss in Sales since 1985 |
|------|-----------------|-------------------------------------|--------------------------|
| 1985 | 74,061 | 2.61 | — |
| 1986 | 59,797 | 1.84 | 19.3% |
| 1987 | 41,322 | 1.31 | 44.2 |
| 1988 | 22,943 | 0.75 | 69.0 |

## TABLE 2

### New versus Used Car Prices, 1985–1988

| | 1985 | 1986 | 1987 | 1988 |
|---|------|------|------|------|
| **New Prices** | | | | |
| Audi 5000 | $18,160 | $19,575 | $20,460 | $22,850 |
| BMW 325i 6 | 21,105 | 20,455 | 22,850 | 25,150 |
| Volvo 740 GLE | 18,585 | 18,980 | 20,610 | 21,850 |
| **Used Car Wholesale Prices in 1989** | | | | |
| Audi 5000 | $ 5,400 | $ 7,650 | $11,175 | $14,550 |
| BMW 325i 6 | 11,300 | 10,300 | 16,600 | 24,500 |
| Volvo 740 GLE | 10,325 | 11,000 | 13,100 | 15,580 |

Note: Figures effective for four-door sedans with automatic transmission.

*Source: Official Used Car Guide* (McLean, VA: National Auto Dealers Association, 1989).

■ Willful and wanton violation of Consumer Fraud and Deceptive Trade Business Practice Act
■ Breach of contract

In addition, many owners filed independent suits against Audi and Volkswagen. By 1988, court fees alone were estimated to have cost Audi over $10 million. More than $4.6 million in payments have been awarded to injured parties throughout the United States, but Audi and Volkswagen continue to face a multitude of unsettled individual lawsuits involving sudden acceleration.

## Audi's Repositioning

With increasingly declining sales and bulging inventories, Audi once again was forced to take drastic action. In the spring of 1988, the firm began to offer $4,000 rebates to previous Audi owners toward the purchase of a new Audi 5000 model. In addition, to control costs, Audi of America reduced its workforce by several hundred in response to the shutdown of an Audi assembly plant in Westmoreland, Pennsylvania. Concurrently, Audi's parent company, Volkswagen of America, executed four major shake-ups in Audi's top management.

Audi continued to run full one- and two-page advertisements directly addressing the issue of sudden acceleration. According to *Automotive News*, "ads captioned 'It's Time We Talked' . . . suggest that Audi erred at first when it decided to let the facts speak for themselves."[2] In February 1989, Audi kicked off the advertising year with the theme "The Alternate Route." Promotions during the year highlighted Audi's longer warranties and four-wheel drive system as standard features of its newest lines. The new marketing approach was budgeted by Audi of America at approximately $60 million, almost twice the amount of previous years' promotional budgets.

In 1989, Audi discontinued the 5000 models and introduced a new 100/200 line to divorce itself from the issues that plagued the 5000 series. The new line represents "a major step in Audi's recovery program, as it refines, upgrades, and improves on the original 5000 series." With a better-built car and longer servicing warranties, Audi hopes its faithful clientele—as well as its own management—will encounter fewer complications and amend their relationship. To entice previous 5000 owners to accept their new offer, Audi provided a resale guarantee, limited to the first through fourth years of ownership, that would pay the customer the entire difference in retail trade-in values between the Audi 5000 and the comparable 260 E Mercedes-Benz, Volvo 740, and BMW 525.

## Case Closed

A March 1989 National Highway Traffic Safety Administration study concluded that sudden acceleration may occur on a number of automobiles for a variety of reasons: "close lateral pedal placements, similarity of pedal force displacement, pedal travel and vertical offset, and vehicle acceleration capability that allows an error to occur before a driver has time to take corrective action." The study also explicitly stated that changes to the pedal design and placement in future models would only reduce the number of occurrences and not eliminate them altogether.

In July 1989, Audi of America took advantage of this conclusion and ran the "Case Closed" advertisement shown in Figure 1.

In the following years, Audi continued to conduct major promotional campaigns. Even though major emphasis rested on the technology advantages of an Audi, rebates still played a major role. In addition, a new three-year, no-worry policy was offered to Audi buyers: The purchase price included all scheduled maintenance down to the windshield wipers. Maintaining an Audi therefore costs only the oil and gas needed to drive. Table 3 shows how sales developed over these years.

In spite of the major drop in sales, used car prices showed a gradual strengthening for the Audi. Table 4 shows these prices in comparison to similar models of BMW and Volvo.

### Questions for Discussion

1. Would a U.S. automaker have responded differently to the CBS *60 Minutes* broadcast?
2. Evaluate the "re-marketing" efforts of Audi of America for 1986–1988 and 1989–1993.
3. Design an alternative response to maintain customer satisfaction.
4. Do you believe the case is closed on the Audi 5000?

---

[2]David Versical, "Audi Reports U.S. Loss, Beefs Up Ad Campaign," *Automotive News (April 4, 1988):3.*

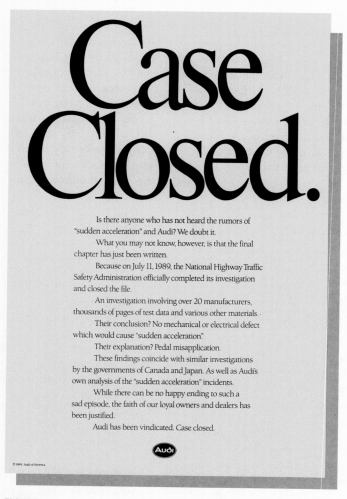

**FIGURE 1**

**Audi Advertisement Announcing Final Decision of the National Highway Traffic Safety Administration**

**TABLE 3**

**Audi Sales in the United States, 1989–1992**

| Year | Number of Sales | Percentage of Imports | Loss in Sales since 1998 |
|------|-----------------|------------------------|----------------------------|
| 1989 | 21,283 | .77 | 7.2% |
| 1990 | 21,106 | .86 | 8.0% |
| 1991 | 12,283 | .58 | 46.5% |
| 1992 | 14,756 | .74 | 35.7% |

*Source:* "1993 Market Databook," *Automotive News* (May 26, 1993):28.

**TABLE 4**

Used Car Prices in 1993 (average trade-in, U.S. $)

|          | 1989   | 1990   | 1991   | 1992   | 1993    |
|----------|--------|--------|--------|--------|---------|
| Audi 100 | 7,125  | 10,225 | 13,200 | 17,900 | 20,700  |
| BMW 325i | 10,475 | 13,225 | 16,550 | 20,775 | 24,050  |
| Volvo 740 GLE | 10,350 | 12,425 | 15,925 | 17,950 | 18,500* |

*940 model

*Source: Official Used Car Guide* (McLean, VA: National Auto Dealers Association, 1994).

# Establishing an Overseas Law Office

Stuffim & Bacom is a 20-year-old, 125-member law firm based in St. Paul, Minnesota. Aside from its home office, the firm maintains offices in Washington, D.C.; Denver, Colorado; and Paris, France. As in any major firm, there are many areas of practice, but the firm's fastest growing section is its international business department. This department is headed by the firm's principal rainmaker and senior Washington partner, Harley Hambone, assisted by an aggressive junior partner, Sylvester Soupspoon, also based in Washington.

Stuffim & Bacom has just begun to acquire business on the African continent. Its biggest client, Safari Air Lines (SAL), is an international airfreight company with corporate headquarters in Abidjan, Ivory Coast. Last year, SAL was the major airfreight carrier for all of east, central, and west Africa. Recently, Hambone, an international finance expert and master salesman, persuaded SAL to drop the law firm of Bend, Spindell & Mutilate, an old-line New York City firm, as the company's U.S. counsel and transfer all of SAL's business to the Stuffim firm. SAL is now almost a $1 million per year account for Stuffim & Bacom, which includes work with airline regulatory

agencies in the United States, as well as general advice regarding international aviation matters.

In addition, Soupspoon, a transportation attorney, recently brought in as a new client Livingstone Tours Inc., a small but burgeoning U.S.–based travel agency specializing in three-month African safaris. Livingstone maintains its only overseas office in Nairobi, Kenya. Stuffim bills Livingstone less than $500,000 per year, mainly for preparing and negotiating agreements with international charter airlines and local tour operators serving east Africa.

Due to their already substantial client obligations, as well as the sudden, unexpected growth in their business on the African continent and the impracticality of handling the work out of their Washington, D.C. office, Hambone and Soupspoon have decided to propose that the firm open an office in Africa to cover its growing client needs in that part of the world. This would not only enable the firm to better serve SAL and Livingstone Tours, but it would also help the firm garner more African business.

SAL and Livingstone Tours are each pressing Stuffim & Bacom to set up an African office as soon as possible, preferably close to their respective African operations. That would require the firm to invest $250,000 to start up an office, as well as yearly expenditures (including related overhead) of $125,000 per U.S. attorney and $75,000 per local attorney to staff it with qualified lawyers.

Establishing a foreign office is nothing new to Stuffim & Bacom. For almost 10 years, the firm has maintained an office in Paris, France. As with many foreign branches of U.S. law firms, the Paris office generates very little profit and is regarded by the firm as something of a prestigious "foreign outpost." The firm continues to maintain the Paris office at a break-even level, mainly for the benefit of one major client, Ali Nord, an Arab- and French-

*SOURCE: This case was written by William E. Casselman II, managing partner in the law firm of Casselman and Associates (Washington office). Reprinted with permission. It is intended only to describe fictional business situations, and any resemblance to real individuals or business organizations is purely coincidental. The various economic, legal, political, and cultural conditions described in the case are for illustration only and do not necessarily reflect the actual conditions prevailing within the regions or countries mentioned.*

owned freight forwarding company with extensive business in the United States, Central America, and the Middle East.

The Paris office's only attorney, Sylvia Souffle, a senior partner and member of the Colorado bar, is qualified under French law to advise clients, such as Ali Nord, on questions of foreign and international law but may not appear in French courts or advise clients regarding French law. After 10 years of general corporate practice in France, she has recently indicated her desire to leave the Paris office and head the proposed office in the Ivory Coast, a former French colony in West Africa. Souffle has many contacts in the Ivory Coast, where French is the official language.

The firm has also opened two other offices abroad, neither of which succeeded. The first office was opened six years ago in Saudi Arabia to represent U.S. engineering and construction firms doing business there. The branch closed after one year due to a lack of business stemming from a decline in the price of oil and threats from Middle East terrorists, who were upset over Stuffim's representation of Ali Nord, which they wrongly believed to be a CIA front. More recently, a heretofore unknown terrorist group announced in the Middle East that it would "go to the ends of the earth" to wreak revenge upon Ali Nord and its "yellow running dog lackeys of Yankee imperialism," including the Stuffim firm.

The second office was opened three years ago in Bangkok, Thailand, to service Torch & Glow Industries, a Colorado corporation and major provider of fire-resistant tiling and roofing materials. Torch & Glow had experienced an unanticipated boom in business in Southeast Asia. Therefore, Stuffim & Bacom opened a regional office in Bangkok with special permission of the Thai government to represent Torch & Glow in Thailand, and then only on matters not requiring appearances in the courts of Thailand. Unfortunately, a massive class action suit was brought against Torch & Glow in both the United States and Thailand for damages caused by the unexplained flammability of the company's products when used in tropical climates. As a result, Torch & Glow recently went out of business, as did Stuffim's office in Bangkok. Both of these failures cost the firm a great deal of money in lost start-up expense and attorney and employee severance payments, and the firm's partners swore never again to open another overseas office.

Undaunted by these past failures, Hambone and Soupspoon want to pursue the concept of a Stuffim & Bacom office in Africa. They have several options, which include,

but are not limited to, the following: First, they could send a contingent of at least three Stuffim lawyers, possibly led by Souffle, to establish an Abidjan office. Unfortunately, none of the firm's current attorneys, other than Souffle, speaks adequate French. Second, they could recruit a group of SAL's in-house Ivory Coast lawyers from its headquarters in Abidjan, make them special partners in the Stuffim firm, and have them run Stuffim's office. Third, they could send one or more lawyers to open an office in Kenya, an English-speaking nation and former British colony, to work principally on the Livingstone account and secondarily on the SAL account. Fourth, they could form a joint venture with a Kenyan law firm to staff and run the Nairobi office.

Soupspoon, aware that Livingstone already employs a local law firm, Amen & Hadafly, to handle some of its legal needs in Kenya, approached that firm about its willingness to form a joint venture with Stuffim to run the Nairobi office. However, Amen & Hadafly, although personal friends of Soupspoon, would agree only on the condition that they received full partnership status, not just a share of the local office profits to which special partners are entitled. In view of this demand, as well as Amen & Hadafly's somewhat questionable reputation in the Kenyan legal community, Hambone was reluctant to accept the offer. On the other hand, because Amen & Hadafly is well connected in the local legal establishment, it is unlikely that any other local firm would agree to such a joint venture. There are no joint venture possibilities in the Ivory Coast, owing to SAL's having its own in-house attorneys and preferring to work only with the Stuffim firm because of its expertise in international transportation law.

In addition to the differences in legal systems and languages, Kenya and the Ivory Coast also have different infrastructure conditions. For example, Nairobi has good telecommunications but a shortage of available office space. Abidjan is known for its modern office buildings but lacks the more up-to-date communications facilities found in Nairobi. Both countries enjoy roughly the same political and economic stability and have a generally favorable attitude toward foreign investment.

Further complicating matters, the laws of both the Ivory Coast and Kenya place serious restrictions on foreign law firms establishing local offices with foreign lawyers, requiring any foreign law firm to employ a majority of local lawyers or to ensure that their local office is managed by a local lawyer. Moreover, any foreign lawyer who wants to practice before the courts of either country has to be certified by the local bar association as being competent to do so (and no Stuffim lawyers are so certified in either the Ivory Coast or Kenya). There is one exception—any lawyer qualified in a comparable legal system can practice without satisfying the formal requirements. The United States common law system has not been recognized in the Ivory Coast, but, because of the Ivory Coast's close ties to France, the French code system has. Conversely, the Kenyan bar recognizes the English and U.S. systems, but not the French system. Of course, it might be possible to persuade either government to create an exception for a single Stuffim & Bacom client, as was done in Thailand for Torch & Glow.

Even if Hambone and Soupspoon could persuade the governments involved to permit them to practice locally without meeting local requirements, they would still have to persuade the rest of Stuffim & Bacom's partners that an African office is a good idea. In light of the two recent overseas office failures, the remaining partners, most of whom are in the St. Paul office, are not expected to enthusiastically embrace Hambone and Soupspoon's idea for an office in Africa.

The time has come for Hambone and Soupspoon to lay their idea on the line. Hambone has arranged meetings with government officials in the Ivory Coast and Kenya to negotiate an office in one of the two countries. Soupspoon must persuade the Stuffim & Bacom partners of the merits of establishing an African office in the country selected by Hambone. You have been asked by Hambone and Soupspoon to prepare them for these crucial meetings.

## Questions for Discussion

1. Advise Hambone of the various business, legal, political, and cultural obstacles standing in the way of opening an office in each country and how he can best overcome them. Also make a recommendation as to where you think the office should be located and how (and by whom) it should be staffed and operated.
2. Advise Soupspoon as to how he can convince his fellow partners that an African office will be profitable for the firm, if not in the short term, then in the long term. This would include the type of representation arrangements that the Stuffim firm should make with its clients in Africa to minimize its financial risk.
3. How do you believe Stuffim & Bacom, as a growing international law firm, should respond to terrorist threats?

# Aston Systems Corporation

Gail Hartley, international regional manager of Aston Systems Corporation, briskly thumbed through the pile of fax transmittals on her desk as she finished her phone conversation and hung up. "I'm going to have to cut this meeting short," she said as she glanced across her office apologetically. "Our attorney is going out of town tonight, and I will be in Europe all next week. It's important that I meet with him to discuss the pending litigation."

As her coworkers left the room, Hartley began to reflect on the recent problems she had faced at Aston. Realizing this wasn't the time for reflection, she gathered her papers and rushed out to make her appointment.

## History

Aston Systems Corporation is a medium-sized computer software company with headquarters located in the eastern United States. The firm was founded in 1983 by a young software engineer named Roger McGuire and his wife, Cynthia Drake. The company's original focus was on marketing software that McGuire had developed to monitor and manage the performance of the IBM mainframe operating system. The initial product was the industry's first complete performance-management system running in CICS,[1] one of IBM's smaller operating systems. By 1986, the company had branched out, developing software that managed a diverse group of larger operating system platforms and subsystems.

Drake made the first sales, but within the first year, Aston hired Jeff Black as vice president of domestic sales. Black began hiring a sales force to meet the growing demand. By 1992, Aston had 230 employees, 95 percent of whom were based at its headquarters, with the other 5 percent based in its California sales office. From its headquarters, Aston's management oversaw domestic and international sales as well as product development and acquisition of other products and companies.

SOURCE: This case was developed by Professor Michael R. Czinkota and MBA candidate Marc S. Gross. Funding support by the U.S. Department of Education is gratefully acknowledged. Names have been disguised to protect proprietary interests.

[1] CICS stands for Customer Information Control System, which acts as transaction processing software. CICS is one of many operating systems for IBM mainframe computer systems.

Aston experienced remarkable growth, with gross revenues climbing from $56,000 in 1983 to more than $50 million in 1992 (see Figure 1). Aston management expected revenues to reach $100 million by 1994. To reach this goal, Aston initiated an aggressive program to acquire complementary products and companies and planned to utilize its established distribution network to add value and thus increase profit.

## Products

Aston sells system software tools for IBM mainframe computer users. The software packages operate in a number of IBM operating environments, including CICS, MVS, DB2, and VTAM. All Aston software products are easily integrated, menu driven, and share a common architecture and format. This means that once a customer has mastered the commands for an Aston software package, the same commands apply to all other Aston software. The user-friendly attributes encourage the purchase of multiple products.

Aston's complete performance-management software systems are designed to monitor IBM mainframe performance and diagnose information system problems quickly, before they affect the user through costly system downtime. The performance-monitoring tools provide users with critical information about memory allocation, bottlenecks, and file utilization through full-color charts, graphs, and real-time access. In addition, the tools provide upper management with an overview of the information system, its response times, number of tasks, and program and transaction codes. This helps users to optimize existing computer resources and plan for hardware upgrades.

The main Aston products as percent of sales both in units and revenues for the first half of 1992 were as follows: Monitor for CICS—45 percent of units sold, 49 percent of revenues; Monitor for MVS—17 percent of units sold, 23 percent of revenues; Monitor for DB2—14 percent of units sold, 17 percent of revenues; Monitor for VTAM—2 percent of units sold, 1 percent of revenues (see Figure 2). The monitor for the VTAM network communication systems was a new product that had been acquired from Cashwell Research, Inc., in 1990 and introduced only recently.

In addition to the software itself, much of the customer value came from Aston's after-sales service and support. Furthermore, Aston offered the finest in English-language brochures and reference manuals as part of the software package.

## International Expansion

Aston was unique in its international expansion. Contrary to the normal patterns of expanding into international markets after establishing domestic sales, Aston had made its first sale to a company in the Netherlands. In 1983, Drake was attending a user-group meeting for Oxford Software Company in Holland. At that meeting, she was introduced to Alex Nagle, one of Oxford's marketing representatives. As Drake told Nagle about Aston's product, he became increasingly enthusiastic about its market potential in Europe. Aston gave Nagle the opportunity to distribute the product, a relationship that proved to be long and prosperous.

As European sales grew, Aston authorized Nagle to establish agent relationships on its behalf. He then established distributorships in Sweden, Switzerland, the United Kingdom, France, Holland, and Germany. All distributors initially reported to Nagle, who maintained records and reported to Aston management.

In the software-production process at Aston, software engineers wrote commands to a master tape. To reduce overhead and administrative costs, Aston shipped master tapes directly to distributors and granted exclusive rights to reproduce and distribute the software and license to end users. End users received the software on floppy disks, which could be installed directly into their computer systems. In addition, the user received numerous English-language brochures and reference manuals.

Sixty percent of sales revenue went to the distributor, who incurred production and marketing costs. Nagle received the remaining 40 percent, retaining 10 percent of gross sales revenue as a fee for managing the relationship with distributors and sending the remaining 30 percent to Aston.

For example, if a German distributor sold an Aston software package for DM 20,000, she would retain DM 12,000 to cover overhead expenses and sales commission. Nagle would receive DM 8,000, of which he would retain DM 2,000 for his management services and forward the dollar equivalent of the remaining DM 6,000 to Aston. Since Aston's distributors set prices in local currency, the dollar value of the revenue Aston received from its 30 percent margin varied as exchange rates fluctuated.

In 1989, a rapid increase in European sales caused Aston management to reconsider its relationship with Nagle. Aston management believed it had enough people employed in its headquarters to effectively manage distributors and wanted higher margins to continue its expansion. At the same time, Nagle no longer wanted to

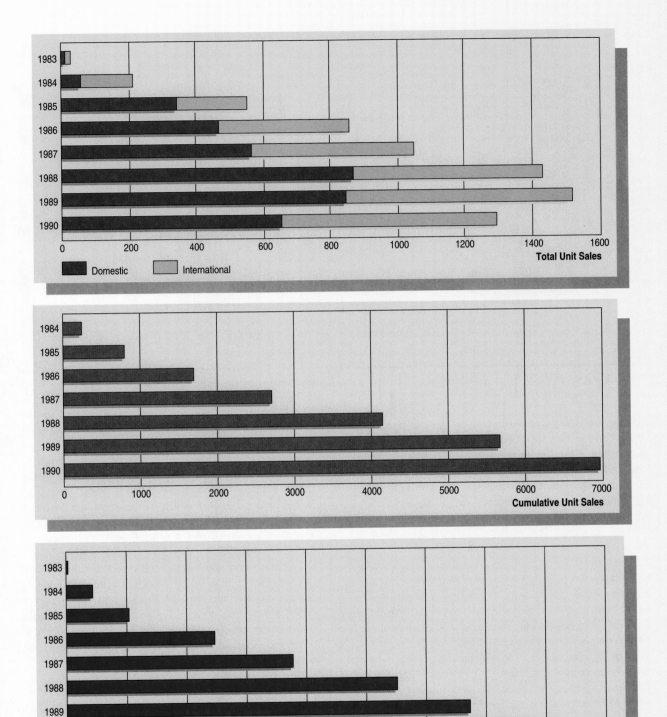

**FIGURE 1**

**Aston Revenues**

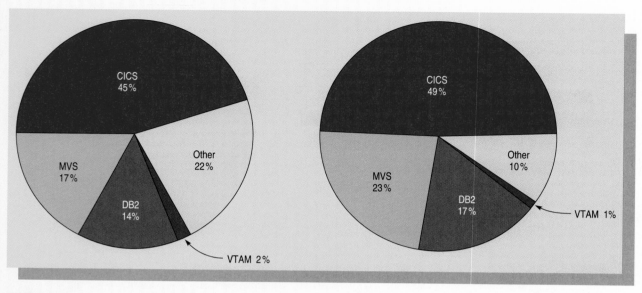

**FIGURE 2**

Aston: Percent of Units Sold First Half of 1992        Aston: Percent of Revenues First Half of 1992

manage the effort, and Aston bought out the remainder of his contract. Aston retained all of its distributors and established direct communication and reporting channels and new contractual distributor agreements to replace the agreements distributors had with Nagle. The agreements granted distributors exclusive geographical marketing rights and provided them the same 60 percent of sales revenue. The remaining 40 percent went to Aston.

The nature of the distribution agreement provided Aston a built-in reporting system as a safeguard against unreported sales. Pursuant to the agreement, Aston provided sales support in terms of seminars, marketing materials, and on-site client visits, as well as in-depth research support directly to clients. Most clients will at one time or another have a problem requiring direct contact with Aston technical support staff. Having an unreported customer contact Aston for technical support could be very embarrassing and ultimately devastating for a distributor. Although Aston responded to both distributor and end-user inquiries from around the globe, there was no formal means of responding to inquiries made in languages other than English.

Currently, Aston has 21 international distributors marketing in more than 70 countries. International sales account for 51 percent of the total. In 1992, Aston's 12 largest distributors in Europe represented more than 60 percent of international income; Japan represented another 16 percent.

In late 1992, Hartley was in the process of finalizing an agreement to establish Aston's first subsidiary in the United Kingdom. Aston had recently acquired Integrated Software Group (ISG), which had developed a software product for the widely used UNIX operating platform. The subsidiary consisted of one full-time sales employee, formerly with ISG, a car, and a cellular telephone. Although Aston management was focused on minimization of overhead, it planned to launch the initial marketing phase of the product through this subsidiary. Although it had not yet been decided how to appoint distributors for the new product, Hartley did not plan to offer distributors exclusive marketing rights to the product as had been the case with other Aston products.

## Distributor Selection

In selecting new distributors, Hartley relies heavily on referrals. She contacts current distributors for referrals as well as a variety of other vendors to find out whom they are using and if a candidate's performance has been satisfactory. After making contact with the prospective distributor, Hartley begins a formal interview process, much like that of hiring someone for a job within the company. Hartley looks to a distributor's financial backing, debt/

equity structure, and business history, ensuring that there are sufficient assets to continue operations and sufficient business experience to minimize the risk of dissolution. In essence, Aston is looking to establish a long-term relationship with its distributors. On the administrative side, Aston analyzes credit reports provided by Dunn and Bradstreet to ensure that prospective distributors are paying creditors on time. In the final analysis, Hartley relies on her gut feeling of whether or not the distributor is hungry to get its hands on the product and sell it. Hartley travels abroad approximately two weeks out of each month to monitor distributor operations, interview potential distributors, and meet with large clients.

## Decision Situation

Despite Aston's rigorous screening process, the firm has encountered problems with distributors. In 1990, Aston's Spanish distributor, Francisco Del Mar, decided to dissolve his company and establish a new company to sell a different range of products. Unbeknownst to Aston, Del Mar, who was based in the Netherlands Antilles, viewed his Spanish operation simply as a tax haven. Del Mar did not provide any advance notice of his intentions and left Aston without representation in Spain.

Recently, Hartley had also encountered problems with the Spanish distributor who replaced Del Mar. The individuals running the company had excellent backgrounds and credentials. They were former Anderson Consulting partners who had been in management consulting for a long time. Despite having met all of Aston's rigorous selection criteria, the company overextended itself, hiring too large a staff too rapidly. After starting with only two employees, the company hired more than 150 within nine months. When the firm encountered difficulties in meeting overhead expense, it began using Aston's royalty share to finance other ventures and pay salaries. Aston had always been willing to work with distributors through legitimate short-term cash flow problems. Normally Aston received payment in full within thirty days of a sale, as was stipulated in the distributor agreement, but it had occasionally extended the payment period. In this case, however, the problem seemed to go beyond the short term. Aston was in the process of terminating the distributor and as yet had no replacement.

## Additional Uncertainties

In addition to the uncertainties with the current Spanish distributor, the challenges associated with the launch of a foreign subsidiary and major exchange rate fluctuation significantly threaten revenues at Aston. Furthermore, a deepening global recession could severely impact cash flow and jeopardize Aston's stated goals of rapid expansion and product acquisition.

**Questions for Discussion**

1. How are Aston's revenues affected by fluctuations in currency exchange rates? Which is better for Aston, a strong or weak dollar? Why?
2. With such a large portion of revenues generated internationally, how should Aston handle inquiries and service requests made from abroad?
3. Should Aston actively pursue recovery of its money from its Spanish distributor?
4. How can Aston avoid distributor problems in the future without placing unreasonable constraints on distributors and market growth? How does the subsidiary relationship fit into Aston's stated long-term goals?

# Crosswell International

It is August 4, 1995, and the Mathieux brothers, Doug and Geoff, were concluding a summer-long effort of developing the Brazilian market for Crosswell International (U.S.). Crosswell's president and CEO, Hector Lans, is convinced that *Precious Ultra Thin Baby Diapers* will be a big seller in Brazil. In their role as brokers for Crosswell, the Mathieuxs have been exploring a number of different distribution channels in the Brazilian market. To date, the distributor response to *Precious* diapers has been enthusiastic, particularly in light of *Precious* diapers' superior quality compared to locally manufactured alternatives. The problem, however, is the price.

Brazilians base many purchasing decisions—at least in regard to disposable diapers—on cost, not on quality. The Mathieuxs find that distributors do not believe they can compete in the market with the relatively high prices offered by Crosswell, even with higher quality diapers. After much debate over how to improve the price competitiveness of *Precious* diapers, the Mathieuxs believe they may have found a solution. Their proposal is to combine extended credit terms to local distributors with Brazil's high domestic interest rates to effectively lower the diapers' price to Brazilian consumers.

## The Brazilian Diaper Market

Until the latter part of the 1980s, most Brazilians had never heard of a disposable diaper, and not surprisingly, the disposable hygiene market in Brazil was virtually nonexistent. By 1995, however, the personal care market was booming. This growth was largely a result of newfound economic stability and a growing middle class. As both the middle class and educational levels about hygiene expand, the personal care market should also expand.

Disposable diapers were first introduced in Brazil in the mid-1980s by U.S.–based multinational Johnson and Johnson (J&J). As J&J promoted its new diapers, Brazilians discovered the advantages of disposable diapers and sales grew steadily in the small upper-class market segment. The diapers were initially very expensive; retailers sold them at a Brazilian currency equivalent price of $1.50–

$2.00 per diaper (depending on size). J&J increased its diaper sales and in the mid-1980s set up manufacturing operations in São Paulo.

Eventually, J&J's large profit margins attracted competitors, so that by 1990 several other players had entered the game. Between 1990 and 1995 the market expanded dramatically, with U.S.–based Procter and Gamble (P&G) and several other major new entrants now manufacturing and distributing in Brazil. The good news for Crosswell is that these diapers are still largely inferior in quality to *Precious* due to technological and capital constraints on domestic producers.

By early 1995 the Brazilian disposable diaper market was growing rapidly as the Brazilian middle class expanded and its purchasing power increased. Competition, however, quickly reduced profit margins as competitors began cutting prices. J&J's leadership position eroded as its market share dropped from 78 percent in 1990 to less than 15 percent in 1995. In an effort to keep its remaining market share, but maintain higher prices in an effort to recover its investment in local manufacturing facilities, J&J has spent freely to promote its premium product image. Table 1 provides an overview of the major players, products, and prices in the Brazilian disposable diaper market in 1995.

**TABLE 1**

**Baby Diaper Prices and Qualities in the Brazilian Market, 1995**

| Company (Country) | Brand | Quality | Prices per Diaper by Size Small | Medium | Large | No. in Package |
|---|---|---|---|---|---|---|
| Bebito (ARG) | Bebito | Low | R$0.198 | R$0.232 | R$0.302 | 24 / 20 / 16 |
| Panales Duffy (ARG) | Duffy | Low | 0.204 | 0.230 | 0.312 | 24 / 20 / 16 |
| Cora Products (BRZ) | Pipita Anatomica | Low | 0.248 | 0.290 | 0.380 | 24 / 20 / 16 |
| Pom Pom (BRZ) | Pom Pom | Low | 0.244 | 0.289 | 0.415 | 12 / 10 / 8 |
| Chansommes (BRZ) | Puppet | Mid | 0.279 | 0.332 | 0.463 | 12 / 10 / 8 |
| Julie Joy (BRZ) | Julie Joy | Mid | 0.265 | 0.301 | 0.437 | 24 / 20 / 16 |
| Kenko (JAP) | Monica Plus | Mid | 0.273 | 0.340 | 0.469 | 24 / 20 / 16 |
| Kenko (JAP) | Tippy | Mid | 0.363 | 0.425 | 0.544 | 24 / 20 / 16 |
| Procter & Gamble (USA) | Pampers Uni | Mid | 0.261 | 0.317 | 0.429 | 24 / 20 / 16 |
| Johnson & Johnson (USA) | Sempre Seca Plus | Mid to High | 0.396 | 0.451 | 0.594 | 24 / 20 / 16 |
| French, Italian, Israeli, Japanese, and U.S. firms | Various | High | Similar to Johnson & Johnson | | | Varies |

*Source:* Authors, 1995. Average exchange rate of R$0.94/US$.

## The Competitors

There were four main groups of competitors in the diaper market in Brazil. The first group, comprised of foreign multinational corporations producing in Brazil, included J&J, P&G, and Kenko do Brasil. These companies commanded 40 percent of the market. J&J had the highest quality diaper produced in Brazil and commanded the highest prices. P&G was viewed as the most efficient manufacturer, producing the midquality *Pampers*. Kenko do Brasil, a Japanese company, entered Brazil by acquiring several local Brazilian diaper producers. The company's brands, *Monica* and *Tippy*, were popular and held a substantial portion of the market. Kenko's quality and price were similar to P&G's *Pampers*.

The second group of competitors consisted of Brazilian companies that produced in-country. These companies generally used simpler manufacturing techniques due to limited financial backing and served the lower quality, lower-price market segment. Some brands, however, such as *Puppet* and *Julie Joy*, competed in the midprice segment. These national brands had captured a 30 percent share of the market by 1995.

The third group of competitors consisted of Argentinian companies with brands such as *Duffy* and *Bebito*. These large diaper producers were taking advantage of the lower import tariffs resulting from the creation of *Mercosur* (as well as favorable exchange rates) by producing in Argentina and selling into Brazil.[1] The production costs of the Argentinians were low, and in the two years prior to 1995 they had captured a 20 percent market share in Brazil by offering low-quality, low-cost diapers.

The final group of competitors includes foreign companies from countries such as France, Italy, Israel, Japan, and the United States. These companies are entering the market with imports of high-quality diapers (at least higher in quality than the majority in the existing Brazilian market). However, they are priced at the high end of the market with prices close to those of J&J and have garnered only a 10 percent share to date. This is the market segment which Crosswell wanted.

Prices for large-size disposable baby diapers in Brazil range from R$0.30 to R$0.60 per diaper (R$ is the symbol for the Brazilian currency, the *Real*). Argentinian companies are at the low end of the range, while J&J commands the highest prices.

In spite of the entry of more and more competitors and increasing production capacity, the Brazilian market was still seen as a high-growth market with excess demand. Brazilian President Fernando Henrique Cardoso's economic recovery plan, the *Real Plan,* is drastically restructuring the Brazilian economy and, in the opinion of most, for the better.[2] Consumers have gained confidence in the economy, and consumer spending is rising. If the plan continues to be a success, the middle class will continue to grow in size and income, resulting in an expanding market for disposable diapers.

## Hospital Specialty Company

Hospital Specialty Company (Hospeco) was the personal care products division of The Tranzonic Companies, a Cleveland, Ohio, based manufacturer and distributor of a wide variety of paper, cloth, and vinyl products. Tranzonic had sales of $131 million in 1994 and was listed on the New York Stock Exchange (symbol TRNZ). Appendix A provides a brief summary of Tranzonic's financial performance in the 1990s. Tranzonic was composed of four major operating divisions, the personal care division (Hospeco), the industrial textiles division, the housewares division, and the industrial packaging division. Hospeco was the largest operating unit within the company, manufacturing and distributing a full line of feminine hygiene products, infant's disposable diapers, adult incontinence products, obstetrical pads, toilet seat covers, and related disposable hygiene products. Hospeco brand names include SAFE & SOFT®, EVERYDAY®, SOFT & THIN®, MAXITHINS®, PRECIOUS®, HEALTH GARDS®, FRESH GARDS®, and AT EASE®. Production facilities were located in Cleveland, Ohio, Lexington, Kentucky, and Phoenix, Arizona.[3]

Although Hospeco faced margin pressures in 1994 (brand product manufacturers had been reducing prices to draw market share from the private label sector), the firm increased its sales and earnings over the 1995 fiscal year. In response to increased competition, the parent company made significant new investments to insure cost-competitive manufacturing of high-quality products. The goal of Tranzonic and Hospeco, was to develop and main-

---

[1]*Mercosur is a regional common market including Argentina, Brazil, Paraguay, and Uruguay. It was implemented on January 1, 1995. This trading agreement set common external tariffs for the four members, while reducing trade barriers and import tariffs for trade within the common market.*

[2]*The* Real Plan, *an economic program combining a new currency with new economic stabilization measures, is described in detail in a following section.*

[3]*The Tranzonic Companies, Annual Report, 1994.*

tain the capacity to offer customers a broad line of products that were equivalent to international brands in terms of quality and performance. Hospeco proved itself adept at leveraging strong customer relationships and introducing new product lines. For example, its adult incontinence product lines and sales continued growing with the "graying of America" and the associated expansion of the elder-care market.

## Hospeco and Crosswell International

Hospeco did not begin to explore market potential outside the United States until 1994. In 1993, Hospeco's president was approached by Hector Lans, a Cuban-born Miami-based businessman, who promised big results if he was allowed to direct a new international sales subsidiary and given the resources to pursue large untapped international markets. Mr. Lans managed to convince Hospeco's directors of the international market potential—particularly in Latin America—for their line of personal care products, and Crosswell International was born. The subsidiary was placed in Miami, Florida, to focus specifically on Latin America.

By May 1995, in a little over eighteen months, Hector Lans had begun developing several Latin American markets, with the glaring omission of Brazil. The lack of any real activity in the Brazilian market was largely a result of the language barrier—Brazil is primarily Portuguese-speaking—and a general lack of familiarity with the market. But Brazil offered enormous potential. Lans sought out two brothers, Doug and Geoff Mathieux, who possessed not only business experience in the Brazilian market but, just as importantly, the language skills necessary to penetrate it (both were fluent in Spanish, French, and most importantly for Brazil, Portuguese). The Mathieux brothers agreed to act as brokers on behalf of Crosswell International in Brazil and to focus on the development of the *Precious Ultra Thin Baby Diaper* product line.

## Economic Situation in Brazil

The economic situation in Brazil improved dramatically after the implementation of President Cardoso's *Real Plan* on July 1, 1994. There were two key elements of the *Real Plan*: (1) the establishment of a new currency, the *Real* (R$), and (2) a commitment to a tight monetary policy that would, once and for all, drive inflation from the Brazilian economic and social fabric. Success to date had been promising. Inflation dropped from a preplan level of 50 percent per month to 2 percent per month, and was ex-

pected to stay at the rate throughout 1995. The new currency, the *Real*, was stable against the dollar and the Brazilian government was committed to maintaining its value.

Interest rates were, however, still high at 3–4 percent per month (not per year) for corporate deposit rates, and 8 percent to 10 percent per month for loan rates, as a result of the tight monetary policy under the *Real Plan* (see Table 2). These rates were expected to remain stable for the next several months, with hope that interest rates may slowly decline over the coming one to two years as inflationary pressures subsided. A continuing influx of foreign capital was also expected to aid in this process of stabilization as inflows would hopefully buoy the *Real* and prevent the currency itself from depreciating and adding to inflationary pressures.

The Brazilian trade balance enjoyed a modest monthly surplus after several months of deficits during the beginning of 1995. Thanks to a large capital account surplus, Brazil was able to increase its volume of foreign reserves to over US$45 billion.[4] Foreign investment once again began flowing into Brazil, indicating that the *Tequila Effect* was wearing off.[5]

---

[4]Brazil Outlook, *Number 9, September 1995, Editora Tama, Ltda., Rio de Janeiro, Brazil.*

[5]*The Tequila Effect refers to the spreading of negative economic impacts to all of Latin America's markets following the devaluation of the Mexican peso in December 1994. Although the devaluation was confined to Mexico alone, international investors withdrew from many Latin American markets in fear that the devaluation might spread. It took over half a year to soothe the anxieties of international investors regarding the stability of the other countries in the region.*

---

**TABLE 2**

**Brazilian Exchange & Money Rates, August 4, 1995**

| Real/US$ Exchange Rates | Bid | Ask |
|---|---|---|
| Commercial | 0.9343 | 0.9357 |
| Parallel | 0.9070 | 0.9220 |
| Tourist | 0.9040 | 0.9270 |

| Deposit Interest Rates | Loan Interest Rates | | |
|---|---|---|---|
| 3.69% per month | 30 days: 8.25% per month | | |
| | 60 days: 8.75% per month | | |
| | 90 days: 9.25% per month | | |

*Source: Brasil FaxLetter, Gilbert o L. DiPierro, August 4, 1995, Miami, Florida.*

The stock market performed quite well during the last quarter, after several difficult months following Mexico's devaluation. These strong results were thought to be indicative of the new consumer and institutional confidence in the economy. After a year of strong growth, consumer spending and retail sales have leveled. Gross domestic product (GDP) growth was expected to reach 6.4 percent in 1995.

With the implementation of the *Real Plan* on June 30, 1994, the Brazilian *Cruzeiro (Crz)* was replaced with the *Real (R$)*, with the official exchange rate changing from approximately Crz2750/US$ to R$1.00/US$. Given the relatively high inflation rates experienced by Brazil after that time, the *Real* should have depreciated against the dollar—but it didn't. The influx of foreign investment became substantial, with benefits to the *Real* itself. In fact, as illustrated in Figure 1, the *Real* appreciated slightly during the first year after the plan, and remained stable through most of 1995.[6] Simultaneously, monthly deposit interest rates dropped precipitously under the *Plan*, stabilizing at 3 to 4 percent per month.[7] Given the apparent health of the economy, the positive trade balance, and

a central bank, which was adding significantly to its foreign exchange reserves, the outlook for maintaining the *Real's* value looked promising.

## Developing the Brazilian Market

When the Mathieux brothers arrived in Brazil in May 1995, they conducted an in-depth analysis of the disposable diaper market. Their primary interest was to isolate what price they believed the market could sustain for Crosswell's *Precious*. The Mathieuxs then completed a detailed import and distribution price analysis for *Precious*. Pricing was constructed in five stages (see Table 3 for the detailed calculation), beginning with Crosswell's price to the Mathieuxs of $32.57 per case, and adding $1.50 per case commission for the Mathieuxs as brokers. The FOB price per case, Miami, was $34.07.[8]

Local freight, loading, documentation, and insurance expenses were incurred in the second stage, resulting in a CIF price to the distributor of $39.25 per case.[9] Although a number of larger firms were increasingly fore-

---

[6] *The Brazilian government had actually intervened in the currency markets to keep the* Real *from appreciating further and making Brazilian exports increasingly expensive and uncompetitive on world markets.*

[7] *Monthly deposit rates averaged between 40 percent and 47 percent for the first six months of 1994, the period just prior to the* Real Plan.

[8] *FOB, "free on board," is an international trade term in which the exporter's quoted price includes the cost of loading goods into transport vessels at a named point.*

[9] *CIF, cost, insurance, and freight is the exporter's quoted price including the cost of packaging, freight or carriage, insurance premium, and other charges paid respecting the goods from the time of loading in the country of export to their arrival at the named port of destination or place of trans-shipment.*

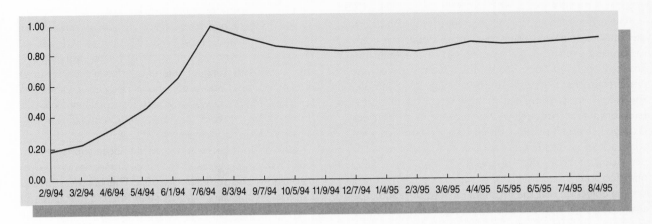

**FIGURE 1**

**Brazilian Real/U.S. Dollar Exchange Rate Under the Real Plan (Feb 1994–Aug 1995)**

*Note:* The Real replaced the Cruzeiro as the Brazilian currency on June 30, 1994. The exchange rate on that date, Crz2750/US$, is used to index the currency rate prior to June 30, resulting in the "falling value" of the Real from February to July 1994 illustrated here. For financial valuation purposes, the exchange rate prior to June 30, 1994 is not directly comparable to the rate in effect after revaluation.

going export insurance expenses—in this case 2.25 percent of CFR price—Doug and Geoff viewed the potential liabilities of a start-up business line such as this as too large, forcing them to incure the added expense. The price to the distributor was invoiced in U.S. dollars. Given the current spot rate of R$0.935/US$, this translated into a price of R$36.70 per case to the Brazilian distributor. The distributor would carry the currency risk, while the U.S. exporter (and broker in this case) were guaranteed their margins on the transfer price without risk of currency movements.

The third stage, the actual logistics of getting the diapers from Miami and through Brazilian customs to the local distributor, was not trivial in either cost or complexity. Given the various fees, tariffs, currency, and brokerage fees, the price in Brazilian Real rose rapidly from a CIF price of R$36.70 to R$40.44 per case, an added 10 percent.

The Brazilian distributor's role, the fourth stage in the pricing saga, added storage costs, inventory financing expenses, and distributor's margin. The price to retailers was now R$52.27 per case. In the fifth and final stage, the retailer paid industrial and merchandise taxes (15 percent and 18 percent, respectively), and added a customary 30 percent markup, resulting in a final price to the consumer of R$92.21. This was a price roughly 2.5 times the price of the diaper prior to hitting the docks of the Brazilian port. Brazilian *Precious* consumers would pay R$0.480 per large, and R$0.524 per extra-large baby diaper. This placed *Precious* in the upper third of the baby diaper price range in Brazil.

The brothers then proceeded to meet with importers, distributors, local representatives of chambers of commerce, and even trade representatives of the American Embassy offices in Brazil. Several useful contacts were established in trade shows in both Rio de Janeiro and São Paulo. Initial discussions with a number of potential distributors were encouraging as a number of distributors displayed strong interest in the diaper product line. Distributors were impressed with the quality of the product, acknowledging the superiority to that of locally-manufactured brands.

The objection that the brothers ran into time and time again, however, was the price. Although all distributors were impressed by the quality, they insisted that *Precious* diapers could not effectively penetrate the Brazilian market at the proposed price (as developed in Table 3). Although the Mathieuxs attempted to impress upon the distributors the changing structure of the Brazilian marketplace, and the opportunity they saw for a high-end

high-quality product at a premium price, distributors insisted that—at least at the time—success would only follow from a price which fell into the midpriced segment of the diaper market. They also commented that "although the Americans saw the Real as stable, only time will convince us."

## Material Hospitalar, Ltd.

In June 1995 the Mathieux brothers were referred to Leonardo Sousa by the local American Chamber of Commerce. Leonardo Sousa was the president of Material Hospitalar, a distributor of health care products with contacts in the hospital and disposable hygiene markets, and one of the largest distributors of hospital supplies in Brazil. Mr. Sousa expressed a strong interest in distributing *Precious* after a demonstration of their superior absorbency, and wished to proceed with the development of a business plan in which he would work with the Mathieuxs in importing and distributing Hospeco's baby diaper products on behalf of Crosswell International.

Mr. Sousa believed that the time was right to enter the baby diaper market, even though competition was intense. The market was currently experiencing growth rates of 25 percent a year, and he was confident that *Precious* could capture one half percent of the potential baby diaper market in Brazil within a year. That represented imports of fifteen containers a month with a value of almost $33,000 per container.[10] The Mathieux brothers provided Leonardo with a price list and outline of a potential representation agreement with payment and credit terms. Payment had to be made in cash in advance or with a confirmed, irrevocable documentary letter of credit with a sight draft. In return they requested financial statements, banking references, foreign commercial references, descriptions of regional sales forces, and sales forecasts. Mr. Sousa was interested in obtaining exclusive distributor rights to all of Brazil, and Crosswell was willing to grant it to the right distributor.

Negotiations between Leonardo Sousa and the Mathieux brothers progressed. Numerous meetings were held throughout the summer of 1995. The brothers visited Material Hospitalar's warehouse in Rio and met three of Leonardo's business associates. They were impressed. The only remaining issue was price. Sousa and his associates insisted that the FOB Miami price offered to Material

---

[10]*Each container held 968 cases of diapers and each case cost $34.07 to Leonardo Sousa (968 * $34.07 = $32,980).*

**TABLE 3**

**Precious Ultra-Thin Pricing**

| | Price / case | Rate | Applied |
|---|---|---|---|
| Cases per container | | 968 | |
| Price/case to Mathieux bros (US$) | $32.57 | | |
| Commission (Mathieux) | 1.50 | 1.50 | US$ per case |
| FOB price per case (US$) | $34.07 | | |
| Freight, loading, & documentation | 4.32 | 4180 | $4180 per container |
| CFR price | $38.39 | | |
| Export insurance | 0.86 | 2.250% | % of CFR |
| CIF/case to distributor (US$) | $39.25 | | |
| Exchange rate (R$/US$) | 0.935 | 0.935 | Average of bid/ask spread |
| CIF price/case to distributor (R$) | 36.70 | | |
| Import duties (ID) | 0.73 | 2.000% | % of CIF |
| Industrial product tax (IPI) | - | 0.000% | % of CIF |
| Merchant marine renovation fee (MMRF) | 1.01 | 25.00% | % of freight |
| Port storage | 0.48 | 1.300% | % of CIF |
| Port handling fees | 0.01 | 10.84 | R$10.84 per container |
| Additional handling tax | 0.10 | 20.000% | % of storage & handling |
| Indemnity for port employees | 0.00 | 0.0407 | R$0.0407 per container |
| Bank currency exchange fees | 0.07 | 0.200% | % of CIF |
| Customs brokerage fees | 0.73 | 2.000% | % of CIF |
| Tax on merc circulation services (ICMS) | - | 0.000% | % of CIF+ID+IPT+MMRF |
| Import license | 0.05 | 50.00 | R$50.0 per container |
| Local transportation | 0.55 | 1.500% | % of CIF |
| Total cost to distributor (R$) | 40.44 | | |
| Storage cost | 0.55 | 1.500% | % of CIF * months |
| Cost of financing diaper inventory | 2.57 | 7.000% | % of CIF * months |
| Distributor's margin | 8.71 | 20.000% | % of price + storage + cc |
| Price to retailer (R$) | 52.27 | | |
| Industrial product tax (IPT−2) | 7.84 | 15.000% | % of price to retailer |
| Tax on merc circulation services (ICMS−2) | 10.82 | 18.000% | % of price + IPT2 |
| Retailer costs and markup | 21.28 | 30.000% | % of price + IPT2 + ICMS2 |
| Price per case to consumer (R$) | 92.21 | | |

| DIAPER PRICES | Bags of 8 per case | Diapers per case | Price to Consumer (R$/diaper) |
|---|---|---|---|
| Small | 44 | 352 | 0.262 |
| Medium | 32 | 256 | 0.360 |
| Large | 24 | 192 | 0.480 |
| Extra Large | 22 | 176 | 0.524 |

Hospitalar was prohibitively high, and would prevent successful market penetration. Sousa was not willing to take the chance of entry failure due to the high price.

Like other distributors, Sousa explained that thrifty Brazilians would not purchase unknown, expensive diapers even if they were higher quality. He wanted Crosswell to cut its diaper prices and fund an advertising campaign to promote the *Precious* name. When the Mathieuxs approached Hector Lans about obtaining funding for promotional efforts, they were told that given Tranzonic/Hospeco's recent financial performance, an ad campaign was out of the question. More specifically, Hector Lans had a limited budget and his superiors at Hospeco were pressuring him to show results for the expenditures related to the establishment of Crosswell. The Mathieuxs concluded that a lower price was the only way to reach an agreement with Sousa. "Once the *Precious* brand is known," he explained, "then you will be able to raise the price of the diaper. But remember, time is of the essence."

Sousa believed that Crosswell's price would have to drop by ten percent or more—the large size diaper needed to be priced at the consumer level at about R$0.43 to R$0.44 per diaper. This would place *Precious* in direct competition with the Brazilian-owned domestic producers, the *Chansommes* and *Julie Joy* brands. Sousa felt that the market shares held by these firms were particularly vulnerable given their inferior quality to that of *Precious*.

As a result, the brothers renewed negotiations with Hector Lans in Miami, explaining that a lower FOB price was necessary for successful market penetration. One suggestion made by the Mathieuxs was for Hospital Specialty to manufacture a cheaper, lower-quality diaper which could more easily fit into the target price range. Although Hector agreed to a small discount—down to $32.07 per case (before commission)—he insisted that Hospeco would not change its manufacturing process for sales to Brazil. The Mathieuxs agreed to cut their commission to three percent ($1 per case). Unfortunately, these changes still only dropped the price to R$89.87 per case, when it needed—in the eyes of Leonardo Sousa— to reach R$83 per case. The Mathieuxs still needed to cut about R$7 out of the price.

## Exploring Alternatives

The Mathieuxs were determined to find a solution to the impasse. They knew that they could not reduce their price further without shrinking their commission to unacceptable levels, and even that would not be enough. One po-tential solution for substantial gains was to find a way to reduce the financing costs of Material Hospitalar. This would enable Sousa to increase his margins and pass the savings on to the retailers.

They first looked into the Foreign Credit Insurance Association (FCIA) and the US Eximbank (Export-Import Bank). They knew that these organizations existed to encourage and facilitate exports from the United States by providing loan guarantees to help finance trade. But the brothers needed to start moving goods immediately. The conditions for entry into the personal care market in Brazil were excellent. Sales were growing and the brothers had identified an excellent potential distributor who was ready to attack the market with Hospeco's premium diapers. These organizations required time to evaluate the loan and verify the background of the companies involved. Obtaining loan guarantees from the FCIA or Eximbank would take too much time (a minimum of three months) and a mountain of paperwork. This was particularly true for a small Brazilian distributorship that had never imported from the United States. Moreover, Crosswell International was unfamiliar with the loan guarantee programs. The Mathieuxs decided that this option was only viable for the long run. Once Crosswell and Material Hospitalar had successfully established the business line, they could consider this as an option for import/export financing.

Another possibility that the Mathieux brothers considered was importing through Uruguay. The import tariffs there were about half as high as Brazilian tariffs. A distributor could import goods into Uruguay, pay the lower import tariffs, and truck the goods into Brazil. Additional tariffs at the Brazilian border would be minimal, thanks to the *Mercosur* regional trade agreement. This option offered the possibility of reduced prices in Brazil but would be very time-consuming, and would require the Mathieuxs to establish an intermediary distributor in Uruguay itself. This would involve either finding an importer or distributor in Uruguay or investing capital there to create an import/export corporation. The latter opinion did not fit Crosswell's strategy, while the former could take a few months of research and negotiation in Uruguay. Importing through Uruguay would also slow the flow of goods into Brazil, as trucking goods from Montevideo to Rio de Janeiro would add an additional two weeks to delivery time. To add to the list, Leonardo Sousa was adamantly against this option because he did not want to lose control of the flow of goods. In addition, some of the gains earned through lower import tariffs would be offset by the higher financing costs (due to the longer delivery time) and inland transportation costs. Finally, this option would be resented by the Brazilian government, which would effectively lose tariff revenues due to the "round-tripping" of Crosswell's goods. The proposal did not look promising.

A third alternative was suggested by Sousa himself. Brazilian regulations required all imports to be preapproved via an import license. To obtain the license, importers had to present a pro forma invoice to the appropriate regulatory agency. It was common practice for exporters to under-invoice merchandise on pro forma invoices to Brazil, and therefore pay significantly lower import tariffs. An importer might typically pay for 50 percent of the purchase price in cash up front (the payment being made to a bank account somewhere outside of Brazil such as Miami). The remaining 50 percent would be paid with a letter of credit, upon which the tariff charges would be levied. And because the layers of tariffs in Brazil were compounded, underinvoicing resulted in substantial savings to the importer. The amount that was saved could then be passed on to the consumer in the form of lower prices. Tranzonic was a publicly traded firm, and underinvoicing for tax evasion purposes in Brazil would violate U.S.–SEC regulations. Underinvoicing was clearly not a justifiable option from either an ethical or legal standpoint.

### Interest Rate Differentials

During a business lunch with the owner of an import-export firm in Rio de Janeiro, the Mathieuxs learned that foreign corporations (i.e., European automobile manufacturers and Chinese textile firms) were successfully undercutting national companies' prices by taking advantage of Brazil's high interest rates. Borrowing rates in the U.S. were substantially lower than deposit rates in Brazil, and given the stable exchange rate, this created an opportunity for uncovered interest rate arbitrage gains.

The basic strategy was premised on the ability to get extended terms from the seller (Crosswell International) and get paid for the goods quickly from the local Brazilian distributor (Leonardo Sousa). If Material Hospitalar could obtain 180-day credit terms, or a standard 180-day letter of credit from Crosswell, the firm could sell the goods into the local market for cash within thirty days of receiving the diapers at port. The cash proceeds from the resale could then be invested in the relatively "high-yielding" Real-denominated deposit rates. At the end of the following four to five months when the payment on the goods to Crosswell was due, the deposits could be closed and the profits taken to offset the cost of financing the purchase. This would reduce the R$2.57 per case financing cost of the distributor as described in the baseline analysis in Table 3. Of course, this was only true if the Real/dollar exchange rate was stable over the period.

The Mathieux brothers were well aware that these interest rate differentials could not persist over the long run. Eventually, interest rates in Brazil would fall (assuming inflation was not reignited). However, in the short run, many international firms were taking advantage of the situation to lower their effective prices and gain market share in Brazil. The Mathieux brothers returned to the United States intent on exploring payment methods and financing with Crosswell.

### Methods of Payment

A contract between an importer and exporter specifies a number of critical transaction details, including the method of payment.[11] There are four methods by which an exporter can sell to a foreign buyer: (1) advanced payment or prepayment, (2) documentary collections, (3) letter of credit (L/C), and (4) open account. The critical differences in the methods primarily involved who assumed the commercial risk and who provided the financing, the importer or exporter.

1. **Advanced payment.** If the importer pays for the goods up front, *prepayment,* the importer assumes all of the risks of nonperformance on the part of the seller. Because the buyer is paying for the goods prior to shipment, the buyer is financing the transaction. This is essentially a cash payment for goods like that of a retail sale.
2. **Documentary collection.** A documentary collection means that payment is due from the buyer upon presentation of certain documents (and explicitly not necessarily upon receipt of the actual goods). Also termed *collection of drafts,* the exporter issues an or-

---

[11] *The common items in a sales contract include: description of merchandise, specifying standards, grade, or quality; exact quantity in units, specific weight, or volume; unit price expressed in a specified currency for payment; trade terms expressed as FOB or CIF, naming of specific ports of exit and entry, individual liabilities associated with individual costs, and risks; packing; identifying markings; extent of insurance coverage and who is to provide it; shipping instructions including method of transportation and consignment, the documents required for shipping, and timing; type of payment method to be used (e.g., L/C).*

der to the importer for payment. This order, the *draft*, may require payment upon demand, a *sight draft*, or may require payment within a set number of days, a *time draft*.[12] A time draft therefore allows a delay in payment by the buyer, and is a form of financing provided by the exporter.[13]

Another subcategory of documentary collection is whether the draft is *clean* or *documentary*. A *clean draft* is very simple and straightforward: the control of the merchandise is turned over to the buyer regardless of the importer's payment or acceptance, very similar to an open account transaction. Multinational firms shipping merchandise to their own foreign affiliates often use clean drafts to effect payment (they trust their own affiliates to make timely payment). A *documentary draft* requires that a number of other shipping documents be attached to the draft, and the buyer must either make payment (sight draft) or acceptance (time draft) in order to obtain possession of the documents needed to take possession of the goods. There is obviously a little less trust involved in a documentary draft transaction.

3. **Documentary letter of credit.** A letter of credit (L/C) is a type of guarantee of payment provided by a bank upon the buyer's request. The issuing bank promises to pay the seller, the exporter, upon presentation of key documents specified in the terms of the credit. The promise to pay by the bank reduces the commercial risk to the exporter. The letter of credit may be confirmed or unconfirmed by the exporter's bank, depending on the contract between importer and exporter. A letter of credit is in many ways a documentary draft with the added safeguard of a bank's guarantee of payment. Although on the surface the cycle appears complex, the process simply involves the exchange of documents and money through intermediaries—normally commercial banks.

4. **Open account.** This is the form of most domestic business transactions where goods are shipped by the seller and a bill or invoice is issued requesting payment within a set number of days. Credit terms associated with an open account method of payment may state a discount if paid within a set number of days and the final date on which payment is due (for example a 2 percent discount if paid within 10 days, with the payment due no later than 30 days, termed "2/10 net 30"). Credit terms internationally vary considerably across borders, and often reflect traditional business habits within a country-market.

## The Proposal

The decision was made to use extended financing as the main selling point to bring Leonardo Sousa on board. The task facing the Mathieuxs was to be clear, yet convincing, when describing the potential benefits and associated risks of their proposed solution. Leonardo Sousa must understand that the success of the strategy was dependent on a stable Real/dollar exchange rate, and his ability to collect as quickly as possible for the diapers. Any significant depreciation of the Real against the dollar would increase the size of Material Hospitalar's obligations to Crosswell, as well as threaten the competitiveness of *Precious* diapers in the Brazilian market.

Doug and Geoff reviewed the financial cycle involved in exporting to Brazil with a 180-day letter of credit.[14] Crosswell would—at least for the first year—require a confirmed letter of credit from the Brazilian's bank in U.S. dollars. The cycle they were currently analyzing was for an order placed August 4, 1995, by Leonardo Sousa. Table 4 details the steps involved if Leonardo Sousa placed the order. Unfortunately, there were no foreign currency futures or forwards available to hedge dollar-denominated accounts payable in the event that the Real did begin to depreciate.[15] The Mathieux brothers grew silent as they both wondered if their proposal would fly.

### Questions for Discussion

1. What actions would you recommend to Crosswell and to Leonardo Sousa that would enable them to hit the target of R$83.00 per case of diapers?

---

[12]*There are two major varieties of time drafts, the* bill of lading draft *and the* fixed maturity draft. A bill of lading draft *requires that payment be made a fixed number of days after the bill of lading date. The fixed maturity draft requires payment on a date specified in the draft.*

[13]*When a time draft is presented to the importer, the buyer stamps a notice of* acceptance *on its face. Once "accepted," it becomes a promise to pay a specified amount of money on a future date like a note or bond. If the draft is drawn upon and accepted by a bank, it becomes a "bankers acceptance."*

[14]*Crosswell International could currently borrow short term in the U.S. dollar market at the following rates: 30 days—8.40 percent, 60 days—8.44 percent, 90 days—8.50 percent, 120 days—8.51 percent, 180 days—8.60 percent (all rates per annum).*

[15]*The Chicago Mercantile Exchange was currently studying the possibility of trading a Brazilian Real/U.S. dollar futures contract, but it was as yet unavailable.*

2. What are the benefits and risks to Mr. Sousa if he uses a U.S. dollar-denominated 180-day letter of credit to finance the import of fifteen containers of *Precious Ultra Thin Baby Diapers*? What are the potential benefits and risks to Crosswell?

3. How much added profit can Mr. Sousa earn from taking advantage of the 180-day letter of credit? (Use the sequence of events and dates described in Table 4. Assume the exchange rate and deposit rates of interest are stable.) Can this be used to reduce the price that Mr. Sousa charges the retailers? Would it be enough?

4. How important is the exchange rate and the exchange rate risk to this product's success in the Brazilian market? Would your answer change if the economy was experiencing hyperinflation as opposed to relative price stability? Would your answer differ if Crosswell had chosen to invoice in Brazilian Reals instead of U.S. dollars?

## TABLE 4

**Proposed Process of Financing With the Letter of Credit**

| | |
|---|---|
| Aug 1 | Importer requests a price from Crosswell |
| Aug 2 | Crosswell responds, via fax, with an FOB price Miami of $34.07 |
| Aug 5 | Importer agrees to terms and faxes a purchase order to Crosswell |
| Aug 6 | Crosswell faxes a pro forma invoice to the importer agreeing to price and terms |
| Aug 7 | Importer makes an application to its bank for a letter of credit (L/C) |
| Aug 8 | Importer's bank issues L/C and sends advice to Crosswell's bank in Miami that a L/C has been opened in its behalf, with instruction as to what documents are required for payment under the L/C. The L/C guarantees payment in U.S. dollars in 180 days upon presentations of specified documents. (The distributor could also request 30-, 60-, 90-, and 120-day credit terms, depending on what is negotiated with Crosswell International at the time of the sale.) |
| Aug 9 | Crosswell's bank confirms the L/C |
| Aug 12 | Crosswell turns the goods over to a freight forwarder for shipment and consigns the goods to the order of the shipper. Crosswell keeps large stocks of diapers in its warehouse so that orders can be shipped immediately upon request. |
| | Crosswell prefers to be paid up front rather than wait 180 days for the total amount. It is standard for the company to add any discount fee to the total amount appearing on the importer's invoice. |
| Aug 13 | Shipping company issues the bill of lading. Crosswell issues a time draft in the name of its bank (since its bank confirmed the L/C) and presents documents to the bank. Crosswell's bank "accepts" the time draft creating a bankers acceptance. |
| | Crosswell can at this point choose to wait to be paid in 180 days, or present the 180-day letter of credit to its bank for payment now. If requesting payment now, the company receives the stated amount less a discount fee set by its bank. The discount rate is equal to the company's short-term borrowing rate in the U.S. on August 4, 1995. The rates vary according to the number of days in the terms of the letter of credit. |
| Aug 14 | The documents are forwarded from the exporter's bank to the importer's bank |
| Sept 6 | Importer receives the goods |
| Sept 10 | Importer sells goods to retailer and is paid cash by the retailer. Importer deposits amount due to Crosswell in a savings account for five months. |
| Feb 10 | Importer pays the Brazilian bank, which then pays Crosswell's bank (180 days after shipment of the goods). |

**Selected Financial Data for The Tranzonic Companies (years ended February 28/29)**

| | 1994 | 1993 | 1992 | 1991 | 1990 |
|---|---|---|---|---|---|
| Sales | 131,182,128 | 119,951,373 | 110,717,585 | 107,333,543 | 96,705,806 |
| Operating earnings | 4,858,423 | 6,816,888 | 7,193,019 | 6,714,882 | 5,541,952 |
| Earnings before income taxes and cum effect | 4,599,265 | 6,785,982 | 7,411,281 | 6,953,690 | 5,914,428 |
| Income taxes | 1,800,000 | 2,572,000 | 2,835,000 | 2,635,000 | 1,746,000 |
| Earnings before cumulative effect of change in acctg | 2,799,265 | 4,213,982 | 4,576,281 | 4,318,690 | 4,168,428 |
| Cum effect of change in acctg | — | — | — | — | 701,500 |
| Net earnings | 2,799,265 | 4,213,982 | 4,576,281 | 4,318,690 | 4,869,928 |
| | | | | | |
| Per share amounts | | | | | |
| Earnings before cum effect | .80 | 1.19 | 1.29 | 1.23 | 1.15 |
| Cum effect of chg in actg | — | — | — | — | .19 |
| Net earnings per common share | .80 | 1.19 | 1.29 | 1.23 | 1.34 |
| | | | | | |
| Cash dividends | | | | | |
| Per Class A Common Share | .18 | .165 | .16 | .16 | .16 |
| Per Class B Common Share | .34 | .325 | .32 | .28 | .28 |
| | | | | | |
| Total assets | 73,537,946 | 63,675,545 | 58,015,061 | 52,515,283 | 49,498,159 |
| Long-term debt | 9,000,000 | 2,900,000 | 195,000 | 195,000 | 1,022,770 |
| Shareholders' equity | 47,479,072 | 46,328,637 | 42,743,659 | 38,848,871 | 36,103,517 |
| Shareholders equity per common share | 13.75 | 13.21 | 12.32 | 11.24 | 10.31 |
| Common shares outstanding | 3,452,038 | 3,507,838 | 3,468,128 | 3,456,934 | 3,500,149 |

Fiscal year 1994 includes a $1,300,000 charge to operating earnings ($792,000 after-tax or 22 cents per share) for costs associated with restructuring the Housewares Division. Fiscal year 1990 includes the cumulative effect of a change in accounting for income taxes.

## APPENDIX B:

**Consolidated Statement of Earnings (years ended February 28, 1994 and 1993, and February 29, 1992)**

| | 1994 | 1993 | 1992 |
|---|---|---|---|
| Sales | $131,182,128 | 119,951,373 | 110,717,585 |
| Costs and expenses: | | | |
| Cost of goods sold | 87,493,123 | 78,470,393 | 71,604,322 |
| Selling, general, and administrative expenses | 37,530,582 | 34,664,092 | 31,920,244 |
| Restructuring cost | 1,300,000 | — | — |
| | 126,323,705 | 113,134,485 | 103,524,566 |
| Operating earnings | 4,858,423 | 6,816,888 | 7,193,019 |
| Interest income | 54,369 | 96,304 | 280,853 |
| Interest expense | (313,527) | (127,210) | (62,591) |
| Earnings before income taxes | 4,599,265 | 6,785,982 | 7,411,281 |
| Income taxes | 1,800,000 | 2,572,000 | 2,835,000 |
| Net earnings | $ 2,799,265 | 4,213,982 | 4,576,281 |
| Net earnings per common share | $ .80 | 1.19 | 1.29 |

# The F-18 Hornet Offset

In May of 1992, the Finnish government's selection of the F/A-18 Hornet over the Swedish JAS-39 Gripen, the French Mirage 2000-5, and fellow American F-16 to modernize the fighter fleet of its air force was a major boost to McDonnell Douglas (MDC) in an otherwise quiet market. The deal would involve the sale of 57 F/A-18 Cs and 7 F/A-18 Ds at a cost of FIM 9.5 billion (approximately $2 billion). Deliveries would take place between 1995 and 2000.

Winning the contract was critical since MDC had been on the losing side of two major aircraft competitions in the United States in 1991. In addition, one of its major projects with the U.S. Navy had been terminated (the A-12), and the government of the Republic of Korea had changed its mind to buy F-16 aircraft after it already had an agreement with MDC for F/A-18 Hornets.

However, the $2 billion will not be earned without strings attached. Contractually, McDonnell Douglas and its main subcontractors (Northrop, General Electric, and General Motor's subsidiary Hughes), the "F-18 Team," are obligated to facilitate an equivalent amount of business for Finnish industry over a ten-year period (1992–2002) using various offset arrangements.

## Offsets

Offsets are various forms of industrial and business activities required as a condition of purchase. They are an obligation imposed on the seller in major (most often military hardware) purchases by or for foreign governments to minimize any trade imbalance or other adverse economic impact caused by the outflow of currency re-

SOURCE: *This case study was written by Ilkka A. Ronkainen and funded in part by a grant from the Business and International Education Program of the U.S. Department of Education. The assistance of the various organizations cited in the case is appreciated. Special thanks to David Danjczek of UNOVA, Inc. For more information, see* **http://www.dac.mdc.com, http://www.ge.com/ geae/military/fighters, http://www.northgrum.com, http:// www.hughes.com.** *Materials used include Maria Jakubik, Irina Kabirova, Tapani Koivunen, Päivi Lähtevänoja, and Denice Stanfors,* Finnish Airforce Buying Fighters, *Helsinki School of Economics, September 24, 1993; Keith Silverang, "Behind the Myth of Offset,"* Style & Steel *2 (Spring 1992): 28–29; and Pompiliu Verzariu, and Paula Mitchell,* International Countertrade: Individual Country Practices *(Washington, D.C.: U.S. Department of Commerce, 1992), Part 1.*

quired to pay for such purchases. In wealthier countries, it is often used for establishing infrastructure. Two basic types of offset arrangements exist: direct and indirect (as seen in Figure 1). Although offsets have long been associated only with the defense sector, there are now increasing demands for offsets in commercial sales where the government is the purchaser or user.

Direct offset consists of product-related manufacturing or assembly either for the purposes of the project in question only or for a longer-term partnership. The purchase, therefore, enables the purchaser to be involved in the manufacturing process. Various Spanish companies produce dorsal covers, rudders, aft fuselage panels, and speed brakes for the F/A-18s designated for the Spanish Air Force. In addition to coproduction arrangements, licensed production is prominent. Examples include Egypt producing U.S. M1-A1 tanks, China producing MDC's MD-82 aircraft, and Korea assembling the F-16 fighter. An integral part of these arrangements is the training of the local employees. Training is not only for production/ assembly purposes but also for maintenance and overhaul of the equipment in the longer term. Some offsets have buyback provisions; that is, the seller is obligated to purchase output from the facility or operations it has set up or licensed. For example, Westland takes up an agreed level of parts and components from the Korean plant that produces Lynx Helicopters under license. In practice, therefore, direct offsets amount to technology transfer.

Indirect offsets are deals that involve products, investments, and so forth which are not to be used in the original sales contract but that will satisfy part of the seller's "local" obligation. Direct purchases of raw materials, equipment, or supplies by the seller or its suppliers from the offset customer country present the clearest case of indirect offsets. These offset arrangements are analogous to counterpurchases and switch trading. Sellers faced with offset obligations work closely with their supplier base, some having goals of increasing supplier participation in excess of 50 percent. Teamwork does make the process more effective and efficient. There are various business activities taking place and procurement decisions being made by one of the sellers or its suppliers without offset needs that others may be able to use as offset credit to satisfy an indirect obligation.

Many governments see offsets as a mechanism to develop their indigenous business and industrial sectors. Training in management techniques may be attractive to both parties. The upgrading of humanware may be seen by the government as more critical for improving international competitiveness than efforts focused only on

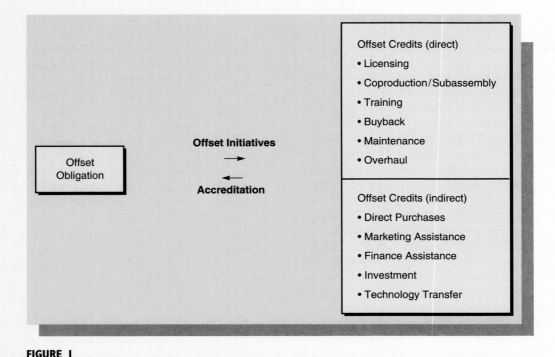

**FIGURE I**

**The Offset Process**

hardware. For the seller, training is relatively inexpensive, but it provides good credits because of its political benefit.

An important dimension of the developmental effort will relate to exports. This may involve the analysis of business sectors showing the greatest foreign market potential, improving organizational and product readiness, conducting market research (e.g., estimating demand or assessing competition), identifying buyers or partners for foreign market development, or assisting in the export process (e.g., company visits, support in negotiations and reaching a final agreement, facilitating trial/sample shipments, handling documentation needs).

Sales are often won or lost on the availability of financing and favorable credit terms to the buyer. Financing packages put together by one of the seller's entities, if it is critical in winning the bid, will earn offset credits.

Buyer nations focusing on industrial development and technology transfer have negotiated contracts that call for offsetting the cost of their purchases through investments. Saudi Arabian purchases of military technology have recently been tied to sellers' willingness to invest in manufacturing plants, defense-related industries, or special interest projects in the country. British Aerospace,

for example, has agreed to invest in factories for the production of farm feed and sanitary ware.

Most often, the final offset deal includes a combination of activities, both direct and indirect vis-à-vis the sale, and no two offset deals are alike. With increasing frequency, governments may require "predeal counterpurchases" as a sign of commitment and ability to deliver should they be awarded the contract. Some companies, such as United Technologies, argue that there is limited advantage in carrying out offset activities in advance of the contract unless the buyer agrees to a firm commitment. While none of the bidders may like it, buyer's market conditions give them very little choice to argue. Even if a bidder loses the deal, it can always attempt to sell its offset credits to the winner or use the credits in conjunction with other sales that one of its divisions may have. Some of the companies involved in the bidding in Finland maintain offset accounts with the Finnish government.

### McDonnell's Deal with the Finnish Air Force

The F/A-18 Hornet is a twin-engine, twin-tail, multimission tactical aircraft that can be operated from aircraft carriers or from land bases (see Table 1). It is both

**TABLE I**

**F/A-18 Hornet Strike Fighter**

| | |
|---|---|
| Prime contractor | McDonnell Douglas |
| Principal subcontractor | Northrop Corporation |
| Type | Single- (C) and two-seat (D), twin-turbofan for fighter and attack missions |
| **Power plant** | Two General Electric F404-GE-402 (enhanced performance engine) |
| Thrust | 4800 kp each (approx.) |
| Afterburning thrust | 8000 kp each (approx.) |
| **Dimensions** | |
| Length | 17.07 m |
| Span | 11.43 m |
| Wing area | 37.16 m$^2$ |
| Height | 4.66 m |
| **Weights** | |
| Empty | 10,455 kg |
| Normal takeoff | 16,650 kg |
| Maximum takeoff | 22,328 kg |
| Wing loading | 450 kg/m$^2$ |
| Fuel (internal) | 6,435 litre (4,925 kg) |
| Fuel (with external tanks) | 7,687 litre |
| **Armament** | |
| Cannon | One General Electric M61A-1 Vulcan rotary-barrel 20-mm |
| Missiles | Six AIM-9 Sidewinder air-to-air |
| | Four AIM-7 Sparrow |
| | Six AIM-120 AMRAAM |
| Radar | AN/APG-73 multi-mode air-to-air and air-to-surface |
| **Performance** | |
| Takeoff distance | 430 m |
| Landing distance | 850 m |
| Fighter-mission radius | > 740 km |
| Maximum speed | 1.8 Mach (1,915 km/h) at high altitude |
| | 1.0 Mach at intermediate power |
| Service ceiling | 15,240 m |
| Payload | 7,710 kg |
| Used since | 1983 |
| Expected manufacturing lifetime | 2000+ |
| Users | USA, Australia, Canada, Spain, and Kuwait |
| Ordered quantity | 1,168 |

a fighter (air-to-air) and an attack (air-to-ground) aircraft. McDonnell Aircraft Company, a division of MDC, is the prime contractor for the F/A-18. Subcontractors include General Electric for the Hornet's smokeless F404 low-bypass turbofan engines, Hughes Aircraft Company for the APG-73 radar, and Northrop Corporation for the airframe. Approximately 1,100 F/A-18s have been delivered worldwide. Although it had been in use by the United States since 1983, it had been (and can continue to be) upgraded during its operational lifetime. Furthermore, it had proven its combat readiness in the Gulf War.

Only since June of 1990 has the F/A-18 been available to countries that are not members of the North Atlantic Treaty Organization (NATO). The change in U.S. government position resulted from the rapidly changed East-West political situation. The attractive deals available in neutral countries such as Switzerland and Finland helped push the government as well. When the Finnish Air Force initiated its program in 1986, MDC was not invited to (and would not have been able to) offer a bid because of U.S. government restrictions.

## The Finnish Government Position

The Finnish government's role in the deal had two critical dimensions: one related to the choice of the aircraft, the other related to managing the offset agreement in a fashion to maximize the benefit to the country's industry for the long term.

### Selecting the Fighter

In 1986, the Finnish Air Force (FAF) decided to replace its aging Swedish-made Drakens and Soviet-made MIG-21s, which made up three fighter squadrons. At that time, the remaining service life of these aircraft was estimated to be fifteen years, calling for the new squadrons to be operational by the year 2000 and to be up-to-date even in 2025. Finland, due to its strategic geographic location, has always needed a reliable air defense system. The position of neutrality adopted by Finland had favored split procurement between Eastern and Western suppliers until the collapse of the Soviet Union in December of 1991 made it politically possible to purchase fighters from a single Western supplier.

The first significant contacts with potential bidders were made in 1988, and in February 1990, the FAF requested proposals from the French Dassault-Breguet, Sweden's Industrigruppen JAS, and General Dynamics in the United States for forty fighters and trainer aircraft. In January 1991, the bid was amended to sixty fighters and seven trainers. Three months later, MDC joined the bidding, and by July 1991, binding bids were received from all of the four manufacturers.

During the evaluative period, the four bidders tried to gain favor for their alternative. One approach was the provision of deals for Finnish companies as "predeal counterpurchases." For example, General Dynamics negotiated for Vaisala (a major Finnish electronics firm) to become a subcontractor of specialty sensors for the F-16. Before the final decision, the Swedish bidder had arranged

for deals worth $250 million for Finnish companies, the French for over $100 million, and General Dynamics for $40 million. MDC, due to its later start, had none to speak of. Other tactics were used as well. The Swedes pointed out to long ties that the countries have had, and especially to the possibilities to develop them further on the economic front. As a matter of fact, offsets were the main appeal of the Swedish bid since the aircraft itself was facing development cost overruns and delays. The French reminded the Finnish government that choosing a European fighter might help in Finland's bid to join the European Union (EU) in 1995. Since the FAF prefers the U.S. AMRAAM missile system for its new fighters, the U.S. government cautioned that its availability depended on the choice of the fighter. The companies themselves also worked on making their bid sweeter: Just before the official announcement, General Dynamics improved its offer to include sixty-seven aircraft for the budgeted sum and a guarantee of 125 percent offsets; that is, the amount of in-country participation would be 125 percent of the sale price paid by the Finnish government for the aircraft.

After extensive flight testing both in the producers' countries and in Finland (especially for winter conditions), the Hornet was chosen as the winner. Despite the high absolute cost of the aircraft (only 57 will be bought versus 60), the Hornet's cost-effectiveness relative to performance was high. The other alternatives were each perceived to have problems: The JAS-39 Gripen had the teething problems of a brand-new aircraft; the Mirage's model 2000-5 has not yet been produced; and the F-16 may be coming to the end of its product life cycle. The MIG-29 from the Soviet Union/Russia was never seriously in the running due to the political turmoil in that country. Some did propose purchasing the needed three squadrons from the stockpiles of the defunct East Germany (and they could have been had quite economically), but the uncertainties were too great for a strategically important product.

### Working out the Offsets

Typically, a specific committee is set up by the government to evaluate which arrangements qualify as part of the offset. In Finland's case, the Finnish Offset Committee (FOC) consists of five members with Ministries of Defense, Foreign Affairs, as well as Industry and Trade represented. Its task is to provide recommendations as to which export contracts qualify and which do not. The Technical Working Group was set up to support its decision making, especially in cases concerning technology transfer. From 1977 to 1991, the procedures and final decisions were made by the Ministry of Defense; since then, the responsibility has been transferred to the Ministry of Trade and Industry (see Figure 2). The transfer was logical given the increased demands and expectations on the trade and technology fronts of the F/A-18 deal.

When the committee was established in 1977 in conjunction with a major military purchase, almost all contracts qualified until an export developmental role for offsets was outlined. The Finnish exporter is required to show that the offset agreement played a pivotal role in securing its particular contract.

Two different approaches are taken by the government to attain its developmental objective. First, the government will not make available (or give offset credit) for counterpurchasing goods that already have established market positions unless the counterpurchaser can show that the particular sale would not have materialized without its support (e.g., through distribution or financing). Second, the government will use compensation "multipliers" for the first time. While previous deals were executed on a one-on-one basis, the government now wants, through the use of multipliers, direct purchases to certain industries or types of companies. For example, in the case of small or medium-sized companies, a multiplier of

two may be used; that is, a purchase of $500,000 from such a firm will satisfy a $1 million share of the counterpurchaser's requirement. Attractive multipliers also may be used, which may generate long-term export opportunities or support Finland's indigenous arms or other targeted industry. Similarly, the seller may also insist on the use of multipliers. In the case of technology transfer, the seller may request a high multiplier because of the high initial cost of research and development that may have gone into the technology licensed or provided to the joint venture as well as its relative importance to the recipient country's economic development.

Finnish industry is working closely with the government on two fronts. The Finnish Industrial Offset Consortium (FINDOC) was established to collaborate with the Finnish Foreign Trade Association (a quasigovernmental organization) on trade development. FINDOC's twenty-one members represent fifteen main business areas (e.g., aircraft, shipbuilding, pulp and paper machinery, and metal and engineering) and are among the main Finnish exporters. Their consortium was set up to take advantage of offset opportunities more efficiently and to provide a focal point for the F-18 Team's efforts. For example, MDC and FINDOC arranged for a familiarization trip to the United States for interested Finnish businesses

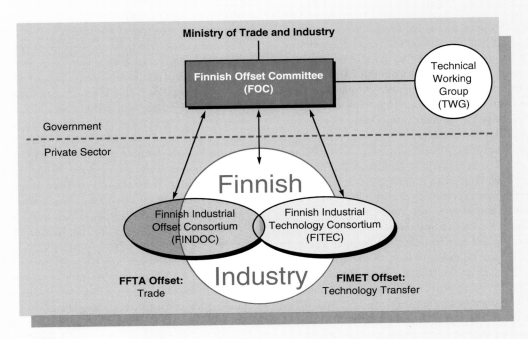

**FIGURE 2**

**Offset: Finnish Industry Input**

in the fall of 1992. For those companies not in FINDOC, it is the task of the FFTA to provide information on possibilities to benefit from the deal. The Finnish Industrial Technology Consortium (FITEC) was established to facilitate technology transfer to and from the Finnish metal and engineering industries.

## The F-18 Team's Position

The monies related to offset management and associated development are not generally allowed as a separate cost in the sales contract. Profit margins for aircraft sales are narrow, and any additional costs must be watched closely. Extraordinary demands by the buyer make bidding more challenging and time consuming. For example, the customer may want extensive changes in the product without changes in the final price. Switzerland wanted major alterations made to the airframe and additional equipment which made its total cost per plane higher than the price in Finland. In the experience of high-tech firms, the add-on for direct offsets range from 3 to 8 percent, which has to be incorporated into the feasibility plans. Offsets have to make good business sense and, once agreed to, successfully executed.

## Competing for the Deal

In accepting the offer to bid for the FAF deal, the F-18 Team believed it had only a 5 percent chance to win the deal but, given its size, decided to go ahead. From the time it received a request to bid from the FAF, MDC had three months to prepare its proposal. The only main negative factor from the short preparation time was MDC's inability to arrange for "prepurchase" deals and generate goodwill with the constituents.

After two fact-finding missions to Finland, MDC established an office in Helsinki in August 1991. The decision to have a full-time office in Finland (compared to the competitors whose representatives were in Helsinki two days a week on the average) was made based on the experiences from Korea and Switzerland. MDC's approach was to be ready and able to help the customer in terms of information and be involved with all the constituents of the process, such as the testing groups of the FAF, the Ministry of Defense (owners of the program), and the Parliament (supporters of the program).

Beyond the technical merits of the Hornet, MDC's capabilities in meeting the pending offset obligations were a critical factor in winning the deal. MDC had by 1992 a total of 100 offset programs in twenty-five countries with

a value of $8 billion, and its track record in administering them was excellent. Another factor in MDC's favor was its long-term relation with Finnair, the national airline. Finnair's aircraft have predominantly come from MDC, starting with the DC-2 in 1941 to the MD-11 aircraft delivered in 1991.

## Satisfying the Offset Obligation

Offset deals are not barter where the seller and the buyer swap products of equal value over a relatively short time period. The F-18 Team members have to complete the offset program by the year 2002 through a number of different elements including marketing assistance, export development, technology transfer, team purchases, and investment financing. One of the major beneficiaries of the offset arrangement is Valmet, the only major aircraft manufacturer in Finland. Valmet will assemble the fifty-seven C-versions in Finland and is also counting on the F-18 Team's connections to open markets for its Redigo trainer aircraft. The F-18 Team works with Finnish companies to develop exports for their products and services by identifying potential buyers and introducing the two parties to each other. Purchases can come from within the contractor companies, suppliers to the F-18 contractors, and third parties. The motivation for completing offset projects is financial penalties for the prime team members if they do not meet contract deadlines.

However, no one in the F-18 Team or among its suppliers is obligated to engage in a given transaction just because Finland purchased fighters from McDonnell Douglas. The key point is that products must meet specifications, delivery dates, and price criteria to be successfully sold in any market. After an appropriate purchase has taken place, the F-18 Team receives offset credit based on the Finnish-manufactured content of the transaction value as approved by the Finnish Offset Committee. For example, when Finnyards won the bid to build a passenger ferry for the Danish Stena Line, Northrop received offset credits due to its role in financing Finnyard's bid.

The offset obligations are not limited to the United States. The Team has offset partners all over the world because the members operate worldwide. As a matter of fact, the F-18 Team companies have to be very careful not to cause U.S. businesses to lose contracts unfairly in pushing for constituents to favor Finnish companies. The so-called Feingold Amendment (named after Senator Russell Feingold of Wisconsin) to the Arms Export Control Act prohibits U.S companies with offset obligations from offering terms and conditions that they would not provide under normal market conditions to secure a deal. Furthermore, given the long time frame involved, there are no pressing time constraints on the members to earn offset credits.

Since 1992, the MDC office in Helsinki has had two officers; one is in charge of the aircraft, the other focused on offsets. Due to the worst recession in recent Finnish history, the response to the offset program has been unprecedented, and the office has been inundated with requests for information.

## One Company's Experience

Hackman, one of Finland's leading exporters in the metal sector, started its cooperation with McDonnell Douglas by putting together a portfolio of Hackman products that offer the best offset potential. The proposal ended up covering a wide range of products ranging from tableware to turnkey cheese plants. Disinfecting machines and food processors created the most interest because of McDonnell Douglas' contracts in the hospital and construction sectors.

The first project identification came in July 1992 when word came from McDonnell Douglas that a $187 million hotel being planned for Denver, Colorado, was a potential offset target. The contractor was seeking export financing (e.g., through GE Finance) in exchange for sourcing products through offset from Finland for which offset credits could be used by MDC. Ideally, the contractor would get attractive financing, the F-18 Team would get offset credits, and Finnish participants would get a shot at a huge deal worth up to $40 million in total.

### Questions for Discussion

1. Why would the members of the F-18 Team, McDonnell Douglas, Northrop, General Electric, and Hughes agree to such a deal rather than insist on a money-based transaction?
2. After the deal was signed, many Finnish companies expected that contracts and money would start rolling in by merely calling up McDonnell Douglas. What are the fundamental flaws of this thinking?
3. Why do Western governments typically take an unsupportive stance on counter-trade arrangements?
4. Comment on this statement: "Offset arrangements involving overseas production that permits a foreign government or producer to, acquire the technical information to manufacture all or part of a U.S.-origin article trade short-term sales for long-term loss of market position."

# Martin Guides, Inc.

If we do nothing to our current products and do not publish a European product, we will experience an increase in sales, though it will be a gradual increase each year. Our European distributors are predicting a surge in CD-ROM equipped computers over the next few years. In order for us to take advantage of the size of the installed base of CD-ROM drives we must adapt our products to the European marketplace. Last year we had sales outside the U.S. of $950,000. At the current rate we will very probably do $1,250,000 this year (maybe $1,500,000). I would project for 1996 $2,100,000 (tops $2,500,000) if we do nothing to our current products.
—Mike Timmons,
European Sales Agent, Martin Guides

As Controller of Martin Guides, Inc. (MG), Cathy McCloud had been assigned by Jeff Martin, the CEO and owner, to research the tax implications of establishing a European sales subsidiary. International tax regulations were not her specialty, but she had invested hours of research and consulted colleagues and was now fairly confident she could outline the firm's main alternatives.

Many changes had taken place at Martin Guides since her arrival there three years before, in 1992. At that time MG was a relatively small company in Duckbay, Massachusetts, that produced guide books for forty-five of the fifty states. A few months after Cathy's arrival, Jeff Martin unveiled plans to make the guides available on CD-ROM. The new format combined video clips, sounds, and user-interactivity with the text information from the paper guides. Jeff Martin's vision turned out to be very good timing as the multimedia boom had just begun. Sales began to grow at 40 percent per year after the launch of several widely acclaimed CD-ROM products.

Suddenly, Martin had begun to attract foreign demand with its *WorldGuide* and *TourUSA* CD-ROM products. While the products were in English, European buyers were attracted by their high-quality content, colorful images, accurate maps, and simple user interface. But no one at the company had true international business experience, and the prospect of expanding into Europe had become the subject of several meetings between department leaders and Jeff Martin.

With five more minutes to go, Cathy trudged across the snowy field to the new annex. She smiled upon entering the room in an attempt to appear at ease, although she knew her boss would not be pleased with the results of her research. At the last meeting, Jeff Martin had been enthusiastic about the prospect of establishing a subsidiary in Ireland or the Netherlands, where he believed the company would face low tax rates. At the meeting, Cathy had expressed doubt that the company could benefit from low tax rates offered in those countries. Now those doubts were confirmed.

Mike Timmons, MG's European sales agent, was back from Germany. He would play an important role in the site selection for the European subsidiary due to his in-depth knowledge of the market. Jeff was genuinely friendly, a good person to work for, but he was demanding. When Jeff had an inspiration, everyone was expected to feel it with him and make it happen.

*Jeff:* Okay, Mike, Cathy, I've only got a few minutes until I have to go over and see the architect for the west building, so let's get down to business. At last month's meeting, Cathy and I had decided that a sales subsidiary in Europe was the best way to address our most imme-diate problems without putting up a large investment. Mike, you had sent us a fax that outlined some problems we're having in Europe. Since you're here now could you recap what the problems are?

*Mike:* Sure. Our European distributors are dissatis-fied with our export teams and with the fact that our products are not adapted to the market there. Last week, we lost a French distributor because he didn't like FOB Duckbay. And that's not just a French reaction. Many dis-tributors are complaining about having to send faxes back and forth to establish an all-in price. He also said sales were low because the product wasn't translated into French. Several people asked me at the CeBIT conven-tion why we were showing the same version of *WorldGuide* for the third year in a row, and when we would have European products. I get the feeling that Eu-ropean customers are getting a bad image of us, one that's totally out of line with our U.S. image of being cus-tomer-oriented. If we have long-term plans in Europe, we shouldn't risk damaging our image before we even really get into the market. It's bad enough we don't have a European product or version. I polled our distri-butors and got their estimates of sales over the next two years for both products (see Table 1.)

*Jeff:* Okay. So really we're dealing with two distinct problems here. One is a marketing problem. Customers aren't totally satisfied with what we're selling. The other

**TABLE 1**

Mike Timmon's Sales Projections for ADAPTED Products

| Country | Pieces | EuroGuide Sales @ $35 | Pieces | WorldGuide Sales @ $42.50 | Combined Sales |
|---|---|---|---|---|---|
| Germany/Austria/Switzerland | 60,000 | $2,100,000 | 70,000 | $2,975,000 | $5,075,000 |
| UK/Ireland | 14,000 | 490,000 | 11,000 | 467,500 | 957,500 |
| France | 10,000 | 350,000 | 11,000 | 467,500 | 817,500 |
| Scandinavia | 7,000 | 245,000 | 4,000 | 170,000 | 415,000 |
| Netherlands | 5,000 | 175,000 | 4,000 | 170,000 | 345,000 |
| Belgium and Luxembourg | 6,000 | 210,000 | 2,000 | 85,000 | 295,000 |
| Spain and Portugal | 2,000 | 70,000 | 1,500 | 63,750 | 133,750 |
| Italy | 9,000 | 315,000 | 3,500 | 148,750 | 463,750 |
| Projected sales, 1996 | 113,000 | $3,955,000 | 107,000 | $4,547,500 | $8,502,500 |
| Projected sales, 1997 | 226,000 | $7,910,000 | 214,000 | $9,095,000 | $17,005,000 |
| Estimated sales, eoy 1995 | $1,500,000 | | | | |
| Project sales in Europe, 1996 | $2,500,000 | | | | |

*Source:* Poll of MB's current distributors.

is an operational problem. Our distributors want simpler, more direct service. Mike, you've mentioned many times before that customers would like to see a European version. I'd like to see those projections for translated products. As I've explained before, we don't have the resources right now to do the translation well. I want to do a good job on that. That's why I've decided to set up a subsidiary in Europe as a sales office and warehousing center, and we'll leave the republishing operation for later. We have more than enough sales in the U.S. to occupy us for now.

*Mike:* So, you're talking about invoicing in Europe for the first time?

*Jeff:* Yes. As you all know, the main reason we have avoided invoicing sales in Europe is to avoid the expense of a European subsidiary. With a mobile agent like Mike, who works out of his house in Germany, we can do everything very inexpensively. We don't have to pay social welfare costs for German staff, and because Mike arranges sales but does not invoice them, we pay no German taxes. This method has worked well for a few years, but now seems inadequate.

*Mike:* Where were you thinking of putting the sales office, Jeff? Germany?

*Jeff:* Well, we talked about this last time, Mike, and we're thinking about putting it somewhere else. I like Ireland. The tax rate in Ireland is 10 percent, guaranteed until 2010. I talked to Sean Ferguson at the Irish Development Agency (IDA), and he said we would qualify for that rate with a sales subsidiary. Also, the IDA offers grants for investment, training and R&D if the operation is large in size. German tax rates—as you know—are higher than 50 percent, and the government there is not offering us any breaks. Am I correct, Cathy? You've been researching this issue.

*Cathy:* Actually, it's a little more complicated than what we've been thinking. Last time I told you I was afraid we wouldn't be able to benefit from the low Irish tax rates, and unfortunately, that's probably the case.

*Jeff:* You mean, the IDA is giving misleading advice?

*Cathy:* Well, no, not really. They were just looking at it from an Irish perspective. You see, our company would pay the Irish government only 10 percent, assuming no withholding tax. Upon repatriation to the U.S. of a dividend from the sales subsidiary, we would pay an additional tax to the U.S. government that would bring the total tax paid up to the same amount we pay now, the U.S. rate.

*Mike:* Why is that?

*Cathy:* The U.S. government taxes U.S. companies on their worldwide income at the U.S. tax rate. That means that whenever a dividend is repatriated to the U.S., it is taxed at 34 percent. Because the U.S. government has treaties with most countries to eliminate double taxation, the U.S. government taxes you only on the amount over and above what you paid in the foreign country on the income before it was repatriated. So in Ireland, you paid $10 on $100 of income, and the U.S. government asks for $24 more, so that in the end, you've paid a total of $34. That's all part of the U.S. tax authorities' goal of tax neutrality. The government doesn't want U.S. domestic companies to pay a higher tax rate than U.S. companies that are operating abroad.

*Mike:* I see, but what about if you have a company in Germany, where the tax rate is higher? Is that where tax credits come in?

*Cathy:* Exactly, Mike. In that case, the Internal Revenue Service (IRS) grants tax credits to the company for the amount of foreign tax over and above what the company would have paid in the United States. So in Germany. . . can I have a piece of paper? Thanks. Okay. Say Martin Guides makes $100. We would pay German tax of $53 and would get tax credits of $19.

*Jeff:* So I pay $53 cash out of my pocket and get only $19 in noncash credits back; doesn't sound like a good deal.

*Cathy:* Right. But the tax credits can be used to cancel out the excess tax the United States government charges for income in countries with a tax rate lower than ours. So if we made the $100 in Ireland, and the $100 in Germany, we could use the $19 of tax credits in Germany to cancel out $19 of the excess tax paid on the Irish dividend. That would mean that we paid $53 to German tax authorities, $10 to Irish tax authorities, and $5 to the IRS. That's a total of $68, which makes for a 34 percent tax rate on income of $200.

*Jeff:* Wait, how are we making money in two places? Now you're talking about two subsidiaries. I don't like this at all. We just decided we only need one subsidiary.

*Cathy:* Actually, Jeff, we could guarantee a 34 percent tax rate in Germany with just one subsidiary if we designated it a branch of MG. Branches pay 34 percent on their earnings because they are considered just an extension of the parent and are outside the German tax jurisdiction.

*Mike:* So in effect, for our purposes, Germany, Ireland, or the Netherlands are on an equal playing field. We end up paying 34 percent regardless.

*Cathy:* Right.

*Jeff:* Isn't there any way to take advantage of the low Irish tax rate? What if we didn't repatriate our earnings from Ireland. Couldn't we defer taxes for as long as we wanted, until we repatriated the dividend? I mean, paying 10 percent now and 24 percent later would be better than paying 34 percent now.

*Cathy:* I am afraid we won't be able to do that with a sales subsidiary.

*Jeff:* Why not? That doesn't make much sense.

*Cathy:* That's a whole deeper level of IRS complexity. Do you have time for it now, Jeff?

*Jeff:* I guess. I really want to hear all this. How can the IDA advertise a 10 percent Irish tax rate if it's not really true?

*Cathy:* Okay. The IRS says that certain companies have to pay taxes on a dividend even if they didn't pay one out.

*Jeff:* Whoa. How does that work?

*Cathy:* Well, I need to start writing some stuff on the board, because it's going to become difficult to remember everything. If the company is classified as a *controlled foreign corporation* (CFC) and earns *Subpart F income,* it will be taxed on a dividend deemed paid on the sub's income for that year, even if there is no dividend actually paid. The normal tax credit rules would then apply on that deemed dividend.

*Jeff:* Would our sales sub fall under those categories?

*Cathy:* Yes, most likely it would. Here's why. Let me define the terms *CFC* and *Subpart F income.* A CFC is a company for which more than 50 percent of the voting power or value of stock is held by U.S. shareholders. In our case, given our concern with control, I doubt we would have less than a 50 percent share in our sales subsidiary. The tax is levied on any shareholder of the CFC who holds at least a 10 percent share. Since we are a small company with few shareholders, I don't think we could get around the tax.

*Jeff:* Could we structure the ownership such that we could hold 50 percent directly, and then hold the other 50 percent indirectly?

*Cathy:* Don't think so, Jeff. Ownership is looked at constructively. The IRS looks at the whole organizational diagram and adds up all the percentages of ownership until it reaches the ultimate shareholder, in order to see who really controls things. Subpart F income is passive income that results from the resale of related party goods. That's actually only the simple definition, since many other types of income fall under that category. For our purposes we've defined Subpart F sufficiently. It means that if we sell our CD guides to our European sub — and it resells them — the sub earns Subpart F income.

*Jeff:* So our sales subsidiary in Ireland would meet the conditions that allow the IRS to tax us on income that

is not remitted. Is that right?

*Cathy:* Right. Our sub would be a CFC that earns Subpart F income.

*Jeff:* That's unbelievable! The IRS taxes you even though the money is still over in Europe?

*Cathy:* Remember, the purpose of the IRS is not to tax you beyond 34 percent, but it will make sure you're paying your fair share. They'll just tax you as if you've remitted all retained earnings as a dividend to the parent. It's true that a lot of U.S. companies used to set up sales subs in low tax areas just to shift profits out of the U.S. tax jurisdiction. They would keep the earnings over there and avoid paying U.S. taxes. So the IRS closed the loophole.

*Jeff:* I guess we have no chance at the Irish tax rate then, even for deferral purposes, unless we can avoid earning Subpart F income and reinvest in European operations.

*Cathy:* Not with a sales subsidiary as we have envisioned it. However, we could escape Subpart F if we resold only to unrelated parties in the country of incorporation of the sub.

*Mike:* For example, if we had a sub in Germany that sold only to the German market.

*Cathy:* Right, but what would be the point? We wouldn't be benefiting from Irish tax rates then.

*Mike:* Oh, yeah.

*Jeff:* If we did establish something in Germany, we'd have to set up a sub somewhere else to offset the excess tax credits. That would be expensive, and not likely to work, since we'll probably earn much more in Germany than in, say, Ireland. We'd still pay at least 34 percent.

*Cathy:* That's exactly right, Jeff. My guess is that we would have trouble setting up such a system, though it would be possible. Besides, there's another major catch. Even if we could avoid earning any sort of Subpart F income, we couldn't retain earnings in the CFC in excess of 25 percent of total assets. So really, deferral would be fairly limited anyway unless we were planning to reinvest in Europe.

*Jeff:* It keeps getting worse. Basically, Cathy, what you're telling us is that there's not really a practical way for MG to get the low Irish rates with a sales subsidiary.

*Cathy:* Unfortunately, no, there isn't. At least not using a sales subsidiary. We would really have to make a much bigger investment in Ireland to take advantage of the 10 percent rate. With a manufacturing sub, we could earn non-Subpart F income and then reinvest the rest back into the Irish sub, or into other European operations.

*Jeff:* I see. And that would allow us to defer paying any taxes until a dividend was remitted from the sub. Hmm . . . that sounds like a possible loophole. Maybe we could just do some very light manufacture. How do they define *manufacture* in the U.S. tax code?

*Cathy:* According to the tax digest I was referring to, *manufacture* was considered adding 20 percent to the market value of the goods.

*Jeff:* Could we work repackaging or translation in such a way that it adds 20 percent more to the value of the product we ship to the subsidiary?

*Cathy:* I wondered the same thing, but I could not find any reference to that type of operation in the digests I was reading, so I asked my friend Jack Vance at Overture Software. Jack is the Tax Directior for Overture, which has a subsidiary in the Netherlands. He has a lot of experience with this sort of question. He said that the IRS doesn't interpret the 20 percent test literally. In fact, to qualify for the manufacturing exclusion, the product shipped from the U.S. cannot be commercially viable. Jack said that the reproduction and translation of software abroad does not constitute *manufacture*. That opinion is based on actual court cases involving the IRS and U.S. firms.

*Jeff:* So basically, the IRS can decide what really constitutes manufacture.

*Cathy:* Yes, if the activity being performed is shaky. If we were writing the software over there, that would probably constitute manufacturing even by their definition. As Jack told me on the phone, the IRS looks at what's really going on, not necessarily what we report to them. In any case, all decisions ultimately go to tax court where they can be decided either way, for us or against us.

*Jeff:* Does the IRS even know anything about what goes into making a software package?

*Cathy:* Actually, yes. Jack was telling me they have special offshore software agents who are quite knowledgeable on the differences between manufacture and packaging for our industry. There's a lot of potential tax revenue at stake.

*Jeff:* So we could probably only benefit from the low Irish tax rate if we located our whole development process over there. Is that the case?

*Cathy:* Right, and remember we would have to reinvest the earnings in the sub anyway in order to avoid accumulating excess passive earnings, which would be currently taxed. So we would want to have something to invest in; a translation operation alone might not provide enough opportunity.

*Jeff:* Well, as we said before, I'm not ready to manufacture there yet. Actually, I'm not sure if I ever want to put the research and development over there. I like the process right here at Duckbay, where I can see it.

Let me see if I've got this all straight. We're back at square one, paying 34 percent unless we locate development in Ireland. Even if we do locate development in Ireland, we can at best defer paying taxes on 24 percent of the income until it's repatriated. On top of it all, we have to reinvest abroad to keep the IRS from levying a tax on the passive earnings.

*Cathy:* You've pretty much summed it up as far as I know. There is one more possibility which might be helpful. The U.S. tax code provides for a special type of subsidiary, a *Foreign Sales Corporation (FSC)*, to help U.S. firms export by giving them permanent exemptions from part of the tax on foreign profits. In other words — this is not a *deferral* — this is permanent *forgiveness*. The firm never has to pay a certain portion of its tax liability.

*Jeff:* How much of an exemption is it?

*Cathy:* That depends on a fairly involved formula, but the results of it are actually quite straightforward. Most companies using FSCs pay around 5 or 6 percent less than the U.S. rate on their foreign profits. Legally, both the FSC and its parent corporation are exempt from taxes on a percentage of their export earnings. The U.S. company may then repatriate the income from the FSC in the form of a dividend that is completely free of U.S. tax.

*Mike:* That's not bad, considering what we've heard today, but what's the catch?

*Cathy:* There isn't much of a catch at all. Setting up an FSC is just a paper transaction. The only requirements are that the FSC is located in a country that has a special treaty with the U.S., and that the U.S. firm meet certain "economic process" requirements. For example, the FSC must have at least one non-U.S. board member, and at least one board meeting per year must be held in the country of the FSC. Those rules are designed to prevent the FSC from being counter to the GATT. In fact they are fairly easy to fulfill. The countries most commonly used are U.S. possessions, such as the U.S. Virgin Islands, because they have little or no income or withholding tax. There are companies, including our own accounting firm, that will arrange the FSC and administer it for a fee of around two or three thousand dollars a year.

*Mike:* It sounds like an offshore operation. I am amazed it's legal. How does it work?

*Cathy:* There are two ways the transaction is structured. Usually, the U.S. parent passes title of the goods to the FSC, which then resells them and takes a fee for the transaction. Sometimes, the transaction is arranged so that the FSC buys the goods outright and resells them for a profit. The transfer prices and fees are set according to special rules in the U.S. tax code so that the parent can't shift all its profits to the FSC. The income of the FSC is partially exempt from U.S. taxes. The earnings of the FSC can then be repatriated to the U.S. parent with no additional tax by the U.S. government. Usually, the country of incorporation of the FSC has no income or withholding taxes and the result is a 5 or 6 percent reduction in the tax rate paid on foreign income.

*Jeff:* Wouldn't selling goods through the Caribbean complicate operations even more?

*Cathy:* Well, the goods aren't actually routed through the FSC. The FSC only takes care of the paperwork. The goods can go directly to distributors.

*Jeff:* That sounds a little better. So we just set up a paper company, pay an annual fee to our accounting firm, and reduce our tax rate to around 28 percent. Amazing. Why don't other companies use this?

*Cathy:* A lot of large firms do use FSCs. I spoke to a friend of mine who is a tax expert at the Department of Commerce who said that many smaller firms just don't know about FSCs.

*Mike:* I have a question, Cathy. Aren't we forgetting the purpose of the meeting here? Don't we really want to improve customer relations in Europe by having a presence there? How does an FSC help us with that?

*Cathy:* I suppose you're right. I mean, we don't want to minimize taxes at the expense of other aspects of the business.

*Jeff:* Can't we use an FSC and a European sales subsidiary? That way we would both lower our tax rate and improve contact with distributors.

*Cathy:* Hmm . . . You know, I really don't know. That would be a very good option if it's possible. The only thing that worries me is that we might be selling from the FSC to another related party, either a branch or a subsidiary.

*Jeff:* Could you find that out for next week? Even if that's not possible, I'd be eager to know how much an FSC would save us over the next few years, if we implemented one.

*Cathy:* Okay. I could have a spreadsheet by then (see Table 2), and the answer to whether the FSC can be used with a sales subsidiary.

*Jeff:* If so, then the right decision appears to be the use of an FSC. If not, then we might have to do without any change for now. We talked a lot about taxes today.

**TABLE 2**

**Calculation of Benefits to Martin Guides of Using a Foreign Sales Corporation (FSC)**

|  | 1995 | 1996 | 1997 |
|---|---|---|---|
| Foreign revenues | $1,500,000 | $2,500,000 | $4,000,000 |
| Foreign cost of goods sold | 259,760 | 432,933 | 692,693 |
| Foreign or other direct & indirect costs | 796,224 | 1,327,040 | 2,123,264 |
| Foreign income before tax | $ 444,016 | $ 740,027 | $1,184,043 |
| *FSC expenses, first year* | | | |
| Formation fee | $ 1,500 | | |
| Incorporation costs: US Virgin Islands | 400 | | |
| Business license: US Virgin Islands | 100 | | |
| *FSC annual expenses* | | | |
| Annual FSC management fee | $ 1,500 | $ 1,500 | $ 1,500 |
| Annual business license USVI | 100 | 100 | 100 |
| Minimum annual franchise tax USVI | 400 | 400 | 400 |
| Estimated exemption as a result of FSC | $ 26,641 | $ 44,402 | $ 71,043 |
| Less expenses to implement FSC | (4,000) | (2,000) | (2,000) |
| Total savings to Martin Guides | $ 22,641 | $ 42,402 | $ 69,043 |
| Tax without FSC | $ 150,965 | $ 251,609 | $ 402,575 |
| Tax rate without FSC | 34% | 34% | 34% |
| Tax with FSC | $ 128,325 | $ 209,208 | $ 333,532 |
| Tax rate with FSC | 29% | 28% | 28% |

But I agree with Mike in that we should also start looking at the other benefits and costs of each location. If we use branches, all three countries are on an equal footing with regard to taxes. If the U.S. tax rate is the best we can do then we'll have to accept that.

# TROLL–AEG[1]

It was late afternoon of January 21, 1992, and Miguel Tey Feliu de la Peña, managing director of J. Feliu de la Peña, S.A., a Spanish manufacturer of lighting elements known for its modern designs marketed under the TROLL brand, was reflecting on the reciprocal commercial distribution contracts which were to be signed the next day with the managers of AEG's Technical Lighting Business Area (AEG Aktiengesellschaft Fachbereich Lichttechnik, or AEG-LT), from Germany.

Basically, these were two "mirror" contracts by which, in one of them, J. Feliu de la Peña, S.A. (JFP) granted AEG a nonexclusive[2] right to distribute its products in Germany while, by virtue of the second contract, AEG granted JFP and its subsidiary TROLL–France a nonexclusive right to distribute its products in Spain and France, respectively. See Table 1 for further information on these contracts.

The simultaneous signature of both contracts, scheduled for the next day, would be marked by a certain degree of solemnity as it would be presided by the Right Honourable Mr. Antoni Subirà i Claus, Councillor for In-

dustry and Energy of the Government of the Generalitat of Catalonia.

Miguel Tey did not doubt that the contracts would be signed. But, reflecting on the matter, several questions came to his mind:

"First, when I review the decisions that have been taken up to this point in time, I wonder if we are doing the right thing in entering into this type of agreement or whether it would have been better to continue following our own fully autonomous growth path, as we have done until now. At the same time, I wonder whether AEG is the best partner for us. Also, when I reread the two contracts, I wonder if something is missing or should not be there, or whether any of the sections should be reworded.

"Second, if we accept everything done until now and do sign the contracts, then there are two major questions with regard to our immediate future that must be answered: What must we decide and do to ensure that this new reciprocal relationship between TROLL and AEG works, and works well? And finally, how will all this end up? In other words, where will our company be three, five or ten years from now? Will these agreements still be in full force?"

No doubt because of the obvious difference in size between JFP and AEG, someone had recently said, only half joking, "In no time at all, we'll all be wearing AEG T-shirts. . . ."

## Background of J. Feliu de la Peña, S.A. (JFP)

Mr. Julio Feliu de la Peña, grandfather of the brothers Xavier and Miguel Tey Feliu de la Peña, started manufacturing "classic" design lamps back in 1929, in Barcelona.[3]

Miguel joined the company as an apprentice in 1960, when he was 15 years old. However, one year later, he was already managing the business. Meanwhile, his elder brother, Xavier, continued his university studies, eventually obtaining a doctorate in industrial engineering.

---

SOURCE: *This case won first prize in the "Joint Ventures and Strategic Alliances" category in the 1995 EFMD European Case Competition Contest, organized by the European Foundation for Management Development.*

[1] *Case of the Research Department of IESE. Prepared by Javier Sarda, MED-1992, under the supervision of Francesc Parés, Lecturer, and Professor Lluís G. Renart, October 1992. Copyright ©1992, by IESE. No part of this publication may be reproduced without the written permission of IESE.*

*As any reader will easily realize, this case was written on the basis of data and interviews granted by managers of JFP, S.A. Therefore, the TROLL-AEG alliance is presented here from the point of view of the Spanish partner.*

[2] *Even though the contracts were formally "nonexclusive" both parties had agreed that, in essence, the spirit of both contracts was of full exclusivity. It is a well known fact that, in case of termination, dissolving exclusive contracts is very difficult and cumbersome.*

[3] *Throughout this case, the words "lamp" or "lighting elements" are used to refer to the lampholder which holds the light source(s), and does not mean the light bulbs or other light sources. "Spot" lights or "accent" lighting elements create a fairly specific field of light, while leaving the surrounding area in comparative darkness.*

**TABLE 1**

## The Reciprocal Distribution Contracts

These were two "mirror" contracts. In one of these, JFP granted AEG a nonexclusive right to distribute certain products in Germany. In the other, AEG Aktiengesellschaft granted JFP a nonexclusive right to distribute certain products in Spain and France. In both cases, the products included were specified in an attachment and the possibility of including new products in the future was left open.

Both contracts specified, in an identical and reciprocal fashion for both companies, a series of rights and obligations. In the opinion of the casewriter, the most important were the following:

The importer should have a sales organization able to satisfactorily sell the other party's products.

The marketing costs would be borne by the importer-distributor, including the obligation to hold sufficient stock to supply its customers and to have a spare parts stock and aftersales service.

In the event of faulty products, the seller would pay the importer 70 percent of the cost of correcting such faults.

The importer would "effectively advertise" the products imported, using the documentation provided by the supplier.

Each party would help the other to sell its products and, after prior agreement, could send specialists to support the importer's sales team, advise its customers or carry out market research. Unless agreed otherwise, the specialist's travelling and living expenses would be paid for by the exporter.

Both parties undertook: to inform the other party in the event that one of them should decide to represent other companies; to keep secret any information it might have received on the other party; to inform the other party on developments in its company and the status of the market and sales; to buy and sell in accordance with the prices included as an attachment to the contract.

The contract's duration would be from the date the contract was signed to December 31, 1993. It could be renewed for successive calendar years, unless one of the parties announced its intention to terminate the contract with a minimum of six months notice.

Both contracts could also be considered terminated in the event of serious breach of the conditions agreed, in the event that the sales targets were not reached, in the event of changes in the other company's ownership or management team, or if either of the two declared themselves to be insolvent or suspended payments.

Finally, a series of articles provided for the steps that would be taken if the contract were to be terminated (return of documents, disposal of stocks, discontinuation in the use of brandnames and marks, . . . ) and an article according to which any possible disputes would be submitted to arbitration, following the Rules of the International Chamber of Commerce.

However, in the casewriter's opinion, there were a few points or details in which the contracts were not exactly symmetrical or "mirror-like":

Brand names: JFP undertook to sell AEG-LT's products in Spain and France under the "AEG" brand while JFP's products sold by AEG-LT in Germany would also be labelled "AEG," although the sales leaflets would also include the indication "designed by TROLL."

The sales targets for products manufactured by JFP and sold by AEG-LT in Germany were more ambitious (approximately 1.6 times higher) than the sum of the sales targets for AEG products in Spain and France together, as shown in the following table in Deutschmarks (accompanied by their exchange rates in the original contracts):

| | 1992 | 1993 | 1994 |
|---|---|---|---|
| AEG purchases | DM2,200,000 | DM4,500,000 | DM7,300,000 |
| JFP purchases | | | |
| In Spain | DM800,000 | DM1,800,000 | DM2,800,000 |
| In France | DM500,000 | DM1,100,000 | DM1,800,000 |
| Total JFP purchases to AEG | DM1,300,000 | DM2,900,000 | DM4,600,000 |

In 1974, when Miguel was 29 years old, they became owners of the business, which at that time operated from a ground floor premises in Bruc Street, on the corner of Valencia Street, that is, very close to the center of Barcelona, and it was legally incorporated as a stock company ("Sociedad Anónima").

"The company was completely outmoded," said Miguel. "It had 15 very old employees, who basically carried out assembly tasks. We were not experts in anything and sold classic design lamps through salesmen who were paid a fixed salary plus commission. Although it was small, the company had a reputation for being reliable and serious. In addition to making its own lamps, the company also had exclusive distribution agreements with other lamp manufacturers. It had one sales outlet for both wholesale and retail sales."

In the same year, 1974, Nordart Industria, S.A. offered them the possibility of selling its products, which were marketed under the TROLL brand. It was a new lighting system made up by spot projectors, power tracks, and adapters (the adapter being the part linking the spot projector to the power carrying track). Miguel saw that the product had a modern design and was very well presented and offered to buy their entire output if he was given exclusive sales rights for Spain. Nordart Industria, S.A. was a small factory without any salesforce and had also been badly stung when a distributor had copied their product and left them in the lurch. Joaquim Masó, the company's owner, accepted to appoint JFP its sole agent after establishing that JFP would operate with a gross margin of 30 percent.

In the remaining six months of 1974, they sold about 16 million pesetas worth of TROLL products. In 1975, sales rose to about 32 million pesetas. In 1976, sales ran at almost 60 million pesetas and by 1977, their TROLL sales had increased to 130 million pesetas. Miguel realised that "the future was TROLL."

In 1978, Joaquim Masó and the Tey brothers agreed to merge both companies with each partner owning one-third of the resulting company, which continued to be called J. Feliu de la Peña, S.A.[4]

"The next decade, 1978–1988, was a period of strong growth for JFP. It stopped manufacturing its classic lamps to manufacture only TROLL lighting elements. After 1981, our products were spotlights, built-in downlights and self-connecting space frames in decorative fluorescence."

During this decade, the company's sales grew at a compound annual rate of slightly more than 50 percent. The workforce increased from 25 to 100 employees and the company became market leader in Spain in this type of accent lighting elements.

JFP's success can be attributed basically to the combination of two success factors: the changes in the distribution channel and the continuous improvement and redesign of its products.

Regarding changes in its distribution policy, JFP ceased selling through traditional (normally classic design) lamp retailers and pioneered the sale of spotlights and downlights through electrical goods wholesalers/stockists.[5]

Miguel Tey considered that this change of distribution policy had only been partly successful as he soon realised that his negotiating power with these wholesalers was very limited:

"I was the 'fellow selling spots,' in other words, a rather unwelcome visitor who was attempting to sell them a very limited range of products, which was relatively new or unusual in their stores and which accounted for only a minute fraction of their total sales. No doubt that was the reason why most often I only got to speak with one of the electrical goods store's sales assistants."

In order to counteract this situation, Miguel sought to create an alliance with other companies who manufactured products that were not directly competitive with each other but which were sold through the same electrical goods stores. Finally, he managed to persuade the general managers of a wire company, a transformer company and a cable fastener company to join forces with him in such an alliance.

The agreement consisted of organizing a network of self-employed representatives who would sell the products of all four manufacturers.

---

[4]*In early 1992, they still had the same shareholding positions.*

[5]*In Spain, this kind of wholesalers/stockists sell mostly to contractors specialising in electrical installations either in new buildings or in building refurbishing jobs. Most of their sales were "counter" sales, made on the spot to contractors who came to their outlet with a list of their immediate needs. Most of them would take the goods with them.*

The first of these representatives was appointed in 1978, in Madrid. The following working procedure was established with this representative: all four manufacturers would place their products on consignment in the representative's warehouse. The representative would then sell and deliver the goods, sending the delivery note to each manufacturer. The manufacturers would then issue the invoice, give credit if applicable and collect payment on the invoice. Should the customer default on payment, the representative would personally assist them in collecting payment.

In exchange for these functions, the representative received a commission that was agreed upon separately with each one of the four manufacturing companies.

Once the Madrid representative was working satisfactorily, the same procedure was followed in Barcelona, appointing a previous TROLL representative. Next came the turn of Palma de Mallorca and when all three were seen to be operating successfully, the process was continued, establishing a total of thirteen joint "branches" covering practically the entire Spanish market.

> "And all that with just paying a commission, that is, a variable cost, and with a minimum investment in stock in all thirteen warehouses. An important point to remember is that thanks to our pioneering role in selling accent lighting elements in Spain, JFP's margins were very high. Our sale price to the electrical goods store was between 2.5 and 3 times our manufacturing cost!"

Initially the least well-known of the four allied companies, J. Feliu de la Peña, S.A. exploited the new situation to the maximum. The higher pooled sales turnover enabled the companies to recruit better representatives and to increase their negotiating power with the electrical goods stores. With the passing of time, JFP became the unofficial leader of the network as the representatives mainly followed Miguel Tey's lead. JFP's young general manager had managed to win them over through a combination of an extremely cordial personal relationship, an excellent service from his company, a product range with skyrocketing sales, and a 10 percent commission, compared with the 5 percent commission or less given to them by the other three companies.

## Changes in the Product Range

The other part of Miguel's enormous success during those years was due to the changes made to the products' design which, in turn, considerably improved the level of service given to the representatives. Until then, each lamp model, of which there were about 50, was manufactured in sixteen colors and consisted of several parts that were specific to each model, plus their variants. In total, there were about 3,200 different stock keeping units (sku's).

Miguel reduced the color range from 16 to 4 (white, black, gold, and stainless steel). The slower-moving designs were dropped from the collection. But the most important change was in the design of the lamp parts, when a new system of universal connector was introduced which allowed all parts to be easily interconnected by simple pressure plus a security screw. This innovation made the four basic parts of the lighting systems manufactured fully interchangeable. This enabled him to cut down the number of sku's to less than 200, leading to a dramatic increase in turnover in all the warehouses in the logistics chain, including, of course, of its immediate customers, that is, the electrical goods stores.

Miguel also implemented major changes in the design process of its lighting elements. Indeed, in the early days, Miguel himself had designed the lighting elements, drawing his inspiration from the designs he saw at the international fairs he attended as a mere visitor. By 1985, Miguel decided that he needed to create an aesthetic consistency and identifying style in his lighting element designs and started to commission original designs from two free lance industrial designers. Miguel wanted his lighting elements to be immediately recognisable:

> "I wanted people to say, when they saw one of our lamps: 'That's TROLL,' without having to read the brandname. Braun was my guiding light in design. I wanted to be the Braun of lighting.'" For that and other reasons, in 1987 the two designers were recruited to the company as full-time, salaried employees."

Thus, the combination of having pioneered accent lighting in Spain (with downlights, spots and tracks), the network of "branches" made up of the thirteen independent representatives, a reasonably well-designed product range, and very ample margins turned the company into one of the most profitable in this industry in Spain. Forecast sales for 1988 were estimated at about 1.5 billion pesetas, with a net income of about 400 million pesetas, and a market share between 25 percent and 30 percent in this kind of product, that is, indoor accent lighting elements.

As Table 2 shows, the company had taken a few tentative steps in exporting, with the recruitment of Josep Sala in 1984. The new factory located in Canovelles, near Granollers (province of Barcelona) was opened in 1985, as described in Table 3. With an initial floor area of 5,000 square meters, it was subsequently expanded to 10,000 square meters.

## 1988: Recruitment of Javier Rocasalbas and the Growth of the Company within Spain

Faced with a strong increase in demand, the company no longer had sufficient capacity to supply all the orders.

Furthermore, Miguel was in serious danger of being overwhelmed by the increasing complexity of the company's management. Consequently, he decided to recruit Javier Rocasalbas as general manager, while he became

managing director and his brother Xavier became president.

In 1988, Javier Rocasalbas was 40 years old. Having initially graduated as an industrial engineer, his early work experience was centered in the engineering-production area, first in a factory making fuel pumps for diesel motors and later in a hydraulic pump manufacturer. Before joining JFP, he had worked in a plastics factory, where, for the first time, his duties had gone beyond the strictly technical.

Javier summarised the company's situation when he joined it in late May, 1989, as follows:

"J. Feliu de la Peña, S.A. was the typical family business where the management style was heavily influenced by the owner's personality. The chief problem was purely industrial. On the one hand, on occasion the lead-times quoted to the customers were very long. Furthermore, there was a clear lack

**TABLE 2**

J. Feliu de la Peña, S.A.

| | Exports Made in the Year | | | | | |
|---|---|---|---|---|---|---|
| | **1986**[1] | **1987** | **1988** | **1989** | **1990** | **1991** |
| To | | | | | | |
| Portugal | 72% = 10.8 $\overline{M}$ | 44% = 9.2 $\overline{M}$ | 5.9% = 3.4 $\overline{M}$ | 14% = 12.6 $\overline{M}$ | * | * |
| United States | 12% = 1.8 $\overline{M}$ | * | * | * | * | * |
| France | 7% = 1.1 $\overline{M}$ | 18% = 3.8 $\overline{M}$ | 80.3% = 46.3 $\overline{M}$ | 45% = 40.5 $\overline{M}$ | 28.9% = 48.9 $\overline{M}$ | 29.6% = 68.1 $\overline{M}$ |
| Saudi Arabia | 6% = 0.9 $\overline{M}$ | 5% = 1.1 $\overline{M}$ | * | * | * | * |
| Belgium-Luxembourg | * ($^2$) | 19% = 4.0 $\overline{M}$ | * | * | * | * |
| United Kingdom | * | * | * | 15% = 13.5 $\overline{M}$ | 14.9% = 25.3 $\overline{M}$ | * |
| Greece | * | * | * | 7% = 6.3 $\overline{M}$ | * | * |
| UEBL | * | * | 8.1% = 4.6 $\overline{M}$ | * | * | * |
| Switzerland | * | * | 3.3% = 1.9 $\overline{M}$ | * | * | * |
| West Germany | * | * | * | * | 15.2% = 25.8 $\overline{M}$ | 25.9% = 59.6 $\overline{M}$ |
| Italy | * | * | * | * | 9.8% = 16.6 $\overline{M}$ | * |
| U.A.E. | * | * | * | * | * | 7.0% = 16.1 $\overline{M}$ |
| Holland | * | * | * | * | * | 12.8% = 29.4 $\overline{M}$ |
| Other countries | 3% = 0.4 $\overline{M}$ | 14% = 2.9 $\overline{M}$ | 2.4% = 1.4 $\overline{M}$ | 19% = 17.1 $\overline{M}$ | 31.2% = 53 $\overline{M}$ | 24.7% = 56.8 $\overline{M}$ |
| Total exports each year | 100% = 15 $\overline{M}$ | 100% = 21 $\overline{M}$ | 100% = 57.6 $\overline{M}$ | 100% = 90 $\overline{M}$ | 100% = 169.6 $\overline{M}$ | 100% = 230 $\overline{M}$ |
| Total JFP, S.A. sales ($^3$) | N.A. | 1,000 $\overline{M}$ | 1,541 $\overline{M}$ | 1,541 $\overline{M}$ | 1,470 $\overline{M}$ | 1,615 $\overline{M}$ |

[1]The "Official Census of the Spanish Exporters—1987," which publishes data on export activity during 1986, indicates that between 1985 and 1986. J. Feliu de la Peña, S.A.'s exports grew 154%. This seems to indicate that exports in 1985 must have amounted to about 6 million pesetas. The 1986 Census did not publish any data on the company, no doubt because the amount of 5,000,000 pesetas was too small and J.F. de la Peña, S.A. was not included in the Census.

[2]An asterisk indicates that in the year in question, we do not know whether or not the company exported to that country, as the Census only gives data on exports to the company's top four importing countries.

In the event that the company had exported to a country marked with an asterisk, this would be included in the line "Other countries" and the amount exported would always be less than that exported to the fourth highest importing country.

For example, if the company exported to the United Kingdom in 1986, it did not export more than the 900,000 pesetas indicated for Saudi Arabia in that year.

**TABLE 3**

**A Visit to the Barcelona Branch**

J. Feliu de la Peña, S.A.'s Barcelona branch was located at No. 68, Numancia Street, relatively near the center of the city. The TROLL logo prominently displayed above the door and a sign with smaller type with the words "Catalonia Branch. Showroom and Projects" clearly stated its identity and purpose.

Any visitor could go there and ask them to draw up a lighting project for a house or apartment, a shop or an industrial premises or an office. This service was free of charge.

From the entrance door, the visitor entered a reception area. Behind the reception, there was a door that gave onto a large room measuring about 100 square meters, divided into various sectors or settings; part of the room portrayed a garden setting; another part represented a stretch of supermarket shelving; another simulated a restaurant table; another, part of an office; two of the walls looked like an art gallery or museum; and another part had a clearly commercial setting, with a large display window with two dummies and some sports accessories, complemented with four display cases measuring 70 by 70 centimeters similar to those that can be found in some jewelers' shops.

Also, in the same room, there was a "lighting robot," a temperature cabinet and a tiny conference area, equipped with about ten or twelve chairs, a projection screen and a lectern.

Each one of the sectors or settings was equipped with different types of lights. The TROLL technician accompanying the visitor could place him in front of a certain setting (for example, the supermarket) and turn on and off different types of lights, equipped with different types of bulbs (incandescent, halogen, dichromatic, fluorescent, etc.) to show the visitor the different lighting effects that could be obtained with the TROLL lighting elements.

Xavier Lopez and Manuel Santos accompanied the casewriter. In the course of the visit, they commented, "Our aim is to show the shopowners that good lighting is good business and profitable, because it helps them to sell more. The products are more attractive and the colors are more vivid and realistic."

The so-called "lighting robot" was not a robot as such. It was a facility consisting basically of an H-shaped metal stand on rails that allowed it to be moved towards and away from a vertical wall.

Different types of lighting elements could be fitted on the stand, each one of them with different types of bulbs, focusing them onto the wall vertically or at an angle. The stand was also fitted with a device for measuring light intensity, which could be read in digital form on a small screen.

The measuring device's cells or sensors were located on the vertical wall in front of the stand. The wall was squared and there was a cell or sensor on each intersection of the grid. Each cell or sensor could be turned on or off individually by switches on the stand.

The "robot" enabled numerical readings of the light intensity impinging on any point of the wall to be obtained each time any of the variables were changed: lamp type, bulb type and wattage, distance from the wall, the light rays' angle of incidence on the wall, etc.

The color temperature cabinet was fitted with a series of windows. Each window had strips of cardboard painted with the main colors from red to violet. All the windows had exactly the same palette of colors and hues. However, the palette in each window was lit by a different type of bulb, which enabled the visitor to clearly see how his or her perception of the colors changed when using one bulb or another.

On his way out, the casewriter walked through a small warehouse also measuring about 100 square meters, which was not open to the public, from which the branch supplied the orders received from the specialty retail stores or distributors.

of internal organization in production, even though JFP was (and still is in 1992) basically a design and assembly company.[6] My first actions were therefore eminently industrial in nature, and included computerising the production process."

Upon turning his attention to design, Rocasalbas realised that the products' aesthetic quality was excellent,

---

[6]*In addition to design and assembly, the company confined itself to carrying out by itself some metal forming work (pressing and cutting) and certain painting and surface finishing tasks. It usually bought or subcontracted to outside suppliers the following: small electrical or electronic items, plastic injection, aluminum injection or extrusion, glass fittings, minor mechanical parts (screws, connectors, etc.), and certain surface finishes other than painting (chrome plating, gold plating, etc.).*

but the technical quality was poor: the electromechanical aspects had been neglected to a considerable extent, which led to difficulties when attempting to assemble the lighting elements on an industrial scale.

Therefore, in 1989, Rocasalbas increased the design team by recruiting Carlos Galán, an industrial engineer and electromechanical designer as its manager. A designer specialised in mechanical functions and a draftsman were also recruited to the team. By the end of 1991, the design and quality department was composed of twelve to fourteen people including Galán.

This team was responsible not only for ensuring that the products performed their function properly as lighting elements but also that they complied with electrical safety standards and that their aesthetic quality made the grade both as individual items and as integral parts of the entire collection. Finally, under Rocasalbas and Galán's management, the company completed the transition from a design process in which the cost price would be known at the end, as a result, to a process in which a cost price was set before starting the design work, as a goal to be achieved, carrying out value analysis processes along the way.

The star products at that time (1988) were the fixed, low-voltage built-in downlight in black or white and the swivelling ball-spot. In total, the company handled less than 300 stock-keeping units.

They were relatively simple products to design, manufacture, assemble and install in the point of use. In fact, they could be considered standard products of average quality and were usually bought by electricians or electrical contractors for installing, without any technical complications, in private homes, shops, offices, etc.

The branches, that is, the thirteen sales representatives with their own warehouse, sold indiscriminately and massively, without distinguishing between different types of customers, JFP published a single price list, which carried a discount that was the same for all JFP's customers, namely, about 45 percent.

## The Model Starts to Suffer Some Tensions

However, from 1988 onwards, this strategy started to encounter increasing difficulties.

On the one hand, competition in Spain became a lot fiercer. A large number of lamp manufacturers sprung up, flooding the market with lighting elements which had designs very similar to those of TROLL, even to the point, in some cases, of using TROLL products to take the photographs for some competitor's catalog. By the end of 1991, Javier Rocasalbas estimated that between 25 and 30 Spanish lamp manufacturers offered virtually identical, standard accent lighting elements.

The resulting price war quickly and severely eroded sales margins, which fell from about 30 percent in 1988 to about 15 percent in 1991.

At the same time, in 1988, Miguel decided that if TROLL products sold well in Spain, they should also be able to attain success in France, which had accounted for almost 4 million pesetas of the company's exports in 1987. Always impulsive and quick off the bat, Miguel went to Lyon and bought an old building near the high-speed train (TGV) station. Although requiring a certain degree of restoration, it had an area of 300 square meters each in a basement, ground floor, and first floor. The operation seemed to be a good buy from the real estate viewpoint as it seemed that the zoning regulations would allow them to build up several additional floors.

Miguel recruited Josep Sitjà as general manager of TROLL-France. A Catalan by birth, he had worked until that time as an electrical contractor in Marseille. As can be seen in Table 2, by 1988, JFP was exporting products to the tune of 46 million pesetas to France.

However, things were not going so smoothly as this might make one believe. On the one hand, part of this export figure included the necessary start-up stock of finished product shipped to Lyon. It also soon became clear that the standard product offered by the company was encountering serious difficulties in being accepted on the French market. The quality was not right, the price was not right, and it was not certified as conforming with the French NF standards. However, on the positive side, they found out that the design's aesthetic aspects were very well accepted and could become the major factor differentiating TROLL lamps, in spite of the lack of electromechanical quality at that time.

In addition to showing them the French market's perception of their products' quality, the experience in France also opened JFP's managers' eyes to another important issue: it was very difficult to achieve a significant level of sales in France without offering an integral, complete, and coherent product range. In other words, the TROLL range was composed solely of interior accent lighting elements, that is, tracks and spots, downlights, and suspended fluorescent lights self-connected by jacks.

However, they had no built-in fluorescent panels (used mainly in offices), industrial lights (for lighting factories), or any type of lighting elements for installation and use outdoors, to light public highways, parks and gardens, tunnels, sports facilities, etc.

## The Reaction

Miguel and Javier's reaction to this setback was to ratify their firm resolve to gain a presence on the European market. They therefore ruled out the option of withdrawing and confining themselves back to the Spanish market.

Therefore, in late 1988 to early 1989, they decided to initiate as soon as possible a change in the composition of their product range, consisting of slowly phasing out their standard products and starting to design, manufacture, and sell technical architectural lighting elements, able to offer special lighting applications in accordance with defined specifications to satisfy the final customer's lighting requirements.

> "We considered that the more sophisticated features of the new generation of lighting elements we wanted to design and launch onto the market would be more difficult for our direct competitors to imitate, most of which were small companies. We were up against companies who were not only limited by their technical skills but also by their financial possibilities, as an 'architectural' lighting element of this type may mean investing about 20

million pesetas in design, tooling, molds, etc.," said Rocasalbas.

> "It was rather an intuitive change; I don't think we really knew what we were letting ourselves in for. Or, at least, at that time, we were not aware that the change in focus of the product range would also necessarily involve a drastic change in the type of final customer, in distribution channels and in the marketing resources to be used to promote our products."

Indeed, when they started to launch the first new-generation lighting elements on the market (see Table 4), they realised that the electrical goods wholesaler/stockist neither bought nor distributed technical architectural lighting products. These were too sophisticated, designed for specific applications, slow-selling, and their installation required a prior analysis to ensure their match with certain specific lighting needs, circumstances, or environments.

In a manner slightly analogous to medicines sold under prescription, technical architectural lighting elements had to be promoted by persuading the prescribers to use them. Within the field of technical lighting, a prescriber could be an architect, an interior decorator, a shop window designer, an engineer, or technician specialised in lighting, an engineering firm, etc.

**TABLE 4**

### The Launching of the New Generation of Technical Architectural Lighting Elements

The first model of this new product policy, focused towards technical architectural lighting elements was the so-called "model 699." It was first introduced on the occasion of the Hannover trade fair, in April 1989.

Model 699 was composed of a certain number of basic bodies, equipped or not with a transformer. Different heads and accessories (such as reflectors, filters, filter holders, or barndoors) could be adapted to the different bodies to obtain different lighting results. This combination of bodies and heads and accessories was done in a way similar to how a professional photographer may use different lenses with different camera bodies.

Soon after that, in 1990, the company redesigned their system of spatial self-connecting lighting structures. Patents were obtained for this so-called "Jack System," composed of different prewired elements and its many accessories.

Further, two more families of versatile projectors were designed and developed: "Vector" and "Delta." Also the "Compact" product range was created, which could be used both as a downlight or as a projector.

The latter three models or families received the "IF" awards, yearly granted by a prestigious international jury on the occasion of the Industrie Forum event in Hannover.

Sometime later, towards the end of 1991, JFP launched a very complete collection of 20 models of professional downlights.

Finally, the latest development had been the "Gallery" model, made up of a family of projectors offering different lighting solutions, expected to be attractive to art galleries, musea, etc.

When faced with certain lighting requirements (a hotel, a stadium, a modern shop, a hospital, etc.), the prescriber studied the lighting needs (light intensity, colorimetry, possible combinations within the surroundings, etc.) and diagnosed the type, quantity, characteristics, and location of each lighting point to be installed in order to obtain the desired decorative and lighting results. In the case of new buildings, it was vital to incline the prescriber in favor of a certain light brand and model while the architectural design was still on the drawing-board.

"The prescriber was a new factor to be reckoned with during the sales process carried out by JFP," said Rocasalbas.

"Until then, we had not taken any steps to influence their decisions because, given the relative simplicity of our products, it was simply not necessary.

"We realised that the image they had of us—if they had any at all—would be something like that of SEAT when it was manufacturing the 600, while now we had decided to make Mercedes Benz!

"Perhaps at that time we might have given other strategic responses to our competitors, such as trying to cut them short by lowering prices or creating a second 'fighting' brand name but the fact is we consciously didn't. This does not mean, however, that we did not fight hard to defend our position in the standard product market, as we were fully aware that the bulk of our sales were precisely composed—and, at the close of 1991, they still are—of these standard products."

Although the need for a change in the sales organization was clearly seen, curiously enough, the first move was made by the Madrid and Barcelona representatives. Apparently, these had secretly come to an agreement in 1988 to propose a change in their manner of functioning, consisting of acting as fully independent and exclusive distributors in their geographical area, buying set quantities and reselling the product on their own account, thus earning a margin instead of a commission.

The proposal had a mixed reception from the four manufacturers in the alliance. The transformer manufacturer accepted the proposed change. However, the cable manufacturer not only rejected the proposal but cancelled the agency agreement with them. Rocasalbas' reaction was more cool-headed: he too turned down the proposal but continued to work with them, trying to get

them to start promoting to prescribers too, while continuing to sell the standard lighting elements.

In order to help them in this, in mid-1990, JFP took on four middle-aged, well-groomed women (two in Madrid and two in Barcelona). These women would start to contact prescribers, introducing them to the company and telling them that JFP was entering the technical architectural lighting market.

"We were not yet out 'project hunting,'" said Rocasalbas. "But we soon realised that 'good grooming' was not enough. We had to be able to solve the prescriber's problem or at least to be able to provide them with all the necessary means for them to solve it themselves. This included providing prescribers with all the necessary technical data, free product samples and to have a showroom where they could handle the lights and test lighting effects.

"We soon found out that the selling process was very complex because the final decision on the light brand and model to be installed not only depends on the prescriber but also on the contractor installing the entire electrical and lighting system and, in the final analysis, on the building's owner, as the person footing the bill.

"Later on, we began to notice certain strange behaviors. In some cases, a certain lighting installation was literally 'auctioned off' to see which manufacturer finally offered the best price. Sometimes, we have suspected that some manufacturers, particularly foreign manufacturers eager to get a foothold in the Spanish market, seemed to be prepared to quote at cost price or even below cost price in order to be able to install its lighting elements in a particularly unique or emblematic building and thus be able to use it as an example and show it. In other cases, a customer's association with a certain corporation tips the balance in favor of a manufacturer of lighting elements who happens to be linked with the same corporation.

"In short, the sale of lighting projects is neither as easy nor as clearcut nor as technically aseptic as we originally, and perhaps rather naively, thought."

Thus, they managed to slowly penetrate the technical architectural lighting market, selling by promoting and carrying out projects for the prescriber. However, in 1990, this market segment only accounted for about 5 percent of JFP's total sales. Quite on the contrary, marketing and sales costs increased substantially.

In an attempt to speed up the change process, in April 1991 they decided to terminate their relationship with the Barcelona representative and open a sales office of their own, complete with a showroom. In December 1991, they did the same thing in Madrid with the result that, by the end of the year, JFP had two branches of its own and eleven independent representatives.

In their Barcelona branch, which was responsible for promotion and sales throughout Catalonia, two sales teams had been created. One team consisted of three full-time employed salesmen who covered the electrical goods wholesalers/stockists and the lamp specialty retailers, mainly selling them the more "standard" product range. At the end of 1991, the other Barcelona-Catalonia sales team targeted the prescription market and was composed of three salaried salesmen who visited prospective customers and another person, who drew up the design projects on the branch's design table.[7]

The first team was much more profitable than the second as, at the end of 1991, sales of standard products continued to account for about 80 percent of the company's total sales.

There was a possibility that, in the future, JFP would open similar fully owned branches in other major Spanish cities, although the decision would depend on two distinct factors: first, the degree of sales and financial success achieved by the two JFP branches already operating (Barcelona and Madrid); second, on the current "old" representatives' attitude and behavior, as they had to show their willingness and effectiveness in promoting the new generation of architectural technical lighting products.

At the end of 1991, Javier Rocasalbas said,

"Perhaps I'm wrong, but I think that even the minimally observant person had realised that lighting in houses and apartments, offices, shops, public areas, etc. had become increasingly sophisticated. Indeed, lighting was becoming an increasingly important part of the building or premise's aesthetics. The challenge for us, then, is to give TROLL lamps the technical capacity to contribute lighting solutions, on the one hand, and to be able to integrate themselves aesthetically with their surroundings, on the other hand. But we also have to explain this to prescribers, without forgetting to 'close the loop,'

that is, acting actively and positively on the contractor and on the building's owner or his purchasing manager. Any one of these people, at any particular time, can act for or against a type, brand or model of lamp. It is crucial to identify new projects at an early stage, in order to mature the final decision in our favor. This selling and 'maturing' process can take several months, with a significant investment in time. And even with all that, we only manage to get one out of every ten projects we bid for!

"To put it another way, when we 'mature' a project, we are not selling 'lighting elements.' We are selling, 'a particular lighting solution.'"

In 1991 the company had spent a total of about 100 million pesetas in advertising expenses, brochures and product catalogs, and attending trade fairs. This amount includes the cost of these expenses by TROLL–France, S.A.

## The Internationalization Process

As has already been mentioned, Josep Sala joined the company in 1984 to create the export department. The result of his efforts over time is shown in Table 2.

TROLL–France S.A., created in Lyon in 1988, was initially under Joseph Sitjà as General Manager. Sitjà organized a sales team whose members were independent sales reps on commission, working for several principals. This was similar to the sales organization in Spain. Quite on the contrary, however, these French reps did not do any warehousing. The only warehouse under the control of the company was that of TROLL–France, S.A., located in Lyon.

Towards the end of 1989, Sitjà opened an office in Paris, in a rented space.

In mid-1990, a new General Manager was hired. Philippe Martínez, of Spanish descent, was very knowledgeable about the lighting element market in France. He was a well-organised manager, with clear ideas about marketing plans and policies (see Table 5).

When he was designated general manager of TROLL–France, S.A., Martínez made a proposal to change the sales organisation. He set up a team of salaried sales reps, exclusively selling TROLL products. This new team would carry out a double selling task: on the one hand, they would sell to electrical goods wholesalers-stockists ("sell in"). On the other hand, the same sales team would carry out promotional tasks to prescribers, with the purpose of selling lighting projects. If they succeeded in "selling"

---

[7] *The yearly cost of each one of these salesmen could be estimated to be about 6.7 million pesetas (including social security), plus another million pesetas spent in travel and miscellaneous expenses.*

## TABLE 5

**Price Lists, Discounts, and Gross Margins**

JFP, S.A., as a privately held company, did not publish its yearly accounts. However, the following figures might be derived from their usual way of operating:

### 1. Sales in Spain

#### 1.1. Sales of TROLL products

| | |
|---|---:|
| Published price list of prices to be charged to final buyers/consumers | 100 |
| Discount made in the invoice[1] | − 50 |
| Net price invoiced by JFP, S.A. to wholesalers | 50 |
| Selling and marketing costs of JFP, S.A.[2] | − 11 |
| Gross margin of JFP, S.A.[3] | 39 |

#### 1.2. Sales of AEG products

Managers of JFP, S.A. had not yet made a final decision regarding the gross margin they would charge to AEG products imported into and sold in Spain (and France) by JFP. However, they were aware of the fact that other independent importer-distributors in the same trade or industry and performing similar sales and marketing functions (purchasing, holding stocks, promotion sales, advertising, after-sales services, etc.) usually charged margins around 30 percent on sales. That means that the difference between the net paid cost to a foreign supplier such as AEG, and the net price collected from wholesalers (that is, after discount in invoice), was about 30 percent of the latter net price collected.

### 2. Exports to AEG or to other countries with an importer-distributor

| | |
|---|---:|
| Net export price invoiced by JFP, S.A.[4] | 40 |
| Export sales and marketing costs[5] | − 4 |
| Gross margin of JFP, S.A.[6] | 36 |

### 3. Exports to TROLL–France, S.A. (own subsidiary)

| | |
|---|---:|
| Net export price invoiced by JFP, S.A. to TROLL-France, S.A.[7] | 36 |
| Export sales and marketing costs[8] | − 3.4 |
| Gross margin of JFP, S.A. (in Spain)[9] | 32.6 |

[1]The total amount of this discount could somehow be shared between the wholesaler-stockist, the contractor, maybe a retailer, if there was one in the channel, and even the final buyer-consumer, if the latter succeeded in negotiating a price which was lower than the official list price as published by JFP, S.A.

[2]Sales and marketing costs of JFP, S.A. would include commissions paid (both to independent reps with warehouse and to salaried reps in the payroll of JFP, S.A., located in Madrid and Barcelona branches); transportation and warehousing; advertising; attending trade shows and organising sales meetings; sales training and seminars; salaries and social security; and travel and accommodation expenses of sales and marketing employees.

[3]Obviously out of this gross margin many other deductions had to be subsequently made, such as cost of goods sold; general overhead and administration costs; financial expenses; etc.

[4]This means that the net selling price collected from foreign importer-distributors (40), was approximately 80 percent of the net selling price collected from wholesalers in Spain (50, as per point 1.1 above).

[5]Advertising, transportation and warehousing in Spain.

[6]Even though the gross margin of JFP, S.A. when selling to AEG or to other foreign importer-distributors was only 36, that is, somewhat lower than the 39 generated when selling to wholesalers-stockists in Spain, managers of JFP, S.A. pointed out that this difference was likely to be partially or fully compensated by the manufacturing economies of scale derived from the fact that orders received from foreign importers-distributors were substantially larger.

[7]This net invoiced price was, in fact, a transfer price between headquarters and its fully owned subsidiary. It may have been unusually low, up to 1991, to help finance the French subsidiary.

[8]These sales and marketing costs included: advertising expenses paid by headquarters; trade show attendance costs; sales seminars and sales training costs; warehousing in Spain.

[9]TROLL–France, S.A, in turn, operated under the following set of figures:

| | |
|---|---:|
| Published price list by TROLL–France to final buyers/consumers | 120 |
| Discount made in the invoice | − 60 |
| Net price invoiced by TROLL–France to wholesalers | 60 |
| Cost of goods sold, as paid by TROLL–France to JFP, S.A. (Spain) | − 36 |
| Gross margin by TROLL–France S.A. (*) | 24 |

(*)Out of this gross margin, TROLL–France S.A. had to pay for the following: transportation costs from Canovelles to Lyon, and from Lyon to wholesalers all over France; all of its sales and marketing expenses; all of its overhead, general and administrative costs, including rent of the Paris office; and, of course, including all salaries, wages and social security costs and travel expenses of all of its employees, including sales reps.

the idea to a prescriber of using TROLL lighting elements in a certain project, they would "transfer" the order to a wholesaler-stockist for him to supply and invoice the goods. In a similar way as in Spain, TROLL–France never sold directly to contractors or to end customers. At the beginning of 1992, TROLL–France, S.A. had six full-time sales reps in its payroll.

In spite of substantial subsidies that had been granted to JFP by ICEX and COPCA (two state and regional agencies devoted to promoting Spanish exports), TROLL–France, S.A had had important losses from the time of its setting up. These losses had amounted to a total of over 120 million pesetas in the period 1988–1991 (four years). Managers of JFF expected TROLL–France, S.A. to reach its break-even point in 1992.

Towards the end of 1991, Miguel Tey and Javier Rocasalbas had had a long conversation. They had tried to share their points of view, and to evaluate all they had done in France up to that point in time.

They were aware of the fact that TROLL–France, S.A. had spent about 250 million Spanish pesetas in start-up funds. Some of these funds had been used to buy and decorate the Lyon building, to the financing of stocks, accounts receivable, etc.

Rocasalbas thought that if the subsidiary had not been set up, this amount of cash would be available in the balance sheet of JFP, S.A., or the level of indebtedness of the company would be so much lower than it was now. This is why he said to Miguel: "From a strictly economical point of view, the economic effort undertaken in France would be highly questionable."

But Miguel retorted:

"First of all, we have to take into account the investment made in the Lyon building, to the amount of some 30 million Spanish pesetas. We have had contacts with prospective buyers of this building, which have led me to estimate its present market value to be around 100 million Spanish pesetas. This would mean that we have potential profits of about 70 million pesetas in that building.

"Furthermore, we have to take into account the fact that we are entering a market which is twice as large as the Spanish market. Our factory will not need any major enlargement, and we shall be able to vastly increase our sales volume. We must see this in a longer time horizon. A businessman cannot evaluate his decisions on purely economic terms. One must also take into account the spirit, the fact of creating and consolidating a new and competitive business venture, the cost of opening up a new market, the amount of shareholder value created as good will, the improved corporate image, etc.

"We must not only maintain Lyon. I have the purpose of changing our Paris Office and turn it into a large showroom.

"If we had not made the good (even if expensive) decision to go out of Spain at the time when the Spanish economy was buoyant, we would find ourselves in a difficult position today, when the Spanish market is stagnant. We would not be able to grow in Spain because the competition in our domestic market is increasing. Quite the contrary, we can now continue growing up."

In other countries, JFP sold to importers-distributors, among which we may mention Ulrich Sattler, in Germany, as we will see further on.

The company regularly attended the Hannover trade fair, which was without doubt the most important fair in the lighting industry. Attendance at this fair provided confirmation of the lessons learnt in France, namely that the European market demanded more quality (look, engineering, certifications, packaging, technical specifications) and that it was easier to sell if a company offered the most comprehensive product range possible, covering all the categories of lighting products.

The growing international presence of JFP on the market and at the trade fairs attracted the attention of several European companies.

## Contacts with Other European Manufacturers of Lighting Elements

Between 1990 and 1991, four European multinational companies approached JFP with the intention of buying or associating with the Catalan company. These companies were one from Austria, one from Belgium, one from Holland, and AEG (Germany).

Curiously enough, all four companies were after virtually the same goal, although by different means: gain access to TROLL products in order to enhance their respective indoor accent lighting lamp collections and thereby to be able to offer the market a more complete product range.

"The first thing that caught our eye was that these four big European companies seemed to want to come to an agreement with TROLL because they did not think that they had neither the economic capacity nor the time nor the human resources required to create their own indoor accent lighting lamp collection," said Rocasalbas.

"This gave us a lot of food for thought because we needed to go the opposite way, that is, with a collection or range of accent lighting elements as our starting point, in order to be able to compete in Europe we would have had to develop the other types of lighting elements that at that time JFP did not manufacture: fluorescent lamp holders, outdoor lighting elements for gardens, sports stadiums, etc.

"Our thoughts were: if they, who are much bigger than us, do not dare to do it, we would neither be able to follow the same business development path the other way around. This made us much more open to listening carefully to their proposals."

## Contacts with the Austrian Company

In late 1990, they had contacts with the owner of a large Austrian company. At the beginning of 1991, JFP's managers visited his factory in Austria and were very impressed by what they interpreted as Far East luxury. The Austrian expressed an interest in buying 30 percent of JFP in order to turn TROLL into its technical indoor decorative lighting division. The owners of the Spanish company did not feel inclined to lose their independence in exchange for a minority holding, so their answer was, "Buy all or nothing."

Contacts were broken off because JFP's shareholders were not interested in selling unless it was for a very high premium.

## Contacts with the Dutch Company

The first contacts were made at the 1990 Hannover trade fair. The Dutch multinational was interested in turning JFP into its workshop, that is, a supplier of accent lighting elements which would then be sold by the Dutch company's marketing organization under its own brand.

The Dutch already had a limited range of indoor accent lighting elements and wanted to expand it.

Although an agreement of this type could generate significant sales for JFP, the managers of the Catalan company did not feel very happy about the loss of identity this could involve. Also, they feared that they might become too dependent on this kind of sales.

Finally, an agreement was reached by which JFP would manufacture a JFP—designed adaptor and a transformer for the Dutch.

This relationship was still in force in early 1992, although it only accounted for a relatively small part of JFP's sales. The managers of the Catalan company did not plan to increase its scope or sales volume:

"Our priority objective is to build and strengthen the TROLL brand. This does not mean that we won't accept manufacturing for another company under their brand but, obviously, it is not our greatest priority," said Rocasalbas.

"For the same reason, we are not actively looking for other customers like the Dutch."

## The Belgian Company

The Belgian company was one of the largest, if not *the* largest, classic lamp manufacturers in Europe. The first contacts with JFP took place at the end of 1991, that is, when negotiations with AEG were already at a fairly advanced stage.

Their proposal was to form an alliance to sell TROLL lamps in the Benelux countries, subsequently expanding the distribution area in gradual stages.

In the end, the conversations with the Belgians were dropped, possibly for two reasons: on the one hand, JFP's managers observed that there were major differences in "lighting culture" between them, as the Belgians had a classic lamp manufacturer mentality. Furthermore, contacts with AEG were already in an advanced stage and JFP's managers felt more in tune with them than with the Belgian managers. Although, as will be explained further on, the agreement with AEG persumably would only cover the German market, neither Miguel Tey nor Javier Rocasalbas felt that it was coherent or desirable to sign two different agreements with two different partners to cover different countries.

## The Contacts and the Negotiation Process with AEG

AEG was a company belonging to the Daimler-Benz Group, which, in turn, was linked with the Deutsche Bank. The Daimler-Benz Group was composed of several companies, including the well-known automobile manufacturer Mercedes-Benz, Deutsche Aerospace A.G., AEG Aktiengesellschaft, etc.

In 1990, AEG Aktiengesellschaft had almost 80,000 employees worldwide. Its sales turnover by divisions was: office and communication techniques, 8 percent; railway systems, 6 percent; automation techniques, 22 percent; electronic equipment and components, 35 percent, microelectronics, 9 percent; and household appliances, 20 percent.

AEG's technical lighting business area (AEG Aktiengesellschaft Fachbereich Lichttechnik) specialised in the manufacture of various types of lighting elements, particularly fluorescent strip lighting. AEG-LT's product range included products in all categories of technical lighting elements, for indoor or for outdoors, with the only exception of elements of accent lighting. It included, for instance, several models for outdoor street lighting, parks, roads and highways, airports, stadiums, etc. Also, for interior lighting, they had lighting elements for offices (inset and suspended fluorescent lighting elements), for factories, warehouses, supermarkets, etc. Its sales amounted to 23 billion pesetas in 1990, of which about two-thirds corresponded to indoor lighting elements and the remaining third, to outdoor lighting elements.

Contacts with JFP were started by Dr. Kappler in April, 1990.

Right from the start, his proposal was crystal-clear in that he was offering JFP a double contract of reciprocal distribution, and that it was not his intention to buy JFP but only to reach a commercial agreement. AEG-LT did not have a range of technical decorative indoor accent lighting elements. Its present customers in Germany were asking for this type of lighting element, but they did not want to develop this new line themselves as the investment required would be too large. They preferred to come to an agreement with a company like JFP that had already developed such a product line.

The German company's managers had been watching the development of JFP since 1987, mainly at the international trade fairs, and considered that the company was following a line which could be interesting for them.

Initially, JFP's management, especially Miguel, was very wary of starting conversations. The early contacts were fairly informal: visits to each other's factory, lunches together, etc.

However, they picked up pace and consolidated significantly when Dr. Kappler was transferred to another area and Dr. Herbert Willmy became the Business Area's new president. Until then, Dr. Willmy had been the area's marketing and sales director (for Germany and foreign markets) and had been involved in the negotiations in that capacity.

"Willmy is overwhelmingly straightforward and clear. He is a person who immediately wins you over with his humanity and honesty," said Rocasalbas.

The negotiator for AEG was Willmy in person. The negotiators for JFP were Miguel Tey and Javier Rocasalbas.

"The negotiation was very much based on the human relationship between both parties and was by no means plain sailing because Miguel had difficulties in following the English," explained Rocasalbas.

Apparently, AEG-LT's managers had been attracted by the following features of JFP: an advanced and original design; a good industrial production capacity; both in-house and subcontracted; good prices; a good range of indoor accent lighting elements; and all this in a company that was effectively managed and economically sound.

"I think that they were aware that JFP was only 'an embryo' AEG distributor in Spain and France. However, even so, we were perhaps the best distributor available to them," commented Rocasalbas.

"Sometimes, the negotiations were even fun. For example, sometimes we were wary and even expressed fears that, should we sign an agreement with AEG-LT, somehow we would be putting ourselves in their power and that 'if they sneezed, we could catch a double pneumonia.'

"On these occasions, in order to get the negotiations out of the rut, Willmy suggested that we do a kind of role-playing, challenging us to put ourselves in his place, as if Miguel or I were the managers of the AEG-LT business area, and try to identify decisions or actions that could harm JFP. As soon as we said something, each time Willmy would come up with the defensive or protective countermeasure that JFP could take, thus effectively knocking down all our objections.

"Willmy caught on very quickly to JFP's way of being and doing business."

For JFP, the single factor that worked most in favor of reaching an agreement with AEG-LT was the possibility of obtaining a high-volume and almost instantaneous distribution of TROLL lighting elements in Germany, through AEG-LT's sales network, composed of about 70 sales engineers; also, the link with the Daimler-Benz Group and the Deutsche Bank could perhaps lead to a certain volume of "captive" or induced sales, thanks to the purchasing priority presumably given to AEG-LT by the other companies in the group. They also hoped that their association with AEG-LT would be a decisive factor in helping them to rapidly obtain the VDE certifications in Germany for their lighting elements.

Another positive factor was the understanding that, wherever AEG had a subsidiary in Europe, JFP could sell through them their accent lighting elements. However, if JFP managers considered that some or any of AEG's subsidiaries were not adequate for this task, they could freely choose any other distributor or marketing channel.

Aside from this, JFP also saw major advantages in distributing AEG-LT's products in Spain and France.

"Obviously, the AEG brand, and its German origin, count for a lot. We realised that AEG-LT's products would be positioned in the high-quality, high-price segment in Spain, so perhaps we might not achieve high sales volumes or high margins for JFP as importers-distributors. However, it was clear to us that the 'partnership' with AEG-LT would give prestige to JFP in Spain and would help us consolidate the image of the TROLL products and our image as a company. This would help us to gain easier access to prescribers.

"Also, it would obviously help us complete the product range we could offer in France and Spain. Now, we would be able to quote virtually all the lighting elements needed for an entire new building or for a complete architectural project. In other words, we would have a complete product range, and we could suggest a solution for any technical lighting need, in the broadest sense."

Rocasalbas expected that distributing AEG-LT lighting elements in Spain and France would not require additional salesmen. Quite on the contrary, he expected to have higher financial expenses due to higher stocks, and higher needs for physical space in their warehouse.

However, negotiating the specific clauses of the contracts had not been without its problems and there had even been moments when it seemed that negotiations would be broken off.

One of those moments was when it came to setting each company's sales targets and purchase commitments for the other company's products.

Another significant difficulty appeared when Miguel Tey said that he was not prepared to stop supplying TROLL lamps to Ulrich Sattler. Ulrich owned an electrical con-

tracting company and a retail store in Stuttgart. He had been JFP's importer-distributor since 1989. In 1991, he had bought about one million deutsche marks.[8] Miguel did not want to lose this sales volume. Also, he thought it would be wise to keep Sattler on, just in case the agreement with AEG did not materialize or work out properly.

In the face of Miguel's adamance, it was finally agreed that Ulrich Sattler would continue to sell the less sophisticated part of JFP's lamp collection under the TROLL brand name, while AEG-LT would concentrate on selling the more sophisticated products—namely, architectural lighting—as AEG products, even though brochures and catalogs would carry the caption: "AEG, designed by TROLL."

Rocasalbas said on that occasion:

"I think we are making a strategic mistake, which will be very difficult to correct. Why don't we impose to Ulrich Sattler that he sell JFP supplied lighting elements under another new brand which isn't TROLL?"

The fact of the matter was that the contract was to be signed with AEG stating that the products sold by AEG-LT in Germany would be labelled "AEG," although sales leaflets would say "AEG, designed by TROLL."

## Reflections in the Late Afternoon of January 21, 1992

Everything seemed to have been taken care of but there were still a number of points that worried Miguel. On the one hand, there was the "big guy will eat the little guy" complex. He felt that if AEG's purchases were to attain very high volumes, the Germans would have too much power over the Catalans and would end up taking them over. Was this a real danger? How could he prevent it? Another point was that he did not know to what extent he should commit himself to this alliance. Should it be a purely commercial alliance or should it include other aspects? How could they get maximum benefit from the alliance? What other synergies were there that might be as yet untapped? He also wondered what he should do with Sattler, the German distributor, and whether AEG had any kind of hidden agenda. With these thoughts running through his mind, Miguel got up, went

---

[8]*One deutsche mark was approximately equivalent to 63 Spanish pesetas in 1991.*

to his desk and started to read, once again, the contracts that had to be signed the next day.

By way of final reflection, it seemed to him that for both companies, the "Spain sells to Germany" flow or relationship was much more important than the "Germany sells to Spain and France" relationship. Out of a hypothetical and speculative total value or sum of both flows or relationships, Miguel would have estimated the weighting of the former as 90 and that of the latter at perhaps only 10.

# Harley-Davidson (B) Hedging Hogs

Harley-Davidson's competitive comeback in the late 1980s is one of the few protectionist success stories. It is the story of a firm that used government protection to adjust to a changing competitive global market. But Harley's success in the late 1980s brought along new problems that threatened to undermine much of the progress already attained. Harley's primary problem was the same problem faced by many undiversified international firms: it produced its motorcycles, hogs,[1] in only one country and exported its product to all foreign markets. But exchange rates change, and prices and earnings originally denominated in foreign currencies end up being worth very different amounts when finding their way back home to the dollar.[2]

## Exporting Hogs

Harley's sales in 1990 were more than $864 million. Of total sales, $268 million, or 31 percent, were international

sales. Harley had been exporting for a very long time: for 50 years to Japan and more than 80 years to Germany. New markets were growing in countries such as Greece, Argentina, Brazil, and even the Virgin Islands. Although international sales were obviously very important to Harley's present profitability, they also represented its future. The domestic market in the United States for motorcycles—any firm's motorcycles—was beginning to decline. This was generally thought to be a result of changing consumer profiles and tastes. International market potential for Harley looked quite promising, but Harley had only 15 percent of the world market. It needed to do better, much better.

Harley's problem was that foreign distributors and dealers needed two things for continued growth and market share expansion: (1) local currency prices and (2) stable prices. First, local currency pricing, whether it be Japanese yen, German marks, Australian dollars, or Canadian dollars, would allow the foreign dealers to compete on price in same currency terms with all competitors. And this competition would not be hindered by the dealers and distributors adding currency surcharges to sticker prices as a result of their own need to cover currency exposure.[3] Harley needed to sell its hogs to foreign dealers and distributorships in local currency, but that would not really solve the problems. First, Harley itself would now be responsible for managing the currency exposure. Second, it still did not assure the foreign dealers of stable prices, not unless Harley intended to absorb all exchange rate changes itself.

Figure 1 illustrates the foreign currency pricing issue for sales of Harleys in Australia and Japan. Australian consumers shop, compare, and purchase in Australian dollars. Starting at the opposite end, however, is the fact that Harley hogs are produced and initially priced in U.S. dollars. Someone must bear the risk of currency exchange, either the parent, the distributor, or the consumer; it rarely will be the consumer.

## Currency Risk Sharing at Harley

John Hevey, manager of international finance, instituted a system that Harley calls "risk sharing." The idea is not new, but it has not been fashionable for some time. The

---

SOURCE: *This case was written by Michael H. Moffett, the University of Michigan, March 1993. The case is intended for class discussion purposes only and does not represent either efficient or inefficient financial management practices. Do not quote without prior permission.*

[1] *The motorcycles produced and sold by Harley-Davidson have traditionally been known as hogs. The nickname is primarily in reference to their traditional large size, weight, and power.*

[2] *This case draws upon several articles including "Harley Uses 'Risk Sharing' To Hedge Foreign Currencies," by Lawrence R. Quinn,* Business International Money Report *(March 16, 1992):105–106; and "Harley: Wheeling and Dealing," by Lawrence Quinn,* Corporate Finance *(April 1992):29–30.*

[3] *For example, an independent Australian dealer who sells and earns Australian dollar revenues but must pay for the Harley hogs shipped from the United States in U.S. dollars will be accepting currency risk. If the Australian dealer then adds a margin to the hog price to cover currency-hedging costs, the product is less competitive.*

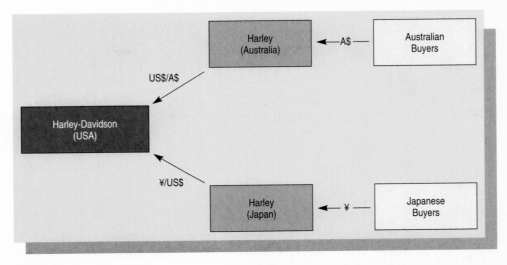

**FIGURE 1**

**Harley-Davidson's Foreign Pricing Flow**

idea is fairly simple: as long as the spot exchange rate does not move a great distance from the rate in effect when Harley quotes foreign currency prices to its foreign dealers, Harley will maintain that single price. This allows the foreign dealers and distributors, both those owned and not owned by Harley, to be assured of predictable and stable prices. The stable prices needed to be denominated in the currency of the foreign dealer and distributor's operations. Harley would then be responsible for managing the currency exposures.

A typical currency risk-sharing arrangement specifies three bands or zones of exchanges: (1) neutral zone, (2) sharing zone, and (3) renegotiation zone. Figure 2 provides an example of how the currency zones may be constructed between a U.S. parent firm and its Japanese dealers or distributors. The neutral zone in Figure 2 is constructed as a band of +/−5 percent change about the central rate specified in the contract, ¥130.00/\$. The central rate can be determined a number of ways, for example, the spot rate in effect on the date of the contract's consummation, the average rate for the past three-month period, or a moving average of monthly rates. In this case, the neutral zone's boundaries are ¥136.84/\$ and ¥123.81/\$.[4] As long as the spot exchange rate between the yen and dollar remains within this neutral zone, the U.S. parent assures the Japanese dealers of a constant price in yen. If a particular product line was priced in the United States at \$4,000, the yen-denominated price would be ¥520,000. This assures the Japanese dealers a constant supply price in their own currency terms. The pre-

dictability of costs reduces the currency risks of the Japanese dealers and allows them to pass on the more predictable local currency prices to their customers.

If, however, the spot rate moves out of the neutral zone into the sharing zone, the U.S. parent and the Japanese dealer will share the costs or benefits of the margin beyond the neutral zone rate. For example, if the Japanese yen depreciated against the dollar to ¥140.00/\$, the spot rate will have moved into the upper sharing zone. If the contract specified that the sharing would be a 50/50 split, the new price to the Japanese dealer would be

$$\$4,000 \times \left[ ¥130.00/\$ + \frac{¥140.00/\$ - ¥136.84/\$}{2} \right]$$
$$= \$4,000 \times ¥131.58/\$ = ¥526,320.$$

Although the supply costs have indeed risen to the Japanese dealers, from ¥520,000 to ¥526,320, the percentage increase is significantly less than the percentage change in the exchange rate.[5] The Japanese dealer is insulated

---

[4]*The upper and lower exchange rates of the band are calculated as:*

$$\frac{¥130.00/\$ - ¥136.84/\$}{¥136.84/\$} \times 100 = -5.0\%.$$

and

$$\frac{¥130.00/\$ - ¥123.81/\$}{¥123.81/\$} \times 100 = +5.0\%.$$

[5]*The yen price has risen only 1.22 percent while the Japanese yen has depreciated 7.14 percent versus the U.S. dollar.*

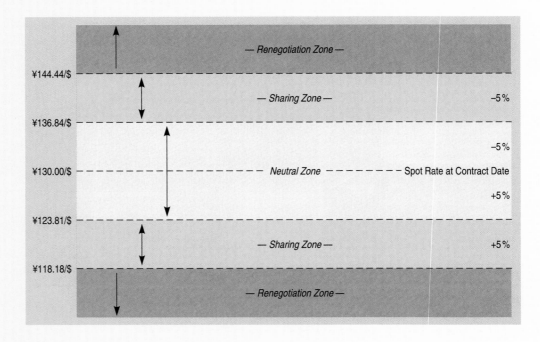

**FIGURE 2**

**Currency Risk Sharing**

*Note:* Percentage changes are in the value of the Japanese yen versus U.S. dollar. For example, a "+ 5%" is a 5 percent appreciation in the value of the yen, from ¥130.00/$ to ¥123.81/$.

against the constant fluctuations of the exchange rate and subsequent fluctuations on supply costs.

Finally, if the spot rate were to move drastically from the neutral zone into the renegotiation zone, the risk-sharing agreement calls for a renegotiation of the price to bring it more in line with current exchange rates and the economic and competitive realities of the market.

## Currency Management at Harley

Harley's risk-sharing program has allowed the firm to increase the stability of prices in foreign markets. But this stability has come about by the parent firm's accepting a larger proportion of the exchange rate risk. Harley's approach to currency management is conservative, both in what it hedges and how it hedges.

The "what," the exposures that Harley actually manages, are primarily its sales, which are denominated in foreign currencies. Although Harley does import some inputs, the volume of imports denominated in foreign currencies (accounts payable) are relatively small compared to the export sales (the accounts receivable).

Harley is a bit more aggressive in its exposure time frame than many other firms, however. Harley will hedge sales that will be made in the near future, anticipated sales, extending about twelve months out. The ability of the firm to hedge sales that have not yet been "booked" is a result of the firm's consistency and predictability of sales in the various markets. Like most firms that hedge future sales, however, Harley will intentionally leave itself a margin of error, therefore hedging less than 100 percent of the expected exposures.

Presently Harley is rather conservative in the "how," the instruments and methods used for currency hedging. Harley uses currency forward contracts for all hedging. Harley will estimate the amount of the various foreign currency payments to be received per period and sell those foreign currency quantities forward (less the percentage margin for error). Like many other firms expanding international operations, Harley is now studying the use of additional currency management approaches, such as the use of foreign currency options. At present, however, Harley executives are satisfied with their currency management program.

## Financial Management's Growing Responsibilities

A third dimension of the new financial/currency management program at Harley is the increased role of financial management with sales. The finance staff keeps in touch with the sales and marketing staffs to work toward the most competitive combinations and packages of pricing. Financial staff also attempts to keep information lines open between its foreign dealers and distributors to help them maintain price competitiveness.

Harley-Davidson is a firm that continues to be unique in many ways. Not only is it one of the true "success stories" for American protectionism, but it has continued to work to improve its international competitiveness by responding to the needs of not only its customers, but also its distributors and dealers.

### Questions for Discussion

1. Why is it so important for Harley-Davidson to both price in foreign currencies in foreign markets and provide stable prices?
2. How effective will "risk sharing" be in actually achieving Harley's stated goals? Is there a better solution?
3. Who is bearing the brunt of the costs of the financial risk management program?

### References

Hufbauer, Gary Clyde, Diane T. Berliner, and Kimberly Ann Elliot. *Trade Protection in the United States: 31 Case Studies.* Washington, D.C.: The Institute for International Economics, 1986.

Pruzin, Daniel R. "Born to be Verrucht." *World Trade* 5, Issue 4 (May 1992): 112–117.

Quinn, Lawrence R. "Harley Uses 'Risk Sharing' to Hedge Foreign Currencies." *Business International Money Report,* March 16, 1992, 105–106.

———, "Harley: Wheeling and Dealing." *Corporate Finance* (April 1992): 29–30.

## Finn-Suklaa Oy

Finn-Suklaa Oy, founded in 1906, is a family-owned medium-sized company in the sweets and biscuit business. Its headquarters is located on the outskirts of Helsinki, Finland. Seppo Jaaskelainen is the treasury manager of the company, and the grandson of Sebastian Jaaskelainen, the founder of the company. Seppo is a typical elder Finn, very conservative and risk-averse in his business dealings. He was now in the process of financing an expansion of the company's Japanese subsidiary and was trying to balance currency of debt denomination, financing costs, and the degree of complexity in the financing arrangement. As always, Seppo was determined to leave a very solid and financially healthy firm as an inheritance to his daughter, Saara Jaaskelainen. In Seppo's eyes, financing was not a part of the business to be taken lightly.

### Finn-Suklaa Oy

Sebastian Jaaskelainen had actually been an unwilling immigrant to Finland in 1940. His family had for generations been manufacturers of sweets and chocolates in the Karelian region of Russia, the province bordering present-day Finland and home of the largest lakes in Europe. At the conclusion of the Russo-Finnish War (1939–1940) in the winter of 1940, also known as the *Winter War,* the Russians had forced thousands of Karelians, the Finnish minority in the region, out of their houses and from their farms with little else than the clothes on their backs. Many, like the Jaaskelainens, also carried with them generations of skill and business experience.

By the early 1950s, the Jaaskelainens had once again opened their own business, now in Finland, and were prospering. Throughout the 1950s, 1960s, and 1970s, the company—then simply called *Jaaskelainen Chocolates* or *Jaaskelainen Suklaa* in Finnish—grew and prospered as a manufacturer and distributor of chocolates. In the early 1970s the company expanded into biscuits and dessert and coffee cookies and restructured into the corporate form seen today, *Finn-Suklaa Oy.* In the 1980s, the company had opened manufacturing operations in Sweden (Mälmo) and Norway (Stavanger) to access those markets from within and to avoid the relatively high import tariffs and restrictions. In 1989, they had established their first truly "foreign" subsidiary, Finn-Suklaa Osaka outside Osaka, Japan. Finn-Suklaa's chocolates had been a particularly big hit with the Japanese, and the business had flourished.

## The Japanese Subsidiary Financing Problem

Finn-Suklaa Osaka produces and sells chocolates and assorted sweets solely in the Japanese market. Although the company has discussed producing for export on a number of occasions, the consensus of management was that the cost of production in Japan currently prevented the operation from being a cost-competitive exporter.

The subsidiary had been quite successful to date, so much so, that the parent company had now decided to invest in a biscuit operation as well. Standard practice within the company was for the Finnish parent to capitalize subsidiaries with minimal equity and maximum debt. And, rather than having the subsidiaries raise their own debt capital in local markets, the parent preferred to raise the capital itself and extend loans to the subsidiaries from the parent company in Helsinki (as was the case with both the Norwegian and Swedish subsidiaries.)

Seppo's immediate problem was to raise approximately ¥883,500,000, about 50 million Finnish markka (FIM) at the current spot exchange rate of ¥17.67/FIM, for the operational expansion of the Japanese subsidiary. Finn-Suklaa Osaka would need the money in six months and would prefer a maturity on the capital of about five years. Seppo believed the five-year maturity would provide a stable funding base, while not putting undue burden on operational cash flows to repay the debt too rapidly.

Interest rates had recently trended upward in Finland, and Seppo was not debating whether he should acquire the funds today and try to lock in lower interest rates.

But, it also depended on whether he borrowed Finnish markka or Japanese yen. The funds were for the subsidiary, and the subsidiary generated 100 percent of its revenue in Japanese yen. Standard practice was to match the currency of denomination of revenues and debt service.

The problem, however, was *access* and *cost.* Since Finn-Suklaa Osaka had not been in the Japanese market for very long, the company was not yet well known in the local markets (at least in the financial markets). After a number of unsuccessful requests, the subsidiary had been offered a five-year loan by Daichi-Kangyo Bank at 4.50 percent. Finn-Suklaa Osaka could obtain the full amount desired on the condition that the parent company guaranteed the debt. After a number of additional calls, Seppo received a quote of 3.50 percent from a competitor bank if the parent was the borrowing unit. After reviewing these two alternatives, Seppo rejected the Daichi-Kangyo Bank offer and concluded that the parent would have to do the borrowing.

## The Back-to-Back Loan Alternative

Seppo has heard through a business associate that a Japanese firm's subsidiary located in Finland, KKI Oy, needs roughly the same amount of capital (in Finnish markka) for its Finnish operations and needs it immediately. Seppo has two days to decide whether he is willing to accept the proposed back-to-back loan, and whether he feels the Japanese firm is a solid counterparty risk. A credit report provided by Seppo's local bank, Kansallis-Osake-Pankki (KOP), describes the Japanese parent company as financially stable, approximately twenty years old, and having expanded internationally slowly and carefully. On this basis, Seppo concludes that the alternative is at least worth considering and collects the relevant interest rates for evaluation (see Table 1).

**TABLE 1**

Interest Rate & Spread Quotes for the Back-to-Back Loan
(basis point spreads over LIBOR)

| Currency | LIBOR | Finn-Suklaa (Finland) | KKI (Japan) |
|---|---|---|---|
| Japanese yen | 2.650% | 85 bp | 35 bp |
| Finnish markka | 6.350% | 65 bp | 165 bp |

According to the interest rate quotes in Figure 1 collected by Seppo, Finn-Suklaa could raise Finnish markka at a floating rate of LIBOR + 65 basis points, or [1]

$$6.350\% - 0.650\% = 7.000\%.$$

Similarly, the Japanese company, KKI, could definitely borrow Japanese yen cheaper than Finn-Suklaa, at a cost of LIBOR + 35 basis points, or

$$2.65\% + 0.350\% = 3.000\%.$$

Finn-Suklaa's comparable cost of yen was 3.500 percent.

The back-to-back loan gets its name from the literally parallel loan structure. In this case, the Finnish parent company of Finn-Suklaa would make a loan to the Finnish subsidiary of the Japanese company—in Finnish markka,

and simultaneously, the Japanese parent company would make a loan of equal size and maturity—but in Japanese yen—to the Japanese subsidiary of Finn-Suklaa Oy. In this way, both subsidiaries could attain the debt capital that they wanted, but at rates that were (hopefully) cheaper than what they themselves could acquire locally. The basic structure and arrangement between the four units is detailed in Figure 1.

Since the swap with KKI would be implemented now, and Finn-Suklaa would not need the funds for another six months, the company could deposit the funds in an interest-bearing account in Japan at a fixed rate, currently quoted at 2.500 percent per annum.[2]

Seppo's treasury assistant, a newly-minted MBA with the traditional MBA-gambling mentality, had advised him to swap the funds with KKI to enjoy the interest differential between the rates. Seppo, however, being of the old school, had little experience with swaps or other derivative instruments and was reluctant. On the other hand,

---

[1] *LIBOR, London InterBank Offer Rate, is the most common base rate for floating rate loans by currency in the world. It is representative of the cost of funds between major banks in the London market and is usually available for 1-, 3-, 6-, and 12-month maturities.*

[2] *The comparable interest-bearing accounts in Finland for Finmarks are currently 6.100 percent per annum.*

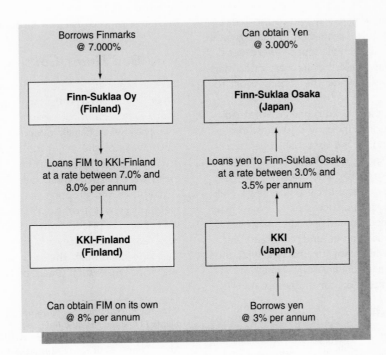

**FIGURE 1**

**The Proposed Back-to-Back Swap between Finn-Suklaa (Finland) & KKI (Japan)**

Seppo had a very good relationship with his banker at KOP in Helsinki, and he now turned to that banker for advice.

### The Bank Swap Alternative

Seppo asked his longtime friend and banker at KOP, Arja Tirronen, if the bank itself would be willing to enter into a similar swap structure. Arja, after checking with her trading-desks and derivatives group, explained that if Finn-Suklaa Oy went ahead with the Finmark loan, the bank could arrange a swap that would lock in the Japanese yen at LIBOR + 72.5 basis points (3.375 percent at the current LIBOR; same spot rate). Seppo thought this seemed much less risky, given that KOP would be the counterparty and he knew exactly what his cost of funds were without negotiating with the Japanese company.

### Market Conditions

The Japanese yen had been rising slowly and steadily for years against the markka, and Seppo felt that this trend would continue. This would mean that he would need to pay more Finnish markkas in the future to obtain the Japanese yen needed for the biscuit line production. Every day he waited, Seppo felt, would only add to the cost of the necessary funds. Although committed to floating-rate debt (fixed rates for firms such as Seppo's were decidedly unattractive), he was afraid that interest rates may also be on their way up a bit over the coming short to medium-term.

The market for sweets and biscuits had grown steadily in spite of the long-enduring Finnish and Japanese recessions (the Japanese economy had essentially been in recession since the early spring of 1990). Finn-Suklaa Osaka's market share in sweets had risen nearly 3 percent per year in the past two years, and it was seemingly well positioned to make a major and successful foray into the biscuit market. Seppo called a meeting to discuss the pros and cons of the various alternatives, and to try and reach a quick consensus on which way to proceed with the Japanese subsidiary's expansion financing. Time was indeed money if interest rates or currencies were rising.

### Questions for Discussion

1. Discuss the pros and cons of the financing alternatives. Prioritize criteria, including the nonquantifiable factors such as company culture and complexity.
2. How do exchange rate and interest rate expectations affect the valuation of the alternatives? How significant

should these expectations be in making the financing decision?
3. Using the numbers quoted in the case, what would you recommend Seppo to do?

# Comeback from a Near-Death Experience: Audi of America 1992–97

In the mid-1980s, Audi was one of the American auto industry's most attractive franchises, selling more vehicles than BMW. Its cars were stylish and technologically sophisticated, especially the 'Quattro' all-wheel-drive models. Negative media coverage suddenly reversed this trend. A report on CBS' newsmagazine *60 Minutes* claimed that Audi's hot-selling 5000 sedan could unexpectedly accelerate out of control. Ultimately, government safety agencies in the United States and Germany cleared the 5000, but Audi of America could not recover from the bad publicity and its own mishandling of the situation, and its sales fell precipitously.

### The Bad Times Continue

In the beginning of the 1990s, most news coverage of Audi still started with the "unintended acceleration" story, although most writers acknowledged that the company was officially exonerated. However, the safety issue was not the only problem Audi faced. Audi's quality was seen as lower than the industry average, and repairs were costly. Some dealers lost interest in the slow-selling cars and dropped the Audi franchise. The public perception was that Audi's products were underpowered and overpriced. Some of Audi's troubles were self-inflicted. The company insisted on maintaining its high prices, even though the cars no longer carried a premium image. Audi's 'Quattro' four-wheel-drive system,

---

*\*SOURCE: This case was prepared by Michael R. Czinkota and Vlado Loukanov based on public sources such as* Advertising Age, Los Angeles Times, Business Week, USA Today, The New York Times, Chicago Tribune, Adweek Southeast, Medical Economics, Ward's Auto World, Investor's Business Daily, Reuters Financial Service, PR Newswire, *and* Marketing and Media Decisions. *See Audi Web sites at* **http://www.audi.com** *and* **http://www.audiusa.com**

unique in the luxury passenger class, was available only in the top-of-the-line models. In addition, automotive analysts insisted that Audi of America lacked the marketing muscle it needed to revitalize its image in the United States.

In 1991–92, Audi offered a new and simplified vehicle lineup, aimed at materializing the company's claim that it offered "German engineering at Japanese prices." What had been the 80/90 series in the smaller-car lineup was now simply the 90; the 100/200 series was now the 100 midsize sedan plus an S4 performance version; at the top was the V8 sedan. (The original 90 and 100 lines had replaced the 5000 series in 1988, offering better overall quality at lower prices.) The new 90CS carried a sticker price of about $25,000, or $2,000 less than the comparable BMW 325i. The all-wheel-drive 90CS Quattro Sport was only available with a five-speed manual transmission.

At the end of 1993, Audi again drew attention to the brand with the introduction of the new Cabriolet and a new station wagon. The Cabriolet was likely to attract new customers because of its stylish design; the wagon offered minivan customers a practical and well-designed alternative. To counter the image of low reliability and high maintenance costs, Audi of America started offering the most extensive warranty in the luxury class, featuring free routine maintenance on all new Audis for three years. The company pioneered the short-term lease, which was marketed as "Audi's three-year test-drive."

U.S. sales remained disappointing, however. In 1991, when Audi sold a record 448,000 vehicles worldwide, Audi of America sold only 12,283 cars, or 42 percent less than in 1990, and 83 percent less than the 1985 peak. In 1992, sales rebounded to 14,756 cars, but fell again the following year to 12,943. On the other hand, Volkswagen, the parent company, as a whole remained the country's top-selling European importer.

Audi of America appeared to be at a dead end, and the rumor that Volkswagen was going to pull the brand from the U.S. market seemed well-grounded. However, VW's new Chairman, Ferdinand Piech, insisted that "if you lose America, you lose the world." Gerd Klauss, the then-new Vice President in charge of Audi of America at Volkswagen of America, enjoyed the full support of parent's management during those hard times. Chairman Piech, whose previous job was CEO of Audi, was facing similar issues globally at Volkswagen. VW was still financially sound, but without a deep-cutting reorganization its plans to become a major global competitor could be jeopardized.

## A New Approach

In 1993, Piech outlined a plan for sweeping reforms, including a "lean manufacturing program" borrowed from the Japanese and a speedup of new-car development. Compared to the Japanese, VW was estimated to take twice as much time to develop a car, and its assembly lines employed four times the amount of labor. Concurrently, Piech started a multibillion dollar spending program to finance corporate growth in Europe and North America. In the spring of 1993, a series of management changes were announced at both Volkswagen of America and Audi of America. Klauss, the new chief executive of Audi, came from Mercedes-Benz of North America where he had been responsible for developing and coordinating the overall corporate strategy as well as the strategic positioning within the parent company's worldwide business. Audi of America also saw new executives appointed to the positions of General Service Manager, Controller, and Director of Marketing and Product Planning. The latter, Ken Moriarty, had served as a senior marketing and promotions manager at Mercedes-Benz of North America.

Audi's new philosophy reflected what company officials called the three "Ps"—lower prices, an emphasis on higher performance, and a range of new products. Klauss realized two important facts about the Audi brand on the U.S. market: first, the company could not support a price positioning similar to BMW and Mercedes, and second, it was not putting sufficient marketing effort behind the benefits of the Quattro four-wheel-drive system.

## Competitive Positioning

Audi began its new strategy by slashing the prices of its 1995 model year cars on the average by several thousand dollars. (At the same time, the stronger yen began driving up prices on Japanese luxury imports.) Audi also strengthened the performance of its automobiles by introducing a range of more powerful engines. Essential in the brand's repositioning, according to marketing director Moriarty, was the new emphasis on all-wheel drive. To make the Quattro more accessible to a wider range of customers, Audi dropped it as standard equipment on the high-end models and offered it as a $1,500 option on its entire product line. The move reduced the effective transaction price of an average Audi car with the system by $5,000. Within one year, the percentage of buyers ordering the Quattro jumped from 2 percent to 50 percent. This pricing strategy provided some momentum for

Audi so it could add a third "P" to *performance* and *pricing* with the introduction of the all-new A line of *products* in 1995–97.

The A4 was to take on such tough import competitors as the Mercedes C-Class, BMW's 3-series, and the Lexus ES300. Audi officials admitted they faced a challenge in attempting to seize share from the better-established nameplates. However, they hoped the new compact sedan would win over buyers with its radically new design and a blend of features, including a new five-speed automatic transmission and a revised four-wheel-drive system. The new 1.8-liter Turbo engine won several "ten best engines of the year" awards. With a base price at about $23,000, the A4 1.8 T, introduced in 1996, became the lowest priced luxury sedan sold in the United States (see Table 1). The A4, with the more powerful 2.8-liter, six-cylinder engine, had been launched the previous year. Audi was luring a new generation of buyers, many of them unaware of the problems the car manufacturer faced ten years earlier. As one automotive analyst on Wall Street put it, "the passage of time has also helped. People have forgotten about the 'unintended acceleration' scare." The aggressive pricing and bold new design of the A4 made it a big hit throughout North America, especially in areas where the company had never been very strong, such as Southern California.

## A Product Breakthrough

The true revolutionary newcomer, however, was the A8, the all-aluminum challenge to the BMW 7-series and the Mercedes S-Class. The A8 was about one-third lighter than comparable steel units and was the first car in the world to offer six airbags—two for each the driver and the front-seat passenger (front and side impact) and one for each rear-seat passenger. The lighter car offered better fuel economy, livelier engine power, and more responsiveness because there was less mass to shift. Audi had achieved lightness without sacrificing strength, rigidity, or crash performance. One automotive writer called the A8 a "rolling testbed for technology." The downside for customers was that aluminum frame repairs and insurance policies were more expensive. Audi's new flagship, which replaced the previous V8 saloon, was also priced significantly lower than its German competitors.

Audi kept surprising its customers and the industry with continuous innovation. When the redesigned A6 sedan came to market in the fall of 1997, industry experts predicted it would duplicate the success of the A4. The A6 featured striking design, a longer wheelbase, and substantial improvements in technology, safety, and equipment levels, including a five-speed automatic transmission with Porsche's "Tiptronic" technology, which allowed the

**TABLE 1**

**Manufacturer Suggested Retail Prices (MSRP) for the 1998 Model Year**

| Audi | MSRP | BMW | MSRP | Mercedes | MSRP |
|---|---|---|---|---|---|
| | | 318ti Coupe | $21,960 | | |
| A4 1.8T | $23,790 | 318i Sedan | $26,720 | | |
| | | 323is Coupe | $29,270 | C230 Sedan | $ 30,450 |
| A4 2.8 | $28,390 | 328i Sedan | $33,670 | C280 Sedan | $ 35,400 |
| | | 328is Coupe | $33,770 | | |
| A4 Avant | $30,465 | | | | |
| Cabriolet | $34,600 | 323i Convertible | $35,270 | SLK230 | $ 39,700 |
| | | 328i Convertible | $42,070 | CLK320 | $ 39,850 |
| A6 | $33,750 | 528i Sedan | $39,470 | E300 TD Sedan | $ 41,800 |
| | | 540i (automatic) | $51,070 | E320 Sedan | $ 45,500 |
| A6 Wagon | $34,600 | | | E320 Wagon | $ 46,500 |
| A8 3.7 | $57,400 | | | S 320 Sedan | $ 64,000 |
| | | 740i Sedan | $62,070 | | |
| A8 4.2 | $65,000 | 740iL Sedan | $66,070 | S420 Sedan | $ 73,900 |
| | | 750iL Sedan | $92,100 | S500 Sedan | $ 87,500 |
| | | | | S600 Sedan | $132,250 |

The table compares all Audi models to most BMW and Mercedes models in relevant classes. BMW's M-3 and the 800 series and Mercedes' SL and CL classes are not shown. Source: Audi, BMW, and Mercedes-Benz.

driver to choose between automatic and manual mode. The new luxury touring car introduced a new interior concept with three different environments called "atmospheres," which customers could choose from at no extra cost. The A6 was aggressively positioned in the $35,000 price range and compared very favorably to the BMW 528i, which started at around $40,000.

## Customer Satisfaction

All cars in the A line came standard with the "Audi Advantage" warranty package, including the luxury market's customary three-year/50,000 mile limited warranty, ten-year limited warranty against corrosion perforation, and twenty-four-hour roadside assistance for three years. The three-year/50,000 miles free scheduled maintenance, however, continued to distinguish Audi from other luxury imports. This feature significantly improved customer satisfaction with dealers, a longtime weak point for Audi. Customer satisfaction rates outranked those of BMW and Mercedes in 1995–97.

In October 1997, the company established Audi Financial Services (AFS), a division of VW Credit, Inc., to serve Audi customers and the 270 dealers throughout the United States. By establishing the new division, corporate management was aiming at better customer satisfaction and higher customer retention rates. A 1997 Consumer Satisfaction Study by J.D. Power and Associates had found that customer retention is 20 percent higher when financing is placed with a captive provider, compared to when financing is placed with a bank.

## Marketing and Advertising

A 1993 corporate study showed that, while rising among Audi owners, Audi's image continued to worsen among U.S. consumers overall. The company fired its longtime advertising agency, DDB Needham, and hired McKinney & Silver to take over the $30 million account. One Audi dealer characterized DDB Needham's work as inconsistent, but added that the blame lay with both the agency and the marketer. Ending the relationship with DDB was a difficult decision for Gerd Klauss, the new chief executive of Audi of America, since the agency was handling VW's and Audi's global accounts. According to some accounts, McKinney & Silver won the account because it convinced company officials that it knew what the Audi should do to lure customers back—in essence, to position Audi as "the single most underrated car in the country."

McKinney launched its face makeover campaign with a four-page spread in many national publications titled, "What Is Audi." Rather than focusing on image, as previous advertising did (DDB's last campaign was carried under the slogan "Take Control"), new ads touted product attributes and value and claimed that Audi gives customers more—for less. An ad by DDB Needham, "Welcome to the '90s," featured a sophisticated-looking working mother. She takes her kids to school, goes to work, and has an exciting nightlife—all on jazzy background music. The new McKinney ad contained a simply laundry list of safety and performance features, including "the safety and traction of the Quattro all-wheel drive [and] child safety seat locks." Unusual for the luxury category, some ads even mentioned rivals BMW and Mercedes and pointed out that the Audi offered better value.

"We are positioning the A-6 midsize sedan as excellent German engineering for a more affordable price." said McKinney's Cameron McNaughton. The 1996 campaign for the A4 sedan, in the words of Ken Moriarty, the marketing director for Audi of America, used more of a human touch. With its A8 luxury sedan, Audi pioneered lending cars to Hollywood celebrities. The company gave free loaners to two dozen entertainment personalities "with active social lives," including Jay Leno, Jerry Seinfeld, and Quincy Jones. "They are extroverted movers and shakers who go out a lot," Moriarty said. "And when they do, they take the car with them." (Seinfeld did actually end up buying an A8.) Following a long sponsoring tradition in Europe, Audi began contributing to the arts in the United States in 1996, when it sponsored the Three Tenors Concert at Giant Stadium. The following year, the company contributed $100,000 to the San Diego opera.

As demand for luxury sport-utility vehicles soared in the mid-1990s, Audi's marketing strengthened its emphasis on the benefits of the Quattro four-wheel-drive system. In 1996, Audi launched a $10 million TV and print advertising campaign based on the "un-SUV" theme. One spot showed a woman struggling to climb down from a towering SUV as another woman drove up in an A6 Quattro wagon and easily got out. The announcer claimed that the Audi is also easy to get in, obviously referring to the price difference with luxury SUVs, such as Lexus and Lincoln-Mercury. The Quattro ad for the 1998 model year, dubbed "Tracks," features an elderly Inuet (native of Alaska) coaching his grandson in the ancient art of tracking caribou and bear. When he comes to a car track, he picks up a bit of snow, smells it and then exclaims, "Quattro." The A6 spot claimed that the model could not be compared to other cars like "apples to apples" because "the A6 is not an apple." The car then speeds up through a discord chorus of apples.

## The Market's Response

Audi's U.S. sales went up by 44 percent in 1995, up again by 52 percent in 1996, and up by 33 percent in the first half of 1997. With these increases, Audi achieved the fastest growth of any brand in the luxury passenger-car market. Sales were so brisk that dealers had to ask customers to wait for weeks and sometimes months to fulfill orders. About half of new Audi buyers had previously owned Japanese brands. Still, the 27,400 vehicles sold in 1996 represented a little more than one-third of the 1985 peak level.

The company hoped that this level would be eclipsed by the year 2000. The A-line clearly identified what Audi represented to the consumer: a provider of boldly styled performance and cars that offer substantial value. With consumer tastes evolving in the direction of its renovated product portfolio, Audi appeared poised for success in the U.S. market. Audi growth reflected in part the gains achieved by European luxury imports in mid '90s, largely at the expense of the Japanese. The resurgence of the former came as they lowered costs and prices, improved customer service and introduced stylish products with more features that affluent Americans wanted. On the average, European luxury car sales grew about 50 percent faster in 1994–97 than Japanese imports.

When in 1992–93 both BMW and Mercedes-Benz announced they were going to open production lines in the United States, Gerd Klauss declared that Audi would follow suit. One of the Audi board members reasoned in the fall of 1995, after the German competitors had built their U.S. plants, that the company "needed to be involved in a dollar base" in order to offset the strong D-mark. Another senior executive noted in early 1996 that a dollar base did not necessarily mean producing in the United States. Gerd Klauss insisted that the company needed a U.S. plant to produce cars geared specifically to the American customers, more interested in safety and comfort than speed like the Germans. If the Audi board said "yes," such a huge investment—likely to top $500 million—had to be approved by Volkswagen. In the spring of 1997, the company leadership was considering possible plant locations in the Sunbelt region of the United States.

## Questions for Discussion

1. What were the problems in the beginning of the '90s that kept Audi of America from regaining its market position of mid-1980s?
2. How did the new management reposition the company on the U.S. market after 1993 and why?
3. What are the major factors that contributed to Audi's increasing sales in the second half of the '90s?
4. Will the prepaid maintenance affect the quality of services performed by Audi dealers?

# An Expatriate Tour in El Salvador

## December 10, 1998: The Job Offer

John and Joanna Lafferty had just opened a bottle of wine to share with friends who had come to see their new apartment in Toronto when the telephone rang. John, a lanky, easygoing development economist, excused himself to answer the phone in the kitchen.

Recently married, John and Joanna were excited to be building a life together in the same city at last. As a development economist specializing in Latin America, John Lafferty's work had taken him to Peru, Bolivia, and Guatemala on a series of three- to four-month assignments over the previous three years. While he loved the challenge and adventure of this fieldwork and had come to love the people and culture, he also wanted a home base and steady presence in Toronto, where Joanna worked as a human resource management consultant. Just before their wedding six months earlier, John accepted a position with a Toronto-based NGO (non-governmental organization) focused on research, fundraising and government lobbying on issues related to Central American political refugees. Throughout the 1980s, tens of thousands of refugees had fled political persecu-

SOURCE: *This case was written by Susan Bartholomew based on personal interviews. Names, dates, and details of situations have been modified for illustrative purposes. The various economic, political, and cultural conditions described are presented as perceptions of the individuals in the case; they do not necessarily reflect the actual conditions in the region. The events described are presented as a basis for classroom discussion rather than to illustrate effective or ineffective handling of a cross-cultural situation. For more information on El Salvador, see* **http://www.yahoo.com/ Regional/Countries/El_Salvador.**

tion and human rights abuse in war-torn Central America to seek political asylum in Canada; John's field experience in Guatemala and his natural diplomacy were invaluable to the Canadian organization. He was passionate about his work and quickly gained a reputation for being a savvy and politically astute advocate of refugees' cases.

As Joanna went to get some wineglasses from the kitchen, she could overhear her husband speaking in Spanish on the phone. Joanna had studied Spanish in college but had difficulty following the rapid, one-sided conversation. However, one phrase, "Me allegre mucho" and John's broad grin as he said it, was impossible to misinterpret. Joanna returned to her guests in the living room:

*"It sounds like good news."*

John's work with refugees in the Canadian NGO had caught the attention of the United Nations High Commission for Refugees, headquartered in Geneva, and he had recently returned from a one-week visit and series of interviews. While John had not been searching for a new job opportunity, the Geneva invitation had been too exciting to resist. John walked back into the living room with a huge smile:

*"Forget the wine, I think we should open some champagne. The U.N. has just offered me the most incredible job."*

*"In Geneva?"* Joanna asked excitedly.

John's smile grew even broader. *"No. In El Salvador."*

## December 17, 1998: The Decision

The El Salvador assignment would be for two years, as a Program Officer responsible for organizing the repatriation of Salvadoran refugees from various refugee camps back to El Salvador and developing programs to ensure the protection and well-being of such refugees in their return to Salvadoran communities. The position would report to the Charge de Mission of the El Salvador office. While this office was based in the capital city, San Salvador, the job would also require frequent travel to various field offices and refugee camps throughout El Salvador, Nicaragua, Guatemala, and Honduras. The challenge of the assignment excited John tremendously; he also believed that this was an exceptional opportunity for him to make a real difference in the lives of the refugees of Central America. He certainly wanted to accept the job; however, he would only go if Joanna would be willing and happy to go with him.

Two questions would weigh heavily on Joanna's mind:

*1. "What about the political instability of the area?"*
The politics of El Salvador were complicated and difficult

to understand, and the story seemed to vary depending on the source. As Joanna gathered, the civil war in El Salvador had come to an end in 1992 with a U.N.–brokered peace treaty between the conservative government of the Republican Nationalist Alliance (Arena) and the Marxist-led Farabundo Marti National Liberation Front (FMLN). Throughout the war, the U.S. had apparently spent more than $4 billion to support the government and military, while the Soviet Bloc supported the FMLN. Human-rights groups alleged that right-wing death squads had murdered 40,000 of the 70,000 people killed during the twelve-year war. However, the peace agreement had significantly reduced the size of the army, disbanded corrupt police forces, purged the country of the most notorious human-rights abusers, and disarmed the FMLN, allowing it to become a legal political party. The country appeared to have made substantial progress towards peace and democracy. The information and briefings they received from Salvadorans and other expatriates who had recently returned from the country suggested that life in the capital San Salvador was quite safe. Economically, the country was becoming more internationally open, with establishment of large export factories, increasing privatization, and reforms aimed at stimulating foreign investment. While certain precautions were required, and the area was still heavily patrolled by armed forces, Joanna was told she could expect a relatively normal lifestyle. They would live in a highly secure part of the city, in the area populated by all the foreign embassies. They would also be living and traveling on a U.N. diplomatic passport ("Laissez-passer"), which would afford them excellent protection.

*2. "What about my career?"*
Moving to El Salvador was the last thing Joanna had imagined when she married John Lafferty six months earlier. Joanna had worked in Toronto for three years as a human resource consultant after graduating with an MBA. She was bright and ambitious, and her career was advancing well. While she was very happy to be married, she also enjoyed her professional and financial independence. Besides, Toronto was not only professionally rewarding, it was also home, friends, and family. However, Joanna was also ready for a change; secretly, she had always envied John the sense of adventure that accompanied his work. Maybe this was an opportunity for her to develop her human resource consulting skills in an international context.

After much discussion, they decided that John would accept the assignment.

## January–March, 1999: Predeparture Arrangements

When John confirmed with the Geneva office that he would take the assignment, it was arranged for him to move to San Salvador at the end of March and for Joanna to follow one month later. It was often recommended in assignments of this kind to send married staff ahead of time to get settled into the job before their spouse and/or family arrived. This option made sense to the Laffertys and had several advantages. First, it would give Joanna more time to finish off her current consulting projects in Toronto and make a graceful exit from her present firm. She had a strong professional reputation and wanted to ensure she was remembered favourably by her corporate clients when she returned to Toronto two years later.

Second, John would be able to get the housing arrangements settled before Joanna's arrival. John's employer would provide ample financial and logistical support to staff in finding housing; however, John also knew from past experience that dealing with local realtors and utility companies in Central America could be highly frustrating. Tasks that were quite simple in Toronto, such as having a lease drawn up and getting a telephone installed, just didn't seem to follow any system or set of procedures. "Tomorrow" could mean next week or even next month. Patience, flexibility, and a good deal of charm were usually required; getting angry rarely helped. While John was used to the inconvenience and unpredictability of local services in Central America, he was uncertain how Joanna would react initially. John held a deep affection for the Central American people and felt hopeful that Joanna would develop an affinity for the culture as well. However, he hoped to at least have the majority of the living arrangements worked out before she arrived to make her transition to El Salvador as smooth as possible.

Finally, the extra time gave Joanna more opportunity to prepare herself for the transition. Joanna had taken a course on International Human Resource Management as an MBA and was familiar with the phenomenon of culture shock in international assignments. She recalled from her course that predeparture preparation and cultural orientation made a significant difference in helping employees and their families adapt to the foreign environment. Joanna was determined to read and learn as much about Salvadoran history and politics as she could. She was also keen to improve her Spanish before she arrived and as soon as the decision was made that they would be going to El Salvador, she enrolled in night courses for six hours a week.

As Joanna walked home from her Spanish class one evening, pleased with her results on her comprehension test, she recalled with amusement a conversation she had had with Joan Taylor. Joan was the wife of a senior executive with Altron, a Canadian firm with offices throughout Latin America. The Taylors had just returned from a two-year assignment in Guatemala City, and Joanna had contacted Joan to get some insight on the practicalities of living in the region.

"My dear Joanna," Joan began, "you will have a very fine life in Central America, or in most developing countries your husband will be sent to, for that matter. You will live better than you ever could anywhere else." Joan gave Joanna a playful nudge "Just watch out for the 'gilded cage syndrome'."

"The what?" Joanna had asked.

"As corporate executives or diplomats in third-world postings, we live a pretty high life, certainly a standard of living far beyond what we could have in our own countries. Everything is there for you and everything is done for you. It's like living in a gilded cage. Some people love it, and get pretty spoiled; after a while you can't imagine even making a sandwich for yourself . . . ."

Humph, Joanna thought to herself at the time. That would certainly never happen to me. I am a professional. This is an incredible learning opportunity and I am going to make the most of it!

## May, 1999: Joanna's Arrival in El Salvador

Joanna arrived on a balmy afternoon, grateful for the warm breeze after a cold Toronto winter. She was excited to see John and only slightly disappointed that their first drive into San Salvador would not be alone, but accompanied by a young Salvadoran named Julio Cesar, who had been assigned as their driver. On the drive from the airport, Joanna tried hard to follow his rapid banter as he pointed out the sights to her. She had felt confident in her Spanish in the classroom in Toronto, but now she could barely understand a word Julio Cesar said. John, sensing her frustration, began to translate, and by the time they reached the house, Joanna was exhausted and discouraged.

John was proud of the house he had found, next door to the Mexican embassy and only a block from a tennis club where most of the members were expatriates. He thought this might provide a good social base for Joanna if she got homesick for North American lifestyle. The large twelve-room house was certainly impressive, with its shining terazzo floors and two large gardens. Joanna wondered what to do with all the space. It was also quite secure, with metal bars on all the windows, and surrounded by twelve-foot walls.

"*This isn't a house, John, it's a fortress,*" Joanna said in amazement.

"*Yeah . . . I know it's a bit much,*" said John. "*But this is the one area of the city we are strongly advised to live in, for security reasons. Smaller homes or apartments just don't exist. Most of the families living here are either expats or very wealthy Salvadorans. Most have live-in help and need the space.*"

"*But I don't want anyone else living with us. . . .*"

"*Come . . . I want you to meet Maria.*" Joanna followed John out to the back of the house, and was introduced to a small, brown woman, vigorously scrubbing clothes. "*Maria worked for the family who lived here before; it only seemed right that she should stay. She only lives a few blocks away, though, so she will go home each evening.*"

After a week, Joanna soon learned Maria's work patterns. Maria would hand wash all their clothes in the cement tub and hang them to dry outside, a chore that would take all day long, as Maria would often wash things three times. The following day she would return to do the ironing, which would take another full day. As Joanna sat in her study upstairs, reading her books and newspapers, she felt an overwhelming sense of guilt thinking of Maria, hand washing every last item of their clothing in the cement tub. Some days Joanna longed to just walk into an empty house and put her own clothes in a washing machine. Then, when Joanna found out that John paid Maria $6.00 per day, she was furious. John explained to Joanna that this was the customary wage for the women from the "barrios marginales" who worked as domestic help for wealthy Salvadorans and expatriates. These "marginal communities" were small groupings of tin shacks located in the ravines that surrounded the city. A few had electricity, but many of the communities, including Maria's, still cooked their meals over fires and lit their homes with candles. Joanna began to slip more money into Maria's pay envelope.

Joanna hoped to make a friend of Maria and looked forward to having lunch each day with her and learning more of the local way of speaking. Joanna realized now that the formal Spanish she had learned in school was vastly different from the language she heard each day on the streets of San Salvador. However, Maria refused to eat at the same table as Joanna and insisted on serving Joanna first in the dining room, and then eating her own lunch on the stone steps in the back room. Joanna was deeply uncomfortable with this and began to eat lunch at the restaurant in her nearby tennis club instead.

Other things began to irritate Joanna as well. For example, one day, she started to wash the car in the driveway. Suddenly, Maria's son appeared and insisted that he do the job for her, horrified that "la Senora" would undertake such a task herself. Another time, Joanna began to dig up some of the plants in the garden for replanting; the following morning, a gardener appeared at the door, saying that he was a cousin of Maria's and would be pleased to take on additional gardening work.

Joanna resented this intrusion into her daily life. If she was going to be spending so much time at home, she wanted privacy to read and study. It was going to be a while, she realized, before she found a job. Joanna was disappointed with the job prospects among local and even international companies. Most available positions were clerical, for which she was vastly overqualified. "*I didn't get an MBA to work as a file clerk!*" she would think to herself angrily. Then, she would think sadly, "*My Spanish probably isn't even good enough to get a job as a file clerk.*"

One day, in frustration, Joanna called her two closest friends in Toronto, colleagues from her old firm.

"*I can't win!*" Joanna complained. "*I feel guilty all the time. I feel guilty because I don't do anything myself. And I feel guilty if I don't hire local people to the housework. They need the money so much. Then I feel guilty that we pay them six dollars a day. We can afford so much more. I feel guilty that I have a maid and she lives in a tin shack in a ravine two blocks from my house. But John says we can't pay her more than the going rate because it would upset the whole balance of her community. He says they have their own economic structure and norms and we have to respect that. My Salvadoran neighbors tell me that if I pay Maria or the gardener more they won't respect me. But I do anyway, and then I feel guilty because I don't tell John. And then our driver, Julio Cesar . . . .*"

The sarcastic response was the same from both. "*Gee, Joanna, sounds tough. Beautiful house, a maid, gardener, and driver, afternoons at the tennis club . . . no wonder you're so miserable?*"

Joanna got off the phone, feeling worse than ever. Had accepting this assignment been a big mistake? She knew how much this job meant to John, and it was a great step forward for his career. But what about her career and her own happiness? This had been a mutual decision. Something was going to have to change or they would be on a plane back to Toronto very soon. The question was . . . what?

## Questions for Discussion

1. Is Joanna suffering from culture shock? What elements of the Salvadoran culture seem most difficult for her to adapt to?
2. Should Joanna have done anything differently in terms of her preparation for moving to El Salvador? What do you think she should do now?
3. How could Joanna further her career as a human resource consultant while living in El Salvador? What skills could she develop? Would these skills be transferrable if she moved back to Toronto? To another country?
4. If you were John, would you have taken the job in El Salvador? If you were Joanna, would you have agreed to go?

5. Do you think international careers are feasible for dual-career couples? What issues are important to consider for the individuals involved?
6. What can companies do to make foreign assignments more successful for couples and families? Is the happiness of the employee's spouse the responsibility of the company?
7. What recommendations would you make to international organizations and companies sending employees to politically unstable regions? Do companies have a responsibility for the physical safety of expatriate employees? Does this responsibility extend to locally hired staff as well?
8. Do you think Joanna should pay her cleaning lady and gardener more than the standard $6.00 per day? Why or why not?

**absolute advantage**   The ability to produce a good or service more cheaply than it can be produced elsewhere.

**accounting diversity**   The range of differences in national accounting practices.

**acculturation**   The process of adjusting and adapting to a specific culture other than one's own.

**adaptability screening**   A selection procedure that usually involves interviewing both the candidate for an overseas assignment and his or her family members to determine how well they are likely to adapt to another culture.

**airfreight**   Transport of goods by air; accounts for less than one percent of the total volume of international shipments, but more than 20 percent of value.

**allocation mentality**   The tradition of acquiring resources based not on what is needed but on what is available.

**American terms**   Quoting a currency rate as the U.S. dollar against a country's currency (e.g., U.S. dollars/yen).

**antidumping**   Laws that many countries use to impose tariffs on foreign imports. They are designed to help domestic industries that are injured by unfair competition from abroad due to imported products being sold at less than fair market value.

**antitrust laws**   Laws that prohibit monopolies, restraint of trade, and conspiracies to inhibit competition.

**arbitration**   The procedure for settling a dispute in which an objective third party hears both sides and makes a decision; a procedure for resolving conflict in the international

business arena through the use of intermediaries such as representatives of chambers of commerce, trade associations, or third-country institutions.

**area expertise**   A knowledge of the basic systems in a particular region or market.

**area structure**   An organizational structure in which geographic divisions are responsible for all manufacturing and marketing in their respective areas.

**area studies**   Training programs that provide factual preparation prior to an overseas assignment.

**arm's length price**   Self sufficiency; a price that unrelated parties would have reached.

**assessment of taxes**   The valuation of property or transactions for purposes of taxation; in countertrade, based on the exact value of the goods exchanged, the time when income was received, and the profitability of the transaction.

**autarky**   Self-sufficiency: a country that is not participating in international trade.

**average cost method**   An accounting principle by which the value of inventory is estimated as the average cost of the items in inventory.

**backtranslation**   The retranslation of text to the original language by a different person than the one who made the first translation. Useful to find translation errors.

**backward innovation**   The development of a drastically simplified version of a product.

**Balance of Payments (BOP)**   A statement of all transactions between one country and the rest of the world during a given period; a

record of flows of goods, services, and investments across borders.

**balance sheet hedge**   The counterbalance of exposed assets with exposed liabilities to reduce translation or transaction exposure.

**bank draft**   A withdrawal document drawn against a bank.

**barter**   A direct exchange of goods of approximately equal value, with no money involved.

**base salary**   Salary not including special payments such as allowances paid during overseas assignments.

**bearer bond**   A bond owned officially by whoever is holding it.

**bilateral negotiations**   Negotiations carried out between two nations focusing only on their interests.

**bill of lading**   A contract between an exporter and a carrier indicating that the carrier has accepted responsibility for the goods and will provide transportation in return for payment.

**black hole**   The situation that arises when an international marketer has a low-competence subsidiary—or none at all—in a highly strategic market.

**boycott**   An organized effort to refrain from conducting business with a particular seller of goods or services; used in the international arena for political or economic reasons.

**brain drain**   A migration of professional people from one country to another, usually for the purpose of improving their incomes or living conditions.

**Bretton Woods Agreement**   An agreement reached in 1944 among finance ministers of 45 Western nations to establish a system of fixed exchange rates.

**bribery**   The use of payments or favors to obtain some right or benefit to which the briber has no legal right; a criminal offense in the United States but a way of life in many countries.

**Buddhism**   A religion that extends through Asia from Sri Lanka to Japan and has 334 million followers, emphasizing spiritual attainment rather than worldly goods.

**buffer stock**   Stock of a commodity kept on hand to prevent a shortage in times of unexpectedly great demand; under international commodity and price agreements, the stock controlled by an elected or appointed manager for the purpose of managing the price of the commodity.

**bulk service**   Ocean shipping provided on contract either for individual voyages or for prolonged periods of time.

**bureaucratic controls**   A limited and explicit set of regulations and rules that outline desired levels of performance.

**buy-back**   A refinement of simple barter with one party supplying technology or equipment that enables the other party to produce goods, which are then used to pay for the technology or equipment that was supplied.

**capital account**   An account in the BOP statement that records transactions involving borrowing, lending, and investing across borders.

**capital budget**   The financial evaluation of a proposed investment to determine whether the expected returns are sufficient to justify the investment expenses.

**capital flight**   The flow of private funds abroad because investors be-

lieve that the return on investment or the safety of capital is not sufficiently ensured in their own countries.

**capital or financial lease**   A lease that transfers all substantial benefits and costs inherent in the ownership of the property to the lessee. The lessee accounts for the lease as if it is an acquisition of an asset or incurrence of a liability.

**capital structure**   The mix of debt and equity used in a corporation.

**capitalizing**   The accounting practice of charging a portion of the cost of a capital equipment purchase over a number of years, thus depreciating its useful life out over time.

**Caribbean Basin Initiative (CBI)**   Extended trade preferences to Caribbean countries and granted them special access to the markets of the United States.

**cartel**   An association of producers of a particular good, consisting either of private firms or of nations, formed for the purpose of suppressing the market forces affecting prices.

**cash pooling**   Used by multinational firms to centralize individual units' cash flows, resulting in less spending or foregone interest unnecessary cash balances.

**central plan**   The economic plan for the nation devised by the government of a socialist state; often a five-year plan that stipulated the quantities of industrial goods to be produced.

**centralization**   The concentrating of control and strategic decision making at headquarters.

**change agent**   A person or institution who facilitates change in a firm or in a host country.

**channel design**   The length and width of the distribution channel.

**Christianity**   The largest world religion with 1.8 billion followers;

Protestantism encourages work and accumulation of wealth.

**clearing account barter**   A refinement of simple barter in which clearing accounts are established to track debits and credits. CAB permits barter transactions to take place over longer time periods.

**code law**   Law based on a comprehensive set of written statutes.

**codetermination**   A management approach in which employees are represented on supervisory boards to facilitate communication and collaboration between management and labor.

**commercial invoice**   A bill for transported goods that describes the merchandise and its total cost and lists the addresses of the shipper and seller and delivery and payment terms.

**Committee on Foreign Investments in the United States (CFIUS)**   A federal committee, chaired by the U.S. Treasury, with the responsibility to review major foreign investments to determine whether national security or related concerns are at stake.

**commodity price agreement**   An agreement involving both buyers and sellers to manage the price of a particular commodity, but often only when the price moves outside a predetermined range.

**common agricultural policy (CAP)**   An integrated system of subsidies and rebates applied to agricultural interests in the European Union.

**common law**   Law based on tradition and depending less on written statutes and codes than on precedent and custom—used in the United States.

**common market**   A group of countries that agree to remove all barriers to trade among members, to establish a common trade policy with respect to nonmembers, and also to allow mobility for factors of production—labor, capital, and technology.

**communication services**  Services that are provided in the areas of videotext, home banking, and home shopping, among others.

**comparative advantage**  The ability to produce a good or service more cheaply, relative to other goods and services, than is possible in other countries.

**compensation arrangement**  Another term for buyback.

**competitive advantage**  The ability to produce a good or service more cheaply than other countries due to favorable factor conditions and demand conditions, strong related and supporting industries, and favorable firm strategy, structure, and rivalry conditions.

**competitive assessment**  A research process that consists of matching markets to corporate strengths and providing an analysis of the best potential for specific offerings.

**competitive devaluation**  Reducing the value of one nation's currency in terms of other currencies to stimulate exports.

**composition of trade**  The ratio of primary commodities to manufactured goods in a country's trade.

**concentration strategy**  The market expansion policy that involves concentrating on a small number of markets.

**confirmed letter of credit**  A letter of credit confirmed by the recipient's bank.

**confiscation**  The forceful government seizure of a company without compensation for the assets seized.

**confucianism**  A code of conduct with 150 million followers throughout Asia, stressing loyalty and relationships.

**consulting services**  Services that are provided in the areas of management expertise on such issues as transportation and logistics.

**container ships**  Ships designed to carry standardized containers, which greatly facilitate loading and unloading as well as intermodal transfers.

**contract manufacturing**  Outsourcing the actual production of goods so that the corporation can focus on research, development, and marketing.

**contractual hedging financial market**  A multinational firm's use of contracts to minimize its transaction exposure.

**contributor**  A national subsidiary with a distinctive competence, such as product development.

**control**  Refers to restrictions on what a foreign investor may own or control in another country.

**convertibility**  The ability to exchange a currency for any other currency without being subject to government restrictions, approvals, or government specified rates of exchange.

**coordinated decentralization**  The providing of overall corporate strategy by headquarters while granting subsidiaries the freedom to implement it within established ranges.

**coordinated intervention**  A currency value management method whereby the central banks of the major nations simultaneously intervene in the currency markets, hoping to change a currency's value.

**Coordinating Committee for Multilateral Export Controls (COCOM)**  A body formed by NATO countries (including Japan, but not Iceland) to continually define those items for which exports need to be controlled, or decontrolled, and to structure national policies to result in a unified and effective export control system; abolished in 1994.

**corporate income tax**  A tax applied to all residual earnings, regardless of what is retained or what is distributed as dividends.

**corruption**  Payments or favors made to officials in return for services.

**correspondent banks**  Banks located in different countries and unrelated by ownership that have a reciprocal agreement to provide services to each other's customers.

**cost and freight (CFR)**  Seller quotes a price for the goods, including the cost of transportation to the named port of debarkation. Cost and choice of insurance are left to the buyer.

**cost, insurance, and freight (CIF)**  Seller quotes a price including insurance, all transportation, and miscellaneous charges to the point of debarkation from the vessel or aircraft.

**cost leadership**  A pricing tactic where a company offers an identical product or service at a lower cost than the competition.

**cost of communications**  The cost of communicating electronically or by telephone with other locations. These costs have been drastically reduced through the use of fiber-optic cables.

**cost of living allowance (COLA)**  An allowance paid during assignment overseas to enable the employee to maintain the same standard of living as at home.

**cost-plus method**  A pricing policy in which there is a full allocation of foreign and domestic costs to the product.

**counterpurchase**  A refinement of simple barter that unlinks the timing of the two transactions.

**coups d'etat**  A forced change in a country's government, often resulting in attacks of foreign firms and policy changes by the new government.

**critical commodities list**  A U.S. Department of Commerce file containing information about products that are either particularly sensitive to national security or controlled for other purposes.

**cross marketing**   Firms may have a reciprocal arrangement whereby each partner provides the other access to its markets for a product.

**cross rates**   Exchange rate quotations which do not include the U.S. dollar as one of the two currencies quoted.

**cross-subsidization of an industry**   The use of resources accumulated in one part of the world to fight a competitive battle in another.

**cultural assimilator**   A program in which trainees for overseas assignments must respond to scenarios of specific situations in a particular country.

**cultural convergence**   Increasing similarity among cultures accelerated by technological advances.

**cultural risk**   The risk of business blunders, poor customer relations, and wasted negotiations that results when firms fail to understand and adapt to the differences between their own and host countries' cultures.

**cultural universals**   Manifestations of the total way of life of any group of people.

**culture shock**   The more pronounced reactions to the psychological disorientation that most people feel when they move for an extended period of time in to a markedly different culture.

**currency flows**   The movement of currency from nation to nation, which in turn determine exchange rates.

**currency swap**   An agreement by which a firm exchanges or swaps its debt service payments in one currency for debt service payments in a different currency. The equivalent of the interest rate swap, only the currency of denomination of the debt is different.

**current account**   An account in the BOP statement that records the results of transactions involving merchandise, services, and unilateral transfers between countries.

**current transfer**   A current account on the Balance of Payments statement that records gifts from the residents of one country to the residents of another.

**customer involvement**   The active participation of customers; a characteristic of services in that customers often are actively involved in the provision of services they consume.

**customer service**   A total corporate effort aimed at customer satisfaction; customer service levels in terms of responsiveness that inventory policies permit for a given situation.

**customer structure**   An organizational structure in which divisions are formed on the basis of customer groups.

**customs union**   Collaboration among trading countries in which members dismantle barriers to trade in goods and services and also establish a common trade policy with respect to nonmembers.

**debt-for-debt swap**   The exchange of a loan held by one creditor for a loan held by another creditor; allows debt holders to consolidate outstanding loans.

**debt-for-education swap**   The exchange of debt for educational opportunities in a foreign country.

**debt-for-equity swap**   An exchange of developing country debts for equity investments in the countries.

**debt-for-nature swap**   The purchase of nonperforming loans at substantial discounts and their subsequent return to the debtor country in exchange for the preservation of natural resources.

**debt-for-product swap**   An exchange of debt for products, often requiring an additional cash payment for the product.

**debt swaps**   An emerging form of countertrade in which debt holders exchange the debt of a less-developed country for some other good or service or financial instrument.

**decentralization**   The granting of a high degree of autonomy to subsidiaries.

**deemed exports**   Addresses people rather than products where knowledge transfer could lead to a breach of export restrictions.

**delivery duty paid (DDP)**   Seller delivers the goods, with import duties paid, including inland transportation from import point to the buyer's premises.

**delivery duty unpaid (DDU)**   Only the destination customs duty and taxes are paid by the consignee.

**Delphi studies**   A research tool using a group of participants with expertise in the area of concern to state and rank major future developments.

**demand pattern analysis**   Analysis that indicates typical patterns of growth and decline in manufacturing.

**density**   Weight-to-volume ratio; often used to determine shipping rates.

**deregulation**   Removal of government regulation.

**differentiation**   Takes advantage of the company's real or perceived uniqueness on elements such as design or after-sales service.

**direct intervention**   The process governments used in the 1970s if they wished to alter the current value of their currency. It was done by simply buying or selling their own currency in the market using their reserves of other major currencies.

**direct investment** An account in the BOP statement that records investments with an expected maturity of more than one year and an investor's ownership position of at least 10 percent.

**direct quotation** A foreign exchange quotation that specifies the amount of home country currency needed to purchase one unit of foreign currency.

**direct taxes** Taxes applied directly to income.

**discriminatory regulations** Regulations that impose larger operating costs on foreign service providers than on local competitors, that provide subsidies to local firms only, or that deny competitive opportunities to foreign suppliers.

**distributed earnings** The proportion of a firm's net income after taxes which is paid out or distributed to the stockholders of the firm.

**diversification** A market expansion policy characterized by growth in a relatively large number of markets or market segments.

**division of labor** The premise of modern industrial production where each stage in the production of a good is performed by one individual separately, rather than one individual being responsible for the entire production of the good.

**domestication** Government demand for partial transfer of ownership and management responsibility from a foreign company to local entities, with or without compensation.

**double-entry bookkeeping** Accounting methodology where each transaction gives rise to both a debit and a credit of the same currency amount. It is used in the construction of the Balance of Payments.

**double taxation** Taxing of the same income twice; taxing of multinational corporations by the home country and the host country.

**dual pricing** Price-setting strategy in which the export price may be based on marginal cost pricing, resulting in a lower export price than domestic price; may open the company to dumping charges.

**dumping** Selling goods overseas at a price lower than in the exporter's home market, or at a price below the cost of production, or both.

**economic and monetary union (EMU)** The ideal among European leaders that economic integration should move beyond the four freedoms; specifically, it entails (1) closer coordination of economic policies to promote exchange rate stability and convergence of inflation rates and growth rates, (2) creation of a European central bank, and (3) replacement of national monetary authorities by the European Central Bank and adoption of the EURO as the European currency.

**economic exposure** The potential for long-term effects on a firm's value as the result of changing currency values.

**economic infrastructure** The transportation, energy, and communication systems in a country.

**economic union** A union among trading countries that has the characteristics of a common market and also harmonizes monetary policies, taxation, and government spending and uses a common currency.

**economies of scale** Production economies made possible by the output of larger quantities.

**education allowance** Reimbursement by company for dependent educational expenses incurred while a parent is assigned overseas.

**effective tax rate** Actual total tax burden after including all applicable tax liabilities and credits.

**embargo** A governmental action, usually prohibiting trade entirely, for a decidedly adversarial or political rather than economic purpose.

**engineering services** Services that are provided in the areas of construction, design, and engineering.

**Enterprise for the Americas Initiative (EAI)** An attempt by the United States to further democracy in Latin America by providing incentives for market development and trade liberalization.

**environmental protection** Actions taken by governments to protect the environment and resources of a country.

**environmental scanning** Obtaining ongoing data about a country.

**equity method** An accounting method used for investments; a method used when a U.S. firm owns a substantial amount of voting stock in a foreign company, meaning more than 10 percent but less than 50 percent.

**estimation by analogy** A method for estimating market potential when data for the particular market do not exist.

**ethics** The local morality that global companies need to recognize as a rule in conducting business.

**ethnocentric** Tending to regard one's own culture as superior; tending to be home-market oriented.

**ethnocentrism** The regarding of one's own culture as superior to others'.

**euro** A single currency proposed for use by the European Union that will eventually replace all the individual currencies of the participating member states.

**Eurobanks** Large international banks comprising the most active participants in the Eurocurrency markets.

**Eurobond**   A bond that is denominated in a currency other than the currency of the country in which the bond is sold.

**Euro commercial paper (ELP)**   A short-term debt instrument, typically 30, 60, 90, or 180 days in maturity, sold in the Eurocurrency markets.

**Eurocurrency**   A bank deposit in a currency other than the currency of the country where the bank is located; not confined to banks in Europe.

**Eurocurrency interest rates**   Loan or deposit rates of interest on foreign currency denominated deposits.

**Eurodollars**   U.S. dollars deposited in banks outside the United States; not confined to banks in Europe.

**Euromarkets**   Money and capital markets in which transactions are denominated in a currency other than that of the place of the transaction; not confined to Europe.

**Euronote**   A short to medium-term debt instrument sold in the Eurocurrency markets. The three major classes of Euronotes are Euro commercial paper, Euro-medium-term notes, and Euronotes.

**European Monetary System (EMS)**   An organization formed in 1979 by eight EC members committed to maintaining the values of their currencies within a 2 1/4 percent of each other's.

**European terms**   Quoting a currency rate as a country's currency against the U.S. dollar (e.g., yen/U.S. dollars).

**European Union**   The January 1, 1994 organization created by the 12 member countries of the European Community (now 15 members).

**exchange controls**   Controls on the movement of capital in and out of a country, sometimes imposed when the country faces a shortage of foreign currency.

**exchange rate mechanism (ERM)**   The acceptance of responsibility by a European Monetary System member to actively maintain its own currency within agreed-upon limits versus other member currencies established by the European Monetary System.

**expatriate**   One living in a foreign land; a corporate manager assigned to an overseas location.

**expensing**   The accounting practice of claiming the entire cost of a purchase as a deductible expense from current income entirely in the present period.

**experiential knowledge**   Knowledge acquired through involvement (as opposed to information, which is obtained through communication, research, and education).

**experimentation**   A research tool to determine the effects of a variable on an operation.

**export complaint systems**   Allow customers to contact the original supplier of a product in order to inquire about products, make suggestions, or present complaints.

**export-control system**   A system designed to deny or at least delay the acquisition of strategically important goods to adversaries; in the United States, based on the Export Administration Act and the Munitions Control Act.

**export license**   A license obtainable from the U.S. Department of Commerce Bureau of Export Administration, which is responsible for administering the Export Administration Act.

**export management companies (EMCs)**   Domestic firms that specialize in performing international business services as commission representatives or as distributors.

**export trading company (ETC)**   The result of 1982 legislation to improve the export performance of

small and medium-sized firms, the export trading company allows businesses to band together to export or offer export services. Additionally, the law permits bank participation in trading companies and relaxes antitrust provisions.

**expropriation**   The government takeover of a company with compensation frequently at a level lower than the investment value of the company's assets.

**external economies of scale**   Lower production costs resulting from the free mobility of factors of production in a common market.

**extraterritoriality**   An exemption from rules and regulations of one country that may challenge the national sovereignty of another. The application of one country's rules and regulations abroad.

**ex-works (EXW)**   Price quotes that apply only at the point of origin; the seller agrees to place the goods at the disposal of the buyer at the specified place on a date or within a fixed period.

**factor intensities**   The proportion of capital input to labor input used in the production of a good.

**factor mobility**   The ability to freely move factors of production across borders, as among common market countries.

**factor proportions theory**   Systematic explanation of the source of comparative advantage.

**factors of production**   All inputs into the production process, including capital, labor, land, and technology.

**factual cultural knowledge**   Knowledge obtainable from specific country studies published by governments, private companies, and universities and also available in the form of background information from facilitating agencies such as banks, advertising agencies, and transportation companies.

**field experience** Experience acquired in actual rather than laboratory settings; training that exposes a corporate manager to a different cultural environment for a limited amount of time.

**FIFO** Method of valuation of inventories for accounting purposes, meaning First-In-First-Out. The principle rests on the assumption that costs should be charged against revenue in the order in which they occur.

**Financial Accounting Standards Board Statement No. 52 (FASB 52)** A 1982 ruling governing accounting for international transactions and operations.

**financial incentives** Monetary offers intended to motivate; special funding designed to attract foreign direct investors that may take the form of land or building, loans, or loan guarantees.

**financial infrastructure** Facilitating financial agencies in a country; for example, banks.

**financial risk management** The management of a firm's cash flows associated with the three basic financial dimensions of interest rates, exchange rates, and commodity prices.

**financing cash flows** The cash flows arising from the firms funding activities.

**fiscal incentives** Incentives used to attract foreign direct investment that provide specific tax measures to attract the investor.

**fixed exchange rate** The government of a country officially declares that its currency is convertible into a fixed amount of some other currency.

**flextime** A modification of work scheduling that allows workers to determine their own starting and ending times within a broad range of available hours.

**floating exchange rate** Under this system, the government possesses no responsibility to declare that its currency is convertible into a fixed amount of some other currency; this diminishes the role of official reserves.

**focus group** A research technique in which representatives of a proposed target audience contribute to market research by participating in an unstructured discussion.

**foreign bond** Bonds that are issued by a country's borrowers in other countries, subject to the same restrictions as bonds issued by domestic borrowers.

**Foreign Corrupt Practices Act** A 1977 act making it a crime for U.S. executives of publicly traded firms to bribe a foreign official in order to obtain business.

**foreign direct investment** The establishment or expansion of operations of a firm in a foreign country. Like all investments, it assumes a transfer of capital.

**foreign policy** The area of public policy concerned with relationships with other countries.

**foreign service premium** A financial incentive to accept an assignment overseas, usually paid as a percentage of the base salary.

**foreign tax credit** Credit applied to home-country tax payments due for taxes paid abroad.

**foreign trade organizations (FTOs)** Organizations authorized to make purchases and sales internationally as specified by the government; in the past, prevalent in the Soviet Union, Eastern Europe, and China.

**foreign trade zones** Special areas where foreign goods may be held or processed without incurring duties and taxes.

**Fortress Europe** Suspicion raised by trading partners of Western Europe, claiming that the integration of the European Union may result in increased restrictions on trade and investment by outsiders.

**forward contracts** Agreements between firms and banks which permit the firm to either sell or buy a specific foreign currency at a future date at a known price.

**forward rates** Contracts that provide for two parties to exchange currencies on a future date at an agreed-upon exchange rate.

**franchising** A form of licensing that allows a distributor or retailer exclusive rights to sell a product or service in a specified area.

**free alongside ship (FAS)** Exporter quotes a price for the goods, including charges for delivery of the goods alongside a vessel at a port. Seller handles cost of unloading and wharfage; loading, ocean transportation, and insurance are left to the buyer.

**free carrier (FCA)** Applies only at a designated inland shipping point. Seller is responsible for loading goods into the means of transportation; buyer is responsible for all subsequent expenses.

**free on board (FOB)** Applies only to vessel shipments. Seller quotes a price covering all expenses up to and including delivery of goods on an overseas vessel provided by or for the buyer.

**free trade area** An area in which all barriers to trade among member countries are removed, although sometimes only for certain goods or services.

**Free Trade Area of the Americas (FTAA)** A hemispheric trade zone covering all of the Americas. Organizers hope for it to be operational by 2005.

**freight forwarders** Specialists in handling international transportation by contracting with carriers on behalf of shippers.

**functional structure** An organizational structure in which departments are formed on the basis of functional areas such as production, marketing, and finance.

**fundamental disequilibrium** A term commonly understood to mean persistent BOP imbalances that are unlikely to correct themselves.

**gap analysis** Analysis of the difference between market potential and actual sales.

**General Agreement on Tariffs and Trade (GATT)** An international code of tariffs and trade rules signed by 23 nations in 1947; headquartered in Geneva, Switzerland; 132 members currently; now part of the World Trade Organization.

**General Agreement on Trade in Services (GATS)** A legally enforceable pact among GATT participants that covers trade and investments in the services sector.

**general license** An export license that provides blanket permission to ship nonsensitive products to most trading partners.

**geocentric** Tending to take a world view; tending to be oriented toward the global marketplace.

**glasnost** The Soviet policy of encouraging the free exchange of ideas and discussion of problems, pluralistic participation in decision making, and increased availability of information.

**global account management** Global customers of a company may be provided with special services including a single point of contact for domestic and international operations and consistent worldwide service.

**global linkages** Worldwide interdependencies of financial markets, technology, and living standards.

**globalization** Awareness, understanding, and response to global developments as they affect a company.

**glocal** A term coined to describe the networked global organization approach to an organizational structure.

**gold standard** A standard for international currencies in which currency values were stated in terms of gold.

**goods trade** An account of the BOP statement that records funds used for merchandise imports and funds obtained from merchandise exports.

**gray market** A market entered in a way not intended by the manufacturer of the goods.

**Group of Five** The United States, Great Britain, Germany, France, and Japan.

**Group of Seven** The United States, Great Britain, Germany, France, Japan, Italy, and Canada. The meeting of finance ministers of these seven countries in Jamaica in 1976 resulted in an agreement to allow their currencies to continue to float.

**Group of Ten** The United States, Great Britain, Germany, France, Japan, Italy, Canada, Sweden, Netherlands, and Belgium.

**hardship allowance** An allowance paid during an assignment to an overseas area that requires major adaptation.

**hedge** To counterbalance a present sale or purchase with a sale or purchase for future delivery as a way to minimize loss due to price fluctuations; to make counterbalancing sales or purchases in the international market as protection against adverse movements in the exchange rate.

**high-context cultures** Cultures in which behavioral and environmental nuances are an important means of conveying information.

**Hinduism** With 750 million followers, a way of life rather than a religion, with economic and other attainment dictated by the caste into which its followers are born.

**housing allowance** An allowance paid during assignment overseas to provide living quarters.

**implementor** The typical subsidiary role, which involves implementing strategy that originates with headquarters.

**import substitution** A policy for economic growth adopted by many developing countries that involves the systematic encouragement of domestic production of goods formerly imported.

**income elasticity of demand** A means of describing change in demand in relative response to a change in income.

**incoterms** International Commerce Terms. Widely accepted terms used in quoting export prices.

**indirect quotation** Foreign exchange quotation that specifies the units of foreign currency that could be purchased with one unit of the home currency.

**indirect taxes** Taxes applied to non-income items, such as value-added taxes, excise taxes, tariffs, and so on.

**industrial policy** Official planning for industry as a whole or for a particular industry; in the United States, occurs only indirectly.

**information system** Can provide the decision maker with basic data for most ongoing decisions.

**infrastructure shortages** Problems in a country's underlying physical structure, such as transportation, utilities, and so on.

**input-output analysis** A method for estimating market activities and potential that measures the factor inflows into production and the resultant outflow of products.

**insurance services** Services that are provided in underwriting, risk evaluation, and operations.

**intangibility** The inability to be seen, tasted, or touched in a conventional sense; the characteristic of services that most strongly differentiates them from products.

**intellectual property rights** Protects the technology and knowledge of multinational firms.

**Interbank interest rates** The interest rate charged by banks to banks in the major international financial centers.

**interest rate swap** A firm uses its credit standing to borrow capital at low fixed rates and exchange its interest payments with a slightly lower credit-rated borrower who has debt-service payments at floating rates.

**intermodal movements** The transfer of freight from one mode or type of transportation to another.

**internal bank** A multinational firm's financial management tool that actually acts as a bank to coordinate finances among its units.

**internal economies of scale** Lower production costs resulting from greater production for an enlarged market.

**internalization** Occurs when a firm establishes its own multinational operation, keeping information that is at the core of its competitiveness within the firm.

**International Bank for Reconstruction and Development (World Bank)** An institution established in 1945 to make loans for reconstruction of war-ravaged countries; now focused on making loans to developing countries.

**International Banking Act of 1978** An act that established a comprehensive federal government role in the regulation of foreign bank operations in the United States.

**International Banking Facility (IBF)** Operations established by U.S. international banks that are free from a number of regulations restraining domestic banks, including deposit insurance and reserve requirements.

**international bond** Bond issued in domestic capital markets by foreign borrowers (foreign bonds) or issued in the Eurocurrency markets in currency different from that of the home currency of the borrower (Eurobonds).

**international competitiveness** The ability of a firm, an industry, or a country to compete in the international marketplace at a stable or rising standard of living.

**international debt load** Total accumulated negative net investment of a nation.

**international investment** Investment by companies from one country in enterprises in other countries.

**international law** The body of rules governing relationships between sovereign states; also certain treaties and agreements respected by a number of countries.

**International Monetary Fund (IMF)** A specialized agency of the United Nations established in 1944. An international financial institution for dealing with Balance of Payment problems; the first international monetary authority with at least some degree of power over national authorities.

**international monetary system** The set of rules or procedures in place for making and receiving international payments.

**International Trade Organization (ITO)** A forwardlooking approach to international trade and investment embodied in the 1948 Havana Charter; due to disagreements among sponsoring nations, its provisions were never ratified.

**interpretative knowledge** An acquired ability to understand and appreciate the nuances of foreign cultural traits and patterns.

**interviews** A face-to-face research tool to obtain in-depth information.

**intrafirm transfers** The sale of goods or services between units of the same firm. For example, the sale of an unfinished product by the U.S. parent firm to its foreign subsidiary in the United Kingdom.

**Intraindustry trade** The simultaneous export and import of the same good by a country. It is of interest due to the traditional theory that a country will either export or import a good, but not do both at the same time.

**Intranet** A process that integrates a company's information assets into a single accessible system using Internet-based technologies such as e-mail, news groups, and the World Wide Web.

**inventory**    Materials on hand for use in the production process; also finished goods on hand.

**inventory carrying costs**    The expense of maintaining inventories.

**investment income**    The proportion of net income that is paid back to a parent company.

**Islam**    A religion that has over 1 billion followers from the west coast of Africa to the Philippines, as well as in the rest of the world and is supportive of entrepreneurism but not of exploitation.

**Jamaica Agreement**    An agreement reached in 1976 by the Group of Seven to continue to allow their currencies to float in response to market pressures.

**joint occurrence**    Occurrence of a phenomenon affecting the business environment in several locations simultaneously.

**Joint Research and Development Act**    A 1984 act that allows both domestic and foreign firms to participate in joint basic-research efforts without fear of U.S. antitrust action.

**just-in-time inventory**    Materials scheduled to arrive precisely when they are needed on a production line.

**lags**    Paying a debt late to take advantage of exchange rates.

**land bridge**    Transfer of ocean freight on land among various modes of transportation.

**Law of One Price**    The theory that the relative prices of any single good between countries, expressed in each country's currency, is representative of the proper or appropriate exchange rate value.

**Leads**    Paying a debt early to take advantage of exchange rates.

**Leontief Paradox**    Wassily Leontief's studies of U.S. trade indicated that the United States was a labor-abundant country, exporting labor-intensive products. This was a paradox because of the general belief that the United States was a capital-abundant country which should be exporting capital-intensive products.

**letter of credit**    Document issued by a bank promising to pay a specified amount of money to an exporter; the most common mechanism for financing international trade.

**LIBOR**    The London InterBank Offer Rate. The rate of interest charged by top-quality international banks on loans to similar quality banks in London. This interest rate is often used in both domestic and international markets as the rate of interest on loans and other financial agreements.

**licensing**    A firm gives a license to another firm to produce or package its product.

**licensing agreement**    An agreement in which one firm permits another to use its intellectual property in exchange for compensation.

**LIFO**    Method of valuation of inventories for accounting purposes, meaning Last-In-First-Out. The principle rests on the practice of recording inventory by "layer" of the cost at which it was incurred.

**liner service**    Ocean shipping characterized by regularly scheduled passage on established routes.

**lingua franca**    The language habitually used among people of diverse speech to facilitate communication.

**lobbyist**    Typically, a well-connected person or firm that is hired by a business to influence the decision making of policymakers and legislators.

**local content**    Regulations to gain control over foreign investment by ensuring that a large share of the product is locally produced or a larger share of the profit is retained in the country.

**location decision**    A decision concerning the number of facilities to establish and where they should be situated.

**logistics platform**    Vital to a firm's competitive position, it is determined by a location's ease and convenience of market reach under favorable cost circumstances.

**London Interbank Offer Rate (LIBOR)**    The rate at which large London banks will lend funds to each other in Eurodollars.

**Louvre Accord**    Another name for the Paris Pact.

**low-context cultures**    Cultures in which most information is conveyed explicitly rather than through behavioral and environmental nuances.

**Maastricht Treaty**    The agreement signed in December 1991 in Maastricht, the Netherlands, in which European Community members agreed to a specific timetable and set of necessary conditions to create a single currency for the EU countries by the end of this century.

**macroeconomic approach**    An approach concerned with total output, income, and employment; an approach to accounting that gives government officials the information they need to take an active role in managing the economy, as occurs in centrally planned economies.

**macroeconomic level**    Level at which trading relationships affect individual markets.

**management contract**    An international business alternative in which the firm sells its expertise in running a company while avoiding the risk or benefit of ownership.

**managerial commitment** The desire and drive on the part of management to act on an idea and to support it in the long run.

**maquiladoras** Mexican border plants that make goods and parts or process food for export back to the United States. They benefit from lower labor costs.

**marginal cost method** This method considers the direct costs of producing and selling goods for export as the floor beneath which prices cannot be set.

**market-differentiated pricing** Price-setting strategy based on demand rather than cost.

**market imperfections** Departure from the strict assumptions of competitive economic theory; rationale for government intervention; for example, market gaps in long-term, high-volume export financing.

**market transparency** Availability of full disclosure and information about key market factors such as supply, demand, quality, service, and prices.

**marketing infrastructure** Facilitating marketing agencies in a country; for example, market research firms, channel members.

**materials management** The timely movement of raw materials, parts, and supplies into and through the firm.

**matrix structure** An organizational structure that uses functional and divisional structures simultaneously.

**maximization of shareholder value** The ultimate goal of the management of a multinational firm is to increase the value of the shareholder's investment as much as possible.

**media strategy** Strategy applied to the selection of media vehicles and the development of a media schedule.

**mercantilism** Political and economic policy in the 17th and early 18th centuries aimed at increasing a nation's wealth and power by encouraging the export of goods in return for gold.

**microeconomic level** Level of business concerns that affect an individual firm or industry.

**mininationals** Newer companies with sales between $200 million and $1 billion that are able to serve the world from a handful of manufacturing bases.

**minority participation** Participation by a group having less than the number of votes necessary for control.

**mixed aid credits** Credits at rates composed partially of commercial interest rates and partially of highly subsidized developmental aid interest rates.

**mixed structure** An organizational structure that combines two or more organizational dimensions; for example, products, areas, or functions.

**money market hedge** The international equivalent of selling accounts receivable. A firm may wish to avoid currency risk by selling at a discount the foreign currency denominated receivable today to obtain the money now, eliminating the exposure.

**Most-Favored Nation (MFN)** A term describing a GATT clause that calls for member countries to grant other member countries the same most favorable treatment they accord any country concerning imports and exports.

**multidomestic strategy** A business strategy where each individual country organization is operated as a profit center.

**multilateral negotiations** Negotiations carried out among a number of countries.

**multilateral netting** The process of settling only the net difference in payments between units of a multinational firm.

**multilateral trade negotiations** Trade negotiations among more than two parties; the intricate relationships among trading countries.

**multinational corporations** Companies that invest in countries around the globe.

**multiple factor indexes** Indexes that measure market potential indirectly by using proxy variables.

**national security** The ability of a nation to protect its internal values from external threats.

**national sovereignty** The supreme right of nations to determine national policies; freedom from external control.

**natural hedging** The structuring of a firm's operations so that cash flows by currency, inflows against outflows, are matched.

**net errors & omissions account** Makes sure the balance of payments (BOP) actually balances.

**net present value (NPV)** The sum of the present values of all cash inflows and outflows from an investment project discounted at the cost of capital.

**netting** Cash flow coordination between a corporation's global units so that only one smaller cash transfer must be made.

**1992 White Paper** A key document developed by the EC Commission to outline the further requirements necessary for a successful integration of the European Union.

**nonfinancial incentives**   Nonmonetary offers intended to motivate; special offers designed to attract foreign direct investors that may take the form of guaranteed government purchases, special protection from competition, or improved infrastructure facilities.

**nontariff barriers**   Barriers to trade, other than tariffs. Examples include buy-domestic campaigns, preferential treatment for domestic bidders, and restrictions on market entry of foreign products such as involved inspection procedures.

**not-invented-here syndrome**   A defensive, territorial attitude that, if held by managers, can frustrate effective implementation of global strategies.

**observation**   A research tool where the subjects' activity and behavior are observed.

**ocean shipping**   The forwarding of freight by ocean carrier.

**official reserves account**   An account in the BOP statement that shows (1) the change in the amount of funds immediately available to a country for making international payments and (2) the borrowing and lending that has taken place between the monetary authorities of different countries either directly or through the International Monetary Fund.

**official settlements balance**   A summary measure of a country's Balance of Payments which is the sum of the current account, long-term and short-term capital accounts, and the net balance on errors and omissions.

**offset**   A form of barter arrangement designed to reduce the Balance of Payment effect of an international transaction. Usually calls for portions of a purchased product to be produced or assembled in the purchasing country; may take the form of coproduction, licensing, subcontracting, or joint venture; mostly used in the context of military sales.

**offshore banking**   The use of banks or bank branches located in low-tax countries, often Caribbean islands, to raise and hold capital for multinational operations.

**one-stop logistics**   Allows shippers to buy all the transportation modes and functional services from a single carrier.

**open account**   A type of trade credit that allows buyers to purchase goods or services and pay for them within a specified period of time without charges or interest.

**operating cash flows**   The cash flows arising from the firm's everyday business activities.

**operating or service lease**   A lease that transfers most but not all benefits and costs inherent in the ownership of the property to the lessee. Payments do not fully cover the cost of purchasing the asset or incurring the liability.

**operating risk**   The danger of interference by governments or other groups in one's corporate operations abroad.

**opportunity cost**   Cost incurred by a firm as the result of foreclosure of other sources of profit; for example, for the licenser in a licensing agreement, the cost of forgoing alternatives such as exports or direct investment.

**order cycle time**   The total time that passes between the placement of an order and the receipt of the merchandise.

**orientation program**   A program that familiarizes new workers with their roles; the preparation of employees for assignment overseas.

**Overseas Private Investment Corporation**   A federal agency that provides insurance to U.S. direct foreign investors.

**ownership risk**   The risk inherent in maintaining ownership of property abroad. The exposure of foreign owned assets to governmental intervention.

**par value**   The face value of a financial instrument.

**parallel barter**   Another term for counterpurchase.

**Paris Convention for the Protection of Industrial Property**   An agreement among 96 countries to set minimum standards of protection for patents, designs, and trademarks.

**Paris Pact**   Agreements reached in 1987 by the Group of Five plus Canada to cooperate closely to foster stability of exchange rates.

**patent**   A government grant to an inventor providing an exclusive right to the invention for 17 years.

**pax Americana**   An American peace between 1945 through 1990 that led to increased international business transactions.

**pax Romana**   Two relatively peaceful centuries in the Roman Empire.

**pegging**   Establishing and maintaining a par value for a currency; usually by linking its value to another currency.

**pension liabilities**   The accumulating obligations of employers to fund the retirement or pension plans of employees.

**perestroika**   A movement to fundamentally reform the Soviet economy by improving the overall technological and industrial base and the quality of life for Soviet citizens through increased availability of food, housing, and consumer goods.

**perishability**   Susceptibility to deterioration; the characteristic of services that makes them difficult to store.

**physical distribution**   The movement of finished products from suppliers to customers.

**Plaza Agreement**   An accord reached in 1985 by the Group of Five that held that the major nations should join in a coordinated effort to bring down the value of the U.S. dollar.

**political risk**   The risk of loss by an international corporation of assets, earning power, or managerial control as a result of political actions by the host country.

**polycentric**   Tending to regard each culture as a separate entity; tending to be oriented toward individual foreign markets.

**population increase**   The effect of changes in countries' populations on economic matters.

**population stabilization**   An attempt to control rapid increases in population and ensure that economic development exceeds population growth.

**portfolio investment**   An account in the BOP statement that records investments in assets with an original maturity of more than one year and where an investor's ownership position is less than 10 percent.

**portfolio models**   Tools that have been proposed for use in market and competitive analysis. They typically involve two measures—internal strength and external attractiveness.

**ports**   Harbor towns or cities where ships may take on or discharge cargo; the lack of ports and port services is the greatest constraint in ocean shipping.

**positioning**   The perception by consumers of a firm's product in relation to competitors' products.

**preferential policies**   Government policies that favor certain (usually domestic) firms; for example, the use of national carriers for the transport of government freight

even when more economical alternatives exist.

**price controls**   Government regulation of the prices of goods and services; control of the prices of imported goods or services as a result of domestic political pressures.

**price escalation**   The establishing of export prices far in excess of domestic prices—often due to a long distribution channel and frequent markups.

**primary data**   Data obtained directly for a specific research purpose through interviews, focus groups, surveys, observation, or experimentation.

**private placement**   The sale of debt securities to private or institutional investors without going through a public issuance like that of a bond issue or equity issue.

**privatization**   A policy of shifting government operations to privately owned enterprises to cut budget costs and ensure more efficient services.

**process structure**   A variation of the functional structure in which departments are formed on the basis of production processes.

**product cycle theory**   A theory that views products as passing through four stages: introduction, growth, maturity, decline; during which the location of production moves from industrialized to lower-cost developing nations.

**product differentiation**   The effort to build unique differences or improvements into products.

**product structure**   An organizational structure in which product divisions are responsible for all manufacturing and marketing.

**production possibilities frontier**   A theoretical method of representing the total productive capabilities of a nation used in the formula-

tion of classical and modern trade theory.

**promotional message**   The content of an advertisement or a publicity release.

**proxy information**   Data used as a substitute for more desirable data that are unobtainable.

**punitive tariff**   A tax on an imported good or service intended to punish a trading partner.

**purchasing power parity (PPP)**   A theory that the prices of tradable goods will tend to equalize across countries.

**quality circles**   Groups of workers who meet regularly to discuss issues related to productivity.

**quality of life**   The standard of living combined with environmental factors, it determines the level of well-being of individuals.

**quality of work life**   Various corporate efforts in the areas of personal and professional development undertaken with the objectives of increasing employee satisfaction and increasing productivity.

**quotas**   Legal restrictions on the import quantity of particular goods, imposed by governments as barriers to trade.

**R&D cost**   Research and development cost; the costs incurred in developing technology.

**reciprocity provisions**   Provisions for the purchase of goods on a preferential basis with the expectation that the seller will in turn also buy on a preferential basis.

**recognizability**   The characteristic of appearing to be previously known; the ability of a product to be recognized even though it has been adapted to local market conditions.

**reference groups** Groups such as the family, co-workers, and professional and trade associations that provide the values and attitudes that influence and shape behavior, including consumer behavior.

**reference zone** Another name for a managed float.

**regiocentric** Tending to be oriented toward regions larger than individual countries as markets.

**reinvoicing** The policy of buying goods from one unit and selling them to a second unit and reinvoicing the sale to the next unit, to take advantage of favorable exchange rates.

**reliability** Dependability; the predictability of the outcome of an action. For example, the reliability of arrival time for ocean freight or airfreight.

**representative office** An office of an international bank established in a foreign country to serve the bank's customers in the area in an advisory capacity; does not take deposits or make loans.

**reverse distribution** A system responding to environmental concerns that ensures a firm can retrieve a product from the market for subsequent use, recycling, or disposal.

**roll-on-roll-off (RORO)** Transportation vessels built to accommodate trucks, which can drive on in one port and drive off at their destinations.

**royalty** The compensation paid by one firm to another under an agreement.

**rules of the game** An expression symbolizing the unwritten rules of the gold standard—a country will allow gold to flow in and out in order to preserve currency values versus gold.

**sanction** A governmental action, usually consisting of a specific coer-cive trade measure, that distorts the free flow of trade for an adversarial or political purpose rather than an economic one.

**scenario building** The identification of crucial variables and determining their effects on different cases or approaches.

**sea bridge** The transfer of freight among various modes of transportation at sea.

**secondary data** Data originally collected to serve another purpose than the one in which the researcher is currently interested.

**securitization** The conversion of developing country bank debt into tradable securities.

**self-management** Independent decision making; a high degree of worker involvement in corporate decision making.

**self-reference criterion** The unconscious reference to one's own cultural values.

**selling forward** A market transaction in which the seller promises to sell currency at a certain future date at a prespecified price.

**sensitivity training** Training in human relations that focuses on personal and interpersonal interactions; training that focuses on enhancing an expatriate's flexibility in situations quite different from those at home.

**service capacity** The maximum level at which a service provider is able to provide services to customers.

**service consistency** Uniform quality of service.

**service trade** The international exchange of personal or professional services, such as financial and banking services, construction, and tourism.

**shipper's order** A negotiable bill of lading that can be bought, sold, or traded while the subject goods are still in transit and that is used for letter of credit transactions.

**Single Europe Act** The legislative basis for the European Integration.

**Smithsonian Agreement** An agreement reached by the Group of Ten in 1971 concerning changes in the Bretton Woods Agreement on currency values.

**Smoot-Hawley Act** A 1930 act that raised import duties to the highest rates ever imposed by the United States; designed to promote domestic production, it resulted in the downfall of the world trading system.

**social infrastructure** The housing, health, educational, and other social systems in a country.

**social stratification** The division of a particular population into classes.

**sogoshosha** A large Japanese general trading company.

**Special Drawing Right (SDR)** International reserves created by the IMF to support growth in international trade and investment; essentially, a currency used only in transactions among central banks.

**specie** Gold and silver.

**spot rates** Contracts that provide for two parties to exchange currencies with delivery in two business days.

**spread** The difference between two amounts; a bank's profit on foreign exchange trading.

**standard of living** The level of material affluence of a group or nation, measured as a composite of quantities and qualities of goods.

**standard worldwide pricing** Price-setting strategy based on average unit costs of fixed, variable, and export-related costs.

**state-owned enterprise** A corporate form that has emerged in non-Communist countries, primarily for reasons of national security and economic security.

**straight bill of lading** A non-negotiable bill of lading usually used in prepaid transactions in which the transported goods involved are delivered to a specific individual or company.

**strategic alliances** A new term for collaboration among firms, often similar to joint ventures.

**strategic leader** A highly competent firm located in a strategically critical market.

**Subpart F income** Passive income as defined by the Tax Reform Act of 1986.

**supply-chain management** Results where a series of value-adding activities connect a company's supply side with its demand side.

**surveys** Typically, the use of questionnaires to obtain quantifiable research information.

**switch-trading** A refinement of clearing account barter in which credits and debits can be sold or transferred to a third party.

**syndicated loan** A loan which is arranged and managed by a small group of 2 to 5 banks and then sold in pieces to other banking institutions worldwide.

**systems concept** A concept of logistics based on the notion that materials-flow activities are so complex that they can be considered only in the context of their interaction.

**tariffs** Taxes on imported goods and services, instituted by governments as a means to raise revenue and as barriers to trade.

**tax equalization** Reimbursement by the company when an employee in an overseas assignment pays taxes at a higher rate than if he or she were at home.

**tax policy** A means by which countries may control foreign investors.

**teaching services** Services that are provided in the areas of training and motivating as well as in teaching of operational, managerial, and theoretical issues.

**team building** A process that enhances the cohesiveness of a department or group by helping members learn how to organize their work and assume responsibility for it.

**technology transfer** The transfer of systematic knowledge for the manufacture of a product, the application of a process, or the rendering of a service.

**"Tentative U.S. tax"** The calculation of U.S. taxes on foreign source incomes to estimate U.S. tax payments.

**total cost concept** A decision concept that uses cost as a basis for measurement in order to evaluate and optimize logistical activities.

**tracking** The capability of a shipper to track goods at any point during the shipment.

**Trade Act of 1974** An act that, among other provisions, expanded the definition of international trade to include trade in services.

**trade creation** A benefit of economic integration; the benefit to a particular country when a group of countries trade a product freely among themselves but maintain common barriers to trade with nonmembers.

**trade diversion** A cost of economic integration; the cost to a particular country when a group of countries trade a product freely among themselves but maintain common barriers to trade with nonmembers.

**trade draft** A withdrawal document drawn against a company.

**trade-off concept** A decision concept that recognizes linkages within the decision system.

**trade policy mechanisms** Measures used to influence and alter trade relationships.

**trademark** The distinctive identification of a product or service in the form of a name, symbol, letter, picture, or other device to distinguish it from similar offerings.

**trademark licensing** A special form of licensing that permits the names or logos of recognizable individuals or groups to be used on products.

**trading blocks** Formed by agreements among countries to establish links through movement of goods, services, capital, and labor across borders.

**tramp service** Ocean shipping via irregular routes, scheduled only on demand.

**transaction exposure** The potential for losses or gains when a firm is engaged in a transaction denominated in a foreign currency.

**transfer cost** All variable costs incurred in transferring technology to a licensee and all ongoing costs of maintaining the licensing agreement.

**transfer prices** The prices at which a firm sells its products to its own subsidiaries and affiliates.

**transfer risk** The danger of having one's ability to transfer profits or products in and out of a country inhibited by governmental rules and regulations.

**transit time** The period between departure and arrival of a carrier.

**translation exposure** The potential effect on a firm's financial statements of a change in currency values.

**transportation modes** Forms of transportation.

**Treaty of Rome** The original agreement that established the foundation for the formation of the European Economic Community.

**triangular arbitrage** The exchange of one currency for a second currency, the second for a third, and the third for the first in order to make a profit.

**trigger mechanisms** Specific acts or stimuli that set off reactions.

**tunnel** A term describing the 1971 Smithsonian Agreement's allowance of a 2 1/4 percent variation from par value for currency exchange rates.

**turnkey operation** A specialized form of management contract between a customer and an organization to provide a complete operational system together with the skills needed for unassisted maintenance and operation.

**undistributed earnings** The proportion of a firm's net income after taxes which is retained within the firm for internal purposes.

**uniform accounting** A system of accounting that follows uniform standards prescribed by law, as in Germany and France.

**United States Trade Representative** A U.S. cabinet position responsible for the area of trade negotiations, as designated in the Trade Act of 1979.

**validated export license** An export license from the Department of Commerce that authorizes shipment of a high-technology product.

**value-added tax (VAT)** A tax on the value added at each stage of the production and distribution process; a tax assessed in most European countries and also common among Latin American countries.

**virtual team** A team of people who are based at various locations around the world and communicate through Intranet and other electronic means to achieve a common goal.

**voluntary agreements** Trade-restraint agreements resulting in self-imposed restrictions not covered by the GATT rules; used to manage or distort trade flows. For example, Japanese restraints on the export of cars to the United States.

**Webb-Pomerene Act** A 1918 statute that excludes from antitrust prosecution U.S. firms cooperating to develop foreign markets.

**Webb-Pomerene association** A group of U.S. firms cooperating to develop foreign markets, as permitted by the Webb-Pomerene Act.

**withholding taxes** Taxes applied to the payment of dividends, interest, or royalties by firms.

**works council** Councils that provide labor a say in corporate decision making through a representative body that may consist entirely of workers or of a combination of managers and workers.

**work redesign programs** Programs that alter jobs to increase both the quality of the work experience and productivity.

**work scheduling** Preparing schedules of when and how long workers are at the workplace.

**working capital management** The management of a firm's current assets (cash, accounts receivable, inventories) and current liabilities (accounts payable, short-term debt).

**World Bank** An international financial institution created to facilitate trade.

**World Trade Organization** The institution that supplanted GATT in 1995 to administer international trade and investment accords.

# CREDITS

Page 8, Global Perspective 1.1. Reprinted by permission of The Wall Street Journal, © 1993, Dow Jones & Company, Inc. All Rights Reserved Worldwide.

Page 11, Global Perspective 1.2. Reprinted by permission of The Wall Street Journal, © 1993, Dow Jones & Company, Inc. All Rights Reserved Worldwide.

Page 12, map. 1998 Houghton Mifflin.

Page 14, Figure 1.3. The World Bank. Reprinted with permission.

Page 17, Global Perspective 1.3. Reprinted by permission of The Wall Street Journal, © 1993, Dow Jones & Company, Inc. All Rights Reserved Worldwide

Page 43, Table 2.2. Gulf Publishing. Reprinted with permission.

Page 44. map. *The World Factbook 1997–98*. Reprinted with permission.

Page 51, Table 2.4. Institute of International Education. Reprinted with permission.

Page 73, Figure 3.2. Tim, Inc. All rights reserved. Reprinted with permission.

Page 76, map. Source: *The 1992 Information Please Environmental Almanac*. Reprinted with permission.

Page 77, map. Source: *Atlas of the Environment*, 1994. Reprinted with permission.

Page 86, Global Perspective 3.4. *The Journal of Commerce*. Reprinted with permission.

Page 102, Global Perspective 4.1. *The Journal of Commerce*. Reprinted with permission.

Page 103, Global Perspective 4.2. *The Journal of Commerce*. Reprinted with permission.

Page 107, Figure 4.2. John Wiley and Sons. Reprinted with permission of the publisher.

Page 115, Global Perspective 4.4.  Reprinted with permission of *The Washington Post*, © 1994.

Page 117, Figure 4.3. Reprinted with permission of *The Washington Post*, © 1997.

Pate 128, Figure 3. Fortune 500, © 1993 Time Inc. All Rights Reserved.

Page 140, Part 1 Case. *National Geographic*. Reprinted with permission.

Page 153, opening vignette. *Financial Times*. Reprinted with permission.

Page 169, Figure 5.4. Source: *Quarterly Journal of Economics*.

Page 176, Figure 5.6. Reprinted with permission.

Page 188, Table 6.1. The International Monetary Fund. Reprinted with permission.

Page 189, Figure 6.1. Source: Based on The International Monetary Fund, *Balance of Payments Statistics Yearbook*, 1996, p. 823. Reprinted with permission.

Page 191, Table 6.2. The International Monetary Fund. Reprinted with permission.

Page 193, Figure 6.2. Source: *International Financial Statistics* The International Monetary Fund, December, 1997. Reprinted with permission.

Page 194, Figure 6.3. Source: Based on The International Monetary Fund, *Balance of Payments Statistics Yearbook*, 1996, p. 823. Reprinted with permission.

Page 197, Table 6.3. The International Monetary Fund. Reprinted with permission.

Page 198, Global Perspective 6.2. *Financial Times*. Reprinted with permission.

Page 203, Figure 6.4. Source: Based on The International Monetary Fund, *Balance of Payments Statistics Yearbook*, 1996, p. 823. Reprinted with permission.

Page 205, Table 6.4. The International Monetary Fund. Reprinted with permission.

Page 215, opening vignette. Copyright, *Los Angeles Times*. Reprinted with permission.

Page 217, Figure 7.1. Reprinted by permission of *The Wall Street Journal*, © 1997, Dow Jones & Company, Inc. All Rights Reserved Worldwide.

Page 220, Figure 7.2. *The Financial Times*. Reprinted with permission.

Page 222, Global Perspective 7.1. Reprinted by permission of *The Wall Street Journal*, © 1996, Dow Jones & Company, Inc. All Rights Reserved Worldwide.

Page 224, Global Perspective 7.2. Reprinted courtesy of The Federal Reserve Bank of NY.

Page 225, Figure 7.3. Reprinted courtesy of The Federal Reserve Bank of NY.

Page 230, Figure 7.4. Source: *The Federal Reserve Bulletin*, U. S. Board of Governors, Federal Reserve Bank of U. S. Monthly.

Page 233, Table 7.3. Source: International Financial Statistics, The International Monetary, December, 1997. Reprinted with permission.

Page 248, Figure 7.7. Dresdner Bank. Reprinted with permission.

Page 250, Global Perspective 7.4. The McGraw-Hill Companies. Reprinted with permission.

Page 256, Table 8.1. South-Western Publishing Company. Reprinted with permission of the publisher.

Page 278, map. *Statesman Yearbook 1997–98*. Reprinted with permission.

Page 287, opening vignette. Reprinted with permission of *The Wall Street Journal*, © 1997 Dow Jones & Company, Inc. All Rights Reserved Worldwide.

Page 291, Figure 9.1. The International Monetary Fund. Reprinted with permission.

Page 296, Global Perspective 9.2. Reprinted from the March 31, 1997 issue of *Business Week* by special permission copyright © 1997 by The McGraw-Hill Companies.

Page 299, Global Perspective 9.3. Reprinted from the May 26, 1997 issue of *Business Week* by special permission copyright © 1997 by The McGraw-Hill Companies.

Page 339, Figure 10.2. *Financial Times*. Reprinted with permission.

Page 343, Global Perspective 10.2. Reprinted with permission of *The Wall Street Journal*, © 1991 Dow Jones & Company, Inc. All Rights Reserved Worldwide.

Page 347, Global Perspective 10.3. *The Journal of Commerce*. Reprinted with permission.

**Mercedes-Benz**
http://www.daimlerbenz.com
Part 1 Cases

**Microsoft**
http://www.microsoft.com
Chapter 4

**Mitsubishi Motors**
http://www.mitsubishi-motors.co.jpl/
Chapter 5

**Mobile Corporation**
http://www.mobil.com
Chapter 14

**Moody's Sovereign Ceilings**
http://www.moodys.com/repldata/
ratings/ratsov.htm
Chapter 6, 7

**Motorola**
http://www.mot.com
Chapter 14, 15

**N**

**NAFTA**
http://www.nafta.org
Chapter 8

**National Association of
Foreign Trade Zones**
http://imex.com.naftz.htm
Chapter 16

**National Trade Data Bank**
http://www.stat-usa.gov
Chapter 3

**Nestlé S. A.**
http://www.nestle.com/html/home.html
Chapter 5, 13

**Nestlé: The World Food Company**
http://www.nestle.com/press/current/
Chapter 19

**NetFRAME Systems Inc.**
http://www.netframe.com
Chapter 20

**Nike**
http://www.nike.com
Chapter 4

**Nike**
http://www.nikeworkers.com
Chapter 11, Part 4 Cases

**Nike**
http://www.nike.com/faq/
http://www.caa.org.au/campaigns/
nike/index.html
Part 4 Cases

**Nokia**
http://www.nokia.com
Chapter 14

**Nortel**
http://www.nortel.com
Chapter 12

**Novartis**
http://www.novartis.com
Chapter 21

**NT&T**
http://www.ntt.co.jp
Chapter 15

**O**

**Office of the U. S. Trade Representative**
http://www.ustr.gov
Chapter 3

**Office for Special Economic Zones of
the PRC State Council**
http://www.sezo.gov.cn
Chapter 16

**Organization for Economic
Cooperation and Development**
http://www.oecd.org
Chapter 4, 8, 10, 11, 15, 18

**Organization for Economic
Cooperation and Development,
Directorate for Financial, Fiscal, and
Enterprise Affairs**
http://www.oecd.org/daf
Chapter 4

**Organization of American States**
http://www.oas.org
Chapter 4

**Otis Elevator**
http://www.otis.com
Chapter 11

**Overseas Private Investment
Corporation**
http://www.opic.gov
Chapter 4

**P**

**Pathfinder**
http://www.pathfinder.com/fortune/
Chapter 11, 19

**Pepsi Co.**
http://www.glas.pepsi.ru
Chapter 18

**Perkin-Elmer Corp**
http://www.perkin-elmer.com
Chapter 13, 20

**Philadelphia Stock Exchange**
http://www.phlx.com/
Chapter 17

**Philips Electronics**
http://www.philips.com
Chapter 21

**Pier 1**
http://www.pier1.com
Part 1 Cases

**Q
R**

**Rank Xerox**
http://www.rankxerox.co.uk
Chapter 21

**Rhône-Polenc**
http://www.rhone-polenc.com
Chapter 2

**Runzheimer International**
http://www.runzheimer.com
Chapter 20

**S**

**Samsung**
http://www.samsung.com
Chapter 2

**Securities and Exchange Commission
Edgar Files**
http://www.sec.gov/cgi-bin/srch-edgar
Chapter 19

**Sea-Land Service, Inc.**
http://www.sealand.com
Chapter 16

**SICE**
http://www.sice.oas.org
Part 3 Cases

**Smith-Kline Beecham**
http://www.sb.com
Chapter 11

**Solvay**
http://www.solvay.com
Chapter 21

**Statistical Office of The European
Communities (EUROSTAT)**
http://europa.eu.int/en/comm/eurostat/
serven/part6/6som.htm
Chapter 10

**T**

**3M**
http://www.3m.com
Chapter 2, 21

**TK Associates International**
http://www.webcom.com/kyc
Chapter 22

**TradePort**
http://www.tradeport.org
Chapter 11

**Transparency International**
http://www.transparency.de
Chapter 4